McDougal Littell
Earth SCIENCE

Earth's
Atmosphere

Space Science

The Changing
Earth

Earth's Waters

Earth's Surface

EARTH SCIENCE

Acknowledgments: Excerpts and adaptations from *National Science Education Standards* by the National Academy of Sciences. Copyright © 1996 by the National Academy of Sciences. Reprinted with permission from the National Academies Press, Washington, D.C.

Excerpts and adaptations from *Benchmarks for Science Literacy: Project 2061.* Copyright © 1993 by the American Association for the Advancement of Science. Reprinted with permission.

ISBN: 0-618-30368-5   3 4 5 6 7 8 VJM 08 07 06 05 04

Internet Web Site: http://www.mcdougallittell.com

Science Consultants

Chief Science Consultant

James Trefil, Ph.D. is the Clarence J. Robinson Professor of Physics at George Mason University. He is the author or co-author of more than 25 books, including *Science Matters* and *The Nature of Science*. Dr. Trefil is a member of the American Association for the Advancement of Science's Committee on the Public Understanding of Science and Technology. He is also a fellow of the World Economic Forum and a frequent contributor to *Smithsonian* magazine.

Rita Ann Calvo, Ph.D. is Senior Lecturer in Molecular Biology and Genetics at Cornell University, where for 12 years she also directed the Cornell Institute for Biology Teachers. Dr. Calvo is the 1999 recipient of the College and University Teaching Award from the National Association of Biology Teachers.

Kenneth Cutler, M.S. is the Education Coordinator for the Julius L. Chambers Biomedical Biotechnology Research Institute at North Carolina Central University. A former middle school and high school science teacher, he received a 1999 Presidential Award for Excellence in Science Teaching.

Instructional Design Consultants

Douglas Carnine, Ph.D. is Professor of Education and Director of the National Center for Improving the Tools of Educators at the University of Oregon. He is the author of seven books and over 100 other scholarly publications, primarily in the areas of instructional design and effective instructional strategies and tools for diverse learners. Dr. Carnine also serves as a member of the National Institute for Literacy Advisory Board.

Linda Carnine, Ph.D. consults with school districts on curriculum development and effective instruction for students struggling academically. A former teacher and school administrator, Dr. Carnine also co-authored a popular remedial reading program.

Sam Miller, Ph.D. is a middle school science teacher and the Teacher Development Liaison for the Eugene, Oregon, Public Schools. He is the author of curricula for teaching science, mathematics, computer skills, and language arts.

Donald Steely, Ph.D. serves as principal investigator at the Oregon Center for Applied Science (ORCAS) on federal grants for science and language arts programs. His background also includes teaching and authoring of print and multimedia programs in science, mathematics, history, and spelling.

Vicky Vachon, Ph.D. consults with school districts throughout the United States and Canada on improving overall academic achievement with a focus on literacy. She is also co-author of a widely used program for remedial readers.

Content Reviewers

John Beaver, Ph.D.
Ecology
Professor, Director of Science Education Center
College of Education and Human Services
Western Illinois University
Macomb, IL

Donald J. DeCoste, Ph.D.
Matter and Energy, Chemical Interactions
Chemistry Instructor
University of Illinois
Urbana-Champaign, IL

Dorothy Ann Fallows, Ph.D., MSc
Diversity of Living Things, Microbiology
Partners in Health
Boston, MA

Michael Foote, Ph.D.
The Changing Earth, Life Over Time
Associate Professor
Department of the Geophysical Sciences
The University of Chicago
Chicago, IL

Lucy Fortson, Ph.D.
Space Science
Director of Astronomy
Adler Planetarium and Astronomy Museum
Chicago, IL

Elizabeth Godrick, Ph.D.
Human Biology
Professor, CAS Biology
Boston University
Boston, MA

Isabelle Sacramento Grilo, M.S.
The Changing Earth
Lecturer, Department of the Geological Sciences
San Diego State University
San Diego, CA

David Harbster, MSc
Diversity of Living Things
Professor of Biology
Paradise Valley Community College
Phoenix, AZ

Richard D. Norris, Ph.D.
Earth's Waters
Professor of Paleobiology
Scripps Institution of Oceanography
University of California, San Diego
La Jolla, CA

Donald B. Peck, M.S.
Motion and Forces; Waves, Sound, and Light;
  Electricity and Magnetism
Director of the Center for Science Education (retired)
Fairleigh Dickinson University
Madison, NJ

Javier Penalosa, Ph.D.
Diversity of Living Things, Plants
Associate Professor, Biology Department
Buffalo State College
Buffalo, NY

Raymond T. Pierrehumbert, Ph.D.
Earth's Atmosphere
Professor in Geophysical Sciences (Atmospheric Science)
The University of Chicago
Chicago, IL

Brian J. Skinner, Ph.D.
Earth's Surface
Eugene Higgins Professor of Geology and Geophysics
Yale University
New Haven, CT

Nancy E. Spaulding, M.S.
Earth's Surface, The Changing Earth, Earth's Waters
Earth Science Teacher (retired)
Elmira Free Academy
Elmira, NY

Steven S. Zumdahl, Ph.D.
Matter and Energy, Chemical Interactions
Professor Emeritus of Chemistry
University of Illinois
Urbana-Champaign, IL

Susan L. Zumdahl, M.S.
Matter and Energy, Chemical Interactions
Chemistry Education Specialist
University of Illinois
Urbana-Champaign, IL

Safety Consultant

Juliana Texley, Ph.D.
Former K–12 Science Teacher and School Superintendent
Boca Raton, FL

English Language Advisor

Judy Lewis, M.A.
Director, State and Federal Programs for reading proficiency
and high risk populations
Rancho Cordova, CA

iv

Teacher Panel Members

Carol Arbour
Tallmadge Middle School,
Tallmadge, OH

Patty Belcher
Goodrich Middle School,
Akron, OH

Gwen Broestl
Luis Munoz Marin Middle School,
Cleveland, OH

Al Brofman
Tehipite Middle School,
Fresno, CA

John Cockrell
Clinton Middle School,
Columbus, OH

Jenifer Cox
Sylvan Middle School,
Citrus Heights, CA

Linda Culpepper
Martin Middle School,
Charlotte, NC

Kathleen Ann DeMatteo
Margate Middle School,
Margate, FL

Melvin Figueroa
New River Middle School,
Ft. Lauderdale, FL

Doretha Grier
Kannapolis Middle School,
Kannapolis, NC

Robert Hood
Alexander Hamilton Middle School,
Cleveland, OH

Scott Hudson
Covedale Elementary School,
Cincinnati, OH

Loretta Langdon
Princeton Middle School,
Princeton, NC

Carlyn Little
Glades Middle School,
Miami, FL

Ann Marie Lynn
Amelia Earhart Middle School,
Riverside, CA

James Minogue
Lowe's Grove Middle School,
Durham, NC

Joann Myers
Buchanan Middle School,
Tampa, FL

Barbara Newell
Charles Evans Hughes Middle School,
Long Beach, CA

Anita Parker
Kannapolis Middle School,
Kannapolis, NC

Greg Pirolo
Golden Valley Middle School,
San Bernardino, CA

Laura Pottmyer
Apex Middle School,
Apex, NC

Lynn Prichard
Booker T. Washington Middle Magnet
School, Tampa, FL

Jacque Quick
Walter Williams High School,
Burlington, NC

Robert Glenn Reynolds
Hillman Middle School,
Youngstown, OH

Stacy Rinehart
Lufkin Road Middle School,
Apex, NC

Theresa Short
Abbott Middle School,
Fayetteville, NC

Rita Slivka
Alexander Hamilton Middle School,
Cleveland, OH

Marie Sofsak
B F Stanton Middle School,
Alliance, OH

Nancy Stubbs
Sweetwater Union Unified School District,
Chula Vista, CA

Sharon Stull
Quail Hollow Middle School,
Charlotte, NC

Donna Taylor
Okeeheelee Middle School,
West Palm Beach, FL

Sandi Thompson
Harding Middle School,
Lakewood, OH

Lori Walker
Audubon Middle School & Magnet Center,
Los Angeles, CA

Teacher Lab Evaluators

Andrew Boy
W.E.B. DuBois Academy,
Cincinnati, OH

Jill Brimm-Byrne
Albany Park Academy,
Chicago, IL

Gwen Broestl
Luis Munoz Marin Middle School,
Cleveland, OH

Al Brofman
Tehipite Middle School,
Fresno, CA

Michael A. Burstein
The Rashi School,
Newton, MA

Trudi Coutts
Madison Middle School,
Naperville, IL

Jenifer Cox
Sylvan Middle School,
Citrus Heights, CA

Larry Cwik
Madison Middle School,
Naperville, IL

Jennifer Donatelli
Kennedy Junior High School,
Lisle, IL

Melissa Dupree
Lakeside Middle School,
Evans, GA

Carl Fechko
Luis Munoz Marin Middle School,
Cleveland, OH

Paige Fullhart
Highland Middle School,
Libertyville, IL

Sue Hood
Glen Crest Middle School,
Glen Ellyn, IL

William Luzader
Plymouth Community Intermediate School,
Plymouth, MA

Ann Min
Beardsley Middle School,
Crystal Lake, IL

Aileen Mueller
Kennedy Junior High School,
Lisle, IL

Nancy Nega
Churchville Middle School,
Elmhurst, IL

Oscar Newman
Sumner Math and Science Academy,
Chicago, IL

Lynn Prichard
Booker T. Washington Middle Magnet
School, Tampa, FL

Jacque Quick
Walter Williams High School,
Burlington, NC

Stacy Rinehart
Lufkin Road Middle School,
Apex, NC

Seth Robey
Gwendolyn Brooks Middle School,
Oak Park, IL

Kevin Steele
Grissom Middle School,
Tinley Park, IL

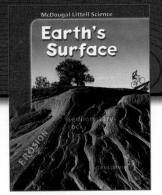

McDougal Littell Science

Earth's Surface

eEdition

UNIT A
Earth's Surface

Why can gold be separated from other minerals and rocks in a river? page A40

Visual Highlights

McDougal Littell Science

The Changing Earth

UNIT B

The Changing Earth

eEdition

What caused these rails to bend, and how long did it take? page B42

How does new land form from molten rock? page B74

Visual Highlights

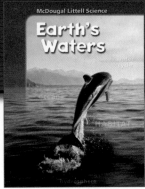

McDougal Littell Science

Earth's Waters

eEdition

UNIT C
Earth's Waters

Unit Features

1 The Water Planet   C6

the BIG idea

Water moves through Earth's atmosphere, oceans, and land in a cycle.

2 Freshwater Resources   C38

the BIG idea

Fresh water is a limited resource and is essential for human society.

In what ways do you depend on water? page C38

What causes these waves? page C72

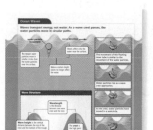

Visual Highlights

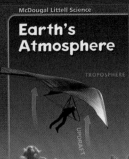

eEdition

UNIT D
Earth's Atmosphere

Unit Features

1 Earth's Changing Atmosphere   D6

the **BIG** idea

Earth's atmosphere is a blanket of gases that supports and protects life.

2 Weather Patterns   D40

the **BIG** idea

Some features of weather have predictable patterns.

What weather conditions do you see in the distance? page D40

What types of weather can move a house? page D76

3 Weather Fronts and Storms D76

4 Climate and Climate Change D114

Visual Highlights

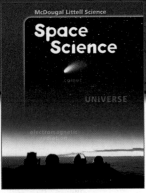

McDougal Littell Science

Space Science

comet

UNIVERSE

electromagnetic radiation

eEdition

UNIT E
Space Science

Unit Features

1 Exploring Space — E6

the **BIG** idea

People develop and use technology to explore and study space.

2 Earth, Moon, and Sun — E40

the **BIG** idea

Earth and the Moon move in predictable ways as they orbit the Sun.

What would you see if you looked at the Moon with a telescope? page E40

This image shows Jupiter with one of its large moons. How big are these objects compared with Earth? page E76

Visual Highlights

Features

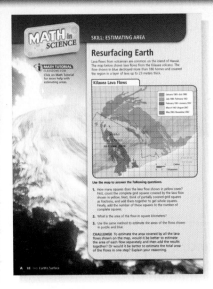

Math in Science

Think Science

Connecting Sciences

Science on the Job

Extreme Science

Frontiers in Science

Timelines in Science

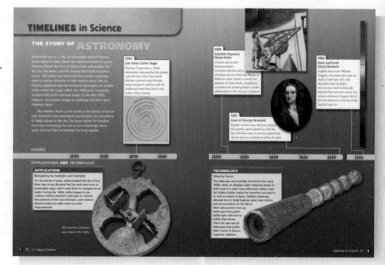

Internet Resources @ ClassZone.com

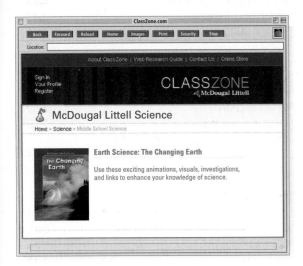

Simulations

Visualizations

Career Centers

Resource Centers

EARTH'S SURFACE
Resources for the following topics may be found at ClassZone.com: *Satellite Mapping, Map Projections, GIS, Precious Metals, Minerals, Gemstones, Meteorites and Impacts, Igneous Rocks, Sedimentary Rocks, Metamorphic Rocks, Earth System Research, Weathering, Soil, Mudflows, Rivers and Erosion, Glaciers.*

THE CHANGING EARTH
Resources for the following topics may be found at ClassZone.com: *Earth's Interior, Effects of Plate Movement, Recent Earthquakes, Seismology, Tsunamis, Historic and Current Volcanic Eruptions, Effects of Volcanic Eruptions, Evidence of an Event in Earth's Past, Fossils, Finding the Ages of Rocks, Fossil Research and Excavation, Natural Resources, Pollution-Digesting Microbes, Renewable Energy Resources.*

EARTH'S WATERS
Resources for the following topics may be found at ClassZone.com: *Water, Evidence of a Water Cycle on Mars, Frozen Fresh Water, Geysers and Hot Springs, Dams, Water Conservation, Ocean Currents, Ocean Waves, Ocean Tides, Ocean Research, Ocean Environments, Coral Reefs, Hydrothermal Vents, Ocean Pollution and Pollution Prevention.*

EARTH'S ATMOSPHERE
Resources for the following topics may be found at ClassZone.com: *Earth's Atmosphere, Ozone Layer, Air Pressure, Global Winds, Clouds, Lightning, Weather Safety, Weather and Weather Forecasting, Atmospheric Research, El Niño, Climate Zones, Climate and Climate Change, Global Warming.*

SPACE SCIENCE
Resources for the following topics may be found at ClassZone.com: *Telescopes, Space Exploration, Seasons, Tides, Advances in Astronomy, Impact Craters, Moons of Giant Planets, Life Cycles of Stars, Galaxies, Galaxy Collisions.*

Math Tutorials

NSTA SciLinks

Codes for use with the NSTA SciLinks site may be found on every chapter opener.

Content Reviews

There is a content review for every chapter at ClassZone.com

Test Practice

There is a standardized test practice for every chapter at ClassZone.com

Explore the Big Idea

Chapter Opening Inquiry

Each chapter opens with hands-on explorations that introduce the chapter's Big Idea.

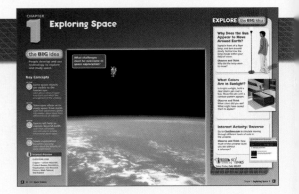

Chapter Investigations

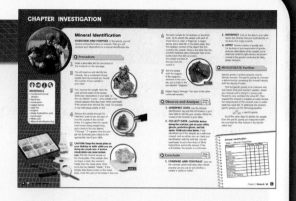

Full-Period Labs

The Chapter Investigations are in-depth labs that let you form and test a hypothesis, build a model, or sometimes design your own investigation.

Explore

Introductory Inquiry Activities

Most sections begin with a simple activity that lets you explore the Key Concept before you read the section.

Earth's Surface

The Changing Earth

Earth's Waters

Earth's Atmosphere

Space Science

Investigate

Skill Labs

Each Investigate activity gives you a chance to practice a specific science skill related to the content that you're studying.

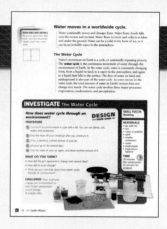

Standards and Benchmarks

Each unit in **Earth Science** addresses some of the learning goals described in the *National Science Education Standards* (NSES) and the Project 2061 *Benchmarks for Science Literacy.* The following National Science Education Standards are also addressed in the book introduction, unit and chapter features, and lab investigations in all the units: A.9 Understandings About Scientific Inquiry, E.6 Understandings About Science and Technology, F.5 Science and Technology in Society, G.1 Science as a Human Endeavor, G.2 Nature of Science, G.3 History of Science.

National Science Education Standards

Content Standards

UNIT A Earth's Surface

A.9.d | Technology is used to gather more detailed and accurate data to help scientists in their investigations.

D.1.a | Earth consists of an inner and outer core, a mantle, and a crust.

D.1.c | Landforms are shaped by weathering and erosion.

D.1.d | In the rock cycle, old rocks at Earth's surface weather and become sediments. The sediments are buried, then compressed and heated to form new rock.

D.1.e | Soil consists of weathered rocks, organic plant and animal matter, and bacteria.

D.1.k | Living organisms have produced some types of rocks and have contributed to the weathering of rocks.

E.6.c | Technology allows scientists to observe or measure phenomena that would otherwise be beyond scientists' reach.

UNIT B The Changing Earth

B.3.f | The Sun is a major source of energy that produces phenomena and changes on Earth's surface.

D.1.b | Lithospheric plates move around Earth, carrying continents and ocean basins with them.

D.1.c | Movements in Earth's crust help build the planet's landforms. Landforms can be built by sudden changes in Earth's crust, including volcanic eruptions

D.2.a | The processes that shape Earth today are similar to those in Earth's past.

E.6.f | All technological solutions have benefits and consequences.

F.3.a | Internal and external processes in the Earth system cause natural hazards such as earthquakes.

F.3.b | Human activities can introduce pollution and other hazards into the environment.

F.4.a | Earthquakes and volcanic explosions present dangers to human and wildlife habitats.

F.4.b | The risks of using different types of energy include air, water, and soil pollution.

UNIT C Earth's Waters

C.4.c | For ecosystems, the major source of energy is sunlight. Energy passes from organism to organism in food webs.

C.4.d | The number of organisms an ecosystem can support depends on the resources available and on factors such as quantity of light and range of temperatures.

D.1.f | Water, which covers the majority of Earth's surface, circulates through Earth's atmosphere, surface, and crust in what is known as the "water cycle."

D.1.g | Water is a solvent. As it passes through the water cycle, it dissolves minerals and gases and carries them to oceans.

D.1.j	Global patterns of atmospheric movement influence local weather. Oceans have a major effect on climate.
D.3.c	Gravity keeps planets in orbit around the Sun, governs motion in the solar system, and explains the phenomenon of tides.
D.3.d	The Sun is the major source of energy for phenomena on Earth's surface, such as the water cycle.

| F.3.b | Human activities can produce hazards and affect the speed of natural changes. |
| F.4.b | Risks are associated with natural hazards such as floods. Risks are also associated with chemical hazards such as pollution in air, water, and soil, as well as with biological hazards, such as bacteria and viruses. |

UNIT D Earth's Atmosphere

D.1.f	Water evaporates from Earth's surface; rises, cools, and condenses in the atmosphere; and falls as rain or snow.
D.1.h	The atmosphere is a mixture of the gases nitrogen and oxygen and small amounts of water vapor and other gases.
D.1.i	Clouds form when water vapor condenses. Clouds affect the weather.

D.1.j	Global patterns of motion in the atmosphere and the oceans and heat energy from oceans affect the weather.
D.2.a	The Earth processes we see today are similar to those that occurred in the past.
F.3.a	Processes of the Earth system, such as storms, can cause hazards that affect humans and wildlife.
F.3.b	Human activities can produce hazards and affect the speed of natural changes.

UNIT E Space Science

A.9.d	Technology allows scientists to be more accurate and to use data.
B.3.a	Energy is associated with heat, light, electricity, motion, sound, nuclei, and the nature of a chemical.
B.3.f	Energy from the Sun has a range of wavelengths, including visible light, infrared radiation, and ultraviolet radiation.
D.3.a	The Sun is the central and largest body in a system of nine planets and their moons and objects such as asteroids and comets.

D.3.b	The regular and predictable motions of objects in the solar system explain such phenomena as the day, the year, phases of the Moon, and eclipses.
D.3.d	Seasons result from varying amounts of the Sun's energy hitting the surface due to the tilt of Earth's axis and the length of the day.
F.5.c	Technology influences society through its products and processes.
G.2.a	Scientists use observations, experiments, and models to test their explanations.

Process and Skill Standards

A.1	Identify questions that can be answered using scientific methods.
A.2	Design and conduct a scientific investigation.
A.3	Use appropriate tools and techniques to gather and interpret data.
A.4	Use evidence to describe, predict, explain, and model.
A.5	Use critical thinking to find relationships between results and interpretations.
A.6	Consider alternative explanations and predictions.

A.7	Communicate procedures, results, and conclusions.
A.8	Use mathematics in scientific inquiry.
E.1	Identify a problem to be solved.
E.2	Design a solution or product.
E.3	Implement the proposed solution.
E.4	Evaluate the solution or design.
F.4.b	Understand the risks associated with natural hazards.

Project 2061 Benchmarks

Content Benchmarks

UNIT A Earth's Surface

1.C.6 | Computers speed up and extend scientists' ability to collect, store, compile, analyze, and prepare data.

4.B.2 | Earth is a rocky planet surrounded by a thin blanket of air, with water covering nearly three-quarters of its surface.

4.B.10 | The ability to recover valuable minerals is just as important as how abundant or rare they are in nature. As minerals are used up, obtaining them becomes more difficult.

4.C.2 | Earth's surface is shaped in part by the motion of wind and water over a long time.

4.C.3 | In the rock cycle, sediments are buried and cemented together by dissolved minerals to form solid rock again.

4.C.4 | Rocks bear evidence of the minerals, temperatures, and forces that formed them in the rock cycle.

4.C.6 | Soil composition, texture, fertility, and resistance to erosion are influenced by plant roots and debris and by organisms living in the soil.

9.C.3 | The spherical Earth is distorted when projected onto a flat map.

9.C.5 | It takes two numbers to locate a point on a map.

11.A.2 | Thinking about things as systems means looking at how each part relates to the others.

UNIT B The Changing Earth

4.B.10 | Recycling and developing synthetic materials can extend natural resources but may also be costly.

4.B.11 | Earth's resources can be reduced by using them wastefully or by destroying them. Cleaning up polluted air and water can be difficult and costly.

4.C.1 | Heat flow and material within Earth create mountains and ocean basins. Gas and dust from volcanoes can change the atmosphere.

4.C.5 | Thousands of layers of sedimentary rock and their fossils confirm the long history of Earth's changing surface and life forms.

4.F.4 | Earthquake waves spread away from the source and move at different speeds through different materials.

8.C.2 | Different ways of obtaining and using energy have different consequences on the environment.

8.C.5 | Energy from the Sun, wind, and water is unlimited, but requires large collection systems to make use of it. Other types of energy are not renewable or are replaced very slowly.

UNIT C Earth's Waters

4.B.2 | Three-fourths of Earth's surface is covered by a relatively thin layer of water, some of it frozen.

4.B.6 | Climates have sometimes changed abruptly. Even relatively small changes in atmospheric or ocean content can have widespread effects.

4.B.7 | Water evaporates from Earth's surface, rises and cools, and condenses into rain or snow. The water falling on land as precipitation collects in rivers and lakes, soil, and porous layers of rock, and much of it flows back into the ocean.

4.B.8 | Fresh water, limited in supply, is essential for life and also for most industrial processes.

4.B.9 | Heat energy carried by ocean currents has a strong influence on climate.

4.B.11 | The benefits of Earth's resources can be reduced by using them wastefully or by destroying them. The atmosphere and oceans have a limited capacity to absorb waste and recycle materials.

4.C.1 | The interior of Earth is hot. Heat flow and movement of material within Earth cause earthquakes and volcanic eruptions and create mountains and ocean basins.

UNIT D Earth's Atmosphere

3.A.2 Technologies are important in science because they let people gather, store, compute, and communicate large amounts of data.

4.B.4 Sunlight falls more intensely on different parts of Earth, and the pattern changes over the year. The differences in heating of Earth's surface produce seasons and other weather patterns.

4.B.6 The atmosphere can change suddenly when a volcano erupts or when Earth is struck by a huge rock from space.

4.B.7 Water is important in the atmosphere. Water evaporates from Earth's surface; rises

4.B.7 *cont'd.* and cools; condenses into rain or snow; and falls back to the surface.

4.E.3 Heat energy can move by the collision of particles, by the motion of particles, or by waves through space.

11.B.1 Models are often used to think about processes that cannot be observed directly or that are too vast or too dangerous to be changed directly. Models can be displayed on a computer and then changed to see what happens.

UNIT E Space Science

4.A.2 Light takes time to travel, so distant objects seen from Earth appear as they were long ago. It takes light a few minutes to reach Earth from the Sun, the closest star, and several billion years to reach Earth from very distant galaxies.

4.A.3 Nine planets that vary in size, composition, and surface features orbit the Sun in nearly circular orbits. Some planets have rings and a variety of moons. Some planets and moons show signs of geological activity.

4.A.4 Chunks of rock that orbit the Sun sometimes impact Earth's atmosphere and sometimes reach Earth's surface. Other

4.A.4 *cont'd.* chunks of rock and ice produce long, illuminated tails when they pass close to the Sun.

4.B.5 Phases of the Moon occur because the Moon's orbit changes the amount of the sunlit part of the Moon that can be seen from Earth.

4.G.2 The Sun's gravitational pull holds Earth in its orbit, just as Earth's gravitational pull holds the Moon in orbit.

11.B.1 Models are often used to think about processes that cannot be observed directly, changed deliberately, or examined safely.

Process and Skill Benchmarks

1.A.3 Some knowledge in science is very old and yet is still used today.

1.B.1 Design an investigation in which you collect evidence, reason logically, and use imagination to devise hypotheses.

3.A.2 Technology is essential to access outer space and remote locations; to collect, use, and share data; and to communicate.

3.B.1 Design requires taking constraints into account.

9.A.3 Write numbers in different forms.

9.B.2 Use mathematics to describe change.

9.B.3 Use graphs to show the relationship between two variables.

9.C.4 Use graphs to show patterns and make predictions.

10.A.2 Use telescopes to observe the stars and the Moon, the Sun, and the planets.

11.A.2 Think about things as systems by looking for the ways each part relates to others.

11.B.1 Use models to think about processes.

11.C.4 Use equations to summarize observed changes.

11.D.2 With complex systems, use summaries, averages, ranges, and examples.

12.B.1 Find what percentage one number is of another.

12.B.2 Use and compare numbers in equivalent forms such as decimals and percents.

12.B.3 Calculate volumes of rectangular solids.

12.B.5 Estimate distances and travel times from maps.

12.B.7 Determine, use, and convert units.

12.B.9 Express numbers like 100, 1000, and 1,000,000 as powers of 10.

12.C.1 Compare amounts proportionally.

12.C.3 Use and read measurement instruments.

12.D.1 Use tables and graphs to organize information and identify relationships.

12.D.2 Read, interpret, and describe tables and graphs.

12.D.4 Understand information in various types of graphs and charts.

12.D.5 Use coordinates to find locations on maps.

12.E.4 Recognize more than one way to interpret a given set of findings.

Introducing Earth Science

Scientists are curious. Since ancient times, they have been asking and answering questions about the world around them. Scientists are also very suspicious of the answers they get. They carefully collect evidence and test their answers many times before accepting an idea as correct.

In this book you will see how scientific knowledge keeps growing and changing as scientists ask new questions and rethink what was known before. The following sections will help get you started.

What Is Earth Science?

Earth science is the study of Earth's interior, its rocks and soil, its atmosphere, its oceans, and outer space. For many years, scientists studied each of these topics separately. They learned many important things. More recently, however, scientists have looked more and more at the connections among the different parts of Earth—its oceans, atmosphere, living things, and rocks and soil. Scientists have also been learning more about other planets in our solar system, as well as stars and galaxies far away. Through these studies they have learned much about Earth and its place in the universe.

The text and pictures in this book will help you learn key concepts and important facts about earth science. A variety of activities will help you investigate these concepts. As you learn, it helps to have a big picture of earth science as a framework for this new information. The four unifying principles listed below will give you this big picture. Read the next few pages to get an overview of each of these principles and a sense of why they are so important.

- **Heat energy inside Earth and radiation from the Sun provide energy for Earth's processes.**

- **Physical forces, such as gravity, affect the movement of all matter on Earth and throughout the universe.**

- **Matter and energy move among Earth's rocks and soil, atmosphere, waters, and living things.**

- **Earth has changed over time and continues to change.**

the **BIG** idea

Each chapter begins with a big idea. Keep in mind that each big idea relates to one or more of the unifying principles.

Heat energy inside Earth and radiation from the Sun provide energy for Earth's processes.

The lava pouring out of this volcano in Hawaii is liquid rock that was melted by heat energy under Earth's surface. Another, much more powerful energy source constantly bombards Earth's surface with energy, heating the air around you, and keeping the oceans from freezing over. This energy source is the Sun. Everything that moves or changes on Earth gets its energy either from the Sun or from the inside of our planet.

What It Means

You are always surrounded by different forms of energy, such as heat energy or light. **Energy** is the ability to cause change. All of Earth's processes need energy to occur. A process is a set of changes that leads to a particular result. For example, **evaporation** is the process by which liquid changes into gas. A puddle on a sidewalk dries up through the process of evaporation. The energy needed for the puddle to dry up comes from the Sun.

Heat Energy Inside Earth

Underneath the cool surface layer of rock, Earth's interior is so hot that the solid rock there is able to flow very slowly—a few centimeters each year. In a process called **convection,** hot material rises, cools, then sinks until it is heated enough to rise again. Convection of hot rock carries heat energy up to Earth's surface, where it provides the energy to build mountains, cause earthquakes, and make volcanoes erupt.

Radiation from the Sun

Earth receives energy from the Sun as **radiation**—energy that travels across distances in the form of certain types of waves. Visible light is one type of radiation. Radiation from the Sun heats Earth's surface, making bright summer days hot. Different parts of Earth receive different amounts of radiation at different times of the year, causing seasons. Energy from the Sun also causes winds to blow, ocean currents to flow, and water to move from the ground to the atmosphere and back again.

Why It's Important

Understanding Earth's processes makes it possible to

- know what types of crops to plant and when to plant them
- know when to watch for dangerous weather, such as tornadoes and hurricanes
- predict a volcano's eruption in time for people to leave the area

Physical forces, such as gravity, affect the movement of all matter on Earth and throughout the universe.

The universe is everything that exists, and everything in the universe is governed by the same physical laws. The same laws govern the stars shown in this picture and the page on which the picture is printed.

What It Means

What do the stars in a galaxy, the planet Earth, and your body have in common? For one thing, they are all made of matter. **Matter** is anything that has mass and takes up space. Rocks are matter. You are matter. Even the air around you is matter. Matter is made of tiny particles called **atoms** that are too small to see through an ordinary microscope.

Everything in the universe is also affected by the same physical forces. A **force** is a push or a pull. Forces affect how matter moves everywhere in the universe.

- One force you experience every moment is **gravity,** which is the attraction, or pull, between two objects. Gravity is pulling you to Earth and Earth to you. Gravity is the force that causes objects to fall downward toward the center of Earth. Gravity is also the force that keeps objects in orbit around planets and stars.

- **Friction** is the force that resists motion between two surfaces that are pressed together. Friction can keep a rock on a hillside from sliding down to the bottom of the hill. If you lightly rub your finger across a smooth page in a book and then across a piece of sandpaper, you can feel how the different surfaces produce different frictional forces. Which is easier to do?

- There are many other forces at work on Earth and throughout the universe. For example, Earth has a magnetic field. A compass needle responds to the force exerted by Earth's magnetic field. Another example is the contact force between a rock and the ground beneath it. A contact force occurs when one object pushes or pulls on another object by touching it.

Why It's Important

Physical forces influence the movement of all matter, from the tiniest particle to you to the largest galaxy. Understanding forces allows people to

- predict how objects and materials move on Earth
- send spacecraft and equipment into space
- explain and predict the movements of Earth, the Moon, planets, and stars

Matter and energy move among Earth's rocks and soil, atmosphere, waters, and living things.

When a wolf eats a rabbit, matter and energy move from one living thing into another. When a wolf drinks water warmed by the Sun, matter and energy move from Earth's waters into one of its living things. These are just two examples of how energy and matter move among different parts of the Earth system.

What It Means

Think of Earth as a huge system, or an organized group of parts that work together. Within this system, matter and energy move among the different parts. The four major parts of Earth's system are the

- **atmosphere,** which includes all the air surrounding the solid planet
- **geosphere,** which includes all of Earth's rocks and minerals, as well as Earth's interior
- **hydrosphere,** which includes oceans, rivers, lakes, and every drop of water on or under Earth's surface
- **biosphere,** which includes all the living things on Earth

Matter in the Earth System

It's easy to see how matter moves within the Earth system. When water in the atmosphere falls as rain, it becomes part of the hydrosphere. When an animal drinks water from a puddle, the water becomes part of the biosphere. When rainwater soaks into the ground, it moves through the geosphere. As the puddle dries up, the water becomes part of the atmosphere again.

Energy in the Earth System

Most of the energy you depend on comes from the Sun and moves among the four major parts of the Earth system. Think again about the puddle that is drying up. Sunlight shines through the water and heats the soil, or geosphere, beneath the puddle. Some of this heat energy goes into the puddle, moving into the hydrosphere. As the water evaporates and becomes part of the atmosphere, it takes the energy that came from the Sun with it. The Sun provides energy for all weather and ocean currents. Without the Sun, life could not exist on Earth's surface.

Why It's Important

Understanding how matter and energy move through the Earth system makes it possible to

- predict how a temperature change in ocean water might affect the weather
- determine how clearing forests might affect rainfall
- explain where organisms on the ocean floor get energy to carry out life processes

Earth has changed over time and continues to change.

You see Earth changing all of the time. Rain turns dirt to mud, and a dry wind turns the mud to dust. Many changes are small and can take hundreds, thousands, or even millions of years to add up to much. Other changes are sudden and can destroy in minutes a house that had stood for many years.

What It Means

Events are always changing Earth's surface. Some events, such as the building or wearing away of mountains, occur over millions of years. Others, such as earthquakes, occur within seconds. A change can affect a small area or even the entire planet.

Records of Change

What was the distant past like? Think about how scientists learn about ancient people. They study what the people left behind and draw conclusions based on the evidence. In a similar way, scientists learn about Earth's past by examining the evidence they find in rock layers and by observing processes now occurring.

By observing that water breaks down rocks and carries the material away to other places, people learned that rivers can slowly carve deep valleys. Evidence from rocks and fossils along the edges of continents shows that all continents were once joined and then moved apart over time. A **fossil** is the trace of a once-living organism. Fossils also show that new types of plants and animals develop, and others, such as dinosaurs, die out.

Change Continues Today

Every year, earthquakes occur, volcanoes erupt, and rivers flood. Continents continue to move slowly. The Himalayan Mountains of Asia push a few millimeters higher. **Climate**—the long-term weather patterns of an area—may also change. Scientists are studying how changes in climates around the world might affect Earth even within this century.

Why It's Important

Understanding the changing Earth makes it possible to

- predict and prepare for events such as volcanic eruptions, landslides, floods, and climate changes
- design buildings to withstand shaking during earthquakes
- protect important environments for plants and animals

The Nature of Science

You may think of science as a body of knowledge or a collection of facts. More important, however, science is an active process that involves certain ways of looking at the world.

Scientific Habits of Mind

Scientists are curious. They ask questions. A scientist who finds an unusual rock by the side of a river would ask questions such as, "Did this rock form in this area?" or "Did this rock form elsewhere and get moved here?" Questions like these make a scientist want to investigate.

Scientists are observant. They look closely at the world around them. A scientist who studies rocks can learn a lot about a rock just by picking it up, looking at its color, and feeling how heavy it is.

Scientists are creative. They draw on what they know to form possible explanations for a pattern, an event, or an interesting phenomenon that they have observed. Then scientists put together a plan for testing their ideas.

Scientists are skeptical. Scientists don't accept an explanation or answer unless it is based on evidence and logical reasoning. They continually question their own conclusions as well as the conclusions suggested by other scientists. Scientists only trust evidence that can be confirmed by other people or other methods.

Scientists use seismographs to observe and measure vibrations that move through the ground.

This scientist is collecting a sample of melted rock from a hot lava flow in Hawaii.

Science Processes at Work

You can think of science as a continuous cycle of asking and seeking answers to questions about the world. Although there are many processes that scientists use, all scientists typically do the following:

- Observe and ask a question
- Determine what is known
- Investigate
- Interpret results
- Share results

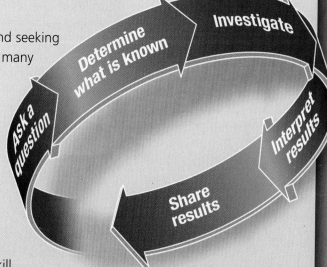

Observe and Ask a Question

It may surprise you that asking questions is an important skill. A scientific investigation may start when a scientist asks a question. Perhaps scientists observe an event or a process that they don't understand, or perhaps answering one question leads to another.

Determine What Is Known

When beginning an inquiry, scientists find out what is already known about a question. They study results from other scientific investigations, read journals, and talk with other scientists. The scientist who is trying to figure out where an unusual rock came from will study maps that show what types of rocks are already known to be in the area where the rock was found.

Investigate

Investigating is the process of collecting evidence. Two important ways of doing this are experimenting and observing.

An **experiment** is an organized procedure to study something under controlled conditions. For example, the scientist who found the rock by the river might notice that it is lighter in color where it is chipped. The scientist might design an experiment to determine why the rock is a different color on the inside. The scientist could break off a small piece of the inside of the rock and heat it up to see if it becomes the same color as the outside. The scientist would need to use a piece of the same rock that is being studied. A different rock might react differently to heat.

A scientist may use photography to study fast events, such as multiple flashes of lightning.

Rocks, such as this one from the Moon, can be subjected to different conditions in a laboratory.

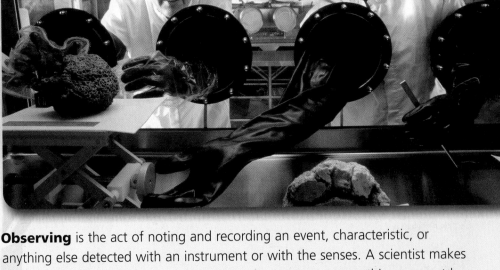

Observing is the act of noting and recording an event, characteristic, or anything else detected with an instrument or with the senses. A scientist makes observations while performing an experiment. However, some things cannot be studied using experiments. For example, streaks of light called meteors occur when small rocks from outer space hit Earth's atmosphere. A scientist might study meteors by taking pictures of the sky at a time when meteors are likely to occur.

Forming hypotheses and making predictions are two other skills involved in scientific investigations. A **hypothesis** is a tentative explanation for an observation or a scientific problem that can be tested by further investigation. For example, the scientist might make the following hypothesis about the rock from the beach:

The rock is a meteorite, which is a rock that fell to the ground from outer space. The outside of the rock changed color because it was heated up from passing through Earth's atmosphere.

A **prediction** is an expectation of what will be observed or what will happen. To test the hypothesis that the rock's outside is black because it is a meteorite, the scientist might predict that a close examination of the rock will show that it has many characteristics in common with rocks that are already known to be meteorites.

Interpret Results

As scientists investigate, they analyze their evidence, or data, and begin to draw conclusions. **Analyzing data** involves looking at the evidence gathered through observations or experiments and trying to identify any patterns that might exist in the data. Scientists often need to make additional observations or perform more experiments before they are sure of their conclusions. Many times scientists make new predictions or revise their hypotheses.

Scientists use computers to gather and interpret data.

Scientists make images such as this computer drawing of a landscape to help share their results with others.

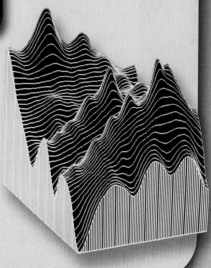

Share Results

An important part of scientific investigation is sharing results of experiments. Scientists read and publish in journals and attend conferences to communicate with other scientists around the world. Sharing data and procedures gives scientists a way to test each others' results. They also share results with the public through newspapers, television, and other media.

The Nature of Technology

When you think of technology, you may think of cars, computers, and cell phones. Imagine having no refrigerator or radio. It's difficult to think of a world without the products of what we call technology. Technology, however, is more than just devices that make our daily activities easier. Technology is the process of using scientific knowledge to design solutions to real-world problems.

Science and Technology

Science and technology go hand in hand. Each depends upon the other. Even a device as simple as a thermometer is designed using knowledge of the ways different materials respond to changes in temperature. In turn, thermometers have allowed scientists to learn more about the world. Greater knowledge of how materials respond to changes in temperature helped engineers to build items such as refrigerators. They have also built thermometers that could be read automatically by computers. New technologies lead to new scientific knowledge and new scientific knowledge leads to even better technologies.

The Process of Technological Design

The process of technological design involves many choices. What, for example, should be done to protect the residents of an area prone to severe storms such as tornadoes and hurricanes? Build stronger homes that can withstand the winds? Try to develop a way to detect the storms long before they occur? Or learn more about hurricanes in order to find new ways to protect people from the dangers? The steps people take to solve the problem depend a great deal on what they already know about the problem as well as what can reasonably be done. As you learn about the steps in the process of technological design, think about the different choices that could be made at each step.

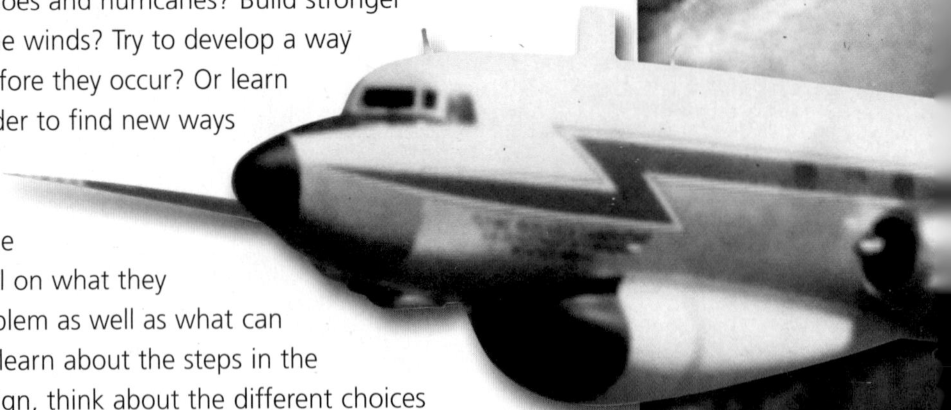

Identify a Need

To study hurricanes, scientists needed to know what happens inside the most dangerous parts of the storm. However, it was not safe for scientists to go near the centers of hurricanes because the winds were too strong and changed direction too fast. Scientists needed a way to measure conditions deep inside the storm without putting themselves in danger.

Design and Develop

One approach was to design a robotic probe to take the measurements. The probe and instruments needed to be strong enough to withstand the fast winds near the center of a hurricane. The scientists also needed a way to send the probe into the storm and to get the data from the instruments quickly.

Scientists designed a device called a dropsonde, which could be dropped from an airplane flying over the hurricane. A dropsonde takes measurements from deep inside the storm and radios data back to the scientists.

Test and Improve

Even good technology can usually be improved. When scientists first used dropsondes, they learned about hurricanes. They also learned what things about the dropsondes worked well and what did not. For example, the scientists wanted better ways to keep track of where the probe moved. Newer dropsondes make use of the Global Positioning System, which is a way of pinpointing any position on Earth by using satellite signals.

Using McDougal Littell Science

Reading Text and Visuals

This book is organized to help you learn. Use these boxed
pointers as a path to help you learn and remember
the **Big Ideas** and **Key Concepts**.

Take notes.

Use the strategies on the
Getting Ready to Learn page.

Read the Big Idea.

As you read **Key Concepts** for
the chapter, relate them to
the Big Idea.

CHAPTER

2 Min

the BIG idea

Minerals are basic
building blocks of Earth.

Key Concepts

SECTION 2.1 Minerals are all around us.
Learn about the characteristics
all minerals share.

SECTION 2.2 A mineral is identified by its properties.
Learn how to identify
minerals by observing and
testing their properties.

SECTION 2.3 Minerals are valuable resources.
Learn how minerals form,
how they are mined, and
how they are used.

Internet Preview

CLASSZONE.COM
Chapter 2 online resources:
Content Review, Visuali-
zation, three Resource
Centers, Math Tutorial,
Test Practice

 40 Unit: Earth's Surface

CHAPTER 2

Getting Ready to Learn

CONCEPT REVIEW

- Earth has four main layers:
  crust, mantle, outer core, and
  inner core.
- Matter exists in the forms of
  gas, liquid, and solid.
- People use maps to show many
  different features of Earth.

VOCABULARY REVIEW

atom *See Glossary.*
geosphere p. 12

CONTENT REVIEW
CLASSZONE.COM
Review concepts and vocabulary.

TAKING NOTES

SUPPORTING MAIN IDEAS

Make a chart to show
each main idea and the
information that supports
it. Copy each blue
heading. Below each
heading, add supporting
information, such as
reasons, explanations,
and examples.

VOCABULARY STRATEGY

Place each vocabulary
term at the center of
a **description wheel**. On
the spokes write some
words explaining it.

See the Note-Taking Handbook
on pages R45–R51.

A 42 Unit: Earth's Surface

SCIENCE NOTEBOOK

Minerals have four characteristics.

→ Minerals form naturally.

→ All minerals are solids.

→ Each mineral is always made of the sam[e]
element or elements.

→ All minerals have crystal structures.

atoms joined in
a repeating 3-D
pattern

formed by
all minerals

CRYSTAL

KEY CONCEPT

2.1 Minerals are all around us.

◄ BEFORE, you learned	► NOW, you will learn
• Earth is made of layers • Earth's outermost rocky layer is the crust	• What the characteristics of minerals are • How minerals are classified into groups • Which mineral group is most common

VOCABULARY

mineral p. 43
element p. 45
crystal p. 46

EXPLORE Minerals

What are some characteristics of a mineral?

PROCEDURE

① Sprinkle some table salt on a sheet of colored paper. Look at a few grains of the salt through a magnifying glass. Then rub a few grains between your fingers.

② In your notebook, describe all the qualities of the salt that you observe.

③ Examine the rock salt in the same way and describe its qualities in your notebook. How do the two differ?

MATERIALS
• colored paper
• table salt
• rock salt
• magnifying glass

WHAT DO YOU THINK?
Salt is a mineral. From your observations of salt, what do you think are some characteristics of minerals?

Minerals have four characteristics.

You use minerals all the time. Every time you turn on a microwave oven or a TV, you depend on minerals. The copper in the wires that carry electricity to the device is a mineral. Table salt, or halite (HAYL-yt), is another mineral that you use in your everyday life.

Minerals have four characteristics. A **mineral** is a substance that

• forms in nature
• is a solid
• has a definite chemical makeup
• has a crystal structure

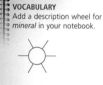

VOCABULARY
Add a description wheel for *mineral* in your notebook.

Chapter 2: **Minerals** 43

Reading Text and Visuals

Study the visuals.

- Read the title.
- Read all labels and captions.
- Figure out what the picture is showing. Notice colors, arrows, and lines.

Minerals in Rocks

Most rocks are made up of minerals.

Quartz

Feldspar

Mica

granite

This piece of granite contains the minerals quartz, feldspar, and mica.

Answer the questions.

Check Your Reading questions will help you remember what you read.

READING TiP

Proportions show relationships between amounts. For example, a quartz crystal always has two oxygen atoms for every silicon atom.

Read one paragraph at a time.

Look for a topic sentence that explains the main idea of the paragraph. Figure out how the details relate to that idea. One paragraph might have several important ideas; you may have to reread to understand.

READING TiP

Molten rock refers to rock that has become so hot that it has melted.

You might think that minerals and rocks are the same things. But a mineral must have the four characteristics listed on page 43. A rock has only two of these characteristics—it is a solid and it forms naturally. A rock usually contains two or more types of minerals.

Two samples of the same type of rock may vary greatly in the amounts of different minerals they contain. Minerals, however, are always made up of the same materials in the same proportions. A ruby is a mineral. Therefore, a ruby found in India has the same makeup as a ruby found in Australia.

CHECK YOUR READING How are minerals different from rocks?

Formed in Nature

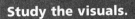 Minerals are formed by natural processes. Every type of mineral can form in nature by processes that do not involve living organisms. As you will read, a few minerals can also be produced by organisms as part of their shells or bones.

Minerals form in many ways. The mineral halite, which is used as table salt, forms when water evaporates in a hot, shallow part of the ocean, leaving behind the salt it contained. Many types of minerals, including the ones in granite, develop when molten rock cools. Talc, a mineral that can be used to make baby powder, forms deep in Earth as high pressure and temperature cause changes in solid rock.

A 44 Unit: **Earth's Surface**

Doing Labs

To understand science, you have to see it in action. Doing labs helps you understand how things really work.

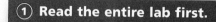

① Read the entire lab first.

② Follow the procedure.

③ Record the data.

CHAPTER INVESTIGATION

Mineral Identification

OVERVIEW AND PURPOSE In this activity, you will observe and perform tests on minerals. Then you will compare your observations to a mineral identification key.

▶ Procedure

1 Make a data table like the one shown in the notebook on the next page.

2 You will examine and identify five minerals. Get a numbered mineral sample from the mineral set. Record the number of your sample in your table.

3 First, observe the sample. Note the color and the luster of the sample. Write your observations in your table. In the row labeled "Luster," write *metallic* if the mineral appears shiny like metal. Write *nonmetallic* if the sample does not look like metal. For example, it may look glassy, pearly, or dull.

step 3

4 Observe the sample through the hand lens. Look to see any signs of how the crystals in the mineral broke. If it appears that the crystals have broken along straight lines, put a check in the row labeled "Cleavage." If it appears that the sample has fractured, put a check in the appropriate row of your table.

step 4

5 **CAUTION: Keep the streak plate on your desktop or table while you are doing the streak test. A broken streak plate can cause serious cuts.** Rub the mineral sample on the streak plate. If the sample does not leave a mark, the mineral is harder than the streak plate. Write *no* in the row labeled "Streak." If the sample does leave a mark on the streak plate, write the color of the streak in that row.

step 5

MATERIALS
- numbered mineral samples
- hand lens
- streak plate
- copper penny
- steel file
- magnet
- dilute hydrochloric acid
- eyedropper
- Mohs scale
- Mineral Identification Key

6 Test each sample for its hardness on the Mohs scale. Try to scratch the sample with each of these items in order: a fingernail, a copper penny, and a steel file. In the Mohs scale, find the hardness number of the object that first scratches the sample. Write in the table that the mineral's hardness value is between that of the hardest item that did not scratch the sample and that of the item that did scratch it.

7 Test the sample with the magnet. If the magnet is attracted to the sample, put a check in the row labeled "Magnetic."

step 7

8 Repeat steps 2 through 7 for each of the other numbered samples.

▶ Observe and Analyze   *Write It Up*

1. **INTERPRET DATA** Use the Mineral Identification Key and the information in your data table to identify your samples. Write the names of the minerals in your table.

2. **COLLECT DATA CAUTION: Before doing the acid test, put on your safety glasses, protective gloves, and lab apron. Acids can cause burns.** If you identified one of the samples as a carbonate mineral, such as calcite, you can check your identification with the acid test. Use the eyedropper to put a few drops of dilute hydrochloric acid on the mineral. If the acid bubbles, the sample is a carbonate.

▶ Conclude   *Write It Up*

1. **COMPARE AND CONTRAST** How are the minerals calcite and halite alike? Which property can you use to test whether a sample is calcite or halite?

2. **INTERPRET** Look at the data in your table. Name any minerals that you could identify on the basis of a single property.

3. **APPLY** Examine a piece of granite rock. On the basis of your examination of granite and your observations of the samples, try to determine what the light-colored, translucent mineral in the granite is and what the flaky, darker mineral is.

▶ INVESTIGATE Further

Specific gravity is another property used to identify minerals. The specific gravity of a mineral is determined by comparing the mineral's density with the density of water.

Find the specific gravity of an unknown mineral chosen from your teacher's samples. Attach your mineral with a string to a spring scale. Record its mass and label this value $M1$. Then suspend the mineral in a beaker of water. Record the measurement of the mineral's mass in water. Label this value $M2$. To determine the mineral's specific gravity, use the following equation:

$$\frac{M1}{M1 - M2} = \text{specific gravity}$$

Do all the other steps to identify the sample. Does the specific gravity you measured match the one listed for that mineral in the identification key?

Mineral Identification

Table 1. Mineral Properties

Property	Sample Number				
	1	2	3	4	5
Color					
Luster					
Cleavage					
Fracture					
Streak					
Hardness					
Magnetic					
Acid test					
Name of mineral					

A 58 Unit: Earth's Surface

Chapter 2: Minerals 59 A

④ Analyze your results.

⑤ Write your lab report.

Using Technology

The Internet is a great source of information about up-to-date science. The ClassZone Website and SciLinks have exciting sites for you to explore. Video clips and simulations can make science come alive.

Look for red banners.

Go to **ClassZone.com** to see simulations, visualizations, resources centers, and content review.

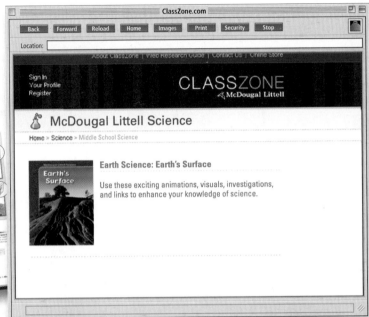

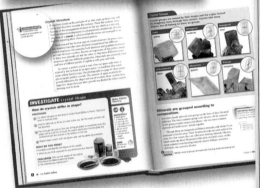

Watch the videos.

See science at work in the **Scientific American Frontiers** video.

Look up SciLinks.

Go to **scilinks.org** to explore the topic.

Atmospheric Pressure and Winds **Code: MDL010**

UNIT A

Earth's Surface

biosphere

sedimentary rock

EROSION

geosphere

Earth's Surface
Contents Overview

Unit Features

1 Views of Earth Today   6

(the **BIG** idea)

Modern technology has changed the
way we view and map Earth.

2 Minerals   40

(the **BIG** idea)

Minerals are basic building
blocks of Earth.

3 Rocks   72

(the **BIG** idea)

Rocks change into other rocks
over time.

4 Weathering and Soil Formation   112

(the **BIG** idea)

Natural forces break rocks apart
and form soil, which supports life.

5 Erosion and Deposition   142

(the **BIG** idea)

Water, wind, and ice shape
Earth's surface.

REMOTE SENSING

Technology high above Earth's surface is giving scientists a whole new look at our planet. This image is of Jasper Ridge, near Palo Alto, California.

SCIENTIFIC AMERICAN FRONTIERS

View the video segment "All That Glitters" to learn how explorers use remote sensing and other methods to find valuable materials.

This research jet aircraft carries instruments to study Earth's land surface, ocean, and atmosphere. It flies at high altitudes, allowing it to collect data and images over large areas during a single flight.

Mapping Earth

You're probably familiar with images of gold prospectors in the Old West. Maybe you've seen them in old movies or read about them in history books. Prospectors wandered through the mountains, looking for signs of ores or gemstones, going here and there in response to rumors or stories, pitching camp in remote canyons on a hunch. People still prospect for minerals today, but they're more likely to fly in airplanes than to ride mules. And stories of fabled mines are just stories and fables. Today's prospectors rely on scientific evidence from remote sensing.

Remote sensing—the use of instruments to gather data from a distance—has two great advantages. The first is that sensors mounted in satellites and airplanes can collect vast amounts of detailed information over large areas. The second is that the sensors can easily collect information about the same area again and again.

For example, scientists use remote sensing to make better and more detailed maps of Earth and to track changes over time. Thanks to remote sensing, scientists now know that Mount Everest, the highest point on Earth, is actually getting higher by about 1 centimeter (0.4 in.) per year. Remote sensors on satellites are also mapping global ocean temperatures and showing how they change over the course of a year.

Uncut diamond

Detecting Minerals from Above

One of the many uses of remote sensing is to find new sources of valuable minerals, such as diamonds. To detect minerals from airplanes or satellites, remote sensors make use of the energy in sunlight. Sunlight reaches Earth as radiation, which travels in the form of waves. All objects absorb some types of radiation and reflect others. The particular wavelengths absorbed or reflected depend upon the materials that make up the objects. Each kind of material has a unique "fingerprint" of the wavelengths it absorbs and the wavelengths it reflects.

When sunlight strikes Earth's surface, some of it is reflected back into the sky. Some of the radiation is absorbed by rocks and other objects and then emitted, or given off, in a different form. Remote sensors in airplanes and satellites collect the reflected and emitted radiation and analyze it to determine which types of rocks and minerals lie on the surface. The remote sensing

Sun

Energy from the Sun reflects at different wavelengths from materials at Earth's surface. Instruments on the jet analyze the reflected energy and map the surface.

systems collect so much data that computer processing and analysis are difficult and expensive. Still, the data are usually clear enough to show the types of minerals located in the regions scanned. However, minerals that are buried cannot be detected by remote sensing from aircraft or satellites. The sensors receive only energy from or near the surface.

SCIENTIFIC AMERICAN FRONTIERS

View the "All that Glitters" segment of your *Scientific American Frontiers* video to see how finding certain common minerals can indicate the presence of a valuable mineral like diamond.

IN THIS SCENE FROM THE VIDEO ▶ a mineral prospector searches for diamonds in a cylinder of rock drilled from beneath Earth's surface.

SEARCHING FOR DIAMONDS People used to think that North America did not have many diamonds. However, northern Canada is geologically similar to the world's major diamond-producing areas:

southern Africa, Russia, and Australia. A few diamond prospectors kept searching, using remote sensing and other techniques. The prospectors looked for more common minerals that form under the same conditions as diamonds. They made maps showing where these minerals were most plentiful and used the maps to search for diamond-rich rock. Once the prospectors realized that the glaciers of the last ice age had moved the minerals, they looked for and found diamonds farther northward. Canada is now a big producer of diamonds.

Remote sensing can show the presence of minerals that occur with diamonds, but people must still use older methods to collect samples for further analysis.

Prospecting for Diamonds

One of the major regions of mineral exploration in which remote sensing is used is in the Northwest Territories of Canada, where the first diamond mine began operating in 1998. The Canada Centre for Remote Sensing has helped develop sensing equipment that can fit easily onto light airplanes and computer equipment to analyze results quickly. The sensing equipment is used to detect certain types of minerals that are often found along with diamonds.

Using remote sensing to locate minerals associated with diamonds or valuable ores is only a beginning. The data cannot show how far the minerals or ores extend underground. Prospectors must still explore the area and take samples. However, remote sensing gives mineral prospectors an excellent idea of where to start looking.

UNANSWERED Questions

As scientists use remote sensing to study Earth's land surface, ocean, and atmosphere, they work to answer new questions.

- Can remote sensing be used to locate sources of iron, platinum, or gold in areas that are difficult to explore on foot?

- How do changes in water temperature at the ocean surface affect long-range weather patterns and the health of ocean organisms?

- How do different types of clouds affect the amount of sunlight reaching Earth's surface and the average temperature of the surface?

UNIT PROJECTS

As you study this unit, work alone or with a group on one of the projects listed below.

Hiker's Guide Video

Like prospectors, wilderness hikers must be able to read maps that show the shape of the land. Prepare a video to teach hikers how to choose hiking and camping areas by reading maps.

- Obtain a topographic map of a wilderness area in a national or state park.

- Write a script outlining what you will teach and how you will videotape it.

- Present your video and display the maps you used.

Diamond Mine Model

Diamonds can be carried toward Earth's surface by kimberlite pipes. Show how diamonds are mined from kimberlite.

- Build a model of a diamond-mine tunnel that passes through kimberlite.

- Present your model to your class. Explain the relationship between kimberlite and diamonds.

Glacier Photo Essay

Make a photo essay showing how glaciers reshape Earth's surface as they move and melt.

- Find images of areas that are or have been affected by glaciers. Write captions for them.

- Present the images as a photo essay on a poster or in a portfolio.

 **CAREER CENTER**
CLASSZONE.COM

Learn more about careers in mineralogy.

Views of Earth Today

the BIG idea

Modern technology has changed the way we view and map Earth.

Key Concepts

SECTION
1.1 Technology is used to explore the Earth system.
Learn how technology has changed people's view of Earth.

SECTION
1.2 Maps and globes are models of Earth.
Learn how to locate any place on Earth and how Earth's sphere is portrayed on flat maps.

SECTION
1.3 Topographic maps show the shape of the land.
Learn about representing the features of Earth's surface on flat maps.

SECTION
1.4 Technology is used to map Earth.
Learn how satellites and computers are used to provide more detailed maps of Earth.

Internet Preview

CLASSZONE.COM

Chapter 1 online resources: Content Review, Simulation, Visualization, three Resource Centers, Math Tutorial, and Test Practice

What do all these views show about Earth?

Swirling clouds over North and South America: NASA Terra satellite data

Warm and cool ocean-surface temperatures: NASA satellite image

Chlorophyll levels (green) on land and sea: SeaStar spacecraft image

Earth's rocky surface without the oceans: NASA satellite data

Earth's Changing Surface

Go outside and find evidence of how wind, water, or living things change the surface of Earth. You might look in alley-ways, parks, wooded areas, or backyards. For example, you might find a path worn through a grassy area near a parking lot.

Observe and Think What changes do you observe? What do you think caused the changes?

Using Modern Maps

Find a map of a city, a bus or rail system, or a state. Study the names, colors, and symbols on the map and any features of interest.

Observe and Think Which direction on the map is north? What do the symbols mean? How do you measure the distance from one point to another?

Internet Activity: Mapping

Go to **ClassZone.com** to learn more about mapping Earth from space. Find out about a NASA mission to develop the most accurate map of Earth ever made.

Observe and Think Why do you think scientists need different maps produced from satellite data?

NSTA
scilinks.org
SCiLINKS

Earth's Spheres **Code: MDL013**

Getting Ready to Learn

CONCEPT REVIEW

- Earth, like all planets, is shaped roughly like a sphere.
- Earth supports a complex web of life.
- The planet consists of many parts that interact with one another.

VOCABULARY REVIEW

See Glossary for definitions.

energy

matter

planet

satellite

 **CONTENT REVIEW**
CLASSZONE.COM
Review concepts and vocabulary.

TAKING NOTES

MAIN IDEA AND DETAIL NOTES

Make a two-column chart. Write the main ideas, such as those in the blue headings, in the column on the left. Write details about each of those main ideas in the column on the right.

VOCABULARY STRATEGY

Draw a **word triangle** diagram for each new vocabulary term. On the bottom line write and define the term. Above that, write a sentence that uses the term correctly. At the top, draw a picture to show what the term looks like.

See the Note-Taking Handbook on pages R45–R51.

SCIENCE NOTEBOOK

MAIN IDEAS	DETAIL NOTES
1. The Earth system has four main parts.	1. Atmosphere = mixture of gases surrounding Earth 1. Hydrosphere = all waters on Earth

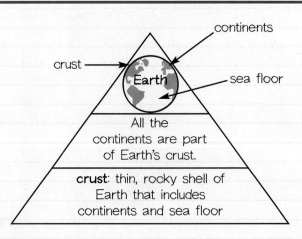

All the continents are part of Earth's crust.

crust: thin, rocky shell of Earth that includes continents and sea floor

Technology is used to explore the Earth system.

 BEFORE, you learned

- Earth has a spherical shape and supports a complex web of life
- Earth's environment is a system with many parts

NOW, you will learn

- About the Earth system and its four major parts
- How technology is used to explore the Earth system
- How the parts of the Earth system shape the surface

VOCABULARY

system p. 9
atmosphere p. 10
hydrosphere p. 10
biosphere p. 11
geosphere p. 12

THINK ABOUT

How do these parts work together?

Look closely at this terrarium. Notice that the bowl and its cover form a boundary between the terrarium and the outside world. What might happen to the entire terrarium if any part were taken away? What might happen if you placed the terrarium in a dark closet?

VOCABULARY
Remember to draw a word triangle in your notebook for each vocabulary term.

The Earth system has four major parts.

A terrarium is a simple example of a **system** —an organized group of parts that work together to form a whole. To understand a system, you need to see how all its parts work together. This principle is true for a small terrarium, and it is true for planet Earth.

Both a terrarium and Earth are closed systems. They are closed because matter, such as soil or water, cannot enter or leave. However, energy can flow into or out of the system. Just as light and heat pass through the glass of the terrarium, sunlight and heat enter and leave the Earth system through the atmosphere.

Within the Earth system are four connected parts: the atmosphere (Earth's air), the hydrosphere (Earth's waters), the biosphere (Earth's living things), and the geosphere (Earth's interior and its rocks and soils). Each of these parts is an open system because both matter and energy move into and out of it. The four open systems work together to form one large, closed system called Earth.

Atmosphere

READING TiP

The names of the Earth system's four parts contain Greek prefixes. *Atmo-* refers to vapor or gas. *Hydro-* refers to water. *Bio-* refers to life, and *geo-* refers to earth.

The **atmosphere** (AT-muh-SFEER) is the mixture of gases and particles that surrounds and protects the surface of Earth. The most abundant gases are nitrogen (about 78%) and oxygen (nearly 21%). The atmosphere also contains carbon dioxide, water vapor, and a few other gases.

Before the 1800s, all studies of the atmosphere had to be done from the ground. Today, scientists launch weather balloons, fly specially equipped planes, and view the atmosphere in satellite images. The data they collect show that the atmosphere interacts with the other parts of the Earth system to form complex weather patterns that circulate around Earth. The more scientists learn about these patterns, the more accurately they can predict local weather.

Hydrosphere

The **hydrosphere** (HY-druh-SFEER) is made up of all the water on Earth in oceans, lakes, glaciers, rivers, and streams and underground. Water covers nearly three-quarters of Earth's surface. Only about 3 percent of the hydrosphere is fresh water. Nearly 70 percent of Earth's fresh water is frozen in glaciers and polar ice caps.

Parts of the Earth System

Atmosphere

Over 400 cones make this weather balloon more stable as it gathers data about the atmosphere.

Hydrosphere

Scientists need special diving equipment to study Earth's oceans.

In the past 50 years, scientists have used deep-sea vehicles, special buoys, satellite images, and diving suits, such as the one shown on page 10, to study the world's oceans. They have discovered that the oceans contain several layers of cold and warm water. As these layers circulate, they form cold and warm ocean currents. The currents interact with wind patterns in the atmosphere and affect Earth's weather.

 CHECK YOUR READING How does the hydrosphere affect the atmosphere?

Biosphere

The **biosphere** (BY-uh-SFEER) includes all life on Earth, in the air, on the land, and in the waters. The biosphere can be studied with a variety of technologies. For example, satellite photos are used to track yearly changes in Earth's plant and animal life. As the photograph below shows, special equipment allows scientists to study complex environments, such as rain forests, without damaging them.

Scientists have learned a lot about how the biosphere interacts with the other parts of the Earth system. For example, large forests act as Earth's "lungs," absorbing carbon dioxide and releasing oxygen into the atmosphere. When dead trees decay, they return nutrients to the soil.

 CHECK YOUR READING Name one way the biosphere and the atmosphere interact.

MAIN IDEA AND DETAILS As you read this section, use this strategy to take notes.

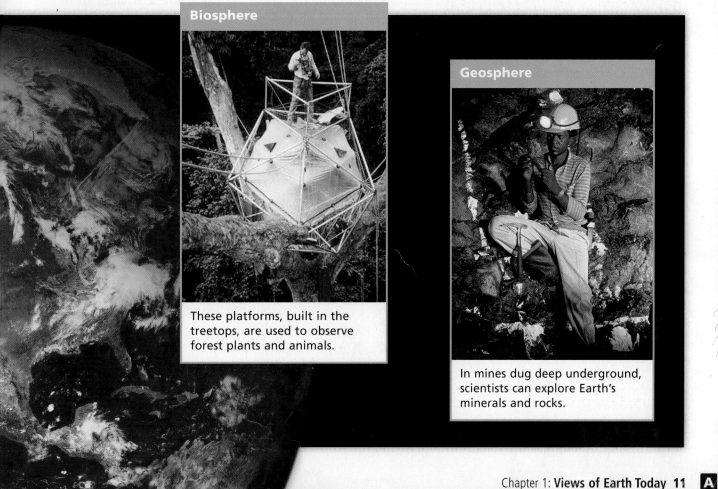

Biosphere

These platforms, built in the treetops, are used to observe forest plants and animals.

Geosphere

In mines dug deep underground, scientists can explore Earth's minerals and rocks.

Geosphere

The **geosphere** (JEE-uh-SFEER) includes all the features on Earth's surface—the continents, islands, and sea floor—and everything below the surface. As the diagram illustrates, the geosphere is made up of several layers: crust, mantle, and outer and inner core.

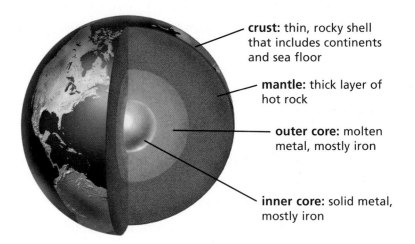

crust: thin, rocky shell that includes continents and sea floor

mantle: thick layer of hot rock

outer core: molten metal, mostly iron

inner core: solid metal, mostly iron

People have studied the surface of the geosphere for centuries. Not until the 1900s, however, were people able to study Earth from space or to explore deep within the planet. Today, scientists use satellite images, sound waves, and computer modeling to develop accurate pictures of features on and below Earth's surface. These images show that Earth constantly changes. Some changes are sudden—a volcano explodes, releasing harmful gases and dust into the air. Other changes, such as the birth of new islands, happen over millions of years.

CHECK YOUR READING Give an example of matter moving from the geosphere to the atmosphere.

Earth's continents have many unique landforms such as these rock towers in Cathedral Valley, Utah.

INVESTIGATE Geosphere's Layers

How can you model the geosphere's layers?

PROCEDURE

1. To model the layers of the geosphere, you will be using a quarter of an apple that your teacher has cut. Note: NEVER eat food in the science classroom.

2. Hold the apple slice and observe it carefully. Compare it with the diagram of the geosphere's layers on page 12.

3. Draw a diagram of the apple and label it with the names of the layers of the geosphere.

WHAT DO YOU THINK?

- What are the four parts of the apple slice?
- What major layer of the geosphere does each part of the apple resemble?

CHALLENGE What other object do you think would make a good model of the geosphere's layers? What model could you build or make yourself?

SKILL FOCUS
Modeling

MATERIALS
apple slice

TIME
15 minutes

All four parts of the Earth system shape the planet's surface.

Earth's surface is worn away, built up, and reshaped every day by the atmosphere, the hydrosphere, the biosphere, and the geosphere. Here are some of the ways they affect the surface.

Atmosphere and Hydrosphere Not even the hardest stone can withstand wind and water. Over millions of years, rain, wind, and flowing water carve huge formations such as the Grand Canyon in Arizona or the rock towers of Utah, shown on page 12.

Geosphere Landmasses pushing together have set off earthquakes and formed volcanoes and mountain ranges around the world.

Biosphere Plants, animals, and human beings have also changed Earth's surface. For instance, earthworms help make soils more fertile. And throughout human history, people have dammed rivers and cleared forests for farmland.

You are part of this process, too. Every time you walk or ride a bike across open land, you are changing Earth's surface. Your feet or the bike's tires dig into the dirt, wearing away plants and exposing soil to sunlight, wind, and water. If you take the same route every day, over time you will wear a path in the land.

READING TiP

Landmass is a compound word made up of the words *land* and *mass*. Landmass means "a large area of land."

Chapter 1: **Views of Earth Today** 13

Mudslide in California

Atmosphere and Hydrosphere Heavy winter rains soak the ground until it cannot absorb any more water.

Biosphere People who build on fragile hillsides remove plants whose roots help hold the soil in place.

Geosphere With nothing to hold the water-soaked ground, it slides downhill, leaving a deep trench.

The photograph above shows a good example of how the four parts can suddenly change Earth's surface. A mudslide like this one can happen in a matter of minutes. Sometimes the side of a mountain may collapse, becoming a river of mud that can bury an entire town.

The four parts of the Earth system continue to shape the surface with every passing year. Scientists will continue to record these changes to update maps and other images of the planet's complex system.

CHECK YOUR READING Find three examples on pages 13 and 14 that show how the parts of the Earth system shape the planet's surface.

1.1 Review

KEY CONCEPTS

1. Define *system.* Compare an open and a closed system.

2. Name the four parts of the Earth system. List one fact about each part that scientists learned through modern technology.

3. Give two examples of how the Earth system's four parts can interact with each other.

CRITICAL THINKING

4. **Apply** One day you see that plants are dying in the class terrarium. What part might be missing from its system?

5. **Infer** You visit a state park and see a thin rock wall with a hole, like a window, worn through it. Which of the four parts of the Earth system might have made the hole? Explain.

◆ CHALLENGE

6. **Predict** Imagine that a meteorite 200 meters wide strikes Earth, landing in a wooded area. Describe one way that this event would affect the biosphere or the geosphere. **Hint:** A meteorite is traveling several thousand kilometers per hour when it strikes the ground.

1.2 Maps and globes are models of Earth.

◀ **BEFORE**, you learned

- The Earth system has four main parts: atmosphere, hydrosphere, biosphere, and geosphere
- Technology is used to study and map the Earth system
- The Earth system's parts interact to shape Earth's surface

▶ **NOW**, you will learn

- What information maps can provide about natural and human-made features
- How to find exact locations on Earth
- Why all maps distort Earth's surface

VOCABULARY

relief map p. 16
map scale p. 17
map legend p. 17
equator p. 18
latitude p. 18
prime meridian p. 19
longitude p. 19
projection p. 20

EXPLORE Mapping

What makes a good map?

PROCEDURE

① Draw a map to guide someone from your school to your home or to a point of interest, such as a park, statue, or store, near your school.

② Trade maps with a classmate. Is his or her map easy to understand? Why or why not?

③ Use feedback from your partner to revise your own map.

WHAT DO YOU THINK?
What visual clues make a map easy to understand and use?

MATERIALS
- paper
- pencil or pen

Maps show natural and human-made features.

Have you ever drawn a map to help someone get to your home? If so, your map is actually a rough model of your neighborhood, showing important streets and landmarks. Any map you use is a flat model of Earth's surface, showing Earth's features as seen from above.

On the other hand, a globe represents Earth as if you were looking at it from outer space. A globe is a sphere that shows the relative sizes and shapes of Earth's land features and waters.

In this section you will learn how maps and globes provide different types of information about Earth's surface. They can show everything from city streets to land features to the entire world.

 How are maps and globes alike? How are they different?

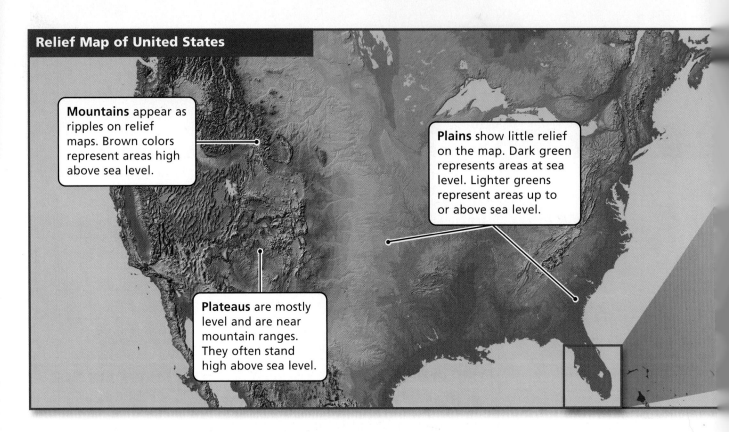

Relief Map of United States

Mountains appear as ripples on relief maps. Brown colors represent areas high above sea level.

Plains show little relief on the map. Dark green represents areas at sea level. Lighter greens represent areas up to or above sea level.

Plateaus are mostly level and are near mountain ranges. They often stand high above sea level.

Land Features on Maps

When scientists or travelers want to know what the landscape of an area actually looks like, they will often use a relief map. A **relief map,** such as the one above, shows how high or low each feature is on Earth. A mapmaker uses photographs or satellite images to build a three-dimensional view of Earth's surface. A relief map shows three main types of land features: mountains, plains, and plateaus.

Mountains stand higher than the land around them. A mountain's base may cover several square kilometers. A group of mountains is called a mountain range. Mountain ranges connected in a long chain form a mountain belt. The Rocky Mountains in the United States are part of a huge mountain belt that includes the Canadian Rockies and the Andes Mountains in South America.

Plateaus have fairly level surfaces but stand high above sea level. Plateaus are often found near large mountain ranges. In the United States, the Colorado Plateau is about 3350 meters (11,000 ft) above sea level. This plateau includes parts of Arizona, Colorado, New Mexico, and Utah.

Plains are gently rolling or flat features. The United States has two types of plains—coastal plains near the eastern and southeastern shores, and interior plains in the center of the nation. The interior Great Plains cover the middle third of the United States.

 CHECK YOUR READING How is a plateau different from either a mountain or a plain?

Southern Florida

Sanford
Spring Hill
Dade City
Orlando
Kissimmee
Melbourne
Clearwater
Winter Haven
St. Petersburg
Tampa
Vero Beach
Bradenton
Sarasota
Arcadia
Fort Pierce
Port St. Lucie
Stuart
Jupiter
Port Charlotte
Pahokee
West Palm Beach
Gulf of Mexico
Fort Myers
Cape Coral
Lake Okeechobee
Coral Springs
Naples
Marco Island
Hollywood
Fort Lauderdale
Coral Gables
Homestead
Miami Beach
Miami

ATLANTIC OCEAN

N W E S

Key Largo
Florida Keys
Islamorada
Marathon
Key West

0   25   50 miles
0   25   50 kilometers

Interstate highway
U.S. highway
State highway

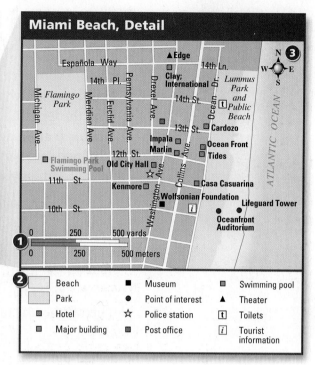

Miami Beach, Detail

Española Way
Edge
14th Ln.
14th Pl.
Clay; International
14th St.
Flamingo Park
Lummus Park and Public Beach
Michigan Ave.
Meridian Ave.
Euclid Ave.
Pennsylvania Ave.
Drexel Ave.
Ocean
13th St.
Cardozo
Impala
Marlin
Ocean Front
Tides
12th St.
Flamingo Park Swimming Pool
Old City Hall
Casa Casuarina
11th St.
Kenmore
Collins Ave.
Washington Ave.
Wolfsonian Foundation
Lifeguard Tower
10th St.
Oceanfront Auditorium

ATLANTIC OCEAN

N W E S

0   250   500 yards
0   250   500 meters

Beach	Museum	Swimming pool
Park	Point of interest	Theater
Hotel	Police station	Toilets
Major building	Post office	Tourist information

Scale and Symbols on Maps

The maps most people use are road and city maps like the ones above. These maps provide information about human-made features as well as some natural features. To use these maps, you need to know how to read a map scale and a map legend, or key.

① A **map scale** relates distances on a map to actual distances on Earth's surface. Notice that on the map of southern Florida above, the scale is in kilometers and miles. On the Miami Beach map, the scale is in meters and yards. The smaller the area a map shows, the more detail it includes.

The scale can be expressed as a ratio, a bar, or equivalent units of distance. For example, a ratio of 1:25,000 means that 1 centimeter on the map represents 25,000 centimeters (0.25 kilometer) on Earth.

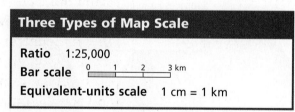

Three Types of Map Scale

Ratio	1:25,000
Bar scale	0 1 2 3 km
Equivalent-units scale	1 cm = 1 km

② A **map legend,** also called a key, is a chart that explains the meaning of each symbol used on a map. Symbols can stand for highways, parks, and other features. The legend on the Miami Beach map shows major points of interest for tourists.

③ A map usually includes a compass rose to show which directions are north, south, east, and west. In general, north on a map points to the top of the page.

What information do map scales and map legends provide?

READING TiP

As used here, *legend* does not refer to a story. It is based on the Latin word *legenda,* which means "to be read."

VISUALIZATION
CLASSZONE.COM

Explore how latitude
and longitude help
you find locations on
Earth's surface.

Latitude and longitude show locations on Earth.

Suppose you were lucky enough to find dinosaur bones in the desert. Would you know how to find that exact spot again? You would if you knew the longitude and latitude of the place. Latitude and longitude lines form an imaginary grid over the entire surface of Earth. This grid provides everyone with the same tools for navigation. Using latitude and longitude, you can locate any place on the planet.

Latitude

READING TiP

Hemi- is a Greek prefix meaning "half."

Latitude is based on an imaginary line that circles Earth halfway between the north and south poles. This line is called the **equator,** and it divides Earth into northern and southern hemispheres. A hemisphere is one half of a sphere.

Latitude is a distance in degrees north or south of the equator, which is 0°. A degree is 1/360 of the distance around a full circle. If you start at one point on the equator and travel all the way around the world back to that point, you have traveled 360 degrees.

The illustration below shows that latitude lines are parallel to the equator and are evenly spaced between the equator and the poles. Also, latitude lines are always labeled north or south of the equator to

Latitude and Longitude

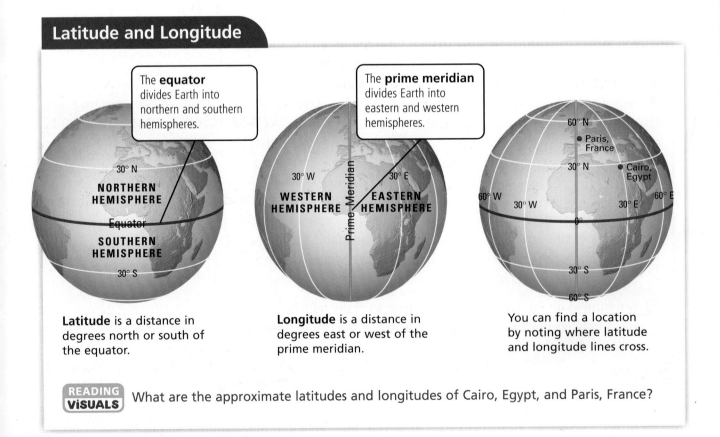

The **equator** divides Earth into northern and southern hemispheres.

The **prime meridian** divides Earth into eastern and western hemispheres.

Latitude is a distance in degrees north or south of the equator.

Longitude is a distance in degrees east or west of the prime meridian.

You can find a location by noting where latitude and longitude lines cross.

READING VISUALS What are the approximate latitudes and longitudes of Cairo, Egypt, and Paris, France?

show whether a location is in the northern or southern hemisphere. For instance, the North Pole is 90° north, or 90°N, while the South Pole is 90° south, or 90°S. Latitude, however, is only half of what you need to locate any spot on Earth. You also need to know its longitude.

Longitude

Longitude is based on an imaginary line that stretches from the North Pole through Greenwich, England, to the South Pole. This line is called the **prime meridian.** Any place up to 180° west of the prime meridian is in the Western Hemisphere. Any place up to 180° east of the prime meridian is in the Eastern Hemisphere.

Longitude is a distance in degrees east or west of the prime meridian, which is 0°. Beginning at the prime meridian, longitude lines are numbered 0° to 180° west and 0° to 180° east.

Longitude lines are labeled east or west to indicate whether a location is in the eastern or western hemisphere. For example, the longitude of Washington, D.C., is about 78° west, or 78°W. The city of Hamburg, Germany, is about 10° east, or 10°E. If you understand latitude and longitude, you can find any spot on Earth's surface.

 CHECK YOUR READING Why do all cities in the United States have a north latitude and a west longitude?

READING TiP
There is an easy way to remember the difference between latitude and longitude. Think of longitude lines as the "long" lines that go from pole to pole.

Global Positioning System

The Global Positioning System (GPS) is a network of satellites that are used to find the latitude, longitude, and elevation, or height above sea level, of any site. Twenty-four GPS satellites circle Earth and send signals that are picked up by receivers on the surface. At least three satellites need to be above the horizon for GPS to work. A computer inside a receiver uses the satellite signals to calculate the user's exact location—latitude, longitude, and elevation. GPS is an accurate, easy method for finding location.

GPS devices are used by many people, including pilots, sailors, hikers, and map makers. Some cars now have GPS receivers and digital road maps stored in their computers. A driver types in an address, and the car's computer finds the best way to get there.

 CHECK YOUR READING Explain how GPS can help someone find their exact location.

Never be lost again. This hiker turns on his GPS unit to find out his current latitude and longitude. He then locates these data on his map to pinpoint his exact location.

Map projections distort the view of Earth's surface.

The most accurate way to show Earth's surface is on a globe. A globe, however, cannot show much detail, and it is awkward to carry. People use flat maps for their detail and convenience. A **projection** is a way of representing Earth's curved surface on a flat map. Mapmakers use different types of projections, all of which distort, or misrepresent, Earth's surface in different ways.

Cylindrical Projection

The Mercator projection shows Earth as if the map were a large cylinder wrapped around the planet. The outlines of the landmasses and seas are then drawn onto the map. As shown in the diagram on page 21, the cylinder is unrolled to form a flat map. Latitude and longitude appear as straight lines, forming a grid of rectangles.

The Mercator projection is useful for navigating at sea or in the air. It shows the entire world, except for regions near the poles, on one map. Sailors and pilots can draw a straight line from one point to

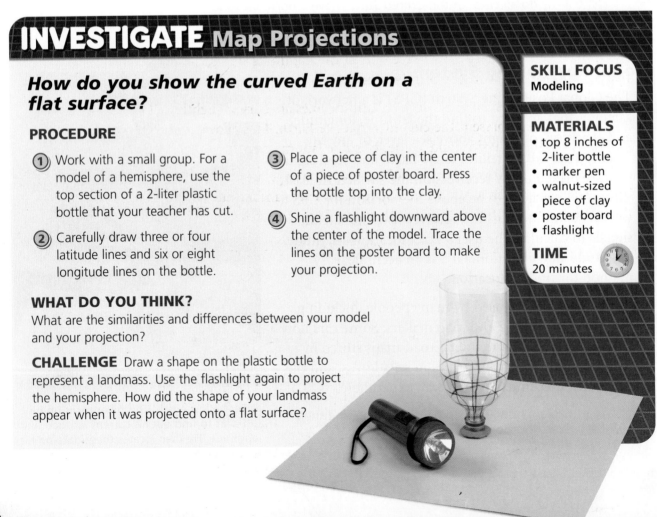

INVESTIGATE Map Projections

How do you show the curved Earth on a flat surface?

PROCEDURE

1. Work with a small group. For a model of a hemisphere, use the top section of a 2-liter plastic bottle that your teacher has cut.

2. Carefully draw three or four latitude lines and six or eight longitude lines on the bottle.

3. Place a piece of clay in the center of a piece of poster board. Press the bottle top into the clay.

4. Shine a flashlight downward above the center of the model. Trace the lines on the poster board to make your projection.

WHAT DO YOU THINK?

What are the similarities and differences between your model and your projection?

CHALLENGE Draw a shape on the plastic bottle to represent a landmass. Use the flashlight again to project the hemisphere. How did the shape of your landmass appear when it was projected onto a flat surface?

SKILL FOCUS
Modeling

MATERIALS
- top 8 inches of 2-liter bottle
- marker pen
- walnut-sized piece of clay
- poster board
- flashlight

TIME
20 minutes

another to plot a course. The problem with Mercator maps is that areas far away from the equator appear much larger than they really are. On the map below, Greenland looks bigger than South America. In reality, South America is about eight times larger than Greenland.

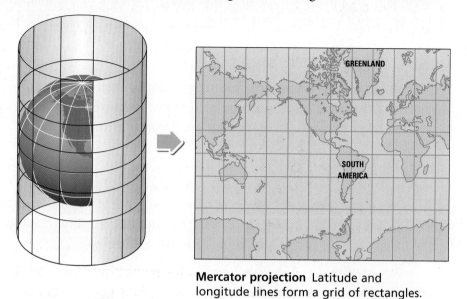

Mercator projection Latitude and longitude lines form a grid of rectangles. Areas away from the equator are distorted.

Conic Projections

Conic projections are based on the shape of a cone. The diagram below shows how a cone of paper might be wrapped around the globe. The paper touches the surface only at the middle latitudes, halfway between the equator and the North Pole.

When the cone is flattened out, the latitude lines are curved slightly. The curved lines represent the curved surface of Earth. This allows the map to show the true sizes and shapes of some landmasses.

Conic projections are most useful for mapping large areas in the middle latitudes, such as the United States. However, landmasses near the equator or near the north or south pole will be distorted.

CHECK YOUR READING What are the main uses of Mercator and conic projections?

Conic projection Latitude lines are slightly curved. Only mid-latitude areas are the correct size and shape.

Planar Projections

Planar projections were developed to help people find the shortest distance between two points. They are drawn as if a circle of paper were laid on a point on Earth's surface. As you look at the diagram below, notice how the shape of the sphere is transferred to the flat map. When a planar map represents the polar region, the longitude lines meet at the center like the spokes of a wheel.

A planar map is good for plotting ocean or air voyages and for showing the north and south polar regions. However, landmasses farther away from the center point are greatly distorted.

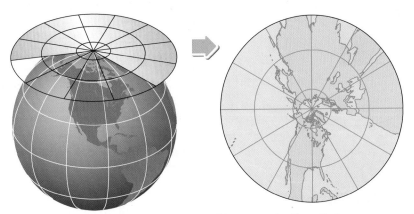

Planar projection Only areas near the center point are the correct size and shape.

The Mercator, conic, and planar projections are all attempts to solve the problem of representing a curved surface on a flat map. Each projection can show certain areas of the world accurately but distorts other areas.

 CHECK YOUR READING What areas does the planar projection show accurately?

1.2 Review

KEY CONCEPTS

1. What natural and human-made features can maps show? Give two examples of each.

2. Explain how latitude and longitude can help you locate any place on Earth.

3. Why do all flat maps distort Earth's surface?

CRITICAL THINKING

4. **Provide Examples** Imagine that your family is on a long car trip. What symbols on a road map would you pay the most attention to? Explain.

5. **Apply** Use a world map to find the approximate latitudes and longitudes of Moscow, Russia; Tokyo, Japan; Denver, Colorado; and La Paz, Bolivia.

◗ CHALLENGE

6. **Apply** Working with a partner or with a small group, select the shortest airline route from Chicago to London, using a globe and a Mercator map. Hint: Notice that as you go farther north on the globe, the longitude lines become closer together.

MATH in SCIENCE

MATH TUTORIAL
CLASSZONE.COM
Click on Math Tutorial for more help with solving proportions.

How Far Is It?

A science class is visiting Chicago and is using the map on the left to walk to the lakefront museums. Remember, a map scale shows how distances on the map compare to actual distances on the ground.

Buckingham Fountain

Example

In this case, the map scale indicates that 1 centimeter on the map represents 300 meters on the ground. The map scale shows this as equivalent units. By using these units to write a proportion, you can use cross products to determine actual distances.

What distance does 3 cm on the map represent? Set up the problem like this:

$$\frac{1 \text{ cm}}{300 \text{ m}} = \frac{3 \text{ cm}}{x}$$

(1) $1 \text{ cm} \cdot x = 3 \text{ cm} \cdot 300 \text{ m}$

(2) $\qquad x = 3 \cdot 300 \text{ m}$

(3) $\qquad x = 900 \text{ m}$

ANSWER 3 centimeters on the map represents 900 meters on the ground.

Use cross products and a metric ruler to answer the following questions.

1. The science class divides into two groups. Each group starts at Buckingham Fountain. How far, in meters, will one group walk to get to the Adler Planetarium if they follow the red dotted line?

2. How far, in meters, will the other group walk to get to the end of Navy Pier if they follow the blue dotted line?

3. The group that walked to Adler decides to take a boat to join the other group at Navy Pier. How far, in meters, is their boat ride along the red dotted line?

CHALLENGE What is the total distance, in kilometers, that the two groups traveled? Set up the problem as a proportion. **Hint:** There are 1000 meters in a kilometer.

0   150   300 meters

1 cm = 300 m

1.3 Topographic maps show the shape of the land.

BEFORE, you learned

- Different maps provide information about natural and human-made features
- Latitude and longitude are used to find places on Earth
- All flat maps distort Earth's surface

NOW, you will learn

- How contour lines show elevation, slope, and relief
- What rules contour lines follow
- What common symbols are used on topographic maps

VOCABULARY

topography p. 24
contour line p. 25
elevation p. 25
slope p. 25
relief p. 25
contour interval p. 26

EXPLORE Topographic Maps

How can you map your knuckles?

PROCEDURE

1. Hold your fist closed, knuckles up, as shown in the photo.

2. Draw circles around the first knuckle. Make sure the circles are the same distance from each other.

3. Flatten out your hand. Observe what happens. Write down your observations.

WHAT DO YOU THINK?

- How does the height of your knuckles change when you clench your fist, then flatten out your hand?
- What do you think the circles represent?

MATERIAL
washable colored pen

Topographic maps use contour lines to show features.

VOCABULARY
Add a word triangle for *topography* to your notebook.

Imagine you are on vacation with your family in a national park. You have a simple trail map that shows you where to hike. But the map does not tell you anything about what the land looks like. Will you have to cross any rivers or valleys? How far uphill or downhill will you have to hike?

To answer these questions, you need to know something about the topography of the area. **Topography** is the shape, or features, of the land. These features can be natural—such as mountains, plateaus, and plains—or human-made—such as dams and roads. To show the topography of an area, mapmakers draw a topographic map.

A topographic map is a flat map that uses lines to show Earth's surface features. Distance and elevation can be given in feet or meters. Take a look at the topographic map of Mount Hood on this page. The wiggly lines on the map are called **contour lines,** and they show an area's elevation, slope, and relief.

1 The **elevation** of a place is how high above sea level it is. An area can range from a few meters to several thousand meters above sea level. The numbers on the contour lines show the elevations of different points in the Mount Hood area.

2 The **slope** of a landform or area is how steep it is. The more gradual the slope, the farther apart the contour lines on the map. The steeper the slope, the closer together the contour lines.

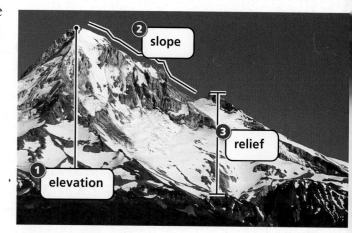

3 The **relief** of an area is the difference between its high and low points. For example, subtracting the lowest elevation on the map from the highest gives you a measure of the area's relief.

 CHECK YOUR READING What is the difference between elevation and slope?

Mount Hood Topographic Map

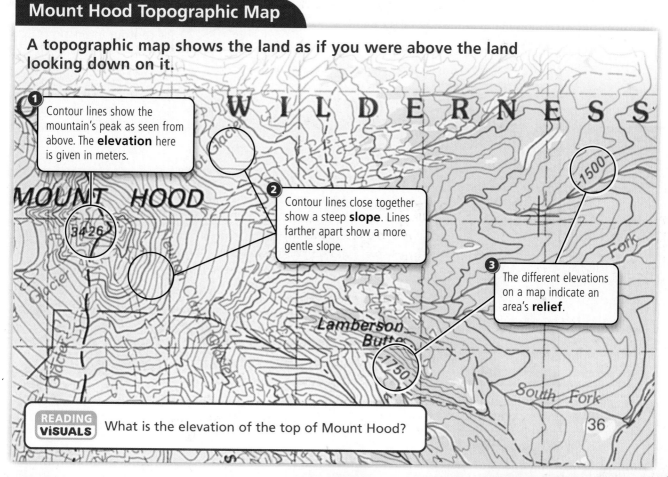

A topographic map shows the land as if you were above the land looking down on it.

1 Contour lines show the mountain's peak as seen from above. The **elevation** here is given in meters.

2 Contour lines close together show a steep **slope**. Lines farther apart show a more gentle slope.

3 The different elevations on a map indicate an area's **relief**.

WILDERNESS

MOUNT HOOD

3426

1500

Fork

Lamberson Butte

1750

South Fork

READING VISUALS What is the elevation of the top of Mount Hood?

36

Contour lines follow certain rules.

MAIN IDEA AND DETAILS
Use your main idea and details chart to take notes on the rules for reading a topographic map.

Contour lines on topographic maps can help you visualize landforms. Think of the following statements as rules for reading such maps:

- **Lines never cross.** Contour lines never cross, because each line represents an exact elevation.

- **Circles show highest and lowest points.** Contour lines form closed circles around mountaintops, hilltops, and the centers of depressions, which are sunken areas in the ground. Sometimes, the elevation of a mountain or hill is written in meters or feet in the middle of the circle.

- **Contour interval is always the same on a map.** The **contour interval** is the difference in elevation from one contour line to the next. For example, the contour interval on the map below is 10 feet. This means that the change in elevation between contour lines is always 10 feet. The contour interval can differ from map to map, but it is always the same on a particular map.

Ely, Minnesota, Topographic Map

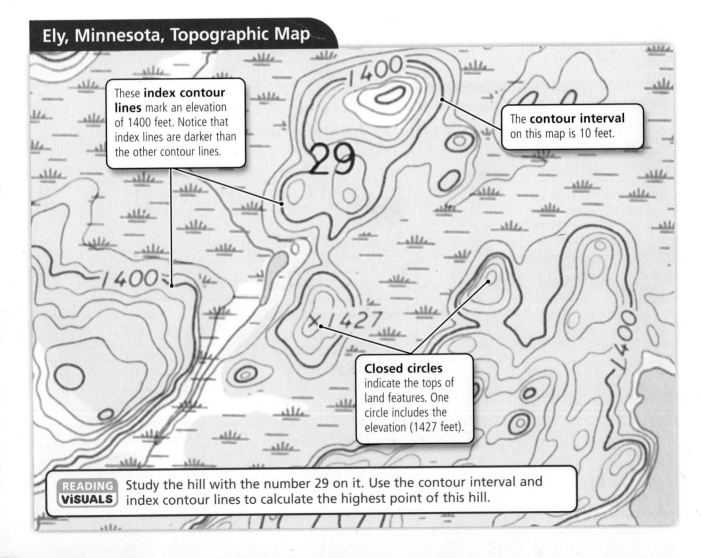

These **index contour lines** mark an elevation of 1400 feet. Notice that index lines are darker than the other contour lines.

The **contour interval** on this map is 10 feet.

Closed circles indicate the tops of land features. One circle includes the elevation (1427 feet).

READING VISUALS Study the hill with the number 29 on it. Use the contour interval and index contour lines to calculate the highest point of this hill.

- **Index contour lines mark elevations.** The darker contour lines on a map are called index contour lines. Numbers that indicate elevations are often written on these lines. To calculate higher or lower elevations, simply count the number of lines above or below an index line. Then multiply that number by the contour interval. For instance, on the Ely map, one index line marks 1400 feet. To find the elevation of a point three lines up from this index line, you would multiply 10 feet (the contour interval) by 3. Add the result, 30, to 1400. The point's elevation is 1430 feet.

Discover the relationship between topographic maps and surface features.

CHECK YOUR READING What information do index contour lines provide?

Besides contour lines, topographic maps also contain symbols for natural and human-made features. Below are some common map symbols that the United States Geological Survey (USGS) uses on its topographic maps.

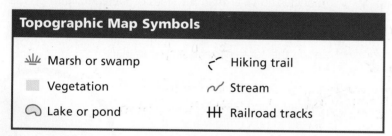

Topographic Map Symbols

ⱱⱳ	Marsh or swamp	↰	Hiking trail
▨	Vegetation	⌁	Stream
◠	Lake or pond	⊬⊬	Railroad tracks

The USGS provides topographic maps for nearly every part of the United States. These maps cover urban, rural, and wilderness areas. Hikers and campers are not the only ones who use topographic maps. Engineers, archaeologists, forest rangers, biologists, and others rely on them as well.

1.3 Review

KEY CONCEPTS

1. How do contour lines show elevation, slope, and relief?

2. Why do contour lines never cross on a topographic map?

3. How would you show the top of a hill, an area of vegetation, or a hiking trail on a topographic map?

CRITICAL THINKING

4. **Apply** For an area with gently sloping hills and little relief, would you draw contour lines close together or far apart? Explain why.

5. **Compare and Contrast** How would a road map and a topographic map of the same area differ? What information would each provide?

CHALLENGE

6. **Synthesize** Work with a group to make a topographic map of the area around your school. First decide how big an area you will include. Then choose a contour interval, a map scale, and symbols for buildings, sports fields, and other features. Let other students test the map's accuracy.

CHAPTER INVESTIGATION

Bright Lake 1391

Investigate Topographic Maps

OVERVIEW AND PURPOSE Topographic maps show the shape of the land. In this lab you will use what you have learned about how Earth's three-dimensional surface is represented on maps to
- make a terrain model out of clay
- produce a topographic map of the model

▶ Procedure

1. Build a simple landscape about 6–8 cm high from modeling clay. Include a variety of land features. Make sure your model is no taller than the sides of the container.

2. Place your model into the container. Stand a ruler upright inside the container and tape it in place.

3. Lay the clear plastic sheet over the container and tape it on one side like a hinge. Carefully trace the outline of your clay model.

   step 3

4. Add 2 cm of colored water to the container.

5. Insert spaghetti sticks into the model all around the waterline. Place the sticks about 3 cm apart. Make sure the sticks are vertical and are no taller than the sides of the container.

6. Lower the plastic sheet back over the container. Looking straight down on the container, make a dot on the sheet wherever you see a spaghetti stick. Connect the dots to trace the contour line accurately onto your map.

7. Continue adding water, 2 cm at a time. Each time you add water, insert the sticks into the model at the waterline and repeat step 6. Continue until the model landscape is underwater. Carefully drain the water when finished.

MATERIALS
- half-gallon cardboard juice container
- scissors
- modeling clay
- clear plastic sheet (transparency or sheet protector)
- cellophane tape
- ruler
- water
- food coloring
- box of spaghetti
- erasable marker pen

step 5

▶ Observe and Analyze

Write It Up

1. Compare your topographic map with the three-dimensional model. Remember that contour lines connect points of equal elevation. What do widely spaced or tightly spaced contour lines mean? What does a closed circle mean?

2. Make a permanent record of your map to keep in your **Science Notebook** by carefully tracing the contour lines onto a sheet of white paper. To make reading the map easier, use a different color for an index contour line.

3. What is the contour interval of your model landscape? For example, each 2 centimeters might represent 20 meters in an actual landscape. Record the elevation of the index contour line on your map.

▶ Conclude

Write It Up

1. **INFER** How would you determine the elevation of a point located halfway between two contour lines?

2. **EVALUATE** Describe any errors that you may have made in your procedure or any places where errors might have occurred.

3. **APPLY** Explain how you would use a topographic map if you were planning a hiking trip or a cross-country bike race.

▶ INVESTIGATE Further

CHALLENGE Choose one feature on a topographic map—such as the map on page 26—to translate into a cross-sectional diagram.

1. Lay a piece of ruled paper across the center of the topographical feature.

2. Mark each of the contour lines on the ruled paper and label each mark with the elevation.

3. Mark the same elevations on the side of the paper, as shown in the example.

4. Use a ruler to draw a straight line down from each mark to the matching elevation on the side of the paper.

5. Connect the points to draw a profile of the landform.

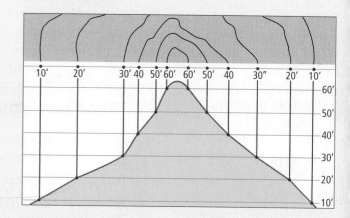

INVESTIGATE TOPOGRAPHIC MAPS

Observe and Analyze

Figure 1. Topographic Map of Model

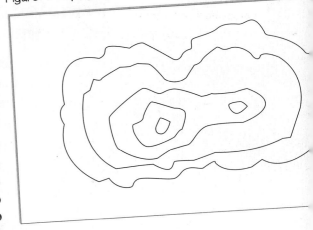

Conclude

Technology is used to map Earth.

BEFORE, you learned

- Contour lines are used on topographic maps to show elevation, slope, and relief
- Contour lines follow certain rules
- Map symbols show many natural and human-made features

NOW, you will learn

- How remote-sensing images can provide detailed and accurate information about Earth
- How geographic data can be displayed in layers to build maps

VOCABULARY

remote sensing p. 30
sensor p. 31
false-color image p. 32
geographic information systems p. 33

THINK ABOUT

What can you see in this image?

Satellites can record all types of information about Earth's surface. This image shows a section of Washington, D.C. The satellite that collected the data is 680 kilometers (420 mi) above Earth. What familiar items can you see in the picture? How might images like this be useful to scientists, mapmakers, and engineers?

Remote sensing provides detailed images of Earth.

If you have ever looked at an object through a pair of binoculars, you have used remote sensing. **Remote sensing** is the use of scientific equipment to gather information about something from a distance. Remote-sensing technology can be as simple as a camera mounted on an airplane or as complex as a satellite orbiting Earth.

To get an idea of how important remote sensing is, imagine you are a mapmaker in the 1840s. You have been asked to draw a map of a state, but you have no cameras, no photographs from airplanes, and no satellites to help you. To get a good view of the land, you have to climb to the highest points and carefully draw every hill, valley, river, and landform below you. It will take you months to map the state.

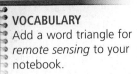

VOCABULARY
Add a word triangle for *remote sensing* to your notebook.

Today, that same map would take far less time to make. Modern mapmakers use remote-sensing images from airplanes and satellites to develop highly detailed and accurate maps of Earth's surface.

Airplane cameras use film to record data, but satellites use sensors to build images of Earth. A **sensor** is a mechanical or electrical device that receives and responds to a signal, such as light. Satellite sensors detect far more than your eyes can see. They collect information about the different types of energy coming from Earth's surface. The satellites then send that information to computers on Earth.

The computers turn the information into images, as shown in the illustration below. Satellite data can be used to build an image of the entire planet, a single continent, or a detail of your area. For example, the image on the right shows a closeup of the Jefferson Memorial in Washington, D.C.

This satellite image includes the Jefferson Memorial, walkways, and roads. See if you can find the memorial in the image on page 30.

 CHECK YOUR READING Explain how remote sensing is used to gather information about Earth.

Satellite Imaging

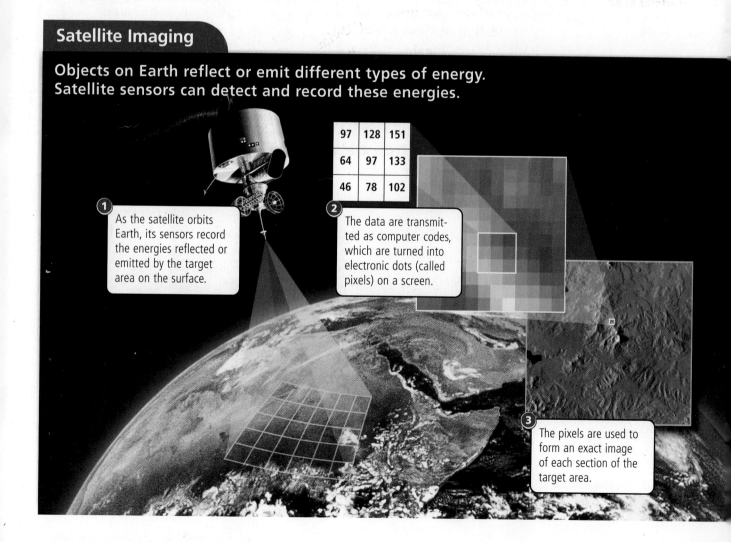

Objects on Earth reflect or emit different types of energy. Satellite sensors can detect and record these energies.

97	128	151
64	97	133
46	78	102

1 As the satellite orbits Earth, its sensors record the energies reflected or emitted by the target area on the surface.

2 The data are transmitted as computer codes, which are turned into electronic dots (called pixels) on a screen.

3 The pixels are used to form an exact image of each section of the target area.

One of the ways scientists study changes is by using false-color images. In one type of **false-color image,** Earth's natural colors are replaced with artificial ones to highlight special features. For example, fire officials used false-color images like the ones below to track the spread of a dangerous wildfire in southern Oregon.

OREGON

July 21, 2002

Small fires
break out.

In this false-color image, vegetation is bright green, burned areas are red, fire is bright pink, and smoke is blue.

August 14, 2002

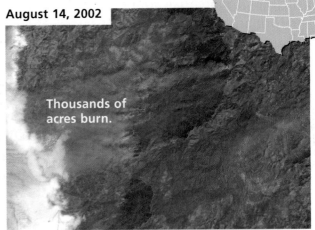

Thousands of
acres burn.

Three weeks later, as this false-color image clearly shows, the fires had spread over a large area.

INVESTIGATE Satellite Imaging

How do satellites send images to Earth?

PROCEDURE

1. Work with a partner. One of you will be the "sensor," and the other will be the "receiving station."

2. The sensor draws the initials of a famous person on a piece of graph paper. The receiving station does NOT see the drawing.

3. The sensor sends the picture to the receiving station. For blank squares, the sensor says "Zero." For filled-in squares, the sensor says "One." Be sure to start at the top row and read left to right, telling the receiving station when a new row begins.

4. The receiving station transfers the code to the graph paper. At the end, the receiver has three tries to guess whose initials were sent.

SKILL FOCUS
Modeling

MATERIALS
- graph paper
- pen or pencil
- *for Challenge:* colored pens or pencils

TIME
25 minutes

WHAT DO YOU THINK?

- What would happen if you accidentally skipped or repeated a row?

- If you increased or decreased the number and size of the squares, how would this affect the picture?

CHALLENGE Use a variety of colors to send other initials or an image. Your code must tell the receiver which color to use for each square.

Geographic information systems display data in layers.

RESOURCE CENTER
CLASSZONE.COM

Find out more about how GIS is used.

Any good city map will show you what is on the surface—buildings, streets, parks, and other features. But suppose you need to know about tunnels under the city. Or maybe you want to know where the most students live. An ordinary map, even one based on remote-sensing images, will not tell you what you want to know.

Instead, you would turn to geographic information systems. **Geographic information systems** (GIS) are computer systems that can store and arrange geographic data and display the data in many different types of maps. Scientists, city planners, and engineers all use GIS maps to help them make decisions. For example, suppose your city wants to build a new airport. It must be away from populated areas and near major highways. The illustration below shows how city officials might use GIS to pick the best site.

Geographic Information Systems

GIS can be used to produce maps that help people make decisions.

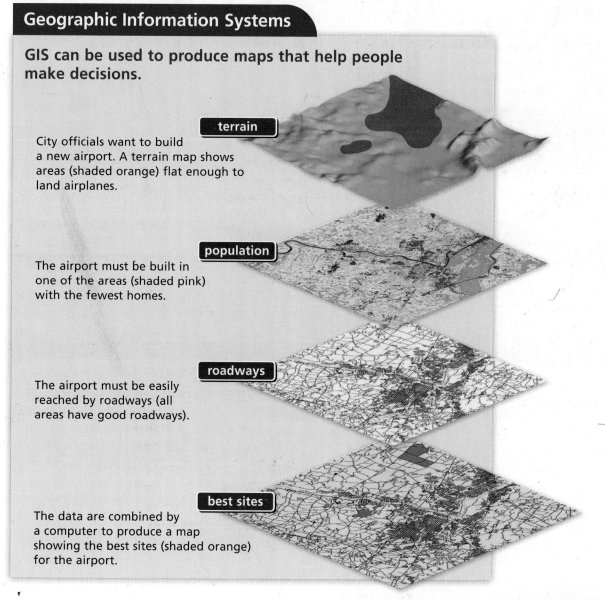

City officials want to build a new airport. A terrain map shows areas (shaded orange) flat enough to land airplanes.

terrain

The airport must be built in one of the areas (shaded pink) with the fewest homes.

population

The airport must be easily reached by roadways (all areas have good roadways).

roadways

The data are combined by a computer to produce a map showing the best sites (shaded orange) for the airport.

best sites

Any geographic information can be entered into GIS and converted into a map. These systems are especially useful in displaying information about changes in the environment.

For example, near Long Valley in California, the volcano known as Mammoth Mountain began giving off carbon dioxide, or CO_2. As the gas rose through the soil, it began killing the roots of trees nearby. Scientists measured the flow of CO_2 around Horseshoe Lake and other areas. They used computer software to build the maps shown below.

CHECK YOUR READING Summarize the ways GIS maps can be helpful to engineers, city planners, and scientists.

Mammoth Mountain

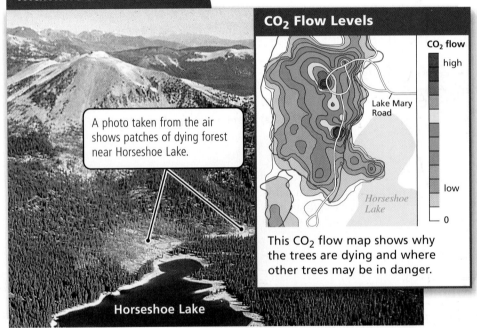

A photo taken from the air shows patches of dying forest near Horseshoe Lake.

Horseshoe Lake

CO₂ Flow Levels

CO₂ flow
high

Lake Mary Road

low

0

Horseshoe Lake

This CO_2 flow map shows why the trees are dying and where other trees may be in danger.

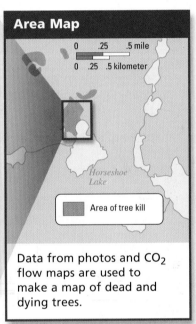

Area Map

0   .25   .5 mile
0   .25   .5 kilometer

Horseshoe Lake

Area of tree kill

Data from photos and CO_2 flow maps are used to make a map of dead and dying trees.

1.4 Review

KEY CONCEPTS

1. How are satellites used to make images of Earth from outer space?

2. What are some of the types of information obtained by remote sensing?

3. Explain in your own words what a GIS map is.

CRITICAL THINKING

4. **Infer** Explain how satellite images might be used to predict what a natural area might look like in 50 or 100 years.

5. **Evaluate** If you wanted to compare a region before and during a flood, how could false-color images help you?

◯ CHALLENGE

6. **Analyze** Work with a small group. Suppose you wanted to ask the city to build a skateboard park. What types of information would you need in order to propose a good site? Draw a map to display each type of information.

Think SCIENCE

Trains and Bus Lines

☰☰☰ Train lines
—— Bus lines

Streets and Freeways

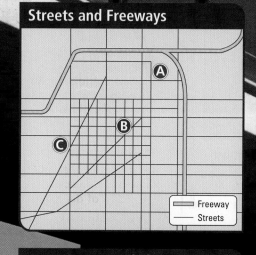

▭▭▭ Freeway
—— Streets

Restaurants and Shopping

▢▦▢ Shops and restaurants

Which Site Is Best for an Olympic Stadium?

Imagine you live in a city that has been chosen to host the Summer Olympics. The only question is where to build the Olympic stadium—in the center of town, in the suburbs, or on the site of an old baseball park. The city government has developed maps to help them decide which is the best site. The planners know that thousands of people will come to see the games. Therefore, they reason, the stadium should be (1) easy to reach by car, (2) close to mass-transit stops, and (3) near restaurants and shops.

▶ Analyzing Map Data

As you study the maps, keep these requirements in mind.

1. Which site(s) is/are easiest to reach by car?
2. Which site(s) is/are closest to bus and train lines?
3. Which site(s) is/are close to shopping areas?

▶ Interpreting Data

In your **Science Notebook,** create a chart like the one below to help you interpret the data displayed on the maps. As you fill in the chart, think about which site offers the greatest benefits to all the people who will attend the Olympic Games.

	Site Ⓐ		Site Ⓑ		Site Ⓒ	
	Yes	No	Yes	No	Yes	No
Near mass transit						
Near highways and roads						
Near shopping areas						

As a group Choose the best site based on your interpretation of the data. Discuss your choice with other groups to see if they agree.

CHALLENGE Once the site is chosen, the planners will start building the stadium. What types of information about the site will they need? Sketch maps displaying the information. **Hint:** The stadium will need electricity, water, and delivery of supplies.

Chapter Review

the BIG idea

Modern technology has changed the way we view and map Earth.

CONTENT REVIEW
CLASSZONE.COM

KEY CONCEPTS SUMMARY

1.1 Technology is used to explore the Earth system.

The atmosphere, hydrosphere, biosphere, and geosphere work together to form one large system called Earth.

VOCABULARY
system p. 9
atmosphere p. 10
hydrosphere p. 10
biosphere p. 11
geosphere p. 12

1.2 Maps and globes are models of Earth.

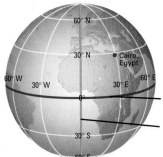

Latitude and longitude are used to locate any point on Earth.

— equator

— prime meridian

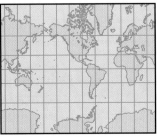

All map projections distort Earth's surface.

VOCABULARY
relief map p. 16
map scale p. 17
map legend p. 17
equator p. 18
latitude p. 18
prime meridian p. 19
longitude p. 19
projection p. 20

1.3 Topographic maps show the shape of the land.

Contour lines show elevation, slope, and relief.

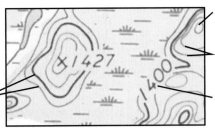

Contour lines never cross.

Closed circles represent hilltops.

Contour lines show steepness of slope.

Index contour lines show elevation.

VOCABULARY
topography p. 24
contour line p. 25
elevation p. 25
slope p. 25
relief p. 25
contour interval p. 26

1.4 Technology is used to map Earth.

Remote-sensing technology gathers accurate data about Earth.

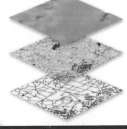

Geographic information systems are computer programs used to merge layers of information.

VOCABULARY
remote sensing p. 30
sensor p. 31
false-color image p. 32
geographic information systems p. 33

Reviewing Vocabulary

Copy and complete the chart below, using vocabulary terms from this chapter.

Term	Use	Appearance
map legend	*to explain map symbols*	*chart of symbols*
1. latitude	to show distance from the equator	
2. longitude		lines going from pole to pole
3.	to show land features	rippled and smooth areas
4. map scale	to represent distances	
5. equator		line at 0° latitude
6. prime meridian	to separate east and west hemispheres	
7.	to show height above sea level	line showing elevation
8. false-color image	to highlight information	

Reviewing Key Concepts

Multiple Choice *Choose the letter of the best answer.*

9. Which Greek prefix is matched with its correct meaning?
- **a.** *hydro* = life
- **b.** *atmo* = gas
- **c.** *bio* = earth
- **d.** *geo* = water

10. What portion of Earth is covered by water?
- **a.** one-quarter
- **b.** one-half
- **c.** three-quarters
- **d.** nine-tenths

11. The continents and ocean basins are part of Earth's
- **a.** crust
- **b.** mantle
- **c.** outer core
- **d.** inner core

12. Which Earth system includes humans?
- **a.** atmosphere
- **b.** biosphere
- **c.** hydrosphere
- **d.** geosphere

13. One way the atmosphere shapes Earth's surface is by
- **a.** winds
- **b.** floods
- **c.** earthquakes
- **d.** tunnels

14. How are the major parts of the Earth system related to each other?
- **a.** They rarely can be studied together.
- **b.** They often are in conflict.
- **c.** They usually work independently.
- **d.** They continually affect each other.

15. A flat map shows Earth's curved surface by means of
- **a.** elevation
- **b.** topography
- **c.** relief
- **d.** projection

16. People use latitude and longitude lines mostly to identify
- **a.** map scales
- **b.** country names
- **c.** exact locations
- **d.** distances

17. The most accurate way to show Earth's surface is a
- **a.** globe
- **b.** conic projection
- **c.** cylindrical projection
- **d.** planar projection

18. One example of remote sensing is the use of
- **a.** contour lines
- **b.** projections
- **c.** GIS
- **d.** binoculars

Short Answer *Write a few sentences to answer each question.*

19. How does the Global Positioning System work? In your answer use each of the following terms. Underline each term in your answer.

24 satellites	computer	longitude
receiver	latitude	elevation

20. How do Mercator maps distort the view of Earth's surface?

21. How do people use sensors in making maps?

Thinking Critically

Use the topographic map below to answer the next seven questions.

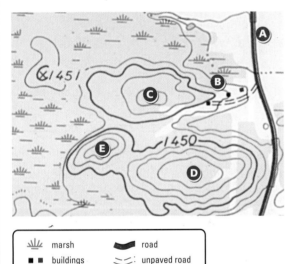

Legend:
- ~~~ marsh
- ▪ ▪ buildings
- road
- unpaved road

22. APPLY Imagine you are hiking through this area. Which hill—C, D, or E—has the steepest slope? How do you know?

23. ANALYZE What is the topography of the land through which the curved road A goes?

24. IDENTIFY CAUSE The squares at B represent buildings. Why do you think the buildings were placed here instead of somewhere else in the area?

25. APPLY The contour interval is 10 meters. What is the elevation of the highest point on the map?

26. SYNTHESIZE Sketch the two hills D and E. What would they look like to someone on the ground?

27. INFER Suppose someone wanted to build a road through the terrain on the far left side of the map. What are the advantages and disadvantages of such a route?

28. EVALUATE Do you think this area would be a good place to ride mountain bikes? Why or why not?

CHART INFORMATION *On a separate sheet of paper, write a word to fill each blank in the chart.*

Feature	Shown on Topographic Maps?	Belongs to Which Major System?
rivers	*yes*	*hydrosphere*
29. slope		
30. winds		
31. plants		
32. lakes		
33. relief		

the BIG idea

34. APPLY Look again at the photographs on pages 6–7. Now that you have finished the chapter, reread the question on the main photograph. What would you change in or add to your answer?

35. SYNTHESIZE Describe some of the types of information that new technology has provided about Earth.

36. DRAW CONCLUSIONS What type of technology do you think has done the most to change the way people view and map Earth? Explain your conclusion.

UNIT PROJECTS

If you are doing a unit project, make a folder for your project. Include in your folder a list of the resources you will need, the date on which the project is due, and a schedule to track your progress. Begin gathering data.

Standardized Test Practice

Analyzing a Diagram

This diagram shows the four major parts of the Earth system. Use it to answer the questions below.

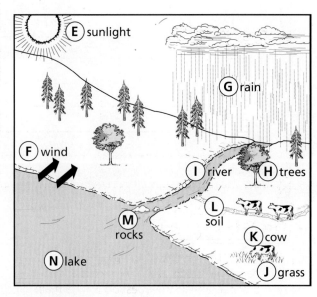

1. Where is the main source of energy for the Earth system?
- **a.** E
- **b.** F
- **c.** G
- **d.** L

2. Where is the biosphere shaping the geosphere?
- **a.** E
- **b.** F
- **c.** L
- **d.** M

3. Where is matter moving from one part of the hydrosphere to another?
- **a.** I to N
- **b.** G to H
- **c.** J to H
- **d.** N to M

4. Which items belong to the geosphere?
- **a.** F and G
- **b.** H and J
- **c.** I and N
- **d.** M and L

5. Which process is occurring at M where water is running over the rocks?
- **a.** The geosphere is shaping the atmosphere.
- **b.** The atmosphere is shaping the biosphere.
- **c.** The hydrosphere is shaping the geosphere.
- **d.** The biosphere is shaping the geosphere.

6. Where is matter moving from the atmosphere to the biosphere?
- **a.** E and F
- **b.** F and M
- **c.** G and H
- **d.** I and G

7. At K, the cow is eating grass. What kind of movement in the Earth system does this represent?
- **a.** from the atmosphere to the hydrosphere
- **b.** from the hydrosphere to the biosphere
- **c.** between two parts of the geosphere
- **d.** between two parts of the biosphere

8. Which is an example of how the hydrosphere is supported by the geosphere?
- **a.** I, because the river receives the rain
- **b.** H, because the trees are rooted in the ground
- **c.** M, because the river drains into the lake
- **d.** N, because the lake is contained by a basin

Extended Response

Answer the two questions below in detail. Include some of the terms shown in the word box. In your answers, underline each term you use.

geosphere	surface	system
atmosphere	hydrosphere	biosphere

9. Rain falls and soaks into the soil. Plants and animals use some of the water. More of the water drains into a river, then enters the ocean. Describe this process as movements among the major parts of the Earth system.

10. Describe an example of how people can shape the surface of the geosphere.

CHAPTER 2 Minerals

the BIG idea

Minerals are basic building blocks of Earth.

Key Concepts

SECTION 2.1
Minerals are all around us.
Learn about the characteristics all minerals share.

SECTION 2.2
A mineral is identified by its properties.
Learn how to identify minerals by observing and testing their properties.

SECTION 2.3
Minerals are valuable resources.
Learn how minerals form, how they are mined, and how they are used.

Internet Preview

CLASSZONE.COM

Chapter 2 online resources: Content Review, Visualization, three Resource Centers, Math Tutorial, Test Practice

Why can gold be separated from other minerals and rocks in a river?

EXPLORE (the BIG idea)

How Do You Turn Water into a Mineral?

Freeze some water into ice cubes. Then compare water, an ice cube, and a penny. Liquid water is not a mineral, but ice is. The surface of the penny is made of the mineral copper.

Observe and Think
How are the water, ice cube, and penny similar? How are they different? What do you think one of the properties of a mineral is?

What Makes Up Rocks?

Find three different rocks near your home or school. Examine them closely with a magnifying glass.

Observe and Think
Describe the rocks. How many materials can you see in each rock? How do you think they got there?

Internet Activity: Minerals

Go to **ClassZone.com** to find out more about minerals that are also precious metals.

Observe and Think
In addition to jewelry, how many different uses can you find for gold?

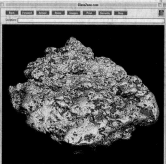

NSTA
scilinks.org
SCi LINKS

Identifying Minerals **Code: MDL014**

Getting Ready to Learn

CONCEPT REVIEW

- Earth has four main layers: crust, mantle, outer core, and inner core.
- Matter exists in the forms of gas, liquid, and solid.
- People use maps to show many different features of Earth.

VOCABULARY REVIEW

atom *See Glossary.*

geosphere p. 12

CONTENT REVIEW
CLASSZONE.COM
Review concepts and vocabulary.

TAKING NOTES

SUPPORTING MAIN IDEAS

Make a chart to show each main idea and the information that supports it. Copy each blue heading. Below each heading, add supporting information, such as reasons, explanations, and examples.

VOCABULARY STRATEGY

Place each vocabulary term at the center of a **description wheel**. On the spokes write some words explaining it.

See the Note-Taking Handbook on pages R45–R51.

SCIENCE NOTEBOOK

Minerals have four characteristics.

→ Minerals form naturally.

→ All minerals are solids.

→ Each mineral is always made of the same element or elements.

→ All minerals have crystal structures.

formed by all minerals

atoms joined in a repeating 3-D pattern

CRYSTAL

2.1 Minerals are all around us.

 BEFORE, you learned

- Earth is made of layers
- Earth's outermost rocky layer is the crust

 NOW, you will learn

- What the characteristics of minerals are
- How minerals are classified into groups
- Which mineral group is most common

VOCABULARY

mineral p. 43
element p. 45
crystal p. 46

EXPLORE Minerals

What are some characteristics of a mineral?

PROCEDURE

1. Sprinkle some table salt on a sheet of colored paper. Look at a few grains of the salt through a magnifying glass. Then rub a few grains between your fingers.

2. In your notebook, describe all the qualities of the salt that you observe.

3. Examine the rock salt in the same way and describe its qualities in your notebook. How do the two differ?

WHAT DO YOU THINK?
Salt is a mineral. From your observations of salt, what do you think are some characteristics of minerals?

MATERIALS
- colored paper
- table salt
- rock salt
- magnifying glass

Minerals have four characteristics.

You use minerals all the time. Every time you turn on a microwave oven or a TV, you depend on minerals. The copper in the wires that carry electricity to the device is a mineral. Table salt, or halite (HAYL-YT), is another mineral that you use in your everyday life.

Minerals have four characteristics. A **mineral** is a substance that

- forms in nature
- is a solid
- has a definite chemical makeup
- has a crystal structure

VOCABULARY
Add a description wheel for *mineral* in your notebook.

Minerals in Rocks

Most rocks are made up of minerals.

Quartz

Feldspar

Mica

granite

This piece of granite contains the minerals quartz, feldspar, and mica.

You might think that minerals and rocks are the same things. But a mineral must have the four characteristics listed on page 43. A rock has only two of these characteristics—it is a solid and it forms naturally. A rock usually contains two or more types of minerals.

Two samples of the same type of rock may vary greatly in the amounts of different minerals they contain. Minerals, however, are always made up of the same materials in the same proportions. A ruby is a mineral. Therefore, a ruby found in India has the same makeup as a ruby found in Australia.

READING TiP

Proportions show relationships between amounts. For example, a quartz crystal always has two oxygen atoms for every silicon atom.

CHECK YOUR READING How are minerals different from rocks?

Formed in Nature

Minerals are formed by natural processes. Every type of mineral can form in nature by processes that do not involve living organisms. As you will read, a few minerals can also be produced by organisms as part of their shells or bones.

Minerals form in many ways. The mineral halite, which is used as table salt, forms when water evaporates in a hot, shallow part of the ocean, leaving behind the salt it contained. Many types of minerals, including the ones in granite, develop when molten rock cools. Talc, a mineral that can be used to make baby powder, forms deep in Earth as high pressure and temperature cause changes in solid rock.

READING TiP

Molten rock refers to rock that has become so hot that it has melted.

Solid

A mineral is a solid—that is, it has a definite volume and a rigid shape. Volume refers to the amount of space an object takes up. For example, a golf ball has a smaller volume than a baseball, and a baseball has a smaller volume than a basketball.

A substance that is a liquid or a gas is not a mineral. However, in some cases its solid form is a mineral. For instance, liquid water is not a mineral, but ice is.

Definite Chemical Makeup

Each mineral has a definite chemical makeup: it consists of a specific combination of atoms of certain elements. An **element** is a substance that contains only one type of atom. In turn, an atom is the smallest particle an element can be divided into.

Everything you can see or touch is made up of atoms. Some substances, including the minerals gold and copper, consist of just one element. All the atoms in gold or copper are of the same type. However, most substances contain atoms of more than one element. Most minerals are compounds, substances consisting of several elements in specific proportions. Halite, for example, has one atom of sodium for every atom of chlorine.

The types of atoms that make up a mineral are part of what makes the mineral unique. The way in which the atoms are bonded, or joined together, is also important. As you will read, many properties of minerals are related to how strong or weak the bonds are.

READING TiP

You may remember *compound* from compound words—words formed by joining together smaller words: *note* + *book* = *notebook*. Likewise, a chemical compound has two or more elements joined together.

Atoms in Minerals

Atoms in Copper

copper

copper

The mineral copper is made up only of copper atoms.

Atoms in Halite

chlorine

halite

sodium

The mineral halite is made up of equal numbers of sodium and chlorine atoms.

READING VISUALS How do the diagrams show that copper consists of only one element and halite is a compound?

Crystal Structure

VISUALIZATION
CLASSZONE.COM

Explore an animation of crystal growth.

If you look closely at the particles of ice that make up frost, you will notice that they have smooth, flat surfaces. These flat surfaces form because of the arrangement of atoms in the ice, which is a mineral. Such an internal arrangement is a characteristic of minerals. It is the structure of a **crystal,** a solid in which the atoms are arranged in an orderly, repeating three-dimensional pattern.

Each mineral has its own type of crystal structure. In some cases, two minerals have the same chemical composition but different crystal structures. For example, both diamond and graphite consist of just one element—carbon. But the arrangements of the carbon atoms in these two minerals are not the same, so they have different crystal structures and very different properties. Diamonds are extremely hard and have a brilliant sparkle. Graphite is soft, gray, and dull.

In nature, a perfect crystal is rare. One can grow only when a mineral is free to form in an open space—a condition that rarely exists within Earth's crust. The photographs on page 47 show examples of nearly perfect crystals. The amount of space available for growth influences the shape and size of crystals. Most crystals have imperfect shapes because their growth was limited by other crystals forming next to them.

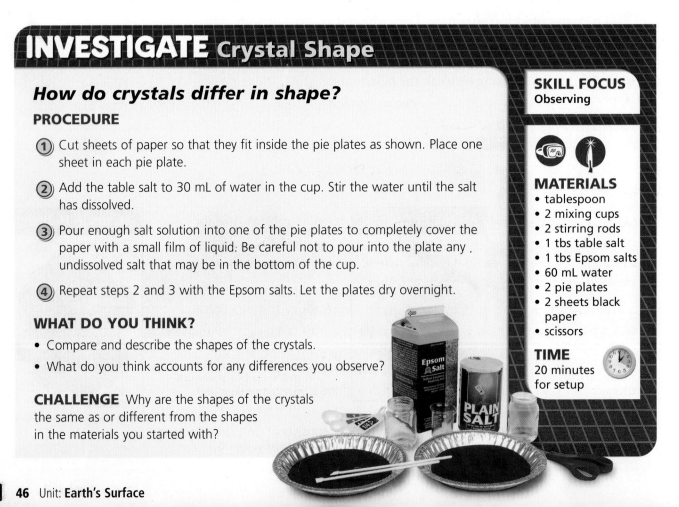

INVESTIGATE Crystal Shape

How do crystals differ in shape?

PROCEDURE

1. Cut sheets of paper so that they fit inside the pie plates as shown. Place one sheet in each pie plate.

2. Add the table salt to 30 mL of water in the cup. Stir the water until the salt has dissolved.

3. Pour enough salt solution into one of the pie plates to completely cover the paper with a small film of liquid. Be careful not to pour into the plate any undissolved salt that may be in the bottom of the cup.

4. Repeat steps 2 and 3 with the Epsom salts. Let the plates dry overnight.

WHAT DO YOU THINK?

• Compare and describe the shapes of the crystals.

• What do you think accounts for any differences you observe?

CHALLENGE Why are the shapes of the crystals the same as or different from the shapes in the materials you started with?

SKILL FOCUS
Observing

MATERIALS
• tablespoon
• 2 mixing cups
• 2 stirring rods
• 1 tbs table salt
• 1 tbs Epsom salts
• 60 mL water
• 2 pie plates
• 2 sheets black paper
• scissors

TIME
20 minutes for setup

Crystal Groups

Crystal groups are named by their shapes and the angles formed by imaginary lines through their centers. Crystals take many shapes, but all belong to these six groups.

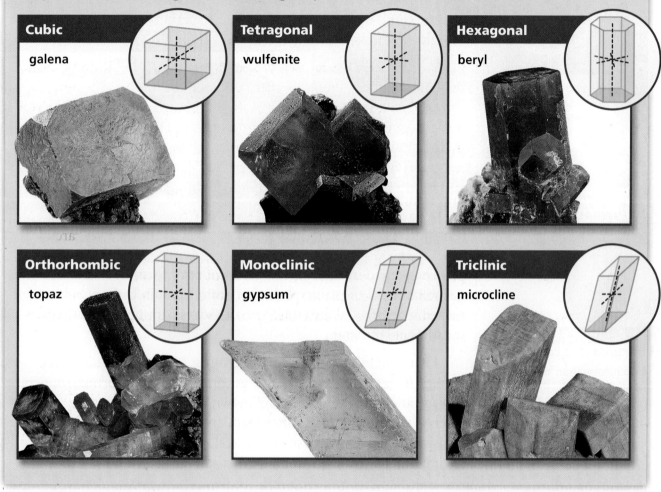

Cubic
galena

Tetragonal
wulfenite

Hexagonal
beryl

Orthorhombic
topaz

Monoclinic
gypsum

Triclinic
microcline

Minerals are grouped according to composition.

Scientists classify minerals into groups on the basis of their chemical makeups. The most common group is the silicates. All the minerals in this group contain oxygen and silicon—the two most common elements in Earth's crust—joined together.

Though there are thousands of different minerals, only about 30 are common in Earth's crust. These 30 minerals make up most rocks in the crust. For that reason, they are called rock-forming minerals. Silicates, which make up about 90 percent of the rocks in Earth's crust, are the most common rock-forming minerals. Quartz, feldspar, and mica (MY-kuh) are common silicates.

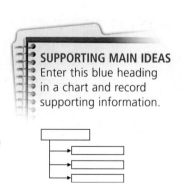

SUPPORTING MAIN IDEAS
Enter this blue heading in a chart and record supporting information.

CHECK YOUR READING Which mineral group do most rock-forming minerals belong to?

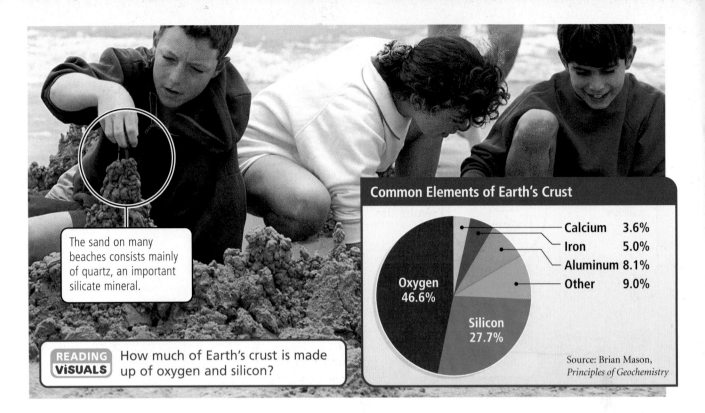

The sand on many beaches consists mainly of quartz, an important silicate mineral.

Common Elements of Earth's Crust

Calcium   3.6%
Iron   5.0%
Aluminum 8.1%
Other   9.0%
Oxygen 46.6%
Silicon 27.7%

Source: Brian Mason, *Principles of Geochemistry*

READING VISUALS How much of Earth's crust is made up of oxygen and silicon?

The second most common group of rock-forming minerals is the carbonates. All the minerals in this group contain carbon and oxygen joined together. Calcite (KAL-SYT), which is common in seashells, is a carbonate mineral.

There are many other mineral groups. All are important, even though their minerals may not be as common as rock-forming minerals. For instance, the mineral group known as oxides contains the minerals from which most metals, such as tin and copper, are refined. An oxide consists of an element, usually a metal, joined to oxygen. This group includes hematite (HEE-muh-TYT), a source of iron.

CHECK YOUR READING Why is the oxide mineral group important?

RESOURCE CENTER CLASSZONE.COM

Find information on minerals.

2.1 Review

KEY CONCEPTS

1. What are the four characteristics of a mineral?

2. On what basis do scientists classify minerals?

3. What is the most common group of minerals? What percentage of the crust do they make up?

CRITICAL THINKING

4. **Classify** Can oil and natural gas be classified as minerals? Why or why not?

5. **Apply** When a piece of quartz is heated to a very high temperature, it melts into a liquid. Is it still a mineral? Why or why not?

CHALLENGE

6. **Interpret** You can see perfect crystals lining the inside of certain rocks when they are broken open. How do you think the crystals were able to form?

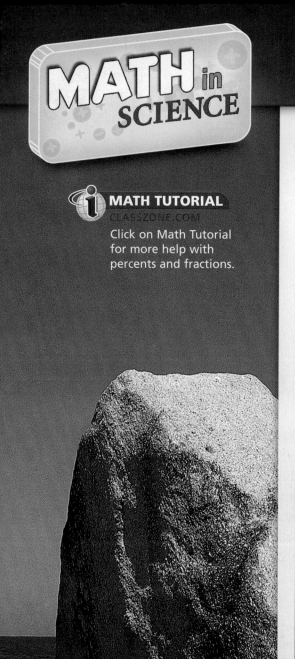

MATH in SCIENCE

MATH TUTORIAL
CLASSZONE.COM

Click on Math Tutorial for more help with percents and fractions.

Minerals in Rocks

Like most rocks, granite is a mixture of several minerals. Each mineral makes up a certain proportion, or fraction, of the granite. You can compare mineral amounts by expressing each mineral's fraction as a percentage.

Granite

Example

To change a fraction to a percentage, you must find an equivalent fraction with 100 as the denominator. Suppose, for example, you want to change the fraction $\frac{1}{5}$ to a percentage. First, divide 100 by the denominator 5, which gives you 20. Then, multiply both the numerator and denominator by 20 to find the percentage.

$$\frac{1}{5} \cdot \frac{20}{20} = \frac{20}{100} \text{ or } 20\% \qquad \frac{1}{5} \text{ is } 20\%$$

The table below shows the fraction of each mineral in a granite sample.

Minerals in Granite Sample

Mineral	Fraction of Granite Sample	Percentage of Granite
Quartz	$\frac{1}{4}$	?
Feldspar	$\frac{13}{20}$	?
Mica	$\frac{3}{50}$	?
Dark minerals	$\frac{1}{25}$	?

Answer the following questions.

1. On your paper, copy the table and fill in the percentage of each mineral in the granite sample above.

2. Which minerals make up the greatest and smallest percentages of the granite?

3. In another granite sample, feldspar makes up $\frac{3}{5}$ and mica makes up $\frac{2}{25}$. What is the percentage of each mineral in the rock?

CHALLENGE The mineral hornblende is often one of the dark minerals in granite. If hornblende makes up $\frac{1}{32}$ of a granite sample, what percentage of the rock is hornblende?

KEY CONCEPT

2.2 A mineral is identified by its properties.

◀ **BEFORE, you learned**

- All minerals have four characteristics
- Most minerals in Earth's crust are silicates

▶ **NOW, you will learn**

- Which mineral properties are most important in identification
- How minerals are identified by their properties

VOCABULARY

streak p. 51
luster p. 52
cleavage p. 53
fracture p. 53
density p. 54
hardness p. 55

THINK ABOUT

What can you tell by looking at a mineral?

The photographs at the right show five pieces of the mineral fluorite (FLUR-YT). As you can see, the pieces are very different in color and size. Fluorite occurs in many colors, even in colorless forms. Its crystals can be well formed or poorly formed. Also, the sides of the crystals may be smooth or rough.

If you came across fluorite while hiking, would you know what it was by just looking at it? Probably not. Read on to find out how you could identify it.

A mineral's appearance helps identify it.

READING TiP

The word *characteristic* is used for a feature that is typical of a person or thing. It can be used as a noun or an adjective.

To identify a mineral, you need to observe its properties—characteristic features that identify it. You might begin by looking at the mineral's color. However, many minerals occur in more than one color, so you would need to examine other properties as well. You might also notice how the mineral reflects light, which determines how shiny or dull it is. Most minerals reflect light in characteristic ways. In this section you will read about how the properties of a mineral—including its appearance—are used to identify it.

 Why do you need to look at properties other than color to identify a mineral?

Color and Streak

Some minerals can be almost any color, but most minerals have a more limited color range. For example, a particular mineral may almost always be brown to black.

Three main factors cause minerals to vary in color. First, a mineral may get its color from tiny amounts of an element that is not part of its normal chemical makeup. For example, a sample of pure quartz is clear and colorless, but tiny amounts of iron can give quartz a violet color. This violet variety of quartz is called amethyst. Second, a mineral's color can change when it is at or near Earth's surface and is in contact with the atmosphere or water. Third, mineral crystals can have defects in their crystal structures that change their color.

Some minerals have a different color when they are ground into a fine powder than when they are left whole. A mineral's **streak** is the color of the powder left behind when the mineral is scraped across a surface. Geologists use a tile of unglazed porcelain, called a streak plate, as a tool to identify minerals by their streaks. Streak is a better clue to a mineral's identity than surface color is. Look at the photographs of hematite below. Even though the mineral samples are different colors, both leave a reddish brown streak when scraped across a streak plate. All samples of the same mineral have the same streak.

 CHECK YOUR READING What is the difference between color and streak?

READING TiP
A geologist is a scientist who studies Earth.

Streak

These samples are of the mineral hematite. They are different colors, but they have the same streak.

This hematite looks dull because it has tiny crystals that reflect light in all directions.

This hematite looks shiny because it has larger crystals.

 READING VISUALS What is a clue that both samples are of the same mineral?

Luster

A mineral's **luster** is the way in which light reflects from its surface. The two major types of luster are metallic and nonmetallic. The mineral pyrite has a metallic luster. It looks as if it were made of metal. A mineral with a nonmetallic luster can be shiny, but it does not appear to be made of metal. An example of a nonmetallic luster is the glassy luster of garnet. Compare the lusters of pyrite and garnet in the photographs below.

Pyrite has a metallic luster.

Garnet crystals in this rock have a nonmetallic luster.

Like a mineral's color, its luster may vary from sample to sample. If a mineral has been exposed to the atmosphere or to water, its surface luster can become dull. However, if the mineral is broken to reveal a fresh surface, its characteristic luster can be seen.

The way a mineral breaks helps identify it.

If you hit a piece of calcite with a hammer, the calcite will break into tilted blocks. You can peel off layers of mica because it splits into thin, flat sheets. Each kind of mineral always breaks in the same way, and this property can help identify a mineral. In fact, the way a mineral breaks is a better clue to its identity than are its color and luster.

Cleavage

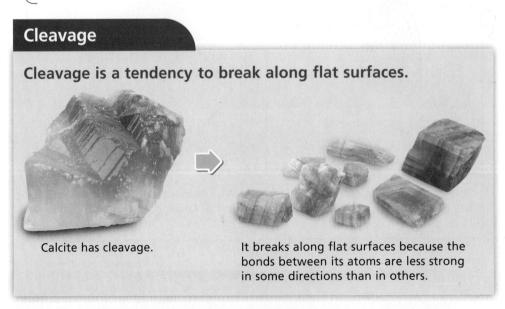

Cleavage is a tendency to break along flat surfaces.

Calcite has cleavage.

It breaks along flat surfaces because the bonds between its atoms are less strong in some directions than in others.

Cleavage

Cleavage is the tendency of a mineral to break along flat surfaces. The way in which a mineral breaks depends on how its atoms are bonded, or joined together. In a mineral that displays cleavage, the bonds of the crystal structure are weaker in the directions in which the mineral breaks.

When geologists describe the cleavage of a mineral, they consider both the directions in which the mineral breaks and the smoothness of the broken surfaces. Mica has cleavage in one direction and breaks into sheets. The photographs on page 52 show that calcite has cleavage in three directions and breaks into tilted blocks. Because the broken surfaces of both mica and calcite are smooth, these minerals are said to have perfect cleavage.

Carbon Bonds in Graphite

strong bonds within layers

weak bonds between layers

carbon atoms

In graphite, carbon atoms are arranged in layers. Graphite has cleavage because the weak bonds between the layers break easily.

Fracture

Fracture is the tendency of a mineral to break into irregular pieces. Some minerals such as quartz break into pieces with curved surfaces, as shown below. Other minerals may break differently—perhaps into splinters or into rough or jagged pieces.

In a mineral that displays fracture, the bonds that join the atoms are fairly equal in strength in all directions. The mineral does not break along flat surfaces because there are no particular directions of weakness in its crystal structure.

VOCABULARY
Add a description wheel for *fracture* in your notebook.

CHECK YOUR READING How does the strength of the bonds between atoms determine whether a mineral displays cleavage or fracture?

Fracture

Fracture is a tendency to break into irregular pieces.

Quartz does not have cleavage. It breaks by fracturing.

It breaks along irregular surfaces because the bonds between its atoms are about the same strength in every direction.

A mineral's density and hardness help identify it.

A tennis ball is not as heavy or as hard as a baseball. You would be able to tell the two apart even with your eyes closed by how heavy and hard they feel. You can identify minerals in a similar way.

Density

READING TiP

The unit of density is grams per cubic centimeter and is abbreviated as g/cm³.

Even though a baseball and a tennis ball are about the same size, the baseball has more mass and so is more dense. A substance's **density** is the amount of mass in a given volume of the substance. For example, 1 cubic centimeter of the mineral pyrite has a mass of 5.1 grams, so pyrite's density is 5.1 grams per cubic centimeter.

Density is very helpful in identifying minerals. For example, gold and pyrite look very similar. Pyrite is often called fool's gold. However, you can tell the two minerals apart by comparing their densities. Gold is much denser than pyrite. The mass of a piece of gold is almost four times the mass of a piece of pyrite of the same size. A small amount of a very dense mineral, such as gold, can have more mass and be heavier than a larger amount of a less dense mineral, such as pyrite. A mineral's density is determined by the kinds of atoms that make up

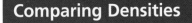

Comparing Densities

Differences in density can be used to tell minerals apart.

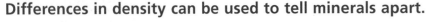

quartz   zincite

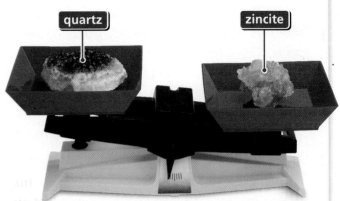

The baseball on the right has more mass, and so is denser, than a tennis ball that is about the same size.

The zincite sample on the right is about twice as dense as the quartz sample.

READING VISUALS Estimate the size a piece of quartz would have to be to balance the zincite sample.

the mineral, as well as how closely the atoms are joined together. An experienced geologist can estimate the density of a mineral by lifting it. But to get an exact measurement, geologists use special scales.

 CHECK YOUR READING Why does a piece of gold weigh much more than a piece of pyrite that is the same size?

Hardness

One way to tell a tennis ball from a baseball without looking at them is to compare their densities. Another way is to test which one is harder. Hardness is another dependable clue to a mineral's identity.

A mineral's **hardness** is its resistance to being scratched. Like a mineral's cleavage, a mineral's hardness is determined by its crystal structure and the strength of the bonds between its atoms. Harder minerals have stronger bonds.

A scale known as the Mohs scale is often used to describe a mineral's hardness. This scale is based on the fact that a harder mineral will scratch a softer one. As you can see in the chart at the right, ten minerals are numbered in the scale, from softest to hardest. Talc is the softest mineral and has a value of 1. Diamond, the hardest of all minerals, has a value of 10.

A mineral can be scratched only by other minerals that have the same hardness or are harder. To determine the hardness of an unknown mineral, you test whether it scratches or is scratched by the minerals in the scale. For example, if you can scratch an unknown mineral with apatite but not with fluorite, the mineral's hardness is between 4 and 5 in the Mohs scale.

In place of minerals, you can use your fingernail, a copper penny, and a steel file to test an unknown mineral. To avoid damage to the minerals, you can test whether the mineral scratches these items. When using a penny to test hardness, make sure its date is 1982 or earlier. Only older pennies are made mainly of copper, which has a hardness of about 3.

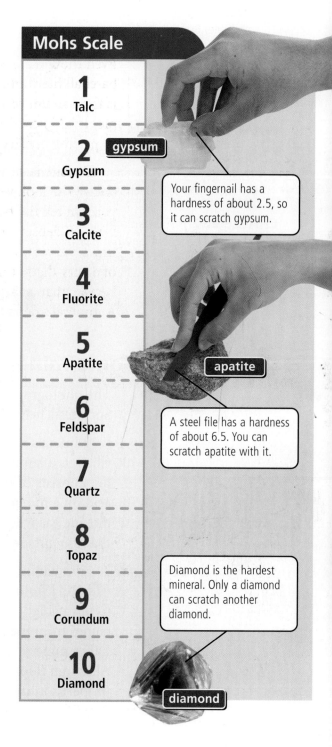

Mohs Scale

1 Talc

2 Gypsum — gypsum

3 Calcite

4 Fluorite

5 Apatite — apatite

6 Feldspar

7 Quartz

8 Topaz

9 Corundum

10 Diamond — diamond

Your fingernail has a hardness of about 2.5, so it can scratch gypsum.

A steel file has a hardness of about 6.5. You can scratch apatite with it.

Diamond is the hardest mineral. Only a diamond can scratch another diamond.

INVESTIGATE Hardness of Minerals

How hard are some common minerals?

PROCEDURE

① Try to scratch each mineral with your fingernail, the penny, and the steel file. Record the results in a chart.

② Assign a hardness range to each mineral.

③ In the last column of your chart, rank the minerals from hardest to softest.

WHAT DO YOU THINK?

• Use your results to assign a hardness range in the Mohs scale to each sample.

• If two minerals have the same hardness range according to your tests, how could you tell which is harder?

CHALLENGE If you had a mineral that could not be scratched by the steel file, what else might you test it with to estimate its hardness?

MATERIALS
• samples of 5 minerals
• copper penny (1982 or earlier)
• steel file

TIME
20 minutes

Some minerals have special properties.

The photographs on page 57 show how geologists test some minerals. Such tests help them identify minerals that have unusual properties.

Minerals in the carbonate group, such as calcite, react with acid. Chalk is a familiar item that is made up of carbonate minerals. The test consists of putting a drop of a weak solution of hydrochloric acid on a mineral sample. If the acid reacts with the mineral, carbon dioxide gas will form and bubble out of the acid. The bubbles show that the mineral is a carbonate.

Some minerals have a property known as fluorescence (flu-REHS-uhns). Fluorescent minerals glow when they are exposed to ultraviolet (UHL-truh-VY-uh-liht) light. The word *fluorescence* comes from the name of the mineral fluorite, which has this property. Other minerals that display fluorescence include calcite and willemite. Although fluorescence is an interesting and sometimes dramatic property, it has limited value in mineral identification. Different samples of the same mineral may or may not display fluorescence, and they may glow in different colors.

CHECK YOUR READING To identify calcite, why would it be more useful to test with dilute hydrochloric acid than to check for fluorescence?

Special Properties

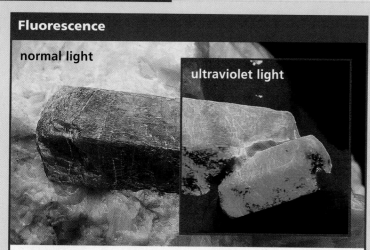

Fluorescence

normal light

ultraviolet light

These minerals look ordinary in normal light but display red and green fluorescence under ultraviolet light.

Acid Test

Acid in contact with carbonate minerals, such as calcite, forms bubbles.

A few minerals respond to magnets. A magnet is pulled toward these minerals. The mineral magnetite strongly attracts magnets, and some other minerals weakly attract magnets. To test a mineral, hold a magnet loosely and bring it close to the mineral. You will be able to notice if there is even a small pull of the magnet toward the mineral. Magnets are commonly used in laboratories and industries to separate magnetic minerals from other minerals.

Some rare minerals have a property known as radioactivity. They contain unstable elements that change into other elements over time. As this happens, they release energy. Geologists can measure this energy and use it to identify minerals that contain unstable elements.

2.2 Review

KEY CONCEPTS

1. Why is color not a reliable clue to the identity of a mineral?

2. What is the difference between cleavage and fracture?

3. Describe what would happen if you rubbed a mineral with a Mohs hardness value of 7 against a mineral with a value of 5.

CRITICAL THINKING

4. **Analyze** Which mineral-identification tests would be easy for a person to perform at home? Which would be difficult?

5. **Draw Conclusions** Diamond and graphite contain only carbon atoms. How can you tell which mineral's atoms are bonded more closely?

● CHALLENGE

6. **Apply** The mineral topaz has perfect cleavage in one direction. It also displays fracture. Explain why a mineral such as topaz can display both cleavage and fracture.

CHAPTER INVESTIGATION

Mineral Identification

OVERVIEW AND PURPOSE In this activity, you will observe and perform tests on minerals. Then you will compare your observations to a mineral identification key.

▶ Procedure

1. Make a data table like the one shown in the notebook on the next page.

2. You will examine and identify five minerals. Get a numbered mineral sample from the mineral set. Record the number of your sample in your table.

step 3

3. First, observe the sample. Note the color and the luster of the sample. Write your observations in your table. In the row labeled "Luster," write *metallic* if the mineral appears shiny like metal. Write *nonmetallic* if the sample does not look like metal. For example, it may look glassy, pearly, or dull.

4. Observe the sample through the hand lens. Look to see any signs of how the crystals in the mineral broke. If it appears that the crystals have broken along straight lines, put a check in the row labeled "Cleavage." If it appears that the sample has fractured, put a check in the appropriate row of your table.

step 4

5. **CAUTION: Keep the streak plate on your desktop or table while you are doing the streak test. A broken streak plate can cause serious cuts.** Rub the mineral sample on the streak plate. If the sample does not leave a mark, the mineral is harder than the streak plate. Write *no* in the row labeled "Streak." If the sample does leave a mark on the streak plate, write the color of the streak in that row.

step 5

MATERIALS
- numbered mineral samples
- hand lens
- streak plate
- copper penny
- steel file
- magnet
- dilute hydrochloric acid
- eyedropper
- Mohs scale
- Mineral Identification Key

DILUTE HCl

6. Test each sample for its hardness on the Mohs scale. Try to scratch the sample with each of these items in order: a fingernail, a copper penny, and a steel file. In the Mohs scale, find the hardness number of the object that first scratches the sample. Write in the table that the mineral's hardness value is between that of the hardest item that did not scratch the sample and that of the item that did scratch it.

7. Test the sample with the magnet. If the magnet is attracted to the sample, put a check in the row labeled "Magnetic."

step 7

8. Repeat steps 2 through 7 for each of the other numbered samples.

Observe and Analyze
Write It Up

1. **INTERPRET DATA** Use the Mineral Identification Key and the information in your data table to identify your samples. Write the names of the minerals in your table.

2. **COLLECT DATA CAUTION: Before doing the acid test, put on your safety glasses, protective gloves, and lab apron. Acids can cause burns.** If you identified one of the samples as a carbonate mineral, such as calcite, you can check your identification with the acid test. Use the eyedropper to put a few drops of dilute hydrochloric acid on the mineral. If the acid bubbles, the sample is a carbonate.

Conclude
Write It Up

1. **COMPARE AND CONTRAST** How are the minerals calcite and halite alike? Which property can you use to test whether a sample is calcite or halite?

2. **INTERPRET** Look at the data in your table. Name any minerals that you could identify on the basis of a single property.

3. **APPLY** Examine a piece of granite rock. On the basis of your examination of granite and your observations of the samples, try to determine what the light-colored, translucent mineral in the granite is and what the flaky, darker mineral is.

▶ INVESTIGATE Further

Specific gravity is another property used to identify minerals. The specific gravity of a mineral is determined by comparing the mineral's density with the density of water.

Find the specific gravity of an unknown mineral chosen from your teacher's samples. Attach your mineral with a string to a spring scale. Record its mass and label this value $M1$. Then suspend the mineral in a beaker of water. Record the measurement of the mineral's mass in water. Label this value $M2$. To determine the mineral's specific gravity, use the following equation:

$$\frac{M1}{M1 - M2} = \text{specific gravity}$$

Do all the other steps to identify the sample. Does the specific gravity you measured match the one listed for that mineral in the identification key?

Mineral Identification

Table 1. Mineral Properties

Property	Sample Number				
	1	2	3	4	5
Color					
Luster					
Cleavage					
Fracture					
Streak					
Hardness					
Magnetic					
Acid test					
Name of mineral					

2.3 Minerals are valuable resources.

 BEFORE, you learned

- Minerals are classified according to their compositions and crystal structures
- A mineral can be identified by its properties

 NOW, you will learn

- How minerals are used in industry and art
- How minerals form
- How minerals are mined

VOCABULARY

magma p. 62
lava p. 62
ore p. 64

EXPLORE Minerals at Your Fingertips

What is an everyday use of minerals?

PROCEDURE

① Observe the core of a wooden pencil. Even though it is called lead, it is made of a mixture of minerals—clay and graphite. A No. 4 pencil has more clay in its lead.

② Use each pencil to draw something, noticing how each marks the page.

WHAT DO YOU THINK?

- How is using a pencil similar to a streak test?
- When would a No. 4 pencil be more useful than a No. 2 pencil?

MATERIALS

- No. 2 wooden pencil
- No. 4 wooden pencil
- paper

Minerals have many uses in industry.

Minerals are necessary to our modern way of life. Mineral deposits are sources of

- metals for cars and airplanes
- quartz and feldspar for glass
- fluorite and calcite for toothpaste
- silver compounds for photographic film
- mica and talc for paint

These examples illustrate just a few of the many ways we depend on minerals.

 CHECK YOUR READING Give three examples of the use of minerals in familiar products.

Minerals have many uses in the arts.

RESOURCE CENTER
CLASSZONE.COM

Learn more about gemstones.

No matter what month you were born in, there is a mineral associated with it—your birthstone. The tradition of birthstones is hundreds of years old. It is one example of the value that people place on the particularly beautiful minerals known as gemstones. In fact, the ancient Egyptians used gems in necklaces and other jewelry at least 4000 years ago.

When gemstones are found, they are usually rough and irregularly shaped. Before a gemstone is used in jewelry, a gem cutter grinds it into the desired shape and polishes it. This process increases the gemstone's beauty and sparkle. The material used to shape and polish a gemstone must be at least as hard as the gemstone itself. Metals, such as gold and silver, also are used in jewelry making and other decorative arts. Both gold and silver are usually combined with copper to increase their hardness.

READING TiP

Corundum and diamond are the two hardest minerals in the Mohs scale. They are often used to grind and polish gemstones.

CHECK YOUR READING How are minerals prepared for use in jewelry? What other questions do you have about how minerals are used?

Uses of Minerals

Common Uses of Minerals	
Mineral	**Products**
Quartz (source of silicon)	Optics, glass, abrasives, gems
Hematite (source of iron)	Machines, nails, cooking utensils
Gibbsite (source of aluminum)	Soda cans, shopping carts
Dolomite (source of magnesium)	Insulators, medicines
Chromite (source of chromium)	Automobile parts, stainless steel
Galena (source of lead)	Batteries, fiber optics, weights
Kaolinite (found in clay)	Ceramics, paper, cosmetics
Beryl (source of beryllium)	Aircraft frames, gems (green form is emerald)

Technology

A clear quartz crystal was sliced to make this computer chip. Minerals such as copper, silver, and gold are commonly used in electronics.

Industry

Diamonds are used as abrasives, as in this drill tip. Minerals are also used in such products as insulators and water filters.

Arts

Cinnabar is ground up to make the pigment known as vermilion. Other minerals are also used as pigments in dyes and paints. Gemstones are used in jewelry, as are platinum and gold.

Minerals form in several ways.

Minerals form within Earth or on Earth's surface by natural processes. Minerals develop when atoms of one or more elements join together and crystals begin to grow. Recall that each type of mineral has its own chemical makeup. Therefore, what types of minerals form in an area depends in part on which elements are present there. Temperature and pressure also affect which minerals form.

Water evaporates. Water usually has many substances dissolved in it. Minerals can form when the water evaporates. For example, when salt water evaporates, the atoms that make up halite, which is used as table salt, join to form crystals. Other minerals form from evaporation too, depending on the substances dissolved in the water. The mineral gypsum often forms as water evaporates.

Hot water cools. As hot water within Earth's crust moves through rocks, it can dissolve minerals. When the water cools, the dissolved minerals separate from the water and become solid again. In some cases, minerals are moved from one place to another. Gold can dissolve in hot water that moves through the crust. As the water cools and the gold becomes solid again, it can fill cracks in rocks. In other cases, the minerals that form are different from the ones that dissolved. Lead from the mineral galena can later become part of the mineral wulfenite as atoms join together into new minerals.

Molten rock cools. Many minerals grow from magma. **Magma**— molten rock inside Earth—contains all the types of atoms that are found in minerals. As magma cools, the atoms join together to form different minerals. Minerals also form as lava cools. **Lava** is molten rock that has reached Earth's surface. Quartz is one of the many minerals that crystallize from magma and lava.

Heat and pressure cause changes. Heat and pressure within Earth cause new minerals to form as bonds between atoms break and join again. The mineral garnet can grow and replace the minerals chlorite and quartz as their atoms combine in new ways. The element carbon is present in some rocks. At high temperatures carbon forms the mineral graphite, which is used in pencils.

Organisms produce minerals. A few minerals are produced by living things. For example, ocean animals such as oysters and clams produce calcite and other carbonate minerals to form their shells. Even you produce minerals. Your body produces one of the main minerals in your bones and teeth—apatite.

CHECK YOUR READING How is the formation of minerals as molten rock cools similar to the formation of minerals as water evaporates?

Mineral Formation

Minerals form at Earth's surface and within Earth.

Water evaporates.

As water evaporates along a shoreline, it leaves behind substances that were dissolved in it. Here, gypsum is forming.

Hot water cools.

Gold dissolved in hot water can fill cracks in rocks as the water cools.

Molten rock cools.

Minerals such as quartz grow as molten rock cools.

Heat and pressure cause changes.

Graphite forms inside Earth when carbon is subjected to great heat.

READING VISUALS Each of the four processes shown involves heat. What is the heat source for rapid evaporation of water at Earth's surface?

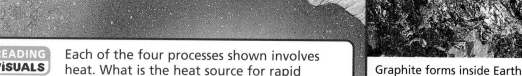

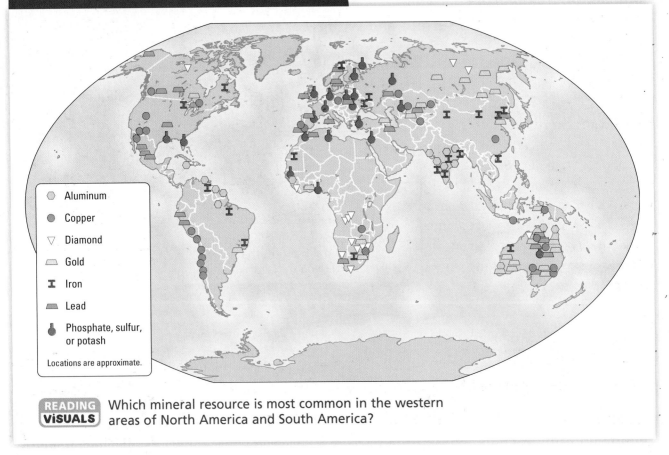

Aluminum
Copper
Diamond
Gold
Iron
Lead
Phosphate, sulfur, or potash

Locations are approximate.

READING VISUALS Which mineral resource is most common in the western areas of North America and South America?

Many minerals are mined.

Before minerals can be used to make products, they must be removed from the ground. Some minerals are found near Earth's surface, while others lie deep underground. Some minerals are found at a wide range of depths, from the surface to deep within Earth.

Most minerals are combined with other minerals in rocks. For any mineral to be worth mining, there must be a fairly large amount of the mineral present in a rock. Rocks that contain enough of a mineral to be mined for a profit are called **ores.**

READING TiP

To make a profit, mine owners must be able to sell ores for more than it cost them to dig the ores out.

Surface Mining

Minerals at or near Earth's surface are recovered by surface mining. Some minerals, such as gold, are very dense. These minerals can build up in riverbeds as less dense minerals are carried away by the water. In a method called panning, a miner uses a pan to wash away unwanted minerals that are less dense. The gold and other dense minerals stay in the bottom of the pan and can then be further separated. In bigger riverbed mining operations, miners use machines to dig out and separate the valuable minerals.

Another method of surface mining is strip mining. Miners strip away plants, soil, and unwanted rocks from Earth's surface. Then they use special machines to dig out an ore.

Like strip mining, open-pit mining involves removing the surface layer of soil. Miners then use explosives to break up the underlying rock and recover the ore. As they dig a deep hole, or pit, to mine the ore, they build roads up the sides of the pit. Trucks carry the ore to the surface. Ores of copper and of iron are obtained by open-pit mining.

If an Olympic-sized swimming pool were filled with rock from this mine, it might contain enough copper to make a solid "beach ball" 146 cm (60 in.) in diameter.

 CHECK YOUR READING How are strip mining and open-pit mining similar? How are they different?

INVESTIGATE Mining

What are the benefits and costs of mining ores?

PROCEDURE

1. Put the birdseed into a pan. Add the beads to the birdseed and mix well.

2. Search through the seeds and separate out the beads and sunflower seeds, placing each kind in a different pile. Take no more than 3 minutes.

3. Assign a value to each of the beads and seeds: red bead, $5; green bead, $4; blue bead, $3; sunflower seed, $2. Count up the value of your beads and seeds. For every yellow bead, subtract $100, which represents the cost of restoring the land after mining.

WHAT DO YOU THINK?

- How does the difficulty of finding the red beads relate to the difficulty of finding the most valuable ores?

- How does the total value of the blue beads and the sunflower seeds compare to the total value of the red and green beads? What can you conclude about deciding which materials to mine?

CHALLENGE The sunflower seeds and the red, green, and blue beads could represent minerals that contain copper, gold, iron, and silver. Which bead or seed is most likely to represent each mineral? Explain your choices.

SKILL FOCUS
Drawing conclusions

MATERIALS
- 1 pound wild-birdseed mix with sunflower seeds
- shallow pan
- 2 small red beads
- 4 small green beads
- 8 small blue beads
- 3 medium yellow beads

TIME

25 minutes

Deep Mining

Deep-mining methods are needed when an ore lies far below Earth's surface. These methods are used to obtain many minerals. Miners dig an opening to reach a deep ore. When the ore is inside a mountain or hill, miners can cut a level passage to reach the mineral they want. Miners dig a vertical passage to reach an ore that lies underground in a flat area or under a mountain.

From the main passage, miners blast, drill, cut, or dig the ore. If the passage is horizontal, they keep digging farther and farther into the hill or mountain. If it is vertical, they remove the ore in layers.

These gold miners are working underground near Carlin, Nevada. The world's deepest gold mine is in South Africa and extends almost 3 km (2 mi) underground.

2.3 Review

KEY CONCEPTS

1. Give two examples of the use of minerals in industry and two examples of the use of minerals in the arts.

2. What are the five ways in which minerals form?

3. What is required for rocks to be considered ores?

CRITICAL THINKING

4. **Infer** Would an ore at Earth's surface or an ore deep underground be more expensive to mine? Explain.

5. **Apply** The mineral quartz has been used as a gemstone for thousands of years. What minerals could jewelry makers use to grind and polish quartz?

● CHALLENGE

6. **Analyze** Both strip mining and open-pit mining are types of surface mining. When might miners choose to use open-pit mining rather than strip mining to obtain an ore?

GEM CUTTER

Geometry for Gems

If you found a gemstone in nature, it would probably look dull and rough. You might want to take it to a gem cutter, who would use a grinding wheel to shape and polish your rough stone into a beautiful gem. You would also discover that a lot of the rough gemstone is ground away into powder.

Gem cutters use geometry to help them choose the best final shapes of gems. Geometry also helps them to shape gems with many small, flat surfaces at specific angles. These surfaces are called facets, and they make the gems sparkle.

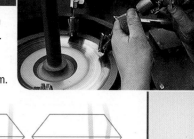

Starred Gems

Some gems—such as certain rubies, sapphires, and forms of quartz—show a six-pointed star when cut in a rounded shape instead of facets. These gems contain tiny flaws aligned at 120-degree angles. When light hits the flaws, it scatters in a star-shaped pattern. The star ruby shown here is a good example of these beautiful gems.

Deeply Colored Gems

Some gems are shaped to show off their rich colors rather than their sparkle. These gems have fewer and larger facets. Also, many brightly colored gems contain lighter and darker areas of color. The gems are shaped so that the richest color is toward the bottom. Light entering one of these gems strikes the bottom and reflects the rich color to the viewer's eye.

Sparkling Gems

How much a gem sparkles depends on the geometric angles at which it is cut. If the overall angle of the bottom part of a gem is too shallow **(A)** or too steep **(C)**, light will go through the gem.

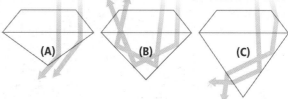

However, if the angles are correct **(B)**, light will bounce around inside the gem as it is reflected to the viewer's eye. The more facets a gem has, the more the light will bounce, and the more the gem will sparkle.

EXPLORE

1. **COMPARE** Table salt, which is the mineral halite, sparkles as light is reflected from its crystal faces. Snow, which is the mineral ice, also sparkles in sunlight. How are the crystal faces of salt and snow similar to facets? How are they different?

2. **CHALLENGE** When would it be best for a gem cutter to split an irregularly shaped crystal into two or more smaller stones before grinding them into finished gems? Remember, one larger stone is usually more valuable than two smaller ones.

the **BIG** idea

Minerals are basic building blocks of Earth.

CONTENT REVIEW
CLASSZONE.COM

◀ KEY CONCEPTS SUMMARY

2.1 Minerals are all around us.

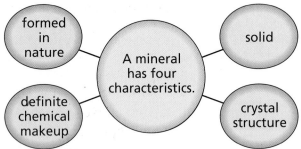

formed in nature — A mineral has four characteristics. — solid

definite chemical makeup — crystal structure

VOCABULARY
mineral p. 43
element p. 45
crystal p. 46

2.2 A mineral is identified by its properties.

Mineral Properties	wulfenite
color	orange
streak	white
luster	nonmetallic
cleavage	yes
density	6.9
hardness	3

VOCABULARY
streak p. 51
luster p. 52
cleavage p. 53
fracture p. 53
density p. 54
hardness p. 55

2.3 Minerals are valuable resources.

copper

Technology

Industry

Arts

Minerals have many uses.

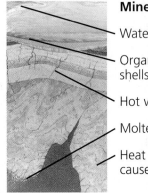

Mineral Formation

Water evaporates.

Organisms form shells or bones.

Hot water cools.

Molten rock cools.

Heat and pressure cause changes.

VOCABULARY
magma p. 62
lava p. 62
ore p. 64

Reviewing Vocabulary

On a separate sheet of paper, write a sentence describing the relationship between the two vocabulary terms.

1. mineral, crystal

2. cleavage, fracture

3. magma, lava

4. element, density

5. mineral, ore

6. element, magma

Reviewing Key Concepts

Multiple Choice *Choose the letter of the best answer.*

7. A mineral is a substance that forms
   - **a.** from rocks
   - **b.** in nature
   - **c.** from one element
   - **d.** in liquid

8. A crystal structure is characteristic of
   - **a.** an element
   - **b.** a rock
   - **c.** magma
   - **d.** a mineral

9. A mineral is made up of one or more
   - **a.** ores
   - **b.** rocks
   - **c.** compounds
   - **d.** elements

10. How is it possible for two different minerals to have the same chemical composition?
    - **a.** They have different crystal structures.
    - **b.** One is formed only by organisms.
    - **c.** Only one is a rock-forming mineral.
    - **d.** They have different appearances.

11. Most minerals in Earth's crust belong to the silicate mineral group because this group contains the
    - **a.** rarest elements on Earth
    - **b.** most common elements on Earth
    - **c.** most valuable metals on Earth
    - **d.** largest crystals on Earth

12. Which of the following is the least reliable clue to a mineral's identity?
    - **a.** color
    - **b.** density
    - **c.** hardness
    - **d.** luster

13. Many properties of a mineral are related to the
    - **a.** number of elements of which it is made
    - **b.** other types of minerals present as it formed
    - **c.** strength of bonds between its atoms
    - **d.** speed at which it formed

14. What types of minerals form in an area depends in part on
    - **a.** which elements are present
    - **b.** the types of rock present
    - **c.** the density of rocks present
    - **d.** whether crystals can form

15. Open-pit mining is used to obtain ores that lie
    - **a.** under flat land
    - **b.** deep in Earth's crust
    - **c.** near the surface of Earth
    - **d.** in riverbeds

16. Gemstones are used in
    - **a.** building materials
    - **b.** paper products
    - **c.** automobile parts
    - **d.** jewelry making

Short Answer *Write a short answer for each question.*

17. Why aren't all solids minerals? Include the term *crystal structure* in your answer.

18. Why is a mineral's streak more useful in identifying it than its color?

19. If you drop dilute hydrochloric acid on the mineral aragonite, it bubbles. What mineral group do you think aragonite belongs to? Why?

20. Describe how the strength of the bonds between atoms in a mineral determines whether the mineral displays cleavage or fracture.

Properties such as hardness and density are used to identify minerals. Use the information from the chart to answer the next five questions.

Mineral	Hardness	Density (g/cm³)
platinum	4.5	19.0
aragonite	4	3
topaz	8	3.5
quartz	7	2.7
arsenic	3.5	5.7

21. COMPARE Platinum can combine with arsenic to form the mineral sperrylite. How do you think the density of sperrylite compares with the densities of platinum and arsenic?

22. APPLY Gems made of topaz are much more valuable than those made of quartz, even though the two minerals can look similar. Describe two methods you could use to identify quartz.

23. APPLY Would a miner be more likely to use the method of panning to find platinum or to find topaz? Why?

24. INFER Aragonite forms very attractive crystals, yet this common mineral is rarely used in jewelry. Why do you think this is?

25. DEDUCE About how many times heavier than a piece of quartz would you expect a piece of platinum of the same size to be? Show your work.

26. HYPOTHESIZE *Halite* is the mineral name for table salt. Thick layers of halite are mined near Detroit, Michigan. At one time, an ocean covered the area. Write a hypothesis that explains how the halite formed there.

27. PREDICT The mineral chromite is the main ore of the metal chromium. What might happen after all the chromite on Earth is mined?

28. PREDICT The mineral apatite is a compound in your bones and teeth. Apatite contains the elements phosphorus and calcium. How might your bones be affected if you do not have enough of these elements in your diet?

29. DRAW CONCLUSIONS You live on the surface of Earth's crust. The average density of the crust is about 2.8 grams per cubic centimeter. Most metal ores have densities greater than 5 grams per cubic centimeter. How common do you think metal ores are in the crust? Why?

the BIG idea

30. ANALYZE Minerals are basic components of planets such as Earth and Mars. Other planets in our solar system, such as Jupiter and Saturn, are called gas giants because they are composed mainly of the gases hydrogen and helium. They do not have solid surfaces. Do you think that minerals are basic components of gas giants? Why or why not?

Mars

Jupiter

31. INFER Minerals make up much of Earth. People use minerals as sources of many materials, such as metals. Some metals are used to make machine parts or build houses. How would your life be different if minerals that contain metals were rare in Earth's crust?

UNIT PROJECTS

If you need to do an experiment for your unit project, gather the materials. Be sure to allow enough time to observe results before the project is due.

Standardized Test Practice

Analyzing a Table

This table shows characteristics of four minerals. Use it to answer the questions below.

Sample	Cleavage or Fracture	Density (g/cm³)	Hardness (in Mohs scale)	Magnetic
E	cleavage	3.7	8.5	no
F	fracture	5.2	5.5	yes
G	fracture	2.7	7.0	no
H	cleavage	2.7	3.0	no

1. Which sample is most dense?

  a. E   **c.** G

  b. F   **d.** H

2. Which sample is hardest?

  a. E   **c.** G

  b. F   **d.** H

3. What will happen if G is rubbed against each of the other samples?

  a. It will scratch only E.

  b. It will scratch only F.

  c. It will scratch only H.

  d. It will scratch F and H.

4. Which statement accurately describes how one of the samples will affect a magnet?

  a. E will attract the magnet.

  b. F will attract the magnet.

  c. G will be pushed away from the magnet.

  d. H will be pushed away from the magnet.

5. Which sample or samples have a crystal structure?

  a. E, F, G, and H   **c.** E and H

  b. only F   **d.** F and G

6. Which samples are likely to break along flat surfaces?

  a. E and G   **c.** G and H

  b. F and G   **d.** E and H

7. An unidentified mineral sample has a density of 2.9 grams per cubic centimeter and a hardness of 6.7. Which mineral is it most like?

  a. E   **c.** G

  b. F   **d.** H

8. Which is true about one-cubic-centimeter pieces of these samples?

  a. Each would have the same weight.

  b. E would be heaviest.

  c. F would be heaviest.

  d. H would be heaviest.

Extended Response

Answer the two questions below in detail. Include some of the terms shown in the word box. In your answers underline each term you use.

chemical makeup	element	compound
crystal structure	Mohs scale	hardness

9. Describe the characteristics of minerals that make them different from rocks.

10. Describe the type of mineral that would work best on the tip of a drill designed to make holes in hard materials.

CHAPTER

3 Rocks

the BIG idea

Rocks change into other rocks over time.

How long will these rocks remain as they are?

Key Concepts

SECTION
3.1 The rock cycle shows how rocks change.
Learn the types of rock and how they change over time.

SECTION
3.2 Igneous rocks form from molten rock.
Learn how igneous rocks form within Earth and at Earth's surface.

SECTION
3.3 Sedimentary rocks form from earlier rocks.
Learn how layers of loose materials develop into sedimentary rocks.

SECTION
3.4 Metamorphic rocks form as existing rocks change.
Learn how one type of rock can change into another.

Internet Preview

CLASSZONE.COM

Chapter 3 online resources: Content Review, Simulation, Visualization, four Resource Centers, Math Tutorial, Test Practice

EXPLORE (the BIG idea)

How Can Rocks Disappear?

Chalk is made of carbonate minerals, as is a type of rock called limestone. Put a piece of chalk in a cup. Pour vinegar over the chalk.

Observe and Think Describe what happens to the chalk. How do you think this change could happen to limestone in nature? **Hint:** Think about the amount of time it might take.

What Causes Rocks to Change?

Make two balls out of modeling clay and freeze them. Take the clay balls out of the freezer and put them on paper. Cover one ball with plastic wrap and stack books on top of it.

Observe and Think Observe how the clay balls change over time. How might rocks respond to changes in temperature, pressure, or both?

Internet Activity: Rocks

Go to **ClassZone.com** to explore how rocks form and change.

Observe and Think Give three examples of the ways in which rocks are continually changing.

NSTA
scilinks.org
SCI *LINKS*

The Rock Cycle **Code: MDL015**

Getting Ready to Learn

◀ CONCEPT REVIEW

- Every mineral has a specific chemical composition.
- A mineral's atoms are arranged in a crystal structure.
- Minerals form under a variety of conditions.

◀ VOCABULARY REVIEW

mineral p. 43

crystal p. 46

magma p. 62

lava p. 62

CONTENT REVIEW
CLASSZONE.COM
Review concepts and vocabulary.

▶ TAKING NOTES

MAIN IDEA WEB

Write each new blue heading in the center box. In the boxes around it, take notes about important terms and details that relate to the main idea.

VOCABULARY STRATEGY

Draw a **magnet word** diagram for each new vocabulary term. Around the "magnet" write words and ideas related to the term.

See the Note-Taking Handbook on pages R45–R51.

SCIENCE NOTEBOOK

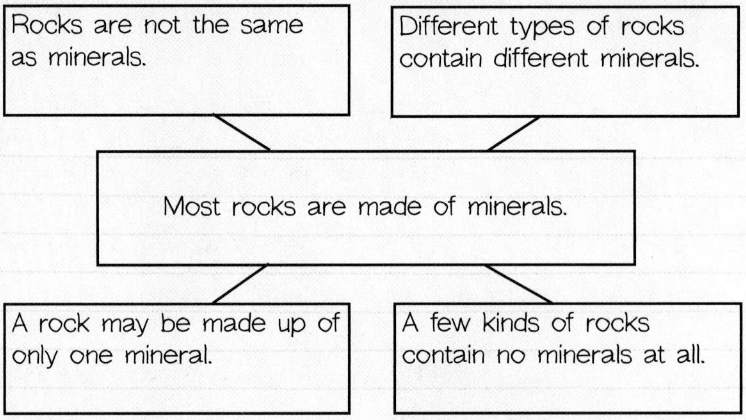

Rocks are not the same as minerals.

Different types of rocks contain different minerals.

Most rocks are made of minerals.

A rock may be made up of only one mineral.

A few kinds of rocks contain no minerals at all.

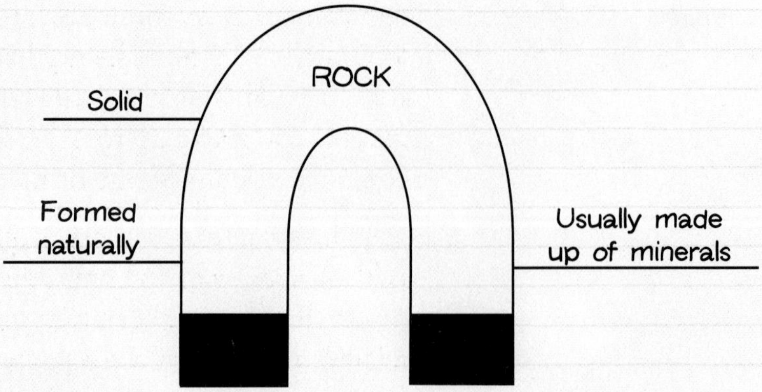

ROCK

Solid

Formed naturally

Usually made up of minerals

3.1 The rock cycle shows how rocks change.

 BEFORE, you learned

- Minerals are basic components of Earth
- Minerals form in many different ways

 NOW, you will learn

- What the three types of rocks are
- How one type of rock can change into another
- How common each rock type is in Earth's crust

VOCABULARY

rock p. 75
rock cycle p. 78
igneous rock p. 78
sedimentary rock p. 78
metamorphic rock p. 78

EXPLORE Rocks and Minerals

How do rocks differ from minerals?

PROCEDURE

1. Closely examine the rock and mineral samples. What do you notice about the forms, shapes, colors, and textures of the rock and the mineral?

2. In your notebook, make lists of the characteristics of the rock and of the mineral.

MATERIALS
- mineral sample
- rock sample
- magnifying glass

WHAT DO YOU THINK?
- What are the similarities and differences between the rock and the mineral?
- What additional observations or tests might help you determine other differences between rocks and minerals?

Most rocks are made of minerals.

If you have ever put together a jigsaw puzzle, you know that each piece is an important part of the final picture. Just as the pieces combine to form the picture, minerals combine to form most rocks. Another way to consider the relationship between minerals and rocks is to compare rocks to words. Just as letters combine to make up words, minerals combine to make up rocks. A **rock** is a naturally formed solid that is usually made up of one or more types of minerals.

The structure of rocks is different from that of minerals. A mineral is always made of the same elements in the same proportions. All minerals have an orderly crystal structure. In contrast, the proportion of different minerals in a particular kind of rock may vary. In addition, the minerals in a rock can be all jumbled together.

A few types of rocks are made up of one kind of mineral, and a few contain no minerals at all. Limestone, for example, can be composed entirely of the mineral calcite. Obsidian (ahb-SIHD-ee-uhn) is a rock that contains no minerals. It consists of natural glass, which is not a mineral because it does not have a crystal structure. Coal is another rock that is not composed of minerals. It is made up of the remains of ancient plants that have been buried and pressed into rock.

Gabbro, like most rocks, is made up of several types of minerals.

Obsidian is an unusual rock because it contains no minerals.

Our world is built of rocks.

Earth is built almost entirely of rock. When you look at Earth's surface, you can see soil, plants, rivers, and oceans. These surface features, however, form only a very thin covering on the planet. Between this thin layer and Earth's metallic core, Earth is made of solid and molten rock.

Because rocks are so common, it is not surprising that people use them for many different purposes, including

- the building of houses and skyscrapers
- the sources of metals, such as iron, aluminum, and copper
- the carving of statues and other works of art
- as a base for pavement for roads and highways

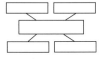

MAIN IDEA WEB
As you read, write each blue heading in a central box and record important details in boxes around it.

These huge cliffs on the coast of the Hawaiian island of Kauai show only a tiny part of the rock that makes up Earth.

People value rocks because rocks last a long time and because some are beautiful. Ancient rock structures and carvings give us a link to our distant past. Many famous monuments and sculptures are made from rocks. Granite blocks form part of the Great Wall of China. Limestone blocks make up the Great Pyramid in Egypt. The faces of four U.S. presidents are carved in the granite of Mount Rushmore.

CHECK YOUR READING · Why do people use rocks for many different purposes?

People study rocks to learn how areas have changed through time. For example, rocks show that North America, as well as most of the rest of the world, has been buried under thick layers of ice many times. You could learn about the types of rocks in your area by collecting and identifying them. You could also examine a map that shows types of rocks and where they are located. This type of map is called a geologic map. The map may be of a large area, such as your state, or a smaller area, such as your county.

This sculptor in Indonesia, like artists throughout the world, shapes rocks into lasting works of art.

INVESTIGATE Classification of Rocks

How can rocks be classified?

Geologists classify rocks by their physical characteristics. Design your own system for classifying rocks, as a scientist might.

PROCEDURE

1. Examine the rock samples. Look at their physical characteristics.
2. Make a list of the differences in the physical characteristics of the rocks.
3. Use your list to decide which characteristics are most important in classifying the rocks into different types. Make a chart in which these characteristics are listed and used to classify the rocks into types.

WHAT DO YOU THINK?

- Which physical characteristic is most helpful in classifying the rocks?
- Which physical characteristic is least helpful in classifying the rocks?

CHALLENGE Is it possible to classify rocks only by the characteristics you can see?

SKILL FOCUS
Classifying

MATERIALS
6 rock samples

TIME
20 minutes

Rocks change as they move through the rock cycle.

VOCABULARY

Add a magnet word diagram for *rock cycle* to your note-book. Then add diagrams for the names of the rock types.

When you want to describe a person you can depend on, you may say that he or she is "like a rock." That's the way people think of rocks—as solid and unchanging. Nevertheless, rocks do change. But the changes usually occur over a huge span of time—thousands to millions of years. The **rock cycle** is the set of natural processes that form, change, break down, and re-form rocks.

A cycle is made up of repeating events that happen one after another. This does not mean that rocks move through the rock cycle in a particular order. As the illustration shows on page 79, a rock at any point in the cycle can change in two or three different ways. Like all cycles, the rock cycle has no beginning or ending but goes on continually.

Rock Types

The three types of rocks are classified by how they form.

- **Igneous rock** (IHG-nee-uhs) forms when molten rock cools and becomes solid. Igneous rock can form within Earth, or it can form on Earth's surface. Igneous rocks that originally formed at great depths can reach Earth's surface over time. Deep rocks may be raised closer to the surface when mountains are pushed up. At the same time, other processes can wear away the rocks that cover the deeper rocks.

- Most **sedimentary rock** (SEHD-uh-MEHN-tuh-ree) forms when pieces of older rocks, plants, and other loose material get pressed or cemented together. Loose material is carried by water or wind and then settles out, forming layers. The lower layers of material can get pressed into rock by the weight of the upper layers. Also, new minerals can grow in the spaces within the material, cementing it together. Some sedimentary rocks form in other ways, as when water evaporates, leaving behind minerals that were dissolved in it.

- **Metamorphic rock** (MEHT-uh-MAWR-fihk) forms when heat or pressure causes older rocks to change into new types of rocks. For example, a rock can get buried deeper in the crust, where pressure and temperature are much greater. The new conditions cause the structure of the rock to change and new minerals to grow in place of the original minerals. The rock becomes a metamorphic rock. Like igneous rocks, metamorphic rocks can be raised to Earth's surface over time.

READING TiP

When material dissolves in water, it breaks into many tiny parts. When the water evaporates, the parts join together and the material becomes solid again.

CHECK YOUR READING What are the three rock types? What questions do you have about how rocks move through the rock cycle?

The Rock Cycle

In the rock cycle, natural processes change each type of rock into other types. Rocks can take many paths through the rock cycle and change into other types in any order.

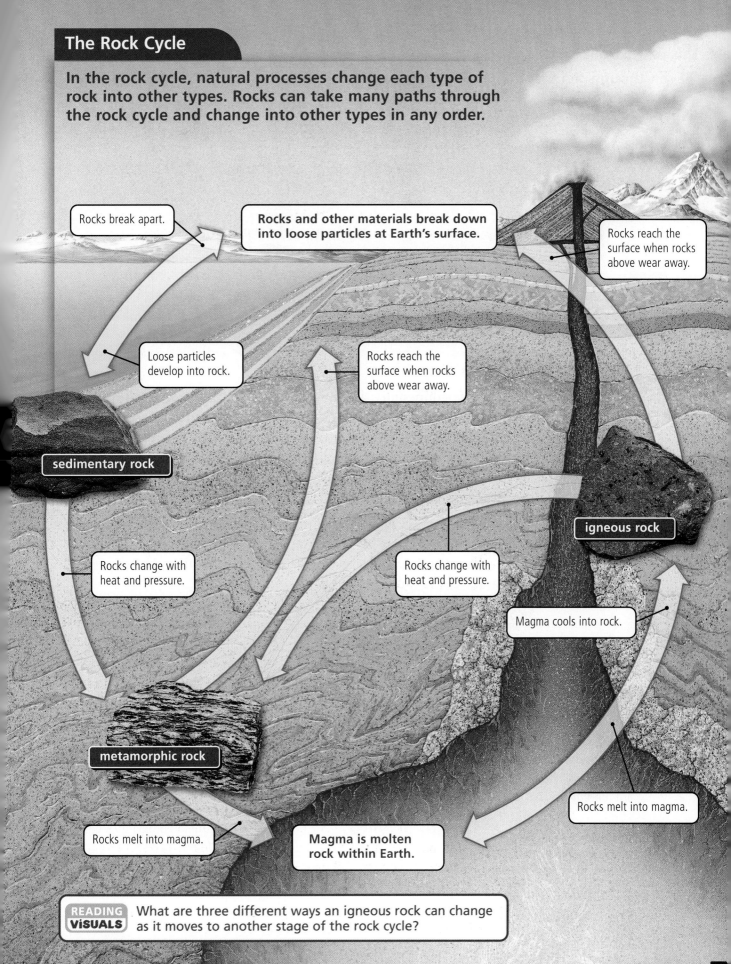

Rocks break apart.

Rocks and other materials break down into loose particles at Earth's surface.

Rocks reach the surface when rocks above wear away.

Loose particles develop into rock.

Rocks reach the surface when rocks above wear away.

sedimentary rock

igneous rock

Rocks change with heat and pressure.

Rocks change with heat and pressure.

Magma cools into rock.

metamorphic rock

Rocks melt into magma.

Rocks melt into magma.

Magma is molten rock within Earth.

READING VISUALS What are three different ways an igneous rock can change as it moves to another stage of the rock cycle?

Rocks in the Crust

Even though sedimentary rock is common at Earth's surface, as a whole the crust consists mainly of igneous and metamorphic rock.

Surface of Crust

Igneous and metamorphic rock 25%

Sedimentary rock 75%

Entire Crust

Sedimentary rock 5%

Igneous and metamorphic rock 95%

Rocks in the Crust

Igneous, sedimentary, and metamorphic rocks are all found in Earth's crust. But these rock types are not evenly distributed. Most of Earth's crust—95 percent of it—consists of igneous rock and metamorphic rock. Sedimentary rock, which forms a thin covering on Earth's surface, makes up only 5 percent of the crust.

The distribution of rock types is a reflection of the rock cycle. Sedimentary rocks are most common at the surface because they are formed by processes that occur at the surface. Most igneous rocks and metamorphic rocks are formed by processes that occur deeper within Earth.

 CHECK YOUR READING Would you expect to find sedimentary rock deep in Earth's crust? Why or why not?

 **3.1 Review**

KEY CONCEPTS

1. How are rocks and minerals different?

2. What are the three types of rock?

3. Which rock types are most common within Earth's crust? Which type is most common at Earth's surface?

CRITICAL THINKING

4. **Analyze** Why is the set of natural processes by which rocks change into other types of rocks called a cycle?

5. **Infer** Which type of rock would you expect to be common on the floor of a large, deep lake? Why?

CHALLENGE

6. **Synthesize** Draw a diagram showing how an igneous rock could change into a metamorphic rock and how the metamorphic rock could change into a sedimentary rock.

Rocks from Space

Earth makes its own rocks. But some rocks come from space and land on Earth's surface. About 30,000 rocks with masses greater than 100 grams (3.5 oz) fall to Earth's surface every year. That's a rate of more than 80 rocks per day!

- A rock from space that reaches Earth's surface after passing through its atmosphere is called a meteorite.
- Most meteorites go unnoticed when they strike Earth. Either they fall in areas where there are few people, or they fall into the ocean.
- The largest rock from space ever found on Earth is called the Hoba meteorite. It weighs 60 tons! It landed in what is now Namibia, Africa, about 80,000 years ago.

A meteorite impact formed Barringer Crater, which is located in the Arizona desert.

This rock is a piece of the meteorite that formed Barringer Crater.

Meteorite Hunters Search Ice

Meteorite hunters search the icy wastes of Antarctica for these rocks. Do more meteorites fall there? No. But they are easy to see against the ice. The cold also helps preserve them in their original condition. In addition, the movements of the ice gather meteorites together in certain locations.

Meteorites Blast Earth

Large meteorites are very rare. This is fortunate, because they hit with great power. About 50,000 years ago, a meteorite that was about 45 meters (150 ft) in diameter slammed into what is now Arizona and blasted a crater 1.2 kilometers (0.75 mi) wide. Craters from ancient impacts may be hard to recognize because the land has been reshaped by geological processes. Evidence can still be found, though. The energy of an impact is so high that some minerals, such as quartz, are permanently altered.

EXPLORE

1. **PREDICT** Oceans cover about 71 percent of Earth's surface. Calculate how many meteorites with masses greater than 100 grams are likely to fall into the ocean each year. How many are likely to fall on land?

2. **CHALLENGE** Use information from the Resource Center to describe how a meteorite impact could have helped cause the dinosaurs to become extinct.

RESOURCE CENTER
CLASSZONE.COM
Learn more about meteorites and meteorite impacts.

A streak of light marks the path of a rock from space through Earth's atmosphere. The rock probably burned up completely before it could land.

3.2 Igneous rocks form from molten rock.

BEFORE, you learned

- Earth's interior is very hot
- Most minerals in Earth's crust are silicates

NOW, you will learn

- Why igneous rocks formed at Earth's surface are different from those formed within Earth
- Why silica content is important in classifying igneous rocks
- Why igneous rocks can make long-lasting landforms

VOCABULARY

intrusive igneous rock
   p. 83
extrusive igneous rock
   p. 83

THINK ABOUT

Why do two rocks made of the same minerals look very different?

Look at a sample of granite and a sample of rhyolite (RY-uh-LYT). These two igneous rocks contain the same minerals, so their chemical compositions are very similar. Yet granite and rhyolite look very different. What do you think might cause this difference?

granite
rhyolite

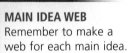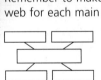

MAIN IDEA WEB
Remember to make a web for each main idea.

Magma and lava form different types of igneous rocks.

Igneous rocks form from molten rock, but where does molten rock come from? The temperature inside Earth increases with depth. That is, the farther down you go, the hotter it gets. Deep within Earth, temperatures are hot enough—750°C to 1250°C (about 1400°F to 2300°F)—to melt rock. This molten rock is called magma. Molten rock that reaches Earth's surface is called lava.

An igneous rock is classified on the basis of its mineral composition and the size of its mineral crystals. A rock formed from magma can have the same composition as a rock formed from lava. The rocks, though, will have different names, because the sizes of their crystals will be very different. You will read why later in this section.

People's decisions about how to use igneous rocks are based in part on the rocks' crystal sizes. For example, rocks with large mineral crystals are often used as building stones because they are attractive.

Origin of Igneous Rocks

Depending on where they form, igneous rocks are classified as intrusive (ihn-TROO-sihv) or extrusive (ihk-STROO-sihv). An **intrusive igneous rock** is one that forms when magma cools within Earth. An **extrusive igneous rock** is one that forms when lava cools on Earth's surface.

Granite is a common intrusive rock in continents. If magma with the same composition reaches the surface, it forms extrusive rocks such as rhyolite and pumice (PUHM-ihs). Basalt (buh-SAWLT) is an extrusive igneous rock that forms the ocean floor. Gabbro is an intrusive rock that has the same composition as basalt.

CHECK YOUR READING How are gabbro and basalt similar? How are they different?

You can see extrusive igneous rocks at Earth's surface. But intrusive igneous rocks form within Earth. How do they reach the surface? Forces inside Earth can push rocks up, as when mountains form. Also, water and wind break apart and carry away surface rocks. Then deeper rocks are uncovered at the surface.

VOCABULARY
Add magnet word diagrams for *intrusive igneous rock* and *extrusive igneous rock* to your notebook.

Types of Igneous Rocks

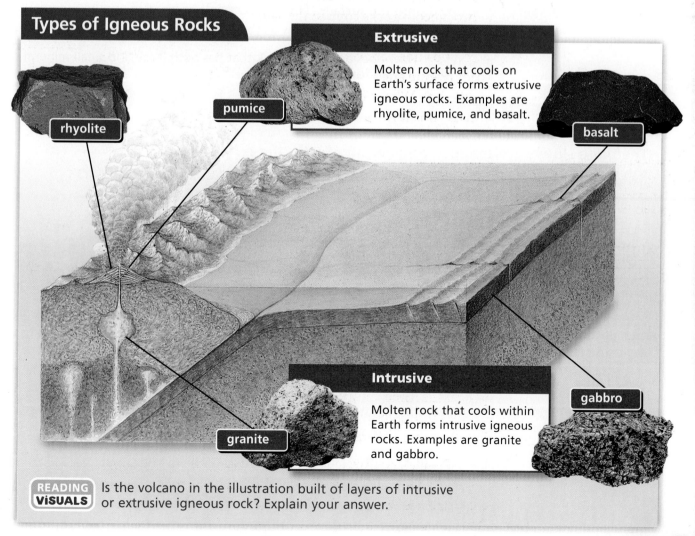

Extrusive

Molten rock that cools on Earth's surface forms extrusive igneous rocks. Examples are rhyolite, pumice, and basalt.

rhyolite

pumice

basalt

Intrusive

Molten rock that cools within Earth forms intrusive igneous rocks. Examples are granite and gabbro.

granite

gabbro

READING VISUALS Is the volcano in the illustration built of layers of intrusive or extrusive igneous rock? Explain your answer.

Textures of Igneous Rocks

VISUALIZATION
CLASSZONE.COM

Explore an animation showing how crystals form as molten rock cools.

The texture of an igneous rock—that is, the size of its mineral crystals—depends on how quickly magma or lava cooled to form it. In an icemaker, crystals form as water freezes into ice. In a similar way, mineral crystals form as molten rock freezes into solid rock.

The magma that forms intrusive igneous rocks stays below the surface of Earth. Large crystals can form in intrusive rocks because

- the interior of Earth is very hot
- the high temperatures allow magma to cool slowly
- slow cooling allows time for large mineral crystals to form

The lava that forms extrusive igneous rocks reaches Earth's surface. Very small crystals form in extrusive rocks because

- the surface of Earth is cooler than Earth's interior
- the lower temperatures cause the lava to cool quickly
- there is no time for large mineral crystals to form

Some igneous rocks contain crystals of very different sizes. These rocks formed from magma that started cooling within Earth and then erupted onto the surface. The large crystals grew as the magma cooled slowly. The small crystals grew as the lava cooled quickly.

CHECK YOUR READING How does an igneous rock that has both large and small mineral crystals form?

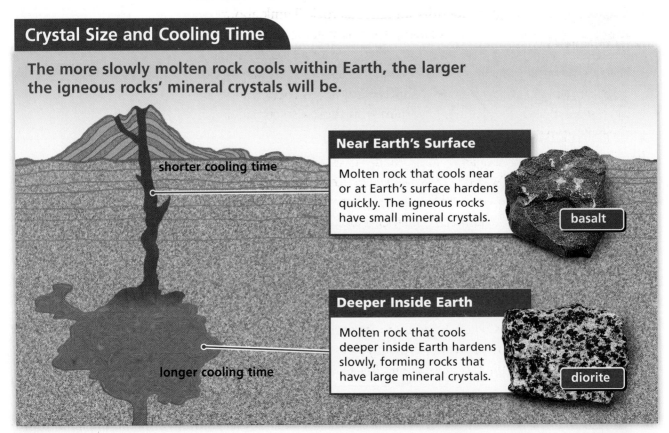

Crystal Size and Cooling Time

The more slowly molten rock cools within Earth, the larger the igneous rocks' mineral crystals will be.

shorter cooling time

Near Earth's Surface

Molten rock that cools near or at Earth's surface hardens quickly. The igneous rocks have small mineral crystals.

basalt

Deeper Inside Earth

Molten rock that cools deeper inside Earth hardens slowly, forming rocks that have large mineral crystals.

diorite

longer cooling time

INVESTIGATE Crystal Size

How does cooling time affect crystal size?

PROCEDURE

1. Look at the Mineral Crystal Diagrams datasheet.

2. Describe your observations of the crystals in each of the igneous-rock diagrams A–C on the lines provided.

3. Describe what is shown in each of graphs 1–3 on the lines provided.

4. Match each igneous-rock diagram with its corresponding graph.

5. On the back of the paper, explain why you matched each crystal diagram with a particular graph.

WHAT DO YOU THINK?

- Which diagram shows an intrusive igneous rock, such as gabbro?
- Where do you think the rock shown in diagram B formed? Explain your answer.

CHALLENGE Write a hypothesis to explain why the rock shown in diagram C might be found at a shallow depth in Earth's crust.

SKILL FOCUS
Analyzing

MATERIALS
Mineral Crystal Diagrams datasheet

TIME
20 Minutes

Composition of Igneous Rocks

Texture is not enough to identify an igneous rock. Think about substances that have similar textures, such as sugar and salt. A spoonful of sugar and a spoonful of salt both consist of small white grains. However, sugar and salt are different materials—that is, they have different compositions. Likewise, different igneous rocks might have similar textures. To identify them, you must also consider their compositions.

Most igneous rocks are mainly made up of silicate minerals, which you read about in the last chapter. The silicate mineral group is the most common group in Earth's crust. Silicate minerals contain varying amounts of silica, a compound of silicon and oxygen. After identifying the texture of an igneous rock, geologists classify the rock on the basis of how rich it is in silica.

Special equipment must be used to determine a rock's exact composition, but you can estimate the level of silica in an igneous rock by looking at its color. Igneous rocks with high levels of silica, such as granite and rhyolite, are typically light in color. Those with low levels of silica, such as gabbro and basalt, are dark in color.

 Would you expect a light gray igneous rock to be rich or poor in silica? Why?

RESOURCE CENTER
CLASSZONE.COM
Find out more about
igneous rocks.

Igneous rocks make long-lasting landforms.

In northwestern New Mexico, a great peak rises out of a flat, barren desert. The Navajo call the peak Tsé Bit'a'í (tseh biht-ah-ih), meaning "rock with wings." In English, it's called Ship Rock, because it looks something like a sailing ship. Ship Rock is an example of the kinds of landforms that are made of igneous rocks. A landform is a natural feature on Earth's land surface.

Intrusive Rock Formations

Ship Rock actually formed about one kilometer below the surface of Earth 30 million years ago. It is all that remains of magma that once fed a volcano. The magma cooled slowly and formed intrusive igneous rock.

As magma pushes up toward Earth's surface, it makes channels and other formations underground. Formations of intrusive igneous rock can be harder and more lasting than other types of rock. Notice in the illustration below how igneous rock has been left at the surface as other, weaker types of rock have been worn away.

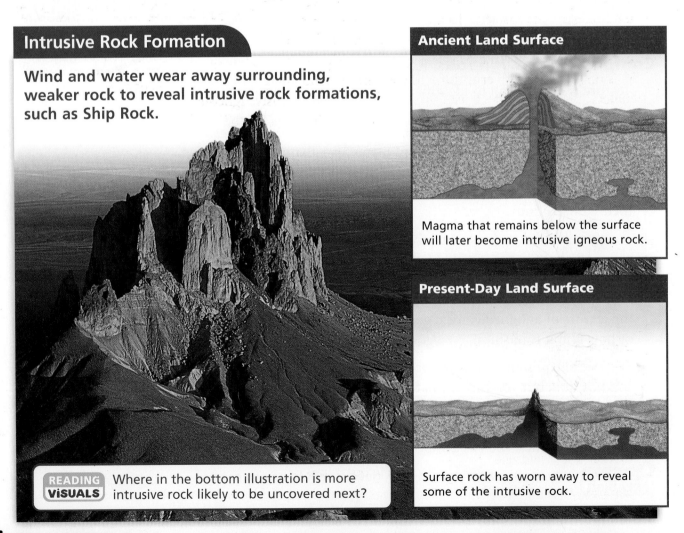

Intrusive Rock Formation

Wind and water wear away surrounding, weaker rock to reveal intrusive rock formations, such as Ship Rock.

Ancient Land Surface

Magma that remains below the surface will later become intrusive igneous rock.

Present-Day Land Surface

Surface rock has worn away to reveal some of the intrusive rock.

READING VISUALS Where in the bottom illustration is more intrusive rock likely to be uncovered next?

Extrusive Rock Formations

When magma makes its way to Earth's surface through a volcano or crack, the lava may erupt in different ways. Some lava can build huge plateaus when it erupts from long cracks in Earth's surface. Lava that is low in silica, such as basalt lava, flows easily and spreads out in thin sheets over great distances. The Columbia Plateau in Oregon and Washington is made of basalt. When lava that is low in silica erupts at a single point, it can build up a huge volcano with gently sloping sides. The Hawaiian Islands are a chain of volcanoes that are built of basalt lava. The volcanoes started erupting on the sea floor and over a very long time grew tall enough to rise above the surface of the ocean as islands.

READING **TiP**

Notice what properties of basalt lava allow it to build large plateaus.

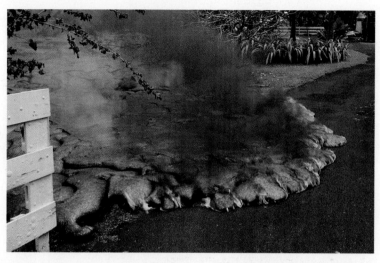

Basalt lava can flow long distances. Here it is spreading over a road in Hawaii.

Lava that contains a greater amount of silica does not flow easily. Silica-rich lava tends to build cone-shaped volcanoes with steep sides. Volcanoes fed by silica-rich magma tend to erupt explosively. Because the magma is thick and sticky, pressure can build up in volcanoes until they explode. An example is Mount St. Helens in the state of Washington. Its 1980 eruption reduced the volcano's height by 400 meters (about 1300 ft). Lava flows are adding new extrusive igneous rock. At the current rate it will take more than 200 years for the volcano to reach its pre-1980 height.

CHECK YOUR READING Why does silica-rich lava tend to build steep volcanoes instead of spreading out?

 Review

KEY CONCEPTS

1. What is the main difference between intrusive and extrusive igneous rocks?

2. What are the two major properties used to classify igneous rocks?

3. Why can intrusive igneous rocks be left behind when surrounding rocks are worn away?

CRITICAL THINKING

4. **Draw Conclusions** If granite within Earth melts and then erupts at the surface, what type of extrusive rock is likely to form?

5. **Analyze** Would you expect extrusive rocks produced by an explosive volcano to be light or dark in color? Why?

CHALLENGE

6. **Synthesize** Why are the names *intrusive* and *extrusive* appropriate for the two types of igneous rocks?

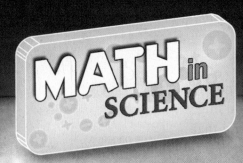

MATH TUTORIAL
CLASSZONE.COM

Click on Math Tutorial for more help with estimating areas.

Resurfacing Earth

Lava flows from volcanoes are common on the island of Hawaii. The map below shows lava flows from the Kilauea volcano. The flow shown in blue destroyed more than 180 homes and covered the region in a layer of lava up to 25 meters thick.

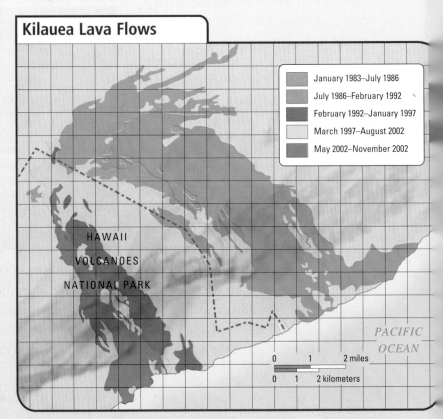

Kilauea Lava Flows

January 1983–July 1986
July 1986–February 1992
February 1992–January 1997
March 1997–August 2002
May 2002–November 2002

HAWAII
VOLCANOES
NATIONAL PARK

PACIFIC OCEAN

0   1   2 miles
0   1   2 kilometers

Use the map to answer the following questions.

1. How many squares does the lava flow shown in yellow cover? First, count the complete grid squares covered by the lava flow shown in yellow. Next, think of partially covered grid squares as fractions, and add them together to get whole squares. Finally, add the number of these squares to the number of complete squares.

2. What is the area of the flow in square kilometers?

3. Use the same method to estimate the areas of the flows shown in purple and blue.

CHALLENGE To estimate the area covered by all the lava flows shown on the map, would it be better to estimate the area of each flow separately and then add the results together? Or would it be better to estimate the total area of the flows in one step? Explain your reasoning.

3.3 Sedimentary rocks form from earlier rocks.

 BEFORE, you learned

- Most rocks are made of minerals
- Some ocean organisms build their shells from minerals
- Dissolved minerals re-form as water evaporates

 NOW, you will learn

- What kinds of materials make up sedimentary rocks
- What the processes that form sedimentary rocks are
- How sedimentary rocks record past conditions

VOCABULARY

sediment p. 89

EXPLORE Particle Layers

What happens as rock particles settle in water?

PROCEDURE

① Pour 2 cups of water into the jar.

② Add the gravel and sand to the water.

③ Shake the jar for a few seconds and then set it down on a counter. Observe and record what happens to the materials in the water.

MATERIALS
- jar
- measuring cup
- water
- 1/3 cup gravel
- 1/3 cup sand

WHAT DO YOU THINK?
- What determines how the materials settle to the bottom of the jar?
- In a lake, how would a mixture of different-sized rock particles settle to the bottom?

Some rocks form from rock particles.

If the sand grains on a beach become naturally cemented together, they form a sedimentary rock called sandstone. Most sedimentary rock forms as sandstone does—from loose material that gets pressed together or cemented into rock. Sedimentary rock forms in other ways, too.

Sedimentary rock takes its name from the word *sediment*, which means "something that settles." **Sediments** are materials that settle out of water or air. In addition to loose pieces of rocks and minerals, pieces of plant and animal remains can also make up sediments. Sedimentary rocks develop from layers of sediments that build up on land or underwater.

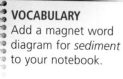

VOCABULARY
Add a magnet word diagram for *sediment* to your notebook.

CHECK YOUR READING What types of material can make up sediments?

Forming and Transporting Rock Particles

A sandy ocean beach, a gravel bar in a river, and a muddy lake bottom all consist mainly of rock particles. These particles were broken away from rocks by the action of water or wind or a combination of both. Such particles may vary in size from boulders to sand to tiny bits of clay.

Just as water washes mud off your hands as it runs over them, rainwater washes away rock particles as it flows downhill. The water carries these rock particles to streams and rivers, which eventually empty into lakes or oceans. Strong winds also pick up sand and rock dust and carry them to distant places.

As winds or water currents slow down, rock particles settle on the land or at the bottom of rivers, lakes, and oceans. The sediments form layers as larger particles settle first, followed by smaller ones.

RESOURCE CENTER
CLASSZONE.COM

Find information on sedimentary rocks.

Forming Loose Sediments into Rocks

If you have ever watched workers building a road, you know that they first put down layers of gravel and other materials. Then they press the layers together, using a huge roller. In a similar way, layers of sediments

Sorting Sediments by Size

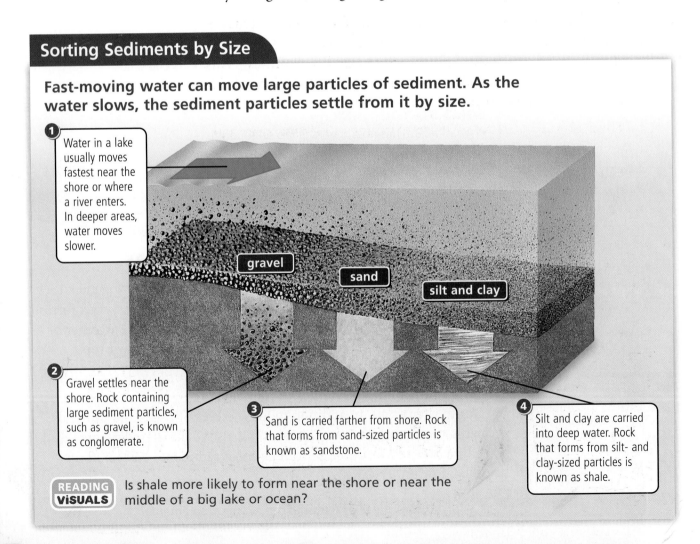

Fast-moving water can move large particles of sediment. As the water slows, the sediment particles settle from it by size.

1 Water in a lake usually moves fastest near the shore or where a river enters. In deeper areas, water moves slower.

gravel

sand

silt and clay

2 Gravel settles near the shore. Rock containing large sediment particles, such as gravel, is known as conglomerate.

3 Sand is carried farther from shore. Rock that forms from sand-sized particles is known as sandstone.

4 Silt and clay are carried into deep water. Rock that forms from silt- and clay-sized particles is known as shale.

READING VISUALS Is shale more likely to form near the shore or near the middle of a big lake or ocean?

composed of rock particles may get pressed together to form rock. One layer gets buried by another, and then another. The overlying layers apply pressure to, or press down on, the sediments underneath.

Small particles of sediment, such as silt and clay, may be formed into rock by pressure alone. In other sedimentary rocks the particles are held together by minerals that have crystallized between them, acting as cement. Over a long time, these processes transform loose sediments into sedimentary rocks.

 CHECK YOUR READING What are two processes that can change sediments into rocks?

Some rocks form from plants or shells.

Processes similar to the ones that produce sedimentary rocks from rock particles also produce rocks from shells or plant remains. These remains are fossils. A fossil is the remains or trace of an organism from long ago.

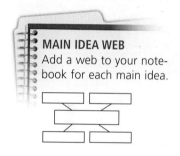
MAIN IDEA WEB
Add a web to your notebook for each main idea.

Coal

If you look at a piece of coal through a magnifying glass, you may be able to make out the shapes of bits of wood or leaves. That is because coal is made up of remains of plants—dead wood, bark, leaves, stems, and roots. Coal is an unusual sedimentary rock because it forms from plants instead of earlier rocks.

The coal people use today started forming millions of years ago in swamps. As plants died, their remains fell upon the remains of earlier plants. Then layers of other sediments buried the layers of plant remains. The weight of the sediments above pressed the plant material into coal.

The dark layer in these rocks is coal.

Here, you can see fossils of ancient plants preserved in coal.

Limestone

Limestone is made up of carbonate minerals, such as calcite. The shells and skeletons of ocean organisms are formed of these minerals. When the organisms die, the shells and skeletons settle on the ocean floor as layers of sediment. Over time, the layers become buried, pressed together, and cemented to form limestone. The photographs below show how loose shells can become limestone.

These shells were made by ocean organisms.

① The shells get cemented together into limestone as some of their minerals dissolve and re-form.

② Individual shells become harder to see as minerals in the limestone continue to dissolve and re-form.

③ Over time, what was once loose sediment becomes limestone with no recognizable shells.

READING TiP

Notice that limestone made up of cemented shells and the limestone in coral reefs were both formed by ocean organisms.

The famous white cliffs of Dover, England, consist of a type of limestone called chalk. The limestone began to form millions of years ago, when the land was under the ocean. The rock developed from shells of tiny organisms that float in the ocean. Most limestone comes from shells and skeletons of ocean organisms. The materials the organisms use to build their shells and skeletons are present in ocean water because they were dissolved from earlier rocks. Like almost all sedimentary rock, limestone forms from material that came from older rocks.

Coral reefs also consist of limestone that comes from organisms. However, in the case of reefs, the limestone is produced directly as coral organisms build their skeletons one on top of another. In the formation of coral, the rock does not go through a loose-sediment stage.

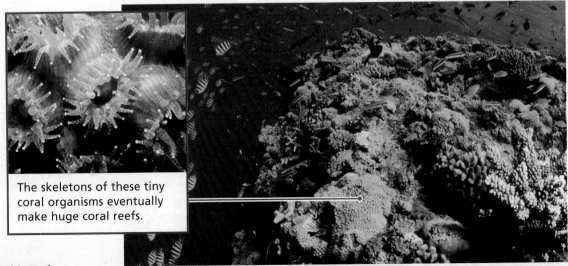

The skeletons of these tiny coral organisms eventually make huge coral reefs.

Some rocks form when dissolved minerals re-form from water.

If you have grown crystals in a container, you know that some substances can dissolve in water and then re-form as the water evaporates. The same process happens in nature. Some sedimentary rocks are made up of minerals that crystallized as water dried up.

The water in oceans, lakes, rivers, and streams contains minerals that came from rocks. Some of these minerals are in solid form. As rainwater washes over rocks, it picks up pieces of minerals and rock particles and carries them into streams and rivers, where many of them settle to the bottom. However, some of the minerals dissolve in the water and are carried along with it.

Water often flows through cracks in rock that is near Earth's surface. As water moves through limestone, some of the rock dissolves. A large open space, or cave, can be left in the rock. As the water flows and drips through the cave, some of it evaporates. The new limestone that forms can take many odd and beautiful shapes.

Sometimes minerals crystallize along the edges of lakes and oceans where the climate is dry and a lot of water evaporates quickly. Over time, the minerals build up and form layers of sedimentary rock. Rock salt and gypsum form in this way. Under the city of Detroit, for example, is a large bed of rock salt that developed when part of an ancient ocean dried up.

Water is shaping this limestone cavern. Water dissolves and transports minerals, then leaves the minerals behind as it evaporates.

CHECK YOUR READING How are the origins of rock salt and some limestone similar?

These limestone towers in Mono Lake, California, formed underwater. They are now above the surface because the lake level has dropped.

INVESTIGATE Rock Layers

How do sedimentary rocks form in layers?

PROCEDURE

1. Prepare the plaster of Paris by mixing it with the water.

2. Mix 2 tablespoons of the gravel with 2 tablespoons of the plaster of Paris and pour the mixture into the paper cup.

3. Mix the sand with 2 tablespoons of the plaster of Paris and the food coloring. Add the mixture to the paper cup, on top of the gravel mixture.

4. Mix the rest of the gravel with the rest of the plaster of Paris. Add the mixture to the paper cup, on top of the sand mixture.

5. After the mixtures harden for about 5 minutes, tear apart the paper cup and observe the layers.

MATERIALS
- 1 paper cup
- 3 mixing cups
- 6 tbs plaster of Paris
- 3 tbs water
- 4 tbs gravel
- 2 tbs sand
- 3 drops food coloring

TIME
20 minutes

WHAT DO YOU THINK?

- How is the procedure you used to make your model similar to the way sedimentary rock forms?
- Describe how similar layers of real rock could form.

CHALLENGE How would you create a model to show the formation of fossil-rich limestone?

Sedimentary rocks show the action of wind and water.

Sedimentary rocks are laid down in layers, with the oldest layers on the bottom. A geologist studying layers of sedimentary rocks can tell something about what conditions were like in the past. For instance, fossils of fish or shells in a layer of rock show that the area was covered by a lake or an ocean long ago.

Fossils are not the only way to tell something about what past conditions were like. The sediments themselves contain a great deal of information. For example, a layer of sedimentary rock may contain sediment particles of different sizes. The largest particles are at the very bottom of the layer. Particles higher in the layer become increasingly smaller. A layer like this shows that the water carrying the sediment was slowing down. The largest particles dropped out when the water was moving quickly. Then smaller and smaller particles dropped out

Crossbeds

The tilted layers in these sandstone rocks are called crossbeds. The layers were once moving sand dunes.

Ripples

The surface of this sandstone preserves ancient sand ripples.

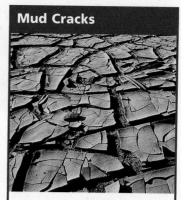

Mud Cracks

As wet silt and clay dry out, cracks develop on the surface of the sediment.

as the water slowed. This type of layer is often created by a flood, when a large amount of water is at first moving quickly.

Sedimentary rocks can give information about the directions in which long-ago wind or water currents were traveling when sediments settled from them. Sand can be laid down in tilted layers on the slopes of sand dunes or sandbars. Sand can also form ripples as water or wind moves over its surface. If the sand has been buried and cemented into sandstone, a geologist can examine it and tell the direction in which the water or wind was moving.

Some rocks made of clay or silt have cracks that developed when the mud from which they formed dried out. Mud cracks show that the rocks formed in areas where wet periods were followed by dry periods.

 CHECK YOUR READING What could a geologist learn by finding rocks that have ripples or mud cracks?

3.3 Review

KEY CONCEPTS

1. What types of material can make up sediments?

2. Describe the three processes by which sedimentary rocks form.

3. Describe how a sedimentary rock can show how fast water was flowing when its sediments were laid down.

CRITICAL THINKING

4. **Infer** Why is coal called a fossil fuel?

5. **Analyze** How could the speed of flowing water change to lay down alternating layers of sand and mud?

△ CHALLENGE

6. **Synthesize** How is it possible for a single sedimentary rock to contain rock particles, animal shells, and minerals that crystallized from water?

3.4 Metamorphic rocks form as existing rocks change.

BEFORE, you learned	NOW, you will learn
• Igneous rocks form as molten rock cools • Sedimentary rocks form from earlier rocks	• How a rock can change into another type of rock • How new minerals can grow in existing rocks

VOCABULARY

metamorphism p. 96
recrystallization p. 97
foliation p. 100

THINK ABOUT

How does a rock change into another kind of rock?

Examine a sample of shale and a sample of schist (shihst). Shale, a sedimentary rock, can change into schist. Think about how this change could occur without the shale's melting or breaking apart. Make a prediction about what process changes shale into schist.

 shale
 schist

Heat and pressure change rocks.

When you cook popcorn, you use heat to increase the pressure within small, hard kernels until they explode into a fluffy snack. Cooking popcorn is just one example of the many ways in which heat and pressure can change the form of things—even things like rocks.

The process in which an existing rock is changed by heat or pressure—or both—is called **metamorphism** (MEHT-uh-MAWR-FIHZ-uhm). The original sedimentary or igneous rock is called the parent rock. The resulting rock is a metamorphic rock. Even a metamorphic rock can be a parent rock for another type of metamorphic rock.

Many of the metamorphic rocks people use were once sedimentary rocks. Limestone is the parent rock of marble, which is used by builders and artists. Shale can be the parent rock of schist, which can be a source of the gemstone garnet. Some schists are a source of the mineral graphite, which is used in pencils.

READING TiP

Rocks change into other rocks by the process of metamorphism. A similar word, *metamorphosis*, refers to what happens when a caterpillar changes into a butterfly.

 CHECK YOUR READING   Give an example of a way people use metamorphic rocks.

During metamorphism, rocks undergo many changes. One type of change occurs when pressure causes a rock's minerals to flatten out in one direction. Other changes can occur in a rock's minerals, but the rock remains solid. Rocks do not melt when they undergo metamorphism. If the temperature gets high enough to melt the rock, the end result is an igneous rock, not a metamorphic rock.

Heat and pressure can break the bonds that join atoms in minerals. Then the atoms can join together differently as new bonds form. This process is called **recrystallization.** It has two main results. First, individual mineral crystals can grow larger as more atoms join their crystal structures. Second, atoms can combine in different ways, and new minerals can form in place of older ones. For example, shale is a sedimentary rock that is formed from silt and clay. During recrystallization, garnet can form from these materials.

How Rocks Change

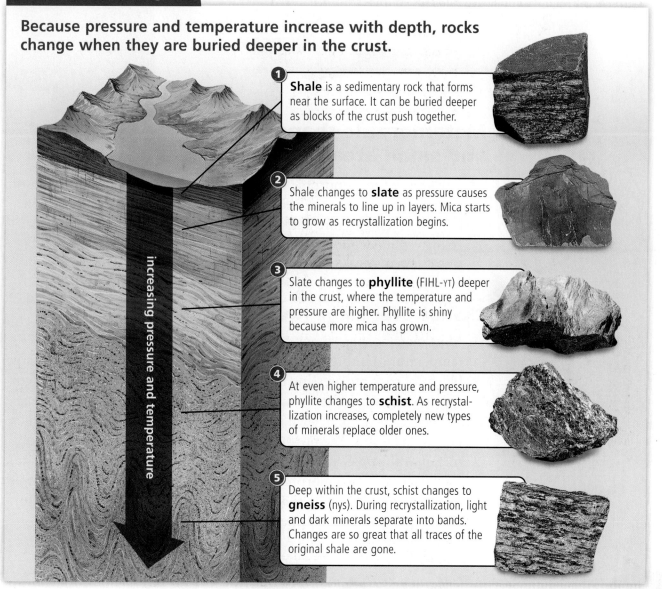

Because pressure and temperature increase with depth, rocks change when they are buried deeper in the crust.

1 **Shale** is a sedimentary rock that forms near the surface. It can be buried deeper as blocks of the crust push together.

2 Shale changes to **slate** as pressure causes the minerals to line up in layers. Mica starts to grow as recrystallization begins.

3 Slate changes to **phyllite** (FIHL-YT) deeper in the crust, where the temperature and pressure are higher. Phyllite is shiny because more mica has grown.

4 At even higher temperature and pressure, phyllite changes to **schist**. As recrystallization increases, completely new types of minerals replace older ones.

5 Deep within the crust, schist changes to **gneiss** (nys). During recrystallization, light and dark minerals separate into bands. Changes are so great that all traces of the original shale are gone.

increasing pressure and temperature

INVESTIGATE Metamorphic Changes

How can pressure and temperature change a solid?

PROCEDURE

(1) Use a vegetable peeler to make a handful of wax shavings of three different colors. Mix the shavings.

(2) Use your hands to warm the shavings, and then squeeze them into a wafer.

WHAT DO YOU THINK?

- Describe what happened to the wax shavings.
- How do the changes you observed resemble metamorphic changes in rocks?

CHALLENGE What changes that occur in metamorphic rocks were you unable to model in this experiment?

SKILL FOCUS
Modeling

MATERIALS
- 3 candles of different colors
- vegetable peeler

TIME
10 minutes

Metamorphic changes occur over large and small areas.

The types of metamorphic changes that occur depend on the types of parent rocks and the conditions of temperature and pressure. When both high temperature and high pressure are present, metamorphic changes can occur over very large areas. When only one of these conditions is present, changes tend to occur over smaller areas.

Change over Large Areas

Most metamorphic changes occur over large areas in which both temperature and pressure are high. An example is a region where large blocks of rock are pressing together and pushing up mountain ranges. This process can affect an area hundreds of kilometers wide and tens of kilometers deep. In such an area, rocks are buried, pressed together, bent, and heated. The pressure and heat cause the rocks to undergo metamorphism. Generally, the deeper below the surface the rocks are, the greater the metamorphic changes that occur in them. For example, a sedimentary rock may change to slate near the surface but become gneiss deep inside a mountain.

CHECK YOUR READING Where can metamorphic changes occur over large areas?

A   **98**   Unit: **Earth's Surface**

Change over Small Areas

Some metamorphic changes occur over small areas. For example, magma can push into rocks underground, or surface rock can be covered by a lava flow. The magma or lava heats the rock it is in contact with, causing recrystallization. These changes are mainly due to high temperature, not pressure. The rocks get roasted but not squeezed. The thickness of rock changed by the heat can range from less than one meter to several hundred meters, depending on the amount and temperature of the molten rock.

Small areas of metamorphic rock can also be formed by high pressure alone. At or near Earth's surface, rocks move and grind past one another during earthquakes. Rocks that grind together in this way can be subjected to high pressures that cause metamorphic changes.

RESOURCE CENTER
CLASSZONE.COM

Find information on metamorphic rocks.

Metamorphic Changes

Changes can occur over hundreds of kilometers or over just a few centimeters.

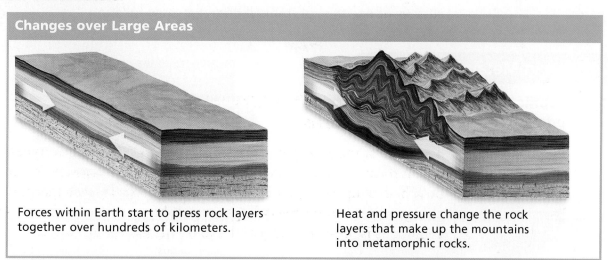

Changes over Large Areas

Forces within Earth start to press rock layers together over hundreds of kilometers.

Heat and pressure change the rock layers that make up the mountains into metamorphic rocks.

Changes over Small Areas

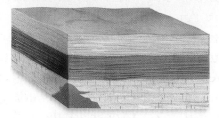

Magma can push into rock layers and cause changes over areas ranging from a few centimeters to tens of meters.

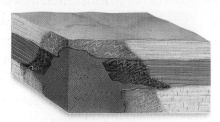

The magma is hot enough to bake the surrounding rocks into metamorphic rocks.

 READING VISUALS Compare how heat and pressure cause changes over the large and small areas shown above.

Most metamorphic rocks develop bands of minerals.

VOCABULARY
Add a magnet word diagram for *foliation* to your notebook.

Some buildings have floors covered with tiles of the metamorphic rock slate. This rock is especially useful for tiles because it displays foliation, a common property of metamorphic rocks. **Foliation** is an arrangement of minerals in flat or wavy parallel bands. Slate can be split into thin sheets along the boundaries between its flat bands of minerals.

You may be familiar with the word *foliage*. Both *foliage* and *foliation* come from the Latin word *folium*, meaning "leaf." Foliated rocks either split easily into leaflike sheets or have bands of minerals that are lined up and easy to see.

Foliated Rocks

Foliation develops when rocks are under pressure. Foliation is common in rocks produced by metamorphic changes that affect large areas. However, as you will see, a metamorphic rock that consists almost entirely of one type of mineral does not show foliation.

Foliation in Metamorphic Rocks

Metamorphic rocks that contain several minerals develop foliation under pressure.

phyllite

Phyllite is a foliated metamorphic rock that contains several types of minerals.

marble

Marble is a nonfoliated metamorphic rock that consists almost entirely of only one mineral.

Foliated

Using a microscope, you can see that the minerals are lined up in bands.

Nonfoliated

The mineral crystals in this rock are not lined up.

READING VISUALS Compare the pictures of the minerals in the foliated rock and the nonfoliated rock. What is different about their arrangements?

Foliation develops when minerals flatten out or line up in bands. At low levels of metamorphism, the bands are extremely thin, as in slate. With higher pressure and temperature, the mineral mica can grow and make the rock look shiny, as is common in phyllite and schist. At even higher levels of metamorphism, the minerals in the rock tend to separate into light and dark bands, like those in gneiss.

 How do rocks change as foliation develops?

Nonfoliated Rocks

Metamorphic rocks that do not show foliation are called nonfoliated rocks. One reason a metamorphic rock may not display foliation is that it is made up mainly of one type of mineral, so that different minerals cannot separate and line up in layers. One common nonfoliated metamorphic rock is marble, which develops from limestone. Marble is used as a decorative stone. It is good for carving and sculpting. Because marble is nonfoliated, it does not split into layers as an artist is working with it. Another example of a nonfoliated rock is quartzite. It forms from sandstone that is made up almost entirely of pieces of quartz.

Another reason that a metamorphic rock may lack foliation is that it has not been subjected to high pressure. Hornfels is a metamorphic rock that can form when a rock is subjected to high temperatures. Hornfels, which often forms when magma or lava touches other rock, is nonfoliated.

 What are two reasons a metamorphic rock might not show foliation?

KEY CONCEPTS

1. What conditions can cause a sedimentary or igneous rock to change into a metamorphic rock?

2. How do new minerals grow within existing rocks?

3. Why do bands of minerals develop in most metamorphic rocks?

CRITICAL THINKING

4. **Draw Conclusions** Would gneiss be more likely to form at shallow depths or at great depths where mountains are being pushed up? Why?

5. **Infer** Would you expect to find foliated or nonfoliated metamorphic rocks next to a lava flow? Why?

CHALLENGE

6. **Synthesize** What features of sedimentary rocks are unlikely to be found in metamorphic rocks? What features of metamorphic rocks do not occur in sedimentary rocks?

CHAPTER INVESTIGATION

Rock Classification

OVERVIEW AND PURPOSE In this activity you will examine rock samples and refer to a rock classification key. You will classify each sample as igneous, sedimentary, or metamorphic.

▶ Procedure

1. Make a data table like the one shown on the **Science Notebook** page.

2. Get a numbered rock sample. Record its number in your data table.

3. Observe the sample as a whole. Then closely examine it with the hand lens. Record in your table all visible properties of the sample. For example, include properties such as mineral or sediment size, layering, or banding.

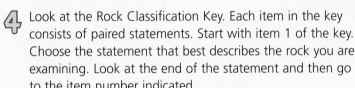

step 3

4. Look at the Rock Classification Key. Each item in the key consists of paired statements. Start with item 1 of the key. Choose the statement that best describes the rock you are examining. Look at the end of the statement and then go to the item number indicated.

MATERIALS
- magnifying glass
- 6–8 rock samples
- Rock Classification Key

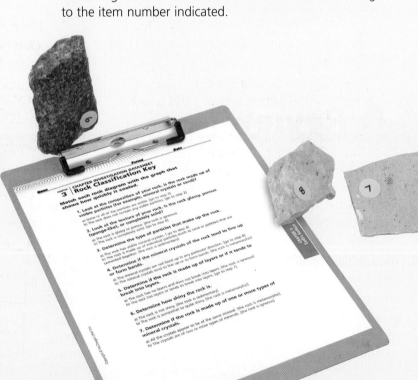

5 Examine the rock sample again and choose the statement that best describes the rock.

6 Continue to work through the key until your choices lead you to a classification that fits your rock. Repeat steps 2–5 for each of the numbered samples.

▶ Observe and Analyze

1. **INTERPRET** Referring to the Rock Classification Key and the observations you recorded, write the type of each rock in your data table.

2. **IDENTIFY LIMITS** What problems, if any, did you experience in applying the key? Which samples did not seem to fit easily into a category? How could you improve the key?

▶ Conclude

1. **COMPARE AND CONTRAST** How are igneous and metamorphic rocks similar? How can you tell them apart?

2. **ANALYZE** Examine a sample of sedimentary rock in which visible particles are cemented together. In addition to sight, what other sense could help you classify this sample?

3. **APPLY** What have you learned from this investigation that would help you make a classification key that someone else could follow? How might you make a key to classify the recordings in a music collection? Write two pairs of numbered statements that would start the classification process.

▶ INVESTIGATE Further

CHALLENGE Make a rock classification key to distinguish between rocks from Earth and rocks from the Moon. Here are some facts to consider. The surface of the Moon was once covered by a thick layer of magma. The Moon has no running water and almost no atmosphere. Minerals on Earth often contain tiny amounts of water. Minerals on the Moon almost never contain any water. The Moon does not have processes that can cause a rock to change into another type of rock.

An astronaut photographed this rock on the Moon. The rock sits in a valley that formed 4 billion years ago. The rock may not have changed or moved since that time.

Rock Classification
Observe and Analyze
Table 1. Rock Sample Properties

Sample Number	Description of Visible Properties	Rock Type

Conclude

Chapter Review

the BIG idea

Rocks change into other rocks over time.

CONTENT REVIEW
CLASSZONE.COM

◄ **KEY CONCEPTS SUMMARY**

3.1 ## The rock cycle shows how rocks change.

Processes at Earth's surface and heat within Earth cause rocks to change into other types of rocks.

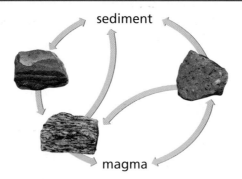

sediment

magma

VOCABULARY
rock p. 75
rock cycle p. 78
igneous rock p. 78
sedimentary rock p. 78
metamorphic rock p. 78

3.2 ## Igneous rocks form from molten rock.

As molten rock cools, minerals crystallize and form igneous rocks.

igneous

Extrusive igneous rocks cool quickly at Earth's surface.

Intrusive igneous rocks cool slowly within Earth.

VOCABULARY
intrusive igneous rock p. 83
extrusive igneous rock p. 83

3.3 ## Sedimentary rocks form from earlier rocks.

Layers of sedimentary rocks form as
• sediments are pressed or cemented together
• dissolved minerals re-form as water evaporates

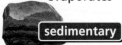
sedimentary

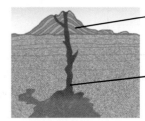

Larger particles of sediment settle faster.

VOCABULARY
sediment p. 89

3.4 ## Metamorphic rocks form as existing rocks change.

Metamorphic rocks form as the structures of the parent rocks change and as their minerals recrystallize.

metamorphic

shale

heat and pressure

schist

VOCABULARY
metamorphism p. 96
recrystallization p. 97
foliation p. 100

Reviewing Vocabulary

Copy and complete the chart below. There may be more than one correct response.

Rock Type	Forms From	Example / Identifying characteristic
intrusive igneous rock	magma	1. large mineral crystals
extrusive igneous rock	2.	basalt 3.
sedimentary rock	4.	conglomerate contains large pieces of earlier rocks
sedimentary rock	ancient plant remains	5. may contain plant fossils
sedimentary rock	6.	limestone 7.
foliated metamorphic rock	parent rock that has several types of minerals	8. minerals are lined up
nonfoliated metamorphic rock	9.	10. 11.

Reviewing Key Concepts

Multiple Choice *Choose the letter of the best answer.*

12. The three groups of rock are sedimentary, metamorphic, and
   a. limestone   **c.** igneous
   b. granite   **d.** coal

13. The rock cycle shows how rocks continually
   a. increase in size
   b. increase in number
   c. become more complex
   d. change over time

14. Which kind of rock forms when molten rock cools?
   a. metamorphic   **c.** igneous
   b. sedimentary   **d.** extrusive

15. An existing rock can change into another type of rock when it is subjected to great
   a. pressure   **c.** flooding
   b. winds   **d.** foliation

16. Which kind of rock forms by recrystallization?
   a. intrusive igneous
   b. extrusive igneous
   c. sedimentary
   d. metamorphic

17. Geologists classify an igneous rock on the basis of its crystal size and the amount of _____ its minerals contain.
   a. carbon   **c.** sediment
   b. silica   **d.** foliation

18. Pieces of rock can settle from water and get cemented into
   a. metamorphic rock
   b. sedimentary rock
   c. igneous rock
   d. extrusive rock

19. Rock salt is an example of a sedimentary rock that develops from dissolved minerals as
   a. water evaporates
   b. magma cools
   c. sediments break down
   d. sand settles in water

Short Answer *Write a short answer to each question.*

20. What is the difference between a rock and a mineral?

21. Compare the distribution of rock types at Earth's surface to their distribution in the entire crust. How are any differences related to processes occurring in the rock cycle?

22. How is the texture of an igneous rock related to the rate at which it cooled?

Thinking Critically

Use the photograph below to answer the next four questions.

23. **INFER** What are the dark markings on the rock?

24. **OBSERVE** Which of the three groups of rocks does this rock belong to? How do you know?

25. **SUMMARIZE** Describe the process by which this rock most likely formed.

26. **PREDICT** If this rock were subjected to metamorphism, how might it change?

27. **APPLY** Copy and complete the concept map below.

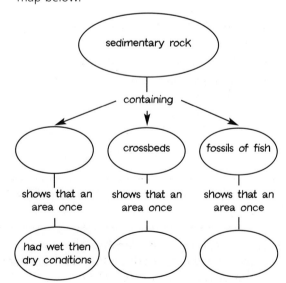

PREDICT Which of the three rock types—igneous, sedimentary, or metamorphic—would you be most likely to find in each area?

Area	Rock Type
28. the bottom of a large lake	
29. older rock surrounding an igneous intrusion	
30. a lava flow from a volcano	
31. a part of the surface that was once deep within a mountain range	
32. the sides of a cave	

the BIG idea

33. **ANALYZE** Look again at the photograph on pages 72–73. Using your knowledge of the rock cycle, draw a diagram showing how sedimentary rocks can form cliffs at Earth's surface. Then add to the diagram by showing how the rocks are likely to change over time.

34. **CONNECT** Describe how material in a rock near the top of a mountain can later be used by an ocean organism in forming its shell.

UNIT PROJECTS

Check your schedule for your unit project. How are you doing? Be sure that you've placed data or notes from your research in your project folder.

Analyzing a Diagram

This diagram shows a simple version of the rock cycle. Use it to answer the questions below.

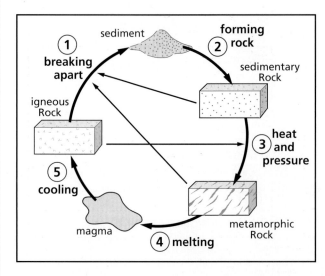

1. Where are loose materials developing into rock?
  a. 1   **c.** 4
  b. 2   **d.** 5

2. Where are sand and other small particles forming from rock?
  a. 1   **c.** 4
  b. 2   **d.** 5

3. Where is magma developing into rock?
  a. 1   **c.** 4
  b. 3   **d.** 5

4. Where is molten rock forming?
  a. 1   **c.** 4
  b. 3   **d.** 5

5. Where are heat and pressure changing solid rock into another type of rock without melting it?
  a. 1   **c.** 4
  b. 3   **d.** 5

6. According to the diagram, what can happen to sedimentary rock?
  a. It can become sediment or magma.
  b. It can become igneous rock or magma.
  c. It can become sediment or metamorphic rock.
  d. It can become sediment, metamorphic rock, or magma.

7. How could you change the diagram to show that igneous rock can become magma again?
  a. Add an arrow from igneous rock to metamorphic rock.
  b. Add an arrow from heat and pressure to igneous rock.
  c. Add an arrow from igneous rock to melting.
  d. Add an arrow from melting to igneous rock.

8. What must happen to rock that formed inside Earth before it can become sediment?
  a. It must reach the surface as rock above it wears away.
  b. It must become magma and erupt from a volcano.
  c. Heat and pressure must change it into sediment.
  d. It must become sedimentary rock while inside Earth.

Extended Response

Answer the two questions below in detail. Include some of the terms shown in the word box. In your answers underline each term you use.

pressed together   buried   mineral crystals
cooling   time

9. Most sedimentary rock forms from pieces of existing rocks. Explain why coal is an unusual sedimentary rock and how coal forms.

10. Melba is trying to decide whether an igneous rock formed deep inside Earth or at the surface. What should she look for? Why?

TIMELINES in Science

HISTORY OF THE EARTH SYSTEM

Systems of air, water, rocks, and living organisms have developed on Earth during the planet's 4.6 billion years of history. More and more scientists have become curious about how these parts of Earth work together. Today, scientists think of these individual systems as part of one large Earth system.

The timeline shows a few events in the history of the Earth system. Scientists have developed special tools and procedures to study this history. The boxes below the timeline show how technology has led to new knowledge about the Earth system and how that knowledge has been applied.

4.6 BYA

Earth Forms in New Solar System

The Sun and nine planets, one of which is Earth, form out of a cloud of gas and dust. Earth forms and grows larger as particles collide with it. While Earth is still young, a slightly smaller object smashes into it and sends huge amounts of material flying into space. Some of this material forms a new object—the Moon.

EVENTS

5 BYA

Billion Years Ago

APPLICATIONS AND TECHNOLOGY

TECHNOLOGY

Measuring Age of Solar System

In 1956, Clair C. Patterson published his estimate that the solar system was 4.55 billion years old. Previously, scientists had learned how to use radioactive elements present in rocks to measure their ages. Patterson used this technology to determine the ages of meteorites that were formed along with the solar system and later fell to Earth. Since 1956, scientists have studied more samples and used new technologies. These studies have generally confirmed Patterson's estimate.

This iron meteorite fell in Siberia in 1947. Data from such meteorites are clues to how and when the solar system formed.

4.4 BYA

Earth Gains Atmosphere, Ocean

Earth's atmosphere forms as volcanoes release gases, including water vapor. Though some gases escape into space, Earth's gravity holds most of them close to the planet. The atmosphere contains no free oxygen. As Earth starts to cool, the water vapor becomes water droplets and falls as rain. Oceans begin to form.

3.5 BYA

Organisms Affect Earth System

Tiny organisms use energy from sunlight to make their food, giving off oxygen as a waste product. The oxygen combines with other gases and with minerals. It may be another billion years before free oxygen starts to build up in the atmosphere.

1.8 BYA

First Supercontinent Forms

All of Earth's continents come together to form one huge supercontinent. The continents and ocean basins are still moving and changing. This supercontinent will break apart in the future. New supercontinents will form and break apart as time goes on.

4 BYA   **3** BYA   **2** BYA   **1** BYA

APPLICATION

Measuring Ozone Levels

In 1924, scientists developed the first instrument to measure ozone, the Dobson spectrophotometer. Ozone is a molecule that consists of three oxygen atoms. In the 1970s, scientists realized that levels of ozone in the upper atmosphere were falling. Countries have taken action to preserve the ozone layer, which protects organisms—including humans—from dangerous ultraviolet radiation. Today, computers process ozone data as they are collected and make them quickly available to researchers around the world.

A Dobson spectrophotometer measures the total amount of ozone in the atmosphere above it.

600 MYA
New Animals Appear
The first multi-celled animals appear in the ocean. Some types of these animals are fastened to the sea floor and get food from particles in water flowing past them. Worms are the most complex type of animals to appear so far.

480 MYA
Plants Appear on Land
The earliest plants appear. These plants, perhaps similar to mosses, join the lichens that already live on land. Through photosynthesis, plants and lichens decrease the amount of carbon dioxide in the air and increase the amount of oxygen. These changes may lead to the eventual development of large, complex animals.

200 MYA
Atlantic Ocean Forms
Earth's continents, which have been combined into the supercontinent Pangaea, start to separate. As what are now the continents of North America and Africa spread apart, the Atlantic Ocean forms.

PANTHALASSA OCEAN

PANGAEA

Tethys Sea

800 MYA   **600 MYA**   **400 MYA**   **200 MYA**

Million Years Ago

TECHNOLOGY
Ocean-Floor Core Samples
In the 1960s, scientists began drilling holes into the sea floor to collect long cores, or columns, of sediment and rock. The cores give clues about Earth's climate, geology, and forms of life for millions of years.

The research ship *JOIDES Resolution* has a drilling rig built into it. Equipment attached to the rig is lowered to the sea floor to collect core samples.

12,000 years ago
Earth Emerges from Ice—Again

Earth's temperature warms slightly. Kilometers-thick ice sheets that formed during the latest of Earth's many ice ages start to melt. Forests and grasslands expand. Sea level rises about 100 meters (330 ft), and the ocean floods the edges of the continents.

1972
New View of Earth

Harrison "Jack" Schmitt, an astronaut traveling 24,000 kilometers (15,000 mi) above Earth, takes a photograph. It is the first to show Earth fully lit by the Sun, and the image is sometimes called the Blue Marble. It helps people see the planet as one system.

RESOURCE CENTER
CLASSZONE.COM

Learn more about the Earth system.

100 MYA   **Today**

APPLICATION

International Space Station

The International Space Station has laboratories in which scientists study Earth, the solar system, and the universe. Also, scientists are doing research to better understand the effects of very low gravity on people. This work is part of an effort to develop the life-support systems needed for people to remain in space a long time. Eventually it might aid in the further exploration of space by humans.

INTO THE FUTURE

In almost every area of life, from music to food to sports, the world has become more connected. Science is no exception. In the past century, scientists have begun to monitor the ozone layer. They have realized that the processes that cause continents to change positions also cause earthquakes and volcanic eruptions to occur.

Changes in technology are likely to help scientists increase their understanding of the Earth system. For example, instruments on artificial satellites measure changes in clouds, ocean life, and land temperatures. These types of data help scientists understand how changes in one part of Earth affect other parts.

ACTIVITIES

Taking a Core Sample

Add layers of damp sand of different colors to a paper cup. Switch cups with a partner. Press a clear straw through the sand, put your finger over the top of the straw, and pull the straw out. Determine the order in which your partner added the sand layers. How would you know if there was a layer of sand that did not go across the entire cup?

Writing About Science

Imagine you are living in microgravity like the astronauts on the International Space Station. Write a detailed description of two hours of your day.

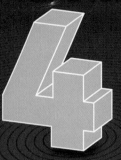

Weathering and Soil Formation

the **BIG** idea

Natural forces break rocks apart and form soil, which supports life.

> **How is rock related to soil?**

Key Concepts

SECTION
4.1 Mechanical and chemical forces break down rocks.
Learn about the natural forces that break down rocks.

SECTION
4.2 Weathering and organic processes form soil.
Learn about the formation and properties of soil.

SECTION
4.3 Human activities affect soil.
Learn how land use affects soil and how soil can be protected and conserved.

Internet Preview

CLASSZONE.COM

Chapter 4 online resources: Content Review, two Visualizations, two Resource Centers, Math Tutorial, Test Practice

Ice Power

Fill a plastic container to the top with water and seal the lid tightly. Place it in the freezer overnight. Check on your container the next morning.

Observe and Think
What happened to the container? Why?

Getting the Dirt on Soil

Remove the top and bottom of a tin can. Be careful of sharp edges. Measure and mark 2 cm from one end of the can. Insert the can 2 cm into the ground, up to the mark. Fill the can with water and time how long it takes for the can to drain. Repeat the procedure in a different location.

Observe and Think
What do you think affects how long it takes for soil to absorb water?

Internet Activity: Soil Formation

Go to **ClassZone.com** to watch how soil forms. Learn how materials break down and contribute to soil buildup over time.

Observe and Think
What do rocks and soil have in common? What do organic matter and soil have in common?

NSTA
scilinks.org
*SCI*LINKS

Soil Conservation **Code: MDL016**

CHAPTER 4

Getting Ready to Learn

CONCEPT REVIEW

- The atmosphere, hydrosphere, biosphere, and geosphere interact to shape Earth's surface.
- Natural processes form, change, break down, and re-form rocks.

VOCABULARY REVIEW

cleavage p. 53
fracture p. 53
rock p. 75
rock cycle p. 78
sediment p. 89

CONTENT REVIEW
CLASSZONE.COM
Review concepts and vocabulary.

TAKING NOTES

COMBINATION NOTES

To take notes about a new concept, first make an informal outline of the information. Then make a sketch of the concept and label it so that you can study it later.

CHOOSE YOUR OWN STRATEGY

Take notes about new vocabulary terms, using one or more of the strategies from earlier chapters—**magnet word, word triangle,** or **description wheel.** Feel free to mix and match the strategies, or use an entirely different vocabulary strategy.

See the Note-Taking Handbook on pages R45–R51.

SCIENCE NOTEBOOK

NOTES

Causes of Mechanical Weathering
- Ice
- Pressure Release
- Plant Roots
- Moving Water

Description Wheel

Word Triangle

Magnet Word

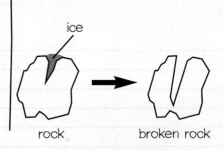

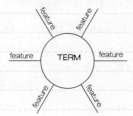

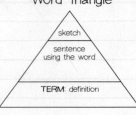

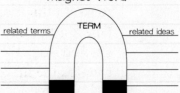

KEY CONCEPT
Mechanical and chemical forces break down rocks.

 BEFORE, you learned

- Minerals make up most rocks
- Different minerals have different properties
- Rocks are broken down to form sediments

 NOW, you will learn

- How mechanical weathering breaks down rocks
- How chemical weathering changes rocks
- What factors affect the rate at which weathering occurs

VOCABULARY

weathering p. 115
mechanical weathering
  p. 116
exfoliation p. 116
abrasion p. 116
chemical weathering
  p. 118

EXPLORE Mechanical Weathering

What causes rocks to break down?

PROCEDURE

1. Place a handful of rocks on a piece of dark-colored construction paper. Observe the rocks and take notes on their appearance.

2. Place the rocks in a coffee can. Put the lid on the can and shake the can forcefully for 2 minutes, holding the lid tightly shut.

3. Pour the rocks onto the construction paper. Observe them and take notes on any changes in their appearance.

WHAT DO YOU THINK?

- What happened to the rocks and why?
- What forces in nature might affect rocks in similar ways?

MATERIALS
- coffee can with lid
- rocks
- dark-colored construction paper

Weathering breaks rocks into smaller pieces.

Think about the tiniest rock you have ever found. How did it get so small? It didn't start out that way! Over time, natural forces break rocks into smaller and smaller pieces. If you have ever seen a concrete sidewalk or driveway that has been cracked by tree roots, you have seen this process. The same thing can happen to rocks.

Weathering is the process by which natural forces break down rocks. In this section you will read about two kinds of weathering. One kind occurs when a rock is physically broken apart—like the cracked sidewalk. Another kind occurs when a chemical reaction changes the makeup of a rock.

VOCABULARY
Remember to add *weathering* to your notebook, using the vocabulary strategy of your choice.

Mechanical weathering produces physical changes in rocks.

RESOURCE CENTER
CLASSZONE.COM

Learn more about
weathering.

READING TiP

The word *expand* means
"to increase in size
or volume."

If you smash a walnut with a hammer, you will break it into a lot
of small pieces, but you will not change what it is. Even though the
pieces of the walnut are no longer connected together, they are still
composed of the same materials. **Mechanical weathering**—the
breaking up of rocks by physical forces—works in much the same
way. In this natural process, physical forces split rocks apart but do
not change their composition—what they are made of. Ice wedging,
pressure release, plant root growth, and abrasion can all cause
mechanical weathering.

① **Ice Wedging** When water freezes, it expands. When water freezes
in the cracks and pores of rocks, the force of its expansion is strong
enough to split the rocks apart. This process, which is called ice
wedging, can break up huge boulders. Ice wedging is common in
places where temperatures rise above and fall below the freezing
point for water, which is 0°C (32°F).

② **Pressure Release** Rock deep within Earth is under great pressure
from surrounding rocks. Over time, Earth's forces can push the rock
up to the surface, or the overlying rocks and sediment can wear away.
In either case, the pressure inside the rock is still high, but the
pressure on the surface of the rock is released. This release of pressure
causes the rock to expand. As the rock expands, cracks form in it,
leading to exfoliation. **Exfoliation** (ehks-FOH-lee-AY-shuhn) is a
process in which layers or sheets of rock gradually break off. This
process is sometimes called onion-skin weathering, because the
rock surface breaks off in thin layers similar to the layers of an onion.

③ **Plant Root Growth** Trees, bushes, and other plants may take
root in cracks in rocks. As the roots of these plants grow, they
wedge open the cracks. The rock—even if it is large—can be split
completely apart.

④ **Abrasion** Water can wear down rocks on riverbeds and along
shorelines by abrasion. **Abrasion** (uh-BRAY-zhuhn) is the process
of wearing down by friction, the rubbing of one object or surface
against another. The force of moving water alone can wear away
particles of rock. Water also causes rocks to tumble downstream.
The tumbling rocks wear down as they grind against the riverbed
and against each other. Ocean waves beating against a rocky shore
also wear down rocks by abrasion.

CHECK YOUR READING How does moving water weather rocks?

Mechanical Weathering

Ice wedging, pressure release, plant root growth, and abrasion can all break apart rocks.

① Ice Wedging

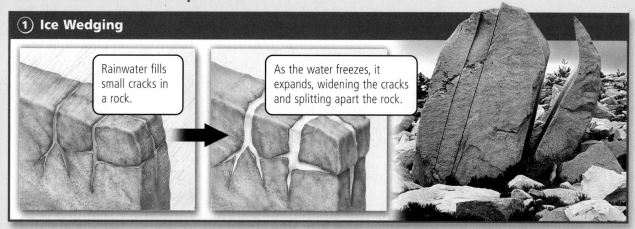

Rainwater fills small cracks in a rock.

As the water freezes, it expands, widening the cracks and splitting apart the rock.

② Pressure Release

Earth's forces can push rock that formed deep underground up to the surface.

The release of pressure causes the rock to expand and crack.

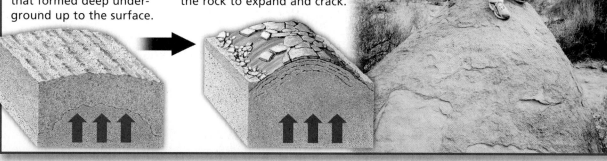

③ Plant Root Growth

When plants grow in cracks in a rock, their roots can widen the cracks and force the rock apart.

④ Abrasion

Flowing water can move rocks, causing them to rub together and wear down into rounded shapes.

READING VISUALS What evidence of mechanical weathering can you see in each photograph above?

Chemical weathering changes the mineral composition of rocks.

VISUALIZATION
CLASSZONE.COM

Watch chemical
weathering in action.

If you have seen an old rusty nail, you have witnessed the result of a chemical reaction and a chemical change. The steel in the nail contains iron. Oxygen in air and water react with the iron to form rust.

Minerals in rocks also undergo chemical changes when they react with water and air. **Chemical weathering** is the breakdown of rocks by chemical reactions that change the rocks' makeup, or composition. When minerals in rocks come into contact with air and water, some dissolve and others react and are changed into different minerals.

Dissolving

Water is the main cause of chemical weathering. Some minerals completely dissolve in ordinary water. The mineral halite, which is the same compound as table salt, dissolves in ordinary water. Many more minerals dissolve in water that is slightly acidic—like lemonade. In the atmosphere, small amounts of carbon dioxide dissolve in rainwater. The water and carbon dioxide react to form a weak acid. After falling to Earth, the rainwater moves through the soil, picking up additional

---

INVESTIGATE Chemical Weathering

What is necessary for rust to form?

PROCEDURE

1. Place a piece of steel wool in a cup filled to the top with water. Place a second piece of steel wool in a cup with a small amount of water. The water should touch but not cover the steel wool. Place a third piece in a cup with no water.

2. Allow the three cups to sit overnight. Observe the appearance of the steel wool in each container the next day.

WHAT DO YOU THINK?
- What happened to the steel wool in each cup?
- Judging by the appearance of the pieces of steel wool, what do you think is necessary for rusting to occur?

CHALLENGE Tear the steel wool that rusted most apart and compare the appearances of the inside and the outside. Why might the inside and the outside look different?

SKILL FOCUS
Identifying variables

MATERIALS
- steel wool
- 3 cups
- water

TIME
15 minutes

About 100 Years Ago

Today

 READING VISUALS **INFER** This ancient stone monument was moved from a desert in Egypt to New York City in 1881. How and why has it changed?

carbon dioxide from decaying plants. The slightly acidic water breaks down minerals in rocks. In the process, the rocks may also break apart into smaller pieces.

Air pollution can make rainwater even more acidic than it is naturally. Power plants and automobiles produce gases such as sulfur dioxide and nitric oxide, which react with water vapor in the atmosphere to form acid rain. Acid rain causes rocks to weather much faster than they would naturally. The photographs above show how acid rain can damage a granite column in just a hundred years.

Rusting

The oxygen in the air is also involved in chemical weathering. Many common minerals contain iron. When these minerals dissolve in water, oxygen in the air and the water combines with the iron to produce iron oxides, or rust. The iron oxides form a coating that colors the weathered rocks like those you see in the photograph of Oak Creek Canyon in Arizona.

The rocks in Oak Creek Canyon are reddish because iron in the rocks reacted with water and air to produce iron oxides.

CHECK YOUR READING How is air involved in chemical weathering?

Weathering occurs at different rates.

COMBINATION NOTES
Record in your notes three factors that affect the rate at which rock weathers.

Most weathering occurs over long periods of time—hundreds, thousands, or even millions of years. It can take hundreds or thousands of years for a very hard rock to wear down only a few millimeters—a few times the thickness of your fingernail. But the rate of weathering is not the same for all rocks. Factors such as surface area, rock composition, and location influence the rate of weathering.

Surface Area The more of a rock's surface that is exposed to air and water, the faster the rock will break down. A greater surface area allows chemical weathering to affect more of a rock.

① Over time, mechanical weathering breaks a rock into smaller pieces.

② As a result, more of the rock's surface is exposed to chemical weathering.

Rock Composition Different kinds of rock break down at different rates. Granite, for example, breaks down much more slowly than limestone. Both of these rocks are often used for tombstones and statues.

Climate Water is needed for chemical weathering to occur, and heat speeds up chemical weathering. As a result, chemical weathering occurs faster in hot, wet regions than it does in cold, dry regions. However, mechanical weathering caused by freezing and thawing occurs more in cold regions than in hot regions.

4.1 Review

KEY CONCEPTS

1. What is weathering?
2. What are four causes of mechanical weathering?
3. How do water and air help cause chemical weathering?
4. Describe three factors that affect the rate at which weathering occurs.

CRITICAL THINKING

5. **Infer** How does mechanical weathering affect the rate of chemical weathering?
6. **Predict** Would weathering affect a marble sculpture inside a museum? Explain your answer.

⚠ CHALLENGE

7. **Infer** The word *weather* is most commonly used to refer to the state of the atmosphere at a certain time. Why do you think the same word is used to refer to the breakdown of rocks?

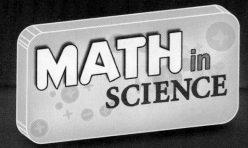

MATH TUTORIAL
CLASSZONE.COM

Click on Math Tutorial for more help with finding the surface areas of rectangular prisms.

Weathering has broken apart these rocks in the Isles of Scilly, England.

Rock Weathering

How quickly a rock weathers depends, in part, on its surface area. The greater the surface area, the more quickly the rock weathers. Do you think a rock will weather more quickly if you break it in half? You can find out by using a rectangular prism to represent the rock.

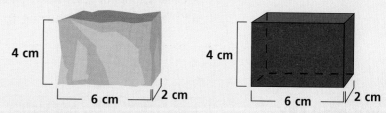

Example

To find the surface area of the prism, add the areas of its faces.

(1) Find the area of each face.

Area of top (or bottom) face: 6 cm $\times$ 2 cm = 12 cm^2
Area of front (or back) face: 6 cm $\times$ 4 cm = 24 cm^2
Area of right (or left) face: 4 cm $\times$ 2 cm = 8 cm^2

(2) Add the areas of all six faces to find the surface area.

Surface area = 12 cm^2 + 12 cm^2 + 24 cm^2 + 24 cm^2
+ 8 cm^2 + 8 cm^2
= 88 cm^2

ANSWER The surface area of the prism is 88 cm^2.

For the rock broken in half, you can use two smaller rectangular prisms to represent the two halves.

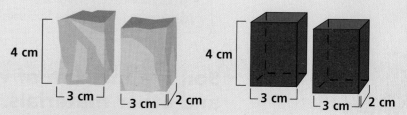

Answer the following questions.

1. What is the surface area of each of the smaller rectangular prisms?

2. How does the total surface area of the two smaller prisms compare with the surface area of the larger prism?

3. Will the rock weather more quickly in one piece or broken in half?

CHALLENGE If the two smaller prisms both broke in half, what would be the total surface area of the resulting four prisms?

4.2 Weathering and organic processes form soil.

◀ BEFORE, you learned	▶ NOW, you will learn
• Weathering processes break down rocks • Climate influences the rate of weathering	• What soil consists of • How climate and landforms affect a soil's characteristics • How the activities of organisms affect a soil's characteristics • How the properties of soil differ

VOCABULARY

humus p. 123
soil horizon p. 124
soil profile p. 124

EXPLORE Soil Composition

What makes soils different?

PROCEDURE

① Spread some potting soil on a piece of white paper. Spread another type of soil on another piece of white paper.

② Examine the two soil samples with a hand lens. Use the tweezers to look for small pieces of rock or sand, humus, and clay. Humus is brown or black, and clay is lighter in color. Record your observations.

MATERIALS

• potting soil
• local soil sample
• white paper (2 pieces)
• hand lens
• tweezers

WHAT DO YOU THINK?

• How do the two soil samples differ? How are they alike?

• What might account for the differences between the two soils?

Soil is a mixture of weathered rock particles and other materials.

Soil may not be the first thing you think of when you wake up in the morning, but it is a very important part of your everyday life. You have spent your whole life eating food grown in soil, standing on soil, and living in buildings built on soil. Soil is under your feet right now—or at least there used to be soil there before the building you are in was constructed. In this section you will learn more about the world of soil beneath your feet.

 Why is soil important?

Soil Composition

Soil is a mixture of four materials: weathered rock particles, organic matter, water, and air. Weathered rock particles are the main ingredient of soil. Soils differ, depending on what types of rock the rock particles came from—for example, granite or limestone.

Water and air each make up about 20 to 30 percent of a soil's volume. Organic matter makes up about 5 percent. The word *organic* (awr-GAN-ihk) means "coming from living organisms." Organic matter in soil comes from the remains and waste products of plants, animals, and other living organisms. For example, leaves that fall to a forest floor decay and become part of the soil. The decayed organic matter in soil is called **humus** (HYOO-muhs).

All soils are not the same. Different soils are made up of different ingredients and different amounts of each ingredient. In the photographs below, the black soil contains much more decayed plant material than the red soil. The black soil also contains more water. The kind of soil that forms in an area depends on a number of factors, including

- the kind of rock in the area
- the area's climate, or overall weather pattern over time
- the landforms in the area, such as mountains and valleys
- the plant cover in the area
- the animals and other organisms in the area
- time

The composition of a soil determines what you can grow in it, what you can build on it, and what happens to the rainwater that falls on it.

VOCABULARY
A description wheel would be a good choice for taking notes about the term *humus.*

READING VISUALS **COMPARE AND CONTRAST** These two soils look different because they contain different ingredients. How would you describe their differences?

Soil Horizons

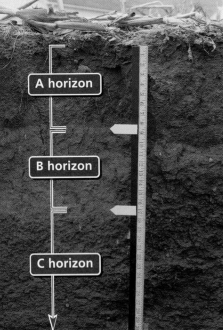

If you dig a deep hole in the ground, you might notice that the deeper soil looks different. As you dig down, you will find larger rock particles that are less weathered. There is also less organic matter in deeper soil.

Soil develops in a series of horizontal layers called soil horizons. A **soil horizon** is a layer of soil with properties that differ from those of the layer above or below it. Geologists label the main horizons A, B, and C. In some places there may also be a layer of dead leaves and other organic matter at the surface of the ground.

- **The A horizon** is the upper layer of soil and is commonly called topsoil. It contains the most organic matter of the three horizons. Because of the humus the A horizon contains, it is often dark in color.

- **The B horizon** lies just below the A horizon. It has little organic matter and is usually brownish or reddish in color. It contains clay and minerals that have washed down from the A horizon.

- **The C horizon** is the deepest layer of soil. It consists of the largest and least-weathered rock particles. Its color is typically light yellowish brown.

The soil horizons in a specific location make up what geologists call a **soil profile.** Different locations can have very different soil profiles. The A horizon, for example, may be very thick in some places and very thin in others. In some areas, one or more horizons may even be missing from the profile. For example, a soil that has had only a short time to develop might be missing the B horizon.

 CHECK YOUR READING What are soil horizons?

Climate and landforms affect soil.

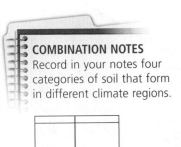
Different kinds of soils form in different climates. The soil that forms in a hot, wet climate is different from the soil of a cold, dry climate. Climate also influences the characteristics and thickness of the soil that develops from weathered rock. Tropical, desert, temperate, and arctic soils are four types of soil that form in different climate regions.

The shape of the land also affects the development of soil. For example, mountain soils may be very different from the soils in nearby valleys. The cold climate on a mountain results in slow soil formation, and the top layer of soil continually washes down off the slopes. As a result, mountain slopes have soils with thin A horizons that cannot support large plants. The soil that washes down the slopes builds up in the surrounding valleys, so the valleys may have soils with thick A horizons that can support many plants.

World Soil Types

Different types of soils form in different climates.

Tropical Soils

Tropical soils form in warm, rainy regions. Heavy rains wash away minerals, leaving only a thin surface layer of humus. Tropical soils are not suitable for growing most crops.

Desert Soils

Desert soils form in dry regions. These soils are shallow and contain little organic matter. Because of the low rainfall, chemical weathering and soil formation occur very slowly in desert regions.

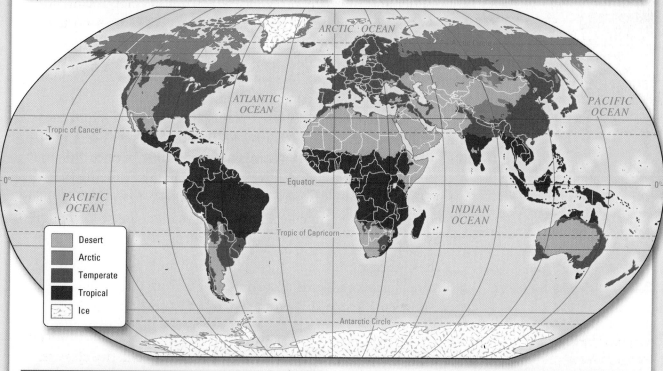

Desert
Arctic
Temperate
Tropical
Ice

Temperate Soils

Temperate soils form in regions with moderate rainfall and temperatures. Some temperate soils are dark-colored, rich in organic matter and minerals, and good for growing crops.

Arctic Soils

Arctic soils form in cold, dry regions where chemical weathering is slow. They typically do not have well-developed horizons. Arctic soils contain a lot of rock fragments.

The activities of organisms affect soil.

COMBINATION NOTES
Record in your notes three types of organisms that affect soil characteristics.

READING **TiP**

A decomposer is an organism that decomposes, or breaks down, dead plants and animals.

Under the ground beneath your feet is a whole world of life forms that are going about their daily activities. The living organisms in a soil have a huge impact on the soil's characteristics. In fact, without them, the soil would not be able to support the wide variety of plants that people depend on to live. The organisms that affect the characteristics of soils include plants, microorganisms (MY-kroh-AWR-guh-NIHZ-uhmz), and animals.

Plants, such as trees and grasses, provide most of the organic matter that gets broken down to form humus. Trees add to the organic matter in soil as they lose their branches and leaves. Trees and other plants also contribute to humus when they die and decompose, or break down.

 CHECK YOUR READING How are plants and humus related?

Microorganisms include decomposers such as bacteria and fungi (FUHN-jy). The prefix *micro-* means "very small." Microorganisms are so small that they can be seen only with a microscope. A spoonful of soil may contain more than a million microorganisms! These microorganisms decompose dead plants and animals and produce nutrients that plants need to grow. Plants absorb these nutrients from the soil through their roots. Nitrogen, for example, is one of the nutrients plants need to grow. Microorganisms change the nitrogen in dead organic matter—and nitrogen in the air—into compounds that plants can absorb and use. Some bacteria also contribute to the formation of soil by producing acids that break down rocks.

The cycling of nutrients through the soil and through plants is a continual process. Plants absorb nutrients from the soil and use those nutrients to grow. Then they return the nutrients to the soil when they die or lose branches and leaves. New plants then absorb the nutrients from the soil and start the cycle over again.

Animals such as earthworms, ants, termites, mice, gophers, moles, and prairie dogs all make their homes in the soil. All of these animals loosen and mix the soil as they tunnel through it. They create spaces in the soil, thereby adding to its air content and improving its ability to absorb and drain water. Burrowing animals also bring partly weathered rock particles to the surface of the ground, where they become exposed to more weathering. Just like plants, animals return nutrients to the soil when their bodies decompose after death.

 CHECK YOUR READING How do animals affect soil? Name at least three ways.

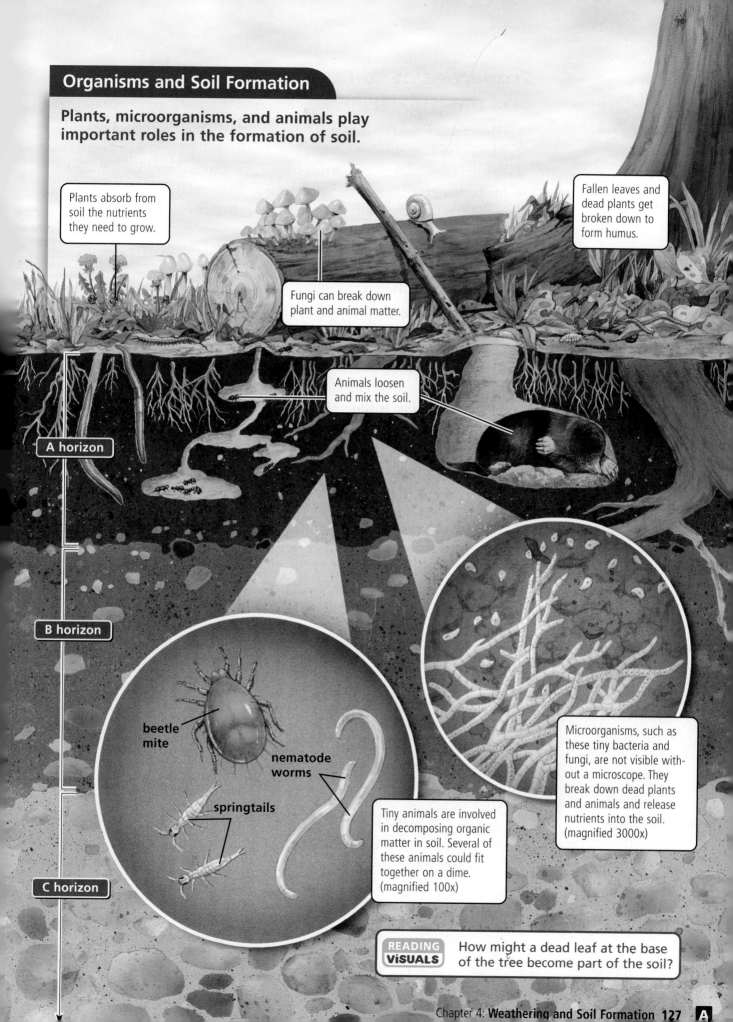

Organisms and Soil Formation

Plants, microorganisms, and animals play important roles in the formation of soil.

Plants absorb from soil the nutrients they need to grow.

Fungi can break down plant and animal matter.

Fallen leaves and dead plants get broken down to form humus.

Animals loosen and mix the soil.

A horizon

B horizon

C horizon

beetle mite

nematode worms

springtails

Tiny animals are involved in decomposing organic matter in soil. Several of these animals could fit together on a dime. (magnified 100x)

Microorganisms, such as these tiny bacteria and fungi, are not visible without a microscope. They break down dead plants and animals and release nutrients into the soil. (magnified 3000x)

READING VISUALS How might a dead leaf at the base of the tree become part of the soil?

Properties of soil can be observed and measured.

Observations and tests of soil samples reveal what nutrients the soils contain and therefore what kinds of plants will grow best in them. Farmers and gardeners use this information to improve the growth of crops and other plants. Soil scientists study many soil properties, including texture, color, pore space, and chemistry.

Texture

The texture of a soil is determined by the size of the weathered rock particles it contains. Soil scientists classify the rock particles in soils into three categories, on the basis of size: sand, silt, and clay. Sand particles are the largest and can be seen without a microscope. Silt particles are smaller than sand particles—too small to be seen without a microscope. Clay particles are the smallest. Most soils contain a mixture of sand, silt, and clay. The texture of a soil influences how easily air and water move through the soil.

Soil Texture

The texture of a soil is determined by the amounts of sand, silt, and clay it contains.

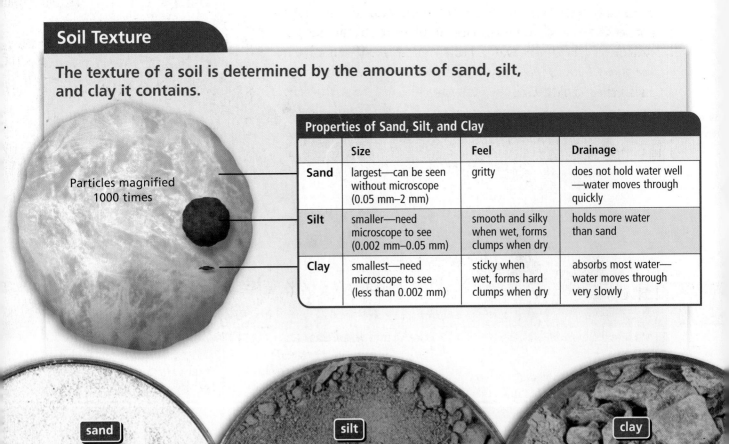

Particles magnified 1000 times

Properties of Sand, Silt, and Clay

	Size	Feel	Drainage
Sand	largest—can be seen without microscope (0.05 mm–2 mm)	gritty	does not hold water well—water moves through quickly
Silt	smaller—need microscope to see (0.002 mm–0.05 mm)	smooth and silky when wet, forms clumps when dry	holds more water than sand
Clay	smallest—need microscope to see (less than 0.002 mm)	sticky when wet, forms hard clumps when dry	absorbs most water—water moves through very slowly

sand

silt

clay

Color

The color of a soil is a clue to its other properties. Soil colors include red, brown, yellow, green, black, and even white. Most soil colors come from iron compounds and humus. Iron gives soil a reddish color. Soils with a high humus content are usually black or brown. Besides indicating the content of a soil, color may also be a clue to how well water moves through the soil—that is, how well the soil drains. Bright-colored soils, for instance, drain well.

RESOURCE CENTER
CLASSZONE.COM

Investigate soil.

Pore Space

Pore space refers to the spaces between soil particles. Water and air move through the pore spaces in a soil. Plant roots need both water and air to grow. Soils range from about 25 to 60 percent pore space. An ideal soil for growing plants has 50 percent of its volume as pore space, with half of the pore space occupied by air and half by water.

This gardener is adding lime to the soil to make it less acidic.

Chemistry

Plants absorb the nutrients they need from the water in soil. These nutrients may come from the minerals or the organic matter in the soil. To be available to plant roots, the nutrients must be dissolved in water. How well nutrients dissolve in the water in soil depends on the water's pH, which is a measure of acidity. Farmers may apply lime to make soil less acidic. To make soil more acidic, an acid may be applied.

 CHECK YOUR READING How does soil acidity affect whether the nutrients in soil are available to plants?

4.2 Review

KEY CONCEPTS

1. What are the main ingredients of soil?
2. How do climate and landforms affect soils' characteristics?
3. How do the activities of organisms affect the characteristics of soil?
4. Describe four properties of soil.

CRITICAL THINKING

5. **Compare and Contrast** How would a soil containing a lot of sand differ from a soil with a lot of clay?
6. **Infer** Which would you expect to be more fertile, the soil on hilly land or the soil on a plain? Why?

CHALLENGE

7. **Synthesize** What kinds of roots might you expect to find on plants that grow in arctic soils? Why?

CHAPTER INVESTIGATION

Testing Soil

OVERVIEW AND PURPOSE Soil is necessary for life. Whether a soil is suitable for farming or construction, and whether it absorbs water when it rains, depends on the particular properties of that soil. In this investigation you will
- test a soil sample to measure several soil properties
- identify the properties of your soil sample

▶ Procedure

PORE-SPACE TEST

1. Measure 200 mL of the dried soil sample in a graduated cylinder. Pour it into the jar.

2. Rinse the graduated cylinder, then fill it with 200 mL of water. Slowly pour the water into the jar until the soil is so soaked that any additional water would pool on top.

3. Record the amount of water remaining in the graduated cylinder. Then determine by subtraction the amount you added to the soil sample. Make a soil properties chart in your **Science Notebook** and record this number in it.

4. Discard the wet soil according to your teacher's instructions, and rinse the jar.

pH TEST AND DRAINAGE TEST

5. Cut off the top of a plastic bottle and use a rubber band to attach a piece of window screening over its mouth. Place the bottle top, mouth down, into the jar.

top of plastic bottle

jar

step 5

window screening

6. Use the graduated cylinder to measure 200 mL of soil, and pour the soil into the inverted bottle top.

7. Rinse the graduated cylinder, and fill it with 100 mL of water. Test the water's pH, using a pH test strip. Record the result in the "before" space in your soil properties chart.

8. Pour the water into the soil. Measure the amount of time it takes for the first drips to fall into the jar. Record the result in your soil properties chart.

MATERIALS
- dried soil sample
- 250 mL graduated cylinder
- 1 qt jar, with lid
- water
- 2 L plastic bottle
- scissors
- window screening
- rubber band
- pH test strips
- clock with second hand
- *for Challenge:* Texture Flow Chart

9 Once the water stops dripping, remove the bottle top. Use a new pH strip to measure the pH of the water in the jar. Record this measurement in the "after" space in your soil properties chart and note any differences in the appearance of the water before and after its filtering through the soil.

10 Discard the wet soil according to your teacher's instructions, and rinse the jar.

PARTICLE-TYPE TEST

11 Add water to the jar until it is two-thirds full. Pour in soil until the water level rises to the top of the jar, then replace the lid. Shake the jar, and set it to rest undisturbed on a countertop overnight.

12 The next day, observe the different soil layers. The sample should have separated into sand (on the bottom), silt (in the middle), and clay (on the top). Measure the height of each layer, as well as the overall height of the three layers. Record your measurements in your soil properties chart.

13 Use the following formula to calculate the percentage of each kind of particle in the sample:

$$\frac{\text{height of layer}}{\text{total height of all layers}} \times 100$$

Record your results and all calculations in your soil properties chart.

▶ Observe and Analyze
Write It Up

1. **RECORD** Complete your soil properties chart.

2. **IDENTIFY** How did steps 1–3 test your soil sample's pore space?

3. **IDENTIFY** How did steps 5–9 test your soil sample's drainage rate?

▶ Conclude
Write It Up

1. **EVALUATE** In step 3 you measured the amount of space between the soil particles in your sample. In step 8 you measured how quickly water passed through your sample. Are these two properties related? Explain your answer.

2. **EVALUATE** Would packing down or loosening up your soil sample change any of the properties you tested? Explain your answer.

3. **INTERPRET** What happened to the pH of the water that passed through the soil? Why do you think that happened?

4. **ANALYZE** Look at the percentages of sand, silt, and clay in your sample. How do the percentages help to explain the properties you observed and measured?

▶ INVESTIGATE Further

CHALLENGE Soil texture depends on the size of the weathered rock particles the soil contains. Use the Texture Flow Chart to determine the texture of your soil sample.

Testing Soil

Observe and Analyze

Table 1. Soil Properties Chart

Property	Result	Notes and Calculations
Pore space	_ mL water added	
pH	before: pH = _ after: pH = _	
Drainage	_ seconds	
Particle type	height of sand = _ cm height of silt = _ cm height of clay = _ cm total height = _ cm	

Conclude

Human activities affect soil.

◀ **BEFORE, you learned**

- Soils consist mainly of weathered rock and organic matter
- Soils vary, depending on climate
- Organisms affect the characteristics of soil
- Soil properties can be measured

▶ **NOW, you will learn**

- Why soil is a necessary resource
- How people's use of land affects soil
- How people can conserve soil

VOCABULARY

desertification p. 133

THINK ABOUT

How does land use affect soil?

Look outside for evidence of ways that people have affected the soil. Make a list of all the things that you can see or think of. Use your list to make a two-column table with the headings "Activity" and "Effects."

Soil is a necessary resource.

Soil helps sustain life on Earth—including your life. You already know that soil supports the growth of plants, which in turn supply food for animals. Therefore, soil provides you with nearly all the food you eat. But that's not all. Many other items you use, such as cotton clothing and medicines, come from plants. Lumber in your home comes from trees. Even the oxygen you breathe comes from plants.

Besides supporting the growth of plants, soil plays other life-sustaining roles. Soil helps purify, or clean, water as it drains through the ground and into rivers, lakes, and oceans. Decomposers in soil also help recycle nutrients by breaking down the remains of plants and animals, releasing nutrients that living plants use to grow. In addition, soil provides a home for a variety of living things, from tiny one-celled organisms to small mammals.

 CHECK YOUR READING Why is soil a necessary resource?

Land-use practices can harm soil.

The way people use land can affect the levels of nutrients and pollution in soil. Any activity that exposes soil to wind and rain can lead to soil loss. Farming, construction and development, and mining are among the main activities that impact soil resources.

Farming

Farming is very important to society because almost all of the world's food is grown on farms. Over the 10,000 years humans have been farming, people have continually improved their farming methods. However, farming has some harmful effects and can lead to soil loss.

Farmers often add nutrients to soil in the form of organic or artificial fertilizers to make their crops grow better. However, some fertilizers can make it difficult for microorganisms in the soil to produce nutrients naturally. Fertilizers also add to water pollution when rainwater draining from fields carries the excess nutrients to rivers, lakes, and oceans.

Over time, many farming practices lead to the loss of soil. All over the world, farmers clear trees and other plants and plow up the soil to plant crops. Without its natural plant cover, the soil is more exposed to rain and wind and is therefore more likely to get washed or blown away. American farmers lose about five metric tons of soil for each metric ton of grain they produce. In many other parts of the world, the losses are even higher.

Another problem is overgrazing. Overgrazing occurs when farm animals eat large amounts of the land cover. Overgrazing destroys natural vegetation and causes the soil to wash or blow away more easily. In many dry regions of the world, overgrazing and the clearing of land for farming have led to desertification. **Desertification** (dih-ZUR-tuh-fih-KAY-shuhn) is the expansion of desert conditions in areas where the natural plant cover has been destroyed.

COMBINATION NOTES
Remember to take notes about how farming affects soil.

Exposed soil can be blown away by wind or washed away by rain.

The top of this hill in San Bernardino County, California, was cleared for a housing development. A house will be built on each flat plot of land.

Construction and Development

To make roads, houses, shopping malls, and other buildings, people need to dig up the soil. Some of the soil at construction sites washes or blows away because its protective plant cover has been removed. The soil that is washed or blown away ends up in nearby low-lying areas, in rivers and streams, or in downstream lakes or reservoirs. This soil can cause problems by making rivers and lakes muddy and harming the organisms that live in them. The buildup of soil on riverbeds raises the level of the rivers and may cause flooding. The soil can also fill up lakes and reservoirs.

Mining

Some methods of mining cause soil loss. For example, the digging of strip mines and open-pit mines involves the removal of plants and soil from the surface of the ground.

By exposing rocks and minerals to the air and to rainwater, these forms of mining speed up the rate of chemical weathering. In mining operations that expose sulfide minerals, the increased chemical weathering causes a type of pollution known as acid drainage. Abandoned mines can fill with rainwater. Sulfide minerals react with the air and the water to produce sulfuric acid. Then the acid water drains from the mines, polluting the soil in surrounding areas.

CHECK YOUR READING How do some methods of mining affect the soil?

To make this open-pit mine in Cananea, Mexico, plants and soil were removed from the surface of the ground.

Soil can be protected and conserved.

Soil conservation is very important, because soil can be difficult or impossible to replace once it has been lost. Soil takes a very long time to form. A soil with well-developed horizons may take hundreds of thousands of years to form! Most soil conservation methods are designed to hold soil in place and keep it fertile. Below are descriptions of a few of the many soil conservation methods that are used by farmers around the world.

Crop rotation is the practice of planting different crops on the same field in different years or growing seasons. Grain crops, such as wheat, use up a lot of the nitrogen—a necessary plant nutrient—in the soil. The roots of bean crops, such as soybeans, contain bacteria that restore nitrogen to the soil. By rotating these crops, farmers can help maintain soil fertility.

Conservation tillage includes several methods of reducing the number of times fields are tilled, or plowed, in a year. The less soil is disturbed by plowing, the less likely it is to be washed or blown away. In one method of conservation tillage, fields are not plowed at all. The remains of harvested crops are simply left on the fields to cover and protect the soil. New seeds are planted in narrow bands of soil.

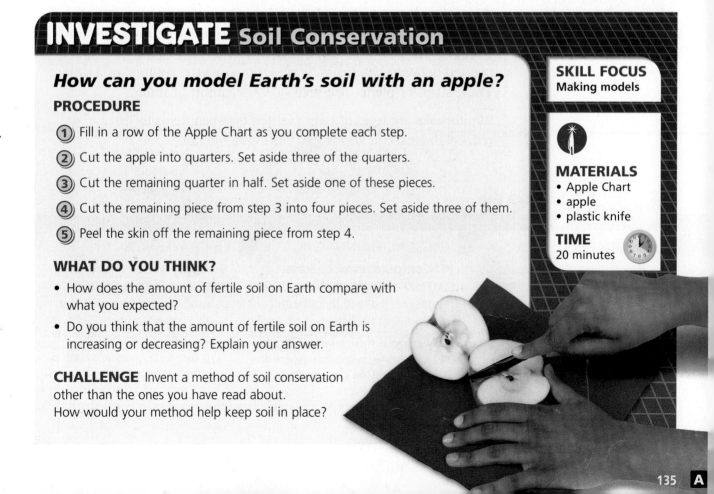

INVESTIGATE Soil Conservation

How can you model Earth's soil with an apple?

PROCEDURE

1. Fill in a row of the Apple Chart as you complete each step.
2. Cut the apple into quarters. Set aside three of the quarters.
3. Cut the remaining quarter in half. Set aside one of these pieces.
4. Cut the remaining piece from step 3 into four pieces. Set aside three of them.
5. Peel the skin off the remaining piece from step 4.

WHAT DO YOU THINK?

- How does the amount of fertile soil on Earth compare with what you expected?
- Do you think that the amount of fertile soil on Earth is increasing or decreasing? Explain your answer.

CHALLENGE Invent a method of soil conservation other than the ones you have read about. How would your method help keep soil in place?

SKILL FOCUS
Making models

MATERIALS
- Apple Chart
- apple
- plastic knife

TIME
20 minutes

Terracing

Contour Plowing

READING VISUALS **COMPARE** Both terracing and contour plowing are soil conservation methods used on sloping land. How does each method help conserve soil?

Terraces are flat, steplike areas built on a hillside to hold rainwater and prevent it from running downhill. Crops are planted on the flat tops of the terraces.

Contour plowing is the practice of plowing along the curves, or contours, of a slope. Contour plowing helps channel rainwater so that it does not run straight downhill, carrying away soil with it. A soil conservation method called strip-cropping is often combined with contour plowing. Strips of grasses, shrubs, or other plants are planted between bands of a grain crop along the contour of a slope. These strips of plants also help slow the runoff of water.

Windbreaks are rows of trees planted between fields to "break," or reduce, the force of winds that can carry off soil.

4.3 Review

KEY CONCEPTS

1. Why is soil a necessary resource?

2. How do land-use practices in farming, construction and development, and mining affect soil?

3. Describe at least three methods of soil conservation.

CRITICAL THINKING

4. **Compare and Contrast** How might the problem of soil loss on flat land be different from that on sloping land?

5. **Apply** If you were building a new home in an undeveloped area, what steps would you take to reduce the impact of construction on the soil?

⬤ CHALLENGE

6. **Apply** You have advised an inexperienced farmer to practice strip-cropping, but the farmer wants to plant all the land in wheat in order to grow as much as possible. What argument would you use to convince the farmer?

SCIENCE on the JOB

LANDSCAPE ARCHITECT

Soil, Water, and Architecture

Landscape architects design the landscapes around buildings and in parks. For example, they decide where to build sidewalks and where to place benches. Since flowing water can wash away soil, they try to control how water moves. They select plants, modify the slope of the land, and install drainage systems that will control the water. The plan below was used to build the park shown in the photographs.

Existing Plants

Large oak trees were already growing on the land. The trees were left in place to provide shade and help protect the soil.

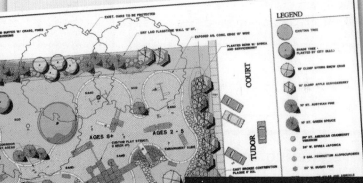

Retaining Wall

The landscape architect added mounds of soil planted with bushes to help divide the inside of the park from the roads around it. Stone walls hold the soil of the mounds in place. Without the walls, the soil would wash down onto the walkways.

Plan for New Park

A landscape architect used a computer program to draw this plan for a park. The program is designed to make the plan look as if it were drawn by hand.

EXPLORE

1. ANALYZE Examine the soil, drainage, plants, and other elements of the landscape of a park or the area around a building. Describe any areas where soil may wash away.

2. CHALLENGE Design a landscape surrounding a new school, stadium, or other building. Draw a sketch and add notes to explain your choices of locations for trees, sidewalks, and other features.

Chapter Review

the BIG idea

Natural forces break rocks apart and form soil, which supports life.

CONTENT REVIEW
CLASSZONE.COM

◀ KEY CONCEPTS SUMMARY

4.1 Mechanical and chemical forces break down rocks.

Over time, **mechanical weathering** breaks a rock into smaller pieces.

Chemical weathering affects exposed rock surfaces.

VOCABULARY
weathering p. 115
mechanical weathering p. 116
exfoliation p. 116
abrasion p. 116
chemical weathering p. 118

4.2 Weathering and organic processes form soil.

Soil has measurable properties, such as color, texture, pore space, and chemistry.

Soil is a mixture of weathered rock, organic matter, water, and air.

Plants, microorganisms, and animals affect soil characteristics.

VOCABULARY
humus p. 123
soil horizon p. 124
soil profile p. 124

4.3 Human activities affect soil.

Soil is essential to life and takes a long time to form. It is difficult or impossible to replace soil that has been lost.

Soil Loss

Farming, construction and development, and mining are three human activities that affect soil.

Soil Conservation

Soil conservation practices help keep soil from blowing or washing away.

VOCABULARY
desertification p. 133

Reviewing Vocabulary

Copy the three-column chart below. Complete the chart for each term. The first one has been done for you.

Term	Definition	Example
EXAMPLE chemical weathering	the breakdown of rocks by chemical reactions that change the rocks' mineral composition	Iron reacts with air and water to form iron oxides or rust.
1. mechanical weathering		
2. abrasion		
3. exfoliation		
4. desertification		

Reviewing Key Concepts

Multiple Choice *Choose the letter of the best answer.*

5. The force of expanding water in the cracks and pores of a rock is an example of
   a. chemical weathering
   b. mechanical weathering
   c. oxidation
   d. desertification

6. The breakdown of a rock by acidic water is an example of
   a. chemical weathering
   b. mechanical weathering
   c. oxidation
   d. desertification

7. Soil is a mixture of what four materials?
   a. granite, limestone, nitrogen, and air
   b. plant roots, iron oxides, water, and air
   c. rock particles, plant roots, humus, and nitrogen
   d. rock particles, humus, water, and air

8. What is the main component of soil?
   a. humus   c. air
   b. water   d. rock particles

9. What is humus?
   a. the decomposed rock particles in soil
   b. the decomposed organic matter in soil
   c. the material that makes up the B horizon
   d. the material that makes up the C horizon

10. Three factors that affect the rate of weathering are
    a. microorganisms, plants, and animals
    b. weather, landforms, and rainfall
    c. surface area, rock composition, and climate
    d. texture, color, and pore space

11. Microorganisms affect the quality of soil by
    a. decomposing organic matter
    b. creating tunnels
    c. absorbing water
    d. increasing mechanical weathering

12. The movement of air and water through a soil is influenced most by the soil's
    a. color and chemistry
    b. texture and pore space
    c. pH and nitrogen content
    d. microorganisms

13. Contour plowing, strip-cropping, and terracing are conservation methods designed to reduce the
    a. runoff of water
    b. activity of microorganisms
    c. acidity of soil
    d. pore space of soil

Short Answer *Write a few sentences to answer each question.*

14. How do farming, construction and development, and mining affect soil?

15. How do ice wedging, pressure release, plant root growth, and abrasion cause mechanical weathering?

16. How do air and water cause chemical weathering?

Thinking Critically

Use the photograph to answer the next three questions.

17. APPLY Make a sketch of the soil profile above, labeling the A, B, and C horizons.

18. OBSERVE What does the color of the top layer indicate about this soil?

19. APPLY Which part of the profile is most affected by chemical and mechanical weathering? Why?

20. APPLY Suppose that you own gently sloping farmland. Describe the methods that you would use to hold the soil in place and maintain its fertility.

21. SYNTHESIZE Describe the composition, color, texture, and amount of pore space of a soil that would be good for growing crops.

22. COMPARE AND CONTRAST How does mechanical weathering differ from chemical weathering? How are the two processes similar?

23. PREDICT What effect will the continued growth of the world's population likely have on soil resources?

24. ANALYZE Soil loss is a problem all over the world. Where might lost soil end up?

25. ANALYZE Can lost soil be replaced? Explain.

26. ANALYZE Copy the concept map below and fill it in with the following terms and phrases.

acidic water	chemical weathering
damaged statue	exfoliation
mechanical weathering	moving water
oxygen and water	pressure release
rounded rocks	rust

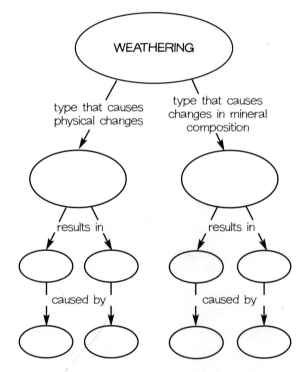

27. ANALYZE Add to the concept map to show the three factors that affect the rate of weathering.

the BIG idea

28. MODEL Draw a diagram that shows an example of a natural force breaking rocks apart to form soil that supports life.

29. SYNTHESIZE A cycle is a series of events or actions that repeats regularly. Describe a cycle that involves soil and living things.

UNIT PROJECTS

If you need to create graphs or other visuals for your project, be sure you have grid paper, poster board, markers, or other supplies.

Analyzing a Table

The table indicates some of the characteristics of four soil samples. Use the table to answer the questions below.

Sample	Color	Ability to Hold Water	Percentage of Pore Space	Percentage of Humus
1	black	average	50%	9%
2	yellowish brown	low	70%	3%
3	reddish brown	average	60%	3%
4	very red	average to low	65%	2%

1. Soils that contain a lot of sand do not hold water very well. Which sample probably contains the most sand?

  a. 1   **c.** 3
  b. 2   **d.** 4

2. Iron gives soil a reddish color. Which sample probably contains the most iron?

  a. 1   **c.** 3
  b. 2   **d.** 4

3. Crops grow best in soils with about half of their volume consisting of pore space. Which soil has an ideal amount of pore space for growing crops?

  a. 1   **c.** 3
  b. 2   **d.** 4

4. What soil color might indicate a high level of organic matter?

  a. black   **c.** red-brown
  b. yellow   **d.** red

5. Imagine you have an additional soil sample. The sample is dark brown, has an average ability to hold water, and has 55% pore space. What percentage of humus would this soil most likely contain?

  a. 1%   **c.** 3%
  b. 2%   **d.** 8%

Extended Response

Answer the two questions below in detail. Include some of the terms shown in the word box. In your answers, underline each term you use.

abrasion	moving water
chemical weathering	plant roots
ice	rusting
mechanical weathering	

6. Jolene is comparing a rock from a riverbed and a rock from deep underground. One is very smooth. The other has very sharp edges. Explain which rock was probably found in each location.

7. In a museum, Hank sees two iron knives that were made in the early 1800s. One has spent 200 years on the top of a fortress wall. The other one has been stored in the museum for 200 years. Why might the two knives look different?

CHAPTER 5

Erosion and Deposition

the BIG idea

Water, wind, and ice shape Earth's surface.

How can ice carve a valley?

Key Concepts

SECTION 5.1
Forces wear down and build up Earth's surface.
Learn how natural forces shape and change the land.

SECTION 5.2
Moving water shapes land.
Learn about the effects of water moving over land and underground.

SECTION 5.3
Waves and wind shape land.
Discover how waves and wind affect land.

SECTION 5.4
Glaciers carve land and move sediments.
Learn about the effect of ice moving over land.

Internet Preview

CLASSZONE.COM

Chapter 5 online resources: Content Review, two Visualizations, three Resource Centers, Math Tutorial, Test Practice

EXPLORE (the BIG idea)

Where Has Water Been?

Think about what water does when it falls and flows on the ground. Go outside your school or home and look at the ground and pavement carefully. Look in dry places for evidence of where water has been.

Observe and Think What evidence did you find? How does it show that water was in a place that is now dry?

How Do Waves Shape Land?

Pile a mixture of sand and gravel on one side of a pie tin to make a "beach." Slowly add water away from the beach until the tin is about one-third full. Use your hand to make waves in the tin and observe what happens.

Observe and Think What happened to the beach? How did the waves affect the sand and gravel?

Internet Activity: Wind Erosion

Go to **ClassZone.com** to learn about one type of wind erosion. See how wind can form an arch in rock.

Observe and Think How long do you think it would take for wind to form an arch?

NSTA
scilinks.org
SCiLINKS

Wind Erosion **Code: MDL017**

Getting Ready to Learn

◀ CONCEPT REVIEW

- Weathering breaks down rocks.
- Water and ice are agents of weathering.
- Soil contains weathered rock and organic material.

◀ VOCABULARY REVIEW

sediment p. 89

weathering p. 115

abrasion p. 116

 CONTENT REVIEW
CLASSZONE.COM
Review concepts and vocabulary.

▶ TAKING NOTES

CHOOSE YOUR OWN STRATEGY

Take notes using one or more of the strategies from earlier chapters—**main idea and detail notes, supporting main ideas, main idea web,** or **combination notes.** Feel free to mix and match the strategies, or use an entirely different note-taking strategy.

VOCABULARY STRATEGY

Write each new vocabulary term in the center of a **four square** diagram. Write notes in the squares around each term. Include a definition, some characteristics, and some examples of the term. If possible, write some things that are not examples of the term.

See the Note-Taking Handbook on pages R45–R51.

SCIENCE NOTEBOOK

Supporting Main Ideas

Main Idea Web

Main Idea and Detail Notes

Definition	Characteristics
process in which weathered particles are picked up and moved	gravity is important part; wind and ice are agents

EROSION

Examples	Nonexamples
mass wasting, mudflow, slump, creep	longshore current, humus

KEY CONCEPT

5.1 Forces wear down and build up Earth's surface.

◀ **BEFORE, you learned**

- Weathering breaks rocks apart
- Weathering forms soil

▶ **NOW, you will learn**

- How erosion moves and deposits rock and soil
- How gravity causes movement of large amounts of rock and soil

VOCABULARY

erosion p. 145
deposition p. 145
mass wasting p. 147

THINK ABOUT

How did natural forces shape this landform?

This valley in Iceland was formed by the action of water. How long might it have taken to form? Where did the material that once filled the valley go?

Natural forces move and deposit sediments.

The valley in the photograph was formed by the movement of water. The water flowed over the land and carried away weathered rock and soil, shaping a valley where the water flows. In this section you will learn about the processes that shape landscapes.

VOCABULARY
Use four square diagrams to take notes about the terms *erosion* and *deposition*.

The process in which weathered particles are picked up and moved from one place to another is called **erosion** (ih-ROH-zhuhn). Erosion has a constant impact on Earth's surface. Over millions of years, it wears down mountains by removing byproducts of weathering and depositing them elsewhere. The part of the erosion process in which sediment is placed in a new location, or deposited, is called **deposition** (DEHP-uh-ZIHSH-uhn).

The force of gravity is an important part of erosion and deposition. Gravity causes water to move downward, carrying and depositing sediment as it flows. Gravity can pull huge masses of ice slowly down mountain valleys. And gravity causes dust carried by the wind to fall to Earth.

Erosion of weathered rock by the movement of water, wind, and ice occurs in three major ways:

- **Water** Rainwater and water from melting snow flow down sloping land, carrying rock and soil particles. The water makes its way to a river, which then carries the sediment along. The sediment gets deposited on the river's bottom, banks, or flood-plain, or near its mouth. Waves in oceans and lakes also carry sediment and deposit it to form beaches and other features.

- **Wind** Strong winds lift tiny particles of dust and carry them long distances. When the wind dies down, the particles drop to the ground. Wind can also push larger particles of sand along the ground.

- **Ice** As ice moves slowly downhill, it transports rock and soil particles that are embedded in it.

CHECK YOUR READING What are the three major ways in which erosion moves sediment?

INVESTIGATE Erosion

How does the effect of rainwater on sloping land differ from its effect on flat land?

DESIGN —YOUR OWN— EXPERIMENT

Streams are one of the main agents of erosion on Earth. Design an experiment to show the effect that rainwater has on sloping land.

PROCEDURE

1. Figure out how to use the soil, water, and trays to test the effects of rainwater on sloping land and on flat land.

2. Write up your procedure.

3. Carry out your experiment.

WHAT DO YOU THINK?

- What were the results of your experiment? Did it work? Why or why not?
- What were the variables in your experiment?
- What does your experiment demonstrate about erosion and running water?

CHALLENGE How would you design an experiment to demonstrate the relationship between floods and erosion?

SKILL FOCUS
Designing experiments

MATERIALS
- soil
- 2 large trays
- pitcher of water

TIME
25 minutes

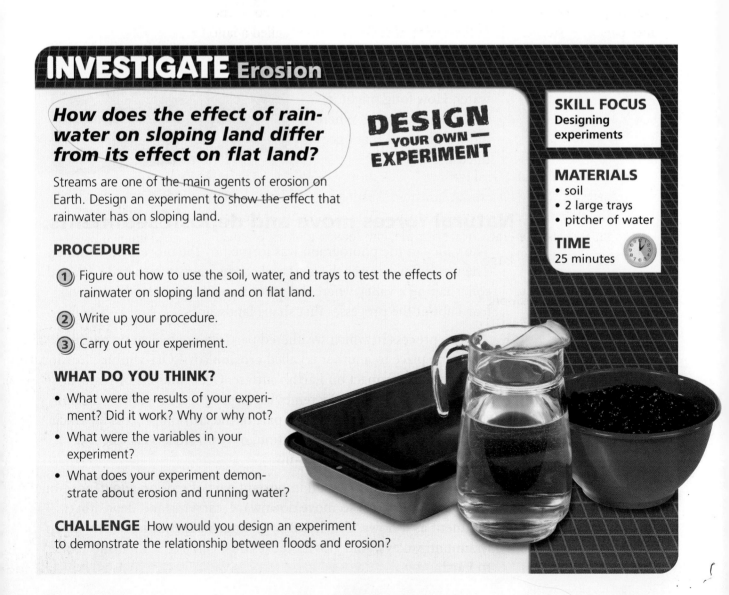

Gravity can move large amounts of rock and soil.

Along the California coast many homes are built atop beautiful cliffs, backed by mountains and looking out to the sea. These homes may seem like great places to live. They are, however, in a risky location.

The California coast region and other mountainous areas have many landslides. A landslide is one type of **mass wasting**—the downhill movements of masses of rock and soil.

In mass wasting, gravity pulls material downward. A triggering event, such as heavy rain or an earthquake, might loosen the rock and soil. As the material becomes looser, it gives way to the pull of gravity and moves downward.

Mass wasting can occur suddenly or gradually. It can involve tons of rock sliding down a steep mountain slope or moving little by little down a gentle hillside. One way to classify an occurrence of mass wasting is by the type of material that is moved and the speed of the movement. A sudden, fast movement of rock and soil is called a landslide. Movements of rock are described as slides or falls. Movement of mud or soil is described as a mudflow.

VOCABULARY
Be sure to make a four square diagram for *mass wasting* in your notebook.

Mass Wasting of Rock

Mass wasting of rock includes rockfalls and rockslides:

- In a rockfall, individual blocks of rock drop suddenly and fall freely down a cliff or steep mountainside. Weathering can break a block of rock from a cliff or mountainside. The expansion of water that freezes in a crack, for example, can loosen a block of rock.

- In a rockslide, a large mass of rock slides as a unit down a slope. A rockslide can reach a speed of a hundred kilometers per hour. Rockslides can be triggered by earthquakes.

Mass wasting of rock often takes place in high mountains. In some places, rocks can fall or slide onto roads. You might also see evidence of rockfalls and rockslides at the base of steep cliffs, where piles of rock slope outward.

Rockslides, such as this one in California, can drop huge amounts of rock onto highways.

Mudflows in 1999 in Venezuela happened very quickly and took as many as 30,000 lives.

RESOURCE CENTER
CLASSZONE.COM

Learn more about mudflows.

Mudflow

Sometimes a mountain slope collapses. Then a mixture of rock, soil, and plants—called debris (duh-BREE)—falls or slides down. Like mass wasting of rock, mass movements of debris are common in high mountains with steep slopes.

A major type of mass wasting of debris is a mudflow. A mudflow consists of debris with a large amount of water. Mudflows often happen in mountain canyons and valleys after heavy rains. The soil becomes so heavy with water that the slope can no longer hold it in place. The mixture of soil, water, and debris flows downward, picking up sediment as it rushes down. When it reaches a valley, it spreads in a thin sheet over the land.

Mudflows also occur on active volcanoes. In 1985, a huge mudflow destroyed the town of Armero, Colombia, and killed more than 20,000 people. When a volcano erupted there, the heat caused ice and snow near the top of the volcano to melt, releasing a large amount of water that mixed with ash from the volcano. The mixture of ash and water rushed down the volcano and picked up debris. It formed gigantic mudflows that poured into all the surrounding valleys.

Mount St. Helens, a volcanic mountain in the state of Washington, is a place where large mudflows have occurred. During an eruption in 1980, some mudflows from the volcano traveled more than 90 kilometers (56 mi) from the mountain.

 CHECK YOUR READING What causes a mudflow to occur?

In this example of slump, at Mesa Verde National Park in Colorado, a huge mass of rock and soil moved downward.

Slumps and Creep

Slumps and creep are two other main types of mass wasting on hilly land. These forms of mass wasting can be much less dramatic than rockslides or mudflows. But they are the types of mass movement that you are most likely to see evidence of.

A slump is a slide of loose debris that moves as a single unit. Slumps can occur along roads and highways where construction has made slopes unstable. They can cover sections of highway with debris. Like other types of mass movement, slumps can be triggered by heavy rain.

The slowest form of mass movement of soil or debris is creep. The soil or debris moves at a rate of about 1 to 10 millimeters a year—a rate too slow to actually be seen. But evidence of creep can be seen on hillsides that have old fences or telephone poles. The fences or poles may lean downward, or some may be out of line. They have been moved by the creeping soil. The soil closer to the surface moves faster than the soil farther down, which causes the fences or poles to lean.

Originally, the fence posts stand vertically in the ground.

Over many years, the soil holding the posts slowly shifts downhill, and the posts lean.

Even the slight slope of this land in Alberta, Canada, caused these posts to tilt because of creep.

Creep can affect buildings as well. The weight of a heavy mass of soil moving slowly downhill can be great enough to crack a building's walls. Creep affects all hillsides covered with soil, but its rate varies. The wetter the soil, the faster it will creep downhill.

5.1 Review

KEY CONCEPTS

1. How does erosion change landscapes?

2. Describe why weathering is important in erosion.

3. How can gravity move large amounts of rock and soil?

CRITICAL THINKING

4. **Compare and Contrast** What is the main difference between erosion and mass wasting?

5. **Infer** What force and what cause can contribute to both erosion and mass wasting?

⬥ CHALLENGE

6. **Rank** Which of the four locations would be the best and worst places to build a house? Rank the four locations and explain your reasoning.

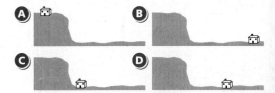

5.2

KEY CONCEPT
Moving water shapes land.

◀ **BEFORE, you learned**

- Erosion is the movement of rock and soil
- Gravity causes mass movements of rock and soil

▶ **NOW, you will learn**

- How moving water shapes Earth's surface
- How water moving underground forms caves and other features

VOCABULARY

drainage basin p. 151
divide p. 151
floodplain p. 152
alluvial fan p. 153
delta p. 153
sinkhole p. 155

EXPLORE Divides

How do divides work?

PROCEDURE

① Fold the sheet of paper in thirds and tape it as shown to make a "ridge."

② Drop the paper clips one at a time directly on top of the ridge from a height of about 30 cm. Observe what happens and record your observations.

WHAT DO YOU THINK?

How might the paper clips be similar to water falling on a ridge?

MATERIALS
- sheet of paper
- tape
- paper clips

Streams shape Earth's surface.

If you look at a river or stream, you may be able to notice something about the land around it. The land is higher than the river. If a river is running through a steep valley, you can easily see that the river is the low point. But even in very flat places, the land is sloping down to the river, which is itself running downhill in a low path through the land.

Running water is the major force shaping the landscape over most of Earth. From the broad, flat land around the lower Mississippi River to the steep mountain valleys of the Himalayas, water running downhill changes the land. Running water shapes a variety of landforms by moving sediment in the processes of erosion and deposition. In this section, you will learn how water flows on land in systems of streams and rivers and how water shapes and changes landscapes. You also will learn that water can even carve out new features underground.

NOTE-TAKING STRATEGY
A main idea and detail notes chart would be a good strategy to use for taking notes about streams and Earth's surface.

Drainage Basins and Divides

When water falls or ice melts on a slope, some of the water soaks into the ground and some of it flows down the slope in thin sheets. But within a short distance this water becomes part of a channel that forms a stream. A stream is any body of water—large or small—that flows down a slope along a channel.

Streams flow into one another to form complex drainage systems, with small streams flowing into larger ones. The area of land in which water drains into a stream system is called a **drainage basin.** In most drainage basins, the water eventually drains into a lake or an ocean. For example, in the Mississippi River drainage basin, water flows into the Mississippi, and then drains into the Gulf of Mexico, which is part of the ocean.

Drainage basins are separated by ridges called divides, which are like continuous lines of high land. A **divide** is a ridge from which water drains to one side or the other. Divides can run along high mountains. On flatter ground, a divide can simply be the the highest line of land and can be hard to see.

Divides are the borders of drainage basins. A basin can be just a few kilometers wide or can drain water from a large portion of a continent. The Continental Divide runs from Alaska to Mexico. Most water that falls west of the Continental Divide ends up draining into the Pacific Ocean. Most water that falls east of it drains into the Gulf of Mexico and Atlantic Ocean.

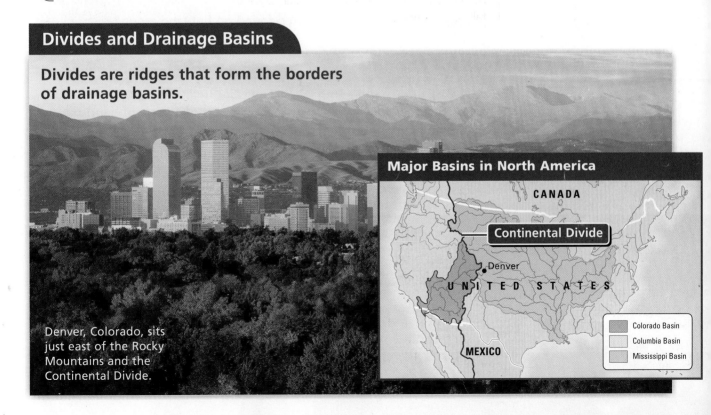

Divides and Drainage Basins

Divides are ridges that form the borders of drainage basins.

Denver, Colorado, sits just east of the Rocky Mountains and the Continental Divide.

Major Basins in North America

CANADA

Continental Divide

Denver

UNITED STATES

MEXICO

Colorado Basin
Columbia Basin
Mississippi Basin

Downtown Davenport, Iowa, sits in the floodplain of the Mississippi River and was covered with water when the river flooded in 1993.

Valleys and Floodplains

As streams flow and carry sediment from the surface of the land, they form valleys. In high mountains, streams often cut V-shaped valleys that are narrow and steep walled. In lower areas, streams may form broad valleys that include floodplains. A **floodplain** is an area of land on either side of a stream that is underwater when the stream floods. The floodplain of a large river may be many kilometers wide.

When a stream floods, it deposits much of the sediment that it carries onto its floodplain. This sediment can make the floodplain very fertile—or able to support a lot of plant growth. In the United States, the floodplains of the Mississippi River are some of the best places for growing crops.

RESOURCE CENTER
CLASSZONE.COM
Find out more about rivers and erosion.

CHECK YOUR READING Why is fertile land often found on flat land around rivers?

Stream Channels

As a stream flows through a valley, its channel may run straight in some parts and curve around in other parts. Curves and bends that form a twisting, looping pattern in a stream channel are called meanders (mee-AN-duhrz). The moving water erodes the outside banks and deposits sediment along the inside banks. Over many years, meanders shift position.

During a flood, the stream may cut a new channel that bypasses a meander. The cut-off meander forms a crescent-shaped lake, which is called an oxbow lake. This term comes from the name of a U-shaped piece of wood that fits under the neck of an ox and is attached to its yoke.

The meanders of this river and oxbow lakes formed as the river deposited sediment and changed course.

Alluvial Fans and Deltas

Besides shaping valleys and forming oxbow lakes, streams also create landforms called alluvial fans and deltas. Both of these landforms are formed by the deposition of sediment.

An **alluvial fan** (uh-LOO-vee-uhl) is a fan-shaped deposit of sediment at the base of a mountain. It forms where a stream leaves a steep valley and enters a flatter plain. The stream slows down and spreads out on the flatter ground. As it slows down, it can carry less sediment. The slower-moving water drops some of its sediment, leaving it at the base of the slope.

A **delta** is an area of land formed by the buildup of sediment at the end, or mouth, of a river. When a river enters the ocean, the river's water slows down, and the river drops much of its sediment. This sediment gradually builds up to form a plain. Like alluvial fans, deltas tend to be fan-shaped. Over a very long time, a river may build up its delta far out into the sea. A large river, such as the Mississippi, can build up a huge delta. Like many other large rivers on Earth, the Mississippi has been building up its delta out into the sea for many thousands of years.

This alluvial fan was formed by a stream flowing into the Jago River in Alaska.

From Divide to Delta

On their path to the ocean, streams and rivers slow down and flatten out.

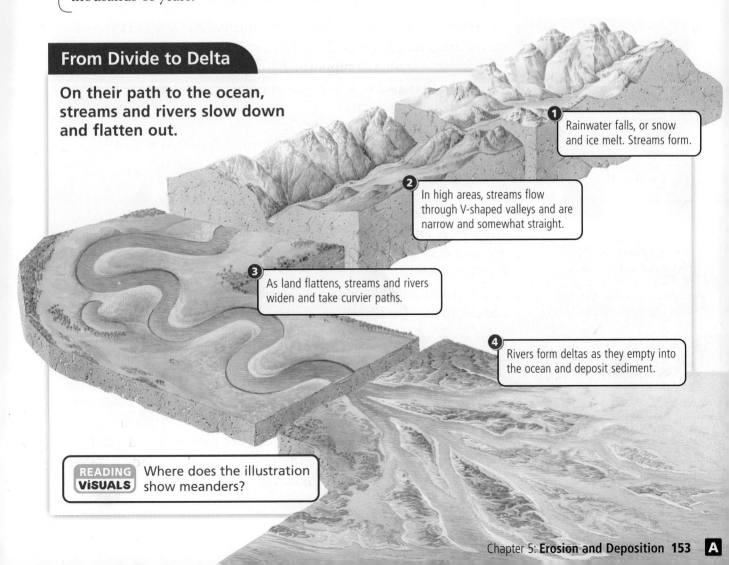

1. Rainwater falls, or snow and ice melt. Streams form.

2. In high areas, streams flow through V-shaped valleys and are narrow and somewhat straight.

3. As land flattens, streams and rivers widen and take curvier paths.

4. Rivers form deltas as they empty into the ocean and deposit sediment.

READING VISUALS Where does the illustration show meanders?

Water moving underground forms caverns.

Not all rainwater runs off the land and flows into surface streams. Some of it evaporates, some is absorbed by plants, and some soaks into the ground and becomes groundwater. At a certain depth below the surface, the spaces in soil and rock become completely filled with water. The top of this water-filled region is called the water table. The water below the water table is called groundwater.

The water table is at different distances below the surface in different places. Its level also can change over time in the same location, depending on changes in rainfall. Below the water table, groundwater flows slowly through underground beds of rock and soil, where it causes erosion to take place.

You have read that chemicals in water and air can break down rock. As you read in Chapter 4, rainwater is slightly acidic. This acidic water can dissolve certain rocks, such as limestone. In some areas, where the underground rock consists of limestone, the groundwater can dissolve some of the limestone and carry it away. Over time, this

VISUALIZATION
CLASSZONE.COM

Observe the process of cave formation.

Cavern Formation

Caves form as water under-ground dissolves limestone, leaving open spaces.

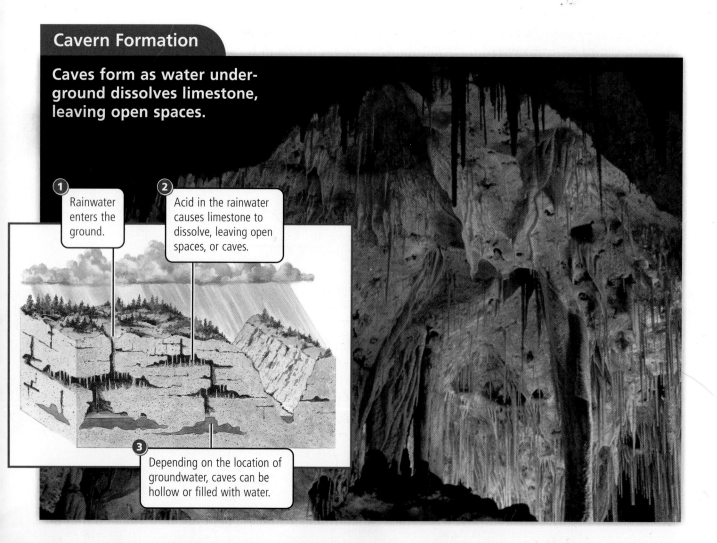

1 Rainwater enters the ground.

2 Acid in the rainwater causes limestone to dissolve, leaving open spaces, or caves.

3 Depending on the location of groundwater, caves can be hollow or filled with water.

This sinkhole took down a large part of a parking lot in Atlanta, Georgia.

process produces open spaces, or caves. Large caves are called caverns. If the water table drops, a cavern may fill with air.

Some caverns have huge networks of rooms and passageways. Mammoth Cave in Kentucky, for example, is part of a cavern system that has more than 560 kilometers (about 350 mi) of explored passageways. Within the cavern are lakes and streams.

A surface feature that often occurs in areas with caverns is a sinkhole. A **sinkhole** is a basin that forms when the roof of a cave becomes so thin that it suddenly falls in. Sometimes it falls in because water that supported the roof has drained away. Landscapes with many sinkholes can be found in southern Indiana, south central Kentucky, and central Tennessee. In Florida, the collapse of shallow underground caverns has produced large sinkholes that have destroyed whole city blocks.

 Why do caverns form in areas with limestone?

 Review

KEY CONCEPTS

1. What is the difference between a drainage basin and a divide?

2. How do streams change as they flow from mountains down to plains?

3. How do caverns form?

CRITICAL THINKING

4. **Sequence** Draw a cartoon with three panels showing how a sinkhole forms.

5. **Compare and Contrast** Make a Venn diagram to compare and contrast alluvial fans and deltas.

CHALLENGE

6. **Apply** During a flood, a river drops the largest pieces of its sediment on the floodplain close to its normal channel. Explain why. (**Hint:** Think about the speed of the water.)

CHAPTER INVESTIGATION

Creating Stream Features

OVERVIEW AND PURPOSE A view from the sky reveals that a large river twists and bends in its channel. But as quiet as it might appear, the river constantly digs and dumps Earth materials along its way. This erosion and deposition causes twists and curves called meanders, and forms a delta at the river's mouth. In this investigation you will

- create a "river" in a stream table to observe the creation of meanders and deltas
- identify the processes of erosion and deposition

Problem

Write It Up

How does moving water create meanders and deltas?

Procedure

1. Arrange the stream table on a counter so that it drains into a sink or bucket. If possible, place a sieve beneath the outlet hose to keep sand out of the drain. You can attach the inlet hose to a faucet if you have a proper adapter. Or you can gently pour water in with a pitcher or use a recirculating pump and a bucket.

2. Place wood blocks beneath the inlet end of the stream table so that the table tilts toward the outlet at about a 20 degree angle. Fill the upper two-thirds of the stream table nearly to the top with sand. Pack the sand a bit, and level the surface with the edge of a ruler. The empty bottom third of the stream table represents the lake or bay into which the river flows.

3. Using the end of the ruler, dig a gently curving trench halfway through the thickness of the sand from its upper to its lower end.

MATERIALS

- stream table, with hose attachment or recirculating pump
- sieve (optional)
- wood blocks
- sand
- ruler
- water
- sink with drain
- pitcher (optional)
- bucket (optional)

4. Direct a gentle flow of tap water into the upper end of the trench. Increase the flow slightly when the water begins to move through the trench. You may have to try this several times before you find the proper rate of flow to soak the sand and fill the stream channel. Avoid adding so much water that it pools at the top before moving into the channel. You can also change the stream table's tilt.

5. Once you are successful in creating a river, observe its shape and any movement of the sand. Continue until the top part of the sand is completely washed away and your river falls apart. Scrape the sand back into place with the ruler and repeat the procedure until you thoroughly understand the stream and sand movements.

▶ Observe and Analyze
Write It Up

1. **RECORD** Diagram your stream-table setup, and make a series of drawings showing changes in your river over time. Be sure to label the river's features, as well as areas of erosion and deposition. Be sure to diagram the behavior of the sand at the river's mouth.

2. **RECORD** Write a record of the development of your river from start to finish. Include details such as the degree of tilt you used, your method of introducing water into the stream table, and features you observed forming.

▶ Conclude
Write It Up

1. **EVALUATE** How do you explain the buildup of sand at the mouth of your river? Use the words *speed, erosion,* and *deposition* in your answer. Did the slope of the stream change over time?

2. **INTERPRET** Where in your stream table did you observe erosion occurring? Deposition? What features did each process form?

3. **INFER** What might have occurred if you had increased the amount or speed of the water flowing into your river?

4. **IDENTIFY LIMITS** In what ways was your setup a simplified version of what would actually occur on Earth? Describe the ways in which an actual stream would be more complex.

5. **APPLY** Drawing on what you observed in this investigation, make two statements that relate the age of a stream to (1) the extent of its meanders and (2) to the size of its delta or alluvial fan.

▶ INVESTIGATE Further

CHALLENGE Revise this activity to test a problem statement about a specific stream feature. You could choose to vary the stream's slope, speed, or volume to test the changes' effects on meanders and deltas, for example. Or you could vary the sediment size and observe the movements of each size. Write a hypothesis and design an experimental procedure. Identify the independent and dependent variables.

Creating stream features
Observe and Analyze
1. Before adding water

2. After one minute

5.3

Waves and wind shape land.

◀ **BEFORE**, you learned

- Stream systems shape Earth's surface
- Groundwater creates caverns and sinkholes

▶ **NOW**, you will learn

- How waves and currents shape shorelines
- How wind shapes land

VOCABULARY

longshore drift p. 159
longshore current p. 159
sandbar p. 160
barrier island p. 160
dune p. 161
loess p. 162

THINK ABOUT

How did these pillars of rock form?

The rock formations in this photograph stand along the shoreline near the small town of Port Campbell, Australia. What natural force created these isolated stone pillars? What evidence of this force can you see in the photograph?

Waves and currents shape shorelines.

The stone pillars, or sea stacks, in the photograph above are a major tourist attraction in Port Campbell National Park. They were formed by the movement of water. The constant action of waves breaking against the cliffs slowly wore them away, leaving behind pillarlike formations. Waves continue to wear down the pillars and cliffs at the rate of about two centimeters (one inch) a year. In the years to come, the waves will likely wear away the stone pillars completely.

The force of waves, powered by wind, can wear away rock and move thousands of tons of sand on beaches. The force of wind itself can change the look of the land. Moving air can pick up sand particles and move them around to build up dunes. Wind can also carry huge amounts of fine sediment thousands of kilometers.

In this section, you'll read more about how waves and wind shape shorelines and a variety of other landforms.

Shorelines

Some shorelines, like the one near Port Campbell, Australia, are made up of steep, rock cliffs. As waves crash against the rock, they wear away the bottom of the cliffs. Eventually, parts of the cliffs above break away and fall into the water, where they are worn down and carried away by the water.

While high, rocky coasts get worn away, low coastlines often get built up. As you read earlier, when a stream flows into an ocean or a lake, it deposits its sediment near its mouth. This sediment mixes with the sediment formed by waves beating against the coast. Waves and currents move this sediment along the shore, building up beaches. Two terms are used to describe the movement of sediment and water along a shore: *longshore drift* and *longshore current*.

- **Longshore drift** is the zigzag movement of sand along a beach. Waves formed by wind blowing across the water far from shore may hit a shoreline at an angle. These angled waves carry sand up onto the shore, and then gravity pulls the water and sand directly back into the water. The sand gradually moves down the beach. The illustration below shows longshore drift.

- A **longshore current** is movement of water along a shore as waves strike the shore at an angle. The direction of the longshore current can change from day to day as the direction of the waves striking the shore changes.

Longshore drift moves large amounts of sand along beaches. It can cause a beach to shrink at one location and grow at another.

Walls of rock extend out into the ocean at Cape May, New Jersey. They were built to keep beaches from being lost to longshore drift.

Longshore Drift

1 Incoming waves push sand up the beach at an angle.

longshore current

2 The sand washes back straight down the beach.

wave direction

INVESTIGATE Longshore Drift

How does sand move along a beach?

PROCEDURE

(1) Prop up a book as shown.

(2) Hold a coin with your finger against the bottom right corner of the book.

(3) Gently flick the coin up the slope of the book at an angle. The coin should slide back down the book and fall off the bottom. If necessary, readjust the angle of the book and the strength with which you are flicking the coin.

(4) Repeat step 3 several times. Observe the path the coin takes. Record your observations. Include a diagram that shows the general path the coin takes as it slides up and down the book.

WHAT DO YOU THINK?

• What path did the coin take on its way up? On its way down?
• In this model of longshore drift, what represents the beach, what represents the sand, and what represents a wave?

CHALLENGE In this model, in which direction will the longshore current move? How could you change the model to change the direction of the current?

MATERIALS
• 2 or 3 books
• coin

TIME
15 minutes

Sandbars and Barrier Islands

As they transport sand, ocean waves and currents shape a variety of coastal landforms. Longshore currents, for example, often deposit sand along shorelines. The sand builds up to form sandbars. A **sandbar** is a ridge of sand built up by the action of waves and currents. A sandbar that has built up above the water's surface and is joined to the land at one end is called a spit. The tip of Cape Cod, Massachusetts, is a spit.

Strong longshore currents that mostly move in one direction may produce sandbars that build up over time into barrier islands. A **barrier island** is a long, narrow island that develops parallel to a coast.

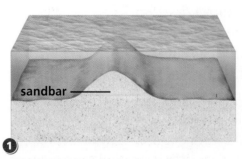

1 Waves and currents move and build up sand deposits to form a sandbar under the water surface.

2 As more sand is deposited, the sandbar rises above the surface to become a barrier island.

This lighthouse on a barrier island in North Carolina had to be moved because of beach erosion. The photograph shows the lighthouse before it was moved.

A barrier island gets its name from the fact that it forms a barrier between the ocean waves and the shore of the mainland. As a barrier island builds up, grasses, bushes, and trees begin to grow on it.

Barrier islands are common along gently sloping coasts around the world. They occur along the coasts of New Jersey and North Carolina and along the coastline of the Gulf of Mexico. Padre Island in Texas is a barrier island about 180 kilometers (110 mi) in length.

Barrier islands constantly change shape. Hurricanes or other storms can speed up the change. During large storms, waves can surge across the land, carrying away huge amounts of sediment and depositing it elsewhere. Houses on beaches can be destroyed in storms.

 How and where do barrier islands form?

Wind shapes land.

At Indiana Dunes National Lakeshore, not far from the skyscrapers of Chicago, you can tumble or slide down huge sand dunes. First-time visitors to the Indiana dunes find it hard to believe that sand formations like these can be found so far from a desert or an ocean. What created this long stretch of dune land along the southern shore of Lake Michigan? The answer: wind. A **dune** is a mound of sand built up by wind.

Like water, wind has the power to transport and deposit sediment. Although wind is a less powerful force of erosion than moving water, it can still shape landforms, especially in dry regions and in areas that have few or no plants to hold soil in place. Wind can build up dunes, deposit layers of dust, or make a land surface as hard as pavement.

wind

sand-particle movement

dune movement

Wind makes sand particles build up and tumble down, causing a dune to migrate, or move.

These hills of sand are at the Great Sand Dunes National Monument in Colorado.

Dune Formation

Even a light breeze can carry dust. A moderate wind can roll and slide grains of sand along a beach or desert, creating ripples. Only a strong wind, however, can actually pick up and carry sand particles. When the wind dies down or hits something—such as a cliff or a hill—it drops the sand. Over time, the deposits of sand build up to create dunes.

Some dunes start out as ripples that grow larger. Others form as wind-carried sand settles around a rock, log, or other obstacle. In climates with enough rainfall, plants begin to grow on dunes a short distance from beaches.

Dunes form only where there are strong winds and a constant supply of loose sand. They can be found on the inland side of beaches of oceans and large lakes, on the sandy floodplains of large rivers, and in sandy deserts.

Dunes can form in a variety of sizes and shapes. They can reach heights of up to 300 meters (about 1000 ft). Some dunes are curved; others are long, straight ridges; still others are mound-shaped hills. A dune usually has a gentle slope on the side that faces the wind and a steeper slope on the side sheltered from the wind.

Loess

Besides forming dunes, wind also changes the soil over large regions of Earth by depositing dust. A strong windstorm can move millions of tons of dust. As the wind dies down, the dust drops to the ground. Deposits of fine wind-blown sediment are called **loess** (LOH-uhs).

In some regions, deposits of loess have built up over thousands and even millions of years. Loess is a valuable resource because it forms good soil for growing crops.

This loess deposit in Iowa built up over many thousands of years.

Loess covers about 10 percent of the land surface of Earth. China has especially large deposits of loess, covering hundreds of thousands of square kilometers. Some of the deposits are more than 300 meters (about 1000 ft) thick. Such thick deposits take a long time to develop. Some of the loess deposits in China are 2 million years old. Winds blowing over the deserts and dry regions of central Asia carried the dust that formed these deposits.

Parts of east central Europe and the Mississippi Valley in the United States also contain significant loess deposits. In the central United States, loess deposits are between 8 and 30 meters (25 and 100 ft) thick.

Desert Pavement

Not only does wind shape land surfaces by depositing dust; it also shapes land surfaces by removing dust. When wind blows away all the smallest particles from a mixture of sand, silt, and gravel, it leaves behind just a layer of stones and gravel. This stony surface is called desert pavement because it looks like a cobblestone pavement. The coarse gravel and rocks are too large to be picked up by wind.

Desert pavement is made up of particles too large to be picked up by wind.

 CHECK YOUR READING How are both loess and desert pavement formed by wind?

5.3 Review

KEY CONCEPTS

1. What kinds of landforms do longshore drift and longshore currents produce?

2. How do dunes form?

3. How does loess form, and why is it important?

CRITICAL THINKING

4. **Identify Cause and Effect** Is longshore drift the cause or effect of a longshore current? Explain.

5. **Predict** What effect would a barrier island have on the shoreline of the mainland?

CHALLENGE

6. **Hypothesize** The south and east shores of Lake Michigan have large areas of sand dunes, but the north and west shores do not. Write a hypothesis that explains why. You might want to use a map and draw the shape of Lake Michigan to explain.

The leaves of American beach grass contain silica, the main component of sand. The leaves are therefore very tough. Why is this important on a dune?

Life on Dunes

Sand dunes are a difficult environment for most organisms. For example, few plants can gather enough nutrition from sand to grow quickly. However, any plant that grows slowly is likely to be buried by the shifting sand. Plants and animals that thrive on dunes generally have unusual traits that help them survive in dune conditions.

American Beach Grass

Among the first plants to grow on new coastal dunes is American beach grass. It grows faster as sand begins to bury it, and it can grow up to 1 meter (more than 3 ft) per year. Its large root system—reaching down as much as 3 meters (about 10 ft)—helps it gather food and water. The roots also help hold sand in place. As the grass's roots make the dunes stable, other plants can begin to grow there.

Sand Food

One of the most unusual plants in desert dunes is called sand food. It is one of the few plants that cannot convert sunlight into energy it can use. Instead, its long underground stem grabs onto the root of another plant and sucks food from it. Most of the plant is the stem. Sand food plants may be more than 2 meters (almost 7 ft) long.

Fowler's Toad

Fowler's toad is one of the animals that can live in coastal dunes. During the day, sunlight can make the top layer of the sand very hot and dry. These toads dig down into the sand, where they are safe, cool, and moist. They are most active at night.

In spring, sand food produces a small head of purple flowers that barely comes out of the ground. How does growing mostly underground help sand food survive?

Fowler's toads have a brownish or greenish color that makes them hard to see against a sandy background. How would this help protect them from animals that want to eat them?

EXPLORE

1. **GENERALIZE** Dune plants often have long roots. Propose an explanation for this.

2. **CHALLENGE** Use library or Internet resources to learn about another plant or animal that lives on dunes. Describe how it has adapted to the conditions in which it lives.

KEY CONCEPT

5.4 Glaciers carve land and move sediments.

BEFORE, you learned

- Running water shapes landscapes
- Wind changes landforms

NOW, you will learn

- How moving ice erodes land
- How moving ice deposits sediment and changes landforms

VOCABULARY

glacier p. 165
till p. 168
moraine p. 168
kettle lake p. 169

EXPLORE Glaciers

How do glaciers affect land?

PROCEDURE

① Flatten the clay on top of a paper towel.

② Drag the ice cube across the clay as shown. Record your observations.

③ Leave the ice cube to melt on top of the clay.

WHAT DO YOU THINK?

- What happened when you dragged the ice cube across the clay?
- What happened to the sand and gravel in the ice cube as it melted?

MATERIALS

- modeling clay
- paper towel
- ice cube containing sand and gravel

Glaciers are moving bodies of ice.

VOCABULARY
Remember to add a four square diagram for *glacier* to your notebook.

You might not think of ice as something that moves. But think about what happens to an ice cube on a table. The cube begins to melt, makes a small puddle, and may slide a little. The water under the cube makes the table surface slippery, which allows the ice cube to slide.

A similar process happens on a much larger scale with glaciers. A **glacier** is a large mass of ice that moves over land. A glacier forms in a cold region when more snow falls than melts each year. As the snow builds up, its weight presses the snow on the bottom into ice. On a mountain, the weight of a heavy mass of ice causes it to flow downward, usually slowly. On flatter land, the ice spreads out as a sheet. As glaciers form, move, and melt away, they shape landscapes.

Chapter 5: **Erosion and Deposition** 165 **A**

Extent of Glaciers

Glaciers can exist only in places where it is cold enough for water to stay frozen year round. Glaciers are found in mountain ranges all over the world and in land regions near the north and south poles.

Today, glaciers cover about 10 percent of Earth's land surface. However, the amount of land surface covered by glaciers has varied greatly over Earth's history. Glaciers have expanded during long cold periods called ice ages and have disappeared during long warm periods. About 30,000 years ago—during the last major ice age—glaciers extended across the northern parts of North America and Eurasia. They covered nearly 30 percent of the present land surface of Earth.

There are two major types of glaciers: alpine glaciers and continental glaciers.

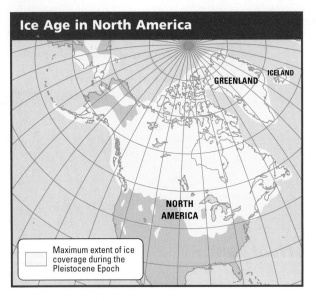

Ice Age in North America

ICELAND
GREENLAND
NORTH AMERICA

Maximum extent of ice coverage during the Pleistocene Epoch

RESOURCE CENTER
CLASSZONE.COM

Learn more about the movement and effects of glaciers.

Alpine Glaciers

Alpine glaciers, also called valley glaciers, form in mountains and flow down through valleys. As these glaciers move, they cause erosion, breaking up rock and carrying and pushing away the resulting sediment. Over time, an alpine glacier can change a V-shaped mountain valley into a U-shaped valley with a wider, flatter bottom.

Some glaciers extend all the way down into the lower land at the bases of mountains. At an alpine glacier's lower end, where temperatures are warmer, melting can occur. The melting glacier drops sediment, and streams flowing from the glacier carry some of the sediment away. If an alpine glacier flows into the ocean, big blocks may break off and become icebergs.

Continental Glaciers

Continental glaciers, also called ice sheets, are much larger than alpine glaciers. They can cover entire continents, including all but the highest mountain peaks. An ice sheet covered most of Canada and the northern United States during the last ice age. This ice sheet melted and shrank about 10,000 years ago.

Today, ice sheets cover most of Greenland and Antarctica. Each of these glaciers is shaped like a wide dome over the land. The ice on Antarctica is as much as 4500 meters (15,000 ft) thick.

 CHECK YOUR READING What are the two major types of glaciers and where do they form?

Types of Glaciers and Movement

A glacier is a large mass of ice that moves over land.

Alpine Glaciers

A glacier, such as this one in Alaska, changes the landscape as it moves down a mountain valley.

Continental Glaciers

Huge sheets of ice cover the continent of Antarctica and other land regions.

Glacier Movement

Gravity causes the ice in a glacier to move downhill. Two different processes cause glaciers to move: flowing and sliding.

Flowing The ice near the surface of a glacier is brittle, and cracks often form in it. However, deep inside a glacier, ice does not break as easily because it is under great pressure from the weight of the ice above it. Instead of breaking, ice inside a glacier flows like toothpaste being squeezed in its tube.

As a glacier moves, it breaks up rock and pushes and carries sediment.

Sliding The weight of a glacier and heat from Earth cause ice at the bottom of a glacier to melt. A layer of water forms under the glacier. The glacier slides along on this layer of water just as an ice cube might slide on a countertop.

READING VISUALS In the illustration, why are cracks shown near the surface of the glacier and not at the bottom?

A moving glacier left visible abrasion lines on this rock.

Glaciers deposit large amounts of sediment.

As glaciers have melted and retreated, they have shaped the landscapes of many places on Earth. As a glacier moves or expands, it transports a vast amount of sediment—a mix of boulders, small rocks, sand, and clay. It acts like a plow, pushing rock and soil and plucking out big blocks of rock. As a glacier moves over rock, it scratches and scrapes the rock in a process called abrasion. Abrasion leaves visible grooves on rock surfaces.

Moraines

When glaciers expand and advance and then melt and retreat, they affect both the land underneath them and the land around them. A glacier pushes huge amounts of sediment to its sides and front. When the glacier retreats, the deposits of sediment remain as visible evidence that ice once moved through. The sediment left directly on the ground surface by a retreating glacier is called **till.**

A deposit of till left behind by a retreating glacier is called a **moraine** (muh-RAYN). The ridges of till deposited at the sides of a glacier are called lateral moraines. The till that marks the farthest advance of a glacier forms a deposit called an end moraine. Moraines formed by continental glaciers, such as those in North America during the ice age, can be huge—many kilometers long.

The blanket of till that a glacier deposits along its bottom is called a ground moraine. Rock deposits from glaciers can often be identified as till because the till rocks are different, in type or age, from the rock that was present before the glacier formed.

CHECK YOUR READING Draw a sketch of a glacier and label where lateral, end, and ground moraines would form.

A glacier scooped out this valley in California and left behind lateral moraines.

Lateral moraines

Lakes

Besides ridges, hills, and blankets of till, melting glaciers also leave behind depressions of various sizes that can become lakes. Landscapes shaped by glaciers are often dotted with small kettle lakes as well as larger lakes. A **kettle lake** is a bowl-shaped depression that was formed by a block of ice from a glacier and then became filled with water.

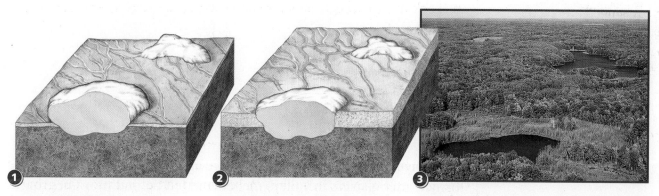

① As a glacier moves away, it leaves huge blocks of ice.

② Over time, sediment builds up around the ice.

③ The ice melts, leaving behind bowls that become kettle lakes. These lakes are in Wisconsin.

The last ice sheet in North America formed many kettle lakes in some regions. Kettle lakes are common in Michigan, Wisconsin, and Minnesota.

INVESTIGATE Kettle Lake Formation

How do kettle lakes form?

DESIGN — YOUR OWN —

Kettle lakes form when sediment builds up around blocks of ice left behind by a retreating glacier. Use what you know about kettle lake formation to design a model of the process.

PROCEDURE

① Use the tray, the ice cubes, and the other materials to model how sediment builds up around ice blocks.

② Write a description of the process you used to make your model.

WHAT DO YOU THINK?

• Describe how your model worked. What did you do first? What happened next?

• Did your model accurately represent the formation of kettle lakes? Did it work? Why or why not?

• What were the limitations of your model? Are there any aspects of kettle lake formation that are not represented? If so, what are they?

SKILL FOCUS
Designing models

MATERIALS
• shallow tray
• ice cubes
• modeling clay
• sand
• gravel
• water

TIME
30 minutes

Great Lakes Formation

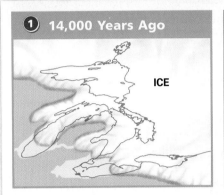

1 **14,000 Years Ago**

ICE

The ice sheet covering a land of river valleys began to retreat.

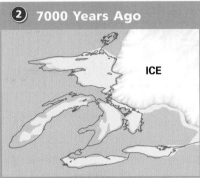

2 **7000 Years Ago**

ICE

Water filled the bowls carved out by the ice.

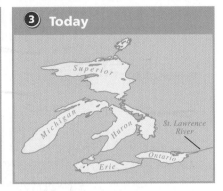

3 **Today**

Superior

Michigan

Huron

St. Lawrence River

Erie

Ontario

The Great Lakes contain 20 percent of the world's fresh lake water.

Many large lakes are the result of ice ages. In some places, lakes formed after glaciers in valleys melted and left behind moraines that dammed the valleys. Many of these lakes are long and narrow, like the Finger Lakes in New York, which are named for their slender shape.

The Great Lakes were formed thousands of years ago as an ice sheet moved over the land and then melted. A million years ago, the region of the Great Lakes had many river valleys. The ice sheet gouged out large depressions in the land and left piles of rock and debris that blocked water from draining out. In some areas, where the deepest Great Lakes are now, the enormous weight of the glacier actually caused the land to sink as much as one kilometer.

The ice sheet started to melt about 14,000 years ago. By about 7000 years ago, it had melted past what would become Lake Erie and Lake Ontario, the lakes farthest to the east.

CHECK YOUR READING What are two ways the ice sheet formed the Great Lakes?

5.4 Review

KEY CONCEPTS

1. Describe the two processes that cause glaciers to move.

2. What are the two major types of glaciers, and where are they found?

3. Describe the land features left behind by glaciers that have melted and shrunk.

CRITICAL THINKING

4. **Compare and Contrast** Identify two ways in which the erosion effects of glaciers differ from those of rivers.

5. **Predict** How would glaciers be affected by changes in climate, such as global warming and global cooling?

⬤ CHALLENGE

6. **Infer** Regions near the equator are generally the warmest on Earth. However, in one small area of Africa, there are glaciers close to the equator. Form a hypothesis to explain why these glaciers exist.

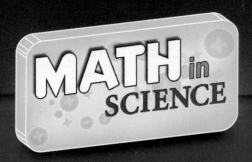

MATH TUTORIAL
CLASSZONE.COM

Click on Math Tutorial for more help with making line graphs.

Snow Line Elevation and Latitude

Glaciers form above the snow line, the lowest elevation at which there is permanent snow in the summer. The snow line elevation depends on temperature and precipitation. In the hot tropics the snow line is high in the mountains, while at the poles it is near sea level. The table shows the snow line elevations at different locations on Earth. The latitude of each location indicates how far the location is from the equator; the latitude of the equator is 0 degrees, and the latitude of the North Pole is 90 degrees.

Location	Latitude (degrees north)	Snow Line Elevation (meters)
North Pole	90	0
Juneau, Alaska	58	1050
Glacier National Park	49	2600
Sierra Nevada	37	3725
Himalayas (East Nepal)	28	5103
Ecuador	0	4788

Follow the steps below to make a line graph of the data.

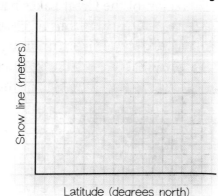

(1) On a sheet of graph paper, draw and label axes. Put latitude on the horizontal axis and snow line elevation on the vertical axis.

(2) Choose and mark a scale for each axis.

(3) Graph each point.

(4) Draw line segments to connect the points.

Use your graph to answer the following questions.

1. Mount Kenya is very close to the equator. Estimate the snow line elevation on Mount Kenya.

2. Mount Rainier is at 47 degrees north latitude and is 4389 meters tall. Can there be glaciers on Mount Rainier? If so, estimate the elevation above which the glaciers form.

3. Mount Washington in New Hampshire is at 45 degrees north latitude and is 1917 meters tall. Can there be glaciers on Mount Washington? If so, estimate their lowest elevation.

CHALLENGE Temperatures are hotter at the equator than at 28 degrees north latitude. Why is the snow line lower at the equator in Ecuador? (**Hint:** The answer involves precipitation.)

Chapter Review

the **BIG** idea

Water, wind, and ice shape Earth's surface.

CONTENT REVIEW
CLASSZONE.COM

◀ KEY CONCEPTS SUMMARY

5.1 Forces wear down and build up Earth's surface.

Water, wind, and ice move sediment in the process called **erosion**. The placement of sediment in a new location is **deposition**, part of the erosion process.

VOCABULARY
erosion p. 145
deposition p. 145
mass wasting p. 147

5.2 Moving water shapes land.

Water drains from land in **drainage basins**, which are separated by **divides.** As water flows over land and underground, it moves sediment and changes land features.

VOCABULARY
drainage basin p. 151
divide p. 151
floodplain p. 152
alluvial fan p. 153
delta p. 153
sinkhole p. 155

5.3 Waves and wind shape land.

The action of water moves sand and builds up new landforms, such as sandbars and barrier islands. Wind forms dunes.

VOCABULARY
longshore drift p. 159
longshore current p. 159
sandbar p. 160
barrier island p. 160
dune p. 161
loess p. 162

5.4 Glaciers carve land and move sediments.

Glaciers are large bodies of ice that change landscapes as they move.

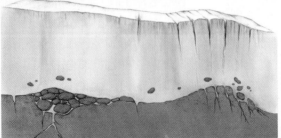

VOCABULARY
glacier p. 165
till p. 168
moraine p. 168
kettle lake p. 169

Reviewing Vocabulary

Copy and complete the chart below. Explain how each landscape feature is formed.

Feature	How It Forms
EXAMPLE delta	A river deposits sediment as it enters the ocean.
1. alluvial fan	
2. sinkhole	
3. sandbar	
4. barrier island	
5. dune	
6. loess	
7. moraine	
8. kettle lake	

Reviewing Key Concepts

Multiple Choice *Choose the letter of the best answer.*

9. The first stage in the erosion process is
   a. deposition
   b. mass wasting
   c. drainage
   d. weathering

10. The main natural force responsible for mass movements of rocks and debris is
    a. rainwater   c. gravity
    b. wind   d. fire

11. A sinkhole is formed by the collapse of
    a. an alluvial fan
    b. a cavern
    c. a moraine
    d. a kettle lake

12. Rivers transport sediment to
    a. drainage basins
    b. oceans and lakes
    c. the water table
    d. moraines

13. Drainage basins are separated by a
    a. moraine   c. tributary
    b. divide   d. barrier island

14. In high mountains, a valley carved by a stream has the shape of a
    a. U   c. plate
    b. crescent   d. V

15. An oxbow lake is formed by the cutting off of a
    a. meander   c. sinkhole
    b. drainage basin d. glacier

16. Sandbars, spits, and barrier islands can all be built up by
    a. glaciers   c. wind
    b. ocean waves   d. mass wasting

17. A dune is a sand mound built up primarily by
    a. gravity   c. glaciers
    b. running water d. wind

18. Strong winds can transport large quantities of
    a. gravel   c. dry sand
    b. wet sand   d. clay

19. A mountain valley carved by a glacier has the shape of a
    a. U   c. bowl
    b. crescent   d. V

Short Answer *Answer each of the following questions in a sentence or two.*

20. How is deposition part of the erosion process?

21. How can rainwater in the Rocky Mountains end up in the ocean?

22. What is the effect of a longshore current on a beach?

23. Why is a mass movement of mud called a flow?

24. What visual evidence is a sign of creep?

25. What is the connection between icebergs and glaciers?

Thinking Critically

This photograph shows two glaciers joining to form one (A). Make a sketch of the glaciers to answer the next three questions.

26. APPLY Place an arrow to show in which direction the main glacier (A) is moving.

27. ANALYZE Mark the places where you think till would be found.

28. APPLY Mark the location of a lateral moraine.

29. ANALYZE Why does the main glacier not have an end moraine?

30. COMPARE AND CONTRAST Compare the main glacier valley in the photograph with the valley at the far right (B). How are the valleys different? Explain why they might be different.

31. APPLY In exploring an area of land, what clues would you look for to determine whether glaciers were once there?

32. COMPARE AND CONTRAST How is a deposit of till from a glacier similar to a river delta? How is it different?

33. EVALUATE If you were growing crops on a field near a slow-moving, curvy river, what would an advantage of the field's location be? What might be a disadvantage?

34. COMPARE AND CONTRAST How are mudflows and mass wasting of rock similar? How are they different? Include references to speed and types of material in your answer.

35. INFER If the wind usually blows from west to east over a large area of land, and the wind usually slows down over the eastern half of the area, where would you be likely to find loess in the area? Explain your answer.

36. APPLY If you were considering a location for a house and were concerned about creep, what two factors about the land would you consider?

37. SYNTHESIZE Describe how the processes of erosion and deposition are involved in the formation of kettle lakes.

the BIG idea

38. SYNTHESIZE Describe how snow falling onto the Continental Divide in the Rocky Mountains can be part of the process of erosion and deposition. Include the words *divide, glacier, stream,* and *ocean* in your answer.

39. PROVIDE EXAMPLES Choose three examples of erosion processes—one each from Sections 5.2, 5.3, and 5.4. Explain how gravity is involved in each of these processes.

UNIT PROJECTS

Evaluate all the data, results, and information in your project folder. Prepare to present your project. Be ready to answer questions posed by your classmates about your results.

Analyzing a Diagram

Use the diagram to answer the questions below.

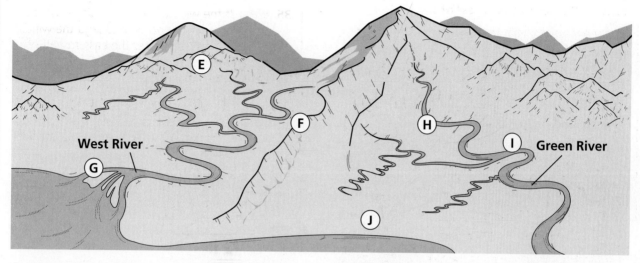

1. Where would a glacier be most likely to form?

   a. E   **c.** G

   b. F   **d.** H

2. Where is a divide?

   a. E   **c.** H

   b. F   **d.** I

3. Where is a delta?

   a. E   **c.** G

   b. F   **d.** J

4. Which process could move sediment from point E to point G?

   a. weathering   **c.** deposition

   b. erosion   **d.** drifting

5. Which word best describes the building up of sediment at point G?

   a. weathering   **c.** deposition

   b. erosion   **d.** drifting

6. Why might the water in the Green River move faster at point H than at point I?

   a. The river at point H is warmer.

   b. The river at point H is smaller.

   c. The slope at point H is steeper.

   d. More rain falls at point H.

Extended Response

Answer the two questions below in detail. Include some of the terms shown in the word box. In your answers, underline each term you use.

ocean waves	currents	barrier island
grass	glaciers	kettle lakes

7. Each year, Clark and his family visit the ocean. Clark notices that a sandbar near the coast is slightly larger each year. Predict what will happen if this trend continues.

8. Annika often goes fishing at one of several small, round lakes that are within 20 miles of her house in Minnesota. How might these lakes have formed?

UNIT B

The Changing Earth

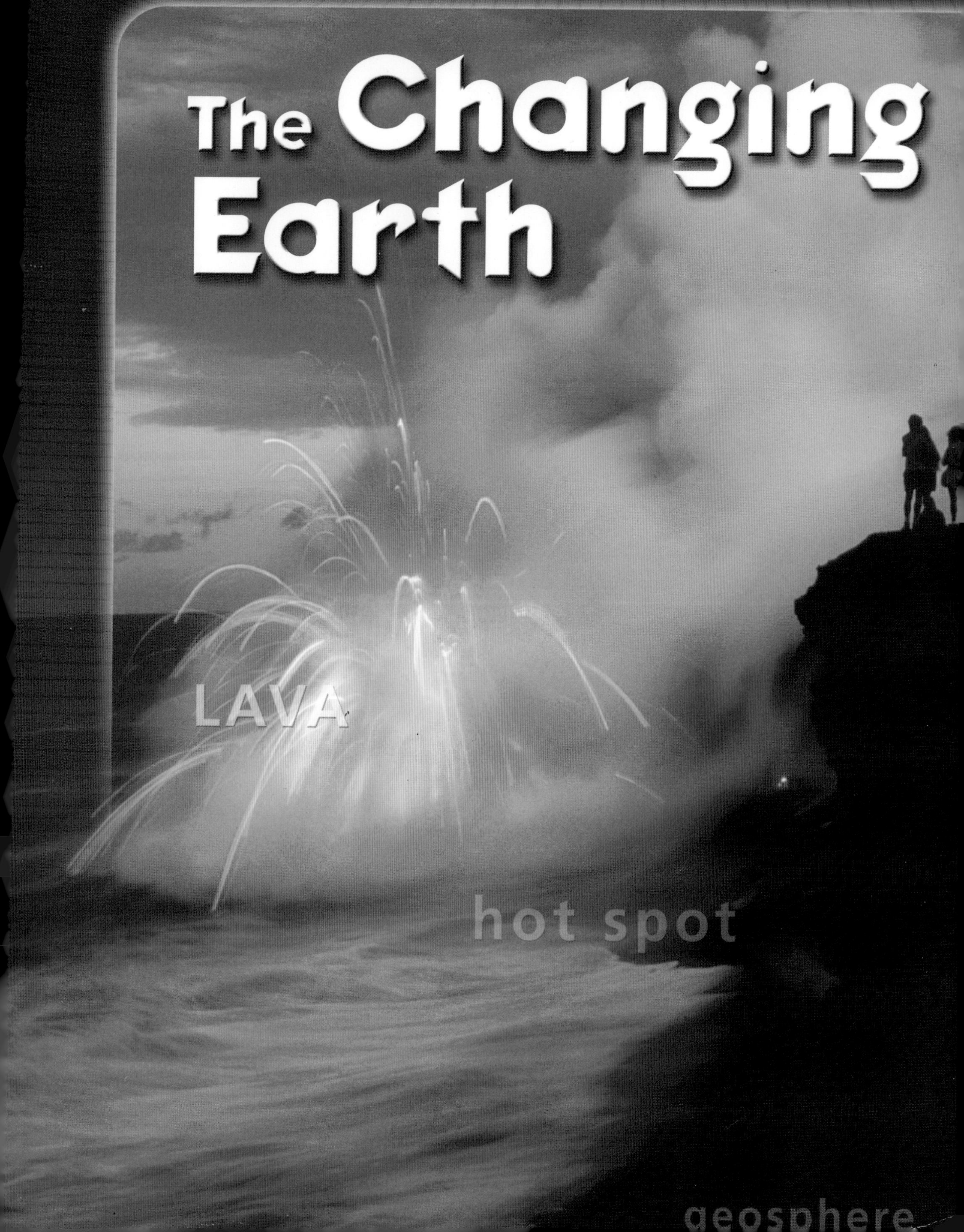
LAVA
hot spot
geosphere

McDougal Littell Science
The Changing Earth

The Changing Earth
Contents Overview

Unit Features

1 Plate Tectonics — 6

(the **BIG** idea)

The movement of tectonic plates
causes geologic changes on Earth.

2 Earthquakes — 42

(the **BIG** idea)

Earthquakes release stress that has
built up in rocks.

3 Mountains and Volcanoes — 74

(the **BIG** idea)

Mountains and volcanoes form as
tectonic plates move.

4 Views of Earth's Past — 108

(the **BIG** idea)

Rocks, fossils, and other types of
natural evidence tell Earth's story.

5 Natural Resources — 144

(the **BIG** idea)

Society depends on natural
resources for energy and materials.

Studying VOLCANOES with Satellites

New ways of viewing Earth are giving scientists powerful tools for learning about and predicting volcanic eruptions.

SCIENTIFIC AMERICAN FRONTIERS

View the video segment "Paradise Postponed" to learn how scientists study volcanoes and predict eruptions.

During a 1997 eruption of the Soufrière Hills volcano on Montserrat, volcanic material flowed all the way to the ocean.

A plume of volcanic ash and gases rises from Soufrière Hills volcano, Montserrat, in this photograph taken from a satellite on October 29, 2002.

Deadly Eruptions

On the island of Montserrat in the West Indies, small eruptions of the Soufrière Hills volcano began in 1995. These early warnings gave people time to move away several months before the first of the large explosions.

People living in the towns near Nevado del Ruiz volcano in Colombia were not so fortunate. On a night in November 1985, a storm hid the snow-covered volcano. No one could see the start of an eruption. Huge amounts of snow and ice melted and mixed with volcanic ash to form mudflows that killed 25,000 people. The flow that buried much of the town of Armero traveled 74 kilometers in just two and one-half hours.

Throughout history volcanic eruptions have caused some of the world's worst disasters. Warnings might have saved hundreds of thousands of lives. But in most cases people had no idea that a rain of rock, a cloud of toxic gases, or other deadly effects of an erupting volcano would soon engulf their area. By the time people realized that a volcano was erupting, it was too late to get away. Today, scientists monitor volcanoes around the world to help avoid such tragedies.

A 1996 eruption of Alaska's Pavlof volcano was the first to be predicted with the use of data from space. The satellite image recorded during the eruption shows an area of hot ground on the volcano in red.

Predicting Volcanic Eruptions

Scientists who study volcanoes paid close attention when an instrument on a weather satellite unexpectedly "saw" hot ground in 1996. The instrument's usual function is to measure cloud temperatures, but it detected an area of increased heat on Alaska's Pavlof volcano. The scientists predicted that the volcano would soon erupt. Three days later, it did. This eruption was the first to be predicted with information from space. Now computers check satellite data as they receive the data. Any unusually hot areas trigger an automatic e-mail alert to scientists.

In 1999, NASA launched the *Terra* satellite as part of a program to study Earth's surface and atmosphere. Among *Terra's* instruments is one that detects heat given off by the planet's surface. When scientists observe an unusual increase in surface temperature, they determine whether magma is rising underground. In some cases unusual heat has been the first sign that a volcano is building toward an eruption.

After an Eruption

Satellites are also used to monitor eruptions as they happen. Lava flows show up clearly, as you can see in the *Terra* image on page 5. In addition, satellites are used to track the locations of volcanic ash and gas clouds. Airplanes flying into this material can be severely damaged, so pilots need to know where it is. Volcanic material in

SCIENTIFIC AMERICAN FRONTIERS

View the "Paradise Postponed" segment of your *Scientific American Frontiers* video to learn how scientists monitor volcanic eruptions.

IN THIS SCENE FROM THE VIDEO ▶
Scientist Barry Voigt examines the effects of a powerful eruption that occurred a few days earlier.

STUDYING VOLCANOES Until 1995, the Caribbean island of Montserrat was a peaceful tourist destination. Then, the island's volcano began to erupt. Over the next two years, the volcano erupted dozens of times, spewing out hot ash, rocks, and gases. These eruptions destroyed most of the island's towns and drove away many residents.

Scientists from around the world have come to Montserrat to find out how well they can predict eruptions. Seismic stations buried near the volcano detect earthquakes, which can be a sign that the volcano is about to erupt. Scientists can also predict an eruption by studying changes in the lava dome that has built up on the volcano. When an eruption does occur, scientists visit the site to collect rocks and measure the volcanic ash flow.

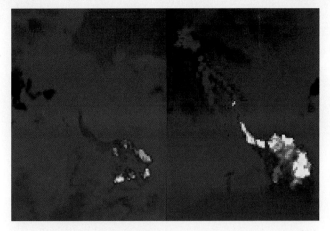

Data collected by the *Terra* satellite show the progress of a Hawaiian lava flow as it enters the ocean on May 13, 2000 (left), and on August 1, 2000 (right).

the air can be difficult to see or to distinguish from normal clouds, especially at night. Satellites are particularly helpful in identifying and tracking eruptions in remote areas where there are few or no observers.

Explosive Neighbors

Satellites such as *Terra* are among the tools scientists use to monitor restless volcanoes near urban areas. Mount Rainier, a volcano in Washington, looms near the large cities of Seattle and Tacoma. In the past, heat from eruptions has melted large amounts of the ice and snow at the top of the volcano, creating mudflows that destroyed everything in their path. Another extremely dangerous volcano is Mount Vesuvius, near Naples, Italy. Timely warnings before eruptions of such volcanoes can allow authorities to safely evacuate the millions of people who live near them.

UNANSWERED Questions

Even when scientists predict that a volcano will erupt soon, many questions still cannot be answered.

- How powerful will the next eruption be?
- On what day (or even during what week) will the volcano erupt?
- How much magma is rising under the volcano, and how fast is it rising? Will it stop?

UNIT PROJECTS

As you study this unit, work alone or with a group on one of the projects listed below.

Review Movie Science

Review a movie that features a volcanic eruption to evaluate how accurate the movie's depiction of a volcano is.

- Visit the U.S. Geological Survey Web site for a list of movies about volcanoes, such as *Dante's Peak*.
- Evaluate one movie and prepare a report on it for a radio or TV spot.

Earthquake Report

Make a map of the volcanic eruptions and earthquakes that occur around the world while you are studying this unit.

- Write a news script and create a graphic to show the events' locations and intensities.
- Present your findings as a special TV report for an evening news program.

Ash-Fall Fossil Exhibit

Prepare an exhibit showing how volcanic ash can preserve fossils of the organisms it buries. You could begin by researching Ashfall Fossil Beds State Historical Park in Nebraska.

- Create a poster that shows the major steps in the formation of fossils of creatures in volcanic ash.
- Make models or tracings of some ash-fall fossils.
- Display the poster and models as a classroom or Web-site exhibit.

CAREER CENTER
CLASSZONE.COM

Learn more about careers in volcanology.

CHAPTER

Plate Tectonics

the BIG idea

The movement of tectonic plates causes geologic changes on Earth.

What might have made this huge crack in the Earth?

Key Concepts

SECTION

1.1 Earth has several layers.
Learn about Earth's interior and its rigid surface plates.

SECTION

1.2 Continents change position over time.
Learn how continental drift and plate tectonics changed the way people view Earth.

SECTION

1.3 Plates move apart.
Learn about the three types of plate boundaries and what happens when plates move apart.

SECTION

1.4 Plates converge or scrape past each other.
Learn what geologic events occur at these plate boundaries.

Internet Preview

CLASSZONE.COM

Chapter 1 online resources: Content Review, two Visualizations, one Resource Center, Math Tutorial, and Test Practice

Watching a Pot Boil

Put a medium-sized pot of water on to boil. Place a small wet sponge on the water. Watch the water and sponge as the water heats.

Observe and Think
What happened to the water as it heated? What happened to the sponge as the water became hotter?

Earth's Moving Surface

Place two halves of a peanut butter and jelly sandwich side by side. Very slowly push them together. Then take one half and very slowly tear it into two pieces.

Observe and Think
What happened when you pushed and pulled on the sandwich halves? What might this activity tell you about the movements of Earth's surface?

Internet Activity: Earth's Interior

Go to **ClassZone.com** to explore the makeup of Earth's layers. Find out how scientists learned what the interior of Earth is like.

Observe and Think
Science fiction books and movies show people traveling to the center of Earth. Do you think this can happen any time soon? Why or why not?

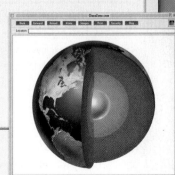

NSTA
scilinks.org
*SCI*LINKS

Plates Code: MDL052

Getting Ready to Learn

CONCEPT REVIEW

- Most rocks are made of minerals.
- Different types of rocks are formed under different temperatures and pressures.
- Earth's surface has changed over millions of years.

VOCABULARY REVIEW

See Glossary for definitions.

density

mineral

rock

CONTENT REVIEW
CLASSZONE.COM
Review concepts and vocabulary.

TAKING NOTES

SUPPORTING MAIN IDEAS

Make a chart to show main ideas and the information that supports them. Copy each blue heading. Below each heading, add supporting information, such as reasons, explanations, and examples.

VOCABULARY STRATEGY

Place each vocabulary term at the center of a **description wheel** diagram. Write some words describing it on the spokes.

See the Note-Taking Handbook on pages R45–R51.

SCIENCE NOTEBOOK

Earth is made up of materials with different densities.

Dense materials—such as iron and nickel—sink toward center

Less dense materials rise toward surface

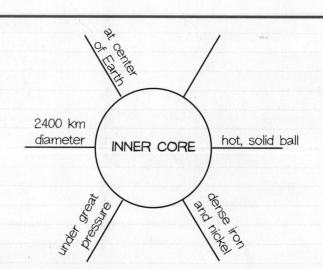

2400 km diameter

at center of Earth

INNER CORE

hot, solid ball

under great pressure

dense iron and nickel

KEY CONCEPT

Earth has several layers.

◀ **BEFORE,** you learned

- Minerals and rocks are the building blocks of Earth
- Different types of rocks make up Earth's surface

▶ **NOW,** you will learn

- About the different properties of Earth's layers
- About the plates that make up Earth's outermost layers

VOCABULARY

inner core p. 10
outer core p. 10
mantle p. 11
crust p. 11
lithosphere p. 11
asthenosphere p. 11
tectonic plate p. 12

EXPLORE Density

Will a denser material sink or float?

PROCEDURE

① Add equal amounts of water to 2 cups. Add 3 spoonfuls of salt to one of the cups and stir until the salt is dissolved.

② Add 10 drops of food coloring to the same cup in which you dissolved the salt.

③ Gently pour about a third of the colored salt water into the cup of fresh water. Observe what happens.

WHAT DO YOU THINK?
- What did you observe when the two types of water were mixed?
- What does this activity tell you about materials of different density?

MATERIALS
- 2 clear plastic cups
- tap water
- table salt
- plastic spoon
- food coloring

Earth is made up of materials with different densities.

SUPPORTING MAIN IDEAS
Support the main ideas about Earth's layers with details and examples.

Scientists think that about 4.6 billion years ago, Earth formed as bits of material collided and stuck together. The planet grew larger as more and more material was added. These impacts, along with radioactive decay and Earth's gravity, produced intense heat. The young planet became a glowing ball of melted rock.

In time, denser materials, such as iron and nickel, sank toward the center of Earth. Less dense materials moved toward the surface. Other materials settled between the planet's center and its surface. Slowly, Earth's main layers formed—the core, the mantle, and the crust.

Earth's layers have different properties.

How do scientists know what Earth's deep interior is like? After all, no one has seen it. To explore the interior, scientists study the energy from earthquakes or underground explosions they set off. The energy travels through Earth somewhat like ripples move through a pond. The energy moves slower through less dense materials or liquids and faster through denser materials or solids. In this way, scientists infer what each layer is made of and how thick the layers are, as shown in the diagram below.

Core, Mantle, Crust

The core is Earth's densest region and is made up of two parts. The **inner core** is a ball of hot, solid metals. There is enormous pressure at the center of Earth. This squeezes the atoms of the metals so closely together that the core remains solid despite the intense heat.

The **outer core** is a layer of liquid metals that surrounds the inner core. The temperature and pressure in the outer core are lower than in the inner core. The lower pressure allows the metals to remain liquid.

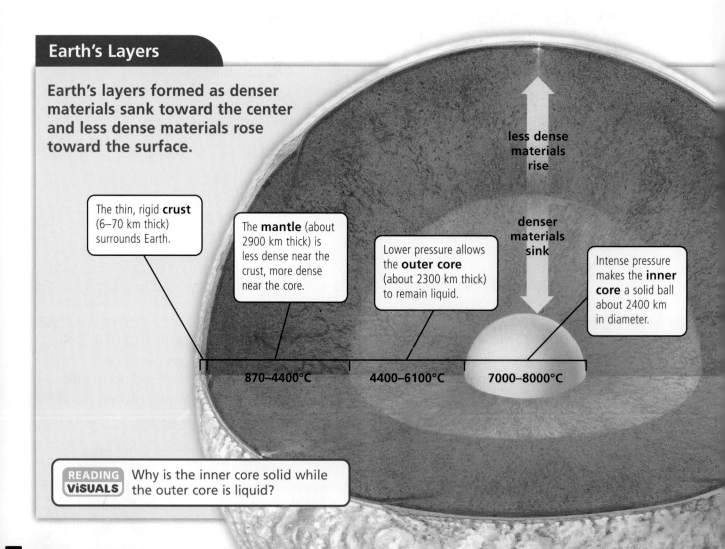

Earth's Layers

Earth's layers formed as denser materials sank toward the center and less dense materials rose toward the surface.

less dense materials rise

denser materials sink

The thin, rigid **crust** (6–70 km thick) surrounds Earth.

The **mantle** (about 2900 km thick) is less dense near the crust, more dense near the core.

Lower pressure allows the **outer core** (about 2300 km thick) to remain liquid.

Intense pressure makes the **inner core** a solid ball about 2400 km in diameter.

870–4400°C   4400–6100°C   7000–8000°C

READING VISUALS Why is the inner core solid while the outer core is liquid?

The **mantle** is Earth's thickest layer, measuring nearly 2900 kilometers (1700 mi). It is made of hot rock that is less dense than the metallic core. The very top part of the mantle is cool and rigid. Just below that, the rock is hot and soft enough to move like a thick paste.

The **crust** is a thin layer of cool rock. It surrounds Earth somewhat like a shell surrounds an egg. There are two basic types of crust. Continental crust includes all continents and some major islands. Oceanic crust includes all the ocean floors. As the diagram below shows, Earth's crust is thinnest under the oceans and thickest under continental mountain ranges. The crust is home to all life on Earth.

Lithosphere and Asthenosphere

Earth's crust and the very top of the mantle together form the **lithosphere** (LIHTH-uh-SFEER). The Greek prefix *litho-* means "stone" or "rock." This layer is the most rigid of all the layers. The lithosphere sits on top of the **asthenosphere** (as-THEHN-uh-SFEER), a layer of hotter, softer rock in the upper mantle. The Greek word *asthenés* means "weak." This layer is not actually weak, but it is soft enough to flow slowly like hot tar. You can imagine the lithosphere as solid pieces of pavement resting on hot tar.

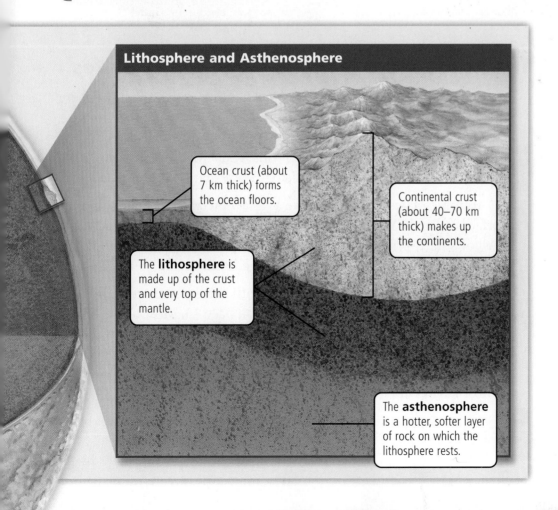

Lithosphere and Asthenosphere

Ocean crust (about 7 km thick) forms the ocean floors.

Continental crust (about 40–70 km thick) makes up the continents.

The **lithosphere** is made up of the crust and very top of the mantle.

The **asthenosphere** is a hotter, softer layer of rock on which the lithosphere rests.

INVESTIGATE Earth's Different Layers

How can you model Earth's layers?

PROCEDURE

1. Put a layer of wooden beads about 1 centimeter thick at the bottom of a clear plastic cup or small jar.

2. Put a layer of gravel about 2 centimeters thick on top of the wooden beads. Stir the beads and gravel until they are well mixed.

3. Put another layer of gravel about 1 centimeter thick on top of the mix. Do NOT mix this layer of gravel.

4. SLOWLY fill the cup about two-thirds full of water. Be sure not to disturb the layers in the cup.

5. Stir the beads and gravel with the stick. Observe what happens.

WHAT DO YOU THINK?

- What happened to the materials when you stirred them?
- How do you think this model represents the layers of Earth?

CHALLENGE What could you add to the model to represent Earth's solid core?

SKILL FOCUS
Modeling

MATERIALS
- clear plastic cup
- small colored wooden beads
- gravel
- stirring stick
- tap water

TIME
15 minutes

The lithosphere is made up of many plates.

READING TIP

The word *tectonic* comes from the Greek *tecktōn*, which means "builder." Tectonic plates are constantly building and changing landforms and oceans around Earth.

As scientists studied Earth's surface, they discovered that the lithosphere does not form a continuous shell around Earth. Instead, they found that the lithosphere is broken into many large and small slabs of rock called **tectonic plates** (tehk-TAHN-ihk). Scientists do not know exactly how or when in Earth's history these giant plates formed.

Tectonic plates fit together like a jigsaw puzzle that makes up the surface of Earth. You could compare the lithosphere to the cracked shell of a hard-boiled egg. The shell may be broken into many pieces, but it still forms a "crust" around the egg itself.

Most large tectonic plates include both continental crust and oceanic crust, as shown in the diagram on page 13. Most of the thicker continental crust rises above the ocean. The rest of the plate is thin oceanic crust, or sea floor, and is underwater. The next time you look at the continents on a world map, remember you are seeing only the part of Earth's crust that rises above the ocean.

CHECK YOUR READING Why do you see only the dry land areas of tectonic plates on a typical world map?

African Plate

Most tectonic plates have both continental and oceanic crust.

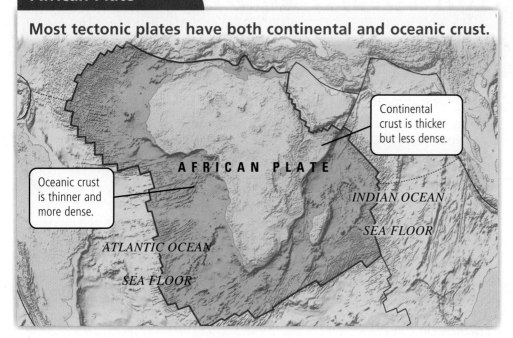

Continental crust is thicker but less dense.

Oceanic crust is thinner and more dense.

AFRICAN PLATE

INDIAN OCEAN

SEA FLOOR

ATLANTIC OCEAN

SEA FLOOR

In the diagram above, notice how much of the African Plate, shaded darker blue, lies underwater. The continent of Africa, which looks large on a world map, is actually about half the size of the entire plate. The plate's oceanic crust forms part of the sea floor of the Atlantic and Indian oceans and of the Mediterranean Sea. The ocean crusts of other plates make up the rest of the sea floors.

Earth's layers and tectonic plates are two of the most important discoveries in geology. They helped solve a mystery that had puzzled people for nearly 400 years. The mystery involved two questions. Have the continents always been where they are today? If not, how did they move to their present positions? In Section 1.2, you will find out how scientists are answering these questions.

 Review

KEY CONCEPTS

1. Briefly describe the inner and outer cores, the mantle, and the crust.

2. In what ways is the lithosphere different from the asthenosphere?

3. Describe the structure of most tectonic plates.

CRITICAL THINKING

4. **Draw Conclusions** Suppose you are looking at a scene that has mountains near an ocean. Where do you think the crust would be the thickest? Why?

5. **Hypothesize** What would Earth look like if most of its crust was above sea level?

⬥ CHALLENGE

6. **Predict** You have learned that Earth's lithosphere is made up of many plates. How do you think this fact might help scientists solve the mystery of the moving continents?

Continents change position over time.

◀ **BEFORE,** you learned

- Earth's main layers are the core, the mantle, and the crust
- The lithosphere and asthenosphere are the topmost layers of Earth
- The lithosphere is made up of tectonic plates

▶ **NOW,** you will learn

- How the continental drift hypothesis was developed
- About evidence for plate movement from the sea floor
- How scientists developed the theory of plate tectonics

VOCABULARY

continental drift p. 14
Pangaea p. 16
mid-ocean ridge p. 16
convection p. 17
convection current p. 17
theory of plate tectonics
p. 18

EXPLORE Movements of Continents

How do you put together a giant continent?

PROCEDURE

① Work with a small group. Draw the outline of a large landmass. Fill in mountains, rivers, lakes, and any other features you like.

② Cut out your landmass, then tear the drawing into several pieces and mix the pieces up. Ask another group to put the puzzle together.

WHAT DO YOU THINK?

- What clues helped you fit the pieces together?
- Do any lands on a world map seem to fit together?

MATERIALS

- sheet of paper
- colored marking pens
- scissors

Continents join together and split apart.

VOCABULARY
Draw a description wheel in your notebook for *continental drift*.

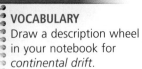

The idea that Earth's surface might be moving is not new. As far back as the 1500s, when mapmakers started including North and South America in their world maps, they noticed something curious. The western coast of Africa and the eastern coast of South America seemed to fit together like pieces in a puzzle. Were these continents joined at one time?

In the late 1800s, German scientist Alfred Wegener (VAY-guh-nuhr) began studying this question. In 1912, he proposed a hypothesis known as **continental drift.** According to Wegener's hypothesis, Earth's continents were once joined in a single landmass and gradually moved, or drifted, apart. For many years, people did not accept Wegener's ideas. Not until the mid-1900s did scientists find new evidence that made them consider continental drift more seriously.

Evidence for Continental Drift

Wegener gathered evidence for his hypothesis from fossils, from studies of ancient climate, and from the geology of continents.

Fossils Wegener learned that the fossils of an ancient reptile, *Mesosaurus* (MEHZ-uh-SAWR-uhs), had been discovered in South America and western Africa. This small reptile lived about 270 million years ago. Its fossils were not found anywhere else in the world. Wegener said this fact could easily be explained if South America and Africa were once joined, as shown in the map below.

Climate Evidence of climate change also supported Wegener's hypothesis. For example, Greenland today lies near the Arctic Circle and is mostly covered in ice. Yet fossils of tropical plants can be found on its shores. In contrast, South Africa today has a warm climate. Yet its rocks were deeply scratched by ice sheets that once covered the area.

Wegener suggested that these continents had moved, carrying their fossils and rocks with them. Greenland, for example, had once been near the equator and had slowly moved to the Arctic Circle. South Africa, once closer to the South Pole, had moved slowly north to a warmer region.

Geology Wegener's best evidence for continental drift came from the kinds of rocks that make up the continents. He showed that the type of rock found in Brazil matched the rock found in western Africa. Also, limestone layers in the Appalachian Mountains of North America were exactly like the limestone in Scotland's Highlands.

READING TiP

Climate refers to a pattern of wind, temperature, and rain or snow that occurs in a region over time. Earth's climates have changed many times in the planet's long history.

CHECK YOUR READING Which evidence for continental drift do you think is the most convincing? Explain your answer.

AFRICA

SOUTH AMERICA

Areas in which *Mesosaurus* fossils have been found

The reptile *Mesosaurus* was about 45 cm (18 in.) long. This fossil was found in Brazil, South America.

VISUALIZATION
CLASSZONE.COM

Examine continental movement over the past 150 million years.

Pangaea and Continental Drift

For Wegener, all the evidence pointed to a single conclusion. The continents had once been joined in a huge supercontinent he called **Pangaea** (pan-JEE-uh). *Pangaea* comes from the Greek word meaning "all lands." This giant continent reached from pole to pole and was centered over the area where Africa lies today.

Pangaea began to split apart some 200 million years ago. In time, the continents moved to where they are today. Yet Wegener could not explain *how* the continents moved. Because of this, his critics called continental drift "a fairy tale" and rejected his hypothesis.

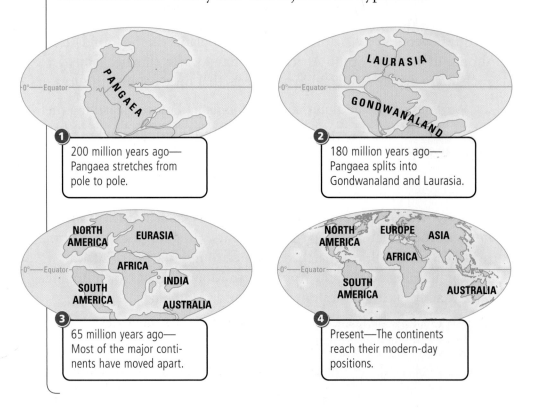

1 200 million years ago— Pangaea stretches from pole to pole.

2 180 million years ago— Pangaea splits into Gondwanaland and Laurasia.

3 65 million years ago— Most of the major continents have moved apart.

4 Present—The continents reach their modern-day positions.

The theory of plate tectonics explains how plates and their continents move.

For many years, Wegener's ideas were pushed aside. Then in the mid-1900s, scientists proved that tectonic plates move. They also offered explanations about how the plates move. Their work eventually led to the theory of plate tectonics, which built on some of Wegener's ideas.

Evidence from the Sea Floor

Scientists began mapping the sea floor in detail in the 1950s. They expected the floor to be smooth and level. Instead, they found huge underwater mountain ranges, called **mid-ocean ridges.** These ridges appeared in every ocean, circling Earth like seams in a baseball.

Sea-Floor Spreading Scientists learned that the ridges form along cracks in the crust. Molten rock rises through these cracks, cools, and forms new oceanic crust. The old crust is pulled away to make room for new material. In this way, the sea floor slowly spreads apart. Scientists call these areas spreading centers. You will read more about spreading centers in Section 1.3.

Age of the Sea Floor Further evidence that the sea floor is spreading apart came from the age of the rocks in the crust. Scientists drilled into the sea floor from a specially equipped vessel called the *Glomar Challenger.* The rock samples revealed that the youngest rock is closest to the ridge, while the oldest rock is farthest away.

The samples also showed that even the oldest ocean floor is young—only 160 to 180 million years old. Continental crust is much older—up to 4 billion years old. These data confirmed that the ocean floor is constantly forming and moving away from the mid-ocean ridges like a conveyor belt. As the sea floor moves, so do the tectonic plates and their continents.

Ocean Trenches Yet, if the sea floor has been spreading for millions of years, why is Earth not getting larger? Scientists discovered the answer when they found huge trenches, like deep canyons, in the sea floor. At these sites, dense oceanic crust is sinking into the asthenosphere. Old crust is being destroyed at the same rate that new crust is forming. Thus, Earth remains the same size.

Scientists now had proof that tectonic plates move. But the same question remained. *How* could the plates move thousands of kilometers around the planet? The asthenosphere provided a possible answer.

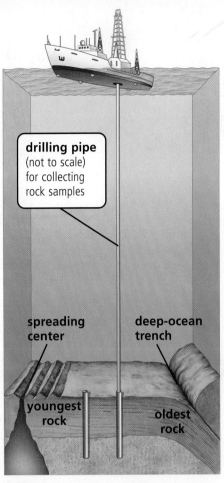

Scientists drill into the sea floor to obtain rock samples. The different ages of the rocks prove that plates move.

⬤ **CHECK YOUR READING** How does the age of the sea floor show that plates move?

Causes of Plate Movement

Tectonic plates rest on the asthenosphere, a layer of soft, hot rock. Rock in this layer and in the mantle just below it moves by convection. **Convection** is energy transfer by the movement of a material. You have seen convection if you have ever boiled a pot of water. The water at the bottom of the pot heats up, becomes less dense, and rises. At the surface, it cools, becomes denser, and sinks, only to be heated and rise again.

The rock in the asthenosphere acts in a similar way. The hot, soft rock rises, cools, and sinks, then is heated and rises again. If this sinking and rising motion continues, it is called a **convection current**—a motion that transfers heat energy in a material.

Convection currents in the mantle are much slower than those in boiling water. The rock creeps only a few centimeters a year. The diagram below shows convection currents circulating. The tectonic plates in the lithosphere are carried on the asthenosphere like long, heavy boxes moved on huge rollers. Over millions of years, convection currents carry the plates thousands of kilometers.

Scientists suspect that two other motions—slab pull and ridge push—help move these huge plates. Slab pull occurs where gravity pulls the edge of a cool, dense plate into the asthenosphere, as shown in the diagram below. Because plates are rigid, the entire plate is dragged along. Ridge push occurs when material from a mid-ocean ridge slides downhill from the ridge. The material pushes the rest of the plate.

Putting the Theory Together

REMINDER

A scientific theory is a well-tested explanation that is consistent with all available evidence.

Geologists combined their knowledge of Earth's plates, the sea floor, and the asthenosphere to develop the **theory of plate tectonics.** The theory states that Earth's lithosphere is made up of huge plates that move over the surface of the Earth.

The map on page 19 shows Earth's major tectonic plates and the directions in which they move. They are the African, the Antarctic, the Australian, the Indian, the Eurasian, the Nazca, the North and South American, and the Pacific plates.

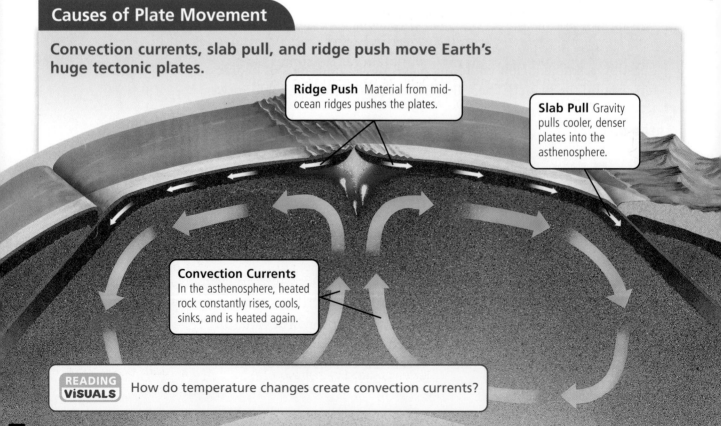

Causes of Plate Movement

Convection currents, slab pull, and ridge push move Earth's huge tectonic plates.

Ridge Push Material from mid-ocean ridges pushes the plates.

Slab Pull Gravity pulls cooler, denser plates into the asthenosphere.

Convection Currents In the asthenosphere, heated rock constantly rises, cools, sinks, and is heated again.

READING VISUALS How do temperature changes create convection currents?

Tectonic Plates

Earth's lithosphere is made up of moving plates.

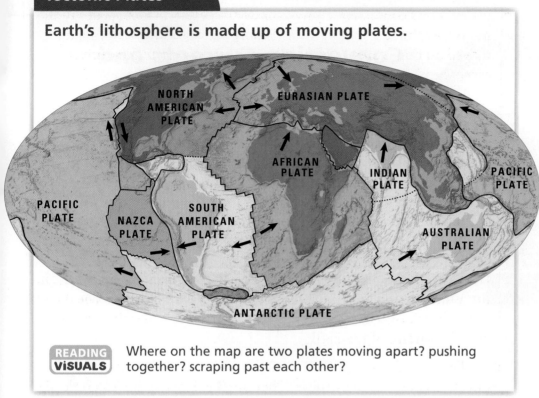

NORTH AMERICAN PLATE

EURASIAN PLATE

AFRICAN PLATE

INDIAN PLATE

PACIFIC PLATE

PACIFIC PLATE

NAZCA PLATE

SOUTH AMERICAN PLATE

AUSTRALIAN PLATE

ANTARCTIC PLATE

READING VISUALS Where on the map are two plates moving apart? pushing together? scraping past each other?

As scientists studied the plates, they realized that one plate could not shift without affecting the others nearby. They found that plates can move apart, push together, or scrape past each other. The arrows on the map above show each type of plate motion.

Plate movements cause great changes in Earth's crust. Most major earthquakes, volcanoes, and mountain ranges appear where tectonic plates meet. You will learn why as you read more about plate movements.

1.2 Review

KEY CONCEPTS

1. What evidence did Wegener gather to support his continental drift hypothesis?

2. Give three types of evidence from the sea floor that prove Earth's tectonic plates move.

3. Explain how motions in the asthenosphere can move tectonic plates around Earth.

CRITICAL THINKING

4. **Apply** A friend tells you he read on a Web site that Earth is getting smaller. What can you tell him that shows Earth's size is not changing?

5. **Evaluate** What other types of scientists, besides geologists, would find the theory of plate tectonics useful in their work?

⬥ CHALLENGE

6. **Infer** Use the arrows on the map above and your knowledge of sea-floor spreading and ocean trenches to answer these questions: What is happening to the size of the Atlantic Ocean? What can you infer is happening to the size of the Pacific Ocean? Explain your answers.

CHAPTER INVESTIGATION

Convection Currents and Plate Movement

OVERVIEW AND PURPOSE South America and Africa are drifting slowly apart. What powerful force could be moving these two plates? In this investigation you will
- observe the movement of convection currents
- determine how convection currents in Earth's mantle could move tectonic plates

▶ Problem

How do convection currents in a fluid affect floating objects on the surface?

▶ Hypothesize

Write a hypothesis to explain how convection currents affect floating objects. Your hypothesis should take the form of an "If . . . , then . . . , because . . ." statement.

▶ Procedure

MATERIALS
- oven-glass lasagna pan
- 2 bread pans or 2 bricks
- water
- liquid food coloring
- 2 small candles
- matches
- 2 sponges
- scissors
- 3–4 pushpins

1. Use two overturned bread pans or two bricks to raise and support the glass lasagna pan. Fill the pan with water to a depth of 4 cm.

2. Hold the food coloring over the middle of the pan. Squeeze several drops into the water. Be careful not to touch or disturb the water with the plastic tip or your hands. Write down your observations.

step 3

3. Light the two candles and place them beneath the center of the pan. Then squeeze several more drops of food coloring into the middle of the pan.

4. Observe what happens for a few minutes, then write down your observations. After you have finished, blow out the candles and wait until the water cools.

5. Moisten the two sponges. Cut one into the shape of South America and the other into the shape of Africa. Insert the pushpins as shown in the photo.

step 5

6 Place the sponges on top of the water in the center of the pan. Fit the two sponges together along their coastlines.

7 Gently hold the sponges together until the water is still, then let go. Observe them for a few minutes and record what you saw.

8 Light the candles again. Place them under the pan and directly beneath the two sponges.

9 Gently hold the sponges together again until the water heats up. Then carefully let go of the sponges, trying not to disturb the water.

10 Observe the sponges for a few minutes, and then record your observations.

▶ Observe and Analyze [Write It Up]

1. **RECORD** Draw diagrams to show how the food coloring and the sponges moved in cold water and in heated water. Use arrows to indicate any motion.

2. **ANALYZE** Did the food coloring and the sponges move more with or without the candles? Use what you have learned about convection to explain the role of the candles.

▶ Conclude [Write It Up]

1. **EVALUATE** Water is a fluid, but the asthenosphere is not. What properties of the asthenosphere allow it to move like a fluid and form convection currents?

2. **COMPARE AND CONTRAST** In what ways is your setup like Earth's asthenosphere and lithosphere? In what ways is your setup different?

3. **ANALYZE** Compare your results with your hypothesis. Do your observations support your hypothesis? Why or why not?

4. **INTERPRET** Write an answer to your problem statement.

5. **IDENTIFY CONTROLS** Did your experiment include controls? If so, what purpose did they serve here?

6. **APPLY** In your own words, explain how the African continent and the South American continent are drifting apart.

7. **APPLY** Suppose you own an aquarium. You want to make sure your fish are warm whether they swim near the top or near the bottom of the aquarium. The pet store sells two types of heaters. One heater extends 5 cm below the water's surface. The other heater rests on the bottom of the aquarium. Based on what you learned in this activity, which heater would you choose, and why?

▶ INVESTIGATE Further

CHALLENGE Design a new version of this experiment that you think would be a better model of the movements in Earth's asthenosphere and lithosphere. What materials will you need? What changes would you make to the procedure? Sketch your version of the lab, and explain what makes it better.

Convection Currents and Plate Movement
Problem How do convection currents in a fluid affect floating objects on the surface?
Hypothesize
Observe and Analyze
Diagram 1. Sponges on Unheated Water

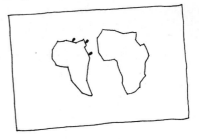

Conclude

Plates move apart.

 BEFORE, you learned

- The continents join and break apart
- The sea floor provides evidence that tectonic plates move
- The theory of plate tectonics helps explain how the plates move

 NOW, you will learn

- About different plate boundaries
- What happens when plates move apart
- How the direction and speed of plates can be measured

VOCABULARY

divergent boundary p. 22
convergent boundary p. 22
transform boundary p. 22
rift valley p. 23
magnetic reversal p. 24
hot spot p. 27

EXPLORE Divergent Boundaries

What happens when plates move apart?

PROCEDURE

① Cut the piece of striped paper into two symmetrical pieces slightly less wide than the slit in the oatmeal box.

② Match up the lines of the two pieces and tape the pieces together at one edge. Push the taped edge into the box until only a few centimeters of the free edges show at the top.

③ Grasp each piece of paper, one in each hand. Slowly pull the two pieces horizontally out of the cylinder, pulling them in opposite directions.

MATERIALS

- scissors
- piece of striped paper
- tape
- small oatmeal box with slit cut in side

WHAT DO YOU THINK?

How is your model similar to the process of sea-floor spreading?

Tectonic plates have different boundaries.

A plate boundary is where the edges of two plates meet. After studying the way plates move, geologists identified three types of boundaries.

- A **divergent boundary** (dih-VUR-juhnt) occurs where plates move apart. Most divergent boundaries are found in the ocean.
- A **convergent boundary** (kuhn-VUR-juhnt) occurs where plates push together.
- A **transform boundary** occurs where plates scrape past each other.

In this section, you will discover what happens at divergent boundaries in the ocean and on land. You will read more about convergent and transform boundaries in Section 1.4.

The sea floor spreads apart at divergent boundaries.

In the ocean, divergent boundaries are also called spreading centers. Mid-ocean ridges mark these sites where the ocean floor is spreading apart. As the ridges continue to widen, a gap called a **rift valley** forms. Here molten material rises to build new crust.

Mid-Ocean Ridges and Rift Valleys

Mid-ocean ridges are the longest chain of mountains on Earth. Most of these ridges contain a rift valley along their center, as shown in the diagram below. When molten material rises from the asthenosphere, cold ocean water cools the rock until it becomes solid. As the plates move apart, new cracks open in the solid rock. More molten material rises and hardens. The growing ridge stands high above the sea floor.

The world's longest ridge, the Mid-Atlantic Ridge, runs the length of the Atlantic Ocean. Here the North and South American plates are moving away from the Eurasian and African plates. The ridge extends nearly 11,000 kilometers (6214 mi) from Iceland to near Antarctica. The rift valley is 24 kilometers (15 mi) wide and 9 kilometers (6 mi) deep—about 7 kilometers (4 mi) deeper than the Grand Canyon!

Divergent Boundary in the Ocean

Mid-ocean ridges, rift valleys, and new crust mark where the sea floor spreads apart.

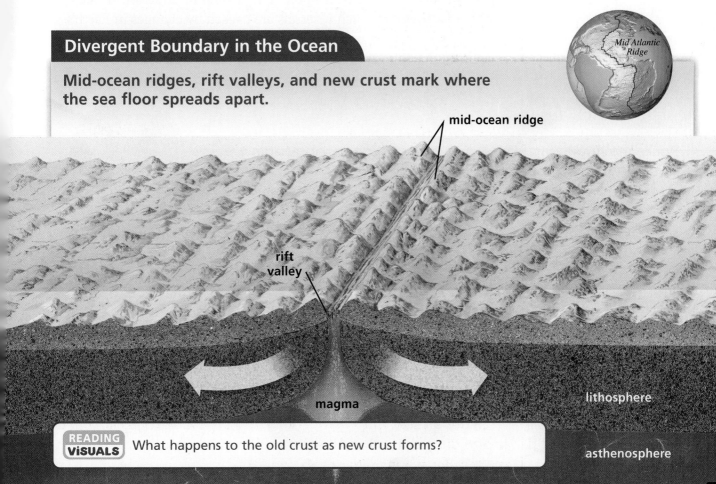

Mid Atlantic Ridge

mid-ocean ridge

rift valley

magma

lithosphere

asthenosphere

READING VISUALS What happens to the old crust as new crust forms?

Sea-Floor Rock and Magnetic Reversals

You read earlier that the sea floor is younger near a mid-ocean ridge and older farther away. As scientists continued to study the sea-floor rock, they made a surprising discovery about Earth's magnetic field.

To understand Earth's magnetic field, you can compare the planet to a bar magnet, which has a north and a south pole. Earth's magnetic field affects the entire planet, as shown in the diagram below. Notice that Earth's geographic and magnetic poles are not in the same place.

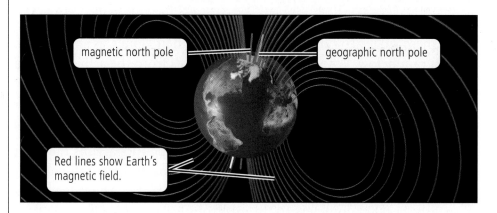

magnetic north pole

geographic north pole

Red lines show Earth's magnetic field.

Unlike a bar magnet, however, Earth's magnetic poles switch places every so often. The north pole becomes the south pole and the south pole becomes the north pole. This switch in direction is called a **magnetic reversal.** Such reversals are caused by changes in Earth's magnetic field. As yet, no one knows why these changes happen. In contrast, Earth's geographic poles never change places.

Magnetic Reversals

Rocks moving away from a mid-ocean ridge carry records of magnetic reversals.

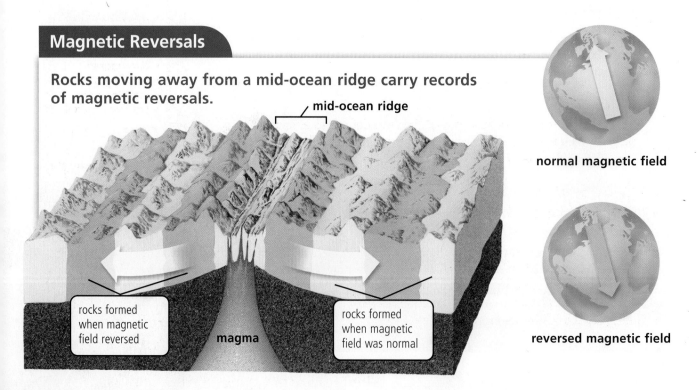

mid-ocean ridge

rocks formed when magnetic field reversed

magma

rocks formed when magnetic field was normal

normal magnetic field

reversed magnetic field

Scientists found that each magnetic reversal is recorded in the sea-floor rock. These records are especially clear at some mid-ocean ridges. As the molten material rises and cools, some magnetic minerals line up with the Earth's magnetic field. When the material hardens, these minerals are permanently fixed like tiny compass needles pointing north and south. Whenever the magnetic field reverses, the cooling minerals record the change.

As shown in the diagram on page 24, the records of magnetic reversals line up like stripes in the rock. As the two plates move away from a mid-ocean ridge, each plate carries a record of magnetic reversals with it. The records are the same on either side of the ridge.

As scientists continued to map the ocean floor, they found more records of these reversals. By dating the rock, scientists had further evidence of plate movement. The youngest rock records the most recent reversal, which happened only about 760,000 years ago. The oldest rock, farthest from the mid-ocean ridge, records reversals that happened more than 150 million years ago.

 CHECK YOUR READING Explain how records of magnetic reversals show that plates move apart.

INVESTIGATE Magnetic Reversals

How can you map magnetic reversals?

PROCEDURE

1. Wrap one end of the string around the middle of the bar magnet. Tape the string in place as shown.

2. Place a small piece of tape on one end of the magnet. Label the tape "N" to represent north.

3. Hold the bar magnet over one end of the sea-floor model as shown. Move the magnet SLOWLY toward the other end of the sea-floor model. Record your observations.

WHAT DO YOU THINK?

- What did the magnet reveal about the sea-floor model? Draw a diagram showing any pattern that you might have observed.

- Which part of the model represents the youngest sea floor? Which part represents the oldest sea floor?

CHALLENGE If Earth's magnetic field had never reversed in the past, how would the sea-floor model be different?

SKILL FOCUS
Modeling

MATERIALS
- string
- bar magnet
- masking tape
- marking pen
- sea-floor model

TIME
20 minutes

Continents split apart at divergent boundaries.

SUPPORTING MAIN IDEAS
Use this diagram to help you take notes on how continents split apart.

Like the sea floor, continents also spread apart at a divergent boundary. The boundary begins to form when hot material rises from deep in the mantle. This heat causes the crust to bulge upward. The crust cracks as it is stretched, and a rift valley forms, as shown in the diagram below. Magma rises through the cracked, thinned crust, forming volcanoes. As the rift valley grows wider, the continent begins to split apart.

If the rift valley continues to widen, the thinned valley floor sinks lower and lower until it is below sea level. Water from nearby oceans or rivers may fill the valley and form a sea or a lake. In the Middle East, for example, the Arabian Plate and African Plate have been moving apart for several million years. Over time, the waters of the Indian Ocean gradually filled the rift valley, forming the Red Sea. This sea is slowly getting wider as the plates continue to move apart.

CHECK YOUR READING What happens when the floor of a rift valley sinks below sea level?

Divergent Boundary on Land

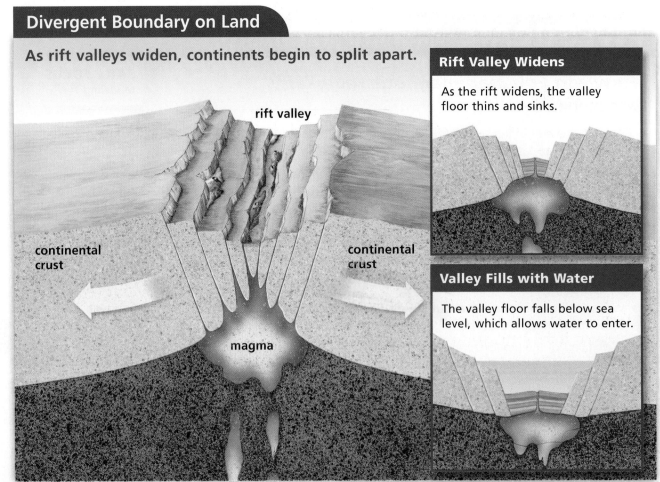

As rift valleys widen, continents begin to split apart.

rift valley

continental crust

continental crust

magma

Rift Valley Widens
As the rift widens, the valley floor thins and sinks.

Valley Fills with Water
The valley floor falls below sea level, which allows water to enter.

Great Rift Valley

The Great Rift Valley in eastern Africa, shown in the photograph above, is a good example of a continental rift valley. It is getting wider as the African Plate splits apart. This huge valley is thousands of kilometers long and as much as 1800 meters (5900 ft) deep.

PREDICT Rift valleys, like the Great Rift Valley in Africa, occur where plates are moving apart. What will happen to the Rift Valley when it gets low enough?

Hot spots can be used to track plate movements.

In some places, called **hot spots,** heated rock rises in plumes, or thin columns, from the mantle. Volcanoes often develop above the plume. Although most hot spots occur far from plate boundaries, they offer a way to measure plate movement. This is because a hot spot generally stays in one place while the tectonic plate above it keeps moving.

At a hot spot, the heat from the plume partly melts some of the rock in the tectonic plate above it. It is like holding a candle under a wax tablet. Eventually, the wax above the flame will melt. Likewise, if the plate stays over the hot spot long enough, the rock above it will melt.

In time, a volcano will form at the surface of the plate. The volcano may become high enough to rise above the sea as an island. For example, the Hawaiian Islands are being built as the Pacific Plate moves slowly over a hot spot.

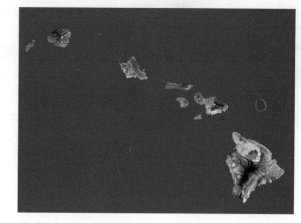

The Hawaiian islands are located in the middle of the Pacific Plate. The largest island, Hawaii, is still over the hot spot.

Hot Spots

Tectonic plates move over hot spots in the mantle.

Oceanic Hot Spot

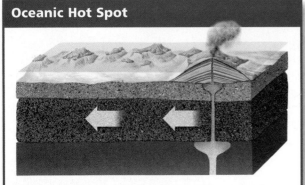

The Pacific Plate carries each Hawaiian island away from the hot spot. Eventually, a new volcano forms over the plume.

Continental Hot Spot

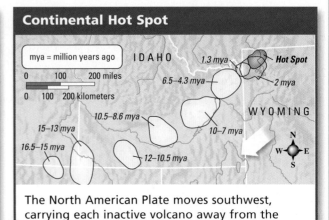

mya = million years ago
0   100   200 miles
0   100   200 kilometers

IDAHO
1.3 mya — Hot Spot
6.5–4.3 mya — 2 mya
WYOMING
10.5–8.6 mya
15–13 mya — 10–7 mya
16.5–15 mya
12–10.5 mya

The North American Plate moves southwest, carrying each inactive volcano away from the Yellowstone hot spot.

READING VISUALS Which island or landform in each diagram was formed first? How do you know?

When the plate moves on, it carries the first volcano away from the hot spot. Heat from the mantle plume will then melt the rock at a new site, forming a new volcano. The diagram on the left shows this process.

Many hot spots provide a fixed point that scientists can use to measure the speed and direction of plate movements. For example, the Yellowstone hot spot under the North American Plate has formed a chain of inactive volcanoes, as shown in the diagram on the right. Scientists estimate that the North American Plate is moving southwest at about 2.3 cm (1 in.) per year.

CHECK YOUR READING How does a hot-spot volcano form?

 Review

KEY CONCEPTS

1. Name and describe the three types of plate movements.

2. Create a two-column chart with the headings: Divergent boundary; Features. Fill in the chart for divergent boundaries at sea and on land.

3. How are hot spots used to track plate motion?

CRITICAL THINKING

4. **Predict** Suppose a magnetic reversal occurred today. How would new rocks at mid-ocean ridges differ from rocks that formed last year?

5. **Infer** A huge crack runs through Iceland, an island that lies above the Mid-Ocean Ridge. What do you think is happening to this country?

⬦ CHALLENGE

6. **Hypothesize** Look carefully at the diagram above and the Hawaiian Islands picture on page 27. Notice that some hot spot islands or landforms are larger than other islands or landforms in the same chain. Develop a hypothesis, based on plate movement, that might explain this fact.

MATH TUTORIAL
CLASSZONE.COM
Click on Math Tutorial for more help with rates.

Arabian Plate

Red Sea

African Plate

This satellite photograph shows where the Arabian Plate and the African Plate are moving apart. As a result, the Red Sea is slowly growing wider.

Tracking Tectonic Plates

Scientists use lasers to track the movements of tectonic plates. They bounce laser light off satellites and measure the distance from each satellite to the ground. As the plates move, the distance changes. With this tracking system, scientists know exactly how much tectonic plates move each year.

You can use equivalent rates to predict how far two divergent plates will move over a given time. A rate is a ratio of two measures expressed in different units, such as

$$\frac{10 \text{ cm}}{4 \text{ yr}}$$

This 0.61-meter-wide satellite is covered with mirrors to reflect laser light back to Earth.

Example

If Boston, Massachusetts, and Lisbon, Portugal, are moving apart at an average rate of 10 cm every 4 years, how much farther apart will they move in 20 years?

Solution

Write an equivalent rate.

> Divide 20 yr by 4 yr to get 5, then multiply 10 cm by 5.

$$\frac{10 \text{ cm}}{4 \text{ yr}} = \frac{?}{20 \text{ yr}}$$

$$20 \div 4 = 5$$

$$10 \times 5 = 50$$

$$\frac{10 \text{ cm}}{4 \text{ yr}} = \frac{50 \text{ cm}}{20 \text{ yr}}$$

ANSWER Boston and Lisbon will move 50 centimeters farther apart in 10 years.

Answer the following questions.

1. If New York, New York, and London, England, are moving apart at an average rate of 5 cm every 2 years, how much farther apart will they move in 8 years?

2. If Miami, Florida, and Casablanca, Morocco, are moving apart at an average rate of 25 cm every 10 years, how much farther apart will they move in 30 years?

3. If Portland, Maine, and Dublin, Ireland, are moving apart at an average rate of 50 cm every 20 years, how much farther apart will they move in 10 years?

CHALLENGE If Halifax, Nova Scotia, and Birmingham, England, are moving apart at an average rate of 5 cm every 2 years, how long will it take them to move 35 cm farther apart?

Plates converge or scrape past each other.

BEFORE, you learned	NOW, you will learn
• Plates move apart at divergent boundaries • In the oceans, divergent boundaries mark where the sea floor spreads apart • On land, continents split apart at divergent boundaries	• What happens when two continental plates converge • What happens when an oceanic plate converges with another plate • What happens when one plate scrapes past another plate

VOCABULARY

subduction p. 30
continental-continental collision p. 31
oceanic-oceanic subduction p. 32
oceanic-continental subduction p. 33

EXPLORE Tectonic Plates

What happens when tectonic plates collide?

PROCEDURE

(1) Arrange six square napkins in two rows.

(2) Slowly push the two rows of napkins together. Observe what happens.

WHAT DO YOU THINK?
• In what ways did the napkin edges move?
• How might your observations relate to the movement of tectonic plates?

MATERIALS
6 square napkins

Tectonic plates push together at convergent boundaries.

You read earlier that new crust forms at divergent boundaries where plates move apart. At convergent boundaries, where plates push together, crust is either folded or destroyed.

When two plates with continental crust collide, they will crumple and fold the rock between them. A plate with older, denser oceanic crust will sink beneath another plate. The crust melts in the asthenosphere and is destroyed. When one plate sinks beneath another, it is called **subduction.** The word is based on the Latin prefix *sub-*, meaning "under," and the Latin *ducere*, meaning "to lead." Therefore, subduction is a process in which one plate is "led under" another.

There are three types of convergent boundaries: where two continental plates meet, where two oceanic plates meet, or where an oceanic plate and a continental plate meet. Major geologic events occur at all three types of boundaries.

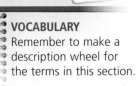

VOCABULARY
Remember to make a description wheel for the terms in this section.

Continental-Continental Collision

A **continental-continental collision** occurs where two plates carrying continental crust push together. Because both crusts are the same density, neither plate can sink beneath the other. If the plates keep moving, their edges crumple and fold, as in the diagram below.

You can see the same effect if you put two blocks of clay on a table and push them together. If you push hard enough, one or both of the blocks will buckle. One cannot sink under the other, so the clay folds under the pressure.

In some cases, the folded crust can be pushed up high enough to form mountains. Some of the world's largest mountains appear along continent-continent boundaries. For instance, the European Alps, shown in the photograph at right, are found where the African and European plates are colliding. The tallest mountains in the world, the Himalayas, first formed when the Indian Plate began colliding with the European Plate.

The Himalayas and the Alps are still forming today. As long as the plates keep moving, these mountains will keep rising higher.

The European Alps began rising nearly 40 million years ago as a section of the African Plate collided with the European Plate.

 CHECK YOUR READING Explain how colliding plates form mountain ranges.

Convergent Boundary—Collision

Rocks crumple and fold to form mountains.

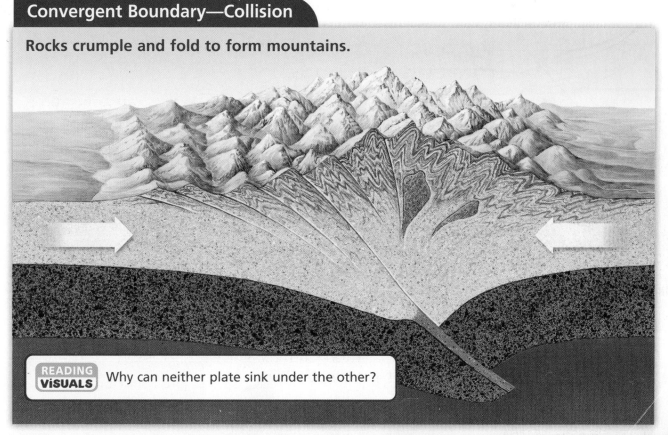

READING VISUALS Why can neither plate sink under the other?

Oceanic-Oceanic Subduction

An **oceanic-oceanic subduction** occurs where one plate with oceanic crust sinks, or subducts, under another plate with oceanic crust. The older plate sinks because it is colder and denser than the younger plate. When the older crust reaches the asthenosphere, it melts in the intense heat. Two main features form at oceanic-oceanic subductions: deep-ocean trenches and island arcs.

Deep-Ocean Trenches These trenches are like deep canyons that form in the ocean floor as a plate sinks. Most deep-ocean trenches are found in the Pacific Ocean. For example, at the Mariana Trench, the Pacific Plate is sinking under the Philippine Plate. This trench is the deepest place in the world's oceans, extending nearly 11,000 meters (36,000 ft) into the sea floor.

Island Arcs There are chains of volcanic islands that form on the top plate, parallel to a deep-ocean trench. As oceanic crust of the sinking plate melts, magma rises through the top plate. Over time, the flows build up a series of islands. Island arcs include the Philippine Islands, the Aleutian Islands of Alaska, and the islands of Japan.

Convergent Boundaries—Subduction

Sinking plates form deep-ocean trenches, island arcs, and coastal mountains.

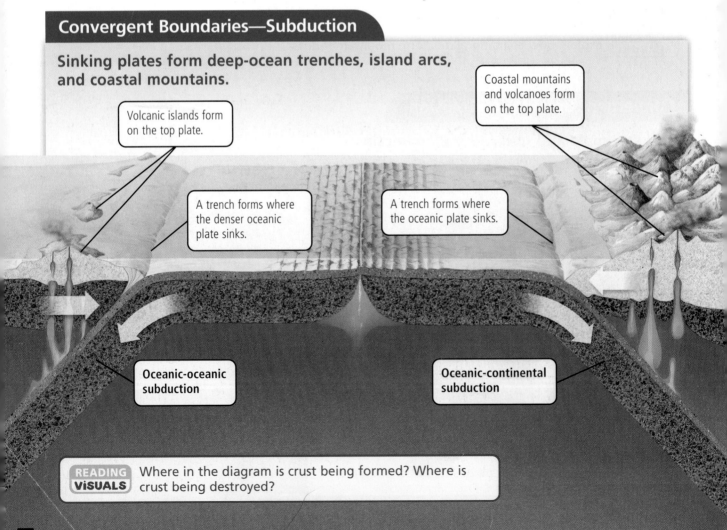

Volcanic islands form on the top plate.

Coastal mountains and volcanoes form on the top plate.

A trench forms where the denser oceanic plate sinks.

A trench forms where the oceanic plate sinks.

Oceanic-oceanic subduction

Oceanic-continental subduction

READING VISUALS Where in the diagram is crust being formed? Where is crust being destroyed?

Oceanic-Continental Subduction

An **oceanic-continental subduction** occurs when ocean crust sinks under continental crust, as shown in the diagram on page 32. The oceanic crust sinks because it is colder and denser than the continental crust. At these sites, deep-ocean trenches also form, along with coastal mountains.

Deep-Ocean Trenches Some of the world's youngest trenches are in the eastern Pacific Ocean. Here, for example, the Pacific Plate is sinking under the North American Plate. As the oceanic crust moves, it often causes underwater earthquakes.

Coastal Mountains As oceanic crust sinks under a continent, the continental crust buckles to form a range of mountains. These mountains, like island arcs, parallel a deep-ocean trench. As the diagram on page 32 shows, some of these mountains are volcanoes, which form as melted oceanic crust rises through the top plate.

The Cascade Mountains in Oregon and Washington are an example of coastal mountains. They began forming as the Juan de Fuca Plate began sinking under the North American Plate. Some of these peaks, such as Mount St. Helens in Washington, are active volcanoes.

VISUALIZATION
CLASSZONE.COM

Explore what happens along plate boundaries.

CHECK YOUR READING Why do deep-ocean trenches form at both types of subduction?

INVESTIGATE Convergent Boundaries

How can you model converging plates?

Tectonic plates move so slowly and are so large that it may be hard to visualize exactly how they move. Use what you know to design models showing how converging plates collide and subduct.

PROCEDURE

DESIGN — YOUR OWN —

1. Design your models using the materials listed. You can use the diagrams on pages 31–32 as a guide.

2. Add more clay to your models if you need it.

WHAT DO YOU THINK?

- Describe how your models worked. You can draw a picture of each model to go along with your description.

- How well did your models represent each type of zone? Did each model work? Why or why not?

- How would you modify your designs now that you have seen the results?

SKILL FOCUS
Designing models

MATERIALS
- clay in three or more colors
- poster board
- marker pens

TIME
30 minutes

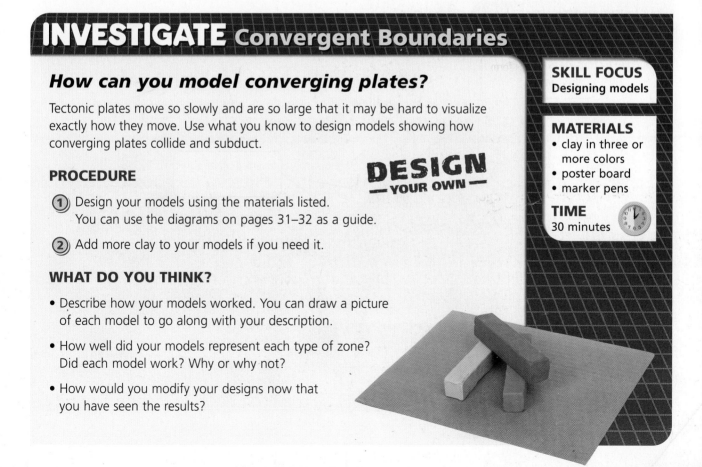

Tectonic plates scrape past each other at transform boundaries.

You learned that crust is formed at a divergent boundary and folded or destroyed at a convergent boundary. However, at a transform boundary, crust is neither formed nor destroyed. Here, two plates move past each other in opposite directions, as shown in the diagram below. As the plates move, their edges scrape and grind against each other.

Transform boundaries occur mostly on the sea floor near mid-ocean ridges. They also occur on land, where some are clearly visible as long cracks in Earth's surface. The San Andreas Fault in California is a transform boundary that runs from the Gulf of California through the San Francisco area. It marks where the Pacific Plate and part of the North American Plate are moving in opposite directions. If the plates keep moving at their present rate, Los Angeles will be a suburb of San Francisco in about 10 million years.

This long crack in the earth reveals the transform boundary known as the San Andreas Fault.

CHECK YOUR READING What makes the San Andreas Fault a transform boundary?

Transform Boundary

Plate edges grind and scrape past each other. Crust is neither formed nor destroyed.

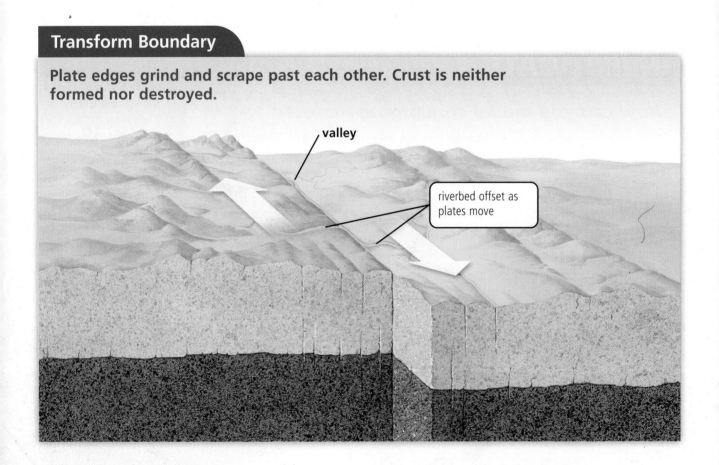

valley

riverbed offset as plates move

Tectonic Plate Boundaries

There are three types of plate boundaries: transform, divergent, and convergent. Major geologic events occur at all three types.

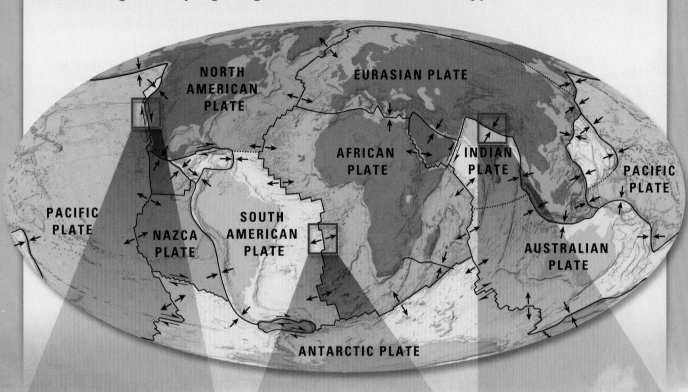

Plates shown:
- NORTH AMERICAN PLATE
- EURASIAN PLATE
- AFRICAN PLATE
- INDIAN PLATE
- PACIFIC PLATE
- NAZCA PLATE
- SOUTH AMERICAN PLATE
- AUSTRALIAN PLATE
- ANTARCTIC PLATE

Transform Boundaries

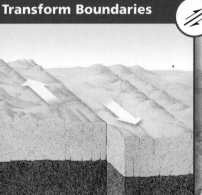

Plates scrape horizontally past each other. Crust is neither formed nor destroyed.

Divergent Boundaries

As plates move apart, new crust is built, forming mid-ocean ridges and rift valleys.

Convergent Boundaries

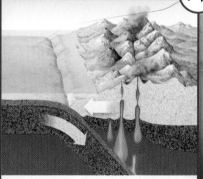

Crust is destroyed where plates subduct. It is folded where plates collide.

READING VISUALS Where else on the map above can you find a transform, divergent, and convergent boundary?

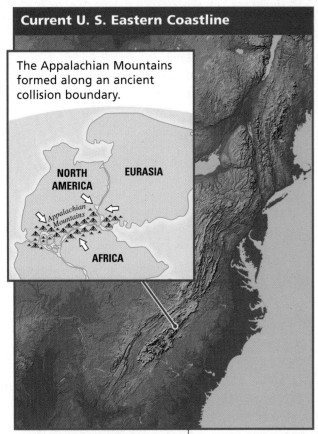

Current U. S. Eastern Coastline

The Appalachian Mountains formed along an ancient collision boundary.

NORTH AMERICA

EURASIA

Appalachian Mountains

AFRICA

The theory of plate tectonics helps geologists today.

The theory of plate tectonics changed the way that scientists view Earth. They learned that the planet's lithosphere has been in motion for millions of years. Today, the theory helps them to explain Earth's past and to predict what might happen along plate boundaries in the future.

By studying rock layers and using the theory, geologists can uncover the history of any region on Earth. For example, in the eastern United States, the deformed and folded rocks in the Appalachian Mountains are evidence of an ancient convergent boundary. Geologists discovered that these rocks are the same type and age as rocks in northwest Africa. These facts reveal that the mountains formed when North America collided with Africa and Eurasia as part of Pangaea. Where the plates eventually pulled apart, the rift valleys formed part of the current U. S. eastern coastline.

The theory of plate tectonics also gives scientists a way to study and predict geologic events. Scientists can predict, for example, that there are likely to be more earthquakes where plates slide past each other. They can look for volcanic activity where plates are sinking beneath other plates. And they can predict that mountains will continue to rise where plates push together.

CHECK YOUR READING What future events can scientists predict using the theory of plate tectonics? Give two examples.

1.4 Review

KEY CONCEPTS

1. What are the three types of convergent boundaries?
2. Describe what happens at a transform boundary.
3. Why is the theory of plate tectonics so important to geologists?

CRITICAL THINKING

4. **Compare and Contrast** Use a Venn diagram to compare and contrast oceanic-oceanic and oceanic-continental subduction boundaries.
5. **Interpreting Visuals** Look again at the map on page 35. Identify the plates and type of boundary that formed the Andes Mountains on the west coast of South America.

CHALLENGE

6. **Synthesize** Sketch a diagram of the following landscape and label all the features. A plate with oceanic crust is sinking beneath a plate with continental crust. Further inland on the continent, a transform boundary can be seen in Earth's crust.

What on Earth Is Happening Here?

When tectonic plates move, they cause major changes in Earth's surface. Among other things, the earth shakes, magma erupts on the surface, crust is built or destroyed, and mountains or islands form. Read the observations about plate movements below, then evaluate the conclusions given.

▶ Observations

Scientists made these observations about a region known for the movement of two major tectonic plates.

a. The region is on the coast of a landmass.

b. Along the coast is a deep-ocean trench.

c. The mountains on the coast are volcanic.

d. A line connecting these mountains is fairly straight.

e. The mountains are getting higher.

f. Far out at sea, a mid-ocean ridge is forming.

▶ Conclusions

Here are three possible conclusions about the movement of tectonic plates in the region.

- One plate is pulling away from the other.
- One plate is sinking under the other.
- One plate is scraping past the other.

▶ Evaluate Each Conclusion

On Your Own Decide how well the observations support each conclusion. Note any observations that indicate that a conclusion is not justified.

As a Group Decide which conclusion is most reasonable. Discuss your ideas in a small group, and see if the group can agree.

CHALLENGE What further observations would support or weaken each conclusion? How could you make these observations? What other phenomena might this conclusion help explain?

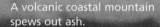

A volcanic coastal mountain spews out ash.

RESOURCE CENTER
CLASSZONE.COM

Learn more about the effects of plate movement.

Chapter Review

the BIG idea

The movement of tectonic plates causes geologic changes on Earth.

CONTENT REVIEW
CLASSZONE.COM

KEY CONCEPTS SUMMARY

1.1 Earth has several layers.

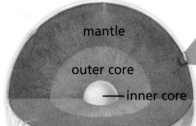
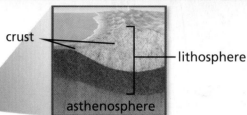

The lithosphere is made up of tectonic plates, which rest on the asthenosphere.

VOCABULARY
inner core p. 10
outer core p. 10
mantle p. 11
crust p. 11
lithosphere p. 11
asthenosphere p. 11
tectonic plate p. 12

1.2 Continents change position over time.

Gravity and motions in the asthenosphere move tectonic plates over Earth's surface.

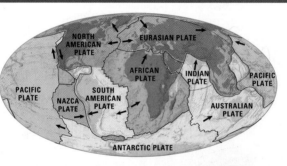

VOCABULARY
continental drift p. 14
Pangaea p. 16
mid-ocean ridge p. 16
convection p. 17
convection current p. 17
theory of plate tectonics p. 18

1.3 Plates move apart.

New crust is formed at divergent boundaries. Features include:
• mid-ocean ridges
• records of magnetic reversals
• rift valleys

VOCABULARY
divergent boundary p. 22
convergent boundary p. 22
transform boundary p. 22
rift valley p. 23
magnetic reversal p. 24
hot spot p. 27

1.4 Plates converge or scrape past each other.

Crust is destroyed or folded at convergent boundaries.
• Subduction boundaries form island arcs, deep-ocean trenches, and coastal mountains.
• Collision boundaries can form mountains.

Crust is neither formed nor destroyed at transform boundaries.

VOCABULARY
subduction p. 30
continental-continental collision p. 31
oceanic-oceanic subduction p. 32
oceanic-continental subduction p. 33

Reviewing Vocabulary

Make a magnet word diagram for each of the vocabulary terms listed below. Write the term in the magnet. Write other terms or ideas related to it on the lines around the magnet.

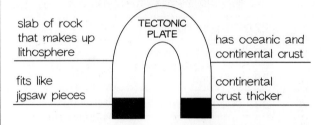

slab of rock that makes up lithosphere

TECTONIC PLATE

has oceanic and continental crust

fits like jigsaw pieces

continental crust thicker

1. mantle

2. lithosphere

3. mid-ocean ridge

4. convection current

5. divergent boundary

6. convergent boundary

Reviewing Key Concepts

Multiple Choice *Choose the letter of the best answer.*

7. Which of the following best describes Earth's mantle?
   a. the densest of Earth's layers
   b. the home of all life on Earth
   c. the thickest layer of hot rock
   d. the thinnest and hottest layer

8. Tectonic plates make up Earth's
   a. lower mantle   **c.** asthenosphere
   b. lithosphere   **d.** inner core

9. Why did many scientists reject Wegener's continental drift hypothesis?
   a. He could not explain how the continents moved.
   b. The geology of continents did not support his hypothesis.
   c. Fossil evidence showed that the continents were never joined.
   d. The climates of the continents have remained the same.

10. What evidence from the sea floor shows that tectonic plates move?
   a. The sea floor is much older than any of the continents.
   b. The sea floor is youngest near a mid-ocean ridge and older farther away.
   c. Mid-ocean ridges circle Earth like seams in a baseball.
   d. The sea floor is thinner than continental crust.

11. A mid-ocean ridge forms where plates
   a. move apart   **c.** scrape past each other
   b. push together   **d.** subduct

12. Plate motion is caused partly by
   a. magnetic reversals
   b. convection currents
   c. continental drift
   d. volcanic hot spots

13. Which of the following is formed at a collision zone?
   a. mountain range
   b. volcanic island chain
   c. deep-ocean trench
   d. continental rift valley

14. What happens when two oceanic plates meet?
   a. Both plates sink into the asthenosphere.
   b. The colder, denser plate sinks.
   c. Both plates fold the rock between them.
   d. One plate slides past the other.

15. Where is crust neither formed nor destroyed?
   a. mid-ocean ridge
   b. continental rift valley
   c. transform boundary
   d. subduction zone

Short Answer *Write a short answer to each question.*

16. How does the theory of plate tectonics help geologists predict future geologic events?

17. How do rocks record changes in Earth's magnetic field?

18. Explain what happens when a continental plate splits apart.

Thinking Critically

Use the diagram to answer the questions below.

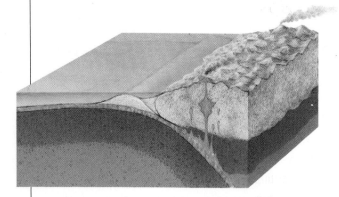

19. ANALYZE Write your own explanation of how the coastal mountains formed.

20. PREDICT Would you expect the volcanoes on this coastline to continue to be active? Why or why not?

21. APPLY Looking at the map above, why do you think the coastal mountains are in a fairly straight line?

22. APPLY On the map above, where would you expect to find a deep ocean trench? Why?

23. APPLY A friend looks at the diagram and tells you that there should be an island arc forming off the coast. Use your own knowledge and the map above to support or reject your friend's statement.

24. SYNTHESIZE On a separate piece of paper, extend the diagram to the left. Draw the type of plate boundary that someone might find far out at sea.

25. PREDICT Will the Andes Mountains on the west coast of South America become taller or shorter in the future? Use the theory of plate tectonics to explain your answer.

APPLY Copy the chart below. Fill in the type of boundary—divergent, convergent, or transform—where each formation is likely to appear.

Formation	Type of Boundary
26. Mid-ocean ridge	
27. Volcanic island arc	
28. Rift valley on land	
29. Mountains	
30. Deep-ocean trench	
31. Hot-spot volcano	

the **BIG** idea

32. IDENTIFY CAUSE AND EFFECT Look again at the photograph on pages 6–7. Now that you have finished the chapter, explain what may be forming this crack in Earth's surface.

33. PREDICT Use the map on page 19, which shows Earth's tectonic plates and the directions in which they are moving. Based on the plate movements, where do you think the continents might be in a few million years? Draw a map that illustrates your prediction. You might want to give your landmasses names.

UNIT PROJECTS

If you are doing a unit project, make a folder for your project. Include in your folder a list of the resources you will need, the date on which the project is due, and a schedule to keep track of your progress. Begin gathering data.

Analyzing a Diagram

The diagram shows several tectonic plates. The arrows indicate the direction each plate is moving. Study the diagram and answer the questions below.

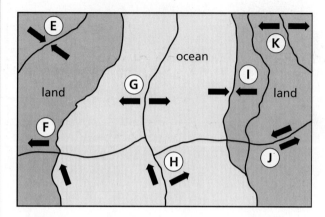

1. Where is an ocean trench most likely to form?

a. F   **c.** H

b. G   **d.** I

2. Where is a continental rift valley most likely to form?

a. E   **c.** J

b. F   **d.** K

3. Where would you find a convergent boundary?

a. E   **c.** H

b. F   **d.** K

4. Where is a mid-ocean ridge most likely to form?

a. G   **c.** I

b. H   **d.** F

5. What is a good example of a transform boundary?

a. E   **c.** J

b. I   **d.** K

6. Which is most likely to happen at I?

a. Island arcs will form parallel to a trench.

b. A spreading center will create a rift valley.

c. Continental crust will be destroyed.

d. Subduction will cause oceanic crust to melt.

7. Why are earthquakes likely to occur at J?

a. Two plates are spreading away from each other.

b. Two plates are colliding with each other.

c. Two plates are scraping past each other.

d. One plate is sliding under another plate.

8. Why are mountains likely to form at E?

a. A rift valley is forming.

b. Two plates are colliding.

c. Magma is flowing upward.

d. One plate is sinking.

9. Which is most likely to happen at G?

a. Rising magma will create new crust.

b. Subduction will cause a deep trench.

c. Colliding plates will cause rocks to crumple.

d. Moving plates will create island arcs.

Extended Response

Answer the two questions below in detail. Include some of the terms shown in the word box. In your answer, underline each term you use.

tectonic plates	subduction	magma	crust
continental drift	hot spot	mantle	

10. Two island chains are separated by a deep ocean trench. Although they are close to each other, the islands have very different fossils and types of rock. Explain why these island chains have such different geologic features.

11. Andrea lives near a chain of mountains located far from plate boundaries. The closest mountain is an active volcano. The other mountains used to be volcanoes. The farther away a mountain is in the chain, the older it is. Explain these facts.

CHAPTER
2 Earthquakes

the BIG idea

Earthquakes release stress that has built up in rocks.

Key Concepts

SECTION 2.1
Earthquakes occur along faults.
Learn how rocks move along different kinds of faults.

SECTION 2.2
Earthquakes release energy.
Learn how energy from an earthquake is used to determine its location and size.

SECTION 2.3
Earthquake damage can be reduced.
Learn how structures are built to better withstand earthquakes.

Internet Preview

CLASSZONE.COM
Chapter 2 online resources: Content Review, two Visualizations, three Resource Centers, Math Tutorial, Test Practice

What caused these rails to bend, and how long did it take?

EXPLORE (the BIG idea)

Can You Bend Energy?

Put a clear glass filled with water on a table. Holding a flashlight at an angle to the glass, shine light through the water so that an oval of light forms on the table.

Observe and Think Did the light, which is a form of energy, travel in a straight line through the layers of air and water? Do you think other forms of energy travel in straight lines through layers inside Earth?

How Can Something Move Forward, Yet Sideways?

Put a stack of cards on a table and hold them as shown in the photograph. Slide the entire stack forward, tilting your fingers from side to side to fan the cards back and forth.

Observe and Think Compare the direction of movement of the entire stack of cards with the directions of movement of individual cards. How might this be similar to how energy can travel in waves?

Internet Activity: Earthquakes

Go to **ClassZone.com** to see maps of recent earthquakes around the world, in the United States, and in your own area.

Observe and Think Where and when did the largest earthquakes occur?

NSTA scilinks.org *SCiLINKS*

Earthquakes **Code: MDL053**

Getting Ready to Learn

◀ CONCEPT REVIEW

- Earth's lithosphere is broken into tectonic plates.
- Tectonic plates pull apart, push together, and scrape past one another.
- Major geologic events occur along tectonic plate boundaries.

◀ VOCABULARY REVIEW

lithosphere p. 11

tectonic plate p. 12

mid-ocean ridge p. 16

subduction p. 30

CONTENT REVIEW
CLASSZONE.COM
Review concepts and vocabulary.

▶ TAKING NOTES

MAIN IDEA AND DETAIL NOTES

Make a two-column chart. Write the main ideas, such as those in the blue headings, in the column on the left. Write details about each of those main ideas in the column on the right.

VOCABULARY STRATEGY

For each vocabulary term, make a **magnet word** diagram. Write other terms or ideas related to that term around it.

See the Note-Taking Handbook on pages R45–R51.

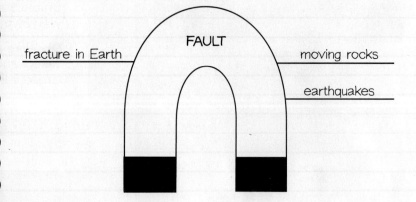

SCIENCE NOTEBOOK

MAIN IDEAS	DETAIL NOTES
1. Rocks move along faults.	1. Blocks of rock can move past one another slowly and constantly.
	1. Blocks of rock can get stuck and then break free, causing earthquakes.
2. Most faults are located along tectonic plate boundaries.	2.
	2.
	2.

fracture in Earth   FAULT   moving rocks

earthquakes

2.1 Earthquakes occur along faults.

◀ **BEFORE,** you learned

- The crust and uppermost mantle make up the lithosphere
- The lithosphere is cold and rigid
- Tectonic plates move over hotter, weaker rock in the asthenosphere

▶ **NOW,** you will learn

- Why earthquakes occur
- Where most earthquakes occur
- How rocks move during earthquakes

VOCABULARY

fault p. 45
stress p. 45
earthquake p. 45

EXPLORE Pressure

How does pressure affect a solid material?

PROCEDURE

① Hold a wooden craft stick at each end.

② Bend the stick very slowly. Continue to put pressure on the stick until it breaks.

WHAT DO YOU THINK?

- How did the stick change before it broke?
- How might rocks react to pressure?

MATERIALS
wooden craft stick

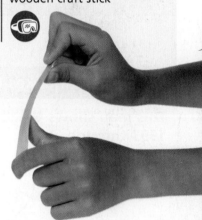

VOCABULARY
Add magnet word diagrams for *fault, stress,* and *earthquake* to your notebook.

Rocks move along faults.

Sometimes when you pull on a drawer, it opens smoothly. At other times, the drawer sticks shut. If you pull hard enough, the drawer suddenly flies open. Rocks along faults behave in a similar way. A **fault** is a fracture, or break, in Earth's lithosphere, along which blocks of rock move past each other.

Along some parts of a fault, the rock on either side may slide along slowly and constantly. Along other parts of the fault, the rocks may stick, or lock together. The rocks bend as stress is put on them. **Stress** is the force exerted when an object presses on, pulls on, or pushes against another object. As stress increases, the rocks break free. A sudden release of stress in the lithosphere causes an earthquake. An **earthquake** is a shaking of the ground caused by the sudden movement of large blocks of rock along a fault.

Most faults are located along tectonic plate boundaries, so most earthquakes occur in these areas. However, the blocks of rock that move during an earthquake are much smaller than a tectonic plate. A plate boundary can be many thousands of kilometers long. During even a very powerful earthquake, blocks of rock might move only a few meters past each other along a distance of several hundred kilometers. The strength of an earthquake depends in part on

- how much stress builds up before the rocks move
- the distance the rocks move along the fault

About 80 percent of all earthquakes occur in a belt around the edges of the Pacific Ocean. In the United States, the best-known fault in this belt is the San Andreas (san an-DRAY-uhs) Fault in California. It forms part of the boundary between the North American Plate and the Pacific Plate. Unlike many other faults, parts of the San Andreas Fault can be seen on the surface of the ground.

A small percentage of earthquakes occur along faults within plates. As you read in Chapter 1, a tectonic plate is rigid. Therefore, stress along a plate's boundary can cause rocks to break and move along weak areas toward the middle of the plate.

Where Earthquakes Occur

This map shows the locations of moderate to intense earthquakes from 1993 through 2002.

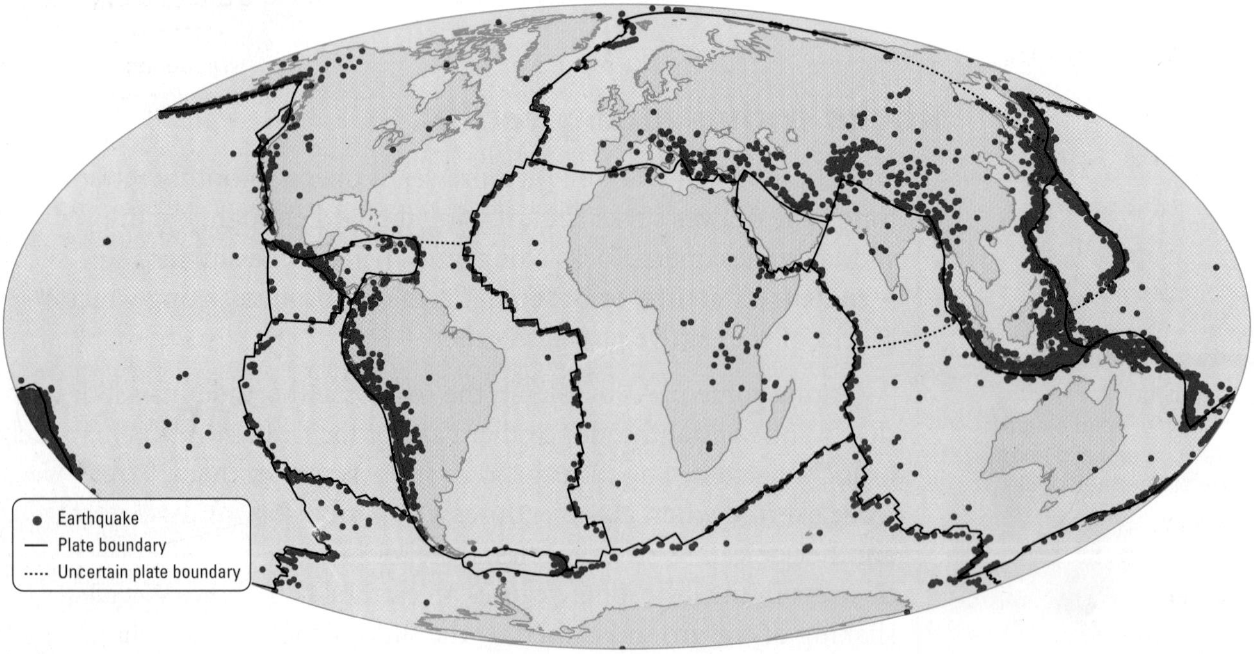

- Earthquake
- Plate boundary
- ..... Uncertain plate boundary

READING VISUALS   Why do most earthquakes in North America and South America occur near the continents' western coasts?

All earthquakes occur in the lithosphere. To understand why, you might compare a tectonic plate to a piece of cold, hard caramel. Like cold caramel, the plate is rigid and brittle. The rocks can break and move suddenly, causing an earthquake. Now compare the asthenosphere below the plate to warm, soft caramel. In the asthenosphere, hot rock bends and flows rather than breaks. A few earthquakes occur far below the normal depth of the lithosphere only because tectonic plates sinking in subduction zones are still cold enough to break.

 CHECK YOUR READING Why don't earthquakes occur in the asthenosphere?

Faults are classified by how rocks move.

The blocks of rock along different types of faults move in different directions, depending on the kinds of stress they are under. Scientists classify a fault according to the way the rocks on one side move with respect to the rocks on the other side.

The three main types of faults are normal faults, reverse faults, and strike-slip faults. More than one type of fault may be present along the same plate boundary. However, the type of fault that is most common along a boundary depends on whether plates are pulling apart, pushing together, or scraping past one another at that boundary.

MAIN IDEA AND DETAILS Record information about each type of fault in your notebook.

INVESTIGATE Faults

How can rocks move along faults?

PROCEDURE

(1) Place one triangular block of wood against the other to form a rectangle.

(2) Put two pieces of masking tape across both blocks. Draw a different pattern on each piece of tape. Break the tape where it crosses the blocks.

(3) Keep the blocks in contact and slide one block along the other.

(4) Repeat step 3 until you find three different ways the blocks can move relative to each other. Draw diagrams showing how the blocks moved. Include the tape patterns.

WHAT DO YOU THINK?

- How can you use the tape patterns to find the relative directions in which the blocks were moved?

- In each case, what sort of stress (such as pulling) did you put on the blocks?

CHALLENGE Compare the ways you moved the blocks with the ways tectonic plates move at their boundaries.

SKILL FOCUS
Modeling

MATERIALS
- 2 triangular blocks of wood
- masking tape
- marker

TIME
15 minutes

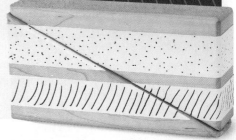

The illustrations on this page and page 49 show that a fault forms a plane that extends both horizontally and vertically. Blocks of rock move along the fault plane during an earthquake. Along a normal or reverse fault, the movement of the blocks is mainly vertical—the blocks move up or down. Along a strike-slip fault, the movement is horizontal—the blocks move sideways.

Normal Faults

Along a normal fault, the block of rock above the fault plane slides down relative to the other block. Stress that pulls rocks apart causes normal faults. Earthquakes along normal faults are common near boundaries where tectonic plates are moving apart, such as in the Great Rift Valley of Africa.

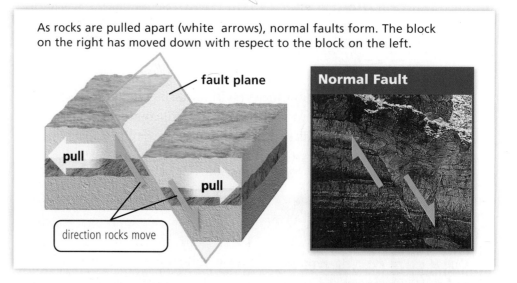

As rocks are pulled apart (white arrows), normal faults form. The block on the right has moved down with respect to the block on the left.

fault plane

pull

pull

direction rocks move

Normal Fault

Reverse Faults

Along a reverse fault, the block of rock above the fault plane moves up relative to the other block. Stress that presses rocks together causes reverse faults. These faults can occur near collision-zone boundaries

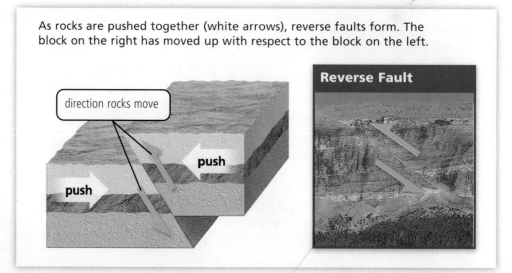

As rocks are pushed together (white arrows), reverse faults form. The block on the right has moved up with respect to the block on the left.

direction rocks move

push

push

Reverse Fault

between plates. The Himalaya Mountains, which rise in the area where the Indian Plate is pushing into the Eurasian Plate, have many earthquakes along reverse faults.

 CHECK YOUR READING What type of stress produces reverse faults?

Strike-Slip Faults

Along a strike-slip fault, blocks of rock move sideways on either side of the fault plane. Stresses that push blocks of rock horizontally cause earthquakes along strike-slip faults. These faults can occur where plates scrape past each other. The San Andreas Fault is a strike-slip fault.

VISUALIZATION
CLASSZONE.COM

Explore animations showing fault motion.

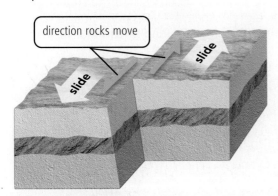

As rocks are pushed horizontally in opposite directions, strike-slip faults form. The block on the right has moved to the right with respect to the block on the left.

direction rocks move

slide

slide

Strike-Slip Fault

Over time, movement of rocks along normal and reverse faults can push up mountains and form deep valleys. As rocks move along strike-slip faults, rocks that were once in continuous layers can become separated by hundreds of kilometers.

2.1 Review

KEY CONCEPTS

1. What causes earthquakes?
2. Why do most earthquakes occur along tectonic plate boundaries?
3. What is the main direction of stress on blocks of rock at normal faults, reverse faults, and strike-slip faults?

CRITICAL THINKING

4. **Compare and Contrast** Make a chart showing the similarities and differences between normal and reverse faults.
5. **Connect** Japan is near a subduction zone. What type of faults would you expect to be responsible for many of the earthquakes there? Explain.

⬤ CHALLENGE

6. **Analyze** What evidence from rock layers could show a scientist that earthquakes had occurred in an area before written records were kept?

EXTREME SCIENCE

When Earth Shakes

Alaskan Earthquake Sinks Louisiana Boats

The most powerful earthquake ever recorded in the United States struck Prince William Sound in Alaska on March 27, 1964. Plates that had been moving a few centimeters per year lurched 9 meters (30 ft), causing the ground to shake for more than three minutes. When energy from the earthquake reached Louisiana, more than 5000 kilometers (3000 mi) away, it caused waves high enough to sink fishing boats in a harbor.

Wall of Water Higher than 20-Story Building

The 1964 Alaskan earthquake caused buildings to crumble and collapse. It also produced tsunamis—water waves caused by a sudden movement of the ground during an earthquake, landslide, or volcanic eruption. In Alaska's Valdez Inlet, a landslide triggered by the earthquake produced a tsunami 67 meters (220 ft) high—taller than a 20-story building.

Missouri Earthquakes Ring Massachusetts Bells

Earthquakes near New Madrid, Missouri, in 1811 and 1812 caused church bells in Boston, Massachusetts—nearly 1600 kilometers (1000 mi) away—to ring.

Five Largest Earthquakes Since 1900		
Location	Date	Moment Magnitude
Off the coast of Chile	1960	9.5
Prince William Sound, Alaska	1964	9.2
Andreanof Islands, Alaska	1957	9.1
Kamchatka Peninsula, Russia	1952	9.0
Off the coast of Ecuador	1906	8.8

Largest Earthquake Ever

The most powerful earthquake ever recorded hit Chile in 1960. This earthquake released almost 10 times as much energy as the 1964 earthquake in Alaska—and about 600 times the energy of the earthquake that destroyed much of San Francisco in 1906.

EXPLORE

1. **EXPLAIN** How were the 1964 Alaskan earthquake and the 1960 Chilean earthquake related to movements along tectonic plate boundaries?
2. **CHALLENGE** An inlet is a narrow body of water connected to a lake or ocean. Why might a tsunami be higher in an inlet than along the coastline around it?

A landslide caused by the 1964 Alaskan earthquake tore this school in Anchorage apart. Fortunately, school was not in session.

In Anchorage, almost 120 km from the center of the earthquake, the ground shook for about three minutes, causing severe damage.

2.2 Earthquakes release energy.

◀ BEFORE, you learned

- Most earthquakes occur along tectonic plate boundaries
- Different directions of stress cause normal, reverse, and strike-slip faults

▶ NOW, you will learn

- How energy from an earthquake travels through Earth
- How an earthquake's location is determined

VOCABULARY

seismic wave p. 51
focus p. 52
epicenter p. 52
seismograph p. 56

EXPLORE Movement of Energy

How does energy travel?

PROCEDURE

1. On a flat surface, hold one end of a spring toy while a partner holds the other end. Stretch the spring, then squeeze some coils together and release them.

2. Again, hold one end of the spring while your partner holds the other end. Shake your end of the spring back and forth.

MATERIALS
spring toy

WHAT DO YOU THINK?
- How did energy travel along the spring when you gathered and released some coils?
- How did energy travel along the spring when you shook one end back and forth?

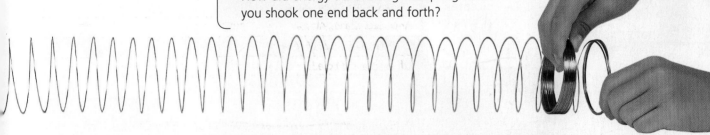

Energy from earthquakes travels through Earth.

MAIN IDEA AND DETAILS
Record information about the energy released by earthquakes.

When you throw a rock into a pond, waves ripple outward from the spot where the rock hits the water. The energy released by an earthquake travels in a similar way through Earth. Unlike the pond ripples, though, earthquake energy travels outward in all directions—up, down, and to the sides. The energy travels as **seismic waves,** (SYZ-mihk) which are vibrations caused by earthquakes. Seismic waves from even small earthquakes can be recorded by sensitive instruments around the world.

All earthquakes start beneath Earth's surface. The **focus** of an earthquake is the point underground where rocks first begin to move. Seismic waves travel outward from the earthquake's focus. The **epicenter** (EHP-ih-SEHN-tuhr) is the point on Earth's surface directly above the focus. Scientists often name an earthquake after the city that is closest to its epicenter.

In general, if two earthquakes of equal strength have the same epicenter, the one with the shallower focus causes more damage. Seismic waves from a deep-focus earthquake lose more of their energy as they travel farther up to Earth's surface.

The depths of earthquakes along tectonic plate boundaries are related to the directions in which the plates move. For example, an earthquake along a mid-ocean spreading center has a shallow focus. There, the plates are pulling apart, and the new crust that forms is thin. Subduction zones have a wide range of earthquake depths, from shallow to very deep. Earthquakes can occur anywhere along the sinking plates.

READING **TiP**

The prefix *epi-* comes from a Greek word meaning "on top of." An earthquake's epicenter is directly over its focus.

Focus and Epicenter

Seismic waves spread out from the focus of an earthquake.

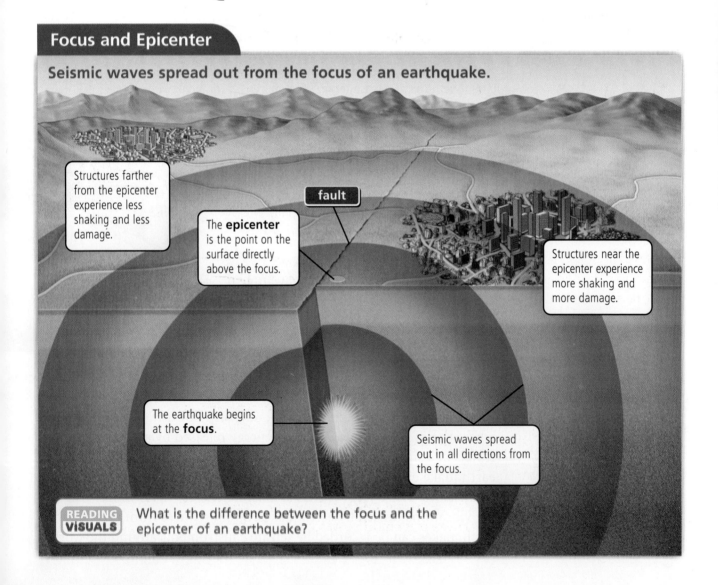

Structures farther from the epicenter experience less shaking and less damage.

The **epicenter** is the point on the surface directly above the focus.

fault

Structures near the epicenter experience more shaking and more damage.

The earthquake begins at the **focus**.

Seismic waves spread out in all directions from the focus.

READING VISUALS   What is the difference between the focus and the epicenter of an earthquake?

INVESTIGATE Subduction-Zone Earthquakes

Why are some earthquakes deeper than others?

PROCEDURE

1. Cut the first string into 4 pieces that are 4 cm long. Cut the second string into 3 pieces that are 8 cm long, and the third string into 4 pieces that are 15 cm long.

2. Use the key on the Earthquake Map to match string lengths with earthquake depths.

3. Tape one end of the pieces of string to the map at the earthquake locations, as shown in the photograph. Always cover the same amount of string with tape.

4. Hold the map upside down, with the strings hanging down. Observe the patterns of earthquake locations and depths.

WHAT DO YOU THINK?

- What patterns among the strings do you observe? How do you explain them?

- How might the earthquake depths relate to the sinking of a tectonic plate in a subduction zone?

CHALLENGE Draw a line on the map, showing where the subduction zone might be at Earth's surface. How might the depths of the earthquakes be different if the subduction zone were on the other side of the island?

Waves and Energy

Waves are part of your everyday life. For example, music reaches your ears as sound waves. All waves, including seismic waves, carry energy from place to place. As a wave moves through a material, particles of the material move out of position temporarily, causing the particles next to them to move. After each particle moves, it returns to its original position. In this way, energy moves through the material, but matter does not.

On October 17, 1989, an earthquake stopped baseball's World Series at Candlestick Park in San Francisco. As the seismic waves arrived, fans heard a low rumble; then for about 15 seconds the stadium shook from side to side and up and down. About 20 minutes after the earthquake was felt at the stadium, the seismic waves had traveled to the other side of Earth. There, the waves did not shake the ground hard enough for people to notice. The waves could be detected only by scientific instruments.

Earthquakes produce three types of seismic waves: primary waves, secondary waves, and surface waves. Each type moves through materials differently. In addition, the waves can reflect, or bounce, off boundaries between different layers. The waves can also bend as they pass from one layer into another. Scientists learn about Earth's layers by studying the paths and speeds of seismic waves traveling through Earth.

Primary Waves

The fastest seismic waves are called primary waves, or P waves. These waves are the first to reach any particular location after an earthquake occurs. Primary waves travel through Earth's crust at an average speed of about 5 kilometers per second (3 mi/s). Primary waves can travel through solids, liquids, and gases. As they pass through a material, the particles of the material are slightly pushed together and pulled apart. Buildings also experience this push and pull as primary waves pass through the ground they are built on.

Secondary Waves

Secondary waves are the second seismic waves to arrive at any particular location after an earthquake, though they start at the same time as primary waves. Secondary waves travel through Earth's interior at about half the speed of primary waves. Secondary waves are also called S waves. As they pass through a material, the material's particles are shaken up and down or from side to side. Secondary waves rock small buildings back and forth as they pass.

Secondary waves can travel through rock, but unlike primary waves they cannot travel through liquids or gases. Look at the illustrations on page 55. As a primary wave passes through a material, the volume and density of the material change slightly. But as a secondary wave passes, the material changes slightly in shape. Liquids and gases do not have definite shapes. These materials flow—that is, particles in them do not return to their original positions after being moved. When scientists learned that secondary waves cannot pass through Earth's outer core, they realized that the outer core is not solid.

 Why can't secondary waves travel through liquids or gases?

Surface Waves

Surface waves are seismic waves that move along Earth's surface, not through its interior. They make the ground roll up and down or shake from side to side. Surface waves cause the largest ground movements and the most damage. Surface waves travel more slowly than the other types of seismic waves.

Seismic Waves

Earthquakes produce three types of seismic waves.

Primary Waves

In primary waves, the particles of materials are slightly pushed together and pulled apart in the direction of the waves' travel.

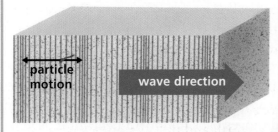

particle motion

wave direction

Secondary Waves

In secondary waves, the particles of materials move at a right angle to the direction of the waves' travel.

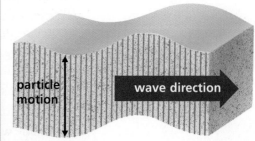

particle motion

wave direction

primary wave

secondary wave

surface wave

Surface Waves

Surface waves are seismic waves trapped near Earth's surface. As depth within Earth increases, motion due to surface waves decreases, then stops.

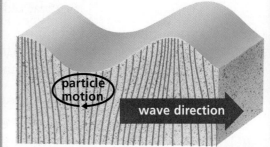

particle motion

wave direction

READING VISUALS How do particles move as primary waves and secondary waves pass through materials?

Seismic waves can be measured.

VOCABULARY
Add a magnet word diagram for *seismograph* to your notebook.

Without listening to the news, scientists at seismic stations all over the world know when an earthquake occurs. Seismic stations are places where ground movements are measured. A **seismograph** (SYZ-muh-GRAF) is an instrument that constantly records ground movements. The recording of an earthquake looks like a group of wiggles in a line. The height of the wiggles indicates the amount of ground movement produced by seismic waves at the seismograph's location.

Using Seismographs

RESOURCE CENTER
CLASSZONE.COM

Learn more about seismology.

Separate seismographs are needed to record side-to-side movements and up-and-down movements. A seismograph that measures side-to-side movements has a heavy weight hanging from a wire. The weight remains almost still as the ground moves back and forth beneath it. A pen attached to the weight records the movements. A seismograph that records up-and-down movements has a heavy weight hanging from a spring. As the ground moves, the weight stays almost still as the spring absorbs the movement by getting longer or shorter. A pen attached to the weight records the changes in distance between the ground and the weight.

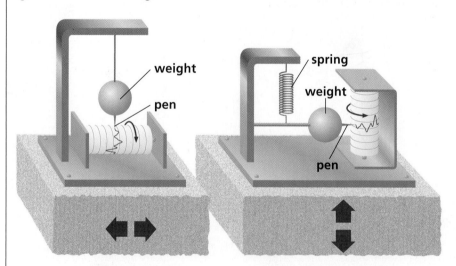

This seismograph records side-to-side movements.

This seismograph records up-and-down movements.

CHECK YOUR READING   Why is more than one kind of seismograph needed to record all the movements of the ground during an earthquake?

Scientists use seismographs to measure thousands of earthquakes, large and small, every year. Some seismographs can detect ground movements as small as one hundred-millionth of a centimeter. The recording produced by a seismograph is called a seismogram. By studying seismograms, scientists can determine the locations and strengths of earthquakes.

Locating an Earthquake

To locate the epicenter of an earthquake, scientists must have seismograms from at least three seismic stations. The procedure for locating an epicenter has three steps:

1 Scientists find the difference between the arrival times of the primary and the secondary waves at each of the three stations.

2 The time difference is used to determine the distance of the epicenter from each station. The greater the difference in time, the farther away the epicenter is.

3 A circle is drawn around each station, with a radius corresponding to the epicenter's distance from that station. The point where the three circles meet is the epicenter.

Finding an Epicenter

Seismograms provide data used to find an earthquake's epicenter.

① Determining Arrival Times

The time difference between the arrival of primary and secondary waves is recorded on a seismogram at each location.

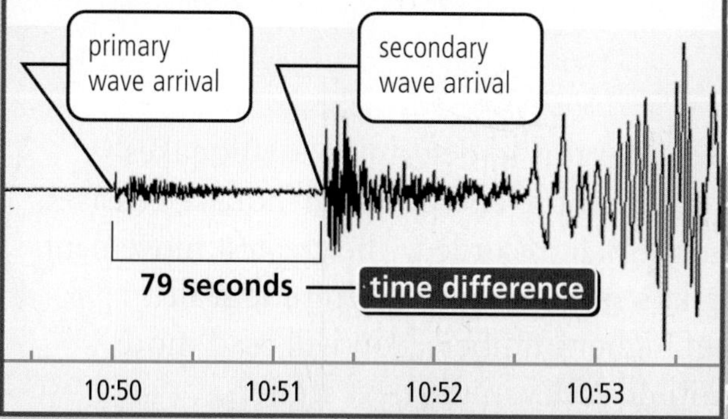

primary wave arrival

secondary wave arrival

79 seconds ── **time difference**

10:50   10:51   10:52   10:53

Minneapolis, MN

Detroit, MI ── 677 km

epicenter

Charleston, SC

| 0 | 250 | 500 miles |
| 0 | 250 | 500 kilometers |

② Calculating Distance

The arrival-time difference is used to determine the distance of the epicenter from the station.

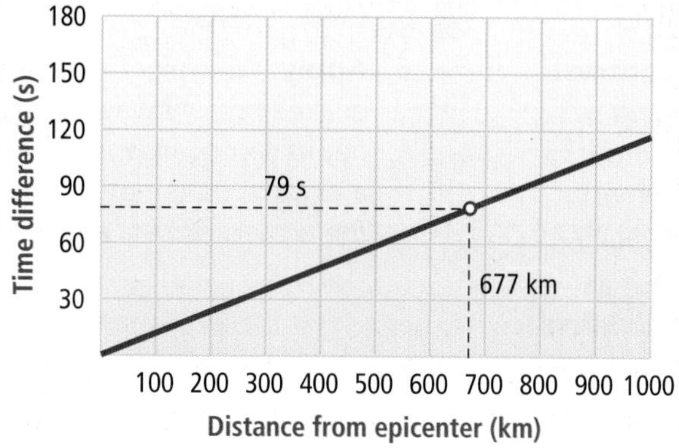

Time difference (s)

180
150
120
90
60
30

79 s

677 km

100 200 300 400 500 600 700 800 900 1000

Distance from epicenter (km)

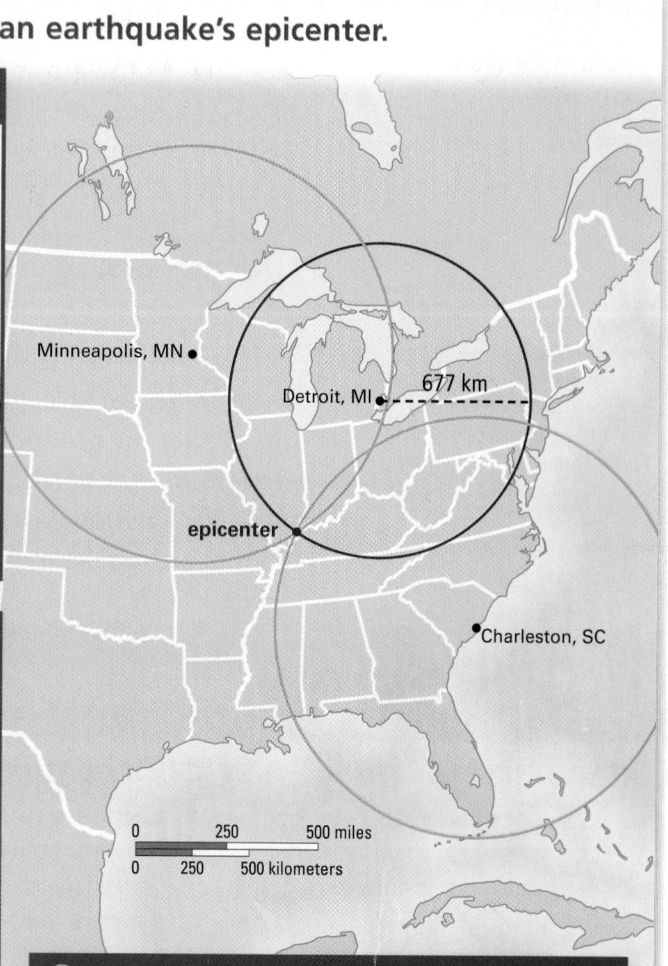

③ Plotting Distance

The distance from the station is used to plot a circle on a map. At least three circles are needed to locate the epicenter.

Scientists can also use seismograph data to locate the focus of an earthquake. They study seismograms to identify waves that have reflected off boundaries inside Earth. Some of these waves help the scientists to determine the earthquake's depth.

A seismogram records the time when the first primary wave arrives. This wave travels by a direct path. The data also show when the first reflected primary wave arrives. After leaving the focus, this wave reflects from Earth's surface and then travels to the seismic station. The reflected wave takes a longer path, so it arrives slightly later. The difference in arrival times indicates the depth of the focus. Scientists can make the necessary calculations, but more commonly a computer is used to calculate the location of an earthquake's epicenter and focus.

An earthquake's depth is determined from the difference in arrival times of direct and reflected seismic waves.

fault

reflected wave

seismic station

focus

direct wave

READING TiP

The word *magnitude* comes from the Latin word *magnitudo,* meaning "greatness."

Scientists also use seismograms to determine earthquakes' magnitudes, or strengths. The more energy an earthquake releases, the greater the ground movement recorded. The greatest movement determines the earthquake's strength on a magnitude scale. Stronger earthquakes get higher numbers. You will read more about earthquake magnitude scales in the next section.

2.2 Review

KEY CONCEPTS

1. Why does the greatest shaking of the ground occur near an earthquake's epicenter?

2. What information do you need to completely describe where an earthquake started?

3. What types of information can a scientist get by studying seismograms?

CRITICAL THINKING

4. **Compare and Contrast** How are primary and secondary waves similar? How are they different?

5. **Apply** What information could you get about an earthquake's location from only two seismic stations' data? Explain.

CHALLENGE

6. **Apply** Why might an earthquake's primary waves, but not its secondary waves, reach a location on the other side of the world from the epicenter?

Earthquake Energy

Seismologists use the moment magnitude scale to describe the energies of earthquakes. Because earthquakes vary from quite weak to very strong, the scale is designed to cover a wide range of energies. Each whole number increase in magnitude represents the release of about 32 times as much energy. For example, a magnitude 5 earthquake releases about 32 times as much energy as a magnitude 4 earthquake.

Magnitude	1	2	3	4	5	6	7	8	9	10
Energy		×32	×32	×32	×32	×32	×32	×32	×32	×32

Similarly, a magnitude 6 earthquake releases about 32 times as much energy as a magnitude 5 earthquake, and a magnitude 7 earthquake releases about 32 times as much energy as a magnitude 6 earthquake. You can use multiplication to compare the energies of earthquakes.

Example

Compare the energy of a magnitude 4 earthquake to the energy of a magnitude 7 earthquake. Give your answer to the nearest 1000.

SOLUTION

Magnitude	1	2	3	4	5	6	7	8	9	10
Energy		×32	×32	×32	×32	×32	×32	×32	×32	×32

(1) Multiply: $32 \times 32 \times 32 =$ **32,768**

(2) Round your answer to the nearest 1000: **33,000**

ANSWER A magnitude 7 earthquake releases about 33,000 times as much energy as a magnitude 4 earthquake.

Compare the energies of two earthquakes:

1. Magnitude 4 and magnitude 6; give your answer to the nearest 100

2. Magnitude 5 and magnitude 9; give your answer to the nearest 100,000

3. Magnitude 3.3 and magnitude 4.3

CHALLENGE What is the magnitude of an earthquake that releases about 1000 times the energy of a magnitude 2 earthquake?

KEY CONCEPT

2.3 Earthquake damage can be reduced.

 BEFORE, you learned

- Seismic waves travel through Earth
- An earthquake's location and magnitude can be determined

 NOW, you will learn

- How an earthquake's magnitude is related to the damage it causes
- How structures are built to withstand most earthquakes
- How scientists estimate the earthquake risk in an area

VOCABULARY

aftershock p. 62
liquefaction p. 62
tsunami p. 62

EXPLORE Shaking

What happens as materials are shaken?

PROCEDURE

1. Pour a pile of sand on a newspaper. Place a metal washer on top of the sand. Shake the paper and observe what happens to the sand and the washer.

2. Now place the washer on top of a flat rock. Shake the rock and observe what happens.

WHAT DO YOU THINK?

- How did the washer, the sand, and the rock react differently to shaking?
- How might the washer, the sand, and the rock model what happens to buildings and land during earthquakes?

MATERIALS

- sand
- newspaper
- flat rock
- washer

Earthquakes can cause severe damage and loss of life.

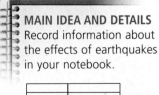

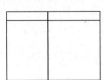

MAIN IDEA AND DETAILS
Record information about the effects of earthquakes in your notebook.

Every year, on average, an extremely powerful earthquake—one with a magnitude of 8 or higher—strikes somewhere on Earth. Such an earthquake can destroy almost all the buildings near its epicenter and cause great loss of life.

Earthquakes are most dangerous when they occur near areas where many people live. Most injuries and deaths due to earthquakes are not directly caused by the movement of the ground. They are caused by collapsing buildings and other structures and by fires. After an earthquake, fires may start due to broken natural-gas lines, broken electrical power lines, or overturned stoves.

Earthquake Magnitude

A very powerful earthquake can release more energy than 1 million weak earthquakes combined. Earthquake magnitude scales give scientists and engineers a simple way to describe this huge range in energy.

The first scale of earthquake magnitude was developed in California during the 1930s by the scientists Charles Richter (RIHK-tuhr) and Beno Gutenberg. In this scale, called the Richter scale, an earthquake's magnitude is based on how fast the ground moves at a seismic station. However, most scientists today prefer to use a newer, more accurate scale: the moment magnitude scale. This scale is based on the total amounts of energy released by earthquakes. The moment magnitude scale is used for all earthquake magnitudes given in this chapter.

Both the Richter scale and the moment magnitude scale are often shown with a top value of 10, but neither actually has a maximum value. On each scale, an increase of one whole number indicates an increase of 32 times more energy. For example, a magnitude 5 earthquake releases 32 times as much energy as a magnitude 4 earthquake and about 1000 times as much energy as a magnitude 3 earthquake.

Magnitude and Effects Near Epicenter

More powerful earthquakes have higher magnitude values.

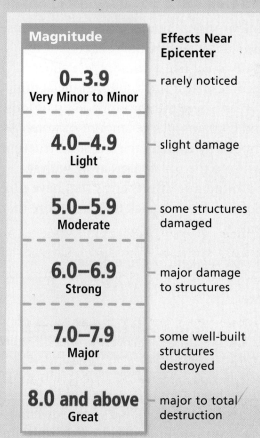

Magnitude	Effects Near Epicenter
0–3.9 Very Minor to Minor	rarely noticed
4.0–4.9 Light	slight damage
5.0–5.9 Moderate	some structures damaged
6.0–6.9 Strong	major damage to structures
7.0–7.9 Major	some well-built structures destroyed
8.0 and above Great	major to total destruction

Damage from Powerful Earthquake

This road collapsed during a magnitude 6.9 earthquake in California on October 17, 1989. About 140 earthquakes with magnitudes of 6 or higher occur each year around the world.

The moment magnitude scale is more accurate for larger earthquakes than the Richter scale. Another advantage of the moment magnitude scale is that it can be used for earthquakes that occurred before seismographs were invented. Geologists can measure the strength of the rocks and the length they moved along a fault to calculate a past earthquake's magnitude. This information is important for geologists to know when they determine an area's earthquake risk.

 What are two advantages of the moment magnitude scale over the Richter scale?

Damage from Earthquakes

Movement of the blocks of rock on either side of a fault can crack roads, buildings, dams, and any other structures on the fault. As blocks of rock move, they can also raise, lower, or tilt the ground surface. Sometimes structures weakened by an earthquake collapse during shaking caused by aftershocks. An **aftershock** is a smaller earthquake that follows a more powerful earthquake in the same area. Also, fires that break out can cause great damage if broken water pipes keep firefighters from getting water. In the 1906 San Francisco earthquake, fires caused more than 90 percent of the building damage.

Earthquakes can cause major damage by affecting the soil and other loose materials. For example, landslides often occur as a result of earthquakes. A landslide is a movement of soil and rocks down a hill or mountain. Earthquakes can cause soil **liquefaction,** a process in which shaking of the ground causes soil to act like a liquid. For a short time the soil becomes like a thick soup. Liquefaction occurs only in areas where the soil is made up of loose sand and silt and contains a large amount of water. As the shaking temporarily changes the wet soil, structures either sink down into the soil or flow away with it. Shaking of the ground also affects areas that have mixtures of soils. Some soil types pack together more than others when shaken.

This building in Venezuela tilted and sank as the ground beneath it collapsed during an earthquake in 1967.

 List five ways in which earthquakes can cause damage.

Damage from Tsunamis

If you sit on an ocean beach, you can watch the depth of the water change as waves come in. If you watch for a longer time, you may notice bigger changes as the tide rises or falls. A special type of wave, however, can make water rise more than the height of a 20-story building. This wave, known as a **tsunami** (tsu-NAH-mee), is a water wave triggered by an earthquake, volcanic eruption, or landslide. Tsunamis are sometimes called tidal waves, but they are not caused by the forces that produce tides. A tsunami may not be a single wave but several waves that can have different heights and can arrive hours apart.

RESOURCE CENTER
CLASSZONE.COM

Explore tsunamis.

Tsunamis move quickly and can travel thousands of kilometers without weakening. In deep water, they can reach speeds of about 700 kilometers per hour (430 mi/h). A tsunami in the deep water of the open ocean may be less than one meter (3 ft) in height at the surface. As a tsunami reaches shallow water around an island or continent, however, it slows down, and its height greatly increases.

A 1946 earthquake on Alaska's coast caused a tsunami that swept across the entire Pacific Ocean. In Alaska the tsunami destroyed a new U.S. Coast Guard lighthouse that otherwise would have been able to send warnings to other areas. In less than five hours, the tsunami reached Hawaii as a series of waves. The highest wave was about 17 meters (55 ft) tall. Because people did not know of the danger, no one had evacuated, and 159 people were killed.

In 1993, a tsunami from a powerful earthquake in Japan threw boats onto land.

Many earthquakes occur around the edges of the Pacific Ocean. Therefore, Hawaii and other areas in and around this ocean are likely to be hit by tsunamis. The Pacific Tsunami Warning Center, located in Hawaii, was established in 1949. The center monitors earthquakes and issues warnings to areas that could be struck by tsunamis.

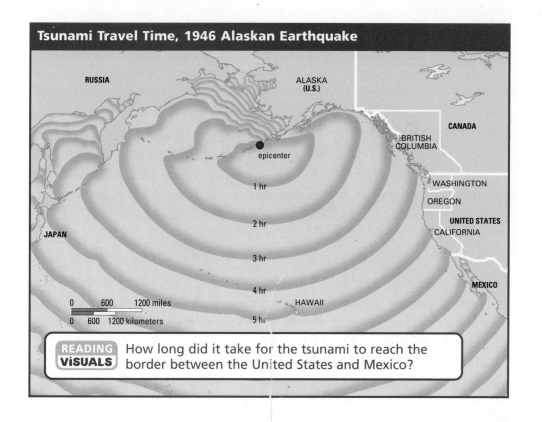

Tsunami Travel Time, 1946 Alaskan Earthquake

READING VISUALS How long did it take for the tsunami to reach the border between the United States and Mexico?

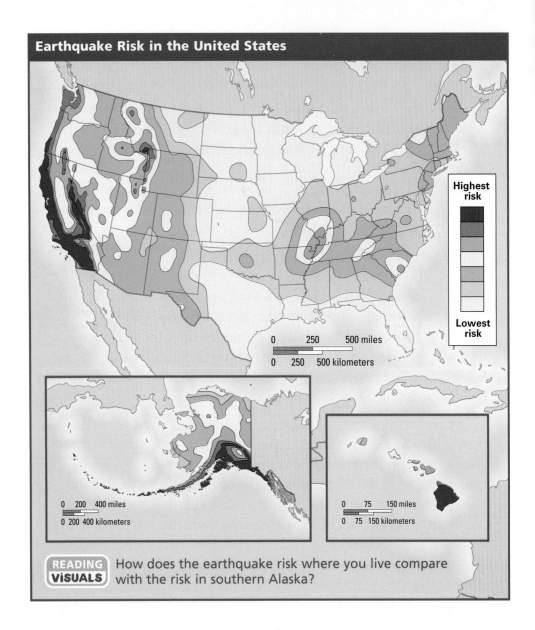

Earthquake Risk in the United States

Highest risk

Lowest risk

0   250   500 miles
0   250   500 kilometers

0   200   400 miles
0   200   400 kilometers

0   75   150 miles
0   75   150 kilometers

READING VISUALS How does the earthquake risk where you live compare with the risk in southern Alaska?

Scientists work to monitor and predict earthquakes.

READING TIP

A prediction is a statement about an event before it occurs. Scientists use their knowledge to make predictions about when earthquakes might occur.

Scientists cannot yet predict the day or even the year when an earthquake will occur. Sometimes there are signs years before an earthquake strikes, and sometimes there are none at all. Usually the best that scientists can do is to give long-term predictions. For example, they might state that an area has a 60 percent chance of being hit by an earthquake with a magnitude 7 or higher within the next 25 years.

The map above shows earthquake risks in the United States for the next 50 years. The map is based on information about earthquakes that have occurred since people began keeping records, along with evidence of earlier earthquakes preserved in rocks. Note that most areas with the highest earthquake risks are near the Pacific Ocean.

To learn more about earthquakes and to find ways of predicting them, scientists all over the world study seismic activity along faults. They monitor whether stress is building up in the rocks along faults. Such signs include

- tilts or changes in the elevation of the ground
- slow movements or stretching in rock
- the development of small cracks in the ground

An increase in small earthquakes can be a sign that stress is building up along a fault and that a large earthquake is likely to occur. But an increase in small earthquakes can also be a sign that a fault is releasing stress bit by bit, decreasing the likelihood of a major earthquake.

Scientists also look for areas where earthquakes have not occurred along an otherwise active fault. They make diagrams in which they plot the locations where earthquakes have started, as shown below. Sometimes such a diagram shows an area of few or no earthquakes that is surrounded by many earthquakes. This area is called a seismic gap. A seismic gap can indicate a location where a fault is stuck. Movement along other parts of the fault can increase stress along the stuck part. This stress could be released by a major earthquake.

 CHECK YOUR READING Why can a lack of earthquakes in an area near an active fault cause concern?

Seismic Gaps

A seismic gap is a section of a fault with few earthquakes compared with sections of the fault on either side of the gap.

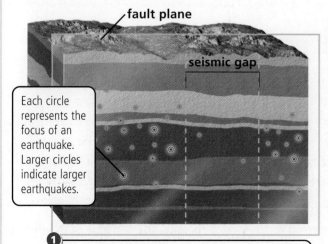

Each circle represents the focus of an earthquake. Larger circles indicate larger earthquakes.

1 Over several years many earthquakes have occurred along this fault. However, one section of the fault has had little earthquake activity. Stress is building up along this section.

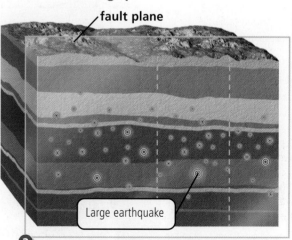

Large earthquake

2 A large earthquake and its aftershocks have occurred, releasing built-up stress. Over just a few weeks the seismic gap has been filled in.

Structures can be designed to resist earthquake damage.

READING TiP

Here, the term *structure* refers to office buildings, homes, bridges, dams, factories—all the things that people build.

For safety, it might be best to be outdoors, far from any buildings, during an earthquake. But there is no way to tell just when or where an earthquake will occur. For this reason, the best way to reduce deaths, injuries, and damage from earthquakes is to build structures able to withstand strong ground shaking. The first step is to understand what the risks from earthquakes are in an area. The second step is to build structures that are appropriate for the area.

Scientists make maps of areas to show the locations of fault zones, past earthquakes, and areas likely to experience flooding, landslides, or liquefaction. In Japan, California, and other areas that have many earthquakes, planners use these maps to develop rules for building new structures and strengthening older ones. The maps are also used to select building locations that are stable—unlikely to experience landslides or liquefaction.

Earthquake damage to small buildings, such as most houses, often occurs when the buildings are shaken off their foundations. Small buildings are better protected when they are firmly fastened to their foundations. Also, their walls need to be strong. Some houses were built before modern safety rules were in place. The walls of these houses can be made stronger by adding supports. Supports are particularly important in brick walls, which can easily collapse in an earthquake. A special type of steel is commonly used for the supports because it is strong and is able to bend, then return to its original shape.

⚠ SAFETY TIPS

Earthquakes

Before

- Fasten heavy objects, such as bookcases, to floors or walls to keep them from falling.
- Put latches on cabinets to keep dishes from falling out.
- Identify safe spots in every room, such as the space under a strong table.
- Keep an emergency supply of bottled water.

During and After

- If you are inside a building, stay inside until the shaking stops. Objects falling from buildings cause many injuries.
- If you are outdoors, move away from buildings, poles, and trees.
- Make a family plan for contacting a person who lives in another town. As people call to say they are safe, this person can pass on the information.

Many of the methods used to make larger buildings and other structures safer are designed to reduce the amount they shake during an earthquake. One method is to use devices called base isolators, as shown in the illustration. Base isolators are placed between a building and its foundation. The isolators are made of flexible materials that are stacked in layers like pancakes. When an earthquake occurs, the isolators absorb much of the ground motion. Any shaking that does reach the building is slower and smoother.

A building may also have an open space, or moat, around it. The moat, which may be covered at the surface with sidewalks and landscaping, lets the building shake more gently than the ground during an earthquake.

Special walls, called shear walls, add strength to a structure. These walls contain steel supports. Shear walls in the center of a building are often built around a stairwell or an elevator shaft. These walls make up a part of the building known as the shear core.

Walls can also be made stronger by adding braces. Pairs of braces that form an **X** shape are called cross braces. They help a structure keep its shape while it is being shaken.

Earthquake-Resistant Building

cross braces

shear wall

shear core

moat

base isolator

CHECK YOUR READING Describe two methods used to make buildings stronger.

2.3 Review

KEY CONCEPTS

1. How is an earthquake magnitude scale related to the amounts of energy released by earthquakes?

2. What are the major dangers to people from an earthquake?

3. Name three methods of improving a building's safety before an earthquake.

CRITICAL THINKING

4. **Apply** What might people living next to the ocean do to protect themselves if they were given a two-hour warning of an approaching tsunami?

5. **Connect** If you lived in an area where earthquakes were common, what could you do to make your room safer?

⬤ CHALLENGE

6. **Analyze** Earthquakes release stress that has built up in rocks. Why do you think aftershocks occur?

CHAPTER INVESTIGATION

How Structures React in Earthquakes

DESIGN —YOUR OWN—

OVERVIEW AND PURPOSE

In 1989 a magnitude 6.9 earthquake struck the San Francisco Bay area, killing 62 people and leaving 12,000 homeless. In 1988 a magnitude 6.9 earthquake occurred near Spitak, Armenia. There, nearly 25,000 people died and 514,000 lost their homes. The difference in the effects of these two earthquakes was largely due to differences in construction methods. In this investigation you will

- build a structure and measure how long it can withstand shaking on a shake table provided by your teacher
- explore methods of building earthquake-resistant structures

MATERIALS
- modeling clay
- stirrer straws
- piece of thin cardboard 15 cm on each side
- scissors
- ruler
- shake table

▶ Problem

How can structures be built to withstand most earthquakes?

▶ Hypothesize

Write a hypothesis to explain how structures can be built to withstand shaking. Your hypothesis should take the form of an "If . . . , then . . . , because . . ." statement.

▶ Procedure

1. Make a data table like the one shown on the next page.

2. Use stirrers joined with clay to build a structure at least 20 cm tall on top of the cardboard. Cut the stirrers if necessary.

3. Make a diagram of your structure.

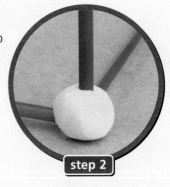

step 2

4 Lift your structure by its cardboard base and place it on the shake-table platform. Pull the platform 2 centimeters to one side and release it.

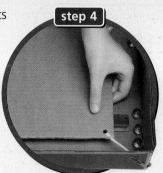

step 4

5 Repeat step 4 until the structure begins to collapse.

Observe and Analyze
Write It Up

1. **RECORD** Complete your data table and make notes about the collapse, including areas of possible weakness in your structure.

2. **INFER** Use your observations to design a structure that will better withstand shaking.

Conclude
Write It Up

1. **INTERPRET** Compare your results with your hypothesis. Do your observations support your hypothesis?

2. **INFER** How would you use the shake table to model earthquakes of different magnitudes?

3. **IDENTIFY VARIABLES** How might your results differ if you always pulled the platform to the same side or if you pulled it to different sides?

4. **IDENTIFY LIMITS** In what ways might a building's behavior during an earthquake differ from the behavior of your structure on the shake table?

5. **COMPARE** Examine the diagrams of the three structures that lasted longest in your class. What characteristics, if any, did they have in common?

6. **APPLY** Based on your results, write a list of recommendations for building earthquake-resistant structures.

INVESTIGATE Further

CHALLENGE Have a contest to see who can build the most earthquake-resistant structure. Design your structure as if you were an earthquake engineer. Make a model of your structure at least 30 centimeters tall, using the types of materials you used in this investigation. Test the structure on the shake table. What design features helped the winning structure to resist shaking the longest?

How Structures React in Earthquakes

Problem How can structures be built to withstand most earthquakes?

Hypothesize

Observe and Analyze

Table 1. Number of Trials Until Collapse of Structure

Trial	Distance Platform Pulled to Side (cm)	Notes
1	2	
2	2	
3	2	
4	2	

Conclude

the BIG idea

Earthquakes release stress that has built up in rocks.

CONTENT REVIEW
CLASSZONE.COM

◀ **KEY CONCEPTS SUMMARY**

2.1 Earthquakes occur along faults.

 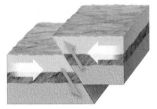 

Normal faults form as rocks are pulled apart.

Reverse faults form as rocks are pushed together.

Strike-slip faults form as rocks are pushed horizontally in opposite directions.

VOCABULARY
fault p. 45
stress p. 45
earthquake p. 45

2.2 Earthquakes release energy.

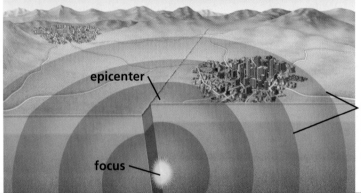

epicenter

focus

Seismic waves move out from the focus in all directions.

VOCABULARY
seismic wave p. 51
focus p. 52
epicenter p. 52
seismograph p. 56

2.3 Earthquake damage can be reduced.

A powerful earthquake releases more energy and causes more shaking of the ground than does a weak earthquake.

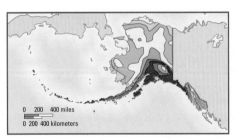

0 200 400 miles
0 200 400 kilometers

An area's risk of earthquakes can be predicted.

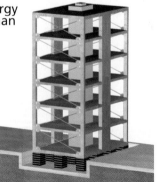

Structures can be designed for greater safety in an earthquake.

VOCABULARY
aftershock p. 62
liquefaction p. 62
tsunami p. 62

Reviewing Vocabulary

On a separate sheet of paper, draw a diagram to show the relationships among each set of words. One set has been done as an example.

seismograph, seismic waves, seismogram

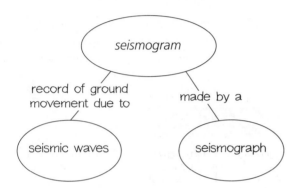

1. earthquake, epicenter, focus

2. earthquake, tsunami, liquefaction

3. fault, stress, earthquake, aftershock

4. tsunami, epicenter, seismogram

Reviewing Key Concepts

Multiple Choice *Choose the letter of the best answer.*

5. What causes an earthquake?
   a. a rise of magma in the mantle
   b. a sudden movement of blocks of rock
   c. a buildup of seismic waves
   d. a change in Earth's magnetic poles

6. Earthquakes release energy in the form of
   a. seismic waves
   b. faults
   c. stress lines
   d. seismograms

7. Most damage from an earthquake usually occurs
   a. below the focus
   b. far from the epicenter
   c. at the focus
   d. near the epicenter

8. To locate the epicenter of an earthquake, scientists need seismograms from at least _____ seismic stations.
   a. two   c. four
   b. three   d. five

9. The seismic waves that usually cause the most damage are
   a. surface waves
   b. tsunami waves
   c. primary waves
   d. secondary waves

10. Earthquakes release _____ that has built up in rocks.
    a. water   c. stress
    b. magnetism   d. electricity

11. About 80 percent of all earthquakes occur in a belt around the
    a. Pacific Ocean
    b. San Andreas Fault
    c. North American Plate
    d. African Rift Valley

12. In a strike-slip fault, blocks of rock move _____ along the fault plane.
    a. up
    b. down
    c. sideways
    d. up and down

13. One method of making a building earthquake resistant is to
    a. add sand under the foundation
    b. reduce the use of steel
    c. make the walls of brick
    d. use cross braces

Short Answer *Write a short answer to each question.*

14. Why do most earthquakes occur at or near tectonic plate boundaries?

15. How do data from seismic waves indicate that Earth's outer core is liquid?

16. What causes most of the injuries and deaths due to earthquakes?

Thinking Critically

Study the illustration below, showing the epicenter and focus of an earthquake, then answer the following six questions.

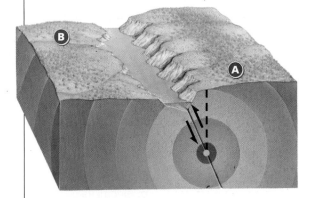

17. APPLY What type of fault is shown in the illustration? How do you know?

18. APPLY Where on the surface is the greatest shaking likely to occur?

19. INFER What does the set of circles around the focus represent?

20. EXPLAIN In what ways would the times of arrival of primary and secondary waves be different at points *A* and *B*?

21. IDENTIFY EFFECTS The land surface to the left of the fault is lower than the land surface to the right. How might this be related to movements along the fault?

22. ANALYZE What are the main directions of stress on the blocks of rock on either side of the fault?

23. APPLY A builder is planning to construct a new house near a fault along which earthquakes are common. Write a list of guidelines that the builder might use to decide where and how to build the house.

24. ANALYZE Identify two areas of the United States where earthquakes are most likely to occur. Explain your choices in terms of plate tectonics.

25. IDENTIFY EFFECTS A town has been struck by an earthquake with a magnitude of 5.8. The epicenter was 10 kilometers (6 mi) away, and the focus was shallow. What sort of damage would you expect to find in the town?

26. ANALYZE What role do earthquakes play in shaping Earth's surface?

27. CALCULATE If primary waves travel at a speed of about 5 kilometers per second, how long would it take them to arrive at a seismic station located 695 kilometers from an earthquake's focus?

the BIG idea

28. CONNECT Look again at the photograph of earthquake damage on pages 42–43. Explain how energy released by an earthquake can travel through rock and cause damage at Earth's surface.

29. SYNTHESIZE The illustration below shows convection in Earth's mantle. What are the relationships among the heat inside Earth, the movements of tectonic plates, and the occurrences of earthquakes?

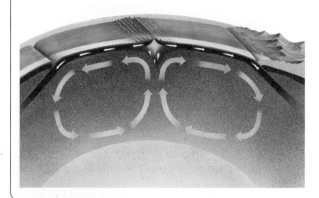

UNIT PROJECTS

If you need to do an experiment for your unit project, gather the materials. Be sure to allow enough time to observe results before the project is due.

Standardized Test Practice

Analyzing Data

The following tables show magnitudes and average numbers of earthquakes in the world per year, and states in which two or more major earthquakes have been recorded. Use the information in the tables to answer the questions below.

Earthquakes in the World per Year

Classification	Magnitude	Average Number per Year
Great	8.0 and higher	1
Major	7.0–7.9	18
Strong	6.0–6.9	120
Moderate	5.0–5.9	800
Light	4.0–4.9	6200
Minor	3.0–3.9	49,000

States That Have Recorded Two or More Major Earthquakes

State	Number of Major Earthquakes
Alaska	74
Arkansas	2
California	16
Hawaii	4
Missouri	2
Nevada	3

1. A major earthquake can have a magnitude of
  a. 6.0–6.9
  b. 6.0 and higher
  c. 7.4
  d. 8.2

2. The most major earthquakes have been recorded in which state?
  a. Arkansas
  b. Hawaii
  c. Missouri
  d. Nevada

3. A magnitude 3.2 earthquake is classified as
  a. major
  b. strong
  c. moderate
  d. minor

4. The world's most powerful earthquakes occur along reverse faults. In which state are reverse faults most likely to be common?
  a. Alaska
  b. California
  c. Hawaii
  d. Nevada

5. In which state is a tectonic plate boundary most likely to be located?
  a. Arkansas
  b. California
  c. Hawaii
  d. Nevada

6. Compared to the number of major earthquakes each year, the number of moderate earthquakes is
  a. about 40 times greater
  b. about 4 times greater
  c. about equal
  d. smaller

7. Alaska has recorded a total of 82 earthquakes with magnitudes of 7.0 and higher. How many of these earthquakes are classified as "great"?
  a. 0
  b. 8
  c. 56
  d. 74

8. An earthquake of which classification releases the most energy?
  a. great
  b. major
  c. strong
  d. minor

Extended Response

Answer the two questions below in detail. Include some of the terms shown in the word box. In your answers underline each term you use.

seismic waves	primary	secondary	surface
stress		fault	plate boundary

9. During an earthquake, Dustin felt a small amount of shaking. About 15 seconds later, he felt some more shaking. Then about 45 seconds later he felt the strongest shaking. Explain what happened.

10. The island of Sumatra is located in an area where the Pacific Plate sinks under the Eurasian Plate. Explain why Sumatra has many earthquakes.

CHAPTER 3
Mountains and Volcanoes

the BIG idea

Mountains and volcanoes form as tectonic plates move.

Key Concepts

SECTION 3.1
Movement of rock builds mountains.
Learn how different types of mountains form.

SECTION 3.2
Volcanoes form as molten rock erupts.
Learn why there are different types of volcanoes and volcanic eruptions.

SECTION 3.3
Volcanoes affect Earth's land, air, and water.
Learn how volcanic eruptions affect land, air, and water.

Internet Preview

CLASSZONE.COM
Chapter 3 online resources: Content Review, Simulation, Visualization, two Resource Centers, Math Tutorial, Test Practice

> How does new land form from molten rock?

EXPLORE (the BIG idea)

Making Mountains

Line up and hold a row of about ten checkers or coins on a table. Tilt the row, then let it go.

Observe and Think What happened to the height, length, and shape of the row? How do you think these changes might be similar to the processes by which some mountains and valleys form?

Under Pressure

Half fill two empty plastic bottles with a fresh carbonated beverage. Screw the caps on the bottles tightly. Put one bottle in hot tap water and one in ice water. Wait three minutes.

Observe and Think Slowly unscrew the caps from the bottles and observe how quickly gas bubbles form and escape. What is the role of pressure? How might gas bubbles cause pressure to build up in magma as they form?

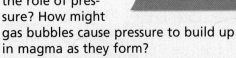

Internet Activity: Volcanoes

Go to **ClassZone.com** to make a volcano erupt.

Observe and Think Why are some volcanic eruptions much more violent than others?

Explore Volcanoes **Code: MDL054**

Getting Ready to Learn

◀ CONCEPT REVIEW

- Earthquakes occur as blocks of rock move along faults.
- Tectonic plates pull apart, push together, or scrape past one another along their boundaries.

◀ VOCABULARY REVIEW

convergent boundary p. 22

subduction p. 30

fault p. 45

earthquake p. 45

magma *See Glossary.*

CONTENT REVIEW
CLASSZONE.COM
Review concepts and vocabulary.

▶ TAKING NOTES

CONTENT FRAME

Organize your notes into a **content frame** for mountains. Make categories at the top that describe their types, features, and how they form. Then fill in the boxes for each type of mountain. Later in the chapter you will make content frames for other topics.

VOCABULARY STRATEGY

Draw a **word triangle** diagram for each new vocabulary term. On the bottom line, write and define the term. Above that, write a sentence that uses the term correctly. At the top, draw a small picture to show what the term looks like.

See the Note-Taking Handbook on pages R45–R51.

SCIENCE NOTEBOOK

TYPE OF MOUNTAINS	CHARACTERISTIC	WHERE THEY FORM	EXAMPLES
folded	rocks bent and folded	at convergent plate boundaries	Appalachians Himalayas
fault-block			

Fault-block mountains form as continental crust is pulled apart.

fault-block mountain: a mountain pushed up or tilted along a fault

Movement of rock builds mountains.

 BEFORE, you learned

- Major geologic events occur at tectonic plate boundaries
- Most faults are located along plate boundaries

 NOW, you will learn

- How the folding of rock can form mountains
- How movement along faults can form mountains

VOCABULARY

folded mountain p. 80
fault-block mountain
p. 82

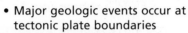

EXPLORE Folding

How does rock fold?

PROCEDURE

1. Make three flat layers of clay on top of a sheet of newspaper. Put a block at either end of the clay.

2. Hold one block still. Push on the other block to slowly bring the blocks closer together.

WHAT DO YOU THINK?

- What happened to the clay when you pushed on the block?
- What shape did the middle layer of clay form?
- If a large block of rock reacted to pressure in a similar way, what kind of landform would result?

MATERIALS

- 2 or 3 colors of modeling clay
- 2 blocks
- newspaper

Most mountains form along plate boundaries.

A shallow sea once covered the area that is now Mount Everest, Earth's tallest mountain. If you were to climb Mount Everest, you would be standing on rocks containing the remains of ocean animals. Mount Everest also contains rocks that formed far away at a spreading center on the sea floor. How can rocks from the sea floor be on top of a mountain on a continent? Plate tectonics provides the answer.

Recall that an oceanic plate sinks when it collides with a continental plate. Some sea-floor material scrapes off the sinking plate and onto the continent. As continental mountains form, material once at the bottom of an ocean can be pushed many kilometers high.

Mountain Ranges and Belts

A mountain is an area of land that rises steeply from the land around it. A single mountain is rare. Most mountains belong to ranges—long lines of mountains that were formed at about the same time and by the same processes. Ranges that are close together make up mountain belts. For example, the Rocky Mountain belt in western North America contains about 100 ranges.

① Mountains rise high above the land around them.

② Most mountains are in groups called mountain ranges.

③ Closely spaced mountain ranges make up mountain belts.

Most of the world's major mountain belts are located along tectonic plate boundaries. But mountain belts like the Appalachians (AP-uh-LAY-chee-uhnz) in eastern North America are in the interior of plates. Mountains such as these were formed by ancient plate collisions that assembled the present-day continents.

Major Mountain Belts

Major mountain belts mark the locations of present or past plate boundaries.

Mountains, Rocks, and Sediment

At the same time that some processes push mountains up, other processes wear them down. At Earth's surface, water and wind break rocks apart and move the pieces away. As long as mountains are pushed up faster than they wear down, they grow taller. For this reason, young mountains tend to be tall and steep. But eventually mountain-building processes slow, then end. Water and wind take over. Given enough time, all mountains become rounded hills, and then they are gone. Countless mountains have formed and worn away throughout Earth's long history.

Rocks break down into loose pieces that can be carried by water or wind. These pieces are called sediments. For example, sand on a beach is sediment. Thick layers of sediments can build up in low-lying areas, such as valleys, lakes, or the ocean. Pieces of sediments form sedimentary rock as they are pressed together or joined by natural cement.

The land becomes flatter as mountains wear down and valleys fill with sediments. If tectonic plates were to stop moving, eventually the surfaces of all the continents would be completely flat.

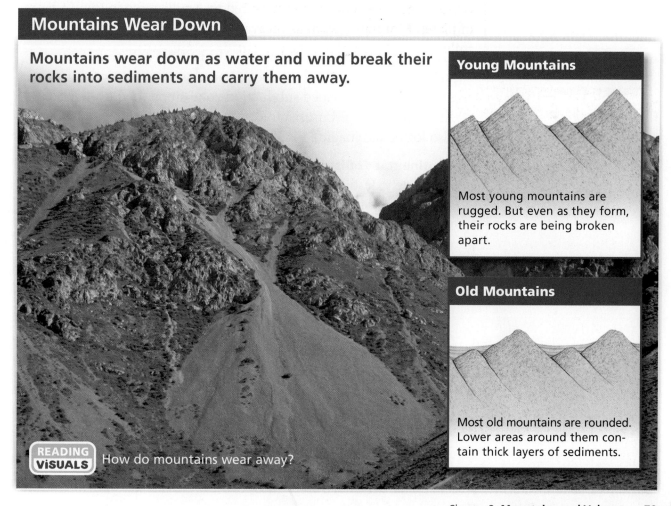

Mountains Wear Down

Mountains wear down as water and wind break their rocks into sediments and carry them away.

Young Mountains

Most young mountains are rugged. But even as they form, their rocks are being broken apart.

Old Mountains

Most old mountains are rounded. Lower areas around them contain thick layers of sediments.

READING VISUALS How do mountains wear away?

Mountains can form as rocks fold.

Though people usually do not think of rocks as being able to bend and fold, they can. Think of a wax candle. If you bend a candle quickly, it will break. If you leave a candle propped up at an angle, over many days it will bend. If the candle is in a warm area, it will bend more quickly. Rocks also bend when stress is applied slowly. Rocks deep in the crust are at high temperatures and pressures. They are particularly likely to bend rather than break.

CHECK YOUR READING Under what conditions are rocks likely to bend and fold?

VOCABULARY
Make a word triangle for *folded mountain* in your notebook.

READING TiP
Eurasia is the landmass consisting of Europe and Asia.

Remember that tectonic plates move only a few centimeters each year. The edge of a continent along a convergent boundary is subjected to stress for a very long time as another plate pushes against it. Some of the continent's rocks break, and others fold. As folding continues, mountains are pushed up. A **folded mountain** is a mountain that forms as continental crust crumples and bends into folds.

Folded mountains form as an oceanic plate sinks under the edge of a continent or as continents collide. One example is the Himalaya (HIHM-uh-LAY-uh) belt, which formed by a collision between India and Eurasia. Its formation is illustrated on page 81.

❶ Convergent Boundary Develops At one time an ocean separated India and Eurasia. As India moved northward, oceanic lithosphere sank in a newly formed subduction zone along the Eurasian Plate. Along the edge of Eurasia, folded mountains formed. Volcanoes also formed as magma rose from the subduction zone to the surface.

❷ Continental Collision Begins Eventually the sea floor was completely destroyed, and India and Eurasia collided. Subduction ended. The volcanoes stopped erupting because they were no longer supplied with magma. Sea-floor material that had been added to the edge of Eurasia became part of the mountains pushed up by the collision.

❸ Collision Continues India and Eurasia continue to push together. Their collision has formed the Himalayas, the world's tallest mountains. They grow even higher as rock is folded and pushed up for hundreds of kilometers on either side of the collision boundary.

Earthquakes can also be important to the upward growth of folded mountains. A great deal of rock in the Himalaya belt has been pushed up along reverse faults, which are common at convergent boundaries.

Formation of Himalayas

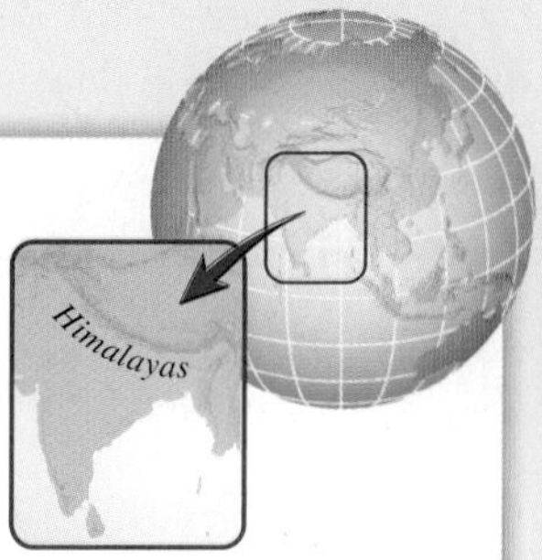

The Himalayas are being pushed higher by an ongoing continental collision.

① Convergent Boundary Develops

As India began moving toward Eurasia 200 million years ago, a convergent boundary developed along the edge of Eurasia. The oceanic lithosphere between the two continents sank into a subduction zone.

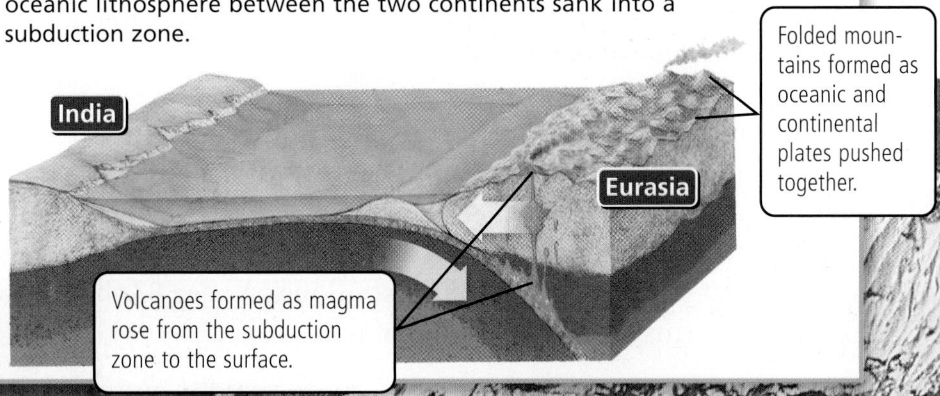

India

Eurasia

Folded mountains formed as oceanic and continental plates pushed together.

Volcanoes formed as magma rose from the subduction zone to the surface.

② Continental Collision Begins

The sea floor was completely destroyed about 50 million years ago, and India and Eurasia collided.

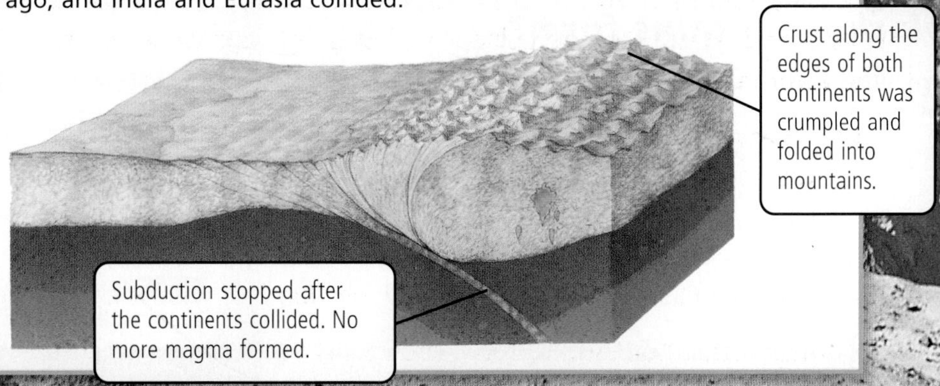

Crust along the edges of both continents was crumpled and folded into mountains.

Subduction stopped after the continents collided. No more magma formed.

③ The Collision Continues

Currently, the Himalayas are growing more than one centimeter higher each year.

Himalayas

As the collision continues, the crust keeps folding. Also, earthquakes are common.

A remnant of sea floor crust remains deep under the mountains.

Himalayas

READING VISUALS In each illustration, where is the boundary between India and Eurasia?

Mountains can form as rocks move along faults.

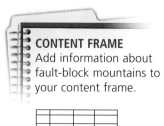

CONTENT FRAME
Add information about fault-block mountains to your content frame.

In the southwestern United States and northwestern Mexico, hundreds of mountain ranges line up in rows. The ranges, as well as the valleys between them, formed along nearly parallel normal faults. Mountains that form as blocks of rock move up or down along normal faults are called **fault-block mountains.**

 CHECK YOUR READING How can the movement of rocks along faults lead to the formation of mountains?

Fault-block mountains form as the lithosphere is stretched and pulled apart by forces within Earth. The rocks of the crust are cool and rigid. As the lithosphere begins to stretch, the crust breaks into large blocks. As stretching continues, the blocks of rock move along the faults that separate them. The illustrations on page 83 show how this process forms fault-block mountains.

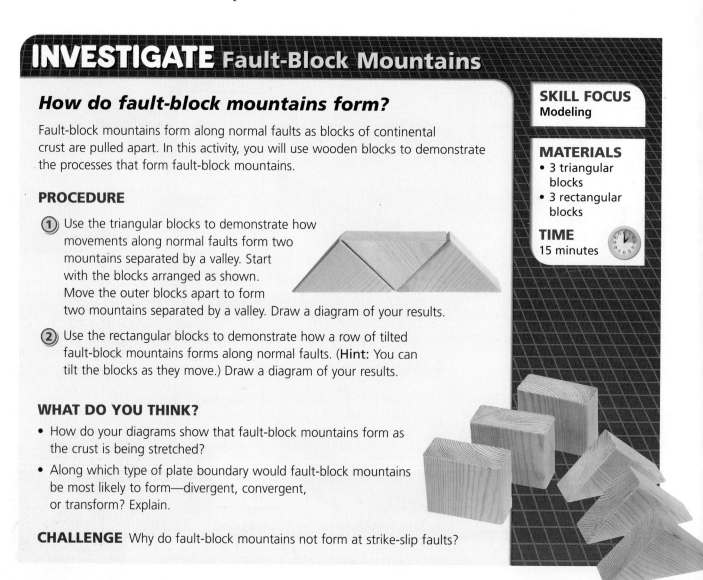

INVESTIGATE Fault-Block Mountains

How do fault-block mountains form?

Fault-block mountains form along normal faults as blocks of continental crust are pulled apart. In this activity, you will use wooden blocks to demonstrate the processes that form fault-block mountains.

PROCEDURE

(1) Use the triangular blocks to demonstrate how movements along normal faults form two mountains separated by a valley. Start with the blocks arranged as shown. Move the outer blocks apart to form two mountains separated by a valley. Draw a diagram of your results.

(2) Use the rectangular blocks to demonstrate how a row of tilted fault-block mountains forms along normal faults. (**Hint:** You can tilt the blocks as they move.) Draw a diagram of your results.

WHAT DO YOU THINK?

- How do your diagrams show that fault-block mountains form as the crust is being stretched?

- Along which type of plate boundary would fault-block mountains be most likely to form—divergent, convergent, or transform? Explain.

CHALLENGE Why do fault-block mountains not form at strike-slip faults?

SKILL FOCUS
Modeling

MATERIALS
- 3 triangular blocks
- 3 rectangular blocks

TIME
15 minutes

1 An area of the lithosphere can arch upward when, for example, it is heated by material rising in the mantle beneath it. As the crust stretches, it breaks into many blocks separated by faults.

2 As the lithosphere is pulled apart, some blocks tilt. The edges of the blocks that tilt upward form mountains, and the edges that tilt downward form valleys. Other blocks drop down between faults, forming valleys. The edges of the blocks next to blocks that drop down are left standing high above the valleys as mountains.

Fault-block mountains form as stress repeatedly builds up in the crust and then is released during earthquakes. Even the most powerful earthquakes can move blocks of rock only a few meters up or down at one time. Fault-block mountains can be kilometers high. Millions of years and countless earthquakes are needed for them to form.

 CHECK YOUR READING Describe two ways that blocks of rock can move along faults and form mountains.

Fault-Block Mountains

Fault-block mountains form as the crust stretches and breaks into blocks that move along faults.

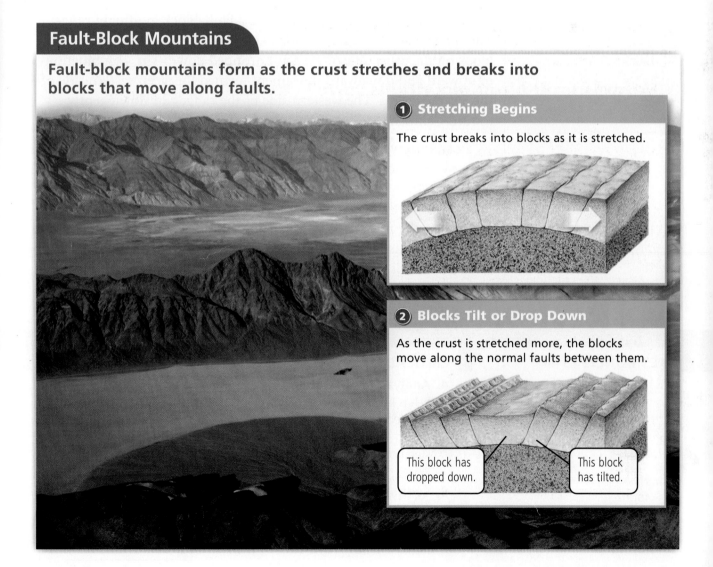

1 Stretching Begins

The crust breaks into blocks as it is stretched.

2 Blocks Tilt or Drop Down

As the crust is stretched more, the blocks move along the normal faults between them.

This block has dropped down.

This block has tilted.

The Sierra Nevada moved up along one side of the fault.

Approximate location of fault

The land on the other side of the fault dropped down.

The Sierra Nevada in California is a fault-block mountain range. The range moved up along a normal fault along its eastern edge. The block on the other side of the fault dropped down. This combination of upward and downward movement formed the steep eastern side of the Sierra Nevada. The western side of the range tilts down gently toward California's Central Valley.

In summary, both folded mountains and fault-block mountains form over millions of years. Folded mountains are pushed up by slow, continual stress that causes rock to gradually bend. Fault-block mountains form, earthquake by earthquake, as stress built up in the crust is released by the movement of rock. Folded mountains form where continental crust is being compressed, and fault-block mountains form where it is being stretched.

3.1 Review

KEY CONCEPTS

1. How is the formation of mountain belts related to tectonic plate boundaries?

2. How do folded mountains form?

3. How do fault-block mountains form?

CRITICAL THINKING

4. **Analyze** The Ural Mountain belt is no longer along the edge of a tectonic plate. Would you expect the Urals to be tall and steep or low and rounded? Why?

5. **Synthesize** How could it be possible for a mountain range to be continually pushed up but not get any higher?

◢ CHALLENGE

6. **Analyze** This graph shows how the heights of two mountains changed as they formed. Which line shows the formation of a folded mountain? a fault-block mountain? Explain.

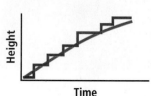

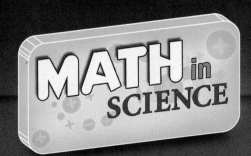

MATH in SCIENCE

 MATH TUTORIAL
CLASSZONE.COM
Click on Math Tutorial
for more help finding
the mean.

Mountain	Height (meters)
McKinley	6194
St. Elias	5489
Foraker	5304
Bona	5029
Blackburn	4996

Mount McKinley, Alaska,
is the tallest mountain in
North America.

**SKILL: CALCULATING THE MEAN
OF A DATA SET**

Comparing Mountain Heights

How do the tallest mountains in the United States compare with the tallest mountains in the world? The table shows the heights of the five tallest mountains in the world. All five are in Asia.

Mountain	Height (meters)
Everest	8850
K2	8611
Kanchenjunga	8586
Lhotse	8516
Makalu	8463

To describe data, you can find their average, or mean. The **mean** of a data set is the sum of the values divided by the number of values.

Example

To find the mean height of the five tallest mountains in the world, first add the heights.

8,850	Then divide by 5, the
8,611	number of mountains.
8,586	$\frac{43,026}{5} = 8605.2$
8,516	
+8,463	Round your result to a
43,026	whole number.

ANSWER The mean height of the five tallest mountains is 8605 meters.

Answer the following questions.

1. The table to the left shows the heights of the five tallest mountains in the United States. All five are in Alaska. Find the mean of the data.

2. What is the difference between the mean height of the three tallest mountains in the world and the mean height of the three tallest mountains in the United States?

3. Suppose Mount Everest were in the United States. What would the mean of the three tallest mountains in the United States then be?

CHALLENGE The mean height of all the land in the United States is 763 meters. Does knowing the mean height help you describe the shape of the land in the United States? Explain why or why not.

KEY CONCEPT

3.2 Volcanoes form as molten rock erupts.

▶ **BEFORE, you learned**

- Magma is molten rock inside Earth
- Magma forms as a plate sinking in a subduction zone starts to melt
- Volcanoes can form over hot spots far from plate boundaries

▶ **NOW, you will learn**

- Where most volcanoes are located
- How volcanoes erupt
- What types of volcanoes there are

VOCABULARY

volcano p. 86
lava p. 87
pyroclastic flow p. 88

EXPLORE Eruptions

What happens when a volcano erupts?

PROCEDURE

① Add water to an empty film canister until it is three-fourths full.

② Drop an antacid tablet in the water and put the lid on the canister. Observe what happens.

WHAT DO YOU THINK?

- What happened to the water and to the canister lid?
- What caused the changes you observed?
- How might the events you observed be similar to the eruption of a volcano?

MATERIALS

- empty film canister
- effervescent antacid tablet
- water

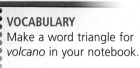

VOCABULARY
Make a word triangle for *volcano* in your notebook.

Volcanoes erupt many types of material.

Earth's thin outer layer is made of cool rock, but most of Earth is made of extremely hot rock and molten metal. Some of the heat inside Earth escapes to the surface through volcanoes. A **volcano** is an opening in Earth's crust through which molten rock, rock fragments, and hot gases erupt. A mountain built up from erupted material is also called a volcano.

A volcano may erupt violently or gently. A violent eruption can cause tremendous destruction even if not much molten rock reaches the surface. For example, a volcano might throw out huge amounts of rock fragments that start fires where they land or fall in thick layers on roofs, causing them to collapse. A volcano can erupt gently yet pour out rivers of molten rock that flow long distances. The violence of an eruption depends mainly on the type of magma feeding the volcano.

Magma

A major portion of all magma is silica, which is a compound of silicon and oxygen. Magma also contains gases, which expand as the magma rises. Magma that is high in silica resists flowing, so expanding gases are trapped in it. Pressure builds up until the gases blast out in a violent, dangerous explosion. Magma that is relatively poor in silica flows easily, so gas bubbles move up through it and escape fairly gently. Though an eruption of silica-poor magma can throw lava high into the air, forming lava fountains, visitors can usually watch safely nearby.

Magma rises toward Earth's surface as long as it is less dense than the surrounding rock. Once magma stops rising, it can collect in areas called magma chambers. Magma can remain in a chamber until it cools, forming igneous rock, or it can erupt. Volcanic eruptions occur when, for example, a chamber is not large enough to hold additional magma that pushes in. When magma erupts, it is called lava. **Lava** is magma that has reached Earth's surface.

CONTENT FRAME
Make a content frame for volcanic materials. Add categories across the top for what they are made of and how they are erupted.

Structure of a Volcano

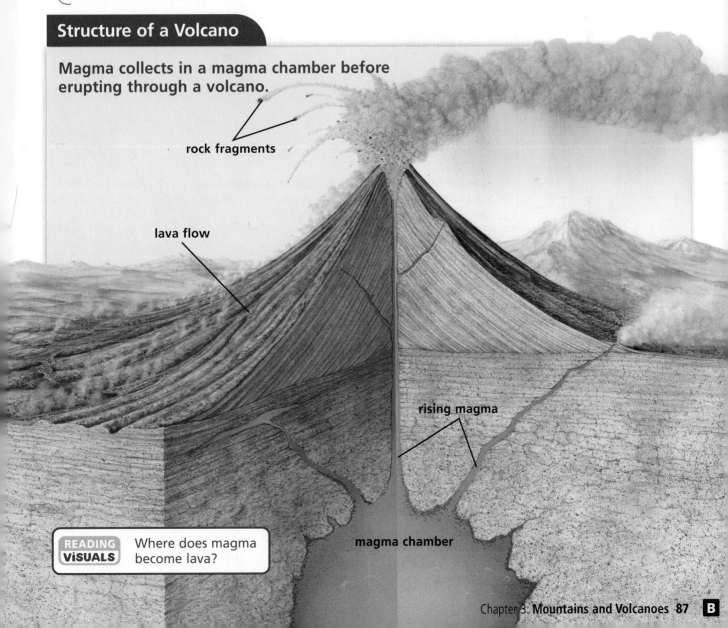

Magma collects in a magma chamber before erupting through a volcano.

rock fragments

lava flow

rising magma

magma chamber

READING VISUALS Where does magma become lava?

Rock Fragments

VISUALIZATION
CLASSZONE.COM

Watch clips of erupted volcanic material.

A great deal of material erupts from volcanoes as rock fragments. The fragments form as

- escaping gas bubbles pop, tearing magma apart
- larger pieces of lava are thrown into the air, cooling and hardening during their flight
- rocks of all sizes rip loose from volcanoes' walls during eruptions

Tiny rock fragments form volcanic ash, which consists of particles ranging from the size of dust to about the size of rice grains. Volcanic cinders are somewhat larger. The largest fragments are volcanic bombs and blocks. Bombs are molten when they are thrown out and often have streamlined shapes. Blocks, which can be the size of houses, erupt as solid pieces of rock. Large rock fragments fall quickly, but ash can be carried long distances by winds—even all the way around Earth.

Volcanic ash is made up of rock fragments less than 2 millimeters in diameter.

Cinders contain holes and tunnels left by escaping gases.

Large fragments are called blocks or bombs.

Volcanic Gases

What looks like smoke rising from a volcano is actually a mixture of ash and gases. The main gases in magma are water vapor and carbon dioxide. Some volcanic gases combine with water in the air to form acids—you will read about these in the next section.

READING TiP

The prefix *pyro-* means "heat," and *clastic* means "made up of rock fragments."

During an eruption, volcanic gases can mix with rock fragments and stay near the ground. The mixture forms a **pyroclastic flow** (PY-roh-KLAS-tihk), which is a dense cloud of superhot gases and rock fragments that races downhill. Such a flow can be as hot as 800°C (1500°F) and can travel faster than 160 kilometers per hour (100 mi/h). Pyroclastic flows are the most dangerous type of volcanic eruption.

CHECK YOUR READING   What are two reasons why pyroclastic flows are dangerous?

Most volcanoes form along plate boundaries.

Volcanoes are common along tectonic plate boundaries where oceanic plates sink beneath other plates. As a plate sinks deep into a subduction zone, it heats and begins to melt, forming magma. If the magma reaches the surface it can build tall volcanic mountains.

Volcanoes are also common along tectonic boundaries where plates pull apart, allowing magma to rise from the mantle. Some of these volcanoes are in Africa's Great Rift Valley. However, much of Earth's volcanic activity takes place underwater. Magma erupts along spreading centers in the ocean and cools to form new lithosphere.

Less commonly, a volcano can form over a hot spot far from a plate boundary. Heat carried by material rising from deep in the mantle melts some of the rock in the lithosphere above it. Eruptions over a hot spot built the Hawaiian Islands.

More than 400 volcanoes—about 80 percent of all active volcanoes above sea level—are along subduction zones in the Pacific Ocean. An active volcano is one that is erupting or has erupted in recorded history. The volcanoes around the Pacific Ocean form a belt called the Ring of Fire. Some of these volcanoes are in the western United States.

Ring of Fire

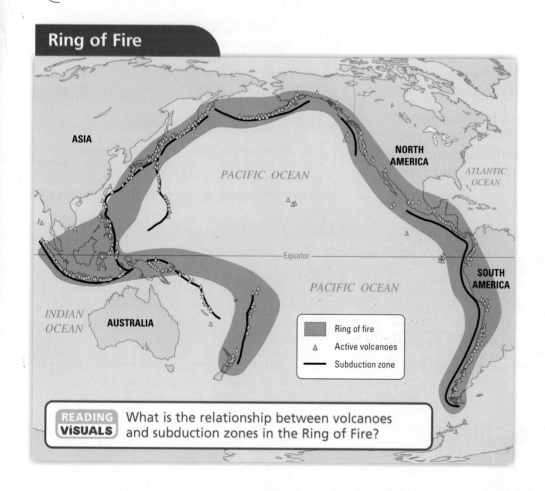

ASIA
NORTH AMERICA
ATLANTIC OCEAN
PACIFIC OCEAN
Equator
SOUTH AMERICA
PACIFIC OCEAN
INDIAN OCEAN
AUSTRALIA

Ring of fire
△ Active volcanoes
— Subduction zone

READING VISUALS What is the relationship between volcanoes and subduction zones in the Ring of Fire?

Volcanoes can have many shapes and sizes.

CONTENT FRAME
Make a content frame for types of volcanoes. Add categories for shape, size, makeup, and examples.

RESOURCE CENTER
CLASSZONE.COM

Learn more about historic and current volcanic eruptions.

Mount St. Helens is a cone-shaped volcano in Washington. Its eruption in 1980 killed 57 people. One side of the volcano exploded, blasting out a mixture of hot rock, ash, and gases that destroyed trees tens of kilometers away. Since 1980, this volcano has had many smaller eruptions.

Volcanoes can have many shapes, including steep cones and nearly flat land. Most volcanoes erupt from openings in bowl-shaped pits called craters. Some volcanoes erupt from long cracks in the ground. The type of magma feeding a volcano determines its shape.

1 **Shield Volcano** A shield volcano is shaped like a broad, flat dome. It is built up by many eruptions of lava that is relatively low in silica and therefore flows easily and spreads out in thin layers. The largest volcano on Earth, Mauna Loa (MOW-nuh LOH-uh), is a shield volcano. It makes up much of the island of Hawaii. The total height of this volcano is about 17 kilometers (10.5 mi), but only about 4 kilometers (2.5 mi) are above sea level. At the top of Mauna Loa is a crater that is 5 kilometers (3 mi) across at its widest point. Mauna Loa is one of Earth's most active volcanoes.

2 **Cinder Cone** A cinder cone is a steep, cone-shaped hill formed by the eruption of cinders and other rock fragments that pile up around

Three Types of Volcanoes

Two types of material form volcanoes: rock fragments that fall close to the openings they erupted from and lava flows that have cooled and hardened.

1 **Shield Volcano**

A shield volcano is built up of many thin layers of hardened lava. Rangitoto, a shield volcano in New Zealand, is broad and has gently sloping sides.

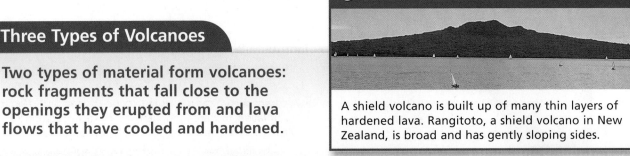

shield volcano

a single crater. Cinders form as gas-rich magma erupts. Escaping gases throw small chunks of lava into the air, where they harden before landing. Cinder cones are tens to hundreds of meters tall. Many of them form on the sides of other types of volcanoes.

❸ Composite Volcano A composite volcano is a cone-shaped volcano built up of layers of lava and layers of rock fragments. Its magma is high in silica, and therefore is pasty. A composite volcano is steep near the top and flattens out toward the bottom. Because hardened lava flows add strength to the structure of a composite volcano, it can grow much larger than a cinder cone.

Composite volcanoes have violent eruptions for two reasons. First, expanding gases trapped in rising magma tend to cause explosions. Second, hardened lava from earlier eruptions often plugs openings in these volcanoes. This rock must be blown out of the way before any more magma can escape. Mount St. Helens is a composite volcano. Though its 1980 eruption was devastating, many composite volcanoes have exploded with much greater power.

READING TiP

The word *composite* comes from a Latin word meaning "put together." Something that is composite is made of distinct parts.

⬤ CHECK YOUR READING
List the three main types of volcanoes. What questions do you have about how they form?

② **Cinder Cone**

A cinder cone, like this one in Arizona, has steep sides and is a loose pile of volcanic rock fragments.

③ **Composite Volcano**

A composite volcano is usually cone-shaped and is built up of layers of hardened lava and of rock fragments. Mount St. Helens is a typical composite volcano.

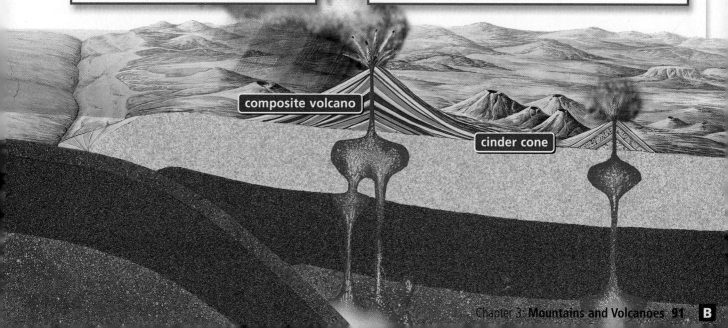

composite volcano

cinder cone

Formation of Crater Lake

Crater Lake fills the caldera of a composite volcano.

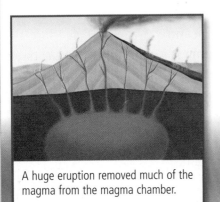

A huge eruption removed much of the magma from the magma chamber.

The volcano collapsed, creating a caldera 8 kilometers in diameter and 1.6 kilometers deep.

New eruptions built a small cone in the caldera. The caldera filled with water from rain and snow.

Both shield volcanoes and composite volcanoes can form features called calderas (kal-DAIR-uhz). A caldera is a huge crater formed by the collapse of a volcano when magma rapidly erupts from underneath it. The crater at the top of Mauna Loa in Hawaii is a caldera. Crater Lake in Oregon fills a caldera formed by a composite volcano about 7700 years ago. A violent eruption emptied much of its magma chamber, and the top of the volcano collapsed into it. The caldera now holds the deepest lake in the United States.

Scientists monitor volcanoes.

CONTENT FRAME
Make a content frame for types of data used to predict eruptions. Include categories for current activity and history.

Before Mount Pinatubo (PIHN-uh-TOO-boh) in the Philippines erupted in 1991, most people living in the area did not realize that it was a composite volcano. It had not erupted in about 500 years, and erosion had changed its shape. Fortunately, scientists in the Philippines knew that the volcano was becoming active months before it exploded. They were able to warn the government and ask people to leave the area. Their efforts probably saved tens of thousands of lives.

As the 1991 eruption of Mount Pinatubo shows, volcanoes can go hundreds of years between eruptions. Before Pinatubo's eruption, scientists noticed warning signs that included the occurrence of many small earthquakes followed by explosions of steam near the volcano's top. Researchers brought in equipment to monitor the volcano's activity. Although they could not stop the eruption, they were able to tell when people should leave.

Scientists monitor volcanoes around the world for signs of eruptions. Indications that magma is moving underneath a volcano include earthquake activity and changes in the tilt of the ground. Scientists also monitor the temperatures at openings, springs, and lakes on volcanoes, as well as the amounts and types of gases given off by the volcanoes. Rising temperatures and changes in volcanic gases can indicate that fresh magma has moved into a shallow magma chamber.

Scientists study the ages and types of volcanic rocks around a volcano to understand the volcano's history, including how much time has passed between eruptions and how violent the eruptions have been. This information gives clues about possible future eruptions.

Even with close monitoring, most property damage from volcanic eruptions cannot be prevented. But warning people to move away from a volcano that is about to erupt can save lives. Many of the active volcanoes that are closely monitored are located near major cities. Among these are Mount Rainier (ruh-NEER), which is near Seattle, Washington, and Mount Vesuvius (vih-SOO-vee-uhs), which is near Naples (NAY-puhlz), Italy.

The robot Dante II is about to enter the crater of Mt. Spurr, Alaska, where it will collect video data as well as water and gas samples.

CHECK YOUR READING What is the purpose of monitoring volcanoes?

3.2 Review

KEY CONCEPTS

1. Where are most volcanoes located, and why are they located there?

2. How does the type of material that erupts from a volcano determine the shape of the volcano?

3. What conditions do scientists examine when they monitor volcanoes?

CRITICAL THINKING

4. **Compare and Contrast** How do the three main types of volcanoes differ?

5. **Infer** Volcanic ash can be deposited in areas many kilometers away from the volcano that produced it. What are two ways in which the ash can reach these areas?

CHALLENGE

6. **Analyze** Draw diagrams showing how a composite volcano might change in shape by getting larger or smaller with repeated eruptions.

CHAPTER INVESTIGATION

Make Your Own Volcanoes

OVERVIEW AND PURPOSE Scientists who have never been to a particular volcano can estimate how steep a climb it would be to its top. All they need to know is what type of volcano it is. Volcanoes vary not only in size but also in slope, or the steepness of their sides. The three main types of volcanoes—cinder cones, shield volcanoes, and composite volcanoes—are very different in size and shape. In this activity you will
- make models of volcanoes and measure their slopes
- determine how the types of materials that form a volcano affect how steep it can get

▶ Problem

What does a volcano's slope reveal about the materials that formed it?

▶ Hypothesize

Write a hypothesis to explain how a volcano's slope is related to the materials it is made of. Your hypothesis should take the form of an "If . . . , then . . . , because . . ." statement.

▶ Procedure

MATERIALS
- 375 mL plaster of Paris
- 180 mL water
- 500 mL gravel
- 3 cardboard pieces
- two 250 mL paper cups
- stirrer
- ruler
- protractor

1. Make a data table like the one shown in the sample notebook on page 95.

2. Mix 125 mL of plaster of Paris with 60 mL of water in a paper cup. Stir the mixture well. Work quickly with the mixture, because it will harden quickly.

3. Pour the mixture onto a piece of cardboard from a height of 2–3 cm. Write "cone A" on the cardboard and set it aside.

step 3

4. Fill another paper cup with gravel. Slowly pour the gravel onto a second piece of cardboard from a height of about 10 cm. Label this model "cone B" and set it aside.

5 In a cup, mix the rest of the plaster of Paris with the rest of the water. Fill the other paper cup with gravel. Pour a small amount of the plaster mixture onto the third piece of cardboard, then pour some gravel on top. Repeat until all the plaster mixture and gravel have been used. Label this model "cone C" and set it aside until the plaster in both cone A and cone C has hardened (about 20 min).

▶ Observe and Analyze
Write It Up

1. **MEASURE** Use the protractor to measure the approximate slope of each cone.

2. **RECORD** Complete your data table.

3. **OBSERVE** Compare the appearances of the cone. Record your observations in your **Science Notebook**.

4. **COMPARE** How different are the slopes of the cones?

▶ Conclude
Write It Up

1. **CONNECT** Which volcanic materials do the plaster mixture and the gravel represent?

2. **IDENTIFY VARIABLES** What is the relationship between the cones' slopes and the materials they are made of?

3. **ANALYZE** Compare your results with your hypothesis. Do your data support your hypothesis?

4. **INTERPRET** Which type of volcano does each model represent?

5. **DRAW CONCLUSIONS** Which of your models represents a volcano that cannot grow as large as the others? Explain.

6. **APPLY** What factors might cause the slopes of real volcanoes to be different from those of your models?

7. **APPLY** If you were a scientist, what information, in addition to slope, might you need in order to determine a volcano's type?

8. **APPLY** How could the method you used to make a model of a cinder cone be used to show how the slope of a hill or mountain contributes to a landslide?

▶ INVESTIGATE Further

CHALLENGE Calculate the slopes of your models using the formula $y = mx + b$. In this formula, y and x are graph coordinates of a point on a straight line. The slope of the line is m. The intersection of the line with the y-axis of the graph is b. For example, if the height of a model is 1.6 cm, and the distance from its edge to its center is 4 cm, then the equation becomes $1.6 = m4 + 0$.
The slope is $\frac{1.6}{4}$, or 0.4.

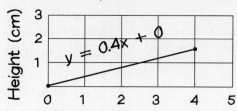

Distance from edge to center (cm)

Make Your Own Volcanoes

Table 1. Volcano Model and Slope

Cone	Drawing of Cone	Slope (degrees)
A.		
B.		
C.		

3.3 Volcanoes affect Earth's land, air, and water.

 BEFORE, you learned

- Rock fragments, lava, and gases erupt from volcanoes
- Some volcanoes have explosive eruptions

 NOW, you will learn

- How volcanic eruptions affect Earth's surface
- How volcanic gases affect the atmosphere
- How volcanic activity affects water

VOCABULARY

acid rain p. 100
geyser p. 101

THINK ABOUT

Which volcano is more dangerous?

Mauna Loa is a shield volcano that forms a large part of the island of Hawaii. It is one of the most active volcanoes on Earth, frequently producing large amounts of lava that flow long distances. Mount Shasta is a composite volcano in California. It has erupted at least once every 600 to 800 years for the past 10,000 years. Mount Shasta can erupt with devastating violence. Which volcano do you think it is more dangerous to live near. Why?

Mauna Loa

Mount Shasta

CONTENT FRAME
Add a content frame for how eruptions affect Earth's land and air. Include categories for what dangers are caused and how long the dangers last.

Volcanic eruptions affect the land.

A volcanic eruption can knock down forests and clog rivers with volcanic ash. Damage can occur far from the volcano. But volcanoes build as well as destroy. Material erupted from volcanoes can form new land. Over time, lava flows can form new, rich soil.

Many towns and cities are located close to volcanoes. The people of Goma in the eastern Democratic Republic of the Congo experienced an eruption of a nearby volcano in 2002. A lava flow cut the city in half and destroyed the homes of tens of thousands of people, either by flowing into the homes or by starting fires. Hilo (HEE-loh), the largest city on the island of Hawaii, is built in part on young lava flows. The city is at high risk from future volcanic activity.

Immediate Effects

The effects of a volcanic eruption largely depend on how much material and what types of material the volcano ejects. Near a volcano, lava flows can cover the land with new rock. A much larger area can be affected by events such as ash falls, landslides, mudflows, pyroclastic flows, and steam explosions.

Lava Flows Most lava moves slowly enough that people can move away and not be hurt. But even a slow-moving lava flow will knock down, cover, or burn nearly everything in its path.

Volcanic Ash Near a volcanic eruption, the weight of fallen volcanic ash can cause the roofs of buildings to collapse. Volcanic ash is heavy because it is made of tiny pieces of rock. Ash makes roads slippery, and it clogs up machinery, including cars and airplanes. Large amounts of falling ash can suffocate plants, animals, and people.

Mudflows Mudflows are landslides that occur when loose rocks and soil are mixed with water. Heat from an eruption melts any ice and snow on the volcano very quickly. Mudflows form as the water mixes with volcanic ash and other loose particles. Mudflows also form as ash mixes into rivers flowing from a volcano. Fast-moving mudflows have buried entire towns tens of kilometers from an eruption.

Pyroclastic flows As a pyroclastic flow rushes downhill, it can knock down or burn everything in its way. Pyroclastic flows tend to follow valleys. However, a particularly fast-moving flow can sweep up and over hills, then race down a neighboring valley. As a flow passes, it can leave a thick layer of volcanic rock fragments. Pyroclastic flows are extremely dangerous. In 1902, a pyroclastic flow from an eruption in the West Indies completely destroyed the city of Saint Pierre (SAYNT PEER). Almost 30,000 people were killed within a few minutes.

Landslides Part of a volcano can collapse and start a landslide— a rapid downhill movement of rock and soil. The collapse may be caused by magma moving underground, an eruption, an earthquake, or even heavy rainfall. A landslide can cause a tsunami if a large amount of material falls into the ocean.

Lava Flow

Trees catch fire as a lava flow moves through a forest in Hawaii in 1999.

Volcanic Ash

Large piles of volcanic ash from the 1991 eruption of Mt. Pinatubo line a street in Olongapo, Philippines, at the start of the cleanup effort.

 REMINDER

A tsunami is a water wave caused by an earthquake, a volcanic eruption, or a landslide.

RESOURCE CENTER
CLASSZONE.COM

Find out more about
the effects of volcanic
eruptions.

Steam Explosions Though relatively uncommon, steam explosions can be devastating. They occur when magma comes near water or into contact with it. A steam explosion may have caused the destruction of a volcanic island in Indonesia. The entire island of Krakatau (KRACK-uh-TOW) exploded in 1883, causing a tsunami that destroyed hundreds of towns and killed more than 36,000 people.

 What are two ways a volcanic eruption can result in damage to areas hundreds of kilometers away?

Long-term Effects

Volcanic eruptions can be tremendously destructive. But even after an eruption ends, a volcano can remain dangerous for many years.

The explosive eruption of Mount Pinatubo in 1991 threw out huge amounts of volcanic ash and rock fragments. The area the volcano is in gets heavy rains each year. Mudflows have formed as large amounts of rainwater mixed with ash and other loose material on the sides of the volcano. Since the eruption, mudflows have destroyed the homes of more than 100,000 people.

This school bus was partly buried by a mudflow from Mount St. Helens. No one was in the bus when the mudflow hit.

Another possible source of water for mudflows was a lake that began filling the volcano's crater. The upper part of the crater is weak, and the lake level was rising. A collapse of the crater could have emptied the lake of much of its water. In 2001, people dug a channel to lower the level of the lake, greatly decreasing the chance of a collapse.

 Why can volcanic ash be dangerous for years after an eruption?

Even though volcanoes are dangerous, over time they can have positive effects. When a lava flow cools, it forms a layer of hard rock on which no plants can grow. However, over many years, this rock can break down to form rich soil. Volcanic ash can smother plants, but the tiny pieces of rock break down quickly and make soil richer. Highly productive farmland surrounds some active volcanoes.

Over time, repeated volcanic eruptions can build a magnificent landscape of mountains and valleys. People may choose to live in a volcanic area in part for its natural beauty. Many other people may visit the area, supporting a tourist industry.

How does the shape of the land affect mudflows?

PROCEDURE

① Look at the map of Mount Rainier mudflows. Observe the relationship between the paths of rivers and the paths of the mudflows.

② Write the number of towns shown within the boundaries of mudflow areas.

③ Write the differences in elevation between the following locations: the top of Mount Rainier and the point where the West Fork joins the White River, the point where the rivers join and the town of Buckley, and the towns of Buckley and Auburn. Where is the land steepest?

④ On the back of the paper, explain why in some areas mudflows have followed rivers and in other areas mudflows have spread out.

WHAT DO YOU THINK?

- What three factors are most important in causing mudflows to start near the top of Mount Rainier and flow long distances?
- How likely are future mudflows to follow the same paths as earlier mudflows?

CHALLENGE The largest mudflow starting on Mount Rainier moved at about 22 kilometers per hour (14 mi/h) and covered the land to an average depth of 6 meters (20 ft). Describe the steps you would take to protect people from a similar mudflow in the same area.

MATERIAL
Map of Mount Rainier Mudflows

TIME
25 minutes

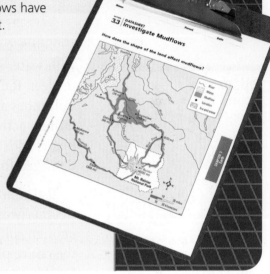

Volcanic gases and ash affect the air.

If you visit a volcano, you might notice some unpleasant odors. These odors come from gases released into the air from magma. Some of these gases contain the element sulfur. Hydrogen sulfide gas smells like rotten eggs. Sulfur dioxide gas is what you smell when you strike a match. The volcano might also be releasing carbon dioxide, a gas you would not notice because it has no color or odor. Volcanoes release gases before, during, and after eruptions.

Many gases from volcanoes are dangerous. They can make breathing difficult and damage the lungs of people and animals. Carbon dioxide can be fatal. In West Africa, a sudden release of carbon dioxide killed 1700 people in 1986. The gas came from a volcano at the bottom of a lake. Carbon dioxide built up in the water until a large amount escaped at once. Pipes are now being used to release carbon dioxide from the bottom of the lake so that the gas will not build up again.

READING **TiP**

An element is a substance that contains only one type of atom.

A cloud of hot gases and ash rises high into the atmosphere during an eruption of Mount Etna in Italy.

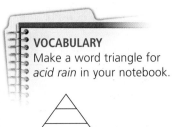

VOCABULARY
Make a word triangle for *acid rain* in your notebook.

Some gases, such as sulfur dioxide, form acids when they mix with water in the air. These acids fall to Earth's surface in rain, snow, or sleet. Rain that contains large amounts of acid is called **acid rain.** Volcanoes are sources of acid-forming gases, but a bigger source is human activity. For example, the burning of coal in electrical power plants adds acid-forming gases to the air. In some areas, acid rain has damaged forests and killed fish in lakes.

Large amounts of volcanic gases in the atmosphere can change weather worldwide. The 1991 eruption of Mount Pinatubo released enough sulfur dioxide to form a haze high in the atmosphere around the entire planet. The haze decreased the amount of sunlight reaching Earth's surface and lowered average world temperatures in 1992 and 1993.

Volcanic gases can lift ash high above an erupting volcano. Winds can then carry the ash far away. During the May 1980 eruption of Mount St. Helens, ash falling 400 kilometers (250 mi) away in Spokane, Washington, blocked so much sunlight that nighttime street-lights were turned on during the day. The smallest ash particles can remain in the air for years, circling Earth many times. These particles also reflect sunlight and can lower Earth's temperature.

CHECK YOUR READING   Describe two ways sulfur dioxide can affect the atmosphere.

Volcanic activity affects water.

Yellowstone National Park in the western United States is famous for its hot springs—places where heated water flows to Earth's surface. Yellowstone is a volcanic region, and its hot springs sit in a huge caldera. The springs' heat comes from a hot spot under the North American Plate.

Geysers

Rainwater can sink through cracks in rock. If it is heated within Earth, it can rise to form hot springs and geysers.

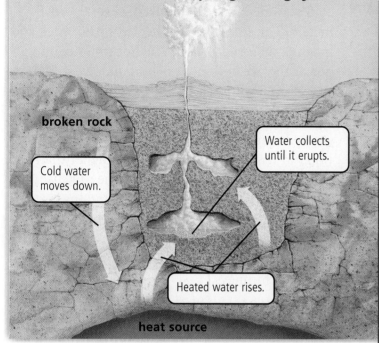

broken rock

Cold water moves down.

Water collects until it erupts.

Heated water rises.

heat source

Old Faithful geyser in Yellowstone National Park erupts more often than any other large geyser. Heated water is forced up into the air through a narrow channel.

Hot Springs, Geysers, and Fumaroles

Most hot springs are in areas where magma or hot rock is near Earth's surface. Water moves down through the ground, gets heated, and rises at a hot spring. At most hot springs, the water flows out into a calm pool. But at a type of hot spring called a **geyser,** water shoots into the air. A geyser forms where water collects in an underground chamber, then erupts through a narrow channel. Old Faithful, a geyser in Yellowstone National Park, erupts every 35 minutes to 2 hours. Most geysers erupt less predictably.

In addition to the United States, countries with many hot springs and geysers include New Zealand and Iceland. Beneath Iceland, which sits on an ocean spreading center, is magma that rises as plates pull apart. People in Iceland use hot underground water as an energy source to heat their capital city, Reykjavík (RAY-kyuh-VEEK).

A feature known as a fumarole (FYOO-muh-ROHL) is similar to a hot spring. Instead of liquid water, though, a fumarole releases steam and other gases. Changes in hot springs and fumaroles located on the sides of a volcano can show that the volcano is becoming more active. As magma moves close to the surface, water temperatures get higher, and fumaroles can release more or different gases.

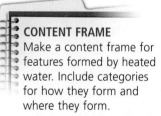

CONTENT FRAME
Make a content frame for features formed by heated water. Include categories for how they form and where they form.

Why might fumaroles and hot springs be monitored?

Deep-Sea Vents

Deep-sea vents are hot springs that form at spreading centers in the ocean. In these places, the ocean floor has many cracks through which cold seawater sinks to depths of several kilometers. The sea water gets heated by hot rock and magma, then rises again. The hot water coming out of the ocean floor is rich in dissolved minerals and gases from the rock and magma.

At some deep-sea vents, warm water flows gently from cracks in the ocean floor. At others, water at temperatures that can be higher than 350°C (660°F) shoots out of chimney-like vents. The water looks black because it contains large amounts of dissolved minerals. As the hot water mixes with cold water, dissolved minerals form into solid minerals again, building up the vent chimneys.

This deep-sea vent is more than 3 kilometers (2 mi) below the surface of the Atlantic Ocean. A black cloud of mineral-rich water rises from the vent.

Deep-sea vents support such unusual life forms as blind crabs and tubeworms that measure up to 3 meters (10 ft) long. These animals feed on one-celled organisms that get their energy from chemicals in the vent water. Unlike other one-celled organisms, these organisms do not need sunlight to make their food.

 CHECK YOUR READING Why do chimneys form around some deep-sea vents?

 Review

KEY CONCEPTS

1. Describe how a heavy ash fall from a volcanic eruption can affect Earth's surface.

2. Describe how large amounts of volcanic gases can affect weather around Earth.

3. Why do hot springs occur in volcanic areas?

CRITICAL THINKING

4. **Compare and Contrast** What do geysers and deep-sea vents that form chimneys have in common? How are they different?

5. **Evaluate** Which is more dangerous, a pyroclastic flow or a mudflow? Explain.

○ CHALLENGE

6. **Analyze** Ice in Greenland and Antarctica contains layers of ash from eruptions that occurred many thousands of years ago. How do you think the ash reached the ice, and why is it preserved?

PARK RANGER

Rangers at Yellowstone

Rangers at Yellowstone National Park help monitor volcanic activity. The hot spot that is now under Yellowstone has powered some of the largest volcanic eruptions on Earth. The amount of volcanic ash and lava produced by Yellowstone's three giant eruptions could fill the Grand Canyon. The last giant eruption occurred 640,000 years ago. At least 30 smaller eruptions have occurred since. Most of Yellowstone's hot springs and geysers sit in the caldera produced by the last giant eruption.

Beware Volcanic Gases

Park rangers must be aware of the effects of volcanic gases given off by hot springs. Here, volcanic gases are bubbling up through mud. Carbon dioxide, a common volcanic gas, is heavier than air. It sinks and fills low areas. Rangers sometimes find the body of a small animal that entered a shallow cave and died for lack of oxygen.

On Thin Ground

It is dangerous to walk up to the edge of Yellowstone's springs, some of which contain scalding hot water. The ground might be a layer of rock too thin to support a person's weight. Park rangers make sure visitors know to stay on safe walkways, and they inform the public about the science of hot springs.

Tracking Yellowstone's Temperature

Park rangers measure the temperatures of hot springs every month. Increases in temperatures or in hot-spring and geyser activity might indicate increasing volcanic activity.

EXPLORE

1. **ANALYZE** Why do you think Yellowstone is sometimes called a supervolcano? What do you think the characteristics of supervolcanoes might be?
2. **CHALLENGE** A geyser's activity often changes after an earthquake. Draw diagrams showing how changes to a geyser's underground system could cause its water to shoot higher when it erupts.

Chapter Review

the **BIG** idea

Mountains and volcanoes form as tectonic plates move.

CONTENT REVIEW
CLASSZONE.COM

KEY CONCEPTS SUMMARY

3.1 Movement of rock builds mountains.

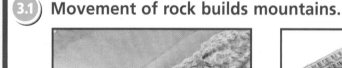

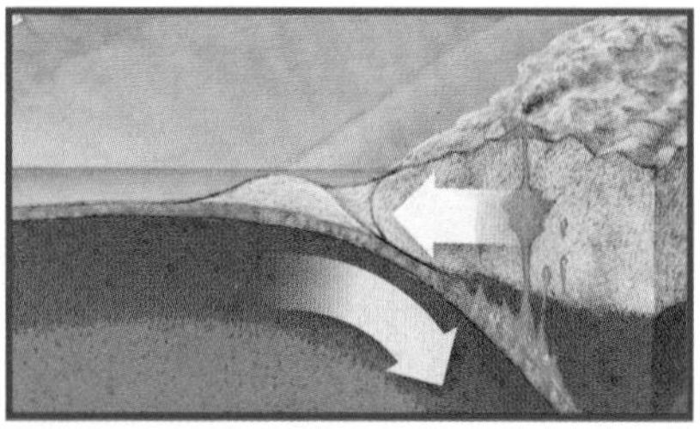

Folded mountains form as plates push together.

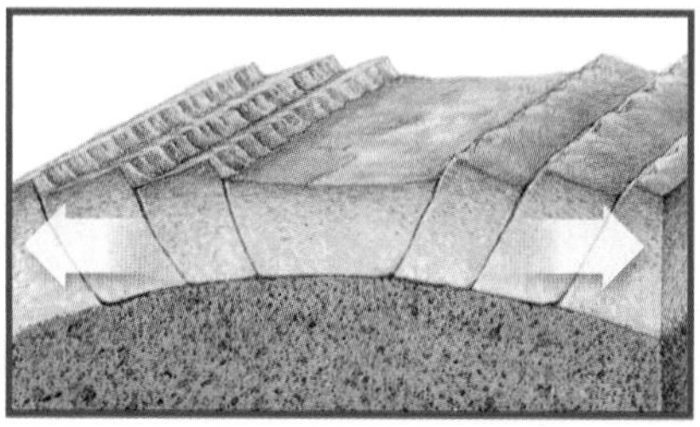

Fault-block mountains form as the lithosphere is stretched.

VOCABULARY
folded mountain p. 80
fault-block mountain
  p. 82

3.2 Volcanoes form as molten rock erupts.

Volcanoes erupt molten rock, rock fragments, and gases. Different types of erupted materials build up different types of volcanoes.

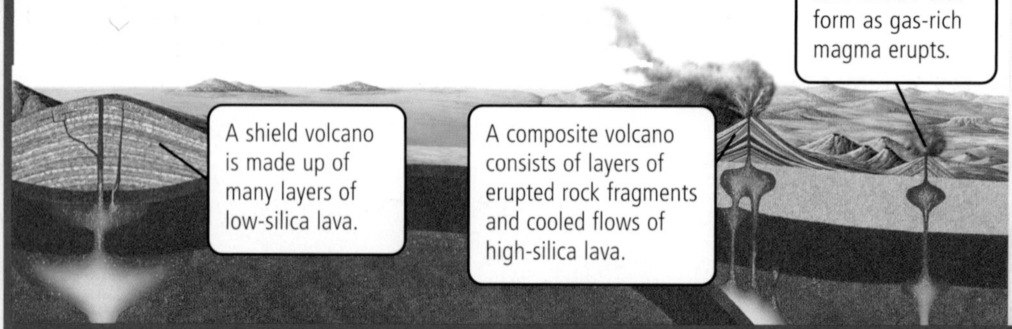

A cinder cone is made up of loose rock fragments and cinders that form as gas-rich magma erupts.

A shield volcano is made up of many layers of low-silica lava.

A composite volcano consists of layers of erupted rock fragments and cooled flows of high-silica lava.

VOCABULARY
volcano p. 86
lava p. 87
pyroclastic flow p. 88

3.3 Volcanoes affect Earth's land, air, and water.

Materials erupted from volcanoes, as well as heat from molten rock underground, affect Earth's surface.

Land	Air	Water
• lava	• poisonous gases	• hot springs
• volcanic ash	• adds to acid rain	• geysers
• landslides	• haze	• fumaroles
• mudflows	• lower temperatures	• deep-sea vents
• pyroclastic flows		

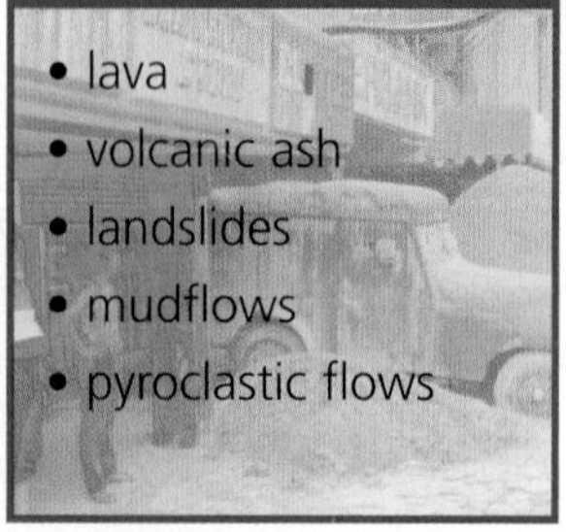

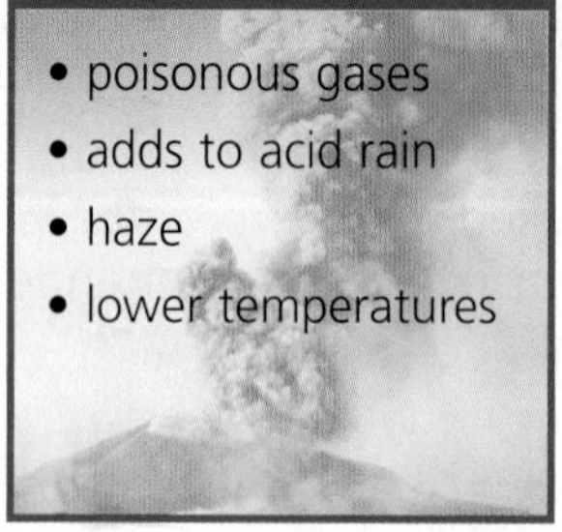

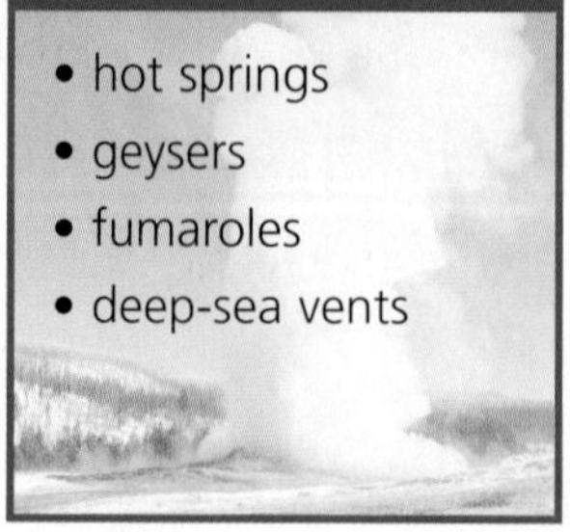

VOCABULARY
acid rain p. 100
geyser p. 101

Reviewing Vocabulary

Draw a Venn diagram to compare and contrast each pair of features. Example:

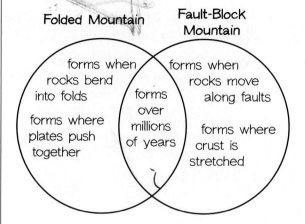

Folded Mountain / Fault-Block Mountain

forms when rocks bend into folds

forms where plates push together

forms over millions of years

forms when rocks move along faults

forms where crust is stretched

1. folded mountain, volcano

2. lava, pyroclastic flow

3. volcano, geyser

Reviewing Key Concepts

Multiple Choice *Choose the letter of the best answer.*

4. In areas where the lithosphere is being pulled apart, the crust
   a. folds and crumples into mountains
   b. breaks into blocks separated by faults
   c. slides down into the mantle
   d. develops a subduction zone

5. When two plates carrying continental crust collide, the rock of the continents
   a. folds   **c.** expands
   b. melts   **d.** stretches

6. The movement of huge blocks of rock along a fault can produce
   a. lava plugs   **c.** fault-block mountains
   b. volcanoes   **d.** folded mountains

7. Volcanoes in the Ring of Fire are supplied with magma rising from
   a. spreading centers   **c.** rift valleys
   b. hot spots   **d.** subduction zones

8. Before magma erupts it collects under a volcano in a
   a. chamber   **c.** crater
   b. caldera   **d.** vent

9. The explosiveness of a volcanic eruption depends mostly on the _____ of the magma.
   a. gas content   **c.** amount
   b. silica content   **d.** temperature

10. The type of magma erupting from a volcano determines the volcano's
   a. size   **c.** shape
   b. age   **d.** location

11. Volcanic ash can be carried thousands of kilometers from an eruption by
   a. lava flows   **c.** landslides
   b. pyroclastic flows   **d.** winds

12. In a volcanic region, water moving through the ground gets _____ by magma or hot rock.
   a. melted   **c.** erupted
   b. dissolved   **d.** heated

Short Answer *Write a short answer to each question.*

13. Describe how an old mountain belt located in the center of a continent most likely formed.

14. How are the locations of volcanoes related to tectonic plate boundaries?

15. What causes a shield volcano to be shaped like a broad dome?

16. By what processes can a volcanic eruption affect temperatures around the world?

Thinking Critically

This photograph shows a volcanic eruption. The volcano produces rivers of lava that flow long distances. Use the photograph to answer the next six questions.

17. INFER What kind of volcano is shown in the photograph? How do you know?

18. APPLY Is this eruption likely to produce large amounts of ash that could lead to dangerous mudflows for many years afterward? Why or why not?

19. IDENTIFY EFFECTS How might volcanic gases affect the health of people and animals living near the volcano?

20. ANALYZE What would be likely to happen if a large amount of water reached the volcano's magma chamber?

21. COMPARE AND CONTRAST How could this volcano affect nearby farmland during the eruption? many years after the eruption?

22. SYNTHESIZE What types of changes would let scientists monitoring the volcano know that an eruption was likely to occur?

23. COMPARE AND CONTRAST How does the stress on continental crust in areas where folded mountains form differ from that in areas where fault-block mountains form?

24. APPLY Draw a diagram showing how one magma chamber can supply magma to a shield volcano and to a cinder cone on the side of the shield volcano.

25. INFER Many of the volcanoes in the Ring of Fire erupt explosively. Would you expect these volcanoes to be cinder cones, shield volcanoes, or composite volcanoes? Explain your answer.

26. PREDICT How might an area with many hot springs and geysers be affected as magma and hot rock near the surface cooled?

27. ANALYZE Why do volcanoes form along boundaries where oceanic plates are pushing into other plates but not along boundaries where continents are pushing together?

28. APPLY Explain why shield volcanoes, composite volcanoes, and cinder cones have different sizes and shapes.

the BIG idea

29. INFER How would you expect tectonic plates to be moving at a plate boundary where folded mountains are being pushed up and volcanoes are erupting?

30. PREDICT If tectonic plates continue to move as they are moving today, the continents of Australia and Antarctica will collide in the far future. What will happen after the sea floor that is now between the continents is destroyed?

UNIT PROJECTS

Check your schedule for your unit project. How are you doing? Be sure that you have placed data or notes from your research in your project folder.

Analyzing Data

The graph below shows the amounts of lava, rock, and other materials released in four large volcanic eruptions. Study the graph, then answer the questions below.

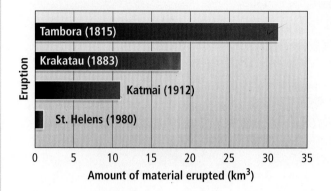

Eruption

Tambora (1815)

Krakatau (1883)

Katmai (1912)

St. Helens (1980)

0   5   10   15   20   25   30   35

Amount of material erupted (km³)

1. How much material did the eruption of Katmai release in 1912?

   a. 12 km³
   b. 17 km³
   c. 29 km³
   d. 41 km³

2. After 1850, which of these eruptions released the greatest amount of material?

   a. Krakatau
   b. Tambora
   c. Katmai
   d. St. Helens

3. About how much more material erupted from Krakatau in 1883 than from Katmai in 1912?

   a. 28 km³
   b. 12 km³
   c. 6 km³
   d. 2 km³

4. Katmai, a large mountain built of layers of hardened lava flows and of rock fragments, is a

   a. cinder cone
   b. shield volcano
   c. pyroclastic cone
   d. composite volcano

5. How much material did the 1815 eruption of Tambora produce compared with the 1883 eruption of Krakatau?

   a. less than one-half the amount
   b. a nearly equal amount
   c. almost two times the amount
   d. almost four times the amount

6. All of the eruptions shown in the graph created calderas—craters formed by the collapse of volcanoes—because the eruptions were large enough to

   a. mostly empty the volcanoes' magma chambers
   b. produce lava that flowed long distances
   c. produce lava that had a low silica content
   d. form dangerous pyroclastic flows and mudflows

7. The average temperature of Earth can decrease for several years when a huge volcanic eruption adds to the atmosphere large amounts of

   a. acid rain
   b. energy
   c. volcanic cinders
   d. volcanic gases

8. A thick layer of volcanic ash can be heavy enough to collapse the roofs of buildings because ash

   a. is produced as rocks burn
   b. is made up of tiny pieces of rock
   c. becomes heavier as it cools
   d. can hold large amounts of water

Extended Response

Answer the two questions below in detail. Include some of the terms shown in the word box. In your answers, underline each term you use.

boundaries	hot spots	rising
subduction	magma	heat
spreading centers		

9. Petra is marking the locations of active volcanoes on a map of the world. Explain how the locations of the volcanoes are related to the locations of tectonic plates.

10. Scientists regularly check the temperature of a lake on a volcano. Explain how this information might help them learn whether the volcano is becoming more active.

CHAPTER 4

Views of Earth's Past

the BIG idea

Rocks, fossils, and other types of natural evidence tell Earth's story.

Key Concepts

SECTION 4.1
Earth's past is revealed in rocks and fossils.
Learn about different kinds of fossils and what they tell about Earth's past.

SECTION 4.2
Rocks provide a timeline for Earth.
Learn how information from rocks tells about Earth's past.

SECTION 4.3
The geologic time scale shows Earth's past.
Learn about 4.6 billion years of Earth's history.

Internet Preview

CLASSZONE.COM

Chapter 4 online resources: Content Review, two Visualizations, three Resource Centers, Math Tutorial, Test Practice

What does this footprint tell you about the animal that left it?

108 Unit: The Changing Earth

How Do You Know What Happened?

Observe an area around your neighborhood to find evidence of a past event. For example, you might see tracks from tires or a stump from a tree. Record your observations.

Observe and Think
What evidence did you find? What does the evidence suggest about the past?

How Long Has That Been There?

Look inside a cabinet or refrigerator and choose one item to investigate. See if you can tell where the item was made, where it was purchased, how long it has been in the cabinet or refrigerator, and when it was last used.

Observe and Think How did you figure out the history of the item?

Internet Activity: Earth's History

Go to **ClassZone.com** to discover how scientists pieced together information to figure out the story of the dinosaurs.

Observe and Think
What kinds of evidence did scientists use?

NSTA scilinks.org
SCiLINKS

Earth's Story **Code: MDL055**

Getting Ready to Learn

◀ CONCEPT REVIEW

- Earth has layers that change over time.
- Movement of rock builds mountains.
- Volcanoes form as molten rock erupts.

◀ VOCABULARY REVIEW

crust p. 11

continental drift p. 15

lava p. 87

CONTENT REVIEW
CLASSZONE.COM
Review concepts and vocabulary.

▶ TAKING NOTES

OUTLINE

As you read, copy the headings on your paper in the form of an outline. Then add notes in your own words that summarize what you read.

CHOOSE YOUR OWN STRATEGY

Take notes about new vocabulary terms, using one or more of the strategies from earlier chapters—**four square, word magnet,** and **word triangle**. Mix and match the strategies, or use an entirely different strategy.

See the Note-Taking Handbook on pages R45–R51.

SCIENCE NOTEBOOK

I. Earth's past is revealed in rocks and fossils.

   A. Rocks, fossils, and original remains give clues about the past.

      1. Original Remains

         a.

         b.

         c.

      2. Fossil Formation

         a.

         b.

         c.

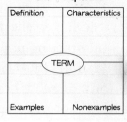

Four Square

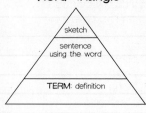

Word Triangle

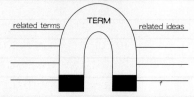

Word Magnet

4.1 Earth's past is revealed in rocks and fossils.

 BEFORE, you learned

- The slow, continuous movement of tectonic plates causes large changes over time
- Molten rock cools to form solid rock

 NOW, you will learn

- How different kinds of fossils show traces of life from Earth's past
- How ice cores and tree rings reveal conditions and changes in the environment

VOCABULARY

fossil p. 111
original remains p. 112
ice core p. 117

EXPLORE Rocks

What can we learn from a rock?

PROCEDURE

1. Use a hand lens to examine the rock sample.
2. Make a sketch of any shapes you see in the rock.

WHAT DO YOU THINK?

- What do you think those shapes are?
- How did they get there?

MATERIALS

- rock sample
- hand lens
- paper and pencil

OUTLINE

Remember to take notes on this section in outline form.

I. Main idea
  A. Supporting idea
    1. Detail
    2. Detail
  B. Supporting idea

Rocks, fossils, and original remains give clues about the past.

You have read about mountain formation, earthquakes, and other ways in which Earth changes over time. Scientists have learned about these changes—even changes that happened long ago—by studying rocks, fossils, and other natural evidence. Two hundred million years ago, for example, huge dinosaurs walked on Earth. These giant reptiles were a major form of animal life on the planet for millions of years. Then, about 65 million years ago, the dinosaurs became extinct, or died out. What happened?

To solve the mystery of why dinosaurs disappeared, scientists look for clues. Fossils, for example, are important clues about past events. **Fossils** are traces or remains of living things from long ago. Dinosaur bones and footprints preserved in stone are examples of fossils.

Using fossils and other natural evidence, scientists have formed a theory about why the dinosaurs disappeared. They now think that some major event, such as the crashing of one or more giant asteroids into Earth, led to rapid changes that caused the dinosaurs to become extinct.

Fossils also tell us about organisms, such as dinosaurs, that are now extinct. Even though no one has ever seen a dinosaur, people have some idea about what dinosaurs looked like and how they behaved because of fossils.

Fossils exist in many different forms. Most fossils are hardened animal remains such as shells, bones, and teeth. Minerals replace the remains, forming a fossil of the hard skeletal body parts. Other fossils are impressions or other evidence of an organism preserved in rock. Sometimes, an actual organism—or part of an organism—can be preserved and become a fossil.

Original Remains

Fossils that are the actual bodies or body parts of organisms are called **original remains.** Usually, soft parts of dead animals and plants decay and disappear. But soft parts can become fossil evidence if they are sealed in a substance that keeps out air and tiny organisms. Original remains are found in places where conditions prevent the decomposition, or breakdown, that normally occurs. Original remains are important because they give direct evidence of forms of life that lived long ago.

1 Ice Ice is one of the best preservers of the remains of prehistoric life. Huge ice fields in Siberia and Alaska contain the bodies of 10,000-year-old mammoths and prehistoric rhinos, with bones, muscle, skin, and even hair still in place. The ice preserved the animals after they died.

2 Amber Another natural substance that preserves the remains of some living things is amber. Amber forms from resin, a sticky substance inside trees that flows like syrup and protects the tree by trapping insects. If the tree gets buried after it dies, the resin can harden into amber. Amber can contain the remains of insects and other small organisms.

3 Tar The original remains of animals have also been found in places where there were pools of tar—a thick, oily liquid. Saber-toothed cats and other animals were trapped in the tar and preserved.

Original Remains

1 Ice

This frozen mammoth body was found in Siberia.

2 Amber

These insects, which are related to flies and mosquitoes, were trapped and preserved in amber 40 million years ago.

3 Tar

This skull of a saber-toothed cat, found in the La Brea Tar Pits in California, was preserved in the tar for 10,000 to 40,000 years.

Fossil Formation

VISUALIZATION
CLASSZONE.COM
Explore how fossils form.

Conditions have to be just right for a fossil to form in rock. The organism or trace of the organism must be preserved before it decomposes or disappears. Usually, the soft parts of an organism decay too quickly to be preserved in rock. For that reason, many rock fossils reveal traces or shapes of only the hard parts of animals or plants. Hard parts, such as shells, bones, teeth, and stems or tree trunks, decompose slowly, so they are more likely to be preserved as fossil evidence. Most organisms that lived in the past died and decomposed without leaving any traces. An organism that has no hard parts, such as a mushroom or a slug, rarely leaves fossil evidence.

Rock fossils form in sedimentary rock. Sedimentary rock forms from layers of sediment, such as sand or mud. Sometimes, the sediment builds up around animal and plant remains, which can leave fossils in the rock. If sedimentary rocks are changed by heat or pressure, their fossils can be destroyed. Igneous rocks never contain fossils. The heat of the molten rock—from which igneous rock cools—destroys any traces of plants or animals.

CHECK YOUR READING Why do rock fossils form in sedimentary rock rather than in igneous rock?

Theropod Fossil

Artist's Drawing of Theropod

CHINA

This 130-million-year-old skeleton of a small theropod dinosaur, found between two slabs of rock in China, contains well-preserved featherlike structures. The fossil is about a meter (3 ft) long.

Fossils in Rocks

If an organism is covered by or buried in sediment, it may become a fossil as the sediments become rock. Many rock fossils are actual body parts, such as bones or teeth, that were buried in sediment and then replaced by minerals and turned to stone.

Some fossils are not original remains or actual body parts that have turned to stone. Instead, these fossils are impressions or traces made of rock and provide indirect evidence that the organisms were there, just as a shoeprint can reveal much about the shoe that made it. Rocks can contain detailed shapes or prints of plants, animals, and even organisms too small to see without a microscope. Fossils in rock include molds and casts, petrified wood, carbon films, and trace fossils.

1 Molds and Casts Some fossils that form in sedimentary rock are mold fossils. A mold is a visible shape that was left after an animal or plant was buried in sediment and then decayed away. In some cases, a hollow mold later becomes filled with minerals, producing a cast fossil. The cast fossil is a solid model in the shape of the organism. If you think of the mold as a shoeprint, the cast would be what would result if sand filled the print and hardened into stone.

2 Petrified Wood The stone fossil of a tree is called petrified wood. In certain conditions, a fallen tree can become covered with sediments. Over time, water passes through the sediments and into the tree's cells. Minerals that are carried in the water take the place of the cells, producing a stone likeness of the tree.

3 Carbon Films Carbon is an element that is found in every living thing. Sometimes when a dead plant or animal decays, its carbon is left behind as a visible layer. This image is called a carbon film. Carbon films can show details of soft parts of animals and plants that are rarely seen in other fossils.

4 Trace Fossils Do you want to know how fast a dinosaur could run? Trace fossils might be able to tell you. These are not parts of an animal or impressions of it, but rather evidence of an animal's presence in a given location. Trace fossils include preserved footprints, trails, animal holes, and even feces. By comparing these clues with what is known about modern animals, scientists can learn how prehistoric animals may have lived, what they ate, and how they behaved. For instance, dinosaur tracks can be studied to learn how fast dinosaurs ran.

RESOURCE CENTER
CLASSZONE.COM
Learn more about fossils.

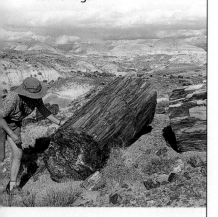

These ancient logs in the Painted Desert Wilderness in Arizona have been preserved as petrified wood for around 225 million years. Minerals replaced the wood to make the stone logs.

CHECK YOUR READING What do carbon film fossils show that trace fossils do not show?

Fossils in Rocks

Rock fossils show shapes and traces of past life.

① Molds and Casts

A mold and cast are formed in the steps below.

An organism dies and falls into soft sediment.

Over time, the sediment becomes rock and the organism decays, leaving a mold.

Minerals fill the mold and make a cast of the organism.

② Petrified Wood

In this close-up, you can see the minerals that replaced the wood, forming petrified wood.

③ Carbon Films

This carbon film of a moth is about 10 million years old. Carbon films are especially useful because they can show details of the soft parts of organisms.

④ Trace Fossils

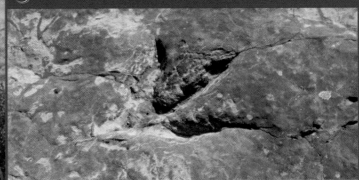

A trace fossil, such as this footprint of a dinosaur in rock, can provide important information about where an animal lived and how it walked and ran.

READING VISUALS What is similar about mold-and-cast fossils and petrified wood?

Fossils and other natural evidence show changes in life and the environment.

Fossils reveal that Earth has undergone many changes over billions of years. Scientists study fossils to learn what organisms and animals once lived in places where the fossils were found. Today the land around the South Pole is mostly covered by ice, but fossils show that crocodiles, dinosaurs, and palm trees once lived on that land. The land was once much closer to the equator.

The earliest fossils are of tiny one-celled organisms that lived in an environment without oxygen. Three billion years ago, humans or the land animals we know today could not have breathed the air on Earth. Fossils also record the disappearance of many species.

Tree Rings

The rings in tree trunks are also a tool for studying the past. The width of tree rings varies, depending on how much the tree grows in various years. In dry years, a tree does not grow very much and the rings for those years are thin. A thick ring is a sign of a good year for growth, with enough rainfall. By analyzing the tree rings of many old trees, scientists can develop an accurate history of overall weather patterns over time.

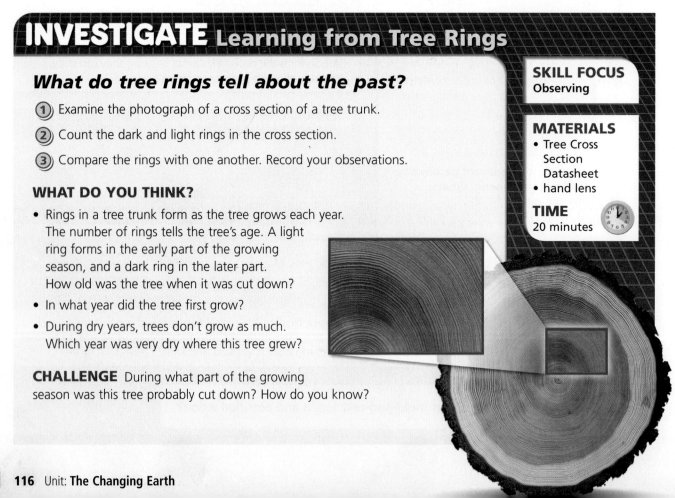

INVESTIGATE Learning from Tree Rings

What do tree rings tell about the past?

1. Examine the photograph of a cross section of a tree trunk.
2. Count the dark and light rings in the cross section.
3. Compare the rings with one another. Record your observations.

WHAT DO YOU THINK?

- Rings in a tree trunk form as the tree grows each year. The number of rings tells the tree's age. A light ring forms in the early part of the growing season, and a dark ring in the later part. How old was the tree when it was cut down?
- In what year did the tree first grow?
- During dry years, trees don't grow as much. Which year was very dry where this tree grew?

CHALLENGE During what part of the growing season was this tree probably cut down? How do you know?

SKILL FOCUS
Observing

MATERIALS
- Tree Cross Section Datasheet
- hand lens

TIME
20 minutes

These scientists are removing an ice core from a thick ice sheet in Antarctica. Ice at the bottom end is oldest.

Scientists study tiny specks of dirt in the ice, looking for signs of past microscopic organisms.

Ice Cores

In Greenland and Antarctica, snowfall has built up gigantic layers of ice that can be much deeper than the height of skyscrapers and as much as 530,000 years old at the bottom. Scientists drill into the ice and remove ice cores for study. An **ice core** is a tubular sample that shows the layers of snow and ice that have built up over thousands of years. The layers serve as a vertical timeline of part of Earth's past.

Scientists analyze air trapped in the ice to learn how the atmosphere has changed. Increases in dust or ash in the ice show when major volcanic eruptions occurred somewhere on Earth. Differences in the air content at different levels of the ice indicate how much temperatures went up and down, showing how long ice ages and warm periods lasted. This information can help scientists understand how Earth's climate might be changing now and how it might change in the future.

CHECK YOUR
READING   How does an ice core provide information about Earth's history?

 Review

KEY CONCEPTS

1. What can rock fossils and original remains show about Earth's past?

2. Why do rock fossils form in sedimentary rock and not in igneous rock?

3. How do tree rings and ice cores help scientists understand how Earth has changed over time?

CRITICAL THINKING

4. **Infer** If you uncovered fossils of tropical fish and palm trees, what could you say about the environment at the time the fossils formed?

5. **Synthesize** Why might ancient lake and sea beds be rich sources of fossils?

CHALLENGE

6. **Rank** Which evidence—a fossil, a tree ring, or an ice core—would be most helpful to a historian studying how the Pilgrims grew food at Plymouth Colony in 1620? Explain your reasoning.

Could *T. Rex* Win a Race?

If you want to know how fast a dinosaur ran, study a chicken. Two scientists, John Hutchinson and Mariano Garcia, did just that. They wanted to know if *Tyrannosaurus rex* was actually as fast on its feet as some people said it was.

To find the answer, the scientists worked to figure out how strong the dinosaur's legs were. What they needed to know was how much muscle the giant dinosaur had in its legs. Yet they couldn't study *T. rex*'s muscle mass directly, because there are no complete remains of dinosaur muscle, just bones. This is where the chicken comes in.

Fossils and Fowls

The bone fossils of dinosaurs suggest that birds and dinosaurs have some similarities. Using the chicken as a model for *T. rex*, the scientists found that a chicken needs at least one-tenth of its body mass to be leg muscle. They measured chickens and found they have even more than that, about one-fifth.

The scientists used a computer program to learn if a chicken the size of a 5900 kilogram (10,000 lb) *T. rex* would be able to run. The computer model showed that a chicken that size would need 90 percent of its body mass in its legs to run fast. By connecting their knowledge of dinosaur fossils and chickens, the two scientists showed that *T. rex* was not a fast runner.

Still, the giant dinosaur was not exactly a slowpoke. The scientists also calculated that with its 2.5 meter (8 ft) legs *T. rex* could travel at a rate of about 24 kilometers per hour (15 mi/h). For many people, that's running speed.

EXPLORE

1. **SYNTHESIZE** Based on what you have read, what might be the relationship between the size of an animal and its speed?

2. **DRAW CONCLUSIONS** Why do you think some scientists think that *T. rex*, a meat eater, mostly ate animals already dead instead of live prey?

4.2 Rocks provide a timeline for Earth.

◀ BEFORE, you learned

- Fossils contain information about the past
- Fossils, ice cores, and tree rings record conditions and changes in the environment

▶ NOW, you will learn

- What the relative ages of rock layers reveal about Earth
- How index fossils are used to determine the ages of rock layers
- How the absolute ages of rocks are determined

VOCABULARY

relative age p. 119
index fossil p. 121
absolute age p. 123
half-life p. 123

THINK ABOUT

How old are these bicycles?

You might not know exactly when each of the bicycles shown was made, but you can probably tell which is the oldest. How could you arrange these bikes in order of their ages without knowing how old each is?

Layers of sedimentary rocks show relative age.

VOCABULARY
Remember to add *relative age* to your notebook, using the vocabulary strategy of your choice.

Fossils are clues in the story of Earth's past. But for the story to make sense, the clues need to be arranged in order. **Relative age** is the age of an event or object in relation to other events or objects. You probably know relative ages for many things in your life. For example, if a friend tells you she has an older brother and a younger brother, you know the relative ages of her brothers even if you don't know their exact ages.

Until the beginning of the 1900s, geologists didn't have a way to determine the exact ages of objects that existed in Earth's past. Instead, they reconstructed Earth's story based on the relative ages of different clues. Today there are still many parts of Earth's history that cannot be given exact ages. Determining relative age continues to be an important way of piecing together the puzzle of Earth's past.

Sedimentary rock layers contain information about the relative ages of events and objects in Earth's history. As you read earlier, sedimentary rocks form from the sediments that fall to the bottom of lakes, rivers, and seas. Over time, the sediments pile up to form horizontal layers of sedimentary rocks. The bottom layer of rock forms first, which means it is oldest. Each layer above that is younger, and the top layer is youngest of all. This ordering is relative because you cannot be sure exactly when each layer formed, only that each layer is younger then the one below it.

When horizontal layers of sedimentary rock are undisturbed, the youngest layer is always on top, as shown in the photograph on the left below. But over millions of years, the movement of tectonic plates can disturb rock layers. A whole set of layers can get turned on its side. Rock layers can get bent, or even folded over, like taco shells that begin as flat tortillas. If a set of rock layers has been disturbed, the youngest layer may no longer be on top. One way scientists determine the original order is to compare the disturbed rock layers with a similar but undisturbed stack of layers.

 CHECK YOUR READING When might the youngest layer in a set of sedimentary rock layers not be on top?

Rock Layers

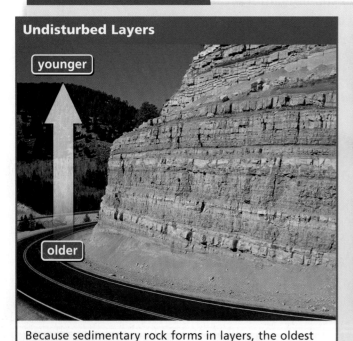
Undisturbed Layers
younger
older
Because sedimentary rock forms in layers, the oldest layer of undisturbed sedimentary rock will be on the bottom and the youngest on top.

Disturbed Layers
older
younger
If the rock layers are bent, they may no longer be in order from oldest to youngest.

READING VISUALS Where are the youngest layers in each photo?

Igneous Rock and Sedimentary Layers

Sedimentary rock layers can also be disturbed by igneous rock. Molten rock from within Earth can force its way up through the layers above it, cooling and forming igneous rock. Because the sedimentary rock layers have to be present before the molten rock cuts through them, the igneous rock must be younger than the layers it cuts through.

VISUALIZATION
CLASSZONE.COM

Watch molten rock cut through layers of sedimentary rock.

① Over time, sand and silt form horizontal layers of sedimentary rock.

② Deep underground, molten rock cuts through the sedimentary rock layers.

③ A river gradually wears away the rock, exposing the younger igneous rock.

If the molten rock erupts and flows onto the surface, it forms a layer of igneous rock on top of the layers of sedimentary rock. Over time, more sedimentary rock layers may form on top of the igneous rock. The igneous rock layer is younger than the sedimentary layers under it and older than the sedimentary layers that form on top of it.

 CHECK YOUR READING Why is igneous rock always younger than any rock it cuts through?

Index Fossils

Fossils contained within sedimentary rock can offer clues about the age of the rock. An organism that was fossilized in rock must have lived during the same time span in which the rock formed. Using information from rocks and other natural evidence, scientists have determined when specific fossilized organisms existed. If people know how long ago a fossilized organism lived, then they can figure out the age of the rock in which the fossil was found.

Fossils of organisms that were common, that lived in many areas, and that existed only during specific spans of time are called **index fossils.** These characteristics of index fossils make them especially useful for figuring out when rock layers formed.

This rock contains the index fossil *Arnioceras semicostatum,* an organism that lived between 206 million and 144 million years ago.

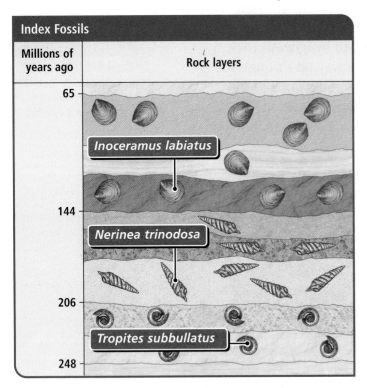

Index Fossils

Millions of years ago	Rock layers
65	Inoceramus labiatus
144	Nerinea trinodosa
206	Tropites subbullatus
248	

Index fossils can be used to estimate the ages of the rocks in which they are found.

The mollusk *Inoceramus labiatus,* for example, is a kind of sea animal that appeared 144 million years ago and went extinct 65 million years ago. So, if you find a rock that contains a fossil of this mollusk, the rock must be between 144 million and 65 million years old because this mollusk lived during that time span.

The chart shows a cross section of rock layers in which *Inoceramus labiatus* and two other index fossils are found. *Nerinea trinodosa* is a kind of sea animal that lived between 206 million and 144 million years ago. *Tropites subbullatus* is a kind of sea animal that lived between 248 million and 206 million years ago.

Remember that one characteristic of index fossils is that they are widespread—they are found in many different parts of the world. Because they are widespread, index fossils can be used to compare the ages of rock layers in different parts of the world.

INVESTIGATE Relative and Absolute Age

How can newspapers model rock layers?

PROCEDURE

1. Have one person in your group arrange the newspapers in a pile with the oldest newspaper on the bottom and the newest on top.

2. After the newspapers are stacked, place one pencil between two newspapers and the other pencil between two different newspapers. Use the model to answer the questions below.

WHAT DO YOU THINK?

- If the newspapers were really placed on the stack on the days they were published, which pencil has probably been there longer?

- Look at the dates on the newspapers. Now what can you say about when the pencils were placed on the stack?

CHALLENGE How does what you could tell about the "ages" of the pencils before looking at the dates differ from what you could tell after looking?

SKILL FOCUS
Making models

MATERIALS
- 5 or more newspapers with different dates
- 2 pencils

TIME
20 minutes

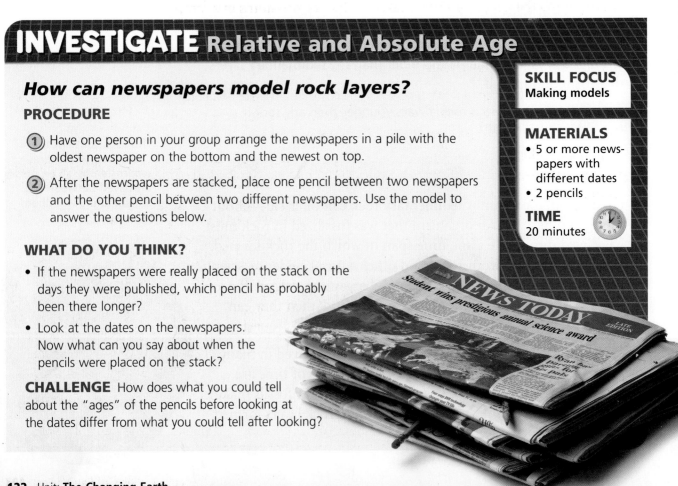

Radioactive dating can show absolute age.

Think again about the friend who tells you that she has two brothers, one older than she is and one younger. You know the order in which they were born—that is, their relative ages. The older brother, however, might be 1 year older or 20 years older. The exact age of the younger brother is also still a mystery. To find out how much older or younger your friend's brothers are, you need to know their actual ages. The actual age of an event or object is called its **absolute age.**

 What is the difference between relative age and absolute age? Use an example in your explanation.

Half-Life

Because scientists can't ask a rock its age, they have had to find a different way of determining the absolute ages of rocks. The solution lies in the smallest unit of matter, the atom. Atoms make up everything on Earth, including you and rocks. The atoms of many chemical elements exist in various forms. Some of these forms are unstable and break down over time into another form. This breakdown—called radioactivity— is a very useful clock because a particular unstable form of an element always breaks down at the same rate into the same other form.

The rate of change of a radioactive element is measured in half-lives. A **half-life** is the length of time it takes for half of the atoms in a sample of a radioactive element to change from an unstable form into another form. Different elements have different half-lives, ranging from fractions of a second to billions of years.

Just as a ruler is not a very useful tool for measuring the distance between planets, elements with very short half-lives are not very useful for measuring the ages of rocks. Instead, elements with half-lives of millions to billions of years are used to date rocks. For example, uranium 235 has a half-life of 704 million years. Uranium 235 is an unstable element found in some igneous rocks. Over time, uranium 235 breaks down into lead 207. Using information from radioactive dating of rocks, scientists estimate that Earth is around 4.6 billion years old.

Over time, a radioactive element breaks down at a constant rate into another form.

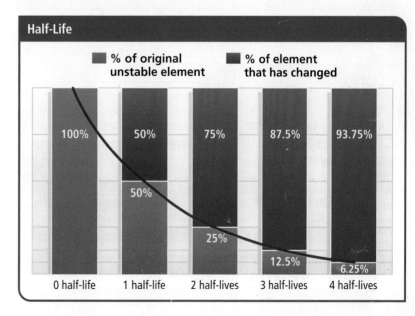

Half-Life

■ % of original unstable element   ■ % of element that has changed

| 100% | 50% | 75% | 87.5% | 93.75% |
| | 50% | 25% | 12.5% | 6.25% |

0 half-life   1 half-life   2 half-lives   3 half-lives   4 half-lives

Radioactive Breakdown and Dating Rock Layers

Igneous rocks contain radioactive elements that break down over time. This breakdown can be used to tell the ages of the rocks.

① 1408 Million Years Ago

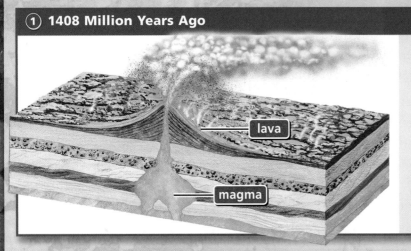

lava

magma

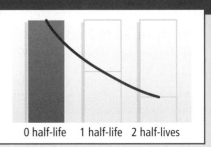

0 half-life   1 half-life   2 half-lives

When magma first hardens into rock, it contains some uranium 235 and no lead 207.

② 704 Million Years Ago

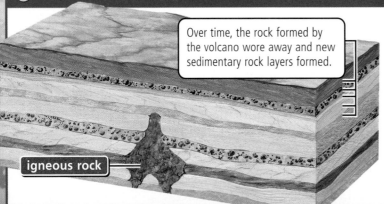

Over time, the rock formed by the volcano wore away and new sedimentary rock layers formed.

igneous rock

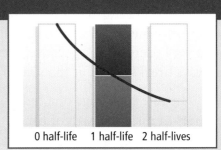

0 half-life   1 half-life   2 half-lives

After 704 million years, or one half-life, half of the uranium 235 in the igneous rock has broken down into lead 207.

③ Today

Radioactive dating shows that this igneous rock is about 1408 million years old.

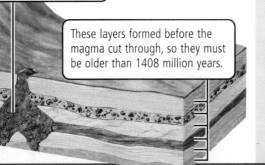

These layers formed before the magma cut through, so they must be older than 1408 million years.

The layers that formed on top of the igneous rock must be younger than 1408 million years.

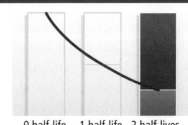

0 half-life   1 half-life   2 half-lives

After 1408 million years, or 2 half-lives, only one-fourth of the uranium 235 in the igneous rock remains.

READING VISUALS How do the relative amounts of uranium 235 and lead 207 in the igneous rock change over time?

Radioactive dating works best with igneous rocks. Sedimentary rocks are formed from material that came from other rocks. For this reason, any measurements would show when the original rocks were formed, not when the sedimentary rock itself formed.

Just as uranium 235 can be used to date igneous rocks, carbon 14 can be used to find the ages of the remains of some things that were once alive. Carbon 14 is an unstable form of carbon, an element found in all living things. Carbon 14 has a half-life of 5730 years. It is useful for dating objects between about 100 and 70,000 years old, such as the wood from an ancient tool or the remains of an animal from the Ice Age.

RESOURCE CENTER
CLASSZONE.COM
Find out more about how scientists date rocks.

Using Absolute and Relative Age

Scientists must piece together information from all methods of determining age to figure out the story of Earth's past.

- Radioactive dating of igneous rocks reveals their absolute age.
- Interpreting layers of sedimentary rock shows the relative order of events.
- Fossils help to sort out the sedimentary record.

You have read that it is not possible to date sedimentary rocks with radioactivity directly. Geologists, however, can date any igneous rock that might have cut through or formed a layer between sedimentary layers. Then, using the absolute age of the igneous rock, geologists can estimate the ages of nearby sedimentary layers.

 CHECK YOUR READING How might the absolute age of an igneous rock layer help scientists to determine the ages of nearby sedimentary rock layers?

4.2 Review

KEY CONCEPTS

1. What can you tell from undisturbed rock layers? Discuss the concept of relative age in your answer.

2. How can index fossils help scientists determine the ages of rock layers?

3. What property of radioactive elements makes them useful for determining absolute age?

CRITICAL THINKING

4. **Provide Examples** What are some things in your life for which you know only their relative ages?

5. **Apply** In your daily life are there index events (like index fossils) that tell you approximate times even when you can't see a clock? What are they?

⬥ CHALLENGE

6. **Apply** A rock contains a radioactive element with a half-life of 100 million years. Tests show that the element in the rock has gone through three half-lives. How old is the rock?

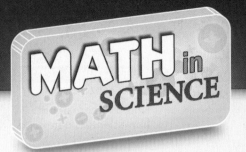

Dating Mammoth Bones

Imagine that scientists find an ancient lakebed with hundreds of well-preserved mammoth bones in it. They are able to measure the amount of carbon 14 that remains in the bones. Carbon 14 has a half-life of approximately 5700 years. How could you use the half-life of carbon 14 to determine how old the bones are?

MATH TUTORIAL
CLASSZONE.COM
Click on Math Tutorial for more help with reading line graphs and multiplying whole numbers.

Mammoths were close relatives of today's elephants. Mammoths lived earlier in the Cenozoic era and are now extinct.

Example

Mammoth bone A has $\frac{1}{4}$ of its original carbon 14. How old is mammoth bone A? Use the half-life of carbon 14 and the graph below.

(1) Find $\frac{1}{4}$ on the vertical axis and follow the line out to the red curved line.

(2) Then follow the line down to the horizontal axis to determine that the carbon 14 in the bone has been through 2 half-lives.

(3) $5700 \times 2 = 11{,}400$

years per half-life   number of half-lives

ANSWER Bone A is 11,400 years old.

Half-Lives

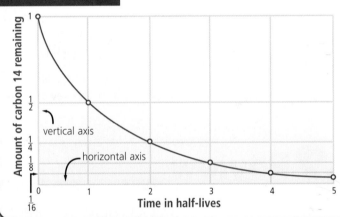

Answer the following questions.

1. Mammoth bone B has $\frac{1}{8}$ of its original carbon 14. How old is mammoth bone B?

2. Mammoth bone C has $\frac{1}{16}$ of its original carbon 14. How old is mammoth bone C?

CHALLENGE Mammoth bone D is 28,500 years old. What fraction of the original carbon 14 remains in bone D?

KEY CONCEPT

4.3 The geologic time scale shows Earth's past.

BEFORE, you learned

- Rocks and fossils give clues about life on Earth
- Layers of sedimentary rocks show relative ages
- Radioactive dating of igneous rocks gives absolute ages

NOW, you will learn

- That Earth is always changing and has always changed in the past
- How the geologic time scale describes Earth's history

VOCABULARY

uniformitarianism p. 128
geologic time scale p. 129

EXPLORE Time Scales

How do you make a time scale of your year?

PROCEDURE

1. Divide your paper into three columns.

2. In the last column, list six to ten events in the school year in the order they will happen. For example, you may include a particular soccer game or a play.

3. In the middle column, organize those events into larger time periods, such as soccer season, rehearsal week, or whatever you choose.

4. In the first column, organize those time periods into even larger ones.

MATERIALS
- pen
- sheet of paper

WHAT DO YOU THINK?
How does putting events into categories help you to see the relationship among events?

Earth is constantly changing.

OUTLINE
Remember to start an outline in your notebook for this section.

I. Main idea
  A. Supporting idea
    1. Detail
    2. Detail
  B. Supporting idea

In the late 1700s a Scottish geologist named James Hutton began to question some of the ideas that were then common about Earth and how Earth changes. He found fossils and saw them as evidence of life forms that no longer existed. He also noticed that different types of fossilized creatures were found in different layers of rocks. Based on his observations of rocks and other natural evidence, Hutton came up with a new theory to explain the story told in the rocks. He was the first to present a hypothesis about Earth's changing over time.

Gradual Change

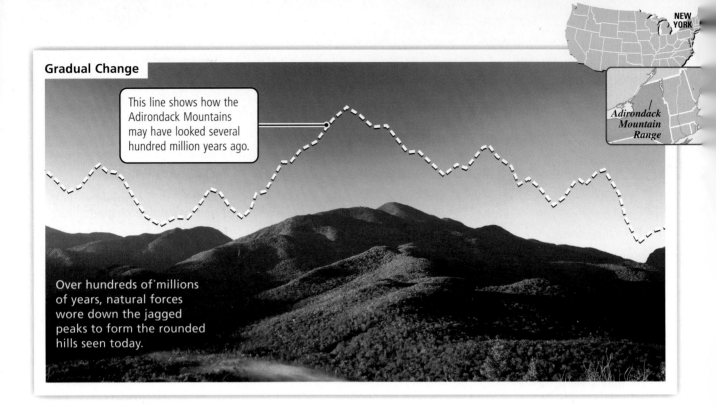

This line shows how the Adirondack Mountains may have looked several hundred million years ago.

Over hundreds of millions of years, natural forces wore down the jagged peaks to form the rounded hills seen today.

NEW YORK

Adirondack Mountain Range

READING TiP

To remember what *uniformitarianism* means, think of the word *uniform,* which means "same."

Hutton recognized that Earth is a constantly changing place. Wind, water, heat, and cold break down rocks. Other processes, such as volcanic eruptions and the building up of sediment, continue to form new rock. Earth's interior is constantly churning with powerful forces that move, fold, raise, and swallow the surface of the planet.

The same processes that changed Earth in the past continue to occur today. A billion years ago a river would have carried particles of rock just as a river does today. Similarly, volcanoes in the past would have erupted just as volcanoes do today. Hutton's theory of **uniformitarianism** (YOO-nuh-fawr-mih-TAIR-ee-uh-nihz-uhm) is the idea that

- Earth is an always-changing place
- the same forces of change at work today were at work in the past

Although this idea may seem simple, it is very important. The theory of uniformitarianism is the basis of modern geology.

Some changes on Earth are gradual. Mountains form and are worn down over many millions of years. Climate and the amount of ice on land can change over hundreds or thousands of years. Other changes are fast. A volcanic eruption, an earthquake, or a flood can cause huge changes over a period of minutes or days. Fast or slow, Earth is always changing.

CHECK YOUR READING What was the new idea that Hutton had about Earth? Describe the idea in your own words.

Fast Change

WASHINGTON

Mount St. Helens

READING ViSUALS **COMPARE AND CONTRAST** These photos show Mount St. Helens before and after it erupted in 1980. What rapid changes occurred during the eruption?

The geologic time scale divides Earth's history.

From a person's point of view, 4.6 billion years is a tremendous amount of time. To help make sense of it, scientists have organized Earth's history in a chart called the geologic time scale. The **geologic time scale** divides Earth's history into intervals of time defined by major events or changes on Earth.

Scientists use information from fossils and radioactive dating to figure out what happened over the 4.6 billion years of Earth's history. The oldest evidence of life is from about 3.8 billion years ago, but life may be even older. Organisms with more than one cell appeared around 1 billion years ago, and modern humans appeared only 100,000 years ago.

Imagine Earth's history compressed into one year. If Earth forms on January 1, the first life we have evidence for appears in the beginning of March. Life with more than one cell appears months later, in the middle of October. Humans do not show up until 11 minutes before midnight on the last day of the year, and they do not understand how old Earth is until about a second before midnight.

first humans

If Earth's history is compared to a calendar year, humans appear just before midnight on December 31.

READING TiP

As you read, find the eons, eras, and periods on the chart below.

Divisions of Geologic Time

The geologic time scale is divided into eons, eras, periods, and epochs (EHP-uhks). Unlike divisions of time such as days or minutes, the divisions of the geologic time scale have no fixed lengths. Instead, they are based on changes or events recorded in rocks and fossils.

Eon The largest unit of time is an eon. Earth's 4.6-billion-year history is divided into four eons.

Era Eons may be divided into eras. The most recent eon is divided into three eras: the Paleozoic, the Mesozoic, and the Cenozoic.

Period Each era is subdivided into a number of periods.

Epoch The periods of the Cenozoic, the most recent era, are further divided into epochs.

Geologic Time Scale

The geologic time scale divides Earth's history into eons, eras, periods, and epochs.

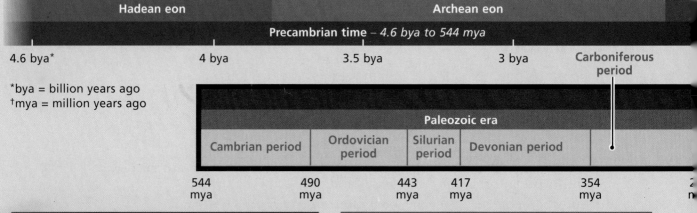

Hadean eon		Archean eon		

Precambrian time – 4.6 bya to 544 mya

4.6 bya*   4 bya   3.5 bya   3 bya   Carboniferous period

*bya = billion years ago
†mya = million years ago

Paleozoic era				
Cambrian period	Ordovician period	Silurian period	Devonian period	

544 mya   490 mya   443 mya   417 mya   354 mya

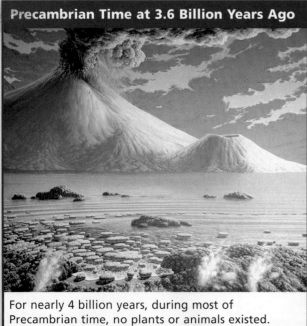

Precambrian Time at 3.6 Billion Years Ago

For nearly 4 billion years, during most of Precambrian time, no plants or animals existed.

Paleozoic Era at 544 Million Years Ago

At the beginning of the Paleozoic era, all life lived in the oceans.

The Hadean, Archean, and Proterozoic eons together are called Precambrian time and make up almost 90 percent of Earth's history. The fossil record for Precambrian time consists mostly of tiny organisms that cannot be seen without a microscope. Other early forms of life had soft bodies that rarely formed into fossils.

The Phanerozoic eon stretches from the end of Precambrian time to the present. Because so many more changes are recorded in the fossil record of this eon, it is further divided into smaller units of time. The smaller time divisions relate to how long certain conditions and life forms on Earth lasted and how quickly they changed or became extinct.

 CHECK YOUR READING What part of geologic time makes up most of Earth's history?

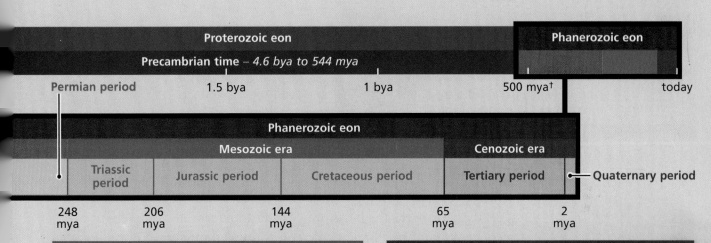

Proterozoic eon			Phanerozoic eon

Precambrian time – 4.6 bya to 544 mya

| Permian period | 1.5 bya | 1 bya | 500 mya† | today |

Phanerozoic eon				
	Mesozoic era		Cenozoic era	
Triassic period	Jurassic period	Cretaceous period	Tertiary period	Quaternary period

| 248 mya | 206 mya | 144 mya | 65 mya | 2 mya |

Mesozoic Era at 195 to 65 Million Years Ago

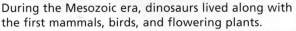
During the Mesozoic era, dinosaurs lived along with the first mammals, birds, and flowering plants.

Cenozoic Era at Present Day

The first humans appeared in the later part of the Cenozoic era, which continues today.

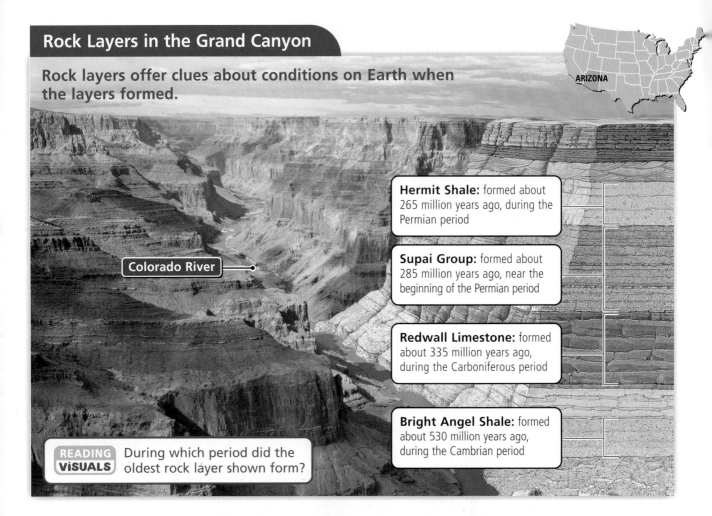

Rock Layers in the Grand Canyon

Rock layers offer clues about conditions on Earth when the layers formed.

ARIZONA

Hermit Shale: formed about 265 million years ago, during the Permian period

Colorado River

Supai Group: formed about 285 million years ago, near the beginning of the Permian period

Redwall Limestone: formed about 335 million years ago, during the Carboniferous period

Bright Angel Shale: formed about 530 million years ago, during the Cambrian period

READING VISUALS During which period did the oldest rock layer shown form?

Phanerozoic Eon

The most recent eon, the Phanerozoic, began around 544 million years ago. Its start marks the beginning of a fast increase in the diversity, or variety, of life. The Phanerozoic eon is divided into three eras:

- the Paleozoic, whose name means "ancient life"
- the Mesozoic, whose name means "middle life"
- the Cenozoic, whose name means "recent life"

READING TiP

As you read, find each era in the geologic time scale on pages 130–131.

The Paleozoic era is the first era of the Phanerozoic eon. At the start of the Paleozoic, all life lived in the ocean. Fish, the first animals with backbones, developed during this time. Toward the end of this era, life moved onto land. Reptiles, insects, and ferns were common. A mass extinction occurred at the end of the Paleozoic era, 248 million years ago. A mass extinction is when many different life forms all die out, or become extinct, at once. The cause of this extinction is not completely understood.

The Mesozoic era spans the next 183 million years and is best known for the dinosaurs that ruled Earth. Mammals, birds, and flowering plants also first appeared during the Mesozoic. For some of this time, parts of North America were covered by a vast sea. The end of the

Mesozoic marks the end of the dinosaurs and many other animals in another mass extinction. This extinction may have been caused by one or more giant asteroids that slammed into Earth, throwing huge amounts of dust into the air. The dust blocked the sunlight, causing plants to die and, along with them, many animals.

The Cenozoic era, the most recent era, began 65 million years ago and continues today. The Cenozoic is often called the Age of Mammals because it marks the time when mammals became a main category of life on Earth.

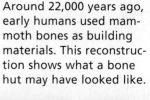

Around 22,000 years ago, early humans used mammoth bones as building materials. This reconstruction shows what a bone hut may have looked like.

The Cenozoic era is divided into two periods: the Tertiary and the Quaternary. The Quaternary period stretches from about 2 million years ago to the present. Most of the Quaternary has been a series of ice ages, with much of Europe, North America, and Asia covered in thick sheets of ice. Mammoths, saber-toothed cats, and other giant mammals were common during the first part of the Quaternary. Fossils of the first modern humans are also from this period; they are about 100,000 years old.

As the amount of ice on land shrank and grew, the ocean levels rose and fell. When the ocean levels fell, exposed land served as natural bridges that connected continents previously separated by water. The land bridges allowed humans and other animals to spread around the planet. It now seems that the end of Quaternary may be defined by the rise of human civilization.

 CHECK YOUR READING How did falling ocean levels lead to the spread of humans and other animals on Earth?

4.3 Review

KEY CONCEPTS

1. Describe the concept of uniformitarianism.
2. What does the geologic time scale measure?
3. What was life like on Earth for most of its history?

CRITICAL THINKING

4. **Apply** What period, era, and eon do you live in?
5. **Evaluate** Some cartoons have shown early humans keeping dinosaurs as pets. From what you know about Earth's history, is this possible? Why or why not?

CHALLENGE

6. **Infer** How might the geologic time scale be different if the event that caused the mass extinction 65 million years ago had never occurred?

CHAPTER INVESTIGATION

Geologic Time

OVERVIEW AND PURPOSE Geologists use information from rocks, fossils, and other natural evidence to piece together the history of Earth. The geologic time scale organizes Earth's history into intervals of time called eons, eras, periods, and epochs. In this investigation you will
- construct a model of the geologic time scale
- place fossil organisms and geologic events in the correct sequence on the timeline

▶ Procedure

1 Complete the geologic time scale conversion chart. Use the conversion 1 mm = 1 million years to change the number of years for each eon, era, period, and epoch on the chart into metric measurements (millimeters, centimeters, and meters).

MATERIALS
- geologic time scale conversion chart
- adding-machine paper 5 meters long
- scissors
- colored markers, pens, or pencils
- metric tape measure or meter stick
- sticky notes

2 Lay the adding-machine paper out in front of you. At the far right end of the strip write "TODAY" lengthwise along the edge.

3 Starting from the TODAY mark, measure back 4.6 meters, or 4600 million years. Label this point "AGE OF EARTH." Cut off excess paper.

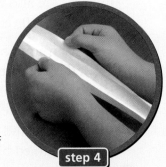
step 4

4 Fold the paper in half lengthwise and then fold it in half lengthwise again. Unfold the paper. The creases should divide your paper into four rows.

5 At the far left end of the strip, label each of the four rows as shown.

step 5

6 Using the numbers from your chart, measure each eon. Start each measurement from the TODAY line and measure back in time. For example, the Archean eon started 3800 million years ago, so measure back 3.8 meters from today. Mark that distance and write "ARCHEAN EON." Do the same for the other eons.

step 6

ARCHEAN EON
3800 million years ago (3.8 meters)

AGE OF EARTH   TODAY

Repeat step 6 to measure and label the eras, periods, and epochs.

 After all the eons, eras, periods, and epochs are measured and labeled, use the same measuring technique to add the fossils and events from the table below.

Table 1. Important Events in Earth's History

Fossils and Events	Time (millions of years ago)
First trilobite	554
First mammal	210
Greatest mass extinction	248
First green algae	1000
Early humans	2
Extinction of dinosaurs	65
First life forms	3800
Flowering plants	130

 Draw pictures of the fossils and events or write the names of the fossils and events on the timeline. If you do not have space to write directly on the timeline, write on sticky notes and then place the sticky notes at the correct positions on the timeline.

▶ Observe and Analyze

Write It Up

1. **COMPARE AND CONTRAST** The time from 4.6 billion years ago up until the beginning of the Phanerozoic eon is called Precambrian time. Find the part of your timeline that represents Precambrian time. How does Precambrian time compare in length with the rest of the geologic time scale?

2. **COMPARE AND CONTRAST** The Cenozoic era is the most recent era, and it includes the present. How does the Cenozoic era compare in length with the other eras?

3. **INTERPRET** Where on the timeline are the two major extinction events?

4. **INFER** What does the location of the two major extinction events suggest about how geologists divided the time scale into smaller units?

▶ Conclude

Write It Up

1. **INTERPRET** Where are most of the life forms that you placed on your time line grouped?

2. **INFER** Judging by the locations of most of the life forms on your timeline, why do you think the shortest era on the timeline—the Cenozoic era—has been divided into so many smaller divisions?

3 **EVALUATE** What limitations or difficulties did you experience in constructing or interpreting this model of the geologic time scale?

4. **APPLY** Think about the relationships among fossils, rock layers, and the geologic time scale. Why do you think the geologists who first constructed the geologic time scale found it difficult to divide the first three eons into smaller time divisions?

▶ INVESTIGATE Further

CHALLENGE Choose several more events or life forms mentioned in the chapter. For each, find either an absolute date or a relative date that will allow you to place it in the correct position in the geologic sequence. Draw or label these new items on your timeline. What new patterns or connections did adding these events or life forms to the timeline reveal?

Geologic Time Scale Conversion Chart

Division of Geologic Time	Millions of Years Ago It Began	Measurement
Eons		4.6 meters
Hadean	4600	
Archean	3800	
Proterozoic	2500	
Phanerozoic	544	
Eras	544	

Chapter Review

the **BIG** idea

Rocks, fossils, and other types of natural evidence tell Earth's story.

CONTENT REVIEW
CLASSZONE.COM

KEY CONCEPTS SUMMARY

4.1 **Earth's past is revealed in rocks and fossils.**

Fossils are traces or remnants of past life. Many fossils are found in rock. Rocks, fossils, and other natural evidence provide information about how Earth and life on Earth have changed over time.

A cast fossil is formed when minerals take the shape of a decayed organism.

VOCABULARY
fossil p. 111
original remains p. 112
ice core p. 117

4.2 **Rocks provide a timeline for Earth.**

Sedimentary rock layers show the order in which rocks formed. The order of the layers is used to determine the **relative ages** of fossils found in the rock.

Radioactive dating can be used to determine the **absolute age** of igneous rock.

Scientists combine information about the relative and absolute ages of rocks and fossils to construct a timeline of Earth.

VOCABULARY
relative age p. 119
index fossil p. 121
absolute age p. 123
half-life p. 123

4.3 **The geologic time scale shows Earth's past.**

The **geologic time scale** divides Earth's history into eons, eras, periods, and epochs. The divisions are based on major changes or events that occurred in Earth's history.

■ Phanerozoic eon ■ Paleozoic era ■ Mesozoic era ■ Cenozoic era

Hadean eon	Archean eon	Proterozoic eon	

Precambrian time

| 4.6 bya* | 3 bya | 2 bya | 1 bya | 500 mya† | today |

*bya = billion years ago   †mya = million years ago

EON → ERA → PERIOD → EPOCH

VOCABULARY
uniformitarianism p. 128
geologic time scale p. 129

Vocabulary

Make a concept definition map for each of the vocabulary terms listed below. Write the term in the center box. Fill in the other boxes by answering the questions. A sample is shown below.

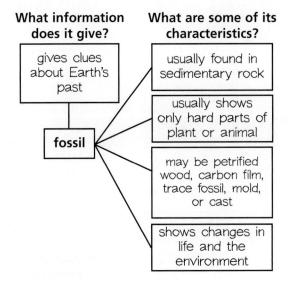

What information does it give?

gives clues about Earth's past

fossil

What are some of its characteristics?

usually found in sedimentary rock

usually shows only hard parts of plant or animal

may be petrified wood, carbon film, trace fossil, mold, or cast

shows changes in life and the environment

1. index fossil

2. ice core

3. original remains

Reviewing Key Concepts

Multiple Choice *Choose the letter of the best answer.*

4. Which of the following might show evidence of a year with low rainfall?
   a. tree rings   **c.** original remains
   b. index fossils   **d.** sedimentary rock

5. In which time span did dinosaurs live?
   a. Cenozoic era   **c.** Paleozoic era
   b. Mesozoic era   **d.** Precambrian time

6. Half-life is a measurement of
   a. fossil age
   b. radioactive breakdown
   c. cold climates
   d. relative age

7. What is the age of Earth?
   a. 570 million years   **c.** 4.6 billion years
   b. 1.1 billion years   **d.** 9.5 billion years

8. What was the earliest form of life?
   a. a fish   **c.** a one-celled organism
   b. a fern   **d.** a reptile

9. Which statement best describes the theory of uniformitarianism?
   a. Earth continues to change as it always has.
   b. Earth is changing, but not as quickly as it used to.
   c. Earth is changing, but faster than it used to.
   d. Earth is no longer changing.

10. How does petrified wood form?
   a. A log falls into water that freezes.
   b. Sedimentary rock forms over a log.
   c. Igneous rock covers a log and heats it.
   d. Water seeps through a log, replacing its cells with minerals.

11. A cast fossil is formed from
   a. igneous rock   **c.** amber
   b. a mold   **d.** wood

12. Which of these substances best preserves soft parts of an organism?
   a. sedimentary rock   **c.** amber
   b. igneous rock   **d.** air

13. Which part of an ancient reptile would you expect to see in a rock fossil?
   a. eye   **c.** heart
   b. bone   **d.** muscle

14. Which type of fossil would be most likely to show the complete outline of a leaf?
   a. petrified wood   **c.** cast fossil
   b. carbon film   **d.** trace fossil

Short Answer *Write a few sentences to answer each question.*

15. Why are no fossils found in igneous rocks?

16. Why is radioactive dating not useful for determining the ages of sedimentary rocks?

APPLY *Refer to the illustration below to answer the next four questions.*

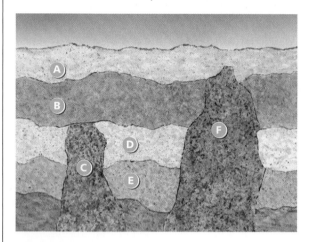

The illustration above is a side view of formations of sedimentary and igneous rock. *C* and *F* are igneous rock.

17. For which of the labeled rock formations could the absolute age be determined? Why?

18. Which of the labeled rock formations is the youngest? How do you know?

19. Which rock is younger, *C* or *D?* Why?

20. Which of the labeled rock layers is the oldest? Why?

21. INFER Why do you think the Hadean, Archean, and Proterozoic eons are not divided into eras, periods, or epochs?

22. COMPARE AND CONTRAST How is the geologic time scale like a calendar? How is it different?

23. CONNECT Copy the concept map below. Use the geologic time scale on pages 130–131 to complete the map.

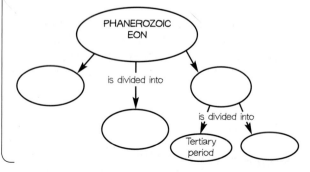

24. APPLY AND GRAPH Copy the graph below on your paper. Plot a point on the graph above each of the half-life numbers to show what percentage of the original unstable element remains. Note that the first point has been placed on the graph to show that all of the original element remains at the beginning, when no half-lives have passed.

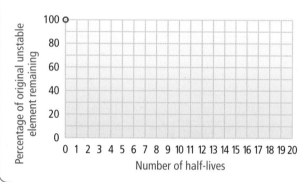

the BIG idea

25. SYNTHESIZE Look at the geologic time scale and think about the major events in the history of Earth and the changes in life forms that it shows. How do rocks, fossils, and other natural evidence tell Earth's story?

26. PREDICT What do you think will remain as evidence of today's world 100,000 years from now? How will the types of evidence differ from those that remain from 100,000 years ago?

UNIT PROJECTS

If you need to create graphs or other visuals for your project, be sure you have grid paper, poster board, markers, or other supplies.

Analyzing a Diagram

This diagram shows a cross section of rock layers. All of the layers are sedimentary, except for the area marked as igneous. Use the diagram to answer the questions below.

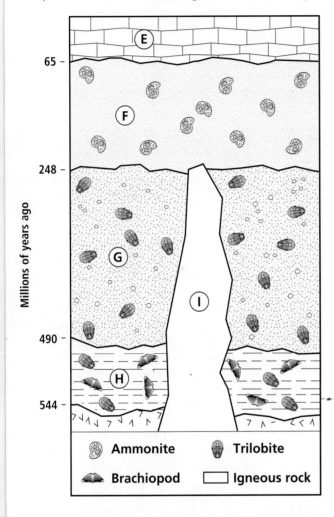

Ammonite   Trilobite

Brachiopod   Igneous rock

1. What is the approximate age of the oldest ammonite fossil shown in the diagram?
   a. 65 million years   **c.** 480 million years
   b. 248 million years   **d.** 540 million years

2. When did trilobites live on Earth?
   a. within the last 65 million years
   b. between 65 million years ago and 248 million years ago
   c. between 248 million years ago and 544 million years ago
   d. more than 544 million years ago

3. Which fossils are most common in the rock that is 500 million years old?
   a. brachiopods   **c.** ammonites
   b. trilobites   **d.** theropods

4. What is the best estimate of the age of rock I?
   a. less than 300 million years old
   b. 300 million years old
   c. more than 300 million years old
   d. more than 544 million years old

5. Which point shows where a fossil that is 500 million years old would most likely be found?
   a. E   **c.** G
   b. F   **d.** H

Extended Response

Answer the two questions below in detail.
Include some of the terms shown in the word box.
In your answers, underline each term you use.

index fossils	original remains	igneous rock
layers	folded	bent
ice core	tree ring	trilobite

6. Azeem is part of a team of scientists studying the natural history of a region. What types of natural evidence might he and his team look for? Why?

7. In studying fossils found in her community, Yvette noticed a pattern in their ages. People found older fossils close to the surface and younger fossils at greater depths. Explain how that might be.

TIMELINES in Science

THE STORY OF FOSSILS

Fossils are an important source of information about the history of life on Earth. The first observer to suggest that fossils provided clues to the past was Xenophanes. He lived in Greece around 500 B.C. Today, knowledge about fossils helps people find deposits of oil and understand changes in weather patterns. Above all, fossils reveal information about plants and animals that lived in the past.

The timeline shows a few events in the history of the study of fossils. Tools, such as radar and CT scanners that were invented for other purposes have helped scientists learn more from fossils. The boxes below the timeline highlight the role of technology, along with applications of knowledge about fossils.

1669

Scientist Notes Importance of Rock Layers

Danish-born scientist Nicolaus Steno recognizes that sediments form new layers of rock on top of old layers. Therefore, digging down provides a way to move back in time. Scientists plan to build on Steno's discovery to determine the ages of fossils found in rock layers.

EVENTS

1640   1660   1680   1700

APPLICATIONS AND TECHNOLOGY

This sandstone formation in Utah displays layers of sediment that were laid down one on top of another.

1799
Siberian Discovers Frozen Mammoth

While hunting for ivory tusks in Siberia, a man discovers a 37,000-year-old mammoth frozen in ice. Unfortunately, before scientists can study the five-ton animal, it thaws and wild animals eat most of it. However, the skeleton and bits of hair still provide clues to Earth's past.

1785
New Theory Suggests Naturalness of Change

James Hutton of Scotland revolutionizes geology with his theory of uniformitarianism. He argues that volcanoes, erosion, and other forces shaped Earth's landscape slowly over a very long period and continue to do so. Hutton's ideas challenge the belief that the landscape is the result of sudden changes and one-time events. His theory leads to a better understanding of the vast ages of Earth and fossils.

1824
Geologist Identifies Bones from Extinct Animal

English geologist William Buckland concludes that a fossilized jawbone comes from an enormous reptilelike animal that is extinct. He names the animal *Megalosaurus*. This is the first dinosaur to be given a scientific name.

| 1720 | 1740 | 1760 | 1780 | 1800 | 1820 | 1840 |

APPLICATION

Mapping Earth's Layers

In the late 1700s, the geologist William Smith helped survey land for canals throughout England and Wales. As workers dug deeper into the ground, Smith noticed that fossils always appeared in the same order. He used this information to create the first map showing the locations of rock layers under surface soil. It was published in 1815. As people began to understand the importance of rock layers, they collected more information from projects that required digging. Maps showing this type of information became more detailed and more useful. Today, geologists combine information collected in the field with data from satellite images to create precise maps of rock layers.

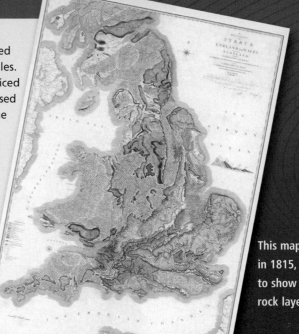

This map, hand-painted in 1815, was the first to show locations of rock layers.

1923
Dinosaur Eggs Show Link with Birds

Researchers in Mongolia find a nest of fossilized dinosaur eggs. The eggs are in a circle. This fact suggests that dinosaurs, like modern birds, moved their eggs and arranged their nests.

1861
Workers Uncover Bird Fossil

Laborers digging up limestone rock in southern Germany find a fossil that looks like a lizard with wings. The fossil is about 150 million years old—the oldest known one of a bird.

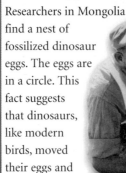

1965
Microfossils Cause Sensation

Two new scientific papers focus attention on Earth's earliest life forms. In these papers scientists describe rocks from Canada that contain microfossils of algae and fungi—traces of life vastly older than any others yet found. These findings trigger huge new efforts in scientific research on ancient life.

1860   1880   1900   1920   1940   1960   1980

TECHNOLOGY
Chemist Creates New Time Scale

In the 1890s, scientists studying radiation began to understand the idea of half-life. The chemist B. B. Boltwood used half-life data to identify the ages of various rocks and create a new geologic time scale. The ages he calculated were in the hundreds of millions or even billions of years—far greater than the ages many scientists had been using. The time scale continues to be modified as new technologies allow for ever more precise measurements.

The half-life of carbon 14 will be used to calculate the ages of the samples this researcher is preparing.

2000

Dinosaur Heart Surprises Many

North Carolina scientists use a medical device called a CT scanner to identify the first known fossilized dinosaur heart. The heart surprises those who thought all dinosaurs were cold-blooded. Its structure suggests that the dinosaur was warm-blooded.

2001

Researchers Find Earliest Mammal

Scientists in China find the oldest known mammal fossil. The 195-million-year-old skull is from an animal that weighed just 2 grams—less than the weight of a penny.

 RESOURCE CENTER
CLASSZONE.COM

Learn more about fossils.

2000

TECHNOLOGY

CT Scans Show That *T. Rex* Could Smell

Computerized tomography (CT) scans are commonly used in medicine to search inside human bodies without surgery. A CT scan of the skull of a *Tyrannosaurus rex* known as Sue showed that it had a large area in its brain for smelling. Its sharp sense of smell, combined with its size and strength, made the tyrannosaur an effective hunter and scavenger.

This skull is part of Sue's skeleton—the largest and most complete *T. rex* yet found.

INTO THE FUTURE

When did life begin on Earth? Fossils have helped scientists answer this question. Many think that the oldest fossils date from 3.5 billion years ago. This date might be pushed back if new techniques identify even older fossils. Or the date might be pushed forward. Some scientists argue that the 3.5-billion-year-old traces in rocks are not really fossils at all. Rather, they argue, the traces are just signs of chemical reactions that did not involve any living organisms.

Research on fossils also helps people evaluate the impact of human activity on the environment. For example, the fossil record shows a pattern of warming and cooling in Earth's history. Human activity, such as burning of coal and oil, has helped cause Earth to get warmer over the past century. Further studies of fossils will help people understand how much of this warming is normal and how much is a result of human action.

ACTIVITIES

Reliving History

Get permission to dig a hole outside. Dig down two feet or more. Draw a sketch showing the layers of soil. Add notes to describe any variations that are not clear in the sketch. Try to explain the differences you notice in the layers.

Writing About Science

Suppose you are an archaeologist who has made one of the fossil discoveries on the timeline. Write a speech to your fellow scientists explaining the importance of your discovery.

CHAPTER

Natural Resources

the BIG idea

Society depends on natural resources for energy and materials.

Key Concepts

SECTION

Natural resources support human activity.
Learn about the costs and benefits of using natural resources to obtain energy and to make products.

SECTION

Resources can be conserved and recycled.
Learn about efforts to conserve and recycle natural resources.

SECTION

Energy comes from other natural resources.
Learn how nuclear power and renewable resources can provide energy to the world.

Internet Preview

CLASSZONE.COM

Chapter 5 online resources: Content Review, Simulation, Visualization, three Resource Centers, Math Tutorial, Test Practice

How do people obtain energy from Earth's resources?

EXPLORE (the BIG idea)

Sunlight as an Energy Source

Tape black paper around two plastic cups. Half fill the cups with water. Fasten plastic wrap over each top with rubber bands. Place one cup in sunlight and one cup in shade. Wait half an hour. Remove the plastic wrap. Place a thermometer in each cup to measure the water temperature.

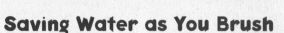

Observe and Think
What happened to the water temperature in each cup? How do you think people might use sunlight as a source of energy?

Saving Water as You Brush

Time how long it takes you to brush your teeth. Then set aside a bucket or large container and a measuring cup. Close the sink's drain; run the water for the same length of time you brushed your teeth. How many cups of water can you bail out of the sink?

Observe and Think
Estimate how much water you could save in a week by turning the water off as you brush.

Internet Activity: Resources

Go to **ClassZone.com** to learn more about natural resources and energy.

Observe and Think
What are the most important natural resources in your state?

Getting Ready to Learn

◀ CONCEPT REVIEW

- Fossils preserve the remains of living things from long ago.
- Fossils and half-lives of elements can be used to determine the age of Earth's rock layers.
- The same forces that have changed Earth in the past are still at work today.

◀ VOCABULARY REVIEW

fossil p. 111
half-life p. 123
See glossary for definitions.

geosphere, mineral

 CONTENT REVIEW
CLASSZONE.COM
Review concepts and vocabulary.

▶ TAKING NOTES

CHOOSE YOUR OWN STRATEGY

As you read, take notes, using one or more of the strategies from earlier chapters—**main idea and detail notes, supporting main ideas, content frame,** or **outline.** Mix and match these strategies, or use an entirely different one.

VOCABULARY STRATEGY

Write each new vocabulary term in the center of a **four-square** diagram. Write notes in the squares around the term. Include a definition, some characteristics, and some examples. If possible, write some things that are not examples.

See the Note-Taking Handbook on pages R45–R51.

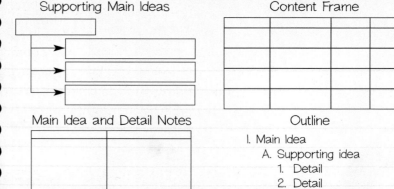

SCIENCE NOTEBOOK

Supporting Main Ideas

Content Frame

Main Idea and Detail Notes

Outline

I. Main Idea
　A. Supporting idea
　　1. Detail
　　2. Detail
　B. Supporting idea

Definition	Characteristics
a natural resource that can be replaced by nature in a fairly short time	
RENEWABLE RESOURCE	
Examples	Non-examples
wind, plant waste, wood	coal, natural gas, oil

Natural resources support human activity.

◀ BEFORE, you learned	▶ NOW, you will learn
• Earth's distant past is revealed in rocks and fossils	• What makes a natural resource renewable or nonrenewable
• Layers of sedimentary rock show relative ages	• About benefits and costs of using fossil fuels
• Living things have inhabited Earth for over 3 billion years	• How people use natural resources in modern life

VOCABULARY

natural resource p. 147
renewable resource p. 148
nonrenewable resource p. 148
fossil fuel p. 150

THINK ABOUT

What resources do you need the most?

Think about all the products you use at school and at home—clothing, books, video games, CDs, backpacks, and other items.

Which ones do you use the most often? What materials are these products made of? Plastic? Cloth? Metal? What would you lose if one of these materials, such as plastic, vanished from Earth overnight?

Natural resources provide materials and energy.

VOCABULARY
Use a four-square diagram for the term *natural resource* in your notebook.

For thousands of years, people have used natural resources to make tools, build cities, heat their homes, and in general make their lives more comfortable. A **natural resource** is any energy source, organism, or substance found in nature that people use.

The four parts of the Earth system—atmosphere, hydrosphere, biosphere, and geosphere—provide all the materials needed to sustain human life. The atmosphere, for instance, provides the air you breathe and the rain that helps living things grow. The hydrosphere contains all of Earth's waters in rivers, lakes, oceans, and underground. The biosphere and the geosphere are sources of food, fuel, clothing, and shelter.

However, people also know that there are costs as well as benefits in using natural resources. For example, burning coal produces heat but also releases smoke that pollutes the air. When forests are cut down, the soil beneath is exposed to the air. Wind and rain can strip away valuable topsoil, making it harder for new trees to grow. The soil can choke streams and rivers and kill fish and other animals living in the waters. As you can see, using resources from one part of Earth's system affects all the other parts.

People are also concerned about saving natural resources. Some resources, such as the water in a river or the wind used to turn a windmill, are constantly being replaced. But others, such as oil, take millions of years to form. If these resources are used faster than they are replaced, they will run out. Today people are more aware of which resources are renewable and which are nonrenewable.

 CHECK YOUR READING Summarize the costs and benefits of using natural resources.

Renewable Resources

The charts on page 149 list some of the most common resources people use in modern life. As you might have guessed, sunlight, wind, water, and trees and other plants are renewable. A **renewable resource** is a natural resource that can be replaced in nature at about the same rate it is used.

For example, a lumber company might plant a new tree for each mature tree it cuts down. Over time, the forest will continue to have the same number of trees. However, if the trees are cut down faster than they can be replaced, even a renewable resource will run out.

Nonrenewable Resources

A **nonrenewable resource** is a natural resource that exists in a fixed amount or that is used up faster than it can be replaced in nature. This means the supply of any nonrenewable resource is limited. In general, all resources produced by geologic forces—coal, natural gas, oil, uranium—are nonrenewable. These resources form over millions of years.

Today people are using coal, oil, and natural gas much faster than they are forming in nature. As a result, these resources are becoming more scarce and expensive. Many countries realize that they must conserve their nonrenewable resources. Some, like the United States, are developing alternative energy sources, such as solar and wind energy.

 CHECK YOUR READING Compare and contrast renewable and nonrenewable resources.

Natural resources can be classified as renewable and nonrenewable resources.

Renewable Resources

Resource	Common Uses
Sunlight	power for solar cells and batteries, heating of homes and businesses, and generating electricity
Wind	power to move windmills that pump water, grind grain, and generate electricity
Water	power to generate electricity, transportation with boats and ships, drinking and washing
Trees and other plants	materials for furniture, clothing, fuel, dyes, medicines, paper, cardboard, and generating electricity
Animal waste	material for fuels

Nonrenewable Resources

Resource	Common Uses
Coal	fuel to generate electricity, chemicals for medicines and consumer products
Oil	fuel for cars, airplanes, and trucks; fuel for heating and generating electricity; chemicals for plastics, synthetic fabrics, medicines, grease, and wax
Natural gas	fuel for heating, cooking, and generating electricity
Uranium	fuel to generate electricity
Minerals and rocks	materials for coins, jewelry, building, computer chips, lasers, household products, paint, and dyes

READING
VISUALS   Read the common uses of each resource. Which of these resources are used to generate electricity?

Fossil fuels supply most of society's energy.

When you turn on the air conditioner, a computer, or a microwave oven, you may use energy from fossil fuels. Millions of people depend on these fuels—coal, oil, and natural gas—for electricity, heat, and fuel.

A **fossil fuel** is a nonrenewable energy source formed from ancient plants and animals buried in Earth's crust for millions of years. The energy in such a fuel represents a form of stored sunlight, since ancient organisms depended on the sun. The buried organisms form layers at the bottom of oceans, ponds, and swamps. Over a long time, this material is compressed and pushed deeper into Earth's crust. High heat and pressure change it chemically into coal, oil, and natural gas.

CHECK YOUR READING Explain how fossil fuels are formed from ancient organisms.

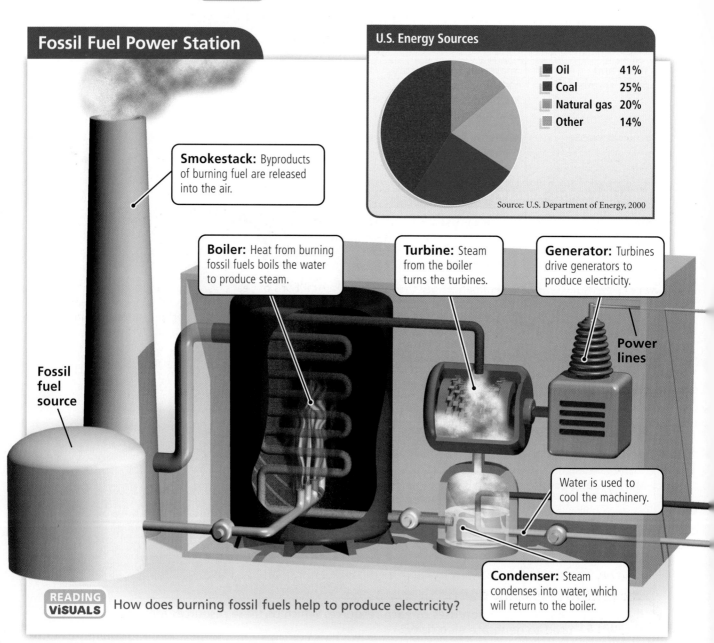

Fossil Fuel Power Station

U.S. Energy Sources

■ Oil	41%
■ Coal	25%
■ Natural gas	20%
▨ Other	14%

Source: U.S. Department of Energy, 2000

Smokestack: Byproducts of burning fuel are released into the air.

Boiler: Heat from burning fossil fuels boils the water to produce steam.

Turbine: Steam from the boiler turns the turbines.

Generator: Turbines drive generators to produce electricity.

Power lines

Fossil fuel source

Water is used to cool the machinery.

Condenser: Steam condenses into water, which will return to the boiler.

READING VISUALS How does burning fossil fuels help to produce electricity?

Fossil fuels burn easily and produce a lot of heat. They are used to run most of the power plants that generate electricity. As shown in the diagram on page 150, heat from a burning fuel is used to change water into steam. The steam turns a turbine. The turbine drives a generator to produce electricity, which is carried through power lines to towns and cities. Electricity runs nearly everything in modern life, from giant factories to the smallest light in your home.

But these resources also harm the environment. Burning fossil fuels produces excess carbon dioxide, harmful acids, and other forms of pollution. Most of this pollution comes from power plants and fossil fuels burned by cars and other vehicles.

READING TiP

Turbine is based on the Latin *turbo,* which means "spinning top." *Generator* is based on the Latin *generāre,* which means "to produce."

Coal

Coal is a solid fossil fuel formed underground from buried and decayed plant material. As shown below, heat and pressure determine the type of coal formed. The hardest coal makes the best energy source. It burns hotter and much cleaner than softer coals. At one time, coal was the main source of energy in the United States.

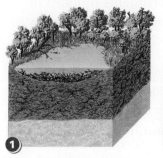

① Swamp plants decay and are compressed to form peat.

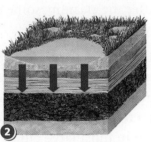

② Sediments bury the peat, and rising pressure and heat change it into soft coal.

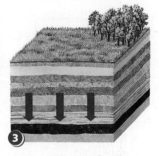

③ Over millions of years, increasing pressure and heat form harder coal.

④ It takes the longest time and the greatest heat and pressure to form the hardest coal.

The world's largest coal deposits are in the United States, Russia, and China. People use surface mining and deep mining to obtain coal. In surface mines, overlying rock is stripped away to expose the coal. In deep mines, miners must go underground to dig out the coal. Most of the world's coal is used to fuel power plants and to run factories that produce steel and cement.

When burned as a fuel, however, coal produces byproducts that pollute air and water. Also, surface mining can destroy entire landscapes. Coal dust in deep mines damages miners' lungs. Yet reducing pollution, restoring landscapes, and protecting miners cost millions of dollars. Society faces a difficult choice—keep the cost of energy low or raise the price to protect the environment and human health.

CHECK YOUR READING   What is the main use of coal?

Oil and Natural Gas

READING TiP

Non- is a Latin prefix meaning "not." Porous rock is full of tiny cracks or holes. Therefore, *nonporous* rock is rock that does not have tiny cracks or holes.

Most oil and natural gas is trapped underground in porous rock. Heat and pressure can push the oil and natural gas upward until they reach a layer of nonporous rock, where they collect. As shown in the illustration below, wells can be drilled through the nonporous rock to bring the oil and natural gas to the surface. Major oil and natural gas deposits are found under the oceans as well as on land.

 CHECK YOUR READING How is oil removed from layers of rock?

Recovered oil is transported by ships, trucks, and pipelines from the wells to refineries. Refineries use heat to break down the oil into its different parts. Each part is used to make different products, from gasoline and jet fuel to cleaning supplies and plastics. Oil and natural gas burn at high temperatures, releasing energy. They are easily transported, which makes them ideal fuels to heat homes and to power vehicles.

There are costs in using oil. When ships that transport oil are damaged, they can spill millions of gallons into the environment. These spills pollute coastlines and waterways, killing many plants and animals. Cleaning up these spills costs governments millions of dollars each year. Even after the cleanup, some of the oil will remain in the environment for years.

Air pollution is another problem. Waste products from the burning of gasoline, jet fuels, and diesel fuels react with sunlight to produce smog—a foglike layer of air pollution. Some countries have passed clean air laws to reduce this pollution. Yet smog continues to be a problem in most large cities.

CHECK YOUR READING What are the benefits and costs of using oil?

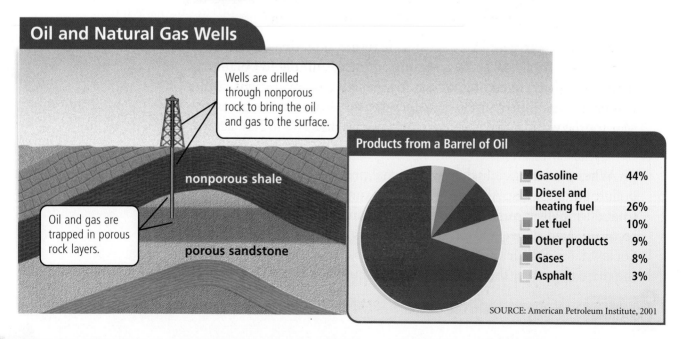

Oil and Natural Gas Wells

Wells are drilled through nonporous rock to bring the oil and gas to the surface.

nonporous shale

Oil and gas are trapped in porous rock layers.

porous sandstone

Products from a Barrel of Oil

Product	Percent
Gasoline	44%
Diesel and heating fuel	26%
Jet fuel	10%
Other products	9%
Gases	8%
Asphalt	3%

SOURCE: American Petroleum Institute, 2001

INVESTIGATE Fossil Fuels

Why does an oil spill do so much harm?

PROCEDURE

① Fill the pan about halfway with water. Using an eyedropper, carefully add 10 drops of oil in the middle of the pan. Rock the pan gently.

② Observe what happens to the drops of oil over the next 2 min. Record your observations in your **Science Notebook.**

③ Place the plastic-foam ball in the oil slick, wait a few seconds, then carefully lift the ball out again. Examine it and record your observations.

WHAT DO YOU THINK?

• What happened when the drops of oil came in contact with the water?

• What might happen to an animal that swims through spilled oil?

CHALLENGE Think of a way to clean up the oil slick on the water. Discuss your ideas with your teacher before you test your cleaning method.

SKILL FOCUS
Modeling

MATERIALS
• water
• vegetable oil
• large pan (at least 22 cm)
• plastic-foam ball (about 5 cm)
• eyedropper

TIME
20 minutes

Fossil fuels, minerals, and plants supply materials for modern products.

Many of the products you use come from fossil fuels. For example, oil is broken down into different chemicals used to make plastics. Plastic materials can be easily shaped, colored, and formed. They are used in electronic and computer equipment, in packaging, in cars and airplanes, and in such personal items as your shoes, toothbrush, and comb.

Minerals are found in cars and airplanes, tools, wires, computer chips, and probably your chair. Minerals such as limestone, gypsum, sand, and salt are used to make building materials and cement. In the United States, it takes 9,720 kilograms (20,000 lbs) of minerals every year to make the products used by just one person.

Plants are used to make another large group of products. For centuries people have used wood to build homes and to make furniture, household utensils, and different types of paper. Plants are also rich sources of dyes, fibers, and medicines. The plant indigo, for example, has been used to dye fabrics since Roman times.

These products benefit people's lives in many important ways, but they also have drawbacks. Fossil fuels must be burned to generate power for the factories and businesses that produce these products.

Consumer Products

Thousands of everyday products are made from natural resources.

Fossil Fuels

Fossil fuels are used to make thousands of products from aspirin to zippers. For example, oil-based plastics are used to make this motocross rider's safety helmet, suit, gloves, and boots. Gasoline powers the motorbike.

Minerals and Rocks

The U.S. Treasury uses zinc, copper, and nickel to mint over 14 billion coins a year. Gold and silver are used in special coins.

Trees and Other Plants

Each year, the United States produces about 400 billion square feet of corrugated cardboard used to make boxes of all sizes.

Factory waste can pollute air, water, and soil. Even making computer chips can be a problem. So much water is needed to clean the chips during manufacture that local water supplies may be reduced.

To maintain modern life and to protect the planet, people must use natural resources wisely. In the next section you will read about ways for every person to conserve resources and reduce pollution.

5.1 Review

KEY CONCEPTS

1. Define *renewable resource* and *nonrenewable resource*. Give four examples of each type of resource.

2. List three advantages and three disadvantages of using fossil fuels.

3. In what ways are natural resources used to make people's lives more comfortable?

CRITICAL THINKING

4. **Infer** Why do you think people are willing to accept the costs as well as the benefits of using fossil fuels?

5. **Predict** If supplies of coal, oil, and natural gas ran out tomorrow, what are some of the ways your life would change?

⚠CHALLENGE

6. **Apply** Suppose you are lost in the woods, miles from any city or town. You have some dried food and matches but no other supplies. What natural resources might you use to survive until you are found?

Got Oil Spills? Call in the Microbes!

You have seen the photographs. A beautiful coastline is fouled by dark, sticky oil. The oil slick coats birds and other animals the same dark color. Hundreds of experts and volunteers appear with buckets, chemicals, shovels, and brooms to clean up the mess.

But did you know that seawater and the world's beaches contain their own natural cleanup crews? These crews consist of tiny microbes that digest oil and other waste products and turn them into gases such as carbon dioxide.

Nature's Disposal Units Do a Great Job . . .

Scientists learned how effective oil-digesting microbes are during the 1989 *Exxon Valdez* oil spill in Alaska. Since then, cleanup crews have been using bacteria and other microbes to help clean up oil spills around the world. Scientists find that areas treated with microbes recover faster than areas treated with chemicals.

. . . But It Is Not All That Simple

Cleaning up oil spills is not as simple as watching millions of microbes munch their way through the mess. Scientists have had to solve a few problems.

- **Problem:** Microbes cannot multiply fast enough to handle a large oil spill. **Solution:** Add nutrients to help them multiply faster.

- **Problem:** There are not enough of the right types of microbes to digest oil. **Solution:** Grow the desired microbes in a laboratory, and add them into the polluted area.

- **Problem:** There is not enough oxygen in the water for all the microbes. **Solution:** Pump in more oxygen to help them work.

Who would have imagined that a partnership between people and microbes would be the best way to clean up oil spills?

EXPLORE

1. **COLLECT DATA** Go to the EPA Web site to learn how the agency uses microbes to clean up different types of pollution. Look under the word *bioremediation,* which means "the correction of a problem through biological means."

2. **CHALLENGE** Do research on bioremediation and find out whether there are any drawbacks to using microbes to clean up pollution.

RESOURCE CENTER Read about microbes that CLASSZONE.COM eat pollutants for lunch.

Above is the oil-eating microbe *Pseudomonas fluorescens,* magnified 17,300 times. Millions of microbes like this swim in the water layer that surrounds soil particles. They digest oil clinging to the particles.

This otter swam through a spill and was covered in black, sticky oil. Animals who try to clean their fur will swallow the oil, which is poisonous.

KEY CONCEPT

5.2 Resources can be conserved and recycled.

 BEFORE, you learned

- Natural resources are either renewable or nonrenewable
- Fossil fuels are used to supply most of society's energy and products, but at a cost to the environment

 NOW, you will learn

- How conservation can help people to reduce waste and reuse natural resources
- How recycling can help people to recover and extend natural resources

VOCABULARY

conservation p. 157
recycling p. 158

EXPLORE Energy Use

What is your EQ (energy quotient)?

PROCEDURE

1. Think about the electrical appliances you use every day at home (TV, computer, room lights, microwave, hair curler, hair dryer). Draw a usage chart like the one in the photo.

2. Estimate the number of hours you use each item every day. Add up all the hours in each column.

3. Multiply the total of each column by 2.5 kilowatts. This is your energy quotient.

WHAT DO YOU THINK?

- Which item(s) do you use the most? How much of the use is necessary?
- What ways can you think of to conserve electricity each day?

MATERIALS

- paper
- pen or pencil
- calculator

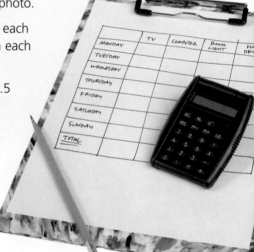

Conservation involves reducing waste and reusing natural resources.

NOTE TAKING
You might want to take main idea and details notes as you read this section.

In the 1960s, each person in the United States produced 1.2 kilograms (2.7 lb) of trash a day. Today, that number has doubled. All together, the nation's households produce nearly 180 million tons of trash each year! Over half of this amount is buried in landfills.

Conservation programs can be used to extend natural resources, to protect human health, and to slow the growing mountain of trash. Read on to find out how much your efforts count.

Conservation means protecting, restoring, and managing natural resources so that they last as long as possible. Conserving resources can also reduce the amount of pollution released into the air, water, and soil. There are two ways every person can help: reducing and reusing.

Reduce You can reduce waste at the source, whether the source is a local retail store or your own home. Here are a few suggestions:

- When choosing between two similar products, choose the one with less packaging. Product packaging is a major source of paper and plastic waste.
- When brushing your teeth or washing your face, turn the water off until you are ready to rinse. You can save 8 to 23 liters (2 to 6 gal.) of water a day, or 2920 to 8395 liters (730 to 2190 gal.) per year.
- When eating in a restaurant or cafeteria, use only the napkins and ketchup and mustard packets that you really need. The less you throw away, the less garbage will be buried in a landfill.
- Where possible, use energy-efficient light bulbs in your home. Turn off lights and appliances when you are not using them.

Reuse Many products can be used more than once. Reusable products and containers conserve materials and resources. Here are some things that you can do:

- Refill plastic water bottles instead of buying new bottles.
- Donate old clothes and other items instead of throwing them away.
- Rinse and reuse plastic sandwich and storage bags.
- Cut the top off a half-gallon container to make a watering can.

VOCABULARY
Add a four-square diagram for the term *conservation* in your notebook.

Reducing Waste

You can reduce paper and plastic waste by choosing products with the least packaging.

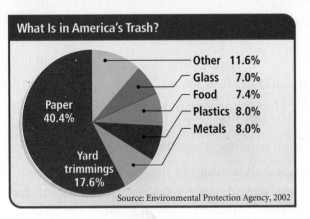

What Is in America's Trash?

Other 11.6%
Glass 7.0%
Food 7.4%
Plastics 8.0%
Metals 8.0%
Paper 40.4%
Yard trimmings 17.6%

Source: Environmental Protection Agency, 2002

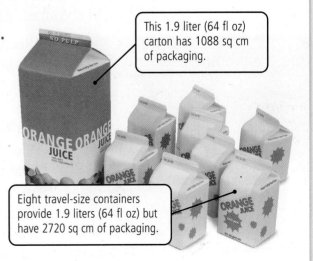

This 1.9 liter (64 fl oz) carton has 1088 sq cm of packaging.

Eight travel-size containers provide 1.9 liters (64 fl oz) but have 2720 sq cm of packaging.

INVESTIGATE Conservation

How can you tell which bulb wastes less energy?

The more heat a light bulb gives off, the more energy it wastes. Use what you know about how to measure the temperature of an object to design an experiment that confirms which type of light bulb wastes less energy.

DESIGN
— YOUR OWN —
EXPERIMENT

MATERIALS
- 2 table lamps
- incandescent light bulb
- fluorescent light bulb
- 2 thermometers
- pen or pencil

PROCEDURE

1. Figure out how you are going to test which light bulb—incandescent or fluorescent—wastes less energy.

2. Write up your procedure.

3. Conduct your experiment and record your results.

WHAT DO YOU THINK?

- What were the variables in your experiment?
- What were the results of your experiment?
- How does your experiment demonstrate which light bulb is less wasteful?

Recycling involves recovering and extending natural resources.

Did you know that recycling one aluminum can saves enough energy to run a television set for three hours? **Recycling** involves recovering materials that people usually throw away. Some common materials you can recycle are glass, aluminum cans, certain plastics, paper, scrap iron, and such metals as gold, copper, and silver. Here are a few statistics that might encourage you to recycle:

- Recycling 90 percent of the newspapers printed in the United States on just one Sunday would save 500,000 trees, equivalent to an entire forest.
- The energy saved by recycling one glass bottle will light a 100-watt bulb for four hours.
- Five 2-liter plastic bottles can be recycled into enough plastic fiber to fill a ski jacket. Thirty-six bottles will make enough fiber for a square yard of synthetic carpet.
- If you recycled all household newspapers, cardboard, glass, and metal, you could reduce the use of fossil fuels. It takes less energy to make products from recycled materials than to make new products.

With every item you recycle, you help to recover and extend limited resources.

Recycled: 500 kilograms (1,102 lb) of cans, glass, plastic, and paper

Buried in landfill: 2500 kilograms (5,512 lb) of garbage

The average family of four generates about 3,000 kilograms (6614 lb) of trash per year. Recycling is catching on, but there is still a long way to go.

It is important to remember that not every item can be recycled or reused. In the photograph above, for instance, only about one-fifth of the family's trash is being recycled. Even some types of plastic and glass items must be thrown away because they cannot be recovered. All the trash in the family's plastic bags will be buried in landfills. You can see why it is important to recycle the items you can and to avoid using items that cannot be recycled.

Recycling is only part of the solution to our resource problems. It takes time, energy, and money to collect waste materials, sort them, remove what can be used, and form new objects. Even with these limitations, however, recycling can help extend available resources and protect human health and the environment.

CHECK YOUR READING What are some of the benefits and drawbacks of recycling?

 **Review**

KEY CONCEPTS

1. Give examples of ways people can reduce waste and conserve natural resources.

2. Explain how recycling can help people recover and extend natural resources.

3. What are some of the limitations of conservation and recycling programs?

CRITICAL THINKING

4. **Evaluate** How can conserving or recycling materials help protect the environment?

5. **Calculate** Your city pays $115 per ton to bury an average of 13 tons of garbage a month in a landfill. A recycling program could reduce that number to 8 tons a month. How much would the city save in landfill fees per month? per year?

⬤ CHALLENGE

6. **Synthesize** Work with a group of classmates to list some of the ways in which you could conserve and recycle resources in your home and at school. Create a graphic—such as a poster or advertisement—to present your ideas to the rest of the class.

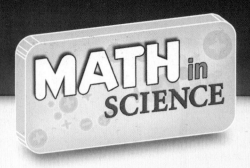

MATH in SCIENCE

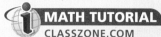

MATH TUTORIAL
CLASSZONE.COM
Click on Math Tutorial for more help with comparing decimals.

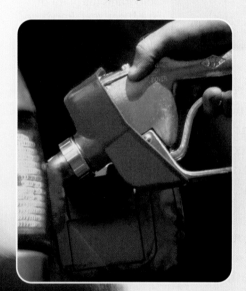

Gas Mileage

An automobile engineer ran tests on new cars to determine their gas mileage in miles per gallon. Her results were in decimals. You can compare two decimals by looking at their place values to determine which is greater.

Steps for comparing decimals

(1) Write the decimals in a column, lining up the decimal points.

(2) If necessary, write zeros to the right of one decimal so that both decimals have the same number of decimal places.

(3) Compare the place values from left to right.

Examples

Example A
For two mid-size sedans, she calculated the following mileages:

The tens digits are the same.
The ones digits are the same.

Car A: 28.450 mi/gal
Car B: 28.502 mi/gal

The tenths digits are different: 5 > 4.

ANSWER:
28.450 mi/gal < 28.502 mi/gal

Example B
For two sport utility vehicles (SUVs), she calculated the following mileages:

The tens digits are the same.
The ones digits are the same.

SUV A: 12.94 mi/gal
SUV B: 12.90 mi/gal

The tenths digits are the same.
The hundredths digits are different: 4 > 0.

ANSWER:
12.94 mi/gal > 12.90 mi/gal

Copy each statement and complete it with <, >, or =.

1. 34.75 mi/gal ___ 34.56 mi/gal

2. 50.5 mi/gal ___ 50.50 mi/gal

3. 52.309 mi/gal ___ 52.311 mi/gal

4. 26.115 mi/gal ___ 26.106 mi/gal

5. 41.75 mi/gal ___ 41.750 mi/gal

CHALLENGE Find a value of n that makes the following statement true:

38.0894 mi/gal > n > 38.08925 mi/gal

5.3

Energy comes from other natural resources.

BEFORE, you learned

- Conservation helps people reduce waste and reuse natural resources
- Recycling helps people recover and extend natural resources

NOW, you will learn

- About the benefits and costs of nuclear power
- How renewable resources are used to generate energy

VOCABULARY

nuclear fission p. 161
hydroelectric energy p. 164
solar cell p. 165
geothermal energy p. 166
biomass p. 168
hydrogen fuel cell p. 168

EXPLORE Nuclear Energy

How can you model splitting atoms?

PROCEDURE

(1) Work in a small group for this activity. Draw a large circle on a piece of paper. Set the paper on the floor or on a countertop.

(2) Put a handful of marbles in the circle (see the photograph). Imagine the circle is an atom and the marbles are particles in its nucleus.

(3) Take turns shooting one marble into the others. Put the marbles back in the circle after each shot. Record your observations.

WHAT DO YOU THINK?

- How many marbles were moved by each shot?
- What does this activity suggest will happen when the center of an atom is struck?

MATERIALS
- marbles
- large piece of paper
- pen or marker

NOTE TAKING

As you read this section, pick a note-taking strategy that will help you list the benefits and limits of each type of energy source.

Nuclear power is used to produce electricity.

Fossil fuels are the most commonly used sources of energy, but they are not the only ones. The United States and many other countries use nuclear power to produce electricity. In the United States, nuclear power plants generate about 10 percent of the total energy used.

You learned that in fossil fuel power plants, water is boiled to make steam that turns a turbine, which drives a generator. In a nuclear power plant, the same process happens. However, the source of energy used to heat the water is nuclear fission. In the process of **nuclear fission,** the nucleus of a radioactive atom is split, forming lighter elements and releasing a huge amount of energy.

A uranium nucleus splits, forming lighter elements and releasing neutrons and a great deal of energy.

neutron

uranium nucleus

lighter elements

energy

Nuclear power plants use uranium atoms as fuel. When a uranium nucleus splits, it forms two smaller nuclei. It also releases two or three neutrons and a large amount of energy in the form of light and heat. The neutrons split other uranium nuclei in a process called a chain reaction. This process is similar to shooting one marble into a group of marbles. Every marble that is hit will strike others nearby.

The power-plant diagram below shows the reactor vessel where the chain reaction takes place. Control rods are used to limit the reaction to provide a safe amount of energy. The chain reaction creates enough heat to produce steam in the reactor vessel. The steam heats a coiled pipe, which is used to boil water in the heat exchanger.

Steam from the exchanger turns the turbines, which drive the generators that produce electricity. The steam condenses into water and is pumped back into the heat exchanger. Water from the cooling tower keeps the equipment from overheating. As you can see, nuclear power plants require an abundant water supply to produce steam and to stay cool.

Nuclear Power Plant

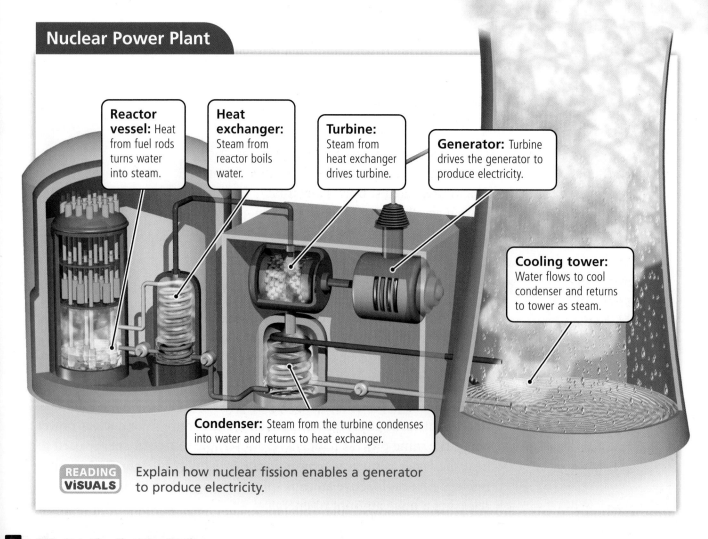

Reactor vessel: Heat from fuel rods turns water into steam.

Heat exchanger: Steam from reactor boils water.

Turbine: Steam from heat exchanger drives turbine.

Generator: Turbine drives the generator to produce electricity.

Cooling tower: Water flows to cool condenser and returns to tower as steam.

Condenser: Steam from the turbine condenses into water and returns to heat exchanger.

READING VISUALS Explain how nuclear fission enables a generator to produce electricity.

cooling towers

reactor buildings

turbine buildings

water source

Splitting just one atom of uranium releases 20 million times more energy than does burning one molecule of natural gas. However, nuclear fission also produces radioactive waste. Radioactivity is a form of energy that can cause death and disease if living things are exposed to it long enough. Nuclear waste from a power plant will remain radioactive for thousands of years. Countries that use nuclear energy face the challenge of storing this waste safely. The storage sites must keep any radioactivity from escaping until the waste material becomes harmless.

A nuclear power plant usually has three main sections: reactor buildings, turbine buildings, and cooling towers.

 CHECK YOUR READING   Explain how fission is used to generate energy.

 SIMULATION
CLASSZONE.COM

Explore how a nuclear power plant produces energy.

Renewable resources are used to produce electricity and fuel.

Moving water, wind, Earth's internal heat, sunlight, living matter, and hydrogen are all sources of renewable energy. Unlike fossil fuels, many of these sources of energy are in unlimited supply. They usually produce electricity or fuel with little or no pollution. Using these clean energy sources helps preserve the environment and protect human health.

So far, however, these resources cannot produce enough energy to pay for the cost of developing them on a large scale. As a result, renewable resources provide only a small percentage of the energy used in the world. In the United States, only about 6 percent of the total energy used comes from these resources.

Scientists and engineers must improve the necessary technologies before renewable resources can supply clean energy to more of the world's people. Imagine if everyone's car ran on hydrogen and produced only water as a byproduct. Or think of solar panels generating enough electricity to light a major city. These visions could come true in your lifetime.

 CHECK YOUR READING   What makes renewable resources attractive as energy sources?

Hydroelectric Energy

Hydroelectric energy is electricity produced by moving water. If you have ever stood near a waterfall or even just turned on a faucet, you have felt the force of moving water. People can use flowing water to generate electricity.

In most cases, a dam is built across a large river, blocking the river's flow and creating an artificial lake, or reservoir. As the illustration below shows, water from the lake enters the dam through intake gates and flows down a tunnel. The fast flowing water turns turbines that drive generators, which produce electricity. Because hydroelectric power does not burn any fuel, it produces no pollution. Dams in the United States generate enough electricity to save 500 million barrels of oil a year.

However, building dams poses problems for the environment. By flooding land to create reservoirs, dams destroy wildlife habitats. In some rivers, such as the Snake and Columbia rivers in the United States, dams interfere with the annual migration of salmon and other fish. Also, areas near the end of the river may receive less water than before, making it harder to raise crops and livestock.

RESOURCE CENTER
CLASSZONE.COM

Learn more about the benefits and costs of renewable energy resources.

Areas with large rivers can use their power to produce electricity. The dam in the photo was built on the Yukon River in Alaska.

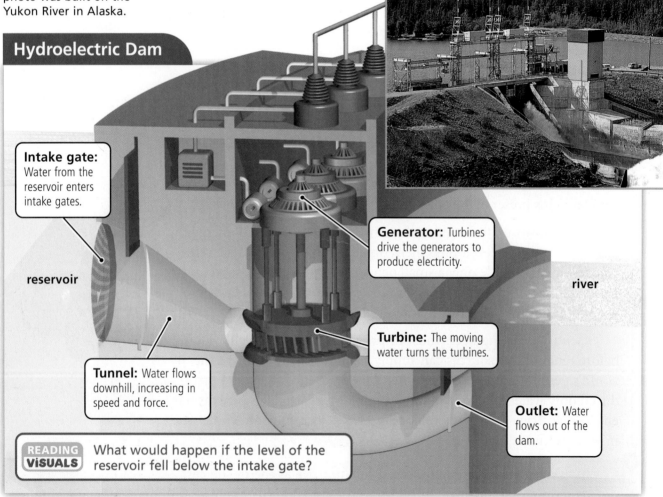

Hydroelectric Dam

Intake gate: Water from the reservoir enters intake gates.

reservoir

Tunnel: Water flows downhill, increasing in speed and force.

Generator: Turbines drive the generators to produce electricity.

Turbine: The moving water turns the turbines.

river

Outlet: Water flows out of the dam.

READING VISUALS What would happen if the level of the reservoir fell below the intake gate?

Solar Energy

Only a small fraction of the sun's energy falls on Earth. Yet even this amount is huge. Every day enough energy from the sun strikes the United States to supply all the nation's energy needs for one and a half years. The problem is how to use this abundant resource to produce electricity.

In an effort to solve the problem, scientists developed solar cells. A **solar cell** is a specially constructed sandwich of silicon and other materials that converts light energy to electricity. As shown in the diagram below, when sunlight strikes the cell, electrons move from the lower to the upper layer, producing an electric current. Individual solar cells can power small appliances, such as calculators and lights.

Solar cells can be wired together in solar panels, which provide heat and electricity for homes and businesses. Solar panels are also used to power some spacecraft and space stations once they are in orbit. To meet the energy needs of some cities, hundreds or even thousands of solar panels are built into large structures called arrays. Many western cities like Barstow, California, receive part of their electricity from solar arrays.

Sunlight is an unlimited source of clean energy. But current methods of collecting sunlight are expensive and somewhat inefficient. As solar technology improves, sunlight is likely to become an important energy source for the world.

VOCABULARY
Add a four-square diagram for the term *solar cell* in your notebook.

READING TiP

Array refers to an arrangement of objects in rows and columns.

CHECK YOUR READING How can people use sunlight to produce electricity?

Sunlight strikes a **solar cell,** and electrons move to produce an electric current.

Solar cells, wired into **panels,** produce more current.

Panels are built into **arrays,** which supply electricity through power plants like the one shown below.

solar arrays

power plant station

Geothermal Energy

READING TiP

Geothermal combines the Greek prefix *geo-*, meaning "earth," and the Greek word *thermē*, meaning "heat."

Imagine tapping into Earth's heat to obtain electricity for your home. In some places, that is exactly what people do. They use **geothermal energy,** or energy produced by heat within Earth's crust.

Geothermal energy comes from underground water that is heated by hot rock. The illustration below shows how hot water is piped from a well into a power plant. This superheated water enters a flash tank and produces enough steam to run turbines, which power generators. Excess water is then pumped back into the ground. Some plants also pipe hot water into homes and businesses for heating.

In the United States, geothermal energy provides electricity for nearly 3.5 million homes. Other major geothermal power plants are in New Zealand and Iceland.

Geothermal energy is clean and renewable. So far, its use is limited to areas where hot water is fairly close to the surface. However, some companies are experimenting with pumping cold water into underground areas of hot rock found in all parts of Earth's crust. The rock heats the water, which is then pumped back to the surface and used

In Iceland, geothermal power plants like the one in the photograph supply nearly all of the country's electricity.

Geothermal Power Plant

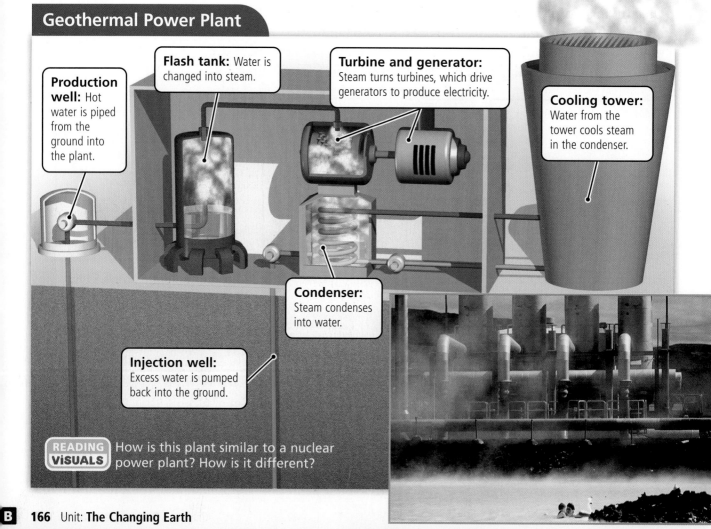

Production well: Hot water is piped from the ground into the plant.

Flash tank: Water is changed into steam.

Turbine and generator: Steam turns turbines, which drive generators to produce electricity.

Cooling tower: Water from the tower cools steam in the condenser.

Condenser: Steam condenses into water.

Injection well: Excess water is pumped back into the ground.

READING ViSUALS How is this plant similar to a nuclear power plant? How is it different?

to generate electricity. This new technique may allow more countries to make use of geothermal energy.

 CHECK YOUR READING What is the source of geothermal energy?

Wind Energy

For thousands of years, people have captured the tremendous energy of wind to move ships, grind grain, and pump water from underground. Today, people also use wind energy—from the force of moving air—to generate electricity.

The modern windmill is made of metal and plastic and can stand as tall as a 40-story building. The blades act as a turbine, turning a set of gears that drives the generator. The amount of electricity a windmill produces depends on the speed and angle of the wind across its blades. The faster the blades turn, the more power the windmill produces.

REMINDER
The generator is the part that produces the electric current, whether it is driven by turbines or gears.

To supply electricity to an area, hundreds of windmills are built on a "wind farm." Wind farms, like the one in the photograph below, are already producing electricity in California, Hawaii, New Hampshire, and several other states. Other countries, such as Denmark and Germany, also use wind farms to supply electricity to some of their cities.

Although wind energy is clean and renewable, it has certain drawbacks. It depends on steady, strong winds blowing most of the time, which are found only in a few places. Wind farms take up a great deal of land, and the turning blades can be noisy. There is also a limit to how much power each windmill can produce. However, in the future, wind farms may become more productive and more widely used.

 CHECK YOUR READING What factor determines how much electricity a windmill produces?

blade

gears

controller

generator

The blades turn the gears, which drive the generator to produce electricity. The controller points the windmill's head into the wind to keep the blades turning rapidly.

Biomass Energy

Biomass is organic matter, such as plant and animal waste, that can be used as fuel. The U.S. Department of Energy works with state and local groups to find ways of converting biomass materials into energy sources.

This wood-burning biomass plant sends electrical energy at a rate of 21 million watts to the San Francisco Bay area. Wood waste products are collected from farms and industries as fuel for the plant.

Each year biomass power stations in the United States burn about 60 million tons of wood and other plant material to generate 37 billion kilowatt hours of electricity. That is more electricity than the state of Colorado uses in an entire year. Small biomass stations are used in rural areas to supply power to farms and towns. Fast-growing trees, grasses, and other crops can be planted to supply a renewable energy source that is cheaper than fossil fuels.

Some plant and animal waste can be converted into liquid fuels. The sugar and starch in corn and potatoes, for example, are made into a liquid fuel called ethanol. Ethanol can be added to gasoline to form gasohol. This fuel can power small cars, farm machinery, and buses. A liquid fuel made from animal waste is used for heating and cooking in many rural areas around the world.

Although biomass is a renewable resource, certain problems limit its use. Burning wood and crops can release as much carbon dioxide into the air as burning fossil fuels does. Biomass crops take up land that could be used to raise food. Also, plant fuels such as ethanol are still too expensive to produce on a large scale. For now, biomass materials provide only a small part of the world's energy.

 CHECK YOUR READING What are the advantages and disadvantages of biomass fuels?

Hydrogen Fuel Cells

VISUALIZATION
CLASSZONE.COM

Watch a hydrogen fuel cell in action.

Scientists are also exploring the use of hydrogen gas as a renewable energy source. Hydrogen is the simplest atom, made up of one proton—the nucleus—and one electron. Scientists have found ways to separate hydrogen from water and from fossil fuels. It is a flammable gas and must be handled with care

Hydrogen is used in a **hydrogen fuel cell,** a device that produces electricity by separating hydrogen into protons and electrons. The diagram on page 169 shows hydrogen fuel entering on one side of the cell while oxygen from the air enters on the other side. Once in the cell, electrons flow out of the cell through wires, forming an electric current that powers the motor. The protons pass through a membrane and combine with oxygen to form water as a byproduct.

Hydrogen fuel cells are used to supply electrical energy on spacecraft and space stations. Fuel-cell buses are being tested in several countries.

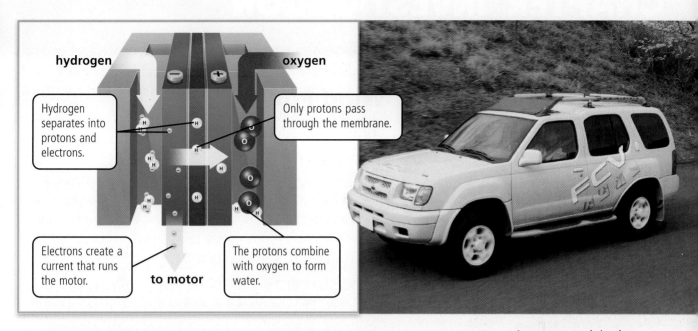

hydrogen

oxygen

Hydrogen separates into protons and electrons.

Only protons pass through the membrane.

Electrons create a current that runs the motor.

to motor

The protons combine with oxygen to form water.

A storage tank in the back of this SUV holds hydrogen fuel. Electrical energy from fuel cells powers the motor and a backup battery.

Also, some fuel-cell cars are now available to the public. Storage tanks in these vehicles carry hydrogen fuel for the cells.

Fuel-cell technology holds great promise for the future. Hydrogen is a clean source of energy, producing only water and heat as byproducts. If every vehicle in the world were powered by hydrogen, the level of air pollution would drop sharply.

However, hydrogen fuel cells are still too expensive to produce in large numbers. Separating hydrogen from water or from fossil fuels takes a great deal of energy, time, and money. Also, there are only a few fueling stations to supply cars and other vehicles that run on hydrogen. The U.S. Department of Energy is working with the automotive industry and other industries to solve these problems.

 CHECK YOUR READING Why is hydrogen considered a promising alternative energy source?

5.3 Review

KEY CONCEPTS

1. List the main advantages and disadvantages of nuclear energy as a power source.

2. Describe the advantages of using sunlight, water, and Earth's heat energy to produce electrical power.

3. What are some factors that limit the use of biomass, wind, and hydrogen as energy sources?

CRITICAL THINKING

4. **Evaluate** Do you think people would use a clean, renewable fuel that cost twice as much as gasoline? Explain.

5. **Calculate** One acre of corn yields 20 gallons of ethanol. A bus gets 20 miles per gallon and travels 9000 miles in one year. How many acres of corn are needed to fuel the bus for a year?

◯ CHALLENGE

6. **Synthesize** Review the energy sources discussed in this section. Then think of ways in which one or more of them could be used to supply electricity to a house in Florida and a house in Alaska. Which energy sources would be suitable in each environment? Describe your ideas in writing, or make sketches of the houses.

CHAPTER INVESTIGATION

Wind Power

OVERVIEW AND PURPOSE Early windmills were used mainly to pump water and grind flour. In this lab, you will use what you have learned about renewable resources to
- build a model windmill and use it to lift a small weight
- improve its performance by increasing the strength of the wind source

▶ Problem

Write It Up

What effect will increasing the wind strength have on the lifting power of a model windmill?

▶ Hypothesize

Write It Up

After completing step 8 of the procedure, write a hypothesis to explain what you think will happen in the next two sets of trials. Your hypothesis should take the form of an "If . . . , then . . . , because . . ." statement.

▶ Procedure

MATERIALS
- half of a file folder
- metric ruler
- quarter
- scissors
- paper punch
- brass paper fastener
- drinking straw
- pushpin
- masking tape
- small paper clip
- pint carton
- 30 cm of string
- clock or stopwatch
- small desktop fan

1. Make a data table in your **Science Notebook,** like the one on page 171.

2. Cut a 15 cm square from a manila file folder. With a ruler, draw lines from the corners toward the center, forming an X. Where the lines cross, use a quarter to draw a circle. Cut inward along the lines from the four corners, stopping at the small circle. Punch a hole in each corner and in the center of the circle.

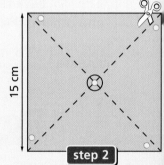
15 cm
step 2

3. Bend the cardboard to align the holes. Push a brass paper fastener through the holes toward the back of the pinwheel. Do not flatten the metal strips of the fastener.

4. Use a pushpin to poke a hole through a straw, about 4 cm from the end. Then push the metal strips through the hole and flatten them at right angles to the straw. Fold the tip of the straw over and tape it to the rest of the straw.

step 4

5. Cut the spout portion off the top of the pint carton. Punch two holes on opposite sides of the carton. Make sure the holes line up and are large enough for the straw to turn easily.

6. Slide the straw through the holes. Tape the string to the end of the straw. Tie a small paper clip (weight) to the other end of the string.

step 6

7. Test the model by blowing on the blades. Describe what happens to the weight.

8. Run three trials of the lifting power of the model windmill as you blow on the blades. Keep the amount of force you use constant. Have a classmate use a stop-watch or clock with a second hand to time the trials. Record the results in your data table. Average your results.

9. Vary the strength of the wind by using a desktop fan at different speeds to turn the windmill's blades. Remember to record your hypothesis explaining what you think will happen in the next two sets of trials.

▶ Observe and Analyze

Write It Up

1. **MODEL** Draw a picture of the completed windmill. What happens to the weight when the blades turn?

2. **IDENTIFY VARIABLES** What method did you use to increase the wind strength? Add a sketch of this method to your picture to illustrate the experimental procedure.

3. **RECORD OBSERVATIONS** Make sure your data table is completed.

4. **COMPARE** How did the average times it took to raise the weight at different wind strengths differ?

▶ Conclude

Write It Up

1. **INTERPRET** Answer the question posed under "problem" on page 170.

2. **ANALYZE** Did your results support your hypothesis?

3. **IDENTIFY LIMITS** What limitations or sources of error could have affected your experimental results?

4. **APPLY** Wind-powered turbines are used to generate electricity in some parts of the country. What might limit the usefulness of wind power as an energy source?

▶ INVESTIGATE Further

CHALLENGE How you can get your model windmill to do more work? You might try differ-ent weights, or you might build a larger windmill and compare it with your original. Create a new data table. Use a bar graph to compare different weights and wind strengths. How much wind power is needed to lift the additional weight?

Wind Power

Problem

Hypothesize

Observe and Analyze

Table 1. Time to Lift Weight

Wind Force Used	Trial Number	Time (sec)
Student powered	1	
	2	
	3	
	Average	
Fan on low speed	1	
	2	
	3	
	Average	
Fan on high speed	1	
	2	
	3	
	Average	

Conclude

Chapter Review

the **BIG** idea

Society depends on natural resources for energy and materials.

CONTENT REVIEW
CLASSZONE.COM

KEY CONCEPTS SUMMARY

5.1 **Natural resources support human activity.**

Renewable Resources
• Sunlight
• Wind
• Water
• Trees, other plants
• Plant and animal waste

Nonrenewable Resources
• Coal
• Oil, natural gas
• Uranium
• Minerals, rocks

Energy

Examples of Products
• Lumber
• Paper
• Clothing

Examples of Products
• Fuels
• Plastics
• Electronic goods

VOCABULARY
natural resource p. 147
renewable resource p. 148
nonrenewable resource p. 148
fossil fuel p. 150

5.2 **Resources can be conserved and recycled.**

People can **conserve** natural resources by reducing waste at the source and reusing products.

Recycling helps people recover materials, reduce the use of fossil fuels, and protect the environment and human health.

VOCABULARY
conservation p. 157
recycling p. 158

5.3 **Energy comes from other natural resources.**

Nuclear power plants
uranium

Hydroelectric dams
flowing water

Solar cells
sunlight

Electrical Energy

Biomass stations
plant and animal waste

Geothermal plants
Earth's heat

Wind farms
moving air

Hydrogen fuel cells
hydrogen

VOCABULARY
nuclear fission p. 161
hydroelectric energy p. 164
solar cell p. 165
geothermal energy p. 166
biomass p. 168
hydrogen fuel cell p. 168

Reviewing Vocabulary

Copy the chart below, and write each word's definition. Use the meaning of the underlined word part to help you.

Word	Meaning of Part	Definition
1. Natural <u>resource</u>	to rise again	
2. <u>Re</u>newable resource	to refresh	
3. <u>Non</u>renewable resource	not to refresh	
4. Fossil <u>fuel</u>	material that burns	
5. <u>Nuclear</u> energy	nut or kernel	
6. <u>Geo</u>thermal energy	heat	

Reviewing Key Concepts

Multiple Choice *Choose the letter of the best answer.*

7. What makes wind a renewable resource?
- **a.** no pollution
- **b.** varied speeds
- **c.** no waste products
- **d.** unlimited supply

8. Which of the following is a nonrenewable resource?
- **a.** trees
- **b.** oil
- **c.** sunlight
- **d.** geothermal energy

9. Fossil fuels provide most of the energy used in the United States because they
- **a.** are found everywhere in the world
- **b.** have no harmful byproducts
- **c.** are easy to transport and burn
- **d.** can be quickly replaced in nature

10. Which part of a power plant actually produces electricity?
- **a.** boiler
- **b.** generator
- **c.** turbine
- **d.** power lines

11. Which of the following is not a problem associated with the use of fossil fuels?
- **a.** air pollution
- **b.** explosions
- **c.** limited supply
- **d.** radiation

12. Which category of products is the most dependent on oil?
- **a.** pottery
- **b.** coins
- **c.** plastics
- **d.** paper

13. How do nuclear power plants generate the heat energy to turn water into steam?
- **a.** by drawing hot water from Earth's crust
- **b.** by producing an electric current
- **c.** by turning a turbine
- **d.** by splitting uranium atoms

14. Hydroelectric energy is produced by using the force of
- **a.** wind
- **b.** sunlight
- **c.** moving water
- **d.** living matter

15. Solar cells produce which of the following?
- **a.** heat energy
- **b.** steam
- **c.** radiation
- **d.** electricity

16. What limits the use of biomass liquid fuels?
- **a.** not enough plant material
- **b.** too expensive to mass-produce
- **c.** not enough energy generated
- **d.** too many harmful byproducts

17. Hydrogen fuel cells produce electricity when
- **a.** electrons from hydrogen leave the cell
- **b.** hydrogen is separated from fossil fuels
- **c.** protons from hydrogen combine with oxygen
- **d.** hydrogen fuel flows into the cell

Short Answer *Write a few sentences to answer each question.*

18. Why is it important to find renewable sources of energy?

19. Why is conservation of natural resources important?

20. How can recycling help reduce the use of fossil fuels?

Thinking Critically

Use the circle graphs below to answer the following questions.

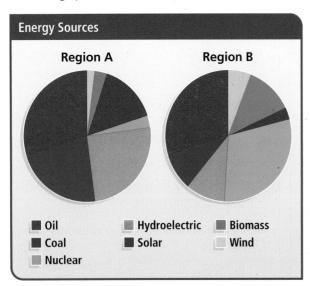

Energy Sources

Region A   Region B

■ Oil   ■ Hydroelectric   ■ Biomass
■ Coal   ■ Solar   ■ Wind
■ Nuclear

21. INTERPRET Which colors represent nonrenewable resources and which ones represent renewable resources?

22. CALCULATE Fossil fuels and nuclear energy together represent about what percentage of the total energy resources in region A? in region B?

23. PREDICT If the price of nonrenewable energy sources rises sharply, which region is likely to be affected more? Why?

24. DRAW CONCLUSIONS What might be one reason that region A uses a greater percentage of fossil fuels and nuclear energy than region B does?

25. INFER Look at the renewable energy sources used in each region. What can you infer about the climate in region A compared with the climate in region B?

26. IDENTIFY CAUSES Why might region B use so much more hydroelectric energy?

27. SYNTHESIZE Region C gets half of its electrical energy from fossil fuels. The region has only 100 days of clear sunlight a year but has abundant plant crops and strong, steady winds. Draw a circle graph for region C, showing the percentage of fossil fuels and the percentage of each renewable energy source the region might use. Explain your choices.

Charting Information

Copy and fill in this chart.

Type of Energy	Produces Energy From	Byproducts
28. uranium		radioactive waste
29. fossil fuel	burning oil, coal	
30.	moving air	none
31. river		
32. sunlight		
33.	burning wood	carbon dioxide
34. hydrogen		

the BIG idea

35. APPLY Look again at the photograph on pages 144–145. Reread the question on the photograph. Now that you have finished the chapter, what would you add to or change about your answer?

36. SYNTHESIZE Imagine that you are a scientist or engineer who is developing a new energy source. What characteristics would you want your energy source to have? List your choices in order of importance, with the most important first—for instance, nonpolluting, inexpensive to mass-produce, and so on.

37. APPLY If you were in charge of your town or city, what measures would you take to conserve natural resources?

UNIT PROJECTS

Evaluate all the data, results, and information in your project folder. Prepare to present your project.

Standardized Test Practice

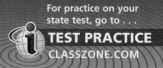

Analyzing a Graph

This graph shows what happens to fuels consumed for energy in the United States. Some of this energy is used and some is lost as heat. Use the graph to answer the questions below.

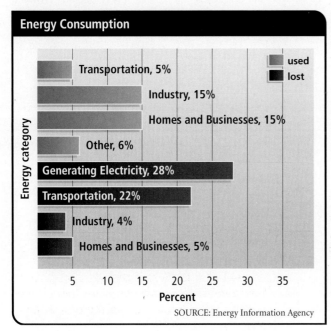

Energy Consumption

- used
- lost

Transportation, 5%
Industry, 15%
Homes and Businesses, 15%
Other, 6%
Generating Electricity, 28%
Transportation, 22%
Industry, 4%
Homes and Businesses, 5%

Energy category

Percent — 5 10 15 20 25 30 35

SOURCE: Energy Information Agency

1. How much energy is used for transportation and industry?
- **a.** 15 percent
- **b.** 20 percent
- **c.** 30 percent
- **d.** 35 percent

2. What is the total amount of energy used and lost in industry?
- **a.** 4 percent
- **b.** 15 percent
- **c.** 19 percent
- **d.** 28 percent

3. What is the largest category of lost energy?
- **a.** transportation
- **b.** homes and businesses
- **c.** generating electricity
- **d.** industry

4. Which category would include energy used to heat a grocery store?
- **a.** used in homes and businesses
- **b.** used in industry
- **c.** used in transportation
- **d.** used in other ways

5. If cars burned fuel more efficiently, which category would probably be smaller?
- **a.** used in homes and businesses
- **b.** used in other ways
- **c.** lost in transportation
- **d.** lost in industry

6. Which statement is true about energy used and lost in transportation?
- **a.** The amount lost is greater than the amount used.
- **b.** The amount used is greater than the amount lost.
- **c.** The amounts used and lost are about the same.
- **d.** The amounts used and lost are very low in comparison to the other categories.

Extended Response

Answer the two questions below in detail. Include some of the terms in the word box. In your answers, underline each term you use.

reusing	recycling	conserve	extends
electricity	hot water	factories	

7. Explain the difference between reusing and recycling products. How does each activity help to reduce the use of natural resources?

8. Give three or more examples of ways in which people in the United States use or rely on energy resources every day.

Earth's Waters

water cycle

ocean

HABITAT

hydrosphere

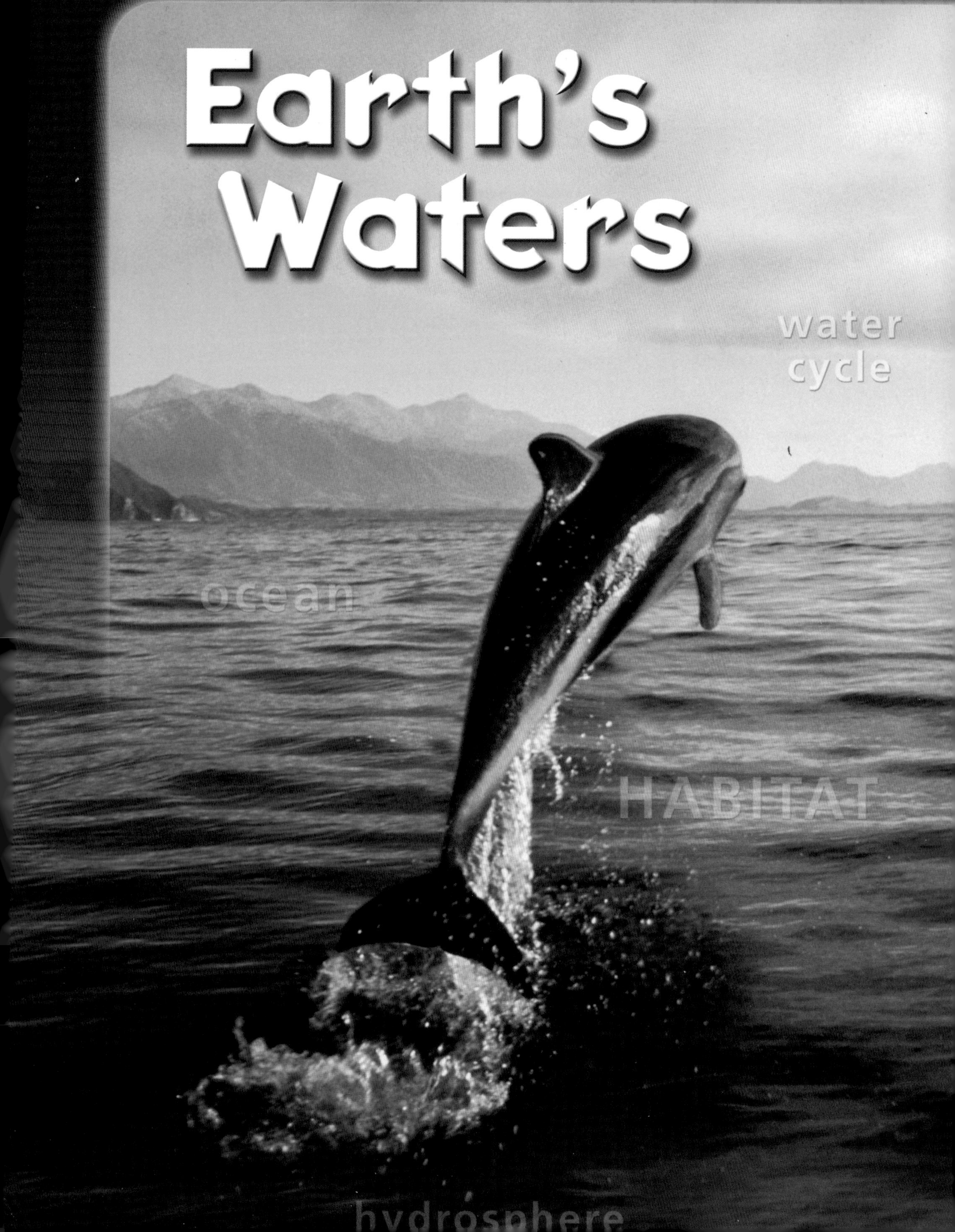

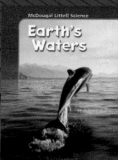

McDougal Littell Science
Earth's Waters

Earth's Waters
Contents Overview

Unit Features

1 The Water Planet   6

> **the BIG idea**
>
> Water moves through Earth's atmosphere, oceans, and land in a cycle.

2 Freshwater Resources   38

> **the BIG idea**
>
> Fresh water is a limited resource and is essential for human society.

3 Ocean Systems   72

> **the BIG idea**
>
> The oceans are a connected system of water in motion.

4 Ocean Environments   110

> **the BIG idea**
>
> The ocean supports life and contains natural resources.

Exploring the Water Planet

Technology allows scientists to see far below the ocean's surface, making exploration easier than ever before.

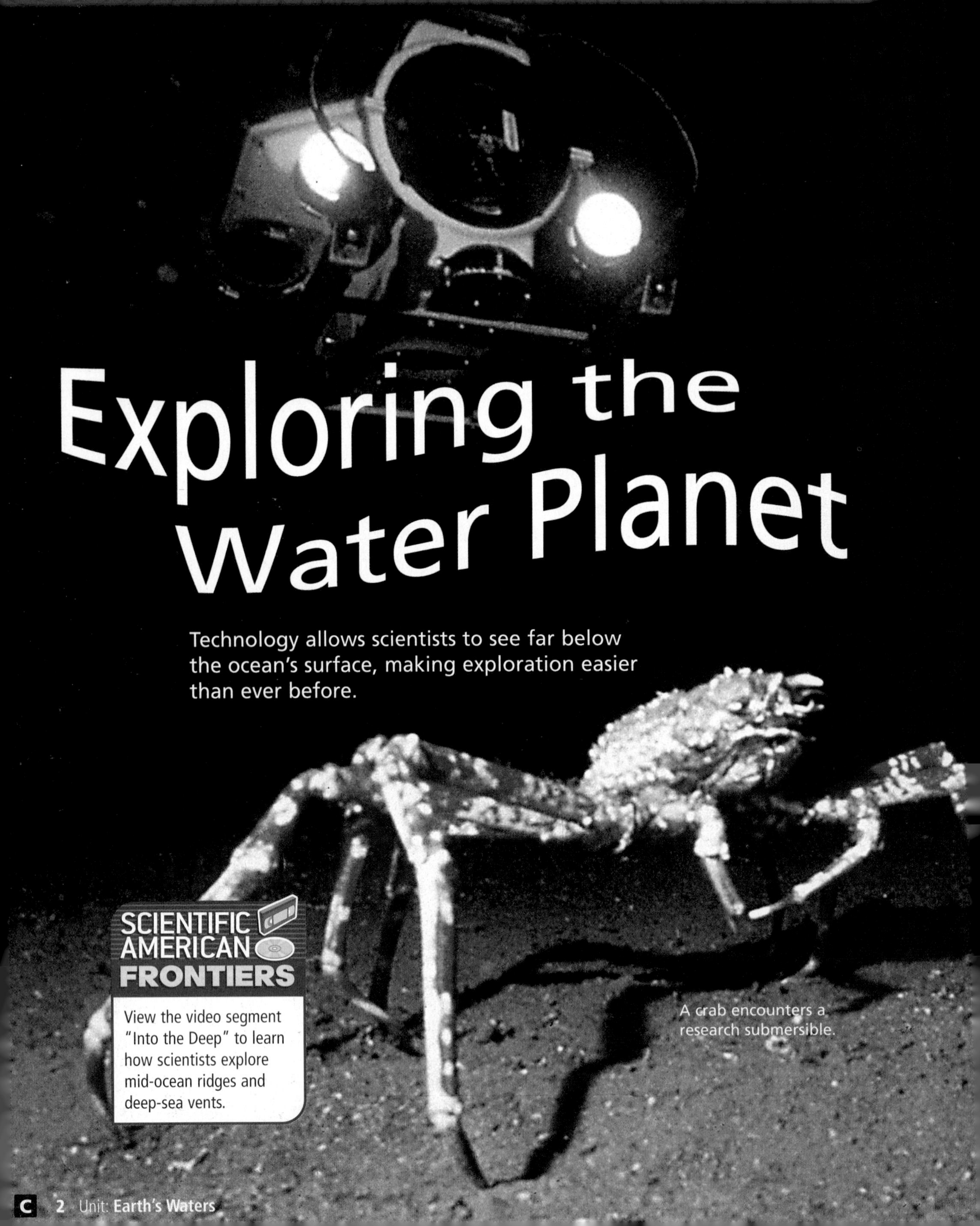

SCIENTIFIC AMERICAN FRONTIERS

View the video segment "Into the Deep" to learn how scientists explore mid-ocean ridges and deep-sea vents.

A crab encounters a research submersible.

Earth's Least-Known Region

What is the least-explored region on Earth? You might guess it's a small area where few things live, perhaps in a vast desert or in high mountains. But this region covers more than 50 percent of the planet and contains almost 98 percent of its living space. It is the deep sea, the part of the ocean sunlight cannot reach, where no plants grow. The deep sea was once thought to be of little interest. Now researchers are studying the organisms living in the deep sea and mapping the resources of the sea floor. Other parts of the ocean are getting more attention, too. For example, researchers are studying how surface water carries nutrients to new areas and how the ocean affects Earth's climate.

As people explore the ocean more thoroughly, they frequently discover new organisms. Many of these organisms are being found in the deep sea. Some, though, are being found in water that is only a few meters deep. One octopus that lives in shallow tropical water was first described in 1998. This brown octopus avoids being eaten by predators by mimicking the appearances and colors of poisonous organisms. For example, the octopus slips six of its arms and much of its body into a hole on the sea floor. Then it waves its other two arms in opposite directions, which makes it look like a banded sea snake. The octopus's colors change to yellow and black, matching the snake's bands. Another organism the octopus mimics is a multicolored lionfish with its poisonous fins spread out.

An octopus (above) changes its colors and hides most of its body and all but two arms to mimic a poisonous sea snake (right).

These scale worms, first described in 1988, live only around deep-sea vents and are thought to feed on the larger tubeworms.

Exploring Deep-Sea Vents

Deep-sea vents support astonishing life forms. These organisms depend on materials dissolved in scalding hot vent water, not on sunlight, for their ultimate source of energy. The superheated vent water contains many dissolved minerals. The minerals become solid as the vent water mixes with cold ocean water. Earth's richest deposits of minerals like copper, silver, and gold may be around some of these vents. To study the minerals that lie beneath thousands of meters of water, researchers use remotely operated devices to collect data and samples.

Exploring the Ocean and Climate

The ocean moves large amounts of heat energy between areas of Earth, affecting the atmosphere and climate. Consider that even though some parts of Alaska and Great Britain are equally close to the North Pole, Great Britain is warmer. Air over the Atlantic Ocean gains heat energy from a warm ocean current, and winds carry this warmth toward Great Britain. In addition to moving across the surface, water also mixes vertically in the ocean. The ocean contains many layers of water, with the warmest generally at the top. But the middle layers of the ocean may now be heating up quickly. Researchers are working to understand how the mixing of water in the ocean affects Earth's atmosphere and climate.

SCIENTIFIC AMERICAN FRONTIERS

View the "Into the Deep" segment of your *Scientific American Frontiers* video to learn how scientists are exploring the deep sea.

IN THIS SCENE FROM THE VIDEO ▶ a deep-sea vent spews out superheated water that is rich in dissolved minerals.

THE DEEPEST DIVES Robert Ballard has made dozens of expeditions in *Alvin*, a three-person submarine. This small vessel can dive deep below the surface to underwater mountain ranges called mid-ocean ridges. Ballard's photographs helped prove that the mountains in a mid-ocean ridge are volcanoes.

While exploring a valley that runs along the top of a mid-ocean ridge, Ballard discovered deep-sea vents. Water that flows out of the vents is very hot and rich in minerals. Ballard was also one of the first scientists to see the giant clams, tubeworms, and other animals that live around the vents. Such life forms are unusual because they depend on energy from within Earth instead of energy from the Sun.

Exploring Ocean Nutrients

Some water masses move in circular or spiral patterns, as you can see in the photograph below. These spinning water masses are called eddies. Water in eddies mixes slowly with the surrounding water. An eddy that contains nutrient-rich water can drift great distances, mixing with nutrient-poor water over a long time, sometimes years. The added nutrients allow populations of tiny plantlike organisms to grow quickly. These organisms are the base of the ocean food chain, and almost all other ocean organisms depend on them. Researchers are studying how changes in the sizes and numbers of eddies affect ocean organisms. Nutrient-rich eddies may be important to fish, such as salmon, that many people eat.

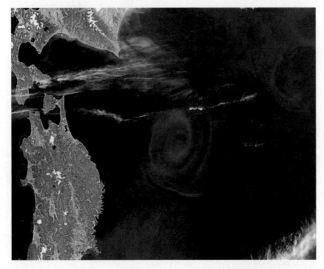

Eddies are mixing seawater from the coast of Japan with water farther from shore.

UNANSWERED Questions

Scientists who study the ocean know that much of it is yet to be explored and that many questions remain.

- How many, and what types of, ocean organisms will be discovered in the next decades?

- How do changes in ocean surface temperatures affect weather?

- What is the best way to maintain populations of fish that people depend on for food?

UNIT PROJECTS

As you study this unit, work alone or with a group on one of the projects listed below.

Track a Drop of Water

Suppose you could follow a drop of surface water as it journeys from your hometown to the ocean.

- Find out which rivers and lakes the drop would travel through, and which ocean it would join.

- Present your findings. You might make a travelogue, a map, or both.

Life in the Water

Investigate the different life forms that live in the water in your area.

- Collect water samples from different sources, such as indoor taps, fountains, puddles, marshes, lakes, and streams.

- Examine a drop from each sample under a microscope. Sketch any living organisms you see.

- Write a lab report to present your findings about the water samples.

Ocean News Report

Imagine that you are part of a news group assigned to report on major discoveries made about the world's oceans over the past 25 years.

- Research the most important or unusual facts uncovered about the oceans. Note what technology was used to gather the data.

- Prepare a special TV or Web-site report about your investigation. Where possible, include photographs or illustrations.

CAREER CENTER
CLASSZONE.COM

Learn more about careers in oceanography.

CHAPTER

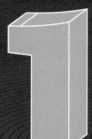

The Water Planet

the BIG idea

Water moves through Earth's atmosphere, oceans, and land in a cycle.

In what forms does water exist on Earth?

Key Concepts

SECTION 1.1
Water continually cycles.
Learn about how water on Earth moves in a world-wide system.

SECTION 1.2
Fresh water flows and freezes on Earth.
Learn about fresh water in rivers, lakes, and ice.

SECTION 1.3
Fresh water flows underground.
Learn about water under the land surface and how it is used.

Internet Preview

CLASSZONE.COM

Chapter 1 online resources: Content Review, Simulation, Visualization, four Resource Centers, Math Tutorial, Test Practice

EXPLORE (the BIG idea)

Where Can You See Water?

Look in your home or school for examples of frozen and liquid water. Go outside and look for the same, plus evidence of water in the air. Record your observations.

Observe and Think
What did you find inside? outside? Did you see evidence of water in the air?

Does the Ice Float?

Place an ice cube in a glass of tap water. Does it float at all? Now add two spoonfuls of salt to the water and stir it in. What happens to the ice cube?

Observe and Think What might the salt do to the water that affects the way the ice cube floats?

Internet Activity: Water

Go to **ClassZone.com** to learn what different forms of water exist on Earth and how water is a part of Earth's systems.

Observe and Think
What are the different ways that water exists on Earth?

NSTA
scilinks.org

SCiLINKS

Water Cycle **Code: MDL018**

Getting Ready to Learn

◀ CONCEPT REVIEW

- Water built up on Earth's surface over time.
- Water is essential for life.
- Earth has an atmosphere of gases.

◀ VOCABULARY REVIEW

See Glossary for definitions.

atmosphere

glacier

system

 CONTENT REVIEW
CLASSZONE.COM
Review concepts and vocabulary.

▶ TAKING NOTES

MAIN IDEA AND DETAIL NOTES

Make a two-column chart. Write the main ideas, such as those in the blue headings, in the column on the left. Write details about each of those main ideas in the column on the right.

VOCABULARY STRATEGY

Write each new vocabulary term in the center of a **four-square** diagram. Write notes in the squares around the term. Include a definition, some characteristics, and some examples. If possible, write some things that are not examples.

See the Note-Taking Handbook on pages R45–R51.

SCIENCE NOTEBOOK

MAIN IDEAS	DETAIL NOTES
1. Water is a unique substance.	1. Only substance in three forms at normal temperatures
	1. Can be solid, liquid, gas
	1. As liquid, can fit any container

Definition	Characteristics
Water that is not salty	Little or no taste, color, or smell

FRESH WATER

Examples	Nonexamples
Liquid in rivers, lakes	Liquid in oceans

1.1 Water continually cycles.

◀ BEFORE, you learned	▶ NOW, you will learn
• The force of running water causes erosion • Water can be solid	• What makes water important • How much of Earth's water is salt water • How water moves throughout Earth and its atmosphere

VOCABULARY

fresh water p. 11
salt water p. 11
water cycle p. 12
evaporation p. 13
condensation p. 13
precipitation p. 13

EXPLORE Water Vapor

Where does the water come from?

PROCEDURE

MATERIALS
• clear glass
• ice
• water

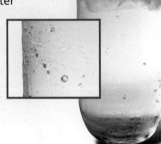

① Put the ice in the glass and fill it with water.

② Observe what happens to the outside of the glass.

WHAT DO YOU THINK?
• Where did the water on the outside of the glass come from?
• What does this activity tell you about the air surrounding you? What conclusion can you draw?

Water is a unique substance.

Seen from outer space, Earth glistens like a beautiful blue and white marble. Welcome to the "water planet," the only planet in our solar system with a surface covered by a vast amount of liquid water. Because of water, a truly amazing substance, life can exist on Earth.

What is so amazing about water? In the temperature ranges we have on Earth, it exists commonly as a solid, a liquid, and a gas. At a low temperature, water freezes. It becomes a solid, which is ice. At a higher temperature, it flows easily in liquid form. Liquid water can become a gas, especially at higher temperatures. If you have ever noticed how something wet dries out in the hot sunlight, you have observed the effect of liquid water changing into a gas. The gas form is the invisible water vapor in our atmosphere.

Liquid water can fit any container. It can hold its shape in a raindrop, then merge with other drops to flow down a hill or slow down and sit for centuries in a lake.

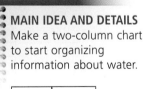

MAIN IDEA AND DETAILS
Make a two-column chart to start organizing information about water.

Water covers most of Earth.

Earth looks bluish from space because most of Earth's surface is ocean. If you look at a globe or a world map, you will see the names of four oceans—Atlantic, Pacific, Indian, and Arctic. If you look more closely or trace the four named oceans with your finger, you will see that they are connected to one another. Together they form one huge ocean. Any part of this ocean is called the sea.

The global ocean covers 71 percent, or almost three-quarters, of Earth's surface. Most of the ocean is in the Southern Hemisphere. The ocean is, on average, 3.8 kilometers (2.4 mi) deep. Although most of the water covering Earth is ocean, water also covers some land areas, as rivers, lakes, and ice.

 CHECK YOUR READING Where is most of Earth's water?

Water-to-Land Ratio

Almost three-quarters of Earth's surface is covered by water.

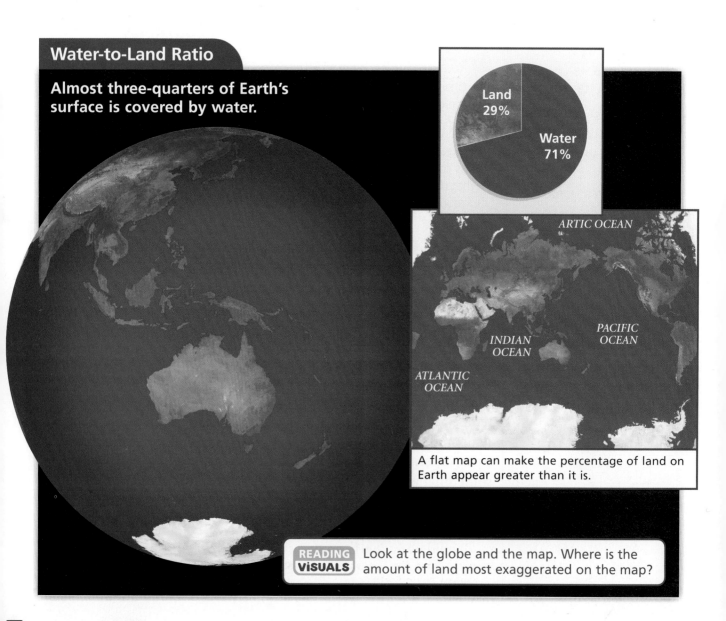

Land 29%

Water 71%

ARTIC OCEAN

PACIFIC OCEAN

INDIAN OCEAN

ATLANTIC OCEAN

A flat map can make the percentage of land on Earth appear greater than it is.

READING VISUALS Look at the globe and the map. Where is the amount of land most exaggerated on the map?

Water and Life

Without water, nothing would live on Earth. Living things need water to function. Your own body is two-thirds water. In your body, your blood—which is mostly water—carries nutrients that give you energy and flushes wastes away. Many forms of life live in water. Oceans, lakes, and rivers are home to fish, mammals, plants, and other organisms. Even a single drop of water may contain tiny forms of life.

Fresh Water and Salt Water

When you hear the word *water*, you might imagine a cool drink that quenches your thirst. The water that you drink and depend on for survival is fresh water. **Fresh water** is water that is not salty and has little or no taste, color, or smell. Most rivers and lakes are fresh water.

The water in the ocean is salt water. **Salt water** is water that contains dissolved salts and other minerals. Human beings and most other land animals cannot survive by drinking salt water, although many other forms of life can live in salt water.

You may be surprised to learn that even though fresh water is important for life, fresh water is actually scarce on Earth. Because most of Earth's water is in the ocean, most of the water on Earth is salt water. The illustration below compares the amounts of fresh water and salt water on Earth. Almost all—about 97 percent—of Earth's water is salt water in the ocean. Only about 3 percent of Earth's water, at any given time, is fresh water.

VOCABULARY
Remember to write the terms *fresh water* and *salt water* in four-square diagrams in your notebook.

CHECK YOUR READING What is the difference between fresh water and salt water?

Salt Water vs. Fresh Water

Most water on Earth is salt water.

3% fresh water

97% salt water

Forms of Fresh Water

- Free flowing   30%
- Frozen   70%

Ice on land and in oceans

Water underground and in rivers, lakes, atmosphere, and plants and animals

Imagine that this glass of water represents all of the water on Earth.

Water moves in a worldwide cycle.

MAIN IDEA AND DETAILS
Record in your notes this main idea and important details about the water cycle.

Water continually moves and changes form. Water from clouds falls over the oceans and on land. Water flows in rivers and collects in lakes and under the ground. Water can be a solid in the form of ice, or it can be an invisible vapor in the atmosphere.

The Water Cycle

Water's movement on Earth is a cycle, or continually repeating process. The **water cycle** is the continuous movement of water through the environment of Earth. In the water cycle, water is constantly changing form, from a liquid on land, to a vapor in the atmosphere, and again to a liquid that falls to the surface. The flow of water on land and underground is also part of the water cycle. As water moves in the water cycle, the total amount of water in Earth's system does not change very much. The water cycle involves three major processes: evaporation, condensation, and precipitation.

INVESTIGATE The Water Cycle

How does water cycle through an environment?

DESIGN —YOUR OWN—

PROCEDURE

1. Construct an environment in a jar with a lid. You can use plants, soil, water, and containers.
2. Find the mass of your closed jar after you construct it.
3. Draw a detailed, colored picture of your jar.
4. Let your jar sit for several days.
5. Find the mass of your jar again, and draw another picture of it.

WHAT DO YOU THINK?

- How did the jar's appearance change over several days?
- How did its mass change?
- What can you conclude about how water cycles through an environment?

CHALLENGE How could you change your environment so that the jar's appearance would change at a faster rate?

SKILL FOCUS
Modeling

MATERIALS
- jar with lid
- soil
- rocks or pebbles
- sand
- smaller containers
- water
- small plants
- triple-beam balance

TIME
30 minutes (for construction; 20 minutes for analysis)

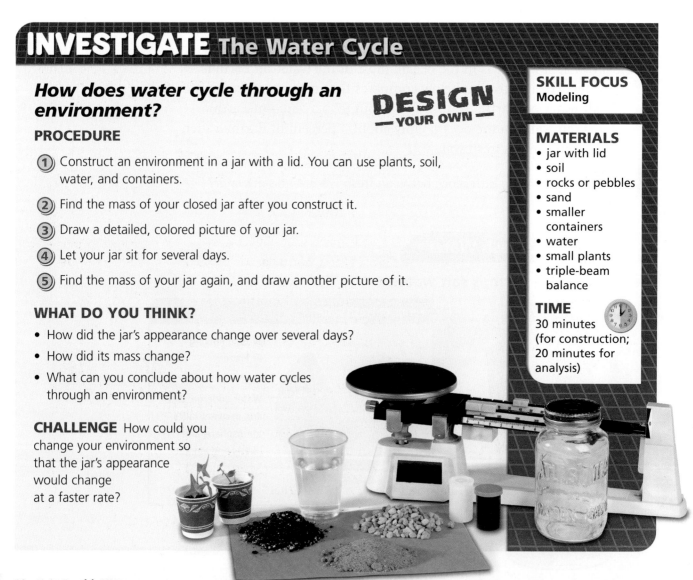

The Water Cycle

Water on Earth moves in a continual cycle.

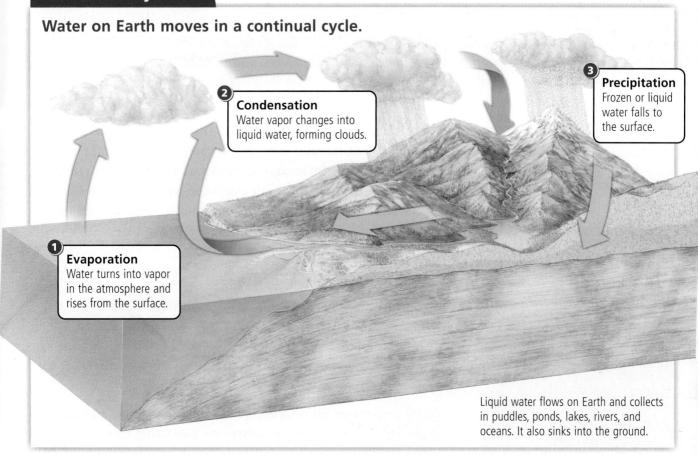

2 Condensation
Water vapor changes into liquid water, forming clouds.

3 Precipitation
Frozen or liquid water falls to the surface.

1 Evaporation
Water turns into vapor in the atmosphere and rises from the surface.

Liquid water flows on Earth and collects in puddles, ponds, lakes, rivers, and oceans. It also sinks into the ground.

1 The process in which water changes from liquid to vapor is called **evaporation.** Heat energy from the Sun warms up the surface of the ocean or another body of water. Some of the liquid water evaporates, becoming invisible water vapor, a gas.

2 The process in which water vapor in the atmosphere becomes liquid is called **condensation.** Condensation occurs as air cools. Because cold air can have less water vapor than warm air, some of the vapor condenses, or turns into droplets of liquid water. These droplets form clouds. At high altitudes clouds are made of ice crystals. Unlike water vapor, clouds are visible evidence of water in the atmosphere.

3 Water that falls from clouds is **precipitation.** Inside a cloud, water droplets bump together and merge into larger droplets. They finally become heavy enough to fall as precipitation—such as rain or sleet. The water from precipitation sinks into the soil or flows into streams and rivers in the process called runoff. The force of gravity pulls the flowing water downward and, in most cases, eventually to the ocean.

VISUALIZATION
CLASSZONE.COM

See how water moves through Earth's system in the water cycle.

 CHECK YOUR READING Why does water vapor in air condense into liquid droplets?

Most of the water that evaporates on Earth—85 percent of it—evaporates from the ocean. (About 75 percent of this condenses into cloud droplets and falls right back into the ocean.) The remaining 15 percent of evaporating water comes from such sources as damp ground, lakes, wet sidewalks, rivers, and sprinklers. Plants are also part of the water cycle. They pull up water from the ground and then release much of it into the air through their leaves.

Even though the water that evaporates into the atmosphere comes from both the salty ocean and from fresh water on land, all the precipitation that falls back to the surface is fresh water. When salt water evaporates, the salt is left behind. Through the water cycle the ocean water that human beings cannot drink becomes a source of fresh water for human beings and other life on Earth.

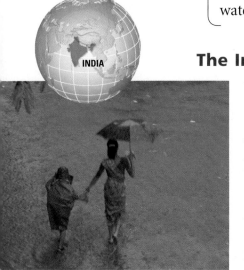

INDIA

Flooding usually occurs during India's annual rainy season.

The Impact of the Water Cycle

The action of the water cycle is easy to spot. When it rains or snows, you can see precipitation in action. When you look at a flowing stream, you see the water cycle returning water to the sea. When a stream dries up, you know that the water cycle in the area has slowed down for a while.

Wet weather can fill reservoirs with drinking water and pour needed water on crops. Wet weather can also bring too much rain. For example, during the wet season in India, winds blow moist air inland from the Indian Ocean. Tremendous rains fall over the land for months. The rain is usually welcome after a long and hot dry season. However, these seasonal rains frequently cause devastating floods, covering acres and acres of land with water.

1.1 Review

KEY CONCEPTS

1. Name three things about water that make it unique or important.

2. How much of Earth's water is fresh water?

3. Explain the three processes that make up the water cycle.

CRITICAL THINKING

4. **Apply** How can a drop of salt water once have been a drop of fresh water?

5. **Compare and Contrast** What are two differences between salt water and fresh water?

○ CHALLENGE

6. **Infer** In 1996, the *Galileo* space probe sent back photographs that showed ice on the surface of one of the moons of Jupiter. Scientists suspected there was water under the ice. Why did this discovery excite some people who thought there was a chance of finding life on that moon?

Does Mars Have a Water Cycle?

Mars once had water flowing on its surface. Today, it is a frozen desert. Most astronomers think that there has been no liquid water on Mars for the past 3.9 billion years. Others, though, think that Mars has had flowing water recently—in the last 10 million years. They suggest that Mars may have a multimillion-year water cycle. According to their hypothesis, occasional volcanic activity melts ice, releasing floods of water. After the water evaporates, condenses, and falls as rain, it becomes ice again. And if Mars does have a water cycle, it could have something else that goes with water on Earth: life.

▶ Issues

For Mars to have a water cycle, it would need several features.

- a source of energy for melting ice into water
- conditions for water to evaporate
- conditions for water vapor to condense

▶ Observations

Astronomers have observed several facts about Mars.

- Mars has water ice at its north and south poles.
- Mars has had very large volcanoes in the past, although it seems to have no active volcanoes today.
- Mars takes about 687 Earth days to orbit the Sun.
- Mars is the fourth planet from the Sun.
- Mars has an atmosphere that is 100 times thinner than the atmosphere of Earth.
- Mars has an average surface air temperature of –55°C (–67°F).
- Mars has features that look like ones shaped by water on Earth: ocean shorelines, river valleys, and gullies.
- Mars has many visible craters—unlike Earth, where most craters get washed away, filled with water, or covered up.

▶ Determine the Relevance of Each Observation

On Your Own Decide whether each observation is relevant in determining whether Mars has a water cycle.

As a Group Discuss the relevance of each observation to the idea of a water cycle on Mars. List other information that might be helpful.

CHALLENGE Research information about Mars. Identify facts that support or oppose the idea of a Martian water cycle.

Mars has features that appear to be like those created by water on Earth.

Icecaps cover the poles of Mars.

ⓘ RESOURCE CENTER

Learn more about evidence that Mars may or may not have a water cycle.

Fresh water flows and freezes on Earth.

 BEFORE, you learned

- Water covers most of Earth's surface
- Water continually cycles
- Water falls to Earth's surface as precipitation

▶ **NOW, you will learn**

- How fresh water flows and collects on land
- How surface water forms lakes
- How frozen water exists on Earth

VOCABULARY

divide p. 17
drainage basin p. 17
turnover p. 19
eutrophication p. 20
iceberg p. 22

EXPLORE Water Collection

How does water flow and collect?

PROCEDURE

① With the open egg carton on a level tray, pour water slowly into the center of the carton until the cups are three-quarters full.

② Empty the carton. Tip it slightly, as shown in the photograph, and pour water into the higher end. Stop pouring when the carton is about to overflow.

WHAT DO YOU THINK?

- How did the water flow when you poured it into the level carton? into the tilted carton? Where did it collect in the carton? Where did it not collect?
- What might your observations tell you about how water flows when it falls on land?

MATERIALS
- plastic-foam egg carton
- tray or pan
- plastic bottle
- water

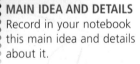
MAIN IDEA AND DETAILS
Record in your notebook this main idea and details about it.

Water flows and collects on Earth's surface.

Imagine you are in a raft on a river, speeding through whitewater rapids. Your raft splashes around boulders, crashing its way downriver. Then the raft reaches a lake. You glide across the surface, slowing down. At the end of the lake, your raft enters a river again and floats down it.

In your raft you are following the path a water drop might take on its way to the ocean. All over the planet, the force of gravity pulls water downhill. Fresh water flows downhill in a series of streams and rivers, collects in lakes and ponds, and eventually flows into the ocean. All of this water flows between high points called divides, in areas called drainage basins.

Divides and drainage basins affect the way water flows on land. A **divide** is a ridge, or continuous line of high land, from which water flows in different directions. If you were on a skateboard and began at the top of a hill, you would ride in one general direction down the hillside. On the other side of the hill, you would ride downhill in a completely different direction. The top of the hill is like a divide. A divide can be a continuous ridge of high mountains. On flatter ground, a divide can simply be the line of highest ground.

A **drainage basin,** or watershed, is an area into which all of the water on one side of a divide flows. If you pour water into the basin of your bathroom sink, it will flow down the side from high points to low, and eventually down the drain, which is at the lowest point. In mountainous areas, hills and mountains form the sides of basins, and valleys form the low points. Flatter regions also have basins. The basins may not be obvious in these regions, but they still drain water.

When it rains in a drainage basin, the water forms streams and rivers or sinks into the ground. Every stream, river, and lake is in a basin. In most places, the water eventually flows to the sea. In a bowl-shaped basin, the water may collect at the bottom of the basin or evaporate.

Divides and Drainage Basins

Divides separate drainage basins.

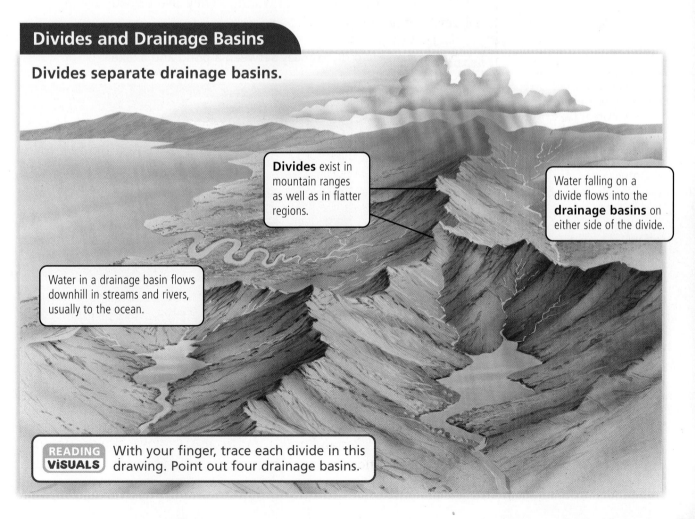

Divides exist in mountain ranges as well as in flatter regions.

Water falling on a divide flows into the **drainage basins** on either side of the divide.

Water in a drainage basin flows downhill in streams and rivers, usually to the ocean.

READING VISUALS With your finger, trace each divide in this drawing. Point out four drainage basins.

Surface water collects in ponds and lakes.

Lakes and ponds form where water naturally collects in low parts of land. Some lakes were formed during the last ice age. For example, the Great Lakes were formed when huge sheets of ice scraped out a series of giant depressions. Other lakes, such as Crater Lake in Oregon, were formed when water collected inside the craters of inactive volcanoes.

Water can fill a lake in several ways. Where the land surface dips below the level of underground water, the low land area fills with water. Rainfall and other precipitation contribute water to all lakes. Water may flow through a lake from a stream or river. Water may also flow away from a lake through a stream running downhill from the lake. Many lakes maintain fairly steady levels because of the balance of flow in and flow out.

The main difference between a pond and a lake is in their overall size. A pond is smaller and shallower than a lake, and there are many plants, such as water lilies and cattails, rooted in its muddy bottom. A lake may have water so deep that sunlight can't reach the bottom. In the deeper part of the lake, plants can't take root, so they grow only around the lake's edges. Ponds and lakes provide homes for many kinds of fish, insects, and other wildlife. They also provide resting places for migrating birds.

CHECK YOUR READING Name two differences between a pond and a lake.

Chicago, Illinois, at the southwest corner of Lake Michigan, is the largest city on a Great Lake. Note that the lake is so wide that from Chicago you cannot see Michigan on the other side.

Lake Michigan

Chicago

Lake Michigan is the third largest of the five Great Lakes, which border eight states and Canada's Ontario province.

Lake Turnover

The water in a lake is not as still as it might appear. The changing temperatures of the seasons affect the water and cause it to move within the lake in a yearly cycle.

In a place with cold winters, ice may form on a lake, so that the wind cannot ruffle the surface. The water temperature in the lake remains steady, and the water stops moving. The water just below the surface ice is near freezing, so the fish move to the bottom, where the water is a bit warmer.

In many lakes the water temperatures at different levels vary as the seasons change. In the spring and summer, sunlight can warm a layer of water at the top of a lake. Because the colder water beneath the top layer is denser than the warmer water above it, the water levels do not mix easily. The warm water contains more oxygen, so fish may be more plentiful in the upper part of the lake.

READING **TiP**

Cold water is denser than (has more mass than the same amount of) warm water.

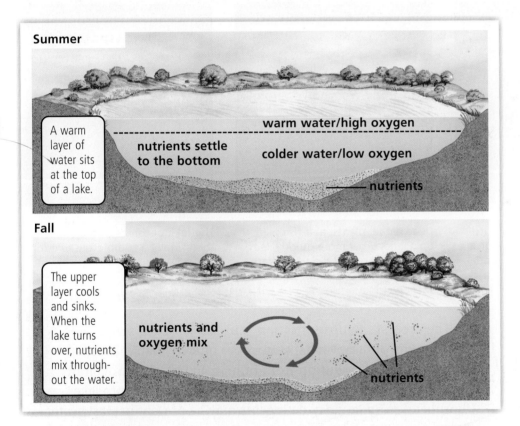

Summer

A warm layer of water sits at the top of a lake.

nutrients settle to the bottom

warm water/high oxygen

colder water/low oxygen

nutrients

Fall

The upper layer cools and sinks. When the lake turns over, nutrients mix through-out the water.

nutrients and oxygen mix

nutrients

In the fall, days cool and the surface water cools too. The upper layer becomes heavy and sinks, so that the lake water "turns over." Nutrients from minerals and from dead plants and organisms are stirred up from the bottom. These nutrients are used by many life forms in the lake. The rising and sinking of cold and warm water layers in a lake is called **turnover**. Turnover occurs twice each year as the seasons change.

⬤ CHECK YOUR READING   What happens to surface water when the weather cools in the fall?

Eutrophication

A lake does not remain a lake forever. Through natural processes that take thousands of years, most lakes eventually are filled in and become meadows—fields covered with grass and other plants. A lake can become filled in as sediments, including the remains of dead fish, plants, and other organisms, pile up on the bottom.

READING TiP

Eutrophication comes from the Greek word *eutrophos,* meaning "well-nourished."

The activity of life in a lake is affected by nutrients. Nutrients are the foods and chemicals that support living things. When the amounts of such nutrients as phosphorus and nitrogen in a lake increase, algae and other organisms in the water grow more rapidly. An increase of nutrients in a lake or pond is called **eutrophication** (yoo-TRAHF-ih-KAY-shuhn). As eutrophication occurs, algae form a thick scum on the water. The amount of oxygen in the water decreases, until fish and other organisms that require oxygen cannot survive. The illustration below shows what happens to a lake when nutrient levels increase.

When the amounts of such nutrients as nitrogen and phosphorus increase, algae grow faster and form a scum layer at the surface.

Dead algae, plants, and fish pile up. Plants grow more quickly, leaving more debris as they die. Water evaporates, and the lake becomes shallower.

The lake becomes a soggy marsh, then finally a completely filled-in meadow.

The process of eutrophication is usually slow. In some cases, however, eutrophication happens more quickly than it normally would because of pollution from human activities. Nitrogen in fertilizers used on farms and gardens may be washed into lakes. Phosphates from laundry detergents may be present in wastewater that reaches lakes. The extra nutrients cause algae and plants in lakes to grow faster and more thickly than they normally would grow. Eutrophication from pollution causes clear lakes to become clogged with algae and plants.

CHECK YOUR READING How does human activity contribute to eutrophication?

Most fresh water on Earth is frozen.

If you want fresh water, take a trip to Greenland or the South Pole. Two-thirds of the world's fresh water is locked up in the ice covering land near the poles.

The ice sheet that covers Antarctica is almost one and a half times as big as the United States and is in places more than a kilometer thick. Ice on Earth's surface contains more than 24 million cubic kilometers of fresh water. Just how much water is that? Imagine that you have three glasses of lemonade. If you take one sip from one of the glasses of lemonade, you have drunk the water in all the lakes and rivers on Earth. The rest of the glass represents liquid ground water. The other two glasses of lemonade represent all the frozen water on the planet.

Ice on Land

In Earth's coldest regions—near both poles and in high mountains—more snow falls each year than melts. This snow builds up to form glaciers. A glacier is a large mass of ice and snow that moves over land. There are two types of glaciers. The ice sheets of Antarctica and Greenland are called continental glaciers because they cover huge landmasses. The other type of glacier is a valley glacier, which builds up in high areas and moves slowly down between mountains.

RESOURCE CENTER
CLASSZONE.COM
Find out more about frozen fresh water.

INVESTIGATE Icebergs

Why do icebergs float?

PROCEDURE

1. Find the masses of the empty graduated cylinder and the ice cube.
2. Add 200 mL of water to the cylinder. Find the volume of the ice cube by measuring how much water it displaces. Make sure the water is extremely cold to prevent the ice cube from melting. Use the point of a paper clip to completely submerge the ice.
3. Remove the water and let the ice melt in the cylinder.
4. Calculate the density (Density = mass/Volume) of the ice cube. Now find the mass and volume of the liquid water from the melted ice and calculate its density.

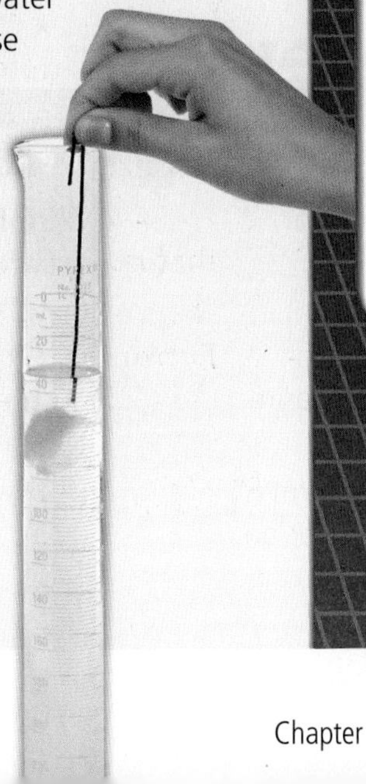

WHAT DO YOU THINK?

- What was the density of the ice cube? the water?
- Why do icebergs float?

CHALLENGE Float a cork in water. How does its behavior compare with that of floating ice?

SKILL FOCUS
Calculating

MATERIALS
- balance
- ice cube
- water
- 250 mL graduated cylinder
- paper clip
- calculator

for Challenge:
- cork

TIME
30 minutes

Icebergs

An **iceberg** is a mass of ice floating in the ocean. An iceberg starts out as part of a glacier. In places such as Antarctica and Greenland, glaciers form ice shelves that extend out over the ocean. When a large chunk of a shelf breaks off and floats away, it becomes an iceberg.

Thousands of icebergs break off from ice sheets each year. In the Northern Hemisphere, ocean currents push icebergs south into the warmer Atlantic Ocean. It may take an iceberg two to three years to float down to the area off the coast of Canada. In that region, it breaks apart and melts in the sea. A North Atlantic iceberg sank the *Titanic*.

Icebergs are masses of frozen fresh water floating in the salt water of the world's oceans.

How big is an iceberg? One iceberg that recently broke off an Antarctic ice shelf was the size of Connecticut. Off the coast of eastern Canada, some icebergs tower 46 meters (150 ft) above the surface of the ocean. This is impressive, because most of a floating iceberg is below the surface. Only about one-eighth of the total weight and volume of the iceberg can be seen above the surface of the sea. When people say "It's only the tip of the iceberg," they mean that a lot of something is unrevealed.

The water in an iceberg may have been frozen for 15,000 years. However, the ice in the center, if melted, can be clean, clear drinking water. And an iceberg can hold a lot of water. An iceberg as big as a city block holds enough drinking water to supply a city of 50,000 people for about ten years. Unfortunately, no one knows how to cheaply move icebergs to cities in order to use the frozen water.

○ **CHECK YOUR READING** How much of an iceberg is below the surface?

1.2 Review

KEY CONCEPTS

1. Why is it important that fresh water flows over Earth's surface?

2. Explain the relationship between a drainage basin and a divide.

3. Where and in what form is most of the fresh water on Earth?

CRITICAL THINKING

4. **Apply** If you were going on a fishing trip in a northern state, why would you want to know about lake turnover?

5. **Connect** Explain the connection between living things in a lake and eutrophication.

○ **CHALLENGE**

6. **Synthesize** How is the water in icebergs involved in the water cycle on Earth?

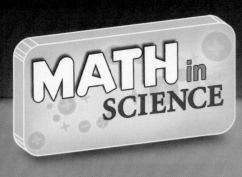

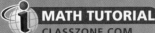

MATH TUTORIAL
CLASSZONE.COM

Click on Math Tutorial for help multiplying fractions and whole numbers.

SKILL: MULTIPLYING FRACTIONS AND WHOLE NUMBERS

How Big Is an Iceberg?

In salt water, the part of an iceberg that is visible above water is only 1/8 of the whole iceberg. The remaining 7/8 of the iceberg is hidden under the water's surface. You can use fractions to estimate how much ice is underwater.

Example

An iceberg is made of 1000 cubic meters of ice. How much of the ice is underwater?

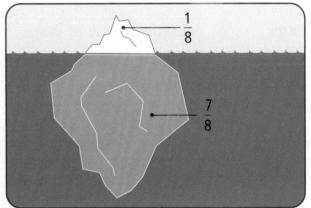

Solution

(1) Write a word equation.

$$\text{Volume of ice underwater} = \text{volume of iceberg} \cdot \text{fraction underwater}$$

(2) Substitute.

$$\text{Volume of ice underwater} = 1000 \text{ m}^3 \cdot \frac{7}{8}$$

(3) Multiply the numerator by the total volume.

$$= \frac{1000 \text{ m}^3 \cdot 7}{8}$$

(4) Calculate and simplify.

$$= \frac{7000 \text{ m}^3}{8} = 875 \text{ m}^3$$

ANSWER About 875 cubic meters of ice are underwater.

Calculate how much ice is underwater.

1. The iceberg is made of 1600 cubic meters of ice.

2. The iceberg is made of 1800 cubic meters of ice.

3. The iceberg is made of 12,000 cubic meters of ice.

CHALLENGE About 500 cubic meters of an iceberg is visible above the water. Estimate the total volume of the iceberg.

1.3 Fresh water flows underground.

◀ **BEFORE, you learned**

- Water flows in river systems on Earth's surface
- Water collects in ponds and lakes on Earth's surface

▶ **NOW, you will learn**

- How water collects and flows underground
- How underground water reaches the surface in springs and by wells

VOCABULARY

groundwater p. 24
permeable p. 24
impermeable p. 25
water table p. 25
aquifer p. 26
spring p. 28
artesian well p. 28

EXPLORE Flow of Water

What does water flow through?

PROCEDURE

1. Fill the cup with water.

2. Have a partner hold the filter open over a sink, bucket, or pan while you pour water into it.

WHAT DO YOU THINK?

- Why did the water remain in the cup before you poured it?
- What route did the water take to pass through the filter?

CHALLENGE What other materials might hold water? allow water to flow through?

MATERIALS
- water
- cup
- paper coffee filter
- bucket, dishpan, or sink

Water fills underground spaces.

After a rainstorm, water does not stay on the ground for long. What happens to this water? It flows along Earth's surface into a river or reservoir, evaporates, or sinks into the soil. Plants use some of the water that sinks into the ground, and the rest of it sinks deeper into Earth. Water held underground is called **groundwater.** The ground under your school may seem too solid to hold water, but it is likely that groundwater sits or moves under the surface.

To understand how groundwater collects, you need to know the difference between permeable and impermeable materials. The ground beneath your feet is made of both permeable and impermeable materials.

A **permeable** substance is a substance that liquids can flow through. Liquids flow through a coffee filter because the filter is permeable. Soil,

VOCABULARY
In your notebook make four-square diagrams for the terms *groundwater* and *permeable*.

sand, and gravel are permeable because there are spaces between the particles. Water flows into and through these spaces. The bigger the particles, the more easily water can flow. Gravel and larger rocks have large spaces between them, so water flows quickly through. Sandy soil also has many pores, or spaces. Some rocks, such as sandstone, are permeable although the spaces in these rocks are extremely small.

An **impermeable** substance is a substance that liquids cannot flow through. A drinking glass holds orange juice because the material of the glass is impermeable. Rocks such as granite are impermeable. Unless granite has cracks, it has no spaces for water to go through. Many impermeable materials are hard, but not all of them. Clay is soft, but it is nearly impermeable. Water can get between its particles, but the overlapping of the particles stops the water from flowing through.

How does groundwater collect? Gravity causes rainwater to sink into the soil. If it rains heavily, all the spaces in the soil fill with water. Eventually the water reaches impermeable rock. There it is held in place or forced to flow in a different direction.

Even when the soil on Earth's surface is dry, huge amounts of groundwater may be stored below. The top of the region that is saturated, or completely filled with water, is called the **water table.** The saturated region below the water table is called the saturation zone.

READING **TiP**

The prefix *im* in *impermeable* means "not."

CHECK YOUR READING What prevents groundwater from sinking farther down?

Groundwater

Pulled down by gravity, water sinks through permeable ground until it reaches an impermeable layer.

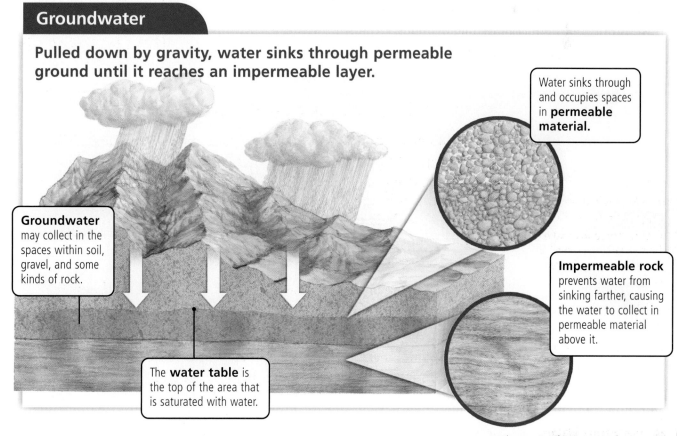

Water sinks through and occupies spaces in **permeable material.**

Groundwater may collect in the spaces within soil, gravel, and some kinds of rock.

Impermeable rock prevents water from sinking farther, causing the water to collect in permeable material above it.

The **water table** is the top of the area that is saturated with water.

Aquifers

An **aquifer** is an underground layer of permeable rock or sediment that contains water. Some aquifers lie deep under layers of impermeable rock. Other aquifers lie just beneath the topsoil.

SIMULATION
CLASSZONE.COM

Explore how groundwater fills in aquifers.

Aquifers can be found all over the world. They lie under deserts as well as wet regions. As the map below shows, they are found in many areas of the United States. An aquifer might be a bed of sand or gravel only a few meters thick. Or it might be an enormous layer of sandstone, several hundred meters thick, holding water in countless pore spaces. The Ogallala Aquifer is the largest aquifer in North America. It covers 450,000 square kilometers (176,000 mi^2), from South Dakota to Texas.

For an aquifer to form, three things are needed:

• A layer of permeable material holds the water. Groundwater is stored in the pore spaces of gravel, sand, or rock.

• A neighboring area of impermeable rock keeps the water from draining away. Sometimes impermeable rock lies both above and below an aquifer.

• A source of water replenishes or refills the aquifer. Like any body of water, an aquifer can be emptied.

You know that fresh water on land flows toward the ocean. Water that is underground acts like slow-motion streams, rivers, and lakes. Underground water moves slowly. The water is under pressure

Aquifers

Water collects underground in layers of permeable material.

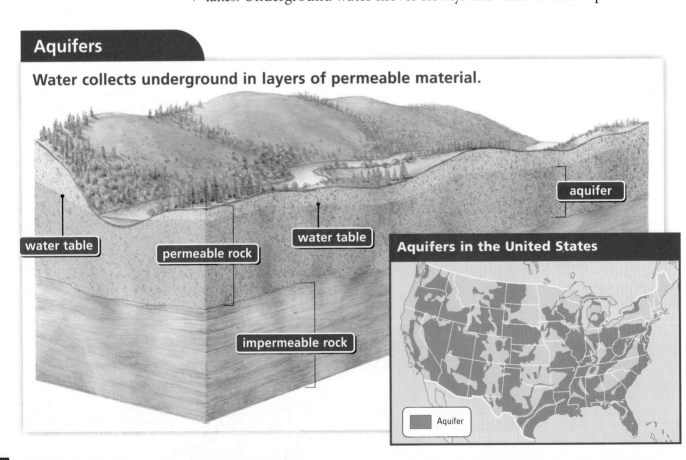

water table

permeable rock

water table

aquifer

impermeable rock

Aquifers in the United States

Aquifer

from all sides, and it must go around endless tiny corners and passageways in rock. Unlike the water in an aboveground river, groundwater moves sideways, down, and even up. In some areas, groundwater is pushed upward so that it flows from a hillside. Because it moves so slowly, much of the water in an aquifer may have been there for thousands of years.

The Importance of Aquifers

When water sinks into land, the ground acts like a giant filter. Stones and sand in the ground can filter out bacteria and other living organisms. This ground filter also removes some harmful chemicals and minerals. The filtering process can make groundwater clear and clean and ready to drink. If it is not polluted, groundwater may not need expensive treatment. It is one of our most valuable natural resources.

Many big cities collect water from rivers and store it in reservoirs above the ground. However, about one-fifth of the people in the United States get their fresh water from underground. Most people who live in rural areas pump groundwater from wells. In many desert regions people depend on sources of underground water.

INVESTIGATE Aquifer Filtration

How can the ground filter water?

PROCEDURE

1. Cap the top of the bottle. Invert it and add to it a layer of gravel, then a layer of sand, then a layer of soil.

2. Slowly pour water onto the soil until a water table becomes visible in the sand beneath it.

3. Add the pollutants pepper, cocoa, and food coloring to the bottle top. Slowly unscrew the cap so that water trickles into the bucket.

4. Observe the water that filtered through.

5. Pour more water onto the soil and let water trickle out.

WHAT DO YOU THINK?

- Which pollutants were filtered out before reaching the "aquifer"? Which ones reached the aquifer?

- What effect does pollution have on drinking water that comes from aquifers?

CHALLENGE What could you do to clean up an aquifer?

SKILL FOCUS
Making models

MATERIALS
- water
- 1L plastic bottle with bottom cut off
- gravel
- sand
- soil
- pepper
- cocoa
- food coloring
- bottle bottom or bucket

TIME
30 minutes

Underground water can be brought to the surface.

MAIN IDEA AND DETAILS
In your notebook, fill out a chart for this main idea.

If you had lived in colonial America or in ancient Greece, your daily chore might have been to haul water home from a well. You would have lowered a bucket into a pit until it reached the water table, then pulled the filled bucket up with a rope. Or you might have worked at digging a well, hacking away at the ground with a shovel until water flowed into the hole you dug.

Today's technology makes it easier to bring groundwater to the surface. Powerful drills bore through rock, and motors pump groundwater to the surface and to kitchen sinks. Scientists study the sizes and areas of aquifers. They know where to get water and how much to expect.

Springs and Wells

Groundwater can be collected from springs and wells. A **spring** is a flow of water from the ground at a place where the surface of the land dips below the water table. In some springs, the water bubbles up, then sinks back into the soil. In others, the water flows into a stream or lake. Spring water has a fresh clean taste, and many water companies bottle this water to sell.

Underground pressure causes this artesian well to shoot water 18 meters (60 ft) into the air.

A well is a hole in the ground that reaches down to the saturation zone—the wet region below the water table. Usually, a pump is used to draw the water out of the ground, and a screen is used to filter out particles of sand and gravel. If the water table is near the surface, a well can be dug by hand. The part of the well beneath the water table will fill with water.

Most modern wells are dug with motorized drills. A drill digs through soil and rock into the saturation zone; then a pipe is lowered into the drill hole. A pump is used to raise the water from the ground. Some wells are more than 300 meters (1000 ft) deep.

One kind of well does not need a pump. An **artesian well** is a well in which water flows to the surface naturally because it is under pressure. In places where impermeable rock dips into an aquifer, the water directly below the rock is pushed to a lower level than the water on either side. When a well is drilled into the water beneath the rock, the weight of the surrounding water pushes the water upward.

 CHECK YOUR READING What makes water flow upward out of an artesian well?

Springs and Wells

Water is brought up from the ground in various ways.

Water flows from an **artesian well** because the water underground is under pressure.

A **spring** occurs where the water table meets the ground surface.

well dug for home

water table

aquifer

How to Make a Well

aquifer

water table

1 Drill into the ground with special machinery.

2 When the drill hole reaches below the water table, lower a pipe into it.

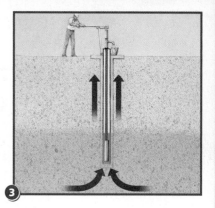

3 At the top of the well, install a pump powered by a motor or human effort to pull up water.

READING VISUALS Look at the top illustration. What would happen if the water table dropped below the bottom end of the well?

The depth of the water table in a particular place can vary from season to season, depending on how much rain falls and how much water is used. When water is taken from an aquifer, the water table might drop. When it rains or snows, some of the water filters back into the aquifer, replacing what has been taken. If water is used faster than it is replaced, wells may run dry. Low groundwater levels can also cause the ground to settle and damage the environment.

As more and more people live on Earth, the amounts of groundwater used to irrigate crops increase. In some states where crops are grown in dry areas, as much as 70 percent of all the groundwater brought to the surface is used for irrigation. Water used for irrigation is recycled back into the water cycle. In some places it sinks back into the ground and filters into aquifers. In other regions much of the water evaporates or flows away, and the groundwater levels are lowered.

Hot Springs

Yellowstone National Park sits atop the remains of an ancient volcano. The rain and melted snow that sink into the ground there eventually reach depths of more than 3000 meters (10,000 feet), where the rocks are extremely hot. The water heats up and reaches the boiling point. Then it becomes even hotter while remaining liquid because it is under such great pressure from the rocks pushing on it from all sides.

The hot water deep underground is like water in an enormous boiling pot—with a lid 3000 meters thick. The water expands the only way that it can, by pushing upward through weak places in the rocks. A place where the water surfaces is a hot spring. A hot spring has a continual flow of hot water.

Vapor rises from these hot springs in Yellowstone National Park in Wyoming.

WYOMING

In a geyser, water heats underground. The diagram shows the underground "plumbing" of a geyser in Iceland.

Hot water and steam are pushed up to the surface where they erupt.

A geyser is a kind of hot spring. The illustrations above show how a geyser works. Beneath the surface, there are underground channels in the rock. The rising hot water is forced to travel through these narrow passages. Like water in a garden hose, the water moves with force because it is under pressure. When it finally reaches Earth's surface, the pressure makes it burst out. It shoots into the air as a dramatic fountain of water and steam. In Yellowstone National Park there are more than 300 geysers. One of the largest, Old Faithful, shoots a jet of hot water and steam about 20 times a day. The eruptions last from 1.5 to 5 minutes, and reach heights of 30 to 55 meters (106 to 184 ft).

RESOURCE CENTER
CLASSZONE.COM

Learn more about geysers and hot springs.

CHECK YOUR READING Why does water shoot out of Old Faithful with such great force?

Review

KEY CONCEPTS

1. Draw a diagram that shows how water collects underground.

2. What is the difference between a spring and a well?

3. What causes water to rise out of the ground in hot springs and geysers?

CRITICAL THINKING

4. **Connect** Is a T-shirt permeable or impermeable? How about a raincoat? Explain why.

5. **Infer** Would you expect to find a spring on the very top of a hill? Why or why not?

⬥ CHALLENGE

6. **Sequence** On a blank sheet of paper, draw a cartoon strip that shows how aquifers collect and store water and how people bring the water to the surface. Show at least five steps in the process. Write captions for your drawing to explain the steps.

CHAPTER INVESTIGATION

Water Moving Underground

OVERVIEW AND PURPOSE
Many people rely on underground aquifers for their drinking water. Some aquifers are small and localized. Others can supply water to huge regions of the United States. Perhaps your own drinking water comes from an underground aquifer. In this investigation you will

DESIGN
— YOUR OWN —
EXPERIMENT

- design an experiment to determine what types of materials best hold and transport water
- infer which types of Earth materials make the best aquifers

▶ Problem

What types of materials will best hold and transport water?

▶ Hypothesize
Write a hypothesis that answers the problem question in "If . . . , then . . . , because . . ." form.

▶ Procedure

1. Design a procedure to test the materials samples to determine which will best hold and transport water. Your procedure should be designed to identify both which material absorbed the most water and which material absorbs water the fastest.

2. Record your procedure in your **Science Notebook.**

MATERIALS
- granite sample
- sandstone sample
- sand
- square piece of cotton muslin or cotton knit, measuring 30 cm per side
- rubber band
- golf ball
- scale
- large jar
- water

3 Create a data table to organize the data you will collect.

4 Be sure that you make both qualitative and quantitative observations.

5 Be sure to include a calculations section in your **Science Notebook.**

▶ Observe and Analyze [Write It Up]

1. **RECORD OBSERVATIONS** Draw a diagram of your experimental setup.

2. **CALCULATE** Which item absorbed the most water?

3. **SCIENTIFIC METHOD** How did you use the golf ball? What did it represent?

▶ Conclude [Write It Up]

1. **INTERPRET** Answer the problem question.

2. **COMPARE** Compare your results with your hypothesis. Do your data support your hypothesis?

3. **IDENTIFY LIMITS** In what ways was this activity limited in demonstrating how water moves underground? How might your experimental setup lead to incorrect conclusions?

4. **APPLY** Look over your data table. Your results should indicate both which material absorbed the most water and which material absorbed water the fastest. How do these two characteristics compare in terms of their importance for an aquifer?

5. **INFER** Which types of Earth materials make the best aquifers?

▶ INVESTIGATE Further

CHALLENGE The data you gathered in this investigation reflect the permeability of each Earth material tested. What qualities and characteristics determine their permeabilities?

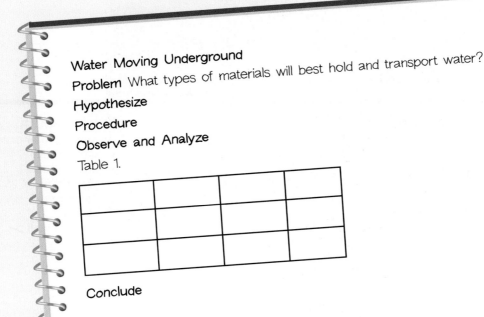

Water Moving Underground
Problem What types of materials will best hold and transport water?
Hypothesize
Procedure
Observe and Analyze
Table 1.

Conclude

Chapter Review

the BIG idea

Water moves through Earth's atmosphere, oceans, and land in a cycle.

CONTENT REVIEW
CLASSZONE.COM

◀ KEY CONCEPTS SUMMARY

1.1 Water continually cycles.
Water moves through Earth's environment in a continuous cycle.

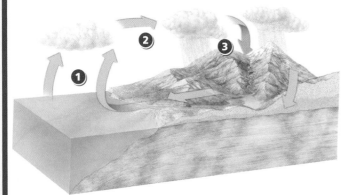

1 **Evaporation** Water becomes vapor.

2 **Condensation** Vapor changes into liquid.

3 **Precipitation** Water falls to the surface.

VOCABULARY
fresh water p. 11
salt water p. 11
water cycle p. 12
evaporation p. 13
condensation p. 13
precipitation p. 13

1.2 Fresh water flows and freezes on Earth.

Water on land collects and flows in rivers and lakes. Much of Earth's fresh water is frozen.

divide

drainage basins

VOCABULARY
divide p. 17
drainage basin p. 17
turnover p. 19
eutrophication p. 20
iceberg p. 22

1.3 Fresh water flows underground.
Water collects and moves beneath the land surface.

Gravity pulls water down through **permeable** materials until it reaches an impermeable layer.

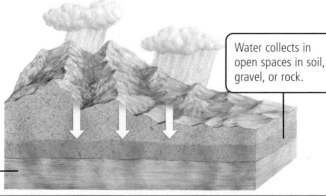

Water collects in open spaces in soil, gravel, or rock.

The **impermeable** layer prevents water from sinking farther down.

VOCABULARY
groundwater p. 24
permeable p. 24
impermeable p. 25
water table p. 25
aquifer p. 26
spring p. 28
artesian well p. 28

Reviewing Vocabulary

Use the terms in the box below to answer the next nine questions.

evaporation	precipitation	water cycle
turnover	eutrophication	artesian
iceberg	groundwater	permeable

1. Which word describes an increase in nutrients in a lake or pond?

2. Which kind of well does not need a pump?

3. Which term describes a seasonal change in a lake?

4. Which term describes a substance through which water can pass?

5. Which term names the continuous movement of water through Earth's environment?

6. What is the name for an enormous chunk of floating ice?

7. What word means the turning of liquid water into a gas?

8. What is the name of water stored in an aquifer?

9. What word is another name for rain, snow, sleet, and hail?

Reviewing Key Concepts

Multiple Choice *Choose the letter of the best answer.*

10. What are the three forms of water on Earth?
- **a.** groundwater, lakes, and clouds
- **b.** liquid water, frozen water, and water vapor
- **c.** gas, steam, and vapor
- **d.** groundwater, oceans, and ice

11. How much of Earth's water is fresh water?
- **a.** almost all
- **b.** about half
- **c.** very little
- **d.** none

12. Which process forms clouds?
- **a.** evaporation
- **b.** precipitation
- **c.** condensation
- **d.** dehydration

13. What ice formation covers Greenland and Antarctica?
- **a.** iceberg
- **b.** landmass
- **c.** valley glacier
- **d.** continental glacier

14. Which is a characteristic of a pond?
- **a.** rooted plants covering the entire bottom
- **b.** plants only near shore
- **c.** a layer of impermeable rock
- **d.** water heated by underground rock

15. How are glaciers like rivers?
- **a.** They are made of liquid water.
- **b.** Their water sinks into the ground.
- **c.** They flow downhill.
- **d.** They are a mile thick.

16. How is water stored in an aquifer?
- **a.** in an open underground lake
- **b.** in cracks and spaces in rocks
- **c.** in impermeable rock
- **d.** in wells and springs

Short Answer *Write a short answer to each question.*

17. Explain why most of the water cycle takes place over the ocean.

18. How does an iceberg form?

19. Why are aquifers valuable?

20. What is the difference between a valley glacier and a continental glacier?

Thinking Critically

Use the photograph to answer the next four questions. There are four liters of water in the jug. The hose has been overflowing for about ten seconds.

21. OBSERVE Describe what the water in the hose is doing.

22. IDENTIFY EFFECTS Explain what effect the water in the jug has on the water in the hose. Why does the water rise in the hose?

23. PREDICT When will the water stop flowing from the hose? Why?

24. COMPARE AND CONTRAST How is what is happening in the hose like and unlike what happens in an artesian well?

25. EXPLAIN Explain why the water cycle matters to humans and animals.

26. CONNECT In a mountainous area, temperatures are lower at higher altitudes. Explain the connection between this fact and the existence of valley glaciers.

27. COMPARE AND CONTRAST Explain the difference between clouds and water vapor in the atmosphere.

28. INFER Explain why water in a bowl-shaped drainage basin does not eventually flow to the ocean.

29. APPLY Name at least two things that you think people could do to lessen eutrophication caused by pollution.

30. APPLY Explain why even though evaporation draws water but not salt from the ocean, the ocean does not become saltier.

PREDICT Fill in the chart with predictions of how water will collect under the stated conditions.

Conditions	Prediction
31. A bed of permeable rock lies atop a bed of impermeable rock; rainfall is plentiful.	
32. Heavy snows fall in a region that has year-round freezing temperatures.	
33. A large depression is left in impermeable rock by a glacier.	
34. Water from farm fields and gardens runs off into ponds.	

the **BIG** idea

35. SYNTHESIZE Explain why a raindrop that falls on your head may once have been water in the Pacific Ocean.

36. MODEL Draw a diagram of two drainage basins, showing how water flows and collects on the surface of Earth. Label the divide, as well as the bodies of water into which water flows.

UNIT PROJECTS

If you are doing a unit project, make a folder for your project. Include in your folder a list of the resources you will need, the date on which the project is due, and a schedule to keep track of your progress. Begin gathering data.

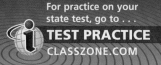
Analyzing Data

In an experiment to study the effect of heating on evaporation, identical pans of water were placed for two hours under different types of lights. The temperature of the air just above each pan was measured with a thermometer every 30 minutes. The amount of evaporation was determined by subtracting the amount of water in the pan at the end of two hours from the amount that was in the pan at the beginning. The data table shows the results. Study the data and answer the questions below.

Pan	Description	Average Air Temperature Above the Water	Evaporation
1	under regular light	22°C (72°F)	30 mL (1.0 oz)
2	under heat lamp on low	25°C (78°F)	40 mL (1.4 oz)
3	under heat lamp on high	28°C (83°F)	50 mL (1.7 oz)

1. What is the relationship between the air temperature and the evaporation rate?

   a. There is no relationship between the temperature and the rate.

   b. As the temperature increases, the rate decreases.

   c. As the temperature increases, the rate stays the same.

   d. As the temperature increases, the rate increases.

2. If the air temperature averaged 27°C (80°F), about how much water would evaporate in two hours?

   a. 28 mL   **c.** 48 mL

   b. 38 mL   **d.** 58 mL

3. The constants in this experiment are the factors that stay the same for all three pans. Which of the following is a constant?

   a. the type of light

   b. the size of the pans

   c. the air temperature above the water

   d. the amount of evaporation

4. The dependent variable in an experiment is the factor that is measured to gather results. Which is the dependent variable in this experiment?

   a. the amount of evaporation

   b. the amount of water in each pan in the beginning

   c. the type of light

   d. the air temperature

5. Which change would make the results of this experiment more reliable?

   a. conducting the experiment for four hours

   b. decreasing the amount of water in the pans

   c. increasing the air temperature for one pan

   d. using a fan to blow air on one of the pans

Extended Response

Answer the two questions below in detail. Include some of the terms shown in the word box. In your answers, underline each term you use.

low	eutrophication	meadow
water table	saturation zone	

6. Kori notices that a pond at his summer camp is filled with more soil and plants each year. Explain how this change fits into the pattern of how ponds change over time.

7. Juanita's family gets water from a well on their ranch. Each time a well has gone dry, they have had to dig a new one that was deeper than the old one. Explain why they have needed to go deeper.

2 Freshwater Resources

the BIG idea

Fresh water is a limited resource and is essential for human society

Key Concepts

SECTION

2.1 Fresh water is an essential resource.
Learn how water is needed for life and how water is used for human activities.

SECTION

2.2 Society depends on clean and safe water.
Learn how water is made safe for drinking and how wastewater is treated.

SECTION

2.3 Water shortages threaten society.
Learn about the causes of water shortages and about ways to conserve water.

 Internet Preview

CLASSZONE.COM

Chapter 2 online resources: Content Review, Simulation, Visualization, two Resource Centers, Math Tutorial, Test Practice

In what ways do you depend on water?

EXPLORE the BIG idea

How Much Water Do You Drink?

From the time you get up to when you finish dinner, keep a list that notes each time you drink a liquid—including water, juice, milk, and soda. Write down what you drank and how much you think you drank.

Observe and Think
How many times did you drink something? From your list, estimate in numbers of medium glassfuls the total amount you drank.

What Happens When Salt Water Evaporates?

Dissolve a spoonful of salt in a cup of water. Put the cup in a warm place, such as a sunny windowsill. Leave it there until the water completely evaporates.

Observe and Think Examine the cup. If you could capture the water that evaporated, would that water be salty? Explain your answer.

Internet Activity: Aquifers

Go to **ClassZone.com** to explore the limits of an aquifer. Review past water usage and try to determine how long the water in an aquifer will last.

Observe and Think
What can be done to slow the use of underground water?

Water Pollution **Code: MDL019**

Getting Ready to Learn

◀ CONCEPT REVIEW

- Water can be a solid, a liquid, or a gas.
- Water continually cycles on Earth.
- Water flows underground.

◀ VOCABULARY REVIEW

fresh water p. 11

water cycle p. 12

groundwater p. 24

aquifer p. 26

 CONTENT REVIEW
CLASSZONE.COM
Review concepts and vocabulary.

▶ TAKING NOTES

SUPPORTING MAIN IDEAS

Make a chart to show main ideas and the information that supports them. Write each blue heading from the chapter in each box. In boxes below it, add supporting information, such as reasons, explanations, and examples.

VOCABULARY STRATEGY

Place each vocabulary term at the center of a **description wheel.** Write some words describing it on the spokes.

See the Note-Taking Handbook on pages R45–R51.

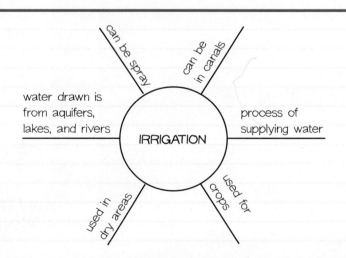

SCIENCE NOTEBOOK

Fresh water supports life.

→ The human body is more than one-half water.

→ Living cells need water.

→ Water is a limited resource.

IRRIGATION

- can be spray
- can be in canals
- water drawn is from aquifers, lakes, and rivers
- process of supplying water
- used for crops
- used in dry areas

2.1 Fresh water is an essential resource.

 BEFORE, you learned

- Fresh water is found on Earth's surface and underground
- People use wells to bring ground water to the surface

▶ **NOW, you will learn**

- How water is required for life
- How water is used for many human activities

VOCABULARY

irrigation p. 43
aquaculture p. 45
dam p. 46
lock p. 46

THINK ABOUT

How valuable is water?

In the United States, fresh water seems plentiful. When you want water for a drink or to wash, you can go to a drinking fountain or turn on the tap to get all the water you want. In some parts of the world, water is scarce and difficult to get. In Port-au-Prince, Haiti, this girl is getting her bucket filled with fresh water so that she can take water home. If you had to get your water this way, how might that change the way you think of water? Would you use water differently than you do now?

Fresh water supports life.

Close your eyes and imagine a beautiful place in nature that is full of life. Maybe you think of trees, flowers, and a waterfall and pools where animals come to drink. Water is important in any scene that involves life.

People have always lived near clean, fresh water. Why is water so important to humans? One reason is that our bodies are more than one-half water. Without the water in your blood, your cells would not receive the nutrients they need. Your skin and tissues hold water in your body, but some water is lost every day. As a result, you get thirsty and drink water or something that contains mostly water, such as milk or juice. Without water, a person cannot live for more than a few days. And without water, people wouldn't be able to grow food.

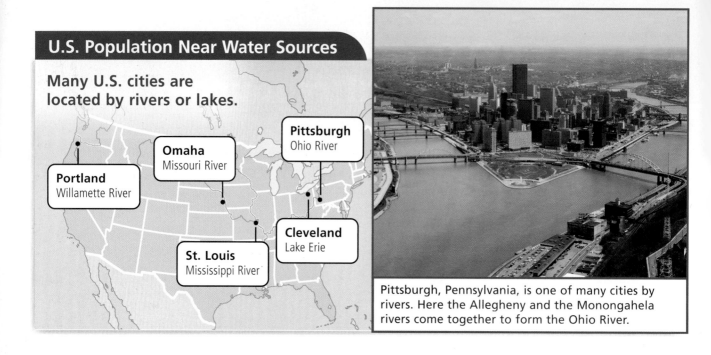

U.S. Population Near Water Sources

Many U.S. cities are located by rivers or lakes.

Portland
Willamette River

Omaha
Missouri River

Pittsburgh
Ohio River

Cleveland
Lake Erie

St. Louis
Mississippi River

Pittsburgh, Pennsylvania, is one of many cities by rivers. Here the Allegheny and the Monongahela rivers come together to form the Ohio River.

You have read that fresh water on Earth is a limited resource. A fixed amount cycles through the atmosphere, flows in rivers, is held in lakes and glaciers, and is stored in aquifers deep under the ground. As more and more people live on the planet every year, our water sources become more precious. If too much water is taken from aquifers, the supply will eventually run out. If the water in rivers and lakes becomes polluted, we can no longer use it.

 CHECK YOUR READING What can happen to water as the world population grows?

Most human activities require water.

SUPPORTING MAIN IDEAS
Record details about how water is important to human activities.

Almost everything you do requires water. When you take a shower or brush your teeth, you use water. Your dishes and clothes are washed with water. You might exercise in water at a pool.

Some of the ways you use water might surprise you. Let's say you do your homework after school. You grab a slice of pizza from the refrigerator, switch on the light, and sit down to read a book in your favorite chair. Have you used any water so far? The answer is yes, many gallons of water.

On farms water was needed to grow the tomatoes and wheat for your pizza. The cheese topping came from a cow that drank water and ate grain grown with water. The paper in your book was produced at a paper plant that used vast amounts of water to wash and mix wood pulp. When you switch on a light, you are probably using energy that was generated by some form of moving water. And the metal in the lamp was mined from underground, using—you guessed it—water.

INVESTIGATE Water Usage

How much water do you use in a week?

PROCEDURE

1. Write down all the ways you use water in a day. Start with the time you get up in the morning. Include things such as brushing your teeth, flushing the toilet, using ice, and taking a shower.

2. Look at the Water Use sheet, and from it, identify other ways that you and others in your household use water.

3. Add up how many liters of water you use in a day, and multiply that by 7. This is how much water you use in a week.

WHAT DO YOU THINK?

- Which of your activities used the most water?
- What are some ways that you could reduce the amount of water you use weekly?

CHALLENGE Based on your weekly water usage, how much water is used by the United States annually? **Hint:** Find the population of the United States in a reference source.

SKILL FOCUS
Analyzing data

MATERIALS
- Water Use sheet
- calculator

TIME
30 minutes

Farming

In the United States, about 40 percent of the water that is used goes to growing crops and raising livestock. Any kind of farm depends on water to grow plants for food and to raise animals. To grow oranges, a farm needs about 0.25 centimeters (0.1 in.) of rainfall a day. To produce one hamburger can require 5000 liters (1300 gal.) of water or more because animals not only drink water but also eat grass and grain that use water.

These green irrigated fields are circular because the metal sprinklers move like clock hands from a center point

In many areas, rainfall does not provide enough water to support crops and animals. In these drier areas, farmers draw water from aquifers, rivers, or lakes to grow crops. The process of supplying water to land to grow crops is **irrigation.**

A common method of irrigation pours water through canals and waterways so that it flows through the fields. A little more than half of U.S. farms that are irrigated use this method, which is called flood irrigation. Most of the other farms that irrigate use spray irrigation, which sprays water onto the fields. You can think of lawn sprinklers as an example of spray irrigation for grass. On farms, the water often is delivered by metal structures that roll around entire fields.

A paper mill uses large quantities of water to process wood pulp.

Industry

The industries that make our cars, notebooks, jeans, sneakers, skateboards, and TVs are major water users. The manufacture of just about any item you can name probably uses water. Consider these examples.

- The process of making one car can require about 50 times the car's weight in water. This process begins with the mining of minerals and ends with the final washing as the car rolls out of the factory.
- In many industries, huge amounts of water are used to cool down machines.
- In a coal mine, water is used to separate chunks of coal from other clumps of dirt and rock.
- A paper mill uses 100 to 300 metric tons of water to manufacture one ton of paper.

Water used in industry can be used again. Factories can clean the water they use and return most of it to lakes and rivers.

○ CHECK YOUR READING How is water used in industry?

Transportation and Recreation

Since the earliest times, rivers and lakes have helped people visit their neighbors and trade food and goods. In the United States, major rivers and the Great Lakes provide an efficient way to transport goods, especially cargo that is bulky and heavy, such as coal. For example, on the Great Lakes, large ships carry iron ore from Minnesota to cities where it is used to make steel. On the Mississippi River, barges haul grain to ports, where the grain may be processed or placed on ships to go overseas.

Great Lakes

This freighter carries cargo on the Great Lakes.

People also use rivers and lakes for recreation. Whitewater rafting, canoeing, and kayaking are popular activities. Many people also like to camp, picnic, swim, and fish along the shores of freshwater rivers and lakes.

Not every section of a river can be navigated by boat. A river may flow too fast or be too shallow for safe travel. To make water transportation easier, people dig channels called canals that bypass rough spots and connect waterways. For example, a 376-kilometer (234-mi) canal lets boats travel between the Tennessee and Tombigbee rivers in Mississippi and Alabama. In Canada, west of Buffalo, New York, the Welland Canal connects two Great Lakes, Ontario and Erie. It is part of the waterway known as the St. Lawrence Seaway, which connects the Great Lakes to the Atlantic Ocean.

Fisheries and Aquaculture

Fresh water is full of life—from tiny one-celled organisms to small shrimp and worms, to trout and salmon. Rivers and lakes provide fish for our food, a living resource that people depend upon. They also provide food for frogs, insects, birds, and larger animals.

When people talk about livestock, do you think of fish? Probably not, but fish farming is a thriving business all over the world. **Aquaculture** is the science and business of raising and harvesting fish in a controlled situation. Freshwater fish farms provide a cheap, ready source of catfish, trout, and salmon. However, aquaculture also causes some problems. The farms can cause excess nutrients and pollution to flow into rivers and lakes.

To help maintain the population of fish in rivers and lakes, fish hatcheries are used to raise fish to release into lakes and rivers. Hatcheries give people who fish something to catch and also help threatened species survive.

An aquaculture worker tends to a fish farm in Nepal.

NEPAL

At a hydroelectric plant, water flowing through a dam spins turbines to produce electricity.

Energy

Not so long ago, water wheels could be seen dotting the rivers of America. The force of the river turned the water wheel, which powered machinery in factories such as grain mills. In dams, electricity is generated in a similar way. A **dam** is a structure that holds back and controls the flow of water in a river or other body of water.

At a hydroelectric dam built across a river, water rushing through the dam turns machines called turbines, generating electricity. Even electric plants that are not powered by rivers use water. For example, many plants use coal or nuclear power to heat water, creating steam that turns the turbines. Nuclear power stations also use water to cool the system.

Dams and other structures alter rivers.

When a dam is built on a river, the landscape and the shape of a river are greatly changed. Below the dam, the speed and volume of water flow may change, making a new ecosystem. Behind the dam, water may collect and form a lake covering what once had been a river valley.

In some locations, a lake behind a dam is used as a source of fresh water. A lake that is used to store water is called a reservoir (REHZ-uhr-VWAHR). Some dams are built solely for the purpose of creating a reservoir, and many communities rely on reservoirs for their water needs. Some reservoirs provide opportunities for boating and other recreational activities.

Dams have purposes in addition to providing hydroelectric power and forming reservoirs. Dams may also be built to control rivers that flow too fast or too unpredictably for boats to use them. These dams might separate a river into sections of different elevations, like steps in a staircase. To allow boats to climb or descend these steps and move to the next river section, locks are built at the dams. A **lock** is a section of waterway, closed off by gates, in which the water level is raised or lowered to move ships through.

In addition to rivers with dams, locks are used in canals and rivers that connect lakes of different elevations. Locks are also used in canals that slope upward and then downward, such as the Panama Canal. The Panama Canal is dug into a strip of land between the Atlantic and Pacific oceans, allowing ships a handy shortcut.

CHECK YOUR READING Why do ships need to use locks?

VOCABULARY
Add a description wheel for *lock* in your notebook.

In some cases dams cause problems as well as solve them. For example, in Egypt's Nile valley the giant Aswan Dam stopped floods that happened every year. However, the dam also blocked the flow of rich soil to the valley below the dam. The soil in the Nile valley was fertile for more than 4000 years. Yet today farmers need to add chemical fertilizers to grow their crops.

Dams can also cause problems for fish. When a dam blocks a river, salmon and steelhead cannot reach their breeding grounds. People have tried to solve this problem by installing fish ladder structures along dams that allow fish to climb up the river.

RESOURCE CENTER
CLASSZONE.COM
Learn more about dams.

Locks and Dams

Locks and dams control the flow of rivers and allow boats to pass through.

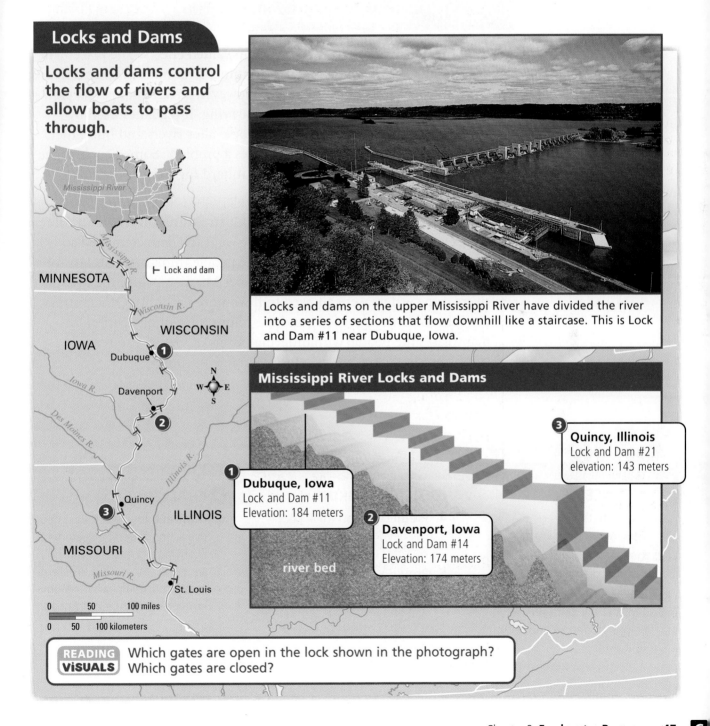

Locks and dams on the upper Mississippi River have divided the river into a series of sections that flow downhill like a staircase. This is Lock and Dam #11 near Dubuque, Iowa.

MINNESOTA

⊢ Lock and dam

Mississippi River

WISCONSIN

IOWA

Dubuque **1**

Davenport

2

Quincy **3**

ILLINOIS

MISSOURI

St. Louis

Iowa R.
Des Moines R.
Illinois R.
Wisconsin R.
Missouri R.

0   50   100 miles
0   50   100 kilometers

Mississippi River Locks and Dams

1 Dubuque, Iowa
Lock and Dam #11
Elevation: 184 meters

2 Davenport, Iowa
Lock and Dam #14
Elevation: 174 meters

3 Quincy, Illinois
Lock and Dam #21
elevation: 143 meters

river bed

READING VISUALS Which gates are open in the lock shown in the photograph? Which gates are closed?

This dammed-up waterway in Texas spilled around its dam during a flood. It formed a new channel that flows to the left of the dam.

Other changes to rivers can have unwanted effects. The placement of locks and the digging of a channel into a river bottom force a river to follow a constant path. In nature, however, a river changes its path depending on how much water it is carrying. It regulates itself by flooding during the wet season. As people alter rivers and build their homes closer to them, flooding becomes a problem. Some people argue that changing the natural flow makes it hard for a river to regulate itself, causing even more flooding.

People have different opinions about structures on rivers. In some places with hydroelectric dams, people want the dams removed so that salmon can swim upstream. Some people think that habitats for wildlife would be improved on the upper Mississippi and the Missouri rivers if the waters were allowed to flow more naturally. Others stress the value of hydroelectricity and the importance of navigation. In many cases the people with differing points of view try to reach compromises so that rivers can serve many purposes.

2.1 Review

KEY CONCEPTS

1. What are three ways that you directly use fresh water daily?

2. Identify a benefit and a possible disadvantage of aquaculture.

3. Explain why dams are both helpful to people and harmful to a river.

CRITICAL THINKING

4. **Predict** Do you think people will need more or less fresh water in the future? Why?

5. **Provide Examples** Explain how water is used in the manufacture of three products that you use every day.

⬤ CHALLENGE

6. **Connect** In some towns near rivers, the federal government is buying houses and paying people to move to a different location. Explain why the government might be doing this.

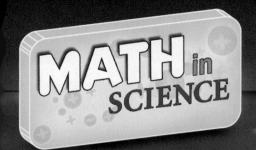

 MATH TUTORIAL
CLASSZONE.COM

Click on Math Tutorial for more help finding the volume of a rectangular prism.

Fish in an Aquarium

A fish requires a certain minimum amount of water to survive. If you plan to keep fish in an aquarium, you can calculate the volume of the aquarium to be sure it will contain enough water.

Example

An aquarium is 50 centimeters long, 30 centimeters wide, and 40 centimeters high. How many liters of water will it hold?

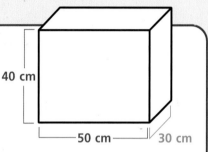

40 cm

50 cm   30 cm

Solution

Use the formula for the volume of a rectangular prism.

Volume = length × width × height	Write a word equation.
$V = lwh$	Replace the words with variables.
= 50 cm × 30 cm × 40 cm	Substitute 50 for l, 30 for w, and 40 for h.
= 60,000 cm^3	Multiply. Note that cm^3 is a cubic centimeter.
= 60,000 mL	Each cubic centimeter holds a milliliter.
= 60 L	Because there are 1000 milliliters in one liter, divide 60,000 by 1000.

ANSWER The aquarium holds 60 liters of water.

Find the volume of each aquarium. Give your answer in liters.

1. The aquarium is 100 centimeters long, 50 centimeters wide, and 80 centimeters high.

2. The aquarium is 50 centimeters long, 20 centimeters wide, and 40 centimeters high.

3. The aquarium is 50 centimeters long, 40 centimeters wide, and 50 centimeters high.

CHALLENGE You are designing an aquarium to house several fish of different species. The aquarium must hold 300 liters of water and fit in a space that is 100 centimeters long and 50 centimeters wide. How high should the aquarium be?

2.2 Society depends on clean and safe water.

 BEFORE, you learned

- Water supports life
- Water is used in many ways

 NOW, you will learn

- How drinking water and wastewater are treated
- How fresh water can become polluted
- How water pollution can be prevented

VOCABULARY

concentration p. 51
sewage system p. 53
septic system p. 54
point-source pollution
  p. 54
nonpoint-source pollution
  p. 54

EXPLORE Concentration

What is one part per million?

PROCEDURE

1. Pour 50 mL of water into the graduated cylinder. This is equal to 1000 drops of water.

2. Add one drop of food coloring to the water in the cylinder. This represents one drop of food coloring to 1000 drops of water, or one part per thousand.

3. Fill the eyedropper from the cylinder.

4. Empty the cylinder and pour 50 mL of new water into the cylinder. Add one drop from the eyedropper to the cylinder. The mixture now contains one part food coloring per thousand thousand parts water, or one part per million (ppm).

MATERIALS
- water
- graduated cylinder
- eyedropper
- food coloring

WHAT DO YOU THINK?
The amount of sodium found in clean spring water is five parts per million. How would you conduct this experiment to make a mixture of food coloring in water of five parts per million?

Treatment makes water safe for drinking.

SUPPORTING MAIN IDEAS
Remember to start a new chart for each main idea.

When you wash your face or brush your teeth, do you ever wonder where the water comes from? It depends on where you live. In many places, water is pumped from a nearby well dug into an underground aquifer. If you live in a big city such as New York City or San Francisco, the water may travel a great distance to arrive at your sink. It is piped to the city from reservoirs that may be many miles away. Then it is stored in tanks or in a local reservoir before flowing through pipes to your home.

Water comes from many different sources, so it may contain impurities or organisms that cause disease. For this reason, drinking water in larger systems is cleaned, or treated, before people can drink it.

Quality Standards

Fresh water can contain a variety of harmful substances and organisms. Certain substances and organisms may be present naturally, but others get into water because of pollution from human activity. Some of the impurities in water are safe for humans to drink in small quantities. However, when impurities reach high concentrations, they can harm people. A **concentration** is the amount of a substance that is in another substance. For example, soft drinks have a high concentration of sugar in water. Concentrations are often expressed in parts per million.

A government agency called the Environmental Protection Agency (EPA) sets standards for safe, clean drinking water. The EPA standards are guidelines for the protection of our natural water sources and the quality of the water that reaches our homes. Government agencies in states and local communities enforce laws based on the EPA standards.

The EPA lists standards for harmful organisms that can cause disease. It also lists safe levels for copper and certain other metals that can be found in water. In addition, the EPA checks for a variety of chemicals and harmful radioactive materials.

Your local water provider regularly tests the water to make sure it meets the EPA requirements. If any concentrations are higher than the EPA standards, the water must be treated. As a result, the United States has one of the safest, cleanest water supplies in the world.

Students test river water in West Virginia for pollutants.

CHECK YOUR READING How does a water provider know that it must treat water?

EPA Standards for Substances in Water		
Substance	Common Source	Maximum Allowed, in Parts per Million
Copper	Natural deposits; household pipes	1.3
Cyanide	Various factories	0.2
Lead	Natural deposits; household pipes	0.015
Mercury	Natural deposits; refineries and factories; landfills; crop fields	0.002
Nitrite	Water running off fertilized fields; sewage leaks; natural deposits	1

Treatment of Drinking Water

VISUALIZATION
CLASSZONE.COM

See a water treatment plant in action.

In a water treatment plant, thousands of gallons of water flow through a series of tanks, where the water is filtered and treated with chemicals to remove harmful substances and kill organisms. The major steps are chemical disinfection and the removal of dirt.

Water Treatment and Distribution

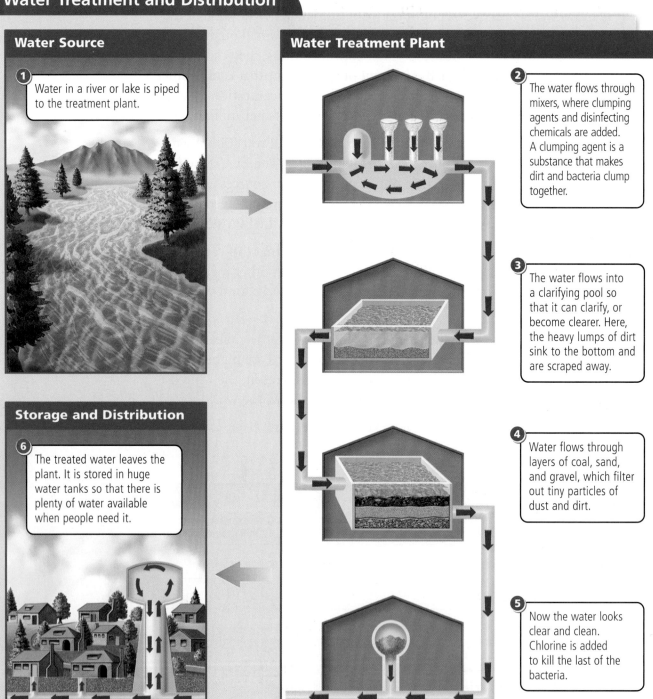

Water Source

1. Water in a river or lake is piped to the treatment plant.

Water Treatment Plant

2. The water flows through mixers, where clumping agents and disinfecting chemicals are added. A clumping agent is a substance that makes dirt and bacteria clump together.

3. The water flows into a clarifying pool so that it can clarify, or become clearer. Here, the heavy lumps of dirt sink to the bottom and are scraped away.

4. Water flows through layers of coal, sand, and gravel, which filter out tiny particles of dust and dirt.

5. Now the water looks clear and clean. Chlorine is added to kill the last of the bacteria.

Storage and Distribution

6. The treated water leaves the plant. It is stored in huge water tanks so that there is plenty of water available when people need it.

Wastewater is treated and released.

Wastewater is the water that runs down the drain. Before wastewater can be released back into the environment, it needs to be treated. Sewage and septic systems are two ways of treating wastewater.

Sewage System

A **sewage system** is a system that collects and treats wastewater from a city or a town. Sewage pipes carry wastewater from homes and businesses to a water treatment plant.

In the first part of treatment, wastewater is strained to remove large objects. Then the water is pumped into a tank, where it sits until the heaviest sludge sinks to the bottom. The sludge is taken away to decompose in another tank. Then chlorine is added to the water to kill the harmful bacteria. This process removes about half of the pollutants.

During the second part of the process, extra oxygen is pumped into the wastewater. The oxygen causes certain kinds of bacteria to grow in great numbers. These bacteria consume much of the sludge and oil that is still in the water. In other words, these tiny organisms help clean the water. More sludge also settles out, and grease is skimmed off the top. Chemicals clean the water one more time and remove any extra chlorine.

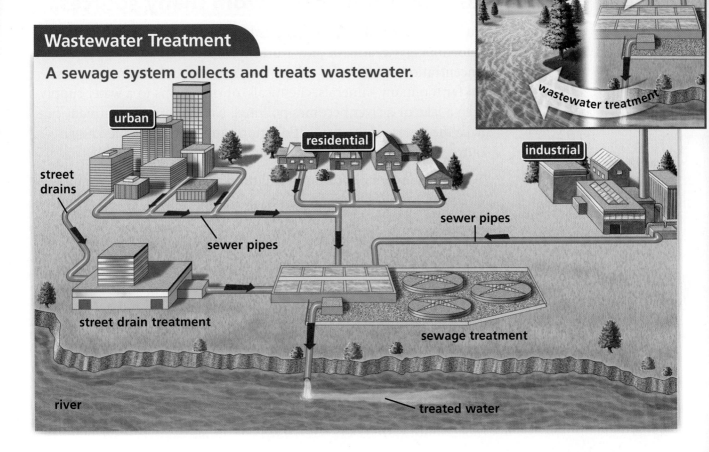

Water Use Cycle

water treatment

wastewater treatment

Wastewater Treatment

A sewage system collects and treats wastewater.

urban

residential

industrial

street drains

sewer pipes

sewer pipes

street drain treatment

sewage treatment

river

treated water

Septic System

A **septic system** is a small wastewater system used by a home or a business. Septic systems are more common in lightly populated areas that do not have central sewage treatment centers. In a house with a septic system, wastewater is carried out through a pipe to an underground tank away from the house. The sludge, or thicker material, in the wastewater settles to the bottom. Much of this sludge is consumed naturally by bacteria, just as in the large sewage treatment plants. Sludge that remains has to be removed from the tank every few years.

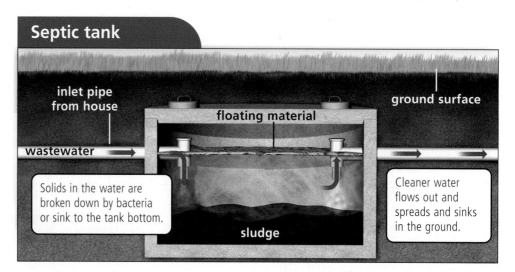

Septic tank

inlet pipe from house

floating material

ground surface

wastewater

Solids in the water are broken down by bacteria or sink to the tank bottom.

Cleaner water flows out and spreads and sinks in the ground.

sludge

Water pollution comes from many sources.

You have learned how fresh water is treated before we drink it. Unfortunately, treatment only works for water that has fairly low concentrations of harmful substances. Sometimes human activities add far too many minerals, chemicals, or organisms to a water supply. Then a lake or a river becomes polluted. No amount of treatment can make the water safe to drink. Pollution can come from one known source, or point, or it can come from many points.

- **Point-source pollution** is pollution that enters water from a known source. It might be sewage flowing from a pipe or chemicals spewing out of a factory. This pollution is easy to spot, and laws can be enforced to stop it.

- **Nonpoint-source pollution** is pollution whose source is hard to find or is scattered. Rain and gravity cause water to wash off streets, lawns, construction sites, and farms. This water, called runoff, can carry oil, gas, pesticides, chemicals, paints, and detergents into storm drains or over land and then to rivers and lakes. If you don't know exactly where pollution comes from, it is hard to enforce laws against it. For this reason, nonpoint-source pollution causes most water pollution.

VOCABULARY
Add a description wheel for *point-source pollution* to your notebook.

Sources of Water Pollution

Human activity can pollute the water supply.

Cities

- Illegal dumping of toxic chemicals
- Water and pollutants running off from streets
- Unsafe disposal of motor oil and other products

Homes

- Improper disposal of household batteries, chemicals, and motor oil
- Use of fertilizers and pesticides
- Poorly functioning septic systems

Sewage

- Improper disposal of factory wastewater
- Poorly functioning sewage systems
- Dumping of raw wastewater when sewage systems cannot handle heavy rainfall

Farms

- Heavy use of fertilizers and pesticides
- Leaks and spills of animal waste
- Animals grazing near rivers and lakes

Shipping, Boating, and Oil Transport

- Spills of oil or other cargo from barges and ships
- Fuel spills and leakage from small boats
- Illegal dumping
- Illegal release of sewage

READING VISUALS Identify three examples of point-source pollution.

Water pollution can be prevented.

Water pollution is a serious problem because water is a limited resource. When water is polluted, there is less water available for use. Water pollution can also endanger people's health. People and businesses can do a number of things to prevent or reduce pollution of water.

Industry and Transportation Operators of factories and of vehicles that haul cargo can take a number of steps to prevent or reduce water pollution. For example, factories can maintain their pipelines and equipment to ensure that harmful chemicals are not leaking into the ground and contaminating groundwater. Transportation companies can inspect and repair their trucks, planes, and ships to prevent oil and fuels from leaking onto pavement or into water.

Industry can prevent or reduce pollution by reducing the amount of toxic waste it generates. Factories can reuse and recycle chemicals and materials used in manufacturing. Companies can also provide ways for their customers to recycle or return certain products—such as used motor oil or batteries—that can pollute water if they are disposed of improperly.

In the construction industry, builders can design their projects to reduce the pollution that new construction can cause. Builders can use less pavement when they build parking areas for malls and office buildings. Less pavement reduces the amount of water that may run off and carry pollutants from cars and other sources to rivers and lakes. And measures to preserve open land, especially wetland areas, can protect a natural water cleansing system and reduce runoff.

READING TiP
A toxic substance is one that is capable of causing harm to health.

⚪ **CHECK YOUR READING** How does pavement contribute to water pollution?

Pollution can make a lake or river dangerous or unusable. In many places, people are cleaning up and restoring freshwater resources.

Agriculture Farming generates chemical and natural waste that can contaminate water. Farmers can follow practices that prevent or reduce pollution from agriculture. On farms with livestock, pastures used by cows and other grazing animals can be fenced off to keep animals away from streams and lakes. Keeping livestock away from water reduces pollution from animal waste. Farms that keep animals in structures can keep waste out of the water supply by storing and disposing of manure properly.

New techniques in farming can reduce pollution. Many farmers grow food without pesticides, which can be toxic and pollute water. The farmers fight insects and other pests by bringing in their natural enemies, such as ladybugs. To fertilize soil, the use of natural substances and the planting of certain crops can take the place of manufactured chemicals. Farming that does not use such chemicals is known as organic.

At home There are a number of things most people can do in their daily lives to prevent or reduce water pollution. People can take their old household chemicals to hazardous waste collection sites. Toxic chemicals should not be poured down the drain or onto the ground. Proper disposal and recycling of electronic devices such as computers can prevent toxic metals contained in them from reaching the water supply.

In shopping for food, consumers can choose organic products to support farming methods that don't use toxic pesticides. People can try to use nontoxic products in their homes. They can also stop using toxic pesticides and weed killers, as well as chemical fertilizers, on lawns and gardens.

These farmers in Vermont use organic methods to produce milk and ice cream.

2.2 Review

KEY CONCEPTS

1. How are EPA standards used to ensure a clean, safe supply of water?

2. What are two ways that wastewater is treated before it can be released?

3. What is the difference between point-source pollution and nonpoint-source pollution?

CRITICAL THINKING

4. **Compare and Contrast** How are sewage systems and septic systems alike? How are they different?

5. **Categorize** Categorize the following as point- or non-point-source pollution: small boat leaking oil; fish farm releasing wastes into a river; person dumping motor oil onto the ground.

CHALLENGE

6. **Compare** What parts of sewage and septic systems are similar to the way water is naturally cleaned by Earth's water cycle?

CHAPTER INVESTIGATION

Monitoring Water Quality

OVERVIEW AND PURPOSE Water pollution in some amount seems to happen wherever people live. That's why water for home drinking is almost always treated. Proper water treatment depends on knowing what forms of pollution water contains. This two-part activity models the process of monitoring for water quality. In this investigation you will

- perform systematic testing procedures similar to those used to test the water supply
- test known samples for common "pollutants," and then identify unknown water samples based on those tests

▶ Procedure

PART ONE

1. Make a data table for Part One like the one shown on the sample **Science Notebook** page on page 59.

2. Test the three different known contaminated water samples with the three types of indicator strips. Dip one of each strip into the solution and instantly remove it. A positive result causes a color change. Make your observations of color changes exactly 30 seconds after dipping the strip. Observe and note the results in your table so you know what a positive result looks like for each contaminant. Do not reuse test strips. You need fresh strips for each water sample.

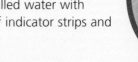

step 2

3. Test the pure distilled water with the three types of indicator strips and note your results.

PART TWO

1. A water-testing company has mixed up four water samples taken from the following locations: a runoff stream from an agricultural field, a river near a factory, a pond on a dairy farm, and a mountain stream. You will test the four unknown samples using the same procedures as above to determine which sample has which contaminant. You will then determine which location the sample most likely came from.

MATERIALS
- 8 each of three types of indicator strips
- watch with second hand
- "pesticide-contaminated" water sample
- "bacteria-contaminated" water sample
- "chemical-contaminated" water sample
- pure distilled water sample
- 4 unknown water samples

2 Make a data table for Part Two like the one shown on the sample **Science Notebook** below.

3 Test each water sample as in step 2, Part One. Record your observations as you test each unknown sample with each indicator strip. Note all color changes you observe.

4 Consult the chart you completed in Part One as you perform tests to determine which type of contaminant each unknown sample contains. From this information determine which location the sample probably came from.

Observe and Analyze   Write It Up

1. **IDENTIFY CONTROLS** Why was it necessary to test the distilled water in Part One?

2. **IDENTIFY** Use what you have learned in this chapter to determine which location corresponds to the types of pollution you learned to identify in Part One.

3. **ANALYZE** Compare your testing results from the unknown water samples with your testing results from the known water samples. Are your results similar?

Conclude   Write It Up

1. **COMPARE** How did your results in Part One compare with your results in Part Two?

2. **EVALUATE** What part of this investigation was the most difficult? Why?

3. **IDENTIFY LIMITS** What limitations does this type of testing pose for real-life water-quality technicians?

4. **APPLY** A runoff pool is contaminated with bacteria, chemicals, and pesticides. How would your water-testing results appear for a sample from this pool?

INVESTIGATE Further

CHALLENGE Design a procedure to test unknown water samples that have numerous contaminants.

Monitoring Water Quality

Table 1. Positive Test Results of Known Water Samples

	Pure distilled water	Chemical-contaminated water	Bacteria-contaminated water	Pesticide-contaminated water
Indicator A				
Indicator B				
Indicator C				

Table 2. Test Results of Unknown Samples with Probable Locations

	Unknown #1	Unknown #2	Unknown #3	Unknown #4
Indicator A				
Indicator B				
Indicator C				
Type of Contaminant				
Location				

2.3 Water shortages threaten society.

 BEFORE, you learned

- Water is treated for drinking
- Wastewater is treated and released
- Pollutants contaminate the water supply

 NOW, you will learn

- How overuse causes water shortages
- How water can be conserved
- How governments and organizations manage water use

VOCABULARY

drought p. 61
desalination p. 66

EXPLORE The Value of Fresh Water

Does water cost more than gasoline?

PROCEDURE

1. Find out the current price of a liter of bottled water.
2. Find out the current price of a gallon of gasoline.
3. To calculate the price of gasoline in liters, multiply the price per gallon by 0.26.

WHAT DO YOU THINK?

- How do the prices of bottled water and gasoline compare?
- What do your results tell you about the value of drinking water?

MATERIALS
calculator

SUPPORTING MAIN IDEAS
Support the main idea of global water shortages with details and examples.

Water shortages are a global problem.

Most nations in the deserts of northern Africa and in the Middle East have severe water shortages. These are some of the driest regions on Earth, but their populations require more and more water as cities grow. Water that could be used to grow food is piped instead to the growing cities, where it is needed in homes and factories.

So how do people in these regions grow enough food? For the most part, they cannot. There is simply not enough water. Jordan imports, or brings in from other countries, about 91 percent of its grain. Israel imports about 87 percent, and Egypt, once a center of agriculture, imports 40 percent.

All over the world, the water supply is dwindling. Populations are growing everywhere, and people must be fed. Farmers draw water from underground aquifers faster than the water can be replaced.

Even places that normally get regular rainfall can face water shortages. **Drought** (drowt) is a long period of abnormally low rainfall. Drought can destroy crops and dry up water supplies. Usually, trees can survive a dry period because their roots reach into the ground for water. However, severe drought can dry out entire forests. Dry trees are more vulnerable to disease, and wildfires are harder to control.

Overuse can cause water shortages.

As the world's population grows, usable fresh water is becoming scarcer in many places. Agriculture uses two-thirds of the world's available fresh water. Unfortunately, only half of that water reaches the roots of the plants. The other half is lost to evaporation and runoff.

Overuse of underground water can cause an aquifer to be depleted, or consumed faster than its water is replaced. In most places where crops require irrigation, farmers water their fields with groundwater. India is using twice as much water from its aquifers as can be replaced. In the United States, farmers are taking so much water that they are draining the huge Ogallala Aquifer. The problem is that underground stores of water can take thousands of years to refill. Draining an aquifer can also destroy it. When water is removed, the ground may settle and close up the storage space.

River water is also being overused in many places. So much water is being taken out that many major rivers now run dry for a large part of the year. These rivers include the Ganges River in South Asia, the Indus River in Pakistan, and the Colorado River in the southwestern United States. People in seven western states use water from the Colorado. As cities in these states have grown, the demand for the river water has increased.

A bridge stands over a dried-out part of a reservoir during a drought in Maryland.

How has overuse of water affected some rivers?

Fresh water can be conserved.

SUPPORTING MAIN IDEAS
Record in your notes the important details about water conservation.

Although water shortages are a serious problem, the situation is not entirely hopeless. Conserving can solve a big part of the problem. Conservation is action taken to protect and preserve the natural world. To conserve water means to use less of it.

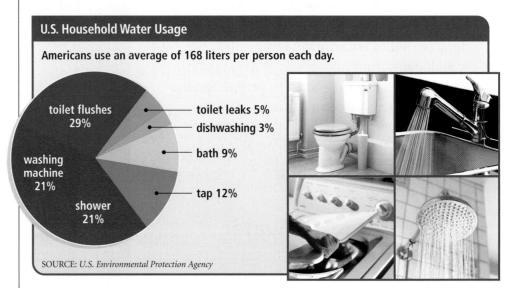

U.S. Household Water Usage

Americans use an average of 168 liters per person each day.

toilet flushes 29%

washing machine 21%

shower 21%

toilet leaks 5%
dishwashing 3%
bath 9%
tap 12%

SOURCE: *U.S. Environmental Protection Agency*

The chart above shows how Americans use water each day. The amount that each American uses on average—168 liters—is higher than in most parts of the world. Note that 5 percent of the amount—more than 8 liters—is wasted by leaking toilets.

The Need for Conservation

Think about what you already know about the water cycle. When aquifers, lakes, and rivers are depleted—or used up faster than the water in them can be replaced naturally—available fresh water from those water supplies decreases. Because water supplies in many regions are being depleted, conservation is an urgent issue.

These water-catching devices are used to collect and store rainwater in Hawaii.

Much of the western United States is mostly desert, and yet the population in dry parts of the West is growing each year. What will happen if the aquifers and rivers that supply this region with water dry up? The less water that people use today, the more water there will be to use in the future.

Water shortages are an increasing problem around the world as the population grows in many regions. About half a billion people in 31 countries—mostly in the Middle East and Africa—currently face water shortages. By 2025, the number of people without enough water will increase five times, to about 2.8 billion people.

Conservation Practices

People conserve water in three ways. The first way is to use less water. Some cities conserve their supply of water simply by repairing leaks in underground pipes. The second way is to reuse water. Many cities reuse treated wastewater for landscaping. The third method is to recycle water, or use water again for the same purpose.

Farmers can conserve water by using drip irrigation instead of spraying water. They can change the grooves in their fields so the water stays in the soil longer. Most industries can use water at least twice before returning it to a river or lake. For example, water used to cool machines can be recycled back through the same system.

At home, people can change their plumbing and their habits. Low-flow toilets and showerheads can cut water use in half. People conserve water by turning off the faucet while brushing their teeth, taking shorter showers, and running the dishwasher only when it is full. Leaking pipes and dripping faucets in homes cause huge amounts of water to be wasted. Repair and maintenance of plumbing systems would reduce water use greatly.

RESOURCE CENTER
CLASSZONE.COM
Learn more about water conservation.

CHECK YOUR READING What are the three main ways in which people conserve water?

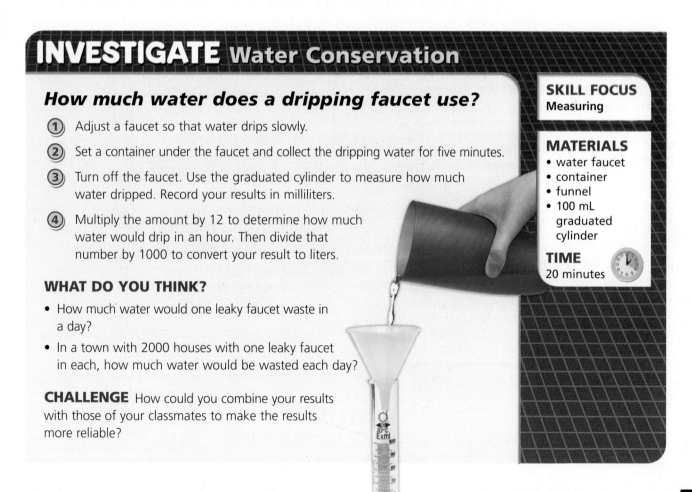

INVESTIGATE Water Conservation

How much water does a dripping faucet use?

1. Adjust a faucet so that water drips slowly.
2. Set a container under the faucet and collect the dripping water for five minutes.
3. Turn off the faucet. Use the graduated cylinder to measure how much water dripped. Record your results in milliliters.
4. Multiply the amount by 12 to determine how much water would drip in an hour. Then divide that number by 1000 to convert your result to liters.

WHAT DO YOU THINK?

- How much water would one leaky faucet waste in a day?
- In a town with 2000 houses with one leaky faucet in each, how much water would be wasted each day?

CHALLENGE How could you combine your results with those of your classmates to make the results more reliable?

SKILL FOCUS
Measuring

MATERIALS
- water faucet
- container
- funnel
- 100 mL graduated cylinder

TIME
20 minutes

People can balance water needs and uses.

People around the world have different views about how water should be used. Americans in the hot Southwest might want water for swimming pools and lawns. Developing countries need water to prevent disease and grow food. In some places, farmers use river water before it can reach others downstream. Some industries want water to make products.

As water becomes scarcer, the arguments become more serious. Public officials and experts can help manage water use and enforce fair laws. For example, what happens when a river flows from one state into another or across a national border? In such a situation, people must agree to share the water rights.

The Rio Grande flows through two states and then between Texas and Mexico. The water in this river is an international issue. In 1939 a legal agreement was made between the states of Colorado, New Mexico, and Texas, and between the United States and Mexico. It listed how much water each region could take.

In the past, water from the Rio Grande was used for farming. However, cities along the river are growing rapidly. All the cities need more water from the Rio Grande, and every year they will need more. The international agreement no longer solves this urgent problem. American and Mexican officials are looking for new solutions.

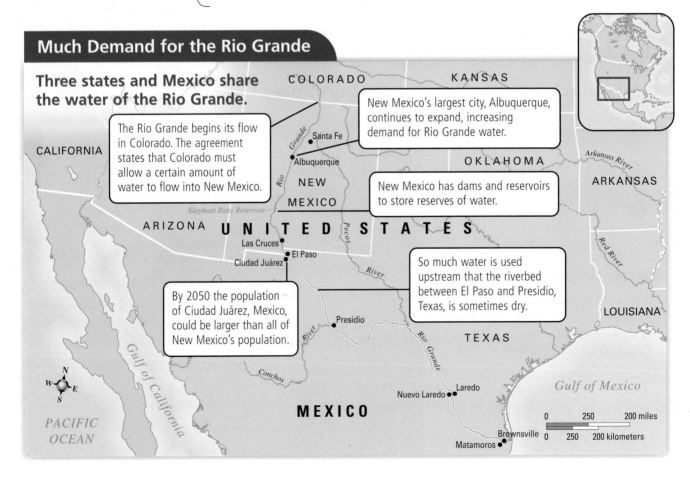

Much Demand for the Rio Grande

Three states and Mexico share the water of the Rio Grande.

The Rio Grande begins its flow in Colorado. The agreement states that Colorado must allow a certain amount of water to flow into New Mexico.

New Mexico's largest city, Albuquerque, continues to expand, increasing demand for Rio Grande water.

New Mexico has dams and reservoirs to store reserves of water.

So much water is used upstream that the riverbed between El Paso and Presidio, Texas, is sometimes dry.

By 2050 the population of Ciudad Juárez, Mexico, could be larger than all of New Mexico's population.

COLORADO · KANSAS · CALIFORNIA · Rio Grande · Santa Fe · Albuquerque · OKLAHOMA · Arkansas River · ARKANSAS · NEW MEXICO · Elephant Butte Reservoir · ARIZONA · UNITED STATES · Pecos · Red River · Las Cruces · El Paso · Ciudad Juárez · River · Presidio · LOUISIANA · TEXAS · Conchos · River · Rio Grande · Laredo · Nuevo Laredo · Gulf of Mexico · MEXICO · Brownsville · Matamoros · PACIFIC OCEAN · Gulf of California

N · W · E · S

0 · 250 · 200 miles
0 · 250 · 200 kilometers

Shortages

When there is not enough water, crops will not grow. And when the crops fail to grow, there is not enough food to eat. The Middle East countries that import most of their grain are, in a way, importing water. Billions of tons of water are used to grow the imported grain.

International organizations help out countries where drought and floods have destroyed the crops. For example, in 2002 the World Food Programme alerted the world to a serious lack of food in southeast Africa. The United Nations agencies arranged for food aid. The shrinking of Lake Chad has also caused hardship for many Africans.

In the future, people may solve some of the problems by sharing water around the world. The governor of Alaska has suggested an undersea pipeline. This line would be between 2200 kilometers (1360 mi) and 3400 kilometers (2100 mi) long. Through this pipe, thousands of liters of fresh water would flow from Alaska to California. Some people have also suggested selling Great Lakes water to Japan. Many people in states and Canadian provinces around the lakes have strongly objected, because they think removing water could damage the lakes.

 CHECK YOUR READING How can Alaska help solve a water shortage in California?

This satellite photograph of Lake Chad in Africa was taken in 1973.

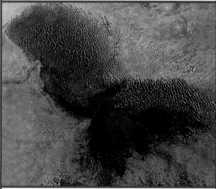

A recent photograph shows how much the lake has shrunk.

Pollution

Where water flows across the boundaries of nations, pollution can flow across as well. One example of this problem is the Danube River in Europe. This river begins in the Black Forest in Germany. It empties into the Black Sea on the coast of Romania. As it flows through the cities of Vienna, Budapest, and Belgrade, more and more pollution is added to the water. Seventeen countries border either the Danube River or the Black Sea. To protect the river and the sea, as well as to manage use of the river water, 11 nations made an agreement among themselves and the European Union. They agreed to cooperate to prevent pollution of the water and to conserve and use water from the Danube sensibly. They also agreed to conserve and protect groundwater.

Some national and international water pollution problems are hard to solve. States in the northeastern United States are concerned about acid rain. Particle pollution from factories to the west is collected in clouds. Then the wind blows the clouds across the Eastern states, and acid rain falls in lakes and rivers that are far from the source. The acid rain can kill plants, as well as fish and other animals.

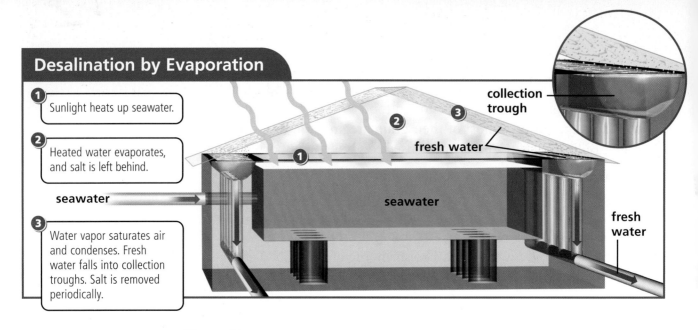

Desalination by Evaporation

1 Sunlight heats up seawater.

2 Heated water evaporates, and salt is left behind.

3 Water vapor saturates air and condenses. Fresh water falls into collection troughs. Salt is removed periodically.

collection trough

fresh water

seawater

seawater

fresh water

New Sources

Can people find new sources of fresh water? The answer, at first, seems obvious. Just remove the salt from seawater. In dry regions, such as Israel, Lebanon, and some coastal towns in California and Florida, people are trying to obtain fresh water this way. The process of removing salt from ocean water is called **desalination** (dee-SAL-ih-NAY-shun). Some treatment plants use a method similar to the natural water cycle. Salt water is evaporated, and salt is left behind. Then water vapor is condensed, or returned to liquid form, as fresh water.

If this process were easy and inexpensive, water shortages might never happen. However, desalination can cost five times as much as normal water treatment. Therefore, it is not a solution that will work for most countries. As technology improves, the cost may go down.

Another possible source of fresh water is icebergs. Icebergs contain millions of liters of fresh water. However, the process of towing an iceberg to a city before it melts is too expensive to be practical.

VOCABULARY
Add a description wheel for *desalination* in your notebook.

2.3 Review

KEY CONCEPTS

1. What is drought and what problems does it cause?

2. How are aquifers and rivers being depleted?

3. Name two ways to help prevent water shortages.

CRITICAL THINKING

4. **Connect** Draw up a plan that suggests three ways to conserve water at your school. Be sure your ideas are practical, and explain how you might convince people to make the changes.

5. **Infer** Why do you think some people object to building a water pipeline from Alaska to California?

○ CHALLENGE

6. **Synthesize** Think about what you have learned about national and international water issues. Then think about what you know about aquifers. What usage problems might occur when one aquifer lies under two countries? How might people solve any problems that arise?

Water and Farming

Farmers have used irrigation, the process of supplying water to crops, for at least 7000 years. Today, about 60 percent of the fresh water used in the world goes for irrigation. However, about one-third of this water does not reach the crops. Some of it runs off the field. By building ditches and ponds, farmers can capture runoff water and pump it back into a field.

Irrigation water can also evaporate before crops can use it. Farmers can reduce this loss by understanding how changes in air temperature, relative humidity, and wind speed affect the evaporation rate. Then farmers can adjust when and how much they irrigate.

Spray Irrigation

In some systems, sprinklers as much as 400 meters (1300 ft) long spray water on crops. Since the water is sprayed into the air, evaporation loss can be high. Spray irrigation is used for many crops in the western United States. Spraying at night can reduce evaporation loss.

Flood Irrigation

Many farmers send water through small ditches between rows of crops, or sometimes farmers flood entire fields. Compared with other systems, flooding results in higher losses from runoff. Flooding is commonly used by rice farmers in eastern Asia.

Drip Irrigation

In drip irrigation, water bubbles out of pipes lying on or just above the ground throughout a field or orchard. The water reaches the ground quickly and in small amounts, so little is lost to runoff or evaporation. Farmers growing fruits and vegetables frequently use this system.

EXPLORE

1. **ANALYZING** Compare the amounts of labor, machinery, and water used in each irrigation system. Which system uses water most efficiently? In what climate regions is this most important? Why would farmers choose a system that uses water less efficiently?

2. **CHALLENGE** Create a model of a flood irrigation system. Use dirt in a pan, with toothpicks to represent crops. Make ditches that send water evenly throughout the "field." As you pour water into your system, note any soil loss that may occur. How can you fix this problem?

2 Chapter Review

the BIG idea

Fresh water is a limited resource and is essential for human society.

CONTENT REVIEW
CLASSZONE.COM

◀ KEY CONCEPTS SUMMARY

2.1 Fresh water is an essential resource.
Fresh water is essential for life and is used for many human activities.

fresh water
- farming
- industry
- transportation and recreation
- fisheries and aquaculture
- energy
- living organisms

VOCABULARY
1 irrigation p. 43
2 aquaculture p. 45
3 dam p. 46
4 lock p. 46

2.2 Society depends on clean and safe water.
Water is treated for safe drinking. Pollution can harm the water supply.

Water is drawn from a river or lake.

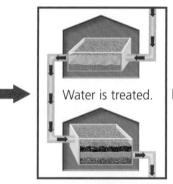

Water is treated.

Water is stored and distributed.

VOCABULARY
5 concentration p. 51
6 sewage system p. 53
7 septic system p. 54
8 point-source pollution p. 54
9 nonpoint-source
10 pollution p. 54

2.3 Water shortages threaten society.
Drought and overuse can cause water shortages.

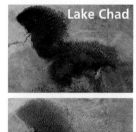

Lake Chad

Americans use an average of 168 liters per person each day.

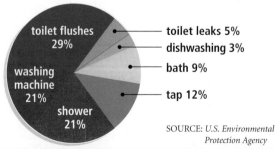

- toilet flushes 29%
- washing machine 21%
- shower 21%
- toilet leaks 5%
- dishwashing 3%
- bath 9%
- tap 12%

SOURCE: *U.S. Environmental Protection Agency*

VOCABULARY
11 drought p. 61
12 desalination p. 66

Reviewing Vocabulary

Use words from the box below to answer the next nine questions.

septic system	nonpoint-source pollution	desalination
concentration	sewage system	point-source pollution
aquaculture	drought	irrigation

1. Which word means "fish farming"?

2. What is the term for a method farmers use to bring water to their fields from rivers and aquifers?

3. Which term can be used to describe the amount of a harmful substance in fresh water?

4. Which term would be used for waste flowing from a factory pipe?

5. Select the term for what a city uses to collect and treat wastewater.

6. Which term would describe oil running off from a parking lot during a rainstorm?

7. What word describes a period when there is little or no rainfall?

8. What process is used to obtain fresh water from seawater?

9. Which term describes a method for treating home wastewater in an underground tank?

Reviewing Key Concepts

Multiple Choice *Choose the letter of the best answer.*

10. Which type of irrigation pours water through canals and waterways?
    a. flood irrigation
    b. spray irrigation
    c. drip irrigation
    d. reservoir irrigation

11. A channel dug to allow boats to travel from one river to another is an example of a
    a. canal
    b. lake
    c. reservoir
    d. sewage system

12. A section of a waterway in which ships are raised or lowered is called a
    a. turbine
    b. fish ladder
    c. dam
    d. lock

13. Concentrations of substances are often expressed as
    a. whole parts
    b. parts per million
    c. parts per thousand
    d. parts per hundred

14. In a sewage plant, sludge and oil are consumed by
    a. chlorine
    b. sand
    c. bacteria
    d. filters

15. In a sewage system, what is added to kill harmful bacteria?
    a. chlorine
    b. sand
    c. bacteria
    d. soap

16. The term for pollution that can be traced to a specific location is
    a. water pollution
    b. point-source pollution
    c. nonpoint-source pollution
    d. runoff pollution

Short Answer *Write a short answer to each question.*

17. How are aquifers depleted?

18. How are EPA standards used to protect fresh water?

19. How does the practice of organic farming help prevent water pollution?

20. What problems do people have sharing water from the Rio Grande?

Thinking Critically

Use the map to answer the next five questions.

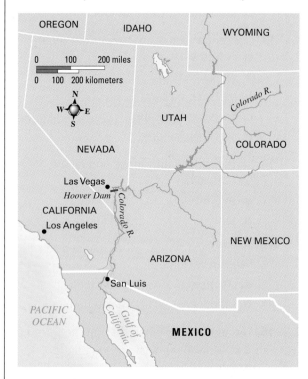

The Colorado River runs from Colorado to the Gulf of California. In California water is needed for 17 million people and also to irrigate 3642 square kilometers (900,000 acres) of farmland. The Colorado provides 60 percent of this water.

21. OBSERVE Through which states and countries does the Colorado River flow?

22. EXAMPLES What are three ways in which water from the Colorado is probably used?

23. INFER What conflicts probably exist between the states of California and Arizona?

24. PREDICT As populations grow in Las Vegas, southern California, and San Luis, Mexico, what problems will arise? How can they be solved?

25. CONNECT Do you think states should receive equal shares of the water in the Colorado River? Explain your answer.

26. IDENTIFY CAUSE Copy the concept map below, and complete it by adding two causes of, and two solutions to, the problem of the water level of an aquifer sinking.

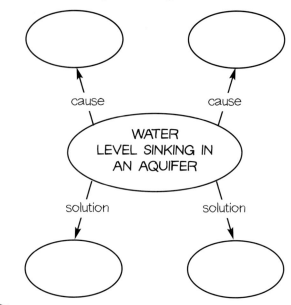

the **BIG** idea

27. PROVIDE EXAMPLES Look again at the photograph on pages 38–39. Now that you have finished the chapter, how would you change your response to the question on the photograph?

28. SEQUENCE Draw a diagram of the path that fresh water travels before and after humans use it. Show where freshwater comes from, how it is treated, how it arrives at our homes, how it leaves our homes as wastewater, how it is treated again, and how it reenters the water cycle.

UNIT PROJECTS

If you need to do an experiment for your unit project, gather the materials. Be sure to allow enough time to observe results before the project is due.

Analyzing a Graph

The line graph below shows the amount of a chemical found in a stream. During the period shown, a factory opened and released water into the stream. Later, a wastewater treatment plant opened and treated water from the factory before it entered the stream. Study the graph and use it to answer the first six questions below.

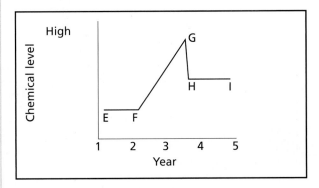

1. Which phrase best describes the concentration of the chemical at Point E?
   - **a.** low
   - **b.** medium
   - **c.** somewhat high
   - **d.** very high

2. A new factory opens during year 2. What immediately happens to the concentration of the chemical?
   - **a.** It does not change.
   - **b.** It decreases sharply.
   - **c.** It decreases slightly.
   - **d.** It increases sharply.

3. Which point probably marks when a new wastewater treatment plant opened?
   - **a.** E
   - **b.** F
   - **c.** G
   - **d.** I

4. Point-source pollution comes from a known source. Which amount is point-source pollution?
   - **a.** the difference between E and F
   - **b.** the difference between F and G
   - **c.** the difference between G and H
   - **d.** the difference between H and I

5. How do the concentrations of E and I compare?
   - **a.** I is higher.
   - **b.** I is lower.
   - **c.** I and E are equal.
   - **d.** The graph does not include enough data to compare concentrations.

6. Which statement best explains the data on the graph?
   - **a.** The factory has less impact than the treatment plant does.
   - **b.** The factory and the treatment plant have little influence on the water.
   - **c.** The factory and the treatment plant balance each other out.
   - **d.** The factory adds more of the chemical than the treatment plant removes.

Extended Response

Answer the two questions below in detail. Include some of the terms shown in the word box. Underline each term you use in your answers.

evaporate	condense	precipitation
groundwater	irrigation	rain

7. Describe the parts of the water cycle that are involved at a desalination plant.

8. For a science fair project, Anthony compared the growth of plants that got their water in different ways. One group grew in soil that he kept moist by providing water through a tube under the surface. For a second group, he poured water on top of the soil each day. In the third group, he sprayed water from a bottle on the plants. How are the three methods Anthony used similar to ways that farmers irrigate crops?

CHAPTER

3

Ocean Systems

the BIG idea

The oceans are a connected system of water in motion.

Key Concepts

SECTION
3.1 The oceans are a connected system.
Learn about ocean water and the ocean floor.

SECTION
3.2 Ocean water moves in currents.
Learn about currents and how they interact with climate and weather.

SECTION
3.3 Waves move through oceans.
Learn how waves form and move through the ocean.

SECTION
3.4 Waters rise and fall in tides.
Learn how tides are related to the Sun and the Moon.

Internet Preview

CLASSZONE.COM

Chapter 3 online resources: Content Review, Simulation, Visualization, three Resource Centers, Math Tutorial, Test Practice

What causes these waves?

EXPLORE (the **BIG** idea)

What Makes Things Float or Sink?

Fill two clear cups with water. Add a heaping spoonful of salt to one cup and stir until it dissolves. Gently squeeze two drops of food coloring into each cup.

Observe and Think What happened to the drops of food coloring in each cup?

How Does Moving Air Affect Water?

Fill a pan with water. Use a straw to blow over the surface of the water.

Observe and Think What happened to the water when you blew on it? Draw a diagram to show what happened.

Internet Activity: The Ocean Floor

Go to **ClassZone.com** to expose the ocean floor by draining all of the water out of the ocean.

Observe and Think How are the features of the ocean floor similar to features on land? How are they different?

NSTA
scilinks.org

SCi
LINKS

Exploring Earth's Oceans **Code: MDL020**

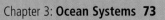

Getting Ready to Learn

◀ CONCEPT REVIEW

- Water covers most of Earth.
- Earth's waters circulate in the water cycle.
- The water in the oceans is salt water.

◀ VOCABULARY REVIEW

salt water p. 11

water cycle p. 12

evaporation p. 13

desalination p. 66

ⓘ CONTENT REVIEW
CLASSZONE.COM
Review concepts and vocabulary.

▶ TAKING NOTES

OUTLINE

As you read, copy the headings into your notebook in the form of an outline. Then add notes in your own words that summarize what you read.

VOCABULARY STRATEGY

Draw a **word triangle** for each new vocabulary term. At the bottom, write and define the term. Above that, write a sentence in which you use the term correctly. At the top, draw a small picture to represent the term.

See the Note-Taking Handbook on pages R45–R51.

SCIENCE NOTEBOOK

OUTLINE

I. The oceans are a connected system.

   A. Ocean water covers much of Earth.

   B. Ocean water contains salts and gases.

      1.

      2.

   C. Ocean temperatures vary.

      1.

      2.

The salinity of ocean water is about 35 grams of salt per 1000 grams of water

salinity: a measure of the saltiness of water

3.1 The oceans are a connected system.

◀ BEFORE, you learned

- Most water on Earth is salt water
- The ocean plays an important role in the water cycle

▶ NOW, you will learn

- What ocean water contains
- What the ocean floor looks like
- How people explore the ocean

VOCABULARY

salinity p. 76
density p. 76
continental shelf p. 80
sonar p. 82

EXPLORE Density

Why do liquids form layers?

PROCEDURE

1. Insert the straw into one of the solutions. Cover the top of the straw with your finger and then remove the straw from the solution. The liquid should stay in the straw.

2. Using this technique, try to layer the three liquids in your straw so that you can see three distinct layers.

3. Experiment with the order in which you place the liquids into the straw. Between trials, empty the contents of the straw into the waste cup.

MATERIALS

- 3 solutions—A, B, and C—provided by your teacher
- clear straw
- waste cup

WHAT DO YOU THINK?

Did it matter in what order you layered the liquids? If so, can you explain why?

Ocean water covers much of Earth.

As land animals, we naturally think of our planet as a rocky and solid place. We even named our planet Earth, which means "land" or "soil." But look at a globe and you will see that oceans cover most of Earth. In fact, 71 percent of Earth is covered in seawater.

Looking at a map of the world, you can see the seven continents spread over our planet. These landmasses divide Earth's global ocean into connected sections. Different sections of the ocean have different names, such as Atlantic, Indian, and Pacific. However, all the sections are connected.

OUTLINE
Remember to start an outline for this section.

I. Main idea
   A. Supporting idea
      1. Detail
      2. Detail
   B. Supporting idea

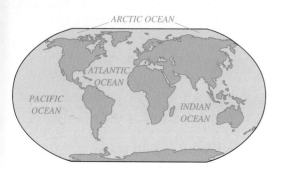

The global ocean is one connected body of water, divided into sections by the continents.

How did Earth become covered by an ocean? Scientists have several theories. The most commonly accepted explanation has to do with how Earth formed. Earth formed about 4.6 billion years ago as a ball of molten rock. Heavier materials sank to the core, and lighter materials floated toward the surface—the same way oil and vinegar in salad dressing separate into layers. Water vapor, a very light substance, rose to the cooler surface. By about 4 billion years ago, Earth had cooled enough for the water vapor to become liquid. At that time, the vapor condensed—just as water vapor condenses into droplets on a cool glass of lemonade—forming liquid water that became the ocean.

Ocean water contains salts and gases.

Despite its name, the salt water that fills the ocean is much more than just salt and water. Ocean water contains many different dissolved substances. Sodium chloride, which is the same compound as ordinary table salt, is the most plentiful of these substances. The ocean also contains other dissolved solids, as well as dissolved molecules of the same gases found in the atmosphere. In fact, the ocean contains all 92 elements that occur in nature, although most are in very tiny amounts.

Salts

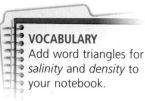

VOCABULARY
Add word triangles for *salinity* and *density* to your notebook.

One taste will convince you that ocean water is salty. Every 1000 grams of seawater contains an average of 35 grams of salt. **Salinity** (suh-LIHN-ih-tee) is a measure of the amount of dissolved salt contained in water. The ocean contains many different kinds of salts. However, sodium chloride accounts for most of the ocean's salinity.

The elements that make up salts are found in rocks and minerals. Over time, rain and rivers wash some of these elements into the sea. The elements that make up salts also enter the ocean when underwater volcanoes erupt. Natural processes also remove salt from the ocean. Because salt is added as well as removed, the ocean's overall salinity does not change much over time. The ocean's salinity has stayed constant for the past 1.5 billion years.

Water that contains dissolved solids, such as salts, is heavier than the same amount of water with no dissolved solids. In other words, salt water has a greater density than fresh water. **Density** is a measure of the amount of matter packed into a given volume.

The higher water's salt content, the greater its density. The denser the water, the more easily things float in it. As you can see in the photograph on page 77, the Dead Sea is so salty (and dense) that people can float easily on the surface.

Salinity and Density

Salt water has a greater density than fresh water.

Fresh Water	Ocean Water	Dead Sea Water
 dissolved solids		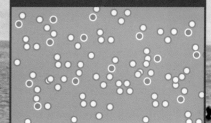
Fresh water has fewer dissolved solids than salt water, so it is less dense than salt water.	Ocean water is more dense than fresh water because it has more dissolved solids.	The Dead Sea is about ten times saltier than the ocean, so Dead Sea water is more dense than ocean water.

Located between Israel and Jordan, the Dead Sea is actually a salty lake and not part of the ocean. Its high salinity, and therefore high density, allows people to float more easily in it than in fresh water or in the ocean.

Dead Sea

Some parts of the ocean are saltier than others. When water evaporates from the ocean, the salts are left behind, causing the remaining water to become even saltier. Ocean water is especially salty in places where water evaporates quickly, such as in shallow areas and warm climates. Salinity is also higher in very cold areas, where the ocean water freezes. When ice forms on the ocean, the salt is left in the water below.

Salinity is lower in areas where the ocean is diluted by fresh water. For example, seawater has lower salinity in places where rivers empty into the ocean. Similarly, the ocean's salinity is lower in areas where a lot of rain falls.

 CHECK YOUR READING How are salinity and density related?

INVESTIGATE Density

How does dense water move?

PROCEDURE

1. Read the instructions below and predict what will happen in steps 3 and 4 before you begin. Record your predictions.

2. Fill one jar with tap water and color it blue. Fill another jar with salt water and color it red. Place an index card over the top of the jar of red salt water.

3. With your hand over the index card, turn the jar over and place it on top of the jar with the blue tap water. Pull out the index card and observe the water movement, if any.

4. Repeat steps 2 and 3, but with the blue tap water on the top.

WHAT DO YOU THINK?

• Describe any ways in which your observations differed from your predictions. On what did you base your predictions?

• Explain why the water moved, if it did, in each of the two setups.

CHALLENGE How do you think water in the ocean might be layered?

MATERIALS
• 2 baby food jars
• blue and red food coloring
• tap water
• 10 percent salt solution
• index cards
• large pan or bucket

TIME
30 minutes

Oxygen and Other Gases

Fish, like other animals, need oxygen to live. Oxygen and other gases dissolve in water, just as sugar dissolves in tea. The ocean contains the same gases as the air, including oxygen, nitrogen, and carbon dioxide. Dissolved gases are essential to ocean life.

You know that when you breathe, you use oxygen and exhale carbon dioxide. Ocean animals also take in oxygen and give off carbon dioxide. Oxygen and carbon dioxide get mixed into the ocean from the air above the ocean surface. Oxygen is also added to the ocean by plants and algae that live near the surface. Plants and algae use sunlight to convert carbon dioxide and water into food, and release oxygen into the water. Besides being used by plants to make food, carbon dioxide is a building block of ocean animals' shells.

Algae use dissolved carbon dioxide to make food, and give off oxygen.

Sea horses take in dissolved oxygen and give off carbon dioxide through their gills.

 CHECK YOUR READING Where does the oxygen in the ocean come from? Name two sources.

Ocean temperatures vary.

Oceanographers—people who study the ocean—divide ocean water into three layers on the basis of temperature.

❶ The surface layer, heated by the Sun and mixed by winds and waves, is the warmest layer. Warm water is less dense than cold water, so the heated water stays at the surface.

❷ The thermocline (THUR-muh-KLYN) lies below the surface layer. The temperature of the water in the thermocline drops fast with depth.

❸ The deep water is cold all year. Almost anywhere on the globe—even in the tropics— the temperature of the water at the ocean's bottom is around 0°C–3°C (32°F–37°F), at or barely above freezing.

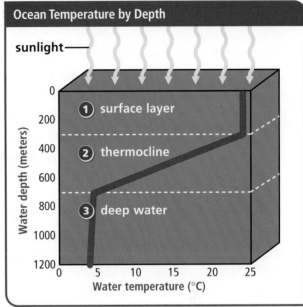

The temperature of the water at the surface of the ocean varies by location and season. As you can see in the map of satellite data below, the surface layer is warmer near the equator than near the poles. Over much of Earth, the surface layer is warmer in the summer and cooler in the winter.

CHECK YOUR READING Why doesn't the warm water at the ocean's surface sink to the bottom?

Surface Temperature

The temperature of the ocean's surface varies by location.

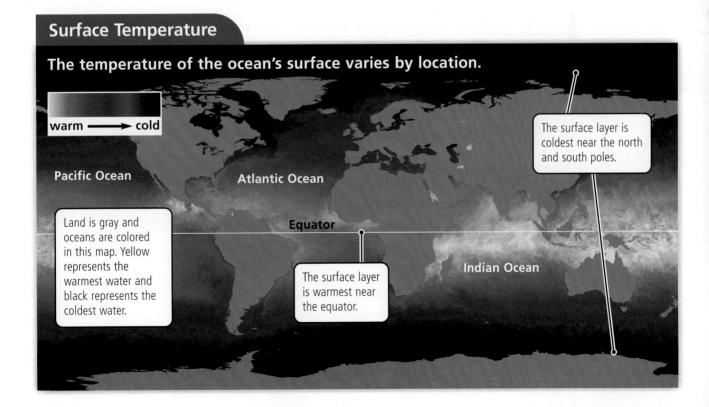

warm ⟶ cold

Pacific Ocean

Atlantic Ocean

Equator

Indian Ocean

Land is gray and oceans are colored in this map. Yellow represents the warmest water and black represents the coldest water.

The surface layer is warmest near the equator.

The surface layer is coldest near the north and south poles.

The ocean floor has many features.

People have sailed the ocean for thousands of years. However, the landscape of most of the ocean floor remained a mystery until the 1950s. Since then, exploration and improvements in mapping techniques have revealed many spectacular features on the ocean floor, including the tallest mountains and deepest canyons on Earth.

A **continental shelf** is the flat or gently sloping land that lies submerged around the edges of a continent and that extends from the shoreline out to a continental slope. Huge submarine canyons, some similar in size to the Grand Canyon, slice through continental shelves and slopes. Farther out, ocean trenches cut deep into the ocean floor. With a bottom over 11,000 meters (36,000 ft) below sea level, the Mariana Trench is the deepest place in the world. Flat abyssal (uh-BIHS-uhl) plains cover huge portions of the deep-ocean floor. Seamounts are undersea mountains. Tall volcanoes that poke above the surface are volcanic islands. Mid-ocean ridges, the world's longest mountain range, run throughout Earth's ocean like the seams on a baseball.

READING **TiP**

Abyss means "a very deep place." Abyssal plains are on the deep-ocean floor.

The Ocean Floor

The ocean floor has canyons, mountains, and many other features.

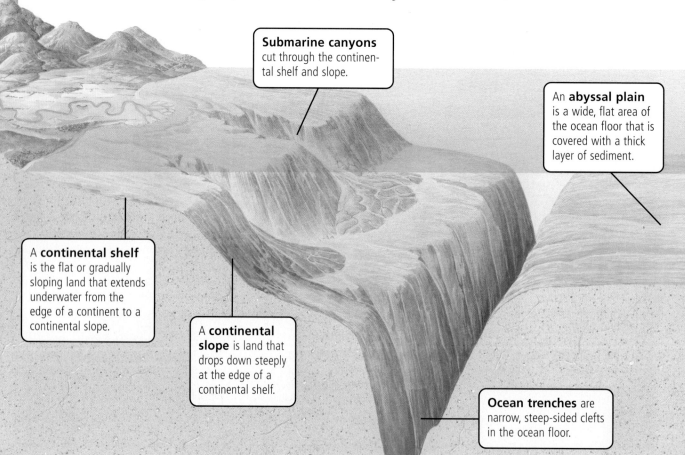

Submarine canyons cut through the continental shelf and slope.

An **abyssal plain** is a wide, flat area of the ocean floor that is covered with a thick layer of sediment.

A **continental shelf** is the flat or gradually sloping land that extends underwater from the edge of a continent to a continental slope.

A **continental slope** is land that drops down steeply at the edge of a continental shelf.

Ocean trenches are narrow, steep-sided clefts in the ocean floor.

Ocean Exploration

Because the majority of Earth's surface is underwater, until recently it remained largely unexplored. If your ears have ever hurt when you dived to the bottom of a pool, you have felt the effects of water pressure. That pressure is multiplied hundreds of times deep in the ocean. The deeper down you go, the more crushing the weight of the water.

Despite the pressure, darkness, lack of air, chilling cold, and other obstacles to ocean exploration, scientists have developed tools that help them discover what lies beneath the surface. Scuba equipment allows a diver to spend about an hour underwater, breathing air carried in a tank on his or her back. Scuba divers can safely reach depths as great as 40 meters (130 ft). To go even deeper, people use small submarines, such as the one pictured here. Robots equipped with cameras offer views of areas too deep or difficult for humans to reach.

Small submarines carry researchers to depths as great as 6500 meters (21,300 ft).

 CHECK YOUR READING What is one obstacle to ocean exploration?

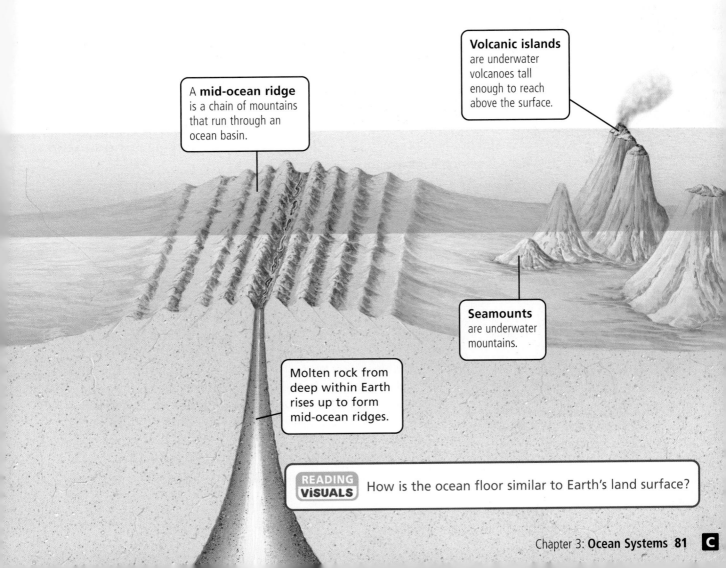

A mid-ocean ridge is a chain of mountains that run through an ocean basin.

Volcanic islands are underwater volcanoes tall enough to reach above the surface.

Molten rock from deep within Earth rises up to form mid-ocean ridges.

Seamounts are underwater mountains.

READING VISUALS How is the ocean floor similar to Earth's land surface?

Mapping the Ocean Floor

VOCABULARY Add a word triangle for *sonar* to your notebook.

Today's detailed maps of the ocean floor would amaze early scientists and sailors, who tested sea-floor depths by dropping weighted lines overboard. Now sailors find depths with **sonar,** a system that uses sound waves to measure distances and locate objects. Ships aim sound waves at the ocean's bottom and measure the time it takes to receive the echo. A fast echo means the bottom is shallow; a slow echo means the bottom is deep.

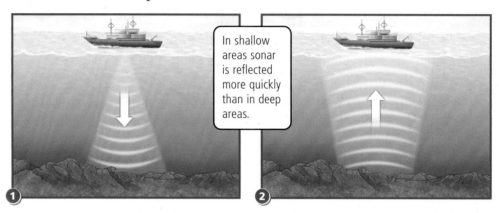

In shallow areas sonar is reflected more quickly than in deep areas.

① To measure sea-floor depth, ships aim sound waves at the ocean floor.

② The time it takes for the echo to return depends on the depth of the ocean floor.

Sonar can provide detailed images of small areas of the ocean floor. For mapping large areas, satellite imaging is much more efficient. Satellites can detect tiny bumps and dips in the ocean's height. These small surface differences reveal the shape of the ocean floor. For example, water levels are slightly higher over seamounts and lower over trenches. Because of its vast size and the challenges of exploring it, the ocean still holds many secrets. Exploration continues to bring new discoveries of geological formations and events.

CHECK YOUR READING What are two methods used in mapping the ocean floor?

3.1 Review

KEY CONCEPTS

1. What substances are contained in ocean water?

2. Describe or draw five features of the ocean-floor landscape.

3. Describe three kinds of technology or equipment used to explore the ocean.

CRITICAL THINKING

4. **Predict** A shallow pan and a deep bowl hold equal amounts of salt water. If you left both containers in the sun for a day and then measured the salinity of the water in each, which would be saltier? Why?

5. **Analyze** Where in the ocean do you think water pressure is greatest? Explain why.

⬤ CHALLENGE

6. **Synthesize** If you wanted to design a submarine to obtain the most information possible during a research voyage, what features would you include and why? First think about what types of information you would like to collect.

Mapping the Ocean Floor

MATH TUTORIAL
CLASSZONE.COM

Click on Math Tutorial for more help with coordinates and line graphs.

Before sonar and satellites, scientists used weighted lines to map the ocean floor. They tied a weight to a cable and dropped the weight overboard. When the weight landed on the ocean floor, the length of the cable indicated the depth of the ocean at that point. By combining many measurements, scientists could make approximate maps of sections of the ocean floor.

The table on the right gives depths at eight positions in the ocean off a coast. The positions are at regular intervals along a straight line. Depths are given as negative numbers.

Ocean-Floor Depths	
Position	Depth
1	−293
2	−302
3	−381
4	−485
5	−593
6	−624
7	−517
8	−204

Example

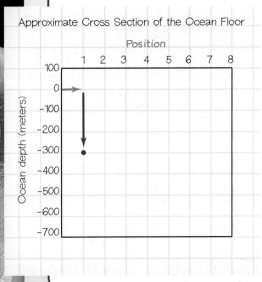

Approximate Cross Section of the Ocean Floor

You can draw an approximate cross section of part of the ocean floor by making a line graph of the data. To graph the data, think of each column in the table as an ordered pair: (**Position, Depth**).

(1) Copy the axes and labels.

(2) Graph each point. The first point has been graphed as an example.

(3) Connect the points with line segments.

Follow the steps above to graph points 2 through 8. Use the data and your graph to answer the following questions.

1. How deep is the ocean at position 2?

2. Which position is the deepest, and what is the depth there?

3. Shade the part of the graph that is underwater.

CHALLENGE Does your graph accurately represent the ocean floor between positions 5 and 6? Explain your reasoning.

The continents are shown in black and the ocean floor is colored in this satellite image. High points are orange and yellow, and the lowest points are deep blue-purple.

KEY CONCEPT

Ocean water moves in currents.

 BEFORE, you learned

- The ocean is explored with sonar and satellite imaging
- The ocean floor is a varied landscape
- The ocean contains dissolved salts and gases

NOW, you will learn

- What causes ocean currents
- How currents distribute heat around the globe
- How currents interact with climate and weather

VOCABULARY

ocean current p. 84
downwelling p. 86
upwelling p. 86
El Niño p. 88

EXPLORE Currents

How does cold water move?

PROCEDURE

1. Stir together cold water, ice, and 3 drops of food coloring in the paper cup. Tape the cup to one inside corner of the plastic box.

2. Fill the plastic box with enough room-temperature water to submerge the bottom of the cup.

3. Use a toothpick to carefully poke a hole in the bottom of the cup. Observe the movement of water.

WHAT DO YOU THINK?

How do you know the water is moving? What do you think is the reason for this movement?

MATERIALS

- cold water
- ice cubes
- food coloring
- paper cup
- masking tape
- clear plastic box
- toothpick
- room-temperature water

The oceans have major currents.

Would you ever want to go rafting on the ocean? Thor Heyerdahl of Norway did it in 1947 to demonstrate how early people might have migrated around the world. He floated on a wood raft from South America to Polynesia, without motor or paddles, powered only by an ocean current. An **ocean current** is a mass of moving water. There are many different currents that move water through the ocean. As they move water, ocean currents distribute heat and nutrients around the globe.

Learn more about the different types of ocean currents.

Surface Currents

Strong winds blowing over the ocean are set in motion by the uneven heating of Earth's surface. These winds cause surface currents to flow. The currents extend only about 100 to 200 meters (300–500 ft) down into the ocean, but they cover large areas. The map below shows the major surface currents.

Earth's rotation curls surface currents into giant clockwise whirlpools in the Northern Hemisphere. In the Southern Hemisphere, currents curl counterclockwise because of Earth's rotation. The shapes of continents also affect the paths of surface currents.

Use your finger to trace a few of the surface currents on the map. Surface currents carry warm water away from the equator and cool water away from the poles. In this way, surface currents moderate global temperatures.

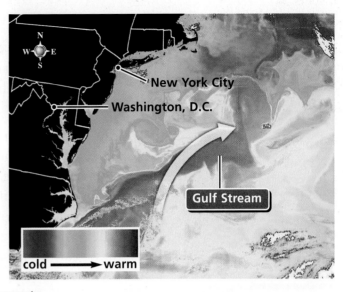

This satellite image shows the Gulf Stream, a surface current that flows along the eastern coast of the United States. The colors indicate the temperature of the water.

CHECK YOUR READING What causes surface currents?

Global Surface Currents

Surface currents are caused by winds. They move warm water away from the equator and cool water away from the poles.

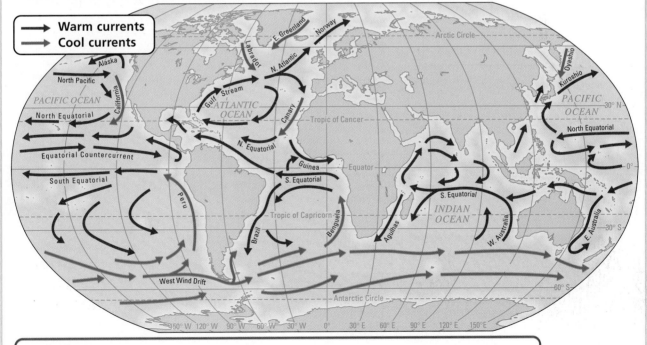

READING VISUALS Which currents could be used for sailing east across the Atlantic Ocean?

Deep Currents

In addition to surface currents, there are also currents flowing deep in the ocean. Deep currents are driven by differences in water density. Dense water sinks in the ocean the same way that dense chocolate syrup sinks in a glass of milk.

Seawater can become more dense because of cooling, an increase in salinity, or both. The densest water is found in the polar regions. For example, as sea ice forms near Antarctica, the salinity of the cold water beneath the ice increases. The highly dense water sinks down the continental slope of Antarctica and then moves slowly across the ocean floor. It may take 1000 years for water from this current to resurface near the equator. Another deep current flows out from the Arctic Ocean.

The movement of water in deep currents involves two processes important to ocean life. **Downwelling** is the movement of water from the surface to greater depths. As the water sinks, it carries oxygen down from the surface. The oxygen allows animals to live in the deep ocean. **Upwelling** is the movement of water up to the surface. Because this process brings up nutrients from the deep ocean, large numbers of ocean animals live in areas where upwelling occurs.

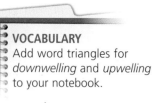

VOCABULARY
Add word triangles for *downwelling* and *upwelling* to your notebook.

How Upwelling Affects Ocean Life

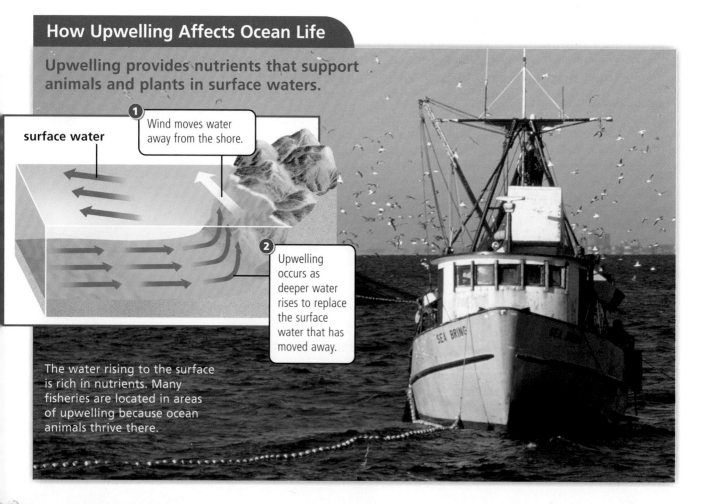

Upwelling provides nutrients that support animals and plants in surface waters.

surface water

1 Wind moves water away from the shore.

2 Upwelling occurs as deeper water rises to replace the surface water that has moved away.

The water rising to the surface is rich in nutrients. Many fisheries are located in areas of upwelling because ocean animals thrive there.

SEA BRING

INVESTIGATE Currents

What happens where bodies of water meet?

PROCEDURE

1. Divide the box into two compartments, using masking tape and aluminum foil.

2. Pour one solution into one side of the box while a partner pours the other solution into the opposite side. Be sure you and your partner pour at the same time in order to keep the barrier from breaking.

3. Sprinkle pepper on the high-salinity side.

4. Use the pencil to poke two holes in the aluminum foil— one just below the water surface and another near the bottom of the box. Observe for 10 minutes.

WHAT DO YOU THINK?

• What did you observe in the box? Did you expect this?

• What forces drove any movements of water you observed?

CHALLENGE Compare what you observed with what you have learned about the actual movements of water in the ocean. How could you change the experiment to better model actual ocean currents?

SKILL FOCUS
Observing

MATERIALS
• clear plastic box
• aluminum foil
• masking tape
• high-salinity water
• low-salinity water
• pepper
• sharp pencil

TIME
30 minutes

HIGH-SALINITY SOLUTION

LOW-SALINITY SOLUTION

BLACK PEPPER
Pure Ground
NET WT 4 OZ   113 g

Currents interact with climate and weather.

Imagine mixing red and blue paint in a cup by blowing through a straw. You can move some paint around, but you cannot predict exactly what pattern will result. Similarly, the ocean and the atmosphere interact in unpredictable ways. Moving air produces movement in the water while the water changes the air above it.

Remember that windblown surface currents help distribute heat around the globe by moving warm water away from the equator and cool water away from the north and south poles. The Gulf Stream, for example, is a surface current that moves warm water northeastward toward Great Britain and Europe. Because of the warm Gulf Stream waters, the British climate is mild. No polar bears wander the streets of Great Britain, as they might in places in Canada that are just as far north.

CHECK YOUR READING How does the Gulf Stream affect Great Britain?

La Scie, Newfoundland

Fowey, England

ATLANTIC OCEAN
La Scie
Fowey

READING VISUALS **COMPARE AND CONTRAST** These two towns are at about the same latitude, or distance from the equator. Ice can be found off the coast of La Scie, Newfoundland. Ice is never found off the coast of Fowey, England, which has mild weather year-round. What might explain this difference? **Hint:** the answer has to do with the Gulf Stream.

A change in even one of Earth's surface currents can result in huge changes in weather patterns. Most years, winds blow westward across the tropical Pacific Ocean. Every three to seven years, however, these winds do not blow as strongly as usual. Without the winds, the movement of currents in the Pacific is disrupted. These changes in air and water movements cause a global weather event called **El Niño,** which may last for 12 to 18 months.

During El Niño years, weather patterns change around the planet. Some places get more or less rain or snow than usual. Temperatures may be warmer or cooler than in other years. By using satellite readings of ocean temperatures and floating measurement devices to study conditions in the Pacific, scientists can often predict when El Niño will occur and how severe, or strong, it will be.

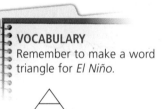

VOCABULARY
Remember to make a word triangle for *El Niño*.

3.2 Review

KEY CONCEPTS

1. What are two causes of currents in the ocean?

2. How do currents distribute heat around the globe?

3. How are climate and weather related to currents? Give two examples.

CRITICAL THINKING

4. **Infer** Describe at least two ways in which upwelled water might differ from the water around it.

5. **Infer** What factor do you think might cause a surface current to change direction?

◐ CHALLENGE

6. **Predict** What would happen if all ocean currents suddenly came to a halt? Describe some effects this change would have.

KEY CONCEPT

Waves move through oceans.

 BEFORE, you learned

- Currents are masses of moving water
- Surface currents are driven mainly by winds
- Deep currents are driven mainly by differences in density

 NOW, you will learn

- How waves form
- How waves move energy through water
- How wave action changes near the shore
- How waves can cause currents near the shore

VOCABULARY

longshore current p. 92
rip current p. 92

EXPLORE Waves

How does wave motion change with depth?

PROCEDURE

① Fill an aquarium or another clear rectangular container about three-fourths full of water.

② Tie several metal washers to each of four corks to make them float at different heights, as shown in the photograph.

③ Using your hand or a piece of cardboard, make steady waves in the water. Experiment with a variety of waves—some small and some large. Observe the cork movements.

WHAT DO YOU THINK?

How does the movement of the corks change with depth?

MATERIALS

- aquarium or clear container
- corks
- string
- metal washers
- water

OUTLINE

Remember to start an outline for this section.

I. Main idea
  A. Supporting idea
    1. Detail
    2. Detail
  B. Supporting idea

Waves form in the open ocean.

If you have ever blown across the surface of hot chocolate, you may have noticed ripples. Each of these ripples is a small wave. A wave is an up-and-down motion along the surface of a body of water. The vast ocean surface is covered with waves of various sizes, which are usually caused by winds. Moving air drags across the water's surface and passes energy to the water, causing waves. Other disturbances—such as earthquakes, landslides, and underwater volcanic eruptions—can also cause waves.

 What can cause waves to form in the ocean?

Wave Action at the Water's Surface

READING TiP

As you read about wave action at the water's surface, look at the illustrations on page 91.

RESOURCE CENTER
CLASSZONE.COM

Explore ocean waves.

A wave in the ocean has the same basic shape as many other waves.

- The **crest** is the high point of the wave.
- The **trough** (trawf) is the low point of the wave.
- **Wave height** is the vertical distance between the top of the crest and the bottom of the trough.
- **Wavelength** is the distance between one wave crest and the next.

You have read that currents move water from one place to another. In contrast, waves do not transport water. Waves move energy. They move through water, but the water stays more or less in the same place. Follow the drawings on page 91 to see how water particles move in a circle as a wave passes through. If waves do not transport water, how do surfers zip toward shore on waves? Surfers are powered by the energy traveling in the waves. Waves transport energy, not water.

Most waves affect only the water near the surface of the ocean. Water particles farther down move in smaller circles than particles near the surface. Below a certain depth, the waves no longer affect the water.

Wave Action near Shore

Waves may pass through the ocean for hundreds or thousands of kilometers before moving into shallow water. Then the waves lose speed and eventually topple over, losing their energy as they break on shore.

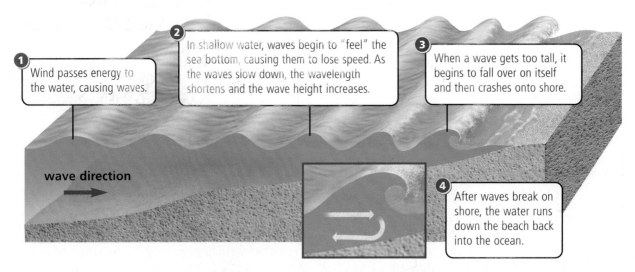

1 Wind passes energy to the water, causing waves.

2 In shallow water, waves begin to "feel" the sea bottom, causing them to lose speed. As the waves slow down, the wavelength shortens and the wave height increases.

3 When a wave gets too tall, it begins to fall over on itself and then crashes onto shore.

4 After waves break on shore, the water runs down the beach back into the ocean.

wave direction

When waves break on a beach, the water runs back down the sand into the ocean. If the shore is steeply sloped toward the water, the water may rush back to sea forcefully. An undertow is the pull of the water as it runs back to sea. Undertows may be dangerous. Some are strong enough to knock a person off his or her feet and into the waves.

Ocean Waves

Waves transport energy, not water. As a wave crest passes, the water particles move in circular paths.

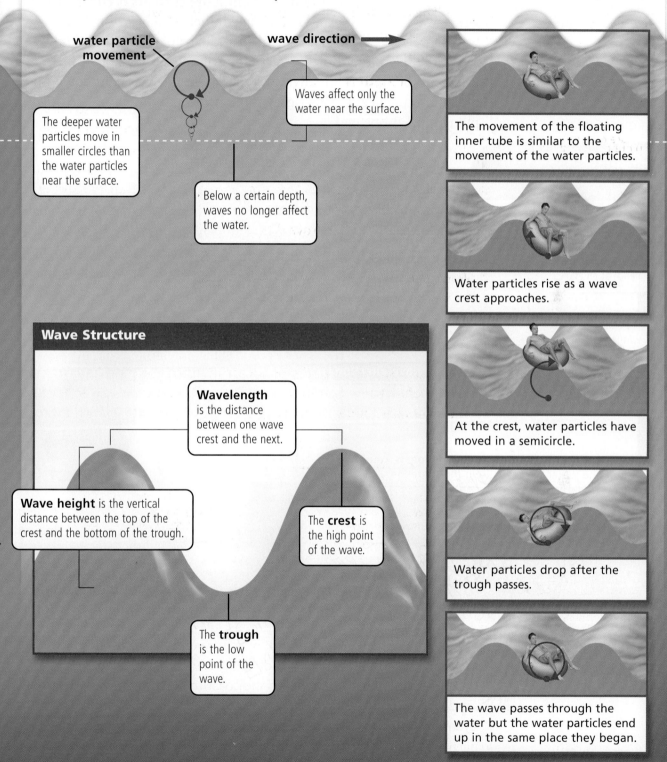

water particle movement

wave direction

Waves affect only the water near the surface.

The deeper water particles move in smaller circles than the water particles near the surface.

Below a certain depth, waves no longer affect the water.

The movement of the floating inner tube is similar to the movement of the water particles.

Water particles rise as a wave crest approaches.

At the crest, water particles have moved in a semicircle.

Water particles drop after the trough passes.

The wave passes through the water but the water particles end up in the same place they began.

Wave Structure

Wavelength is the distance between one wave crest and the next.

Wave height is the vertical distance between the top of the crest and the bottom of the trough.

The **crest** is the high point of the wave.

The **trough** is the low point of the wave.

READING VISUALS What happens to water particles as a wave passes through?

Waves cause currents near shore.

Sometimes swimmers notice that without trying, they have drifted far down a beach. Their drifting is due to a **longshore current,** which moves water parallel to the shore. Longshore currents occur in places where waves meet the land at an angle rather than head-on. Since waves rarely meet the land exactly head-on, or perpendicular to the shore, there is a longshore current along almost every shore. The waves hit the shore at an angle and then wash back straight down the beach into the ocean. This zigzag motion moves sand along the beach, piling it up at one end.

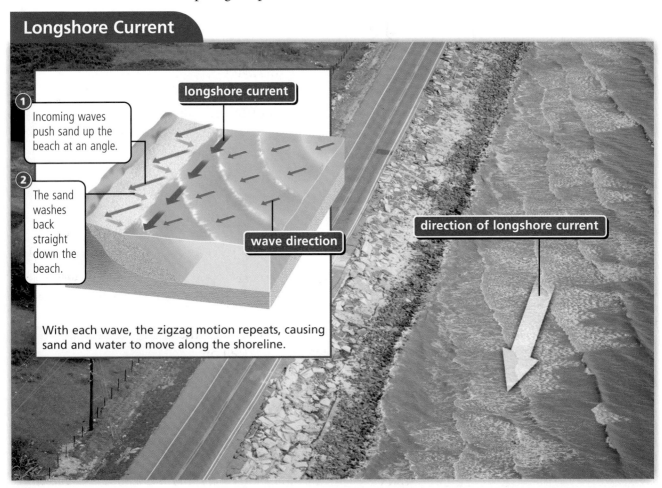

Longshore Current

longshore current

1 Incoming waves push sand up the beach at an angle.

2 The sand washes back straight down the beach.

wave direction

direction of longshore current

With each wave, the zigzag motion repeats, causing sand and water to move along the shoreline.

The movement of waves and longshore currents can build up sandbars in the waters near a shore. Sandbars are long ridges or piles of sand that can form parallel to the coastline. As waves wash over the sandbars and onto shore, water may collect behind the sandbars. Eventually, the pooled water will break through. **Rip currents** are narrow streams of water that break through sandbars and drain rapidly back to sea. Rip currents occur when high winds or waves cause a larger-than-usual amount of water to wash back from the shore.

⚠ CHECK YOUR READING   What role does a sandbar play in the formation of a rip current?

Rip Current

Signs such as this one on a beach in Hawaii warn swimmers of dangerous currents.

1 High winds or waves cause a larger-than-usual amount of water to collect behind a sandbar.

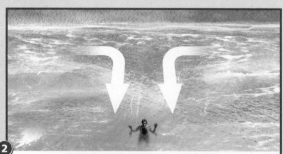
2 The water breaks through the sandbar and washes rapidly out to sea in a rip current.

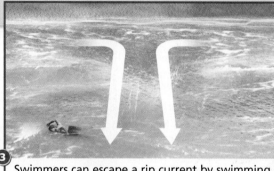
3 Swimmers can escape a rip current by swimming parallel to shore, out of the narrow current.

Like undertows, rip currents can be dangerous for swimmers. In the United States, around 100 people drown in rip currents each year. Most rescues made by lifeguards on U.S. beaches involve swimmers caught in rip currents.

Rip currents are too strong to swim against, but as you can see in the diagram, they are narrow. Swimming parallel to the shore is the best way to escape a rip current. Of course, it is better to avoid rip currents altogether! Many beaches offer daily rip-current forecasts based on information about wind and wave conditions.

Review

KEY CONCEPTS

1. How does moving air form waves in water?

2. Describe the movement of a water particle as a wave passes through.

3. What happens to waves near shore?

4. Name and describe two kinds of currents that wave action can cause near shore.

CRITICAL THINKING

5. **Compare and Contrast** Describe the similarities and differences between surface currents and waves.

6. **Apply** Imagine you find a piece of wood on the beach. The next day, the wood is 100 meters farther north. How might it have moved? Your answer should refer to currents.

⬤ CHALLENGE

7. **Infer** Some coastlines are more steeply sloped than others. How might wave action on a steeply sloped coastline differ from that on a gently sloped coastline?

CHAPTER INVESTIGATION

Wave Movement

OVERVIEW AND PURPOSE The particles in liquid water are constantly moving. Surfers, boaters, and people in inner tubes enjoy the effects of this motion—even though they never see what is happening at the particle level. How do water particles move in waves? In this investigation you will

- observe the movements of a floating object as waves pass through water
- use your observations to draw conclusions about how water particles move in waves

▶ Problem

What does the motion of a floating object reveal about the movement of water particles in a passing wave?

▶ Hypothesize

Write a hypothesis to explain what the motion of a floating object might reveal about how water particles move in a wave. Your hypothesis should take the form of an "If . . . , then . . . , because . . ." statement.

MATERIALS
- small aquarium or clear, shoebox-size container
- water
- small plastic dropping bottle or plastic spice container, with cap
- salt

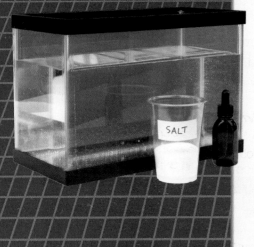

▶ Procedure

1. Fill the aquarium or clear container with cold tap water until it is three-quarters full.

2. Make the small bottle float with its top just below the surface of the water. You can accomplish this in several ways. First, try adding warm water to the bottle, then securely capping it without air bubbles. See if it will float. You can add salt to the bottle to move the bottle lower in the water. If the bottle is too low, you can trap a small air bubble under the cap to move the bottle higher in the water. Adjust these factors until you successfully float the bottle. The investigation will also work if the top of the bottle just touches the water's surface.

step 2

3. Remove the bottle from the water. Make sure the cap is tightly sealed.

4. Push your hand back and forth in the water at one end of the aquarium for about 30 seconds, to produce waves.

5. Gently place the small bottle back into the center of the aquarium. With your eyes level with the water surface, observe the motion of the waves and the bottle. Repeat as many times as needed until you notice the bottle behaving the same way with each passing wave.

▶ Observe and Analyze | Write It Up

1. **RECORD** Make a diagram showing the aquarium setup, including the water, the waves, and the small bottle. Use arrows to show how the bottle moved as waves passed. Or you may draw several diagrams of the aquarium, showing the bottle at different locations as waves passed. Label the various parts of the waves.

2. **ANALYZE** Did the bottle travel with the wave? Why or why not?

▶ Conclude | Write It Up

1. **INTERPRET** Compare your results with your hypothesis. Do your data support your hypothesis?

2. **INTERPRET** Answer the problem question.

3. **INFER** What do your observations tell you about particle movement in waves? Did the results surprise you? Explain.

4. **EVALUATE** Why was it necessary to float the bottle just under the surface of the water rather than letting it float right on top?

5. **IDENTIFY PROBLEMS** What problems, if any, did you encounter in carrying out the procedure?

6. **IDENTIFY LIMITS** In what ways was this experiment limited in showing particle movement? Identify possible sources of error.

7. **PREDICT** How do you think particle motion in a wave with a tall wave height might differ from that in a wave with a short wave height?

8. **SYNTHESIZE** In this lab you made waves with your hand. In the ocean, most waves are caused by wind. Earthquakes, landslides, and other events also cause waves in the ocean. What do earthquakes, landslides, wind, and your hand have in common that allows all of them to make waves?

▶ INVESTIGATE Further

CHALLENGE Redesign this experiment in a way you think will better demonstrate the particle motion in a water wave. You need not limit yourself to the materials you used in this lab. Why will your version of the experiment work better?

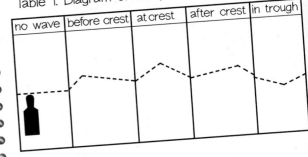

Wave Movement

Problem What does the motion of a floating object reveal about the movement of water particles in a passing wave?

Hypothesize

Observe and Analyze

Table 1. Diagram of Setup

no wave	before crest	at crest	after crest	in trough

Conclude

3.4 Waters rise and fall in tides.

 BEFORE, you learned

- Wind provides the energy to form waves in the ocean
- Ocean waves change near shore
- The ocean is a global body of water

 NOW, you will learn

- What causes tides
- How tides affect coastlines
- How tides can be used to generate electricity

VOCABULARY

tide p. 96
tidal range p. 98
spring tide p. 99
neap tide p. 99

THINK ABOUT

What causes water levels to change in the ocean?

These two photographs were taken on the same day at the boat harbor in Lympstone, England. The change in water level in the harbor occurs every day on a regular and predictable basis. What forces cause shifts in such huge volumes of water? How can we explain the clocklike regularity of the flow?

Coastal waters rise and fall each day.

Have you ever spent a day at a beach along the ocean? Perhaps you placed your blanket and beach chairs in the sand close to the water's edge. An hour later, you may have needed to move your blanket and chairs to keep the advancing waves from washing them away. The water level on coastlines varies with the time of day. This periodic rising and falling of the water level of the ocean is called the **tide.** The water level along a coast is highest at high tide, submerging parts of the coastline. The water level is lowest at low tide, exposing more of the coastline.

What in the world could cause such dramatic changes in the ocean's level? The answer is, nothing in this world. Read on to find out how out-of-this-world objects cause tides.

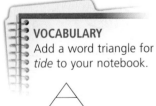

VOCABULARY
Add a word triangle for *tide* to your notebook.

 CHECK YOUR READING How does the water level along a coast differ at high tide and at low tide?

The gravity of the Moon and the Sun causes tides.

Over 2000 years ago, people knew that the Moon and the tide were related. But 1700 years passed before the connection was explained in the terms of modern science. In 1687, Sir Isaac Newton developed his theories of gravity and linked the tide to the Moon's gravitational pull. Gravity is a force of attraction between objects. Earth's gravity pulls things toward its center—including you.

The gravity of the Sun and the gravity of the Moon also pull on objects on Earth. In response to the Moon's gravitational pull, Earth's water bulges on the side facing the Moon. The Moon's gravity also pulls on Earth itself. Earth gets pulled toward the Moon, leaving a second bulge of water on the side of Earth facing away from the Moon. The Sun's gravity pulls too, but with less effect because the Sun is so far away.

Daily Tides

The diagram below shows the two bulges of ocean water: one on the side of Earth closest to the Moon, and the other on the opposite side of Earth. At these bulges, it is high tide. Between the two bulges are dips. At these dips, it is low tide. As Earth rotates, different parts of it pass through the bulges and the dips. As a result, most places experience two high tides and two low tides each day.

VISUALIZATION
CLASSZONE.COM

Watch daily tides in action.

Daily Tides

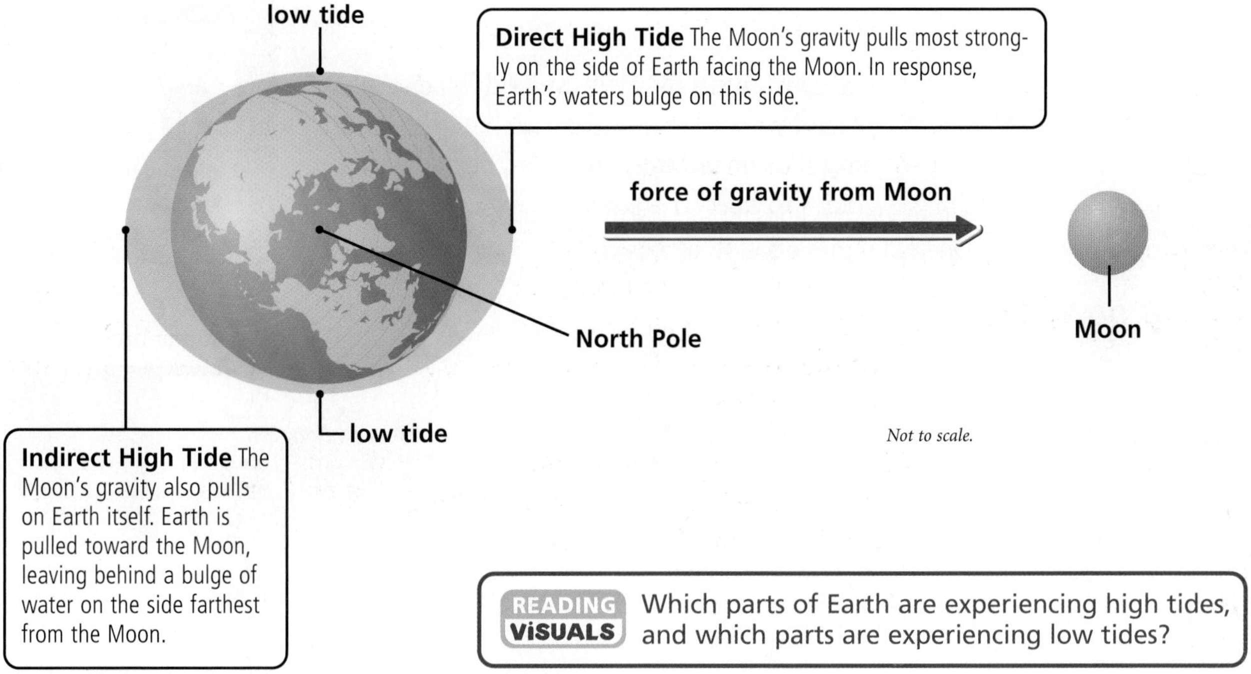

low tide

Direct High Tide The Moon's gravity pulls most strongly on the side of Earth facing the Moon. In response, Earth's waters bulge on this side.

force of gravity from Moon

North Pole

Moon

low tide

Not to scale.

Indirect High Tide The Moon's gravity also pulls on Earth itself. Earth is pulled toward the Moon, leaving behind a bulge of water on the side farthest from the Moon.

READING VISUALS Which parts of Earth are experiencing high tides, and which parts are experiencing low tides?

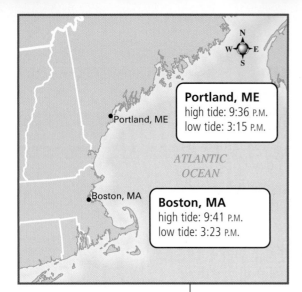

Portland, ME
high tide: 9:36 P.M.
low tide: 3:15 P.M.

ATLANTIC OCEAN

Boston, MA
high tide: 9:41 P.M.
low tide: 3:23 P.M.

A place farther east along a coastline experiences high and low tides earlier in the day, because it passes through the tidal bulge first. Times for high and low tides change daily.

The timing of high and low tides at one location on a coast may differ from the timing at other locations along that coast. As you can see on the map of the coastline of New England, the tides occur later as you move west along the coastline. As Earth rotates, the easternmost points on a coastline will pass through the tidal bulge before places farther west on the same coastline.

The timing of high and low tides is not the only way that tides can differ along a coastline. Some places experience higher high tides and lower low tides than other places. The shape of the land above and below the water affects tidal ranges. A **tidal range** is the difference in height between a high tide and the next low tide. The tidal range is greater in a narrow bay than on a wide-open shore. For example, the narrow harbor of Lympstone, England, shown in the photographs on page 96, has a very large tidal range. A coastline with a steeply sloped ocean floor has a larger tidal range than a coastline with a gradually dropping floor. For example, the coasts of Texas and western Florida have very small tidal ranges because of the gradual slope of the ocean floor there.

CHECK YOUR READING — In what two ways does the shape of the land affect the tidal range? What sentences tell you this?

INVESTIGATE Tides

How does the Moon make tides?

PROCEDURE

1. Cut the Tides datasheet in two, along the dotted line. Cut out the map of Earth on the bottom half of the sheet.

2. Use a paper fastener to connect the two pieces as shown in the photograph.

3. Now you are ready to model the tides. Rotate Earth one full turn in the direction of the arrow. One full turn is equal to one day.

WHAT DO YOU THINK?

- How does the model demonstrate the Moon's role in tides?

- How many times does each place in the ocean experience high tide and low tide each day?

CHALLENGE One full rotation of Earth takes place in a day, or 24 hours. About how much time passes between one high tide and the next high tide at any location on Earth?

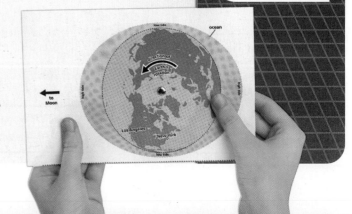

Monthly Tides

The Moon is the main cause of tides, but the Sun affects tides as well. The Moon takes about a month to move around Earth. Twice during this month-long journey—at the new moon and the full moon—the Moon, the Sun, and Earth line up. The gravity of the Sun and the gravity of the Moon combine to pull Earth's waters in the same directions. The result is an extra-high tidal bulge and an extra-low tidal dip, called a **spring tide.**

During first- and third-quarter moons, the Sun and the Moon are not lined up with Earth. The gravity of each pulls from a different direction. The result is a smaller tidal bulge and tidal dip, called a **neap tide.** During a neap tide, high and low tides are less extreme.

Changes in the timing and the height of tides occur in a regular cycle. The timing of tides may be important to people who live near a coast or use coasts for fishing or boating. In many coastal communities, tide tables printed in newspapers give the exact times and heights of the tides.

RESOURCE CENTER
CLASSZONE.COM
Find out more about ocean tides.

READING TiP

Spring tides occur twice a month all year long, not just in spring. This use of the word *spring* is related to its meaning "to jump."

Monthly Tides

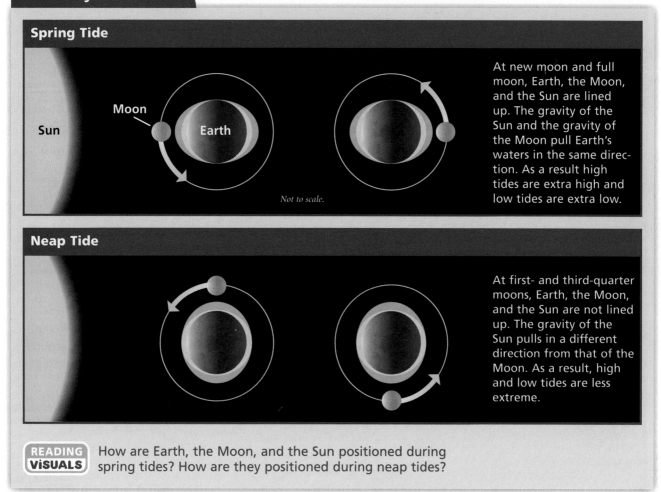

Spring Tide

Sun · Moon · Earth · Not to scale.

At new moon and full moon, Earth, the Moon, and the Sun are lined up. The gravity of the Sun and the gravity of the Moon pull Earth's waters in the same direction. As a result high tides are extra high and low tides are extra low.

Neap Tide

At first- and third-quarter moons, Earth, the Moon, and the Sun are not lined up. The gravity of the Sun pulls in a different direction from that of the Moon. As a result, high and low tides are less extreme.

READING VISUALS How are Earth, the Moon, and the Sun positioned during spring tides? How are they positioned during neap tides?

Tides can be used to generate electricity.

The energy of tides can be used to generate electricity. A tidal dam is built near a coast in the path of tidal waters. The water flows in during high tide and is trapped behind the gates of the dam. Then, when the tide is low, the gates open and the trapped water rushes out. As the water flows out, it spins turbines that power electric generators.

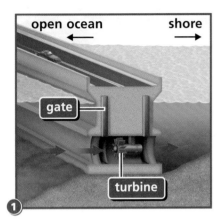

The dam's gates are open as the tide rises. Notice that the water level is the same on both sides.

When the tide begins to lower, the gates close, trapping water behind the dam.

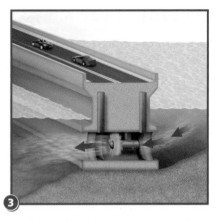

At low tide, the gates open and the water rushes out, spinning turbines that generate electricity.

Tidal dams cause much less pollution than many other methods of generating electricity. Also, tides are a renewable source of energy; the tides are not used up in the process. However, tidal dams have some drawbacks. Few places in the world are actually suitable for such dams. Another problem is that the times of day when tidal dams generate electricity might not be the times of day when people most need electricity. Tidal dams also sometimes block the paths of migrating fish and might hurt marine life by altering the regular flow of water.

CHECK YOUR READING What are the benefits and drawbacks of tidal power plants?

3.4 Review

KEY CONCEPTS

1. Describe the appearance of tidal changes at a coastline.
2. Explain the difference between the Sun's role and the Moon's role in creating tides.
3. How are tides used to generate electricity?

CRITICAL THINKING

4. **Synthesize** Contrast the daily and monthly patterns of tides. What role does the Moon's orbit around Earth play in both?
5. **Compare** Tidal range is the daily difference in high and low water levels. Compare the tidal ranges of neap and spring tides.

○ CHALLENGE

6. **Draw Conclusions** How would the tides be different if the Moon revolved around Earth twice a month instead of once a month?

Tidal Energy

Tidal power plants can work only in a few locations in the world. The best locations for tidal energy plants are ones with large differences between high and low tides. Why can't tides make electricity just anywhere?

The first and largest tidal energy plant in the world is in northern France, where the Rance River enters the English Channel. The plant opened in 1966.

Under Pressure

Each of these jugs contains the same amount of water. Water sprays out of the hole at the bottom of each—but why does it spray farther out of the narrow jug? The water pressure is greater in the tall, narrow jug because the water is deeper. The width of the jug does not matter—just the depth. The deeper the water, the greater the water pressure. The higher the water pressure, the faster the water comes out of the hole—and the farther the water sprays.

From Pressure to Power

Tidal dams use moving water to turn turbines that power generators. Turning turbines requires work. Work is the use of force to move an object. In this case, the force of the water is doing work on the turbines. The faster the water moves, the more work it can do.

Location, Location, Location

Think again about the two jugs. The water moves faster out of the hole in the tall, narrow jug—the one with the higher water pressure. Tidal power plants work best in places where high water pressure moves the water fast enough to turn the turbines. Remember that deeper water makes for higher water pressure. So tidal power plants work best in places with a large tidal range—the difference between high and low tide.

EXPLORE

1. **APPLY** When the water trapped behind a dam is released, it is channeled through openings in the dam and spins the turbines. From what you've learned about water pressure, where do you think the openings are, toward the top of the dam or toward the bottom? Explain your reasoning.

2. **CHALLENGE** Make a model of a tidal-energy plant. Use the side of a milk jug as a base, modeling clay to make the basin, and pieces of plastic for the dam and gates. Try different shapes for your basin and different sizes of gates to see how fast you can get the water to flow.

Chapter Review

the **BIG** idea

The oceans are a connected system of water in motion.

CONTENT REVIEW
CLASSZONE.COM

 KEY CONCEPTS SUMMARY

3.1 The oceans are a connected system.

- Much of Earth is covered by ocean water, which contains dissolved salts and gases.

- Ocean temperatures decrease with depth.
- The ocean floor has canyons, mountains, and many other features.

VOCABULARY
salinity p. 76
density p. 76
continental shelf p. 80
sonar p. 82

3.2 Ocean water moves in currents.

- Surface currents are set in motion by winds and carry heat around the globe.

- Deep currents are caused by differences in water density. Dense water sinks at the poles and very slowly flows toward the equator.

VOCABULARY
ocean current p. 84
upwelling p. 86
downwelling p. 86
El Niño p. 88

3.3 Waves move through oceans.

- Ocean waves transport energy, not water. When a wave passes, water particles end up in the same places they began.

- Longshore currents occur when waves hit shores at angles.
- Rip currents are narrow streams of water that break through sandbars.

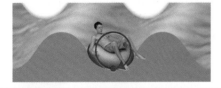

VOCABULARY
longshore current p. 92
rip current p. 92

3.4 Waters rise and fall in tides.

The Moon's gravity pulls Earth's waters into bulges and dips. As Earth rotates, its movement through these bulges and dips causes tides.

indirect high tide — Earth   direct high tide / → Moon

VOCABULARY
tide p. 96
tidal range p. 98
spring tide p. 99
neap tide p. 99

Reviewing Vocabulary

Make a description wheel like the one below for each of the following terms. Write the term in the circle. On the spokes, write words or phrases that describe the term.

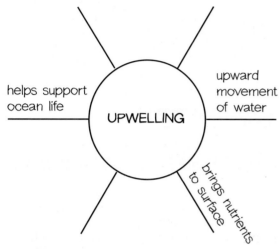

helps support ocean life

upward movement of water

UPWELLING

brings nutrients to surface

1. El Niño

2. longshore current

3. rip current

Reviewing Key Concepts

Multiple Choice *Choose the letter of the best answer.*

4. Warm water stays at the ocean surface because
   a. it is less dense than cold water
   b. it is more dense than cold water
   c. it is saltier than cold water
   d. it has more carbon dioxide than cold water

5. Sonar measures ocean depth by means of
   a. weighted lines   c. sound waves
   b. light waves   d. magnets

6. Surface currents are caused by
   a. waves   c. density
   b. winds   d. heat

7. El Niño is caused by changes in
   a. wave speed   c. salinity
   b. currents   d. tides

8. Deep currents are caused by differences in
   a. location   c. depth
   b. wind speed   d. density

9. Tides are caused by the gravitational pull of
   a. Earth and the Sun
   b. the Sun and the Moon
   c. Earth alone
   d. Earth and the Moon

10. What does wave action involve?
    a. the transfer of water molecules across the ocean surface
    b. the transfer of energy across the ocean surface
    c. oscillations generated by tides
    d. rip currents

Short Answer *Write a short answer to each question.*

11. What is the connection between salinity and density?

12. Explain why Earth's oceans are actually parts of one connected body of water.

13. Describe the relationship between ocean temperature and depth.

14. What are the characteristics of a wave? Copy the drawing below onto your paper, and label each part.

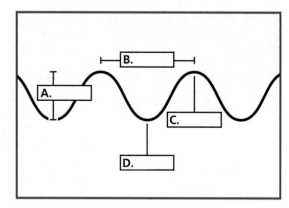

15. SYNTHESIZE One of these cups contains salt water, and the other contains fresh water. Without tasting the water, how could you figure out which sample is which? Describe two methods. You may specify tools or materials you would need to carry out the two methods. **Hint:** Think about the water cycle and density when considering the two methods.

16. INFER After the development of sonar, oceanographic researchers discovered much about the features of the ocean floor. How would the sonar readings of a research ship be affected as it passes above a mid-ocean ridge?

17. COMPARE AND CONTRAST How are space exploration and ocean exploration similar? How are they different?

18. PROVIDE EXAMPLES How could a change in the direction of a surface current in the ocean affect weather? Give examples of the weather in an area before and after the change.

19. INFER If global winds were to change, which ocean motions would be affected?

20. APPLY During a violent storm that causes huge waves to form on the ocean's surface, a submarine glides deep underwater, unaffected by the waves above. Explain why.

21. COMPARE AND CONTRAST Copy and fill in the Venn diagram below. In the overlapping section, list at least one characteristic that is shared by waves and tides. In the outer sections, list characteristics that are not shared. Then write a short summary of the information in the Venn diagram.

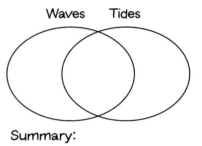

Summary:

22. APPLY Maria and her friends like to play soccer on a beach. Sometimes the water is very low at low tide, and there is plenty of room to play. At other times, the water does not get as low at low tide, and there is not enough room to play. What does Maria need to know about monthly tidal cycles so that she can plan to have the soccer games when there is plenty of room on the beach?

the BIG idea

23. IDENTIFY CAUSE AND EFFECT Look again at the photograph on pages 72–73. Now that you have finished the chapter, explain what is causing the waves in the photograph. Also explain what might cause the water level to rise and cover the area where the surfer is standing.

24. SYNTHESIZE One system can interact with another system. The oceans are a connected system of water in motion. The solar system is the Sun and its family of orbiting planets, moons, and other objects. Describe a connection between the solar system and the ocean system.

UNIT PROJECTS

Check your schedule for your unit project. How are you doing? Be sure that you have placed data or notes from your research in your project folder.

Standardized Test Practice

Analyzing a Table

The table below shows the times of high and low tides at a location on the Atlantic Ocean coast. Use the table to answer the questions below.

	Low Tide	High Tide	Low Tide	High Tide
Monday	12:01 A.M.	5:33 A.M.	11:58 A.M.	5:59 P.M.
Tuesday	12:57 A.M.	6:33 A.M.	12:51 P.M.	6:54 P.M.
Wednesday	1:51 A.M.	7:30 A.M.	1:45 P.M.	7:48 P.M.
Thursday	2:43 A.M.	8:25 A.M.	2:38 P.M.	8:40 P.M.

1. On which day was there a high tide at 7:48 P.M.?

  a. Monday   **c.** Wednesday

  b. Tuesday   **d.** Thursday

2. Low tide is a good time to find shells along the beach. What time would be best for finding shells on Wednesday?

  a. 8:00 A.M.   **c.** noon

  b. 10:00 A.M.   **d.** 2:00 P.M.

3. What was happening to the water level along the beach between 12:00 A.M. and 5:33 A.M. on Monday?

  a. The water level was getting higher.

  b. The water level was getting lower.

  c. The water level was at its lowest.

  d. The water level was at its highest.

4. Which of the following graphs best represents the tides during one day?

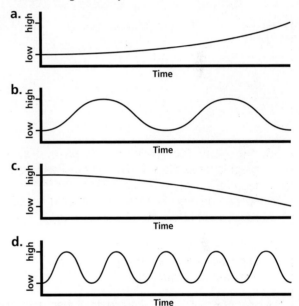

Extended Response

Answer the two questions below in detail.

5. How could you use a cork and a tank of water to demonstrate that waves transport energy, not water? You may include a diagram as part of your response if you wish.

6. The beaker contains both salt water and fresh water. Why do the two liquids form layers? Use the words *salinity* and *density* in your response.

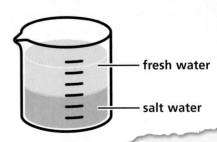

fresh water

salt water

TIMELINES in Science

EXPLORING THE OCEAN

People have been studying ocean waves and currents at least since Egyptians sailed in the Mediterranean Sea more than 5000 years ago. Almost 3000 years ago, Phoenicians in the Mediterranean and Polynesians in the South Pacific understood enough to sail the open sea with confidence. More than 2000 years ago, people developed special gear to provide divers with oxygen so that they could explore the undersea world.

The timeline shows some historical events in the study of the ocean. The boxes below the timeline show how technology has made this study possible and useful.

345 B.C.

Alexander Goes Undersea?

According to legend, Macedonia's powerful ruler Alexander the Great has himself lowered into the ocean in a glass ball so that he can explore what lies underwater.

EVENTS

360 B.C.   320 B.C.

APPLICATIONS AND TECHNOLOGY

APPLICATION

Measuring Ocean Depth

Around 85 B.C., the Greek philosopher Posidonius used a simple method to answer a simple question. He wanted to know the depth of the Mediterranean Sea. So he and a crew sailed out into the sea near Italy. There, they dropped a weight tied to a very long rope into the water. When the weight struck bottom, they measured how much rope they had let out. It was almost 2 kilometers (about 1 mi). This was the standard method for measuring depth for almost 2000 years. Today, instruments on ships emit sound waves that bounce off the sea floor. The instruments then calculate depth according to how long the sound waves take to return to the surface.

A sailor in 1916 prepares to lower a weight on a rope to measure the ocean's depth.

1775
Submarines Allow Undersea Travel

Connecticut inventor David Bushnell designs and builds a wooden submarine. It holds enough air for a person to stay underwater for 30 minutes. The *Turtle*, as his vessel is known, is among the first to allow people to travel underwater.

1797
Explorer Designs First Diving Suit

German mechanic Karl Heinrich Klingert combines waterproof clothes and a helmet with two tubes, one for inhaling and one for exhaling. He calls his outfit a diving machine. It allows people to stay underwater for longer periods than ever before.

1876
Expedition Surveys the Oceans

The sailing ship *Challenger* completes one of the great scientific research efforts of the 1800s, and returns home to Great Britain. In 362 locations around the world, the crew recorded data on ocean depth, currents, temperature, and water chemistry. They identified more than 4000 previously unknown species of plants and animals.

A.D. **1760**   **1800**   **1840**   **1880**

APPLICATION

Charting the Ocean Floor

In the 1800s, sailors began recording measurements of the deep Atlantic Ocean floor. The U.S. Navy lieutenant Matthew Maury collected 200 of these measurements and created the first chart showing water depths in such a large region. His chart, completed in 1855, provided the first evidence of mountains in the middle of the Atlantic. A decade later, Maury's studies of the ocean floor guided those who were laying the first telegraph cable connecting the United States and Europe.

1943

Explorer Breathes Underwater

In 1943, Jacques Cousteau, the most famous of 20th-century undersea explorers, helps develop scuba—a *s*elf-*c*ontained *u*nderwater *b*reathing *a*pparatus. The breathing gear allows divers to explore depths of 30 meters and beyond without having to wear heavy suits and metal helmets.

1938

Fish with Elbows Caught

Among the day's catch of the South African fisherman Hendrick Goosen is an odd five-foot-long fish with joints in its fins, like elbows and knees. Surprised scientists identify it as a coelacanth, a creature they thought had been extinct for 60 million years. The catch spurs people's imaginations about what else the ocean might contain.

1951

Exploration as Entertainment

Improvements in underwater breathing gear in the 1940s make recreational scuba diving possible. Then, a 1951 movie about scuba-wearing soldiers, *The Frogmen,* spurs popular interest in the activity. The movie inspires more people than ever before to start exploring the underwater world for themselves.

1953

Robotic Probe Searches Ocean

POODLE, the first remote operated vehicle (ROV), is invented. Since ROVs carry no people, they allow more research to be done in deep areas that are difficult for people to travel to.

| 1900 | 1920 | 1940 | 1960 | 1980 |

TECHNOLOGY

Sonar

In 1914, Reginald Fessenden developed the first practical instrument for using the echo of a sound to measure distances underwater. This technique, later named sonar, for "*s*ound *n*avigation *a*nd *r*anging," allows scientists to study the undersea world without the expense and danger of going underwater. Sonar has been a valuable tool for measuring the depth of the ocean and the landforms along the bottom. Because temperature and salt concentration affect how sound travels, oceanographers can use sonar to measure these properties as well. One of sonar's most important early uses was to help sailors spot icebergs. Today, industry uses sonar to identify schools of fish, places likely to have oil, and other features.

This sonar image, recorded in October 1999, shows a shipwreck at the bottom of Delaware Bay.

1998

Aquarius *Keeps Researching*

After renovation, the 12-year-old *Aquarius* lab settles on the ocean floor in the Florida Keys. Its crew is investigating a nearby coral reef. They have studied the impact of sewage, the effects of ultraviolet radiation, and chemicals produced by organisms in the reef.

1994

Life Thrives Under Ocean

The discovery of microorganisms thriving in rock pulled up from 500 meters (1600 ft) below the ocean floor raises new questions for scientists. How did the bacteria get there? How do they survive? How many are there? Scientists call the region the deep biosphere.

RESOURCE CENTER
CLASSZONE.COM

Learn more about exploring the ocean.

2000

TECHNOLOGY

Ocean Buoys

Starting in 2000, scientists scattered in the ocean 3000 buoys equipped with the latest developments in floating technology. These Argo floats then started collecting information on water temperature and salinity. They transmitted data by satellite every 15 days. With this more detailed information about ocean water, scientists may be able to make weather predictions more accurate than ever before.

INTO THE FUTURE

Over the past 5000 years, people have learned more and more about the ocean. This knowledge has helped scientists understand how ocean systems work, how Earth has changed, and what factors influence the weather. Continuing research is expanding knowledge in these areas. New findings could be just as surprising as the previous discovery of a fish considered extinct or of microorganisms deep under the ocean floor.

People will probably continue to catch fish and to drill for oil in the ocean for many decades. In addition, people might find it profitable to use other ocean resources. For example, they might mine gold or manganese. Or they might use the tremendous energy in ocean tides or waves—or in the winds that blow over the ocean—to generate electricity. The ocean is so large that many possibilities for using its resources remain.

ACTIVITIES

Mapping the Sea Floor

Suppose you are in a boat that is traveling in a straight line. You take a sonar reading every one-half minute. Your readings, which show how long sound waves take to reach bottom and return to the surface, are as follows:

1. 2 seconds   **3.** 3 seconds
2. 0.5 second   **4.** 3 seconds

Sound travels at about 1500 meters per second (4900 ft/s) in seawater.

From this information, draw what the sea floor looks like under the path of your boat.

Writing About Science

Technology has been used for centuries to study the ocean. Trace the history of one piece of technology, such as a submarine, diving gear, sonar, or a depth gauge. Write a short history of that device.

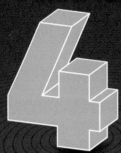

CHAPTER

4

Ocean Environments

the BIG idea

The ocean supports life and contains natural resources.

Key Concepts

SECTION 4.1
Ocean coasts support plant and animal life.
Learn about conditions in coastal environments and about the plants and animals that live there.

SECTION 4.2
Conditions differ away from shore.
Learn how conditions change as you move away from the shore and deeper into the ocean.

SECTION 4.3
The ocean contains natural resources.
Learn about the ocean's living and nonliving resources and how pollution affects the ocean.

Internet Preview

CLASSZONE.COM

Chapter 4 online resources: Content Review, Simulation, Visualization, three Resource Centers, Math Tutorial, Test Practice

How is the deep ocean different from the shore?

EXPLORE (the BIG idea)

It's Alive!

Carefully observe a fish in a fish tank. Pay attention to all of the fish's movements. Record what the fish does and what the fish's environment is like.

Observe and Think All animals, including fish, need oxygen to live. Where does the fish get its oxygen?

Beneath the Surface

What forms of life would you expect to see underwater in the ocean near shore? Draw a picture to show your ideas.

Observe and Think What do you need to know in order to make your picture more accurate? Write five questions you have about the ocean environment near shore.

Internet Activity: Ocean Environments

Go to **ClassZone.com** to learn more about organisms in the ocean. See which plants and animals live in different ocean environments.

Observe and Think What factors or conditions might affect the kinds of organisms that can live in each part of the ocean?

NSTA
scilinks.org

SCILINKS

Ocean Resources **Code: MDL021**

Getting Ready to Learn

◄ CONCEPT REVIEW

- The ocean contains oxygen and other gases.
- Deep currents carry oxygen from the surface to the ocean floor.
- Upwelling carries nutrients from the bottom of the ocean to the surface.

◄ VOCABULARY REVIEW

point-source pollution p. 54
nonpoint-source pollution p. 54
continental shelf p. 80
ocean current p. 84

 CONTENT REVIEW
CLASSZONE.COM
Review concepts and vocabulary.

▶ TAKING NOTES

MAIN IDEA WEB

Write each new blue heading—a main idea—in a box. Then put notes with important terms and details into boxes around the main idea.

CHOOSE YOUR OWN STRATEGY

Take notes about new vocabulary terms, using one or more of the strategies from earlier chapters—**four square, description wheel,** or **word triangle.** Feel free to mix and match the strategies, or use an entirely different vocabulary strategy.

See the Note-Taking Handbook on pages R45–R51.

SCIENCE NOTEBOOK

Different parts of the ocean have different characteristics.	Almost 95 percent of the ocean is still unexplored.

Ocean waters contain many environments.

	Swimmers, floaters, and bottom dwellers are three groups of ocean life.

Four Square
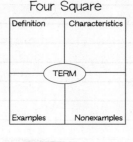

Description Wheel
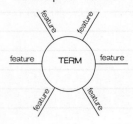

Word Triangle

Ocean coasts support plant and animal life.

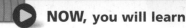

◀ BEFORE, you learned

- Ocean water contains gases such as oxygen
- Salinity is a measure of the amount of salt in water
- Coastal waters rise and fall each day because of tides

▶ NOW, you will learn

- What the intertidal zone is
- What coastal environments exist where fresh water and salt water meet
- How human activity affects shoreline environments

VOCABULARY

habitat p. 114
intertidal zone p. 114
estuary p. 116
wetland p. 116

THINK ABOUT

What are the characteristics of shoreline environments?

This map shows the migration route of the osprey, a type of bird. Each fall ospreys fly south to warmer weather. In the spring they fly north. Each dot on the map represents a place where ospreys stop along the way. What do you notice about where the birds stop? What resources might shoreline environments provide for birds?

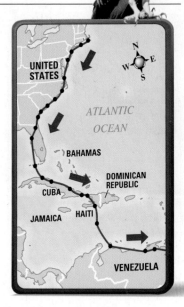

Ocean waters contain many environments.

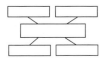

MAIN IDEA WEB
Remember to start a main idea web in your notebook for this blue heading.

Where on Earth can you find a living animal that is larger than the largest dinosaur that ever lived? Where can you find birds that use their wings to fly underwater, or animals that can eject their internal organs—and grow another set? Where can you find warm tropical zones thick with plants, or cold, empty plains where no plant can grow? The ocean contains all these and more.

Like the land, the ocean contains many different environments, each with its own special characteristics. Although scientists have learned a lot about the ocean and its environments, almost 95 percent of the ocean remains unexplored. It is possible that many millions more species of ocean life are yet to be discovered.

The many known ocean organisms are organized in three groups according to the way the organisms live. Bottom dwellers include plantlike organisms called algae (AL-jee) and other organisms that live on the ocean bottom—for example, seaweeds, crabs, corals, starfish, and shellfish. Swimmers are animals such as fish, dolphins, whales, and octopuses that swim in the ocean. Floaters are organisms that do not swim but float at or near the ocean surface. Some floaters, such as jellyfish, are large, but most are so small you need a microscope to see them. These tiny living things include plants, animals, bacteria, and single-celled organisms called protists (PROH-tihsts).

CHECK YOUR READING What are the three groups of ocean life?

The shoreline supports many plants and animals.

READING TiP

Word parts can help you remember the meaning of *intertidal zone*. The prefix *inter-* means "between." The root *tidal* means "relating to the tides." The *intertidal zone* is the area between high and low tides.

An environment that has all the necessary requirements for an organism to live is called a **habitat.** In this chapter you will explore some of the many different ocean habitats. Your journey begins on the coastline, where the ocean meets the land. The habitat at the edge of the ocean is the **intertidal zone** (IHN-tuhr-TYD-uhl)—the narrow ocean margin between the high tide mark and the low tide mark. The conditions constantly change in the intertidal zone. Organisms that live here must be able to survive both wet and dry periods. Plants and animals must also withstand the force of waves that constantly crash onto shore.

① At **low tide,** the intertidal zone is dry and exposed to direct sunlight. Organisms must be able to live out of water. They must also be able to tolerate the air temperature, which may differ from the temperature of the water.

② At **high tide,** the intertidal zone is covered with water, so it is not exposed to direct sunlight. Organisms must be able to live completely underwater and tolerate the temperature of the water.

Tidal pools are areas along the shore where water remains at low tide. Plants and animals that live in tidal pools must survive drastic changes in salinity, or salt content. When sunlight causes water to evaporate, the salinity increases. When rain falls, the salinity decreases.

Organisms have different ways of surviving the conditions of the intertidal zone. For example, crabs can move around and seek cover in the sand or in between rocks. Mussels attach themselves to rocks and close their shells to keep from drying out during low tide. Some seaweeds dry out at low tide but are able to regain moisture at high tide.

Intertidal Zone

The intertidal zone is the area along the coastline between the high tide mark and the low tide mark.

intertidal zone

① Low Tide

At low tide, the intertidal zone is exposed to the air.

Tidal pools are areas where water remains at low tide.

Some seaweeds can dry out during low tide and absorb water at high tide.

At low tide, mussels close their shells tightly to keep from drying out.

② High Tide

At high tide, the intertidal zone is covered with water.

Plants and animals must survive the constant crashing of waves against the shore.

At high tide, mussels open their shells to eat and take in oxygen.

READING VISUALS What organisms can you see in the photograph of low tide?

How do mussels survive?

Most intertidal zone organisms require water to survive, and they must endure long dry periods during low tides. Mussels close their shells tightly during low tide and open them during high tide.

DESIGN
— YOUR OWN —
EXPERIMENT

PROCEDURE

① Using the materials listed, design an experiment to demonstrate why mussels close their shells during low tide.

② Write up your procedure.

③ Test your experiment.

WHAT DO YOU THINK?

• How does your experiment demonstrate why mussels close their shells?

• What were the variables in your experiment?

CHALLENGE How could you redesign your experiment to better model what happens during low tide? What other variables would you include?

SKILL FOCUS
Designing experiments

MATERIALS
• small plastic containers with lids
• sponges
• water

TIME
30 minutes

WATER

Fresh water and salt water meet on coasts.

This aerial photograph shows the Pawcatuck River estuary in the northeastern United States. Fresh water from the river mixes with salt water from the ocean.

You have read that rivers flow to the sea. What happens when they get there? The fresh water from rivers mixes with salt water from the ocean in shoreline areas called **estuaries** (EHS-choo-EHR-eez), which include bays, inlets, and harbors. The water in estuaries is not as salty as ocean water, nor as fresh as river water. The salinity changes as the tide flows in and out. Sometimes the water at the surface is fresh, while denser salt water remains below.

Estuaries are bursting with life. Plants and animals thrive on nutrients washed in by rivers. Worms and shellfish live along the bottom. Plants and animals too small to see without a microscope float in the water. Many different kinds of birds and sea animals breed in estuaries. Roots and grasses offer protection for young fish and other animals. These small fish and other animals are an important food source for larger fish and for birds.

Coastal wetlands form along the edges of estuaries. As the name suggests, **wetlands** are wet, swampy areas that are often flooded with water. There are two kinds of coastal wetlands. Away from the equator, in cooler regions, coastal wetlands are salt marshes. Closer to the equator, in tropical regions, coastal wetlands are mangrove forests.

CHECK YOUR READING How are coastal wetlands related to estuaries?

Salt Marshes

Away from the equator, in cooler regions, grassy salt marshes are found along the edges of estuaries. In the United States, salt marshes are found along the coasts of the Atlantic and Pacific oceans and the Gulf of Mexico. Salt marshes help keep the shoreline from washing away. They also provide an important habitat for fish, birds, and other wildlife.

The rivers that flow into estuaries carry nutrient-rich soil. When the rivers reach the sea, they drop the soil. This rich soil supports thick grasses. The grasses form a protective barrier against waves, tides, and storms. Thick root systems hold the muddy bottom together. Tiny organisms decompose, or break down, dead grasses and return the nutrients the grasses contained to the marsh.

Crabs, snails, and minnows thrive among the grasses. Ospreys and other fish-eating birds find food in salt marshes. Birds that migrate use salt marshes as rest stops when they fly back and forth each season.

In the past, people did not understand the importance of wetlands. Over the last 200 years, about half of all wetlands in the United States were destroyed. Many were drained or filled in with soil to provide solid ground to build on or to farm. In the 1970s, people started working to protect and restore coastal wetlands.

CHECK YOUR READING Why are grasses an important part of the salt marsh environment?

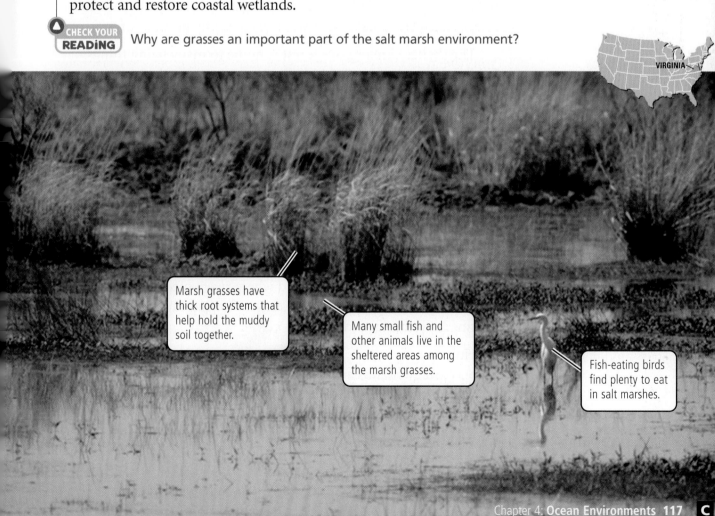

VIRGINIA

Marsh grasses have thick root systems that help hold the muddy soil together.

Many small fish and other animals live in the sheltered areas among the marsh grasses.

Fish-eating birds find plenty to eat in salt marshes.

This is an underwater view of mangrove roots.

INFER This photograph shows mangrove plants along the coast of Florida. How do the roots brace the mangroves against waves and storms?

Mangrove Forests

In tropical regions, the main coastal wetland is the mangrove forest. In the United States, mangrove forests are found along the coast of southern Florida. A mangrove forest is a thick group of mangrove shrubs and trees. The mangrove plants' roots brace them against storms and waves. Without the protection of these plants, shorelines in tropical areas would be drastically changed by heavy storms.

The sheltered mangrove forest is home to many living things. Fiddler crabs may live in the shallow waters among the mangrove roots. You may find seaweeds, oysters, shrimp, and snails. You may even see tree-climbing fish! These fish, called mudskippers, climb mangrove roots to catch insects and crabs.

Human activity affects shorelines.

MAIN IDEA WEB
Remember to start a main idea web in your notebook for this blue heading.

Coastal environments are home not only to many plants and animals, but to many humans as well. About half of the world's population lives within 80 kilometers (50 mi) of a coastline. Big cities and important commercial ports are often located where rivers meet the sea. Many people use coastlines and estuaries for recreation, such as boating, swimming, and fishing.

Human activity can harm the estuary environment. For example, some coastal wetlands are cleared for shrimp farms and for raising crops. Other areas are filled in to make new land for houses and other development. Industry and shipping can disturb wildlife and alter the estuary habitat. In some places, human waste and other sewage drains directly into the water.

About half of the world's population lives near a coastline, such as this one in Mexico.

Even pollution that occurs far away from the shore can affect the coast. The rivers that empty into estuaries pass through farms and cities. Along the way, the rivers may pick up pollutants such as pesticides, fertilizers, oil, and other chemicals. Pollution that washes into the river—even kilometers away from the shore—will eventually end up in the estuary.

Governments, local organizations, and individuals work to protect and preserve shoreline environments in many states. Improved sewage treatment plants reduce the amount of human waste that ends up in shoreline environments. Laws that restrict dumping help reduce pollution along shorelines. Many states have shoreline sanctuaries where plants and animals are protected.

  What are three ways shorelines are protected?

4.1 Review

KEY CONCEPTS

1. Describe the characteristics of the intertidal zone.

2. Name and describe two coastal environments that border estuaries.

3. What human activities are harmful to shoreline environments?

CRITICAL THINKING

4. **Compare and Contrast** What similarities exist between salt marshes and mangrove forests? How are they different?

5. **Infer** Sometimes estuaries are called nursery areas. Why do you think estuaries may have been given that name?

⬤ CHALLENGE

6. **Identify Cause** A salinity meter placed in a tidal pool shows a dramatic decrease in salinity between 2 A.M. and 3 A.M. This decrease is followed by a gradual rise in salinity from 11 A.M. until 4 P.M. the next day. What might explain these changes?

MATH TUTORIAL
CLASSZONE.COM
Click on Math Tutorial for more help with bar graphs.

Machines mounted on boats drill down into the ocean floor to collect sediment cores.

This tube contains a sediment core.

Tracking Contaminants

The layered sediments at the bottom of the ocean have formed over time. The particles in the deeper layers settled to the floor long ago, while those in the top layers settled out of the water more recently. By studying the amounts of pollutants in different layers of sediment, scientists can see how the water quality has changed over time. In 1991, scientists collected sediment cores north of Dash Point in Puget Sound. The table below shows levels of two pollutants, lead and arsenic, in the sediment layers for 1880, 1960, and 1990. The levels are measured in milligrams per kilogram dry weight (mg/kg d.w.).

Levels of Lead and Arsenic in Sediments		
Year	Lead (mg/kg d.w.)	Arsenic (mg/kg d.w.)
1880	10	6
1960	62	22
1990	45	17

You can use a double bar graph to analyze the data. A double bar graph shows two sets of data on the same graph. The first two bars of the graph are drawn for you below.

Example

(1) Copy the axes and labels.

(2) Draw bars for the lead data. Use the scale to determine the height of each bar, as shown.

(3) Draw the arsenic bars next to the lead bars.

(4) Shade the bars in different colors. Include a key.

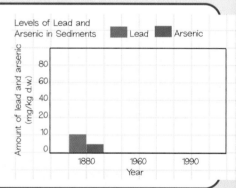

Make a double bar graph of the data by following the steps above. Use your graph to answer the following questions.

1. What happened to the levels of lead and arsenic between 1880 and 1960?

2. What happened to the levels of lead and arsenic between 1960 and 1990?

CHALLENGE Because lead can be harmful to humans, the use of leaded gasoline in new cars was banned in 1975 and the sale of lead-based paint was banned in 1978. How might these bans have affected the amount of lead in Puget Sound? Use evidence from your graph to support your answer.

4.2

KEY CONCEPT

Conditions differ away from shore.

 BEFORE, you learned

- Coasts support plants and animals
- Estuaries and intertidal zones are coastal environments

NOW, you will learn

- About ocean environments away from the coast
- How ocean environments change with depth
- How hydrothermal vents support life in the ocean

VOCABULARY

coral reef p. 122
kelp forest p. 124
phytoplankton p. 126
hydrothermal vent p. 128

EXPLORE Air Bladders

How can air make things float?

PROCEDURE

MATERIALS
- clear container
- soda water
- 5 raisins

① Fill the container halfway with soda water.

② Add raisins to the container, one by one.

③ Observe for 5 minutes. Record your observations.

WHAT DO YOU THINK?

- How did the air bubbles control the movement of the raisins?
- Many ocean fish have an air-filled organ called an air bladder. The fish can control the amount of air in the bladder. How might the amount of air in the bladder change as a fish dives from the ocean surface to the bottom and then returns to the surface?

Ocean environments change with depth and distance from shore.

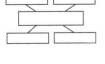

MAIN IDEA WEB
Remember to start a main idea web in your notebook for the blue heading.

Your journey through ocean environments continues as you leave the intertidal zone and move farther out into the ocean. First, you will visit the habitats found in the waters near shore. Next you will move out into the open ocean.

Near shore—in the waters over the continental shelf—sunlight reaches most of the way to the ocean bottom. Nutrients wash in from land. Temperature and salinity are nearly constant from the surface to the bottom. These conditions support many kinds of living things.

 CHECK YOUR READING What are some characteristics of the environment near shore?

The waters near shore support diverse life forms.

More kinds of ocean life live in the waters near shore than in any other ocean environment. Microscopic organisms including bacteria, protists, plants, and animals live there. They share the waters near shore with plants as tall as ten-story buildings and animals larger than elephants. Each organism is part of a delicate and complex food web. You become part of this food web when you eat a fish from the waters near shore. In fact, most of the world's fish are caught in this ocean environment.

Two important habitats near shore are the kelp forest and the coral reef. Kelp forests are found in cooler waters, and coral reefs are found in tropical warm waters.

Coral Reefs

In warm, tropical regions of the globe, the waters near shore support coral reefs. **Coral reefs** are built-up limestone deposits formed by large colonies of ant-sized organisms called corals. Corals produce a hard limestone covering that remains after the corals die. New generations of corals grow on top of older limestone coverings. Although individual corals are small, coral reefs can be huge. Australia's Great Barrier Reef is about 2000 kilometers (1250 mi) long—as long as the distance from Chicago, Illinois, to San Antonio, Texas.

Corals rely on a special relationship with a kind of algae for almost all of their food needs. Tiny algae live inside individual corals. Like plants, the algae use sunlight to produce food through photosynthesis. The food algae produces provides the coral with most of its nutrition. In return, the coral provides some nutrients to the algae. Because the algae need sunlight to survive, coral reefs exist only in the ocean environment near shore, where sunlight reaches all the way to the ocean floor.

Coral reefs, which contain over 25 percent of all of the species of ocean life, help protect shorelines from wave and storm damage.

Coral Reefs

The nutrient-rich, sunlit waters near shore support a greater variety of life than any other part of the ocean.

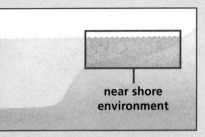

near shore environment

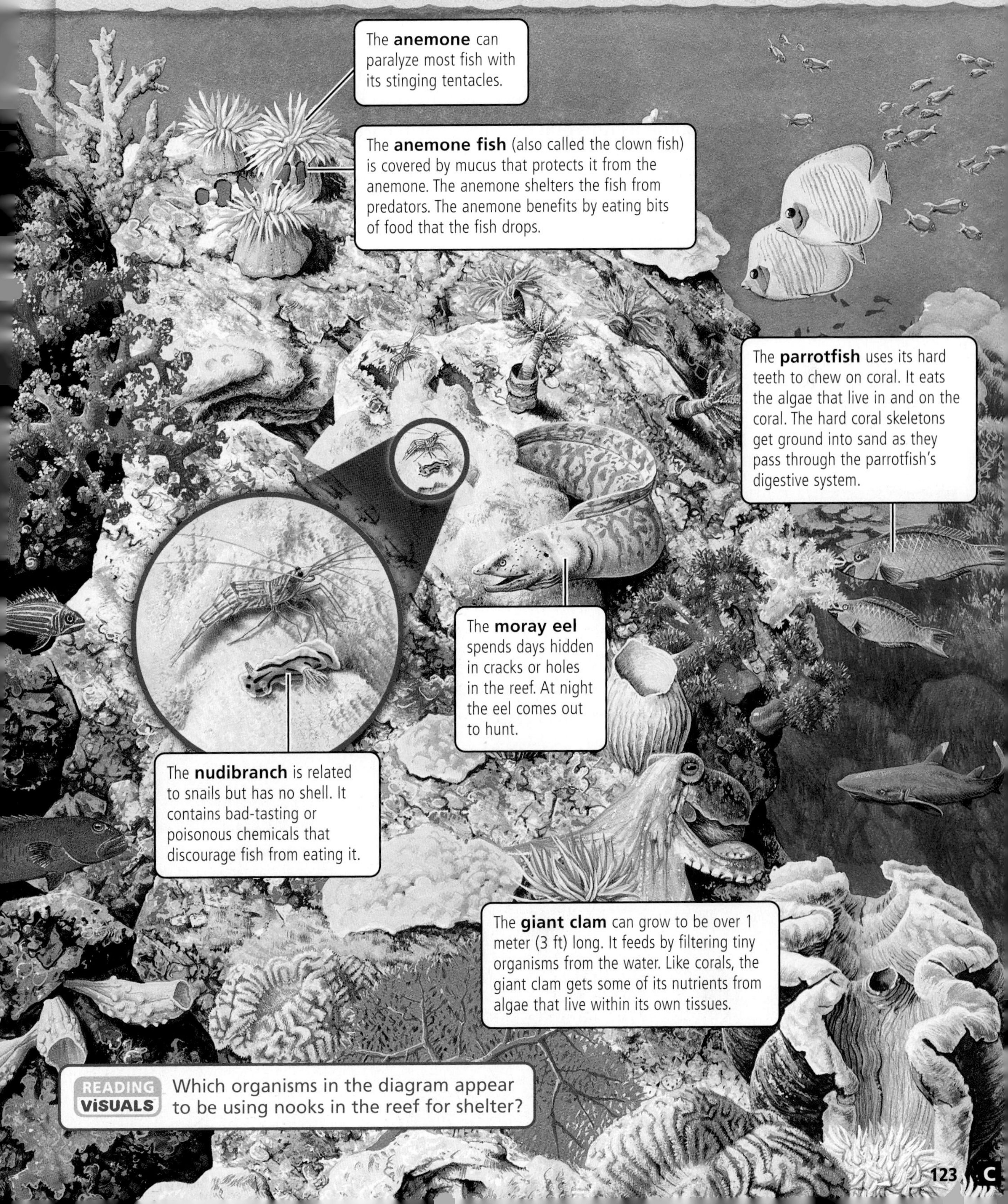

The **anemone** can paralyze most fish with its stinging tentacles.

The **anemone fish** (also called the clown fish) is covered by mucus that protects it from the anemone. The anemone shelters the fish from predators. The anemone benefits by eating bits of food that the fish drops.

The **parrotfish** uses its hard teeth to chew on coral. It eats the algae that live in and on the coral. The hard coral skeletons get ground into sand as they pass through the parrotfish's digestive system.

The **moray eel** spends days hidden in cracks or holes in the reef. At night the eel comes out to hunt.

The **nudibranch** is related to snails but has no shell. It contains bad-tasting or poisonous chemicals that discourage fish from eating it.

The **giant clam** can grow to be over 1 meter (3 ft) long. It feeds by filtering tiny organisms from the water. Like corals, the giant clam gets some of its nutrients from algae that live within its own tissues.

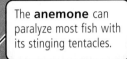

READING VISUALS Which organisms in the diagram appear to be using nooks in the reef for shelter?

123 C

RESOURCE CENTER
CLASSZONE.COM

Explore coral reefs.

The huge amount and variety of life found at coral reefs compares with that found in rain forests. In fact, coral reefs contain over 25 percent of all the species of ocean life. Some reef inhabitants use nooks and crannies in the reef for shelter. Other inhabitants eat corals or feed on seaweed that grows on the corals. Clown fish, sea anemones, (uh-NEHM-uh-neez), sea urchins, starfish, giant clams, and parrotfish are some of the many colorful reef inhabitants.

Coral reefs are now endangered habitats. Pollution that drains off land or that is dumped directly into the water harms coral reefs. Some fishing practices also harm corals and other life at reefs.

 Why are coral reefs endangered?

Kelp Forests

In cold waters, a seaweed called kelp attaches itself to the ocean floor and grows as tall as 40 meters (130 ft)—about the length of an airline jet. Air-filled bulbs on the seaweed's stalks help it to float up toward the surface and remain upright underwater. Large communities of this seaweed form **kelp forests.** Like plants, kelps use sunlight to produce food. Because kelps need sunlight and grow in the ocean, kelp forests

Kelp forests, such as this one in California, provide food and shelter for many living things.

Kelp is an ingredient in many common products including ice cream. Kelp can grow up to 33 cm (13 in) each day.

A sea otter off the coast of California wraps itself in kelp.

are found only in the waters near shore, where sunlight reaches to the ocean floor. Thick kelp forests provide habitats for many organisms. Worms, starfish, lobsters, crabs, abalones, and octopuses are some of the animals that live among the crowded stands of kelp. Fish find shelter and food there. Sea otters dining on sea urchins anchor themselves to the thick mats that the kelps form on the surface.

 CHECK YOUR READING Why are kelp forests found only in waters near shore?

INVESTIGATE Floating

How do plankton float?

DESIGN — YOUR OWN —

Plankton are microscopic organisms that drift in the ocean, where they are moved about by wind, waves, and currents. They must stay near the sunlit surface in order to live. Because plankton have no muscles, they cannot swim to stay afloat. In this lab, you will construct different-shaped clay models to determine how shape helps plankton stay near the ocean surface.

SKILL FOCUS
Modeling

MATERIALS
• clear container
• water
• modeling clay
• watch with a second hand

TIME
30 minutes

PROCEDURE

1. Fill the clear container with tap water.

2. Use the clay to make several different shapes that you think will stay afloat.

3. One by one, place your clay models on the surface of the water. Time how long each piece takes to reach the bottom. Record your observations.

WHAT DO YOU THINK?

• What were the characteristics of the clay shape that sank the slowest?

• What factors affected how fast your clay shape sunk?

CHALLENGE Some kinds of floating organisms release oil droplets or air bubbles to help them stay afloat. How could oil or air help them float?

Environments in the open ocean change with depth.

Out in the open ocean, conditions are different from these found in the waters near shore. Sunlight reaches through only the very top part of the open ocean. Nutrients sink down to the dark depths. There are no rocks, reefs, or big plants to provide shelter from predators. The open ocean covers a huge area but contains fewer living things than the waters near shore. Life is more spread out in the open ocean.

Surface Zone

The surface zone of the open ocean is the sunlit top 200 meters (650 ft). Microscopic floating organisms called **phytoplankton** (FY-toh-PLANGK-tuhn) live at or near the sunlit surface. Like plants, phytoplankton convert sunlight and carbon dioxide into food and oxygen. In fact, phytoplankton convert about as much carbon dioxide into oxygen as all land plants combined. Phytoplankton are an important source of the oxygen that you are breathing right now. Tiny floating animals called zooplankton eat phytoplankton. Zooplankton and phytoplankton then become food for fish, squids, and ocean mammals, such as whales.

READING TiP

Word parts can help you remember the meaning of *phytoplankton* and *zooplankton*. The prefix *phyto-* means "plant" and the prefix *zoo-* means "animal."

Inhabitants of the surface zone must keep from sinking. To stay afloat, phytoplankton bodies have big surface areas and may use air bubbles or oil droplets to stay near the ocean surface. Many fish have an air-filled organ called an air bladder that helps the fish change depth. Changing the amount of air in the bladder allows these fish to move up and down in the water. When the bladder fills with air, the fish floats up toward the surface. Releasing air from the bladder allows the fish to dive down into deeper water.

Deep Zone

The dark and cold deep zone of the open ocean lies under the surface zone. Because sunlight does not reach the deep zone, no plants can live there. Without plants for food, many deep-sea animals must either eat each other or rely on food drifting down from above.

The anglerfish in the photograph on page 127 has many of the common features of deep-sea animals. Its huge mouth and sharp teeth are typical of predators—animals that hunt and eat other animals. Many deep-sea animals glow in the dark, as fireflies do. A glowing extension sticks out from the head of the anglerfish and acts as bait to attract prey. Animals of the deepest waters often have small eyes—and some have no eyes at all. Among the animals found in the deep zone are lantern fish, squids, octopuses, and shrimp.

Life in the Open Ocean

The open ocean consists of a sunlit surface zone and a dark deep zone.

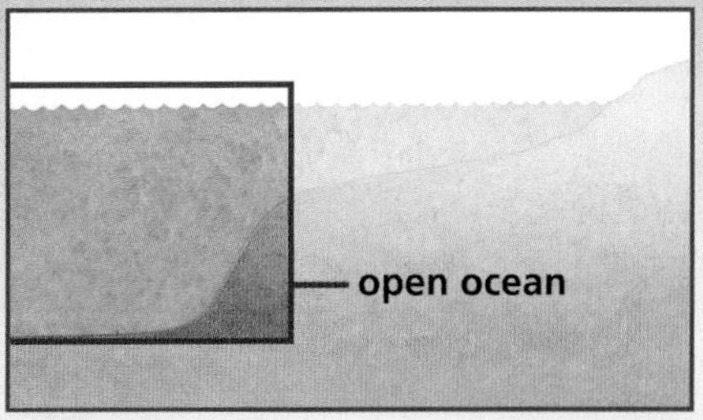

open ocean

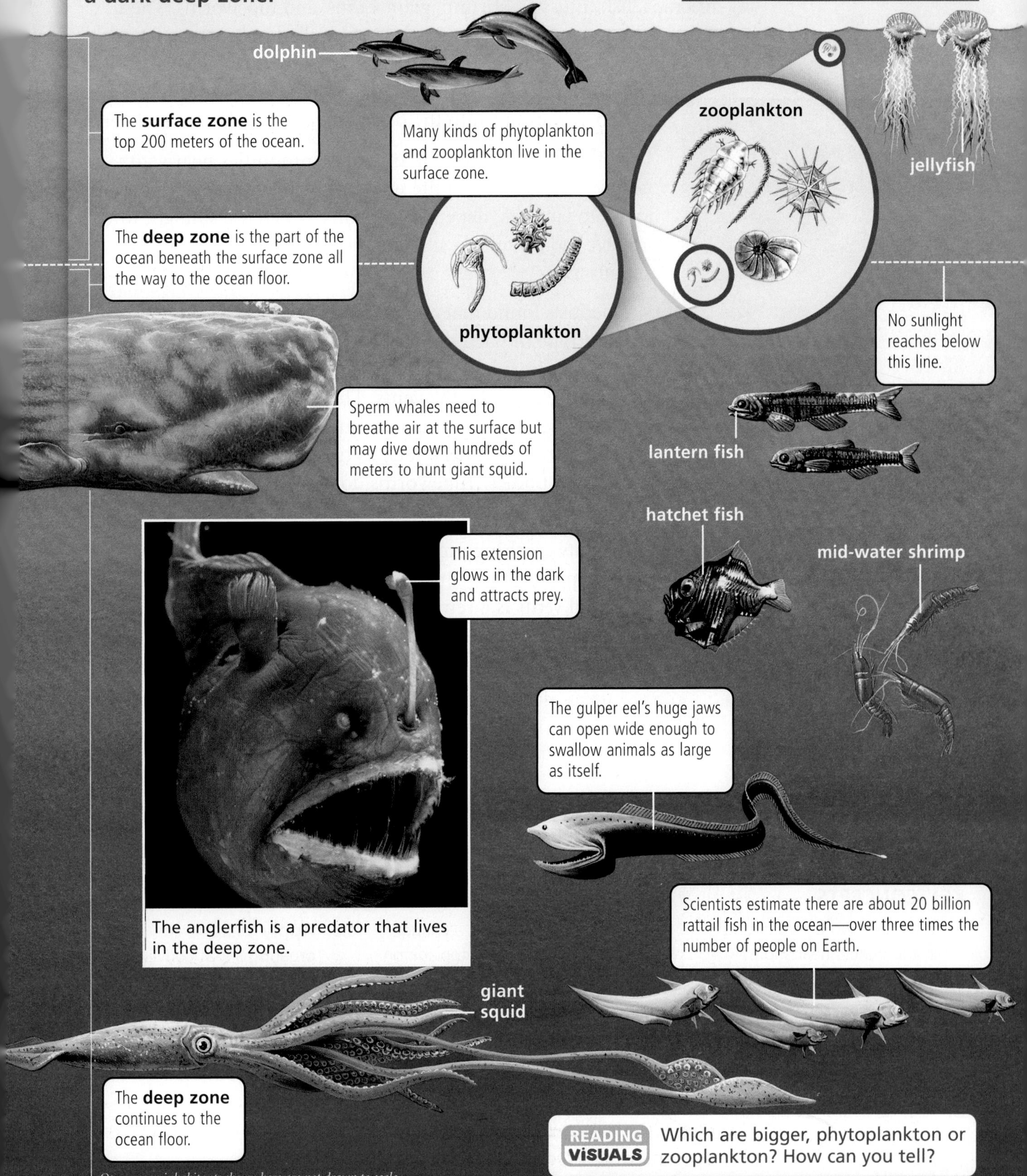

dolphin

The **surface zone** is the top 200 meters of the ocean.

Many kinds of phytoplankton and zooplankton live in the surface zone.

zooplankton

jellyfish

The **deep zone** is the part of the ocean beneath the surface zone all the way to the ocean floor.

phytoplankton

No sunlight reaches below this line.

Sperm whales need to breathe air at the surface but may dive down hundreds of meters to hunt giant squid.

lantern fish

hatchet fish

mid-water shrimp

This extension glows in the dark and attracts prey.

The gulper eel's huge jaws can open wide enough to swallow animals as large as itself.

The anglerfish is a predator that lives in the deep zone.

Scientists estimate there are about 20 billion rattail fish in the ocean—over three times the number of people on Earth.

giant squid

The **deep zone** continues to the ocean floor.

Open ocean inhabitants shown here are not drawn to scale.

READING VISUALS Which are bigger, phytoplankton or zooplankton? How can you tell?

New discoveries about ocean life continue.

VISUALIZATION
CLASSZONE.COM
Examine the life found at hydrothermal vents.

While investigating deep-sea sediments in 1977, scientists got quite a surprise. On the deep-ocean floor they found thriving communities of crabs, fish, mussels, shrimp, giant clams, and tubeworms. These animals live near openings in Earth's crust called **hydrothermal vents**. Cold ocean water that seeps into cracks in the ocean floor gets heated deep underground by hot magma. The heated water then rises up and gushes out into the ocean, forming hydrothermal vents.

Before the discovery of animal communities near vents, most scientists thought life was impossible on the dark ocean floor. On land, life depends on plants, which use sunlight to produce food. Without sunlight, how could these deep sea animals live?

Scientists found that animals at hydrothermal vents depend on a special type of bacteria. Instead of making food from sunlight and carbon dioxide, like plants, these bacteria make food from chemicals released by the vents. The bacteria thus form the base of the food chain at the vents. Some of the animals living there eat the bacteria. Other animals, such as tubeworms, have the bacteria living within their bodies. Tubeworms do not eat and have no digestive system—they absorb all their food directly from the bacteria.

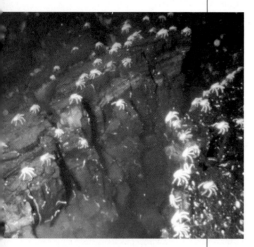

Hydrothermal vents support many kinds of life, including clams, crabs, fish, tubeworms, and bacteria.

Because of its crushing pressure, darkness, and huge size, the deep ocean remains mostly unexplored. The discovery of animal communities at hydrothermal vents is a reminder that life may be possible even in seemingly impossible places. In fact, more recent explorations have even found life deep within the sediments of the ocean floor.

CHECK YOUR READING Why were scientists surprised to find life at hydrothermal vents?

4.2 Review

KEY CONCEPTS

1. What are two environments in the waters near shore? Describe the characteristics of each.

2. How does the surface zone of the open ocean differ from the deep zone?

3. How do hydrothermal vents support life on the deep-ocean floor?

CRITICAL THINKING

4. **Predict** How might a change in the amount of phytoplankton in the ocean affect the world's atmosphere?

5. **Evaluate** Suppose you are seeking a site for a submarine station where scientists could live for months at a time. Which ocean environment would you choose, and why?

CHALLENGE

6. **Apply** Diatoms are tiny ocean organisms that convert carbon dioxide to oxygen. Describe the depth at which diatoms live and where they fit into the ocean food chain.

(magnified 200x)

EXTREME SCIENCE

RESOURCE CENTER
CLASSZONE.COM

Learn more about hydrothermal vents.

When the hot water from the vent hits the nearly freezing ocean water, it cools rapidly. The minerals dissolved in the water settle out, sometimes creating a chimney around the vent. Some chimneys are as tall as 15-story buildings.

Undersea Hot Spots

Deep within Earth, volcanic activity heats up water. When this water shoots out through a crack in the ocean floor, it forms a hydrothermal vent. These vents are among the world's strangest environments.

- The pressure of the ocean water is so high that the water emerging from the vents does not boil—even though it is as hot as 400°C (750°F).

- The water from the vents is so filled with minerals, particularly hydrogen sulfide, that it would poison most animals.

- Sunlight is so dim that the vents exist in near total darkness. However, they often glow slightly, perhaps due to heat radiation.

Home Sweet Home

Organisms that live anywhere else on Earth would not be able to survive the combination of pressure, heat, poisonous water, and darkness that exists near vents. Yet scientists have identified 300 species living near vents.

Tubeworms may grow up to 3 meters (10 ft) in length.

- Bacteria convert the sulfur in the water into energy. This is one of the few places on Earth where the living things at the base of a food chain get energy from chemicals rather than from sunlight.

- Tubeworms that grow up to 3 meters (10 ft) long and oversized clams thrive on the sulfur-eating bacteria.

- Crabs with gigantic legs that make them look like enormous spiders from a horror movie survive by eating the worms and other creatures.

Life Far Away

Organisms that live around the vents are like no others on Earth. However, could a different planet with a sulfur-rich environment support similar life forms? As scientists explore the possibility of life on other planets, they will look to hydrothermal vents for lessons on unusual life.

EXPLORE

1. **SEQUENCE** Create a diagram showing the relationship on the hydrothermal vent food chain between bacteria, crabs, and tubeworms.

2. **CHALLENGE** In 1997 scientists discovered features on Jupiter's moon Europa that look like icebergs floating on an ocean. Why did this discovery suggest that life might exist on Europa?

4.3 The ocean contains natural resources.

 BEFORE, you learned

- The waters near shore support diverse life forms
- The ocean environment changes with depth

▷ **NOW, you will learn**

- What living resources the ocean contains
- What mineral, energy, and other resources the ocean contains
- How pollution affects the ocean

VOCABULARY

overfishing p. 131
by-catch p. 132

EXPLORE Ocean Pollution

How do oil spills affect birds?

PROCEDURE

① Fill the bowl with water.

② Carefully place the feather on top of the water in the bowl.

③ Holding the end of the feather, blow on it to try to make the feather rise up out of the bowl. Record your observations.

④ Remove the feather and place three spoonfuls of oil into the bowl.

⑤ Repeat steps 2 and 3.

WHAT DO YOU THINK?

- How did the oil in the water affect the feather?
- Based on your findings, how do you think oil spills might affect birds?

MATERIALS

- bowl
- water
- feather
- spoon
- cooking oil

The ocean supports living resources.

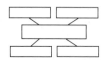

MAIN IDEA WEB
Remember to start a main idea web in your notebook for the blue heading.

The ocean's many algae and animals are important food sources for people in many areas of the world, including the United States. In fact, the United States is the third largest consumer of seafood in the world. The ocean also supports living resources you do not eat for dinner. You have already read about phytoplankton, tiny ocean organisms. Phytoplankton are a very important resource because they produce much of the oxygen in Earth's air. Chemicals from other ocean organisms are used in medicines—including some that treat cancer. As research continues, scientists may find even more useful chemicals in ocean organisms.

Seafood and Algae

Across the United States, supermarkets sell ocean fish and shellfish. Most people, whether they realize it or not, eat seaweeds, too. These ocean algae are commonly used to thicken cheese, ice cream, and pudding. Seaweeds are also ingredients in nonfood products such as shaving cream and pesticides.

When you think of fishing, you might think of a person with a fishing pole catching one fish at a time. This method of fishing, however, is far too slow and inefficient for the commercial fishing industry to use. Instead, the fishing industry uses huge nets bigger than football fields or lines of fishing hooks kilometers long to catch large amounts of fish at a time. As you read this sentence, tens of thousands of nets and fishing lines trail in the ocean. The fishing industry uses sonar, satellites, airplanes, and other technology to find areas in the ocean that contain large numbers of fish.

Overfishing and By-Catch

Over the years, people have noticed that there are fewer and fewer fish than there once were. The main cause of the decrease in fish populations is **overfishing,** or catching fish at a faster rate than they can reproduce. Cod is one popular food fish that was nearly killed off by overfishing. Cod were once common in the North Atlantic, but now the cod population is very small. All of the world's fisheries, or main fishing areas of the ocean, are either overfished or very close to being overfished. Overfishing is a major threat to ocean environments.

VOCABULARY
You can use a description wheel to take notes about the term *overfishing.*

Overfishing

The bar graph shows data from fishing boats that use longlines of baited hooks. The data show how many yellowfin tuna were caught in the subtropical Atlantic Ocean for every 100 hooks used.

SOURCE: *Census of Marine Life*

READING VISUALS What can you conclude about the number of yellowfin tuna left by 1999?

Everything except the shrimp will be thrown away as by-catch from this boat in the Gulf of Mexico.

Fishing nets catch nearly everything in their path. A net that is being used to catch shrimp, for example, may also catch fish, turtles, sharks, dolphins, and other sea animals. The extra catch—everything besides the shrimp—gets tossed back into the ocean either dead or dying. **By-catch,** or by-kill, is the portion of animals that are caught in a net and then thrown away. Sometimes the by-catch is greater than the portion of fish or other animals the net is meant to catch.

To help reduce by-catch, fisheries started using nets designed to prevent animals such as turtles and dolphins from getting caught. Although these efforts have lessened the number of turtles and dolphins caught in fishing nets, fisheries worldwide still throw away about 30 percent of the fish they catch.

CHECK YOUR READING   What harm does overfishing cause?

Saltwater Aquaculture

A shrimp farm extends out into the water off the island of Bora Bora in French Polynesia.

SOCIETY ISLANDS, FRENCH POLYNESIA

As you read in Chapter 2, aquaculture is the farming of both freshwater and ocean organisms. Saltwater farmers may raise fish, oysters, mussels, shrimp, seaweeds, or other organisms.

Most aquaculture harms the environment. Huge amounts of fish waste are often released into the ocean waters surrounding fish farms, causing damage to plants and animals. Nutrients and chemicals added to water at fish farms may also end up in the ocean. Sometimes plants and animals are cleared from an area to make space for aquaculture. About half of the world's mangrove forests have been cleared for shrimp farms and similar uses.

Some methods of aquaculture cause more damage than others. For 4000 years, farmers in China have raised fish without causing much harm. Chinese fish farms are often small, so they release less waste than larger farms.

The ocean contains nonliving resources.

Ocean water itself is a valuable resource for people living in regions with little fresh water. As you read in Chapter 2, desalination is the process by which salt is removed from seawater. Desalinated seawater is a major portion of the fresh water used by many Middle Eastern countries, such as Saudi Arabia.

Many of the natural resources found on land are also found in the ocean. It is often less expensive to remove resources from the land than from the ocean, so many of the ocean's resources are not currently mined. However, as resources on land are used up and new technology makes ocean exploration and mining easier, ocean mining may increase.

Energy Resources

Oil and gas form from the remains of living organisms. In the ocean, organisms are concentrated in the waters over the continental shelf. Oil deposits, therefore, are found near shore. Oil and gas are pumped from the continental shelf of every continent but Antarctica. About 30 percent of the world's oil is pumped from deposits under the ocean floor.

Huge anchored platforms serve as artificial islands that house workers and the necessary equipment for drilling offshore oil wells. The platforms are built to withstand ocean currents, tides, and weather conditions such as storms. Underwater pipelines carry the oil to shore.

Oil is pumped from the ocean floor at huge anchored platforms such as this one in the North Sea.

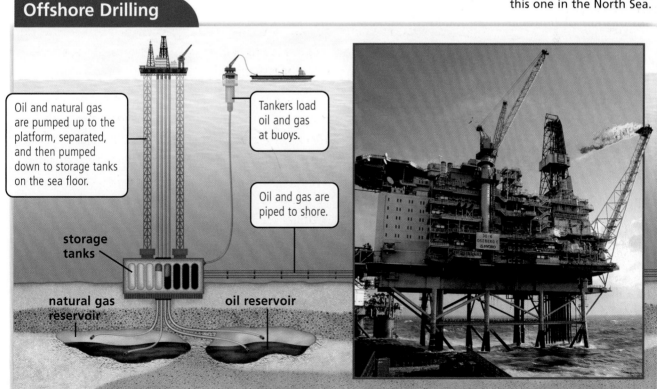

Offshore Drilling

Oil and natural gas are pumped up to the platform, separated, and then pumped down to storage tanks on the sea floor.

Tankers load oil and gas at buoys.

Oil and gas are piped to shore.

storage tanks

natural gas reservoir

oil reservoir

Minerals and Rocks

When rivers empty into the sea, sediments carried by the rivers drop to the bottom. These sediments may contain phosphorite, iron, copper, lead, gold, tin, diamonds, and other minerals. Because these minerals wash into the ocean from land, most of them are found in areas near shore. It is currently too expensive to mine many of these minerals.

Some minerals are found away from shore. Nodules (NAHJ-oolz) are lumps of minerals that are scattered across the deep-ocean floor. The nodules are small at first, but they can build up over millions of years to a size of as much as a meter across. Nodules contain valuable manganese, iron,

Nodules are found away from the coast on the deep-ocean floor.

and cobalt, which are used to make metals such as steel. Nodules are not mined because it would be very expensive to remove them from the ocean floor. In the future, however, nodules may be removed—perhaps with giant vacuums.

The Ocean's Energy and Mineral Resources

The ocean floor contains valuable energy and mineral resources.

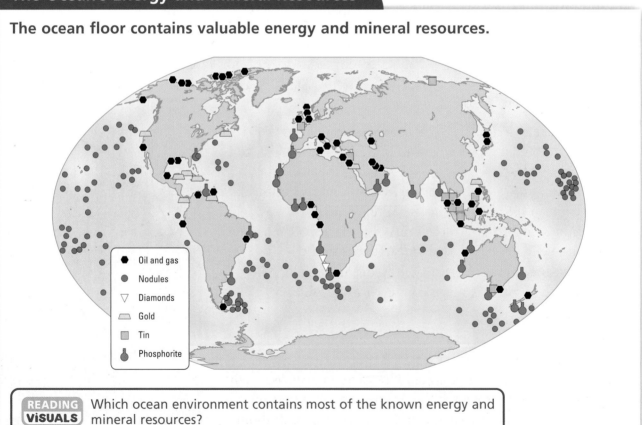

Legend:
- ● Oil and gas
- ● Nodules
- ▽ Diamonds
- ⬟ Gold
- ▢ Tin
- ⬤ Phosphorite

READING VISUALS Which ocean environment contains most of the known energy and mineral resources?

When ocean water evaporates, salt is left behind.

Each of these mounds is a pile of salt harvested from ocean water in Thailand.

A mineral you eat is also removed from the ocean. About one-third of the world's table salt comes from the ocean. Ocean water is left to evaporate in flat, shallow areas. As the water evaporates, salts are left behind.

Sand and gravel might not be the first things you think of when you think of important resources. However, they are building materials used in concrete and cement. Sand and gravel are currently scraped off the sea floor in many locations near shore.

Pollution affects the ocean.

Every part of the ocean is polluted. Solid waste—such as plastic garbage, tar balls, and hypodermic needles—is a visible form of pollution along ocean shorelines. Trash washes up on beaches worldwide, even on the beaches of remote islands. Sea animals may mistake trash for food and eat plastic that can block their digestive systems. Animals also get tangled in and even strangled by plastic waste.

Although you may not see this much garbage on every beach, trash washes up on beaches all over the world—even on remote islands.

Most ocean pollution is harder to see than solid waste. Chemical pollutants, nuclear wastes, and heavy metals like mercury and lead are found in all parts of the ocean. These pollutants are known to harm and kill ocean life. They are also harmful to humans. Pregnant women are sometimes advised not to eat tuna and other fish because the fish may contain low levels of toxic mercury. Although the small amounts of mercury may not harm an adult, they could damage the developing child.

Human waste, sewage, and fertilizers have caused dead zones in the ocean—areas where no plants or animals can live. These pollutants contain nutrients and cause a huge increase in the amount of algae that live in an area. When the algae die, bacteria consume them. The large numbers of bacteria use up all the oxygen in an area of ocean. Without oxygen, the animals in the area cannot survive.

Sources of Ocean Oil Pollution

■ Runoff from land 44%

■ Air pollution 33%

■ Shipping and oil spills 12%

■ Ocean dumping 10%

□ Offshore drilling 1%

SOURCE: *Joint Group of Experts on the Scientific Aspects of the Marine Environment, The State of the Marine Environment, UNEP Regional Seas Reports and Studies No. 115 (Nairobi: U.N. Environment Programme, 1990)*

Oil spills are dramatic and disastrous events. However, most oil pollution in the ocean is washed in from land.

Some pollutants are dumped directly into the ocean. Many other pollutants wash from the land into the ocean or into rivers that flow into the ocean. Although oil spills are dramatic events that kill many animals, they account for only a small percentage of the oil pollution in the ocean. More oil enters the ocean by washing off the land than by being spilled. In addition to oil, pesticides, fertilizers, and many other pollutants wash into the ocean from land.

 CHECK YOUR READING What is the source of most of the ocean's oil pollution?

Preventing Ocean Pollution

RESOURCE CENTER
CLASSZONE.COM

Find out more about ocean pollution and pollution prevention.

Ocean pollution can be prevented or reduced. In 1988, for example, the United States government restricted the use of a harmful chemical that had been used in ship paint. As a result, levels of the chemical dropped in certain areas of the ocean, and the health of some types of sea life, such as oysters, improved. Government organizations have also banned the dumping of some chemicals into the ocean. These bans have successfully reduced some kinds of pollution.

Individuals can help prevent or reduce ocean pollution. Many people may not realize that oil or other chemicals dumped in a drain or sewer or on the ground can end up in the ocean. The proper disposal of household chemicals and other toxic substances could reduce ocean pollution. The Environmental Protection Agency (EPA) has information about the proper disposal of many common chemicals.

Some oyster populations recovered after the use of a toxic chemical in ship paint was restricted. This photo shows an oyster farm in Washington State.

oyster

Global Pollution Problems

Remember that the ocean is a connected global body of water. Ocean currents circulate water around the globe and carry pollutants to all parts of the ocean. Pollution that occurs in any part of the world can affect the whole ocean.

The United Nations, through its 1994 Law of the Sea, attempts to manage ocean resources and to conserve ocean environments. The law calls on all countries to enforce pollution controls. It also sets pollution rules for ships operating in international waters, regulates fishing, and attempts to divide rights to undersea resources. This international law is an important step toward protecting the ocean and its resources for future generations.

 Why is ocean pollution a global problem?

KEY CONCEPTS

1. Describe one living resource contained in the ocean and how its use affects the ocean environment.

2. Describe one nonliving resource contained in the ocean and how its use affects the ocean environment.

3. How does pollution affect the ocean?

CRITICAL THINKING

4. **Connect** How could ocean pollution affect your life?

5. **Sequence** Describe how oil from a car many miles away from the shore could reach the ocean.

CHALLENGE

6. **Evaluate** Most of the ocean does not belong to any country or government. Who do you think should be responsible for limiting pollution in areas outside country borders? Who should be able to claim ownership of resources in these areas?

CHAPTER INVESTIGATION

Population Sampling

OVERVIEW AND PURPOSE Scientists have found that overfishing is decreasing the population of many organisms. They have also found that the population of some other organisms are increasing. How do scientists know this? They count the number of individuals in a small measured area, called a quadrat, then estimate from their counts how many organisms live in a larger area. Repeated samplings over time allow them to determine whether populations are growing or decreasing. In this investigation you will

- count the number of items in a "population" using a quadrat technique
- use small and large quadrats to form two different estimates for the size of a "population"

MATERIALS
- calculator
- removable tape

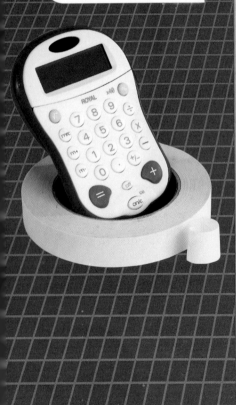

▶ Procedure

1 As a class, brainstorm some objects that you might find in your classroom—for example: pencil, protractor, calculator, or ball cap. Choose one of those objects to count. You will estimate the population at your school of this object.

2 Remove all of the objects that your class decided to count from bags and drawers. For example, if your class is counting pencils, everyone should remove all of their pencils from their bags and place them on their desks.

3 Divide your classroom into four equal-sized pieces. Use removable tape to mark the boundaries of each quadrat. Label the quadrats A, B, C, and D.

4 Count the items in one of the quadrats—either A, B, C, or D. Record the number of objects in your **Science Notebook.**

5 Find the total classroom population of your object by combining your data with the data from groups who counted other quadrats. Record the total classroom population.

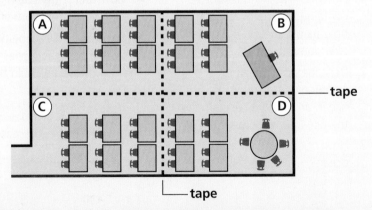

▶ Observe and Analyze

1. **RECORD** Make a data table like the one in the notebook.

2. **CALCULATE** Multiply the number of each item you counted in your quadrat by four. This will give you an estimate of the number of each item in your classroom. Record your answer.

3. **CALCULATE** For this investigation, assume that each classroom in your school is the same size as your classroom. Your teacher will provide you with the number of classrooms in your entire school. Multiply your answer from question 2 by the number of classrooms in your school. This will give you an estimate of the number of each item in your school. Record your answer.

4. **CALCULATE** Now estimate the population of the object in the whole school using the total count from the classroom. Multiply the total classroom population by the number of classrooms in your school. This will give you a second estimate for the population of each item in your school. Record your answer.

▶ Conclude

1. **COMPARE** How does your school population estimate based on your small quadrat count compare with your school population estimate based on your total classroom estimate?

2. **INFER** If there was a difference between your two total population estimates, what do you think could explain the difference?

3. **INFER** Do you think your total population estimate for your object in the school is accurate? Explain.

4. **COMPARE** How would your population estimate compare to one done the same way ten years ago? ten years from now? Explain your reasoning.

5. **IDENTIFY LIMITS** What possible limitations or sources of error could have affected your results?

6. **CONNECT** How would you need to change your procedure if you were sampling an ocean fish population? Give at least two examples.

▶ INVESTIGATE Further

CHALLENGE Suppose your quadrat size was one square meter. How would this have affected your accuracy? Imagine that you were given a wooden frame measuring one square meter in size. How would you change your procedure to best sample the school "population" using this smaller quadrat?

Population Sampling
Observe and Analyze
Table 1. Population Data

Quadrat	Number of Items	Classroom Population Estimate	School Population Estimate (No. in classroom × No. of classrooms in school)
A	7	7 × 4 = 28	
B			
C			
D			
Total: classroom count			

the **BIG** idea

the **BIG** idea

The ocean supports life and contains natural resources.

CONTENT REVIEW
CLASSZONE.COM

◀ KEY CONCEPTS SUMMARY

4.1 Ocean coasts support plant and animal life.

Organisms in the intertidal zone are covered by water during high tide and exposed to the air during low tide.

high tide mark

low tide mark

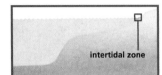

intertidal zone

- Fresh water and salt water mix in estuaries.
- Salt marshes and mangrove forests form along coasts.

VOCABULARY
habitat p. 114
intertidal zone p. 114
estuary p. 116
wetland p. 116

4.2 Conditions differ away from shore.

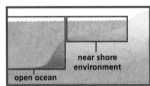

near shore environment

open ocean

Life in the open ocean is more spread out. The surface zone is lit by the Sun. The deep zone is dark.

The waters near shore support more life than any other part of the ocean.

VOCABULARY
coral reef p. 122
kelp forest p. 124
phytoplankton p. 126
hydrothermal vent p. 128

4.3 The ocean contains natural resources.

Living ocean resources include seafood and algae. Overfishing and pollution threaten ocean environments.

Nonliving ocean resources include oil, natural gas, and minerals.

VOCABULARY
overfishing p. 131
by-catch p. 132

Reviewing Vocabulary

Copy and complete the chart below. In the middle column, list characteristics of each environment. In the last column, list examples of organisms that live in each environment.

Vocabulary Term	Characteristics	Organisms
1. intertidal zone		
2. estuary		
3. coral reef		
4. kelp forest		
5. hydrothermal vent		

Reviewing Key Concepts

Multiple Choice *Choose the letter of the best answer.*

6. An environment that contains all the necessary requirements for an organism to live is called
   a. the surface zone   c. a habitat
   b. a nodule   d. an estuary

7. Where would you expect to find ocean organisms that are able to survive out of water and withstand drastic changes in salinity?
   a. the intertidal zone   c. the open ocean
   b. a coral reef   d. a hydrothermal vent

8. Two kinds of wetlands that border estuaries are
   a. coral reefs and mangrove forests
   b. salt marshes and mangrove forests
   c. tidal pools and salt marshes
   d. mangrove forests and tidal pools

9. Tiny plantlike organisms that float at the surface of the ocean are called
   a. phytoplankton   c. corals
   b. kelps   d. bottom dwellers

10. Where are hydrothermal vents located?
    a. in the intertidal zone
    b. on the deep-ocean floor
    c. on coral reefs
    d. in kelp forests

11. The bacteria that form the base of the food chain at hydrothermal vents convert
    a. dim sunlight that filters down into food
    b. heat from the vents into food
    c. phytoplankton that drift down into food
    d. chemicals released by the vents into food

12. Overfishing is best described as catching
    a. more fish than people can eat
    b. fish at a faster rate than they can reproduce
    c. other kinds of fish than the ones intended
    d. fish with huge nets and long lines of hooks

13. Why are 30 percent of the fish that are caught by commercial fishing boats thrown away?
    a. Fishing nets catch everything in their path.
    b. Smaller fish are thrown back into the ocean.
    c. Oil pollution has damaged many of the fish.
    d. Large phytoplankton interfere with nets and lines.

Short Answer *Write a short answer to each question.*

14. How does human activity affect shoreline environments?

15. Name the three categories of ocean life, and give an example of an organism for each category.

16. What resources does the ocean contain?

17. What kinds of pollution are found in the ocean?

18. Why is ocean pollution a global problem?

Thinking Critically

Use the maps shown below to answer the next three questions.

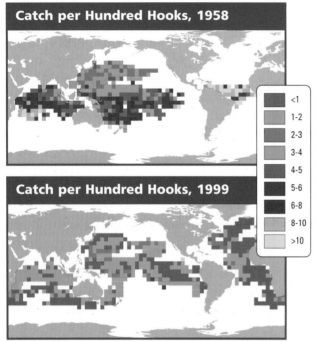

SOURCE: *Census of Marine Life*

These maps show data from Japanese fishing boats of the total numbers of fish that were caught in 1958 and 1999. The color code shows the number of fish caught per 100 hooks on longlines.

19. INTERPRET What do these data show about how ocean fish populations have changed between 1958 and 1999?

20. INFER The data for 1999 were collected over a wider area than were the data for 1958. What might explain the wider area for the 1999 data?

21. PREDICT What would you expect a map with data for the current year to look like? Describe it in terms of color and the extent of the data.

22. COMPARE AND CONTRAST What similarities exist between kelp forests and coral reefs? How are they different?

23. INFER It is believed that life on Earth first appeared in the oceans. In which ocean zone might life have first appeared? Explain your reasoning.

24. APPLY The sargassum frogfish lives among sargassum algae, a type of algae that grows attached to the ocean floor. In which ocean zones could this species of frogfish possibly live? In which could it not live? Explain.

25. SYNTHESIZE A marine sanctuary is an area of the ocean that is protected from fishing and most human use. An environmental organization is trying to decide whether to establish a marine sanctuary. Based on what you have learned, write a short letter telling the organization whether you think a marine sanctuary is a good idea and in which ocean zone the sanctuary should be established.

the BIG idea

26. COMPARE AND CONTRAST Look again at the photograph on pages 110–111. Now that you have finished the chapter, make a Venn diagram to answer the question on the photograph in more detail. For information about Venn diagrams, see page R49.

27. PROVIDE EXAMPLES What types of habitats and resources does the ocean contain? To answer, copy the concept map below into your notebook and add to it. For information about concept maps, see page R49.

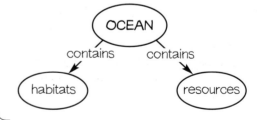

UNIT PROJECTS

Check your schedule for your unit project. How are you doing? Be sure that you've placed data or notes from your research in your project folder.

Standardized Test Practice

Analyzing a Diagram

The diagram below shows a side view of part of the ocean. Use the diagram to answer the questions below.

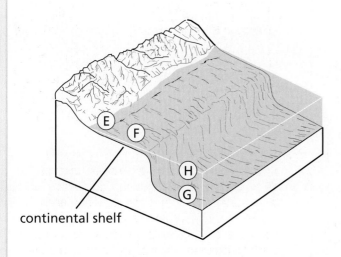

continental shelf

1. Which area is most affected by tides?

  a. E   **c.** G

  b. F   **d.** H

2. Kelps are plantlike algae that grow attached to the ocean bottom. At which points could kelps live?

  a. H and F   **c.** F and G

  b. F only   **d.** G only

3. Where is water the coldest?

  a. E   **c.** G

  b. F   **d.** H

4. Which statement best explains why plantlike algae do not live at G?

  a. The water is too salty at position G.

  b. The water is too cold at position G.

  c. There is not enough oxygen at position G.

  d. There is not enough sunlight at position G.

5. Which trait is most useful for fish in position H as they try to escape predators?

  a. the ability to hide in rocks

  b. the ability to blend in with plants

  c. the ability to swim very fast

  d. the ability to swim without sunlight

6. A limpet is an ocean snail whose flat shape allows it to remain attached to rocks even when waves are pounding against the rocks. Where does the limpet probably live?

  a. E   **c.** G

  b. F   **d.** H

Extended Response

The illustration on the right shows part of an ocean food web. Use the illustration to answer the next two questions in detail.

7. Describe how the killer whale, salmon, and zooplankton in the illustration are linked.

8. What would happen if overfishing caused herring to be removed from the food web? Describe how the other organisms would be affected.

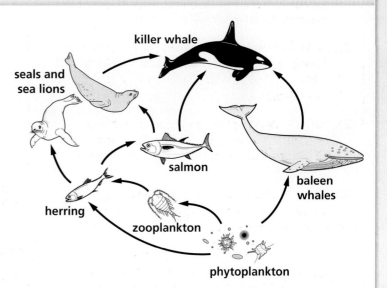

killer whale

seals and sea lions

salmon

baleen whales

herring

zooplankton

phytoplankton

UNIT D

Earth's Atmosphere

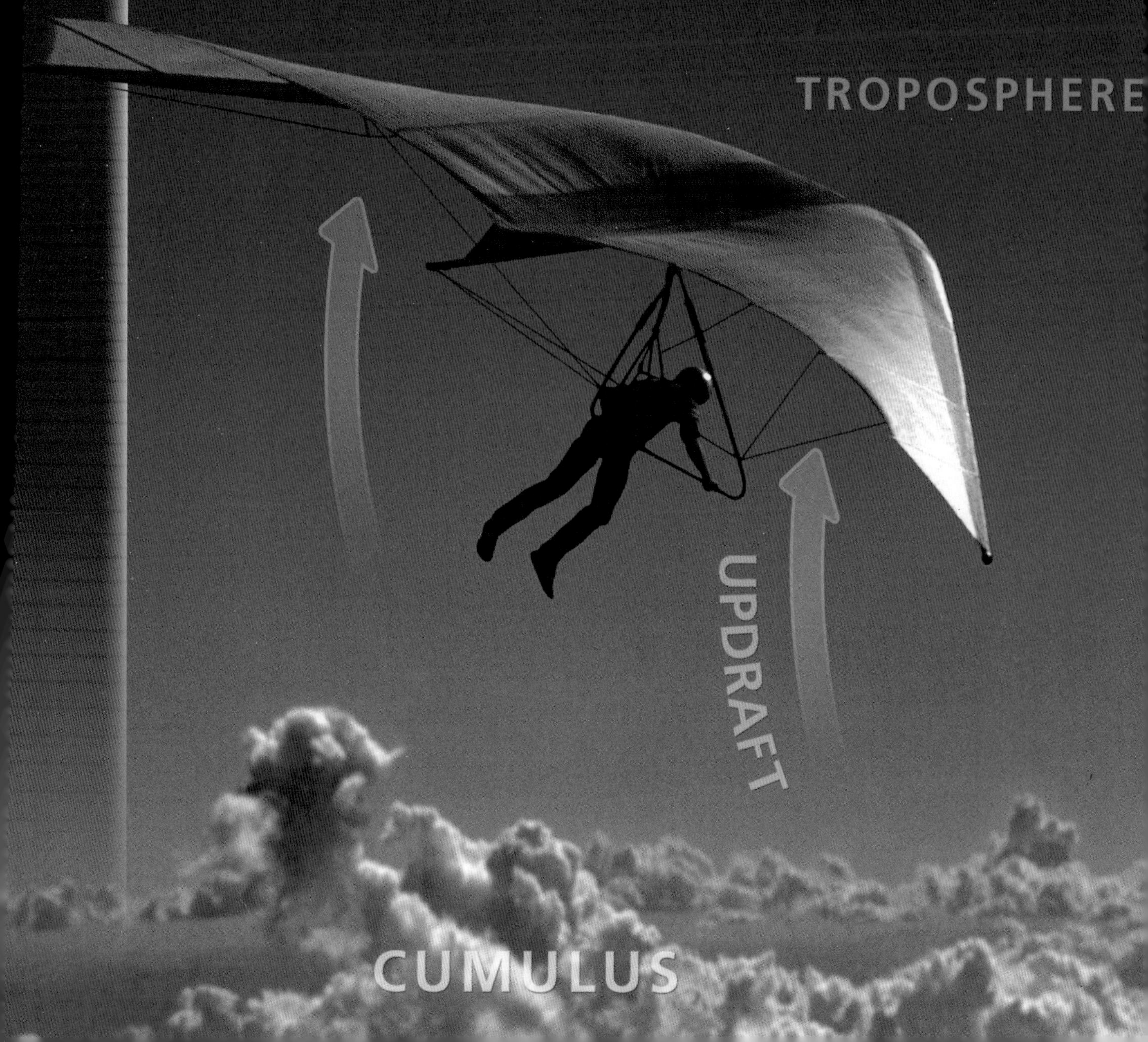
TROPOSPHERE
UPDRAFT
CUMULUS

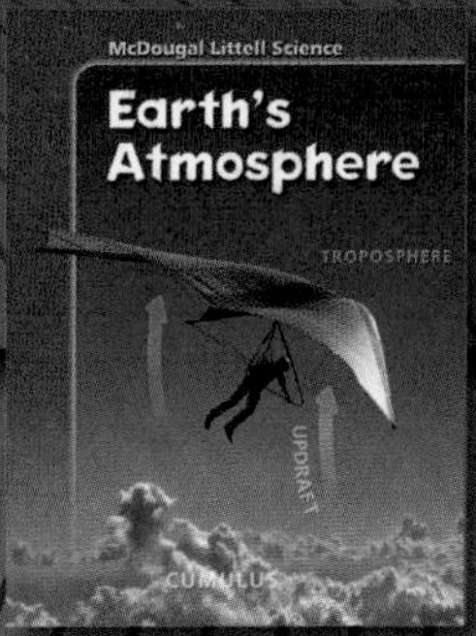

Earth's Atmosphere
Contents Overview

Unit Features

1 Earth's Changing Atmosphere   6

(the **BIG** idea)

Earth's atmosphere is a blanket of
gases that supports and protects life.

2 Weather Patterns   40

(the **BIG** idea)

Some features of weather have predictable patterns.

3 Weather Fronts and Storms   76

(the **BIG** idea)

The interaction of air masses causes
changes in weather.

4 Climate and Climate Change   114

(the **BIG** idea)

Climates are long-term weather patterns
that may change over time.

/

DUST in the AIR

What happens around this beautiful island in the Caribbean when dust from an African storm travels thousands of kilometers across the ocean?

SCIENTIFIC AMERICAN FRONTIERS

Learn more about the scientists studying dust in the atmosphere. See the video "Dust Busting."

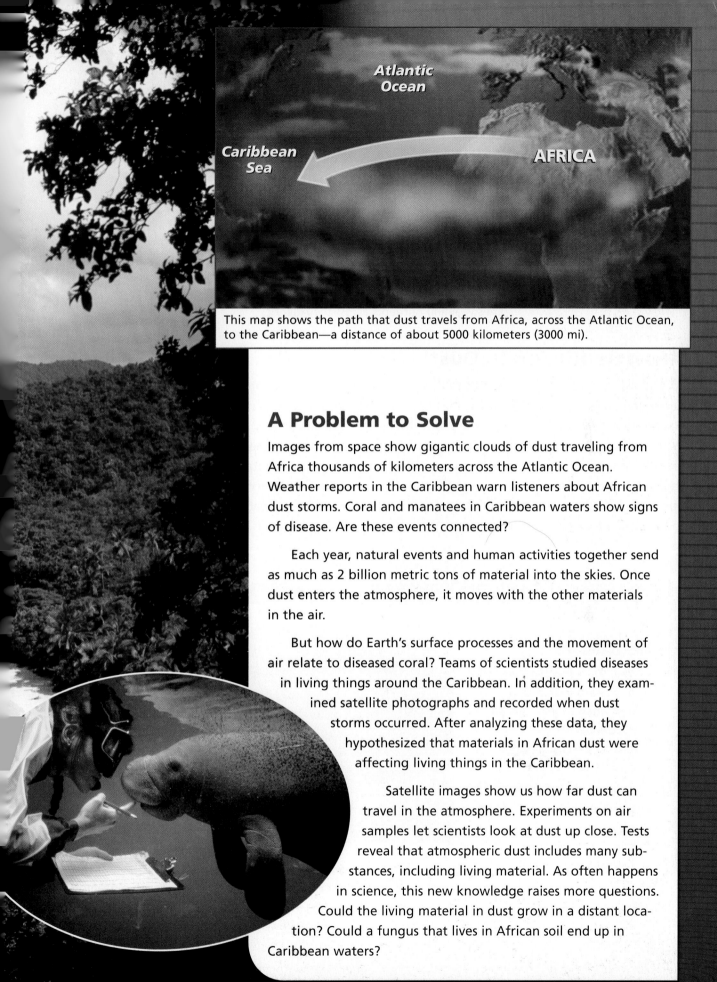

Atlantic
Ocean

Caribbean
Sea

AFRICA

This map shows the path that dust travels from Africa, across the Atlantic Ocean,
to the Caribbean—a distance of about 5000 kilometers (3000 mi).

A Problem to Solve

Images from space show gigantic clouds of dust traveling from
Africa thousands of kilometers across the Atlantic Ocean.
Weather reports in the Caribbean warn listeners about African
dust storms. Coral and manatees in Caribbean waters show signs
of disease. Are these events connected?

Each year, natural events and human activities together send
as much as 2 billion metric tons of material into the skies. Once
dust enters the atmosphere, it moves with the other materials
in the air.

But how do Earth's surface processes and the movement of
air relate to diseased coral? Teams of scientists studied diseases
in living things around the Caribbean. In addition, they examined satellite photographs and recorded when dust
storms occurred. After analyzing these data, they
hypothesized that materials in African dust were
affecting living things in the Caribbean.

Satellite images show us how far dust can
travel in the atmosphere. Experiments on air
samples let scientists look at dust up close. Tests
reveal that atmospheric dust includes many substances, including living material. As often happens
in science, this new knowledge raises more questions.
Could the living material in dust grow in a distant location? Could a fungus that lives in African soil end up in
Caribbean waters?

bromeliad plant

Wind-borne dust provides nutrients for this bromeliad plant growing on a tree trunk high in the rain forest of South America.

dust storm

Atlantic Ocean

AFRICA

The huge dust storm shown in this satellite image carries both destructive fungus spores and life-sustaining nutrients across the Atlantic.

sea fan

Fungus spores carried on dust particles have infected sea-fan corals growing on this reef near the island of St. John in the Caribbean Sea.

Answers Hidden in Dust

To explore these questions, scientists in the Caribbean gather air samples during dust storms. They collect dust from high in the air and from locations closer to Earth's surface. To collect the samples, scientists pull air through a paper filter, trapping the dust. Once they have caught the dust, the scientists are ready to perform tests to see what's really in the tiny particles.

In the laboratory, researchers place dust samples on top of nutrients in petri dishes. Then they see if anything in the dust grows. Recent studies have shown that dust samples collected over the Caribbean contained African fungi and bacteria. More importantly, scientists saw that, even after their long voyage through the atmosphere, the living materials were able to grow.

SCIENTIFIC AMERICAN FRONTIERS

View the "Dust Busting", segment of your *Scientific American Frontiers* video to learn about the detective work that went into solving the mystery of sea-fan disease.

IN THIS SCENE FROM THE VIDEO ▶ Biologist Ginger Garrison shows diseased coral to host Alan Alda.

MYSTERY SOLVED Sea fans are an important part of the Caribbean coral-reef community, but in the 1970s they began to die off. Recently marine biologist Garriet Smith was surprised to discover that a common soil fungus, called aspergillus, was killing the sea fans. But how could a soil fungus reach an undersea reef?

The answer came from geologist Gene Shinn, who knew that global winds carry dust from Africa to the Caribbean. When Shinn read about Smith's research, he hypothesized that aspergillus might be arriving with African dust. Shinn teamed up with Smith and biologist Ginger Garrison to test the hypothesis. They collected Caribbean air samples during an African dust event and cultured dust from the samples. Aspergillus grew in their very first cultures.

Dust from Africa also contains tiny bits of metals, such as iron. The soil and atmosphere in the Caribbean are enriched by iron carried in African dust. Beautiful plants called bromeliads get the iron they need directly from the atmosphere.

Unfortunately, some of the materials found in the dust samples could be harmful to living things, such as manatees and corals. One of the fungi found in Caribbean dust samples is *Aspergillus sydowii,* which may cause diseases in sea fans and other corals. In addition, the dust contains bacteria that may speed the growth of toxic red algae, which can be harmful to manatees and other ocean animals.

Strong Connections

Dust storms affect the entire planet. On April 6–8, 2001, soils from the Gobi Desert in Mongolia and China blew into the air, creating a massive dust cloud. Satellite images showed the cloud traveling eastward. A few days later people in the western United States saw the sky turn a chalky white.

Such observations of atmospheric dust show us how events in one part of the planet can affect living and nonliving things thousands of kilometers away in ways we might not have imagined.

UNANSWERED Questions

Tiny particles of atmospheric dust may have huge effects. Yet the more we learn about the makeup and nature of dust, the more questions we have.

- How do dust storms affect human health?
- What can dust tell us about climate change?
- How can we use information about dust storms to predict climate change?
- How do materials in dust change ecosystems?

UNIT PROJECTS

As you study this unit, work alone or with a group on one of these projects.

TV News Report

Prepare a brief news report on recent dust storms, using visuals and a script.

- Research dust storms that have occurred recently. Find out how they were related to the weather.
- Copy or print visuals, and write and practice delivering your report. Then make your presentation.

Map the Dust

Make a map showing how dust arrives in your area or another location.

- Find out what the dust contains and how it moved there. Collect information from atlases, the Internet, newspapers, and magazines.
- Prepare your map, including all the areas you need to show. Include a key, a title, and a compass rose.

Design an Experiment

Design an experiment to explore how the atmosphere has changed in the past or how it is changing today. Research the forms of evidence scientists gather about the state of our atmosphere.

- Pick one question to investigate in an experiment. Write a hypothesis.
- List and assemble materials for your experiment. Create a data table and write up your procedure.
- Demonstrate or describe your experiment for the class.

CAREER CENTER
CLASSZONE.COM
Learn about careers in meteorology.

CHAPTER

1

Earth's Changing Atmosphere

the BIG idea

Earth's atmosphere is a blanket of gases that supports and protects life.

Key Concepts

SECTION

1.1 Earth's atmosphere supports life.
Learn about the materials that make up the atmosphere.

SECTION

1.2 The Sun supplies the atmosphere's energy.
Learn how energy from the Sun affects the atmosphere.

SECTION

1.3 Gases in the atmosphere absorb radiation.
Learn about the ozone layer and the greenhouse effect.

SECTION

1.4 Human activities affect the atmosphere.
Learn about pollution, global warming, and changes in the ozone layer.

Internet Preview

CLASSZONE.COM

Chapter 1 online resources: Content Review, two Visualizations, two Resource Centers, Math Tutorial, Test Practice

What will make this kite soar?

EXPLORE (the BIG idea)

How Heavy Is Paper?

Put a ruler on a table with one end off the edge. Tap on the ruler lightly and observe what happens. Then cover the ruler with a sheet of paper as shown. Tap again on the ruler and observe what happens.

Observe and Think
What happened to the ruler when you tapped lightly on it with and without the sheet of paper? Was the paper heavy enough by itself to hold the ruler down?

How Does Heating Affect Air?

Stretch the lip of a balloon over the neck of a small bottle. Next, fill a bowl with ice water and a second bowl with hot tap water. Place the bottle upright in the hot water. After 5 minutes, move the bottle to the cold water.

Observe and Think What changes did you observe in the balloon? What might have caused these changes?

Internet Activity: Atmosphere

Go to **ClassZone.com** to learn about Earth's atmosphere.

Observe and Think How does the thickness of the atmosphere compare with the height of a mountain or the altitude of the space shuttle in orbit?

NSTA
scilinks.org
SCI LINKS

Composition of the Atmosphere **Code: MDL009**

Getting Ready to Learn

CONCEPT REVIEW

- Matter is made up of atoms.
- All things on or near Earth are pulled toward Earth by its gravity.
- Heating or cooling any material changes some of its properties.

VOCABULARY REVIEW

See Glossary for definitions.

atom   **mass**

gas   **molecule**

gravity

CONTENT REVIEW
CLASSZONE.COM
Review concepts and vocabulary.

► TAKING NOTES

SUPPORTING MAIN IDEAS

Make a chart to show main ideas and the information that supports them. Write each blue heading from the chapter in a separate box. In boxes below it, add supporting information, such as reasons, explanations, and examples.

VOCABULARY STRATEGY

Write each new vocabulary term in the center of a **frame game** diagram. Decide what information to frame the term with. Use examples, descriptions, pictures, or sentences in which the term is used in context. You can change the frame to fit each term.

See the Note-Taking Handbook on pages R45–R51.

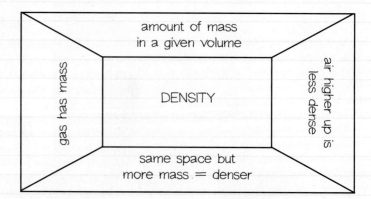

SCIENCE NOTEBOOK

The atmosphere makes life on Earth possible.

Living things use gases in the air.

The atmosphere keeps Earth warm.

The atmosphere protects life.

amount of mass in a given volume

gas has mass

DENSITY

air higher up is less dense

same space but more mass = denser

KEY CONCEPT
Earth's atmosphere supports life.

◀ **BEFORE, you learned**

- Living things need food, water, and air
- Matter can be solid, liquid, or gas

▶ **NOW, you will learn**

- Why the atmosphere is important to living things
- What the atmosphere is made of
- How natural cycles affect the atmosphere

VOCABULARY

atmosphere p. 9
altitude p. 10
density p. 10
cycle p. 12

EXPLORE Air Resistance

How does air affect falling objects?

PROCEDURE

MATERIALS
- metal washer
- coffee filter
- tape

① Drop the washer from shoulder height.

② Tape the metal washer to the center of the coffee filter. The filter will act as a parachute.

③ Drop the washer with the parachute from shoulder height.

WHAT DO YOU THINK?
- What difference did the parachute make?
- What do your results tell you about air?

VOCABULARY
Remember to make a frame game diagram for the term *atmosphere*.

The atmosphere makes life on Earth possible.

Every time you breathe in, your lungs fill with air, which is a mixture of gases. Your body uses materials from the air to help you stay alive. The **atmosphere** is a whole layer of air that surrounds Earth. The atmosphere supports life and protects it. The gases of the atmosphere keep Earth warm and transport energy to different regions of the planet. Without the atmosphere, the oceans would not exist, life would not survive, and the planet would be a cold, lifeless rock.

Even though the atmosphere is very important to life, it is surprisingly thin. If the solid part of Earth were the size of a peach, most of the atmosphere would be no thicker than the peach fuzz surrounding the fruit. The atmosphere is a small but important part of the Earth system.

 CHECK YOUR READING How does the atmosphere make life possible? Find three examples in the text above.

Characteristics of the Atmosphere

In 1862 two British balloonists reached the highest **altitude,** or distance above sea level, any human had ever reached. As their balloon rose to 8.8 kilometers (5.5 mi), one balloonist fainted and the other barely managed to bring the balloon back down. They found that the air becomes thinner as altitude increases.

The thickness or thinness of air is measured by its density. **Density** is the amount of mass in a given volume of a substance. If two objects take up the same amount of space, then the object with more mass has a greater density than the one with less mass. For example, a bowling ball has a higher density than a soccer ball.

The atmosphere's density decreases as you travel upward. The air on top of a mountain is less dense than the air at sea level. A deep breath of mountain air fills your lungs but contains less mass—less gas—than a deep breath of air at sea level. Higher up, at altitudes where jets fly, a breath of air would contain only about one-tenth the mass of a breath of air at sea level. The air farther above Earth's surface contains even less mass. There is no definite top to the atmosphere. It just keeps getting less dense as you get farther from Earth's surface. However, altitudes 500 kilometers (300 mi) or more above Earth's surface can be called outer space.

The decrease of density with greater altitude means that most of the mass of the atmosphere is close to Earth's surface. In fact, more than 99 percent of the atmosphere's mass is in the lowest 30 kilometers (20 mi).

INFER This climber has reached the top of Mount Everest, 8850 m (29,000 ft) above sea level in Nepal. Why does he need an oxygen mask?

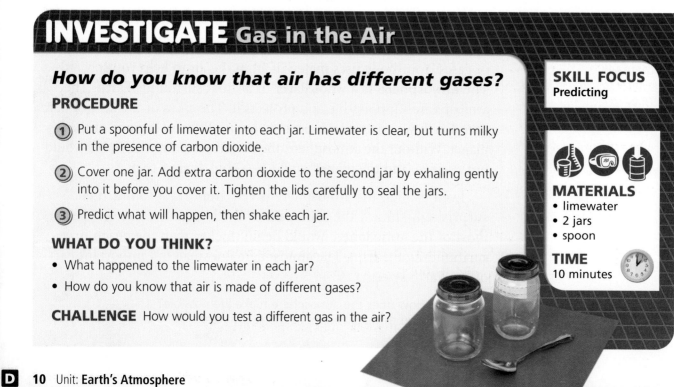

INVESTIGATE Gas in the Air

How do you know that air has different gases?

PROCEDURE

1. Put a spoonful of limewater into each jar. Limewater is clear, but turns milky in the presence of carbon dioxide.

2. Cover one jar. Add extra carbon dioxide to the second jar by exhaling gently into it before you cover it. Tighten the lids carefully to seal the jars.

3. Predict what will happen, then shake each jar.

WHAT DO YOU THINK?

- What happened to the limewater in each jar?
- How do you know that air is made of different gases?

CHALLENGE How would you test a different gas in the air?

SKILL FOCUS
Predicting

MATERIALS
- limewater
- 2 jars
- spoon

TIME
10 minutes

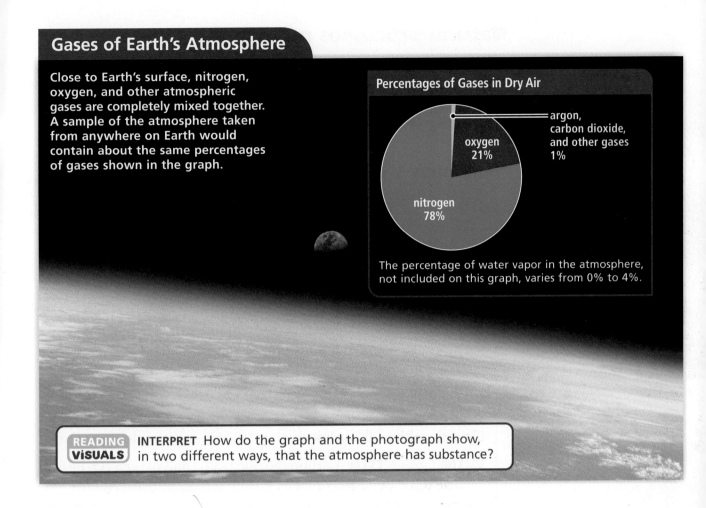

Gases of Earth's Atmosphere

Close to Earth's surface, nitrogen, oxygen, and other atmospheric gases are completely mixed together. A sample of the atmosphere taken from anywhere on Earth would contain about the same percentages of gases shown in the graph.

Percentages of Gases in Dry Air

argon, carbon dioxide, and other gases 1%

oxygen 21%

nitrogen 78%

The percentage of water vapor in the atmosphere, not included on this graph, varies from 0% to 4%.

READING VISUALS INTERPRET How do the graph and the photograph show, in two different ways, that the atmosphere has substance?

Materials in the Atmosphere

Most of the materials in the atmosphere are gases. However, the atmosphere also contains tiny particles of solid or liquid material such as dust, sea salt, and water droplets. Perhaps you have sat by an open window and noticed some of these particles on the window sill.

If you were to write a recipe for air, you would include nitrogen gas as the main ingredient. In dry air, about 78 percent of the gas is nitrogen. The next most common ingredient is oxygen gas, which makes up about 21 percent of the atmosphere. Argon, carbon dioxide, and other gases make up about 1 percent of the atmosphere. Unlike the amounts of nitrogen and other gases, the amount of water vapor varies a great deal. In some places at some times, water vapor can make up as much as 4 percent of the air.

READING TiP

As you read about the amounts of gases, find each gas on the graph above.

The atmosphere's gases provide materials essential for living things. Nitrogen promotes plant growth and is an important ingredient in the chemicals that make up living things. Oxygen is necessary for animals and plants to perform life processes. Plants use carbon dioxide and water to make food.

CHECK YOUR READING Which gas is the most common material in the air around you?

Natural processes modify the atmosphere.

The exact amounts of some gases in the air change depending on location, time of day, season, and other factors. Water vapor, carbon dioxide, and other gases in the atmosphere are affected by both ongoing processes and sudden changes.

Ongoing Processes

SUPPORTING MAIN IDEAS
Make a chart about processes that modify the atmosphere.

You and all other living things participate in ongoing processes. For example, each day you breathe in and out about 13,000 liters (3,000 gal) of air—about as much air as would fill five school buses. When you breathe, your body exchanges gases with the atmosphere. The air you inhale is a slightly different mixture of gases than the air you exhale.

Living things take part in a repeated process of gas exchange with the atmosphere. In addition, living things continually exchange materials in solid and liquid form with the environment. Processes like these that repeat over and over are called **cycles.**

Three of the most important cycles that affect the atmosphere are the carbon cycle, the nitrogen cycle, and the water cycle.

1 The Carbon Cycle Carbon dioxide (CO_2) and oxygen (O_2) gases constantly circulate, or cycle, among plants, animals, and the atmosphere. For example,

- Animals inhale air, use some of its oxygen, and exhale air that has less oxygen but more carbon dioxide and water
- Plants take in carbon dioxide and release oxygen as they make food in the process of photosynthesis

2 The Nitrogen Cycle Different forms of nitrogen cycle among the atmosphere, the soil, and living organisms. For example,

- Tiny organisms remove nitrogen gas (N_2) from the air and transform it into other chemicals, which then enter the soil
- Plants and animals use solids and liquids that contain nitrogen, which returns to the soil when the organisms die and decay
- The soil slowly releases nitrogen back into the air as nitrogen gas

3 The Water Cycle Different forms of water (H_2O) cycle between Earth's surface and the atmosphere. For example,

- Liquid water from oceans and lakes changes into gas and enters the atmosphere
- Plants release water vapor from their leaves
- Liquid water falls from the atmosphere as rain

READING TiP
In the diagrams on page 13, color is used to show particular materials.

 O_2 is red.

 CO_2 is purple.

 N_2 is aqua.

 H_2O is blue.

Cycles and the Atmosphere

A tiger breathing, leaves decaying, trees growing—all are involved in cycles that affect our atmosphere. The diagrams to the right show how materials move in three important cycles.

1 Carbon Cycle

▶ The tiger exhales carbon dioxide (CO_2). Carbon dioxide is taken in by the tree.
▶ The tree releases oxygen (O_2). Oxygen is taken in by the tiger.

2 Nitrogen Cycle

▶ Tiny organisms convert nitrogen gas (N_2) to other forms used by the tree.
▶ Decaying leaves release nitrogen gas (N_2) back into the atmosphere.

3 Water Cycle

▶ Water vapor (H_2O gas) turns to liquid and rains down to Earth's surface.
▶ Water from the lake changes to gas and returns to the atmosphere.

READING VISUALS COMPARE AND CONTRAST How are the three cycles similar? How are they different?

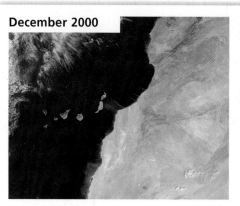

December 2000

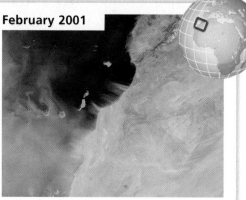

February 2001

READING VISUALS **COMPARE AND CONTRAST** These satellite images show north-western Africa before and during a dust storm. How does the second image differ from the first?

Sudden Changes

In addition to ongoing processes, dramatic events may cause changes in the atmosphere. When sudden events occur, it takes time before the atmosphere is able to restore balance.

- **Volcanic Eruptions** Volcanoes shoot gases and huge amounts of ash into the atmosphere. Certain gases produce a haze that may affect the air for many months and lower temperatures worldwide.

- **Forest Fires** When forests burn, the carbon that makes up each tree combines with oxygen and enters the atmosphere as carbon dioxide. Wood ash also enters the atmosphere.

- **Dust Storms** Wind, water, or drought can loosen soil. Powerful windstorms may then raise clouds of this eroded soil, as in the second picture above. These storms add huge amounts of particles to the air for a time.

1.1 Review

KEY CONCEPTS

1. How is the atmosphere important to living things?

2. What substances make up air?

3. Draw a diagram to show how one natural cycle affects the atmosphere.

CRITICAL THINKING

4. **Apply** Give three examples from everyday life of how the atmosphere supports and protects life.

5. **Predict** How would the atmosphere in your area change if a disease killed all the plants?

⬧ CHALLENGE

6. **Compare** Carbon dioxide enters the oceans from the air. Some carbon becomes stored in shells, and then in rocks. Eventually, it can be released back into the air by volcanoes in the form of carbon dioxide. How are these slow processes similar to the cycles shown on page 13?

CONNECTING SCIENCES

EARTH SCIENCE AND PHYSICAL SCIENCE

Carbon Cycle Chemistry

The atmosphere is keeping you alive. Every time you breathe, you take in the oxygen that you need to live. But that's not the end of the story. The food you eat would not exist without the carbon dioxide in the air that you, and every other animal on Earth, breathe out.

A Closer Look at Oxygen and Carbon Dioxide

Gases in air are tiny molecules that are much too small to see, even if you look through a microscope. Chemists use diagrams to represent these molecules. Oxygen gas (O_2) is made of two atoms of oxygen, so a diagram of an oxygen gas molecule shows two red balls stuck together. A diagram of a carbon dioxide molecule (CO_2) looks similar, but it has one black carbon atom in addition to two red oxygen atoms.

oxygen

carbon dioxide

The Carbon Cycle

carbon in food

oxygen in air

carbon dioxide in air

1 The tree takes carbon from the air.

2 You move carbon from food back into the air.

The Carbon Connection

1 The orange tree takes in carbon dioxide from the air. Molecules of carbon dioxide are broken apart, and some carbon atoms become part of other more complex molecules in the growing orange.

2 You take carbon-containing molecules into your body when you eat the orange. Later, your body uses the food to carry out life processes. Some of the carbon atoms become part of carbon dioxide molecules, which you exhale into the air.

The carbon dioxide you exhale may be taken in again by the tree. This time, the carbon may become part of the trunk of the tree, and then return to the air when the tree dies and decays. Carbon keeps going around and around among living things and the atmosphere.

EXPLORE

1. **COMPARE AND CONTRAST** What is the difference between a carbon dioxide molecule and an oxygen molecule?

2. **CHALLENGE** Draw a diagram showing how carbon can move into and out of the air when a tree grows and then later dies and decays.

The Sun supplies the atmosphere's energy.

◀ **BEFORE, you learned**

- The atmosphere supports and protects life
- The atmosphere contains a mixture of gases
- The atmosphere is affected by natural processes

▶ **NOW, you will learn**

- How solar energy heats Earth's surface and atmosphere
- How the atmosphere moves heat energy around
- About the layers of the atmosphere

VOCABULARY

radiation p. 17
conduction p. 18
convection p. 19

THINK ABOUT

Can you feel sunlight?

If you have been on a hot beach, you have felt energy from sunlight. Perhaps you felt sunlight warming your skin or hot sand underneath your feet. It is easy to notice the energy of sunlight when it makes the ground or your skin warm. Where else does the energy from sunlight go?

Energy from the Sun heats the atmosphere.

SUPPORTING MAIN IDEAS
Write the blue heading into your notes to begin a new chart. Add supporting details.

It may seem hard to believe, but almost all the energy around you comes from the Sun. That means that food energy, fires, and even the warmth of your own body can be traced back to energy from the Sun. A lot of this energy reaches Earth in a form you can see—visible light.

Two main things happen to the sunlight that reaches Earth. Some is reflected, or sent in a new direction. You see most of the objects around you by reflected light. The sand in the picture above looks light in color because it reflects much of the sunlight that hits it. Some of the sunlight that reaches Earth's surface is absorbed. The energy from this light heats the substance that absorbs it. The sand can become warm or even hot as it absorbs some of the sunlight that hits it. Some objects, such as the striped shirts above, have bright parts that reflect more light and dark parts that absorb more light.

CHECK YOUR READING What two things happen to the sunlight that reaches Earth?

The light that you can see is one type of radiation. **Radiation** (RAY-dee-AY-shuhn) is energy that travels across distances in the form of certain types of waves. Visible light and other types of radiation can be absorbed or reflected.

The diagram shows the average amounts of solar radiation, or radiation from the Sun, that are absorbed and reflected by Earth's atmosphere, clouds, and surface. Each arrow in the diagram represents 5 percent of the solar radiation that reaches Earth. As you can see, about 30 percent of the solar energy that reaches Earth is reflected. Clouds and snow-covered ground are white, so they reflect a lot of the radiation that hits them. Air also reflects some radiation. The energy of the reflected radiation goes back into outer space.

The other 70 percent of solar radiation that reaches Earth is absorbed. Most of this energy is absorbed by oceans, landforms, and living things. The absorbed energy heats Earth's surface. In the same way, energy that is absorbed by gas molecules, clouds, and dust particles heats the atmosphere.

Solar Radiation

Arrows show the average global reflection and absorption of solar radiation.

About 5% of solar energy is reflected by Earth's surface.

About 25% of solar energy is reflected by clouds and Earth's atmosphere.

About 20% of solar energy is absorbed by clouds and the atmosphere.

About 50% of solar energy is absorbed by Earth's surface.

The atmosphere is much smaller than shown.

INVESTIGATE Solar Radiation

How does reflection affect temperature?

PROCEDURE

1. Cover the top of one cup with plastic wrap. Cover the second cup with paper. Secure the plastic wrap and paper with tape.

2. Poke a small slit in each cup's cover. Insert a thermometer through each slit.

3. Place the cups in direct sunlight. Record their temperature every minute for 15 minutes.

WHAT DO YOU THINK?

• How did the temperature change inside each cup?

• How did the coverings contribute to these changes?

CHALLENGE What does the paper represent in this model?

SKILL FOCUS
Measuring

MATERIALS
• 2 cups
• plastic wrap
• white paper
• tape
• 2 short thermometers
• watch

TIME

25 minutes

The atmosphere moves energy.

If you walk along a sunny beach, you may be comfortably warm except for the burning-hot soles of your feet. The sand may be much hotter than the air. The sand absorbs solar energy all day and stores it in one place. The air also absorbs solar energy but moves it around and spreads it out. Radiation, conduction, and convection are processes that move energy from place to place.

Radiation You have already read that solar radiation warms a sandy beach. You may be surprised to learn that radiation also transfers energy from the sand to the air. Earth's surface gives off a type of invisible radiation, called infrared radiation, that can be absorbed by certain gases. The energy from the radiation warms the air. The air also gives off infrared radiation. You will read more about this cycle of radiation in Section 1.3.

Conduction Another way that sand warms the air is through conduction. When you walk barefoot on a hot beach, rapidly moving molecules in the hot sand bump against molecules in your feet. This process transfers energy to your feet, which get hot. **Conduction** is the transfer of heat energy from one substance to another by direct contact. Earth's surface transfers energy to the atmosphere by conduction, such as when hot beach sand warms the air above it. Molecules of air can

VOCABULARY
Add new terms to your notebook.

Transfer of Energy

Radiation, conduction, and convection move energy from place to place.

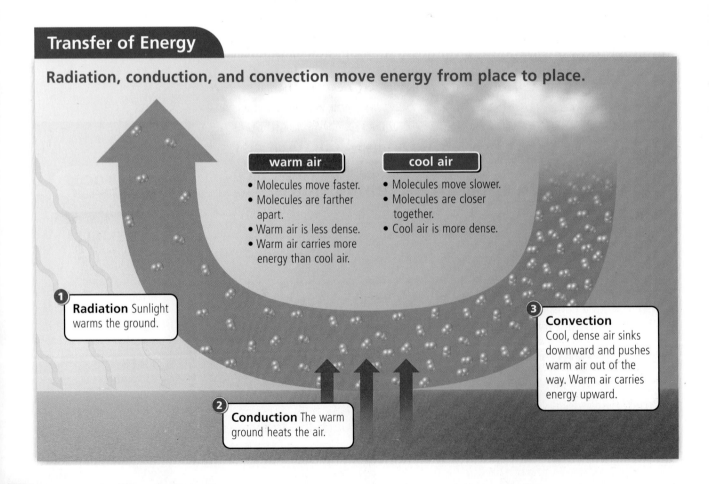

warm air
- Molecules move faster.
- Molecules are farther apart.
- Warm air is less dense.
- Warm air carries more energy than cool air.

cool air
- Molecules move slower.
- Molecules are closer together.
- Cool air is more dense.

1 **Radiation** Sunlight warms the ground.

2 **Conduction** The warm ground heats the air.

3 **Convection** Cool, dense air sinks downward and pushes warm air out of the way. Warm air carries energy upward.

gain energy when they collide with molecules in grains of hot sand. The air just above the sand gets warm. Energy can also spread slowly through the air by conduction as air molecules bump into one another.

Convection Heated air can move easily from place to place. When a heated liquid or gas moves, it carries energy along with it. **Convection** is the transfer of energy from place to place by the motion of gas or liquid. When scientists talk about convection in the atmosphere, they usually mean the motion of gases up and down rather than side to side. The heat energy comes from below and is moved upward. Think once more about the beach. First, radiation from the Sun warms the sand. Second, the hot sand conducts energy to the air. Third, the warm air carries energy upward in convection. Follow this cycle of radiation, conduction, and convection in the diagram on page 18.

Moving hot air near the flames makes the mountain behind appear distorted.

 Compare conduction and convection. How are they similar?

Differences in density produce the motion of air convection. You have read that the atmosphere is less dense at higher altitudes. At any particular altitude, however, the density of air depends mostly on its temperature. Warm air has more energy, so the molecules move faster than they do in cool air. The motion makes the molecules collide more, so they stay farther apart. When there is more space between molecules, the air is less dense.

Imagine a box full of warm air and another box of the same size full of cool air. If you could see air molecules, you would find more molecules—more mass—in the box of cool air. Cool, dense air is heavier, so it tends to sink and push warm, less dense air upward.

As it moves upward, warm air carries energy away from the ground. The air can cool as it rises. Eventually, the air can become cool enough—dense enough—to sink back to the ground, where it may heat up again.

 REMINDER
Density is the amount of mass in a given volume of a substance.

 **VISUALIZATION**
CLASSZONE.COM

See radiation, conduction, and convection in action.

The atmosphere has temperature layers.

Density is not the only characteristic of the atmosphere that changes with altitude. Different parts of the atmosphere absorb and move energy in different ways. As a result, the air's temperature changes with altitude. Scientists use the patterns of these temperature changes to define four layers of the atmosphere. To explore these layers, turn the page and ride an imaginary elevator up through the atmosphere.

Temperature Layers

Explore the atmosphere's temperature layers by riding an imaginary elevator up from the ground.

Thermosphere
Continue through the thermosphere. The air thins out until you reach outer space.

Mesosphere
Reach the mesosphere after rising 50 km (31 mi) off the ground. You are now above 99.9% of the molecules of Earth's air.

Stratosphere
Pass through the stratosphere, which includes the ozone layer. The air gets thinner as you move up through the atmosphere.

Troposphere
Board the elevator at ground level, which is also the bottom of the troposphere.

④

③

②

START HERE

①

−85°C (−120°F)

0°C (32°F)

−60°C (−76°F)

15°C (59°F)

ozone

sea level

Thermosphere
Radiation from the Sun heats the thermosphere, causing the temperature to rise as you move upward.

90 km (56 mi) and up

Mesosphere
This layer is heated from below by the stratosphere, and the temperature falls as you move upward.

50–90 km (31–56 mi)

Stratosphere
Ozone in this layer absorbs energy from the Sun and heats the stratosphere. The temperature rises as you move upward.

10–50 km (6–31 mi)

Troposphere
This layer is heated by the ground. The temperature falls as you move upward.

0–10 km (0–6 mi)

READING VISUALS How does the temperature change as you move up through the atmosphere?

① Troposphere (TROH-puh-SFEER) The layer of the atmosphere nearest Earth's surface is called the troposphere because convection seems to turn the air over. This layer contains about 80 percent of the total mass of the atmosphere, including almost all of the water vapor present in the atmosphere. The troposphere is warmed from below by the ground. The temperature is highest at ground level and generally decreases about 6.5°C for each kilometer you rise.

② Stratosphere (STRAT-uh-SFEER) Above the troposphere lies a clear, dry layer of the atmosphere called the stratosphere. Within the stratosphere are molecules of a gas called ozone. These molecules absorb a type of solar radiation that is harmful to life. The energy from the radiation raises the temperature of the air. The temperature increases as you rise high in the stratosphere.

③ Mesosphere (MEHZ-uh-SFEER) The air in the mesosphere is extremely thin. In fact, this layer contains less than 0.1 percent of the atmosphere's mass. Most meteors that enter the atmosphere burn up within the mesosphere. The mesosphere, like the troposphere, is heated from below, so the temperature in the mesosphere decreases as you rise.

④ Thermosphere (THUR-muh-SFEER) The thermosphere starts about 90 kilometers (56 mi) above Earth's surface. It grows less and less dense over hundreds of kilometers until it becomes outer space. The air high in this layer becomes very hot because the molecules absorb a certain type of solar radiation. However, even the hottest air in this layer would feel cold to you because the molecules are so spread out that they would not conduct much energy to your skin. The temperature in the thermosphere increases as you rise.

READING TiP
You can use the word parts to help you recall the temperature layers.
tropo-"turning"
strato-"spreading out"
meso-"middle"
thermo-"heat"

CHECK YOUR READING How does the temperature change in each layer of the atmosphere?

1.2 Review

KEY CONCEPTS

1. What two things happen to solar radiation that reaches Earth?

2. Describe the three processes that transport energy.

3. What characteristic do scientists use to define four layers of Earth's atmosphere?

CRITICAL THINKING

4. **Draw Conclusions** How might a thick, puffy cloud reflect a different amount of the Sun's radiation than a thin, wispy one?

5. **Apply** Jet planes fly near the top of the troposphere. Is it more important to heat or to cool the passenger cabins? Explain your reasoning.

◯ CHALLENGE

6. **Analyze** Earth loses about the same amount of energy as it absorbs from the Sun. If it did not, Earth's temperature would increase. Does the energy move from Earth's surface and atmosphere out to space through radiation, conduction, or convection? Give your reasons.

KEY CONCEPT

Gases in the atmosphere absorb radiation.

BEFORE, you learned

- Solar radiation heats Earth's surface and atmosphere
- Earth's surface and atmosphere give off radiation
- The ozone layer is in the stratosphere

NOW, you will learn

- More about how radiation and gases affect each other
- About the ozone layer and ultraviolet radiation
- About the greenhouse effect

VOCABULARY

ultraviolet radiation p. 23
infrared radiation p. 23
ozone p. 23
greenhouse effect p. 24
greenhouse gas p. 24

EXPLORE Radiation

Can you feel radiation?

PROCEDURE

① Turn on the lamp and wait for it to become warm. It gives off visible and infrared radiation.

② Hold one hand a short distance from the bulb. Record your observations.

③ Turn the lamp off. The bulb continues to give off infrared radiation. Hold your other hand a short distance from the bulb.

WHAT DO YOU THINK?

- What did you see and feel?
- How did radiation affect each hand?

MATERIALS

- lamp

Gases can absorb and give off radiation.

SUPPORTING MAIN IDEAS
Remember to make a chart for each main idea.

On a sunny day, objects around you look bright. Earth's atmosphere reflects or absorbs some sunlight, but allows most of the visible light to pass through to Earth's surface. A cloudy day is darker because clouds reflect and absorb much of the sunlight, so less light passes through to the ground.

The atmosphere can affect light in four ways. It can absorb light, reflect it, or let it pass through. Air can also emit, or give off, light. Although air does not emit much visible light, certain gases absorb and emit radiation that is similar to visible light.

 List four ways that the atmosphere can affect light.

Just as there are sounds humans cannot hear, there are forms of radiation that humans cannot see. Sounds can be too high to hear. In a similar way, waves of **ultraviolet radiation** (UHL-truh-VY-uh-liht) have more energy than the light you can see. Ultraviolet radiation can cause sunburn and other types of damage. Sounds can also be too low for humans to hear. In a similar way, waves of **infrared radiation** (IHN-fruh-REHD) have less energy than visible light. Infrared radiation usually warms the materials that absorb it. Different gases in the atmosphere absorb these two different types of radiation.

The ozone layer protects life from harmful radiation.

In Section 1.2, you read about a gas called ozone that forms in the stratosphere. An **ozone** molecule (O_3) is made of three atoms of the element oxygen. Your body uses regular oxygen gas (O_2), which has two atoms of oxygen. In the stratosphere, ozone and regular oxygen gases break apart and form again in a complex cycle. The reactions that destroy and form ozone normally balance each other, so the cycle can repeat endlessly. Even though ozone is mixed with nitrogen and other gases, the ozone in the stratosphere is called the ozone layer.

The ozone layer protects life on Earth by absorbing harmful ultraviolet radiation from the Sun. Too much ultraviolet radiation can cause sunburn, skin cancer, and damaged eyesight. Ultraviolet radiation can harm crops and materials such as plastic or paint. Ozone absorbs ultraviolet radiation but lets other types of radiation, such as visible light, pass through.

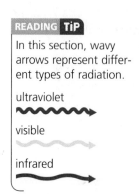

READING TiP

In this section, wavy arrows represent different types of radiation.

ultraviolet

visible

infrared

Ozone in the Stratosphere

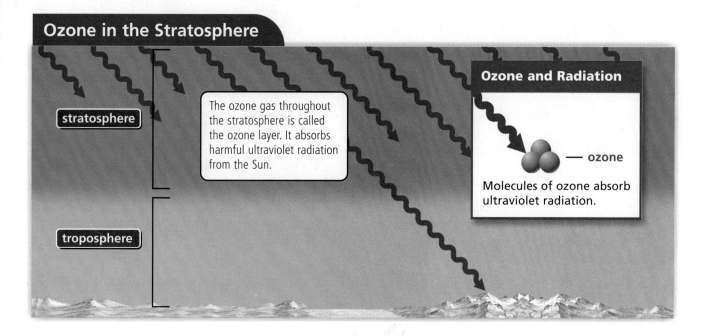

stratosphere

The ozone gas throughout the stratosphere is called the ozone layer. It absorbs harmful ultraviolet radiation from the Sun.

troposphere

Ozone and Radiation

— ozone

Molecules of ozone absorb ultraviolet radiation.

The greenhouse effect keeps Earth warm.

VISUALIZATION
CLASSZONE.COM

See how the greenhouse effect works.

▽ **REMINDER**

Ozone absorbs ultraviolet radiation in the stratosphere. Greenhouse gases absorb and emit infrared radiation in the troposphere.

A jacket helps keep you warm on a cool day by slowing the movement of heat energy away from your body. In a similar way, certain gases in the atmosphere slow the movement of energy away from Earth's surface. The gases absorb and emit infrared radiation, which keeps energy in Earth's system for a while. This process was named the **greenhouse effect** because it reminded scientists of the way glass traps warmth inside a greenhouse.

Carbon dioxide, methane, water vapor, nitrous oxide, and other gases that absorb and give off infrared radiation are known as **greenhouse gases.** Unlike the glass roof and walls of a greenhouse, the greenhouse gases do not form a single layer. They are mixed together with nitrogen, oxygen, and other gases in the air. The atmosphere is densest in the troposphere—the lowest layer—so most of the greenhouse gas molecules are also in the troposphere.

Radiation from the Sun, including visible light, warms Earth's surface, which then emits infrared radiation. If the atmosphere had no greenhouse gases, the infrared radiation would go straight through the atmosphere into outer space. Earth's average surface temperature would be only about −18°C (0°F). Water would freeze, and it would be too cold for most forms of life on Earth to survive.

INVESTIGATE Greenhouse Gases

How have levels of greenhouse gases changed?

Scientists have used ice cores from Antarctica to calculate prehistoric carbon dioxide levels and temperatures. The CO_2 data table has the results for you to plot.

PROCEDURE

① Plot the CO_2 levels on the graph sheet using a regular pencil. Draw line segments to connect the points.

② Plot the temperatures on the same graph using a red pencil. Draw red line segments to connect the points.

WHAT DO YOU THINK?

• How many times during the past 400,000 years were average temperatures in Antarctica above −56°C?

• Do these changes seem to be connected to changes in levels of carbon dioxide? Explain.

CHALLENGE Is it possible to tell from the graph whether temperature affected carbon dioxide levels or carbon dioxide levels affected temperature? Why or why not?

SKILL FOCUS
Graphing

MATERIALS
• Carbon Dioxide Table
• regular pencil
• red pencil

TIME
30 minutes

The Greenhouse Effect

Greenhouse gas molecules absorb and emit infrared radiation.

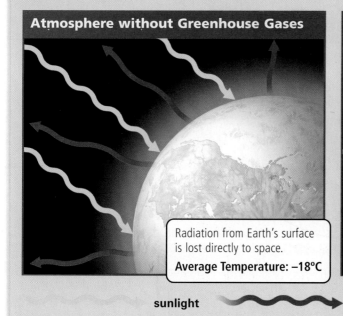

Atmosphere without Greenhouse Gases

Radiation from Earth's surface is lost directly to space.
Average Temperature: –18°C

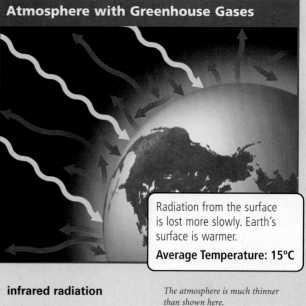

Atmosphere with Greenhouse Gases

Radiation from the surface is lost more slowly. Earth's surface is warmer.
Average Temperature: 15°C

sunlight ➤ infrared radiation

The atmosphere is much thinner than shown here.

Earth's atmosphere does have greenhouse gases. These gases absorb some of the infrared radiation emitted by Earth's surface. The greenhouse gases can then give off this energy as infrared radiation. Some of the energy is absorbed again by the surface, while some of the energy goes out into space. The greenhouse effect keeps Earth's average surface temperature around 15°C (59°F). The energy stays in Earth's system longer with greenhouse gases than without them. In time, all the energy ends up back in outer space. If it did not, Earth would grow warmer and warmer as it absorbed more and more solar radiation.

 **Review**

KEY CONCEPTS

1. Name and describe two of the ways gases can affect radiation.

2. What type of radiation does the ozone layer affect?

3. How do greenhouse gases keep Earth warm?

CRITICAL THINKING

4. **Infer** What would happen if gases in the atmosphere absorbed visible light?

5. **Compare and Contrast** How are ozone and greenhouse gases alike? How are they different?

⚠ CHALLENGE

6. **Predict** How would the temperature on Earth be affected if the amount of greenhouse gases in the atmosphere changed?

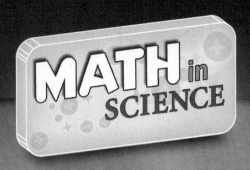

MATH TUTORIAL
CLASSZONE.COM

Click on Math Tutorial for
more help with equations.

SKILL: ALGEBRAIC EQUATIONS

Solar Radiation

The amount of sunlight that reaches Earth's surface varies from day to day. On a cloudy day, for example, clouds may absorb or reflect most of the sunlight before it reaches Earth's surface. You can use equations to determine how much incoming solar radiation is absorbed by Earth's surface on each day.

Example

On a particular cloudy day, 50% of the solar radiation coming into Earth is reflected by clouds and the atmosphere, 40% is absorbed by clouds and the atmosphere, and 1% is reflected by Earth's surface. How much is absorbed by Earth's surface?

Write a verbal model:

radiation reflected by clouds & atmosphere	+	radiation absorbed by clouds & atmosphere	+	radiation reflected by Earth's surface	+	radiation absorbed by Earth's surface	=	total incoming radiation

Substitute into the model: $50\% + 40\% + 1\% + x = 100\%$

Simplify the left side: $91\% + x = 100\%$

Subtract: $-91\% \qquad -91\%$

Simplify: $x = 9\%$

ANSWER 9% of the incoming solar radiation is absorbed by Earth's surface.

Determine the amount of incoming solar radiation that is absorbed by Earth's surface on each day.

1. On a sunny day, 15% is reflected by clouds and the atmosphere, 20% is absorbed by clouds and the atmosphere, and 10% is reflected by Earth's surface.

2. On a partly cloudy day, 25% is reflected by clouds and the atmosphere, 20% is absorbed by clouds and the atmosphere, and 5% is reflected by Earth's surface.

CHALLENGE On a particular day, how much incoming solar radiation is absorbed by Earth's surface if 60% is reflected (either by clouds and the atmosphere or by Earth's surface), and half that amount is absorbed by the atmosphere?

sunny day

partly cloudy day

Human activities affect the atmosphere.

 BEFORE, you learned

- The atmosphere has gases that absorb and give off radiation
- The ozone layer absorbs ultraviolet radiation
- The greenhouse effect keeps Earth warm

NOW, you will learn

- What the types and effects of pollution are
- About the effect of human activities on greenhouse gases
- How the ozone layer is changing

VOCABULARY

air pollution p. 27
particulate p. 28
fossil fuel p. 28
smog p. 28

EXPLORE Air Pollution

Where does smoke go?

PROCEDURE

1. Light the candle and let it burn for a minute or two. Observe the air around the candle.

2. Blow out the candle and observe the smoke until you cannot see it anymore.

MATERIALS
- candle in holder
- matches

WHAT DO YOU THINK?
- How far did the smoke from the candle travel?
- A burning candle produces invisible gases. Where do you think they went?

Human activity can cause air pollution.

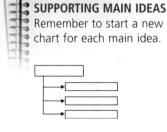

SUPPORTING MAIN IDEAS
Remember to start a new chart for each main idea.

If someone in your kitchen burns a piece of toast, and if a fan is blowing in the hallway, everyone in your home will smell the smoke. That means that everyone will breathe some air containing smoke. Smoke and other harmful materials that are added to the air are called **air pollution.** Outdoors, wind can spread air pollution from place to place the way a fan does within your home.

When toast burns, you may be able to see smoke. If smoke drifts in from another room, it may be too thin to see, but you may be able to smell it. There are other types of air pollution that you cannot see or smell. Like smoke, they can be spread around by wind. Air pollution from one place can affect a wide area. However, most types of pollution leave the air or become thin enough to be harmless after a time.

 How is air pollution moved around?

Types of Pollution

READING **TiP**

Pollution and *pollutant* have the same root, *pollute*—"to make unfit."

Scientists classify the separate types of air pollution, called pollutants, as either gases or particles. Gas pollutants include carbon monoxide, methane, ozone, sulfur oxides, and nitrogen oxides. Some of these gases occur naturally in the atmosphere. These gases are considered pollutants only when they are likely to cause harm. For example, ozone gas is good in the stratosphere but is harmful to breathe. When ozone is in the troposphere, it is a pollutant.

Particle pollutants can be easier to see than gas pollutants. **Particulates** are tiny particles or droplets that are mixed in with air. Smoke contains particulates. The wind can pick up other particulates, such as dust and dirt, pollen, and tiny bits of salt from the oceans. Some sources of pollutants are listed below.

 CHECK YOUR READING What are the two types of pollutants? Give an example of each.

In cities and suburbs, most air pollution comes from the burning of fossil fuels such as oil, gasoline, and coal. **Fossil fuels** are fuels formed from the remains of prehistoric animals and plants. In London in the 1800s, burning coal provided much of the heat and energy for homes and factories. The resulting smoke and local weather conditions often produced a thick fog or cloud. The word **smog** describes this combination of smoke and fog. A newer type of air pollution is also called smog. Sunlight causes the fumes from gasoline, car exhaust, and other gases to react chemically. The reactions form new pollutants, such as ozone, which together are called smog. In cities, there can be enough smog to make a brownish haze.

Sources of Pollution

The burning of fossil fuels in power plants, cars, factories, and homes is a major source of pollution in the United States.

Human Activities

- fossil fuels: gases and particles
- unburned fuels: smog
- manufacturing: gases and particles
- tractors/construction equipment: dust and soil
- farming: fertilizers and pesticides

Natural Sources

- dust, pollen, soil, salt
- volcanoes and forest fires: gases and particles

Effects of Pollution

Air pollution can cause health problems. Polluted air may irritate your eyes, nose, throat, and lungs. It can smell bad or make it hard to breathe. Gases or chemicals from particulates can move from your lungs to other parts of your body. Exercising in polluted air can be dangerous because you take more air into your lungs when you exercise. Over time, people who breathe polluted air can develop lung disease and other health problems. Air pollution can cause extra problems for young children, older adults, and people who suffer from asthma.

A man in Mexico City wears a gas mask while he sells newspapers. The green sign behind him warns people of a high ozone level.

 CHECK YOUR READING Describe three of the ways in which pollution can affect people.

Particulates can stick to surfaces and damage plants, buildings, and other objects outdoors. Dusty air or a dust storm can darken the day and make it difficult to see. Particulates can be carried high into the atmosphere, where they can reflect or absorb sunlight and even affect the weather. Rain clears the air by removing particles and some polluting gases from the air. However, some pollutants are still harmful when rain moves them from the air to the ground, lakes, and oceans.

Controlling Pollution

You may have experienced a smog or ozone alert. In some cities, smog becomes so bad that it is dangerous to exercise outdoors. Weather reports may include smog alerts so that people will know when to be careful. Cities may ask people not to drive cars when the weather conditions are likely to produce smog.

National, state, and local governments work together to reduce air pollution and protect people from its effects. Countries may come to agreements when the air pollution from one country affects another. Within the United States, Congress has passed laws to reduce air pollution. The Clean Air Act limits the amount of air pollution that factories and power plants are allowed to release. The act also sets rules for making car exhaust cleaner. The Environmental Protection Agency measures air pollution and works to enforce the laws passed by Congress.

Human activities are increasing greenhouse gases.

A source of air pollution usually affects areas close to it. In contrast, some natural processes and human activities change the amounts of gases throughout Earth's atmosphere.

Sources of Greenhouse Gases

REMINDER

Plants remove carbon dioxide from the air and store the carbon in solid forms.

You read in Section 1.1 how natural cycles move gases into and out of the atmosphere. Plant growth, forest fires, volcanoes, and other natural processes affect the amounts of carbon dioxide and other greenhouse gases in the atmosphere. The amounts of greenhouse gases then affect temperatures on Earth. In turn, the temperatures affect plant growth and other processes that produce or reduce greenhouse gases.

CHECK YOUR READING How do life and the atmosphere affect each other?

Most greenhouse gases occur naturally. They have helped keep temperatures within a range suitable for the plants and animals that live on Earth. However, human activities are producing greenhouse gases faster than natural processes can remove these gases from the

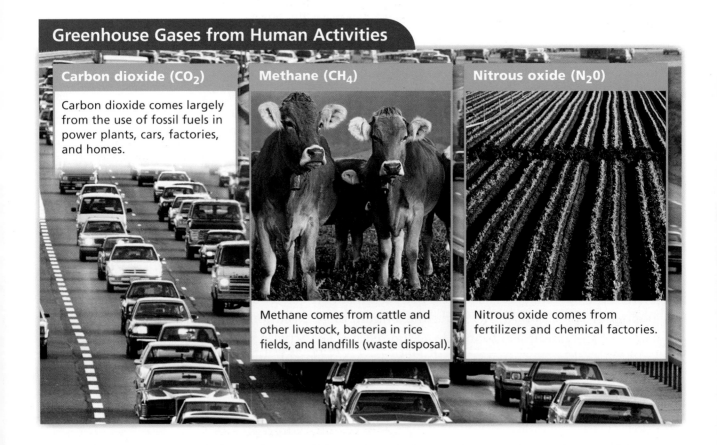

Greenhouse Gases from Human Activities

Carbon dioxide (CO$_2$)

Carbon dioxide comes largely from the use of fossil fuels in power plants, cars, factories, and homes.

Methane (CH$_4$)

Methane comes from cattle and other livestock, bacteria in rice fields, and landfills (waste disposal).

Nitrous oxide (N$_2$O)

Nitrous oxide comes from fertilizers and chemical factories.

atmosphere. Some activities that produce greenhouse gases are shown on page 30. Water vapor is also a greenhouse gas, but the amount of water vapor in the air depends more on weather than on human activity.

Global Warming

Many people are concerned about the amounts of greenhouse gases that humans are adding to the air. Carbon dioxide, for example, can stay in the atmosphere for more than 100 years, so the amounts keep adding up. The air contains about 30 percent more carbon dioxide than it did in the mid-1700s, and the level of carbon dioxide is now increasing about 0.4 percent per year.

 CHECK YOUR READING How are carbon dioxide levels changing?

As the graph below shows, temperatures have risen in recent decades. Earth's atmosphere, water, and other systems work together in complex ways, so it is hard to know exactly how much greenhouse gases change the temperature. Scientists make computer models to understand the effects of greenhouse gases and explore what might happen in the future. The models predict that the average global temperature will continue to rise another 1.4–5.8°C (2.5–10.4°F) by the year 2100. This may not seem like a big change in temperature, but it can have big effects. Global warming can affect sources of food, the amount of water and other resources available, and even human health. You will read more about the possible effects of global warming in Chapter 4.

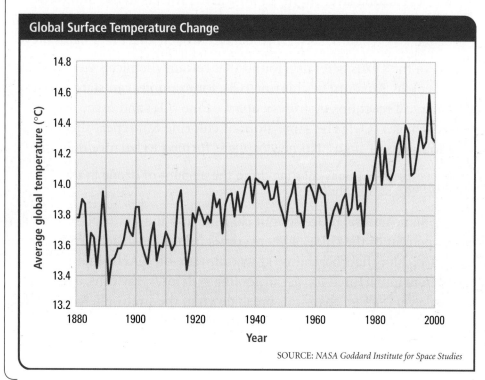

Global Surface Temperature Change

Earth's average temperature has risen over the last century.

SOURCE: *NASA Goddard Institute for Space Studies*

Reducing Greenhouse Gases

Global warming is not a local issue. It affects the atmosphere around the entire planet. An international agreement to limit the amounts of greenhouse gases, called the Kyoto Protocol, would require developed nations to release no more greenhouse gases each year than they did in 1990. The Kyoto Protocol could take effect only if the nations releasing the most greenhouse gases accept the agreement. In 1990, more than one-third of the amount of greenhouse gases released came from the United States, which has not accepted the agreement.

New technologies may help fight the problem of global warming. Scientists are developing ways to heat and cool buildings, transport people and goods, and make products using less energy. Using less energy saves resources and money and it also reduces greenhouse gases. Scientists are also developing ways to produce energy without using any fossil fuels at all.

This commuter is traveling to work without burning fossil fuels.

 How can technology help reduce global warming?

Human activities produce chemicals that destroy the ozone layer.

RESOURCE CENTER
CLASSZONE.COM

Examine the current state of the ozone layer.

At ground level, ozone is a pollutant, but at higher altitudes it benefits life. The ozone layer in the stratosphere protects living things by absorbing harmful ultraviolet radiation. You read in Section 1.3 that ozone is constantly being formed and broken apart in a natural cycle.

In the 1970s, scientists found that certain chemicals were disrupting this cycle. An atom of chlorine (Cl), for example, can start a series of chemical reactions that break apart ozone (O_3) and form regular oxygen gas (O_2). The same atom of chlorine can repeat this process thousands of times. No new ozone is formed to balance the loss.

 What does chlorine do to the amount of ozone in the stratosphere?

Some natural processes put chlorine into the stratosphere, but about 85 percent of the chlorine there comes from human activity. Chemicals called chlorofluorocarbons (KLAWR-oh-FLUR-oh-KAHR-buhnz) have been manufactured for use in cooling systems, spray cans, and foam for packaging. These chemicals break down in the stratosphere and release chlorine and other ozone-destroying chemicals.

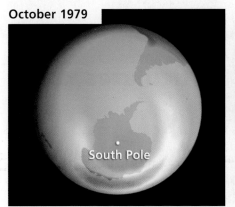
October 1979

South Pole

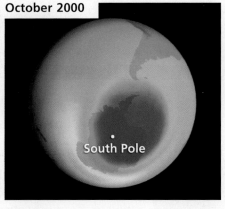
October 2000

South Pole

The size of the dark blue area of little ozone increased from 1979 to 2000.

less ozone — more ozone

SOURCE: *Goddard Space Flight Center/NASA*

READING VISUALS Compare the color at one location on both maps. How has the amount of ozone changed?

The amount of ozone in the stratosphere varies from place to place and changes with the seasons. Cold temperatures and sunshine make the ozone over Antarctica—the South Pole—especially sensitive to the chemicals that destroy ozone. The amount of ozone over Antarctica decreased by half from the 1970s to the mid-1990s. The maps above show the loss of ozone over Antarctica. Smaller but important changes were measured in other regions.

The ozone layer affects the whole world. Since 1987, more than 180 nations have signed an agreement called the Montreal Protocol. They have agreed on a plan to stop making and using chemicals that harm the ozone layer. Experts study the ozone layer and recommend changes to the agreement. The Montreal Protocol has been updated several times. Less harmful chemicals are now used instead of chlorofluorocarbons, but gases from past human activities are still in the ozone layer. If countries continue to follow the Montreal Protocol, ozone levels will return to normal in about 50 years.

1.4 Review

KEY CONCEPTS

1. Describe two of the sources of air pollution.

2. What are three human activities that increase the levels of greenhouse gases?

3. How do human activities affect the ozone layer?

CRITICAL THINKING

4. **Classify** List the following pollutants as either gases or particles: dust, ozone, pollen, carbon monoxide, methane.

5. **Predict** How might global warming affect the way you live in the future?

◊ CHALLENGE

6. **Synthesize** In North America, winds typically blow from west to east. Where might pollution from your community end up? Use a map to help you answer the question.

CHAPTER INVESTIGATION

Observing Particulates

OVERVIEW AND PURPOSE Many of us go through life unaware of particulates in the air, but allergy or asthma sufferers may become uncomfortably aware of high particulate levels. Certain particles, such as dust mite casings, can trigger asthma attacks. Particles that cling to surfaces can make them look dirty or even damage them. Some colors of surfaces may hide the dirt. In this investigation you will

- compare the number and types of particles that settle to surfaces in two different locations
- learn a method of counting particles

▶ Problem

How do the types and numbers of particles in two different locations compare?

▶ Hypothesize

You should decide on the locations in step 3 before writing your hypothesis. Write a hypothesis to explain how particulates collected at two different locations might differ. Your hypothesis should take the form of an "If . . . , then . . . , because . . ." statement.

▶ Procedure

MATERIALS
- 2 index cards
- ruler
- scissors
- transparent packing tape
- magnifying glass
- white paper
- black paper
- graph paper
- calculator

1. Use the ruler to mark on each index card a centered square that is 3 cm per side. Carefully cut out each square.

2. On each card, place a piece of tape so that it covers the hole. Press the edges of the tape to the card, but do not let the center of the tape stick to anything. You should have a clean sticky window when you turn the card over.

3. Choose two different collecting locations where you can safely leave your cards—sticky side up—undisturbed overnight. You might place them on outside and inside windowsills, on the ground and in a tree, or in different rooms.

4. Mark each card with your name, the date, and the location. Tape the cards in place or weigh them down so they will not blow away. Write your hypothesis. Collect your cards the next day.

▶ Observe and Analyze

Write It Up

1. **OBSERVE** Use the magnifying glass to inspect each card closely. Can you identify any of the particles? Try using white paper and black paper behind the card to help you see dark and light particles better. Describe and draw in your **Science Notebook** the types of particles from each card. How does the background affect the type or number of particles you see?

2. **RECORD** Make a data table like the one shown on the notebook page below. Then, place each card onto a piece of graph paper. Line up the top and left edges of each card's center square with the grid on the graph paper and tape the card down. Choose four graph-paper squares and count the number of visible particles in each square. Use the magnifying glass. Record your results on the data table.

3. **CALCULATE**

   AVERAGE Calculate the average number of particles per square for each card.

   $$\text{average} = \frac{\text{sum of particles in 4 squares}}{4}$$

   CONVERT Use the formula below to convert from particles per square to particles per square centimeter. If your squares were half a centimeter wide, then use 0.5 cm in the denominator below.

   $$\frac{\text{particles}}{\text{per cm}^2} = \frac{\text{particles}}{\text{per square}} \times \left(\frac{1\ \text{square}}{\text{width (in cm) of square}}\right)^2$$

▶ Conclude

Write It Up

1. **COMPARE** Compare the types of particles found on the cards. List similarities and differences. Compare the numbers of particles found on the cards.

2. **INTERPRET** Compare your results with your hypothesis. Do your data support your hypothesis?

3. **INFER** What can you infer about where the particles came from or how they reached each location? What evidence did you find to support these inferences?

4. **IDENTIFY LIMITS** What possible limitations or sources of error might have affected your results? Why was it necessary to average the number of particles from several squares?

5. **EVALUATE** Do you think the color of the graph paper affected the number of particles you were able to count?

6. **APPLY** What color would you choose for playground equipment in your area? Explain your choice.

▶ INVESTIGATE Further

CHALLENGE Design an experiment to find out how fast particles in one location are deposited.

Observing Particulates

Problem How do the types and numbers of particles in two different locations compare?

Hypothesize

Observe and Analyze

Table 1. Number of Particles

	Number of Particles						Notes
	Sq. 1	Sq. 2	Sq. 3	Sq. 4	Ave./ sq.	Ave./ cm²	
Card 1							
Card 2							

Conclude

Chapter Review

the **BIG** idea

Earth's atmosphere is a blanket of gases that supports and protects life.

CONTENT REVIEW
CLASSZONE.COM

KEY CONCEPTS SUMMARY

1.1 Earth's atmosphere supports life.

The **atmosphere** is a thin layer surrounding Earth. Gases in the atmosphere provide substances essential for living things. Natural **cycles** and sudden changes affect the atmosphere.

VOCABULARY
atmosphere p. 9
altitude p. 10
density p. 10
cycle p. 12

1.2 The Sun supplies the atmosphere's energy.

Energy from the Sun moves through Earth's atmosphere in three ways.

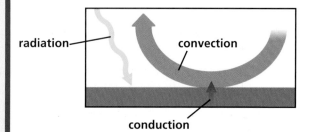

radiation
convection
conduction

Density and temperature change with altitude. The layers, from top to bottom, are

- thermosphere
- mesosphere
- stratosphere
- troposphere

VOCABULARY
radiation p. 17
conduction p. 18
convection p. 19

1.3 Gases in the atmosphere absorb radiation.

Ozone molecules in the stratosphere absorb harmful ultraviolet radiation.

Greenhouse gases in the troposphere keep Earth warm by absorbing and emitting infrared radiation.

VOCABULARY
ultraviolet radiation p. 23
infrared radiation p. 23
ozone p. 23
greenhouse effect p. 24
greenhouse gas p. 24

1.4 Human activities affect the atmosphere.

Human activities have added pollutants and ozone-destroying chemicals to the atmosphere.

The amounts of greenhouse gases have been increasing and global temperatures are rising.

 ozone

 carbon dioxide

VOCABULARY
air pollution p. 27
particulate p. 28
fossil fuel p. 28
smog p. 28

Reviewing Vocabulary

Draw a word triangle for each of the vocabulary terms listed below. Define the term, use it in a sentence, and draw a picture to help you remember the term. A sample is shown below.

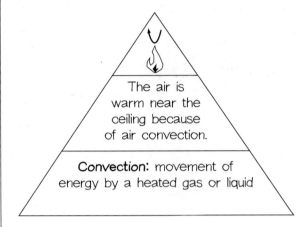

The air is warm near the ceiling because of air convection.

Convection: movement of energy by a heated gas or liquid

1. conduction
2. atmosphere
3. density
4. air pollution
5. altitude
6. radiation
7. cycle
8. particulate

Reviewing Key Concepts

Multiple Choice *Choose the letter of the best answer.*

9. Which of the following represents a sudden change in Earth's atmosphere?
   a. the carbon cycle
   b. the nitrogen cycle
   c. a rain shower
   d. a dust storm

10. The gas that makes up the largest percentage of the atmosphere's substance is
    a. nitrogen
    b. oxygen
    c. water vapor
    d. carbon dioxide

11. Which of the cycles below involves oxygen gas?
    a. the carbon cycle
    b. the water cycle
    c. the density cycle
    d. the argon cycle

12. What process moves energy from Earth's surface to high in the troposphere?
    a. solar energy
    b. conduction
    c. convection
    d. the nitrogen cycle

13. In which of the atmosphere's layers does temperature decrease as the altitude increases?
    a. the troposphere and the stratosphere
    b. the troposphere and the mesosphere
    c. the stratosphere and the mesosphere
    d. the stratosphere and the thermosphere

14. What keeps Earth's surface warm?
    a. conduction
    b. the ozone layer
    c. convection
    d. the greenhouse effect

15. Which gas absorbs ultraviolet radiation?
    a. carbon dioxide
    b. methane
    c. ozone
    d. water vapor

16. Which type of pollution includes harmful droplets?
    a. particulate
    b. gas
    c. dust
    d. smoke

Short Answer *Write a short answer to each question.*

17. Explain why ozone is helpful to life in the stratosphere but harmful in the troposphere.

18. Describe three of the ways human activities affect the atmosphere.

19. Write a brief paragraph describing how the photograph below provides evidence that Earth's atmosphere is in motion.

Thinking Critically

Use the photographs to answer the next two questions.

cold water   hot water

In the demonstration pictured above, hot water has been tinted red with food coloring, and cold water has been tinted blue. View B shows the results after the divider has been lifted and the motion of the water has stopped.

20. OBSERVE Describe how the hot water and the cold water moved when the divider was lifted.

21. APPLY Use your understanding of density to explain the motion of the water.

22. CALCULATE The top of Mount Everest is 8850 meters above sea level. Which layer of the atmosphere contains the top of this mountain? Use the information from page 20 and convert the units.

23. APPLY Why is radiation from Earth's surface and atmosphere important for living things?

24. PREDICT Dust is often light in color, while soot from fires is generally dark. What would happen to the amounts of solar radiation reflected and absorbed if a large amount of light-colored dust was added to the air? What if a large amount of dark soot was added?

25. IDENTIFY EFFECT When weather conditions and sunlight are likely to produce smog, cities may ask motorists to refuel their cars at night instead of early in the day. Why would this behavior make a difference?

26. COMPARE How are the processes in the diagram on page 18 similar to those in the illustration below?

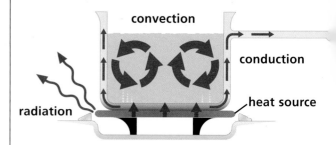

27. CONNECT Give an example from everyday life that shows that the atmosphere has substance.

28. EVALUATE If you had a choice between burning natural gas to cook or using electricity from a power plant, which would you choose? Explain the issues involved. **Hint:** Where does the power plant get energy?

the BIG idea

29. SYNTHESIZE Write one or more paragraphs describing the specific ways that the atmosphere supports and protects life. In your description, use each of the terms below. Underline each term in your answer.

carbon dioxide	solar radiation
water	ozone
oxygen	stratosphere
cycle	

30. APPLY Look again at the photograph on pages 6–7. Now that you have finished the chapter, how would you change or add details to your answer to the question on the photograph?

UNIT PROJECTS

If you are doing a unit project, make a folder for your project. Include in your folder a list of the resources you will need, the date on which the project is due, and a schedule to track your progress. Begin gathering data.

Interpreting Graphs

The following three graphs show the amounts of three types of air pollutants
released into the atmosphere in the United States each year from 1950 to 1990.
Study the graphs closely and use the information to answer the first four questions.

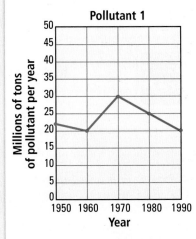

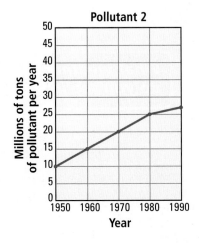

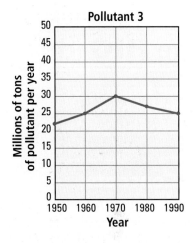

1. What conclusion can you make about pollutant 1?

   a. The release of pollutant 1 has steadily decreased
since 1970.

   b. More pollutant 1 has been released since 1990.

   c. More pollutant 1 has been released since 1970.

   d. The release of pollutant 1 has not changed.

2. Based on the graph for pollutant 2, which of the
following is true?

   a. The release of pollutant 2 declined after 1950.

   b. The release of pollutant 2 has increased
since 1970.

   c. The release of pollutant 2 declined and then rose.

   d. About 15 million tons of pollutant 2 were
released in 1990.

3. Compare the graphs for pollutants 1 and 2.
Which of the following statements is
supported by the graphs?

   a. In 1950, more pollutant 1 was released than
pollutant 2.

   b. Since 1980, no pollutant 1 has been released.

   c. In 1990, twice as much pollutant 2 was
released as pollutant 1.

   d. Since 1950, no pollutant 1 has been released.

4. About how many million tons of pollutant 3
entered the atmosphere in the United States
in 1990?

   a. 10   **c.** 25

   b. 15   **d.** 30

Extended Response

Answer the next two questions in detail. Use in your
answers some of the terms from the word box. In
your answer, underline each term you use.

oxygen	nitrogen	energy
water	air density	carbon dioxide
altitude	absorption	

5. Luz builds a terrarium for her class science fair.
She puts her pet slug in with the plants. She
covers the terrarium with clear plastic that has
vent holes. She places it in a sunlit window. How
do the soil, plants, slug, sunlight, and plastic affect
the air in Luz's terrarium?

6. Mile High Stadium in Denver, Colorado, makes
bottled oxygen available to its players. Players at
lower altitudes do not need extra oxygen.
Explorers pack bottled oxygen when they climb tall
mountains, such as Mount Everest. Explain why
extra oxygen might be necessary for players in Mile
High Stadium and climbers on tall mountains.

CHAPTER

2 Weather Patterns

the BIG idea

Some features of
weather have
predictable patterns.

**What weather conditions
do you see in the distance?**

Key Concepts

 Internet Preview

CLASSZONE.COM

Chapter 2 online resources:
Content Review, two
Visualizations, four Resource
Centers, Math Tutorial, Test
Practice

EXPLORE (the BIG idea)

Are You Stronger Than Air?

Line a wide-mouthed jar with a plastic bag. Secure the bag tightly with a rubber band. Reach in and try to pull the bag out of the jar.

Observe and Think
How easy was it to move the plastic bag? What was holding the bag in place?

How Does Air Motion Affect Balloons?

Tie two balloons to a pencil 5 centimeters apart as shown. Gently blow air between the balloons.

Observe and Think
How did the balloons move? Why did the air make them move this way?

Internet Activity: Wind

Go to **ClassZone.com** to explore how breezes blowing over land and water change over the course of an entire day.

Observe and Think
What patterns can you see in winds that occur near water?

NSTA
scilinks.org
*sci*LINKS

Atmospheric Pressure and Winds **Code: MDL010**

Getting Ready to Learn

◉ CONCEPT REVIEW

- The Sun supplies the atmosphere's energy.
- Energy moves throughout the atmosphere.
- Matter can be solid, liquid, or gas.

◉ VOCABULARY REVIEW

atmosphere p. 9
altitude p. 10
density p. 10
convection p. 19

ⓘ **CONTENT REVIEW**
CLASSZONE.COM
Review concepts and vocabulary.

▶ TAKING NOTES

COMBINATION NOTES

To take notes about a new concept, first make an informal outline of the information. Then make a sketch of the concept and label it so that you can study it later.

VOCABULARY STRATEGY

Place each vocabulary term at the center of a **description wheel**. Write some words describing it on the spokes.

See the Note-Taking Handbook on pages R45–R51.

SCIENCE NOTEBOOK

NOTES

Air pressure
- is the force of air molecules pushing on an area
- pushes in all directions

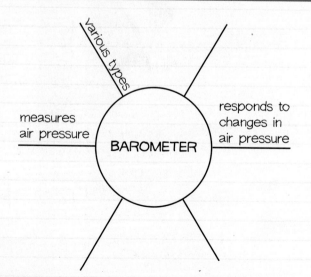

various types
measures air pressure
BAROMETER
responds to changes in air pressure

2.1 The atmosphere's air pressure changes.

◀ **BEFORE, you learned**

- Density is the amount of mass in a given volume of a substance
- Air becomes less dense as altitude increases
- Differences in density cause air to rise and sink

▶ **NOW, you will learn**

- How the movement of air molecules causes air pressure
- How air pressure varies
- How differences in air pressure affect the atmosphere

VOCABULARY

air pressure p. 43
barometer p. 46

EXPLORE Air Pressure

What does air do to the egg?

PROCEDURE

① Set a peeled hard-boiled egg in the mouth of a bottle. Make sure that the egg can't slip through.

② Light the matches. Remove the egg, and drop the matches into the bottle. Quickly replace the egg.

③ Watch carefully, and record your observations.

WHAT DO YOU THINK?

- What happened when you placed the egg back on top of the bottle?
- What can your observations tell you about the air in the bottle?

MATERIALS

- peeled hard-boiled egg
- glass bottle
- 2 wooden matches

Air exerts pressure.

Air molecules move constantly. As they move, they bounce off each other like rubber balls. They also bounce off every surface they hit. As you read this book, billions of air molecules are bouncing off your body, the book, and everything else around you.

Each time an air molecule bounces off an object, it pushes, or exerts a force, on that object. When billions of air molecules bounce off a surface, the force is spread over the area of that surface. **Air pressure** is the force of air molecules pushing on an area. The greater the force, the higher the air pressure. Because air molecules move in all directions, air pressure pushes in all directions.

VOCABULARY
Add a description wheel for *air pressure* to your notebook.

CHECK YOUR READING How does the number of air molecules relate to air pressure?

Air pressure is related to altitude and density.

COMBINATION NOTES
Record details about how
air pressure varies.

REMINDER

Density is the amount of
mass in a given volume of
a substance.

The air pressure at any area on Earth depends on the weight of the air above that area. If you hold out your hand, the force of air pushing down on your hand is greater than the weight of a bowling ball. So why don't you feel the air pushing down on your hand? Remember that air pushes in all directions. The pressure of air pushing down is balanced by the pressure of air pushing up from below.

Air pressure decreases as you move higher in the atmosphere. Think of a column of air directly over your body. If you stood at sea level, this column would stretch from where you stood to the top of the atmosphere. The air pressure on your body would be equal to the weight of all the air in the column. But if you stood on a mountain, the column of air would be shorter. With less air above you, the pressure would be lower. At an altitude of 5.5 kilometers (3.4 mi), air pressure is about half what it is at sea level.

Air pressure and density are related. Just as air pressure decreases with altitude, so does the density of air. Notice in the illustration that air molecules at sea level are closer together than air molecules over the mountain. Since the pressure is greater at sea level, the air molecules are pushed closer together. Therefore, the air at sea level is denser than air at high altitudes.

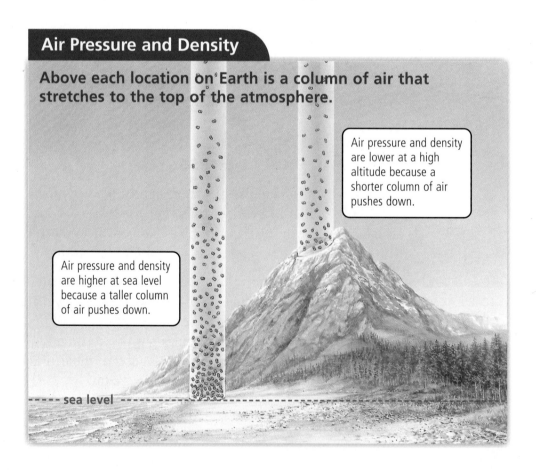

Air Pressure and Density

Above each location on Earth is a column of air that stretches to the top of the atmosphere.

Air pressure and density are lower at a high altitude because a shorter column of air pushes down.

Air pressure and density are higher at sea level because a taller column of air pushes down.

----- sea level -----

Pressure and Air Motion

You've read that air pressure decreases as you move to higher altitudes. Air pressure also often varies in two locations at the same altitude. You can observe how such pressure differences affect air when you open a new can of tennis balls. You may hear a hiss as air rushes into the can. The air inside the sealed can of tennis balls is at a lower pressure than the air outside the can. When you break the seal, air moves from outside the can toward the lower pressure inside it.

Air pressure differences in the atmosphere affect air in a similar way. If the air pressure were the same at all locations, air wouldn't move much. Because of differences in pressure, air starts to move from areas of higher pressure toward areas of lower pressure. The air may move only a short distance, or it may travel many kilometers. You will learn more about how air moves in response to pressure differences in Section 2.2.

RESOURCE CENTER
CLASSZONE.COM

Find out more about air pressure.

CHECK YOUR READING   How do differences in air pressure affect the movement of air?

INVESTIGATE Air Pressure

How can you measure changes in air pressure?

PROCEDURE

1. Cut open a balloon along one side until you get close to the end. Stretch the balloon across the open top of the can. Secure it tightly in place with a rubber band.

2. Cut the straw on an angle to make a pointer. Tape the other end of the straw to the center of the balloon.

3. Tape a ruler against a wall or a box so that the end of the pointer almost touches the ruler. Record the position of the pointer against the ruler.

4. Record the position of the pointer at least once a day for the next five days. Look for small changes in its position. For each day, record the air pressure printed in a local newspaper.

WHAT DO YOU THINK?

- In what direction did the pointer move when the air pressure went up? when the air pressure went down?
- Explain how your instrument worked.

CHALLENGE Predict what would happen to the pointer if you repeated this experiment but poked some small holes in the balloon.

SKILL FOCUS
Collecting data

MATERIALS
- scissors
- round balloon
- metal can
- rubber band
- thin straw
- tape
- ruler

TIME
15 minutes

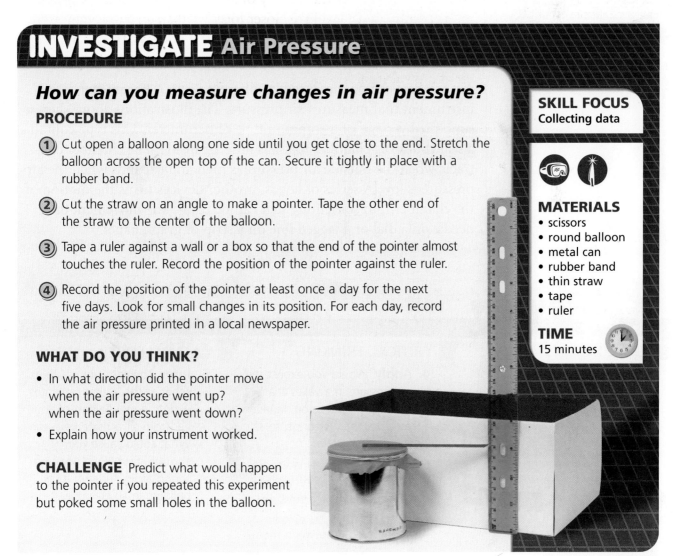

How a Barometer Works

High Air Pressure

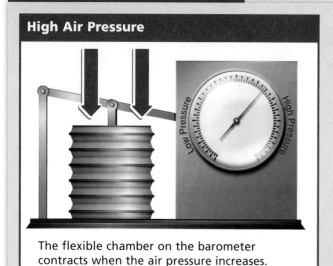

The flexible chamber on the barometer contracts when the air pressure increases.

Low Air Pressure

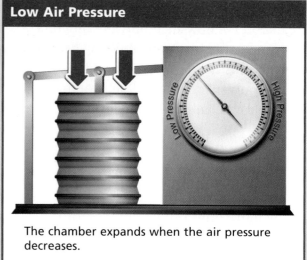

The chamber expands when the air pressure decreases.

READING VISUALS Which of these barometer readings would be the more likely one on a mountain? Explain why.

Barometers and Air Pressure

Air pressure can be measured in different ways. A **barometer** is any instrument that measures air pressure. The illustrations above show a simplified version of a common type of barometer. This type contains a sealed flexible chamber that has little air inside. The chamber contracts when the outside air pressure is high and expands when the air pressure is low. A series of levers or other devices turns the motion of the chamber into something that can be read—the movement of a needle on a dial or a jagged line on a strip of graph paper.

2.1 Review

KEY CONCEPTS

1. How does the movement of air molecules cause pressure?

2. How does altitude affect air pressure?

3. How is air density related to air pressure?

CRITICAL THINKING

4. **Apply** Would you expect the air pressure in a valley that's below sea level to be higher or lower than air pressure at sea level? Explain.

5. **Predict** Two barometers are placed one kilometer apart. One shows higher pressure than the other. What will happen to air between them?

⬥ CHALLENGE

6. **Infer** The eardrum is a thin sheet of tissue that separates air in the middle part of your ear from air outside your ear. What could cause your eardrum to make a popping sound as you ride up a tall building in an elevator?

The atmosphere has wind patterns.

◀ **BEFORE,** you learned

- Solar energy heats Earth's surface and atmosphere
- Differences in density cause air to move
- Air pressure differences set air in motion

▶ **NOW,** you will learn

- About forces that affect wind
- About global winds
- About patterns of heating and cooling

VOCABULARY

weather p. 47
wind p. 47
global wind p. 48
Coriolis effect p. 49
jet stream p. 52
monsoon p. 54

EXPLORE Solar Energy

How does Earth's shape affect solar heating?

PROCEDURE

1. Place a globe on a desk in a darkened room.

2. Point a flashlight at the equator on the globe from a distance of about 15 centimeters. Keep the flashlight level. Observe the lighted area on the globe.

3. Keeping the flashlight level, raise it up and point it at the United States. Observe the lighted area.

WHAT DO YOU THINK?
- How were the two lighted areas different?
- What might have caused the difference?

MATERIALS
- globe
- flashlight
- ruler

Uneven heating causes air to move.

On local news broadcasts, weather forecasters often spend several minutes discussing what the weather will be like over the next few days. **Weather** is the condition of Earth's atmosphere at a particular time and place. Wind is an important part of weather. You will read about other weather factors later in this chapter.

Wind is air that moves horizontally, or parallel to the ground. Remember that air pressure can differ from place to place at the same altitude. Uneven heating of Earth's surface causes such pressure differences, which set air in motion. Over a short distance, wind moves directly from higher pressure toward lower pressure.

▼ **REMINDER**

Remember that air pressure is the force that air molecules exert on an area.

What is the relationship between air pressure and wind?

VISUALIZATION
CLASSZONE.COM

View an animation of the Coriolis effect.

How Wind Forms

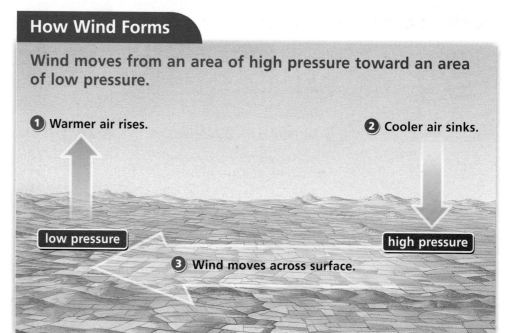

Wind moves from an area of high pressure toward an area of low pressure.

1 Warmer air rises.

2 Cooler air sinks.

low pressure

high pressure

3 Wind moves across surface.

The illustration above shows a common pattern of air circulation caused by uneven heating of Earth's surface:

1 Sunlight strongly heats an area of ground. The ground heats the air. The warm air rises, and an area of low pressure forms.

2 Sunlight heats an area of ground less strongly. The cooler, dense air sinks slowly, and an area of high pressure forms.

3 Air moves as wind across the surface, from higher toward lower pressure.

When the difference in pressure between two areas is small, the wind may move too slowly to be noticeable. A very large pressure difference can produce wind strong enough to uproot trees.

CHECK YOUR READING What factor determines the strength of wind?

The distance winds travel varies. Some winds die out quickly after blowing a few meters. In contrast, **global winds** travel thousands of kilometers in steady patterns. Global winds last for weeks.

Uneven heating between the equator and the north and south poles causes global winds. Notice in the illustration at left how sunlight strikes Earth's curved surface. Near the equator, concentrated sunlight heats the surface to a high temperature. Warm air rises, producing low pressure.

In regions closer to the poles, the sunlight is more spread out. Because less of the Sun's energy reaches these regions, the air above them is cooler and denser. The sinking dense air produces high pressure that sets global winds in motion.

Sunlight is concentrated near the equator because it strikes the surface directly.

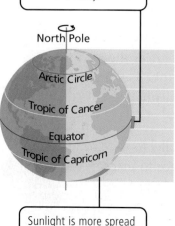

North Pole

Arctic Circle

Tropic of Cancer

Equator

Tropic of Capricorn

Sunlight is more spread out near the poles because it strikes at a lower angle.

Earth's rotation affects wind direction.

If Earth did not rotate, global winds would flow directly from the poles to the equator. However, Earth's rotation changes the direction of winds and other objects moving over Earth. The influence of Earth's rotation is called the **Coriolis effect** (KAWR-ee-OH-lihs). Global winds curve as Earth turns beneath them. In the Northern Hemisphere, winds curve to the right in the direction of motion. Winds in the Southern Hemisphere curve to the left. The Coriolis effect is noticeable only for winds that travel long distances.

Because the Coriolis effect causes global winds to curve, they cannot flow directly from the poles to the equator. Instead, global winds travel along three routes in each hemisphere. These routes, which circle the world, are called global wind belts.

direction of Earth's rotation

How wind actually blows

Path wind would take without Coriolis effect

 CHECK YOUR READING In which direction do winds curve in the Northern Hemisphere?

INVESTIGATE Coriolis Effect

How does Earth's rotation affect wind?

PROCEDURE

1. Blow up a balloon and tie it off.

2. Have a classmate slowly rotate the balloon to the right. Draw a line straight down from the top of the balloon to the center as the balloon rotates.

3. Now draw a line from the bottom of the balloon straight up to the center as the balloon rotates.

WHAT DO YOU THINK?

• How did the rotation affect the lines that you drew?

• How does this activity demonstrate the Coriolis effect?

CHALLENGE How might changing the speed at which the balloon is rotated affect your results? Repeat the activity to test your prediction.

SKILL FOCUS
Modeling

MATERIALS
• round balloon
• felt-tip pen

TIME
10 minutes

Bands of calm air separate global wind belts.

RESOURCE CENTER
CLASSZONE.COM

Learn more about
global winds.

Earth's rotation and the uneven heating of its surface cause a pattern
of wind belts separated by calm regions. Each calm region is a zone
of either high pressure or low pressure. The illustration on page 51
shows how each wind belt and the calm regions that border it form
a giant loop of moving air. These loops are called circulation cells.
The section of a cell that flows along Earth's surface is global wind.
Notice that the direction of airflow changes from one circulation cell
to the next.

Calm Regions

READING TiP

As you read about each
region or wind belt,
locate it in the diagram
on page 51.

The air usually stays calm in high-pressure and low-pressure zones.
Winds are light, and they often change direction.

1 **The doldrums** are a low-pressure zone near the equator. There,
warm air rises to the top of the troposphere, which is the atmosphere's lowest layer. Then the air spreads out toward the poles.
The rising, moist air produces clouds and heavy rain. During the
hottest months, heavy evaporation from warm ocean water in the
region fuels tropical storms.

2 **The horse latitudes** are high-pressure zones located about 30°
north and 30° south of the equator. Warm air traveling away from
the equator cools and sinks in these regions. The weather tends to
be clear and dry.

Wind Belts

As dense air sinks to Earth's surface in the horse latitudes and other
high-pressure zones, it flows out toward regions of low pressure.
This pattern of air movement produces three global wind belts in each
hemisphere. Because of the Coriolis effect, the winds curve toward the
east or toward the west. Some global winds are named for the directions from which they blow. The westerlies, for example, blow from
west to east.

3 **The trade winds** blow from the east, moving from the horse
latitudes toward the equator. These strong, steady winds die out
as they come near the equator.

4 **The westerlies** blow from the west, moving from the horse
latitudes toward the poles. They bring storms across much of the
United States.

5 **The easterlies** blow from the east, moving from the polar regions
toward the mid-latitudes. Stormy weather often occurs when the
cold air of the easterlies meets the warmer air of the westerlies.

Belts of global wind circle Earth. Because of the Coriolis effect, the winds in these belts curve to the east or the west. Between the global wind belts are calm areas of rising or falling air.

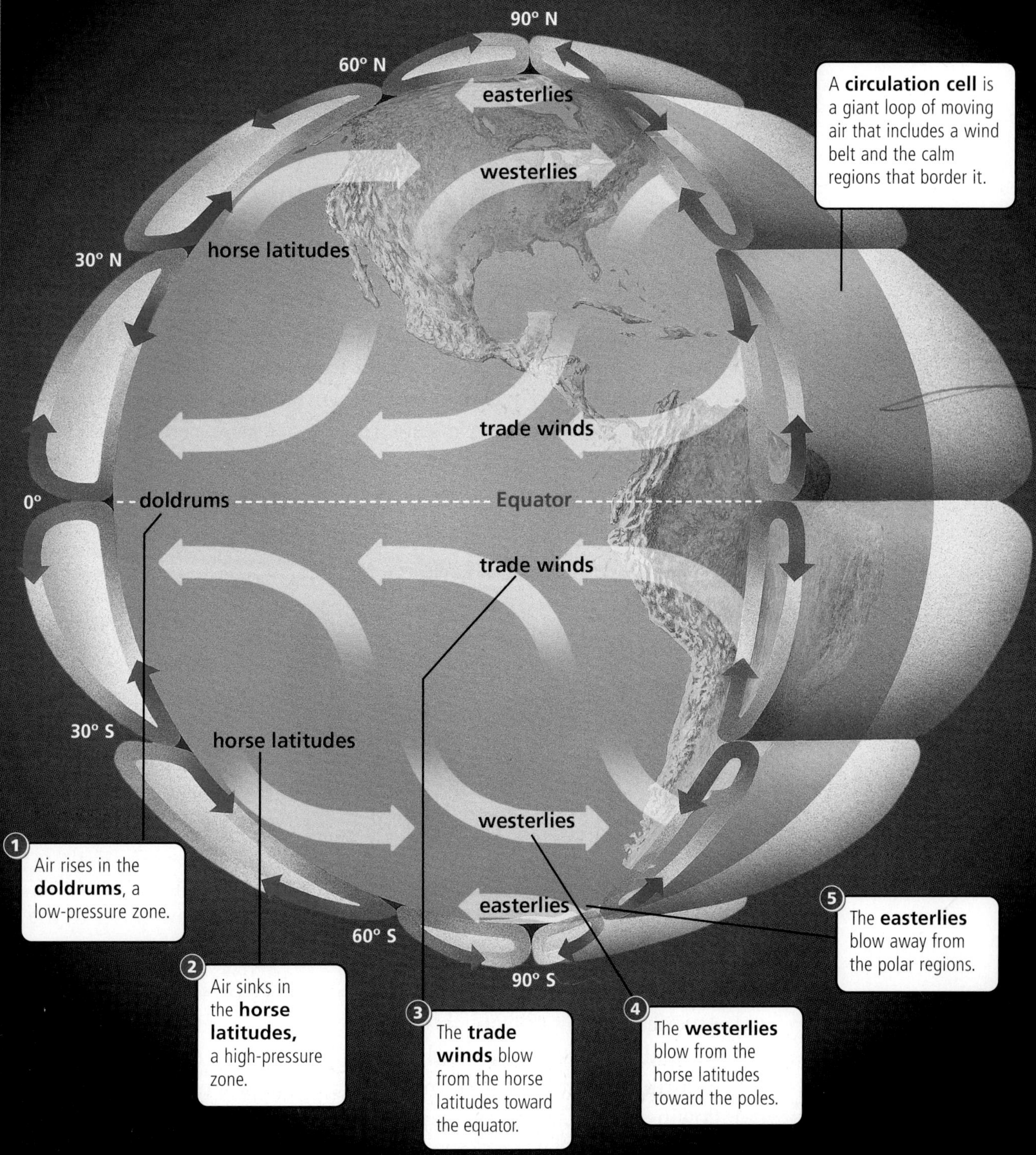

90° N

60° N

easterlies

westerlies

30° N

horse latitudes

A **circulation cell** is a giant loop of moving air that includes a wind belt and the calm regions that border it.

trade winds

0°   doldrums --------------- Equator ------------

trade winds

30° S   horse latitudes

westerlies

(1) Air rises in the **doldrums**, a low-pressure zone.

easterlies

60° S

90° S

(5) The **easterlies** blow away from the polar regions.

(2) Air sinks in the **horse latitudes,** a high-pressure zone.

(3) The **trade winds** blow from the horse latitudes toward the equator.

(4) The **westerlies** blow from the horse latitudes toward the poles.

READING VISUALS What are the positions of the calm regions and the wind belts in the circulation cells?

Effects of Wind on Travel

Before the invention of steam engines, sailors used to dread traveling through the doldrums and the horse latitudes. There often wasn't enough wind to move their sailing ships. A ship might stall for days or even weeks, wasting precious supplies of food and fresh water.

To avoid the calm regions, sailors sought out global wind belts. The trade winds got their name because traders used them to sail from east to west. For centuries, sailors relied on the trade winds to reach North America from Europe. They would return by sailing north to catch the westerlies and ride them across the Atlantic.

Jet streams flow near the top of the troposphere.

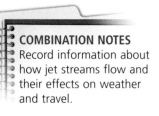

COMBINATION NOTES
Record information about how jet streams flow and their effects on weather and travel.

Not all long-distance winds travel along Earth's surface. **Jet streams** usually flow in the upper troposphere from west to east for thousands of kilometers. Air often moves in jet streams at speeds greater than 200 kilometers per hour (124 mi/hr). Like global winds, jet streams form because Earth's surface is heated unevenly. Instead of following a straight line, jet streams loop north and south, as shown on the globe below.

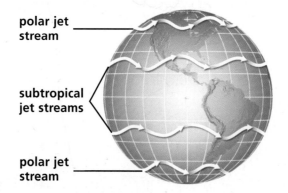

polar jet stream

subtropical jet streams

polar jet stream

Jet streams flow in a wavy pattern from west to east around the world. They change positions during the year.

Each hemisphere usually has two jet streams, a polar jet stream and a subtropical jet stream. The polar jet streams flow closer to the poles in summer than in winter.

The polar jet stream has a strong influence on weather in North America. It can pull cold air down from Canada into the United States and pull warm air up toward Canada. In addition, strong storms tend to form along its loops. Scientists must know where the jet stream is flowing to make accurate weather predictions.

Jet streams also affect air-travel times. They usually flow 10 to 15 kilometers (6–9 mi) above Earth's surface. Since airplanes often fly at these altitudes, their travel times can be lengthened or shortened by the strong wind of a jet stream.

Patterns of heating and cooling cause local winds and monsoons.

Have you ever noticed how the wind can change in predictable ways? For example, at the beach on a hot day you will often feel a cool breeze coming off the water. At night a breeze will flow in the opposite direction. The change in the breeze occurs because water and land heat up and cool down at different rates.

Local Winds

Some winds change daily in a regular pattern. These local winds blow within small areas.

- Sea breezes and land breezes occur near shorelines. During the day, land heats up faster than water. The air over the land rises and expands. Denser ocean air moves into the area of low pressure, producing a sea breeze. As the illustration below shows, this pattern is reversed at night, when land cools faster than water. Warm air rises over the ocean, and cooler air flows in, producing a land breeze.

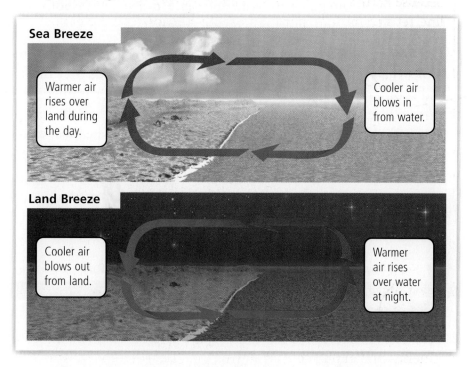

Sea Breeze

Warmer air rises over land during the day.

Cooler air blows in from water.

Land Breeze

Cooler air blows out from land.

Warmer air rises over water at night.

▼ **REMINDER**

Red arrows stand for warmer air. Blue arrows stand for cooler air.

- Valley breezes and mountain breezes are caused by a similar process. Mountain slopes heat up and cool faster than the valleys below them. During the day, valley breezes flow up mountains. At night mountain breezes flow down into valleys.

⬆ **CHECK YOUR READING** How do mountains and bodies of water affect patterns of heating and cooling?

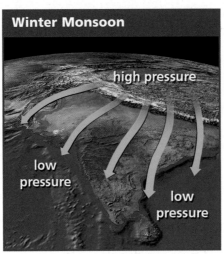

Winter Monsoon

high pressure

low pressure

low pressure

Dry air blows from the high-pressure area over the continent to the low-pressure areas over the ocean.

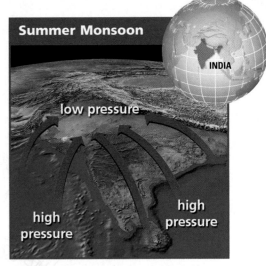

Summer Monsoon

low pressure

high pressure

high pressure

INDIA

Moist air blows from the high-pressure areas over the ocean to the low-pressure area over the continent.

Monsoons

VOCABULARY
Add a description wheel for *monsoon* to your notebook.

Winds that change direction with the seasons are called **monsoons.** Like sea breezes and land breezes, monsoons are caused by the different heating and cooling rates of land and sea. However, monsoons flow longer distances and affect much larger areas.

Winter monsoons occur in regions where the land becomes much cooler than the sea during winter. High pressure builds over the land, and cool, dry wind blows out toward the sea. During summer this pattern reverses as the land becomes much warmer than the sea. Moist wind flows inland, often bringing heavy rains. The most extreme monsoons occur in South Asia and Southeast Asia. Farmers there depend on rain from the summer monsoon to grow crops.

 CHECK YOUR READING How do monsoon winds affect rainfall?

2.2 Review

KEY CONCEPTS

1. How does the uneven heating of Earth's surface cause winds to flow?

2. How does Earth's rotation influence the movement of global winds?

3. Why do some winds change direction in areas where land is near water?

CRITICAL THINKING

4. **Compare and Contrast** How are global winds and local winds similar? How are they different?

5. **Analyze** Make a table that shows the causes and effects of local winds and monsoons.

○ CHALLENGE

6. **Predict** Suppose that a city is located in a valley between the sea and a mountain range. What kind of wind pattern would you predict for this area?

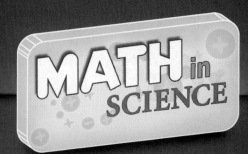

MATH TUTORIAL

CLASSZONE.COM

Click on Math Tutorial for more help with adding measures of time.

High clouds show the location of the jet stream in this satellite image.

Navigate the Jet Stream

When an airplane is flying in the same direction as a jet stream, the airplane gets a boost in its speed. Pilots can save an hour or more if they fly with the jet stream. On the other hand, flying against the jet stream can slow an airplane down.

Example

To determine the total flight time between San Francisco and Chicago, with a stop in Denver, you need to add the hours and minutes separately. Set up the problem like this:

San Francisco to Denver:	2 h	10 min
Denver to Chicago:	1 h	45 min
Total flight time:	3 h	55 min

ANSWER The total flight time is 3 hours 55 minutes.

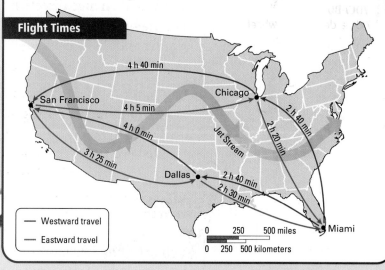

Flight Times

4 h 40 min

San Francisco

Chicago

4 h 5 min

2 h 40 min

4 h 0 min

2 h 20 min

Jet Stream

3 h 25 min

Dallas 2 h 40 min

2 h 30 min

Miami

— Westward travel
— Eastward travel

0   250   500 miles
0   250   500 kilometers

Use the map to answer the following questions.

1. What is the total flight time for an airliner flying from San Francisco to Miami through Chicago?

2. What is the total flight time for an airliner flying from San Francisco to Miami through Dallas?

3. How much time will the fastest possible trip from Miami to San Francisco take?

4. Compare the flight time from Chicago to San Francisco with the flight time from San Francisco to Chicago.

CHALLENGE What is the total flight time from Miami to San Francisco through Chicago? Convert minutes to hours if necessary.

2.3 Most clouds form as air rises and cools.

◀ **BEFORE,** you learned

- Water vapor circulates from Earth to the atmosphere
- Warm air is less dense than cool air and tends to rise

▶ **NOW,** you will learn

- How water in the atmosphere changes
- How clouds form
- About the types of clouds

VOCABULARY

evaporation p. 56
condensation p. 56
precipitation p. 57
humidity p. 58
saturation p. 58
relative humidity p. 58
dew point p. 58

EXPLORE Condensation

How does condensation occur?

PROCEDURE

① Observe the air as a classmate breathes out.

② Observe a mirror as a classmate breathes onto it.

WHAT DO YOU THINK?

- What changes did you observe on the mirror?
- Why could you see water on the mirror but not in the air when your classmate breathed out?

MATERIALS
hand mirror

Temperature affects water in the air.

Water is always in the atmosphere. You may see water in solid form, such as falling snow. Water may also be present as liquid water droplets. Even if you can't see any water, it is still part of the air as water vapor, an invisible gas. When temperatures change, water changes its form.

- **Evaporation** is the process by which a liquid changes into a gas. For water to evaporate, it needs extra energy.

- **Condensation** is the process by which a gas, such as water vapor, changes into a liquid. Condensation occurs when moist air cools.

The picture on the left shows the processes of evaporation and condensation at work. Water in a teakettle absorbs heat. It gets enough energy to evaporate into water vapor. The invisible water vapor rises and escapes from the kettle. When the vapor hits the cooler air outside the kettle, it cools and condenses into tiny but visible water droplets.

droplets

vapor

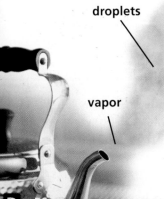

Water in the Air

Vast amounts of Earth's water are recycled. The oceans hold most of the water. Water is also stored in lakes, rivers, and ice sheets; in plants; and underground. Energy from sunlight causes molecules to evaporate from the surface of a body of water. These molecules become part of the air in the form of water vapor.

As air rises in the atmosphere, it cools. The loss of heat causes water vapor to condense into tiny water droplets or ice crystals. If the droplets or crystals grow and become heavy enough, they fall as rain, snow, sleet, or hail. Any type of liquid or solid water that falls to Earth's surface is called **precipitation.** Earth's water goes through a never-ending cycle of evaporation, condensation, and precipitation.

Water vapor can also condense on solid surfaces. Have you ever gotten your shoes wet while walking on grass in the early morning? The grass was covered with dew, which is water that has condensed on cool surfaces at night. If the temperature is cold enough, water vapor can change directly into a covering of ice, called frost.

CHECK YOUR READING Summarize the way water moves in the water cycle. For each part of the cycle, specify whether water exists as a gas, liquid, or solid.

> **VOCABULARY**
> Add a description wheel for *precipitation* to your notebook.

Water Cycle

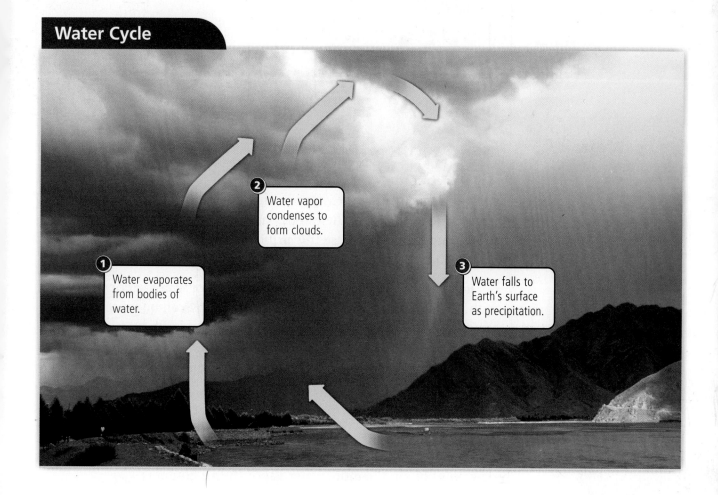

1 Water evaporates from bodies of water.

2 Water vapor condenses to form clouds.

3 Water falls to Earth's surface as precipitation.

Humidity and Relative Humidity

On a warm summer day, evaporation of moisture from your skin can help you feel comfortable. However, a lot of water vapor in the air can cause less moisture to evaporate from your skin. With less evaporation, the air will seem hotter and damper. **Humidity** is the amount of water vapor in air. Humidity varies from place to place and from time to time.

The illustration shows how humidity increases in a sealed container. As water molecules evaporate into the air, some start to condense and return to the water. For a while the air gains water vapor because more water evaporates than condenses. But eventually the air reaches **saturation,** a condition in which the rates of evaporation and condensation are equal. Any additional water that evaporates is balanced by water that condenses.

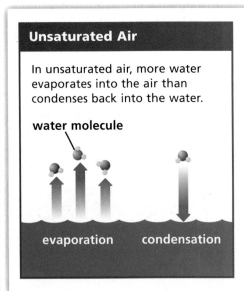

Unsaturated Air

In unsaturated air, more water evaporates into the air than condenses back into the water.

water molecule

evaporation   condensation

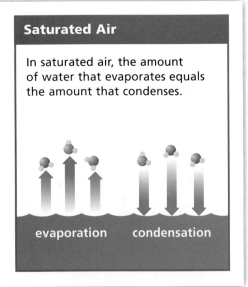

Saturated Air

In saturated air, the amount of water that evaporates equals the amount that condenses.

evaporation   condensation

READING TiP

Relative means "considered in comparison with something else."

The amount of water vapor in air at saturation depends on the temperature of the air. The warmer air is, the more water vapor it takes to saturate it. Scientists use this principle to describe the humidity of air in two different ways: relative humidity and dew point.

Relative humidity compares the amount of water vapor in air with the maximum amount of water vapor that can be present at that temperature. For example, air with 50 percent relative humidity has half the amount of water needed for saturation. If the amount of water vapor in air stays the same, relative humidity will decrease as the air heats up and increase as the air cools.

Dew point is the temperature at which air with a given amount of water vapor will reach saturation. For example, air with a dew point of 26°C (79°F) will become saturated if it cools to 26°C. The higher the dew point of air, the more water vapor the air contains.

Water vapor condenses and forms clouds.

Clouds are made of condensed water vapor. As warm air rises in the atmosphere, it cools. When the air cools to its dew point—the temperature at which air reaches saturation—water vapor condenses into tiny droplets or ice crystals. These droplets and crystals are so light that they either float as clouds on rising air or fall very slowly.

level where condensation begins

Rising warm air can produce clouds. Water vapor begins to condense when the air cools to its dew point.

Recall how dew condenses on grass. Water must condense on something solid. There are no large solid surfaces in the air. However, the air is filled with tiny particles such as dust, smoke, and salt from the ocean. Water vapor condenses on these particles.

INVESTIGATE Condensation

How does a cloud form?

PROCEDURE

1. Add a spoonful of water to the bottle to increase the humidity inside it.

2. Lay the bottle on its side. Light a match, blow it out, and then stick the match into the bottle for a few seconds to let smoke flow in. Replace the cap.

3. Squeeze the bottle quickly and then release it. Observe what happens when the bottle is allowed to expand.

WHAT DO YOU THINK?

• What happened to the water vapor inside the bottle when you squeezed the bottle and then let it expand?

• How did the smoke affect what happened to the water vapor?

CHALLENGE How would the cloud change if you raised or lowered the temperature inside the bottle?

SKILL FOCUS
Observing

MATERIALS
• clear 1-liter plastic bottle with cap
• water at room temperature
• tablespoon
• matches

TIME
10 minutes

Characteristics of Clouds

If you watch the sky over a period of time, you will probably observe clouds that do not look alike. Clouds have different characteristics because they form under different conditions. The shapes and sizes of clouds are mainly determined by air movement. For example, puffy clouds form in air that rises sharply or moves straight up and down. Flat, smooth clouds covering large areas form in air that rises gradually.

Location affects the composition of clouds. Since the troposphere gets colder with altitude, clouds that form at high altitudes are made of tiny ice crystals. Closer to Earth's surface, clouds are made of water droplets or a mixture of ice crystals and water droplets.

CHECK YOUR READING How are clouds that form at high altitudes different from clouds that form close to Earth's surface?

In the illustration on page 61, notice that some cloud names share word parts. That is because clouds are classified and named according to their altitudes, the ways they form, and their general characteristics. The three main types of clouds are cirrus, cumulus, and stratus. These names come from Latin words that suggest the clouds' appearances.

COMBINATION NOTES
Record information about
the three main cloud types.

- **Cirrus** (SEER-uhs) means "curl of hair." Cirrus clouds appear feathery or wispy.
- **Cumulus** (KYOOM-yuh-luhs) means "heap" or "pile." Cumulus-type clouds can grow to be very tall.
- **Stratus** (STRAT-uhs) means "spread out." Stratus-type clouds form in flat layers.

Word parts are used to tell more about clouds. For example, names of clouds that produce precipitation contain the word part *nimbo-* or *nimbus*. Names of clouds that form at a medium altitude have the prefix *alto-*.

cirrus clouds

Cirrus Clouds

Cirrus clouds form in very cold air at high altitudes. Made of ice crystals, they have a wispy or feathery appearance. Strong winds often blow streamers or "tails" off cirrus clouds. These features show the direction of the wind in the upper troposphere. You will usually see cirrus clouds in fair weather. However, they can be a sign that a storm is approaching.

Cloud Types

The three main cloud types are cirrus, cumulus, and stratus. These names can be combined with each other and with other word parts to identify more specific cloud types.

cirrus

cirrocumulus

high altitude

cumulonimbus

cirrostratus

6000 m
20,000 ft

Clouds that produce precipitation often have names containing the word part *nimbo-* or *nimbus*.

altocumulus

medium altitude

altostratus

Clouds that form at a medium altitude have names with the prefix *alto-*.

2000 m
6500 ft

nimbostratus

low altitude

cumulus

stratus

READING VISUALS   Which cloud names are combinations of names of two main cloud types?

Cumulus Clouds

READING TiP

As you read each description of a main cloud type, look back at the visual on page 61. Notice the different clouds that have the main cloud type as part of their names.

Cumulus clouds are puffy white clouds with darker bases. They look like cotton balls floating in the sky. There are several varieties of cumulus clouds. Usually they appear in the daytime in fair weather, when warm air rises and its water vapor condenses. Cooler air sinks along the sides of the clouds, keeping cumulus clouds separate from one another.

cumulus clouds

If cumulus clouds keep growing taller, they can produce showers. The precipitation usually lasts less than half an hour because there are spaces between the clouds. The tallest clouds are cumulonimbus clouds, or thunderheads. These clouds produce thunderstorms that

cumulonimbus clouds

drop heavy rainfall. A cumulonimbus cloud can tower 18 kilometers (11 mi) above Earth's surface. By comparison, jet planes usually fly at about 10 kilometers (6 mi). Strong high-altitude winds often cause the top of the cloud to jut out sharply.

 CHECK YOUR READING How are cumulonimbus clouds different from other cumulus clouds?

Stratus Clouds

Have you ever noticed on some days that the whole sky looks gray? You were looking at stratus clouds. They form in layers when air cools over a large area without rising or when the air is gently lifted. Stratus clouds are smooth because they form without strong air movement.

stratus clouds

Some low stratus clouds are so dark that they completely block out the Sun. These clouds produce steady, light precipitation—unlike the brief showers that come from cumulus clouds. Stratus clouds that form at high altitudes are much thinner than low stratus clouds. You can see the Sun and the Moon through them. The ice crystals in high stratus clouds can make it seem as if there's a circle of colored light around the Sun or the Moon.

This fog formed around Castleton Tower in Utah. The land cooled overnight, causing water vapor in the air above it to condense.

Fog

Fog is a cloud that rests on the ground or a body of water. Like stratus clouds, fog has a smooth appearance. It usually forms when a surface is colder than the air above it. Water vapor in the air condenses as it cools, forming a thick mist. Fog on land tends to be heaviest at dawn, after the ground has cooled overnight. It clears as the ground is heated up by sunlight.

Fog can look beautiful rolling over hills or partly covering structures such as bridges. However, it often makes transportation dangerous by limiting visibility. In the United States close to 700 people die each year in automobile accidents that occur in dense fog.

 Review

KEY CONCEPTS

1. Describe the three forms in which water is present in the atmosphere.

2. How does altitude affect the composition of clouds?

3. How are clouds classified?

CRITICAL THINKING

4. **Summarize** Describe the main characteristics of cirrus, cumulus, and stratus clouds.

5. **Draw Conclusions** Why might cumulonimbus clouds be more likely to form on sunny days than on days with little sunlight?

◯ CHALLENGE

6. **Apply** Imagine that the sky has turned very cloudy after a hot morning. You notice that the bread in your sandwich is soggy and the towels on the towel rack won't dry. Explain why these things are happening. Use the following terms in your answer: *condensation, evaporation, relative humidity.*

CHAPTER INVESTIGATION

Relative Humidity

OVERVIEW AND PURPOSE Finding out the relative humidity can help you predict how comfortable you will feel on a hot day or whether dew will form on the ground. You can use a psychrometer to measure relative humidity. A psychrometer is a device made from two thermometers—one with a wet bulb and the other with a dry bulb. In this activity you will
- make a milk-carton psychrometer
- use it to measure the relative humidity of the air at two locations in your school

▶ Problem

Write It Up

Which location will have the greater relative humidity?

▶ Hypothesize

Write It Up

Write a hypothesis in "If . . . , then . . . , because . . ." form to answer the problem.

▶ Procedure

MATERIALS
- 2 thermometers
- cotton or felt cloth
- 3 rubber bands
- plastic bowl
- water at room temperature
- scissors
- pint milk carton
- ruler
- Relative Humidity Chart

1. Make a table like the one shown on the sample notebook page to record your data.

2. Check the two thermometers that you are using in this experiment to make sure they read the same temperature. Wrap a piece of cotton or felt cloth around the bulb of one thermometer. Hold the cloth in place with a rubber band as shown in the photograph. Dip this wet-bulb thermometer into a bowl of room-temperature water until the cloth is soaked.

step 3

3. Use scissors to cut a small hole in one side of the milk carton, 2 centimeters from the bottom of the carton. Place the wet-bulb thermometer on the same side as the hole that you made in the milk carton, and attach it with a rubber band. Push the tail of the cloth through the hole. Attach the dry-bulb thermometer as shown.

4 Fill the carton with water to just below the hole so that the cloth will remain wet. Empty the bowl and place the completed psychrometer inside it.

5 Write "science room" under the heading "Location 1" in your data table. Take your first readings in the science classroom about 10 minutes after you set up your psychrometer. Read the temperatures on the two thermometers in degrees Celsius. Record the temperature readings for the first location in the first column of your table.

6 Choose a second location in your school, and identify it under the heading "Location 2" in the data table. Take a second set of temperature readings with your psychrometer in this location. Record the readings in the second column of your table.

7 Subtract the wet-bulb reading from the dry-bulb reading for each location. Record this information in the third row of your data table.

8 Use the relative humidity table your teacher provides to find each relative humidity (expressed as a percentage). In the left-hand column, find the dry-bulb reading for location 1 that you recorded in step 5. Then find in the top line the number you recorded in step 7 (the difference between the dry-bulb and wet-bulb readings). Record the relative humidity in the last row of your data table. Repeat these steps for location 2.

▶ Observe and Analyze 　 Write It Up

1. **RECORD OBSERVATIONS** Draw the setup of your psychrometer. Be sure your data table is complete.

2. **IDENTIFY** Identify the variables and constants in this experiment. List them in your **Science Notebook.**

3. **COMPARE** How do the wet-bulb readings compare with the dry-bulb readings?

4. **ANALYZE** If the difference between the temperature readings on the two thermometers is large, is the relative humidity high or low? Explain why.

▶ Conclude 　 Write It Up

1. **INTERPRET** Answer the question in the problem. Compare your results with your hypothesis.

2. **IDENTIFY LIMITS** Describe any possible errors that you made in following the procedure.

3. **APPLY** How would you account for the differences in relative humidity that you obtained for the two locations in your school?

▶ INVESTIGATE Further

CHALLENGE Use the psychrometer to keep track of the relative humidity in your classroom over a period of one week. Make a new chart to record your data. What do you notice about how the changes in relative humidity relate to the weather conditions outside?

Relative Humidity

Problem Which location will have the greater relative humidity?

Hypothesize

Observe and Analyze

Table 1. Relative Humidity at Two Locations

	Location 1	Location 2
Dry-bulb temperature		
Wet-bulb temperature		
Difference between dry-bulb and wet-bulb readings		
Relative humidity		

Conclude

Water falls to Earth's surface as precipitation.

BEFORE, you learned

- Water moves between Earth's surface and the atmosphere
- Water vapor condenses into clouds

NOW, you will learn

- How precipitation forms
- How precipitation is measured
- About acid rain

VOCABULARY

freezing rain p. 68
sleet p. 68
hail p. 68
acid rain p. 70

THINK ABOUT

Why does steam from a shower form large drops?

When you run a hot shower, the bathroom fills up with water vapor. The vapor condenses into tiny droplets that make it seem as if you are standing in fog. You may also see larger drops running down cool surfaces, such as a mirror. Why do some drops fall while others remain suspended?

Precipitation forms from water droplets or ice crystals.

All precipitation comes from clouds. For example, rain occurs when water droplets in a cloud fall to the ground. Then why doesn't every cloud produce precipitation? Cloud droplets are much smaller than a typical raindrop. They weigh so little that it takes only a slight upward movement of air to hold them up. In order for rain to fall from a cloud and reach Earth's surface, the cloud droplets must become larger and heavier.

One way that precipitation can form is through the combining of cloud droplets. The tiny droplets of water move up and down in clouds. Some collide with each other and combine, forming slightly bigger droplets. As the droplets continue to combine, they grow larger and larger. Eventually they become heavy enough to fall. It takes about a million droplets to make a single raindrop.

Water droplets combining to form a raindrop

Another way that precipitation can form is through the growth of ice crystals. When the temperature inside a cloud is below freezing, water vapor changes into tiny ice crystals. The crystals grow by collecting more water vapor or by colliding and merging with one another. When the crystals become heavy enough, they fall from the cloud. Snow isn't the only type of precipitation that forms this way. Most rain in the United States actually starts out as falling ice crystals. Before the crystals reach the ground, they melt in a layer of warm air.

 CHECK YOUR READING How do cloud droplets become large enough to fall as precipitation?

Measuring Precipitation

Scientists use a rain gauge to measure rainfall. A funnel or opening at the top of the gauge allows rain to flow into a cylinder. By measuring the water collected, you can find out how much rain fell in a storm or over a period of time.

Snow depth can be measured with a long ruler. Because the amount of water in snow varies, scientists use a special gauge to find out how much water the snow contains. A built-in heater melts the snow so that it can be measured just like rain.

READING TiP

A gauge (gayj) is an instrument used for measuring or testing.

INVESTIGATE Precipitation

How much rain falls during a storm?

PROCEDURE

(1) Cut off the top third of the bottle. Set this part aside.

(2) Put some gravel at the bottom of the bottle to keep it from tipping over. Add water to cover the gravel. Draw a horizontal line on the bottle at the top of the water. Use a ruler to mark off centimeters on the bottle above the line that you drew. Now take the part of the bottle that you set aside and turn it upside down. Fit it inside the bottle to create a funnel.

(3) Place the bottle outside when a rainstorm is expected. Make sure that nothing will block rain from entering it. Check your rain gauge after 24 hours. Observe and record the rainfall.

WHAT DO YOU THINK?

• How much rain fell during the time period?

• How do the measurements compare with your observations?

CHALLENGE Do you think you would measure the same amount of rain if you used a wider rain gauge? Explain.

SKILL FOCUS
Measuring

MATERIALS
• scissors
• 1-liter plastic bottle
• gravel
• water
• permanent marker
• ruler

TIME
15 minutes

When you watch weather reports on television, you often see storm systems passing across a weather map. Some of these images are made with Doppler radar. The radar shows which areas are getting precipitation and how fast it is falling. Forecasters use this information to estimate the total amount of precipitation an area will receive.

Types of Precipitation

Precipitation reaches Earth's surface in various forms. Some precipitation freezes or melts as it falls through the atmosphere.

1 **Rain and Drizzle** Rain is the most common type of precipitation. Raindrops form from liquid cloud droplets or from ice crystals that melt as they fall. A light rain with very small drops is called drizzle. Drizzle usually comes from stratus clouds, which don't have enough air movement to build up larger raindrops.

2 **Freezing Rain** Raindrops may freeze when they hit the ground or other surfaces in cold weather. **Freezing rain** covers surfaces with a coating of ice. During an ice storm, roads become slippery and dangerous. The weight of ice can also bring down trees and power lines.

3 **Sleet** When rain passes through a layer of cold air, it can freeze before hitting the ground. The small pellets of ice that form are called **sleet.**

4 **Snow** As ice crystals grow and merge in clouds, they become snowflakes. Snowflakes come in many different shapes and sizes. Usually they have six sides or branches. When snow falls through moist air that is near freezing, the flakes tend to join together in clumps. When snow falls through colder and drier air, snowflakes don't join together, and the snow is powdery.

5 **Hail** Surprisingly, the largest type of frozen precipitation often arrives in warm weather. Lumps or balls of ice that fall from cumulonimbus clouds are called **hail.** During a thunderstorm, violent air currents hurl ice pellets around the cloud. These pellets grow as water droplets freeze onto them at high elevations. Some start to fall and then are pushed back up again. They may repeat this process several times, adding a layer of ice each time. Eventually they fall to the ground.

Large hailstones can damage property and injure people and animals. The biggest hailstone ever found in the United States weighed 1.7 pounds and was about as wide as a compact disc.

 CHECK YOUR READING Which forms of precipitation undergo a change after they leave a cloud?

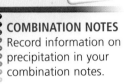
COMBINATION NOTES
Record information on precipitation in your combination notes.

Most snowflakes have six branches or sides.

How Precipitation Forms

All precipitation forms from water droplets or ice crystals in clouds. Some precipitation freezes or melts after it falls from the clouds.

⑤ Hail forms when ice pellets move up and down in clouds, growing larger as they gain layers of ice.

① Rain and **drizzle** form from water droplets or ice crystals that melt as they fall.

② Freezing rain is rain that freezes when it hits the ground or other surfaces.

③ Sleet is rain that freezes into ice pellets while falling through cold air.

④ Snow forms from ice crystals that merge in clouds.

freezing rain

hail

READING VISUALS What forms of precipitation occur most often where you live?

These trees have few needles because acid rain has damaged the trees.

Precipitation can carry pollution.

VOCABULARY
Add a description wheel for *acid rain* to your notebook.

Rainwater is naturally a little acidic. **Acid rain** is rain that has become much more acidic than normal because of pollution. Factories, power plants, automobiles, and some natural sources release sulfur dioxide and nitrogen oxides into the air. These gases can combine with water vapor to form sulfuric acid and nitric acid. The acids mix with cloud droplets or ice crystals that eventually fall to Earth's surface as precipitation.

Because wind can blow air pollution hundreds of kilometers, acid rain may fall far from the source of the pollution. Acid rain harms trees and raises the acidity of lakes, making it difficult for fish to live in them. Acid rain also damages the surfaces of buildings and sculptures.

CHECK YOUR READING How does acid rain form? Your answer should mention water vapor.

2.4 Review

KEY CONCEPTS

1. What are the two ways that rain can form?

2. How are rain and snow measured?

3. What human activities cause acid rain?

CRITICAL THINKING

4. **Compare and Contrast** How are sleet and freezing rain similar? How are they different?

5. **Draw Conclusions** When a large hailstone is cut open, four layers can be seen. What conclusions can you draw about the formation of the hailstone?

▲ CHALLENGE

6. **Predict** Temperatures in a cloud and on the ground are below freezing. A warmer layer of air lies between the cloud and the ground. What type of precipitation do you predict will occur? Explain.

Caught Inside a Thunderhead

In 1959, engine failure forced Lieutenant Colonel William Rankin to eject from his plane at a high altitude. When his parachute opened, he thought he was out of danger. However, he soon realized that he was caught inside a cumulonimbus cloud during a fierce thunderstorm.

As Rankin hung by his parachute, violent air movement inside the cloud tossed him "up, down, sideways, clockwise." The rain was so heavy that he feared he would drown in midair. Lightning flashed all around him. Rankin finally landed 40 minutes after his adventure began. He had many injuries, including bruises from hailstones. Fortunately, none of the storm's lightning had struck him.

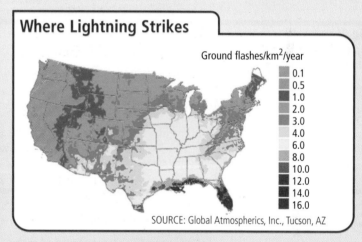

Where Lightning Strikes

Ground flashes/km²/year

| 0.1 |
| 0.5 |
| 1.0 |
| 2.0 |
| 3.0 |
| 4.0 |
| 6.0 |
| 8.0 |
| 10.0 |
| 12.0 |
| 14.0 |
| 16.0 |

SOURCE: Global Atmospherics, Inc., Tucson, AZ

Water, Wind, Hail, and Lightning

- A cumulonimbus cloud, or thunderhead, can rise to over 18 kilometers above Earth's surface. That's about twice the elevation of Mount Everest.

- A cumulonimbus cloud may contain 500,000 tons of water.

- Thunderstorm clouds cause 8 million lightning flashes each day.

EXPLORE

1. **ANALYZE** Find where you live on the map. Use the color key to figure out how often lightning strikes each square kilometer in your area.

2. **CHALLENGE** Use information from the Resource Center to propose an explanation for the pattern of lightning frequencies shown on the map.

RESOURCE CENTER
CLASSZONE.COM
Learn more about lightning.

Lightning flashes to the ground from a thunderhead, or cumulonimbus cloud.

Chapter Review

the BIG idea

Some features of weather have predictable patterns.

CONTENT REVIEW
CLASSZONE.COM

KEY CONCEPTS SUMMARY

2.1 The atmosphere's air pressure changes.

Air pressure is the force of air molecules pushing on an area. Air pressure decreases as you move higher in the atmosphere. Air pressure can also differ in two locations at the same altitude.

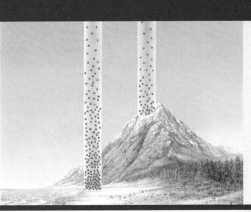

VOCABULARY
air pressure p. 43
barometer p. 46

2.2 The atmosphere has wind patterns.

Wind blows from areas of high pressure toward areas of low pressure. Earth's rotation causes long-distance winds to curve.

area of high pressure   *wind direction* →   **area of low pressure**

VOCABULARY
weather p. 47
wind p. 47
global wind p. 48
Coriolis effect p. 49
jet stream p. 52
monsoon p. 54

2.3 Most clouds form as air rises and cools.

Clouds are made of tiny water droplets or ice crystals that condense from water vapor in rising air.

VOCABULARY
evaporation p. 56
condensation p. 56
precipitation p. 57
humidity p. 58
saturation p. 58
relative humidity p. 58
dew point p. 58

2.4 Water falls to Earth's surface as precipitation.

Water droplets in clouds merge to form raindrops.

Ice crystals in clouds can form snow, rain, and other types of precipitation.

VOCABULARY
freezing rain p. 68
sleet p. 68
hail p. 68
acid rain p. 70

Reviewing Vocabulary

Write a definition of each term. Use the meaning of the underlined root to help you.

Word	Root Meaning	Definition
EXAMPLE air <u>press</u>ure	to apply force	the force of air molecules pushing on an area
1. <u>baro</u>meter	weight	
2. <u>satur</u>ation	to fill	
3. <u>glob</u>al wind	sphere	
4. <u>monsoon</u>	season	
5. e<u>vapor</u>ation	steam	
6. con<u>dens</u>ation	thick	
7. <u>humid</u>ity	moist	
8. <u>precipit</u>ation	thrown down	

Reviewing Key Concepts

Multiple Choice *Choose the letter of the best answer.*

9. The movement of air molecules causes
   a. air density
   b. air pressure
   c. humidity
   d. relative humidity

10. Winds curve as they move across Earth's surface because of
   a. the Coriolis effect
   b. air pressure
   c. humidity
   d. relative humidity

11. Jet streams generally flow toward the
   a. north
   b. south
   c. east
   d. west

12. Condensation increases with greater
   a. relative humidity
   b. air temperature
   c. air pressure
   d. wind speed

13. Any type of liquid or solid water that falls to Earth's surface is called
   a. precipitation
   b. dew
   c. a monsoon
   d. humidity

14. What are low-altitude clouds composed of?
   a. snowflakes
   b. raindrops
   c. water droplets
   d. water vapor

15. Clouds made of ice crystals form under conditions of
   a. strong winds
   b. high altitude
   c. low humidity
   d. high pressure

16. Which type of cloud is most likely to bring thunderstorms?
   a. stratus
   b. altostratus
   c. cumulonimbus
   d. cirrus

17. Over short distances wind blows toward areas of
   a. high pressure
   b. high density
   c. low temperature
   d. low pressure

18. The doldrums and the horse latitudes are both regions of
   a. high air pressure
   b. light winds
   c. heavy rains
   d. low temperatures

19. As altitude increases, air pressure usually
   a. decreases
   b. increases
   c. varies more
   d. varies less

Short Answer *Write a short answer to each question.*

20. What causes land breezes to flow at night?

21. Why does hair take longer to dry after a shower on days with high relative humidity?

22. How does air pressure affect air density?

23. Why are dust and other particles necessary for precipitation?

24. How did global wind belts and calm regions affect transportation in the past?

Thinking Critically

The soil in this terrarium was soaked with water two weeks ago. Then the box was sealed so that no moisture could escape. Use the diagram to answer the next six questions.

25. IDENTIFY EFFECTS How does sunlight affect conditions inside the terrarium?

26. ANALYZE Draw a diagram of the water cycle inside the terrarium.

27. INFER What do the water drops on the glass indicate about the temperatures inside and outside the terrarium?

28. PREDICT Explain how long you think the plants will live without being watered.

29. PREDICT What would happen if you placed the terrarium on top of a block of ice?

30. HYPOTHESIZE How would conditions inside the terrarium change if there were a hole in one side of it?

31. COMPARE AND CONTRAST How are sea breezes and monsoon winds alike, and how are they different?

32. PREDICT A cumulus cloud is growing taller. What will happen to the density of the air beneath it? Explain.

33. INFER Imagine that a group of factories and power plants lies 200 kilometers to the west of a forest where trees are dying. Describe three steps in a process that could be causing the trees to die.

IDENTIFY EFFECTS Write the type of precipitation that would form under each set of conditions.

Conditions	Precipitation
34. above-freezing air inside a cloud and freezing air beneath it	
35. above-freezing air beneath a cloud and freezing temperatures on the ground	
36. below-freezing air inside a cloud and above-freezing temperatures in the air beneath it and on the ground	
37. below-freezing air inside a cloud and beneath it	
38. ice pellets hurled around by air currents inside a cloud	

the BIG idea

39. APPLY Look again at the photograph on pages 40–41. Now that you have finished the chapter, how would you change your response to the question on the photograph?

40. WRITE Write one or more paragraphs explaining how energy from the Sun influences the weather. In your discussion, include at least three of the following topics:

- global wind belts
- high- and low-pressure areas
- local winds
- monsoons
- the water cycle
- cloud formation

UNIT PROJECTS

If you need to do an experiment for your unit project, gather the materials. Be sure to allow enough time to observe results before the project is due.

Analyzing a Diagram

This diagram shows the water cycle. Use it to answer the questions below.

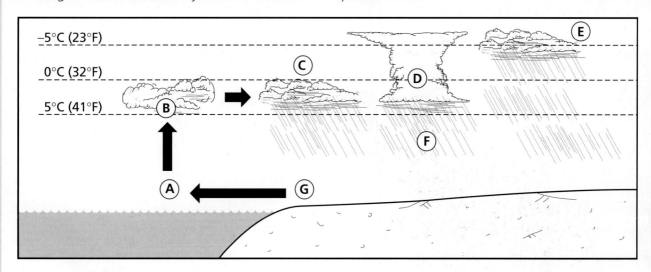

1. Where is evaporation occurring?

   a. A   **c.** F

   b. D   **d.** G

2. Where is condensation occurring?

   a. A   **c.** F

   b. B   **d.** G

3. Where is precipitation shown?

   a. A   **c.** E

   b. C   **d.** F

4. Where is hail most likely to form?

   a. C   **c.** E

   b. D   **d.** F

5. From which cloud will precipitation fall as snow and then turn to rain?

   a. B   **c.** D

   b. C   **d.** E

6. Which is the best estimate for the temperature in B?

   a. 8°C (46°F)   **c.** −3°C (27°F)

   b. 3°C (37°F)   **d.** −8°C (17°F)

7. What does the arrow pointing up between A and B indicate?

   a. the movement of moisture

   b. the direction of the wind

   c. a low pressure area

   d. a reflection off the water

Extended Response

Answer the two questions below in detail. Include some of the terms shown in the word box. In your answers underline each term you use.

low air pressure	cool air	west
high air pressure	warm air	east
Coriolis effect		

8. Whenever Richard rides in an elevator to the top of a skyscraper, he feels a pop inside his ears. Explain what is happening in the air to produce the pop in Richard's ears.

9. Winds tend to blow from west to east across the United States. If Earth spun in the other direction, how might the winds across the United States be different? Use the terms *east, west,* and *Coriolis effect* in your answer.

CHAPTER

3

Weather Fronts and Storms

the BIG idea

The interaction of air masses causes changes in weather.

> **What types of weather can move a house?**

Key Concepts

SECTION 3.1
Weather changes as air masses move.
Learn about air masses, fronts, and high- and low-pressure systems.

SECTION 3.2
Low-pressure systems can become storms.
Learn about hurricanes and winter storms.

SECTION 3.3
Vertical air motion can cause severe storms.
Learn about thunderstorms, lightning, and tornadoes.

SECTION 3.4
Weather forecasters use advanced technologies.
Learn about different types of weather data and how forecasters predict weather.

Internet Preview

CLASSZONE.COM

Chapter 3 online resources: Content Review, two Visualizations, two Resource Centers, Math Tutorial, Test Practice

How Does Cold Air Move?

Hold one hand near the top of a refrigerator door and the other hand near the bottom. Open the refrigerator door just a little bit.

Observe and Think How did each hand feel before and after you opened the door? How did the air move?

How Does Weather Move?

Collect newspaper weather maps for three consecutive days. Identify at least one flagged line on a map (identifying a weather front) and track the line's movement over the three days.

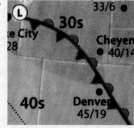

Observe and Think What type of weather did you find each day where the line passed? Why did this line move the way it did?

Internet Activity: Weather Safety

Go to **ClassZone.com** to find information about weather safety. Find out the types of dangerous weather that may affect your region.

Observe and Think What can you do ahead of time to be ready for severe weather?

NSTA
scilinks.org

SCi LINKS

Severe Weather **Code: MDL011**

Getting Ready to Learn

◄ CONCEPT REVIEW

- Air temperature decreases as you rise in the troposphere.
- Temperature affects air density.
- Pressure differences make air move.
- Uneven heating of Earth's surface produces winds.
- Clouds form as air rises, expands, and cools.

◄ VOCABULARY REVIEW

altitude p. 10

convection p. 19

evaporation p. 56

condensation p. 56

relative humidity p. 58

CONTENT REVIEW
CLASSZONE.COM
Review concepts and vocabulary.

▶ TAKING NOTES

MAIN IDEA WEB

Write each new blue heading—a main idea—in a box. Then put notes with important terms and details into boxes around the main idea.

VOCABULARY STRATEGY

Draw a **word triangle** diagram for each new vocabulary term. In the bottom row write and define the term. In the middle row, use the term correctly in a sentence. At the top, draw a small picture to help you remember the term.

See the Note-Taking Handbook on pages R45–R51.

SCIENCE NOTEBOOK

Marine air masses form over water.

Continental air masses form over land.

Air masses are large bodies of air.

Tropical air masses are warm.

Polar air masses are cold.

Yesterday the temperature fell as a cold front passed us.

front: the boundary between two air masses

3.1 Weather changes as air masses move.

 BEFORE, you learned

- Air pressure changes with location and altitude
- Water vapor in the atmosphere condenses when air rises

 NOW, you will learn

- What air masses are
- What happens when air masses meet
- How pressure systems affect the weather

VOCABULARY

air mass p. 79
front p. 82
high-pressure
  system p. 84
low-pressure system p. 85

EXPLORE Air Masses

How does an air mass form?

PROCEDURE

① Put ice into one bowl and warm water into a second bowl. Leave the third bowl empty.

② Place each bowl in a different box and cover the box with plastic wrap. Wait a few minutes.

③ Put your hand into each box in turn.

WHAT DO YOU THINK?
- How would you describe the air in each box?
- Which box's air feels the most humid? Why?

MATERIALS
- 3 bowls
- ice
- warm water
- 3 shoeboxes
- plastic wrap

Air masses are large bodies of air.

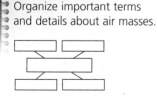

MAIN IDEA WEB
Organize important terms and details about air masses.

You have probably experienced the effects of air masses—one day is hot and humid, and the next day is cool and pleasant. The weather changes when a new air mass moves into your area. An **air mass** is a large volume of air in which temperature and humidity are nearly the same in different locations at the same altitude. An air mass can cover many thousands of square kilometers.

An air mass forms when the air over a large region of Earth sits in one place for many days. The air gradually takes on the characteristics of the land or water below it. Where Earth's surface is cold, the air becomes cold. Where Earth's surface is wet, the air becomes moist. As an air mass moves, it brings its temperature and moisture to new locations.

 Explain how the weather can change with the arrival of a new air mass. Your answer should include two ways that weather changes.

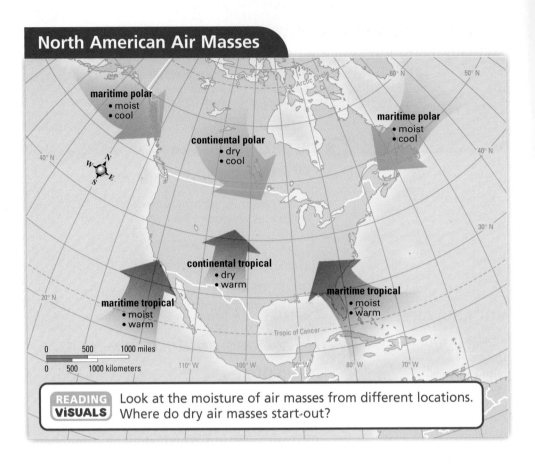

North American Air Masses

maritime polar
• moist
• cool

maritime polar
• moist
• cool

continental polar
• dry
• cool

continental tropical
• dry
• warm

maritime tropical
• moist
• warm

maritime tropical
• moist
• warm

0   500   1000 miles
0   500   1000 kilometers

READING VISUALS Look at the moisture of air masses from different locations. Where do dry air masses start out?

Characteristics of an Air Mass

Some regions of Earth's surface, such as those shown in the map above, produce air masses again and again. The characteristics of an air mass depend on the region where it forms. A hot desert produces dry, hot air masses, while cool ocean waters produce moist, cool air masses. Scientists classify air masses into categories according to the characteristics of regions. Each category name is made of two words—one for moisture, one for temperature.

The first word of an air mass's category name tells whether the air mass formed over water or dry land. It describes the moisture of the air mass.

- **Continental** air masses form over land. Air becomes dry as it loses its moisture to the dry land below it.
- **Maritime** (MAR-ih-TYM) air masses form over water. Air becomes moist as it gains water vapor from the water below it.

The second word of a category name tells whether an air mass formed close to the equator. It describes the air mass's temperature.

- **Tropical** air masses form near the equator. Air becomes warm as it gains energy from the warm land or water.
- **Polar** air masses form far from the equator. Air becomes cool as it loses energy to the cold land or water.

READING TiP

The word *maritime* has the same root as the word *marine*. Both come from the Latin word *mare*, which means "sea."

The combination of words gives the characteristics of the air mass. A maritime tropical air mass is moist and warm, while a continental polar air mass is dry and cold.

 CHECK YOUR READING What can you tell from each word of an air mass's name?

Movement of an Air Mass

Air masses can travel away from the regions where they form. They move with the global pattern of winds. In most of the United States, air masses generally move from west to east. They may move along with the jet stream in more complex and changing patterns.

When an air mass moves to a new region, it carries along its characteristic moisture and temperature. As the air moves over Earth's surface, the characteristics of the surface begin to change the air mass. For example, if a continental polar air mass moves over warm water, the air near the surface will become warmer and gain moisture. These changes begin where the air touches the surface. It may take days or weeks for the changes to spread upward through the entire air mass. An air mass that moves quickly may not change much. If it moves quickly enough, a continental polar air mass can move cold air from northern Canada all the way to the southern United States.

INVESTIGATE Air Masses

What happens when air masses collide?

PROCEDURE

1. Cut the cardboard to create a snug barrier that divides your beaker in half.

2. Mix about 5 mL of salt, 50 mL of water, and a drop of blue food coloring in one cup. This dense mixture represents a cold air mass.

3. Mix 50 mL of water with a drop of red food coloring in the other cup. This less-dense mixture represents a warm air mass.

4. Carefully pour the red water into one side of your divided beaker and the blue saltwater into the other side. As you look through the side of the beaker, quickly remove the barrier.

WHAT DO YOU THINK?

- What happened when the two liquids met?
- To what extent did the liquids mix together?

CHALLENGE How are the liquids like air masses?

SKILL FOCUS
Inferring

MATERIALS
- 500 mL beaker
- stiff cardboard
- scissors
- 2 cups
- small beaker for measuring
- salt
- water
- food coloring

TIME
25 minutes

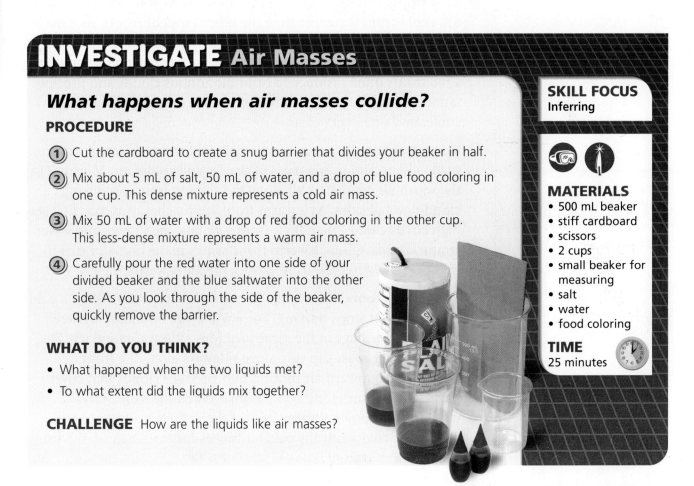

Weather changes where air masses meet.

When a new air mass moves over your area, you can expect the weather to change. Perhaps you have heard a weather forecaster talk about fronts. A **front** is a boundary between air masses. The weather near a front can differ from the weather inside the rest of an air mass. As one air mass pushes another, some of the air at the boundary will be pushed upward. Clouds can form in this rising air. The weather often becomes cloudy or stormy as a front passes. Afterward, you experience the temperature and humidity of the air mass that has moved in.

Fronts and Weather

MAIN IDEA WEB
Organize the notes you take about fronts.

Different types of fronts produce different patterns of weather. When a cold, dense air mass pushes warmer air, it produces a cold front. When a warm air mass pushes colder air, it produces a warm front. These names tell you which way the temperature will change but not how much it will change. A cold front can turn a heat wave into normal summer weather or turn cold winter air into very cold weather.

 CHECK YOUR READING How would the weather change if a cold front moved into your area?

① **Cold fronts** can move into regions quickly. As you can see on page 83, a cold front is steeper than the other types of fronts. As a mass of cold, dense air moves forward, warmer air ahead of it is pushed upward. Water vapor in the warm air condenses as the air rises. Cold fronts often produce tall cumulonimbus clouds and precipitation. Brief, heavy storms are likely. After the storms, the air is cooler and often very clear.

② **Warm fronts** move more slowly than cold fronts. Warm air moves gradually up and over a mass of denser and colder air. Moisture in the warm air condenses all along the sloping front, producing cloud-covered skies. As a warm front approaches, you may first see high cirrus clouds, then high stratus clouds, then lower and lower stratus clouds. Often, a warm front brings many hours of steady rain or snow. After the front passes, the air is warmer.

VISUALIZATION
CLASSZONE.COM

See how the air moves in warm fronts and cold fronts.

③ **Stationary fronts** occur when air masses first meet or when a cold or warm front stops moving. For a while, the boundary between the air masses stays in the same location—it stays stationary. The air in each air mass can still move sideways along the front or upward. The upward air motion may produce clouds that cover the sky, sometimes for days at a time. When the front starts moving, it becomes a warm front if the warm air advances and pushes the cold air. If the cold air moves forward instead, the front becomes a cold front.

Fronts and Weather

As fronts move across Earth's surface, they produce changes in the weather.

1 Cold Front

A **cold front** forms when a cold air mass pushes a warm air mass and forces the warm air to rise. As the warm air rises, its moisture condenses and forms tall clouds.

Triangles show the direction that a cold front moves.

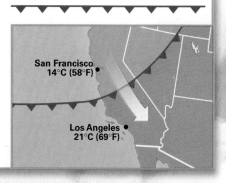

San Francisco
14°C (58°F)

Los Angeles
21°C (69°F)

2 Warm Front

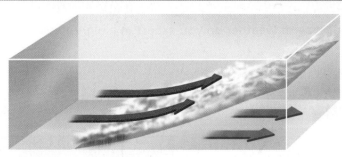

A **warm front** forms when a warm air mass pushes a cold air mass. The warm air rises slowly over the cold air and its moisture condenses into flat clouds.

Semicircles show the direction that a warm front moves.

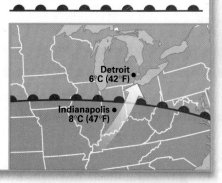

Detroit
6°C (42°F)

Indianapolis
8°C (47°F)

3 Stationary Front

A **stationary front** occurs when two air masses push against each other without moving. A stationary front becomes a warm or cold front when one air mass advances.

Alternating triangles and semicircles show a stationary front.

Atlanta
17°C (62°F)

Orlando
27°C (80°F)

READING VISUALS **PREDICT** Which city will the cold front affect next?

High-Pressure Systems

You may have seen the letters H and L on a weather map. These letters mark high-pressure centers and low-pressure centers, often simply called highs and lows. Each center is the location of the highest or lowest pressure in a region. The pressure differences cause air to move in ways that may make a high or low become the center of a whole system of weather.

READING TiP

A *system* includes different parts that work together.

At a high-pressure center, air sinks slowly down. As the air nears the ground, it spreads out toward areas of lower pressure. In the Northern Hemisphere, the Coriolis effect makes the air turn clockwise as it moves outward. A **high-pressure system** is formed when air moves all the way around a high-pressure center. Most high-pressure systems are large and change slowly. When a high-pressure system stays in one location for a long time, an air mass may form. The air—and resulting air mass—can be warm or cold, moist or dry.

A high-pressure system generally brings clear skies and calm air or gentle breezes. This is because as air sinks to lower altitudes, it warms up a little bit. Water droplets evaporate, so clouds often disappear.

CHECK YOUR READING What type of weather do you expect in a high-pressure system?

Weather Systems in the Northern Hemisphere

High-pressure systems and low-pressure systems produce patterns of weather across Earth's surface.

A spiral of clouds often shows the location of a low-pressure system.

Air sinks at a high-pressure center and spreads out toward locations with low pressure. The spreading air moves slowly clockwise.

Air circles into a low-pressure center and moves upward. The motion is counterclockwise and can be quick.

READING VISUALS With your finger, trace the motion of air, starting above the high. Where have you seen similar patterns in earlier chapters?

Low-Pressure Systems

A small area of low pressure can also develop into a larger system. A **low-pressure system** is a large weather system that surrounds a center of low pressure. It begins as air moves around and inward toward the lowest pressure and then up to higher altitudes. The upward motion of the air lowers the air pressure further, and so the air moves faster. The pattern of motion strengthens into a low-pressure weather system. The rising air produces stormy weather. In the Northern Hemisphere, the air in a low-pressure system circles in a counterclockwise direction.

A low-pressure system can develop wherever there is a center of low pressure. One place this often happens is along a boundary between a warm air mass and a cold air mass. The diagram shows an example of this process.

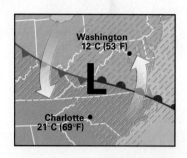

Washington
12°C (53°F)

Charlotte
21°C (69°F)

- Part of the boundary between the air masses moves south and becomes a cold front.
- Part of the boundary moves north and becomes a warm front.
- A center of low pressure forms where the ends of the two fronts meet.

The low-pressure center and fronts become parts of a whole system of weather. Rising air at the fronts and at the low can cause very stormy weather.

The diagram on page 84 shows how air moves between pressure centers. Air moves down, out, and around a high-pressure center. Then it swirls around and into a low-pressure center and moves upward. Highs and lows affect each other as they move across the surface. Large weather systems generally move with the pattern of global winds—west to east over most of North America. But, within a weather system, winds can blow in different directions.

3.1 Review

KEY CONCEPTS

1. What are the two characteristics of an air mass that you need to know in order to classify it?

2. What happens when a warmer air mass pushes a cooler air mass?

3. What type of weather system brings calm, clear weather?

CRITICAL THINKING

4. **Compare and Contrast** Explain how air moves differently in low- and high-pressure systems.

5. **Apply** If the weather becomes stormy for a short time and then becomes colder, which type of front has passed?

⬤ CHALLENGE

6. **Synthesize** You check a barometer and observe that the air pressure has been dropping all day. Is tonight's weather more likely to be calm or stormy?

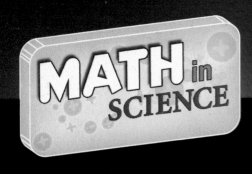

SKILL: DETERMINING RATES

Movement of a Front

Scientists measure the speeds of weather fronts to forecast weather conditions. The speed at which a front moves is an example of a rate. A rate can be written as a ratio. For example, the rate of a front that moves a distance of 500 kilometers in 1 day can be written as follows:

500 kilometers : 1 day

The map below shows the movement of a cold front over four consecutive days. Use the map scale to determine the distance that the front moves on each day.

MATH TUTORIAL
CLASSZONE.COM
Click on Math Tutorial for more help with rates as ratios.

Cold Front Movement

Answer the following questions.

1. What was the front's rate of movement between Wednesday and Thursday? Express your answer as a ratio.

? : 1 day

2. What was the front's rate of movement between Friday and Saturday? Express your answer as a ratio.

3. What was the mean rate of the front's movement from Wednesday to Saturday? Remember, *mean* means "average." Express your answer as a ratio.

CHALLENGE Use the rate from Wednesday to Saturday to estimate the day on which the front must have moved through San Francisco.

3.2 Low-pressure systems can become storms.

BEFORE, you learned

- Moving air masses cause changes in weather
- A low-pressure system brings stormy weather

NOW, you will learn

- How hurricanes develop
- About the dangers of hurricanes
- About different types of winter storms

VOCABULARY

tropical storm p. 87
hurricane p. 87
storm surge p. 89
blizzard p. 90

EXPLORE Hurricanes

What things make hurricanes lose strength?

PROCEDURE

1. Crumple a piece of paper, then flatten it out. Crumple and flatten it out again.

2. Spin the top on the flattened paper. Count the seconds until it stops spinning.

3. Spin the top on a smooth surface. Count the seconds until it stops spinning.

MATERIALS
- sheet of paper
- top

WHAT DO YOU THINK?
How does the texture of the surface affect the rate at which the top loses energy?

Hurricanes form over warm ocean water.

MAIN IDEA WEB
Remember to make notes about hurricanes.

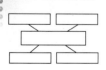

Near the equator, warm ocean water provides the energy that can turn a low-pressure center into a violent storm. As water evaporates from the ocean, energy moves from the ocean water into the air. This energy makes warm air rise faster. Tall clouds and strong winds develop. As winds blow across the water from different directions into the low, the Coriolis effect bends their paths into a spiral. The winds blow faster and faster around the low, which becomes the center of a storm system.

A **tropical storm** is a low-pressure system that starts near the equator and has winds that blow at 65 kilometers per hour (40 mi/h) or more. A **hurricane** (HUR-ih-KAYN) is a tropical low-pressure system with winds blowing at speeds of 120 kilometers per hour (74 mi/h) or more—strong enough to uproot trees. Hurricanes are called typhoons or cyclones when they form over the Indian Ocean or the western Pacific Ocean.

Formation of Hurricanes

VISUALIZATION
CLASSZONE.COM

Watch the progress of
a hurricane.

In the eastern United States, hurricanes most often strike between August and October. Energy from warm water is necessary for a low-pressure center to build into a tropical storm and then into a hurricane. The ocean water where these storms develop only gets warm enough—26°C (80°F) or more—near the end of summer.

Tropical storms and hurricanes generally move westward with the trade winds. Near land, however, they will often move north, south, or even back eastward. As long as a storm stays above warm water, it can grow bigger and more powerful. As soon as a hurricane moves over land or over cooler water, it loses its source of energy. The winds lose strength and the storm dies out. If a hurricane moves over land, the rough surface of the land reduces the winds even more.

The map below shows the progress of a storm. The tropical storm gained energy and became a hurricane as it moved westward. When the hurricane moved north, the storm lost energy and was called a tropical storm again as its winds slowed.

CHECK YOUR READING What is the source of a hurricane's energy?

Structure of a Hurricane

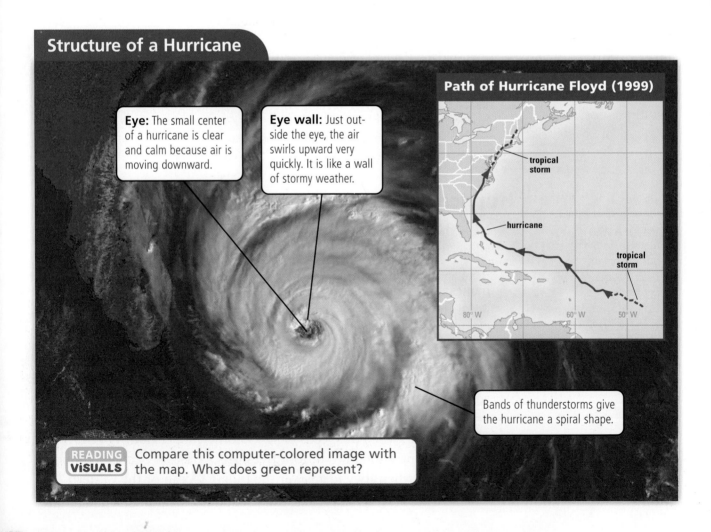

Eye: The small center of a hurricane is clear and calm because air is moving downward.

Eye wall: Just outside the eye, the air swirls upward very quickly. It is like a wall of stormy weather.

Path of Hurricane Floyd (1999)

tropical storm

hurricane

tropical storm

80° W   60° W   50° W

Bands of thunderstorms give the hurricane a spiral shape.

READING VISUALS Compare this computer-colored image with the map. What does green represent?

At the center of a hurricane is a small area of clear weather, 20–50 kilometers (10–30 mi) in diameter, called the eye. The storm's center is calm because air moves downward there. Just around the eye, the air moves very quickly around and upward, forming a tall ring of cumulonimbus clouds called the eye wall. This ring produces very heavy rains and tremendous winds. Farther from the center, bands of heavy clouds and rain spiral inward toward the eye.

Effects of Hurricanes

A hurricane can pound a coast with huge waves and sweep the land with strong winds and heavy rains. The storms cause damage and dangerous conditions in several ways. Hurricane winds can lift cars, uproot trees, and tear the roofs off buildings. Hurricanes may also produce tornadoes that cause even more damage. Heavy rains from hurricanes may make rivers overflow their banks and flood nearby areas. When a hurricane moves into a coastal area, it often pushes a huge mass of ocean water known as a **storm surge.** In a storm surge, the sea level rises several meters, backing up rivers and flooding the shore. A storm surge can be destructive and deadly. Large waves add to the destruction. A hurricane may affect an area for a few hours or a few days, but the damage may take weeks or even months to clean up.

CHECK YOUR READING What are the effects of hurricanes? Make a list for your answer.

The National Hurricane Center helps people know when to prepare for a hurricane. The center puts out a tropical-storm or hurricane watch when a storm is likely to strike within 36 hours. People may be evacuated, or moved away for safety, from areas where they may be in danger. As the danger gets closer—24 hours or less— the center issues a tropical-storm or hurricane warning. The warning stays in effect until the danger has passed.

SAFETY TIPS

HURRICANES

- Before a storm, prepare a plan to leave the area. Gather emergency supplies.
- Listen to weather reports for storm updates.
- Secure loose objects outside, and cover windows.
- If ordered to evacuate, leave immediately.
- During a storm, stay indoors and away from windows.
- After a storm, be aware of power lines, hanging branches, and flooded areas.

NORTH CAROLINA

Topsail Island

COMPARE AND CONTRAST These pictures show a shoreline in North Carolina before and after Hurricane Fran in 1996. Compare the houses, road, and water in the two pictures.

Winter storms produce snow and ice.

Most severe winter storms in the United States are part of low-pressure systems. Unlike hurricanes, the systems that cause winter storms form when two air masses collide. A continental polar air mass that forms over snow-covered ground is especially cold, dry, and dense. It can force moist air to rise very quickly, producing a stormy low-pressure system.

The National Weather Service (NWS) alerts people to dangerous weather. The NWS issues a winter storm watch up to 48 hours before a storm is expected. A winter storm warning means that dangerous conditions are already present or will affect an area shortly.

Blizzards Strong winds can blow so much snow into the air at once that it becomes difficult to see and dangerous to travel. **Blizzards** are blinding snowstorms with winds of at least 56 kilometers per hour (35 mi/h) and low temperatures—usually below –7°C (20°F). Blizzards occur in many parts of the northern and central United States. Wind and snow can knock down trees and power lines. Without heat, buildings can become very cold, and water in pipes may freeze. Schools, hospitals, and businesses may have to close. Deep, heavy snow on top of a building may cause the roof to cave in.

Lake-Effect Snowstorms Some of the heaviest snows fall in the areas just east and south of the Great Lakes. Cold air from the northwest gains moisture and warmth as it passes over the Great Lakes. Over cold land, the air cools again and releases the moisture as snow. The lake effect can cover areas downwind of the Great Lakes with clouds and snow even when the rest of the region has clear weather.

VOCABULARY
Remember to add a word triangle diagram for *blizzard*.

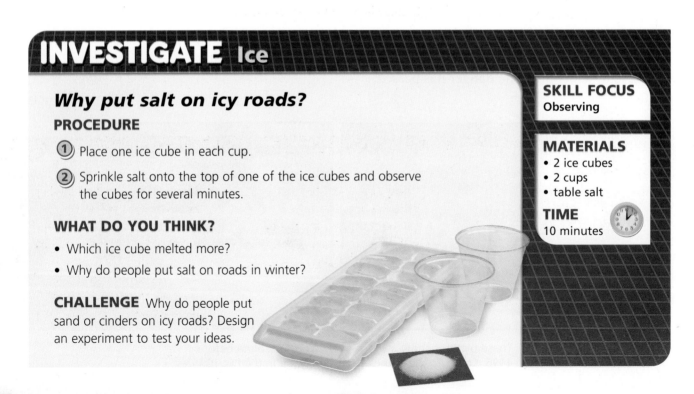

INVESTIGATE Ice

Why put salt on icy roads?
PROCEDURE
1. Place one ice cube in each cup.
2. Sprinkle salt onto the top of one of the ice cubes and observe the cubes for several minutes.

WHAT DO YOU THINK?
- Which ice cube melted more?
- Why do people put salt on roads in winter?

CHALLENGE Why do people put sand or cinders on icy roads? Design an experiment to test your ideas.

SKILL FOCUS
Observing

MATERIALS
- 2 ice cubes
- 2 cups
- table salt

TIME
10 minutes

Ice Storms When rain falls onto freezing-cold ground, conditions can become dangerous. The cold rain freezes as it touches the ground and other surfaces. This freezing rain covers everything with heavy, smooth ice. The ice-covered roads become slippery and dangerous. Drivers may find it hard to steer and to stop their cars. Branches or even whole trees may break from the weight of ice. Falling branches can block roads, tear down power and telephone lines, and cause other damage. Damage from ice storms can sometimes shut down entire cities.

 CHECK YOUR READING What type of precipitation occurs in each type of winter storm?

3.2 Review

KEY CONCEPTS

1. Where and when do hurricanes form?
2. In what two ways can hurricanes cause floods?
3. List three of the possible dangers from winter storms.

CRITICAL THINKING

4. **Compare and Contrast** What are the differences between the eye and the eye wall of a hurricane?
5. **Compare** What do hurricanes and winter storms have in common?

● CHALLENGE

6. **Apply** If the wind is blowing from the west and the conditions are right for lake-effect snow, will the snow fall to the north, south, east, or west of a lake? Drawing a diagram may help you work out an answer.

Vertical air motion can cause severe storms.

BEFORE, you learned

- Fronts produce changes in weather
- Rising moist air can produce clouds and precipitation

NOW, you will learn

- How thunderstorms develop
- About the effects of thunderstorms
- About tornadoes and their effects

VOCABULARY

thunderstorm p. 92
tornado p. 95

EXPLORE Lightning

Does miniature lightning cause thunder?

PROCEDURE

1. Use a thumbtack to attach the eraser to the center of a piece of foil.

2. Rub the foam tray quickly back and forth several times on the wool. Set the tray down.

3. Using the eraser as a handle, pick up the foil and set it onto the tray. Slowly move your finger close to the foil.

WHAT DO YOU THINK?
What happened when you touched the foil?

MATERIALS
- thumbtack
- eraser
- aluminum foil
- plastic foam tray
- wool fabric

Thunderstorms form from rising moist air.

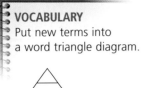

VOCABULARY
Put new terms into a word triangle diagram.

If you have ever shuffled your shoes on a carpet, you may have felt a small shock when you touched a doorknob. Electrical charges collected on your body and then jumped to the doorknob in a spark of electricity.

In a similar way, electrical charges build up near the tops and bottoms of clouds as pellets of ice move up and down through the clouds. Suddenly, a charge sparks from one part of a cloud to another or between a cloud and the ground. The spark of electricity, called lightning, causes a bright flash of light. The air around the lightning is briefly heated to a temperature hotter than the surface of the Sun. This fast heating produces a sharp wave of air that travels away from the lightning. When the wave reaches you, you hear it as a crack of thunder. A **thunderstorm** is a storm with lightning and thunder.

Is thunder a cause or an effect of lightning?

Formation of Thunderstorms

Thunderstorms get their energy from humid air. When warm, humid air near the ground moves vertically into cooler air above, the rising air, or updraft, can build a thunderstorm quickly.

  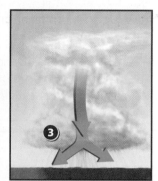

❶ Rising humid air forms a cumulus cloud. The water vapor releases energy when it condenses into cloud droplets. This energy increases the air motion. The cloud continues building up into the tall cumulonimbus cloud of a thunderstorm.

❷ Ice particles form in the low temperatures near the top of the cloud. As the ice particles grow large, they begin to fall and pull cold air down with them. This strong downdraft brings heavy rain or hail—the most severe stage of a thunderstorm.

❸ The downdraft can spread out and block more warm air from moving upward into the cloud. The storm slows down and ends.

Thunderstorms can form at a cold front or within an air mass. At a cold front, air can be forced upward quickly. Within an air mass, uneven heating can produce convection and thunderstorms. In some regions, the conditions that produce thunderstorms occur almost daily during part of the year. In Florida, for example, the wet land and air warm up during a long summer day. Then, as you see in the diagram, cool sea breezes blow in from both coasts of the peninsula at once. The two sea breezes together push the warm, humid air over the land upward quickly. Thunderstorms form in the rising air.

In contrast, the summer air along the coast of California is usually too dry to produce thunderstorms. The air over the land heats up, and a sea breeze forms, but there is not enough moisture in the rising warm air to form clouds and precipitation.

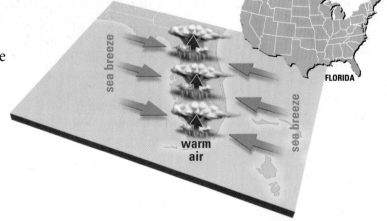

INVESTIGATE Updrafts

How do updrafts form?

PROCEDURE

1. Set up the cardboard, the cups, the container, and the cool water as shown in the photograph. Wait for the water to become still.

2. Use the eyedropper to place 2–3 drops of coloring at the bottom of the water.

3. Slide a cup of hot water (about 70°C) beneath the food coloring.

WHAT DO YOU THINK?

In what ways was the motion of the water like the air in a thunderstorm?

CHALLENGE How could you observe updrafts in air?

SKILL FOCUS
Inferring

MATERIALS
- 4 cardboard squares
- 5 foam cups
- clear container
- cool water
- food coloring
- eyedropper
- hot tap water

TIME
20 minutes

Effects of Thunderstorms

A thunderstorm may provide cool rain at the end of a hot, dry spell. The rain can provide water for crops and restore lakes and streams. However, thunderstorms are often dangerous.

Flash floods can be strong enough to wash away people, cars, and even houses. One thunderstorm can produce millions of liters of rain. If a thunderstorm dumps all its rain in one place, or if a series of thunderstorms dump rain onto the same area, the water can cover the ground or make rivers overflow their banks.

Winds from a thunderstorm can be very strong. They can blow in bursts that exceed 270 kilometers per hour (170 mi/hr). Thunderstorm winds once knocked down a stretch of forest in Canada that was about 16 kilometers (10 mi) wide and 80 kilometers (50 mi) long. Thunderstorms can also produce sudden, dangerous bursts of air that move downward and spread out.

Hail causes nearly $1 billion in damage to property and crops in the United States every year. Hail can wipe out entire fields of a valuable crop in a few minutes. Large hailstones can damage roofs and kill livestock.

Lightning can kill or seriously injure any person it hits. It can damage power lines and other equipment. Lightning can also spark dangerous forest fires.

SAFETY TIPS

THUNDERSTORMS

- Stay alert when storms are predicted or dark, tall clouds are visible.
- If you hear thunder, seek shelter immediately and stay there for 30 minutes after the last thunder ends.
- Avoid bodies of water, lone trees, flagpoles, and metal objects.
- Stay away from the telephone, electrical appliances, and pipes.
- If flash floods are expected, move away from low ground.
- Do not try to cross flowing water, even if it looks shallow.

 CHECK YOUR READING In what ways are thunderstorms dangerous? Did any surprise you?

Tornadoes form in severe thunderstorms.

Under some conditions, the up-and-down air motion that produces tall clouds, lightning, and hail may produce a tornado. A **tornado** is a violently rotating column of air stretching from a cloud to the ground. A tornado moves along the ground in a winding path underneath the cloud. The column may even rise off the ground and then come down in a different place.

READING TiP

A spinning column of air is not called a tornado unless it touches the ground. If it touches water instead, it is called a waterspout.

You cannot see air moving. A tornado may become visible when water droplets appear below the cloud in the center of the rotating column. A tornado may lift dust and debris from the ground, so the bottom of the column becomes visible, as you see in the photographs below. Water droplets and debris may make a tornado look like an upright column or a twisted rope.

CHECK YOUR READING What makes a tornado become visible?

More tornadoes occur in North America than anywhere else in the world. Warm, humid air masses move north from the Gulf of Mexico to the central plains of the United States. There, the warm air masses often meet cold, dense air and form thunderstorms. In the spring, the winds in this region often produce the conditions that form tornadoes. A thunderstorm may form a series of tornadoes or even a group of tornadoes all at once.

Tornado Formation

As a tornado forms, a funnel cloud seems to stretch down from the cloud above.

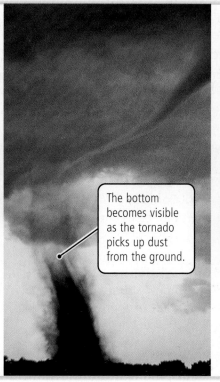

The bottom becomes visible as the tornado picks up dust from the ground.

The tornado moves along the ground before it dies out.

SAFETY TIPS

TORNADOES

- Listen for tornado warnings when severe weather is predicted.
- If you are in a car or mobile home, get out and go into a sturdy building or a ditch or depression.
- Go to the basement if possible.
- Avoid windows and open areas.
- Protect your head and neck.

Effects of Tornadoes

The powerful winds of a tornado can cause damage as the bottom of the tornado moves along the ground. Tornado winds can also pick up and slam dirt and small objects into buildings or anything else in the tornado's path.

The most common tornadoes are small and last only a few minutes. Their winds may be strong enough to break branches off trees, damage chimneys, and tear highway billboards. A typical path along the ground may be 100 meters (300 ft) wide and 1.5 kilometers (1 mi) long.

Larger tornadoes are less common but have stronger winds and last longer. About 20 percent of tornadoes are strong enough to knock over large trees, lift cars off the ground, and tear the roofs off houses. Very few—about 1 percent of all tornadoes—are violent enough to lift or completely demolish sturdy buildings. These huge tornadoes may last more than two hours. You can find more details about tornadoes in the Appendix.

Paths of Tornadoes

A tornado moves along with its thunderstorm. It travels at the same pace and weaves a path that is impossible to predict. A tornado may appear suddenly and then disappear before anyone has time to report it. However, the conditions that form tornadoes may persist, so citizens' reports are still useful. The National Weather Service issues a tornado watch when the weather conditions might produce tornadoes. A tornado warning is issued when a tornado has been detected.

3.3 Review

KEY CONCEPTS

1. What conditions produce thunderstorms?
2. How can rain from thunderstorms become dangerous?
3. How do tornadoes cause damage?

CRITICAL THINKING

4. **Compare** What do hail and tornadoes have in common? **Hint:** Think about how each forms.
5. **Synthesize** Which type of front is most likely to produce thunderstorms and tornadoes? Explain why.

⬤ CHALLENGE

6. **Compare and Contrast** If you saw the photograph above in a newspaper, what details would tell you that the damage was due to a tornado and not a hurricane?

What Type of Weather Buried This Truck?

This picture was taken soon after a weather event partly buried this truck in Britannia Beach, British Columbia.

▶ Observations and Inferences

One observer made this analysis.

a. The truck, the tree, and two fences in the background were partly buried by sand and stones.

b. No stones are visible inside the truck.

c. The rounded stones must have come from an ocean or river.

d. The tree near the truck has green leaves. The wind must have been too weak to tear off the leaves.

e. The area is near the Pacific Ocean. It is far from the equator. There is a very large island between the location and the ocean.

▶ Hypotheses

The observer made the following hypotheses.

a. A storm surge carried sand and stones from the Pacific Ocean. The material covered a large area. The truck floated, so it was not filled with material.

b. A tornado picked up the truck with other material. It dumped everything together, and the material partly buried the truck, fences, and tree.

c. Thunderstorms produced a flash flood that carried sand and stones from a riverbed to this area. The flood receded and left material that covered the area.

d. The truck was parked on a pile of snow during a blizzard. When the snow melted, the area under the truck collapsed and the truck sank into the ground.

A waterway leads south and west from Britannia Beach to a bay, around an island, to the Pacific Ocean.

▶ Evaluate Each Hypothesis

Review each hypothesis and think about whether the observations support it. Some facts may rule out some hypotheses. Some facts may neither support nor weaken some hypotheses.

CHALLENGE How could you model one or more of the hypotheses with a toy truck, sand, and a basin of water?

Weather forecasters use advanced technologies.

 BEFORE, you learned

- Weather changes when air masses move
- High-pressure systems bring fair weather
- Fronts and low-pressure systems bring stormy weather

 NOW, you will learn

- How weather data are collected
- How weather data are displayed
- How meteorologists forecast the weather

VOCABULARY

meteorologist p. 98
isobar p. 101

EXPLORE Weather Maps

What does a weather map show?

PROCEDURE

① Look at the weather outside. Write down the conditions you observe.

② Use the map to check the weather conditions for your region.

WHAT DO YOU THINK?

- What symbols on the map do you recognize?
- How does the information on the weather map compare with the weather you observed outside?

MATERIALS

newspaper
weather map

Weather data come from many sources.

Looking at the weather outside in the morning can help you decide what to wear. Different things give you clues to the current weather. If you see plants swaying from side to side, you might infer that it is windy. If you see a gray sky and wet, shiny streets, you might decide to wear a raincoat.

You might also check a weather report to get more information. A weather report can show conditions in your area and also in the region around you. You can look for weather nearby that might move into your area during the day. More detailed predictions of how the weather will move and change may be included in a weather report by a meteorologist. A **meteorologist** (MEE-tee-uh-RAHL-uh-jihst) is a scientist who studies weather.

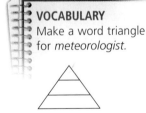

VOCABULARY
Make a word triangle for *meteorologist*.

 What information can a weather report show?

In order to predict the weather, meteorologists look at past and current conditions. They use many forms of technology to gather data. The illustration below shows how weather information is gathered. For example, radar stations and satellites use advanced technologies to gather data for large areas at a time.

Instruments within the atmosphere can make measurements of local weather conditions. Newer instruments can make measurements frequently and automatically and then report the results almost instantly. Instruments are placed in many ground stations on land and weather buoys at sea. Instruments can also be carried by balloons, ships, and planes. These instruments report a series of measurements along a path within the atmosphere.

RESOURCE CENTER
CLASSZONE.COM

Learn more about weather forecasting and your local weather.

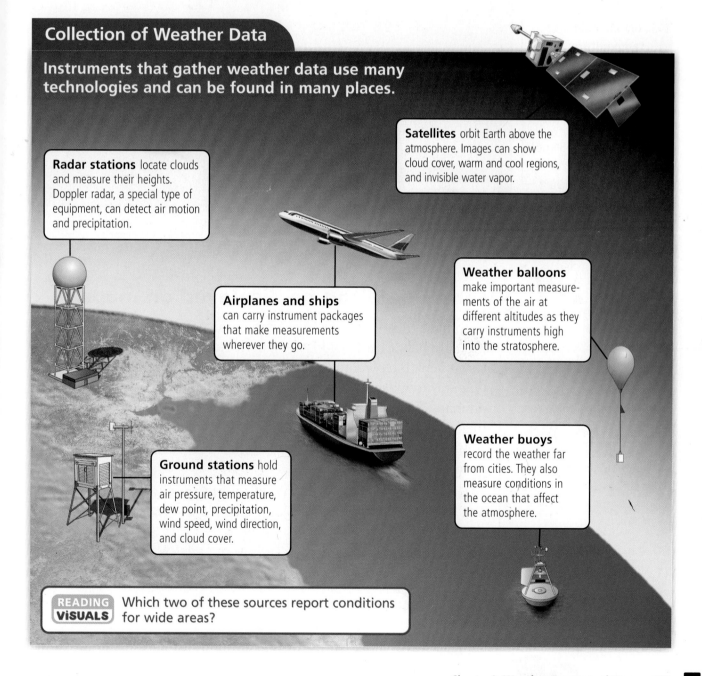

Collection of Weather Data

Instruments that gather weather data use many technologies and can be found in many places.

Satellites orbit Earth above the atmosphere. Images can show cloud cover, warm and cool regions, and invisible water vapor.

Radar stations locate clouds and measure their heights. Doppler radar, a special type of equipment, can detect air motion and precipitation.

Airplanes and ships can carry instrument packages that make measurements wherever they go.

Weather balloons make important measurements of the air at different altitudes as they carry instruments high into the stratosphere.

Ground stations hold instruments that measure air pressure, temperature, dew point, precipitation, wind speed, wind direction, and cloud cover.

Weather buoys record the weather far from cities. They also measure conditions in the ocean that affect the atmosphere.

READING VISUALS Which two of these sources report conditions for wide areas?

Information on a Weather Map

Meteorologists use maps to display a lot of weather information at once.

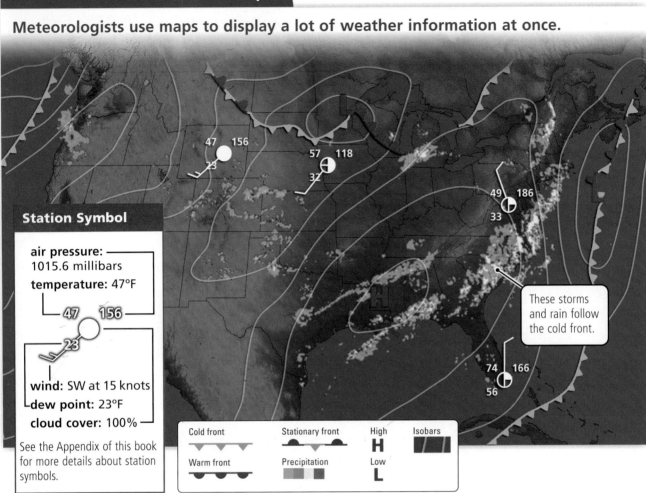

Station Symbol

air pressure:
1015.6 millibars

temperature: 47°F

47   156

23

wind: SW at 15 knots

dew point: 23°F

cloud cover: 100%

See the Appendix of this book for more details about station symbols.

These storms and rain follow the cold front.

| Cold front | Stationary front | High **H** | Isobars |
| Warm front | Precipitation | Low **L** | |

Weather data can be displayed on maps.

MAIN IDEA WEB
Add to your notebook information about weather data.

Automatic measurements from many sources constantly pour in to the National Oceanic and Atmospheric Administration. Scientists use computers to record and use the enormous amount of data gathered. One way to make the information easier to understand is to show it on maps. A single map can show many different types of data together to give a more complete picture of the weather. The map above combines information from ground stations with Doppler radar measurements of precipitation.

- Precipitation is shown as patches of blue, green, yellow, and red. The colors indicate the amounts of rain or other precipitation.
- Station symbols on the map show data from ground stations. Only a few stations are shown.
- Symbols showing fronts and pressure patterns are added to the map to make the overall weather patterns easier to see.

CHECK YOUR READING   How is information from Doppler radar shown?

Computer programs are used to combine information from many ground stations. The resulting calculations give the highs, lows, and fronts that are marked on the map. The cold front near the East Coast has triangles to show that the front is moving eastward. This cold front produced the heavy rain that is visible in the Doppler radar data.

Air Pressure on Weather Maps

The map below shows conditions from the same date as the map on page 100. Thin lines represent air pressure. An **isobar** (EYE-suh-BAHR) is a line that connects places that have the same air pressure. Each isobar represents a different air pressure value. All the isobars together, combined with the symbols for highs and lows, show the patterns of air pressure that produce weather systems.

Each isobar is labeled with the air pressure for that whole line in units called millibars (MIHL-uh-BAHRZ). A lower number means a lower air pressure. As you read earlier, differences in pressure cause air to move. Meteorologists use isobars to understand air motion.

Sometimes air-pressure measurements are listed in inches of mercury. This unit comes from an old type of barometer that measures how high the air pressure pushes a column of mercury, a liquid metal. Computer-controlled instruments are used more often today, but the measurements may be converted to inches of mercury.

READING **TiP**

Iso- means "equal," and *bar* means "pressure."

Understanding Isobars

Isobars show pressure patterns, which determine winds.

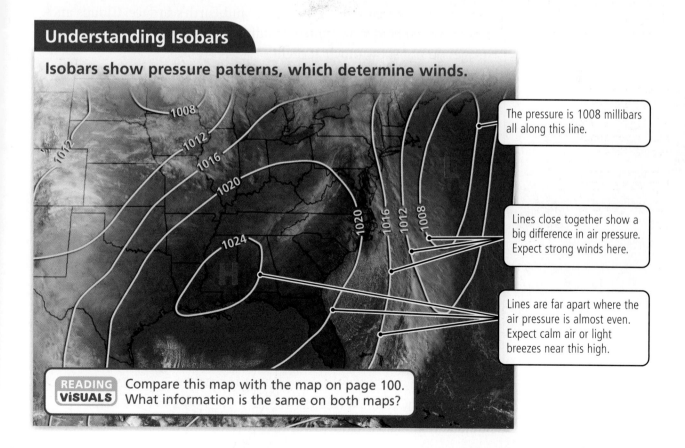

The pressure is 1008 millibars all along this line.

Lines close together show a big difference in air pressure. Expect strong winds here.

Lines are far apart where the air pressure is almost even. Expect calm air or light breezes near this high.

READING VISUALS Compare this map with the map on page 100. What information is the same on both maps?

Satellite Images

Visible Light

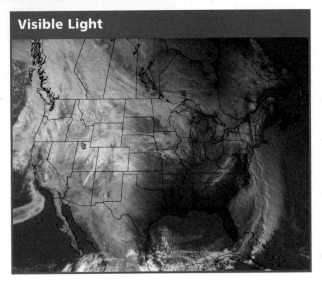

This visible-light satellite image shows clouds from above. The patches of white are clouds.

Infrared Radiation

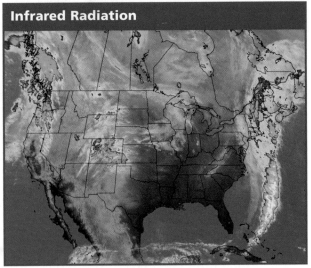

This infrared satellite image also shows clouds, but uses colors to show where there are tall clouds.

READING VISUALS Find a location on these maps and the map on page 100. What were the weather conditions?

Satellite Images and Special Maps

Satellites take different types of images from space. Some images record the visible light that reflects off clouds and Earth's surface. Clouds and snow-covered land look white in sunlight. Unfortunately, visible-light images do not show much at night.

Another type of image shows infrared radiation given off by the warm surface and cooler clouds. These infrared images can show cloud patterns even at night because objects with different temperatures show up differently. Air temperatures change with altitude, so infrared images also show which clouds are low and which are high or tall. You can see in the maps above how visible and infrared satellite images show similar clouds but different details. Outlines of the states have been added to make the images easier to understand.

Data from ground stations and other sources can be used to make other types of maps. The map at left shows the pattern of temperatures on the same date as the images above and the map on page 100. Other maps may show winds or amounts of pollution. A map can be made to show any type of measurement or weather prediction. Different types of maps are often used together to give a more complete picture of the current weather.

The colors on this map represent different ranges of temperature (°F).

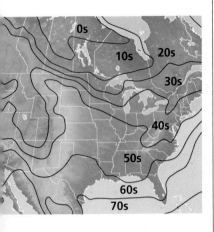

CHECK YOUR READING Why would a weather report show more than one map?

Forecasters use computer models to predict weather.

Instruments can only measure the current weather conditions. Most people want to know what the weather will be like in the future.

Forecasters can make some predictions from their own observations. If they see cirrus clouds above and high stratus clouds to the west, they might infer that a warm front is approaching. They would predict weather typical for a warm front—more clouds, then rain, and eventually warmer weather. If they also have information from other places, the forecasters might be able to tell where the warm front is already and how fast it is moving. They might be able to predict how soon it will arrive and even how warm the weather will be after the front passes.

Computers have become an important tool for forecasting weather. When weather stations send in data, computers can create maps right away. Computer models combine many types of data to forecast what might happen next. Different computer models give different types of forecasts. Scientists study the computer forecasts, then apply their knowledge and experience to make weather predictions.

Forecasting the weather is complicated. As a result, some forecasts are more dependable than others. The farther in advance a forecast is made, the more time there is for small differences between the predicted and the actual weather to add up. For this reason, short-range forecasts—up to three days in advance—are the most accurate. Forecasts of fast-changing weather, such as severe storms, are less accurate far in advance. It is best to watch for new predictions close to the time the storm is forecast.

Forecasters use maps and satellite images to communicate weather conditions and predictions.

 **Review**

KEY CONCEPTS

1. List three of the sources of weather data.

2. What does a map with isobars show?

3. How do meteorologists use computers?

CRITICAL THINKING

4. **Draw Conclusions** Why do meteorologists not combine all their weather information into one map?

5. **Analyze** How is the information from radar and satellites different from the information from ground stations?

⚫ CHALLENGE

6. **Apply** Suppose you are planning an afternoon picnic a week in advance. Fair weather is forecast for that day, but a storm is expected that night. What will you do? Explain your reasoning.

CHAPTER INVESTIGATION

Design a Weather Center

DESIGN
— YOUR OWN —

OVERVIEW AND PURPOSE The accuracy of a weather forecast depends largely on the type and quality of the data that it is based on. In this lab, you will use what you have learned about weather to
- observe and measure weather conditions
- record and analyze the weather-related data

▶ Procedure

1. Survey the possible sources of weather data in and around your classroom. You can use a thermometer to record the outside air temperature. You can observe cloud types and the amount of cloud cover from a window or doorway. You can also observe precipitation and notice if it is heavy or light. If there is a flag in view, use it to find the wind direction and to estimate wind speed.

2. Assemble or make tools for your observations. You may want to make a reference chart with pictures of different cloud types or other information. Decide if you wish to use homemade weather instruments. You may have made a barometer, a psychrometer, and a rain gauge already. If not, see the instructions on pages 45, 64, and 67. You may also wish to do research to learn how to make or use other weather instruments.

3. Make an initial set of observations. Write down the date and time in your **Science Notebook.** Record the readings from the thermometer and other instruments.

MATERIALS
- thermometer
- magnetic compass
- other weather instruments
- graph paper

4. Decide how to record your observations of the clouds, the wind, and any precipitation. Organize your notes to make it easy for you to record later observations in a consistent way.

5. Create a chart with a row for each type of observation you are making. You might darken fractions of circles to record amounts of cloud cover, as in the station symbols on page 100. Make sure each row has a heading and enough room for numbers, words, or sketches. Include a row for notes that do not belong in the data rows.

6. Record your observations every day at the same time. Try to make the observations exactly the same way each time. If you have to redraw your chart, copy the information carefully.

▶ Observe and Analyze
Write It Up

1. **GRAPH** Graph the data you collected that represent measurable quantities. Use graphs that are appropriate to your data. Often a simple line graph will work. Choose an appropriate scale and interval based on the range of your data. Make the *x*-axis of each graph the same so that you can compare the different types of data easily.

2. **COMPARE AND CONTRAST** Look at your graphs for patterns in your data. Some aspects of weather change at the same time because they are related to each other. Did one type of change occur before a different type of change? If so, this pattern may help you predict weather.

▶ Conclude
Write It Up

1. **INTERPRET** Did a front pass through your area during the period you observed? What observations helped you answer this question?

2. **EVALUATE** Why was it necessary to observe at the same time each day?

3. **APPLY** If you predicted that each day's weather would be repeated the next day, how often would you be right?

▶ INVESTIGATE Further

CHALLENGE Locate a newspaper weather page for the period during which you were making your weather observations. How do the weather data reported for your area compare with your measurements? How do you account for any differences you notice in the data?

Design a Weather Center

Table 1. Daily Weather Chart

Date/time of observations			
Temperature (°C)			
Cloud types			
Cloud coverage	○	○	○
Precipitation (cm) and notes			
Wind direction			
Other notes			

Chapter Review

the BIG idea

The interaction of air masses causes changes in weather.

CONTENT REVIEW
CLASSZONE.COM

KEY CONCEPTS SUMMARY

3.1 Weather changes as air masses move.

Air masses meet and produce **fronts,** which can bring lowered pressure and stormy weather. Fronts can be cold, warm, or stationary.

VOCABULARY
air mass p. 79
front p. 82
high-pressure system p. 84
low-pressure system p. 85

3.2 Low-pressure systems can become storms.

Hurricanes and winter storms develop from low-pressure systems.

Hurricanes form over warm ocean water.

VOCABULARY
tropical storm p. 87
hurricane p. 87
storm surge p. 89
blizzard p. 90

3.3 Vertical air motion can cause severe storms.

Rising moist air can produce **thunderstorms.** The up-and-down motion of air in a thunderstorm can produce a **tornado.**

VOCABULARY
thunderstorm p. 92
tornado p. 95

3.4 Weather forecasters use advanced technologies.

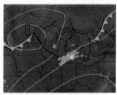

Weather information comes from many sources.

Meteorologists use weather data and computer models to forecast weather.

VOCABULARY
meteorologist p. 98
isobar p. 101

Reviewing Vocabulary

Describe each term below, using the related term as part of the description.

Term	Related Term	Description
EXAMPLE hurricane	low-pressure system	a low-pressure system in the tropics with winds at least 120 km/h
1. front	air mass	
2. low-pressure system	low-pressure center	
3. storm surge	hurricane	
4. tropical storm	low-pressure system	
5. air mass	humidity	
6. thunderstorm	convection	
7. tornado	thunderstorm	
8. blizzard	low-pressure system	

Reviewing Key Concepts

Multiple Choice *Choose the letter of the best answer.*

9. What qualities are nearly the same at different locations in a single air mass?
  a. temperature and pressure
  b. temperature and humidity
  c. air pressure and wind speed
  d. air pressure and humidity

10. Which is the name for an air mass that forms over the ocean near the equator?
  a. maritime tropical   **c.** continental tropical
  b. maritime polar   **d.** continental polar

11. A meteorologist is a scientist who
  a. predicts meteor showers
  b. studies maps
  c. studies the weather
  d. changes the weather

12. An isobar shows locations with the same
  a. temperature   **c.** air pressure
  b. rainfall   **d.** wind speed

13. Which is produced when a warm air mass pushes a colder air mass?
  a. a stationary front   **c.** a warm front
  b. a cold front   **d.** a thunderstorm

14. Which can be measured in inches of mercury?
  a. air pressure   **c.** hail
  b. temperature   **d.** lightning

15. Which source provides measurements for just one location?
  a. ground station   **c.** weather balloon
  b. radar station   **d.** satellite

16. Compared with warm fronts, cold fronts are
  a. faster moving   **c.** more cloudy
  b. less dense   **d.** less steep

17. Which statement is usually true of high-pressure systems in North America?
  a. They bring fair weather.
  b. They change quickly.
  c. The air in them is cold and dense.
  d. The air in them moves counterclockwise.

18. Thunderstorms often begin with the rising of
  a. cool, dry air   **c.** warm, dry air
  b. cool, humid air   **d.** warm, humid air

19. What is the relationship between lightning and thunder?
  a. They have separate causes.
  b. They have the same cause.
  c. Lightning causes thunder.
  d. Thunder causes lightning.

Short Answer *Write a short answer to each question.*

20. Why are hurricanes in the eastern United States more likely in autumn than in spring?

21. What causes lake-effect snow?

22. In what four ways can thunderstorms be dangerous?

Thinking Critically

Use this weather map to answer the next six questions. The numbers under each city name are the highest and the lowest temperature for the day in degrees Fahrenheit.

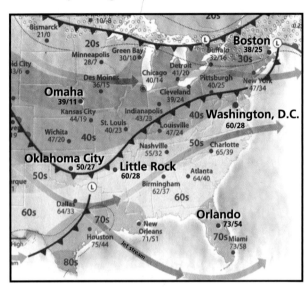

23. **INFER** Name and describe the air mass that has moved south to Omaha from Canada.

24. **IDENTIFY EFFECTS** How are two low-pressure systems affecting the weather near Boston?

25. **PREDICT** Explain whether Washington, D.C., or Orlando is more likely to have a big change in weather in the next two days.

26. **COMPARE AND CONTRAST** Explain the difference in temperature between Oklahoma City and Little Rock.

27. **PREDICT** How will the weather in Little Rock change in the next day or two?

28. **APPLY** Does this map indicate that it is hurricane season? Explain your reasoning.

29. **CONNECT** Describe today's weather and explain what fronts and pressure systems might be influencing it.

30. **COMPARE AND CONTRAST** Use a Venn diagram to compare images from visible light and infrared radiation.

PREDICT *For each set of conditions listed in the chart, write a weather prediction.*

Conditions	Prediction
31. A cold front is moving into an area that has warm, moist air.	
32. A warm front is moving into an area that has cold, dense air.	
33. A cool sea breeze is blowing inland, causing warm, humid air to rise.	
34. Air pressure is falling and the temperature is rising.	
35. Air pressure is increasing and the temperature is steady.	
36. A thunderstorm is developing spinning winds at its center.	
37. A low-pressure center is over the Atlantic Ocean where the water temperature is above 27°C (81°F).	
38. Cold air is pushing warm air where the air is 2°C (36°F) and the ground is -3°C (27°F).	

39. **COMPARE** How is the air motion in the eye of a hurricane similar to the air motion at a high-pressure center?

40. **EVALUATE** Which type of storm is most dangerous? Explain your reasoning.

the **BIG** idea

41. **APPLY** Look again at the photograph on pages 76–77. Now that you have finished the chapter, how would you change your response to the question on the photograph?

42. **SEQUENCE** Draw a storyboard with at least four sketches to show how cool, sunny weather might change into warm, rainy weather.

UNIT PROJECTS

Check your schedule for your unit project. How are you doing? Be sure that you have placed data or notes from your research in your project folder.

Analyzing a Map

Use this weather map to answer the questions below.

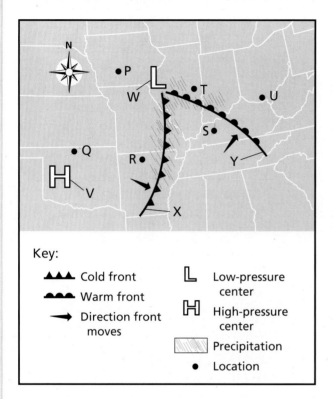

Key:

▲▲▲ Cold front

●●● Warm front

→ Direction front moves

L Low-pressure center

H High-pressure center

░ Precipitation

● Location

1. Which letter labels a cold front?

  a. Q   **c.** X

  b. U   **d.** Y

2. Which word best describes the general movement of the fronts?

  a. to the north   **c.** clockwise

  b. to the east   **d.** counterclockwise

3. A warm front occurs where warm air moves into colder air. Which of these locations is probably warmest?

  a. R   **c.** T

  b. S   **d.** U

4. Temperatures usually change quickly near a front and more slowly away from a front. The temperature at Q is 10°C (50°F). The temperature at S is 20°C (68°F). Which is the best estimate for the temperature at R?

  a. 6°C (43°F)   **c.** 20°C (68°F)

  b. 11°C (52°F)   **d.** 24°C (75°F)

5. If the fronts continue to move as shown, which location will get warmer soon?

  a. Q   **c.** S

  b. R   **d.** T

6. Low pressure often brings stormy weather, and high pressure often brings fair weather. Which of these locations is most likely to have clear skies?

  a. Q   **c.** S

  b. R   **d.** U

Extended Response

Use the map above to answer the two questions below in detail. Include some of the terms shown in the word box. Underline each term you use in your answers.

cold front	humid	west
warm front	east	prevailing winds

7. Along which front on the weather map above would you expect to find cumulonimbus clouds? Explain why.

8. The weather system shown on the map above is in the continental United States. In which direction do you expect it to move? Explain why.

TIMELINES in Science

OBSERVING THE ATMOSPHERE

The atmosphere is always changing, and scientists are developing better ways to observe these changes. Accurate weather forecasts help people make everyday decisions, such as what kind of clothing to wear. Forecasts also allow us to plan for dangerous storms and other natural disasters. Scientists are now warning of long-term changes to the atmosphere that can affect the entire world. These predictions are possible because of the work of scientists and observers over hundreds of years.

The timeline shows some historical events in the study of Earth's air and weather. The boxes below the timeline show how technology has led to new knowledge about the atmosphere and show how that knowledge has been applied.

1686

Trade Winds Are Linked to Sun's Energy

Sailors have used trade winds for centuries to sail from Europe to the Americas. Now, Edmund Halley, a British astronomer, explains global winds in a new theory. He argues that trade winds blowing toward the equator replace air that rises due to solar heating.

EVENTS

1640   1660   1680

APPLICATIONS AND TECHNOLOGY

TECHNOLOGY

Measuring Air Pressure

The mercury barometer was invented in 1643 to measure air pressure. Changes in outside air pressure cause the level of mercury to rise and fall in a tall glass tube. This remarkably accurate type of barometer was used for centuries. Now, most air-pressure measurements are taken with aneroid barometers, which are easier to use.

1804
Atmosphere Explorations Pass 7000 Meters

French chemist Joseph Louis Gay-Lussac rises to an altitude of 7016 meters in a balloon to study the atmosphere. His studies show that the atmosphere's composition remains the same up to that altitude.

1827
Atmospheric Greenhouse Warms Earth

French scientist Jean-Baptiste Fourier coins a new term, "greenhouse effect." He suggests that the atmosphere slows the movement of energy from Earth's surface out toward space. Fourier compares this effect to the way heat is trapped in a greenhouse.

1743
Franklin Tracks Storms

Benjamin Franklin tries to look at an eclipse of the Moon, but a storm blocks his view. Meanwhile, a friend in another city has a clear view during the eclipse, and soon afterward the storm arrives there. Franklin concludes that storms travel instead of forming and dying in the same place.

1740   **1760**   **1780**   **1800**   **1820**

APPLICATION

Telegraphing the Weather

The development of the telegraph in the 1800s was important for weather forecasting because it allowed observers to quickly send data to distant locations. In 1870, the U.S. government organized a system of weather observers who communicated by telegraph. This was the beginning of the National Weather Service, which at first focused on providing storm warnings for coastal regions. However, the weather reporting service was soon extended to cover the entire nation. The National Weather Service has become a crucial information agency.

1942
Pilots Find Jet Streams
Wartime pilots discover very fast winds called jet streams at high altitudes. Pilots find that the jet streams are like narrow rivers of air moving at speeds that average 180 kilometers per hour (110 mi/h).

1958
Greenhouse Gas Monitored
Carbon dioxide and other greenhouse gases are measured at Mauna Loa Observatory on the Big Island of Hawaii, 11,000 feet above sea level. Accurate measurements can be obtained from this location because it is far from cities and other human influences.

1918
Storm Fronts Explained
Norway's Jacob Bjerknes explains how large storm systems develop at the boundaries between masses of air. He calls the boundaries "fronts," comparing them to battlefronts between armies.

1900	**1920**	**1940**	**1960**

TECHNOLOGY

Picturing the Weather

Ground-based weather stations cannot collect data from high altitudes or from areas between stations. The development of weather technology helped fill the gaps. In the 1930s, weather balloons carried instruments to different altitudes. In 1953, the development of Doppler radar showed raindrop sizes and speeds. Scientists later began using Doppler radar to measure precipitation for a wide area all at once.

In 1960, weather satellites began to provide images of weather from space. Satellites can show hurricanes long before they hit the shore. Fifteen years later, scientists began to use instruments on satellites to detect radiation other than visible light. Infrared cameras showed clouds at night and made detailed measurements that improved forecasts.

1985

Hole Found in Ozone Layer

Using data from a ground-based instrument in Antarctica, scientists discover a large area where the protective layer of ozone is very thin. They call it the ozone hole. The discovery confirms earlier predictions that certain industrial chemicals can result in ozone destruction.

RESOURCE CENTER
CLASSZONE.COM

Learn more about current research on the atmosphere.

1980   2000

APPLICATION

Computer Modeling

Scientists use computers not only to collect data but also to make models of the atmosphere. Models show how the atmosphere changed in the past and how it may change in the future. As computers become faster and better, the models can be made more detailed and therefore more reliable.

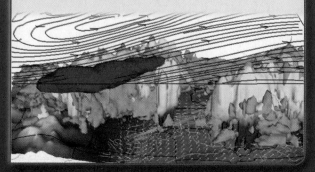

INTO THE FUTURE

With frequent measurements of much of Earth's atmosphere, scientists can now understand a lot more about weather. Supercomputers let scientists make models of ordinary weather and complicated storms.

In the future, scientists will better understand the way the oceans and the atmosphere affect one another. They will make models of complex patterns that involve long-term changes in the oceans and the atmosphere.

Researchers will use models of Earth's past weather to understand the changes happening today. They will make more detailed predictions about future changes. People will be able to make better decisions about human activities that affect Earth's atmosphere. Researchers will continue to improve and use their understanding of the atmospheres of other worlds to understand Earth.

ACTIVITIES

Reliving History

Ancient peoples made simple weather instruments, such as wind vanes. You can make a wind vane and then map the wind directions in your neighborhood.

Push a straight pin through the middle of a drinking straw and then into an eraser at the end of a pencil. Tape a square of cardboard vertically to one end of the straw. Put a small piece of clay on the other end so that the wind vane is balanced. The straw will turn so that the clay end of the straw points into the wind.

Use your wind vane and a magnetic compass to find the wind direction in several places in your neighborhood. Record the results on a copy of a map. Do you notice any patterns?

Writing About Science

Suppose scientists learn to control the weather. What factors have to be considered in choosing the weather? Write a conversation in which opposing viewpoints are debated.

Climate and Climate Change

the **BIG** idea

Climates are long-term weather patterns that may change over time.

Key Concepts

Internet Preview

CLASSZONE.COM

Chapter 4 online resources: Content Review, Simulation, four Resource Centers, Math Tutorial, Test Practice

What evidence of different types of climate can you see in this photo?

EXPLORE (the BIG idea)

Why Are Climates Different?

Look at a newspaper weather map. Find some cities that usually have very different weather from the weather in your area.

Observe and Think
Where are those cities located on the map? Are they north or south of your location? What geographical differences might help make the weather in those cities different from the weather in your area?

How Do Microclimates Form?

Go outside with a thermometer and take temperature readings in four different places. Repeat your observations at a later time of day.

Observe and Think
What temperature readings did you observe? Did the readings stay the same later in the day?

Internet Activity: El Niño

Go to **ClassZone.com** to find out information about El Niño.

Observe and Think
How does El Niño affect temperature and precipitation patterns in your region?

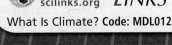

NSTA
scilinks.org
SCiLINKS

What Is Climate? **Code: MDL012**

Getting Ready to Learn

CONCEPT REVIEW

- Earth's atmosphere supports life.
- In a system that consists of many parts, the parts usually influence one another.
- Human activities are increasing greenhouse gases.

VOCABULARY REVIEW

altitude p. 10

greenhouse gas p. 24

weather p. 47

precipitation p. 57

CONTENT REVIEW
CLASSZONE.COM
Review concepts and vocabulary.

TAKING NOTES

MAIN IDEA AND DETAIL NOTES

Make a two-column chart. Write the main ideas, such as those in the blue headings, in the column on the left. Write details about each of those main ideas in the column on the right.

CHOOSE YOUR OWN STRATEGY

Take notes about new vocabulary terms, using one or more of the strategies from earlier chapters—**frame game, description wheel,** or **word triangle.** Feel free to mix and match the strategies, or use an entirely different vocabulary strategy.

See the Note-Taking Handbook on pages R45–R51.

SCIENCE NOTEBOOK

MAIN IDEAS	DETAIL NOTES
1. Latitude affects climate.	1. Places close to the equator are usually warmer than places close to the poles.
	1. Latitude has the same effect in both hemispheres.
2. Altitude affects climate.	2. Temperature decreases with altitude.
	2. Altitude can overcome the effect of latitude on temperature.

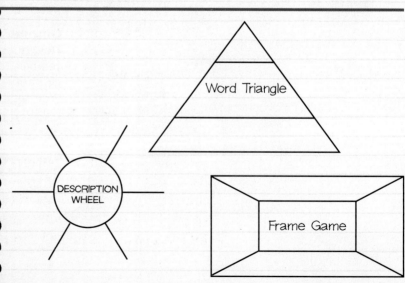

4.1

Climate is a long-term weather pattern.

 BEFORE, you learned

- The Sun's energy heats Earth's surface unevenly
- The atmosphere's temperature changes with altitude
- Oceans affect wind flow

NOW, you will learn

- How climate is related to weather
- What factors affect climate
- About seasonal patterns of temperature and precipitation

VOCABULARY

climate p. 117
latitude p. 118
marine climate p. 120
continental climate p. 120
ocean current p. 121
season p. 122

EXPLORE Solar Energy

How does the angle of light affect heating?

PROCEDURE

1. Tape a black square over the bulb of each thermometer. Then tape the thermometers to the cardboard tube as shown.

2. Place the arrangement on a sunny windowsill or under a lamp. One square should directly face the light. Record the temperatures.

3. Wait 10 minutes. Record the temperature changes.

WHAT DO YOU THINK?

- How did the temperature readings change?
- How did the angle of light affect the amount of heat absorbed?

MATERIALS

- tape
- 2 black paper squares
- 2 thermometers
- 1 cardboard tube from a paper towel roll
- sunny windowsill or lamp

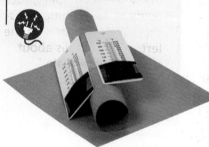

Geography affects climate.

You can check your current local weather simply by looking out a window. Weather conditions may not last very long; they can change daily or even hourly. In contrast, the climate of your area changes over much longer periods of time. **Climate** is the characteristic weather conditions in a place over a long period. Climate influences the kind of clothes you own, the design of your home, and even the sports you play.

All parts of weather make up climate, including wind, humidity, and sunshine. However, meteorologists usually focus on patterns of temperature and precipitation when they classify climates. Four key geographical factors affect temperature and precipitation: latitude, altitude, distance from large bodies of water, and ocean currents.

VOCABULARY
You could use a frame game diagram to take notes about the term *climate*.

Latitude and Temperature

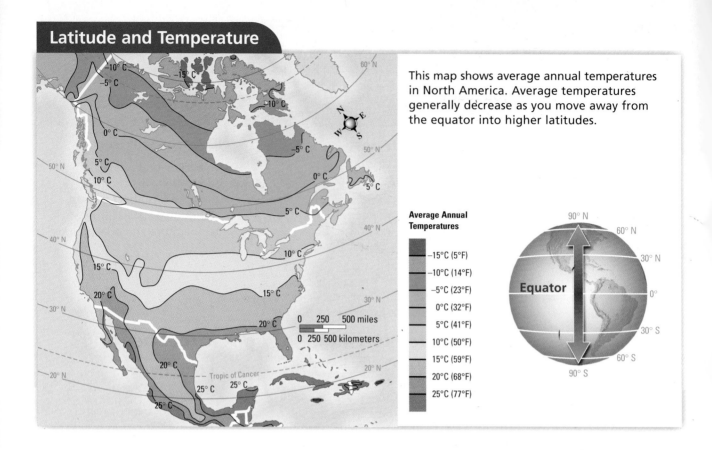

This map shows average annual temperatures in North America. Average temperatures generally decrease as you move away from the equator into higher latitudes.

Average Annual Temperatures

- −15°C (5°F)
- −10°C (14°F)
- −5°C (23°F)
- 0°C (32°F)
- 5°C (41°F)
- 10°C (50°F)
- 15°C (59°F)
- 20°C (68°F)
- 25°C (77°F)

Latitude

READING TiP

Notice on the globe in the illustration that latitude numbers get higher as you move away from the equator.

One factor that affects temperature is latitude. **Latitude** is the distance in degrees north or south of the equator, which is 0°. Each degree equals 1/360 of the distance around the world.

As you read in Chapter 2, the Sun heats Earth's curved surface unevenly. Sunlight strikes Earth's surface directly near the equator. Near the poles, sunlight strikes the surface at a lower angle, so it is more spread out. In addition, the polar regions receive little or no solar energy during winter.

Because of this pattern of uneven heating, average annual temperatures generally decrease as you move closer to the poles. For example, Belém, Brazil, which is almost on the equator, has an average temperature of about 26°C (79°F). Qaanaaq, Greenland, located close to the North Pole, has an average temperature of only −11°C (12°F).

Latitude has the same effect on temperature in both hemispheres. Suppose one city is located at 45° N and another city is located at 45° S. The first city is in the Northern Hemisphere, and the second is in the Southern Hemisphere. However, they are both nearly 5000 kilometers (3100 mi) from the equator, so they would receive about the same amount of sunlight over a year.

CHECK YOUR READING What is the connection between latitude and temperature?

Altitude

Altitude, the height above sea level, is another geographical factor that affects temperature. If you rode a cable car up a mountain, the temperature would decrease by about 6.5°C (11.7°F) for every kilometer you rose in altitude. Why does it get colder as you move higher up? The troposphere is mainly warmed from below by Earth's surface. As convection lifts the warmed air to higher altitudes, the air expands and cools.

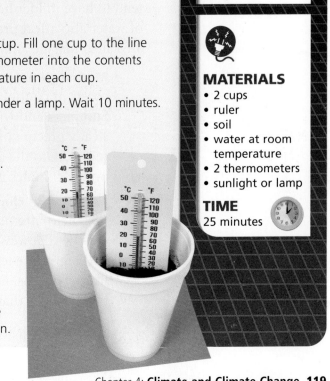

snow line

tree line

Even at the equator, a mountain peak can be covered with snow and ice.

Temperatures are too cold above this elevation for trees to grow.

Because altitude changes sharply on a mountain, different climates can exist within a small area.

Altitude increases can overcome the effect of lower latitudes on temperature. The temperature at the peak of a tall mountain is low regardless of the mountain's latitude. One example is Mount Stanley, near the border of Uganda and the Democratic Republic of the Congo in central Africa. Although it lies just a short distance from the equator, Mount Stanley has ice sheets and a permanent covering of snow. Notice in the illustration how one mountain can have several types of climates.

SIMULATION
CLASSZONE.COM

Explore the effects of latitude and altitude.

INVESTIGATE Heating and Cooling Rates

How quickly do soil and water heat and cool?

PROCEDURE

1. Mark a line 3 centimeters from the top of each cup. Fill one cup to the line with water and the other with soil. Place a thermometer into the contents of each cup. Wait 2 minutes. Record the temperature in each cup.

2. Place the cups side by side in bright sunlight or under a lamp. Wait 10 minutes. Record the temperature in each cup.

3. Move the cups into a shaded area to cool. Wait 10 minutes. Record the temperature in each cup.

WHAT DO YOU THINK?

- Which heats up faster, soil or water?
- Which cools faster?
- How might the heating and cooling rates of inland areas compare with those of coastal areas?

CHALLENGE Will adding gravel to the soil change your results? Repeat the activity to test your prediction.

SKILL FOCUS
Comparing

MATERIALS
- 2 cups
- ruler
- soil
- water at room temperature
- 2 thermometers
- sunlight or lamp

TIME
25 minutes

How Oceans Affect Climate

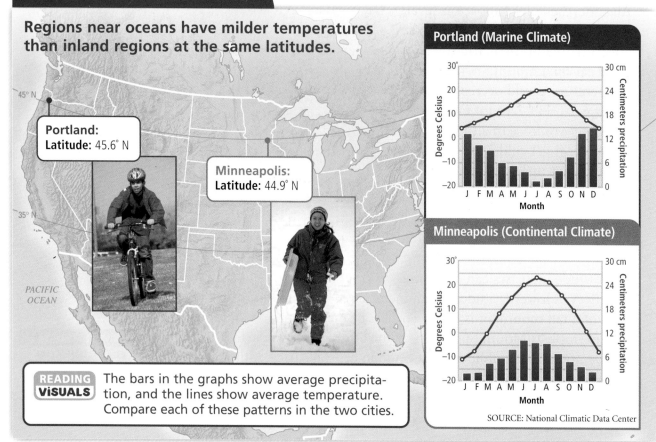

Regions near oceans have milder temperatures than inland regions at the same latitudes.

Portland:
Latitude: 45.6° N

Minneapolis:
Latitude: 44.9° N

45° N

35° N

PACIFIC
OCEAN

Portland (Marine Climate)

Minneapolis (Continental Climate)

SOURCE: National Climatic Data Center

READING VISUALS The bars in the graphs show average precipitation, and the lines show average temperature. Compare each of these patterns in the two cities.

Large Bodies of Water

Land heats up and cools off faster than water. Because oceans and large lakes slow down heating and cooling of the air, coastal regions tend to have milder temperatures than areas far inland. Large bodies of water also affect precipitation. Climates influenced by these factors are called marine and continental climates.

- **Marine climates** occur near the ocean, usually along the west coasts of continents. Temperatures do not drop very far at night. Summers and winters are mild. Many marine climates receive steady precipitation because winds blowing off the ocean bring moisture to the atmosphere. Large lakes can have a similar effect on the climates near their shores.

- **Continental climates** occur in the interior of continents. Weather patterns vary in the different types of continental climates. However, most have large differences between daytime and nighttime temperatures because they lack the influence of nearby oceans. For the same reason, winter months are usually much colder than summer months.

CHECK YOUR READING How are marine climates different from continental climates?

Ocean Currents

Ocean currents are streams of water that flow through oceans in regular patterns. They influence climates by transferring energy from one part of an ocean to another. In general, warm-water currents carry warmth from the tropics to higher latitudes, where they help keep coastal regions warm. Cold-water currents have the opposite effect. They cool coastal regions by carrying cold water from polar regions toward the equator.

The illustration below shows the paths of ocean currents in the North Atlantic. Find the Gulf Stream on the illustration. The Gulf Stream is a major warm-water current. As the waters that feed the Gulf Stream pass near the Caribbean Sea and the Gulf of Mexico, the concentrated solar rays that strike there warm its water. Water flowing in the Gulf Stream can be 6°C to 10°C (11–18°F) warmer than the surrounding water. The Gulf Stream warms the winds that blow over it. In turn, those winds warm coastal regions.

Like altitude, ocean currents can overcome the effects of latitude. For example, London, England, has an average annual temperature of nearly 11°C (52°F). Natashquan, a town in eastern Canada at about the same latitude and altitude, has an average annual temperature of only 1°C (34°F). London's milder climate is the result of an ocean current carrying warm water to Europe's west coast.

Ocean Currents

Ocean currents can cause two places at the same latitude to have different climates.

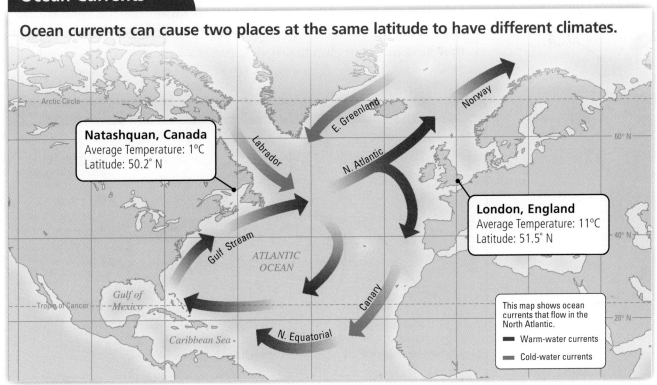

Natashquan, Canada
Average Temperature: 1°C
Latitude: 50.2° N

London, England
Average Temperature: 11°C
Latitude: 51.5° N

This map shows ocean currents that flow in the North Atlantic.
— Warm-water currents
— Cold-water currents

Seasonal changes are part of climate.

What marks the change of seasons where you live? In the Midwest and New England, there are four distinct seasons. Mild spring and autumn months come between hotter summers and colder winters. In Florida and other southern states, the seasonal changes are much less extreme. **Seasons** are periods of the year associated with specific weather conditions, such as cold temperatures or frequent rain. These periods are part of the overall pattern that makes up a climate.

Temperature Patterns

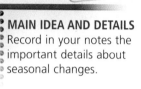

MAIN IDEA AND DETAILS
Record in your notes the important details about seasonal changes.

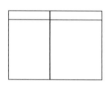

Seasons occur because the amounts of energy that the Northern Hemisphere and the Southern Hemisphere receive from the Sun change over the course of a year. Winter begins in the Northern Hemisphere around December 21, when the daytime is shortest. Summer begins around June 21, when the daytime is longest. Spring begins around March 21, and autumn begins around September 22. On the first day of spring and of autumn, day and night are equal in length. There are 12 hours of daylight and 12 hours of darkness.

CHECK YOUR READING Which seasons have the longest and the shortest periods of daytime?

Temperature patterns are an important feature of climate. The graph below shows the average monthly temperatures in Half Moon Bay, California, and Bloomington, Indiana. Each city has an average annual temperature of about 12°C (54°F). However, Bloomington has hot summers and cold winters, while Half Moon Bay has mild weather all year. Although their average annual temperatures are the same, they have different climates.

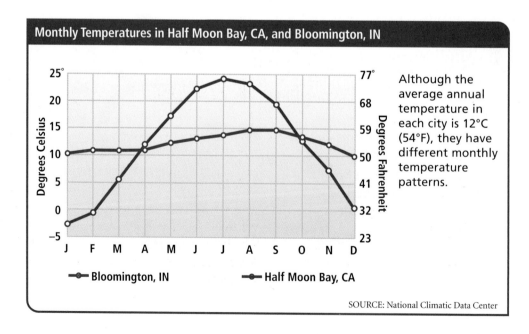

Monthly Temperatures in Half Moon Bay, CA, and Bloomington, IN

Although the average annual temperature in each city is 12°C (54°F), they have different monthly temperature patterns.

— Bloomington, IN   — Half Moon Bay, CA

SOURCE: National Climatic Data Center

Dry Season

Wet Season

INDIA

These photos show the same rice fields in India at different times of the year.

Precipitation Patterns

Like temperature patterns, seasonal patterns of precipitation vary among different climates. For example, Connecticut's precipitation is distributed fairly evenly throughout the year. In contrast, nearly half of Montana's precipitation falls during May, June, and July. Many tropical regions have wet and dry seasons. These regions stay warm all year long, but certain months are much rainier than other months.

The seasonal pattern of precipitation can determine the types of plants that grow in a region and the length of the growing season. Although Montana is a fairly dry state, much of its precipitation falls during the growing season. This pattern allows the state to be a major grain producer.

 Review

KEY CONCEPTS

1. Explain the difference between climate and weather.

2. Make a chart showing how latitude, altitude, large bodies of water, and ocean currents affect climate.

3. How does the length of daytime change with each season?

CRITICAL THINKING

4. **Predict** How would a region's climate change if a cold-water ocean current stopped flowing past it?

5. **Identify Cause** What geographical factors might cause a region to have a narrow temperature range and mild weather all year?

○ CHALLENGE

6. **Infer** Suggest specific climate characteristics that might make the owners of a vacation resort decide to advertise the average annual temperature rather than provide temperature averages for each month or season.

ARCHITECT

Climate and Architecture

When architects design houses, office towers, and other buildings, they think about how the climate will affect the structures and the people who will use them. For example, when planning a house for a cold climate, an architect will consider ways to keep warm air inside. He or she might call for energy-efficient glass in the windows, thick insulation in walls, and an extra set of inside doors to close off entryways.

Snow

Snow is very heavy. Because of snow's weight, architects usually design slanted roofs on houses built in snowy climates. The sharper the slant, the easier snow slides off. This church was built in Norway around 1150.

Heat

In the 1960s, Houston wanted to get a major league baseball team. City officials asked architects to design a stadium suitable for Houston's hot, rainy climate. They created the first domed, air-conditioned ballpark, the Astrodome.

Floods

Intense rains and high winds combine to make floods common in many places. To protect themselves, some people who live on the shores of large rivers, lakes, and oceans build their homes on stilts. This home is in the Northern Territory of Australia. It was designed by the architect Glenn Murcutt and completed in 1994.

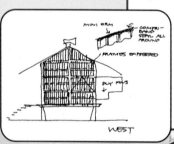

EXPLORE

1. **ANALYZING** Bring to class photos of buildings located in various climate regions. Discuss whether the architecture reflects the influence of the climate.

2. **CHALLENGE** Use building blocks to make a model of a house for a warm climate in which the wind usually blows from the west. Place doors, windows, and walls to get the best flow of air through the house. To check the airflow, dust your model with a light powder. Blow lightly and note how much powder moves.

4.2 Earth has a variety of climates.

◀ **BEFORE, you learned**

- The main factors that affect climate are latitude, altitude, distance from large bodies of water, and ocean currents
- Seasonal changes in temperature and precipitation are part of climate

▶ **NOW, you will learn**

- How scientists classify climates
- About the characteristics of different climate zones
- How natural features and human activity affect climate

VOCABULARY

climate zone p. 125
microclimate p. 128
urban heat island p. 128
rain shadow p. 129

THINK ABOUT

What does ground cover reveal about climate?

For trees and bushes to grow, they must have enough precipitation and at least a few months of mild temperatures each year. Lichens and some small plants can grow in harsher climates. The photograph shows typical ground cover along Greenland's rocky coast. What does the ground cover tell you about Greenland's long-term weather patterns?

Scientists have identified six major climate zones.

Classification systems can help you see patterns. For example, communities are often classified as cities, towns, and villages. This classification system organizes communities on the basis of size. Two cities in different parts of a country might have more in common than a village and a nearby city.

To show patterns in climate data, scientists have developed systems for classifying climates. A **climate zone** is one of the major divisions in a system for classifying the climates of different regions based on characteristics they have in common. The most widely used system groups climates by temperature and precipitation. The six major climate zones of this classification system are (1) humid tropical, (2) dry, (3) moist mid-latitude with mild winters, (4) moist mid-latitude with severe winters, (5) polar, and (6) highland.

RESOURCE CENTER
CLASSZONE.COM

Find out more about climate zones.

The chart on page 127 summarizes information about the different climate zones. Each climate zone has a specific set of characteristics. For example, humid tropical climates are hot and rainy. Many areas close to the equator have this type of climate.

Notice that most of the climate zones are further divided into subclimates. When scientists identify a subclimate, they choose one characteristic that makes it different from other subclimates within the same climate zone. For example, the humid tropical climate zone includes tropical wet climates and tropical wet and dry climates. The difference between them is that tropical wet climates have abundant rainfall every month, while tropical wet and dry climates have a few months of dry weather.

The climate map below shows that many regions scattered throughout the world have similar climates. When you use the map, keep in mind that climates do not change suddenly at the borders of the colored areas. Instead, each climate gradually blends into neighboring ones.

READING TiP

The colors on the map below correspond to the colors in the chart on page 127. As you read descriptions on the chart, look back to the map to find examples.

World Climates

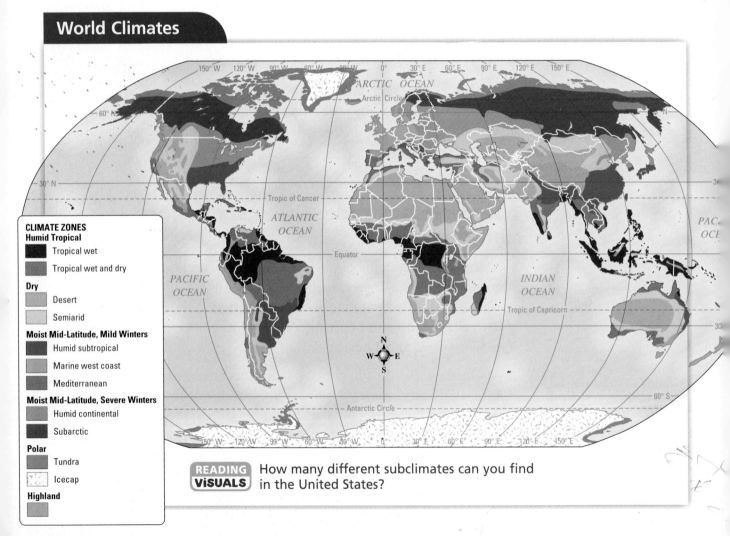

CLIMATE ZONES

Humid Tropical
- Tropical wet
- Tropical wet and dry

Dry
- Desert
- Semiarid

Moist Mid-Latitude, Mild Winters
- Humid subtropical
- Marine west coast
- Mediterranean

Moist Mid-Latitude, Severe Winters
- Humid continental
- Subarctic

Polar
- Tundra
- Icecap

Highland

READING VISUALS How many different subclimates can you find in the United States?

Climate Classification

Climate Zone	Subclimate	Description
Humid tropical	**Tropical wet** Example: Amazon rain forest in South America	Temperatures remain high throughout the year. Rising hot, humid air causes heavy cloud cover and abundant rainfall, with no dry season. Annual rainfall usually is more than 2.5 meters (8 ft).
	Tropical wet and dry Example: Miami, Florida	Like tropical wet climates, these climates are hot and rainy, but they have a dry season in winter.
Dry	**Desert** Example: Phoenix, Arizona	Precipitation is infrequent and scanty—usually less than 20 centimeters (8 in.) per year. Deserts include the hottest places on Earth, but they can be cool, especially at night. In most deserts high daytime temperatures lead to rapid evaporation, which increases the dryness.
	Semiarid Example: Denver, Colorado	These regions are found next to deserts. They have wider temperature ranges than deserts and are not as dry. Most of the Great Plains region in North America is semiarid.
Moist mid-latitude with mild winters	**Humid subtropical** Example: Charlotte, North Carolina	Summers are hot and muggy. Winters are usually mild. Precipitation is fairly even throughout the year.
	Marine west coast Example: Seattle, Washington	These regions have mild temperatures year-round and steady precipitation. Low clouds and fog are common.
	Mediterranean Example: San Francisco, California	Dry summers and mild, wet winters are typical of these regions. Some coastal areas have cool summers and frequent fog.
Moist mid-latitude with severe winters	**Humid continental** Example: Des Moines, Iowa	These regions have hot summers and cold winters. Precipitation is fairly even throughout the year. Snow covers the ground for 1 to 4 months in winter.
	Subarctic Example: Fairbanks, Alaska	Temperatures usually stay below freezing for 6 to 8 months each year. Summers are brief and cool. The amount of precipitation is low, but snow remains on the ground for long periods because of the cold.
Polar	**Tundra** Example: Barrow, Alaska	The average temperature of the warmest month is below 10°C (50°F). A deep layer of soil is frozen year-round. During summer a shallow layer at the surface thaws out and turns muddy.
	Icecap Example: Antarctica	The surface is permanently covered with ice and snow. Temperatures rarely rise above freezing, even in summer.
Highland	**Highland** Example: Rocky Mountains	Because temperature drops as altitude increases, mountain regions can contain many climates. Tall mountains may have a year-round covering of ice and snow at their peaks.

Tropical wet

Desert

Marine west coast

Humid continental

Tundra

Natural features and human activity can affect local climates.

The climate map on page 126 shows three subclimates in Madagascar, a large island off the east coast of Africa. But if you went to Madagascar, you would probably notice a greater variety of climates. A meadow might be warmer than a nearby wooded area, and a city block might be warmer than a meadow.

READING TiP

You can use word parts to help you recall the meaning of climate terms. The prefix *sub-* can indicate a part of a larger unit. The prefix *micro-* means "very small."

The climates of smaller areas within a subclimate are called **microclimates.** The area of a microclimate can be as large as a river valley or smaller than a garden. Forests, beaches, lakes, valleys, hills, and mountains are some of the features that influence local climates. For example, sea breezes often make beaches cooler than nearby inland areas on warm afternoons.

Shade from the tree produces a cooler microclimate where snow takes longer to melt.

Urban Heat Islands

Humans create artificial surfaces that can also affect local climates. Cities are usually warmer than surrounding rural areas. The warmer body of air over a city is called an **urban heat island.** At certain times the air temperature may be as much as 12°C (22°F) higher in a large city than in the nearby countryside. The following factors contribute to this effect:

- During the day, buildings and streets absorb more solar energy than do grass, trees, and soil. These artificial surfaces release the additional stored energy at night, which warms the air over a city.

- Evaporation of moisture helps cool areas. Because artificial surfaces absorb less water than most natural surfaces, there is less cooling from evaporation in cities than in rural areas.

- Cities use a lot of energy for cooling, transportation, and other activities. The use of energy releases heat into the atmosphere.

CHECK YOUR READING How do cities influence local temperature?

How Rain Shadows Form

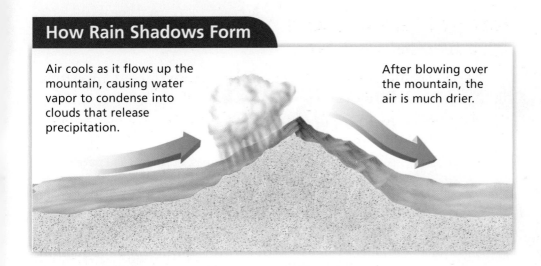

Air cools as it flows up the mountain, causing water vapor to condense into clouds that release precipitation.

After blowing over the mountain, the air is much drier.

Rain Shadows

Mountains have a strong effect on climate in places where steady winds blow inland from oceans. The illustration above shows how mountains can affect precipitation:

- Air is forced to rise as it flows over a mountain.
- As the air rises and cools, it condenses into clouds. Areas near the side of a mountain that faces wind may get heavy precipitation.
- After passing over the mountain, the air is much drier because it has lost moisture through condensation and precipitation.

The dry area on the downwind side of a mountain where this process occurs is called a **rain shadow.** Mountains do not affect only local climates. Many dry climate zones that extend over large regions are found in the rain shadows of mountain ranges.

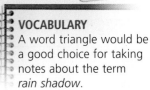

VOCABULARY
A word triangle would be a good choice for taking notes about the term *rain shadow*.

Review

KEY CONCEPTS

1. What two weather characteristics do meteorologists usually focus on when they determine climate zones?

2. Why do highland climate zones contain more than one climate?

3. How do mountains affect precipitation patterns?

CRITICAL THINKING

4. **Compare and Contrast** How are tundra and icecap subclimates similar? How are they different?

5. **Infer** In which climates would you expect to find the most vacation resorts? Explain.

⚠ CHALLENGE

6. **Apply** What is the subclimate of the region where you live? What microclimates exist in your local area?

Microclimates

OVERVIEW AND PURPOSE Microclimates are local variations within a region's climate. Natural and artificial features such as beaches, hills, wooded areas, buildings, and pavement can cause such variations. Even trees planted around a house or parking lot may influence the climate of that small area. In this lab, you will use what you have learned about weather and climate to

- measure weather factors, such as air temperature, in two different microclimates
- discover how natural and artificial features affect local climate

▶ Problem

How do natural and artificial features affect the climate of a small area?

▶ Hypothesize

Write a hypothesis to explain how you expect the microclimates of two nearby locations to be affected by the different natural and artificial features in those areas. Your hypothesis should take the form of an "If . . . , then . . . , because . . ." statement. You should complete steps 1–3 of the procedure before writing your hypothesis.

▶ Procedure

MATERIALS
- 2 thermometers
- 2 other weather instruments of the same kind

1. Work in a group of four students. You will use a thermometer to record air temperature. Choose another weather instrument that you have made or that is available to you. You might use a psychrometer to measure relative humidity, a barometer to measure air pressure, or an anemometer to measure wind speed.

2. Make data tables similar to the ones in the sample notebook page. The label in the second row of each table should identify what you will measure with the instrument you chose in step 1.

3. Go outside the school with your teacher, taking your instruments and notebook. Choose two locations near the school with different features for your group to study. For example, you might choose a grassy area and a paved area, or one area with trees and another area without trees.

4. Divide your group into two pairs. Each pair of students should have one thermometer and the other instrument you have chosen. You and your partner will study one location. The other pair will study the second location.

5. Decide ahead of time how you will control for variables. For example, both pairs might take measurements at a set height above the ground.

6. Draw pictures of the location you are studying in your notebook. Write a description of the natural and artificial features in this area.

7. Set up the instruments in your location. Record the air temperature. Take follow-up readings five and ten minutes later. Take a reading with the other weather instrument each time you take a temperature reading.

8. Record data gathered by the other two members of your group in your data table. Calculate the average temperature for each location. Then calculate the average reading for the other weather factor that you measured.

▶ Observe and Analyze   Write It Up

1. **IDENTIFY VARIABLES AND CONSTANTS** Identify the variables and constants in the investigation. List these factors in your **Science Notebook**.

2. **COMPARE AND CONTRAST** Which average measurements in the two locations were the same? What differences did your investigations reveal? For example, was one area cooler or less windy than the other?

▶ Conclude   Write It Up

1. **INFER** Answer the question posed in the problem.

2. **INTERPRET** Compare your results with your hypothesis. Did the results support your hypothesis? Did the natural and artificial features have the effects you expected?

3. **EVALUATE** What were the limitations of your instruments? What other sources of error could have affected the results?

4. **APPLY** How could you apply the results of your investigation to help you make landscaping or building decisions? For example, what could you do to make a picnic area more comfortable?

▶ INVESTIGATE Further

CHALLENGE Return to the locations you investigated at the same time of day on three consecutive days. Take readings with the same weather instruments that you used before. Are these new readings consistent with the patterns you observed on the first day? If not, how would you alter your earlier conclusions?

Microclimates

Problem How do natural and artificial features affect the climate of a small area?

Hypothesize

Observe and Analyze

Table 1. Weather Factors Within Microclimates

Time (min)	Location 1		Location 2	
	Temp (°C)	Wind Speed	Temp (°C)	Wind Speed
0				
5				
10				

Conclude

KEY CONCEPT

Climates can change suddenly or slowly.

◀ BEFORE, you learned	▶ NOW, you will learn
• Earth absorbs and reflects solar energy • Greenhouse gases help keep Earth warm • Human activities are contributing to global warming	• How climates can cool when particles block sunlight • About climate changes that repeat over time • How climates may change because of global warming

VOCABULARY

ice age p. 135
El Niño p. 136

THINK ABOUT

How do particles affect light?

If you shine a light through foggy air, you may notice that the beam of light is dimmer than usual. The droplets, or liquid particles, that make up fog block some of the light from reaching objects in the beam's path. Which natural events can suddenly add many particles to the atmosphere?

Climates cool when particles block sunlight.

Our atmosphere contains many particulates—tiny solid and liquid particles mixed in with air. Particulates block some of the Sun's energy, preventing it from reaching Earth's surface. Occasionally a natural event will suddenly release enormous amounts of particulates. Such an event may cause a temporary change in climates around the world.

Large volcanic eruptions can send huge clouds of gas and dust into the stratosphere. When these clouds enter the stratosphere, they spread out and drift around the world. Volcanoes affect global climate mainly by releasing sulfur dioxide gas. The gas combines with water to form sulfuric acid droplets, which block sunlight. Because Earth absorbs less solar energy, average global temperatures may decrease for up to several years.

 CHECK YOUR READING How can a sudden release of particles affect climate?

In 1991, Mount Pinatubo erupted in the Philippines. The eruption, one of the largest of the last century, affected climates for about two years. During the summer of 1992, parts of North America were more than 3°C (5.4°F) cooler than usual. Over that entire year, global temperatures dropped by 0.5°C (0.9°F).

The impact of rocky objects from space can also release particles into the atmosphere. Earth is often hit by space objects. Most are too small to have much of an effect. However, objects 3 kilometers (2 mi) in diameter strike Earth about once every million years. These powerful collisions can suddenly change climates.

When a large space object strikes Earth, it explodes and leaves behind a crater, or pit, in the surface. The explosion throws dust into the atmosphere. The largest impacts may have raised so much dust that temperatures around the world dropped sharply for months. They may also have caused changes in the atmosphere by setting off forest fires. A space object that hit Earth 65 million years ago blasted out a crater about 200 kilometers (120 mi) in diameter in what is now Mexico. Many scientists think that climate changes following this impact led to the extinction of the dinosaurs and other species.

PHILIPPINES

The eruption of Mount Pinatubo in 1991 affected temperatures around the world for about two years.

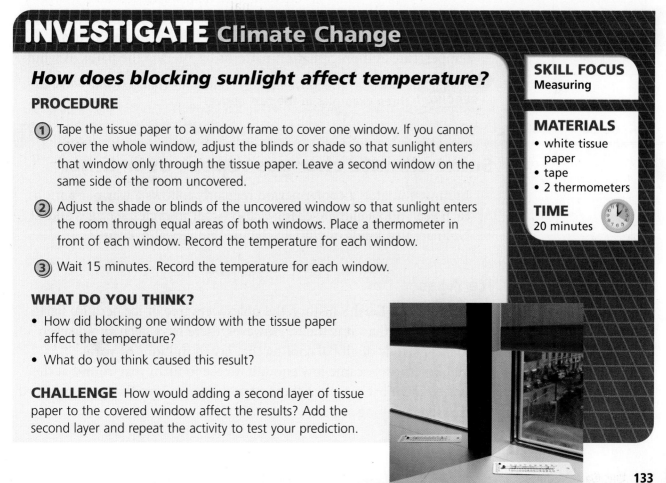

INVESTIGATE Climate Change

How does blocking sunlight affect temperature?

PROCEDURE

1. Tape the tissue paper to a window frame to cover one window. If you cannot cover the whole window, adjust the blinds or shade so that sunlight enters that window only through the tissue paper. Leave a second window on the same side of the room uncovered.

2. Adjust the shade or blinds of the uncovered window so that sunlight enters the room through equal areas of both windows. Place a thermometer in front of each window. Record the temperature for each window.

3. Wait 15 minutes. Record the temperature for each window.

WHAT DO YOU THINK?

- How did blocking one window with the tissue paper affect the temperature?

- What do you think caused this result?

CHALLENGE How would adding a second layer of tissue paper to the covered window affect the results? Add the second layer and repeat the activity to test your prediction.

SKILL FOCUS
Measuring

MATERIALS
- white tissue paper
- tape
- 2 thermometers

TIME
20 minutes

Climates change as continents move.

Climates can change suddenly for brief periods after a volcanic eruption. In contrast, the movement of continents causes steady climate changes over many millions of years. The maps below show two stages of this movement in the distant past.

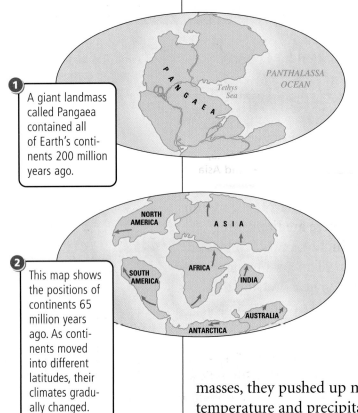

1 A giant landmass called Pangaea contained all of Earth's continents 200 million years ago.

2 This map shows the positions of continents 65 million years ago. As continents moved into different latitudes, their climates gradually changed.

1 Earth's continents were once joined together in a gigantic landmass called Pangaea (pan-JEE-uh). This giant landmass began to break up about 200 million years ago.

2 By 65 million years ago, the continents had moved closer to their present positions. As the continents moved, their climates gradually changed in different ways. Some continents cooled as they moved toward higher latitudes. Other continents grew warmer as they moved toward the equator.

The movement of continents had other effects on climate. As they drifted apart, the continents changed the paths of ocean currents that help warm coastal regions. When landmasses collided with other landmasses, they pushed up mountain ranges. Mountains influence temperature and precipitation patterns by altering the paths of winds.

CHECK YOUR READING How does the movement of continents change climate? Find three examples in the text above.

Some climate changes repeat over time.

In most climates, a cooler period regularly follows a warmer period each year. Some climate changes also occur in cycles. Ice ages and El Niño are two kinds of climate change that repeat over time.

Ice Ages

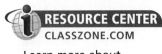

RESOURCE CENTER
CLASSZONE.COM

Learn more about climate change.

For much of Earth's history, the poles were free of ice because Earth was warmer than it is today. However, there have been about seven major periods of global cooling that lasted millions of years. Temperatures became low enough for ice to form year-round at the poles. The most recent of these periods began 2 million years ago and is still continuing.

How Ice Expands in an Ice Age

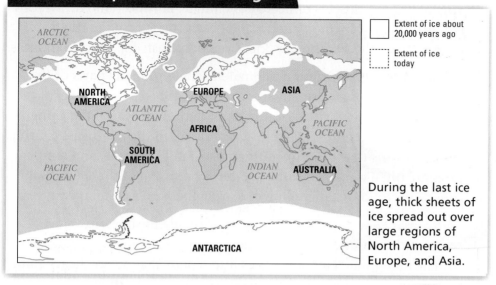

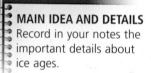 Extent of ice about 20,000 years ago

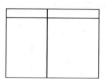 Extent of ice today

During the last ice age, thick sheets of ice spread out over large regions of North America, Europe, and Asia.

During major periods of global cooling, there are times when polar ice expands. **Ice ages** are periods in which huge sheets of ice spread out beyond the polar regions. The map above shows how far the ice sheets reached in the last ice age, which ended between 14,000 and 10,000 years ago. These sheets were several kilometers thick and covered nearly a third of Earth's land area.

Ice ages usually last tens of thousands of years. They are separated by warmer periods in which ice sheets shrink back toward the poles. We are living in one of these warmer periods. Average global temperatures are now 5°C to 10°C (9–18°F) higher than they were during the last ice age. Only Greenland and Antarctica have large ice sheets today.

Various sources of evidence show that ice ages occurred. Scientists study polar ice and the ocean floor to estimate past changes in temperature. Geological features that formed during ice ages, such as scratches on rocks, can reveal the movement of ice sheets. Some of the evidence also provides clues about what causes ice ages. Most scientists think that there are two main causes:

- Ice ages are closely linked to changes in how Earth moves around the Sun. These changes may have caused ice sheets to grow by altering the temperature patterns of the seasons.

- As you learned in Chapter 1, carbon dioxide is a greenhouse gas. Levels of carbon dioxide in the atmosphere dropped during ice ages. Lower carbon dioxide levels may have caused global cooling by weakening the greenhouse effect.

Other factors probably play a role in the development of ice ages. Scientists are still trying to understand how different factors work in combination to cause global cooling.

MAIN IDEA AND DETAILS
Record in your notes the important details about ice ages.

El Niño

The oceans are closely connected to climate. **El Niño** (ehl NEEN-yoh) is a disturbance of wind patterns and ocean currents in the Pacific Ocean. It usually occurs every 3 to 7 years and lasts for 12 to 18 months.

El Niño causes temporary climate changes in many parts of the world. It can cause unusually dry conditions in the western Pacific region and unusually heavy rainfall in South America. In the United States, El Niño tends to bring heavier rainfall to the Southeast. During winter, storms may be stronger than usual in California, and temperatures are often milder in some northern states. All of these unusual conditions follow changes in wind strength and ocean temperatures.

1 **Normal Year** Strong trade winds normally push warm water toward the western Pacific, where an area of low pressure develops. The rising warm air condenses into clouds that release heavy rain. Cooler water flows near the west coast of South America.

2 **El Niño Year** Weak trade winds allow warm water to flow back toward the central and eastern Pacific. The clouds and heavy rain also shift eastward, toward South America. The effects of El Niño vary, depending on how much warming occurs in the eastern Pacific.

How El Niño Forms

Weak trade winds during El Niño cause changes in ocean temperature and precipitation.

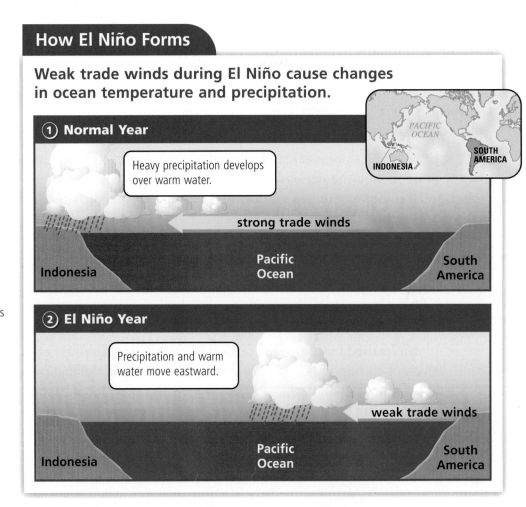

1 **Normal Year**

Heavy precipitation develops over warm water.

strong trade winds

Indonesia — Pacific Ocean — South America

PACIFIC OCEAN

INDONESIA — SOUTH AMERICA

2 **El Niño Year**

Precipitation and warm water move eastward.

weak trade winds

Indonesia — Pacific Ocean — South America

1983

2002

This ice sheet on a mountain in Peru has shrunk 820 meters (2690 ft) in 19 years.

Human activities are changing climate.

Most climate experts predict that by 2100, there will be a rise in global temperature of 1.4°C to 5.8°C (2.5–10.4°F). As you read in Chapter 1, human activities release greenhouse gases. Higher levels of greenhouse gases in the atmosphere cause global warming. Earth hasn't warmed so rapidly at any time in at least the last 10,000 years. Even a small temperature increase could have a great impact on climate.

REMINDER

Remember that greenhouse gases are gases that absorb infrared energy.

Predictions of Climate Change

Although scientists expect all land areas to warm up by 2100, the rate of warming will be uneven. The greatest warming is expected to occur in the high latitudes of the Northern Hemisphere. The increase in Greenland's temperature, for example, may be two or three times the global average. Higher temperatures have recently started to melt the ice sheet that covers much of Greenland. Ice is also melting in the Arctic Ocean and on mountains in many parts of the world.

The effects of global warming on precipitation will also vary. Scientists predict an overall increase in precipitation, because more water will evaporate from Earth's warmer surface. Precipitation will tend to fall more heavily in short periods of time, which will increase flooding. However, some areas where water is already scarce may get even less precipitation. Lower precipitation in those areas will make droughts more frequent and severe.

CHECK YOUR READING Summarize how global warming is expected to affect temperature and precipitation.

Impact of Global Warming

MAIN IDEA AND DETAILS
Record in your notes the important details about the impact of global warming.

RESOURCE CENTER
CLASSZONE.COM

Find out more about the effects of global warming.

Global warming affects many of Earth's systems. Because these systems work together in complex ways, it is difficult to predict the full impact of global warming. Most climate scientists predict that global warming will probably cause the following changes.

Sea Levels As temperatures warm, the oceans will expand. They will also gain additional water from melting ice. Scientists expect the average sea level to rise 9 to 88 centimeters (4–35 in.) over the next century. Higher sea levels will damage coastal regions and increase flooding. These problems could be severe in small island nations.

Wildlife Global warming will endanger many plant and animal species by altering natural habitats. Some species will die out or move to cooler areas. Other species, such as warm-water fishes, will benefit from an expansion of their habitats.

Agriculture Changes in temperature and precipitation can affect crops and livestock. If Earth warms more than a few degrees Celsius, most of the world's agriculture will be harmed. More moderate warming will help agriculture in some regions by lengthening the growing season. However, even moderate warming will harm agriculture in other regions.

Human Health Warmer temperatures could increase heat-related deaths and deaths from some diseases, such as malaria, especially in areas near the equator. On the other hand, deaths caused by extreme cold could decrease at higher latitudes.

Some scientists predict more dangerous changes beyond 2100 if humans continue to add greenhouse gases to the atmosphere at current levels. However, the harmful effects of global warming can be limited if we reduce emissions of greenhouse gases.

4.3 Review

KEY CONCEPTS

1. How can volcanic eruptions and impacts of large objects from space change climate?

2. What changes in climate occur during an ice age?

3. Give two examples of ways in which global warming will probably affect life on Earth.

CRITICAL THINKING

4. **Connect** What is the connection between latitude, the movement of continents, and climate change?

5. **Compare and Contrast** Compare and contrast the effects of El Niño and ice ages on climate.

⚠ CHALLENGE

6. **Infer** Discuss why some countries might be more reluctant than others to take steps to reduce levels of greenhouse gases.

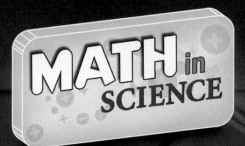

Carbon Dioxide Levels

MATH TUTORIAL
GLASSZONE.COM

Click on Math Tutorial for more help with interpreting line graphs.

Since the 1950s, carbon dioxide levels have been measured in air samples collected at the Mauna Loa Observatory in Hawaii. The graphs below show the carbon dioxide data plotted in two different ways. In the graph on the left, the scale showing carbon dioxide levels starts at 0 parts per million (ppm) and goes up to 400 ppm. The graph on the right offers a close-up view of the same data. The scale on the right-hand graph is broken to focus on the values from 310 ppm to 380 ppm.

Amount of Carbon Dioxide in the Air

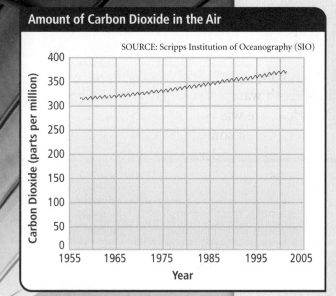

Amount of Carbon Dioxide in the Air

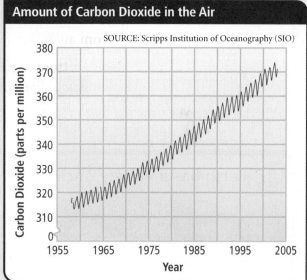

Use the graphs to answer the following questions.

1. What was the carbon dioxide level at the beginning of 1995?

2. The data show a 17 percent increase in the carbon dioxide level in the air from 1958 through 2001. Which graph shows this increase more clearly? Why?

3. In both graphs, the line that shows carbon dioxide levels is jagged, because carbon dioxide levels rise and fall regularly as the seasons change. In some years, the seasonal rise and fall is greater than in other years. Which graph emphasizes these variations more? Why?

CHALLENGE The carbon dioxide level in the air starts falling in May or June each year and continues to fall through October. What do you think causes this change to occur?

Chapter Review

the BIG idea

Climates are long-term weather patterns that may change over time.

CONTENT REVIEW
CLASSZONE.COM

KEY CONCEPTS SUMMARY

4.1 Climate is a long-term weather pattern.

The main factors that influence climate are

- latitude
- altitude
- distance from large bodies of water
- ocean currents

Seasonal changes are also part of climate patterns.

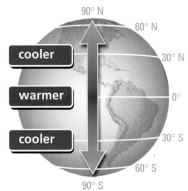

Temperatures usually decrease as latitude increases.

VOCABULARY
climate p. 117
latitude p. 118
marine climate p. 120
continental climate p. 120
ocean current p. 121
season p. 122

4.2 Earth has a variety of climates.

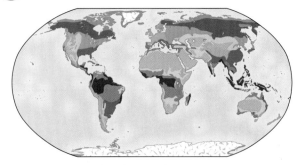

Each color on the map shows a different subclimate.

Scientists usually group climates by temperature and precipitation. There are six major climate zones. Climate zones can be divided into subclimates. Microclimates are smaller areas within subclimates.

VOCABULARY
climate zone p. 125
microclimate p. 128
urban heat island p. 128
rain shadow p. 129

4.3 Climates can change suddenly or slowly.

Natural events, such as eruptions of volcanoes, can change climate. Human activities that release greenhouse gases are also changing climate.

VOCABULARY
ice age p. 135
El Niño p. 136

Reviewing Vocabulary

Make a magnet word diagram for each of the vocabulary terms listed below. Write the term in the magnet. Write other terms or ideas related to it on the lines around the magnet.

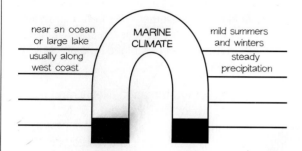

near an ocean or large lake

usually along west coast

MARINE CLIMATE

mild summers and winters

steady precipitation

1. continental climate
2. ocean current
3. microclimate
4. urban heat island
5. rain shadow
6. ice age

Reviewing Key Concepts

Multiple Choice *Choose the letter of the best answer.*

7. Compared with weather patterns, climate patterns are more
   a. severe
   c. local
   b. long-term
   d. unusual

8. Climates are usually classified by
   a. plant cover and animal life
   b. altitude and latitude
   c. bodies of water and ocean currents
   d. temperature and precipitation

9. Which latitude receives the least amount of solar energy?
   a. 30° N
   c. 30° S
   b. 0°
   d. 90° S

10. What is El Niño?
    a. a change in wind patterns and ocean currents
    b. an increase in carbon dioxide levels
    c. a decrease in global temperature
    d. a change in solar energy

11. Which effect is a likely result of global warming?
    a. fewer droughts
    b. lower sea levels
    c. more flooding
    d. more cold-related deaths

12. Volcanoes can cool the climate by
    a. increasing wind speeds
    b. using up Earth's energy
    c. releasing gas and particles
    d. raising air pressure

13. A large coastal city probably has cooler summers than a city at the same latitude that is
    a. on a mountain
    c. near a volcano
    b. much smaller
    d. far inland

14. Which carries warmth from the tropics toward the polar regions?
    a. urban heat islands
    b. warm-water currents
    c. cold-water currents
    d. trade winds

15. Several different climates can exist within a small area in
    a. marine climates
    b. continental climates
    c. polar climates
    d. highland climates

16. Day and night are equal in length on the first day of
    a. spring
    c. winter
    b. summer
    d. El Niño

Short Answer *Write a short answer to each question.*

17. How can changes caused by the movement of continents affect climate?

18. Identify the two main causes of ice ages.

19. Describe how a space object might have helped kill off the dinosaurs.

20. How is the climate of a city usually different from the climate of a nearby rural area?

Thinking Critically

Use the climate graphs to answer the next four questions.

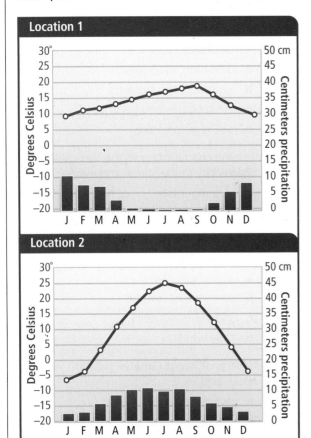

Location 1

Location 2

21. **COMPARE AND CONTRAST** Compare and contrast the seasonal precipitation patterns shown in the graphs.

22. **COMPARE AND CONTRAST** Contrast the seasonal temperature patterns shown in the graphs.

23. **HYPOTHESIZE** Which of the four main geographical factors that affect climate is the most likely cause of the difference in temperature patterns in the two locations? Explain.

24. **SYNTHESIZE** Suppose you want to plant a crop that requires a long growing season. Which location would you choose? Why?

25. **IDENTIFY EFFECTS** Describe the possible effect on the microclimate of a city if people planted grass lawns on the roofs of buildings.

26. **SYNTHESIZE** Would you expect to find a greater variety of climates on a tall mountain at 10° N or at 65° N? Explain.

27. **APPLY** In the evening after a hot summer day, the temperature at a beach stays higher longer than it does farther inland. Explain why this happens.

28. **APPLY** Both Kathmandu, Nepal, and Fuzhou, China, are located at about 25° N. Kathmandu is far inland and high in the mountains. Fuzhou is a seaport. How would you expect their climates to differ?

29. **PREDICT** What might be the impact of global warming in the area where you live?

the BIG idea

30. **APPLY** Look again at the photograph on pages 114–115. Now that you have finished the chapter, how would you change your response to the question on the photograph?

31. **EVALUATE** Describe a place that has what you consider to be a perfect climate. Explain how the following geographical factors affect the climate of that place:
    • latitude
    • altitude
    • distance from large bodies of water
    • ocean currents

UNIT PROJECTS

Evaluate all the data, results, and information in your project folder. Prepare to present your project.

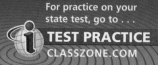
Analyzing Data

The following tables show the average temperatures in four cities and the temperature characteristics of four climate zones. Use the information in the tables to answer the questions below.

City	Avg. Temperature in Coldest Month	Avg. Temperature in Warmest Month
Miami, Florida	20°C	29°C
Minneapolis, Minnesota	–11°C	23°C
Little Rock, Arkansas	4°C	28°C
Barrow, Alaska	–26°C	4°C

Climate Zone	Characteristics
Polar	Average temperature of warmest month is below 10°C.
Moist mid-latitude with severe winters	Average temperature of coldest month is below –2°C.
Moist mid-latitude with mild winters	Average temperature of coldest month is between –2°C and 18°C.
Humid tropical	Average temperature of every month is greater than 18°C.

1. What is the average temperature in Miami in the coldest month?
   a. –11°C   **c.** 20°C
   b. 4°C   **d.** 29°C

2. What is the average temperature in Little Rock in the warmest month?
   a. 4°C   **c.** 28°C
   b. 23°C   **d.** 29°C

3. Which city has a moist mid-latitude climate with mild winters?
   a. Miami   **c.** Little Rock
   b. Minneapolis   **d.** Barrow

4. Which city has a humid tropical climate?
   a. Miami   **c.** Little Rock
   b. Minneapolis   **d.** Barrow

5. Which city has a moist mid-latitude climate with severe winters?
   a. Miami   **c.** Little Rock
   b. Minneapolis   **d.** Barrow

6. In which climate zone would Little Rock be if its average temperature in the coldest month were 10° colder?
   a. polar
   b. moist mid-latitude with severe winters
   c. moist mid-latitude with mild winters
   d. humid tropical

Extended Response

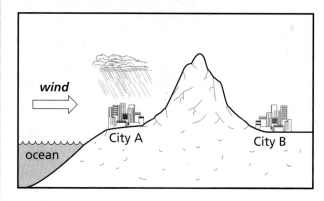

Use information in the diagram to answer the two questions below in detail.

7. City A receives 165 centimeters of rain each year. Explain why its climate is so moist. Use the words *wind, evaporate, condense,* and *precipitation* in your answer.

8. City B receives an average of 22 centimeters of rain each year. Explain why city B is much drier than city A. Use the term *rain shadow* in your answer.

UNIT E

Space Science

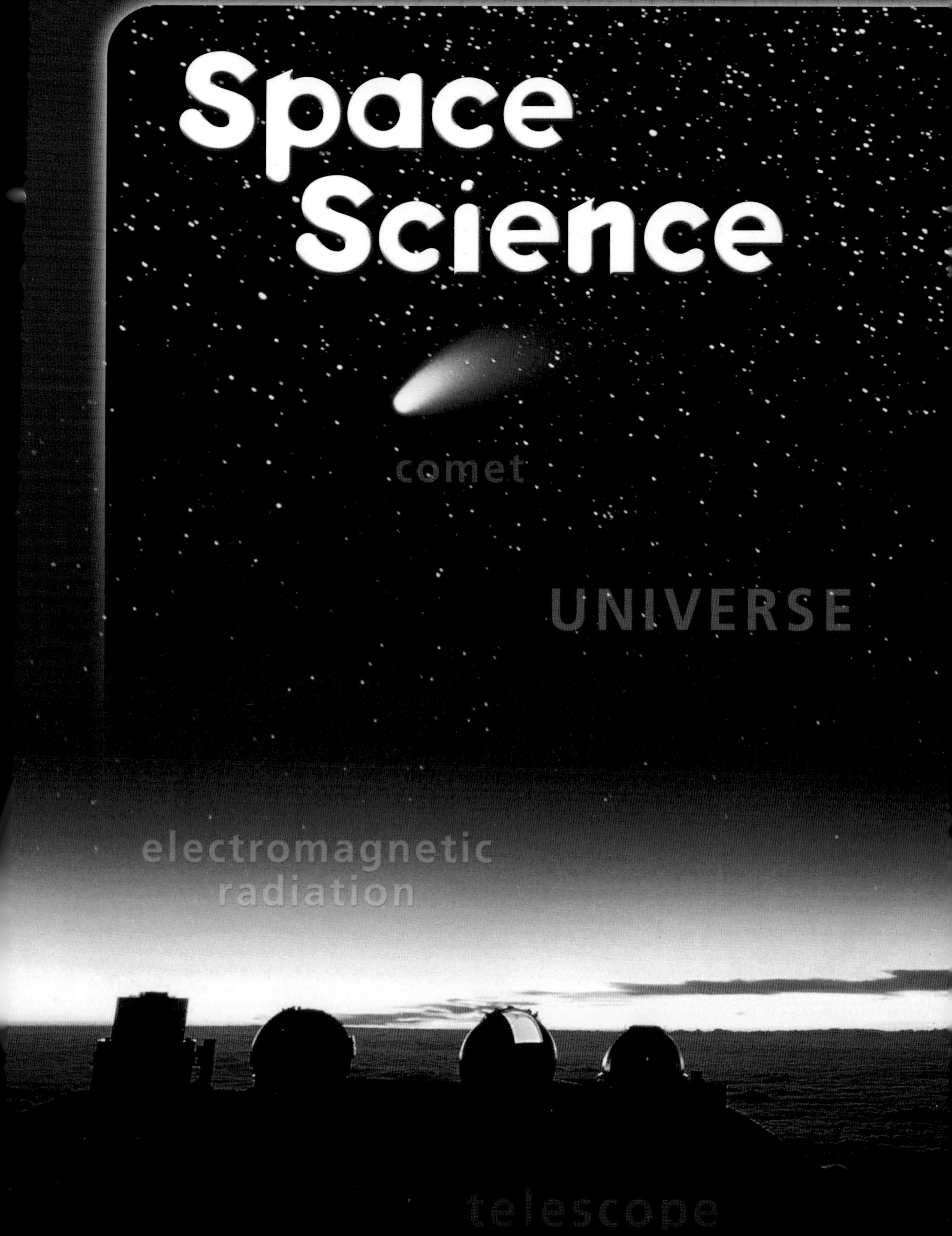
comet
UNIVERSE
electromagnetic radiation
telescope

Space Science
Contents Overview

Unit Features

DANGER from the Sky

How can astronomers find out whether a large object from space is going to strike our planet?

SCIENTIFIC AMERICAN FRONTIERS

View the video segment "Big Dish" to learn how astronomers use the largest radio telescope on Earth.

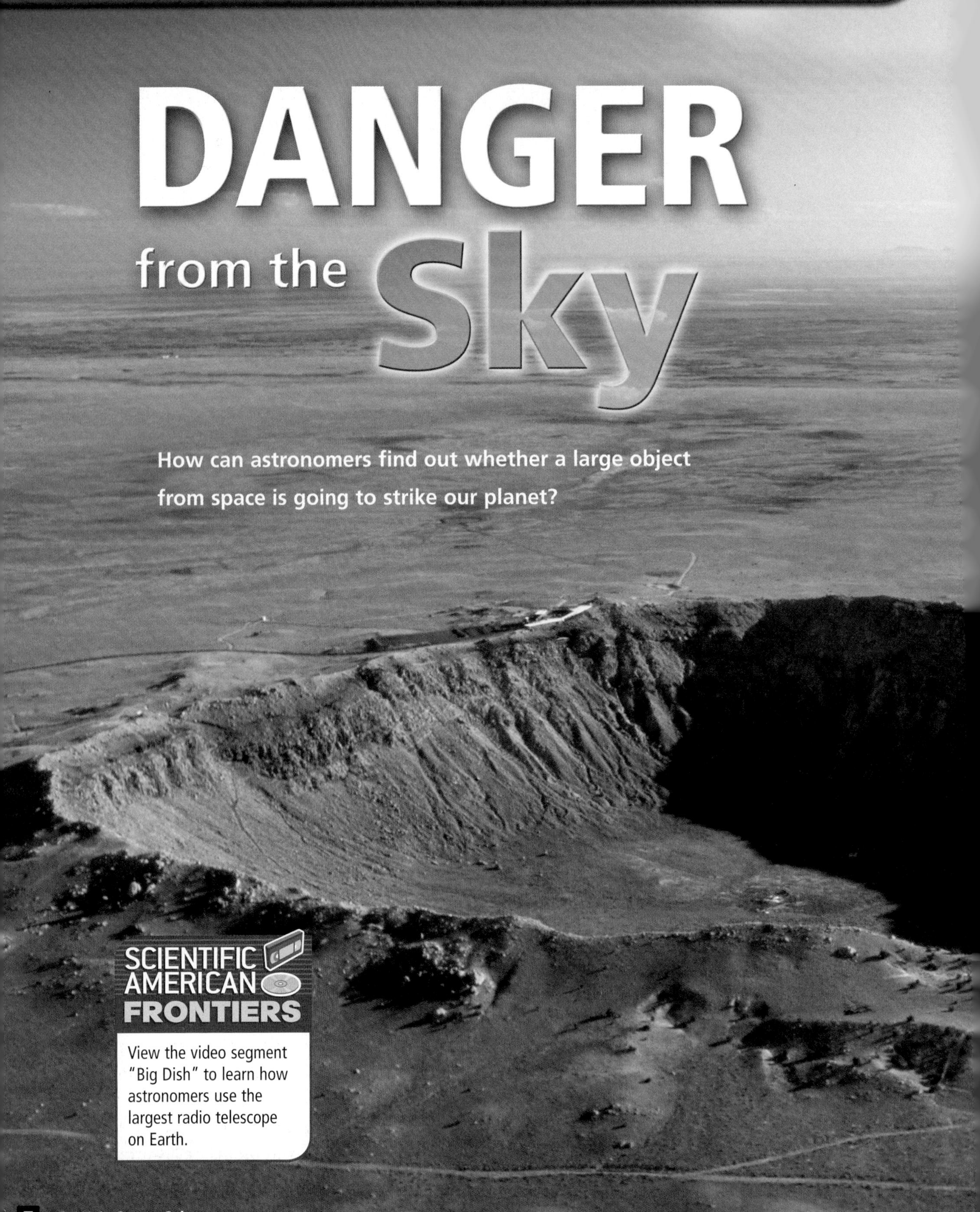

The streak of light in the photograph above was produced by a tiny particle from space burning up in Earth's atmosphere. Shown to the left is Barringer Crater in Arizona.

Collisions in Space

In the summer of 1994, telescopes all over the world were aimed at Jupiter. For the first time in history, astronomers had warning of a collision in space. Jupiter's gravity had split a comet named Shoemaker-Levy 9 into more than 20 large pieces. As the rocky objects collided with Jupiter's atmosphere, they exploded spectacularly.

Astronomers have found evidence of impacts closer to home. The craters that cover much of the Moon's surface were caused by collisions with space objects billions of years ago. In 1953 an astronomer even caught on film the bright flash of an object hitting the Moon. Other solid bodies in space also have impact craters. Little evidence of impacts remains on Earth because its surface is always changing. Fewer than 200 craters are still visible.

Earth's atmosphere protects us from collisions with small objects, which burn up in the air. However, when a large object strikes Earth, the atmosphere can spread the effects of the impact far beyond the crater. A large collision may throw dust high into the air, where it can be carried around the globe. The dust can block sunlight for months and sharply lower global temperatures.

About 65 million years ago, a large space object struck Earth. The dust from this collision can be found around the world in a layer of rock that was forming at the time. At about the same time, most species of organisms died out, including the dinosaurs. Many scientists think that the collision caused this global devastation.

The Risk of a Major Collision

When will the next space object hit Earth? A collision is probably occurring as you read this sentence. Tiny particles hit Earth's atmosphere all the time. Some of these particles have enough mass to make it through the atmosphere. Objects that reach Earth's surface are called meteorites. Most meteorites splash harmlessly into the ocean or hit unpopulated areas. Every few years a meteorite damages a home or other property. However, there is no known case of a meteorite's killing a person.

Collisions that cause widespread damage happen less often because the solar system contains fewer large objects. In 1908 a large object from space exploded above a remote region of Russia. The explosion knocked down trees across an area more than half the size of Rhode Island. Even this impact was small in comparison with major collisions that affect the entire world. Such collisions happen on average about twice every million years. Events that kill off many species occur even less often.

Tracking Asteroids

Although Earth is unlikely to have a major collision with a space object anytime soon, the danger is too great to ignore. Scientists are using telescopes to find large, rocky space objects called asteroids. After locating an asteroid, they use computer models to predict its path centuries into the future. Scientists expect that by 2008 they will have found almost all of the asteroids that could cause global devastation on Earth.

Locating objects that may threaten life on Earth is just the first step. Scientists also want to

View the "Big Dish" segment of your *Scientific American Frontiers* video to learn how astronomers are using the giant Arecibo radio telescope to explore the universe.

IN THIS SCENE FROM THE VIDEO ⏵

You see a close-up of the Arecibo telescope's dome and one of its antennas.

EXPLORING ASTEROIDS An asteroid's crashing into Earth may seem like the subject of a science fiction movie. Yet asteroids pose a real danger to humans. Some asteroids could cause widespread destruction if they struck our planet.

Astronomers are tracking these asteroids to determine how close they will pass to Earth in the future.

Asteroids are too faint to be viewed clearly with optical telescopes on Earth. However, radio telescopes can provide detailed images of asteroids. Inside the dome of the Arecibo telescope is the world's most powerful radar transmitter. The transmitter can bounce a beam of radio waves off the telescope's dish to reach an asteroid millions of miles away. The telescope picks up returning signals, which are converted into images.

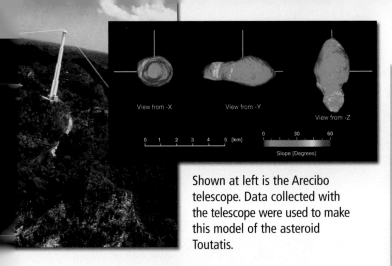

Shown at left is the Arecibo telescope. Data collected with the telescope were used to make this model of the asteroid Toutatis.

learn about the characteristics of asteroids. The Arecibo telescope in Puerto Rico is an important tool for studying asteroids. The largest radio dish in the world, it allows scientists to determine the motions and shapes of asteroids. Computer models and tests with real materials provide additional information about the mass, materials, and structure of each asteroid.

If scientists ever find an asteroid headed toward Earth, these studies may help us change the asteroid's course safely. Remember the comet that struck Jupiter in many pieces? If an asteroid broke apart before reaching Earth, pieces hitting different locations could cause even more damage than a single impact. Before using a bomb or laser to change the course of an asteroid, governments must make sure that the asteroid will not break apart. Fortunately, scientists would have decades to study a dangerous asteroid and figure out what action to take.

UNANSWERED Questions

Scientists are learning about the risk of an asteroid's colliding with Earth. The more we learn about collisions in space, the more questions we have.

• What methods can be used to change the course of an asteroid that threatens Earth?

• How can we make sure that an asteroid will not break apart because of our efforts to change its course?

• How many smaller but still dangerous objects may be headed toward Earth?

UNIT PROJECTS

As you study this unit, work alone or with a group on one of these projects.

Observe the Sky

Choose a space object or part of the distant sky to observe over a month. Keep an observation journal of what you see and think.

• Pay special attention to any changes relative to other objects in the sky.

• Look up information or construct tools to help you observe.

• Copy your best drawings for a display board. Explain your observations.

Multimedia Presentation

The Arecibo telescope is not used only for studying asteroids. Prepare a multimedia presentation on other research that is being carried out with the giant radio telescope.

• Find information about the research from Internet sites and other sources.

• Prepare both audio and visual components for your presentation.

Map a Space Object

Use a large potato to represent a newly explored space object. Draw lines of latitude and longitude. Then identify features, and make a flat map.

• Use roller-ball pens to mark poles, an equator, and lines of longitude and latitude. Try not to pierce the potato's skin.

• Do the potato's eyes seem like craters or volcanoes? Decide how to name the different types of features.

• Make a flat map of the space object.

CAREER CENTER
CLASSZONE.COM
Learn about careers in astronomy.

CHAPTER

1 Exploring Space

the BIG idea

People develop and use technology to explore and study space.

Key Concepts

SECTION
1.1 **Some space objects are visible to the human eye.**
Learn about views of space from Earth and about the arrangement of the universe.

SECTION
1.2 **Telescopes allow us to study space from Earth.**
Learn how astronomers gather information about space from different kinds of radiation.

SECTION
1.3 **Spacecraft help us explore beyond Earth.**
Learn how astronauts and instruments provide information about space.

SECTION
1.4 **Space exploration benefits society.**
Learn about the benefits of space exploration.

Internet Preview

CLASSZONE.COM

Chapter 1 online resources: Content Review, Simulation, Visualization, two Resource Centers, Math Tutorial, Test Practice

What challenges must be overcome in space exploration?

EXPLORE (the BIG idea)

Why Does the Sun Appear to Move Around Earth?

Stand in front of a floor lamp, and turn around slowly. Notice how the lamp moves within your field of vision.

Observe and Think Why did the lamp seem to move?

What Colors Are in Sunlight?

In bright sunlight, hold a clear plastic pen over a box. Move the pen until a rainbow pattern appears.

Observe and Think What colors did you see? What might have caused them to appear?

Internet Activity: Universe

Go to **ClassZone.com** to simulate moving through different levels of scale in the universe.

Observe and Think How much of the universe could you see without a telescope?

NSTA
scilinks.org
SCI LINKS

Space Probes **Code: MDL057**

Getting Ready to Learn

◀ CONCEPT REVIEW

- There are more stars in the sky than anyone can easily count.
- Telescopes magnify the appearance of distant objects in the sky.
- Once an invention exists, people are likely to think up new ways of using it.

◀ VOCABULARY REVIEW

See Glossary for definitions.

data

energy

gravity

technology

CONTENT REVIEW
CLASSZONE.COM
Review concepts and vocabulary.

▶ TAKING NOTES

MAIN IDEA WEB

Write each new blue heading, or main idea, in the center box. In the boxes around it, take notes about important terms and details that relate to the main idea.

VOCABULARY STRATEGY

Think about a vocabulary term as a **magnet word** diagram. Write the other terms or ideas related to that term around it.

See the Note-Taking Handbook on pages R45–R51.

SCIENCE NOTEBOOK

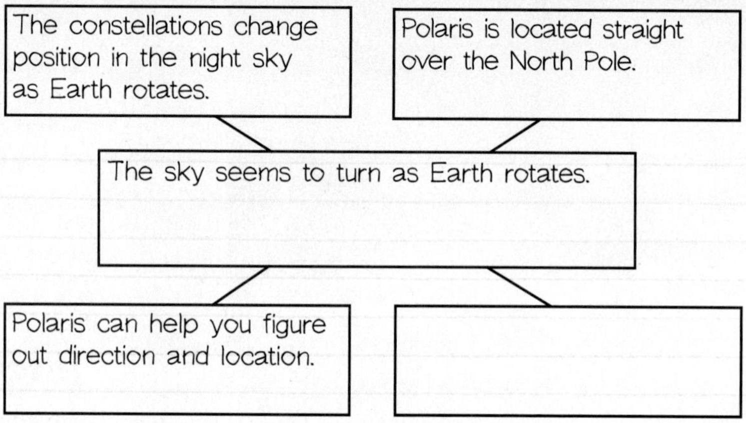

The constellations change position in the night sky as Earth rotates.

Polaris is located straight over the North Pole.

The sky seems to turn as Earth rotates.

Polaris can help you figure out direction and location.

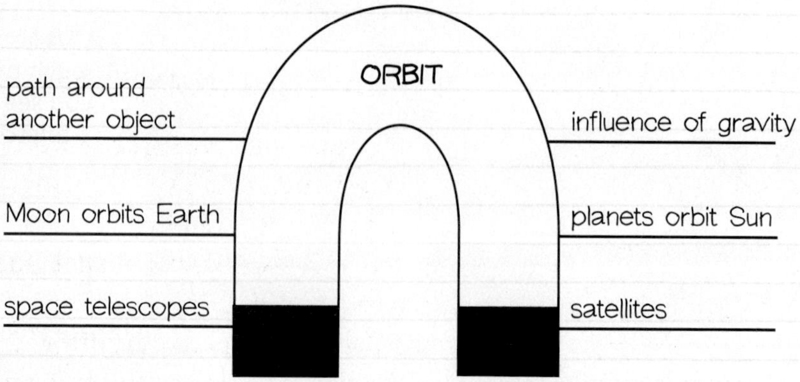

ORBIT

path around another object

influence of gravity

Moon orbits Earth

planets orbit Sun

space telescopes

satellites

Some space objects are visible to the human eye.

◀ **BEFORE,** you learned

- Earth is one of nine planets that orbit the Sun
- The Moon orbits Earth
- Earth turns on its axis every 24 hours

▶ **NOW,** you will learn

- How the universe is arranged
- How stars form patterns in the sky
- How the motions of bodies in space appear from Earth

VOCABULARY

orbit p. 10
solar system p. 10
galaxy p. 10
universe p. 10
constellation p. 12

EXPLORE Distance

How far is the Moon from Earth?

PROCEDURE

① Tie one end of the string around the middle of the tennis ball. The tennis ball will represent Earth.

② Wrap the string 9.5 times around the tennis ball, and make a mark on the string at that point. Wrap the aluminum foil into a ball around the mark. The foil ball will represent the Moon.

③ Stretch out the string to put the model Moon and Earth at the right distance compared to their sizes.

MATERIALS

- tennis ball
- aluminum foil (5 cm strip)
- string (250 cm)
- felt marker

WHAT DO YOU THINK?

- How does the scale model compare with your previous idea of the distance between Earth and the Moon?
- How many Earths do you estimate would fit between Earth and the Moon?

We see patterns in the universe.

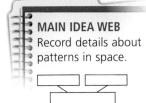

MAIN IDEA WEB
Record details about patterns in space.

For most of history, people had very limited knowledge of space. They saw planets and stars as points of light in the night sky. However, they did not know how far those bodies were from Earth or from each other. Early observers made guesses about planets and stars on the basis of their appearance and the ways they seemed to move in the sky. Different peoples around the world connected the patterns they saw in the sky with stories about imaginary beings.

We still have much to learn about the universe. Within the last few hundred years, however, new tools and scientific theories have greatly increased our knowledge. In this chapter you will learn about the arrangement of planets and stars. You will also learn about the ways in which astronomers explore and study space.

Arrangement of the Universe

If you look up at the sky on a clear night, you will see only a tiny fraction of the planets and stars that exist. The number of objects in the universe and the distances between them are greater than most people can imagine. Yet these objects are not spread around randomly. Gravity causes objects in space to be grouped together in different ways.

The images on page 11 show some basic structures in the universe. Like a camera lens zooming out, the images provide views of space at different levels of size.

READING TiP
The word *orbit* can be a noun or a verb.

1 Earth Our planet's diameter is about 13,000 kilometers (8000 mi). This is almost four times the diameter of the Moon, which orbits Earth. An **orbit** is the path of an object in space as it moves around another object because of gravity.

2 Solar System Earth and eight other major planets orbit the Sun. The Sun, the planets, and various smaller bodies make up the **solar system.** The Sun is about 100 times greater in diameter than Earth. You could fit more than 4000 bodies the size of the Sun between the Sun and the solar system's outermost planet at its average distance from the Sun. The Sun is one of countless stars in space. Astronomers have detected planets orbiting some of these other stars.

3 The Milky Way Our solar system and the stars you can see with your bare eyes are part of a galaxy called the Milky Way. A **galaxy** is a group of millions or billions of stars held together by their own gravity. If the solar system were the size of a penny, the Milky Way would stretch from Chicago to Dallas. Most stars in the Milky Way are so far away that our galaxy appears to us as a hazy band of light.

4 The Universe The **universe** is everything—space and all the matter and energy in it. The Milky Way is just one of many billions of galaxies in the universe. These galaxies extend in all directions.

Astronomers study space at each of these different levels. Some focus on planets in the solar system. Other astronomers study distant galaxies. To learn how the universe formed, astronomers even study the smallest particles that make up all matter.

CHECK YOUR READING What is the relationship between the solar system and the Milky Way?

Structures in the Universe

Gravity causes objects to be grouped together in space.

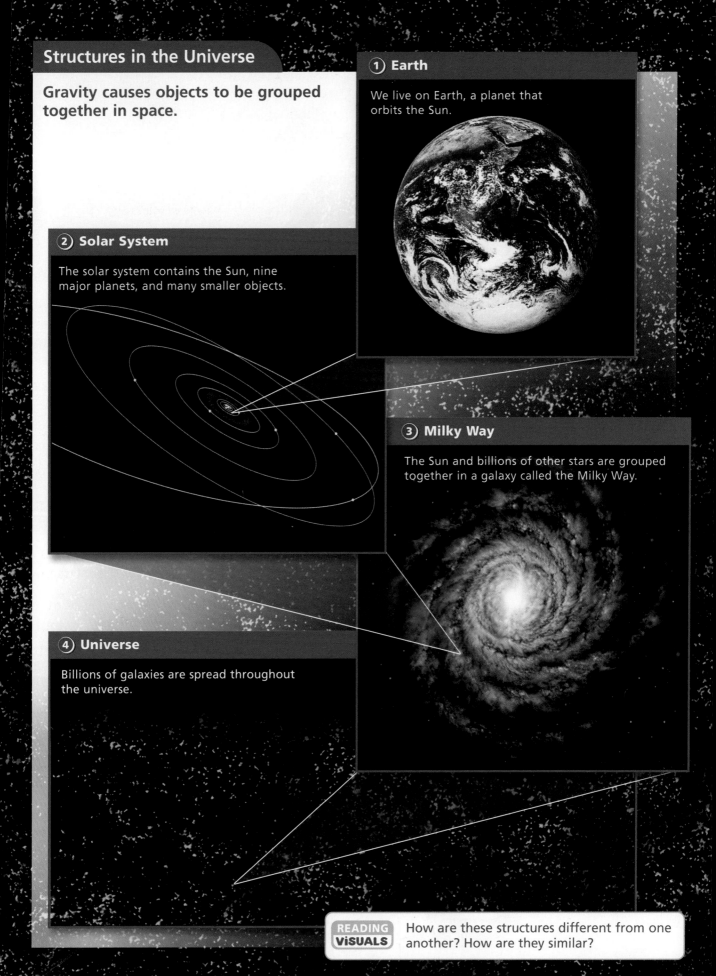

① Earth

We live on Earth, a planet that orbits the Sun.

② Solar System

The solar system contains the Sun, nine major planets, and many smaller objects.

③ Milky Way

The Sun and billions of other stars are grouped together in a galaxy called the Milky Way.

④ Universe

Billions of galaxies are spread throughout the universe.

READING VISUALS How are these structures different from one another? How are they similar?

Constellation Patterns

The stars of a constellation are often far apart from one another, but they appear grouped together when viewed from Earth.

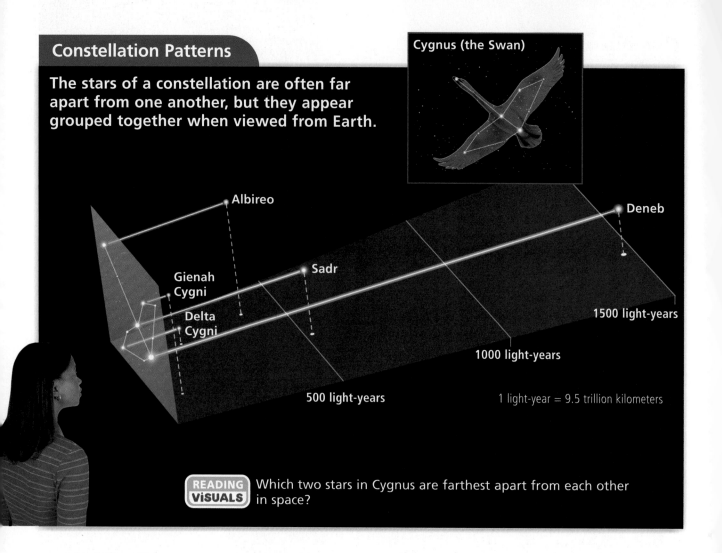

Cygnus (the Swan)

Albireo

Deneb

Gienah Cygni

Sadr

Delta Cygni

1500 light-years

1000 light-years

500 light-years

1 light-year = 9.5 trillion kilometers

READING VISUALS Which two stars in Cygnus are farthest apart from each other in space?

Constellations

If you want to find a particular place in the United States, it helps to know the name of the state it is in. Astronomers use a similar system to describe the locations of objects in the sky. They have divided the sky into 88 areas named for the constellations.

A **constellation** is a group of stars that form a pattern in the sky. In the constellation Cygnus, for example, a group of bright stars form the shape of a flying swan. Any other objects in that area of the sky, such as galaxies, are said to be located in Cygnus, even if they are not parts of the swan pattern. The ancient Greeks named many of the constellations for animals and imaginary beings.

Unlike the planets in the solar system, the stars in a constellation are usually not really close to each other. They seem to be grouped together when viewed from Earth. But as the illustration above shows, you would not see the same pattern in the stars if you viewed them from another angle.

VISUALIZATION
CLASSZONE.COM

View images of the night sky taken throughout the year.

CHECK YOUR READING What relationship exists among the stars in a constellation?

The sky seems to turn as Earth rotates.

You cannot see all of the constellations at once, because Earth blocks half of space from your view. However, you can see a parade of constellations each night as Earth rotates. As some constellations slowly come into view over the eastern horizon, others pass high in the sky above you, and still others set at the western horizon. Throughout the ages, many peoples have observed these changes and used them to help in navigation and measuring time.

If you extended the North Pole into space, it would point almost exactly to a star called Polaris, or the North Star. If you were standing at the North Pole, Polaris would be directly over your head. As Earth rotates through the night, the stars close to Polaris seem to move in circles around it. Although not the brightest star in the sky, Polaris is fairly bright and easy to find. You can use Polaris to figure out direction and location.

The stars in this image were photographed over several hours to show how they move across the night sky.

 CHECK YOUR READING What causes constellations to change positions during the night?

INVESTIGATE Constellation Positions

How does time of day affect the positions of constellations?

PROCEDURE

1. Cut out both diagrams on the Constellation Wheel Sheet and assemble them as shown.

2. Rotate the wheel so that the current month is aligned with 9 P.M. Observe the positions of the constellations.

3. Align the current month with other times to determine how the positions of the constellations change during the night.

WHAT DO YOU THINK?

- How do the positions of the constellations change during the night?
- In which direction does the northern sky seem to turn?

CHALLENGE Earth's rotation makes the sky seem to turn. What does the model tell you about the direction of Earth's rotation?

SKILL FOCUS
Analyzing

MATERIALS
- Constellation Wheel Sheet
- scissors
- brass fastener

TIME
20 minutes

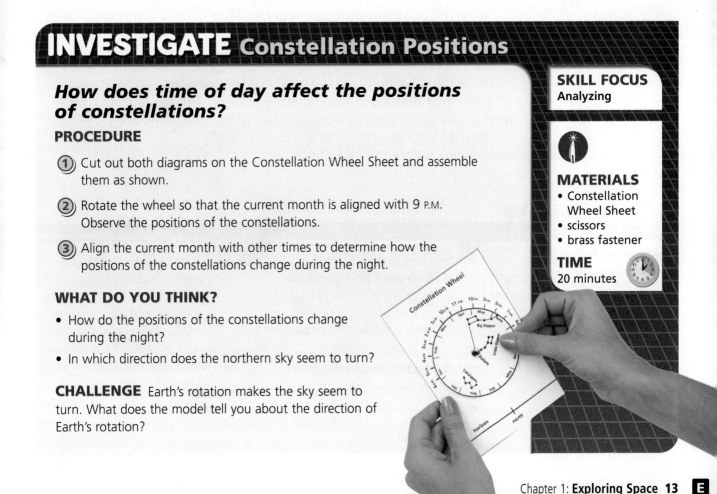

The movements of planets and other nearby objects are visible from Earth.

A jet plane travels at a greater speed and altitude than a bird. Yet if a bird and a plane flew overhead at the same time, you might think that the bird was faster. You would have this impression because the farther away a moving object is from you, the less it seems to move.

Stars are always moving, but they are so far away that you cannot see their movements. Observers have seen the same constellation patterns for thousands of years. Only over a much longer period does the motion of stars gradually change constellation patterns.

By contrast, the Moon moves across the star background a distance equal to its width every hour as it orbits Earth. The Moon is our closest neighbor. The planets are farther away, but you can see their gradual movements among the constellations over a period of weeks or months.

Planet comes from a Greek word that means "wanderer." Ancient Greek astronomers used this term because they noticed that planets move among the constellations. It is easiest to see the movements of Venus and Mars, the two planets closest to Earth. They change their positions in the sky from night to night.

The apparent movement of the sky led early astronomers to believe that Earth was at the center of the universe. Later astronomers discovered that Earth and the other planets orbit the Sun. The time-line on pages 72–75 introduces some of the astronomers who helped discover how planets really move in the solar system.

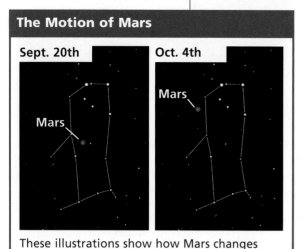

The Motion of Mars

Sept. 20th   Oct. 4th

Mars   Mars

These illustrations show how Mars changes positions in the constellation Gemini over a period of two weeks.

1.1 Review

KEY CONCEPTS

1. What are the basic structures in which objects are grouped together in space?

2. What is a constellation?

3. How does Earth's rotation affect our view of stars?

CRITICAL THINKING

4. **Compare and Contrast** How is the grouping of stars in a constellation different from the grouping of planets in the solar system?

5. **Apply** The planet Jupiter is farther than Mars from Earth. Which planet seems to move faster when viewed from Earth? Explain.

◯ CHALLENGE

6. **Predict** Suppose that you are standing at the North Pole on a dark night. If you keep turning clockwise at the same speed as Earth's rotation, how would your movement affect your view of the stars?

KEY CONCEPT

Telescopes allow us to study space from Earth.

◀ BEFORE, you learned

- Objects in the universe are grouped together in different ways
- The motions of planets and other nearby objects are visible from Earth

▶ NOW, you will learn

- About light and other forms of radiation
- How astronomers gather information about space

VOCABULARY

electromagnetic radiation
  p. 15
spectrum p. 16
wavelength p. 16
telescope p. 17

EXPLORE Distortion of Light

How can light become distorted?

PROCEDURE

① Place a white sheet of paper behind a glass filled with plain water. Shine a flashlight through the glass, and observe the spot of light on the paper.

② Pour a spoonful of salt into the water. Stir the water, and observe the spot of light.

WHAT DO YOU THINK?

- How did the spot of light change after you mixed the salt into the water?
- How could Earth's atmosphere cause similar changes in light from space?

MATERIALS

- flashlight
- glass filled with water
- sheet of white paper
- spoon
- salt

Light and other forms of radiation carry information about space.

VOCABULARY
Add a magnet word diagram for *electromagnetic radiation* to your notebook.

When you look at an object, your eyes are gathering light from that object. Visible light is a form of **electromagnetic radiation** (ih-LEHK-troh-mag-NEHT-ihk), which is energy that travels across distances as certain types of waves. There are other forms of electromagnetic radiation that you cannot see directly, such as radio waves and x-rays. Scientists have developed instruments to detect these other forms.

Electromagnetic radiation travels in all directions throughout space. Almost everything we know about the universe has come from our study of radiation. Astronomers can often learn about the size, distance, and movement of an object by studying its radiation. Radiation can also reveal what an object is made of and how it has changed.

The Electromagnetic Spectrum

The different forms of electromagnetic radiation vary in their wavelengths.

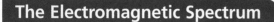

wavelength

visible light

| radio waves | microwaves | infrared | ultraviolet | x-rays | gamma rays |

Radio Waves

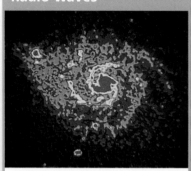

This image of a galaxy shows where radio waves are emitted.

Visible Light

Visible light is the only form of radiation our eyes can detect.

X-Rays

This image shows where the same galaxy emits x-rays.

READING TiP

A prism is a transparent object that is used to separate the wavelengths of light.

If you shine a flashlight through a prism, the beam of white light will separate into a range of colors called a **spectrum** (SPEHK-truhm). The colors that make up visible light are red, orange, yellow, green, blue, indigo, and violet. These are the colors in a rainbow, which appears when light spreads out as it passes through raindrops.

In a spectrum, the colors of visible light appear in the order of their wavelengths. **Wavelength** is the distance between one wave peak and the next wave peak. Red light has the longest wavelength. Violet light has the shortest.

As you can see in the illustration above, visible light is just a tiny part of a larger spectrum called the electromagnetic spectrum. The electromagnetic spectrum includes all the forms of electromagnetic radiation. Notice that the wavelength of infrared radiation is longer than the wavelength of visible light but not as long as the wavelength of microwaves or radio waves. The wavelength of ultraviolet radiation is shorter than the wavelength of visible light but not as short as the wavelength of x-rays or gamma rays.

 CHECK YOUR READING How is visible light different from other forms of electromagnetic radiation?

Astronomers use telescopes to collect information about space.

A **telescope** is a device that gathers electromagnetic radiation. If you have ever looked through a telescope, it was probably one that gathers visible light. Such telescopes provide images that are much clearer than what is seen with the naked eye. Images from other types of telescopes show radiation that your eyes cannot detect. Each form of radiation provides different information about objects in space.

Astronomers usually record images from telescopes electronically, which allows them to use computers to analyze images. Different colors or shades in an image reveal patterns of radiation. For example, in the right-hand image on page 16, the colors yellow and red indicate where the galaxy is emitting large amounts of x-rays.

Most types of telescopes gather radiation with a glass lens or a reflecting surface, such as a mirror. Larger lenses and reflecting surfaces produce brighter and more detailed images. You can magnify an image from a telescope to any size. However, enlarging an image will not bring out any more details of an object. If the image is fuzzy at a small size, it will remain fuzzy no matter how much it is enlarged.

Visible-Light, Infrared, and Ultraviolet Telescopes

There are two types of visible-light telescopes: reflecting telescopes and refracting telescopes. Reflecting telescopes can also be built to gather infrared or ultraviolet radiation.

- **Reflecting Telescope** This type of telescope has a curved mirror that gathers light. The image comes into focus in front of the mirror. Many reflecting telescopes have a second mirror that reflects the image to recording equipment or to a lens called an eyepiece.

- **Refracting Telescope** This type of telescope has an objective lens, or curved piece of glass, at one end of a long tube. The lens gathers light and focuses it to form an image near the other end of the tube. An eyepiece magnifies this image.

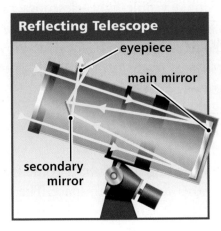

Reflecting Telescope

eyepiece

main mirror

secondary mirror

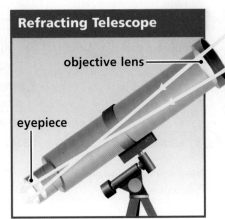

Refracting Telescope

objective lens

eyepiece

Most powerful visible-light telescopes are built on mountaintops in rural areas. Rural areas offer a much better view of the night sky than cities do, because the many electric lights in cities make dim space objects hard to see. By locating telescopes on mountaintops, astronomers reduce problems caused by Earth's atmosphere. The atmosphere interferes with light coming in from space. In fact, movements of the air are what make stars appear to twinkle. At high altitudes there is less air above the ground to interfere with light.

Radio Telescopes

Radio telescopes show where radio waves are being emitted by objects in space. A radio telescope has a curved metal surface, called a dish, that gathers radio waves and focuses them onto an antenna. The dish works in the same way as the main mirror of a reflecting telescope. Some radio telescopes have dishes made of metal mesh rather than solid metal.

Because radio waves are so long, a single radio telescope must be very large to produce useful images. To improve the quality of images, astronomers often aim a group of radio telescopes at the same object. Signals from the telescopes are combined and then converted into an image. Groups of radio telescopes, like the Very Large Array in New Mexico, can show more detail than even the largest single dish.

Unlike visible-light telescopes, radio telescopes are not affected by clouds or bad weather. They even work well in daylight. In addition, radio telescopes can be located at low altitudes because most radio waves pass freely through Earth's atmosphere.

Radio Telescope

Signals from these radio telescopes in New Mexico can be combined to produce clearer images.

○ CHECK YOUR READING   What is the function of the dish in a radio telescope?

RESOURCE CENTER
CLASSZONE.COM

Find out more about telescopes.

Telescopes in Space

Many exciting images have come from the Hubble Space Telescope and other telescopes in space. The Hubble telescope is a reflecting telescope. It was placed in orbit around Earth in 1990. Astronomers operate it from the ground, although astronauts have visited it to make repairs and improvements. The telescope sends images and measurements back to Earth electronically.

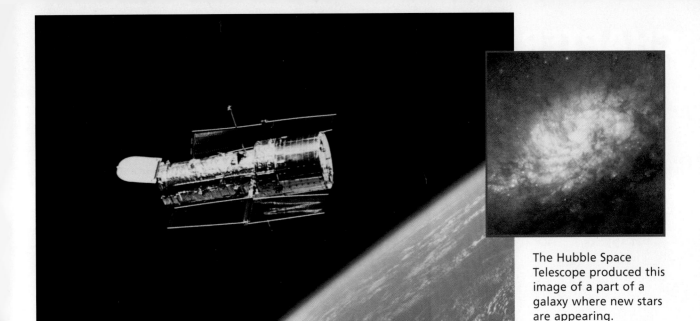

The Hubble Space Telescope produced this image of a part of a galaxy where new stars are appearing.

Because the Hubble telescope is located in space, Earth's atmosphere does not interfere with light from objects the telescope is aimed at. This lack of interference allows it to obtain clearer images than ground-based telescopes with much larger mirrors. In addition to collecting visible light, the Hubble telescope produces images of ultraviolet and infrared radiation.

The Hubble Space Telescope is part of a group of telescopes that orbit Earth. The telescopes allow astronomers to gain information from the full range of electromagnetic radiation. The Compton Gamma-Ray Observatory was sent into orbit in 1991. The Chandra X-Ray Observatory was launched eight years later. These telescopes were placed in space because Earth's atmosphere blocks most x-rays and gamma rays.

 CHECK YOUR READING Why does the Hubble telescope produce clearer images than a telescope of the same size on Earth?

1.2 Review

KEY CONCEPTS

1. How are visible light, radio waves, and other forms of electromagnetic radiation different from each other?

2. What function do mirrors serve in reflecting telescopes?

3. Why are some telescopes placed on mountains or in orbit around Earth?

CRITICAL THINKING

4. **Compare and Contrast** What are the similarities and differences between refracting telescopes and reflecting telescopes?

5. **Analyze** Why would it be difficult to build radio telescopes if they did not work well at low altitudes?

CHALLENGE

6. **Analyze** Why might astronomers use different types of telescopes to obtain images of the same object in space?

CHAPTER INVESTIGATION

Observing Spectra

OVERVIEW AND PURPOSE Visible light is made up of different colors that can be separated into a rainbow band called a spectrum. Astronomers gain information about the characteristics of stars by spreading their light into spectra (*spectra* is the plural form of *spectrum*). A spectroscope is a device that produces spectra. In most spectroscopes, diffraction gratings are used to separate light into different colors. The colors with the longest wavelengths appear farthest from the slit in a spectroscope. The colors with the shortest wavelengths appear closest to the slit. In this investigation you will

- build a spectroscope and observe the spectra of three different light sources
- identify ways in which the spectra of light sources differ

MATERIALS
- shoebox with lid
- ruler
- scissors
- diffraction grating
- tape
- index card
- pencils or markers in a variety of colors
- incandescent light
- fluorescent light
for Challenge:
- cellophane in several colors

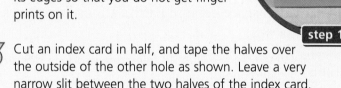

▶ Procedure

1. Cut a hole measuring 3 cm by 1.5 cm in each end of a shoebox. Make sure that the holes line up.

2. On the inside of the box, tape a piece of diffraction grating over one of the holes. Handle the diffraction grating by its edges so that you do not get fingerprints on it.

step 1

3. Cut an index card in half, and tape the halves over the outside of the other hole as shown. Leave a very narrow slit between the two halves of the index card.

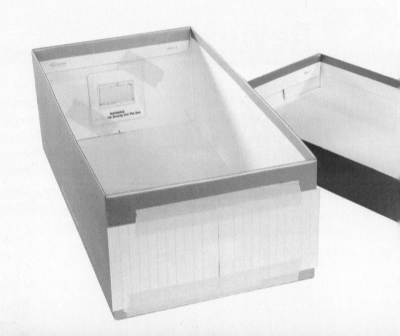

4 Put the lid on the shoebox. Then turn off the overhead lights in the classroom.

5 Look through the hole covered with the diffraction grating, aiming the spectroscope's slit at the sky through a window. **Caution:** *Never look directly at the Sun.* Observe the spectrum you see to the left of the slit.

step 5

6 Repeat step 5 while aiming the spectroscope at an incandescent light and then at a fluorescent light.

▶ Observe and Analyze

Write It Up

1. **RECORD OBSERVATIONS** For each light source, draw in your data table the spectrum you see to the left of the slit. Describe the colors and patterns in the spectrum, and label the light source.

2. **IDENTIFY LIMITS** What problems, if any, did you experience in observing the spectra? Why was it important to turn off overhead lights for this activity?

▶ Conclude

Write It Up

1. **COMPARE AND CONTRAST** How did the spectra differ from one another? Did you notice any stripes of color that were brighter or narrower than other colors in the same spectrum? Did you notice any lines or spaces separating colors?

2. **ANALYZE** The shorter the wavelength of a color, the closer it appears to the slit in a spectroscope. On the basis of your observations, which color has the shortest wavelength? Which color has the longest wavelength?

3. **INFER** How might the spectra look different if the slit at the end of the spectroscope were curved instead of a straight line?

▶ INVESTIGATE Further

CHALLENGE Cover the slit on your spectroscope with a piece of colored cellophane. Aiming the spectroscope at a fluorescent light or another light source, observe and draw the resulting spectrum. Then repeat with cellophane of other colors. List the colors that each piece of cellophane transmitted. Did these results surprise you? If so, why?

Observing Spectra

Observe and Analyze

Table 1. Spectra of Different Light Sources

Light Source	Drawing	Description

Conclude

1.3 Spacecraft help us explore beyond Earth.

◀ BEFORE, you learned

- The motions of planets and other nearby objects are visible from Earth
- Light and other forms of radiation carry information about the universe

▶ NOW, you will learn

- How astronauts explore space near Earth
- How different types of spacecraft are used in exploration

VOCABULARY

satellite p. 23
space station p. 24
lander p. 28
probe p. 29

EXPLORE Viewing Space Objects

How do objects appear at different distances?

PROCEDURE

① Crumple the paper into a ball and place it on your desk.

② Sketch the ball at the same time as another student sketches it. One of you should sketch it from a distance of 1 m. The other should sketch it from 5 m away.

WHAT DO YOU THINK?

- How do the details in the two drawings compare?
- What details might be easier to see on a planet if you were orbiting the planet?

MATERIALS

- paper
- pencils

Astronauts explore space near Earth.

RESOURCE CENTER
CLASSZONE.COM

Learn more about space exploration.

Space travel requires very careful planning. Astronauts take everything necessary for survival with them, including air, water, and food. Spacecraft need powerful rockets and huge fuel tanks to lift all their weight upward against Earth's gravity. The equipment must be well designed and maintained, since any breakdown can be deadly.

Once in space, astronauts must get used to a special environment. People and objects in an orbiting spacecraft seem to float freely unless they are fastened down. This weightless condition occurs because they are falling in space at the same rate as the spacecraft. In addition, to leave their airtight cabin, astronauts must wear special protective suits. Despite these conditions, astronauts have managed to perform experiments and make important observations about space near Earth.

Moon Missions

For about a decade, much of space exploration was focused on a race to the Moon. This race was driven by rivalry between the United States and the Soviet Union, which included Russia. In 1957 the Soviet Union launched the first artificial satellite to orbit Earth. A **satellite** is an object that orbits a more massive object. The Soviet Union also sent the first human into space in 1961. Although the United States lagged behind in these early efforts, it succeeded in sending the first humans to the Moon.

Preparation Many steps had to be taken before astronauts from the United States could visit the Moon. The National Aeronautics and Space Administration (NASA) sent spacecraft without crews to the Moon to find out whether it was possible to land on its surface. NASA also sent astronauts into space to practice important procedures.

Landings The NASA program to reach the Moon was called Apollo. During early Apollo missions, astronauts tested spacecraft and flew them into orbit around the Moon. On July 20, 1969, crew members from *Apollo 11* became the first humans to walk on the Moon's surface. NASA achieved five more Moon landings between 1969 and 1972. During this period, the Soviet Union sent spacecraft without crews to get samples of the Moon's surface.

Scientific Results The Apollo program helped scientists learn about the Moon's surface and interior. Much of the information came from 380 kilograms (weighing 840 lb) of rock and soil that astronauts brought back to Earth. These samples are still being studied.

Powerful booster rockets were used to launch the Apollo spacecraft. Beginning with *Apollo 15*, astronauts rode in lunar roving vehicles to explore greater areas of the Moon's surface.

Orbiting Earth

VOCABULARY
Add a magnet word diagram for *space station* to your notebook.

A **space station** is a satellite in which people can live and work for long periods. The United States and the Soviet Union launched the first space stations in the early 1970s. After the breakup of the Soviet Union in 1991, the Russian space agency and NASA began to act as partners rather than rivals. Russian and U. S. astronauts carried out joint missions aboard *Mir* (meer), the Russian space station.

The *Mir* missions helped prepare for the International Space Station (ISS). The United States, Russia, and 15 other nations are working together to build the ISS. When completed, it will cover an area about as large as two football fields. The ISS is too large to launch into space in one piece. Instead, sections of the space station are being launched separately and assembled in orbit over a period of years.

Construction of the ISS began in 1998. The first three-member crew arrived at the station in 2000. In addition to constructing the station, crew members make observations of Earth and perform experiments. Some experiments are much more effective when they are performed in space, where gravity affects them differently. For example, scientists can grow cell tissue more easily in space than they can on Earth. Research on cell tissue grown in space may increase our understanding of cancer and other diseases.

International Space Station

Each section of the space station has a specific function.

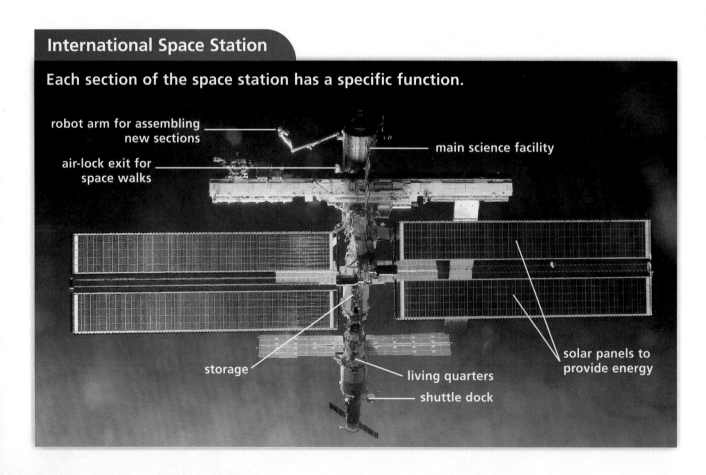

robot arm for assembling new sections

air-lock exit for space walks

main science facility

storage

living quarters

shuttle dock

solar panels to provide energy

Research and technological advances from the space station may lay the groundwork for new space exploration. ISS crew members study how living in space affects the human body over long periods. This research may provide useful information for future efforts to send astronauts to other planets.

Most crews have flown to the ISS aboard space shuttles. Unlike earlier spacecraft, a space shuttle can be used again and again. At the end of a mission, it reenters Earth's atmosphere and glides down to a runway. The large cargo bay of a space shuttle can carry satellites, equipment, and laboratories.

NASA has launched space shuttles more than 100 times since 1981. Space shuttles are much more sophisticated than the Apollo spacecraft that carried astronauts to the Moon. However, space travel remains a dangerous activity.

Two booster rockets and an external fuel tank are needed to lift a space shuttle into orbit.

 CHECK YOUR READING Why might some researchers choose to perform experiments aboard a space station rather than on Earth?

INVESTIGATE Launch Planning

How does Earth's rotation affect launches of spacecraft?

PROCEDURE

1. Tightly wad 14 sheets of paper into balls, and place the balls in a small bucket.

2. Stand 1.5 m away from a large bucket placed on a desk. Try tossing 7 balls into the bucket.

3. While turning slowly, try tossing the remaining 7 balls into the bucket.

WHAT DO YOU THINK?

- How much more difficult was it to toss the paper balls into the bucket while you were turning than when you were standing still?

- Why does Earth's rotation make launching rockets into space more complicated?

CHALLENGE How would you design an experiment to show the variables involved in a launch from Earth toward another rotating body in space, such as the Moon?

SKILL FOCUS
Identifying variables

MATERIALS
- paper
- small bucket
- large bucket

TIME
10 minutes

Spacecraft carry instruments to other worlds.

Currently, we cannot send humans to other planets. One obstacle is that such a trip would take years. A spacecraft would need to carry enough air, water, and other supplies needed for survival on the long journey. Another obstacle is the harsh conditions on other planets, such as extreme heat and cold. Some planets do not even have surfaces to land on.

Because of these obstacles, most research in space is accomplished through the use of spacecraft without crews aboard. These missions pose no risk to human life and are less expensive than missions involving astronauts. The spacecraft carry instruments that test the compositions and characteristics of planets. Data and images are sent back to Earth as radio signals. Onboard computers and radio signals from Earth guide the spacecraft.

Spacecraft have visited all the major planets in our solar system except Pluto. NASA has also sent spacecraft to other bodies in space, such as comets and moons. Scientists and engineers have designed different types of spacecraft to carry out these missions.

CHECK YOUR READING What questions do you still have about space exploration?

Flybys

The first stage in space exploration is to send out a spacecraft that passes one or more planets or other bodies in space without orbiting them. Such missions are called flybys. After a flyby spacecraft leaves Earth's orbit, controllers on Earth can use the spacecraft's small rockets to adjust its direction. Flyby missions may last for decades. However, because a spacecraft flies by planets quickly, it can collect data and images from a particular planet only for a brief period.

As a flyby spacecraft passes a planet, the planet's gravity can be used to change the spacecraft's speed or direction. During the flyby of the planet, the spacecraft can gain enough energy to propel it to another planet more quickly. This method allowed *Voyager 2* to fly past Saturn, Uranus, and Neptune, even though the spacecraft left Earth with only enough energy to reach Jupiter.

Many complex mathematical calculations are needed for a flyby mission to be successful. Experts must take into account Earth's rotation and the positions of the planets that the spacecraft will pass. The period of time when a spacecraft can be launched is called a launch window.

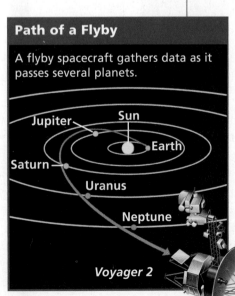

Path of a Flyby

A flyby spacecraft gathers data as it passes several planets.

Jupiter

Sun

Earth

Saturn

Uranus

Neptune

Voyager 2

Orbiters

The second stage in space exploration is to study a planet over a long period of time. Spacecraft designed to accomplish this task are called orbiters. As an orbiter approaches its target planet, rocket engines are fired to slow the spacecraft down. The spacecraft then goes into orbit around the planet.

In an orbiter mission, a spacecraft orbits a planet for several months to several years. Since an orbiter remains near a planet for a much longer period of time than a flyby spacecraft, it can view most or all of the planet's surface. An orbiter can also keep track of changes that occur over time, such as changes in weather and volcanic activity.

Orbiters allow astronomers to create detailed maps of planets. Most orbiters have cameras to photograph planet surfaces. Orbiters may also carry other instruments, such as a device for determining the altitudes of surface features or one for measuring temperatures in different regions.

Some orbiters are designed to explore moons or other bodies in space instead of planets. It is also possible to send a spacecraft to orbit a planet and later move it into orbit around one of the planet's moons.

⬥ **REMINDER**

Remember that objects orbit, or move around, other objects in space because of the influence of gravity.

⬥ **CHECK YOUR READING** What is the main difference between a flyby spacecraft and an orbiter?

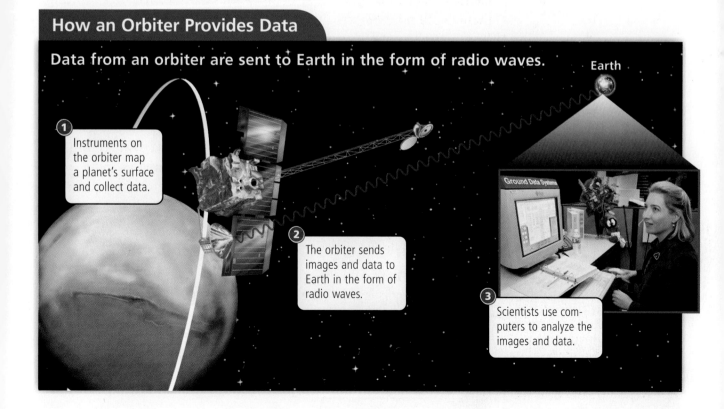

How an Orbiter Provides Data

Data from an orbiter are sent to Earth in the form of radio waves.

Earth

1. Instruments on the orbiter map a planet's surface and collect data.

2. The orbiter sends images and data to Earth in the form of radio waves.

Ground Data System

3. Scientists use computers to analyze the images and data.

Landers and Probes

The third stage in space exploration is to land instruments on a planet or to send instruments through its atmosphere. Such a mission can tell us more about the features and properties of a planet. It can also provide clues to what the planet was like in the past.

A **lander** is a craft designed to land on a planet's surface. After a lander touches down, controllers on Earth can send it commands to collect data. Landers have been placed successfully on the Moon, Venus, and Mars. Some have operated for months or years at a time.

The images taken by a lander are more detailed than those taken by an orbiter. In addition to providing close-up views of a planet's surface, a lander can measure properties of the planet's atmosphere and surface. A lander may have a mechanical arm for gathering soil and rock samples. It may also contain a small vehicle called a rover, which can explore beyond the landing site.

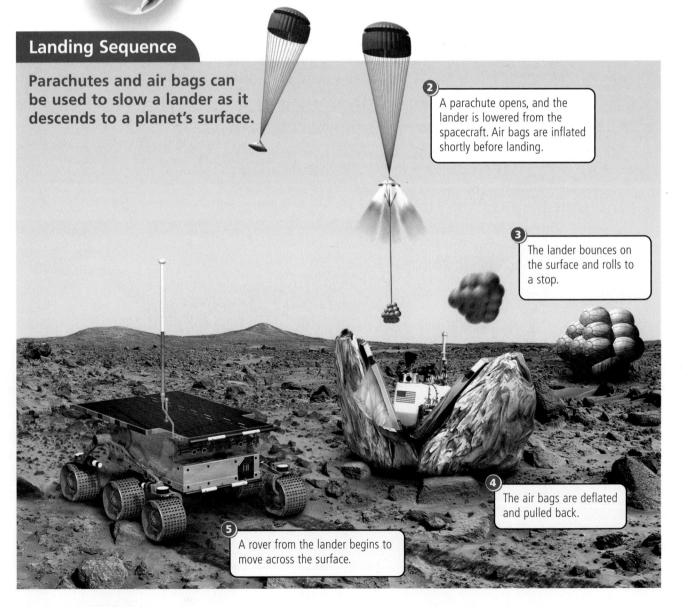

1 The spacecraft slows down as it moves through the atmosphere.

Landing Sequence

Parachutes and air bags can be used to slow a lander as it descends to a planet's surface.

2 A parachute opens, and the lander is lowered from the spacecraft. Air bags are inflated shortly before landing.

3 The lander bounces on the surface and rolls to a stop.

4 The air bags are deflated and pulled back.

5 A rover from the lander begins to move across the surface.

One of the most successful space missions was that of *Mars Pathfinder*, which landed on Mars in 1997. *Mars Pathfinder* and its rover sent back thousands of photographs. These images provided evidence that water once flowed over the surface of Mars. Unfortunately, another lander, sent two years later, failed to work after it reached Mars.

Some spacecraft are designed to work only for a short time before they are destroyed by conditions on a planet. The term **probe** is often used to describe a spacecraft that drops into a planet's atmosphere. As the probe travels through the atmosphere, its instruments identify gases and measure properties such as pressure and temperature. Probes are especially important for exploring the deep atmospheres of giant planets, such as Jupiter.

 CHECK YOUR READING What is the difference between a probe and a lander?

Combining Missions

A lander or a probe can work in combination with an orbiter. For example, in 1995 the orbiter *Galileo* released a probe into Jupiter's atmosphere as it began orbiting the planet. The probe sent data back to the orbiter for nearly an hour before it was destroyed. The orbiter passed the data on to Earth. *Galileo* continued to orbit Jupiter for eight years.

Future space missions may involve even more complex combinations of spacecraft. Planners hope to send groups of landers to collect soil and rock samples from the surface of Mars. A rocket will carry these samples to an orbiter. The orbiter will then bring the samples to Earth for study.

 **Review**

KEY CONCEPTS

1. Why are space stations important for scientific research?

2. How is information sent between Earth and a spacecraft?

3. What are the three main stages in exploring a planet?

CRITICAL THINKING

4. **Analyze** Why is most space exploration accomplished with spacecraft that do not have astronauts on board?

5. **Infer** Why is it important to map a planet's surface before planning a lander mission?

○ CHALLENGE

6. **Predict** Early space exploration was influenced by political events, such as the rivalry between the United States and the Soviet Union. What circumstances on Earth might interfere with future space missions?

MATH TUTORIAL
CLASSZONE.COM
Click on Math Tutorial for more help with powers and exponents.

Distances in Space

Astronomers often deal with very large numbers. For example, the planet Venus is about 100 million kilometers from the Sun. Written out, 100 million is 100,000,000. To use fewer zeros and to make the number easier to write and read, you could write 100 million as 10^8, which is the same value in exponent form.

Example

PROBLEM Write 1000 km, using an exponent.

To find the exponent of a number, you can write the number as a product. For example,

$$1000 \text{ km} = 10 \times 10 \times 10 \text{ km}$$

This product has 3 factors of 10. When whole numbers other than zero are multiplied together, each number is a factor of the product. To write a product that has a repeated factor, you can use an exponent. The exponent is the number of times the factor is repeated. With factors of 10, you can also determine the exponent by counting the zeros in the given number.

There are 3 zeros in 1000.   The factor 10 is repeated 3 times.

$$1000 = 10 \times 10 \times 10$$

ANSWER The exponent form of 1000 km is 10^3 km.

Write each distance, using an exponent.

1. 10,000 km

2. 1,000,000 km

3. 100,000,000,000 km

4. 10,000,000,000,000 km

5. 100,000,000,000,000,000 km

6. 10 km

CHALLENGE The galaxy shown on this page is about 10^{18} kilometers across. Write the value of 10^{18} without using an exponent.

Galaxy M83, which is roughly the same size as the Milky Way, has a diameter of about 10^{18} kilometers.

KEY CONCEPT

Space exploration benefits society.

 BEFORE, you learned

- Light and other radiation carry information about space
- Astronauts explore space near Earth

 NOW, you will learn

- How space exploration has helped us to learn more about Earth
- How space technology is used on Earth

VOCABULARY

impact crater p. 32

THINK ABOUT

How does Earth look from space?

This photograph of Earth over the Moon was taken by the crew of *Apollo 8*. The Apollo missions provided the first images of our planet as a whole. What do you think we can learn about Earth from photographs taken from space?

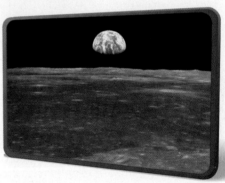

Space exploration has given us new viewpoints.

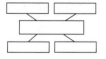

MAIN IDEA WEB
Record in your notes important information that space exploration has provided about Earth.

Space exploration enriches us in many ways. Throughout history, the study of stars and planets has inspired new ideas. As we meet the challenges of space exploration, we gain valuable technology. Space exploration is also an exciting adventure.

Space science has advanced knowledge in other scientific fields, such as physics. For example, observations of the Moon and other bodies in space helped scientists understand how gravity works. Scientists figured out that the same force that causes an object to fall to the ground causes the Moon to orbit Earth.

Finally, the study of other worlds can teach us about our own. Earth has changed considerably since its formation. By comparing Earth with different worlds, scientists can learn more about the history of Earth's surface features and atmosphere.

 Identify some benefits of space exploration.

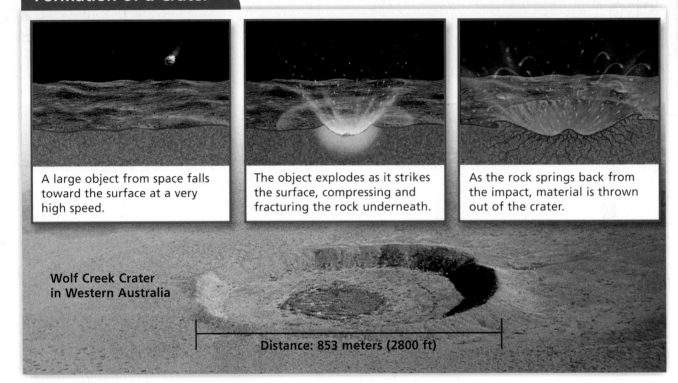

Formation of a Crater

A large object from space falls toward the surface at a very high speed.

The object explodes as it strikes the surface, compressing and fracturing the rock underneath.

As the rock springs back from the impact, material is thrown out of the crater.

Wolf Creek Crater in Western Australia

Distance: 853 meters (2800 ft)

Surface Features

Exploration of other worlds has helped us learn about the impacts of space objects. When an object strikes the surface of a larger object in space, it explodes and leaves behind a round pit called an **impact crater.** The illustration above shows how an impact crater forms.

Earth has little evidence of impacts because its surface is constantly being worn down by wind and water and altered by forces beneath the surface. However, impact craters remain on the Moon, Mercury, and many other bodies that have no wind or liquid water.

Atmosphere

We are also learning about Earth's atmosphere from space exploration. Earth's temperature allows liquid water to remain on the surface. Mars and Venus, the planets closest to Earth, have no liquid water on their surfaces. By comparing Earth with those planets, we can see how liquid water has affected the development of Earth's atmosphere.

Another area of study involves the energy Earth receives from the Sun. Many scientists think that small changes visible on the Sun's surface can affect weather on Earth. These changes may have caused periods of cooling in Earth's atmosphere.

 CHECK YOUR READING   What have scientists learned about Earth's past from studying bodies in space?

INVESTIGATE Weathering

How does weather affect evidence of impacts on Earth?

PROCEDURE

1. Fill a shoebox lid halfway with sand, and smooth the surface with a ruler.
2. Create three craters by dropping a golf ball into the sand from a height of 70 cm. Remove the ball carefully. Leave the lid inside the classroom.
3. Repeat steps 1 and 2 outdoors, leaving the lid in an area where it will be exposed to the weather.
4. Check both lids after 24 hours. Observe changes in each one.

WHAT DO YOU THINK?

- How did the craters in the sand that you left outdoors differ in appearance from the craters in the sand that remained inside?
- What aspect of weather caused any differences you observed?

CHALLENGE What natural processes besides weather can affect evidence of impacts from space objects on Earth?

SKILL FOCUS
Predicting

MATERIALS
- 2 shoebox lids
- sand
- ruler
- golf ball

TIME
30 minutes

Space technology has practical uses.

Space exploration has done more than increase our knowledge. It has also provided us with technology that makes life on Earth easier. Each day you probably benefit from some material or product that was developed for the space program.

Satellite Views of Earth

One of the most important benefits of space exploration has been the development of satellite technology. Satellites collect data from every region of our planet. The data are sent to receivers on Earth and converted into images. Scientists have learned from the space program how to enhance such images to gain more information.

Weather satellites show conditions throughout Earth's atmosphere. Images and data from weather satellites have greatly improved weather forecasting. Scientists can now provide warnings of dangerous storms long before they strike populated areas.

Other satellites collect images of Earth's surface to show how it is being changed by natural events and human activity. Satellite data are also used for wildlife preservation, conservation of natural resources, and mapping.

Technology Spinoffs

Have you ever come up with a new way to use something that was designed for a different purpose? NASA often creates advanced technology to meet the special demands of space travel. Many spinoffs of technology from the space program can be found in homes, offices, schools, and hospitals.

Everything on a spacecraft must be as small and lightweight as possible because the heavier a spacecraft is, the more difficult it is to launch. Design techniques developed to meet this need have improved devices used on Earth, such as tools for diagnosing diseases and devices that help people overcome disabilities.

NASA designers helped develop a system that allows this boy to communicate by using eye movements.

Materials and parts on a spacecraft have to endure harsh conditions, such as extreme heat and cold. Many new homes and buildings contain fire-resistant materials developed for the space program. Firefighters wear protective suits made from fabric originally used in space suits. NASA has also helped design devices that allow firefighters to avoid injury from inhaling smoke.

Humans need a safe environment in spacecraft and space stations. NASA has developed systems for purifying air, water, and food. These systems now help protect people on Earth as well as in space.

1.4 Review

KEY CONCEPTS

1. How has space exploration helped us learn about impacts of space objects on Earth?
2. How do satellites provide images of Earth's surface and atmosphere?
3. Give two examples of technology we use on Earth that is a result of space exploration.

CRITICAL THINKING

4. **Infer** Hurricanes form in the middle of the ocean. Why would satellites be useful in tracking hurricanes?
5. **Apply** What space-technology spinoffs might be used in a school?

⬥ CHALLENGE

6. **Predict** It takes over a year for a spacecraft to reach Mars and return to Earth. If astronauts ever travel to Mars, they will need a spacecraft that can recycle air and water. How might such technology be adapted for use on Earth?

How Earth's Gravity Affects Plants

One of the most important issues in biology is understanding how plants grow. By applying the results of research on this issue, American farmers now grow twice as much food as they did 50 years ago.

One aspect of plant growth is the direction in which plants grow. After a plant sprouts from a seed, some of its cells form a shoot that grows upward. Other cells grow downward, becoming roots. How does this happen? Biologists think that plants usually respond to signals from the Sun and from the force of gravity.

Gravity and Plant Growth

To test the importance of sunlight, biologists can grow plants in the dark on Earth. Testing the impact of gravity, though, is more difficult. In 1997, a space shuttle carried moss plants into space. The plants grew for two weeks in microgravity, an environment in which objects are almost weightless. When the shuttle returned the plants to Earth, biologists studied how they had grown.

Prediction

Biologists had predicted that the moss would grow randomly. They expected that without signals from sunlight or the force of gravity, the moss would grow in no particular pattern.

Results

The biologists were surprised by what they saw. The moss had not grown randomly. Instead, the plants had spread out in a clear pattern. Each plant had formed a clockwise spiral.

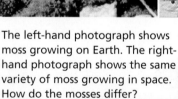

The left-hand photograph shows moss growing on Earth. The right-hand photograph shows the same variety of moss growing in space. How do the mosses differ?

Significance

The moss experiment may be important for future space exploration. Can plants provide the food and oxygen that astronauts will need on long voyages to other planets? Experiments with moss are among the first steps in finding out.

EXPLORE

1. **PROVIDE EXAMPLES** Make a list of other spiral formations that occur in nature. Discuss why spirals may be common.
2. **CHALLENGE** Use library or Internet resources to learn about other experiments that test the effects of microgravity on plants and seeds.

the **BIG** idea

People develop and use technology to explore and study space.

CONTENT REVIEW
CLASSZONE.COM

◀ KEY CONCEPTS SUMMARY

1.1 Some space objects are visible to the human eye.

- Gravity causes objects in space to be grouped together in different ways.
- Stars form patterns in the sky.
- The sky seems to turn as Earth rotates.

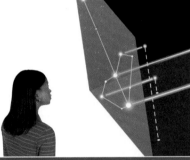

VOCABULARY
orbit p. 10
solar system p. 10
galaxy p. 10
universe p. 10
constellation p. 12

1.2 Telescopes allow us to study space from Earth.

Each form of electromagnetic radiation provides different information about objects in space. Astronomers use different types of telescopes to gather visible light and other forms of radiation.

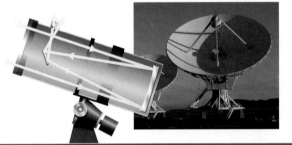

VOCABULARY
electromagnetic radiation p. 15
spectrum p. 16
wavelength p. 16
telescope p. 17

1.3 Spacecraft help us explore beyond Earth.

Astronauts can explore space near Earth. Spacecraft without crews carry instruments to other worlds. A flyby mission usually provides data from several bodies in space. Orbiters, landers, and probes gather data from one planet or body.

VOCABULARY
satellite p. 23
space station p. 24
lander p. 28
probe p. 29

1.4 Space exploration benefits society.

Space exploration has taught us about Earth's development. It has also provided technology that has important uses on Earth.

VOCABULARY
impact crater p. 32

Reviewing Vocabulary

Write a definition of each word. Use the meaning of the underlined word part to help you.

Word	Root Meaning	Definition
EXAMPLE <u>satellite</u>	person of lesser rank	an object that orbits a more massive object
1. <u>orbit</u>	circle	
2. <u>solar</u> system	Sun	
3. <u>uni</u>verse	one	
4. con<u>stell</u>ation	star	
5. electro-<u>magnetic</u> <u>radiation</u>	to emit rays	
6. <u>spect</u>rum	to look at	
7. <u>probe</u>	test	
8. impact <u>crater</u>	bowl	

Reviewing Key Concepts

Multiple Choice *Choose the letter of the best answer.*

9. Stars in a galaxy are held together by
   a. light
   b. radiation
   c. gravity
   d. satellites

10. Astronomers use constellations to
    a. locate objects in the sky
    b. calculate the distances of objects
    c. calculate the masses of objects
    d. classify spectra

11. Stars rise and set in the night sky because
    a. Earth orbits the Sun
    b. Earth rotates
    c. the North Pole points toward Polaris
    d. the stars are moving in space

12. In the electromagnetic spectrum, different forms of radiation are arranged according to their
    a. colors
    b. distances
    c. wavelengths
    d. sizes

13. Astronomers often locate telescopes on mountains to
    a. lessen the interference of Earth's atmosphere
    b. save money on land
    c. keep their discoveries secret
    d. get closer to space objects

14. A reflecting telescope gathers light with a
    a. lens
    b. eyepiece
    c. refractor
    d. mirror

15. What was the goal of the Apollo program?
    a. to view Earth from space
    b. to explore the Sun
    c. to explore the Moon
    d. to explore other planets

16. Which type of mission produces detailed maps of a planet?
    a. flyby
    b. orbiter
    c. lander
    d. probe

17. What causes an impact crater to form on a planet's surface?
    a. Gravity pulls soil and rock downward.
    b. Wind and water wear away the surface.
    c. Forces beneath the surface push upward.
    d. An object from space strikes the surface.

Short Answer *Write a short answer to each question.*

18. Why is it easier to see the motions of planets than to see the motions of stars?

19. How do astronomers obtain most of their information about space?

20. How does the size of a telescope's main lens or mirror affect its performance?

21. Why have lightweight materials been developed for space travel?

Copy the Venn diagram below, and use it to help you answer the next two questions.

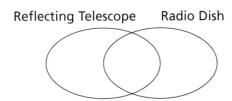

Reflecting Telescope   Radio Dish

22. COMPARE AND CONTRAST Fill in the Venn diagram to show similarities and differences between a reflecting telescope and a radio dish.

23. APPLY Suppose that you live in an area that has frequent storms. Which would be more suitable for your location, a reflecting telescope or a radio dish? Explain.

24. COMPARE AND CONTRAST What are the similarities and differences between visible light and radio waves?

25. HYPOTHESIZE Many of the constellations named by ancient peoples are now hard to see from populated areas. Why might it have been easier to see them hundreds or thousands of years ago?

26. ANALYZE What may be the advantages of electronically recording an image from a telescope instead of looking at the object directly through the telescope's eyepiece?

27. SYNTHESIZE Suppose it became possible to send astronauts to explore a nearby planet. What concerns would need to be taken into account before deciding whether to send a spacecraft with astronauts or a spacecraft with no crew aboard?

28. COMPARE AND CONTRAST Compare and contrast the development of the International Space Station with the Apollo missions to the Moon.

29. ANALYZE If you were designing a medical device to be implanted in a patient's body, why might you seek help from designers of space technology?

30. EVALUATE Do you think that the United States should continue to maintain its own space program, or should it combine its space program with the programs of other nations? Explain.

31. SEQUENCE Astronomers have learned that some stars other than the Sun have planets orbiting them. Imagine that you are planning a program to explore one of these planet systems. Copy the chart below. Use the chart to identify stages in the exploration of the system and to describe what would occur during each stage.

Stage of Exploration	Description

the BIG idea

32. PROVIDE EXAMPLES Look again at the photograph on pages 6–7. Now that you have finished the chapter, how would you change your response to the question on the photograph?

33. EVALUATE In the United States billions of dollars are spent each year on space exploration. Do you think that this expense is justified? Why or why not?

UNIT PROJECTS

If you are doing a unit project, make a folder for your project. Include in your folder a list of the resources you will need, the date on which the project is due, and a schedule to track your progress. Begin gathering data.

Standardized Test Practice

For practice on your
state test, go to . . .

TEST PRACTICE
CLASSZONE.COM

Analyzing a Star Map

Use the star map to answer the next five questions.

1. Constellations are represented on the map as dots that are

a. surrounded by planets

b. grouped in a spiral pattern

c. connected by lines

d. scattered in a random pattern

2. How would a map showing the same portion of the sky two hours later compare with the map above?

a. Almost all the space objects would have changed position noticeably.

b. No space objects would have changed position.

c. Only the moon would have changed position.

d. Only the planets would have changed position.

3. Why would the map for two hours later be different from this map?

a. The Moon is rotating on its axis.

b. Earth is rotating on its axis.

c. The solar system is part of the Milky Way.

d. The planets move in relation to the stars.

4. A map showing the same portion of the sky exactly one year later would look very similar to this map. What would probably be different?

a. the shapes of the constellations

b. the names of the constellations

c. the positions of the Moon and the planets

d. the radiation of the stars

5. Which statement best describes the location of the stars shown on the map?

a. They are outside the solar system but within the Milky Way galaxy.

b. They are within the solar system.

c. They are outside the Milky Way galaxy but within the universe.

d. They are outside the universe.

Extended Response

Answer the two questions below in detail. Include some of the terms shown in the word box. In your answer, underline each term you use.

electromagnetic radiation	solar system
Milky Way	radio waves
universe	visible light

6. What is the relationship between Earth, our solar system, the Milky Way, and the universe?

7. What do visible-light telescopes and radio telescopes have in common? How are they different?

Chapter 1: **Exploring Space** 39 **E**

CHAPTER

Earth, Moon, and Sun

the BIG idea

Earth and the Moon move in predictable ways as they orbit the Sun.

Key Concepts

SECTION 2.1
Earth rotates on a tilted axis and orbits the Sun.
Learn what causes day and night and why there are seasons.

SECTION 2.2
The Moon is Earth's natural satellite.
Learn about the structure and motion of Earth's Moon.

SECTION 2.3
Positions of the Sun and Moon affect Earth.
Learn about phases of the Moon, eclipses, and tides.

Internet Preview

CLASSZONE.COM

Chapter 2 online resources: Content Review, two Visualizations, two Resource Centers, Math Tutorial, Test Practice

What would you see if you looked at the Moon with a telescope?

EXPLORE (the BIG idea)

How Do Shadows Move?

Place a small sticky note on a window that sunlight shines through. At several different times of day, sketch the location of the note's shadow in the room.

Observe and Think
Does the shadow move in a clockwise or counterclockwise direction? Does the shadow's distance from the window change?

What Makes the Moon Bright?

On a day when you see the Moon in the sky, compare it with a round object. Hold the object in line with the Moon. Make sure that your hand does not block the sunlight. Notice the part of the object that is bright.

Observe and Think
How does the sunlight on the object compare with the light on the Moon?

Internet Activity: Seasons

Go to **ClassZone.com** to explore seasons. Find out how sunlight affects the temperature in different places at different times of year.

Observe and Think
Does the picture show Earth in June or in December?

NSTA
scilinks.org

SCi LINKS

The Moon **Code: MDL058**

Getting Ready to Learn

◀ CONCEPT REVIEW

- The sky seems to turn as Earth rotates.
- The motions of nearby space objects are visible from Earth.
- Light and other radiation carry information about space.

◀ VOCABULARY REVIEW

orbit p. 10

electromagnetic radiation p. 15

satellite p. 23

See Glossary for definitions.

force, gravity, mass

CONTENT REVIEW
CLASSZONE.COM
Review concepts and vocabulary.

▶ TAKING NOTES

COMBINATION NOTES

To take notes about a new concept, first make an informal outline of the information. Then make a sketch of the concept and label it so you can study it later.

VOCABULARY STRATEGY

Write each new vocabulary term in the center of a **frame game** diagram. Decide what information to frame the term with. Use examples, descriptions, pictures, or sentences in which the term is used in context. You can change the frame to fit each term.

See the Note-Taking Handbook on pages R45–R51.

SCIENCE NOTEBOOK

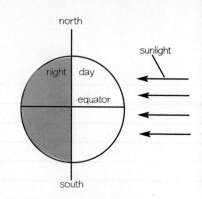

NOTES

Earth turns.
- It turns on an imaginary axis.
  - Poles are ends of axis.
  - Equator is halfway.
- Rotation takes 24 hours.
- Sun shines on one side only.
  - Light side is daytime.
  - Dark side is night.

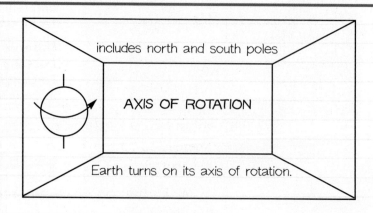

includes north and south poles

AXIS OF ROTATION

Earth turns on its axis of rotation.

2.1

Earth rotates on a tilted axis and orbits the Sun.

◄ **BEFORE, you learned**

- Stars seem to rise, cross the sky, and set because Earth turns
- The Sun is very large and far from Earth
- Earth orbits the Sun

▶ **NOW, you will learn**

- Why Earth has day and night
- How the changing angles of sunlight produce seasons

VOCABULARY

axis of rotation p. 44
revolution p. 45
season p. 46
equinox p. 46
solstice p. 46

EXPLORE Time Zones

What time is it in Iceland right now?

PROCEDURE

1. Find your location and Iceland on the map. Identify the time zone of each.

2. Count the number of hours between your location and Iceland. Add or subtract that number of hours from the time on your clock.

MATERIAL
time zone map

WHAT DO YOU THINK?

- By how much is Iceland's time earlier or later than yours?
- Why are clocks set to different times?

Earth's rotation causes day and night.

When astronauts explored the Moon, they felt the Moon's gravity pulling them down. Their usual "down"—Earth—was up in the Moon's sky.

As you read this book, it is easy to tell which way is down. But is down in the same direction for a person on the other side of Earth? If you both pointed down, you would be pointing toward each other. Earth's gravity pulls objects toward the center of Earth. No matter where you stand on Earth, the direction of down will be toward Earth's center. There is no bottom or top. Up is out toward space, and down is toward the center of the planet.

As Earth turns, so do you. You keep the same position with respect to what is below your feet, but the view above your head changes.

 CHECK YOUR READING In what direction does gravity pull objects near Earth?

The globe and the flat map show the progress of daylight across Earth in two ways. This location is experiencing sunrise.

noon

night moves westward

midnight

The directions north, south, east, and west are based on the way the planet rotates, or turns. Earth rotates around an imaginary line running through its center called an **axis of rotation.** The ends of the axis are the north and south poles. Any location on the surface moves from west to east as Earth turns. If you extend your right thumb and pretend its tip is the North Pole, then your fingers curve the way Earth rotates.

At any one time, about half of Earth is in sunlight and half is dark. However, Earth turns on its axis in 24 hours, so locations move through the light and darkness in that time. When a location is in sunlight, it is daytime there. When a location is in the middle of the sunlit side, it is noon. When a location is in darkness, it is night there, and when the location is in the middle of the unlit side, it is midnight.

CHECK YOUR READING   If it is noon at one location, what time is it at a location directly on the other side of Earth?

INVESTIGATE Rotation

What causes day and night?

In this model the lamp represents the Sun, and your head represents Earth. The North Pole is at the top of your head. You will need to imagine locations on your head as if your head were a globe.

PROCEDURE

1. Face the lamp and hold your hands to your face as shown in the photograph. Your hands mark the horizon. For a person located at your nose, the Sun would be high in the sky. It would be noon.

2. Face away from the lamp. Determine what time it would be at your nose.

3. Turn to your left until you see the lamp along your left hand.

4. Continue turning to the left, through noon, until you just stop seeing the lamp.

WHAT DO YOU THINK?

- What times was it at your nose in steps 2, 3, and 4?
- When you face the lamp, what time is it at your right ear?

CHALLENGE How can a cloud be bright even when it is dark on the ground?

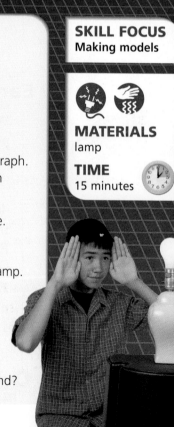

Earth's tilted axis and orbit cause seasons.

Just as gravity causes objects near Earth to be pulled toward Earth's center, it also causes Earth and other objects near the Sun to be pulled toward the Sun's center. Fortunately, Earth does not move straight into the Sun. Earth moves sideways, at nearly a right angle to the Sun's direction. Without the Sun's gravitational pull, Earth would keep moving in a straight line out into deep space. However, the Sun's pull changes Earth's path from a straight line to a round orbit about 300 million kilometers (200,000,000 mi) across.

Just as a day is the time it takes Earth to rotate once on its axis, a year is the time it takes Earth to orbit the Sun once. In astronomy, a **revolution** is the motion of one object around another. The word *revolution* can also mean the time it takes an object to go around once.

Earth's rotation and orbit do not quite line up. If they did, Earth's equator would be in the same plane as Earth's orbit, like a tiny hoop and a huge hoop lying on the same tabletop. Instead, Earth rotates at about a 23° angle, or tilt, from this lined-up position.

READING TiP

Use the second vowel in each word to help you remember that an object rot_a_tes on its own _a_xis, but rev_o_lves around another _o_bject.

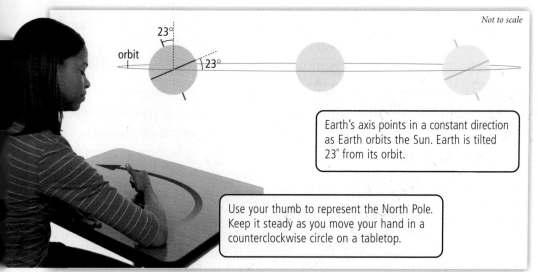

Not to scale

23°

orbit

23°

Earth's axis points in a constant direction as Earth orbits the Sun. Earth is tilted 23° from its orbit.

Use your thumb to represent the North Pole. Keep it steady as you move your hand in a counterclockwise circle on a tabletop.

As Earth moves, its axis always points in the same direction in space. You could model Earth's orbit by moving your right fist in a circle on a desktop. You would need to point your thumb toward your left shoulder and keep it pointing that way while moving your hand around the desktop.

Earth's orbit is not quite a perfect circle. In January, Earth is about 5 million kilometers closer to the Sun than it is in July. You may be surprised to learn that this distance makes only a tiny difference in temperatures on Earth. However, the combination of Earth's motion around the Sun with the tilt of Earth's axis does cause important changes of temperature. Turn the page to find out how.

July

153,000,000 km

148,000,000 km

January   *Not to scale*

Earth's orbit is almost a circle. Earth's distance from the Sun varies by only about 5,000,000 km—about 3%—during a year.

Seasonal Patterns

Most locations on Earth experience **seasons,** patterns of temperature changes and other weather trends over the course of a year. Near the equator, the temperatures are almost the same year-round. Near the poles, there are very large changes in temperatures from winter to summer. The temperature changes occur because the amount of sunlight at each location changes during the year. The changes in the amount of sunlight are due to the tilt of Earth's axis.

Look at the diagram on page 47 to see how the constant direction of Earth's tilted axis affects the pattern of sunlight on Earth at different times of the year. As Earth travels around the Sun, the area of sunlight in each hemisphere changes. At an **equinox** (EE-kwuh-NAHKS), sunlight shines equally on the northern and southern hemispheres. Half of each hemisphere is lit, and half is in darkness. As Earth moves along its orbit, the light shifts more into one hemisphere than the other. At a **solstice** (SAHL-stihs), the area of sunlight is at a maximum in one hemisphere and a minimum in the other hemisphere. Equinoxes and solstices happen on or around the 21st days of certain months of the year.

READING TiP
The positions and lighting can be hard to imagine, so you might use a model as well as the diagram on the next page to help you understand.

1 September Equinox When Earth is in this position, sunlight shines equally on the two hemispheres. You can see in the diagram that the North Pole is at the border between light and dark. The September equinox marks the beginning of autumn in the Northern Hemisphere and of spring in the Southern Hemisphere.

2 December Solstice Three months later, Earth has traveled a quarter of the way around the Sun, but its axis still points in the same direction into space. The North Pole seems to lean away from the direction of the Sun. The solstice occurs when the pole leans as far away from the Sun as it will during the year. You can see that the North Pole is in complete darkness. At the same time, the opposite is true in the Southern Hemisphere. The South Pole seems to lean toward the Sun and is in sunlight. It is the Southern Hemisphere's summer solstice and the Northern Hemisphere's winter solstice.

3 March Equinox After another quarter of its orbit, Earth reaches another equinox. Half of each hemisphere is lit, and the sunlight is centered on the equator. You can see that the poles are again at the border between day and night.

4 June Solstice This position is opposite the December solstice. Earth's axis still points in the same direction, but now the North Pole seems to lean toward the Sun and is in sunlight. The June solstice marks the beginning of summer in the Northern Hemisphere. In contrast, it is the winter solstice in the Southern Hemisphere.

 In what month does winter begin in the Southern Hemisphere?

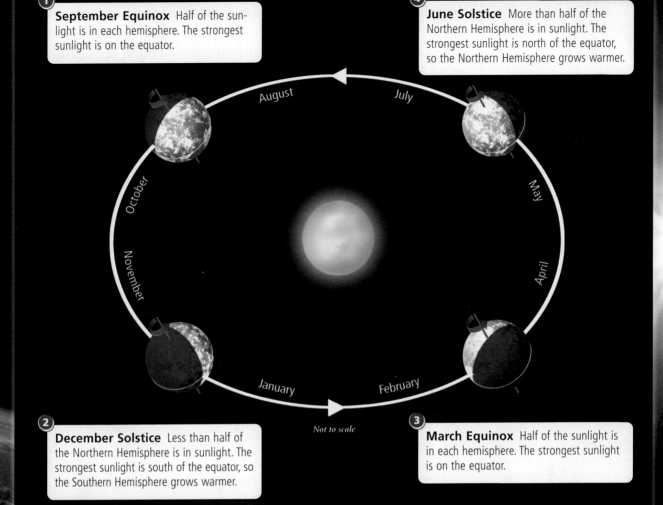

September Equinox Half of the sunlight is in each hemisphere. The strongest sunlight is on the equator.

June Solstice More than half of the Northern Hemisphere is in sunlight. The strongest sunlight is north of the equator, so the Northern Hemisphere grows warmer.

August

July

October

May

November

April

January

February

Not to scale

2 **December Solstice** Less than half of the Northern Hemisphere is in sunlight. The strongest sunlight is south of the equator, so the Southern Hemisphere grows warmer.

3 **March Equinox** Half of the sunlight is in each hemisphere. The strongest sunlight is on the equator.

View from the Sun

If you could stand on the Sun and look at Earth, you would see different parts of Earth at different times of year.

fall — spring — **1** September Equinox

winter — summer — **2** December Solstice

spring — fall — **3** March Equinox

summer — winter — **4** June Solstice

The equinoxes and solstices mark the beginnings of seasons in the two hemispheres. Warmer seasons occur when more of a hemisphere is in sunlight.

READING VISUALS Look at the poles to help you see how each hemisphere is lit. When is the South Pole completely in sunlight?

Angles of Sunlight

RESOURCE CENTER
CLASSZONE.COM

Learn more about
seasons.

You have seen that seasons change as sunlight shifts between hemispheres during the year. On the ground, you notice the effects of seasons because the angle of sunlight and the length of daylight change over the year. The effects are greatest at locations far from the equator. You may have noticed that sunshine seems barely warm just before sunset, when the Sun is low in the sky. At noon the sunshine seems much hotter. The angle of light affects the temperature.

When the Sun is high in the sky, sunlight strikes the ground at close to a right angle. The energy of sunlight is concentrated. Shadows are short. You may get a sunburn quickly when the Sun is at a high angle. When the Sun is low in the sky, sunlight strikes the ground at a slant. The light is spread over a greater area, so it is less concentrated and produces long shadows. Slanted light warms the ground less.

Near the equator, the noonday Sun is almost overhead every day, so the ground is warmed strongly year-round. In the middle latitudes, the noon Sun is high in the sky only during part of the year. In winter the noon Sun is low and warms the ground less strongly.

CHECK YOUR READING How are temperatures throughout the year affected by the angles of sunlight?

Sun Height and Shadows

Winter Solstice, 12 P.M.

Winter shadows are long because sunlight is spread out. The Sun appears low in the sky even at noon.

location on Earth

Spring Equinox, 12 P.M.

Spring and fall shadows are of medium length, and the noon Sun appears higher in the sky.

Summer Solstice, 12 P.M.

Summer shadows are short because the light is concentrated in a small area. The noon Sun appears high in the sky.

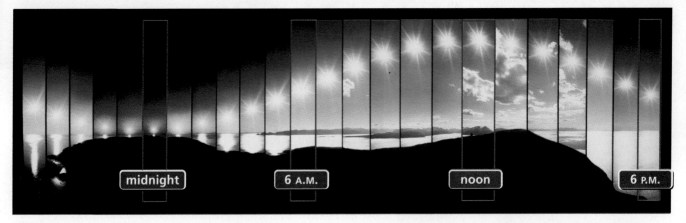

midnight   6 A.M.   noon   6 P.M.

Lengths of Days

Seasonal temperatures depend on the amount of daylight, too. In Chicago, for example, the summer Sun heats the ground for about 15 hours a day, but in winter there may be only 9 hours of sunlight each day. The farther you get from the equator, the more extreme the changes in day length become. As you near one of the poles, summer daylight may last for 20 hours or more.

Very close to the poles, the Sun does not set at all for six months at a time. It can be seen shining near the horizon at midnight. Tourists often travel far north just to experience the midnight Sun. At locations near a pole, the Sun sets on an equinox and then does not rise again for six months. Astronomers go to the South Pole in March to take advantage of the long winter night, which allows them to study objects in the sky without the interruption of daylight.

Very near the equator, the periods of daylight and darkness are almost equal year-round—each about 12 hours long. Visitors who are used to hot weather during long summer days might be surprised when a hot, sunny day ends suddenly at 6 P.M. At locations away from the equator, daylight lasts 12 hours only around the time of an equinox.

Near the pole in the summer, the Sun stays above the horizon, so there is no night. This series of photographs was taken over the course of a day.

READING **TiP**

Equinox means "equal night"—daylight and nighttime are equal in length.

2.1 Review

KEY CONCEPTS

1. What causes day and night?
2. What happens to Earth's axis of rotation as Earth orbits the Sun?
3. How do the areas of sunlight in the two hemispheres change over the year?

CRITICAL THINKING

4. **Apply** If you wanted to enjoy longer periods of daylight in the summertime, would you head closer to the equator or farther from it? Why?
5. **Compare and Contrast** How do the average temperatures and the seasonal changes at the equator differ from those at the poles?

⚫ CHALLENGE

6. **Infer** If Earth's axis were tilted so much that the North Pole sometimes pointed straight at the Sun, how would the hours of daylight be affected at your location?

Chapter 2: **Earth, Moon, and Sun** 49 **E**

CHAPTER INVESTIGATION

Modeling Seasons

OVERVIEW AND PURPOSE Why is the weather in North America so much colder in January than in July? You might be surprised to learn that it has nothing to do with Earth's distance from the Sun. In fact, Earth is closest to the Sun in January. In this lab, you will model the cause of seasons as you
- orient a light source at different angles to a surface
- determine how the angles of sunlight at a location change as Earth orbits the Sun

▶ Problem

Write It Up

How does the angle of light affect the amount of solar energy a location receives at different times of year?

▶ Hypothesize

Write It Up

After performing step 3, write a hypothesis to explain how the angles of sunlight affect the amounts of solar energy your location receives at different times of year. Your hypothesis should take the form of an "If . . . , then . . . , because . . ." statement.

▶ Procedure

PART A

MATERIALS
- graph paper
- flashlight
- meter stick
- protractor
- globe
- stack of books
- sticky note

1. Mark an X near the center of the graph paper. Shine the flashlight onto the paper from about 30 cm straight above the X—at an angle of 90° to the surface. Observe the size of the spot of light.

2. Shine the flashlight onto the X at different angles. Keep the flashlight at the same distance. Write down what happens to the size of the spot of light as you change angles.

3. Repeat step 2, but observe just one square near the X. Write down what happens to the brightness of the light as you change the angle. The brightness shows how much energy the area receives from the flashlight.

step 2

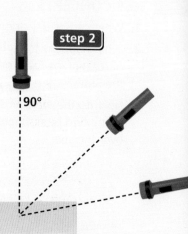

90°

4. Think about the temperatures at different times of year at your location, then write your hypothesis.

PART B

5 Set up the globe, books, and flashlight as shown in the photograph. Point the globe's North Pole to the right. This position represents solstice A.

solstice A

6 Find your location on the globe. Place a folded sticky note onto the globe at your location as shown in the photograph. Rotate the globe on its axis until the note faces toward the flashlight.

7 The flashlight beam represents noonday sunlight at your location. Use the protractor to estimate the angle of the light on the surface.

light
steps 6–7

8 Move the globe to the left side of the table and the flashlight and books to the right side of the table. Point the North Pole to the right. This position represents solstice B.

9 Repeat step 7 for solstice B.

solstice B

Observe and Analyze
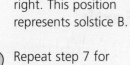

1. **RECORD** Draw the setup of your materials in each part of the investigation. Organize your notes.

2. **ANALYZE** Describe how the angle of the flashlight in step 2 affected the area of the spot of light. Which angle concentrated the light into the smallest area?

3. **EVALUATE** At which angle did a square of the graph paper receive the most energy?

4. **COMPARE** Compare the angles of light in steps 7 and 9. In which position was the angle of light closer to 90°?

Conclude
Write It Up

1. **EVALUATE** How did the angle of sunlight at your location differ at the two times of year? At which position is sunlight more concentrated at your location?

2. **APPLY** The amount of solar energy at a location affects temperature. Which solstice—A or B—represents the summer solstice at your location?

3. **INTERPRET** Do your results support your hypothesis? Explain why or why not.

INVESTIGATE Further

CHALLENGE What happens in the other hemisphere at the two times of year? Use the model to find out.

Modeling Seasons
Problem How does the angle of light affect the amount of solar energy a location receives at different times of year?

Hypothesize

Observe and Analyze

Table 1. Solstices A and B

	Solstice A	Solstice B
Drawing		
Angle of light (°)		
Observations		

Conclude

2.2 The Moon is Earth's natural satellite.

 BEFORE, you learned

- Earth turns as it orbits the Sun
- The day side of Earth is the part in sunlight
- The Moon is the closest body to Earth

 NOW, you will learn

- How the Moon moves
- What the Moon's dark-colored and light-colored features are
- About the inside structure of the Moon

VOCABULARY

mare p. 53

EXPLORE The Moon's Motion

How much does the Moon turn?

PROCEDURE

1. Draw a circle to represent the Moon's orbit with Earth at the center. The compass represents the Moon.

2. Move the compass around the circle. Keep the side of the compass marked *E* always facing Earth.

3. Observe the positions of the *E* and the compass needle at several positions on the circle.

WHAT DO YOU THINK?

What does the model tell you about the Moon's motion?

MATERIALS
- paper
- magnetic compass

The Moon rotates as it orbits Earth.

When you look at the disk of the Moon, you may notice darker and lighter areas. Perhaps you have imagined them as features of a face or some other pattern. People around the world have told stories about the animals, people, and objects they have imagined while looking at the light and dark areas of the Moon. As you will read in this chapter, these areas tell a story to scientists as well.

The pull of gravity keeps the Moon, Earth's natural satellite, in orbit around Earth. Even though the Moon is Earth's closest neighbor in space, it is far away compared to the sizes of Earth and the Moon.

The Moon's diameter is about 1/4 Earth's diameter, and the Moon is about 30 Earth diameters away.

● Earth ─────────────────────────────── • Moon

The distance between Earth and the Moon is roughly 380,000 kilometers (240,000 mi) —about a hundred times the distance between New York and Los Angeles. If a jet airliner could travel in space, it would take about 20 days to cover a distance that huge. Astronauts, whose spaceships traveled much faster than jets, needed about 3 days to reach the Moon.

You always see the same pattern of dark-colored and light-colored features on the Moon. Only this one side of the Moon can be seen from Earth. The reason is that the Moon, like many other moons in the solar system, always keeps one side turned toward its planet. This means that the Moon turns once on its own axis each time it orbits Earth.

 Why do you see only one side of the Moon?

The Moon's craters show its history.

The half of the Moon's surface that constantly faces Earth is called the near side. The half that faces away from Earth is called the far side. Much of the Moon's surface is light-colored. Within the light-colored areas are many small, round features. There are also dark-colored features, some of which cover large areas. Much of the near side of the Moon is covered with these dark-colored features. In contrast, the far side is mostly light-colored with just a few of the darker features.

Just as on Earth, features on the Moon are given names to make it easier to discuss them. The names of the larger surface features on the Moon are in the Latin language, because centuries ago scientists from many different countries used Latin to communicate with one another. Early astronomers thought that the dark areas might be bodies of water, so they used the Latin word for "sea." Today, a dark area on the Moon is still called a lunar **mare** (MAH-ray). The plural form is *maria* (MAH-ree-uh).

The maria are not bodies of water, however. All of the features that can be seen on the Moon are different types of solid or broken rock. The Moon has no air, no oceans, no clouds, and no life.

Moon

The side of the Moon that constantly faces Earth has large, dark areas called maria.

Mass 1% of Earth's mass
Diameter 27% of Earth's diameter
Average distance
  from Earth 380,000 km
Orbits in 27.3 Earth days
Rotates in 27.3 Earth days

READING TIP

Lunar means "having to do with the Moon." The word comes from *luna*, the Latin word for the Moon.

Craters and Maria

The light-colored areas of the Moon are higher—at greater altitudes—than the maria, so they are called the lunar highlands. The ground of the lunar highlands is rocky, and some places are covered with a powder made of finely broken rock.

The highlands have many round features, called impact craters, that formed when small objects from space hit the Moon's surface. Long ago, such collisions happened more often than they do today. Many impact craters marked the surfaces of the Moon, Earth, and other bodies in space. On Earth, however, most craters have been worn away by water and wind. On the dry, airless Moon, impact craters from a long time ago are still visible.

Long ago, some of the largest craters filled with molten rock, or lava, that came from beneath the Moon's surface. The lava filled the lowest areas and then cooled, forming the large, flat plains called maria. Smaller impacts have continued to occur, so the dark plains of the maria do contain some craters. Most of the large maria are on the near side of the Moon. However, the widest and deepest basin on the Moon is on the far side, near the Moon's south pole.

CHECK YOUR READING How did the maria form? List the steps.

Lunar Map

Light-colored highlands and dark maria form a familiar pattern on the near side of the Moon and a very different pattern on the far side.

Near Side

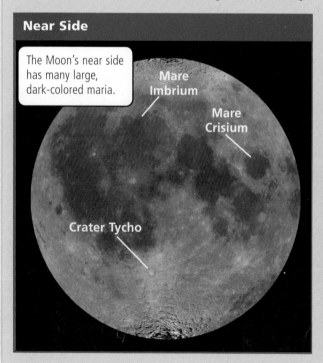

The Moon's near side has many large, dark-colored maria.

Mare Imbrium

Mare Crisium

Crater Tycho

Far Side

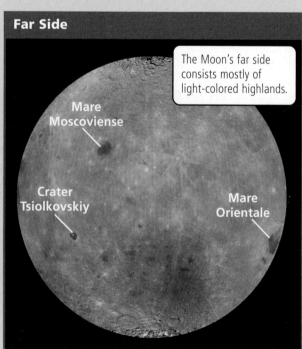

The Moon's far side consists mostly of light-colored highlands.

Mare Moscoviense

Crater Tsiolkovskiy

Mare Orientale

INVESTIGATE Moon Features

How did the Moon's features form?

In this model, you will use a paper towel to represent the Moon's surface and gelatin to represent molten rock from inside the Moon.

PROCEDURE

1. Pour about 1 cm of partly cooled liquid gelatin into the cup.

2. Hold the paper towel by bringing its corners together. Push the towel into the cup until the center of the towel touches the bottom of the cup. Open the towel slightly.

3. Place the cup in the bowl of ice, and allow the gelatin time to solidify.

WHAT DO YOU THINK?

- What part of the towel did the gelatin affect?
- When you look down into the cup, what can the smooth areas tell you about heights?

CHALLENGE Early astronomers thought there might be oceans on the Moon. How does your model lava resemble an ocean?

SKILL FOCUS
Inferring

MATERIALS
- liquid gelatin
- clear plastic cup
- paper towel
- bowl of ice

TIME
20 minutes

Moon Rocks

Moon rocks have different ages. Some of the surface rock of the Moon is about 4.5 billion years old—as old as the Moon itself. This very old rock is found in the lunar highlands. The rock in the maria is younger because it formed from lava that solidified later, 3.8–3.1 billion years ago. These two main types of rock and their broken pieces cover most of the Moon's surface. Astronauts explored the Moon and brought back samples of as many different types of material as they could.

Impacts from space objects leave craters, and they also break the surface material into smaller pieces. This breaking of material is called weathering, even though it is not caused by wind and water. Weathered material on the Moon forms a type of dry, lifeless soil. The lunar soil is more than 15 meters (50 ft) deep in some places. Impacts can also toss lunar soil into different places, compact it into new rocks, or melt it and turn it into a glassy type of rock.

The dark-colored rock that formed from lava is called basalt (buh-SAWLT). Lunar basalt is similar to the rock deep beneath Earth's oceans. The basalt of the lunar maria covers large areas but is often only a few hundred meters in depth. However, the basalt can be several kilometers deep at the center of a mare, a depth similar to that of Earth's oceans.

Almost 400 kg (weighing more than 800 lb) of Moon rocks and soil were collected and brought back to Earth by astronauts.

highland rock

basalt

The Moon has layers.

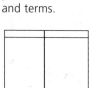
Scientists on Earth have analyzed the lunar rocks and soil to determine their ages and materials. These results told scientists a story about how the Moon changed over time. During an early stage of the Moon's history, impacts happened often and left craters of many different sizes. That stage ended about 3.8 billion years ago, and impacts have happened much less often since then. The highland rocks and soil come from the original surface and impacts. Shortly after the impacts slowed, lava flooded the low-lying areas and formed the maria. Then the flooding stopped. During the last 3 billion years, the Moon has gained new impact craters from time to time but has remained mostly unchanged.

Structure

The Moon's interior resembles Earth's interior in several ways.

Scientists have used information from lunar rocks and other measurements to figure out what is inside the Moon. Beneath its thin coating of crushed rock, the Moon has three layers—a crust, a mantle, and a core. As on Earth, the crust is the outermost layer. It averages about 70 kilometers (about 40 mi) thick and contains the least dense type of rock.

Beneath the crust is a thick mantle that makes up most of the Moon's volume. The mantle is made of dense types of rock that include the elements iron and magnesium. The basalt on the lunar surface contains these same elements, so scientists infer that the material of the basalt came from the mantle.

In the middle of the Moon is a small core, approximately 700 kilometers (400 mi) across. Although dense, it makes up only a tiny fraction of the Moon's mass. Scientists have less information about the core than the mantle because material from the core did not reach the Moon's surface. The core seems to consist of iron and other metals.

CHECK YOUR READING What are your own questions about the Moon?

Formation

Scientists develop models to help them understand their observations, such as the observed similarities and differences between Earth and the Moon. The two objects have similar structures and are made of similar materials. However, the materials are in different proportions. The Moon has more materials like Earth's crust and mantle and less material like Earth's core.

Scientists have used these facts to develop models of how the Moon formed. A widely accepted model of the Moon's origin involves a giant collision. In this model, an early version of Earth was hit by a

Formation of the Moon

Collision

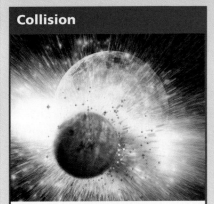

An early version of Earth is struck by a slightly smaller space body.

Re-Forming

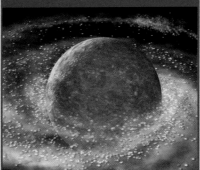

The many pieces pull each other into orbits. Most of the material forms a new version of Earth.

Earth and Moon

The Moon forms from material that orbits the new version of Earth.

smaller space body. Much of the material from both bodies, especially the cores, combined to form a new version of Earth. The energy of the collision also threw material out, away from Earth. Bits of material from the crusts and mantles of both bodies went into orbit around the new Earth. Much of this orbiting material clumped together and became the Moon. Computer simulations of these events show that the Moon may have formed quickly—perhaps within just one year.

Evidence from fossils and rocks on Earth show that, whether the Moon formed from a giant collision or in some other way, it was once much closer to Earth than it is today. The Moon has been moving slowly away from Earth. It now moves 3.8 centimeters (1.5 in.) farther from Earth each year. However, this change is so slow that you will not notice any difference in your lifetime.

2.2 Review

KEY CONCEPTS

1. How many times does the Moon rotate on its axis during one trip around Earth?

2. What are the dark spots and the light areas on the Moon called?

3. Describe the Moon's layers.

CRITICAL THINKING

4. **Compare and Contrast** How are the Moon's dark-colored areas different from its light-colored areas?

5. **Draw Conclusions** How have the Moon rocks that astronauts brought back to Earth helped scientists understand the history of the Moon?

⚪ CHALLENGE

6. **Analyze** Scientists use indirect methods to learn about the cores of Earth and the Moon. Imagine you have several Styrofoam balls, some with steel balls hidden inside. Without breaking a ball open, how might you tell whether it contains a steel ball?

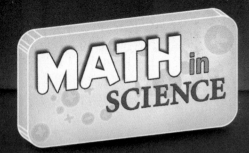

Graphing Sunlight

The location of the Moon and the Sun in the sky depend on your location on Earth and when you look. In summer, the noon Sun is at a greater angle above the horizon—closer to 90°—than it is in winter. In summer, the Sun rises earlier and sets later than in winter. Longer days and steeper angles of sunlight combine to make summer days much warmer than winter days. Plot the data for Washington, D.C. (latitude 39° N) to see the changing patterns of sunlight.

MATH TUTORIAL
CLASSZONE.COM

Click on Math Tutorial for more help with line graphs.

Washington, D.C.

Month	Sunlight Each Day (h)	Angle of Sun at Noon (°)
Jan.	9.9	31.4
Feb.	11.0	40.8
Mar.	12.2	51.6
Apr.	13.5	63.2
May	14.5	71.4
June	14.9	74.6
July	14.5	71.4
Aug.	13.5	63.0
Sept.	12.2	51.6
Oct.	11.0	40.2
Nov.	9.9	31.1
Dec.	9.5	27.7

This is a series of images of the Sun photographed at exactly the same time of day every few days over most of a year. The bottom of the photograph is from just one of the days and includes a stone circle calendar.

Example

You can make a double line graph to see patterns in the data. Use a colored pencil to label the second y-axis.

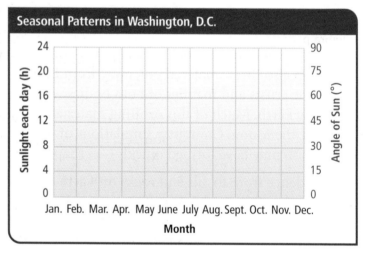

(1) Copy all three graph axes onto graph paper.

(2) Use the y-axis on the left to plot the data for the hours of daylight. Draw line segments to connect the points.

(3) Use the y-axis on the right and a colored pencil to plot the data for the angle of the Sun. Draw line segments to connect the points.

Answer the following questions.

1. During which time period do days get shorter?

2. About how many degrees higher in the sky is the noon Sun in June than in December? About how many more hours of sunlight are there each day in June than in December?

3. Does the angle of the Sun change more quickly between June and July or between September and October? How can you tell?

CHALLENGE Copy the axes again, then graph the data your teacher gives you for a location near the North Pole. Use your graphs to compare daylight patterns at the two latitudes.

KEY CONCEPT

2.3 Positions of the Sun and Moon affect Earth.

 BEFORE, you learned

- The Moon orbits Earth
- Sunlight shines on Earth and the Moon

▶ **NOW, you will learn**

- Why the Moon has phases
- What causes eclipses
- Why Earth's oceans have tides

VOCABULARY

eclipse p. 63
umbra p. 63
penumbra p. 63

THINK ABOUT

Have you seen the Moon in daylight?

Many people think that the Moon is visible only at night. This idea is not surprising, because the Moon is the brightest object in the sky at night. In the daytime the Moon is only as bright as a tiny, thin cloud. It is easy to miss, even in a cloudless blue sky. You can see the Moon sometimes in the day-time, sometimes at night, often at both times, and sometimes not at all. Why does the Moon sometimes disappear from view?

Phases are different views of the Moon's sunlit half.

What you see as moonlight is really light from the Sun reflected by the Moon's surface. At any time, sunlight shines on half of the Moon's surface. Areas where sunlight does not reach look dark, just as the night side of Earth looks dark from space. As the Moon turns on its axis, areas on the surface move into and out of sunlight.

When you look at the Moon, you see a bright shape that is the lit part of the near side of the Moon. The unlit part is hard to see. Lunar phases are the patterns of lit and unlit portions of the Moon that you see from Earth. It takes about a month for the Moon to orbit Earth and go through all the phases.

COMBINATION NOTES
Use the blue heading to start a new set of notes.

 CHECK YOUR READING
Why do you sometimes see only part of the near side of the Moon?

The Moon's position in its monthly orbit determines how it appears from Earth. The diagram on page 61 shows how the positions of the Moon, the Sun, and Earth affect the shapes you see in the sky.

Waxing Moon

First Week The cycle begins with a new moon. From Earth, the Moon and the Sun are in the same direction. If you face a new moon, you face the Sun. Your face and the far side of the Moon are in sunlight. The near side of the Moon is unlit, so you do not see it. During a new moon, there appears to be no Moon.

As the Moon moves along its orbit, sunlight begins falling on the near side. You see a thin crescent shape. During the first week, the Moon keeps moving farther around, so more of the near side becomes lit. You see thicker crescents as the Moon waxes, or grows.

Second Week When half of the near side of the Moon is in sunlight, the Moon has completed one-quarter of its cycle. The phase is called the first quarter, even though you might describe the shape as a half-moon. You can see in the diagram that the Moon is 90 degrees—at a right angle—from the Sun. If you face the first-quarter moon when it is high in the sky, sunlight will shine on the right side of your head and the right side of the Moon.

You see more of the Moon as it moves along its orbit during the second week. The phase is called gibbous (GIHB-uhs) when the near side is more than half lit but not fully lit. The Moon is still waxing, so the phases during the second week are called waxing gibbous moons.

 CHECK YOUR READING Why does the Moon sometimes seem to have a crescent shape?

Waning Moon

Third Week Halfway through its cycle, the whole near side of the Moon is in sunlight—a full moon. You might think of it as the second quarter. Viewed from Earth, the Moon and the Sun are in opposite directions. If you face a full moon at sunset, sunlight from behind you lights the back of your head and the near side of the Moon.

As the Moon continues around during the third week, less and less of the near side is in sunlight. The Moon seems to shrink, or wane, so these phases are called waning gibbous moons.

Fourth Week When the near side is again only half in sunlight, the Moon is three-quarters of the way through its cycle. The phase is called the third quarter. The Moon is again 90 degrees from the Sun. If you face the third-quarter moon when it is high in the sky, sunlight will shine on the left side of your head and the left side of the Moon.

Lunar Phases

The appearance of the Moon depends on the positions of the Sun, Moon, and Earth.

If you could watch the Moon from high above its pole, you would always see half the Moon in sunlight and half in darkness.

sunlight

WAXING (GROWING)

WANING (SHRINKING)

new moon

1 first week

2 second week

Earth

line of sight

Not to scale

fourth week **4**

3 third week

full moon

waning gibbous

direction from Earth

This lit portion is visible from Earth.

View from Earth

Viewed from Earth, the Moon's shape seems to change.

1 first week

new moon

waxing crescent

2 second week

first quarter

waxing gibbous

3 third week

full moon

waning gibbous

4 fourth week

third quarter

waning crescent

READING VISUALS **COMPARE** How are the sunlit portions alike in the image and the diagram of the waning gibbous moon?

As the Moon continues to move around Earth during the fourth week, less and less of the near side is in sunlight. The waning crescent moon grows thinner and thinner. At the end of the fourth week, the near side is again unlit, and the new moon begins a new cycle.

Crescent and Gibbous Moons

Think through the waxing lunar phases again. The Moon waxes from new to crescent to gibbous during the first half of its cycle. Then it wanes from full to gibbous to crescent during the second half of its cycle.

The amount of the Moon that you see from Earth depends on the angle between the Moon and the Sun. When this angle is small, you see only a small amount of the Moon. Crescent moons occur when the Moon appears close to the Sun in the sky. As a result, they are visible most often in the daytime or around the time of sunrise or sunset. When the angle between the Sun and the Moon is large, you see a large amount of the Moon. Gibbous and full moons appear far from the Sun in the sky. You may see them in the daytime, but you are more likely to notice them at night.

CHECK YOUR READING What shape does the Moon appear to be when it is at a small angle to the Sun?

INVESTIGATE Phases of the Moon

Why does the Moon seem to change shape?
PROCEDURE

1. Place the ball on the stick, which will act as a handle. The ball will represent the Moon, and your head will represent Earth.

2. Hold the ball toward the light, then move it to your left until you see a bright edge. Draw what you see.

3. Move the ball farther around until half of what you see is lit. Draw it.

4. Keep moving the ball around to your left until the side you see is fully lit, then half lit, then lit only a little bit. Each time, face the ball and draw it.

WHAT DO YOU THINK?

- In step 2, which side of the ball was lit? Explain why.
- How are your drawings like the photographs of the Moon's phases? Label each drawing with the name of the corresponding lunar phase.

CHALLENGE When the Moon is a crescent, sometimes you can dimly see the rest of the Moon if you look closely. Where might the light that makes the darker part of the Moon visible come from?

SKILL FOCUS
Making models

MATERIALS
- foam ball
- stick
- lamp

TIME
20 minutes

Shadows in space cause eclipses.

Sunlight streams past Earth and the Moon, lighting one side of each body. Beyond each body is a long, thin cone of darkness where no sunlight reaches—a shadow in space. The two bodies are far apart, so they usually miss each other's shadow as the Moon orbits Earth. However, if the Moon, the Sun, and Earth line up exactly, a shadow crosses Earth or the Moon. An **eclipse** occurs when a shadow makes the Sun or the Moon seem to grow dark. In a lunar eclipse, the Moon darkens. In a solar eclipse, the Sun seems to darken.

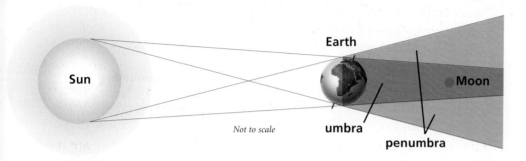

Sun

Earth

Moon

Not to scale

umbra

penumbra

Lunar Eclipses

The Moon becomes dark during a lunar eclipse because it passes through Earth's shadow. There are two parts of Earth's shadow, as you can see in the diagram above. The **umbra** is the darkest part. Around it is a spreading cone of lighter shadow called the **penumbra.**

Just before a lunar eclipse, sunlight streaming past Earth produces a full moon. Then the Moon moves into Earth's penumbra and becomes slightly less bright. As the Moon moves into the umbra, Earth's dark shadow seems to creep across and cover the Moon. The entire Moon can be in darkness because the Moon is small enough to fit entirely within Earth's umbra. After an hour or more, the Moon moves slowly back into the sunlight that is streaming past Earth.

A total lunar eclipse occurs when the Moon passes completely into Earth's umbra. If the Moon misses part or all of the umbra, part of the Moon stays light and the eclipse is called a partial lunar eclipse.

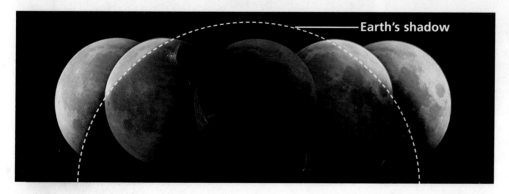

Earth's shadow

The Moon starts getting dark on one side as it passes into Earth's umbra. Even when the Moon is completely within Earth's umbra, some red sunlight, bent by Earth's atmosphere, may still reach the Moon.

Solar Eclipses

In a solar eclipse, the Sun seems to darken because the Moon's shadow falls onto part of Earth. Imagine that you are in the path of a solar eclipse. At first, you see a normal day. You cannot see the dark Moon moving toward the Sun. Then part of the Sun seems to disappear as the Moon moves in front of it. You are in the Moon's penumbra. After several hours of growing darkness, the Moon covers the Sun's disk completely. The sky becomes as dark as night, and you may see constellations. In place of the Sun is a black disk—the new moon—surrounded by a pale glow. You are in the Moon's umbra, the darkest part of the shadow, experiencing a total solar eclipse. After perhaps a minute, the Sun's bright surface starts to appear again.

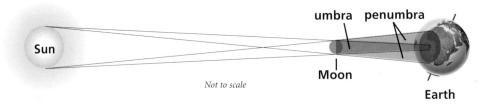

Sun

umbra penumbra

Moon

Earth

Not to scale

A solar eclipse occurs when the Moon passes directly between Earth and the Sun. As you can see in the diagram above, the side of the Moon that faces Earth is unlit, so solar eclipses occur only during new moons.

If you could watch a solar eclipse from space, it might seem more like a lunar eclipse. You would see the Moon's penumbra, with the dark umbra in the center, move across Earth's daylight side. However, the Moon is smaller than Earth, so it casts a smaller shadow. As you can see in the diagram above, the Moon's umbra covers only a fraction of Earth's surface at a time.

June 21, 2001, Eclipse

total eclipse

In this time-lapse photograph, the Sun's disk appears darker as the Moon passes in front. When the Moon is exactly in front of the Sun, the sky grows as dark as night.

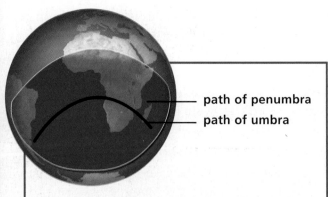

path of penumbra

path of umbra

Path of June 21, 2001, Eclipse Only locations along the thin central path of the shadow experience a total eclipse. Other locations experience a partial eclipse.

Only locations in the path of the Moon's shadow experience a solar eclipse. Some people travel thousands of miles to be in the thin path of the Moon's umbra so that they can experience a total solar eclipse. Locations near the path of the umbra get an eclipse that is less than total. If only the penumbra moves over your location, you experience a partial solar eclipse. The Moon covers just part of the Sun.

Bright light from the Sun's disk can damage your eyes if you look directly at it. The Sun is unsafe to look at even when the Moon covers most of the Sun's disk. If you have the chance to experience a solar eclipse, use a safe method to view the Sun.

COMBINATION NOTES
Remember to make notes about new ideas.

CHECK YOUR READING Where is the Moon during a solar eclipse? Find a way to remember the difference between the two types of eclipses.

The Moon's gravity causes tides on Earth.

If you have spent time near an ocean, you may have experienced the usual pattern of tides. At first, you might see dry sand that slopes down to the ocean. Then, waves creep higher and higher onto the sand. The average water level rises slowly for about 6 hours. The highest level is called high tide. Then the water level slowly drops for about 6 hours. The lowest level is called low tide. Then the water level rises and falls again. The entire pattern—two high tides and two low tides—takes a little more than 24 hours.

In areas with tides, the water generally reaches its lowest level twice a day and its highest level twice a day.

CHECK YOUR READING How many high tides do you expect per day?

Tides occur because the Moon's gravity changes the shape of Earth's oceans. The Moon pulls on different parts of Earth with different amounts of force. It pulls hardest on the side of Earth nearest it, a little less hard on the center of Earth, and even less hard on the farthest side of Earth. If Earth were flexible, it would be pulled into a football shape. Earth's crust is hard enough to resist being pulled into a different shape, but Earth's oceans do change shape.

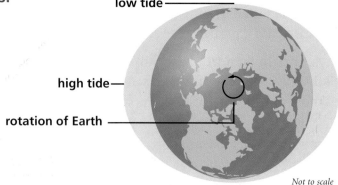

The Moon's gravity changes the shape of Earth's oceans.

low tide

high tide

rotation of Earth

Moon

Not to scale

The diagram above shows what would happen if Earth were covered with a thick layer of water. The Moon's pull produces a bulge of thicker ocean water on the side of Earth nearest the Moon. Another bulge of water is produced on the side of Earth farthest from the Moon because the Moon pulls the center of Earth away from that side. The layer of water is thinnest in the middle, between the bulges.

A location moves past different thicknesses of water as Earth turns on its axis. As a result, the water level there rises and falls. The thickest water produces the highest level, which is high tide. A quarter of a rotation—6 hours—later, the location has moved to the thinnest layer of water, or low tide. Another high tide and low tide complete the cycle. Because the Moon is orbiting while Earth is turning, the cycle takes a little longer than the 24 hours in a day.

 CHECK YOUR READING Why does a cycle of tides take about 24 hours?

2.3 Review

KEY CONCEPTS

1. When the Moon is full, where is it in its orbit around Earth?

2. Where is the Moon in its orbit at the time of a solar eclipse?

3. If it is high tide where you are, is the tide high or low on the side of Earth directly opposite you?

CRITICAL THINKING

4. **Apply** If you were on the Moon's near side during a new moon, how much of the side of Earth facing you would be sunlit?

5. **Predict** If Earth did not turn, how would the pattern of tides be affected?

◯ CHALLENGE

6. **Predict** Would we see lunar phases if the Moon did not rotate while it orbits Earth?

Astronomy in Archaeology

In order to understand how people lived and thought long ago, archaeologists study the buildings and other physical remains of ancient cultures. Archaeologists often think about what needs people had in order to figure out how they used the things they built. For example, people needed to know the time of year in order to decide when to plant crops, move to a different location for winter, or plan certain ceremonies.

Archaeologists can use their knowledge about objects in the sky to hypothesize about the purpose of an ancient structure. They can also use knowledge and models from astronomy to test their hypotheses. For example, archaeologists found some structures at Chimney Rock that were built at times of special events in the sky.

Antikythera Computer

A device with gears and dials was found in an ancient Greek shipwreck. While examining the device, a scientist noticed terms, patterns, and numbers from astronomy. These observations led him to form a hypothesis that ancient Greeks used the instrument to calculate the positions of the Sun, Moon, and other bodies in space. Gamma-ray images of the instrument's interior later supported this hypothesis.

Chimney Rock

Chimney Rock, in Colorado, is topped by two natural pillars of rock. The Moon appears to rise between the pillars under special circumstances that happen about every 18 years. Near the pillars are ruins of buildings of the Anasazi people. In order to construct the buildings and live here, the builders had to haul materials and water much farther than was usual. Some archaeologists hypothesize that the Anasazi built here in order to watch or celebrate special events in the sky.

Stonehenge

Stonehenge is an arrangement of stones in Britain. The first stones were placed there around 3100 B.C. The way that the Sun and Moon line up with the stones has led some archaeologists to think that they were designed to help people predict solstices and eclipses. Solstices tell people the time of year, so Stonehenge has sometimes been called a calendar.

path of rising Sun on solstice

Stonehenge as seen from above

EXPLORE

1. **COMPARE** How is each archaeological example related to astronomy?

2. **CHALLENGE** Make a list of five print or television advertisements that feature the Sun or other objects in the sky. Bring in copies of the advertisements if you can. Why might the advertisers have chosen these objects?

Ruins of buildings were found on a high, narrow ridge at Chimney Rock.

the BIG idea

Earth and the Moon move in predictable ways as they orbit the Sun.

KEY CONCEPTS SUMMARY

2.1 Earth rotates on a tilted axis and orbits the Sun.

Earth's rotation in sunlight causes day and night.

The changing angles of sunlight on Earth cause seasons.

VOCABULARY
axis of rotation p. 44
revolution p. 45
season p. 46
equinox p. 46
solstice p. 46

2.2 The Moon is Earth's natural satellite.

Dark-colored maria formed from lava-filled craters.

Light-colored highlands are old and cratered.

The Moon's near side always faces Earth.

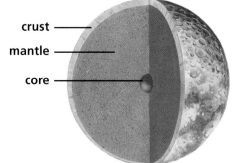

crust
mantle
core

VOCABULARY
mare p. 53

2.3 Positions of the Sun and Moon affect Earth.

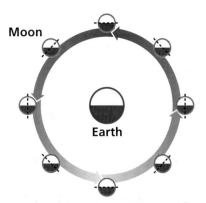

Moon

Earth

Lunar phases are different views of the Moon's sunlit half.

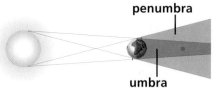

penumbra

umbra

Shadows cause eclipses.

The Moon's gravity causes tides as Earth turns.

VOCABULARY
eclipse p. 63
umbra p. 63
penumbra p. 63

Reviewing Vocabulary

Use words and diagrams to show the relationship between the terms in each the following pairs. Underline the two terms in each answer.

1. revolution, rotation

2. revolution, season

3. solstice, equinox

4. mare, impact crater

5. eclipse, umbra

6. umbra, penumbra

Reviewing Key Concepts

Multiple Choice *Choose the letter of the best answer.*

7. How long does it take Earth to turn once on its axis of rotation?
   a. an hour   c. a month
   b. a day   d. a year

8. How long does it take Earth to orbit the Sun?
   a. an hour   c. a month
   b. a day   d. a year

9. About how long does it take the Moon to revolve once around Earth?
   a. an hour   c. a month
   b. a day   d. a year

10. Why is it hotter in summer than in winter?
    a. Earth gets closer to and farther from the Sun.
    b. Sunlight strikes the ground at higher angles.
    c. Earth turns faster in some seasons.
    d. Earth revolves around the Sun more times in some seasons.

11. The dark maria on the Moon formed from
    a. dried-up seas
    b. finely-broken rock
    c. large shadows
    d. lava-filled craters

12. The lunar highlands have more impact craters than the maria, so scientists know that the highlands
    a. are older than the maria
    b. are younger than the maria
    c. are flatter than the maria
    d. are darker than the maria

13. Why is just one side of the Moon visible from Earth?
    a. The Moon does not rotate on its axis as it orbits Earth.
    b. The Moon rotates once in the same amount of time that it orbits.
    c. Half of the Moon is always unlit by the Sun.
    d. Half of the Moon does not reflect light.

14. Why does the Moon seem to change shape from week to week?
    a. Clouds block part of the Moon.
    b. The Moon moves through Earth's shadow.
    c. The Moon is lit in different ways.
    d. Different amounts of the dark-colored side of the Moon face Earth.

15. Which words describe the different shapes that the Moon appears to be?
    a. waning and waxing
    b. waning and crescent
    c. waxing and gibbous
    d. crescent and gibbous

16. During a total eclipse of the Moon, the Moon is
    a. in Earth's umbra
    b. in Earth's penumbra
    c. between Earth and the Sun
    d. casting a shadow on Earth

Short Answer *Write a short answer to each question.*

17. What motion produces two high tides in a day? Explain your answer.

18. How are the structure of the Moon and the structure of Earth similar?

Thinking Critically

Use the lunar map below to answer the next four questions.

Near Side

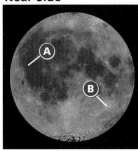

Far Side

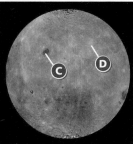

19. APPLY Which points are at higher elevations? Explain how you know.

20. COMPARE During a first-quarter moon, will point A, point B, both, or neither be in sunlight? **Hint:** Use the diagram on page 61.

21. INFER During a total lunar eclipse, which points will be in darkness?

22. INFER During a total solar eclipse, the Moon is new. Which points will be in darkness?

23. CONNECT Use your knowledge of the motions of Earth and the Moon to determine how long it takes the Moon to travel once around the Sun.

24. ANALYZE Which two parts of the Moon have important chemical elements in common? Choose from the following: core, mantle, crust, maria, highlands.

25. APPLY If it is noon for you, what time is it for someone directly on the opposite side of Earth?

26. CLASSIFY On what part or parts of Earth are winter and summer temperatures the most different from each other?

27. APPLY If it is the winter solstice in New York, what solstice or equinox is it in Sydney, Australia, in the Southern Hemisphere?

28. PREDICT If Earth stayed exactly the same distance from the Sun throughout the year, would the seasons be different? Explain what you think would happen.

29. PREDICT If Earth's axis were not tilted with respect to the orbit, would the seasons be different? Explain what you think would happen.

30. PROVIDE EXAMPLES How do the positions of the Sun and the Moon affect what people do? Give three examples of the ways that people's jobs or other activities are affected by the positions of the Sun, the Moon, or both.

31. PREDICT Which shape of the Moon are you most likely to see during the daytime? **Hint:** Compare the directions of the Sun and Moon from Earth in the diagram on page 61.

32. CLASSIFY What types of information have scientists used to make inferences about the Moon's history?

South Pole

33. ANALYZE The photograph above shows the side of Earth in sunlight at a particular time. The location of the South Pole is indicated. Was the photograph taken in March, in June, in September, or in December?

the BIG idea

34. APPLY Look again at the photograph on pages 40–41. Now that you have finished the chapter, how would you change your response to the question on the photograph?

35. SYNTHESIZE If you were an astronaut in the middle of the near side of the Moon during a full moon, how would the ground around you look? How would Earth, high in your sky, look? Describe what is in sunlight and what is in darkness.

UNIT PROJECTS

If you need to do an experiment for your unit project, gather the materials. Be sure to allow enough time to observe results before the project is due.

Analyzing a Diagram

*The sketches show the phases of the Moon one week apart. The diagram
shows the Moon's orbit around Earth. Use the diagram and the sketches to
answer the questions below.*

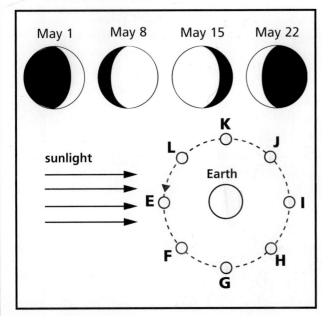

1. At which letter on the diagram might a full moon
occur?

a. E   c. I

b. G   d. J

2. Which letter on the diagram shows the position of
the Moon on May 8?

a. E   c. G

b. F   d. H

3. Approximately when was the Moon full?

a. May 4   c. May 18

b. May 11   d. May 29

4. At which letter on the diagram might a solar
eclipse occur?

a. E   c. I

b. H   d. L

5. How much of the sunlit part of the Moon was
visible from Earth on May 8?

a. None of the sunlit part was visible.

b. About one-quarter of the sunlit part was visible.

c. About three-quarters of the sunlit part
was visible.

d. All of the sunlit part was visible.

6. Which of these sketches show Earth's shadow on
the Moon?

a. those for May 1 and May 22

b. those for May 8 and May 15

c. all 4 of them

d. none of them

7. Which factor is most directly responsible for
determining how often a full moon appears?

a. the size of the Moon

b. the size of Earth

c. how quickly the Moon orbits Earth

d. how quickly the Moon turns on its axis

Extended Response

*Answer the two questions below in detail. A diagram
may help you to answer.*

8. The Moon was once much closer to Earth. What
effect do you think that this distance had
on eclipses?

9. What do you think would happen to tides on
Earth if Earth stopped rotating? Why?

TIMELINES in Science

THE STORY OF ASTRONOMY

Around the year A.D. 140, an astronomer named Ptolemy wrote down his ideas about the motion of bodies in space. Ptolemy shared the view of many Greek astronomers that the Sun, the Moon, and the planets orbit Earth in perfect circles. The Greeks had observed that planets sometimes seem to reverse direction in their motion across the sky. Ptolemy explained that the backward movements are smaller orbits within the larger orbits. For 1400 years, Europeans accepted this Earth-centered model. In the mid-1500s, however, astronomers began to challenge and then reject Ptolemy's ideas.

The timeline shows a few events in the history of astronomy. Scientists have developed special tools and procedures to study objects in the sky. The boxes below the timeline show how technology has led to new knowledge about space and how that knowledge has been applied.

1543

Sun Takes Center Stage

Nicolaus Copernicus, a Polish astronomer, proposes that the planets orbit the Sun rather than Earth. His Sun-centered model shocks many because it conflicts with the traditional belief that Earth is the center of the universe.

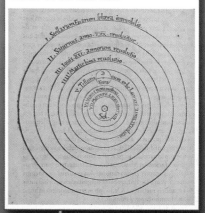

EVENTS

| 1500 | 1520 | 1540 | 1560 |

APPLICATIONS AND TECHNOLOGY

APPLICATION

Navigating by Sunlight and Starlight

For thousands of years, sailors studied the sky to find their way at sea. Because the Sun and stars move in predictable ways, sailors used them to navigate across water. During the 1400s, sailors began to use a device called a mariner's astrolabe to observe the positions of the Sun and stars. Later devices allowed sailors to make more accurate measurements.

This mariner's astrolabe was made in the 1600s.

1609

Scientist Pinpoints Planet Paths

German astronomer Johannes Kepler concludes that the orbits of planets are not circles but ellipses, or flattened circles. Kepler, formerly the assistant of Tycho Brahe, reached his conclusion by studying Brahe's careful observations of the motions of planets.

1863

Stars and Earth Share Elements

English astronomer William Huggins announces that stars are made of hydrogen and other elements found on Earth. Astronomers had traditionally believed that stars were made of a unique substance. Huggins identified the elements in stars by studying their spectra.

1687

Laws of Gravity Revealed

English scientist Isaac Newton explains that gravity causes planets to orbit the Sun. His three laws of motion explain how objects interact on Earth as well as in space.

| 1600 | 1620 | 1640 | 1660 | 1680 | 1860 |

TECHNOLOGY

Viewing Space

The telescope was probably invented in the early 1600s, when an eyeglass maker attached lenses to both ends of a tube. Soon afterward, Italian scientist Galileo Galilei copied the invention and used it to look at objects in space. Galileo's telescope allowed him to study features never seen before, such as mountains on the Moon. Most astronomers now use telescopes that gather visible light with mirrors rather than lenses. There are also special telescopes that gather other forms of electro-magnetic radiation.

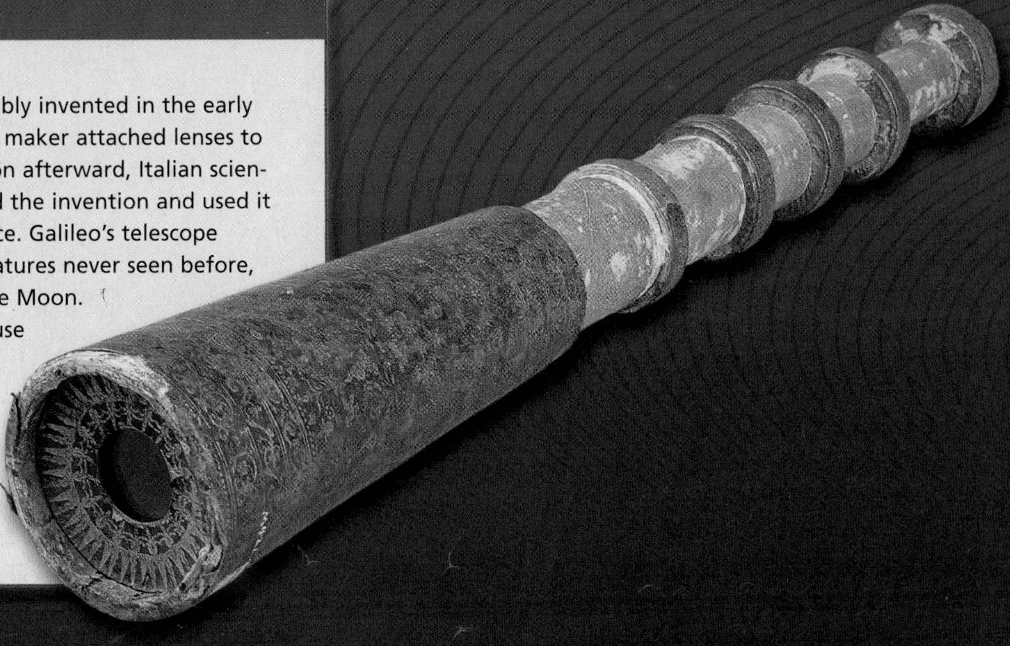

1912
Cycles of Stars Are Key to Distances

Certain types of stars, called Cepheid variables, get brighter and then dimmer in a regular cycle. Astronomer Henrietta Leavitt finds that brighter stars have longer cycles. This discovery will allow the distances to these stars to be calculated.

1916
Time, Space, and Mass Are Connected

The general theory of relativity expands Newton's theory of gravitation. Albert Einstein shows that mass affects time and space. According to this theory, gravity will affect the light we receive from objects in space.

1929
Big Is Getting Bigger

Edwin Hubble has already used Cepheid variables to show that some objects in the sky are actually distant galaxies. Now he finds that galaxies are generally moving apart, at rates that increase with distance. Many astronomers conclude that the universe is expanding.

| 1880 | 1900 | 1920 | 1940 | 1960 |

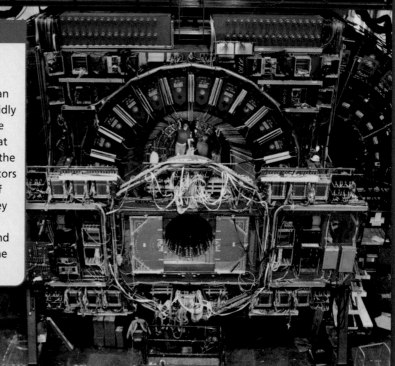

TECHNOLOGY

Colliding Particles Give Details About the Start of the Universe

Scientists think that all matter and energy was in an extremely hot, dense state and then exploded rapidly in an event called the big bang. Some scientists are attempting to re-create some of the conditions that existed during the first billionth of a second after the big bang. They use devices called particle accelerators to make tiny particles move almost at the speed of light. When the particles crash into each other, they produce different types of particles and radiation. Scientists use what they learn from the particles and the radiation to develop models of conditions at the beginning of the universe.

1998

Fast Is Getting Faster

Two groups of astronomers studying exploding stars called supernovae come to the same remarkable conclusion. Not only is the universe expanding, but the rate of expansion is increasing. In the diagram below, the rate of expansion is shown by the distances between rings and between galaxies.

The expanding universe

Present

Expansion slows down | Expansion speeds up

Big Bang

Farthest supernova

~15 billion years

RESOURCE CENTER
CLASSZONE.COM
Learn more about current advances in astronomy.

1980   2000

TECHNOLOGY

Measuring the Big Bang

In 1965 two researchers noticed radio waves that came from all directions instead of from just one direction, like a signal from a space object. They inferred that the radiation was left over from the big bang. In 1989 and again in 2001, NASA launched spacecraft to study the radiation. Data gathered using these telescopes in space are still being used to test different models of the big bang, including the arrangement of matter in the universe. In this map of the sky, red and yellow show the areas that were hottest after the big bang.

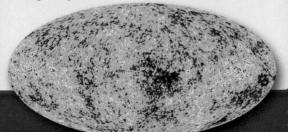

INTO THE FUTURE

Throughout history, people have learned about the universe from visible light and other radiation. New and better measurements have been made as technologies improved. Better and more complex models are filling in details that cannot be measured directly. In the future, improvements will continue. Computers, telescopes in space, and other instruments will allow astronomers to collect better data and make better models.

Some matter in the universe does not give off or reflect any detectable radiation. This is called dark matter. Astronomers infer its existence from its effects on matter that is detected. In the future, astronomers hope to determine what dark matter is, exactly where it is, and how it moves in the universe. In a similar way, astronomers will learn more about why the universe is expanding faster with time and what energy is involved in this acceleration.

ACTIVITIES

Reliving History

Some early astronomers observed the Moon in order to develop and test their ideas about space. For two weeks or more, make frequent observations of the Moon and keep your notes, sketches, and thoughts in a notebook. You might look for the Moon at a certain time each day or night or perhaps record the direction in which the Moon sets. A newspaper may list the times of moonrise and moonset for your location.

Compare your observations and thoughts with those of other students. You might also find out what people in other cultures thought of the patterns of change they saw in the Moon.

Writing About Science

Choose one of these famous astronomers and research his or her story. Write a biographical profile or an imaginary interview with that person.

CHAPTER

Our Solar System

the BIG idea

Planets and other objects form a system around our Sun.

Key Concepts

SECTION
3.1 **Planets orbit the Sun at different distances.**
Learn about the sizes and the distances of objects in the solar system and about its formation.

SECTION
3.2 **The inner solar system has rocky planets.**
Learn about the processes that shape Earth and other planets.

SECTION
3.3 **The outer solar system has four giant planets.**
Learn about the largest planets.

SECTION
3.4 **Small objects are made of ice and rock.**
Learn about moons, asteroids, and comets.

Internet Preview

CLASSZONE.COM

Chapter 3 online resources: Content Review, Visualization, two Resource Centers, Math Tutorial, Test Practice

This image shows Jupiter with one of its large moons. How big are these objects compared with Earth?

EXPLORE (the BIG idea)

How Big Is Jupiter?

Measure 1.4 mL of water (about 22 drops) into an empty 2 L bottle to represent Earth. Use a full 2 L bottle to represent Jupiter. Lift each one.

Observe and Think How big is Jupiter compared with Earth? Using this scale, you would need more than nine hundred 2 L bottles to represent the Sun. How big is the Sun compared with Jupiter?

How Round Is an Orbit?

Tie a loop 10 cm long in a piece of string. Place two thumbtacks 2 cm apart in the center of a piece of paper. Loop the string around the thumbtacks and use a pencil to draw an oval the shape of Pluto's orbit. Remove one thumbtack. The remaining thumbtack represents the Sun.

Observe and Think How would you describe the shape of this orbit? How different is it from a circle?

Internet Activity: Spacing

Go to **ClassZone.com** to take a virtual spaceflight through the solar system. Examine distances between planets as your virtual spaceship travels at a constant speed.

Observe and Think What do you notice about the relative distances of the planets?

NSTA
scilinks.org
SCiLINKS

The Solar System **Code: MDL059**

Getting Ready to Learn

◀ CONCEPT REVIEW

- The planets we see are much closer than the stars in constellations.
- The Sun, the planets, and smaller bodies make up the solar system.
- Scientists observe different types of electromagnetic radiation from space objects.

◀ VOCABULARY REVIEW

orbit p. 10

solar system p. 10

satellite p. 23

impact crater p. 32

axis of rotation p. 44

 CONTENT REVIEW
CLASSZONE.COM
Review concepts and vocabulary.

▶ TAKING NOTES

MAIN IDEA AND DETAILS

Make a two-column chart. Write **main ideas,** such as those in the blue headings, in the column on the left. Write **details** about each of those main ideas in the column on the right.

VOCABULARY STRATEGY

Draw a **word triangle** diagram for each new vocabulary term. In the bottom row write and define the term. In the middle row, use the term correctly in a sentence. At the top, draw a small picture to help you remember the term.

See the Note-Taking Handbook on pages R45–R51.

SCIENCE NOTEBOOK

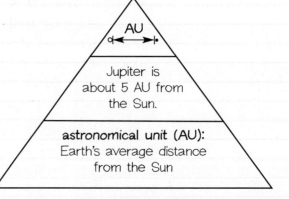

MAIN IDEAS	DETAIL NOTES
1. Planets have different sizes and distances.	1. Objects in the solar system • Sun • planets • moons • comets and asteroids
2.	2.

AU

Jupiter is about 5 AU from the Sun.

astronomical unit (AU): Earth's average distance from the Sun

3.1 Planets orbit the Sun at different distances.

 BEFORE, you learned

- Earth orbits the Sun
- The Moon is Earth's natural satellite
- The Moon's features tell us about its history

 NOW, you will learn

- What types of objects are in the solar system
- About sizes and distances in the solar system
- How the solar system formed

VOCABULARY

astronomical unit (AU) p. 81
ellipse p. 81

EXPLORE Planet Formation

How do planets form?

PROCEDURE

1. Fill the bowl about halfway with water.
2. Stir the water quickly, using a circular motion, and then remove the spoon.
3. Sprinkle wax pieces onto the swirling water.

WHAT DO YOU THINK?

- In what direction did the wax move?
- What else happened to the wax?

MATERIALS
- bowl
- water
- spoon
- wax pieces

Planets have different sizes and distances.

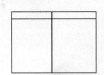

MAIN IDEA AND DETAILS
Put sizes and distances in the solar system into a chart.

You may have seen some planets in the sky without realizing it. They are so far from Earth that they appear as tiny dots of light in the darkened sky. If you have seen something that looks like a very bright star in the western sky in the early evening, you have probably seen the planet Venus. Even if you live in a city, you may have seen Mars, Jupiter, or Saturn but thought that you were seeing a star. Mercury is much more difficult to see. You need a telescope to see three of the planets in our solar system—Uranus, Neptune, and Pluto.

Like the Moon, planets can be seen because they reflect sunlight. Planets do not give off visible light of their own. Sunlight is also reflected by moons and other objects in space, called comets and asteroids. However, these objects are usually too far away and not bright enough to see without a telescope.

 Why do planets look bright?

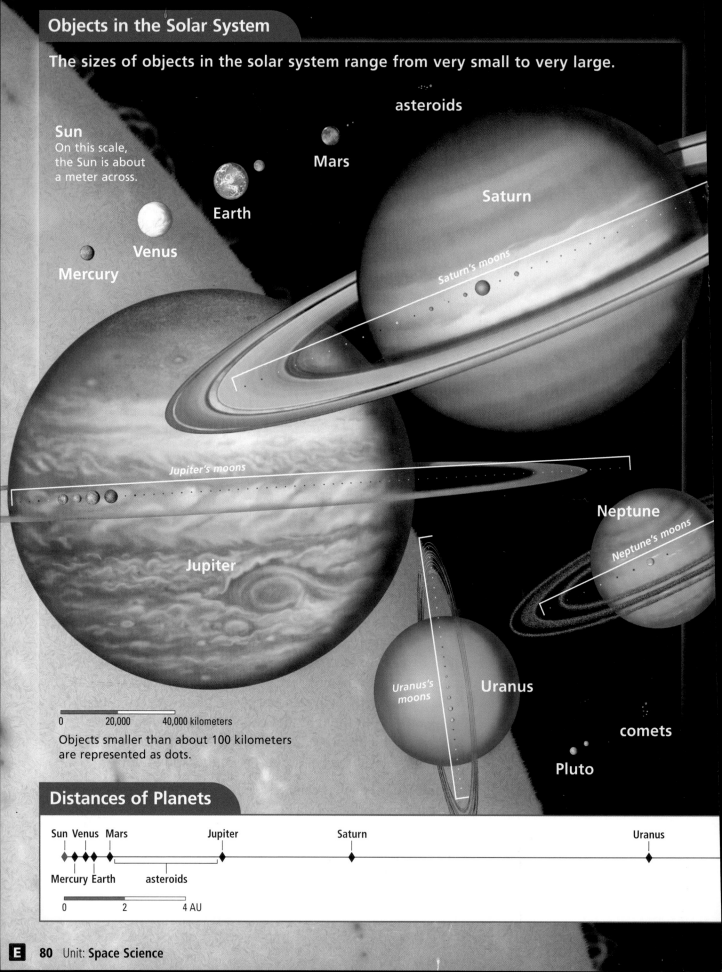

Objects in the Solar System

The sizes of objects in the solar system range from very small to very large.

asteroids

Sun
On this scale,
the Sun is about
a meter across.

Mars

Earth

Saturn

Venus

Saturn's moons

Mercury

Jupiter's moons

Neptune

Neptune's moons

Jupiter

Uranus's
moons

Uranus

0   20,000   40,000 kilometers

Objects smaller than about 100 kilometers
are represented as dots.

comets

Pluto

Distances of Planets

Sun	Venus	Mars		Jupiter		Saturn		Uranus

Mercury Earth   asteroids

0   2   4 AU

Objects in the solar system have very different sizes. An asteroid may be as small as a mountain, perhaps 1/1000 Earth's diameter. In contrast, the largest planets are about 10 Earth diameters across. The Sun's diameter is about 100 times Earth's. If the planets were the sizes shown on page 80, the Sun would be about a meter across.

Distances

The distances between most objects in space are huge in comparison with the objects' diameters. If Earth and the Sun were the sizes shown on page 80, they would be more than 100 meters from each other.

Astronomers understand huge distances by comparing them with something more familiar. One **astronomical unit,** or AU, is Earth's average distance from the Sun. An AU is about 150 million kilometers (93 million mi). Mercury is less than 0.5 AU from the Sun, Jupiter is about 5 AU from the Sun, and Pluto gets nearly 50 AU from the Sun at times. You can use the diagram at the bottom of pages 80–81 to compare these distances. However, the planets are not arranged in a straight line—they move around the Sun.

VOCABULARY
Draw word triangles in your notebook for new terms.

You can see that the planets are spaced unevenly. The first four planets are relatively close together and close to the Sun. They define a region called the inner solar system. Farther from the Sun is the outer solar system, where the planets are much more spread out.

 CHECK YOUR READING What are the two regions of the solar system?

Orbits

More than 99 percent of all the mass in the solar system is in the Sun. The gravitational pull of this huge mass causes planets and most other objects in the solar system to move around, or orbit, the Sun.

The shape of each orbit is an **ellipse**—a flattened circle or oval. A circle is a special type of ellipse, just as a square is a special type of rectangle. Most of the planets' orbits are very nearly circles. Only one planet—Pluto—has an orbit that looks a little flattened instead of round.

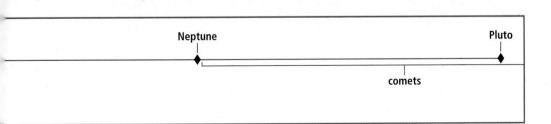

Neptune

Pluto

comets

INVESTIGATE Distances

How far apart are the planets?

PROCEDURE

1. Mark one sheet from the end of the roll of paper as the location of the Sun. Mark an *X* and write the word *Sun* with dots rather than lines.

2. Use the Distance Table data sheet to mark the distances for the rest of the solar system. Count sheets and estimate tenths of a sheet as necessary. Re-roll or fold the paper neatly.

3. Go to a space where you can unroll the paper. Compare the distances of planets as you walk along the paper and back again.

WHAT DO YOU THINK?

• How does the distance between Earth and Mars compare with the distance between Saturn and Uranus?

• How would you use the spacing to sort the planets into groups?

CHALLENGE If it took two years for the *Voyager 2* spacecraft to travel from Earth to Jupiter, about how long do you think it took for *Voyager 2* to travel from Jupiter to Neptune?

SKILL FOCUS
Using models

MATERIALS
• roll of toilet paper
• felt-tipped pen
• Distance Table

TIME
30 minutes

The solar system formed from a swirling cloud of gas and dust.

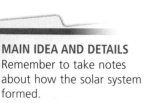

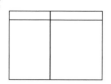

MAIN IDEA AND DETAILS
Remember to take notes about how the solar system formed.

The planets orbit the Sun in similar ways. Their paths are almost in a flat plane, like the rings of a target. They all orbit the Sun in the same direction—counterclockwise as seen from above Earth's North Pole. Most of the planets rotate on their axes in this direction, too. Many other objects in the solar system also orbit and rotate in this same direction. These similar motions have given scientists clues about how the solar system formed.

According to the best scientific model, the solar system formed out of a huge cloud of different gases and specks of dust. The cloud flattened into a disk of whirling material. Most of the mass fell to the center and became a star—the Sun. At the same time, tiny bits of dust and frozen gases in the disk stuck together into clumps. The clumps stuck together and became larger. Large clumps became planets. They moved in the same direction that the flat disk was turning.

Not all the clumps grew big enough to be called planets. However, many of these objects still orbit the Sun the same way that planets orbit. Some of the objects close to the Sun are like rocks or mountains in space and are called asteroids. Other objects, farther from the Sun, are more like enormous snowballs or icebergs. They are called comets.

Formation of the Solar System

The Sun and other objects formed out of material in a flat disk.

① Nebula

Part of a huge cloud of material, called a nebula, collapsed into a flattened disk.

② Disk

The Sun formed at the center of the disk. Other objects formed from the whirling material of the disk.

③ Solar System

Much of the material was cleared away. The Sun, planets, and other objects remained.

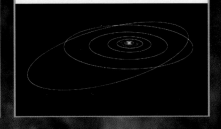

Some objects orbit planets instead of orbiting the Sun directly, so they are considered moons. You will read more about asteroids, comets, and moons in Section 3.4.

You can tell a little bit about the size of an object in space from its shape. Lumpy objects are usually much smaller than round objects. As a space object starts to form, the clumps come together from many directions and produce an uneven shape. The gravity of each part affects every other part. The pieces pull each other closer together. When an object has enough mass, this pulling becomes strong enough to make the object round. Any parts that would stick far out are pulled in toward the center until the object becomes a sphere.

 CHECK YOUR READING Why do planets and large moons have a spherical shape?

3.1 Review

KEY CONCEPTS

1. What are the types of space objects in the solar system?

2. Why is the unit of measurement used for the distances of planets from the Sun different from the unit used for their sizes?

3. How did planets and other objects in the solar system form out of material in a disk?

CRITICAL THINKING

4. **Analyze** Why do the planets all orbit in one direction?

5. **Infer** Which of the two moons below has more mass? Explain why you think so.

⬥ CHALLENGE

6. **Apply** Could you model all the sizes of objects in the solar system by using sports balls? Explain why or why not.

This picture of Buzz Aldrin on the Moon was taken by Neil Armstrong, who can be seen reflected in Aldrin's helmet.

MATH TUTORIAL
CLASSZONE.COM
Click on Math Tutorial for more help with the percent equation.

How Much Would You Weigh on Other Worlds?

When astronauts walked on the Moon, they felt much lighter than they felt when they were on Earth. Neil Armstrong's total mass—about 160 kilograms with space suit and backpack—did not change. However, the Moon did not pull as hard on him as Earth did, so he weighed less on the Moon. At the surface, the Moon's gravitational pull is only 17% of Earth's gravitational pull. You can use percentages to calculate Neil Armstrong's weight on the Moon.

Example

On Earth, with his heavy space suit and backpack, Neil Armstrong weighed about 1600 newtons (360 lb). To calculate his weight on the Moon, find 17% of 1600 newtons.

"Of" means "multiply."   17% of 1600 N = 17% × 1600 N

Change the percent to a decimal fraction.   = 0.17 × 1600 N

Simplify.   = 272 N

ANSWER With his suit and backpack, Neil Armstrong weighed about 270 newtons on the Moon.

Use the percentages in the table to answer the following questions.

1. A backpack weighs 60 newtons (13 lb) on Earth. **(a)** How much would it weigh on Jupiter? **(b)** How much would it weigh on Jupiter's moon Io?

2. **(a)** How much would a student weighing 500 newtons (110 lb) on Earth weigh on Saturn? **(b)** on Venus?

3. On which planet or moon would you be lightest?

CHALLENGE A pencil weighs 0.3 newtons (1 oz) on Earth. How much would it weigh on the Moon? If an astronaut let go of the pencil on the Moon, would the pencil fall? Explain.

Percent of Weight on Earth	
Planet or Moon	**%**
Mercury	38
Venus	91
Earth	100
Moon (Earth)	17
Mars	38
Jupiter	236
Io (Jupiter)	18
Europa (Jupiter)	13
Ganymede (Jupiter)	15
Callisto (Jupiter)	13
Saturn	92
Titan (Saturn)	14
Uranus	89
Neptune	112
Triton (Neptune)	8.0
Pluto	6.7
Charon (Pluto)	2.8

3.2 The inner solar system has rocky planets.

 BEFORE, you learned

- Planets are closer together in the inner solar system than in the outer solar system
- Planets formed along with the Sun
- Gravity made planets round

NOW, you will learn

- How four processes change the surfaces of solid planets
- How atmospheres form and then affect planets
- What the planets closest to the Sun are like

VOCABULARY

terrestrial planet p. 85
tectonics p. 86
volcanism p. 86

EXPLORE Surfaces

How does a planet's mantle affect its surface?

PROCEDURE

1. Dampen a paper towel and place it on top of two blocks to model a crust and a mantle.

2. Move one block. Try different amounts of motion and different directions.

WHAT DO YOU THINK?

- What happened to the paper towel?
- What landforms like this have you seen?

MATERIALS

- 2 blocks
- paper towel
- newspaper

The terrestrial planets have rocky crusts.

Scientists study Earth to learn about other planets. They also study other planets to learn more about Earth. The **terrestrial planets** are Mercury, Venus, Earth, and Mars—the four planets closest to the Sun. They all have rocky crusts and dense mantles and cores. Their insides, surfaces, and atmospheres formed in similar ways and follow similar patterns. One planet—Earth—can be used as a model to understand the others. In fact, the term *terrestrial* comes from *terra*, the Latin word for Earth.

Earth

Most of Earth's rocky surface is hidden by water. More details about Earth and other planets are listed in the Appendix at the back of this book.

Mass 6×10^{24} kg
Diameter 12,800 km
Average distance from Sun 1 AU

Orbits in 365 days
Rotates in 24 hours

Processes and Surface Features

All terrestrial planets have layers. Each planet gained energy from the collisions that formed it. This energy heated and melted the planet's materials. The heaviest materials were metals, which sank to the center and formed a core. Lighter rock formed a mantle around the core. The lightest rock rose to the surface and cooled into a crust.

Four types of processes then shaped each planet's rocky crust. The processes acted to different extents on each planet, depending on how much the crust and inside of the planet cooled.

READING TiP

Compare what you read about each type of feature with the pictures and diagrams on page 87.

① Tectonics Earth's crust is split into large pieces called tectonic plates. These plates are moved by Earth's hot mantle. Mountains, valleys, and other features form as the plates move together, apart, or along each other. The crusts of other terrestrial planets are not split into plates but can be twisted, wrinkled up, or stretched out by the mantle. **Tectonics** is the processes of change in a crust due to the motion of hot material underneath. As a planet cools, the crust gets stiffer and the mantle may stop moving, so this process stops.

② Volcanism A second process, called **volcanism,** occurs when molten rock moves from a planet's hot interior onto its surface. The molten rock is called lava when it reaches the surface through an opening called a volcano. On Earth, lava often builds up into mountains. Volcanoes are found on Earth, Venus, and Mars. Lava can also flow onto large areas and cool into flat plains like the lunar maria. When the inside of a planet cools enough, no more molten rock reaches the surface.

③ Weathering and Erosion You have read about weathering on Earth and the Moon. Weather or small impacts break down rocks. The broken material is moved by a group of processes called erosion. The material may form dunes, new layers of rock, or other features. On Earth, water is important for weathering and erosion. However, similar things happen even without water. Wind can carry sand grains that batter at rocks and form new features. Even on a planet without air, rock breaks down from being heated in the daylight and cooled at night. The material is pulled downhill by gravity.

RESOURCE CENTER
CLASSZONE.COM

Find out more about impact craters on Earth and other space objects.

④ Impact Cratering A small object sometimes hits a planet's surface so fast that it causes an explosion. The resulting impact crater is often ten times larger than the object that produced it. On Earth, most craters have been erased by other processes. Impact craters are easier to find on other planets. If a planet or part of a planet is completely covered with impact craters, then the other processes have not changed the surface much in billions of years.

CHECK YOUR READING What processes affect the surfaces of terrestrial planets?

Features of Rocky Planets

The processes that shape features on a planet's surface can be divided into four types. The features can tell you different things about the planet.

① Tectonics

A hot mantle can move and distort the crust above it. This system of mountains and valleys on **Earth** formed as the crust was stretched.

② Volcanism

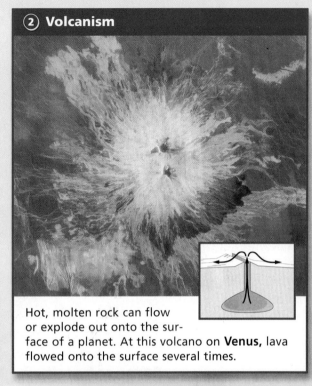

Hot, molten rock can flow or explode out onto the surface of a planet. At this volcano on **Venus,** lava flowed onto the surface several times.

③ Weathering and Erosion

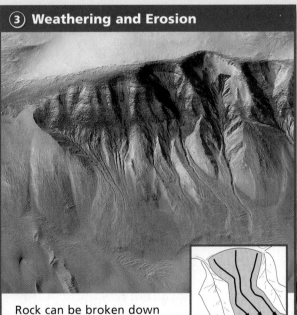

Rock can be broken down and moved. In this region of **Mars,** material broken from a cliff was moved by erosion into new slopes and dunes.

④ Impact Cratering

A small space object can hit a planet's surface and leave a crater. Because the other processes on **Mercury** are weak, newer craters can be seen on a background of older, more eroded craters.

READING VISUALS Which two processes happen because of hot material beneath the surface?

INVESTIGATE Layers

How do the layers inside of planets form?

In this model, the materials you use represent different rocks and metals that make up the solid planets.

PROCEDURE

1. Put pieces of gelatin into the container until it is about one-quarter full.

2. Mix in a spoonful each of sand and wax. Use the spoon to break the gelatin into small pieces as you mix. Remove the spoon.

3. Place the container in a bowl of hot tap water (about 70°C) and observe what happens as the gelatin melts.

WHAT DO YOU THINK?

• What happened to each of the materials when the gelatin melted?

• How do the results resemble the core, mantle, and crust of Earth and other planets?

CHALLENGE How might you improve this model?

SKILL FOCUS
Using models

MATERIALS
• container
• spoon
• firm gelatin
• sand
• wax pieces
• bowl of hot tap water

TIME
40 minutes

Atmospheres

Atmospheres on terrestrial planets mainly formed from gases that poured out of volcanoes. If a planet's gravity is strong enough, it pulls the gases in and keeps them near the surface. If a planet's gravity is too weak, the gases expand into outer space and are lost.

Venus, Earth, and Mars each had gravity strong enough to hold heavy gases such as carbon dioxide. However, the lightest gases—hydrogen and helium—escaped into outer space. The atmospheres of Venus and Mars are mostly carbon dioxide.

An atmosphere can move energy from warmer places to cooler places. This movement of heat energy makes temperatures more uniform between a planet's day side and its night side and between its equator and its poles. An atmosphere can also make a planet's whole surface warmer by slowing the loss of energy from the surface.

After Earth formed, its atmosphere of carbon dioxide kept the surface warm enough for water to be liquid. Oceans covered most of Earth's surface. The oceans changed the gases of the atmosphere, and living organisms caused even more changes. Earth's atmosphere is now mostly nitrogen with some oxygen.

 CHECK YOUR READING Why is the solid Earth surrounded by gases?

Craters cover the surface of Mercury.

Mercury, like the Moon, has smooth plains and many craters. The processes at work on Earth also affected Mercury.

Tectonics Long, high cliffs stretch across Mercury's surface. Scientists think that Mercury's huge core of iron shrank when it cooled long ago. The crust wrinkled up, forming cliffs, as the planet got a little smaller.

Volcanism Parts of the surface were covered with lava long ago. Large, smooth plains formed. The plains are similar to lunar maria.

Weathering and Erosion Small impacts and temperature changes have broken rock. Gravity has moved broken material downhill.

Impact Cratering Round features cover much of the surface. These craters show that the other processes have not changed Mercury's surface very much for a long time.

Mercury has the longest cycle of day and night of the terrestrial planets—three months of daylight and three months of darkness. There is no atmosphere to move energy from the hot areas to the cold areas. In the long daytime, it can get hotter than 420°C (about 800°F)—hot enough to melt lead. During the long, cold night, the temperature can drop lower than –170°C (about –280°F).

—no data

Mercury

This map of Mercury was made from many images taken by one spacecraft. The blank patches show areas that were not mapped by the spacecraft.

Mass 6% of Earth's mass

Diameter 38% of Earth's diameter

Average distance from Sun 0.39 AU

Orbits in 88 Earth days

Rotates in 59 Earth days

CHECK YOUR READING How is Mercury similar to the Moon?

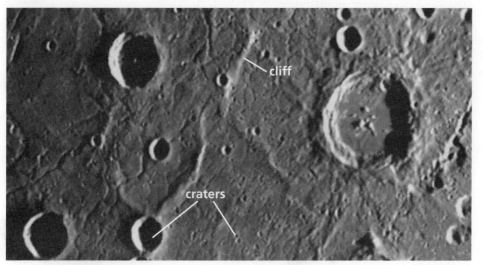
cliff

craters

Craters of all sizes cover Mercury's surface, but there are also flat lava plains and cliffs from long ago.

Volcanoes shape the surface of Venus.

The planet Venus is only a little smaller than Earth and orbits a little closer to the Sun. As a result, Venus is sometimes called Earth's sister planet. However, Venus is different from Earth in important ways.

Venus takes about eight months to turn just once on its axis. Unlike most other planets, Venus rotates and orbits in opposite directions. The rotation and orbit together produce very long days and nights—two months of daylight followed by two months of darkness.

The atmosphere of Venus is very dense. Air pressure on Venus is 90 times that on Earth. Venus's atmosphere is mostly carbon dioxide. This gas slows the loss of energy and makes the surface very hot. The ground temperature on Venus is about 470°C (about 870°F). The atmosphere of Venus moves energy around so well that the long nights are as hot as the days and the poles are as hot as the equator. In addition, there are droplets of sulfuric acid, a corrosive chemical, in the atmosphere. These droplets form thick white clouds that completely cover the planet and hide the surface.

Like Mercury, Venus is affected by the same four types of processes that change Earth's surface. Scientists think that tectonics and volcanism may still be changing Venus's surface today.

Tectonics Patterns of cracks and cliffs have formed as movements of the hot mantle have stretched, wrinkled, and twisted the surface.

Volcanism Most of the surface of Venus has been covered with lava in the last billion years or so. Volcanoes and flat lava plains are found all over the surface.

Thick clouds make it impossible to see Venus's surface in visible light. This inset shows a map of Venus that scientists made using radio waves.

Venus

Venus is nearly the size of Earth but has a thicker atmosphere and is much hotter than Earth. The surface is rocky, as you can see in the image below.

Mass 82% of Earth's mass
Diameter 95% of Earth's diameter
Average distance from Sun 0.72 AU

Orbits in 225 Earth days
Rotates in 243 Earth days

weathered and eroded rock

spacecraft

Weathering and Erosion Venus is too hot to have liquid water, and the winds do not seem to move much material. Erosion may be slower on Venus than on Earth.

Impact Cratering Round craters mark the surface here and there. Older craters have been erased by the other processes. Also, Venus's thick atmosphere protects the surface from small impacts.

 Why is Venus not covered with craters?

Erosion changes the appearance of Mars.

Mars is relatively small, with a diameter about half that of Earth. The orange color of some of the surface comes from molecules of iron and oxygen—rust. Mars has two tiny moons. They were probably once asteroids that were pulled into orbit around Mars.

Surface of Mars

The same processes that affect the other terrestrial planets affect Mars.

Tectonics Valleys and raised areas formed on Mars as the mantle moved. One huge system of valleys, called Valles Marineris, is long enough to stretch across the United States.

Volcanism Most of the northern hemisphere has smooth plains of cooled lava. Several volcanoes are higher than any mountain on Earth. The lava must have built up in the same spot for a long time, so scientists have inferred that the crust of Mars has cooled more than Earth's crust. On Earth, the tectonic plates move, so chains of smaller volcanoes form instead of single larger volcanoes.

Weathering and Erosion Fast winds carry sand that breaks down rocks. Wind and gravity move the broken material, forming new features such as sand dunes. There are also landforms that look like the results of gigantic flash floods that happened long ago.

Impact Cratering Round craters cover much of the southern hemisphere of Mars. Many craters are very old and eroded. A few impact craters on the volcanoes make scientists think that the volcanoes have not released lava for a long time.

Mars

The atmosphere of Mars is thin but causes weathering and erosion.

Mass 11% of Earth's mass
Diameter 53% of Earth's diameter
Average distance from Sun 1.5 AU
Orbits in 1.9 Earth years
Rotates in 25 hours

volcanoes

Valles Marineris

red dust carried by wind

distant hills

weathered and eroded rock

The sky of Mars is made red by dust that the wind picks up and carries to new places.

Gases and Water on Mars

The atmosphere of Mars is mostly carbon dioxide. The air pressure is only about 1 percent of the air pressure on Earth. The gas is not dense enough to keep the surface warm or to move much energy from cold areas to warmer areas. Therefore, temperatures may reach almost 20°C (about 60°F) in the daytime and −90°C (−130°F) at night. The large differences in temperature produce fast winds. The winds cause gigantic dust storms that sometimes cover most of the planet.

Like Earth, Mars has polar caps that grow in winter and shrink in summer. However, the changing polar caps of Mars are made mostly of frozen carbon dioxide—dry ice. The carbon dioxide of the atmosphere can also form clouds, fog, and frost on the ground.

There is no liquid water on the surface of Mars today. Any water would quickly evaporate or freeze. However, there were floods in the past, and there is still frozen water in the ground and in one polar cap. Water is important for life and will also be needed to make rocket fuel if humans are ever to make trips to Mars and back.

 CHECK YOUR READING In what ways is Mars different from Earth?

3.2 Review

KEY CONCEPTS

1. What are the four types of processes that shape planets' surfaces? For each, give one example of a feature that the process can produce.

2. How can an atmosphere affect the temperature of a planet's surface?

3. Which terrestrial planet has the oldest, least-changing surface?

CRITICAL THINKING

4. **Compare and Contrast** Make a chart with columns for the four types of processes and for an atmosphere. Fill out a row for each planet.

5. **Apply** If a planet had a surface with craters but no other features, what could you say about the inside of the planet?

● CHALLENGE

6. **Infer** Describe how a hot mantle can affect a planet's atmosphere. **Hint**: Which of the four processes is involved?

What Shapes the Surface of Mars?

Many features on Mars, when seen close up, look a lot like features found on Earth. Astronomers use their knowledge of the four types of processes that affect the terrestrial planets to hypothesize about the features on Mars. Using what you know about the processes, make your own hypotheses to explain the features in the image to the left.

▶ Results of Research

- Small objects hit the surface, producing craters.
- Volcanoes erupt, creating mountains and flows of lava.
- The mantle moves the crust, producing mountains and valleys.
- Wind, water, and gravity move material on the surface, eroding some places and building up others.

▶ Observations

- Dark, raised triangles point roughly east.
- Patterns of light stripes run mostly north-south between the dark hills.
- The features are inside a huge impact crater.

dark hills

light stripes

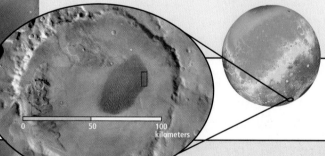

The large image shows details of the area in the red rectangle.

The black oval on the globe shows the location of the crater.

0   50   100 kilometers

▶ Form a Hypothesis

On Your Own Consider one or more processes that might produce the hills and stripes seen in the image at left.

As a Group With a small group discuss possible hypotheses to explain the formation of these features. See if the group can agree on which one is most reasonable.

CHALLENGE Create a model that you can use to test your hypothesis. What will you use to represent the surface of Mars and the forces acting on it?

0   0.5   1.0 kilometers

KEY CONCEPT

3.3 The outer solar system has four giant planets.

BEFORE, you learned	NOW, you will learn
• Planets formed along with the Sun • Vast distances separate planets • The gravity of a terrestrial planet may be strong enough to hold the heavier gases	• About the four giant planets in the solar system • What the atmospheres of giant planets are like • About the rings of giant planets

VOCABULARY

gas giant p. 94
ring p. 97

THINK ABOUT

What is Jupiter like inside?

Most of Jupiter's huge mass is hidden below layers of clouds. Scientists learn about Jupiter by studying its gravity, its magnetic field, its motions, and its radiation. Scientists also use data from other space bodies to make models, from which they make predictions. Then they observe Jupiter to test their predictions. What might it be like under Jupiter's clouds?

The gas giants have very deep atmospheres.

VOCABULARY
Remember to draw a word triangle when you read a new term.

You have already read about the four rocky planets in the inner solar system, close to the Sun. Beyond Mars stretches the outer solar system, where the four largest planets slowly orbit the Sun. The **gas giants**— Jupiter, Saturn, Uranus (YUR-uh-nuhs), and Neptune—are made mainly of hydrogen, helium, and other gases.

When you think of gases, you probably think of Earth's air, which is not very dense. However, the giant planets are so large and have such large amounts of these gases that they have a lot of mass. The huge gravitational force from such a large mass is enough to pull the gas particles close together and make the atmosphere very dense. Inside the giant planets, the gases become more dense than water. The outermost parts are less dense and more like Earth's atmosphere.

 CHECK YOUR READING Why are the gas giants dense inside?

The atmosphere of a giant planet is very deep. Imagine traveling into one. At first, the atmosphere is thin and very cold. There may be a haze of gases. A little lower is a layer of clouds that reflect sunlight, just like clouds on Earth. There are strong winds and other weather patterns. Lower down, it is warmer and there are layers of clouds of different materials. As you go farther, the atmosphere gradually becomes dense enough to call a liquid. It also gets thousands of degrees hotter as you get closer to the center of the planet. The materials around you become more and more dense until they are solid. Scientists think that each of the four gas giants has a solid core, larger than Earth, deep in its center.

Interior of a Giant Planet

Jupiter

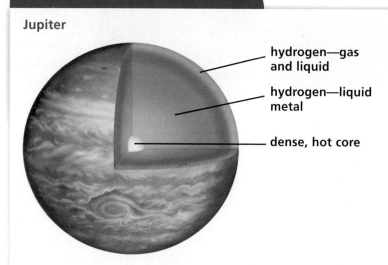

hydrogen—gas and liquid

hydrogen—liquid metal

dense, hot core

Jupiter is a world of storms and clouds.

Jupiter is the largest planet in the solar system. It is more than 10 times larger than Earth in diameter and more than 1200 times larger in volume. A jet plane that could circle Earth in about 2 days would take 23 days to circle Jupiter. If you could weigh the planets on a cosmic scale, all the other planets put together would weigh less than half as much as Jupiter.

Jupiter is more than five times farther from the Sun than Earth is. It moves more slowly through space than Earth and has a greater distance to travel in each orbit. Jupiter takes 12 Earth years to go once around the Sun.

Even though it is big, Jupiter takes less than 10 hours to turn once on its axis. This fast rotation produces fast winds and stormy weather. Like Earth, Jupiter has bands of winds that blow eastward and westward, but Jupiter has many more bands than Earth does.

Jupiter

Jupiter's colorful stripes are produced by clouds at different levels in Jupiter's deep atmosphere.

Mass 318 Earth masses
Diameter 11 Earth diameters
Average distance from Sun 5.2 AU
Orbits in 12 Earth years
Rotates in 9.9 hours

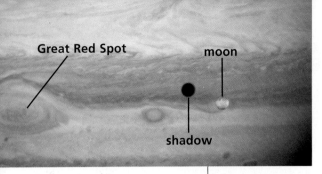

Great Red Spot

moon

shadow

This image shows one of Jupiter's moons casting a shadow on Jupiter. If you were in that shadow, you would experience a solar eclipse.

Stripes of cold clouds form along the bands. The clouds look white because they are made of crystals that reflect sunlight. The crystals in these high white clouds are frozen ammonia rather than frozen water, as on Earth. Between Jupiter's white bands of clouds, you can see down to the next layer. The lower clouds are brown or red and made of different chemicals. Sometimes there are clear patches in the brown clouds, where the next layer of bluish clouds shows through.

CHECK YOUR READING What are Jupiter's white stripes?

Storms can form between bands of winds that blow in opposite directions. Because Jupiter has no land to slow the storms, they can last for a long time. The largest of these storms is the Great Red Spot, which is twice as wide as Earth and at least 100 years old. Its clouds rise even higher than the white ammonia-ice clouds. Scientists are trying to find out which chemicals produce the spot's reddish color.

Saturn has large rings.

REMINDER

Density is the amount of mass in a given volume. An object of low density can still have a great total mass if it has a large volume.

The sixth planet from the Sun is Saturn. Saturn is only a little smaller than Jupiter, but its mass is less than one-third that of Jupiter. Because there is less mass, the gravitational pull is weaker, so the gas particles can spread out more. As a result, Saturn has a much lower density than Jupiter. The storms and stripes of clouds form deeper in Saturn's atmosphere than in Jupiter's, so the details are harder to see.

Saturn

Saturn has an average density less than that of liquid water on Earth. The diameter of Saturn's ring system is almost as great as the distance from Earth to the Moon.

Mass 95 Earth masses

Diameter 9 Earth diameters

Average distance from Sun 9.5 AU

Orbits in 29 Earth years

Rotates in 11 hours

Saturn was the first planet known to have rings. A planetary **ring** is a wide, flat zone of small particles that orbit a planet. All four gas giants have rings around their equators. Saturn's rings are made of chunks of water ice the size of a building or smaller. Larger chunks, considered to be tiny moons, orbit within the rings. Saturn's main rings are very bright. The outermost ring is three times as wide as the planet, but it is usually too faint to see. Saturn's rings have bright and dark stripes that change over time.

You can use Saturn's rings to see the planet's seasons. Like Earth's axis of rotation, Saturn's axis is tilted. The angle is 27 degrees. When the image on this page was taken, sunlight shone more on the northern hemisphere, so the north side of the rings was bright. The shadow of the rings fell on the southern hemisphere. Winter started in Saturn's northern hemisphere in May 2003 and will last more than seven Earth years. Saturn is almost ten times farther from the Sun than Earth is, so Saturn takes almost 30 Earth years to go around the Sun once.

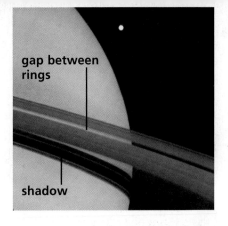

gap between rings

shadow

Sunlight shines from the upper right of this image. The rings cast shadows on Saturn's clouds.

INVESTIGATE Giant Planets

Why do Saturn's rings seem to change size?

PROCEDURE

1. Poke the stick through the plate and cut off the plate's rim. Shape the clay onto both sides of the plate to make a model of a planet with rings.

2. Model Saturn's orbit for your partner. Stand between your partner and the classroom clock. Point one end of the stick at the clock. Hold the model at the same height as your partner's eyes. Have your partner watch the model with just one eye open.

3. Move one step counterclockwise around your partner and point the stick at the clock again. Make sure the model is as high as your partner's eyes. Your partner may need to turn to see the model.

4. Continue taking steps around your partner and pointing the stick at the clock until you have moved the model all the way around your partner.

5. Switch roles with your partner and repeat steps 2, 3, and 4.

WHAT DO YOU THINK?

- How did your view of the rings change as the model planet changed position?

- How many times per orbit do the rings seem to vanish?

CHALLENGE How do Saturn's axis and orbit compare with those of Earth?

SKILL FOCUS
Observing

MATERIALS
- ice-cream stick
- disposable plate
- scissors
- clay

TIME
20 minutes

Uranus and Neptune are extremely cold.

The seventh and eighth planets from the Sun are Uranus and Neptune. These planets are similar in size—both have diameters roughly one-third that of Jupiter. Unlike Jupiter and Saturn, Uranus and Neptune are only about 15 percent hydrogen and helium. Most of the mass of each planet is made up of heavier gases, such as methane, ammonia, and water. As a result, Uranus and Neptune are more dense than Jupiter.

Uranus looks blue-green, and Neptune appears deep blue. The color comes from methane gas, which absorbs certain colors of light. Each planet has methane gas above a layer of white clouds. Sunlight passes through the gas, reflects off the clouds, then passes through the gas again on its way out. The gas absorbs the red, orange, and yellow parts of sunlight, so each planet's bluish color comes from the remaining green, blue, and violet light that passes back out of the atmosphere.

Uranus is a smooth blue-green in visible light. The small infrared image shows that the pole facing the Sun is warmer than the equator.

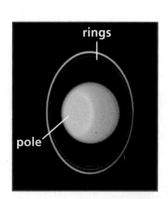

rings

pole

Uranus

Uranus is about twice Saturn's distance from the Sun. The farther a planet is from the Sun, the more slowly it moves along its orbit. The greater distance also results in a larger orbit, so it takes Uranus 84 Earth years to travel around the Sun.

Like the other gas giants, Uranus has a system of rings and moons around its equator. The ring particles and moons orbit Uranus in the same direction as the planet's spin. Unlike the other planets, Uranus has an axis of rotation that is almost in the plane of its orbit. As a result, Uranus seems to spin on its side. During a solstice, one pole of Uranus points almost straight toward the Sun.

Some scientists think that there was a large collision early in Uranus's history. The result left the planet and its system spinning at an unusual angle.

Uranus

Each pole of Uranus experiences more than 40 years of sunlight and then more than 40 years of darkness as the planet orbits the Sun.

Mass 15 Earth masses

Diameter 4 Earth diameters

Average distance from Sun 19 AU

Orbits in 84 Earth years

Rotates in 17 hours

Neptune

Neptune orbits about 10 AU farther from the Sun than Uranus, so you would expect it to be colder. However, Neptune has about the same outside temperature as Uranus because it is hotter inside.

Uranus is usually one smooth color, but light and dark areas often appear on Neptune. Clouds of methane ice crystals can form high enough in the atmosphere of Neptune to look white.

Storm systems can appear in darker shades of blue than the rest of the planet. One storm, seen during the flyby of the *Voyager 2* spacecraft in 1989, was named the Great Dark Spot. Unlike the huge storm on Jupiter, the Great Dark Spot did not stay at the same latitude. It moved toward Neptune's equator. The winds there may have broken up the storm. Images of Neptune obtained a few years later with the Hubble Space Telescope showed no sign of the Great Dark Spot.

CHECK YOUR READING What are the white patches often seen on Neptune?

Neptune

Neptune has a large moon that orbits in a direction opposite to Neptune's rotation. Scientists think a giant collision might have occurred in Neptune's past.

Mass 17 Earth masses
Diameter 4 Earth diameters
Average distance from Sun 30 AU
Orbits in 164 Earth years
Rotates in 16 hours

High clouds cast shadows on the layer below.

cloud

shadow

3.3 Review

KEY CONCEPTS

1. Which planet has a greater mass than all the other planets put together?
2. What do you see instead of a solid surface when you look at an image of a giant planet?
3. Which planets have rings?

CRITICAL THINKING

4. **Compare and Contrast** Why do Jupiter and Saturn show a lot of white, while Uranus and Neptune are more blue in color?
5. **Analyze** Most of Saturn is much less dense than most of Earth. Yet Saturn's mass is much greater than Earth's mass. How can this be so?

◯ CHALLENGE

6. **Apply** If Uranus had areas of ice crystals high in its atmosphere, how would its appearance change?

3.4 Small objects are made of ice and rock.

 BEFORE, you learned

- Smaller bodies formed with the Sun and planets
- Planets in the inner solar system consist of rock and metal
- The outer solar system is cold

 NOW, you will learn

- About Pluto and the moons of the giant planets
- How asteroids and comets are similar and different
- What happens when tiny objects hit Earth's atmosphere

VOCABULARY

asteroid p. 103
comet p. 104
meteor p. 105
meteorite p. 105

THINK ABOUT

Do small space bodies experience erosion?

Very small bodies in space often have potato-like shapes. Some are covered with dust, boulders, and craters. Solar radiation can break down material directly or by heating and cooling a surface. Broken material can slide downhill, even on a small asteroid. What other processes do you think might act on small and medium-sized bodies in space?

Pluto and most objects in the outer solar system are made of ice and rock.

READING TIP

The name of Earth's satellite is the Moon, but the word *moon* is also used to refer to other satellites.

The materials in a space body depend on where it formed. The disk of material that became the solar system was cold around the outside and hottest in the center, where the Sun was forming. Far from the center, chemicals such as carbon dioxide, ammonia, and water were frozen solid. These ices became part of the material that formed bodies in the outer solar system. Bodies that formed near the center of the solar system are made mostly of rock and metal. Bodies that formed far from the center are mostly ice with some rock and a little metal.

Some of the bodies had enough mass to become rounded. Some even melted and formed cores, mantles, and crusts. Many of these bodies have mountains and valleys, volcanoes, and even winds and clouds. The processes at work on Earth also affect other space bodies.

 CHECK YOUR READING What do the proportions of ice, rock, and metal show about a space object?

Pluto and Charon

Many space bodies of ice and rock orbit the Sun at the distance of Neptune and beyond. Since 1992, scientists have been using sophisticated equipment to find and study these bodies. However, one body has been known since 1930. Because Pluto was discovered decades before the other objects, it is considered one of the nine major planets.

Pluto is the smallest of the nine planets. It is smaller than the Moon. Pluto's mass is less than 0.3 percent of Earth's mass, so its gravitational pull is weak. However, Pluto is round and probably has a core, mantle, and crust. Pluto also has a thin atmosphere. No spacecraft has passed close to Pluto, so scientists do not have clear images of the planet's surface.

CHECK YOUR READING Why do scientists know less about Pluto than about other planets?

Pluto's moon, Charon, has a diameter half that of Pluto and a mass about 15 percent of Pluto's. Because Pluto and Charon orbit each other, they are sometimes called a double planet. Just as the Moon always has the same side facing Earth, Pluto and Charon always keep the same sides turned toward each other.

Pluto and Charon also move together around the Sun. Pluto's path around the Sun is not as round as the orbits of the rest of the planets, so its distance from the Sun changes a lot as it orbits. Pluto gets closer to the Sun than Neptune's distance of 30 AU. At the other side of its orbit, Pluto is about 50 AU from the Sun. Pluto's orbit is at an angle with respect to Neptune's, as you can see in the diagram below, so the two paths do not cross and the planets will not collide.

Pluto

This map of Pluto's surface shows only bright and dark areas because Pluto is very distant from Earth and no spacecraft has been close enough to see Pluto's surface in detail.

Mass 0.2% Earth's mass
Diameter 18% Earth's diameter
Average distance from Sun 40 AU
Orbits in 248 Earth years
Rotates in 6 Earth days

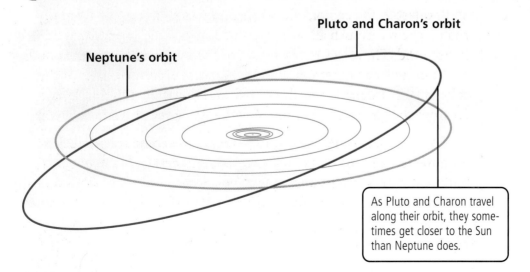

Pluto and Charon's orbit

Neptune's orbit

As Pluto and Charon travel along their orbit, they sometimes get closer to the Sun than Neptune does.

Moons of Gas Giants

RESOURCE CENTER
CLASSZONE.COM

Learn more about the different moons of giant planets.

Each giant planet has a system of moons. Six of the moons are larger than Pluto. Their features are formed by the same processes that shape the terrestrial planets. Saturn's largest moon, Titan, has a dense atmosphere of nitrogen, as Earth does, although a haze hides Titan's surface. Neptune's largest moon, Triton, has a thin atmosphere and ice volcanoes. Jupiter has four large moons—Io, Europa, Ganymede, and Callisto. Io (EYE-oh) is dotted with volcanoes, which continue to erupt, so Io has few impact craters. Europa (yu-ROH-puh) has long ridges where the crust has been pushed and pulled by the material beneath it. The outer two moons have craters over most of their surfaces.

The other moons of the gas giants are all smaller than Pluto, with diameters ranging from about 1600 kilometers (1000 mi) down to just a few kilometers. The smallest moons have irregular shapes, and some may be bodies that were captured into orbit.

CHECK YOUR READING What processes are at work on the largest moons?

Some Moons of Gas Giants

Moons in the outer solar system are shaped by the same processes that produce features on the terrestrial planets.

Saturn's moon **Titan** has a dense atmosphere of cold nitrogen gas. A thick haze hides this moon's surface.

haze

Jupiter's moon **Europa** has a crust of frozen water shaped by tectonics. Warm material below has broken the crust into many pieces.

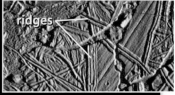

ridges

Neptune's moon **Triton** has dark streaks that show where ice volcanoes have erupted. Winds in the thin atmosphere blow material to one side of an eruption.

ice volcano

streak

Jupiter's moon **Io** has a surface constantly being changed by volcanoes. New material covers the surface and then changes color over time.

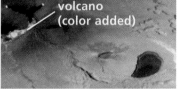

volcano (color added)

READING VISUALS Which images show volcanoes?

Asteroids and comets orbit the Sun.

Objects called asteroids and comets formed along with the Sun, planets, and moons. These objects still orbit the Sun at different distances. Most of the objects are much smaller than planets and had too little mass to become round. The objects that formed far from the Sun are made mostly of ice, with some rock and metal. The objects that formed closer to the Sun, where it was warmer, have little or no ice.

MAIN IDEA AND DETAILS
Remember to take notes to help you study later.

Asteroids

Small, solid, rocky bodies that orbit close to the Sun are called **asteroids.** They range from almost 1000 kilometers (600 mi) in diameter down to a kilometer or less. Except for the largest, their gravity is too weak to pull them into round spheres. Therefore, most asteroids have irregular shapes. Some asteroids are the broken pieces of larger, rounded asteroids.

Most asteroids have paths that keep them between the orbits of Mars and Jupiter. This huge region is called the asteroid belt, and contains more than 10,000 asteroids. However, the asteroids are so far apart that spacecraft from Earth have passed completely through the belt without danger of collision. The mass of all the asteroids put together is estimated to be less than the mass of our Moon.

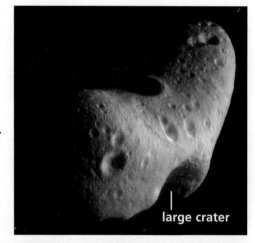

large crater

This asteroid is small compared with a planet, but it is large compared with a person. The large crater at the bottom is about the size of a small city.

The surfaces of asteroids are covered with craters, broken rock, and dust. Even though asteroids are far apart, smaller objects do hit them from time to time. Impacts from very long ago are still visible because most asteroids are not massive enough to have formed cores, mantles, and crusts. Therefore, they do not have volcanism or tectonics to erase the craters. Most asteroids do not have atmospheres, so their surfaces change only when impacts happen or when gravity pulls material downhill.

 Why do asteroids have craters?

Some asteroids have collided with Earth in the past. The collisions left impact craters, some of which can still be seen today. Scientists have found evidence that an asteroid 10 kilometers (6 mi) in diameter hit Earth 65 million years ago. A cloud of dust from the collision spread around the world and probably affected surface temperatures. Many forms of life, including dinosaurs, died off at about that time, and the impact may have been part or all of the reason. Today astronomers are working to study all asteroids larger than 1 kilometer (0.6 mi) in diameter to determine whether any could hit Earth.

Comets

Sometimes, a fuzzy spot appears in the night sky. It grows from night to night as it changes position against the background stars. The fuzzy spot is a cloud of material, called a coma (KOH-muh), around a small space object. An object that produces a coma is called a **comet.** A comet without its coma is a small, icy object that is difficult to see even with a powerful telescope. Scientists use the number of comets that have become visible to infer that vast numbers of comets exist.

Comets formed far from the Sun, so they are made of different ices as well as rock and some metal. Their orbits are usually more oval than the paths of planets. A comet's orbit may carry it from regions far beyond Pluto's orbit to the inner solar system.

When a comet gets close to the Sun, solar radiation warms the surface and turns some of the ice into gas. A coma forms as the gas moves outward, often carrying dust with it. High-speed particles and radiation from the Sun push this material into one or more tails that can stretch for millions of kilometers. A comet's tails point away from the Sun no matter which way the comet is moving. The coma and tails look bright because sunlight shines on them, even though they may be less dense than Earth's atmosphere.

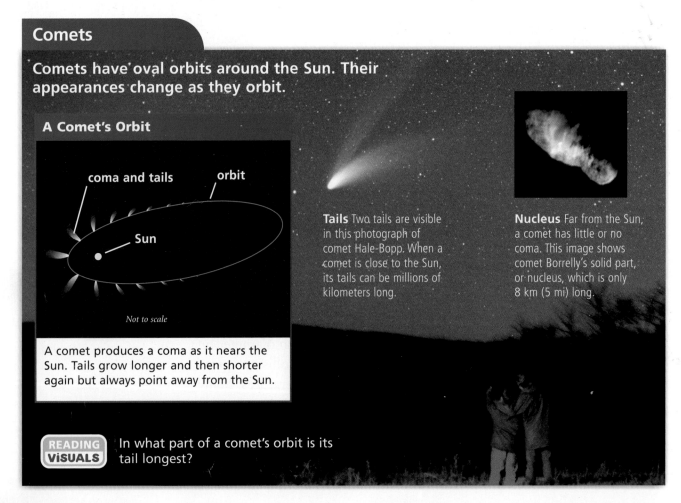

Comets

Comets have oval orbits around the Sun. Their appearances change as they orbit.

A Comet's Orbit

coma and tails

orbit

Sun

Not to scale

A comet produces a coma as it nears the Sun. Tails grow longer and then shorter again but always point away from the Sun.

Tails Two tails are visible in this photograph of comet Hale-Bopp. When a comet is close to the Sun, its tails can be millions of kilometers long.

Nucleus Far from the Sun, a comet has little or no coma. This image shows comet Borrelly's solid part, or nucleus, which is only 8 km (5 mi) long.

READING VISUALS In what part of a comet's orbit is its tail longest?

Most comets are too faint to be noticed easily from Earth. Many years can go by between appearances of bright comets, such as the one in the photograph on page 104.

 CHECK YOUR READING What makes a comet visible?

Meteors and Meteorites

Earth collides constantly with particles in space. Earth orbits the Sun at about 100,000 kilometers per hour (70,000 mi/h), so these particles enter Earth's thin upper atmosphere at very high speeds. The particles and the air around them become hot enough to glow, producing brief streaks of light called **meteors.** You may be able to see a few meteors per hour on a clear, dark night. Several times during the year, Earth passes through a stream of orbiting particles left by a comet. In the resulting meteor shower, you can see many meteors per hour.

A meteor produced by a particle from a comet may last less than a second. Bits of rock or metal from asteroids may produce brighter, longer-lasting meteors. Rarely, a very bright meteor, called a fireball, lights up the sky for several seconds.

An object with greater mass, perhaps 10 grams or more, may not be destroyed by Earth's atmosphere. A **meteorite** is a space object that reaches Earth's surface. The outside of a meteorite is usually smooth from melting, but the inside may still be frozen. Most meteorites come from the asteroid belt, but a few are rocky fragments that have been blasted into space from the Moon and Mars.

This piece of iron is part of a huge meteorite. The energy of the impact melted the metal and changed its shape.

 CHECK YOUR READING What is the difference between a meteor and a meteorite?

 **Review**

KEY CONCEPTS

1. How are Pluto and most moons of the gas giant planets similar?
2. List two differences between asteroids and comets.
3. What causes meteors?

CRITICAL THINKING

4. **Apply** Of the four types of processes that shape terrestrial worlds, which also shape the surfaces of moons of giant planets?
5. **Compare and Contrast** How is a comet different from a meteor?

● CHALLENGE

6. **Predict** What do you think Pluto would look like if its orbit brought it close to the Sun?

CHAPTER INVESTIGATION

Exploring Impact Craters

DESIGN —YOUR OWN— EXPERIMENT

OVERVIEW AND PURPOSE Nearly 50,000 years ago, an asteroid plummeted through Earth's atmosphere and exploded near what is now Winslow, Arizona. The photograph at left shows the resulting impact crater, which is about 1.2 kilometers (0.7 mi) wide. Most of the other craters on Earth have been erased. However, some planets and most moons in the solar system have surfaces that are covered with craters. In this investigation you will

- use solid objects to make craters in a flour surface
- determine how one variable affects the resulting crater

▶ Problem

Write It Up

How does one characteristic of an impact or a colliding object affect the resulting crater?

▶ Hypothesize

Write It Up

Complete steps 1–5 before writing your problem statement and hypothesis. Once you have identified a variable to test, write a hypothesis to explain how changing this variable will affect the crater. Your hypothesis should take the form of an "If . . . , then . . . , because . . ." statement.

▶ Procedure

MATERIALS
- newspapers
- container
- flour
- colored powder
- several objects
- meter stick
- ruler
- balance

1. Place the container on newspapers and add flour to a depth of 2–4 cm. Stir the flour to break up any lumps, and then smooth the surface with a ruler. Sprinkle the top with colored powder.

2. Drop an object into the flour from waist height, then carefully remove it without disturbing the flour. Use the diagram to identify the various parts of the impact crater you made.

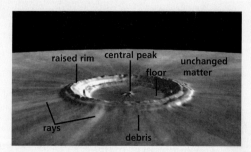

raised rim   central peak   unchanged matter   floor   rays   debris

3. To help you design your experiment, try several cratering methods. Make each new crater in a different location in the container. If your container becomes too full of craters, stir the flour, smooth it, and sprinkle on more colored powder.

4. Design an experiment to test the effects of a variable. Choose just one variable to change—the height, the size or mass of the object, or perhaps the fluffiness of the flour. Determine how much you need to change your variable in order to get results different enough to see.

5. Experiment to find some part of the crater that is affected by changing your variable, such as the depth, the size of the blanket of debris, or the number of rays. Design your experiment so that you measure the part of the crater that changes the most.

6. Write a specific problem statement by completing the question, How does _____ affect _____? Write a hypothesis to answer your problem statement.

7. Perform your experiment. Do not change any factors except your chosen variable.

8. Make several trials for each value of your variable, because there are some factors you cannot control.

9. Record measurements and other observations and make drawings as you go along.

▶ Observe and Analyze
Write It Up

1. RECORD Use a diagram to show how you measure the craters. Organize your data into a table. Include spaces for averages.

2. IDENTIFY VARIABLES List the variables and constants. The independent variable is the factor that you changed. The dependent variable is affected by this change. Use these definitions when you graph your results.

3. CALCULATE Determine averages by adding all of your measurements at each value of your independent variable, then dividing the sum by the number of measurements.

4. GRAPH Make a line graph of your average results. Place the independent variable on the horizontal axis and the dependent variable on the vertical axis. Why should you use a line graph instead of a bar graph for these data?

▶ Conclude
Write It Up

1. ANALYZE Answer your problem statement. Do your data support your hypothesis?

2. EVALUATE Did you identify a trend in your results? Is your experiment a failure if you did not identify a trend? Why or why not?

3. IDENTIFY LIMITS How would you modify the design of your experiment now that you have seen the results?

4. APPLY What do you think would happen if a colliding object hit water instead of land?

▶ INVESTIGATE Further

CHALLENGE How do the craters in this model differ from real impact craters? Design, but do not attempt, an experiment to simulate the cratering process more realistically.

Exploring Impact Craters
Problem How does _____ affect _____?
Hypothesize
Observe and Analyze
Table 1. Data and Averages

Conclude

the BIG idea

Planets and other objects form a system around our Sun.

CONTENT REVIEW
CLASSZONE.COM

KEY CONCEPTS SUMMARY

3.1 Planets orbit the Sun at different distances.

The planets have different sizes and distances from the Sun. The solar system formed from a disk of dust and gas. Massive objects became round.

inner solar system
Mercury, Venus, Earth, Mars, asteroids

outer solar system
Jupiter, Saturn, Uranus, Neptune, Pluto, comets

VOCABULARY
astronomical unit
(AU) p. 81
ellipse p. 81

3.2 The inner solar system has rocky planets.

- The terrestrial planets are round and have layers.
- Atmospheres came from volcanoes and impacts.
- Four processes produce surface features.

   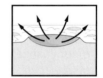

tectonics   volcanism   weathering and erosion   impact cratering

VOCABULARY
terrestrial planet p. 85
tectonics p. 86
volcanism p. 86

3.3 The outer solar system has four giant planets.

- The gas giants have very dense, deep atmospheres with layers of clouds.
- All four giant planets have ring systems.

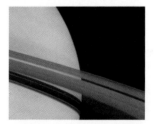

Close-up of Saturn's rings

VOCABULARY
gas giant p. 94
ring p. 97

3.4 Small objects are made of ice and rock.

- Objects in the inner solar system are rocky.
- Pluto and most other objects in the outer solar system are made of ice and rock.
- Rocky asteroids and icy comets orbit the Sun and produce tiny fragments that may become meteors.

The asteroid Eros

VOCABULARY
asteroid p. 103
comet p. 104
meteor p. 105
meteorite p. 105

Reviewing Vocabulary

Make a Venn diagram for each pair of terms. Put an important similarity in the overlapping part. Use the rest of the diagram to show an important difference.

Example:

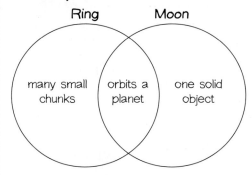

Ring | Moon

many small chunks | orbits a planet | one solid object

1. terrestrial planet, gas giant

2. volcanism, impact cratering

3. erosion, tectonics

4. asteroid, comet

5. meteor, meteorite

6. comet, meteor

Reviewing Key Concepts

Multiple Choice *Choose the letter of the best answer.*

7. Even though orbits are ellipses, what shape is a typical planet's orbit most like?
   a. a short rectangle
   b. an egg-shape with a pointy end
   c. a long, narrow oval
   d. a circle

8. How is a moon different from a planet?
   a. A moon is smaller than any planet.
   b. A moon is less massive than any planet.
   c. A moon is in orbit around a planet.
   d. A moon is unable to have an atmosphere.

9. Which of these appears in Earth's atmosphere?
   a. a moon   **c.** a meteor
   b. an asteroid   **d.** a comet

10. How did planets and other objects in the solar system form?
    a. After the Sun formed, it threw off hot pieces that spun and cooled.
    b. The Sun captured objects that formed in other places in the galaxy.
    c. Two stars collided, and the broken pieces went into orbit around the Sun.
    d. Material in a disk formed large clumps as the Sun formed in the center of the disk.

11. Which process occurs only when a small space object interacts with a larger space body?
    a. tectonics   **c.** erosion
    b. volcanism   **d.** impact cratering

12. Which processes occur because a planet or another space body is hot inside?
    a. tectonics and volcanism
    b. volcanism and erosion
    c. erosion and impact cratering
    d. impact cratering and tectonics

13. What do all four gas giants have that terrestrial planets do not have?
    a. atmospheres   **c.** moons
    b. solid surfaces **d.** rings

14. What are the white stripes of Jupiter and the white spots of Neptune?
    a. clouds high in the atmosphere
    b. smoke from volcanoes
    c. continents and islands
    d. holes in the atmosphere

Short Answer *Write a short answer to each question.*

15. The solid part of a comet is small in comparison with a planet. However, sometimes a comet appears to be larger than the Sun. What makes it seem so large?

16. Why do all nine major planets orbit the Sun in the same direction?

Use the image of Jupiter's moon Ganymede to answer the next five questions.

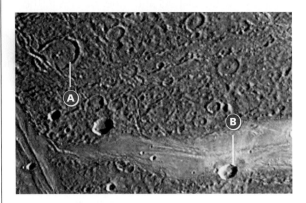

17. OBSERVE Which crater, A or B, is more eroded? Explain why you think so.

18. COMPARE AND CONTRAST Describe the differences between the surface in the upper half of the image and the long, triangular area near the bottom of the image.

19. INFER Explain which area of the surface, the smooth part or the heavily cratered part, is probably older.

20. APPLY The lighter area was produced by tectonic processes and may have been covered with molten material. What can you infer about the inside of this moon?

21. SEQUENCE A crack runs through part of crater A. Explain how you can tell whether the crack or the crater formed first. **Hint:** Think about what would have happened if the other feature had formed first.

22. PREDICT Suppose the Moon were hotter inside. How might its surface be different?

23. IDENTIFY CAUSE Mercury's surface is not as hot as Venus's, even though Mercury is closer to the Sun. In addition, the night side of Mercury gets very cold, while the night side of Venus is about as hot as the day side. Why are the temperature patterns on these two planets so different?

24. EVALUATE Would it be easier to design a lander mission for the surface of Venus or the surface of Mercury? Explain your reasoning.

25. INFER Some comets orbit in a direction opposite to that of the planets. Why might this make some scientists wonder if they formed with the rest of the solar system?

26. HYPOTHESIZE Scientists calculate the mass of a planet from the effects of its gravity on other objects, such as moons. However, Mercury and Venus have no moons. What other objects in space could have been used to determine the planets' masses?

27. COMPARE AND CONTRAST Images of Earth from space show white clouds above darker land and water. In what ways are they like and unlike images of Jupiter?

Earth   **Jupiter**

28. ANALYZE Scientists sometimes use round numbers to compare quantities. For example, a scientist might say that the Sun's diameter is about 100 times Earth's diameter, even though she knows that the precise value is 109 times. Why might she use such an approximation?

the BIG idea

29. APPLY Look back at pages 76–77. Think about the answer you gave to the question about the large image of a planet and moon. How would you answer this question differently now?

30. SYNTHESIZE Ice is generally less dense than rock, which is generally less dense than metal. Use what you know about materials in the solar system to estimate whether a moon of Mars, a moon of Uranus, or the planet Mercury should be the least dense.

UNIT PROJECTS

Check your schedule for your unit project. How are you doing? Be sure that you have placed data or notes from your research in your project folder.

Interpreting a Passage

Read the following passage. Then answer the questions that follow.

Life in Extreme Environments

Could living organisms survive in the crushing, hot atmosphere of Venus? Could they thrive on a waterless asteroid or get their energy from tides in the dark ocean that might be beneath the surface of Europa? Scientists are looking for answers to these questions right here on Earth. They study extremophiles, which are life forms that can survive in extreme environments—very high or low temperatures or other difficult conditions. These environments have conditions similar to those on other planets, and those on moons, asteroids, and comets.

Scientists have found tiny organisms that grow in the scalding water of hot vents on the ocean floor, deep inside rock, and in miniature ponds within glaciers. Scientists have also found organisms that were dormant because they were frozen solid for thousands of years but that were still capable of living and growing after warming up. By studying extremophiles, scientists learn more about the conditions needed to support life.

Choose from the following four environments to answer each of the next three questions.

- the dark ocean that might be underneath Europa's surface
- the flood channels on Mars, which have been dry and frozen for a long time
- the very hot, high-pressure environment of Venus
- the dry rock of an asteroid that alternately heats and cools

1. Some organisms survive deep underwater, where photosynthesis does not occur because little or no sunlight reaches those depths. Which environment can these organisms teach about?

a. under Europa's surface   c. Venus
b. Martian flood channels   d. an asteroid

2. Some organisms survive in very deep cracks in rocks, where they are protected from changing temperatures. Where else might scientists look for these types of organisms?

a. under Europa's surface   c. Venus
b. Martian flood channels   d. an asteroid

3. Where might scientists look for tiny organisms that are dormant but that might revive if given warmth and water?

a. under Europa's surface   c. Venus
b. Martian flood channels   d. an asteroid

4. Where, outside Earth, should scientists look for tiny ponds of water within solid ice?

a. the other terrestrial planets
b. the gas giants
c. small space objects in the inner solar system
d. small space objects in the outer solar system

Extended Response

Answer the two questions in detail.

5. A class was given a sample of ordinary dormant, dry yeast that had been exposed to an extreme environment. Describe ways the students might test the yeast to see if it remained undamaged, or even survived, the conditions.

6. Imagine that scientists have found extremophiles in clouds of frozen water crystals high in Earth's atmosphere. How might this discovery affect a search for organisms on the gas giants?

CHAPTER

4

Stars, Galaxies, and the Universe

the **BIG** idea

Our Sun is one of billions of stars in one of billions of galaxies in the universe.

Key Concepts

SECTION
4.1 **The Sun is our local star.**
Learn how the Sun produces energy and about the Sun's layers and features.

SECTION
4.2 **Stars change over their life cycles.**
Learn how stars form and change.

SECTION
4.3 **Galaxies have different sizes and shapes.**
Learn how galaxies are classified.

SECTION
4.4 **The universe is expanding.**
Learn about the formation and expansion of the universe.

Internet Preview

CLASSZONE.COM

Chapter 4 online resources: Visualization, Simulation, three Resource Centers, Math Tutorial, Test Practice

What could be present in the light and dark areas in this galaxy?

EXPLORE (the BIG idea)

How Can Stars Differ?

Look at the sky at night and find three stars that differ in appearance. Try to identify the locations of these stars, using the star maps in the Appendix at the back of this book.

Observe and Think How did the characteristics of the stars differ?

How Do Galaxies Move Apart?

Blow air into a balloon until it is partially inflated. Use a felt-tip pen to make 12 dots on the round end. Then stand in front of a mirror and observe the dots as you completely inflate the balloon.

Observe and Think What caused the dots to move apart? What might cause galaxies to move apart in the universe?

Internet Activity: Galaxy Shapes

Go to **ClassZone.com** to explore the different shapes of galaxies in the universe.

Observe and Think How do the types of galaxies differ from one another?

NSTA
scilinks.org

SCLINKS

The Sun Code: MDL060

Getting Ready to Learn

◀ CONCEPT REVIEW

- Electromagnetic radiation carries information about space.
- Our solar system is in the Milky Way galaxy.
- A galaxy is a group of millions or billions of stars.

◀ VOCABULARY REVIEW

solar system p. 10

galaxy p. 10

universe p. 10

electromagnetic radiation p. 15

wavelength p. 16

CONTENT REVIEW
CLASSZONE.COM
Review concepts and vocabulary.

▶ TAKING NOTES

CHOOSE YOUR OWN STRATEGY

Take notes using one or more of the strategies from earlier chapters—**main idea web, combination notes,** or **main idea and details.** Feel free to mix and match the strategies, or use an entirely different note-taking strategy.

VOCABULARY STRATEGY

Place each vocabulary term at the center of a **description wheel** diagram. Write some words describing it on the spokes.

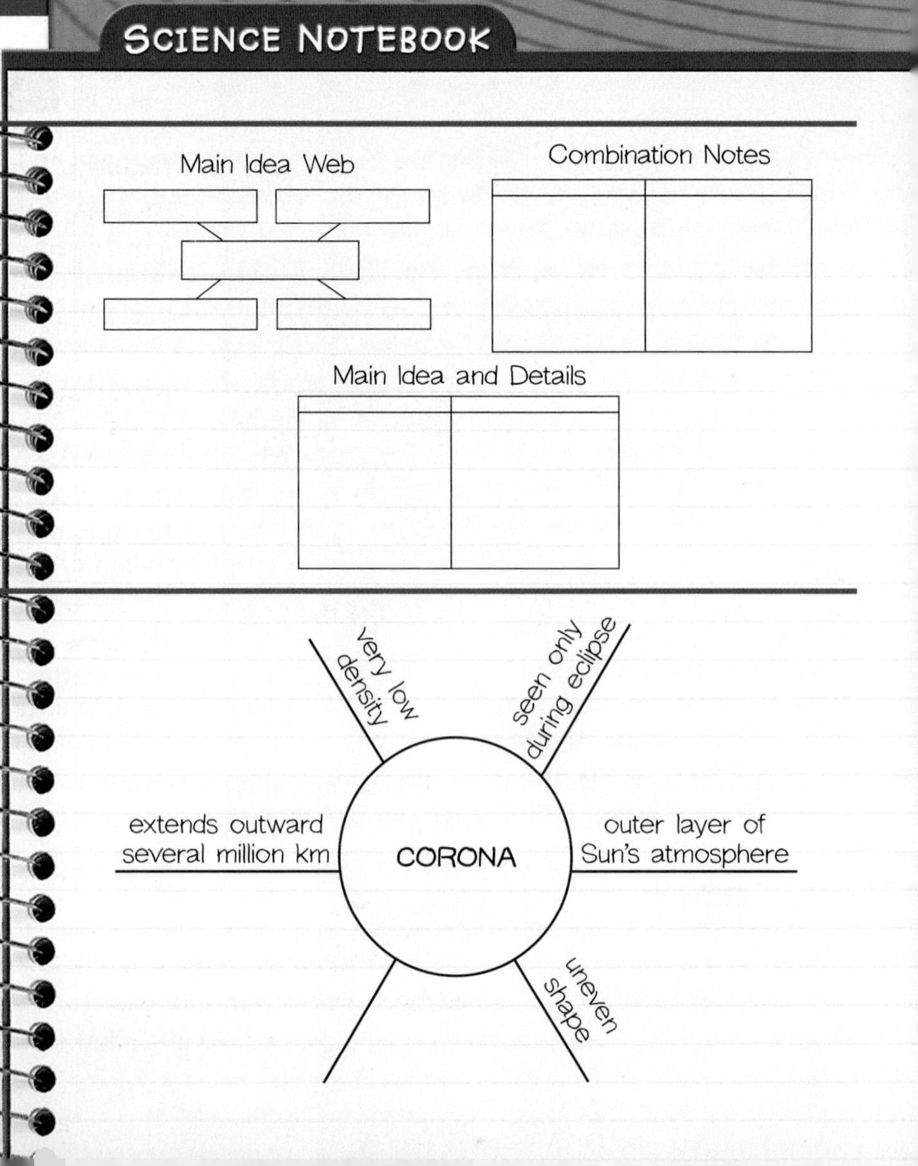

See the Note-Taking Handbook on pages R45–R51.

SCIENCE NOTEBOOK

Main Idea Web

Combination Notes

Main Idea and Details

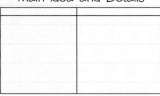

very low density

seen only during eclipse

extends outward several million km

CORONA

outer layer of Sun's atmosphere

uneven shape

KEY CONCEPT

The Sun is our local star.

4.1

◀ **BEFORE,** you learned

- There are different wavelengths of electromagnetic radiation
- The Sun provides light in the solar system

▶ **NOW,** you will learn

- How the Sun produces energy
- How energy flows through the Sun's layers
- About solar features and solar wind

VOCABULARY

fusion p. 116
convection p. 116
corona p. 116
sunspot p. 118
solar wind p. 119

EXPLORE Solar Atmosphere

How can blocking light reveal dim features?

PROCEDURE

① Unbend the paper clip and use it to make a tiny hole in the center of the card.

② Turn on the lamp, and briefly try to read the writing on the bulb.

③ Close one eye, and hold the card in front of your other eye. Through the hole, try to read the writing on the bulb.

WHAT DO YOU THINK?

- How did looking through the hole affect your view of the writing?
- How might a solar eclipse affect your view of the Sun's dim outermost layer?

MATERIALS

- small paper clip
- index card
- lamp with 45-watt bulb

The Sun produces energy from hydrogen.

MAIN IDEA AND DETAILS
You could record information about the Sun by using a main idea and details table.

The Sun is the only star in our solar system. Astronomers have been able to study the Sun in more detail than other stars because it is much closer to Earth. As a result, they have learned a great deal about its size and composition and the way it produces energy.

The Sun is far larger than any of the planets. It contains 99.9 percent of the mass of the entire solar system. For comparison, imagine that Earth had the mass of a sparrow; then the Sun would have the mass of an elephant.

The Sun consists mostly of hydrogen gas. Energy is produced when hydrogen in the Sun's interior turns into helium. This energy is the source of light and warmth that make life possible on Earth.

Energy flows through the Sun's layers.

Although the Sun is made entirely of gas, it does have a structure. Energy produced in the center of the Sun flows out through the Sun's layers in different forms, including visible light.

The Sun's Interior

The Sun's interior generally becomes cooler and less dense as you move away from the center.

1 Core The center of the Sun, called the core, is made of very dense gas. Temperatures reach about 15 million degrees Celsius. Under these extreme conditions, some hydrogen particles collide and combine to form helium in a process called **fusion.** The process releases energy that travels through the core by radiation.

Remember that radiation is energy that travels across distances as electromagnetic waves.

2 Radiative Zone Energy from the core moves by radiation through a thick layer called the radiative zone. Although this layer is very hot and dense, conditions in the radiative zone are not extreme enough for fusion to occur.

3 Convection Zone In the convection zone, energy moves mainly by convection. **Convection** is the transfer of energy from place to place by the motion of heated gas or liquid. Rising currents of hot gas in the convection zone carry energy toward the Sun's surface.

 CHECK YOUR READING Where does the Sun's energy come from?

SIMULATION
CLASSZONE.COM

View the Sun at different wavelengths.

The Sun's Atmosphere

The Sun's outer layers are called its atmosphere. These layers are much less dense than the interior. The atmosphere generally becomes hotter and less dense as you move outward.

4 Photosphere Visible light moves by radiation out into space from the photosphere. It takes about eight minutes for the light to reach Earth. Since the photosphere is the layer you see in photographs of the Sun, it is often called the Sun's surface. Convection currents beneath the photosphere cause it to have a bumpy texture.

5 Chromosphere The chromosphere is the thin middle layer of the Sun's atmosphere. It gives off a pinkish light.

6 Corona The Sun's outermost layer is called the **corona.** The corona, which varies in shape, extends outward several million kilometers. Both the chromosphere and the corona are much hotter than the photosphere. However, they have such low densities that you can see their light only during a total eclipse of the Sun, when the Moon blocks the much brighter light from the photosphere.

Layers of the Sun

Energy produced by fusion in the Sun's core flows out through its layers.

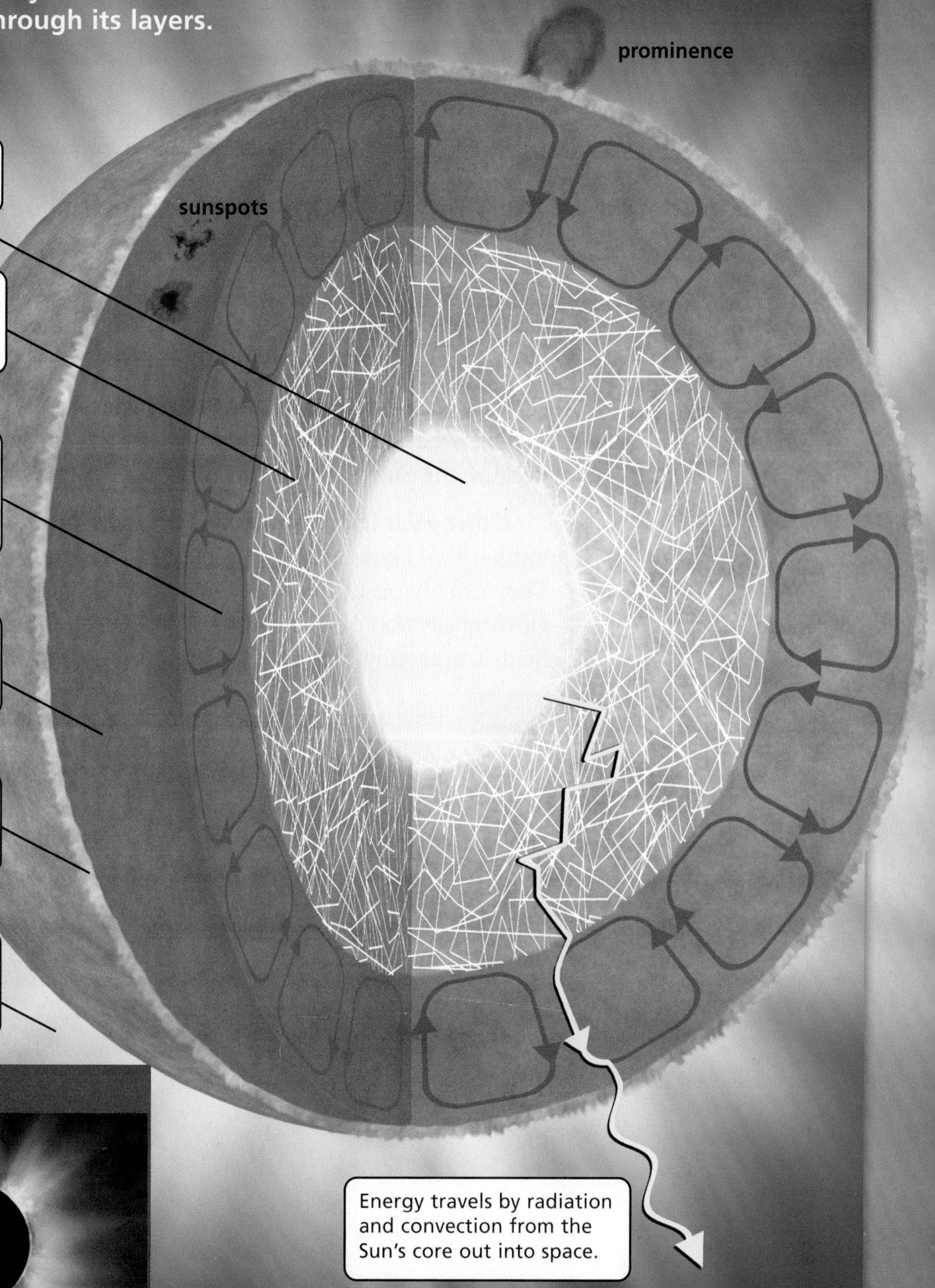

prominence

1 Energy is produced in the Sun's **core**.

2 Energy moves by radiation through the **radiative zone.**

3 Currents of hot gas in the **convection zone** carry energy outward.

4 The **photosphere** is the visible layer of the Sun.

5 The **chromosphere** is the middle layer of the Sun's atmosphere.

6 The **corona**, the Sun's outermost layer, has a very low density.

sunspots

Energy travels by radiation and convection from the Sun's core out into space.

Corona

During a solar eclipse, the corona becomes visible because the much brighter photosphere is hidden. The corona varies in shape.

Features on the Sun

Astronomers have observed features on the Sun that vary over time. Near the Sun's surface there are regions of magnetic force called magnetic fields. These magnetic fields get twisted into different positions as the Sun rotates. Features appear on the surface in areas where strong magnetic fields are located.

Sunspots are spots on the photosphere that are cooler than surrounding areas. Although they appear dark, sunspots are actually bright. They only seem dim because the rest of the photosphere is so much brighter.

Sunspot activity follows a pattern that lasts about 11 years. At the peak of the cycle, dozens of sunspots may appear. During periods of low activity, there may not be any sunspots.

Sunspots move across the Sun's surface as it rotates. Astronomers first realized that the Sun rotates when they noticed this movement. Because the Sun is not solid, some parts rotate faster than others.

Other solar features include flares and prominences (PRAHM-uh-nuhn-sihz). Flares are eruptions of hot gas from the Sun's surface. They usually occur near sunspots. Prominences are huge loops of glowing gas that extend into the corona. They occur where magnetic fields connecting sunspots soar into the outer atmosphere.

 CHECK YOUR READING How are sunspots different from other areas of the photosphere?

Solar Features

Features on the Sun appear in areas where a magnetic field is strong.

Sunspots

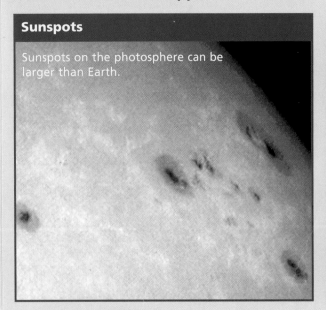

Sunspots on the photosphere can be larger than Earth.

Prominences

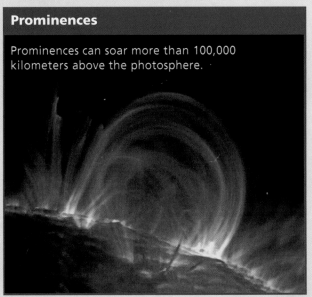

Prominences can soar more than 100,000 kilometers above the photosphere.

Solar Wind

Material in the Sun's corona is continually streaming out into space. The electrically charged particles that flow out in all directions from the corona are called the **solar wind.** The solar wind extends throughout our solar system.

This circular green aurora occurred over Alaska when particles from the solar wind entered the atmosphere.

Most of the solar wind flowing toward Earth is safely guided around the planet by Earth's magnetic field. When solar-wind particles do enter the upper atmosphere, they release energy, which can produce beautiful patterns of glowing light in the sky. Such displays of light are called auroras (uh-RAWR-uhz), or the northern and southern lights. Auroras often occur near the poles.

Earth's atmosphere usually prevents charged particles from reaching the surface. However, during the peak of the sunspot cycle, flares and other kinds of solar activity release strong bursts of charged particles into the solar wind. These bursts, called magnetic storms, can disrupt electric-power delivery across large regions by causing surges in power lines. They can also interfere with radio communication.

Magnetic storms are much more harmful above the protective layers of Earth's atmosphere. Bursts of particles in the solar wind can damage or destroy orbiting satellites. The solar wind also poses a danger to astronauts during space flights.

CHECK YOUR READING What causes auroras to form?

4.1 Review

KEY CONCEPTS

1. How does the Sun produce energy?
2. How does energy move from the Sun's core to the photosphere?
3. How does the solar wind normally affect Earth?

CRITICAL THINKING

4. **Analyze** Why is the core the only layer of the Sun where energy is produced?
5. **Compare and Contrast** Make a diagram comparing sunspots, flares, and prominences.

⬤ CHALLENGE

6. **Infer** A communications satellite stops working while in orbit, and a surge in an electric power line causes blackouts in cities across a large region. What probably happened in the Sun's atmosphere shortly before these events?

CHAPTER INVESTIGATION

Temperature, Brightness, and Color

OVERVIEW AND PURPOSE Think of the metal heating surface on a hot plate. How can you tell whether the hot plate is fully heated? Is the metal surface brighter or dimmer than when it is just starting to get warm? Does the color of the surface change as the hot plate gets hotter? You may already have an idea of how temperature, brightness, and color are related—at least when it comes to heated metal. Do the same relationships apply to electric lights? to stars? This investigation is designed to help you find out. You will

- construct a wax photometer to compare the brightnesses and colors of different light sources
- determine how the temperature of a light source affects its brightness and color

MATERIALS

- 2 paraffin blocks
- aluminum foil
- 2 rubber bands
- 2 light-bulb holders
- 2 miniature light bulbs
- 3 AA batteries
- 4 pieces of uninsulated copper wire 15 cm long
- masking tape

for Challenge:
- incandescent lamp
- dimmer switch

▶ **Problem** Write It Up

How are brightness and color related to temperature?

▶ **Hypothesize** Write It Up

Write a hypothesis to explain how brightness and color are related to temperature. Your hypothesis should take the form of an "If . . . , then . . . , because . . ." statement.

▶ **Procedure**

1. An instrument called a photometer makes it easier to compare the brightnesses and colors of different light sources. Assemble the wax photometer as shown on page 121. The aluminum foil between the wax blocks should be folded so that the shiny side faces out on both sides.

2. Hold the photometer so that you can see both blocks. Bring it to different locations in the classroom, and observe how the brightnesses and colors of the blocks change as the two sides of the photometer are exposed to different light conditions.

3. Tape a piece of copper wire to each end of a battery, and connect the wires to a light-bulb holder. The battery will provide electricity to heat up the wire inside a light bulb.

step 3

4. Tape the negative terminal, or flat end, of one battery to the positive terminal of another battery. Tape a piece of copper wire to each end, and connect the wires to a light-bulb holder. Because two batteries will provide electricity to the bulb in this holder, the wire in the bulb will be hotter than the wire in the bulb powered by one battery.

step 4

5. With the room darkened, insert a bulb into each light-bulb holder. If the bulb connected to two batteries does not light up, you may need to press the two batteries together with your fingers.

6. Place the photometer halfway between the two light bulbs. Compare the brightnesses of the two light sources. Record your observations in your **Science Notebook.**

7. Move the photometer closer to the cooler bulb until both sides of the photometer are equally bright. Compare the colors of the two light sources. Record your observations in your **Science Notebook**. To avoid draining the batteries, remove the bulbs from the holders when you have completed this step.

step 6

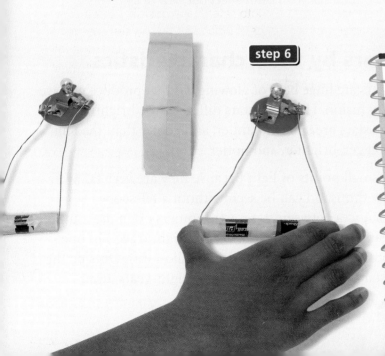

▶ Observe and Analyze Write It Up

1. **RECORD OBSERVATIONS** Draw the setup of your photometer and light sources. Be sure your data table is complete with descriptions of brightness and color.

2. **IDENTIFY** Identify the variables in this experiment. List them in your **Science Notebook.**

▶ Conclude Write It Up

1. **INTERPRET** Answer the question in the problem. Compare your results with your hypothesis.

2. **ANALYZE** How does distance affect your perception of the brightness of an object?

3. **APPLY** Judging by the results of the investigation, would you expect a red star or a yellow star to be hotter? Explain why.

▶ INVESTIGATE Further

CHALLENGE Connect an incandescent lamp to a dimmer switch. Write a procedure to show how you would use a photometer to show the relationship between the color and the temperature of the bulb as it fades from brightest to dimmest. Then carry out your procedure.

Temperature, Brightness, and Color

Observe and Analyze

Table 1. Properties of Light from Two Sources

	Cooler Bulb (one battery)	Warmer Bulb (two batteries)
Brightness		
Color		

4.2 Stars change over their life cycles.

 BEFORE, you learned

- The Sun is our local star
- The other stars are outside our solar system
- There are huge distances between objects in the universe

 NOW, you will learn

- How stars are classified
- How stars form and change

VOCABULARY

light-year p. 122
parallax p. 123
nebula p. 125
main sequence p. 126
neutron star p. 126
black hole p. 126

EXPLORE Characteristics of Stars

How does distance affect brightness?

PROCEDURE

1. In a darkened room, shine a flashlight onto a dark surface from 30 cm away while your partner shines a flashlight onto the surface from the same distance. Observe the two spots of light.

2. Move one of the flashlights back 15 cm and then another 15 cm. Compare the two spots of light each time you move the flashlight.

MATERIALS
- 2 flashlights
- meter stick
- dark surface

WHAT DO YOU THINK?
- How did distance affect the brightness of the light on the dark surface?
- How does the distance of a star from Earth affect our view of it?

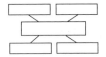

MAIN IDEA WEB
A main idea web would be a good choice for taking notes about the characteristics of stars.

We classify stars by their characteristics.

Like our Sun, all stars are huge balls of glowing gas that produce or have produced energy by fusion. However, stars differ in size, brightness, and temperature. Some stars are smaller, fainter, and cooler than the Sun. Others are much bigger, brighter, and hotter.

Stars look like small points of light because they are very far away. At most, only a few thousand can be seen without a telescope. To describe the distances between stars, astronomers often use a unit called the light-year. A **light-year** is the distance light travels in one year, which is about 9.5 trillion kilometers (6 trillion mi). Outside the solar system, the star closest to Earth is about 4 light-years away.

Brightness and Distance

If you look at stars, you will probably notice that some appear to be brighter than others. The amount of light a star gives off and its distance from Earth determine how bright it appears to an observer. A star that gives off a huge amount of light can appear faint if it is far away. On the other hand, a star that gives off much less light can appear bright if it is closer to Earth. Therefore, to determine the true brightness of a star, astronomers must measure its distance from Earth.

One way astronomers measure distance is by using **parallax,** which is the apparent shift in the position of an object when viewed from different locations. Look at an object with your right eye closed. Now quickly open it and close your left eye. The object will seem to move slightly because you are viewing it from a different angle. The same kind of shift occurs when astronomers view stars from different locations.

To measure the parallax of a star, astronomers plot the star's position in the sky from opposite sides of Earth's orbit around the Sun. They then use the apparent shift in position and the diameter of Earth's orbit to calculate the star's distance.

 CHECK YOUR READING What factors affect how bright a star appears from Earth?

INVESTIGATE Parallax

How does the distance of an object affect parallax?

PROCEDURE

1. Stand 1 m away from a classmate. Have the classmate hold up a meter stick at eye level.

2. With your left eye closed, hold a capped pen up close to your face. Look at the pen with your right eye, and line it up with the zero mark on the meter stick. Then open your left eye and quickly close your right eye. Observe how many centimeters the pen seems to move. Record your observation.

3. Repeat step 2 with the pen held at arm's length and then with the pen held at half your arm's length. Record your observation each time.

WHAT DO YOU THINK?

• How many centimeters did the pen appear to move each time you observed it?

• How is parallax affected when you change the distance of the pen from you?

CHALLENGE How could you use this method to estimate distances that you cannot measure directly?

SKILL FOCUS
Measuring

MATERIALS
• meter stick
• capped pen

TIME
10 minutes

Size

It is hard to get a sense of how large stars are from viewing them in the sky. Even the Sun, which is much closer than any other star, is far larger than its appearance suggests. The diameter of the Sun is about 100 times greater than that of Earth. A jet plane flying 800 kilometers per hour (500 mi/h) would travel around Earth's equator in about two days. If you could travel around the Sun's equator at the same speed, the trip would take more than seven months.

Some stars are much larger than the Sun. Giant and supergiant stars range from ten to hundreds of times larger. A supergiant called Betelgeuse (BEET-uhl-JOOZ) is more than 600 times greater in diameter than the Sun. If Betelgeuse replaced the Sun, it would fill space in our solar system well beyond Earth's orbit. Because giant and supergiant stars have such huge surface areas to give off light, they are very bright. Betelgeuse is one of the brightest stars in the sky, even though it is 522 light-years away.

There are also stars much smaller than the Sun. Stars called white dwarfs are about 100 times smaller in diameter than the Sun, or roughly the size of Earth. White dwarfs cannot be seen without a telescope.

A star the size of the Sun
Diameter = 1.4 million kilometers (900,000 mi)

White dwarf
1/100 the Sun's diameter

Giant star
10–100 times the Sun's diameter

Supergiant star
100–1000 times the Sun's diameter

Color and Temperature

If you observe stars closely, you may notice that they vary slightly in color. Most stars look white. However, a few appear slightly blue or red. The differences in color are due to differences in temperature.

You can see how temperature affects color by heating up metal. For example, if you turn on a toaster, the metal coils inside will start to glow a dull red. As they get hotter, the coils will turn a brighter orange. The illustration on page 125 shows changes in the color of a metal bar as it heats up.

Like the color of heated metal, the color of a star indicates its temperature. Astronomers group stars into classes by color and surface temperature. The chart on page 125 lists the color and temperature range of each class of star. The coolest stars are red. The hottest stars are blue-white. Our Sun—a yellow, G-class star—has a surface temperature of about 6000°C.

Stars of every class give off light that is made up of a range of colors. Astronomers can spread a star's light into a spectrum to learn about the star's composition. The colors and lines in a spectrum reveal which gases are present in the star's outer layers.

CHECK YOUR READING How does a star's temperature affect its appearance?

Objects that radiate light change color as they heat up.

Classification of Stars		
Class	Color	Surface Temperature (°C)
O	blue-white	above 25,000
B	blue-white	10,000–25,000
A	white	7500–10,000
F	yellow-white	6000–7500
G	yellow	5000–6000
K	orange	3500–5000
M	red	below 3500

Stars are classified according to their colors and temperatures. The Sun is a G-class star.

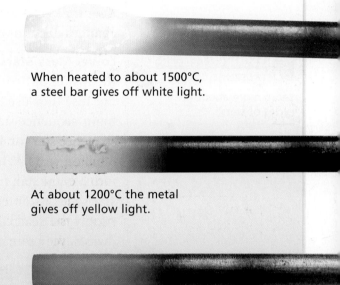

When heated to about 1500°C, a steel bar gives off white light.

At about 1200°C the metal gives off yellow light.

A steel bar glows red when heated to about 600°C.

Stars have life cycles.

Although stars last for very long periods, they are not permanent. Like living organisms, stars go through cycles of birth, maturity, and death. The life cycle of a star varies, depending on the mass of the star. Higher-mass stars develop more quickly than lower-mass stars. Toward the end of their life cycles, higher-mass stars also behave differently from lower-mass stars.

Stars form inside a cloud of gas and dust called a **nebula** (NEHB-yuh-luh). Gravity pulls gas and dust closer together in some regions of a nebula. As the matter contracts, it forms a hot, dense sphere. The sphere becomes a star if its center grows hot and dense enough for fusion to occur.

When a star dies, its matter does not disappear. Some of it may form a nebula or move into an existing one. There, the matter may eventually become part of new stars.

Colors have been added to this photograph of the Omega Nebula in order to bring out details.

CHECK YOUR READING How is gravity involved in the formation of stars?

Stages in the Life Cycles of Stars

The diagram on page 127 shows the stages that stars go through in their life cycles. Notice that the length of a cycle and the way a star changes depend on the mass of the star at its formation.

RESOURCE CENTER
CLASSZONE.COM

Learn more about life cycles of stars.

Lower-Mass Stars The stage in which stars produce energy through the fusion of hydrogen into helium is called the **main sequence.** Because they use their fuel slowly, lower-mass stars can remain in the main-sequence stage for billions of years. The Sun has been a main-sequence star for 4.6 billion years and will remain one for about another 5 billion years. When a lower-mass star runs out of hydrogen, it expands into a giant star, in which helium fuses into carbon. Over time a giant star sheds its outer layers and becomes a white dwarf. A white dwarf is simply the dead core of a giant star. Although no fusion occurs in white dwarfs, they remain hot for billions of years.

Higher-Mass Stars Stars more than eight times as massive as our Sun spend much less time in the main-sequence stage because they use their fuel rapidly. After millions of years, a higher-mass star expands to become a supergiant star. In the core of a supergiant, fusion produces heavier and heavier elements. When an iron core forms, fusion stops and gravity causes the core to collapse. Then part of the core bounces outward, and the star erupts in an explosion called a supernova.

For a brief period, a supernova can give off as much light as a galaxy. The outer layers of the exploded star shoot out into space, carrying with them heavy elements that formed inside the star. Eventually this matter may become part of new stars and planets.

Neutron Stars and Black Holes

The collapsed core of a supergiant star may form an extremely dense body called a **neutron star.** Neutron stars measure only about 20 kilometers (12 mi) in diameter, but their masses are one to three times that of the Sun.

Neutron stars emit little visible light. However, they strongly emit other forms of radiation, such as x-rays. Some neutron stars emit beams of radio waves as they spin. These stars are called pulsars because they seem to pulse as the beams rotate.

Sometimes a supernova leaves behind a core with a mass more than three times that of the Sun. In such a case, the core does not end up as a neutron star. Instead, it collapses even further, forming an invisible object called a **black hole.** The gravity of a black hole is so strong that no form of radiation can escape from it.

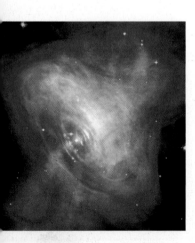

A pulsar emits beams of radio waves as it spins rapidly. The pulsar seems to pulse as the beams rotate toward and away from Earth.

 CHECK YOUR READING   How do lower-mass stars differ from higher-mass stars after the main-sequence stage?

Life Cycles of Stars

A star forms inside a cloud of gas and dust called a nebula.
The life cycle of a star depends on its mass.

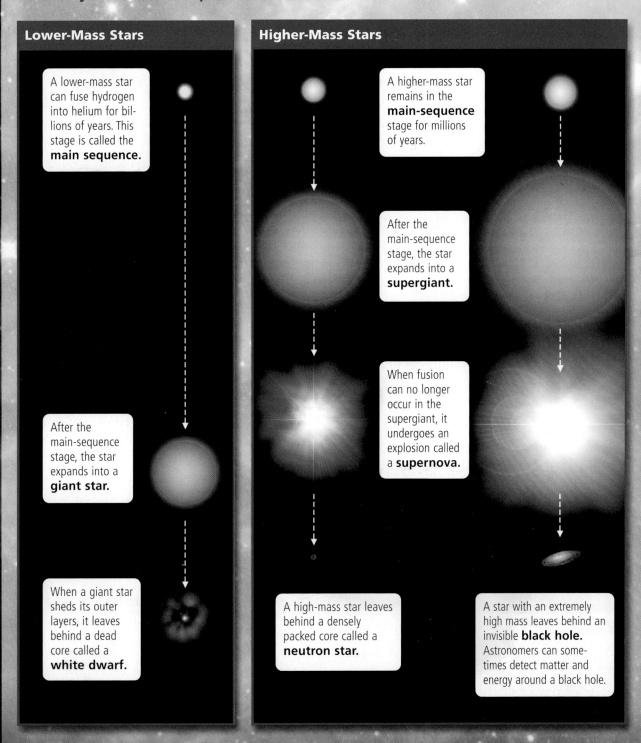

Lower-Mass Stars

A lower-mass star can fuse hydrogen into helium for billions of years. This stage is called the **main sequence.**

After the main-sequence stage, the star expands into a **giant star.**

When a giant star sheds its outer layers, it leaves behind a dead core called a **white dwarf.**

Higher-Mass Stars

A higher-mass star remains in the **main-sequence** stage for millions of years.

After the main-sequence stage, the star expands into a **supergiant.**

When fusion can no longer occur in the supergiant, it undergoes an explosion called a **supernova.**

A high-mass star leaves behind a densely packed core called a **neutron star.**

A star with an extremely high mass leaves behind an invisible **black hole.** Astronomers can sometimes detect matter and energy around a black hole.

READING VISUALS How do the stars shown in this illustration differ in the main-sequence stage of their life cycles?

Star Systems

Unlike our Sun, most stars do not exist alone. Instead, they are grouped with one or more companion stars. The stars are held together by the force of gravity between them. A binary star system consists of two stars that orbit each other. A multiple star system consists of more than two stars.

In many star systems, the stars are too close together to be seen individually. However, astronomers have developed ways of detecting such systems. For example, in a binary star system, one of the stars may orbit in front of the other when viewed from Earth. The star that orbits in front will briefly block some of the other star's light, providing a clue that more than one star is present. The illustration at right shows a binary star system that can be detected this way. Sometimes astronomers can also figure out whether a star is really a star system by studying its spectrum.

Star systems are an important source of information about star masses. Astronomers cannot measure the mass of a star directly. However, they can figure out a star's mass by observing the effect of the star's gravity on a companion star.

Binary Star System

Some binary star systems appear to dim briefly when one star orbits in front of the other and blocks some of its light.

When neither star is in front of the other, the star system appears to give off more light.

 Why are star systems important to astronomers?

4.2 Review

KEY CONCEPTS

1. Why must astronomers figure out a star's distance to calculate its actual brightness?

2. How are color and temperature related in stars?

3. How does a star's mass affect its life cycle?

CRITICAL THINKING

4. **Analyze** Some of the brightest stars are red supergiants. How can stars with cooler red surfaces be so bright?

5. **Infer** Will the Sun eventually become a black hole? Why or why not?

⬤ CHALLENGE

6. **Infer** At what stage in the life cycle of the Sun will it be impossible for life to exist on Earth? Explain.

MATH in SCIENCE

MATH TUTORIAL
CLASSZONE.COM
Click on Math Tutorial for more help with scatter plots.

Brightness and Temperature of Stars

A star's brightness, or luminosity, depends on the star's surface temperature and size. If two stars have the same surface temperature, the larger star will be more luminous. The Hertzsprung-Russell (H-R) diagram below is a scatter plot that shows the relative temperatures and luminosities of various stars.

Example

Describe the surface temperature and luminosity of Spica.

(1) Surface temperature: Without drawing on the graph, imagine a line extending from Spica down to the temperature axis. Spica is one of the hottest stars.

(2) Luminosity: Imagine a line extending from Spica across to the luminosity axis. Spica has a high luminosity.

ANSWER Spica is one of the hottest and most luminous stars.

Hertzsprung-Russell (H-R) Diagram

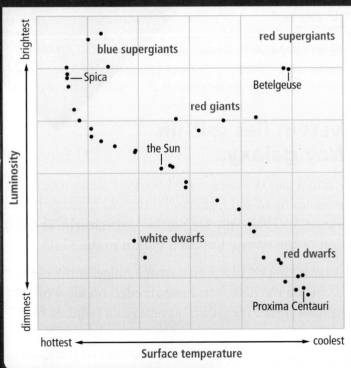

Use the diagram to answer the questions.

1. Describe the surface temperature and luminosity of Proxima Centauri.

2. Compare the surface temperature and luminosity of the Sun with the surface temperature and luminosity of Betelgeuse.

3. Compare the surface temperature and luminosity of the red dwarfs with the surface temperature and luminosity of the blue supergiants.

CHALLENGE When an old red giant star loses its outer atmosphere, all that remains is the very hot core of the star. Because the core is small, it does not give off much light. What kind of star does the red giant star become after it loses its outer atmosphere? How can you tell from the diagram?

KEY CONCEPT

4.3 Galaxies have different sizes and shapes.

◀ **BEFORE, you learned**

- Our solar system is part of a galaxy called the Milky Way
- Stars change over their life cycles

▶ **NOW, you will learn**

- About the size and shape of the Milky Way
- How galaxies are classified
- About the centers of galaxies

VOCABULARY

quasar p. 133

EXPLORE The Milky Way

Why does the Milky Way look hazy?

PROCEDURE

① Use a white gel pen to make 50 small dots close together on a piece of black paper.

② Tape the paper to a wall, and move slowly away from it until you have difficulty seeing the individual dots.

WHAT DO YOU THINK?

- At what distance did the dots become hazy?
- Why might some of the stars in the Milky Way appear hazy from Earth?

MATERIALS
- white gel pen
- black paper
- tape

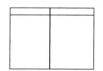

COMBINATION NOTES
You could record information about the Milky Way in a combination notes table.

Our solar system lies within the Milky Way galaxy.

The Sun lies within a galaxy called the Milky Way. Remember that a galaxy is a huge grouping of stars, gas, and dust held together by gravity. Without a telescope, you can only see nearby stars clearly. Those stars are a tiny fraction of the several hundred billion in the Milky Way.

The Milky Way is shaped like a disk with a bulge in the center. Because Earth is inside the disk, you have an edge-on view of part of the galaxy. On a dark night, the galaxy appears as a band of blended starlight. The Milky Way got its name from the hazy, or milky, appearance of this band of stars. You cannot see the center of the galaxy because it is hidden by dust.

 Why can't we see all of the Milky Way from Earth?

The Milky Way

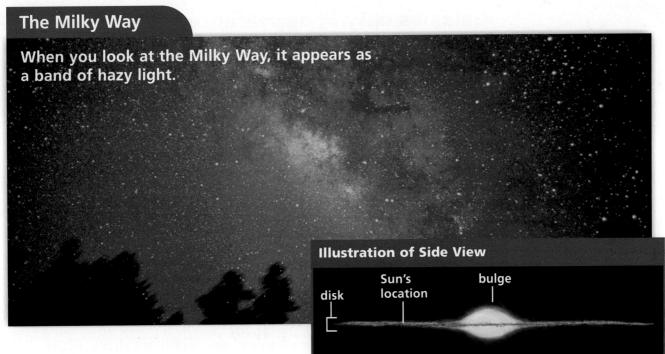

When you look at the Milky Way, it appears as a band of hazy light.

Illustration of Side View

disk   Sun's location   bulge

The Milky Way is about 100,000 light-years in diameter.

The disk of the Milky Way measures more than 100,000 light-years in diameter. The bulge of densely packed stars at the center is located about 26,000 light-years from the Sun. A large but very faint layer of stars surrounds the disk and bulge. In addition to stars, the Milky Way contains clouds of gas and dust called nebulae.

The stars and nebulae in the Milky Way orbit the galaxy's center at very high speeds. However, the galaxy is so large that the Sun takes about 250 million years to complete one orbit.

INVESTIGATE Galaxy Shapes

How can you classify galaxies according to shape?

PROCEDURE

① Cut out the photographs of galaxies on the Galaxy Photo Sheet.

② Sort the galaxies into different groups according to their shapes. You may need a group for galaxies that do not fit in other groups.

WHAT DO YOU THINK?

• How many groups did you sort the galaxies into?

• Describe each group briefly, and list which galaxies you put in each group.

CHALLENGE What is the connection between the apparent shape of a galaxy and the galaxy's relationship to the viewer? **Hint:** Think about how an edge-on view of a compact disc differs from a view of it lying flat on a table.

SKILL FOCUS
Classifying

MATERIALS
• Galaxy Photo Sheet
• scissors

TIME
15 minutes

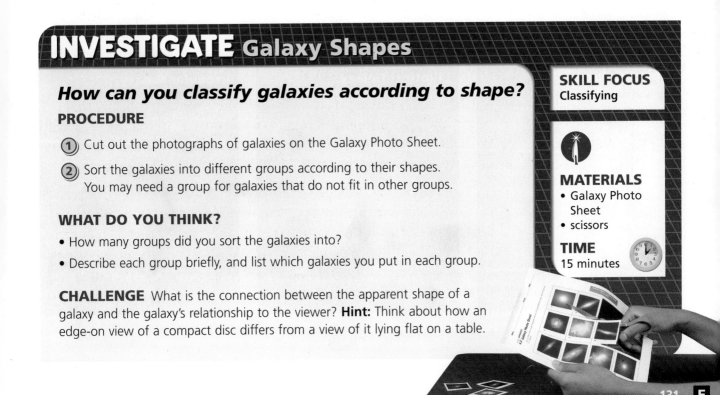

Galaxies vary in appearance.

Galaxies differ greatly in size. Some contain as few as a hundred million stars, but the biggest have more than a trillion stars. Galaxies also vary in shape. Astronomers have classified galaxies into three main types based on their shape.

 CHECK YOUR READING What are two ways in which galaxies can differ from one another?

Types of Galaxies

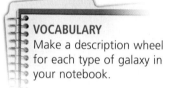
VOCABULARY
Make a description wheel for each type of galaxy in your notebook.

The three main types of galaxies are spiral, elliptical, and irregular. Most galaxies are either spiral or elliptical.

Spiral galaxies have arms of stars, gas, and dust that curve away from the center of the galaxy in a spiral pattern. The Milky Way is a spiral galaxy. Like the Milky Way, other spiral galaxies are disk-shaped and have a central bulge. Most of the stars in the disk and the bulge are old stars. However, the dense spiral arms within the disk contain many young, bright stars.

Elliptical galaxies are shaped like spheres or eggs. Unlike spiral galaxies, elliptical galaxies have almost no dust or gas between stars, and all of their stars are old.

Irregular galaxies are faint galaxies without a definite shape. They are smaller than the other types of galaxies and have many fewer stars.

Galaxies sometimes collide with other galaxies. These collisions can cause changes in their shapes. The Extreme Science feature on page 134 describes such collisions.

Spiral Galaxy

Elliptical Galaxy

Irregular Galaxy

Centers of Galaxies

Most large galaxies seem to have supermassive black holes at their centers. The mass of a supermassive black hole can be millions or even billions of times greater than that of the Sun. At the center of the Milky Way, for example, is a black hole with a mass about three million times that of the Sun.

Like all black holes, a supermassive black hole is invisible. Astronomers can identify the presence of a black hole by the behavior of matter around it. The gravity of a supermassive black hole is so strong that it draws in a huge whirlpool of gas from nearby stars. As gases are pulled toward the black hole, they become compressed and extremely hot, so they give off very bright light. The motions of stars orbiting the black hole can also reveal its presence.

If the center of a galaxy is very bright, it may look like a star from a great distance. The very bright centers of some distant galaxies are called **quasars.** *Quasar* is a shortened form of *quasi-stellar,* which means "seeming like a star." The galaxy surrounding a quasar is often hard to see because the quasar is so much brighter than it.

Evidence of a Supermassive Black Hole

disk of gas swirling around the black hole

gas being drawn into the black hole

 CHECK YOUR READING How can astronomers detect the presence of a supermassive black hole at the center of a galaxy?

 Review

KEY CONCEPTS

1. What is the shape of the Milky Way?

2. Why does the Milky Way look like a hazy band of stars in the sky?

3. What keeps the stars in galaxies from moving apart?

CRITICAL THINKING

4. **Compare and Contrast** Make a diagram showing similarities and differences among the three main types of galaxies.

5. **Infer** How might our view of the Milky Way be different if the Sun were located inside the central bulge?

CHALLENGE

6. **Predict** If two spiral galaxies collide, what might eventually happen to the supermassive black holes at their centers?

EXTREME SCIENCE

When Galaxies Collide

A small galaxy is moving through our galaxy, the Milky Way, right now!

- The small galaxy may be destroyed by the collision, but the Milky Way is not in danger.
- The same galaxy seems to have moved through the Milky Way ten times before.
- Other galaxies may also be moving through the Milky Way.

Not to Worry!

Galaxies containing many billions of stars are colliding all the time. What are the chances that their stars will crash into one another? The chances are very small, because there is so much empty space between stars.

Galactic Cannibals

When galaxies collide, a larger galaxy can "eat up" a smaller one.

- The stars of the smaller galaxy become part of the larger one.
- The collision of two spiral galaxies may form a new elliptical galaxy.

Bent Out of Shape

Sometimes galaxies pass very close to each other without actually colliding. In these near misses, gravity can produce some interesting new shapes. For example, the Tadpole Galaxy (left) has a long tail of dust and gas pulled out by the gravity of a passing galaxy.

Model Galaxies

Astronomers use computer simulations to predict how the stars and gas in galaxies are affected by a collision. To understand galaxy collisions better, they then compare the simulations with images of actual galaxies.

EXPLORE

1. **PREDICT** Draw the shape of the new galaxy that the two in the photograph on the left might form.

2. **CHALLENGE** Look at online images and simulations of galaxy collisions. Make a chart showing how these collisions can differ.

 **RESOURCE CENTER**
CLASSZONE.COM
Find out more about galaxy collisions.

Come back in a few billion years and you may see that these two spiral galaxies have become one elliptical galaxy.

The universe is expanding.

◀ **BEFORE,** you learned

- Galaxies contain millions or billions of stars
- Electromagnetic radiation carries information about space

▶ **NOW,** you will learn

- How galaxies are moving apart in the universe
- What scientists are discovering about the development of the universe

VOCABULARY

Doppler effect p. 136
big bang p. 138

EXPLORE Large Numbers

How much is a billion?

PROCEDURE

1. Guess how thick a billion-page book would be. Write down your guess.

2. Count how many sheets of paper in a book add up to a millimeter in thickness. Multiply by 2 to calculate the number of pages.

3. Then divide 1 billion (1,000,000,000) by that number to determine how many millimeters thick the book would be. Divide your result by 1,000,000 to convert to kilometers.

MATERIALS
- book
- ruler
- calculator

WHAT DO YOU THINK?
- How thick would a billion-page book be?
- How close was your guess?

Galaxies are moving farther apart in the universe.

COMBINATION NOTES
You could record information about the expansion of the universe in a combination notes table.

The universe is unbelievably huge. It consists of all space, energy, and matter. The Milky Way is just one of about 100 billion galaxies. These galaxies occur in groups that together form superclusters. Between the superclusters are huge areas of nearly empty space.

Because the universe is so huge, you might think that the most distant regions of the universe are very different from space near Earth. However, by looking at the spectra of light from stars and galaxies, astronomers have determined that the same elements are found throughout the universe. Scientific observations also indicate that the same physical forces and processes operate everywhere.

Looking Back in Time

Light from the Andromeda Galaxy takes 2 million years to reach Earth.

When we look far out into space, we see galaxies by the light they gave off long ago. This light has traveled millions or even billions of years before reaching telescopes on Earth. The Andromeda Galaxy, for example, is the closest large galaxy. The light of its stars takes over 2 million years to reach Earth. When we view this galaxy through a telescope, we are seeing what happened in it 2 million years ago. To see what is happening there now, we would have to wait 2 million years for the light to arrive.

As astronomers look at galaxies farther and farther away, they see how the universe looked at different times in the past. These views are like photographs in an album that show someone at various stages of life. Astronomers can see how the universe has developed over billions of years.

 CHECK YOUR READING Why can astronomers learn about the past by looking at distant galaxies?

The Motion of Galaxies

Have you ever noticed that the sound of an ambulance siren changes as it travels toward and then away from you? The pitch of the siren seems to be higher as the ambulance approaches. As the ambulance passes you and starts moving away, the pitch of the siren seems to get lower. The shifting pitch of the siren is an example of the **Doppler effect,** which is a change in the observed wavelength or frequency of a wave that occurs when the source of the wave or the observer is moving.

The Doppler effect occurs with light as well as sound. If a galaxy is moving toward Earth, the light we receive will seem compressed to shorter wavelengths. This change is called a blue shift because the light shifts toward the blue end of the spectrum. If a galaxy is moving away from Earth, the light we receive will seem stretched to longer wavelengths. This change is called a red shift because the light shifts toward the red end of the spectrum.

In the early 1900s, astronomers discovered that light from distant galaxies is stretched to longer wavelengths. This fact indicates that the galaxies are moving apart. By analyzing the spectra of galaxies, astronomers also discovered that the galaxies are moving apart faster the farther away they are. These observations led astronomers to conclude that the universe has been expanding throughout its history.

Evidence of an Expanding Universe

The Doppler effect can show how galaxies are moving in relation to Earth.

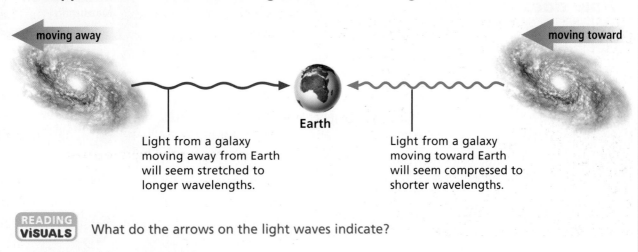

moving away

moving toward

Earth

Light from a galaxy moving away from Earth will seem stretched to longer wavelengths.

Light from a galaxy moving toward Earth will seem compressed to shorter wavelengths.

READING VISUALS What do the arrows on the light waves indicate?

The illustration of raisin-bread dough rising will help you imagine this expansion. Suppose you were a raisin. You would observe that all the other raisins are moving away from you as the dough expands. The raisins are being moved apart by the expanding dough. Furthermore, you would observe that distant raisins are moving away faster than nearby raisins. They move away faster because there is more dough expanding between you and those raisins.

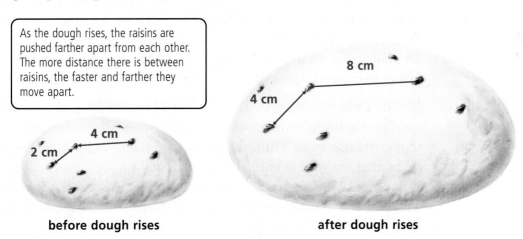

As the dough rises, the raisins are pushed farther apart from each other. The more distance there is between raisins, the faster and farther they move apart.

2 cm
4 cm
4 cm
8 cm

before dough rises

after dough rises

Like the dough that expands and moves raisins apart, space in the universe is expanding and moving galaxies apart. The universe does not expand into anything, since there is nothing outside the universe. Rather, the universe itself is expanding.

CHECK YOUR READING How are galaxies moving in relation to each other?

INVESTIGATE Galaxies

How does the universe expand?

PROCEDURE

1. Spread the cut rubber band against the ruler without stretching it. Mark off every centimeter for 6 centimeters.

2. Align the first mark on the rubber band with the 1-centimeter mark on the ruler and hold it in place tightly. Stretch the rubber band so that the second mark is next to the 3-centimeter mark on the ruler.

3. Observe how many centimeters each mark has moved from its original location against the ruler.

WHAT DO YOU THINK?

- How far did each mark on the rubber band move from its original location?

- What does this activity demonstrate about the expansion of the universe?

CHALLENGE How could you calculate the rates at which the marks moved when you stretched the rubber band?

SKILL FOCUS
Measuring

MATERIALS
- thick rubber band cut open
- ballpoint pen
- ruler

TIME
20 minutes

Scientists are investigating the origin of the universe.

After astronomers learned that galaxies are moving apart, they developed new ideas about the origin of the universe. They concluded that all matter was once merged together and then the universe suddenly began to expand. The evidence for this scientific theory is so strong that almost all astronomers now accept it.

The **big bang** is the moment in time when the universe started to expand out of an extremely hot, dense state. Astronomers have calculated that this event happened about 14 billion years ago. The expansion was very rapid. In a tiny fraction of a second, the universe may have expanded from a size much smaller than a speck of dust to the size of our solar system.

VOCABULARY
Add a description wheel for *big bang* in your notebook.

Evidence of the Big Bang

Evidence for the big bang comes from various sources. One important source of evidence is microwave radiation. Astronomers predicted in 1948 that the universe would still be filled with microwaves emitted shortly after the big bang. In 1965 researchers detected this kind of radiation streaming through space in all directions.

Besides the presence of microwave radiation and the motions of galaxies, scientists have found other evidence of the big bang by observing space. For example, images of very distant galaxies provide information about the universe's development. Additional evidence of the big bang has come from experiments and computer models.

Development of the Universe

Immediately after the big bang, the universe was incredibly dense and hot—much hotter than the core of the Sun. Matter and energy behaved very differently than they do under present conditions. As the universe rapidly expanded, it went through a series of changes.

Scientists do not fully understand what conditions were like in the early universe. However, they are gaining a clearer picture of how the universe developed. One way that scientists are learning about this development is by performing experiments in particle accelerators. These huge machines expose matter to extreme conditions.

Scientists have found that the earliest stages in the universe's development occurred in a tiny fraction of a second. However, it took about 300,000 years for the first elements to form. Stars, planets, and galaxies began to appear within the next billion years. Some evidence suggests that the first stars formed only a few hundred million years after the big bang.

This Hubble telescope image of very distant galaxies has helped scientists learn what the universe was like about 13 billion years ago.

 CHECK YOUR READING What happened to the universe shortly after the big bang?

 **4.4 Review**

KEY CONCEPTS

1. How are distant regions of the universe similar to space near Earth?

2. What does the Doppler effect indicate about the motion of galaxies?

3. How do scientists explain the origin of the universe?

CRITICAL THINKING

4. **Apply** If a star 100 light-years from Earth is beginning to expand into a giant star, how long will it take for astronomers to observe this development? Explain.

5. **Analyze** Why do scientists need to perform experiments to learn about the earliest stages of the universe?

CHALLENGE

6. **Infer** Galaxy A and galaxy B both give off light that appears stretched to longer wavelengths. The light from galaxy B is stretched to even longer wavelengths than the light from galaxy A. What can you infer from these data?

the BIG idea

Our Sun is one of billions of stars in one of billions of galaxies in the universe.

CONTENT REVIEW
CLASSZONE.COM

KEY CONCEPTS SUMMARY

4.1 The Sun is our local star.

The Sun produces energy from hydrogen. Energy flows through the Sun's layers. Features appear on the Sun's surface.

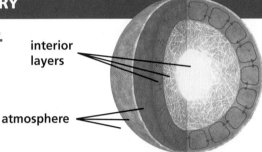

interior layers

atmosphere

VOCABULARY
fusion p. 116
convection p. 116
corona p. 116
sunspot p. 118
solar wind p. 119

4.2 Stars change over their life cycles.

Stars vary in brightness, size, color, and temperature. The development of a star depends on the mass of the star. Most stars are grouped with one or more companion stars.

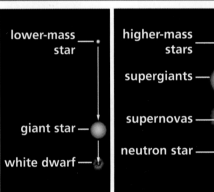

lower-mass star

giant star

white dwarf

higher-mass stars

supergiants

supernovas

neutron star

black hole

VOCABULARY
light-year p. 122
parallax p. 123
nebula p. 125
main sequence p. 126
neutron star p. 126
black hole p. 126

4.3 Galaxies have different sizes and shapes.

Our galaxy, the Milky Way, is a spiral galaxy. Galaxies can also be elliptical or irregular. Irregular galaxies have no definite shape.

Spiral Galaxy

Elliptical Galaxy

Irregular Galaxy

VOCABULARY
quasar p. 133

4.4 The universe is expanding.

Galaxies are moving farther apart in the universe. Scientists are investigating the origin and development of the universe.

VOCABULARY
Doppler effect p. 136
big bang p. 138

Reviewing Vocabulary

Make a frame for each of the vocabulary words listed below. Write the word in the center. Decide what information to frame it with. Use definitions, examples, descriptions, parts, or pictures. An example is shown below.

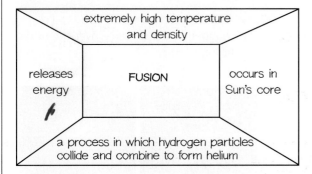

extremely high temperature and density

releases energy

FUSION

occurs in Sun's core

a process in which hydrogen particles collide and combine to form helium

1. convection

2. corona

3. sunspot

4. solar wind

5. nebula

6. black hole

7. Doppler effect

8. big bang

Reviewing Key Concepts

Multiple Choice *Choose the letter of the best answer.*

9. Which layer do you usually see in photographs of the Sun?
   a. convection zone   **c.** chromosphere
   b. photosphere   **d.** corona

10. Which statement is true of sunspots?
   a. They are permanent features on the Sun's surface.
   b. They are caused by solar wind.
   c. They are where fusion occurs.
   d. They are cooler than surrounding areas.

11. Which unit is usually used to describe the distances of stars?
   a. astronomical units   **c.** kilometers
   b. light-years   **d.** miles

12. Which example best shows the relationship between color and temperature?
   a. A rainbow forms when sunlight strikes raindrops.
   b. A flashlight beam looks red when passed through a red plastic filter.
   c. A chemical light-stick glows a yellow-green color.
   d. A metal rod in a fireplace changes in color from red to orange.

13. How do lower-mass stars differ from higher-mass stars?
   a. They develop more quickly.
   b. They develop more slowly.
   c. They end up as black holes.
   d. They have too little mass to produce energy.

14. Which term describes the Milky Way?
   a. spiral galaxy   **c.** irregular galaxy
   b. elliptical galaxy   **d.** quasar

15. The Doppler effect is used to determine
   a. the number of stars in a galaxy
   b. the number of galaxies in the universe
   c. the size of the universe
   d. whether a galaxy is moving toward or away from Earth

16. What is the big bang?
   a. the collision of galaxies
   b. the formation of the solar system
   c. the beginning of the universe's expansion
   d. the time when stars began to form

Short Answer *Write a short answer to each question.*

17. Why can't we see the Sun's corona under normal conditions?

18. How do astronomers use parallax to calculate a star's distance?

19. Where do heavy elements, such as iron, come from?

20. How can astronomers tell whether a black hole exists in the center of a galaxy?

The table below shows the distances of some galaxies and the speeds at which they are moving away from the Milky Way. Use the table to answer the next three questions.

Galaxy	Distance (million light-years)	Speed (kilometers per second)
NGC 7793	14	241
NGC 6946	22	336
NGC 2903	31	472
NGC 6744	42	663

21. COMPARE AND CONTRAST How do the speed and distance of NGC 7793 compare with the speed and distance of NGC 2903?

22. ANALYZE What general pattern do you see in these data?

23. APPLY What would you estimate to be the speed of a galaxy located 60 million light-years away? **Hint:** Notice the pattern between the first and third rows and the second and fourth rows in the chart.

24. INFER Why might the solar wind have a stronger effect on inner planets than on outer planets in the solar system?

25. PREDICT The core of a particular star consists almost entirely of helium. What will soon happen to this star?

26. ANALYZE Planets shine by reflected light. Why do some planets in our solar system appear brighter than stars, even though the stars give off their own light?

27. IDENTIFY CAUSE A star dims for a brief period every three days. What could be causing it to dim?

28. COMPARE AND CONTRAST Describe the similarities and differences between the life cycles of lower-mass stars and higher-mass stars.

29. EVALUATE If you wanted to study a neutron star, would you use a visible-light telescope or an x-ray telescope? Explain why.

30. INFER Suppose that astronomers find evidence of iron and other heavy elements in a galaxy. On the basis of this evidence, what can you assume has already occurred in that galaxy?

31. ANALYZE Why did the discovery that galaxies are moving farther apart help scientists conclude that all matter was once merged together?

32. PREDICT What changes do you predict will happen in the universe over the next 10 billion years?

33. COMPARE AND CONTRAST The photographs above show a spiral galaxy and an elliptical galaxy. What similarities and differences do you see in these two types of galaxies?

the BIG idea

34. INFER Look again at the photograph on pages 112–113. Now that you have finished the chapter, how would you change your response to the question on the photograph? What else might be present?

35. SYNTHESIZE Think of a question that you still have about the universe. What information would you need to answer the question? How might you obtain this information?

UNIT PROJECTS

Evaluate all the data, results, and information in your project folder. Prepare to present your project.

Standardized Test Practice

Analyzing a Chart

Use the chart and diagram to answer the next six questions.

Classification of Stars

Class	Color	Surface Temperature (°C)
O	blue–white	above 25,000
B	blue–white	10,000–25,000
A	white	7500–10,000
F	yellow–white	6000–7500
G	yellow	5000–6000
K	orange	3500–5000
M	red	below 3500

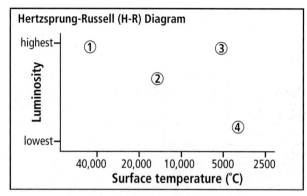

1. Which class of star has the lowest surface temperature?

a. O   **c.** G

b. B   **d.** M

2. Which class of star has the highest surface temperature?

a. O   **c.** G

b. B   **d.** M

3. What would be the color of a star with a surface temperature of 8000°C?

a. blue–white   **c.** orange

b. white   **d.** red

4. Toward the end of their life cycles, very massive stars expand in size, and their surface temperature becomes lower. Which of the following is an example of this change?

a. A white star becomes a blue-white star.

b. A blue-white star becomes a red star.

c. A red star becomes a blue-white star.

d. A yellow star becomes a yellow-white star.

5. The H-R diagram above shows the surface temperatures and luminosities, or true brightnesses, of four stars. Which of the stars is a type O?

a. 1   **c.** 3

b. 2   **d.** 4

6. Which two stars on the H-R diagram have the most similar surface temperatures?

a. 1 and 2   **c.** 2 and 3

b. 1 and 3   **d.** 3 and 4

Extended Response

Answer the two questions below in detail.

7. Why is looking at a star in the night sky like seeing back into time?

8. How could you use two flashlights to demonstrate the concept that the apparent brightness of a star is affected by its distance from Earth? You can include a diagram as part of your answer.

Student Resource Handbooks

Scientific Thinking Handbook

Making Observations

An **observation** is an act of noting and recording an event, character-istic, behavior, or anything else detected with an instrument or with the senses.

Observations allow you to make informed hypotheses and to gather data for experiments. Careful observations often lead to ideas for new experiments. There are two categories of observations:

- **Quantitative observations** can be expressed in numbers and include records of time, temperature, mass, distance, and volume.

- **Qualitative observations** include descriptions of sights, sounds, smells, and textures.

EXAMPLE

A student dissolved 30 grams of Epsom salts in water, poured the solution into a dish, and let the dish sit out uncovered overnight. The next day, she made the following observations of the Epsom salt crystals that grew in the dish.

Table 1. Observations of Epsom Salt Crystals

Quantitative Observations	Qualitative Observations
• mass = 30 g • mean crystal length = 0.5 cm • longest crystal length = 2 cm	• Crystals are clear. • Crystals are long, thin, and rectangular. • White crust has formed around edge of dish.

To determine the mass, the student found the mass of the dish before and after growing the crystals and then used subtraction to find the difference.

The student measured several crystals and calculated the mean length. (To learn how to calculate the mean of a data set, see page R36.)

Photographs or sketches are useful for recording qualitative observations.

Epsom salt crystals

MORE ABOUT OBSERVING

- Make quantitative observations whenever possible. That way, others will know exactly what you observed and be able to compare their results with yours.

- It is always a good idea to make qualitative observations too. You never know when you might observe something unexpected.

Predicting and Hypothesizing

A **prediction** is an expectation of what will be observed or what will happen. A **hypothesis** is a tentative explanation for an observation or scientific problem that can be tested by further investigation.

EXAMPLE

Suppose you have made two paper airplanes and you wonder why one of them tends to glide farther than the other one.

1. Start by asking a question.

2. Make an educated guess. After examination, you notice that the wings of the airplane that flies farther are slightly larger than the wings of the other airplane.

3. Write a prediction based upon your educated guess, in the form of an "If . . . , then . . ." statement. Write the independent variable after the word *if,* and the dependent variable after the word *then.*

4. To make a hypothesis, explain why you think what you predicted will occur. Write the explanation after the word *because*.

1. Why does one of the paper airplanes glide farther than the other?

2. The size of an airplane's wings may affect how far the airplane will glide.

3. Prediction: If I make a paper airplane with larger wings, then the airplane will glide farther.

To read about independent and dependent variables, see page R30.

4. Hypothesis: If I make a paper airplane with larger wings, then the airplane will glide farther, because the additional surface area of the wing will produce more lift.

Notice that the part of the hypothesis after *because* adds an explanation of why the airplane will glide farther.

MORE ABOUT HYPOTHESES

- The results of an experiment cannot prove that a hypothesis is correct. Rather, the results either support or do not support the hypothesis.

- Valuable information is gained even when your hypothesis is not supported by your results. For example, it would be an important discovery to find that wing size is not related to how far an airplane glides.

- In science, a hypothesis is supported only after many scientists have conducted many experiments and produced consistent results.

Inferring

An **inference** is a logical conclusion drawn from the available evidence and prior knowledge. Inferences are often made from observations.

SCIENTIFIC THINKING HANDBOOK

EXAMPLE

A student observing a set of acorns noticed something unexpected about one of them. He noticed a white, soft-bodied insect eating its way out of the acorn.

The student recorded these observations.

Observations

- There is a hole in the acorn, about 0.5 cm in diameter, where the insect crawled out.
- There is a second hole, which is about the size of a pinhole, on the other side of the acorn.
- The inside of the acorn is hollow.

Here are some inferences that can be made on the basis of the observations.

Inferences

- The insect formed from the material inside the acorn, grew to its present size, and ate its way out of the acorn.
- The insect crawled through the smaller hole, ate the inside of the acorn, grew to its present size, and ate its way out of the acorn.
- An egg was laid in the acorn through the smaller hole. The egg hatched into a larva that ate the inside of the acorn, grew to its present size, and ate its way out of the acorn.

When you make inferences, be sure to look at all of the evidence available and combine it with what you already know.

MORE ABOUT INFERENCES

Inferences depend both on observations and on the knowledge of the people making the inferences. Ancient people who did not know that organisms are produced only by similar organisms might have made an inference like the first one. A student today might look at the same observations and make the second inference. A third student might have knowledge about this particular insect and know that it is never small enough to fit through the smaller hole, leading her to the third inference.

Identifying Cause and Effect

In a **cause-and-effect relationship,** one event or characteristic is the result of another. Usually an effect follows its cause in time.

There are many examples of cause-and-effect relationships in everyday life.

Cause	Effect
Turn off a light.	Room gets dark.
Drop a glass.	Glass breaks.
Blow a whistle.	Sound is heard.

Scientists must be careful not to infer a cause-and-effect relationship just because one event happens after another event. When one event occurs after another, you cannot infer a cause-and-effect relationship on the basis of that information alone. You also cannot conclude that one event caused another if there are alternative ways to explain the second event. A scientist must demonstrate through experimentation or continued observation that an event was truly caused by another event.

EXAMPLE

Make an Observation

Suppose you have a few plants growing outside. When the weather starts getting colder, you bring one of the plants indoors. You notice that the plant you brought indoors is growing faster than the others are growing. You cannot conclude from your observation that the change in temperature was the cause of the increased plant growth, because there are alternative explanations for the observation. Some possible explanations are given below.

- The humidity indoors caused the plant to grow faster.

- The level of sunlight indoors caused the plant to grow faster.

- The indoor plant's being noticed more often and watered more often than the outdoor plants caused it to grow faster.

- The plant that was brought indoors was healthier than the other plants to begin with.

To determine which of these factors, if any, caused the indoor plant to grow faster than the outdoor plants, you would need to design and conduct an experiment.

See pages R28–R35 for information about designing experiments.

Recognizing Bias

Television, newspapers, and the Internet are full of experts claiming to have scientific evidence to back up their claims. How do you know whether the claims are really backed up by good science?

Bias is a slanted point of view, or personal prejudice. The goal of scientists is to be as objective as possible and to base their findings on facts instead of opinions. However, bias often affects the conclusions of researchers, and it is important to learn to recognize bias.

When scientific results are reported, you should consider the source of the information as well as the information itself. It is important to critically analyze the information that you see and read.

SOURCES OF BIAS

There are several ways in which a report of scientific information may be biased. Here are some questions that you can ask yourself:

1. **Who is sponsoring the research?**

   Sometimes, the results of an investigation are biased because an organization paying for the research is looking for a specific answer. This type of bias can affect how data are gathered and interpreted.

2. **Is the research sample large enough?**

   Sometimes research does not include enough data. The larger the sample size, the more likely that the results are accurate, assuming a truly random sample.

3. **In a survey, who is answering the questions?**

   The results of a survey or poll can be biased. The people taking part in the survey may have been specifically chosen because of how they would answer. They may have the same ideas or lifestyles. A survey or poll should make use of a random sample of people.

4. **Are the people who take part in a survey biased?**

   People who take part in surveys sometimes try to answer the questions the way they think the researcher wants them to answer. Also, in surveys or polls that ask for personal information, people may be unwilling to answer questions truthfully.

SCIENTIFIC BIAS

It is also important to realize that scientists have their own biases because of the types of research they do and because of their scientific viewpoints. Two scientists may look at the same set of data and come to completely different conclusions because of these biases. However, such disagreements are not necessarily bad. In fact, a critical analysis of disagreements is often responsible for moving science forward.

Identifying Faulty Reasoning

Faulty reasoning is wrong or incorrect thinking. It leads to mistakes and to wrong conclusions. Scientists are careful not to draw unreasonable conclusions from experimental data. Without such caution, the results of scientific investigations may be misleading.

EXAMPLE

Scientists try to make generalizations based on their data to explain as much about nature as possible. If only a small sample of data is looked at, however, a conclusion may be faulty. Suppose a scientist has studied the effects of the El Niño and La Niña weather patterns on flood damage in California from 1989 to 1995. The scientist organized the data in the bar graph below.

The scientist drew the following conclusions:

1. The La Niña weather pattern has no effect on flooding in California.

2. When neither weather pattern occurs, there is almost no flood damage.

3. A weak or moderate El Niño produces a small or moderate amount of flooding.

4. A strong El Niño produces a lot of flooding.

Flood and Storm Damage in California

Estimated damage (millions of dollars) vs. Starting year of season (July 1–June 30): Weak–moderate El Niño; Strong El Niño

SOURCE: *Governor's Office of Emergency Services, California*

For the six-year period of the scientist's investigation, these conclusions may seem to be reasonable. However, a six-year study of weather patterns may be too small of a sample for the conclusions to be supported. Consider the following graph, which shows information that was gathered from 1949 to 1997.

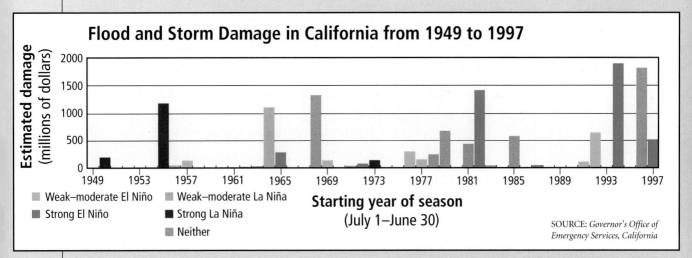

Flood and Storm Damage in California from 1949 to 1997

Estimated damage (millions of dollars) vs. Starting year of season (July 1–June 30)

Weak–moderate El Niño; Strong El Niño; Weak–moderate La Niña; Strong La Niña; Neither

SOURCE: *Governor's Office of Emergency Services, California*

The only one of the conclusions that all of this information supports is number 3: a weak or moderate El Niño produces a small or moderate amount of flooding. By collecting more data, scientists can be more certain of their conclusions and can avoid faulty reasoning.

Analyzing Statements

To **analyze** a statement is to examine its parts carefully. Scientific findings are often reported through media such as television or the Internet. A report that is made public often focuses on only a small part of research. As a result, it is important to question the sources of information.

Evaluate Media Claims

To **evaluate** a statement is to judge it on the basis of criteria you've established. Sometimes evaluating means deciding whether a statement is true.

Reports of scientific research and findings in the media may be misleading or incomplete. When you are exposed to this information, you should ask yourself some questions so that you can make informed judgments about the information.

1. **Does the information come from a credible source?**

   Suppose you learn about a new product and it is stated that scientific evidence proves that the product works. A report from a respected news source may be more believable than an advertisement paid for by the product's manufacturer.

2. **How much evidence supports the claim?**

   Often, it may seem that there is new evidence every day of something in the world that either causes or cures an illness. However, information that is the result of several years of work by several different scientists is more credible than an advertisement that does not even cite the subjects of the experiment.

3. **How much information is being presented?**

   Science cannot solve all questions, and scientific experiments often have flaws. A report that discusses problems in a scientific study may be more believable than a report that addresses only positive experimental findings.

4. **Is scientific evidence being presented by a specific source?**

   Sometimes scientific findings are reported by people who are called experts or leaders in a scientific field. But if their names are not given or their scientific credentials are not reported, their statements may be less credible than those of recognized experts.

Differentiate Between Fact and Opinion

Sometimes information is presented as a fact when it may be an opinion. When scientific conclusions are reported, it is important to recognize whether they are based on solid evidence. Again, you may find it helpful to ask yourself some questions.

1. **What is the difference between a fact and an opinion?**

   A **fact** is a piece of information that can be strictly defined and proved true. An **opinion** is a statement that expresses a belief, value, or feeling. An opinion cannot be proved true or false. For example, a person's age is a fact, but if someone is asked how old they feel, it is impossible to prove the person's answer to be true or false.

2. **Can opinions be measured?**

   Yes, opinions can be measured. In fact, surveys often ask for people's opinions on a topic. But there is no way to know whether or not an opinion is the truth.

HOW TO DIFFERENTIATE FACT FROM OPINION

Human Activities and the Environment

Unfortunately, human use of fossil fuels is one of the most significant developments of the past few centuries. Humans rely on fossil fuels, a non-renewable energy resource, for more than 90 percent of their energy needs.

This careless misuse of our planet's resources has resulted in pollution, global warming, and the destruction of fragile ecosystems. For example, oil pipelines carry more than one million barrels of oil each day across tundra regions. Transporting oil across such areas can only result in oil spills that poison the land for decades.

Opinions

Notice words or phrases that express beliefs or feelings. The words *unfortunately* and *careless* show that opinions are being expressed.

Opinion

Look for statements that speculate about events. These statements are opinions, because they cannot be proved.

Facts

Statements that contain statistics tend to be facts. Writers often use facts to support their opinions.

Lab Handbook

Safety Rules

Before you work in the laboratory, read these safety rules twice. Ask your teacher to explain any rules that you do not completely understand. Refer to these rules later on if you have questions about safety in the science classroom.

Directions

- Read all directions and make sure that you understand them before starting an investigation or lab activity. If you do not understand how to do a procedure or how to use a piece of equipment, ask your teacher.
- Do not begin any investigation or touch any equipment until your teacher has told you to start.
- Never experiment on your own. If you want to try a procedure that the directions do not call for, ask your teacher for permission first.
- If you are hurt or injured in any way, tell your teacher immediately.

Dress Code

goggles

apron

gloves

- Wear goggles when
  — using glassware, sharp objects, or chemicals
  — heating an object
  — working with anything that can easily fly up into the air and hurt someone's eye
- Tie back long hair or hair that hangs in front of your eyes.
- Remove any article of clothing—such as a loose sweater or a scarf—that hangs down and may touch a flame, chemical, or piece of equipment.
- Observe all safety icons calling for the wearing of eye protection, gloves, and aprons.

Heating and Fire Safety

fire safety

heating safety

- Keep your work area neat, clean, and free of extra materials.
- Never reach over a flame or heat source.
- Point objects being heated away from you and others.
- Never heat a substance or an object in a closed container.
- Never touch an object that has been heated. If you are unsure whether something is hot, treat it as though it is. Use oven mitts, clamps, tongs, or a test-tube holder.
- Know where the fire extinguisher and fire blanket are kept in your classroom.
- Do not throw hot substances into the trash. Wait for them to cool or use the container your teacher puts out for disposal.

Electrical Safety

electrical safety

- Never use lamps or other electrical equipment with frayed cords.
- Make sure no cord is lying on the floor where someone can trip over it.
- Do not let a cord hang over the side of a counter or table so that the equipment can easily be pulled or knocked to the floor.
- Never let cords hang into sinks or other places where water can be found.
- Never try to fix electrical problems. Inform your teacher of any problems immediately.
- Unplug an electrical cord by pulling on the plug, not the cord.

Chemical Safety

chemical safety

poison

fumes

- If you spill a chemical or get one on your skin or in your eyes, tell your teacher right away.
- Never touch, taste, or sniff any chemicals in the lab. If you need to determine odor, waft. Wafting consists of holding the chemical in its container 15 centimeters (6 in.) away from your nose, and using your fingers to bring fumes from the container to your nose.
- Keep lids on all chemicals you are not using.
- Never put unused chemicals back into the original containers. Throw away extra chemicals where your teacher tells you to.
- Pour chemicals over a sink or your work area, not over the floor.
- If you get a chemical in your eye, use the eyewash right away.
- Always wash your hands after handling chemicals, plants, or soil.

Wafting

LAB HANDBOOK

Glassware and Sharp-Object Safety

sharp objects

- If you break glassware, tell your teacher right away.
- Do not use broken or chipped glassware. Give these to your teacher.
- Use knives and other cutting instruments carefully. Always wear eye protection and cut away from you.

Animal Safety

- Never hurt an animal.
- Touch animals only when necessary. Follow your teacher's instructions for handling animals.
- Always wash your hands after working with animals.

Cleanup

disposal

- Follow your teacher's instructions for throwing away or putting away supplies.
- Clean your work area and pick up anything that has dropped to the floor.
- Wash your hands.

Using Lab Equipment

Different experiments require different types of equipment. But even though experiments differ, the ways in which the equipment is used are the same.

Beakers

- Use beakers for holding and pouring liquids.
- Do not use a beaker to measure the volume of a liquid. Use a graduated cylinder instead. (See page R16.)
- Use a beaker that holds about twice as much liquid as you need. For example, if you need 100 milliliters of water, you should use a 200- or 250-milliliter beaker.

Test Tubes

- Use test tubes to hold small amounts of substances.
- Do not use a test tube to measure the volume of a liquid.
- Use a test tube when heating a substance over a flame. Aim the mouth of the tube away from yourself and other people.
- Liquids easily spill or splash from test tubes, so it is important to use only small amounts of liquids.

Test-Tube Holder

- Use a test-tube holder when heating a substance in a test tube.
- Use a test-tube holder if the substance in a test tube is dangerous to touch.
- Make sure the test-tube holder tightly grips the test tube so that the test tube will not slide out of the holder.
- Make sure that the test-tube holder is above the surface of the substance in the test tube so that you can observe the substance.

Test-Tube Rack

- Use a test-tube rack to organize test tubes before, during, and after an experiment.

- Use a test-tube rack to keep test tubes upright so that they do not fall over and spill their contents.

- Use a test-tube rack that is the correct size for the test tubes that you are using. If the rack is too small, a test tube may become stuck. If the rack is too large, a test tube may lean over, and some of its contents may spill or splash.

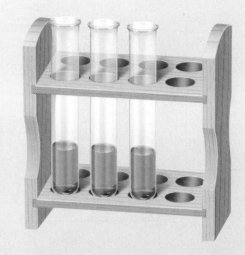

Forceps

- Use forceps when you need to pick up or hold a very small object that should not be touched with your hands.

- Do not use forceps to hold anything over a flame, because forceps are not long enough to keep your hand safely away from the flame. Plastic forceps will melt, and metal forceps will conduct heat and burn your hand.

Hot Plate

- Use a hot plate when a substance needs to be kept warmer than room temperature for a long period of time.

- Use a hot plate instead of a Bunsen burner or a candle when you need to carefully control temperature.

- Do not use a hot plate when a substance needs to be burned in an experiment.

- Always use "hot hands" safety mitts or oven mitts when handling anything that has been heated on a hot plate.

Microscope

Scientists use microscopes to see very small objects that cannot easily be seen with the eye alone. A microscope magnifies the image of an object so that small details may be observed. A microscope that you may use can magnify an object 400 times—the object will appear 400 times larger than its actual size.

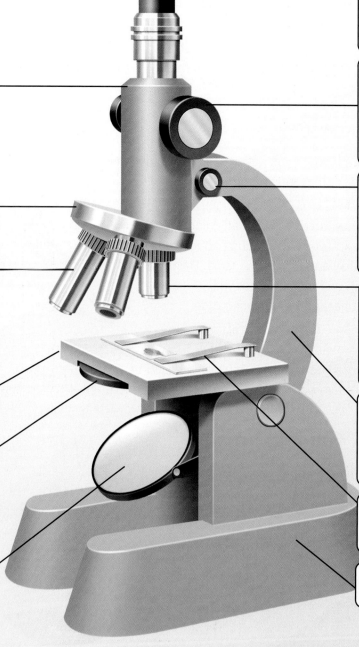

Eyepiece Objects are viewed through the eyepiece. The eyepiece contains a lens that commonly magnifies an image 10 times.

Coarse Adjustment This knob is used to focus the image of an object when it is viewed through the low-power lens.

Fine Adjustment This knob is used to focus the image of an object when it is viewed through the high-power lens.

Low-Power Objective Lens This is the smallest lens on the nosepiece. It magnifies an image approximately 10 times.

Arm The arm supports the body above the stage. Always carry a microscope by the arm and base.

Stage Clip The stage clip holds a slide in place on the stage.

Base The base supports the microscope.

Body The body separates the lens in the eyepiece from the objective lenses below.

Nosepiece The nosepiece holds the objective lenses above the stage and rotates so that all lenses may be used.

High-Power Objective Lens This is the largest lens on the nosepiece. It magnifies an image approximately 40 times.

Stage The stage supports the object being viewed.

Diaphragm The diaphragm is used to adjust the amount of light passing through the slide and into an objective lens.

Mirror or Light Source Some microscopes use light that is reflected through the stage by a mirror. Other microscopes have their own light sources.

VIEWING AN OBJECT

1. Use the coarse adjustment knob to raise the body tube.

2. Adjust the diaphragm so that you can see a bright circle of light through the eyepiece.

3. Place the object or slide on the stage. Be sure that it is centered over the hole in the stage.

4. Turn the nosepiece to click the low-power lens into place.

5. Using the coarse adjustment knob, slowly lower the lens and focus on the specimen being viewed. Be sure not to touch the slide or object with the lens.

6. When switching from the low-power lens to the high-power lens, first raise the body tube with the coarse adjustment knob so that the high-power lens will not hit the slide.

7. Turn the nosepiece to click the high-power lens into place.

8. Use the fine adjustment knob to focus on the specimen being viewed. Again, be sure not to touch the slide or object with the lens.

MAKING A SLIDE, OR WET MOUNT

① Place the specimen in the center of a clean slide.

② Place a drop of water on the specimen.

③ Place a cover slip on the slide. Put one edge of the cover slip into the drop of water and slowly lower it over the specimen.

④ Remove any air bubbles from under the cover slip by gently tapping the cover slip.

⑤ Dry any excess water before placing the slide on the microscope stage for viewing.

Spring Scale (Force Meter)

- Use a spring scale to measure a force pulling on the scale.
- Use a spring scale to measure the force of gravity exerted on an object by Earth.
- To measure a force accurately, a spring scale must be zeroed before it is used. The scale is zeroed when no weight is attached and the indicator is positioned at zero.
- Do not attach a weight that is either too heavy or too light to a spring scale. A weight that is too heavy could break the scale or exert too great a force for the scale to measure. A weight that is too light may not exert enough force to be measured accurately.

Graduated Cylinder

- Use a graduated cylinder to measure the volume of a liquid.
- Be sure that the graduated cylinder is on a flat surface so that your measurement will be accurate.
- When reading the scale on a graduated cylinder, be sure to have your eyes at the level of the surface of the liquid.
- The surface of the liquid will be curved in the graduated cylinder. Read the volume of the liquid at the bottom of the curve, or meniscus (muh-NIHS-kuhs).
- You can use a graduated cylinder to find the volume of a solid object by measuring the increase in a liquid's level after you add the object to the cylinder.

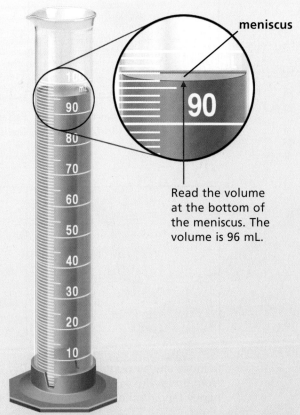

meniscus

Read the volume at the bottom of the meniscus. The volume is 96 mL.

LAB HANDBOOK

Metric Rulers

- Use metric rulers or meter sticks to measure objects' lengths.

- Do not measure an object from the end of a metric ruler or meter stick, because the end is often imperfect. Instead, measure from the 1-centimeter mark, but remember to subtract a centimeter from the apparent measurement.

- Estimate any lengths that extend between marked units. For example, if a meter stick shows centimeters but not millimeters, you can estimate the length that an object extends between centimeter marks to measure it to the nearest millimeter.

- **Controlling Variables** If you are taking repeated measurements, always measure from the same point each time. For example, if you're measuring how high two different balls bounce when dropped from the same height, measure both bounces at the same point on the balls—either the top or the bottom. Do not measure at the top of one ball and the bottom of the other.

EXAMPLE

How to Measure a Leaf

1. Lay a ruler flat on top of the leaf so that the 1-centimeter mark lines up with one end. Make sure the ruler and the leaf do not move between the time you line them up and the time you take the measurement.

2. Look straight down on the ruler so that you can see exactly how the marks line up with the other end of the leaf.

3. Estimate the length by which the leaf extends beyond a marking. For example, the leaf below extends about halfway between the 4.2-centimeter and 4.3-centimeter marks, so the apparent measurement is about 4.25 centimeters.

4. Remember to subtract 1 centimeter from your apparent measurement, since you started at the 1-centimeter mark on the ruler and not at the end. The leaf is about 3.25 centimeters long (4.25 cm – 1 cm = 3.25 cm).

Triple-Beam Balance

This balance has a pan and three beams with sliding masses, called riders. At one end of the beams is a pointer that indicates whether the mass on the pan is equal to the masses shown on the beams.

1. Make sure the balance is zeroed before measuring the mass of an object. The balance is zeroed if the pointer is at zero when nothing is on the pan and the riders are at their zero points. Use the adjustment knob at the base of the balance to zero it.

2. Place the object to be measured on the pan.

3. Move the riders one notch at a time away from the pan. Begin with the largest rider. If moving the largest rider one notch brings the pointer below zero, begin measuring the mass of the object with the next smaller rider.

4. Change the positions of the riders until they balance the mass on the pan and the pointer is at zero. Then add the readings from the three beams to determine the mass of the object.

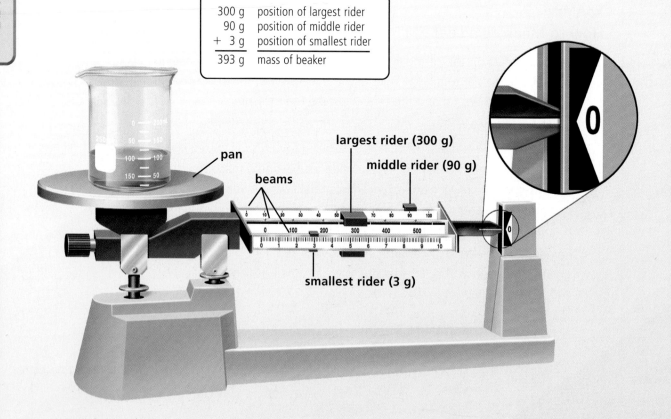

300 g	position of largest rider
90 g	position of middle rider
+ 3 g	position of smallest rider
393 g	mass of beaker

Double-Pan Balance

This type of balance has two pans. Between the pans is a pointer that indicates whether the masses on the pans are equal.

1. Make sure the balance is zeroed before measuring the mass of an object. The balance is zeroed if the pointer is at zero when there is nothing on either of the pans. Many double-pan balances have sliding knobs that can be used to zero them.

2. Place the object to be measured on one of the pans.

3. Begin adding standard masses to the other pan. Begin with the largest standard mass. If this adds too much mass to the balance, begin measuring the mass of the object with the next smaller standard mass.

4. Add standard masses until the masses on both pans are balanced and the pointer is at zero. Then add the standard masses together to determine the mass of the object being measured.

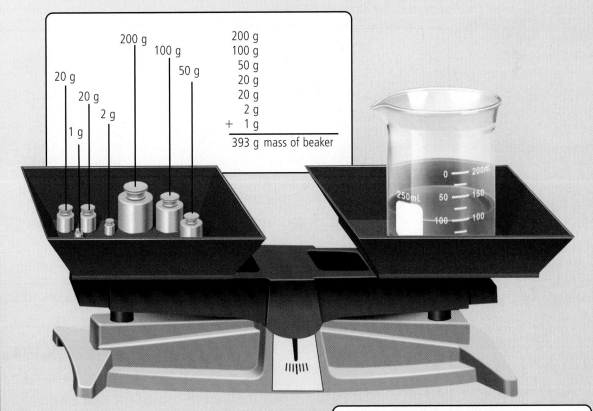

```
          200 g        200 g
                100 g  100 g
                        50 g
  20 g          50 g    20 g
                        20 g
     20 g                2 g
          2 g      +     1 g
                       _____
  1 g                   393 g  mass of beaker
```

Never place chemicals or liquids directly on a pan. Instead, use the following procedure:

1. Determine the mass of an empty container, such as a beaker.

2. Pour the substance into the container, and measure the total mass of the substance and the container.

3. Subtract the mass of the empty container from the total mass to find the mass of the substance.

The Metric System and SI Units

Scientists use International System (SI) units for measurements of distance, volume, mass, and temperature. The International System is based on multiples of ten and the metric system of measurement.

Basic SI Units		
Property	**Name**	**Symbol**
length	meter	m
volume	liter	L
mass	kilogram	kg
temperature	kelvin	K

SI Prefixes		
Prefix	**Symbol**	**Multiple of 10**
kilo-	k	1000
hecto-	h	100
deca-	da	10
deci-	d	$0.1 \left(\frac{1}{10}\right)$
centi-	c	$0.01 \left(\frac{1}{100}\right)$
milli-	m	$0.001 \left(\frac{1}{1000}\right)$

Changing Metric Units

You can change from one unit to another in the metric system by multiplying or dividing by a power of 10.

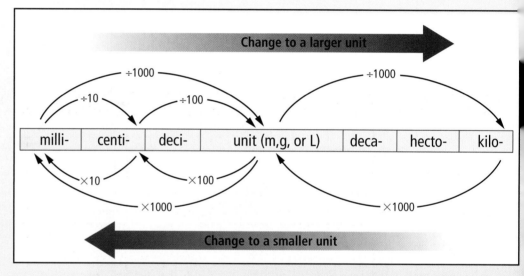

Example

Change 0.64 liters to milliliters.

(1) Decide whether to multiply or divide.

(2) Select the power of 10.

ANSWER 0.64 L = 640 mL

Change to a smaller unit by multiplying.

mL ← × 1000 — L

0.64 × 1000 = **640.**

Example

Change 23.6 grams to kilograms.

(1) Decide whether to multiply or divide.

(2) Select the power of 10.

ANSWER 23.6 g = 0.0236 kg

Change to a larger unit by dividing.

g — ÷ 1000 → kg

23.6 ÷ 1000 = **0.0236**

Temperature Conversions

Even though the kelvin is the SI base unit of temperature, the degree Celsius will be the unit you use most often in your science studies. The formulas below show the relationships between temperatures in degrees Fahrenheit (°F), degrees Celsius (°C), and kelvins (K).

$$°C = \frac{5}{9}(°F - 32)$$

$$°F = \frac{9}{5}°C + 32$$

$$K = °C + 273$$

See page R42 for help with using formulas.

Examples of Temperature Conversions		
Condition	**Degrees Celsius**	**Degrees Fahrenheit**
Freezing point of water	0	32
Cool day	10	50
Mild day	20	68
Warm day	30	86
Normal body temperature	37	98.6
Very hot day	40	104
Boiling point of water	100	212

Converting Between SI and U.S. Customary Units

Use the chart below when you need to convert between SI units and U.S. customary units.

SI Unit	From SI to U.S. Customary			From U.S. Customary to SI		
Length	**When you know**	**multiply by**	**to find**	**When you know**	**multiply by**	**to find**
kilometer (km) = 1000 m	kilometers	0.62	miles	miles	1.61	kilometers
meter (m) = 100 cm	meters	3.28	feet	feet	0.3048	meters
centimeter (cm) = 10 mm	centimeters	0.39	inches	inches	2.54	centimeters
millimeter (mm) = 0.1 cm	millimeters	0.04	inches	inches	25.4	millimeters
Area	**When you know**	**multiply by**	**to find**	**When you know**	**multiply by**	**to find**
square kilometer (km²)	square kilometers	0.39	square miles	square miles	2.59	square kilometers
square meter (m²)	square meters	1.2	square yards	square yards	0.84	square meters
square centimeter (cm²)	square centimeters	0.155	square inches	square inches	6.45	square centimeters
Volume	**When you know**	**multiply by**	**to find**	**When you know**	**multiply by**	**to find**
liter (L) = 1000 mL	liters	1.06	quarts	quarts	0.95	liters
	liters	0.26	gallons	gallons	3.79	liters
	liters	4.23	cups	cups	0.24	liters
	liters	2.12	pints	pints	0.47	liters
milliliter (mL) = 0.001 L	milliliters	0.20	teaspoons	teaspoons	4.93	milliliters
	milliliters	0.07	tablespoons	tablespoons	14.79	milliliters
	milliliters	0.03	fluid ounces	fluid ounces	29.57	milliliters
Mass	**When you know**	**multiply by**	**to find**	**When you know**	**multiply by**	**to find**
kilogram (kg) = 1000 g	kilograms	2.2	pounds	pounds	0.45	kilograms
gram (g) = 1000 mg	grams	0.035	ounces	ounces	28.35	grams

Precision and Accuracy

When you do an experiment, it is important that your methods, observations, and data be both precise and accurate.

low precision

precision, but not accuracy

precision and accuracy

Precision

In science, **precision** is the exactness and consistency of measurements. For example, measurements made with a ruler that has both centimeter and millimeter markings would be more precise than measurements made with a ruler that has only centimeter markings. Another indicator of precision is the care taken to make sure that methods and observations are as exact and consistent as possible. Every time a particular experiment is done, the same procedure should be used. Precision is necessary because experiments are repeated several times and if the procedure changes, the results will change.

EXAMPLE

Suppose you are measuring temperatures over a two-week period. Your precision will be greater if you measure each temperature at the same place, at the same time of day, and with the same thermometer than if you change any of these factors from one day to the next.

Accuracy

In science, it is possible to be precise but not accurate. **Accuracy** depends on the difference between a measurement and an actual value. The smaller the difference, the more accurate the measurement.

EXAMPLE

Suppose you look at a stream and estimate that it is about 1 meter wide at a particular place. You decide to check your estimate by measuring the stream with a meter stick, and you determine that the stream is 1.32 meters wide. However, because it is hard to measure the width of a stream with a meter stick, it turns out that you didn't do a very good job. The stream is actually 1.14 meters wide. Therefore, even though your estimate was less precise than your measurement, your estimate was actually more accurate.

Making Data Tables and Graphs

Data tables and graphs are useful tools for both recording and communicating scientific data.

Making Data Tables

You can use a **data table** to organize and record the measurements that you make. Some examples of information that might be recorded in data tables are frequencies, times, and amounts.

EXAMPLE

Suppose you are investigating photosynthesis in two elodea plants. One sits in direct sunlight, and the other sits in a dimly lit room. You measure the rate of photosynthesis by counting the number of bubbles in the jar every ten minutes.

1. Title and number your data table.
2. Decide how you will organize the table into columns and rows.
3. Any units, such as seconds or degrees, should be included in column headings, not in the individual cells.

Table 1. Number of Bubbles from Elodea

Time (min)	Sunlight	Dim Light
0	0	0
10	15	5
20	25	8
30	32	7
40	41	10
50	47	9
60	42	9

Always number and title data tables.

The data in the table above could also be organized in a different way.

Table 1. Number of Bubbles from Elodea

Light Condition	Time (min)						
	0	10	20	30	40	50	60
Sunlight	0	15	25	32	41	47	42
Dim light	0	5	8	7	10	9	9

Put units in column heading.

Making Line Graphs

You can use a **line graph** to show a relationship between variables. Line graphs are particularly useful for showing changes in variables over time.

EXAMPLE

Suppose you are interested in graphing temperature data that you collected over the course of a day.

Table 1. Outside Temperature During the Day on March 7

	Time of Day						
	7:00 A.M.	9:00 A.M.	11:00 A.M.	1:00 P.M.	3:00 P.M.	5:00 P.M.	7:00 P.M.
Temp (°C)	8	9	11	14	12	10	6

1. Use the vertical axis of your line graph for the variable that you are measuring—temperature.

2. Choose scales for both the horizontal axis and the vertical axis of the graph. You should have two points more than you need on the vertical axis, and the horizontal axis should be long enough for all of the data points to fit.

3. Draw and label each axis.

4. Graph each value. First find the appropriate point on the scale of the horizontal axis. Imagine a line that rises vertically from that place on the scale. Then find the corresponding value on the vertical axis, and imagine a line that moves horizontally from that value. The point where these two imaginary lines intersect is where the value should be plotted.

5. Connect the points with straight lines.

Be sure to add a number and a title to your graph.

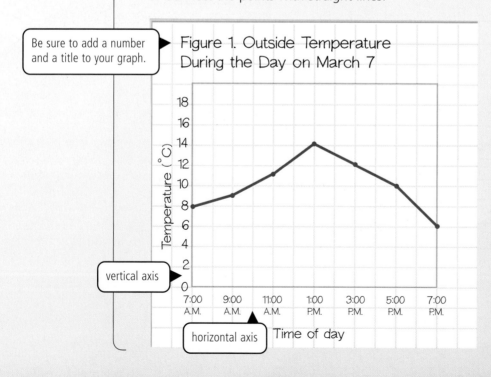

Figure 1. Outside Temperature During the Day on March 7

vertical axis

horizontal axis

Time of day

Making Circle Graphs

You can use a **circle graph,** sometimes called a pie chart, to represent data as parts of a circle. Circle graphs are used only when the data can be expressed as percentages of a whole. The entire circle shown in a circle graph is equal to 100 percent of the data.

EXAMPLE

Suppose you identified the species of each mature tree growing in a small wooded area. You organized your data in a table, but you also want to show the data in a circle graph.

1. To begin, find the total number of mature trees.

   $56 + 34 + 22 + 10 + 28 = 150$

2. To find the degree measure for each sector of the circle, write a fraction comparing the number of each tree species with the total number of trees. Then multiply the fraction by 360°.

   Oak: $\frac{56}{150} \times 360° = 134.4°$

3. Draw a circle. Use a protractor to draw the angle for each sector of the graph.

4. Color and label each sector of the graph.

5. Give the graph a number and title.

Table 1. Tree Species in Wooded Area

Species	Number of Specimens
Oak	56
Maple	34
Birch	22
Willow	10
Pine	28

Figure 1. Tree Species in Wooded Area

Willow 10
Birch 22
Pine 28
Oak 56
Maple 34

Instead of labeling each sector, you could make a color key.

Oak 56
Maple 34
Pine 28
Birch 22
Willow 10

Bar Graph

A **bar graph** is a type of graph in which the lengths of the bars are used to represent and compare data. A numerical scale is used to determine the lengths of the bars.

EXAMPLE

To determine the effect of water on seed sprouting, three cups were filled with sand, and ten seeds were planted in each. Different amounts of water were added to each cup over a three-day period.

Table 1. Effect of Water on Seed Sprouting

Daily Amount of Water (mL)	Number of Seeds That Sprouted After 3 Days in Sand
0	1
10	4
20	8

1. Choose a numerical scale. The greatest value is 8, so the end of the scale should have a value greater than 8, such as 10. Use equal increments along the scale, such as increments of 2.

2. Draw and label the axes. Mark intervals on the vertical axis according to the scale you chose.

3. Draw a bar for each data value. Use the scale to decide how long to make each bar.

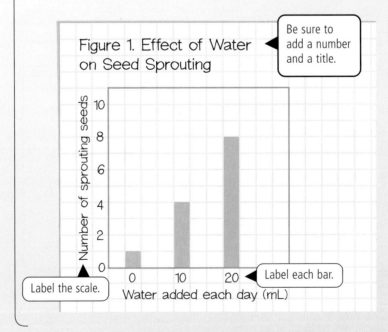

Figure 1. Effect of Water on Seed Sprouting

Be sure to add a number and a title.

Label the scale.

Label each bar.

Double Bar Graph

A **double bar graph** is a bar graph that shows two sets of data. The two bars for each measurement are drawn next to each other.

EXAMPLE

The seed-sprouting experiment was done using both sand and potting soil. The data for sand and potting soil can be plotted on one graph.

1. Draw one set of bars, using the data for sand, as shown below.

2. Draw bars for the potting-soil data next to the bars for the sand data. Shade them a different color. Add a key.

Table 2. Effect of Water and Soil on Seed Sprouting

Daily Amount of Water (mL)	Number of Seeds That Sprouted After 3 Days in Sand	Number of Seeds That Sprouted After 3 Days in Potting Soil
0	1	2
10	4	5
20	8	9

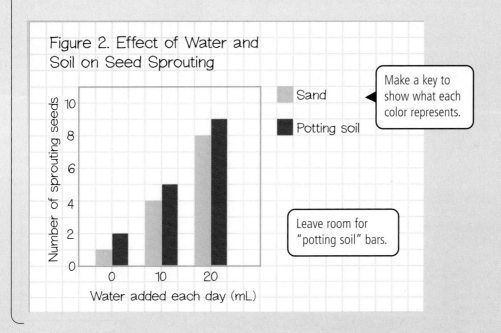

Figure 2. Effect of Water and Soil on Seed Sprouting

Make a key to show what each color represents.

Leave room for "potting soil" bars.

Designing an Experiment

Use this section when designing or conducting an experiment.

Determining a Purpose

You can find a purpose for an experiment by doing research, by examining the results of a previous experiment, or by observing the world around you. An **experiment** is an organized procedure to study something under controlled conditions.

1. Write the purpose of your experiment as a question or problem that you want to investigate.

2. Write down research questions and begin searching for information that will help you design an experiment. Consult the library, the Internet, and other people as you conduct your research.

> Don't forget to learn as much as possible about your topic before you begin.

EXAMPLE

Middle school students observed an odor near the lake by their school. They also noticed that the water on the side of the lake near the school was greener than the water on the other side of the lake. The students did some research to learn more about their observations. They discovered that the odor and green color in the lake

came from algae. They also discovered that a new fertilizer was being used on a field nearby. The students inferred that the use of the fertilizer might be related to the presence of the algae and designed a controlled experiment to find out whether they were right.

Problem

How does fertilizer affect the presence of algae in a lake?

Research Questions

- Have other experiments been done on this problem? If so, what did those experiments show?
- What kind of fertilizer is used on the field? How much?
- How do algae grow?
- How do people measure algae?
- Can fertilizer and algae be used safely in a lab? How?

> **Research**
> As you research, you may find a topic that is more interesting to you than your original topic, or learn that a procedure you wanted to use is not practical or safe. It is OK to change your purpose as you research.

Writing a Hypothesis

A **hypothesis** is a tentative explanation for an observation or scientific problem that can be tested by further investigation. You can write your hypothesis in the form of an "If . . . , then . . . , because . . ." statement.

Hypothesis

If the amount of fertilizer in lake water is increased, then the amount of algae will also increase, because fertilizers provide nutrients that algae need to grow.

Hypotheses
For help with hypotheses, refer to page R3.

Determining Materials

Make a list of all the materials you will need to do your experiment. Be specific, especially if someone else is helping you obtain the materials. Try to think of everything you will need.

Materials

- 1 large jar or container
- 4 identical smaller containers
- rubber gloves that also cover the arms
- sample of fertilizer-and-water solution
- eyedropper
- clear plastic wrap
- scissors
- masking tape
- marker
- ruler

Determining Variables and Constants

EXPERIMENTAL GROUP AND CONTROL GROUP

An experiment to determine how two factors are related always has two groups—a control group and an experimental group.

1. Design an experimental group. Include as many trials as possible in the experimental group in order to obtain reliable results.

2. Design a control group that is the same as the experimental group in every way possible, except for the factor you wish to test.

> **Experimental Group:** two containers of lake water with one drop of fertilizer solution added to each
>
> **Control Group:** two containers of lake water with no fertilizer solution added

Go back to your materials lis and make sure you have enough items listed to cover both your experimental grou and your control group.

VARIABLES AND CONSTANTS

Identify the variables and constants in your experiment. In a controlled experiment, a **variable** is any factor that can change. **Constants** are all of the factors that are the same in both the experimental group and the control group.

1. Read your hypothesis. The **independent variable** is the factor that you wish to test and that is manipulated or changed so that it can be tested. The independent variable is expressed in your hypothesis after the word *if*. Identify the independent variable in your laboratory report.

2. The **dependent variable** is the factor that you measure to gather results. It is expressed in your hypothesis after the word *then*. Identify the dependent variable in your laboratory report.

Hypothesis
If the amount of fertilizer in lake water is increased, then the amount of algae will also increase, because fertilizers provide nutrients that algae need to grow.

> Table 1. Variables and Constants in Algae Experiment
>
> | Independent Variable | Dependent Variable | Constants |
> |---|---|---|
> | Amount of fertilizer in lake water | Amount of algae that grow | • Where the lake water is obtained
• Type of container used
• Light and temperature conditions where water will be stored |
>
> Set up your experiment so that you will test only one variable.

MEASURING THE DEPENDENT VARIABLE

Before starting your experiment, you need to define how you will measure the dependent variable. An **operational definition** is a description of the one particular way in which you will measure the dependent variable.

Your operational definition is important for several reasons. First, in any experiment there are several ways in which a dependent variable can be measured. Second, the procedure of the experiment depends on how you decide to measure the dependent variable. Third, your operational definition makes it possible for other people to evaluate and build on your experiment.

EXAMPLE 1

An operational definition of a dependent variable can be qualitative. That is, your measurement of the dependent variable can simply be an observation of whether a change occurs as a result of a change in the independent variable. This type of operational definition can be thought of as a "yes or no" measurement.

Table 2. Qualitative Operational Definition of Algae Growth

Independent Variable	Dependent Variable	Operational Definition
Amount of fertilizer in lake water	Amount of algae that grow	Algae grow in lake water

A qualitative measurement of a dependent variable is often easy to make and record. However, this type of information does not provide a great deal of detail in your experimental results.

EXAMPLE 2

An operational definition of a dependent variable can be quantitative. That is, your measurement of the dependent variable can be a number that shows how much change occurs as a result of a change in the independent variable.

Table 3. Quantitative Operational Definition of Algae Growth

Independent Variable	Dependent Variable	Operational Definition
Amount of fertilizer in lake water	Amount of algae that grow	Diameter of largest algal growth (in mm)

A quantitative measurement of a dependent variable can be more difficult to make and analyze than a qualitative measurement. However, this type of data provides much more information about your experiment and is often more useful.

Writing a Procedure

Write each step of your procedure. Start each step with a verb, or action word, and keep the steps short. Your procedure should be clear enough for someone else to use as instructions for repeating your experiment.

> If necessary, go back to your materials list and add any materials that you left out.

Procedure

1. Put on your gloves. Use the large container to obtain a sample of lake water.

2. Divide the sample of lake water equally among the four smaller containers.

> **Controlling Variables**
> The same amount of fertilizer solution must be added to two of the four containers.

3. Use the eyedropper to add one drop of fertilizer solution to two of the containers.

4. Use the masking tape and the marker to label the containers with your initials, the date, and the identifiers "Jar 1 with Fertilizer," "Jar 2 with Fertilizer," "Jar 1 without Fertilizer," and "Jar 2 without Fertilizer."

5. Cover the containers with clear plastic wrap. Use the scissors to punch ten holes in each of the covers.

> **Controlling Variables**
> All four containers must receive the same amount of light.

6. Place all four containers on a window ledge. Make sure that they all receive the same amount of light.

7. Observe the containers every day for one week.

8. Use the ruler to measure the diameter of the largest clump of algae in each container, and record your measurements daily.

Recording Observations

Once you have obtained all of your materials and your procedure has been approved, you can begin making experimental observations. Gather both quantitative and qualitative data. If something goes wrong during your procedure, make sure you record that too.

> **Observations**
> For help with making qualitative and quantitative observations, refer to page R2.

> For more examples of data tables, see page R23.

Table 4. Fertilizer and Algae Growth

Date and Time	Experimental Group		Control Group		Observations
	Jar 1 with Fertilizer (diameter of algae in mm)	Jar 2 with Fertilizer (diameter of algae in mm)	Jar 1 without Fertilizer (diameter of algae in mm)	Jar 2 without Fertilizer (diameter of algae in mm)	
5/3 4:00 P.M.	0	0	0	0	condensation in all containers
5/4 4:00 P.M.	0	3	0	0	tiny green blobs in jar 2 with fertilizer
5/5 4:15 P.M.	4	5	0	3	green blobs in jars 1 and 2 with fertilizer and jar 2 without fertilizer
5/6 4:00 P.M.	5	6	0	4	water light green in jar 2 with fertilizer
5/7 4:00 P.M.	8	10	0	6	water light green in jars 1 and 2 with fertilizer and in jar 2 without fertilizer
5/8 3:30 P.M.	10	18	0	6	cover off jar 2 with fertilizer
5/9 3:30 P.M.	14	23	0	8	drew sketches of each container

> Notice that on the sixth day, the observer found that the cover was off one of the containers. It is important to record observations of unintended factors because they might affect the results of the experiment.

> Use technology, such as a microscope, to help you make observations when possible.

Drawings of Samples Viewed Under Microscope on 5/9 at 100x

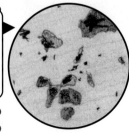
Jar 1 with Fertilizer

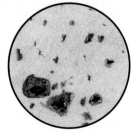
Jar 2 with Fertilizer

Jar 1 without Fertilizer

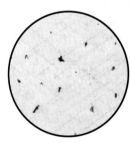
Jar 2 without Fertilizer

Summarizing Results

To summarize your data, look at all of your observations together. Look for meaningful ways to present your observations. For example, you might average your data or make a graph to look for patterns. When possible, use spreadsheet software to help you analyze and present your data. The two graphs below show the same data.

EXAMPLE 1

Always include a number and a title with a graph.

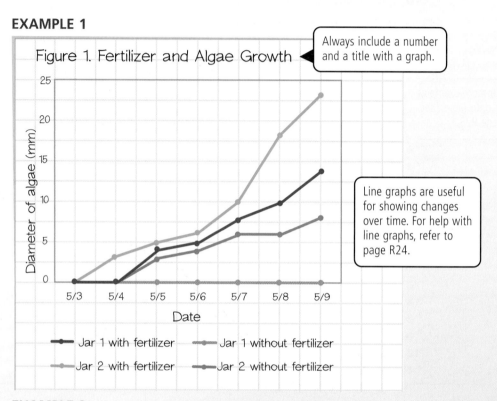

Figure 1. Fertilizer and Algae Growth

Line graphs are useful for showing changes over time. For help with line graphs, refer to page R24.

Bar graphs are useful for comparing different data sets. This bar graph has four bars for each day. Another way to present the data would be to calculate averages for the tests and the controls, and to show one test bar and one control bar for each day.

EXAMPLE 2

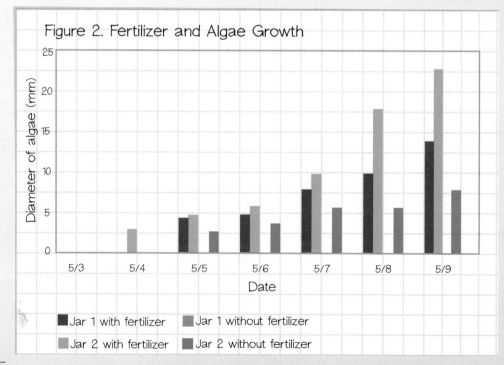

Figure 2. Fertilizer and Algae Growth

Drawing Conclusions

RESULTS AND INFERENCES

To draw conclusions from your experiment, first write your results. Then compare your results with your hypothesis. Do your results support your hypothesis? Be careful not to make inferences about factors that you did not test.

> For help with making inferences, see page R4.

Results and Inferences

The results of my experiment show that more algae grew in lake water to which fertilizer had been added than in lake water to which no fertilizer had been added. My hypothesis was supported. I infer that it is possible that the growth of algae in the lake was caused by the fertilizer used on the field.

> Notice that you cannot conclude from this experiment that the presence of algae in the lake was due only to the fertilizer.

QUESTIONS FOR FURTHER RESEARCH

Write a list of questions for further research and investigation. Your ideas may lead you to new experiments and discoveries.

Questions for Further Research

- What is the connection between the amount of fertilizer and algae growth?
- How do different brands of fertilizer affect algae growth?
- How would algae growth in the lake be affected if no fertilizer were used on the field?
- How do algae affect the lake and the other life in and around it?
- How does fertilizer affect the lake and the life in and around it?
- If fertilizer is getting into the lake, how is it getting there?

Math Handbook

Describing a Set of Data

Means, medians, modes, and ranges are important math tools for describing data sets such as the following widths of fossilized clamshells.

13 mm   25 mm   14 mm   21 mm   16 mm   23 mm   14 mm

Mean

The **mean** of a data set is the sum of the values divided by the number of values.

> #### Example
>
> To find the mean of the clamshell data, add the values and then divide the sum by the number of values.
>
> $$\frac{13 \text{ mm} + 25 \text{ mm} + 14 \text{ mm} + 21 \text{ mm} + 16 \text{ mm} + 23 \text{ mm} + 14 \text{ mm}}{7} = \frac{126 \text{ mm}}{7} = 18 \text{ mm}$$
>
> **ANSWER** The mean is 18 mm.

Median

The **median** of a data set is the middle value when the values are written in numerical order. If a data set has an even number of values, the median is the mean of the two middle values.

> #### Example
>
> To find the median of the clamshell data, arrange the values in order from least to greatest. The median is the middle value.
>
> 13 mm   14 mm   14 mm   16 mm   21 mm   23 mm   25 mm
>
> **ANSWER** The median is 16 mm.

Mode

The **mode** of a data set is the value that occurs most often.

> ## Example
>
> To find the mode of the clamshell data, arrange the values in order from least to greatest and determine the value that occurs most often.
>
> 13 mm   14 mm   14 mm   16 mm   21 mm   23 mm   25 mm
>
> **ANSWER** The mode is 14 mm.

A data set can have more than one mode or no mode. For example, the following data set has modes of 2 mm and 4 mm:

2 mm   2 mm   **3 mm**   4 mm   4 mm

The data set below has no mode, because no value occurs more often than any other.

2 mm   3 mm   4 mm   5 mm

Range

The **range** of a data set is the difference between the greatest value and the least value.

> ## Example
>
> To find the range of the clamshell data, arrange the values in order from least to greatest.
>
> 13 mm   14 mm   14 mm   16 mm   21 mm   23 mm   25 mm
>
> Subtract the least value from the greatest value.
>
> 13 mm is the least value.
> 25 mm is the greatest value.
>
> 25 mm − 13 mm = 12 mm
>
> **ANSWER** The range is 12 mm.

Using Ratios, Rates, and Proportions

You can use ratios and rates to compare values in data sets. You can use proportions to find unknown values.

Ratios

A **ratio** uses division to compare two values. The ratio of a value a to a nonzero value b can be written as $\frac{a}{b}$.

> ### Example
>
> The height of one plant is 8 centimeters. The height of another plant is 6 centimeters. To find the ratio of the height of the first plant to the height of the second plant, write a fraction and simplify it.
>
> $$\frac{8 \text{ cm}}{6 \text{ cm}} = \frac{4 \times \overset{1}{\cancel{2}}}{3 \times \underset{1}{\cancel{2}}} = \frac{4}{3}$$
>
> **ANSWER** The ratio of the plant heights is $\frac{4}{3}$.

You can also write the ratio $\frac{a}{b}$ as "a to b" or as $a:b$. For example, you can write the ratio of the plant heights as "4 to 3" or as $4:3$.

Rates

A **rate** is a ratio of two values expressed in different units. A unit rate is a rate with a denominator of 1 unit.

> ### Example
>
> A plant grew 6 centimeters in 2 days. The plant's rate of growth was $\frac{6 \text{ cm}}{2 \text{ days}}$. To describe the plant's growth in centimeters per day, write a unit rate.
>
> *Divide numerator and denominator by 2:* $\quad \frac{6 \text{ cm}}{2 \text{ days}} = \frac{6 \text{ cm} \div 2}{2 \text{ days} \div 2}$
>
> *Simplify:* $\quad\quad\quad\quad = \frac{3 \text{ cm}}{1 \text{ day}}$
>
> You divide 2 days by 2 to get 1 day, so divide 6 cm by 2 also.
>
> **ANSWER** The plant's rate of growth is 3 centimeters per day.

Proportions

A **proportion** is an equation stating that two ratios are equivalent. To solve for an unknown value in a proportion, you can use cross products.

Example

If a plant grew 6 centimeters in 2 days, how many centimeters would it grow in 3 days (if its rate of growth is constant)?

$$\textit{Write a proportion:} \quad \frac{6 \text{ cm}}{2 \text{ days}} = \frac{x}{3 \text{ days}}$$

$$\textit{Set cross products:} \quad 6 \text{ cm} \cdot 3 = 2x$$

$$\textit{Multiply 6 and 3:} \quad 18 \text{ cm} = 2x$$

$$\textit{Divide each side by 2:} \quad \frac{18 \text{ cm}}{2} = \frac{2x}{2}$$

$$\textit{Simplify:} \quad 9 \text{ cm} = x$$

ANSWER The plant would grow 9 centimeters in 3 days.

Using Decimals, Fractions, and Percents

Decimals, fractions, and percentages are all ways of recording and representing data.

Decimals

A **decimal** is a number that is written in the base-ten place value system, in which a decimal point separates the ones and tenths digits. The values of each place is ten times that of the place to its right.

Example

A caterpillar traveled from point *A* to point *C* along the path shown.

A   **36.9 cm**   B   **52.4 cm**   C

ADDING DECIMALS To find the total distance traveled by the caterpillar, add the distance from *A* to *B* and the distance from *B* to *C*. Begin by lining up the decimal points. Then add the figures as you would whole numbers and bring down the decimal point.

```
  36.9 cm
+ 52.4 cm
_____
  89.3 cm
```

ANSWER The caterpillar traveled a total distance of 89.3 centimeters.

Example *continued*

SUBTRACTING DECIMALS To find how much farther the caterpillar traveled on the second leg of the journey, subtract the distance from *A* to *B* from the distance from *B* to *C*.

$$
\begin{array}{r}
52.4 \text{ cm} \\
- \ 36.9 \text{ cm} \\
\hline
15.5 \text{ cm}
\end{array}
$$

ANSWER The caterpillar traveled 15.5 centimeters farther on the second leg of the journey.

Example

A caterpillar is traveling from point *D* to point *F* along the path shown. The caterpillar travels at a speed of 9.6 centimeters per minute.

D _____ E _____ **33.6 cm** _____ F

MULTIPLYING DECIMALS You can multiply decimals as you would whole numbers. The number of decimal places in the product is equal to the sum of the number of decimal places in the factors.

For instance, suppose it takes the caterpillar 1.5 minutes to go from *D* to *E*. To find the distance from *D* to *E*, multiply the caterpillar's speed by the time it took.

9.6	1	decimal place
$\times$ 1.5	+ 1	decimal place
480		
96		
14.40	2	decimal places

Align as shown.

ANSWER The distance from *D* to *E* is 14.4 centimeters.

DIVIDING DECIMALS When you divide by a decimal, move the decimal points the same number of places in the divisor and the dividend to make the divisor a whole number.

For instance, to find the time it will take the caterpillar to travel from *E* to *F*, divide the distance from *E* to *F* by the caterpillar's speed.

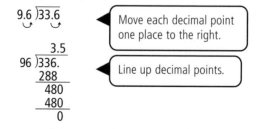

9.6)33.6   ◄ Move each decimal point one place to the right.

$$
\begin{array}{r}
3.5 \\
96 \overline{)336.} \\
\underline{288} \\
480 \\
\underline{480} \\
0
\end{array}
$$

◄ Line up decimal points.

ANSWER The caterpillar will travel from *E* to *F* in 3.5 minutes.

Fractions

A **fraction** is a number in the form $\frac{a}{b}$, where b is not equal to 0. A fraction is in **simplest form** if its numerator and denominator have a greatest common factor (GCF) of 1. To simplify a fraction, divide its numerator and denominator by their GCF.

Example

A caterpillar is 40 millimeters long. The head of the caterpillar is 6 millimeters long. To compare the length of the caterpillar's head with the caterpillar's total length, you can write and simplify a fraction that expresses the ratio of the two lengths.

$$\text{Write the ratio of the two lengths:} \quad \frac{\text{Length of head}}{\text{Total length}} = \frac{6 \text{ mm}}{40 \text{ mm}}$$

$$\text{Write numerator and denominator as products of numbers and the GCF:} \quad = \frac{3 \times 2}{20 \times 2}$$

$$\text{Divide numerator and denominator by the GCF:} \quad = \frac{3 \times \overset{1}{\cancel{2}}}{20 \times \underset{1}{\cancel{2}}}$$

$$\text{Simplify:} \quad = \frac{3}{20}$$

ANSWER In simplest form, the ratio of the lengths is $\frac{3}{20}$.

Percents

A **percent** is a ratio that compares a number to 100. The word *percent* means "per hundred" or "out of 100." The symbol for *percent* is %.

For instance, suppose 43 out of 100 caterpillars are female. You can represent this ratio as a percent, a decimal, or a fraction.

Percent	Decimal	Fraction
43%	0.43	$\frac{43}{100}$

Example

In the preceding example, the ratio of the length of the caterpillar's head to the caterpillar's total length is $\frac{3}{20}$. To write this ratio as a percent, write an equivalent fraction that has a denominator of 100.

$$\text{Multiply numerator and denominator by 5:} \quad \frac{3}{20} = \frac{3 \times 5}{20 \times 5}$$

$$= \frac{15}{100}$$

$$\text{Write as a percent:} \quad = 15\%$$

ANSWER The caterpillar's head represents 15 percent of its total length.

Using Formulas

A **formula** is an equation that shows the general relationship between two or more quantities.

The term *variable* is also used in science to refer to a factor that can change during an experiment.

In science, a formula often has a word form and a symbolic form. The formula below expresses Ohm's law.

Word Form

$$\text{Current} = \frac{\text{voltage}}{\text{resistance}}$$

Symbolic Form

$$I = \frac{V}{R}$$

In this formula, I, V, and R are variables. A mathematical **variable** is a symbol or letter that is used to represent one or more numbers.

Example

Suppose that you measure a voltage of 1.5 volts and a resistance of 15 ohms. You can use the formula for Ohm's law to find the current in amperes.

Write the formula for Ohm's law: $I = \dfrac{V}{R}$

Substitute 1.5 volts for V and 15 ohms for R: $I = \dfrac{1.5 \text{ volts}}{15 \text{ ohms}}$

Simplify: $I = 0.1 \text{ amp}$

ANSWER The current is 0.1 ampere.

If you know the values of all variables but one in a formula, you can solve for the value of the unknown variable. For instance, Ohm's law can be used to find a voltage if you know the current and the resistance.

Example

Suppose that you know that a current is 0.2 amperes and the resistance is 18 ohms. Use the formula for Ohm's law to find the voltage in volts.

Write the formula for Ohm's law: $I = \dfrac{V}{R}$

Substitute 0.2 amp for I and 18 ohms for R: $0.2 \text{ amp} = \dfrac{V}{18 \text{ ohms}}$

Multiply both sides by 18 ohms: $0.2 \text{ amp} \cdot 18 \text{ ohms} = V$

Simplify: $3.6 \text{ volts} = V$

ANSWER The voltage is 3.6 volts.

MATH HANDBOOK

Finding Areas

The area of a figure is the amount of surface the figure covers.

Area is measured in square units, such as square meters (m²) or square centimeters (cm²). Formulas for the areas of three common geometric figures are shown below.

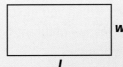

Area = (side length)²
$A = s^2$

Area = length × width
$A = lw$

Area = $\frac{1}{2}$ × base × height
$A = \frac{1}{2} bh$

Example

Each face of a halite crystal is a square like the one shown. You can find the area of the square by using the steps below.

Write the formula for the area of a square: $A = s^2$

3 mm

3 mm

Substitute 3 mm for s: $= (3 \text{ mm})^2$

Simplify: $= 9 \text{ mm}^2$

ANSWER The area of the square is 9 square millimeters.

Finding Volumes

The volume of a solid is the amount of space contained by the solid.

Volume is measured in cubic units, such as cubic meters (m³) or cubic centimeters (cm³). The volume of a rectangular prism is given by the formula shown below.

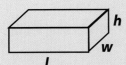

Volume = length × width × height
$V = lwh$

Example

A topaz crystal is a rectangular prism like the one shown. You can find the volume of the prism by using the steps below.

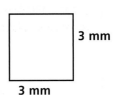

10 mm

12 mm

20 mm

Write the formula for the volume of a rectangular prism: $V = lwh$

Substitute dimensions: $= 20 \text{ mm} \times 12 \text{ mm} \times 10 \text{ mm}$

Simplify: $= 2400 \text{ mm}^3$

ANSWER The volume of the rectangular prism is 2400 cubic millimeters.

Using Significant Figures

The **significant figures** in a decimal are the digits that are warranted by the accuracy of a measuring device.

When you perform a calculation with measurements, the number of significant figures to include in the result depends in part on the number of significant figures in the measurements. When you multiply or divide measurements, your answer should have only as many significant figures as the measurement with the fewest significant figures.

Example

Using a balance and a graduated cylinder filled with water, you determined that a marble has a mass of 8.0 grams and a volume of 3.5 cubic centimeters. To calculate the density of the marble, divide the mass by the volume.

Write the formula for density: $\text{Density} = \dfrac{\text{mass}}{\text{Volume}}$

Substitute measurements: $= \dfrac{8.0 \text{ g}}{3.5 \text{ cm}^3}$

Use a calculator to divide: $\approx 2.285714286 \text{ g/cm}^3$

ANSWER Because the mass and the volume have two significant figures each, give the density to two significant figures. The marble has a density of 2.3 grams per cubic centimeter.

Using Scientific Notation

Scientific notation is a shorthand way to write very large or very small numbers. For example, 73,500,000,000,000,000,000,000 kg is the mass of the Moon. In scientific notation, it is 7.35×10^{22} kg.

Example

You can convert from standard form to scientific notation.

Standard Form	Scientific Notation
720,000	7.2×10^5
5 decimal places left	Exponent is 5.
0.000291	2.91×10^{-4}
4 decimal places right	Exponent is −4.

You can convert from scientific notation to standard form.

Scientific Notation	Standard Form
4.63×10^7	46,300,000
Exponent is 7.	7 decimal places right
1.08×10^{-6}	0.00000108
Exponent is −6.	6 decimal places left

MATH HANDBOOK

Note-Taking Handbook

Note-Taking Strategies

Taking notes as you read helps you understand the information. The notes you take can also be used as a study guide for later review. This handbook presents several ways to organize your notes.

Content Frame

1. Make a chart in which each column represents a category.
2. Give each column a heading.
3. Write details under the headings.

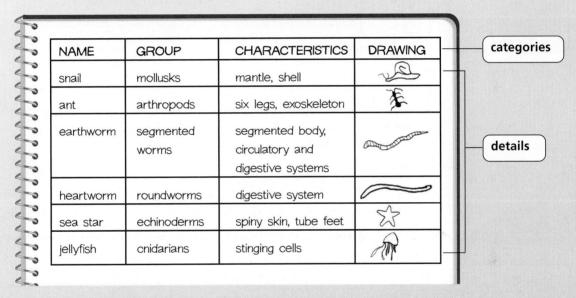

NAME	GROUP	CHARACTERISTICS	DRAWING
snail	mollusks	mantle, shell	
ant	arthropods	six legs, exoskeleton	
earthworm	segmented worms	segmented body, circulatory and digestive systems	
heartworm	roundworms	digestive system	
sea star	echinoderms	spiny skin, tube feet	
jellyfish	cnidarians	stinging cells	

categories

details

Combination Notes

1. For each new idea or concept, write an informal outline of the information.
2. Make a sketch to illustrate the concept, and label it.

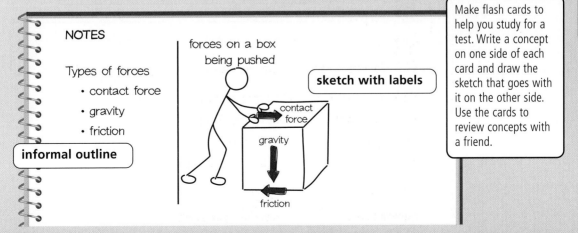

NOTES

Types of forces

- contact force
- gravity
- friction

informal outline

forces on a box being pushed

sketch with labels

contact force

gravity

friction

Make flash cards to help you study for a test. Write a concept on one side of each card and draw the sketch that goes with it on the other side. Use the cards to review concepts with a friend.

Main Idea and Detail Notes

1. In the left-hand column of a two-column chart, list main ideas. The blue headings express main ideas throughout this textbook.

2. In the right-hand column, write details that expand on each main idea.

You can shorten the headings in your chart. Be sure to use the most important words.

When studying for tests, cover up the detail notes column with a sheet of paper. Then use each main idea to form a question—such as "How does latitude affect climate?" Answer the question, and then uncover the detail notes column to check your answer.

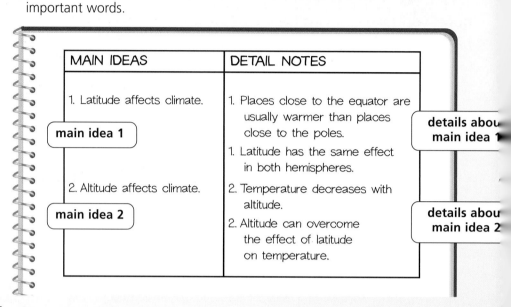

MAIN IDEAS	DETAIL NOTES
1. Latitude affects climate. **main idea 1**	1. Places close to the equator are usually warmer than places close to the poles. 1. Latitude has the same effect in both hemispheres.
2. Altitude affects climate. **main idea 2**	2. Temperature decreases with altitude. 2. Altitude can overcome the effect of latitude on temperature.

details about main idea 1

details about main idea 2

Main Idea Web

1. Write a main idea in a box.

2. Add boxes around it with related vocabulary terms and important details.

You can find definitions near highlighted terms.

definition of *work*

Work is the use of force to move an object.

formula

Work = force · distance

main idea

Force is necessary to do work.

The joule is the unit used to measure work.

definition of *joule*

Work depends on the size of a force.

important detail

Mind Map

1. Write a main idea in the center.
2. Add details that relate to one another and to the main idea.

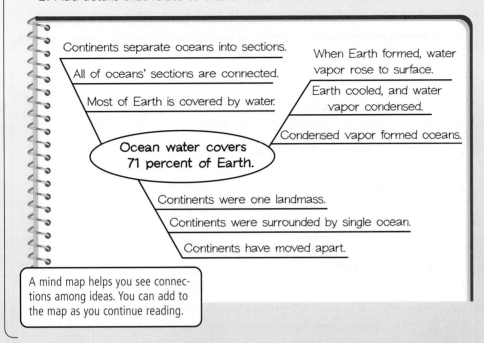

Continents separate oceans into sections.

All of oceans' sections are connected.

Most of Earth is covered by water.

When Earth formed, water vapor rose to surface.

Earth cooled, and water vapor condensed.

Condensed vapor formed oceans.

Ocean water covers 71 percent of Earth.

Continents were one landmass.

Continents were surrounded by single ocean.

Continents have moved apart.

A mind map helps you see connections among ideas. You can add to the map as you continue reading.

Supporting Main Ideas

1. Write a main idea in a box.
2. Add boxes underneath with information—such as reasons, explanations, and examples—that supports the main idea.

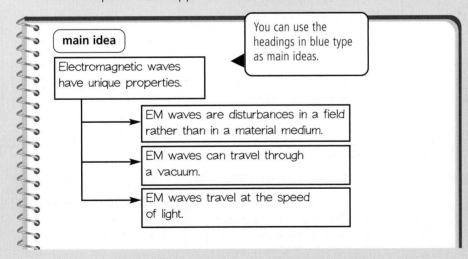

main idea

Electromagnetic waves have unique properties.

You can use the headings in blue type as main ideas.

EM waves are disturbances in a field rather than in a material medium.

EM waves can travel through a vacuum.

EM waves travel at the speed of light.

Outline

1. Copy the chapter title and headings from the book in the form of an outline.

2. Add notes that summarize in your own words what you read.

Cell Processes

1st key idea

I. Cells capture and release energy.

1st subpoint of I

  A. All cells need energy.

2nd subpoint of I

  B. Some cells capture light energy.

1st detail about B

    1. Process of photosynthesis

2nd detail about B

    2. Chloroplasts (site of photosynthesis)
    3. Carbon dioxide and water as raw materials
    4. Glucose and oxygen as products

  C. All cells release energy.
    1. Process of cellular respiration
    2. Fermentation of sugar to carbon dioxide
    3. Bacteria that carry out fermentation

II. Cells transport materials through membranes.

  A. Some materials move by diffusion.
    1. Particle movement from higher to lower concentrations
    2. Movement of water through membrane (osmosis)

  B. Some transport requires energy.
    1. Active transport
    2. Examples of active transport

Correct Outline Form

Include a title.

Arrange key ideas, subpoints, and details as shown.

Indent the divisions of the outline as shown.

Use the same grammatical form for items of the same rank. For example, if A is a sentence, B must also be a sentence.

You must have at least two main ideas or subpoints. That is, every A must be followed by a B, and every 1 must be followed by a 2.

Concept Map

1. Write an important concept in a large oval.

2. Add details related to the concept in smaller ovals.

3. Write linking words on arrows that connect the ovals.

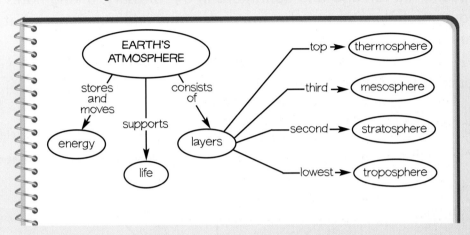

The main ideas or concepts can often be found in the blue headings. An example is "The atmosphere stores and moves energy." Use nouns from these concepts in the ovals, and use the verb or verbs on the lines.

Venn Diagram

1. Draw two overlapping circles, one for each item that you are comparing.

2. In the overlapping section, list the characteristics that are shared by both items.

3. In the outer sections, list the characteristics that are peculiar to each item.

4. Write a summary that describes the information in the Venn diagram.

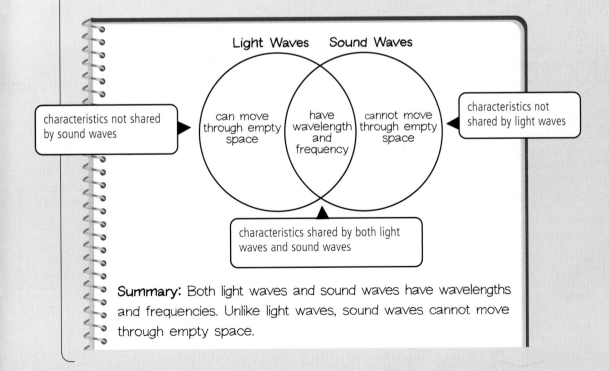

Summary: Both light waves and sound waves have wavelengths and frequencies. Unlike light waves, sound waves cannot move through empty space.

Vocabulary Strategies

Important terms are highlighted in this book. A definition of each term can be found in the sentence or paragraph where the term appears. You can also find definitions in the Glossary. Taking notes about vocabulary terms helps you understand and remember what you read.

Description Wheel

1. Write a term inside a circle.
2. Write words that describe the term on "spokes" attached to the circle.

When studying for a test with a friend, read the phrases on the spokes one at a time until your friend identifies the correct term.

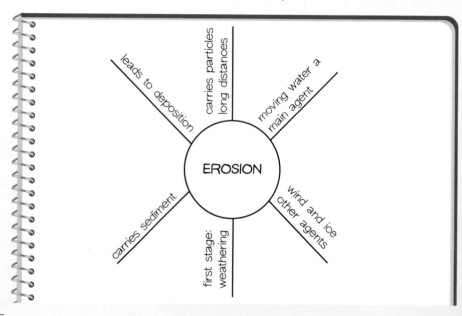

Four Square

1. Write a term in the center.
2. Write details in the four areas around the term.

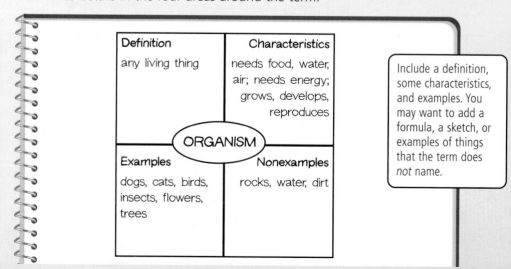

Include a definition, some characteristics, and examples. You may want to add a formula, a sketch, or examples of things that the term does *not* name.

NOTE-TAKING HANDBOOK

Frame Game

1. Write a term in the center.
2. Frame the term with details.

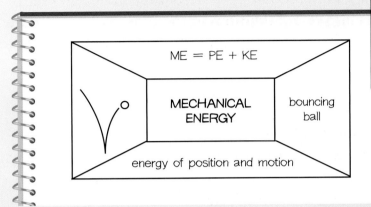

Include examples, descriptions, sketches, or sentences that use the term in context. Change the frame to fit each new term.

Magnet Word

1. Write a term on the magnet.
2. On the lines, add details related to the term.

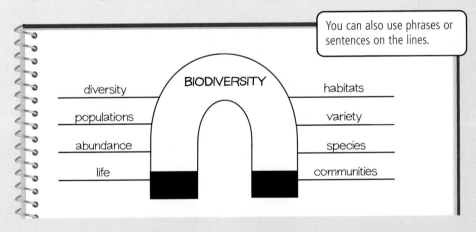

You can also use phrases or sentences on the lines.

Word Triangle

1. Write a term and its definition in the bottom section.
2. In the middle section, write a sentence in which the term is used correctly.
3. In the top section, draw a small picture to illustrate the term.

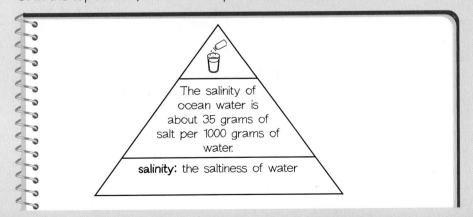

Appendix

Properties of Common Minerals

In this table, minerals are arranged alphabetically, and the most useful properties for identification are printed in *italic* type. Most minerals can be identified by means of two or three of the properties listed below. For some minerals, density is important; for others, cleavage is characteristic; and for others, the crystal shapes identify the minerals. The colors listed are the most common for each mineral.

Name	Hardness	Color	Streak	Cleavage	Remarks
Apatite	5	Green, brown	White	Poor in one direction	Nonmetallic (glassy) luster. Sp. gr. 3.1 to 3.2.
Augite	5–6	Dark green to black	Greenish	*Two directions, nearly at 90°*	Nonmetallic (glassy) luster. *Stubby four- or eight-sided crystals.* Common type of pyroxene. Sp. gr. 3.2 to 3.4.
Beryl	7.5–8	*Bluish-green, yellow, pink, colorless*	White	Imperfect in one direction	Nonmetallic (glassy) luster. *Hardness, greenish color, six-sided crystals.* Aquamarine and emerald are gem varieties. Sp. gr. 2.6 to 2.8.
Biotite mica	2.5–3	Black, brown, dark green	White	*Perfect in one direction*	Nonmetallic (glassy) luster. *Thin elastic films peel off easily.* Sp. gr. 2.8 to 3.2.
Calcite	3	White, colorless	White	*Perfect, three directions, not at 90° angles*	Nonmetallic (glassy to dull) luster. *Fizzes in dilute hydrochloric acid.* Sp. gr. 2.7.
Chalcopyrite	3.5–4	*Golden yellow*	Greenish black	Poor in one direction	Metallic luster. *Hardness distinguishes from pyrite.* Sp. gr. 4.1 to 4.3.
Chlorite	2–2.5	*Greenish*	Pale green to gray or brown	Perfect in one direction	Nonmetallic (glassy to pearly) luster. *Nonelastic flakes.* Sp. gr. 2.6 to 3.3.
Copper	2.5–3	*Copper red*	Copper	None	*Metallic luster on fresh surface. Dense.* Sp. gr. 8.9.
Corundum	9	Brown, pink, blue	White	None, parting resembles cleavage	Nonmetallic (glassy to brilliant) luster. *Barrel-shaped, six-sided crystals with flat ends.* Sp. gr. 4.0.
Diamond	10	Colorless to pale yellow	White	Perfect, four directions	Nonmetallic (brilliant to greasy) luster. *Hardest of all minerals.* Sp. gr. 3.5.

Sp. gr. = specific gravity

Name	Hardness	Color	Streak	Cleavage	Remarks
Dolomite	3.5–4	Pinkish, colorless, white	White	*Perfect, three directions, not at 90° angles*	Nonmetallic luster. *Scratched surface fizzes in dilute hydrochloric acid. Cleavage surfaces curved.* Sp. gr. 2.8 to 2.9.
Feldspar (Orthoclase)	*6*	*Salmon pink,* red, *white, light gray*	White	*Good, two directions, 90° intersection*	Nonmetallic (glassy) luster. *Hardness, color, and cleavage taken together are diagnostic.* Sp. gr. 2.6.
Feldspar (Plagioclase)	6	*White to light gray,* can be salmon pink	White	*Good, two directions, about 90°*	Nonmetallic (glassy to pearly) luster. *If striations are visible, they are diagnostic.* Sp. gr. 2.6 to 2.8.
Fluorite	4	Varies	White	*Perfect, four directions*	Nonmetallic (glassy) luster. In cubes or octahedrons as crystals. Sp. gr. 3.2.
Galena	2.5	*Lead gray*	Lead gray	*Perfect, three directions, at 90° angles*	*Metallic luster.* Occurs as crystals and masses. *Dense.* Sp. gr. 7.4 to 7.6.
Gold	2.5–3	*Gold*	Gold	None	Metallic luster. *Dense.* Sp. gr. 15.0 to 19.3.
Graphite	1–2	*Dark gray to black*	Grayish black	*Perfect in one direction*	Metallic or nonmetallic (earthy) luster. *Greasy feel, marks paper.* This is the "lead" in a pencil (mixed with clay). Sp. gr. 2.2.
Gypsum	*2*	Colorless, white, gray, yellowish, reddish	White	*Perfect in one direction*	Nonmetallic (glassy to silky) luster. *Can be scratched easily by a fingernail.* Sp. gr. 2.3.
Halite	2–2.5	Colorless, white	White	*Perfect, three directions, at 90° angles*	Nonmetallic (glassy) luster. *Salty taste.* Sp. gr. 2.2.
Hematite	5–6 (may appear softer)	*Reddish-brown, gray, black*	*Reddish*	None	Metallic or nonmetallic (earthy) luster. *Dense.* Sp. gr. 5.3.
Hornblende	5–6	*Dark green to black*	Brown to gray	*Perfect, two directions at angles of 56° and 124°*	Nonmetallic (glassy to silky) luster. Common type of amphibole. Long, slender, six-sided crystals. Sp. gr. 3.0 to 3.4.
Kaolinite	2	White, gray, yellowish	White	*Perfect in one direction*	Nonmetallic (dull, earthy) luster. Claylike masses. Sp. gr. 2.6.
Limonite group	4–5.5	*Yellow, brown*	*Yellowish brown*	None	Nonmetallic (earthy) luster. Rust stains. Sp. gr. 2.9 to 4.3.
Magnetite	5.5–6.5	*Black*	Black	None	Metallic luster. Occurs as eight-sided crystals and granular masses. *Magnetic. Dense.* Sp. gr. 5.2.

Sp. gr. = specific gravity

Properties of Common Minerals *continued*

Name	Hardness	Color	Streak	Cleavage	Remarks
Muscovite mica	2–2.5	Colorless in thin films; silvery, yellowish, and greenish in thicker pieces	*White*	Perfect in one direction	Nonmetallic (glassy to pearly) luster. *Thin elastic films peel off readily.* Sp. gr. 2.8 to 2.9.
Olivine	6.5–7	*Yellowish, greenish*	White	*None*	*Nonmetallic (glassy) luster. Granular.* Sp. gr. 3.3 to 4.4.
Opal	5–6.5	Varies	White	None	*Nonmetallic (glassy to pearly) luster. Conchoidal fracture.* Sp. gr. 2.0 to 2.2.
Pyrite	6–6.5	*Brass yellow*	Greenish black	None	Metallic luster. *Cubic crystals and granular masses. Dense.* Sp. gr. 5.0 to 5.1.
Quartz	7	*Colorless, white; varies*	White	None	Nonmetallic (glassy) luster. *Conchoidal fracture. Six-sided crystals common.* Many varieties. Sp. gr. 2.6.
Serpentine	3–5	*Greenish (variegated)*	White	None or good in one direction, depending on variety	*Nonmetallic (greasy, waxy, or silky) luster. Conchoidal fracture.* Sp. gr. 2.5 to 2.6.
Sphalerite	3.5–4	*Yellow, brown, black*	Yellow to light brown	*Perfect, six directions*	*Nonmetallic (brilliant to resinous) luster.* Sp. gr. 3.9 to 4.1.
Sulfur	1.5–2.5	*Yellow*	Yellow	Poor, two directions	Nonmetallic (glassy to earthy) luster. Granular. Sp. gr. 2.0 to 2.1.
Talc	1	Apple-green, gray, white	White	Perfect in one direction	Nonmetallic (pearly to greasy) luster. Nonelastic flakes, *greasy feel.* Sp. gr. 2.7 to 2.8.
Topaz	8	Varies	White	Perfect in one direction	Nonmetallic (brilliant to glassy) luster. *Crystals commonly striated length-wise.* Sp. gr. 3.4 to 3.6.
Tourmaline	7–7.5	*Black; varies*	White	None	Nonmetallic (glassy) luster. *Crystals often have triangular cross sections. Conchoidal fracture.* Sp. gr. 3.0 to 3.3.

Sp. gr. = specific gravity

Topographic Map Symbols

The U.S. Geological Survey uses the following symbols to mark human-made and natural features on all of the topographic maps the USGS produces.

Primary highway, hard surface ....
Secondary highway, hard surface ....
Light-duty road, hard or improved surface ...
Unimproved road ....
Trail ....
Railroad: single track ....
Railroad: multiple track ....
Bridge ....
Drawbridge ....
Tunnel ....
Footbridge ....
Overpass—Underpass ....
Power transmission line with located tower ..
Landmark line (labeled as to type) .... TELEPHONE

Dam with lock ....
Canal with lock ....
Large dam ....
Small dam: masonry—earth ....
Buildings (dwelling, place of employment, etc.) ...
School—Church—Cemeteries ....
Buildings (barn, warehouse, etc.) ....
Tanks; oil, water, etc. (labeled only if water) ...
Wells other than water (labeled as to type) ... Oil   Gas
U.S. mineral or location monument—Prospect ...   X
Quarry—Gravel pit   X
Mine shaft—Tunnel or cave entrance ....
Campsite—Picnic area ....
Located or landmark object—Windmill ....
Exposed wreck ....
Rock or coral reef ....
Foreshore flat ....
Rock: bare or awash ....

Benchmarks .... BM×671   ×672
Road fork—Section corner with elevation ...   +58
Checked spot elevation .... × 5970
Unchecked spot elevation .... × 5970

Boundary: national ....
State ....
county, parish, municipio ....
civil township, precinct, town, barrio ....
incorporated city, village, town, hamlet .
reservation, national or state ....
small park, cemetery, airport, etc. ....
land grant ....
Township or range line, U.S. land survey ....
Section line, U.S. land survey ....
Township line, not U.S. land survey ....
Section line, not U.S. land survey ....
Fence line or field line ....
Section corner: found—indicated .... +   +
Boundary monument: land grant—other ... ⊡   ⊡

Index contour   Intermediate contour
Supplementary cont   Depression contours
Cut—Fill   Levee
Mine dump   Large wash
Dune area   Distorted surface
Sand area   Gravel beach

Glacier   Intermittent streams
Seasonal streams   Aqueduct tunnel
Water well—Spring   Falls
Rapids   Intermittent lake
Channel   Small wash
Sounding—   Marsh (swamp)
Depth curve   Land subject to
Dry lake bed   controlled flooding

Woodland   Mangrove
Submerged marsh   Scrub
Orchard   Wooded marsh
Vineyard   Many buildings
Areas revised since previous edition

Source: U.S. Geological Survey

Properties of Rocks and Earth's Interior

Scheme for Sedimentary Rock Identification

TEXTURE	GRAIN SIZE	COMPOSITION	COMMENTS	ROCK NAME	MAP SYMBOL
Clastic (fragmental)	Pebbles, cobbles, and/or boulders embedded in sand, silt, and/or clay	Mostly quartz, feldspar, and clay minerals; may contain fragments of other rocks and minerals	Rounded fragments	Conglomerate	
			Angular fragments	Breccia	
	Sand (0.2 to 0.006 cm)		Fine to coarse	Sandstone	
	Silt (0.006 to 0.0004 cm)		Very fine grain	Siltstone	
	Clay (less than 0.0004 cm)		Compact; may split easily	Shale	

CHEMICALLY AND/OR ORGANICALLY FORMED SEDIMENTARY ROCKS

TEXTURE	GRAIN SIZE	COMPOSITION	COMMENTS	ROCK NAME	MAP SYMBOL
Crystalline	Varied	Halite	Crystals from chemical precipitates and evaporites	Rock Salt	
	Varied	Gypsum		Rock Gypsum	
	Varied	Dolomite		Dolostone	
Bioclastic	Microscopic to coarse	Calcite	Cemented shell fragments or precipitates of biologic origin	Limestone	
	Varied	Carbon	From plant remains	Coal	

Scheme for Metamorphic Rock Identification

TEXTURE	GRAIN SIZE	COMPOSITION	TYPE OF METAMORPHISM	COMMENTS	ROCK NAME	MAP SYMBOL
FOLIATED — MINERAL ALIGNMENT	Fine	MICA QUARTZ FELDSPAR AMPHIBOLE GARNET PYROXENE	Regional (Heat and pressure increase with depth)	Low-grade metamorphism of shale	Slate	
	Fine to medium			Foliation surfaces shiny from microscopic mica crystals	Phyllite	
				Platy mica crystals visible from metamorphism of clay or feldspars	Schist	
FOLIATED — BANDING	Medium to coarse			High-grade metamorphism; some mica changed to feldspar; segregated by mineral type into bands	Gneiss	
NONFOLIATED	Fine	Variable	Contact (Heat)	Various rocks changed by heat from nearby magma/lava	Hornfels	
	Fine to coarse	Quartz	Regional or Contact	Metamorphism of quartz sandstone	Quartzite	
		Calcite and/or dolomite		Metamorphism of limestone or dolostone	Marble	
	Coarse	Various minerals in particles and matrix		Pebbles may be distorted or stretched	Metaconglomerate	

Scheme for Igneous Rock Identification

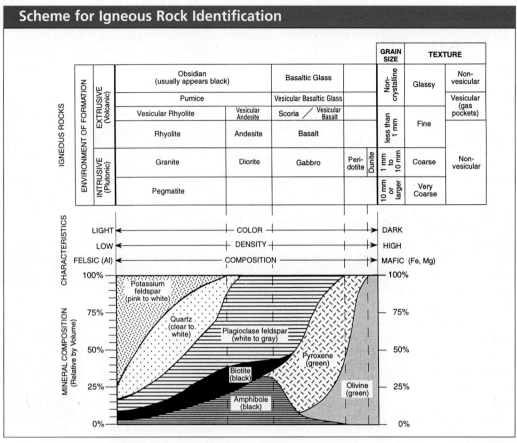

		GRAIN SIZE	TEXTURE	

IGNEOUS ROCKS

ENVIRONMENT OF FORMATION

EXTRUSIVE (Volcanic)

Obsidian (usually appears black)		Basaltic Glass	Non-crystalline	Glassy	Non-vesicular
Pumice		Vesicular Basaltic Glass			Vesicular (gas pockets)
Vesicular Rhyolite	Vesicular Andesite	Scoria / Vesicular Basalt	less than 1 mm	Fine	
Rhyolite	Andesite	Basalt			

INTRUSIVE (Plutonic)

| Granite | Diorite | Gabbro | Peri-dotite | Dunite | 1 mm to 10 mm | Coarse | Non-vesicular |
| Pegmatite | | | | | 10 mm or larger | Very Coarse | |

CHARACTERISTICS

LIGHT	————— COLOR —————	DARK
LOW	—————— DENSITY ——————	HIGH
FELSIC (Al)	————— COMPOSITION —————	MAFIC (Fe, Mg)

MINERAL COMPOSITION (Relative by Volume)

Potassium feldspar (pink to white)

Quartz (clear to white)

Plagioclase feldspar (white to gray)

Biotite (black)

Amphibole (black)

Pyroxene (green)

Olivine (green)

Inferred Properties of Earth's Interior

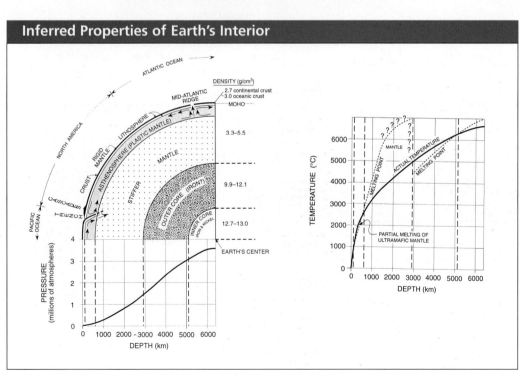

United States Physical Map

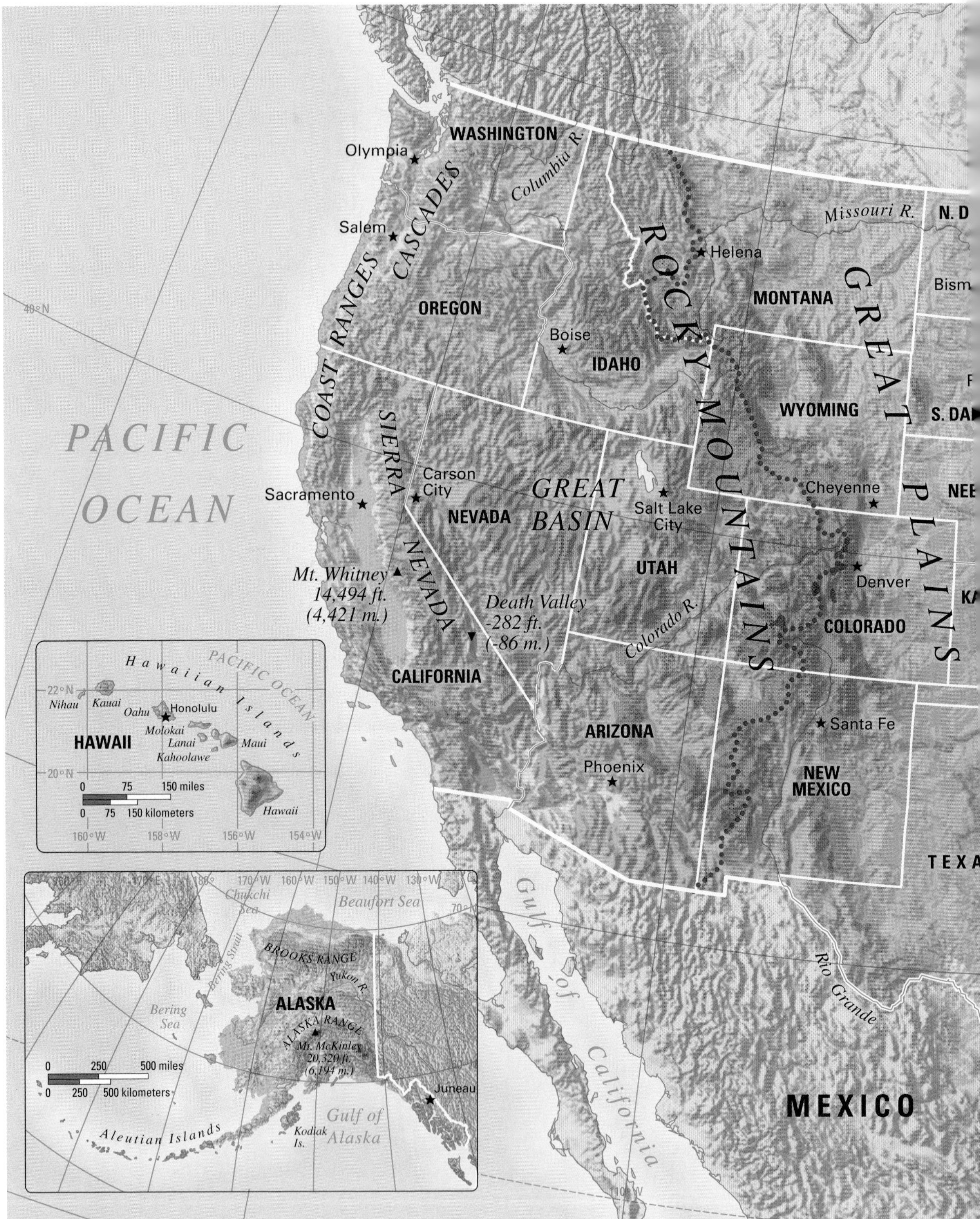

Olympia

WASHINGTON

Columbia R.

Salem

CASCADES

COAST RANGES

OREGON

Boise

IDAHO

ROCKY MOUNTAINS

Helena

MONTANA

Missouri R.

N. D

Bism

GREAT PLAINS

WYOMING

S. DA

PACIFIC

OCEAN

SIERRA NEVADA

Sacramento

Carson City

NEVADA

GREAT BASIN

Salt Lake City

UTAH

Cheyenne

NEE

Mt. Whitney 14,494 ft. (4,421 m.)

Death Valley -282 ft. (-86 m.)

Colorado R.

Denver

COLORADO

KA

CALIFORNIA

ARIZONA

Phoenix

Santa Fe

NEW MEXICO

TEXA

Hawaiian Islands

PACIFIC OCEAN

22°N

Nihau Kauai Oahu Honolulu

Molokai Lanai Kahoolawe

Maui

HAWAII

20°N

0   75   150 miles

0   75   150 kilometers

Hawaii

160°W   158°W   156°W   154°W

160°E 170°E 180° 170°W 160°W 150°W 140°W 130°W

Chukchi Sea

Beaufort Sea

70°

BROOKS RANGE

Bering Strait

Yukon R.

Bering Sea

ALASKA

ALASKA RANGE

Mt. McKinley 20,320 ft. (6,194 m.)

Juneau

0   250   500 miles

0   250   500 kilometers

Aleutian Islands

Kodiak Is.

Gulf of Alaska

Gulf of California

Rio Grande

MEXICO

100°W

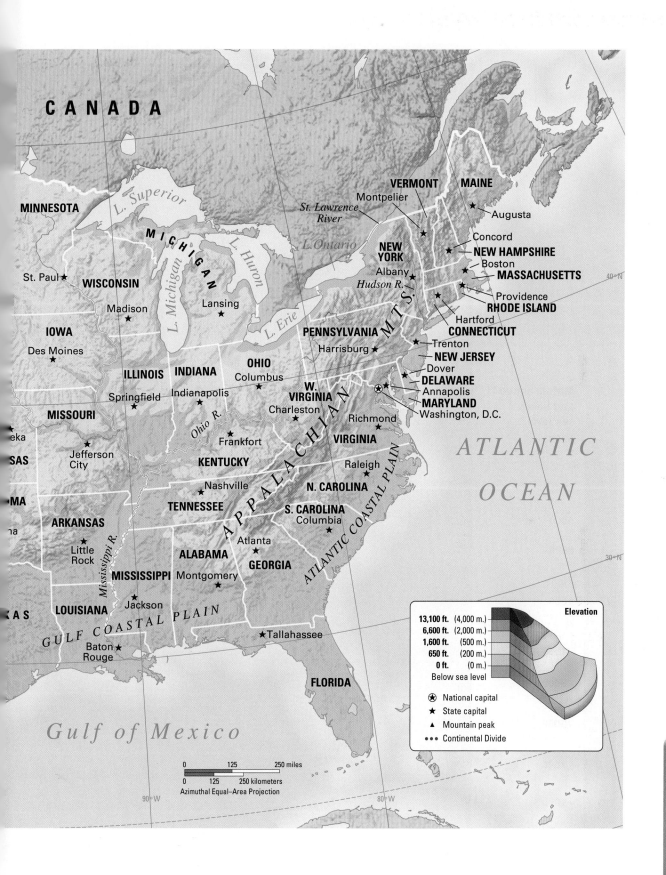

CANADA

MINNESOTA

L. Superior

MICHIGAN

L. Michigan

L. Huron

St. Paul ★ WISCONSIN

Madison ★

Lansing ★

IOWA

Des Moines ★

ILLINOIS INDIANA

Springfield ★ Indianapolis ★

MISSOURI

ika ★

Jefferson City ★

SAS

MA

ARKANSAS

Little Rock ★

KAS

LOUISIANA

Mississippi R.

Jackson ★

Baton Rouge ★

VERMONT MAINE

Montpelier Augusta ★

St. Lawrence River

L. Ontario

Concord

NEW YORK NEW HAMPSHIRE

Boston

Albany ★ MASSACHUSETTS 40° N

Hudson R.

Providence

RHODE ISLAND

Hartford

PENNSYLVANIA CONNECTICUT

Harrisburg ★ Trenton

NEW JERSEY

Dover

DELAWARE

Annapolis

MARYLAND

Washington, D.C.

Richmond ★

W. VIRGINIA

Charleston ★

Frankfort ★

KENTUCKY VIRGINIA

Nashville ★ Raleigh ★

Ohio R.

Columbus ★

L. Erie

OHIO

APPALACHIAN MTS.

ATLANTIC COASTAL PLAIN

ATLANTIC

OCEAN

N. CAROLINA

TENNESSEE

S. CAROLINA

Columbia ★

Atlanta ★

ALABAMA

GEORGIA

MISSISSIPPI Montgomery ★

GULF COASTAL PLAIN

★ Tallahassee

FLORIDA

Gulf of Mexico

30° N

	Elevation
13,100 ft. (4,000 m.)	
6,600 ft. (2,000 m.)	
1,600 ft. (500 m.)	
650 ft. (200 m.)	
0 ft. (0 m.)	
Below sea level	

⊛ National capital
★ State capital
▲ Mountain peak
••• Continental Divide

0   125   250 miles
0   125   250 kilometers
Azimuthal Equal–Area Projection

90° W   80° W

World Physical Map

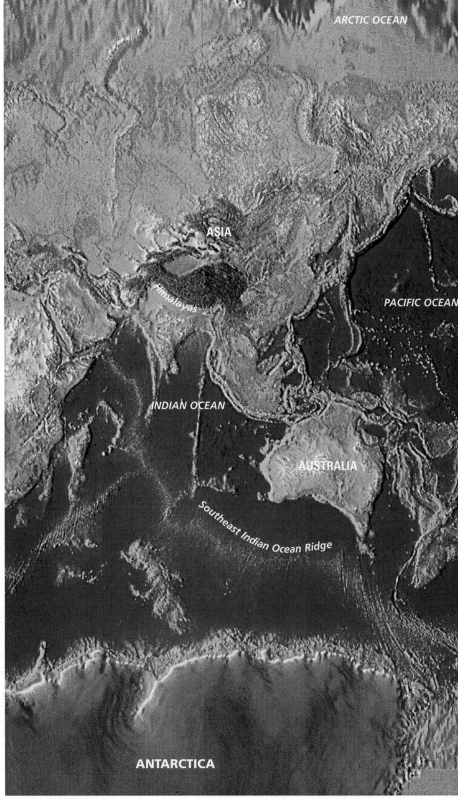

Meters above
and below
sea level

9000

5000

3500

2000

1000

0

Sea
level

−1500

−3000

−5000

−7000

−9000

−11000

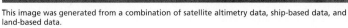

This image was generated from a combination of satellite altimetry data, ship-based data, and land-based data.

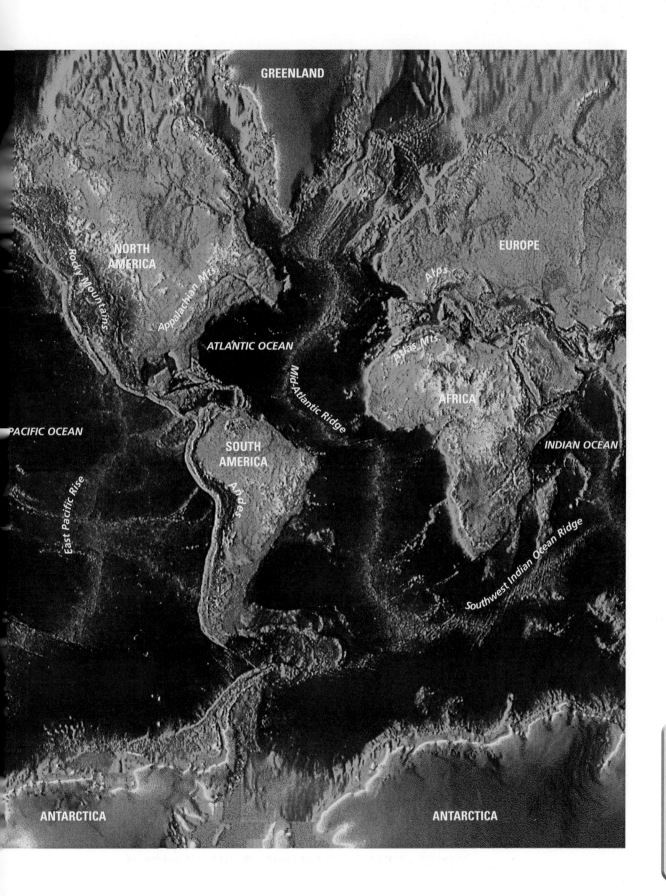

GREENLAND

NORTH
AMERICA

EUROPE

Rocky Mountains

Appalachian Mts.

Alps

ATLANTIC OCEAN

Atlas Mts.

AFRICA

Mid-Atlantic Ridge

PACIFIC OCEAN

INDIAN OCEAN

SOUTH
AMERICA

East Pacific Rise

Andes

Southwest Indian Ocean Ridge

ANTARCTICA

ANTARCTICA

Tectonic Plates

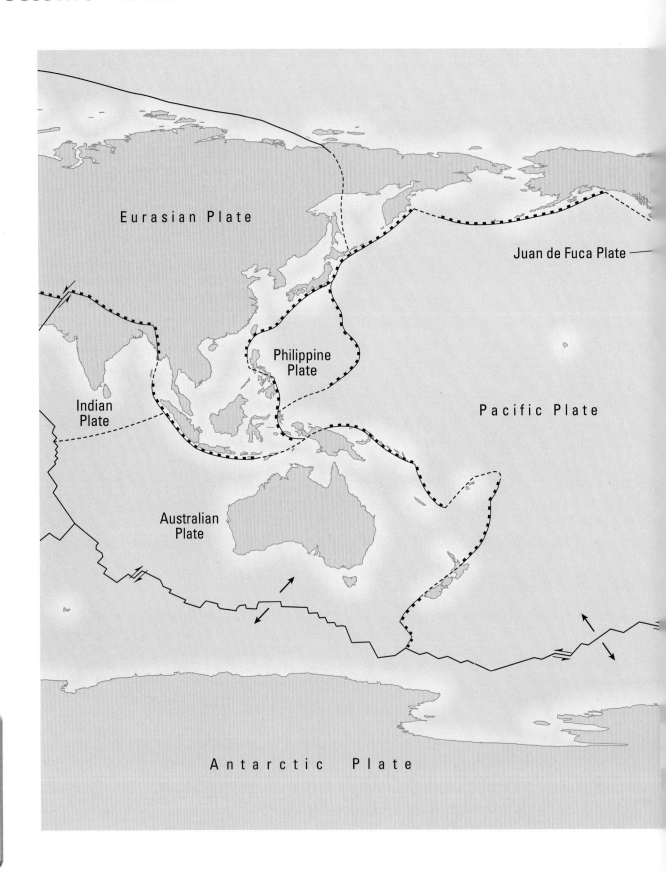

Eurasian Plate

Juan de Fuca Plate

Philippine Plate

Indian Plate

Pacific Plate

Australian Plate

Antarctic Plate

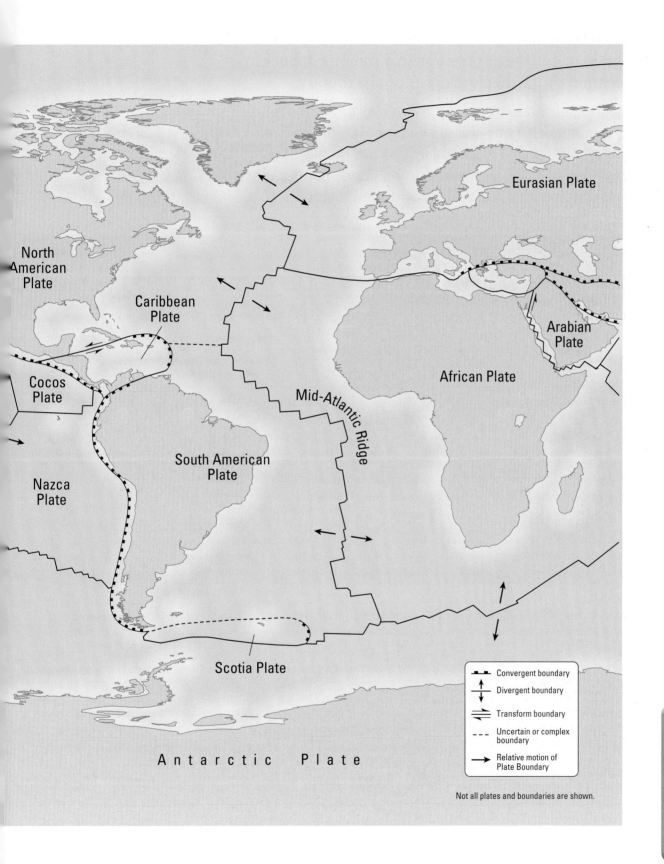

North
American
Plate

Caribbean
Plate

Cocos
Plate

Nazca
Plate

South American
Plate

Mid-Atlantic Ridge

Eurasian Plate

African Plate

Arabian
Plate

Scotia Plate

Antarctic   Plate

	Convergent boundary
	Divergent boundary
	Transform boundary
	Uncertain or complex boundary
	Relative motion of Plate Boundary

Not all plates and boundaries are shown.

Station Symbols

Meteorologists use station symbols to condense the weather data they receive from ground stations. The symbols are displayed on maps. The information in a station symbol can be understood by the meteorologists of any country.

In the symbol, air pressure readings are shortened by omitting the initial 9 or 10 and the decimal point. For numbers greater than 500, place a 9 to the left of the number and divide by 10 to get the air pressure in millibars. For numbers less than 500, place a 10 to the left and then divide by 10.

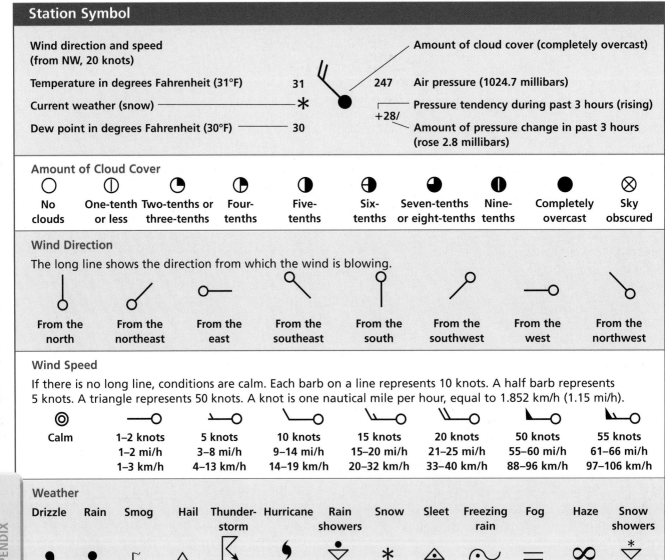

Station Symbol

Wind direction and speed (from NW, 20 knots)

Temperature in degrees Fahrenheit (31°F) 31

Current weather (snow) — ✳

Dew point in degrees Fahrenheit (30°F) — 30

Amount of cloud cover (completely overcast)

247 **Air pressure (1024.7 millibars)**

+28/ **Pressure tendency during past 3 hours (rising)**

Amount of pressure change in past 3 hours (rose 2.8 millibars)

Amount of Cloud Cover

No clouds	One-tenth or less	Two-tenths or three-tenths	Four-tenths	Five-tenths	Six-tenths	Seven-tenths or eight-tenths	Nine-tenths	Completely overcast	Sky obscured

Wind Direction

The long line shows the direction from which the wind is blowing.

From the north	From the northeast	From the east	From the southeast	From the south	From the southwest	From the west	From the northwest

Wind Speed

If there is no long line, conditions are calm. Each barb on a line represents 10 knots. A half barb represents 5 knots. A triangle represents 50 knots. A knot is one nautical mile per hour, equal to 1.852 km/h (1.15 mi/h).

Calm	1–2 knots 1–2 mi/h 1–3 km/h	5 knots 3–8 mi/h 4–13 km/h	10 knots 9–14 mi/h 14–19 km/h	15 knots 15–20 mi/h 20–32 km/h	20 knots 21–25 mi/h 33–40 km/h	50 knots 55–60 mi/h 88–96 km/h	55 knots 61–66 mi/h 97–106 km/h

Weather

Drizzle	Rain	Smog	Hail	Thunder-storm	Hurricane	Rain showers	Snow	Sleet	Freezing rain	Fog	Haze	Snow showers

Relative Humidity

You can find the relative humidity by calculating the difference between the two readings on a psychrometer. First look up the dry-bulb temperature in the left-hand column of the relative humidity chart. Then find in the top line the difference between the wet-bulb temperature and the dry-bulb temperature.

Relative Humidity (%)

Dry-Bulb Tempera-ture (°C)	Difference Between Wet-Bulb and Dry-Bulb Temperatures (°C)															
	0	1	2	3	4	5	6	7	8	9	10	11	12	13	14	15
−20	100	28														
−18	100	40														
−16	100	48														
−14	100	55	11													
−12	100	61	23													
−10	100	66	33													
−8	100	71	41	13												
−6	100	73	48	20												
−4	100	77	54	32	11											
−2	100	79	58	37	20	1										
0	100	81	63	45	28	11										
2	100	83	67	51	36	20	6									
4	100	85	70	56	42	27	14									
6	100	86	72	59	46	35	22	10								
8	100	87	74	62	51	39	28	17	6							
10	100	88	76	65	54	43	33	24	13	4						
12	100	88	78	67	57	48	38	28	19	10	2					
14	100	89	79	69	60	50	41	33	25	16	8	1				
16	100	90	80	71	62	54	45	37	29	21	14	7	1			
18	100	91	81	72	64	56	48	40	33	26	19	12	6			
20	100	91	82	74	66	58	51	44	36	30	23	17	11	5		
22	100	92	83	75	68	60	53	46	40	33	27	21	15	10	4	
24	100	92	84	76	69	62	55	49	42	36	30	25	20	14	9	4
26	100	92	85	77	70	64	57	51	45	39	34	28	23	18	13	9
28	100	93	86	78	71	65	59	53	47	42	36	31	26	21	17	12
30	100	93	86	79	72	66	61	55	49	44	39	34	29	25	20	16

Wind Speeds

Descriptive names, such as *fresh gale,* were used by sailors and other people to describe the strength of winds. Later, ranges of wind speeds were determined. The table below lists the wind speeds and conditions you might observe around you on land.

Beaufort Scale of Wind Speeds

Beaufort Number	Wind Speed	Description
0	0 km/h (0 mi/h)	**Calm or Still** Smoke will rise vertically
1	2–5 km/h (1–3 mi/h)	**Light Air** Rising smoke drifts, weather vane is inactive
2	6–12 km/h (4–7 mi/h)	**Light Breeze** Leaves rustle, can feel wind on your face, weather vane moves
3	13–20 km/h (8–12 mi/h)	**Gentle Breeze** Leaves and twigs move around, lightweight flags extend
4	21–30 km/h (13–18 mi/h)	**Moderate Breeze** Thin branches move, dust and paper raised
5	31–40 km/h (19–24 mi/h)	**Fresh Breeze** Small trees sway
6	41–50 km/h (25–31 mi/h)	**Strong Breeze** Large tree branches move, open wires (such as telegraph wires) begin to "whistle," umbrellas are difficult to keep under control
7	51–61 km/h (32–38 mi/h)	**Moderate Gale** Large trees begin to sway, noticeably difficult to walk
8	62–74 km/h (39–46 mi/h)	**Fresh Gale** Twigs and small branches are broken from trees, walking into the wind is very difficult
9	75–89 km/h (47–54 mi/h)	**Strong Gale** Slight damage occurs to buildings, shingles are blown off of roofs
10	90–103 km/h (55–63 mi/h)	**Whole Gale** Large trees are uprooted, building damage is considerable
11	104–119 km/h (64–72 mi/h)	**Storm** Extensive, widespread damage. These typically occur only at sea, rarely inland.
12	120 km/h or more (74 mi/h or more)	**Hurricane** Extreme damage, very rare inland

Tornado Intensities

The Fujita scale describes the strength of a tornado based on the damage it does. The scale is useful for classifying tornadoes even though it is not exact. For example, a tornado can strengthen and then weaken before it dies out. The wind speeds are estimates of the strongest winds near the ground. Most tornadoes are F0 or F1. One-quarter to one-third of tornadoes are F2 or F3. Only a few percent of tornadoes are F4 or F5.

Fujita Scale for Tornadoes

F-Scale	Wind Speed	Type of Damage
F0	64–116 km/h (40–72 mi/h)	**Light Damage** Some damage to chimneys; branches broken off trees; shallow-rooted trees pushed over; sign boards damaged
F1	117–180 km/h (73–112 mi/h)	**Moderate Damage** Surface peeled off roofs; mobile homes pushed off foundations or overturned; moving autos blown off roads
F2	181–253 km/h (113–157 mi/h)	**Considerable Damage** Roofs torn off frame houses; mobile homes demolished; boxcars overturned; large trees snapped or uprooted; light-object missiles generated; cars lifted off ground
F3	254–332 km/h (158–206 mi/h)	**Severe Damage** Roofs and some walls torn off well-constructed houses; trains overturned; most trees in forest uprooted; heavy cars lifted off the ground and thrown
F4	333–418 km/h (207–260 mi/h)	**Devastating Damage** Well-constructed houses leveled; structures with weak foundations blown away some distance; cars thrown and large missiles generated
F5	419–512 km/h (261–318 mi/h)	**Incredible Damage** Strong frame houses leveled off foundations and swept away; automobile-sized missiles fly through the air in excess of 100 meters (109 yds); trees debarked; incredible phenomena will occur

Time Zones

Because Earth rotates, noon can occur in one location at the same moment that the Sun is setting in another location. To avoid confusion in transportation and communication, officials have divided Earth into 24 time zones. Within a time zone, clocks are set to the same time of day.

Time zones are centered on lines of longitude, but instead of running straight, their boundaries often follow political boundaries. The starting point for the times zones is centered on the prime meridian (0°). The time in this zone is generally called Greenwich Mean Time (GMT), but it is also called Universal Time (UT) by astronomers and Zulu Time (Z) by meteorologists. The International Date Line is centered on 180° longitude. The calendar date to the east of this line is one day earlier than the date to the west.

In the map below, each column of color represents one time zone. The color beige shows areas that do not match standard zones. The labels at the top show the times at noon GMT. Positive and negative numbers at the bottom show the difference between the local time in the zone and Greenwich Mean Time.

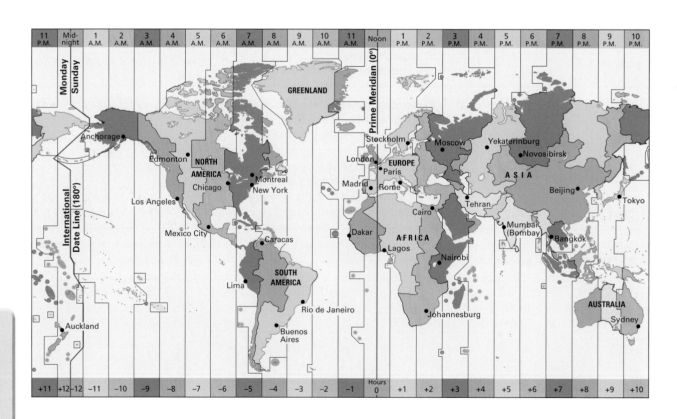

Characteristics of Planets

Some data about the planets and Earth's satellite, the Moon, are listed below. Some data, such as the tilt of Mercury and the mass of Pluto, are not known as well as other data. One astronomical unit (AU) is Earth's average distance from the Sun, or 149,597,870 kilometers. For comparison, Earth's mass is 5.97×10^{24} kilograms, and Earth's diameter is 12,756 kilometers.

Eccentricity is a measure of how flattened an ellipse is. An ellipse with an eccentricity of 0 is a circle. An ellipse with an eccentricity of 1 is completely flat.

Venus, Uranus, and Pluto rotate backward compared to Earth. If you use your left thumb as one of these planets' north pole, your fingers curve in the direction the planet turns.

Characteristics of Planets

Characteristic	Mercury	Venus	Earth	Mars	Jupiter	Saturn	Uranus	Neptune	Pluto	Moon
Mean distance from Sun (AU)	0.387	0.723	1.00	1.52	5.20	9.55	19.2	30.1	39.5	
Period of revolution (Earth years)	0.241 (88 Earth days)	0.615 (225 Earth days)	1.00	1.88	11.9	29.4	83.7	164	248	0.075 (27.3 Earth days)
Eccentricity of orbit	0.206	0.007	0.017	0.093	0.048	0.056	0.046	0.009	0.249	0.055
Diameter (Earth = 1)	0.382	0.949	1.00	0.532	11.21	9.45	4.01	3.88	0.180	0.272
Volume (Earth = 1)	0.06	0.86	1.00	0.15	1320	760	63	58	0.006	0.02
Period of rotation	58.6 Earth days	243 Earth days	23.9 hours	24.6 hours	9.93 hours	10.7 hours	17.2 hours	16.1 hours	6.39 Earth days	27.3 Earth days
Tilt of axis (°) (from perpendicular to orbit)	0.1 (approximate)	2.6	23.45	25.19	3.12	26.73	82.14	29.56	60.4	6.67
Mass (Earth = 1)	0.0553	0.815	1.00	0.107	318	95.2	14.5	17.1	0.002	0.0123
Mean density (g/cm^3)	5.4	5.2	5.5	3.9	1.3	0.7	1.3	1.6	2	3.3

Seasonal Star Maps

Your view of the night sky changes as Earth orbits the Sun. Some constellations appear throughout the year, but others can be seen only during certain seasons. And over the course of one night, the constellations appear to move across the sky as Earth rotates.

When you go outside to view stars, give your eyes time to adjust to the darkness. Avoid looking at bright lights. If you need to look toward a bright light, preserve your night vision in one eye by keeping it closed.

The star maps on pages R71–R74 show parts of the night sky in different seasons. If you are using a flashlight to view the maps, you should attach a piece of red balloon over the lens. The balloon will dim the light and also give it a red color, which affects night vision less than other colors. The following steps will help you use the maps:

1. Stand facing north. To find this direction, use a compass or turn clockwise 90° from the location where the Sun set.

2. The top map for each season shows some constellations that appear over the northern horizon at 10 P.M. During the night, the constellations rotate in a circle around Polaris, the North Star.

3. Now turn so that you stand facing south. The bottom map for the season shows some constellations that appear over the southern horizon at 10 P.M.

WINTER SKY to the NORTH, *January 15*

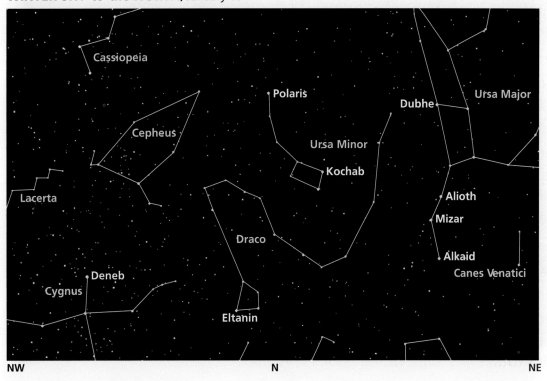

NW   N   NE

WINTER SKY to the SOUTH, *January 15*

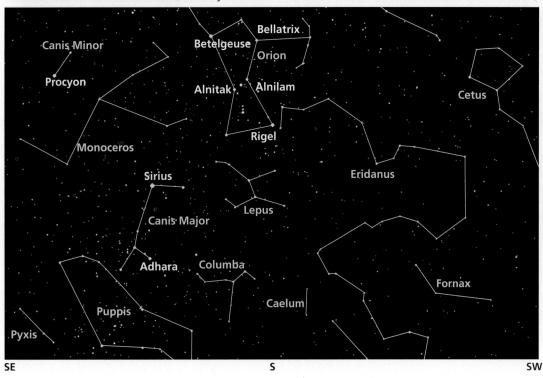

SE   S   SW

Seasonal Star Maps *continued*

SPRING SKY to the NORTH, *April 15*

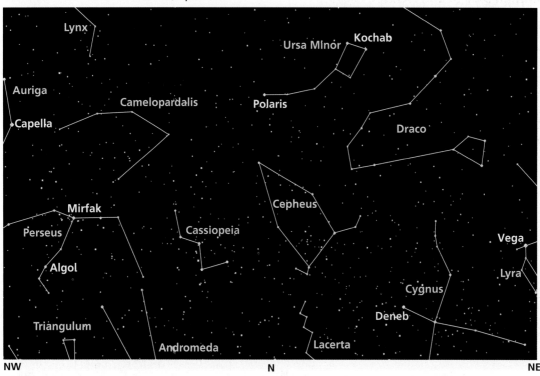

SPRING SKY to the SOUTH, *April 15*

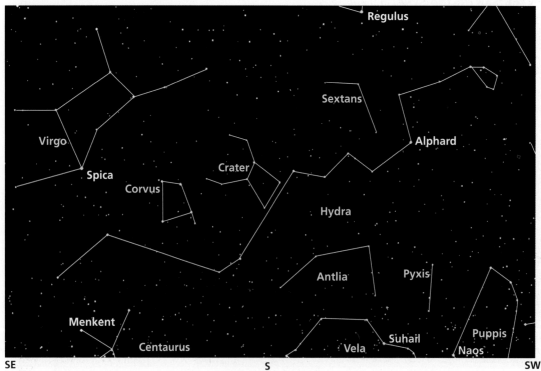

SUMMER SKY to the NORTH, *July 15*

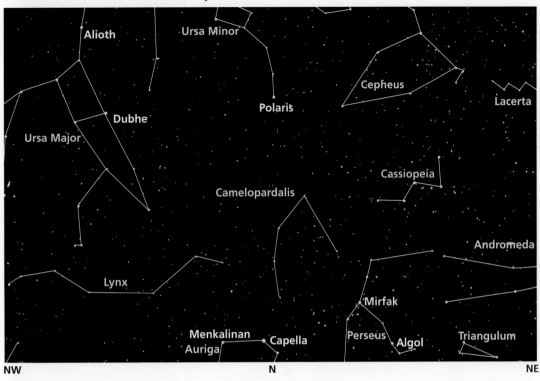

Alioth
Ursa Minor
Cepheus
Lacerta
Polaris
Dubhe
Ursa Major
Cassiopeia
Cameleopardalis
Andromeda
Lynx
Mirfak
Menkalinan
Capella
Perseus
Algol
Triangulum
Auriga

NW   N   NE

SUMMER SKY to the SOUTH, *July 15*

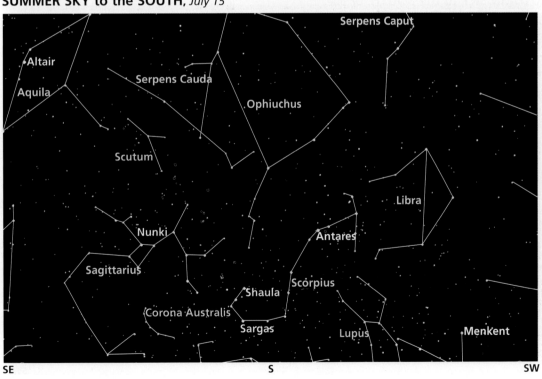

Serpens Caput
Altair
Serpens Cauda
Aquila
Ophiuchus
Scutum
Libra
Nunki
Antares
Sagittarius
Scorpius
Shaula
Corona Australis
Lupus
Menkent
Sargas

SE   S   SW

Seasonal Star Maps *continued*

AUTUMN SKY to the NORTH, *October 15*

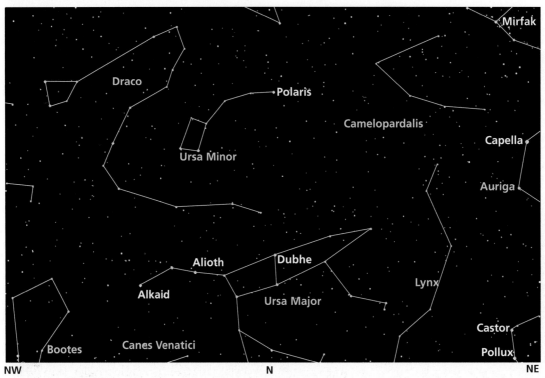

Mirfak

Draco

Polaris

Camelopardalis

Capella

Ursa Minor

Auriga

Alioth

Dubhe

Lynx

Alkaid

Ursa Major

Castor

Bootes

Canes Venatici

Pollux

NW   N   NE

AUTUMN SKY to the SOUTH, *October 15*

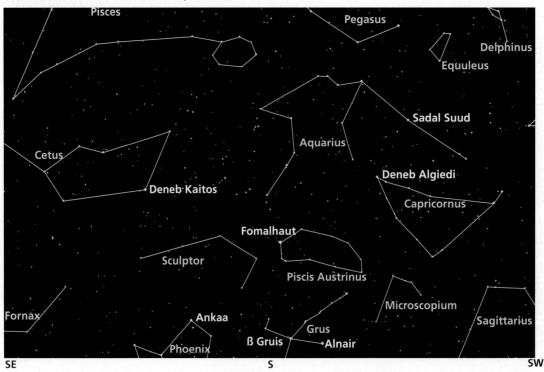

Pisces

Pegasus

Delphinus

Equuleus

Sadal Suud

Cetus

Aquarius

Deneb Algiedi

Deneb Kaitos

Capricornus

Fomalhaut

Sculptor

Piscis Austrinus

Microscopium

Fornax

Sagittarius

Ankaa

Grus

Phoenix

ß Gruis

Alnair

SE   S   SW

The Hertzsprung-Russell Diagram

The Hertzsprung-Russell (H-R) Diagram is a graph that shows stars plotted according to brightness and surface temperature. Most stars fall within a diagonal band called the main sequence. In the main-sequence stage of a star's life cycle, brightness is closely related to surface temperature. Red giant and red supergiant stars appear above the main sequence on the diagram. These stars are bright in relation to their surface temperatures because their huge surface areas give off a lot of light. Dim white dwarfs appear below the main sequence.

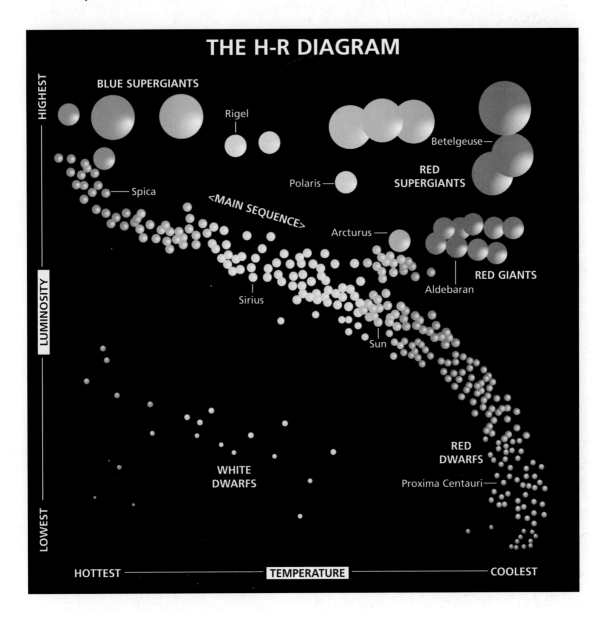

Glossary

GLOSSARY

A

abrasion (uh-BRAY-zhuhn)
The process of wearing something down by friction. (p. A116)

> **abrasión** El proceso de desgaste de algo por efecto de la fricción.

absolute age
The actual age in years of an event or object. (p. B123)

> **edad absoluta** La edad real en años de un evento u objeto.

acid rain
Rain that has become more acidic than normal due to pollution. (pp. B100, D70)

> **lluvia ácida** Lluvia que se ha vuelto más ácida de lo normal debido a la contaminación.

aftershock
A smaller earthquake that follows a more powerful earthquake in the same area. (p. B62)

> **réplica** Un terremoto más pequeño que ocurre después de uno más poderoso en la misma área.

air mass
A large volume of air that has nearly the same temperature and humidity at different locations at the same altitude. (p. D79)

> **masa de aire** Un gran volumen de aire que tiene casi la misma temperatura y humedad en distintos puntos a la misma altitud.

air pollution
Harmful materials added to the air that can cause damage to living things and the environment. (p. D27)

> **contaminación de aire** Materiales nocivos añadidos al aire que pueden causar daño a los seres vivos y al medio ambiente.

air pressure
The force of air molecules pushing on an area. (p. D43)

> **presión de aire** La fuerza de las moléculas de aire empujando sobre un área.

alluvial fan (uh-LOO-vee-uhl)
A fan-shaped deposit of sediment at the base of a slope, formed as water flows down the slope and spreads at the bottom. (p. A153)

> **abanico aluvial** Un depósito de sedimentos en forma de abanico situado en la base de una pendiente; se forma cuando el agua baja por la pendiente y se dispersa al llegar al pie de la misma.

altitude
The distance above sea level. (p. D10)

> **altitud** La distancia sobre el nivel del mar.

aquaculture
The science and business of raising and harvesting fish in a controlled situation. (p. C45)

> **acuacultura** La ciencia y el negocio de criar y cosechar peces en una situación controlada.

aquifer
An underground layer of permeable rock that contains water. (p. C26)

> **acuífero** Una capa subterránea de roca permeable que contiene agua.

artesian well
A well in which pressurized water flows upward to the surface. (p. C28)

> **pozo artesiano** Un pozo en el cual el agua bajo presión fluye hacia arriba hasta la superficie.

asteroid
A small, solid, rocky body that orbits the Sun. Most asteroids orbit in a region between Mars and Jupiter called the asteroid belt. (p. E103)

> **asteroide** Un pequeño cuerpo sólido y rocoso que orbita alrededor del Sol. La mayoría de los asteroides orbitan en una región entre Marte y Júpiter denominada cinturón de asteroides.

asthenosphere (as-THEHN-uh-SFEER)
The layer in Earth's upper mantle and directly under the lithosphere in which rock is soft and weak because it is close to melting. (p. B11)

> **astenosfera** La capa del manto superior de la Tierra situada directamente bajo la litosfera en la cual la roca es blanda y débil por encontrarse próxima a su punto de fusión.

astronomical unit AU

Earth's average distance from the Sun, which is approximately 150 million kilometers (93 million mi). (p. E81)

unidad astronómica ua La distancia promedio de la Tierra al Sol, la cual es de aproximadamente 150 millones de kilómetros (93 millones de millas).

atmosphere (AT-muh-SFEER)

The outer layer of gases of a large body in space, such as a planet or star; the mixture of gases that surrounds the solid Earth; one of the four parts of the Earth system. (pp. A10, D9)

atmósfera La capa externa de gases de un gran cuerpo que se encuentra en el espacio, como un planeta o una estrella; la mezcla de gases que rodea la Tierra sólida; una de las cuatro partes del sistema terrestre.

atom

The smallest particle of an element that has the chemical properties of that element. (p. xxxiii)

átomo La partícula más pequeña de un elemento que tiene las propiedades químicas de ese elemento.

axis of rotation

An imaginary line about which a turning body, such as Earth rotates. (p. E44)

eje de rotación Una línea imaginaria alrededor de la cual gira un cuerpo, como lo hace la Tierra.

B

barometer

An instrument that measures air pressure in the atmosphere. (p. D46)

barómetro Un instrumento que mide la presión del aire en la atmósfera.

barrier island

A long, narrow island that develops parallel to a coast as a sandbar builds up above the water's surface. (p. A160)

isla barrera Una isla larga y angosta que se desarrolla paralelamente a la costa al crecer una barra de arena hasta rebasar la superficie del agua.

big bang

The moment in time when the universe started to expand out of an extremely hot, dense state, according to scientific theory. (p. E138)

la gran explosión De acuerdo a la teoría científica, el momento en el tiempo en el cual el universo empezó a expandirse a partir de un estado extremadamente caliente y denso.

biomass

Organic matter that contains stored energy from sunlight and that can be burned as fuel. (p. B168)

biomasa Materia orgánica que contiene energía almacenada proveniente de la luz del Sol y que puede ser usada como combustible.

biosphere (BY-uh-SFEER)

All living organisms on Earth in the air, on the land, and in the waters; one of the four parts of the Earth system. (p. A11)

biosfera Todos los organismos vivos de la Tierra, en el aire, en la tierra y en las aguas; una de las cuatro partes del sistema de la Tierra.

black hole

The final stage of an extremely massive star, which is invisible because its gravity prevents any form of radiation from escaping. (p. E126)

hoyo negro La etapa final de una estrella de enorme masa, la cual es invisible porque su gravedad evita que cualquier tipo de radiación escape.

blizzard

A blinding snowstorm with winds of at least 56 kilometers per hour (35 mi/h), usually with temperatures below −7°C (20°F). (p. D90)

ventisca Una cegadora tormenta de nieve con vientos de por lo menos 56 kilómetros por hora (35 mi/h), usualmente con temperaturas menores a −7°C (20°F).

by-catch

The portion of animals that are caught in a net and then thrown away as unwanted. (p. C132)

captura incidental La porción de los animales que se capturan en una red y luego se desechan como no deseados.

C

chemical weathering

The breakdown or decomposition of rock that takes place when minerals change through chemical processes. (p. A118)

meteorización química La descomposición de las rocas que ocurre cuando los minerales cambian mediante procesos químicos.

cleavage

The property of a mineral that describes its tendency to break along flat surfaces. (p. A53)

clivaje La propiedad de un mineral que describe su tendencia a romperse a lo largo de una superficie plana.

climate
The characteristic weather conditions in an area over a long period of time. (p. D117)

clima Las condiciones meteorológicas características de un lugar durante un largo período de tiempo.

climate zone
One of the major divisions in a system for classifying the climates of different regions based on characteristics they have in common. (p. D125)

zona climática Una de las mayores divisiones en un sistema de clasificación de climas de diferentes regiones, basado en las características que tienen en común.

comet
A body that produces a coma of gas and dust; a small, icy body that orbits the Sun. (p. E104)

cometa Un cuerpo que produce una coma de gas y polvo; un cuerpo pequeño y helado que se mueve en órbita alrededor del Sol.

compound
A substance made up of two or more different types of atoms bonded together.

compuesto Una sustancia formada por dos o más diferentes tipos de átomos enlazados.

concentration
The amount of a substance that is contained in another substance—such as dissolved sugar in water—often expressed as parts per million or parts per billion. (p. C51)

concentración La cantidad de una sustancia contenida en otra sustancia, como el azúcar disuelto en agua; a menudo se expresa como partes por millón o partes por mil millones.

condensation
The process by which a gas changes into a liquid. (pp. C13, D56)

condensación El proceso por el cual un gas se transforma en líquido.

conduction
The transfer of heat energy from one substance to another through direct contact without obvious motion. (p. D18)

conducción La transferencia de energía calorífica de una sustancia a otra a través de contacto directo, sin que haya movimiento obvio.

conservation
The process of saving or protecting a natural resource. (p. B157)

conservación El proceso de salvar o proteger un recurso natural.

constellation
A group of stars that form a pattern in the sky. (p. E12)

constelación Un grupo de estrellas que forman un patrón en el cielo.

continental climate
A climate that occurs in the interior of a continent, with large temperature differences between seasons. (p. D120)

clima continental El clima que se presenta en el interior de un continente, con grandes diferencias de temperatura entre estaciones.

continental-continental collision
A boundary along which two plates carrying continental crust push together. (p. B31)

colisión continente-continente Un límite a lo largo del cual dos placas de corteza continental empujan contra sí.

continental drift
The hypothesis that Earth's continents move on Earth's surface. (p. B14)

deriva continental La hipótesis que postula que los continentes de la Tierra se mueven sobre la superficie del planeta.

continental shelf
The flat or gently sloping land that lies submerged around the edges of a continent and that extends from the shoreline out to the continental slope. (p. C80)

plataforma continental La tierra plana o ligeramente inclinada que está sumergida alrededor de las orillas de un continente y que se extiende desde la costa hasta el talud continental.

contour interval
On a topographic map, the difference in elevation from one contour line to the next. (p. A26)

equidistancia entre curvas de nivel En un mapa topográfico, la diferencia en elevación de una curva de nivel a la siguiente.

contour line
A line on a topographic map that joins points of equal elevation. (p. A25)

curva de nivel Una línea en un mapa topográfico que une puntos de igual elevación.

convection

The transfer of energy from place to place by the motion of heated gas or liquid; in Earth's mantle, convection is thought to transfer energy by the motion of solid rock, which when under great heat and pressure can move like a liquid. (pp. B17, D19, E116)

convección La transferencia de energía de un lugar a otro por el movimiento de un líquido o gas calentado; se piensa que en el manto terrestre la convección transfiere energía mediante el movimiento de roca sólida, la cual puede moverse como un líquido cuando está muy caliente y bajo alta presión.

convection current

A circulation pattern in which material is heated and rises in one area, then cools and sinks in another area, flowing in a continuous loop. (p. B17)

corriente de convección Un patrón de circulación en el cual el material se calienta y asciende en un área, luego se enfría y se hunde en otra área, fluyendo en un circuito continuo.

convergent boundary (kun-VUR-juhnt)

A boundary along which two tectonic plates push together, characterized either by subduction or a continental collision. (p. B22)

límite convergente Un límite a lo largo del cual dos placas tectónicas se empujan mutuamente; este límite se caracteriza por una zona de subducción o una colisión entre continentes.

coral reef

A built-up limestone deposit formed by small ant-sized organisms called corals. (p. C122)

arrecife de coral Un depósito de piedra caliza formado por organismos pequeños del tamaño de una hormiga llamados corales.

Coriolis effect (KAWR-ee-OH-lihs)

The influence of Earth's rotation on objects that move over Earth. (p. D49)

efecto Coriolis La influencia de la rotación de la Tierra sobre objetos que se mueven sobre la Tierra.

corona

The outer layer of the Sun's atmosphere. (p. E116)

corona La capa exterior de la atmósfera del Sol.

crust

A thin outer layer of rock above a planet's mantle, including all dry land and ocean basins. Earth's continental crust is 40 kilometers thick on average and oceanic crust is 7 kilometers thick on average. (p. B11)

corteza Una delgada capa exterior de roca situada sobre el manto de un planeta que incluye toda la tierra seca y todas las cuencas oceánicas. La corteza continental de la Tierra tiene un grosor promedio de 40 kilómetros y la corteza oceánica tiene un grosor promedio de 7 kilómetros.

crystal

A solid substance in which the atoms are arranged in an orderly, repeating, three-dimensional pattern. (p. A46)

cristal Una sustancia sólida en la cual los átomos están organizados en un patrón tridimensional y ordenado que se repite.

cycle

n. A series of events or actions that repeat themselves regularly; a physical and/or chemical process in which one material continually changes locations and/or forms. Examples include the water cycle, the carbon cycle, and the rock cycle.

v. To move through a repeating series of events or actions.

ciclo s. Una serie de eventos o acciones que se repiten regularmente; un proceso físico y/o químico en el cual un material cambia continuamente de lugar y/o forma. Ejemplos: el ciclo del agua, el ciclo del carbono y el ciclo de las rocas.

D

dam

A structure that holds back and controls the flow of water in a river or other body of water. (p. C46)

presa Una estructura que retiene y controla el flujo de agua en un río u otro cuerpo de agua.

data

Information gathered by observation or experimentation that can be used in calculating or reasoning. *Data* is a plural word; the singular is *datum.*

datos Información reunida mediante observación o experimentación y que se puede usar para calcular o para razonar.

delta

An area of land at the end, or mouth, of a river that is formed by the buildup of sediment. (p. A153)

delta Un área de tierra al final, o en la desembocadura, de un río y que se forma por la acumulación de sedimentos.

density
A property of matter representing the mass per unit volume. (pp. A54, D10)

 densidad Una propiedad de la materia que representa la masa por unidad de volumen.

deposition (DEHP-uh-ZISH-uhn)
The process in which transported sediment is laid down. (p. A145)

 sedimentación El proceso mediante el cual se deposita sedimento que ha sido transportado.

desalination (de-SAL-ih-nay-shun)
The process of removing salt from ocean water. Desalination is used to obtain fresh water. (p. C66)

 desalinización El proceso de eliminar la sal del agua de mar. La desalinización se usa para obtener agua dulce.

desertification (dih-ZUR-tuh-fih-KAY-shuhn)
The expansion of desert conditions in areas where the natural plant cover has been destroyed. (p. A133)

 desertificación La expansión de las condiciones desérticas en áreas donde la vegetación natural ha sido destruida.

dew point
The temperature at which air with a given amount of water vapor will reach saturation. (p. D58)

 punto de rocío La temperatura a la cual el aire con una cantidad determinada de vapor de agua alcanzará la saturación.

divergent boundary (dih-VUR-juhnt)
A boundary along which two tectonic plates move apart, characterized by either a mid-ocean ridge or a continental rift valley. (p. B22)

 límite divergente Un límite a lo largo del cual dos placas tectónicas se separan; este límite se caracteriza por una dorsal oceánica o un valle de rift continental.

divide
A continuous high line of land—or ridge—from which water drains to one side or the other. (pp. A151, C17)

 línea divisoria de aguas Una línea continua de tierra alta, o un cerro, desde donde el agua escurre hacia un lado o hacia el otro.

Doppler effect
A change in the observed frequency of a wave, occurring when the source of the wave or the observer is moving. Changes in the frequency of light are often measured by observing changes in wavelength, whereas changes in the frequency of sound are often detected as changes in pitch. (p. E136)

 efecto Doppler Un cambio en la frecuencia observada de una onda que ocurre cuando la fuente de la onda o el observador están en movimiento. Los cambios en la frecuencia de la luz a menudo se miden observando los cambios en la longitud de onda, mientras que los cambios en la frecuencia del sonido a menudo se detectan como cambios en el tono.

downwelling
The movement of water from the surface to greater depths. (p. C86)

 sumergencia El movimiento de agua de la superficie hacia mayores profundidades.

drainage basin
An area of land in which water drains into a stream system. The borders of a drainage basin are called divides. (pp. A151, C17)

 cuenca tributaria Un área de tierra en la cual el agua escurre a un sistema de corrientes. Los límites de una cuenca tributaria se denominan líneas divisorias de aguas.

drought (drowt)
A long period of abnormally low amounts of rainfall. (p. C61)

 sequía Un período largo con cantidades inusualmente bajas de lluvia.

dune
A mound of sand built up by wind. (p. A161)

 duna Un montículo de arena formado por el viento.

E

earthquake
A shaking of the ground caused by the sudden movement of large blocks of rocks along a fault. (p. B45)

 terremoto Un temblor del suelo ocasionado por el movimiento repentino de grandes bloques de rocas a lo largo de una falla.

eclipse

An event during which one object in space casts a shadow onto another. On Earth, a lunar eclipse occurs when the Moon moves through Earth's shadow, and a solar eclipse occurs when the Moon's shadow crosses Earth. (p. E63)

eclipse Un evento durante el cual un objeto en el espacio proyecta una sombra sobre otro. En la Tierra, un eclipse lunar ocurre cuando la Luna se mueve a través de la sombra de la Tierra, y un eclipse solar ocurre cuando la sombra de la Luna cruza la Tierra.

electromagnetic radiation

(ih-LEHK-troh-mag-NEHT-ihk RAY-dee-AY-shuhn) Energy that travels across distances as certain types of waves. Types of electromagnetic radiation are radio waves, microwaves, infrared radiation, visible light, ultraviolet radiation, x-rays, and gamma rays. (p. E15)

radiación electromagnética Energía que viaja a través de las distancias en forma de ciertos tipos de ondas. Las ondas de radio, las microondas, la radiación infrarroja, la luz visible, la radiación ultravioleta, los rayos X y los rayos gama son tipos de radiación electromagnética.

element

A substance that cannot be broken down into a simpler substance by ordinary chemical changes. An element consists of atoms of only one type. (p. A45)

elemento Una sustancia que no puede descomponerse en otra sustancia más simple por medio de cambios químicos normales. Un elemento consta de átomos de un solo tipo.

elevation

A measure of how high something is above a reference point, such as sea level. (p. A25)

elevación Una medida de lo elevado que está algo sobre un punto de referencia, como el nivel del mar.

ellipse

An oval or flattened circle. (p. E81)

elipse Un óvalo o círculo aplanado.

El Niño (ehl NEEN-yoh)

A disturbance of wind patterns and ocean currents in the Pacific Ocean that causes temporary climate changes in many parts of the world. (pp. C88, D136)

El Niño Un disturbio en los patrones de viento y las corrientes oceánicas del océano Pacifico que causa cambios climáticos temporales en muchas partes del mundo.

energy

The ability to do work or to cause a change. For example, the energy of a moving bowling ball knocks over pins; energy from food allows animals to move and to grow; and energy from the Sun heats Earth's surface and atmosphere, which causes air to move. (p. xxxi)

energía La capacidad para trabajar o causar un cambio. Por ejemplo, la energía de una bola de boliche en movimiento tumba los pinos; la energía proveniente de su alimento permite a los animales moverse y crecer; la energía del Sol calienta la superficie y la atmósfera de la Tierra, lo que ocasiona que el aire se mueva.

epicenter (EHP-ih-SEHN-tuhr)

The point on Earth's surface directly above the focus of an earthquake. (p. B52)

epicentro El punto en la superficie de la Tierra situado directamente sobre el foco sísmico.

equator

An imaginary east-west line around the center of Earth that divides the planet into the Northern Hemisphere and the Southern Hemisphere; a line set at 0° latitude. (p. A18)

ecuador Una línea imaginaria de este a oeste alrededor del centro de la Tierra y que divide al planeta en hemisferio norte y hemisferio sur; la línea está fijada a latitud 0°.

equinox (EE-kwhu-NAHKS)

In an orbit, a position and time in which sunlight shines equally on the Northern Hemisphere and the Southern Hemisphere; a time of year when daylight and darkness are nearly equal for most of Earth. (p. E46)

equinoccio En una órbita, la posición y el tiempo en los cuales la luz del Sol incide de la misma manera en el Hemisferio Norte y en el Hemisferio Sur; una época del año en la cual la luz del día y la oscuridad son casi iguales para la mayor parte de la Tierra.

erosion

The process in which sediment is picked up and moved from one place to another. (p. A145)

erosión El proceso en el cual el sedimento es recogido y transportado de un lugar a otro.

estuary (EHS-choo-EHR-ee)

A shoreline area where fresh water from a river mixes with salt water from the ocean. (p. C116)

estuario Un litoral donde se mezcla agua dulce de un río con agua salada del océano.

eutrophication (yoo-TRAF-ih-KAY-shun)
An increase in nutrients in a lake or pond. Eutrophication can occur naturally or as a result of pollution, and causes increased growth of algae and plants. (p. C20)

> **eutrofización** Un aumento en los nutrientes de un lago o una laguna. La eutrofización puede ocurrir de manera natural o como resultado de la contaminación y ocasiona un aumento en el crecimiento de algas y plantas.

evaporation
The process by which liquid changes into gas. (pp. C13, D56)

> **evaporación** El proceso por el cual un líquido se transforma en gas.

exfoliation (ex-FOH-lee-AY-shuhn)
In geology, the process in which layers or sheets of rock gradually break off. (p. A116)

> **exfoliación** En geología, el proceso en el cual capas u hojas de roca se desprenden gradualmente.

experiment
An organized procedure to study something under controlled conditions. (p. xl)

> **experimento** Un procedimiento organizado para estudiar algo bajo condiciones controladas.

extrusive igneous rock
(ihk-STROO-sihv IHG-nee-uhs)
Igneous rock that forms as lava cools on Earth's surface. (p. A83)

> **roca ígnea extrusiva** Roca ígnea que se forma al enfriarse la lava sobre la superficie de la Tierra.

F

false-color image
A computer image in which the colors are not what the human eye would see. A false-color image can assign different colors to different types of radiation coming from an object to highlight its features. (p. A32)

> **imagen de color falso** Una imagen computacional en la cual los colores no son los que el ojo humano observaría. Una imagen de color falso puede asignar diferentes colores a los diferentes tipos de radiación que provienen de un objeto para hacer destacar sus características.

fault
A fracture in Earth's lithosphere along which blocks of rock move past each other. (p. B45)

> **falla** Una fractura en la litosfera de la Tierra a lo largo de la cual bloques de roca se mueven y pasan uno al lado de otro.

fault-block mountain
A mountain that forms as blocks of rock move up or down along normal faults in areas where the lithosphere is being pulled apart. (p. B82)

> **montaña de bloques de falla** Una montaña que se forma cuando bloques de roca se mueven hacia arriba o hacia abajo a lo largo de fallas normales en las áreas donde la litosfera está siendo separada.

floodplain
A flat area of land on either side of a stream that becomes flooded when a river overflows its banks. (p. A152)

> **planicie de inundación** Un área plana de tierra en cualquier costado de un arroyo que se inunda cuando un río se desborda.

focus
In an earthquake, the point underground where the rocks first begin to move. (p. B52)

> **foco sísmico** En un terremoto, el punto subterráneo donde comienza el movimiento de las rocas.

folded mountain
A mountain that forms as continental crust is compressed and rocks bend into large folds. (p. B80)

> **montaña plegada** Una montaña que se forma cuando la corteza continental es comprimida y las rocas se doblan en grandes pliegues.

foliation
The arrangement of minerals within rocks into flat or wavy parallel bands; a characteristic of most metamorphic rocks. (p. A100)

> **foliación** La organización de minerales en bandas paralelas planas u onduladas en las rocas; una característica de la mayoría de las rocas metamórficas.

force
A push or a pull; something that changes the motion of an object. (p. xxxiii)

> **fuerza** Un empuje o un jalón; algo que cambia el movimiento de un objeto.

fossil
A trace or the remains of a once-living thing from long ago. (pp. B111, C111)

> **fósil** Un rastro o los restos de un organismo que vivió hace mucho tiempo.

fossil fuels
Fuels formed from the remains of prehistoric organisms that are burned for energy. (pp. B150, D28)

> **combustibles fósiles** Combustibles formados a partir de los restos de organismos prehistóricos que son consumidos para obtener energía.

fracture
The tendency of a mineral to break into irregular pieces. (p. A53)

fractura La tendencia de un mineral a romperse en pedazos irregulares.

freezing rain
Rain that freezes when it hits the ground or another surface and coats the surface with ice. (p. D68)

lluvia helada Lluvia que se congela cuando cae a la tierra o cualquier otra superficie y cubre la superficie con hielo.

fresh water
Water that is not salty and has little or no taste, color, or smell. Most lakes and rivers are made up of fresh water. (p. C11)

agua dulce Agua que no es salada y que tiene muy poco o ningún sabor, color u olor. La mayoría de los lagos y los ríos están compuestos de agua dulce.

friction
A force that resists the motion between two surfaces in contact. (p. xxxvii)

fricción Una fuerza que resiste el movimiento entre dos superficies en contacto.

front
The boundary between air masses. (p. D82)

frente El limite entre masas de aire.

fusion
A process in which particles of an element collide and combine to form a heavier element, such as the fusion of hydrogen into helium that occurs in the Sun's core. (p. E116)

fusión Un proceso en el cual las partículas de un elemento chocan y se combinan para formar un elemento más pesado, como la fusión de hidrógeno en helio que ocurre en el núcleo del Sol.

G

galaxy
Millions or billions of stars held together in a group by their own gravity. (p. E10)

galaxia Millones o miles de millones de estrellas unidas en un grupo por su propia gravedad.

gas
A state of matter different from liquid and solid, with no definite volume and no definite shape.

gas Un estado de la material, que no es sólido ni líquido, en el cual la sustancia se puede expandir o contraer para llenar un recipiente.

gas giant
A large planet that consists mostly of gases in a dense form. The four large planets in the outer solar system—Jupiter, Saturn, Uranus, and Neptune—are gas giants. (p. E94)

gigante de gas Un planeta grande compuesto principalmente de gases en forma densa. Los cuatro planetas grandes en el sistema solar exterior—Júpiter, Saturno, Urano y Neptuno —son gigantes de gas.

geographic information systems
Computer systems that can store, arrange, and display geographic data in different types of maps. (p. A33)

sistemas de información geográfica Sistemas computarizados que pueden almacenar, organizar y mostrar datos geográficos en diferentes tipos de mapas.

geologic time scale
The summary of Earth's history, divided into intervals of time defined by major events or changes on Earth. (p. B129)

escala de tiempo geológico El resumen de la historia de la Tierra, dividido en intervalos de tiempo definidos por los principales eventos o cambios en la Tierra.

geosphere (JEE-uh-SFEER)
All the features on Earth's surface—continents, islands, and seafloor—and everything below the surface—the inner and outer core and the mantle; one of the four parts of the Earth system. (p. A12)

geosfera Todas las características de la superficie de la Tierra, es decir, continentes, islas y el fondo marino, y de todo bajo la superficie, es decir, el núcleo externo e interno y el manto; una de las cuatro partes del sistema de la Tierra.

geothermal energy
Heat energy that originates from within Earth and drives the movement of Earth's tectonic plates. Geothermal energy can be used to generate electricity. (p. B166)

energía geotérmica Energía calorífica que se origina en el interior de la Tierra y que impulsa el movimiento de las placas tectónicas de planeta. La energía geotérmica puede usarse para generar electricidad.

geyser
A type of hot spring that shoots water into the air. (p. B100)

géiser Un tipo de fuente termal que dispara agua al aire.

glacier (GLAY-shuhr)
A large mass of ice that exists year-round and moves over land. (p. A165)

> **glaciar** Una gran masa de hielo que existe durante todo el año y se mueve sobre la tierra.

global winds
Winds that travel long distances in steady patterns over several weeks. (p. D48)

> **vientos globales** Vientos que viajan grandes distancias en patrones fijos por varias semanas.

gravity
The force that objects exert on each other because of their mass. (p. xxxiii)

> **gravedad** La fuerza que los objetos ejercen entre sí debido a su masa.

greenhouse effect
The process by which certain gases in a planet's atmosphere absorb and emit infrared radiation, resulting in an increase in surface temperature. (p. D24)

> **efecto invernadero** El proceso mediante el cual ciertos gases en la atmósfera de un planeta absorben y emiten radiación infrarroja, resultando en un incremento de la temperatura superficial del planeta.

greenhouse gases
Gases, such as carbon dioxide and methane, that absorb and give off infrared radiation as part of the greenhouse effect. (p. D24)

> **gases invernadero** Gases, como el dióxido de carbono y el metano, que absorben y emiten radiación infrarroja como parte del efecto invernadero.

groundwater
Water that collects and is stored underground. (p. C24)

> **agua subterránea** Agua que se acumula y almacena bajo tierra.

habitat
The natural environment in which a living thing gets all that it needs to live; examples include a desert, a coral reef, and a freshwater lake. (p. C114)

> **hábitat** El medio ambiente natural en el cual un organismo vivo consigue todo lo que requiere para vivir; ejemplos incluyen un desierto, un arrecife coralino y un lago de agua dulce.

hail
Layered lumps or balls of ice that fall from cumulonimbus clouds. (p. D68)

> **granizo** Trozos de hielo que caen de nubes cumulonimbos.

half-life
The length of time it takes for half of the atoms in a sample of a radioactive element to change from an unstable form into another form. (p. B123)

> **vida media** El tiempo que tardan la mitad de los átomos de una muestra de un elemento radiactivo en cambiar de una forma inestable a otra forma.

hardness
The resistance of a mineral or other material to being scratched. (p. A55)

> **dureza** La resistencia de un mineral o de otro material a ser rayado.

high-pressure system
A generally calm and clear weather system that occurs when air sinks down in a high-pressure center and spreads out toward areas of lower pressure as it nears the ground. (p. D84)

> **sistema de alta presión** Un sistema climático generalmente claro y calmo que se presenta cuando el aire desciende en un centro de alta presión y se esparce hacia áreas de baja presión conforme se acerca al suelo.

hot spot
An area where a column of hot material rises from deep within a planet's mantle and heats the lithosphere above it, often causing volcanic activity at the surface. (p. B27)

> **punto caliente** Un área donde una columna de material caliente surge del interior del manto de un planeta y calienta la litosfera situada sobre él, con frecuencia ocasionando actividad volcánica en la superficie.

humidity
The amount of water vapor in air. (p. D58)

> **humedad** La cantidad de vapor de agua en el aire.

humus (HYOO-muhs)
The decayed organic matter in soil. (p. A123)

> **humus** La materia orgánica en descomposición del suelo.

hurricane (HUR-ih-KAYN)
A tropical low-pressure system with sustained winds of 120 kilometers per hour (74 mi/h) or more. (p. D87)

> **huracán** Un sistema tropical de baja presión con vientos sostenidos de 120 kilómetros por hora (74 mi/h) o más.

hydroelectric energy

Electricity that is generated by the conversion of the energy of moving water. (p. B164)

energía hidroeléctrica Electricidad que se genera por la conversión de la energía del agua en movimiento.

hydrogen fuel cell

A device that uses hydrogen and oxygen to produce electricity. The byproducts are heat and water. (p. B168)

celda de combustible de hidrógeno Un aparato que usa hidrógeno y oxígeno para producir electricidad. Los subproductos son calor y agua.

hydrosphere (HY-druh-SFEER)

All water on Earth—in the atmosphere and in the oceans, lakes, glaciers, rivers, streams, and underground reservoirs; one of the four parts of the Earth system. (p. A10)

hidrosfera Toda el agua de la Tierra: en la atmósfera y en los océanos, lagos, glaciares, ríos, arroyos y depósitos subterráneos; una de las cuatro partes del sistema de la Tierra.

hydrothermal vent

An opening in the sea floor from which heated water rises and mixes with the ocean water above. (p. C128)

abertura hidrotermal Una salida en el fondo marino desde la cual asciende agua caliente que se mezcla con el agua del océano.

hypothesis

A tentative explanation for an observation or phenomenon. A hypothesis is used to make testable predictions. (p. xl)

hipótesis Una explicación provisional de una observación o de un fenómeno. Una hipótesis se usa para hacer predicciones que se pueden probar.

ice age

A period of time during which surface temperatures drop significantly and huge ice sheets spread out beyond the polar regions. (p. D135)

edad de hielo Un período de tiempo durante el cual las temperaturas superficiales disminuyen significativamente y grandes capas de hielo se extienden más allá de las regiones polares.

iceberg

A mass of floating ice that broke away from a glacier. (p. C22)

iceberg Una masa de hielo flotante que se separó de un glaciar.

ice core

A tubular sample that shows the layers of snow and ice that have built up over the years. (p. B117)

núcleo de hielo Una muestra tubular que presenta las capas de nieve y hielo que se han acumulado con los años.

igneous rock (IHG-nee-uhs)

Rock that forms as molten rock cools and becomes solid. (p. A78)

roca ígnea Roca que se forma al enfriarse la roca fundida y hacerse sólida.

impact crater

A round pit left behind on the surface of a planet or other body in space after a smaller object strikes the surface. (p. E32)

cráter de impacto Un pozo circular en la superficie de un planeta u otro cuerpo en el espacio que se forma cuando un objeto más pequeño golpea la superficie.

impermeable

Resistant to the passage of water. (p. C25)

impermeable Resistente al paso del agua.

index fossil

A fossil of an organism that was common, lived in many areas, and existed only during a certain span of time. Index fossils are used to help determine the age of rock layers. (p. B121)

fósil indicador Un fósil de un organismo que era común, vivió en muchas áreas y existió sólo durante cierto período de tiempo. Los fósiles indicadores se usan para ayudar a determinar la edad de las capas de roca.

infrared radiation (IHN-fruh-REHD RAY-dee-AY-shuhn)

Radiation of lower frequencies than visible light. (p. D23)

radiación infrarroja Radiación de frecuencia más baja que la luz visible.

inner core

A solid sphere of metal, mainly nickel and iron, at Earth's center. (p. B10)

núcleo interno Una esfera sólida de metal, principalmente níquel y hierro, que se encuentra en el centro de la Tierra.

intertidal zone

The narrow ocean margin between the high-tide mark and the low-tide mark. (p. C114)

zona intermareal El estrecho margen oceánico entre el límite de la marea alta y el límite de la marea baja.

intrusive igneous rock (ihn-TROO-sihv IHG-nee-uhs)
Igneous rock that forms as magma cools below Earth's surface. (p. A83)

   roca ígnea intrusiva Roca ígnea que se forma al enfriarse el magma bajo la superficie de la Tierra.

irrigation
The process of supplying water to land to grow crops. (p. C43)

   irrigación El proceso de suministrar agua a las tierras de cultivo.

isobar (EYE-suh-BAHR)
A line on a weather map connecting places that have the same air pressure. (p. D101)

   isobara Una línea en un mapa climático que conecta lugares que tienen la misma presión de aire.

J

jet stream
A wind that flows in the upper troposphere from west to east over vast distances at great speeds. (p. D52)

   corriente de chorro Un viento que sopla vastas distancias en la troposfera superior de oeste a este a grandes velocidades.

K

kelp forest
A large community of kelp, a type of seaweed that can attach to the ocean floor. (p. C124)

   bosque de kelp Una comunidad grande de kelp, un tipo de alga marina que puede adherirse al fondo marino.

kettle lake
A bowl-shaped lake that was formed as sediment built up around a block of ice left behind by a glacier. (p. A169)

   lago kettle Un lago en forma de tazón que se formó al acumularse sedimento alrededor de un bloque de hielo que quedó tras el paso de un glaciar.

L

lander
A craft designed to land on a planet's surface. (p. E28)

   módulo de aterrizaje Una nave diseñada para aterrizar en la superficie de un planeta.

latitude
The distance in degrees north or south from the equator. (pp. A18, D118)

   latitud La distancia en grados norte o sur a partir del ecuador.

lava
Molten rock that reaches a planet's surface through a volcano. (pp. A62, B87)

   lava Roca fundida que llega a la superficie de un planeta a través de un volcán.

law
In science, a rule or principle describing a physical relationship that always works in the same way under the same conditions. The law of conservation of energy is an example.

   ley En las ciencias, una regla o un principio que describe una relación física que siempre funciona de la misma manera bajo las mismas condiciones. La ley de la conservación de la energía es un ejemplo.

light-year
The distance light travels in one year, which is about 9.5 trillion kilometers (6 trillion mi). (p. E122)

   año luz La distancia que viaja la luz en un año, la cual es de casi 9.5 billones de kilómetros (6 billones de millas).

liquefaction
A process in which the shaking of ground causes loose, wet soil to act like a liquid. (p. B62)

   licuación Un proceso en el cual el temblor del suelo ocasiona que la tierra húmeda y suelta actúe como un líquido.

lithosphere (LIHTH-uh-SFEER)
The layer of Earth made up of the crust and the rigid rock of the upper mantle, averaging about 40 kilometers thick and broken into tectonic plates. (p. B11)

   litosfera La capa de la Tierra compuesta por la corteza y la roca rígida del manto superior, con un promedio de 40 kilómetros de grosor y fracturada en placas tectónicas.

lock

A section of a waterway, closed off by gates, in which the water level is rasied or lowered to move ships through. (p. C46)

esclusa Una sección de un canal cerrado con compuertas, en la cual se eleva o se baja el nivel del agua para que pasen barcos.

loess (LOH-uhs)

Deposits of fine-grained, wind-blown sediment. (p. A162)

loes Depósitos de sedimento de grano fino transportado por el viento.

longitude

The distance in degrees east or west of the prime meridian. Longitude lines are numbered from 0° to 180°. (p. A19)

longitud La distancia en grados al este o al oeste del primer meridiano. Las líneas de longitud están numeradas de 0° a 180°.

longshore current

The overall direction and movement of water as waves strike the shore at an angle. (pp. A159, C92)

corriente litoral La dirección y el movimiento general del agua conforme las olas golpean la costa en ángulo.

longshore drift

The zigzag movement of sand along a beach, caused by the action of waves. (p. A159)

deriva litoral El movimiento en zigzag de la arena a lo largo de una playa, ocasionado por la acción de las olas.

low-pressure system

A large and often stormy weather system that occurs when air moves around and into a low-pressure center, then moves up to higher altitudes. (p. D85)

sistema de baja presión Un sistema climático grande y usualmente lluvioso que se presenta cuando el aire se mueve alrededor de y hacia un centro de baja presión, y luego se mueve hacia mayores altitudes.

luster

The property of a mineral that describes the way in which light reflects from its surface. Major types of luster are metallic and nonmetallic. (p. A52)

brillo La propiedad de un mineral que describe la manera en la cual la luz se refleja en su superficie. Los principales tipos de brillo son metálico y no metálico.

M

magma

Molten rock beneath Earth's surface. (p. A62)

magma Roca fundida que se encuentra bajo la superficie de la Tierra.

magnetic reversal

A switch in the direction of Earth's magnetic field so that the magnetic north pole becomes the magnetic south pole and the magnetic south pole becomes the magnetic north pole. (p. B24)

inversión magnética Un cambio en la dirección del campo magnético de la Tierra, de modo que el polo norte magnético se convierte en el polo sur magnético y el polo sur magnético se convierte en el polo norte magnético.

main sequence

The stage in which stars produce energy through the fusion of hydrogen into helium. (p. E126)

secuencia principal La etapa en la cual las estrellas producen energía mediante la fusión de hidrógeno en helio.

mantle

The layer of rock between Earth's outer core and crust, in which most rock is hot enough to flow in convection currents; Earth's thickest layer. (p. B11)

manto La capa de roca situada entre el núcleo externo y la corteza de la Tierra, en la cual la mayor parte de la roca es lo suficientemente caliente para fluir en corrientes de convección; la capa más gruesa de la Tierra.

map legend

A chart that explains the meaning of each symbol used on a map; also called a key. (p. A17)

clave del mapa Una tabla que explica el significado de cada símbolo usado en un mapa.

map scale

The comparison of distance on a map with actual distance on what the map represents, such as Earth's surface. Map scale may be expressed as a ratio, a bar scale, or equivalent units. (p. A17)

escala del mapa La comparación de la distancia en un mapa con la distancia real en lo que el mapa representa, como la superficie de la Tierra. La escala del mapa puede expresarse como una azón, una barra de escala o en unidades equivalentes.

mare (MAH-ray)

A large, dark plain of solidified lava on the Moon. The plural form of mare is maria (MAH-ree-uh). (p. E53)

mare Una planicie grande y oscura de lava solidificada en la Luna. El plural de mare es maría.

marine climate

A climate influenced by a nearby ocean, with generally mild temperatures and steady precipitation. (p. D120)

clima marino El clima influido por un océano cercano, y que generalmente tiene temperaturas moderadas y precipitación poco variable.

mass

A measure of how much matter an object is made of.

masa Una medida de la cantidad de materia de la que está compuesto un objeto.

mass wasting

The downhill movement of loose rock or soil. (p. A147)

movimiento de masa El desplazamiento cuesta abajo de suelo o de roca suelta.

matter

Anything that has mass and volume. Matter exists ordinarily as a solid, a liquid, or a gas. (p. xxxiii)

materia Todo lo que tiene masa y volumen. Generalmente la materia existe como sólido, líquido o gas.

mechanical weathering

The breakdown of rock into smaller pieces of the same material without any change in its composition. (p. A116)

meteorización mecánica El desmoronamiento de las rocas en pedazos más pequeños del mismo material, sin ningún cambio en su composición.

metamorphic rock (MEHT-uh-MAWR-fihk)

Rock formed as heat or pressure causes existing rock to change in structure, texture, or mineral composition. (p. A78)

roca metamórfica Roca formada cuando el calor o la presión ocasionan que la roca existente cambie de estructura, textura o composición mineral.

metamorphism (MEHT-uh-MAWR-FIHZ-uhm)

The process by which a rock's structure or mineral composition is changed by pressure or heat. (p. A96)

metamorfismo El proceso mediante el cual la estructura o la composición mineral de una roca cambia debido a la presión o al calor.

meteor

A brief streak of light produced by a small particle entering Earth's atmosphere at a high speed. (p. E105)

meteoro Un breve rayo luminoso producido por una partícula pequeña que entra a la atmósfera de la Tierra a una alta velocidad.

meteorite

A small object from outer space that passes through Earth's atmosphere and reaches the surface. (p. E105)

meteorito Un pequeño objeto del espacio exterior que pasa a través de la atmósfera de la Tierra y llega a la superficie.

meteorologist (MEE-tee-uh-RAHL-uh-jihst)

A scientist who studies weather. (p. D98)

meteorólogo Un científico que estudia el clima.

microclimate

The climate of a smaller area within a subclimate. (p. D128)

microclima El clima de un área más pequeña dentro de un subclima.

mid-ocean ridge

A long line of sea-floor mountains where new ocean crust is formed by volcanic activity along a divergent boundary. (p. B16)

dorsal oceánica Una larga línea de montañas en el fondo marino donde se forma nueva corteza oceánica debido a la actividad volcánica a lo largo de un límite divergente.

mineral

A substance that forms in nature, is a solid, has a definite chemical makeup, and has a crystal structure. (p. A43)

mineral Una sustancia sólida formada en la naturaleza, de composición química definida y estructura cristalina.

molecule

A group of atoms that are held together by covalent bonds so that they move as a single unit.

molécula Un grupo de átomos que están unidos mediante enlaces covalentes de tal manera que se mueven como una sola unidad.

monsoon

A wind that changes direction with the seasons. (p. D54)

monzón Un viento que cambia de dirección con las estaciones.

moraine (muh-RAYN)

A deposit of till left behind by a retreating glacier. Moraines can form along a glacier's sides and at its end. (p. A168)

morrena Un depósito de sedimentos glaciares dejado por un glaciar que retrocede. Las morrenas pueden formarse en los costados de un glaciar o en su extremo.

N

natural resource

Any type of matter or energy from Earth's environment that humans use to meet their needs. (p. B147)

recurso natural Cualquier tipo de materia o energía del medio ambiente de la Tierra que usan los humanos para satisfacer sus necesidades.

neap tide

A tide of small range occurring during the first- and third-quarter phases of the Moon. (p. C99)

marea muerta Una marea de poco rango que ocurre durante las fases cuarto menguante y cuarto creciente de la Luna.

nebula (NEHB-yuh-luh)

A cloud of gas and dust in space. Stars form in nebulae. (p. E125)

nebulosa Una nube de gas y polvo en el espacio. Las estrellas se forman en las nebulosas.

neutron star

A dense core that may be left behind after a higher-mass star explodes in a supernova. (p. E126)

estrella de neutrones Un núcleo denso que puede resultar después de que una estrella de mayor masa explota en una supernova.

nonpoint-source pollution

Pollution with a source that is hard to find or scattered. (p. C56)

contaminación por fuentes difusas Contaminación de fuentes que son dispersas o difíciles de encontrar.

nonrenewable resource

A resource that exists in a fixed amount or is used up more quickly than it can be replaced in nature. (p. B148)

recurso no renovable Un recurso que existe en una cantidad fija o se consume más rápidamente de lo que puede reemplazarse en la naturaleza.

nuclear fission (FIHSH-uhn)

The process of splitting the nuclei of radioactive atoms, which releases huge amounts of energy mainly in the form of radiation and heat energy. (p. B161)

fisión nuclear El proceso de rotura de los núcleos de átomos radioactivos, el cual libera inmensas cantidades de energía, principalmente en forma de radiación y energía calorífica.

ocean current

A mass of moving ocean water. (pp. C84, D121)

corriente oceánica Una masa de agua oceánica en movimiento.

oceanic-continental subduction

A boundary along which a plate carrying oceanic crust sinks beneath a plate with continental crust. (p. B33)

subducción océano-continente Un límite a lo largo del cual una placa de corteza oceánica se hunde bajo una placa de corteza continental.

oceanic-oceanic subduction

A boundary along which a plate carrying oceanic crust sinks beneath another plate with oceanic crust. (p. B32)

subducción océano-océano Un límite a lo largo del cual una placa de corteza oceánica se hunde bajo otra placa de corteza oceánica.

orbit

n. The path of an object in space as it moves around another object due to gravity; for example, the Moon moves in an orbit around Earth. (p. E10)

v. To revolve around, or move in an orbit; for example, the Moon orbits Earth.

órbita *s.* La trayectoria de un objeto en el espacio a medida que se mueve alrededor de otro objeto debido a la gravedad; por ejemplo, la Luna se mueve en una órbita alrededor de la Tierra.

orbitar *v.* Girar alrededor de algo, o moverse en una órbita; por ejemplo, la Luna orbita la Tierra.

ore

A rock that contains enough of a valuable mineral to be mined for a profit. (p. A64)

mena Una roca que contiene suficiente mineral valioso para ser extraído con fines lucrativos.

original remains

A fossil that is the actual body or body parts of an organism. (p. B112)

restos originales Un fósil que es en realidad el cuerpo o partes del cuerpo de un organismo.

outer core

A layer of molten metal, mainly nickel and iron, that surrounds Earth's inner core. (p. B10)

núcleo externo Una capa de metal fundido, principalmente níquel y hierro, que rodea al núcleo interno de la Tierra.

overfishing

The catching of fish at a faster rate than they can reproduce. (p. C131)

sobrepesca La captura de peces a un ritmo mayor a la que pueden reproducirse.

ozone
A gas molecule that consists of three oxygen atoms. (p. D23)

ozono Una molécula de gas que consiste en tres átomos de oxígeno.

P

Pangaea (pan-JEE-uh)
A hypothetical supercontinent that included all of the landmasses on Earth. It began breaking apart about 200 million years ago. (p. B16)

Pangea Un supercontinente hipotético que incluía todas las masas continentales de la Tierra. Empezó a fracturarse aproximadamente hace 200 millones de años.

parallax
The apparent shift in the position of an object when viewed from different locations. (p. E123)

paralaje El cambio aparente en la posición de un objeto cuando se observa desde diferentes puntos.

particulates
Tiny particles or droplets, such as dust, dirt, and pollen, that are mixed in with air. (p. D28)

particulados Diminutas partículas o gotas, como por ejemplo de polvo, tierra o polen, que están mezcladas con el aire.

penumbra
A region of lighter shadow that may surround an umbra; for example, the spreading cone of lighter shadow cast by a space object. (p. E63)

penumbra Una región de sombra más tenue que puede rodear a una umbra; por ejemplo, la sombra más tenue cónica proyectada por un objeto espacial.

permeable
Allowing the passage of water. (p. C24)

permeable Que permite el paso del agua.

phytoplankton (fy-toh-PLANGK-tuhn)
Microscopic floating organisms that live in water and, like plants, convert sunlight and carbon dioxide into food. (p. C126)

fitoplancton Organismos microscópicos que flotan y viven en el agua y, al igual que las plantas, convierten la luz del Sol y el dióxido de carbono en alimento.

planet
A spherical body, larger than a comet or asteroid, that orbits the Sun, or a similar body that orbits a different star.

planeta Un cuerpo esférico, más grande que un cometa o un asteroide, que orbita alrededor del Sol, o un cuerpo similar que orbita alrededor de una estrella distinta.

point-source pollution
Pollution that enters water from a known source. (p. C54)

contaminación por fuentes puntuales Contaminación que entra al agua proveniente de una fuente conocida.

precipitation
Any type of liquid or solid water that falls to Earth's surface, such as rain, snow, or hail. (pp. C13, D57)

precipitación Cualquier tipo de agua líquida o sólida que cae a la superficie de la Tierra, como por ejemplo lluvia, nieve o granizo.

prime meridian
An imaginary north-south line that divides the planet into the Eastern Hemisphere and the Western Hemisphere. The prime meridian passes through Greenwich, England. (p. A19)

primer meridiano Una línea imaginaria de norte a sur que divide al planeta en hemisferio oriental y hemisferio occidental. El primer meridiano pasa a través de Greenwich, Inglaterra.

probe
A spacecraft that is sent into a planet's atmosphere or onto a solid surface. (p. E29)

sonda espacial Una nave espacial enviada a la atmósfera de un planeta o a una superficie sólida.

projection
A representation of Earth's curved surface on a flat map. (p. A20)

proyección Una representación de la superficie curva de la Tierra en un mapa plano.

pyroclastic flow (PY-roh-KLAS-tihk)
A dense cloud of superheated gases and rock fragments that moves quickly downhill from an erupting volcano. (p. B88)

corriente piroclástica Una nube densa de gases sobrecalentados y fragmentos de rocas que desciende rápidamente de un volcán en erupción.

Q

quasar
The very bright center of a distant galaxy. (p. E133)

quásar El centro muy brillante de una galaxia distante.

R

radiation (RAY-dee-AY-shuhn)
Energy that travels across distances as certain types of waves. (p. D17)

radiación Energía que viaja a través de la distancia en forma de ciertos tipos de ondas.

rain shadow
An area on the downwind side of a mountain that gets less precipitation than the side that faces the wind. (p. D129)

sombra de lluvia Un área viento abajo de una montaña que recibe menos precipitación que el lado de la montaña que hace frente al viento.

recrystallization
The process by which bonds between atoms in minerals break and re-form in new ways during metamorphism. (p. A97)

recristalización El proceso mediante el cual los enlaces entre los átomos de los minerales se rompen y se vuelven a formar de diferentes maneras durante el metamorfismo.

recycling
The reusing of materials that people would otherwise throw away, such as paper, glass, plastics, and certain metals. (p. B158)

reciclaje El reutilizar los materiales que la gente de otra forma desecharía, como el papel, el vidrio, los plásticos y ciertos metales.

relative age
The age of an event or object in relation to other events or objects. (p. B119)

edad relativa La edad de un evento u objeto en relación a otros eventos u objetos.

relative humidity
The comparison of the amount of water vapor in air with the maximum amount of water vapor that can be present in air at that temperature. (p. D58)

humedad relativa La comparación entre la cantidad de vapor de agua en el aire y la cantidad máxima de vapor de agua que puede estar presente en el aire a esa temperatura.

relief
In geology, the difference in elevation between an area's high and low points. (p. A25)

relieve En geología, la diferencia en elevación entre los puntos altos y bajos de un área.

relief map
A map that shows the differences in elevation in an area. Relief maps can show elevations through the use of contour lines, shading, colors, and, in some cases, three-dimensional materials. (p. A16)

mapa de relieve Un mapa que muestra las diferencias en elevación de un área. Los mapas de relieve pueden mostrar elevaciones mediante del uso de curvas de nivel, sombreado, colores y, en algunos casos, materiales tridimensionales.

remote sensing
A method of using scientific equipment to gather information about something from a distance. Most remote-sensing methods make use of different types of electromagnetic radiation. (p. A30)

sensoramiento remoto Un método de reunir información sobre algo a distancia usando equipo científico. La mayoría de los métodos de sensoramiento remoto hacen uso de diferentes tipos de radiación electromagnética.

renewable resource
A natural resource that can be replaced in nature at about the same rate as it is used. (p. B148)

recurso renovable Un recurso natural que puede reemplazarse en la naturaleza casi al mismo ritmo al que es utilizado.

revolution
The motion of one body around another, such as Earth in its orbit around the Sun; the time it takes an object to go around once. (p. E45)

revolución El movimiento de un cuerpo alrededor de otro, como la Tierra en su órbita alrededor del Sol; el tiempo que le toma a un objeto dar la vuelta una vez.

rift valley
A deep valley formed as tectonic plates move apart, such as along a mid-ocean ridge. (p. B23)

valle de rift Un valle profundo formado cuando las placas tectónicas se separan, como a lo largo de una dorsal oceánica.

ring
In astronomy, a wide, flat zone of small particles that orbit around a planet's equator. (p. E97)

anillo En astronomía, una zona ancha y plana de pequeñas partículas que orbitan alrededor del ecuador de un planeta.

rip current

A narrow stream of water that breaks through sandbars and drains rapidly back into deeper water. (p. C92)

corriente de retorno Una estrecha corriente de agua que atraviesa barras de arena y drena rápidamente hacia aguas más profundas.

rock

A naturally formed solid that is usually made up of one or more types of minerals. (p. A75)

roca Un sólido formado de manera natural y generalmente compuesto de uno o más tipos de minerales.

rock cycle

The set of natural, repeating processes that form, change, break down, and re-form rocks. (p. A78)

ciclo de las rocas La serie de procesos naturales y repetitivos que forman, cambian, descomponen y vuelven a formar rocas.

S

salinity (suh-LIHN-ih-tee)

The measure of the amount of dissolved salt contained in water. (p. C76)

salinidad La medida de la cantidad de sal disuelta en el agua.

salt water

Water that contains dissolved salts and other minerals. Oceans consist of salt water. (p. C11)

agua salada Agua que contiene sales disueltas y otros minerales. Los océanos están compuestos de agua salada.

sandbar

A ridge of sand built up by the action of waves and currents. (p. A160)

barra de arena Una colina de arena que se forma por la acción de las olas y las corrientes.

satellite

An object that orbits a more massive object. (p. E23)

satélite Un objeto que orbita un objeto de mayor masa.

saturation

A condition of the atmosphere in which the rates of evaporation and condensation are equal. (p. D58)

saturación Una condición de la atmósfera en la cual las tasas de evaporación y condensación son iguales.

season

One part of a pattern of temperature changes and other weather trends over the course of a year. Astronomical seasons are defined and caused by the position of Earth's axis relative to the direction of sunlight. (pp. D122, E46)

estación Una parte de un patrón de cambios de temperatura y otras tendencias meteorológicas en el curso de un año. Las estaciones astronómicas se definen y son causadas por la posición del eje de la Tierra en relación a la dirección de la luz del Sol.

sediment

Solid materials such as rock fragments, plant and animal remains, or minerals that are carried by water or by air and that settle on the bottom of a body of water or on the ground. (p. A89)

sedimento Materiales sólidos como fragmentos de rocas, restos de plantas y animales o minerales que son transportados por el agua o el aire y que se depositan en el fondo de un cuerpo de agua o en el suelo.

sedimentary rock (SEHD-uh-MEHN-tuh-ree)

Rock formed as pieces of older rocks and other loose materials get pressed or cemented together or as dissolved minerals re-form and build up in layers. (p. A78)

roca sedimentaria Roca que se forma cuando los pedazos de rocas más viejas y otros materiales sueltos son presionados o cementados o cuando los minerales disueltos vuelven a formarse y se acumulan en capas.

seismic wave (SYZ-mihk)

The vibrations caused by an earthquake. (p. B51)

onda sísmica Las vibraciones ocasionadas por un terremoto.

seismograph (SYZ-muh-GRAF)

An instrument that constantly records ground movements. (p. B56)

sismógrafo Un instrumento que registra constantemente los movimientos del suelo.

sensor

A mechanical or electronic device that receives and responds to a signal, such as light. (p. A31)

sensor Un dispositivo mecánico o electrónico que recibe y responde a una señal, como la luz.

septic system

A small sewage system, often for one home or business, that uses an underground tank to treat wastewater. (p. C54)

sistema séptico Un pequeño sistema de aguas residuales, a menudo para un hogar o un negocio, que usa un tanque subterráneo para tratar las aguas de desecho.

sewage system
A system that collects and treats wastewater from a city or a town. (p. C53)

sistema de aguas residuales Un sistema que recolecta y trata las aguas de desecho de una ciudad o población.

sinkhole
An open basin that forms when the roof of a cavern becomes so thin that it falls in. (p. A155)

sumidero Una cuenca abierta que se forma cuando el techo de una caverna se vuelve tan delgado que se desploma.

sleet
Small pellets of ice that form when rain passes through a layer of cold air and freezes before hitting the ground. (p. D68)

aguanieve Pequeñas bolitas de hielo que se forman cuando la lluvia pasa a través de una capa de aire frío y se congela antes de caer al suelo.

slope
A measure of how steep a landform is. Slope is calculated as the change in elevation divided by the distance covered. (p. A25)

pendiente Una medida de lo inclinada de una formación terrestre. La pendiente se calcula dividiendo el cambio en la elevación por la distancia recorrida.

smog
The combination of smoke and fog; a type of air pollution that occurs when sunlight causes unburnt fuels, fumes, and other gases to react chemically, often seen as a brownish haze. (p. D28)

smog La combinación de humo y neblina; un tipo de contaminación de aire que se presenta cuando la luz solar provoca la reacción química de combustibles no consumidos, humos y otros gases, que a menudo se ve como una bruma parda.

soil horizon
A soil layer with physical and chemical properties that differ from those of soil layers above or below it. (p. A124)

horizonte del suelo Una capa del suelo con propiedades físicas y químicas que difieren de las de las capas del suelo superior e inferior a la misma.

soil profile
The soil horizons in a specific location; a cross section of soil layers that displays all soil horizons. (p. A124)

perfil del suelo Los horizontes del suelo en un lugar específico; una sección transversal de las capas del suelo que muestra todos los horizontes del suelo.

solar cell
A device that converts the energy of sunlight into electrical energy. (p. B165)

celda solar Un aparato que convierte la energía de la luz del Sol en energía eléctrica.

solar system
The Sun and its family of orbiting planets, moons, and other objects. (p. E10)

sistema solar El Sol y su familia de planetas, lunas y otros objetos en órbita.

solar wind
A stream of electrically charged particles that flows out in all directions from the Sun's corona. (p. E119)

viento solar Una corriente de partículas eléctricamente cargadas que fluye hacia fuera de la corona del Sol en todas las direcciones.

solstice (SAHL-stihs)
In an orbit, a position and time during which one hemisphere gets its maximum area of sunlight, while the other hemisphere gets its minimum amount; the time of year when days are either longest or shortest, and the angle of sunlight reaches its maximum or minimum. (p. E46)

solsticio En una órbita, la posición y el tiempo durante los cuales un hemisferio obtiene su área máxima de luz del Sol, mientras que el otro hemisferio obtiene su cantidad mínima; la época del año en la cual los días son los más largos o los más cortos y el ángulo de la luz del Sol alcanza su máximo o su mínimo.

sonar (SO-NAHR)
A system that uses underwater sound waves to measure distance and locate objects. (p. C82)

sonar Un sistema que usa ondas sonoras subacuáticas para medir distancias y ubicar objetos.

space station
A satellite in which people can live and work for long periods. (p. E24)

estación espacial Un satélite en el cual la gente puede vivir y trabajar durante períodos largos.

spectrum (SPEHK-truhm)
1. Radiation from a source separated into a range of wavelengths. 2. The range of colors that appears in a beam of visible light when it passes through a prism. *See also* electromagnetic radiation. (p. E16)

espectro 1. Radiación de una fuente separada en una gama de longitudes de onda. 2. La gama de colores que aparece en un haz de luz visible cuando éste pasa a través de un prisma. Ver también radiación electromagnética.

spring

A flow of water from the ground at a place where the surface of the land dips below the water table. (p. C28)

manantial Un flujo de agua proveniente del suelo en un punto donde la superficie de la tierra desciende por debajo del nivel freático.

spring tide

A tide of large range occurring during the new and full moons, resulting in an extra-high tidal bulge and an extra-low tidal dip. (p. C99)

marea viva Una marea de amplio rango que ocurre durante la luna nueva y la luna llena y que resulta en una protuberancia mareal más alta de lo normal y un descenso de la marea más bajo de lo normal.

storm surge

A rapid rise in water level in a coastal area that occurs when a hurricane pushes a huge mass of ocean water, often leading to flooding and widespread destruction. (p. D89)

marea de tormenta Un rápido aumento del nivel del agua en un área costera que ocurre cuando un huracán empuja una gran masa de agua oceánica, muchas veces provocando inundaciones y destrucción extensa.

streak

The color of a mineral powder left behind when a mineral is scraped across a surface; a method for classifying minerals. (p. A51)

raya El color del polvo que queda de un mineral cuando éste se raspa a lo largo de una superficie; un método para clasificar minerales.

stress

The force applied by an object pressing on, pulling on, or pushing against another object. (p. B45)

tensión La fuerza aplicada por un objeto que presiona, jala o empuja contra otro objeto.

subduction

The process by which an oceanic tectonic plate sinks under another plate into Earth's mantle. (p. B30)

subducción El proceso mediante el cual una placa tectónica oceánica se hunde bajo otra placa y entra al manto de la Tierra.

sunspot

A darker spot on the photosphere of the Sun. A sunspot appears dark because it is cooler than the surrounding area. (p. E118)

mancha solar Una mancha oscura en la fotosfera del Sol. Una mancha solar se ve oscura porque es más fría que el área que la rodea.

system

A group of objects or phenomena that interact. A system can be as simple as a rope, a pulley, and a mass. It also can be as complex as the interaction of energy and matter in the four parts of the Earth system.

sistema Un grupo de objetos o fenómenos que interactúan. Un sistema puede ser algo tan sencillo como una cuerda, una polea y una masa. También puede ser algo tan complejo como la interacción de la energía y la materia en las cuatro partes del sistema de la Tierra.

T

technology

The use of scientific knowledge to solve problems or engineer new products, tools, or processes.

tecnología El uso de conocimientos científicos para resolver problemas o para diseñar nuevos productos, herramientas o procesos.

tectonic plate (tehk-TAHN-ihk)

One of the large, moving pieces into which Earth's lithosphere is broken and which commonly carries both oceanic and continental crust. (p. B13)

placa tectónica Una de las grandes piezas en movimiento en las que la litosfera de la Tierra se rompe y que comúnmente lleva corteza oceánica y continental.

tectonics (tehk-TAHN-ihks)

The processes in which the motion of hot material under a crust changes the crust of a space body. Earth has a specific type of tectonics called plate tectonics. (p. E86)

tectónica Los procesos en los cuales el movimiento del material caliente bajo una corteza cambia la corteza de un cuerpo espacial. La Tierra tiene un tipo específico de tectónica denominado tectónica de placas.

telescope

A device that gather visible light or another form of electromagnetic radiation. (p. E17)

telescopio Un aparato que reúne luz visible u otra forma de radiación electromagnética.

terrestrial planet

Earth or a planet similar to Earth that has a rocky surface. The four planets in the inner solar system—Mercury, Venus, Earth, and Mars—are terrestrial planets. (p. E85)

planeta terrestre La Tierra o un planeta parecido a la Tierra que tiene una superficie rocosa. Los cuatro planetas en el sistema solar interior — Mercurio, Venus, la Tierra y Marte — son planetas terrestres.

theory
In science, a set of widely accepted explanations of observations and phenomena. A theory is a well-tested explanation that is consistent with all available evidence.

teoría En las ciencias, un conjunto de explicaciones de observaciones y fenómenos que es ampliamente aceptado. Una teoría es una explicación bien probada que es consecuente con la evidencia disponible.

theory of plate tectonics
A theory stating that Earth's lithosphere is broken into huge plates that move and change in size over time.

Teoría de la tectónica de placas Una teoría que establece que la litosfera de la Tierra está formada por enormes placas que se mueven y cambian de tamaño con el tiempo.

thunder
The sound wave created by intensely heated air around a lightning bolt. (p. D92)

trueno La onda sonora creada por el aire calentado intensamente alrededor de un relámpago.

thunderstorm
A storm with lightning and thunder. (p. D92)

tormenta eléctrica Una tormenta con relámpagos y truenos.

tidal range
The difference in height between high tide and low tide. (p. C98)

rango de marea La diferencia en altura entre la marea alta y la marea baja.

tide
The periodic rising and falling of the water level of the ocean due to the gravitational pulls of the Moon and the Sun. (p. C96)

marea La subida y caída periódica del nivel del agua del océano debido a las atracciones gravitacionales de la Luna y del Sol.

till
Sediment of different sizes left directly on the ground by a melting, or retreating, glacier. (p. A168)

sedimentos glaciares Sedimentos de diferentes tamaños depositados directamente en el suelo por un glaciar que se derrite o retrocede.

topography
All natural and human-made surface features of a particular area. (p. A24)

topografía Todas las características de superficie de origen natural y humano en un área particular.

tornado
A violently rotating column of air stretching from a cloud to the ground. (p. D95)

tornado Una columna de aire que gira violentamente y se extiende desde una nube hasta el suelo.

transform boundary
A boundary along which two tectonic plates scrape past each other, and crust is neither formed nor destroyed. (p. B22)

límite transcurrente Un límite a lo largo del cual dos placas tectónicas se rozan y no se forma corteza ni se destruye.

tropical storm (TRAHP-ih-kuhl)
A low-pressure system that starts in the tropics with winds of at least 65 kilometers per hour (40 mi/h) but less than 120 kilometers per hour (74 mi/h). (p. D87)

tormenta tropical Un sistema de baja presión que inicia en los trópicos con vientos de por lo menos 65 kilómetros por hora (40 mi/h) pero menores a 120 kilómetros por hora (74 mi/h).

tsunami (tsu-NAH-mee)
A water wave caused by an earthquake, volcanic eruption, or landslide. (p. B62)

tsunami Una ola de agua ocasionada por un terremoto, erupción volcánica o derrumbe.

turnover
The yearly rising and sinking of cold and warm water layers in a lake. (p. C19)

renovación La ascensión y el hundimiento anual de las capas de agua fría y agua cálida en un lago.

U

ultraviolet radiation
(UHL-truh-VY-uh-liht RAY-dee-AY-shuhn)
Radiation of higher frequencies than visible light, which can cause sunburn and other types of damage. (p. D23)

radiación ultravioleta Radiación de frecuencia más alta que la luz visible que puede causar quemaduras de sol y otros tipos de daño.

umbra
The dark, central region of a shadow, such as the cone of complete shadow cast by an object. (p. E63)

umbra La región central y oscura de una sombra, como la sombra completa cónica proyectada por un objeto.

uniformitarianism
(yoo-nuh-fawr-mih-TAIR-ee-uh-nihz-uhm)
A theory stating that processes shaping Earth today, such as erosion and deposition, also shaped Earth in the past, and that these processes cause large changes over geologic time. (p. B128)

uniformismo Una teoría que afirma que los procesos que le dan forma a la Tierra hoy en día, como la erosión y la sedimentación, también le dieron forma a la Tierra en el pasado; además, afirma que estos procesos ocasionan grandes cambios en tiempo geológico.

universe
Space and all the matter and energy in it. (p. E10)

universo El espacio y toda la materia y energía que hay dentro de él.

upwelling
The vertical movement of deep water up to the surface. (p. C86)

surgencia El movimiento vertical del agua profunda a la superficie.

urban heat island
The warmer body of air over a city. (p. D128)

isla de calor urbana La masa de aire más cálida que se encuentra sobre una ciudad.

V

variable
Any factor that can change in a controlled experiment, observation, or model. (p. R30)

variable Cualquier factor que puede cambiar en un experimento controlado, en una observación o en un modelo.

volcanism
The process of molten material moving from a space body's hot interior onto its surface. (p. E86)

vulcanismo El proceso del movimiento de material fundido del interior caliente de un cuerpo espacial a su superficie.

volcano
An opening in the crust through which molten rock, rock fragments, and hot gases erupt; a mountain built up from erupted materials. (p. B86)

volcán Una abertura en la corteza a través de la cual la roca fundida, fragmentos de roca y gases calientes hacen erupción; una montaña formada a partir de los materiales que surgen de una erupción.

volume
An amount of three-dimensional space, often used to describe the space that an object takes up.

volumen Una cantidad de espacio tridimensional; a menudo se usa este término para describir el espacio que ocupa un objeto.

W, X, Y, Z

water cycle
The continuous movement of water on Earth, through its atmosphere, and in the living things on Earth. (p. C12)

ciclo del agua El movimiento continuo de agua sobre la Tierra, por su atmósfera y dentro de los organismos vivos de la Tierra.

water table
The highest part in the ground that is saturated, or completely filled with water. (p. C25)

nivel freático La parte más alta del suelo que está saturada, o completamente llena de agua.

wavelength
The distance between one peak and the next peak on a wave. (p. E16)

longitud de onda La distancia entre una cresta y la siguiente cresta en una onda.

weather
The condition of Earth's atmosphere at a particular time and place. (p. D47)

estado del tiempo La condición de la atmósfera terrestre en un lugar y momento particular.

weathering
The process by which natural forces break down rocks. (p. A115)

meteorización El proceso por el cual las fuerzas naturales fragmentan las rocas.

wetland
A wet, swampy area that is often flooded with water. (p. C116)

humedal Un área húmeda y pantanosa que a menudo está inundada de agua.

wind
The horizontal movement of air caused by differences in air pressure. (p. D47)

viento El movimiento horizontal de aire provocado por diferencias en la presión de aire.

Index

Page numbers for definitions are printed in **boldface** type.
Page numbers for illustrations, maps, and charts are printed in *italics*.

INDEX

F

M

INDEX

oxygen, A11, A109, C78, C86, C135. *See also* ozone.
  animals' use of, D12, D*13*, D15
  atmospheric (gas), D*11*, D14, D*15*, D23, D24, D32
  elemental, D23
  life processes and, D12, D*13*, D15
ozone, A109, D*20*, D21, D**23**, D*23*, D32. *See also* ozone layer.
  absorption of ultraviolet radiation by, D*20*, D21, D*23*, D32, D*36*
  chlorine reaction with, D32
  as pollutant, D28
  smog formation and, D28
  stratosphere and, D*20*, D21, D*23*, D*23*
  troposphere and, D28
ozone alert, D*29*
ozone layer, D*20*, D21, D*23*, D28
  absorption of ultraviolet radiation by, D*20*, D21, D*23*, D*23*, D32, D*36*
  destruction of, by human activities, D32–33, D*33*, D*36*

P

Pacific Ocean
  El Niño and, D*136*
  storms in western, D87
Pacific Plate, B46
Pacific Tsunami Warning Center, B63
packing foam, chlorofluorocarbons in, D32
Paleozoic era, B130–32
Panama Canal, C46
Pangaea, B16, B**16**, B*16*, D*134*
Panthalassa Ocean, D*134*
paper, B153
parallax, E**123**
parent rocks, A96
parrotfish, C*123*, C124
particulates, D**28**, D29, D132–133. *See also* air pollution.
  absorption and reflection of sunlight, D29, D132, D*133*
Pathfinder, E29
Patterson, Clair C., A108
penumbra, E**63**, E*63–64*
percents, **R41**
periods, geologic, B130, B136
permeable materials, C**24**, C*24–25*, C*25*, C34
Permian period, B130–31
pesticides, C57, C119
petrified wood, B114, B*115*
Phanerozoic eon, B131–33
phases of the Moon, E59–62, E*61*, E68
Philippine Islands, B32
phosphorus, C20
photosynthesis, D12
phyllite, A*97*, A*100*
physical forces, xxxii–xxxiii
physical laws, xxxii
phytoplankton, C**126**, C*127*
Pinatubo, Mount (Philippines)
  eruption of, D*133*
  global climate and, D*133*
plains, A**16**, A*16*
planar projections, A22
planetary rings, E**97**, E*97*, E108

planets, C9, C15, E14, E*14*, E26, E79–82, E*80*. *See also* Solar System; specific planets, e.g. Mars.
  characteristics of, R*69*
  cores, E85
  distances, E*80*, E81
  doubles, E101
  exploration, E27, E29
  gas giants, E**94**, E94–99, E102, E*102*
  landers, E**28**, E*28*, E28–29
  mantles, E85
  moons, E98, E101–102, E*102*
  orbits of Sun, E81–82, E108
  processes and surface features, E86, E*87*
  rocky crusts, E85–92
  sizes, E79–81, E*80*
  terrestrial, E85–92
plants, B148–50, B153, B168, B172, C14, C**78**. *See also* ocean environments.
  air pollution effect on, D29
  carbon dioxide, oxygen and, D12, D*13*, D15
  greenhouse effect and, D30
  growth, E35
  nitrogen and, D12, D*13*
  and soil formation, A116, A*117*, A126, A*127*
  water cycle role of, D12, D*13*
plastic, B153
plateaus, A**16**, A*16*
plate tectonics, B6–41, B*37*. *See also* tectonics.
  asthenosphere, B**11**, B*11*, B38
  boundaries, B22–37, B46, B*46*, B52, B89
  causes of movement, B17–18
  Chapter Investigation, B20–21
  coastal mountains, B*32*, B33, B38
  continental-continental collision, B31, B*31*, B38, B80
  continental drift, B**14**, B14–19, B*16*, B38
  convection, B**17**
  convection currents, B**17**, B17–18, B*18*, B20–21
  convergent boundaries, B**22**, B30–33, B*31*, B*32*, B*35*, B38, B80
  core, B10, B*10*
  crust, B10, B**11**, B38
  deep-ocean trenches, B*32*, B*32*, B33, B38
  density of materials, B9
  disturbed layers of rock, B120, B*120*
  divergent boundaries, B**22**, B22–28, B*23*, B*35*, B38
  hot spots, B**27**, B27–28, B*28*, B89
  inner core, B**10**, B*10*, B38
  Internet Activities, B7
  island arcs, B**32**, B*32*, B38
  layers of Earth, B*10*, B10–12, B38
  lithosphere, B**11**, B*11*, B11–12, B38
  magnetic reversals, B**24**, B*24*, B24–25, B38
  mantle, B*10*, B**11**, B38
  mountain formation, B77
  oceanic-continental subduction, B*32*, B**33**, B38, B80, B*80*, B*81*
  oceanic-oceanic subduction, B**32**, B*32*, B38, B80, B*80*, B*81*, B89
  outer core, B**10**, B*10*, B38
  Pangaea, B16, B*16*, B**16**
  ridge push, B18, B*18*
  rift valleys, B26–27, B*26*, B*27*, B38, B89
  slab pull, B18, B*18*
  spreading centers, B17, B23
  subduction, B**30**, B30–33, B38

INDEX

Acknowledgments

Photography

Cover © Grafton Marshall Smith/Corbis; **i** © Grafton Marshall Smith/Corbis; **iii** *left (top to bottom)* Photograph of James Trefil by Evan Cantwell; Photograph of Rita Ann Calvo by Joseph Calvo; Photograph of Linda Carnine by Amilcar Cifuentes; Photograph of Sam Miller by Samuel Miller; *right (top to bottom)* Photograph of Kenneth Cutler by Kenneth A. Cutler; Photograph of Donald Steely by Marni Stamm; Photograph of Vicky Vachon by Redfern Photographics; **vi** © Steve Starr, Boston Inc./PictureQuest; **viii** © Robert Patrick/Corbis Sygma; **ix** © Douglas Peebles; **x** © Photographer's Choice/Getty Images; **xi** © Darrell Jones/Getty Images; **xii** © Catherine Karnow/Corbis; **xiii** AP/WideWorld Photos; **xiv** © Roger Ressmeyer/Corbis; **xv** Courtesy of NASA/JPL/Caltech; **xx** *bottom* Bike Map courtesy of Chicagoland Bicycle Federation. **xx–xxi** Photographs by Sharon Hoogstraten; **xxx–xxxi** Doug Scott/age fotostock; **xxxii–xxxiii** © Aflo Foto Agency; **xxxiv–xxxv** © Tim Fitzharris/Masterfile; **xxxvi–xxxvii** AP/Wide World Photos; **xxxviii** © Vince Streano/Corbis; **xxxix** © Roger Ressmeyer/Corbis; **xl** *left* University of Florida Lightning Research Laboratory; *center* © Roger Ressmeyer/Corbis; **xli** *center* © Mauro Fermariello/ Science Researchers; *bottom* © Alfred Pasieka/Photo Researchers; **xlii–xliii** © Stocktrek/ Corbis; *center* NOAA; **xliii** *top* © Alan Schein Photography/Corbis; *right* Vaisala Oyj, Finland; **xlviii** © The Chedd-Angier Production Company.

Earth's Surface

Divider © Per Breiehagen/Getty Images; **A2–A3** Courtesy of NASA/JPL/Caltech; **A3** *top* Carla Thomas/NASA; *bottom* Diamonds North Resources, Ltd.; **A4** *top* Carla Thomas/NASA; *bottom* © The Chedd-Angier Production Company; **A5** © William Whitehurst/Corbis; **A6–A7** NASA; **A7** *top left* © NASA; *center left* SeaWiFS Project/NASA Goddard Space Flight Center; *bottom left* National Air & Space Museum/Smithsonian Institution; *top right* Courtesy of L. Sue Baugh; *center right* Bike Map courtesy of Chicagoland Bicycle Federation. Photograph by Sharon Hoogstraten; *bottom right* NASA Goddard Space Flight Center; **A9** Photograph by Sharon Hoogstraten; **A10–A11** NASA; **A10** *bottom left* © David Parker/Photo Researchers; *bottom center* © R. Wickllund/ OAR/National Undersea Research Program; **A11** *bottom center* University of Victoria, Victoria, British Columbia, Canada; *bottom right* © Peter and Georgina Bowater/Stock Connection/PictureQuest; **A12** © Photodisc/Getty Images; **A13** Photograph by Sharon Hoogstraten; **A14** © A. Ramey/PhotoEdit/PictureQuest; **A15** Photograph by Sharon Hoogstraten; **A16** U.S. Geological Survey; **A19** © David Parker/Photo Researchers; **A20** Photograph by Sharon Hoogstraten; **A23** © Jerry Driendl/Getty Images; **A24** Photograph by Sharon Hoogstraten; **A25** *top* © Stan Osolinski/Getty Images; *bottom* U.S. Geological Survey; **A26, A28** *top left* U.S. Geological Survey; *bottom left, center right, bottom right* Photographs by Sharon Hoogstraten; **A30, A31** *top right* © Space Imaging; *bottom background* © Paul Morrell/Getty Images; *bottom left* National Oceanic and Atmospheric Administration/Department of Commerce; **A32** *top left, top center* Eros Data Center/U.S. Geological Survey; *bottom right* Photograph by Sharon Hoogstraten; **A34** Photo courtesy of John D. Rogie, 1997; **A35** © Lynn Radeka/SuperStock Images; **A36** *top* NASA; *lower center* U.S. Geological Survey; *bottom left, background,* © Paul Morrell/Getty Images; *bottom left* National Oceanic and Atmospheric Administration/ Department of Commerce; **A38** U.S. Geological Survey; **A40–A41** © Steve Starr, Boston Inc./ PictureQuest; **A41** *top right, center right* Photographs by Sharon Hoogstraten; *bottom right* © Dan Suzio/Photo Researchers; **A43** Photograph by Sharon Hoogstraten; **A44** © Andrew J. Martinez/Photo Researchers; **A45** *left* © Astrid & Hanns-Freider/Photo Researchers; *center* © Charles D. Winters/Photo Researchers; **A46** Photograph by Sharon Hoogstraten; **A47** *top left, center* © Charles D. Winters/Photo Researchers; *top right* Photograph by Malcolm Hjerstedt. Courtesy of F. John Barlow/SANCO Publishing; *bottom left* © Biophoto Associates/Photo Researchers; *bottom center* © Dorling Kindersley; *bottom right* © Phil Degginger/Color Pic, Inc.; *top* © David Young Wolff/PhotoEdit; *bottom* © Doug Martin/Photo Researchers; **A49** *background* © Joyce Photographics/Photo Researchers; *top* © Dorling Kindersley; **A50, A51** Photographs by Sharon Hoogstraten; **A52** *top left* © Charles D. Winters/Photo Researchers; *top right* © Mark A. Schneider/Photo Researchers; *bottom* Photograph by Sharon Hoogstraten; **A53, A54** Photographs by Sharon Hoogstraten; **A55** *top, center right* Photographs by Sharon Hoogstraten; *bottom right* © Thomas Hunn/Visuals Unlimited; **A56** Photograph by Sharon Hoogstraten; **A57** *top left, center* © Mark A. Schneider/Visuals Unlimited; *top right* Photograph by Sharon Hoogstraten; **A58** *top left* © Martin Miller/Visuals Unlimited; *bottom left, right* Photographs by Sharon Hoogstraten; **A59, A60** Photographs by Sharon Hoogstraten; **A61** *top left* © Geoff Tompkinson/PhotoResearchers; *center left* © A.J. Copely/Visuals Unlimited; *bottom left* © Charles D. Winters/Photo Researchers; *top right* © Charles Falco/Photo Researchers; *center right, bottom right* © Dorling Kindersley; **A63** *top right, center left* © Mark A. Schneider/Photo Researchers; *center right* © Andrew J. Martinez/Photo Researchers; *bottom right* © M. Claye/Photo Researchers; **A65** *top* © Mervyn P. Lawes/Corbis; *bottom* Photograph by Sharon Hoogstraten; **A66** Newmont Mining Corp.; **A67** *top left* © Dorling Kindersley; *top right* © Louis Goldman/Photo Researchers; *center left, bottom left* © Dorling Kindersley; **A68** *center* © Charles D. Winters/Photo Researchers; *bottom left* © Astrid & Hanns-Freider/ Photo Researchers; *bottom right top* © Photodisc/Getty Images; *bottom right middle* © Dorling Kindersley; *bottom right* © Photodisc/Getty Images; **A70** *left* NASA/Science Photo Library; *right* NASA; **A72–A73** Stephen Alvarez/NGS Image Collection; **A73** *top, center* Photographs by Sharon Hoogstraten; *bottom* Courtesy of L. Sue Baugh; **A75** Photograph by Sharon Hoogstraten; **A76** *top left* © Dorling Kindersley; *top right* © Doug Martin/Photo Researchers; *bottom* © The Image Bank/Getty Images; **A77** *top* © James Lyon/Lonely Planet Images; *bottom* Photograph by Sharon Hoogstraten; **A79** *center left, bottom* © Andrew J. Martinez/Photo

Researchers; *center right* © Arthur R. Hill/Visuals Unlimited; **A81** *background* Arne Danielsen, Norway; *left* © Charles O'Rear/ Corbis; *right* © Detlev Van Ravenswaay/ Photo Researchers; **A82** Photograph by Sharon Hoogstraten; **A83** *top left* © Arthur R. Hill/Visuals Unlimited; *top center, top right* © Joyce Photographics/Photo Researchers; *bottom center* © Mark Schneider/Visuals Unlimited;*bottom right* © Dorling Kindersley; **A84** *top* © Andrew J. Martinez/Photo Researchers; *bottom* © Breck P. Kent; **A85** Photograph by Sharon Hoogstraten; **A86, A87** © Francois Gohier/Photo Researchers; **A88** *background* © Dr. Juero Aleon/Photo Researchers; **A89** Photograph by Sharon Hoogstraten; **A91** *left* © Carolyn Iverson/Photo Researchers; *right* © Ted Clutter/Pennsylvania State Museum Collection/Photo Researchers; **A92** *top left* Photograph by Sharon Hoogstraten; *center* Courtesy of L. Sue Baugh; *bottom right* © Norbert Wu/Norbert Wu Productions/ PictureQuest; *bottom left;* National Oceanic and Atmospheric Administration **A93** *top* © Look GMBH/eStockPhotography/ PictureQuest; *bottom* © Corbis; **A94** Photograph by Sharon Hoogstraten; **A95** *left* © 1991 Ned Haines/ Photo Researchers; *center* © Wayne Lawler/Photo Researchers; *right* © Jim Steinberg/Photo Researchers; **A96** Photograph by Sharon Hoogstraten; **A97** *right (top to bottom)* © Andrew J. Martinez 1995/Photo Researchers; © Andrew J. Martinez 1995/Photo Researchers; Boltin Picture Library; © Breck P. Kent; © 1996 Andrew J. Martinez/Photo Researchers; **A98** Photograph by Sharon Hoogstraten; **A100** *top left* The Boltin Picture Library; *top right* Photograph courtesy of John Longshore; *bottom left* © E.R. Degginger/Color-Pic, Inc.; *bottom right* © Patricia Tye/Photo Researchers; **A102** *top* Will Hart/PhotoEdit; *center, bottom* Photographs by Sharon Hoogstraten; **A103** © Corbis; **A104** *top left, top center* © Andrew J. Martinez/Photo Researchers; *upper center section left* Arthur R. Hill/Visuals Unlimited; *lower center section, left* © Andrew J. Martinez/Photo Researchers; *right* Photograph by Sharon Hoogstraten; *bottom left, center* © Andrew J. Martinez/Photo Researchers; *bottom right* © Breck P. Kent; **A106** © G.R. Roberts Photo Library; **A108** *top* © Chris Butler/Photo Researchers; *bottom* © Detlev van Ravenswaay/Photo Researchers; **A109** *top* © Jim Brandenburg/Minden Pictures; *center* J.W. Schopf/University of California, Los Angeles; *bottom* Japan Meteorological Agency; **A110** *top left* © Simon Fraser/Photo Researchers; *top right* © Chase Studios/Photo Researchers; *bottom* Courtesy of the Ocean Drilling Program; **A111** *top* NASA Goddard Space Flight Center; *bottom* STS-113 Shuttle Crew/NASA; **A112–A113** © Wendy Conway/Alamy Images; **A113** *top right, center* Photographs by Sharon Hoogstraten; **A115** Photograph by Sharon Hoogstraten; **A117** *background* © Photodisc/Getty Images; *inset top* © Susan Rayfield/Photo Researchers; *inset center, bottom left* Photographs courtesy of Sara Christopherson; *inset bottom right* © Kirkendall-Spring Photographer; **A118** Photograph by Sharon Hoogstraten; **A119** *top left* © Bettmann/Corbis; *top right* © Runk/Schoenberger/ Grant Heilman Photography; *bottom* © Cheyenne Rouse/Visuals Unlimited; **A121** *background* © Ecoscene/Corbis; *inset* © Michael Nicholson/Corbis; **A122** Photograph by Sharon Hoogstraten; **A123** *left* © Joel W. Rogers/Corbis; *right* © Barry Runk/Grant Heilman Photography; **A124** © Barry Runk/Grant Heilman Photography; **A125** *top left* © Sally A. Morgan/Corbis; *top right* © Peter Falkner/Photo Researchers; *bottom left* © Tony Craddock/ Photo Researchers; *bottom left* © Tui de Roy/Bruce Coleman, Inc.; **A128** © Barry Runk/Grant Heilman Photography; **A129** © Jim Strawser/Grant Heilman Photography; **A130** *top left* © Larry Lefever/Grant Heilman Photography; *center right, bottom left* Photograph by Sharon Hoogstraten; **A132** © Cameron Davidson/Stock Connection, Inc./Alamy Images; **A133** AP/Wide World Photos; **A134** *top* © Steve Strickland/ Visuals Unlimited; *bottom* Betty Wald/Aurora; **A135** Photograph by Sharon Hoogstraten; **A136** *left* © Charles O'Rear/Corbis; *right* © Larry Lefever/Grant Heilman Photography; **A137** *center inset* Courtesy of Teska Associates, Evanston. Illinois; **A138** *top right* © Runk/Schoenberger/Grant Heilman Photography; *bottom* © Larry Lefever/Grant Heilman Photography; **A140** © Barry Runk/Grant Heilman Photography; **A142–A143** © A.C. Waltham/Robert Harding Picture Library/Alamy Images; **A143** *center right* Photograph by Sharon Hoogstraten; **A145** © Bernhard Edmaier/Photo Researchers; **A146** Photograph by Sharon Hoogstraten; **A147** AP/Wide World Photos; **A148** *top* Photograph by L.M. Smith, Waterways Experiment Station, U.S. Army Corps of Engineers. Courtesy, USGS; *bottom* © Thomas Rampton/Grant Heilman Photography; **A149** © Troy and Mary Parlee/Alamy Images; **A150** Photograph by Sharon Hoogstraten; **A151** © Bill Ross/Corbis; **A152** *top* © Kevin Horan/Stock Boston /PictureQuest; *bottom* © Yann Arthus-Bertrand/Corbis; **A153** © 1992 Tom Bean; **A154** © Charles Kennard/Stock Boston/PictureQuest; **A155** © Reuters NewMedia, Inc./Corbis; **A156** © Peter Bowater/Alamy Images; **A158** © John and Lisa Merrill/Getty Images; **A159** © Robert Perron; **A160** Photograph by Sharon Hoogstraten; **A161** © Tim Barnwell/Picturesque/ PictureQuest; **A162** © John Shaw/Bruce Coleman, Inc.; **A163** *top* © 1994 Tom Bean; *right* © Goodshoot/Alamy Images; **A164** *background* © Gustav Verderber/Visuals Unlimited; *inset left* © Gary Meszaros/Bruce Coleman, Inc.; *inset right* © Lee Rentz/Bruce Coleman, Inc.; **A165** Photograph by Sharon Hoogstraten; **A167** *left* © Bernard Edmaier/Photo Researchers; *right* © ImageState-Pictor/PictureQuest ; **A168** *top* © Norman Barett/Bruce Coleman, Inc.; *bottom* © Jim Wark/Airphoto; **A169** *top* © 1990 Tom Bean; *bottom* Photograph by Sharon Hoogstraten; **A171** © Charles W. Campbell/ Corbis; **A172** *top* © Bernhard Edmaier/Photo Researchers; *center* © John and Lisa Merrill/Getty Images; **A174** © Tom Bean.

The Changing Earth
Divider © Roger Ressmeyer/Corbis; **B2–B3** © Stephen and Donna O'Meara/Photo Researchers; **B3** *top* NASA/GSFC/METI/ERSDAC/JAROS, and U.S./Japan ASTER Science Team; **B4** *top left* U.S. Geological Survey; *inset* Photograph by T. Miller/U.S. Geological Survey; *bottom* The Chedd-Angier Production Company; **B5** NASA/GSFC/METI/ ERSDAJAROS, and U.S./Japan ASTER Science Team; **B6–B7** Tony Waltham/Geophotos; **B7, B9, B12, B14** Photographs by Sharon Hoogstraten; **B15** © 1995–2002 Geoclassics. All rights reserved.; **B20** Worldsat International/Photo Researchers; **B22, B25** Photographs by Sharon Hoogstraten; **B27** *top* © Christophe Ratier/NHPA/Photo Researchers; *bottom* © NASA/Photo Researchers; **B29** *left* © Dr. John Brackenbury/Photo Researchers; *right* NASA; **B30** Photograph by Sharon Hoogstraten; **B31** © John Coletti/Stock Boston/ PictureQuest; **B33** Photograph by Sharon Hoogstraten; **B34** © Lloyd Cluff/Corbis; **B35** © Paul Chesley/Getty Images; **B37** *left* © Albrecht G. Schaefer/Corbis; *right* © Mitch Diamond/Index Stock/PictureQuest;

B42–B43 © Robert Patrick/Corbis Sygma; **B43, B45, B47** Photographs by Sharon Hoogstraten; **B48** © Martin Miller/University of Oregon, Eugene, Oregon; **B49** NOAA/National Geophysical Data Center; **B50** *left* U.S. Geological Survey; *inset* © Bettmann/Corbis; **B51, B53** Photograph by Sharon Hoogstraten; **B59** AP/Wide World Photos; **B60** Photograph by Sharon Hoogstraten; **B61** © Mark Downey; **B62** U.S. Geological Survey; **B63** Commander Dennis J. Sigrist acting Director of the International Tsunami Information Center/NOAA; **B66** © Roger Ressmeyer/Corbis; **B68** *top* © Michael S. Yamashita/Corbis; *bottom left, bottom right* Photograph by Sharon Hoogstraten; **B69** Photograph by Sharon Hoogstraten; **B74–B75** © Douglas Peebles; **B75, B77** Photographs by Sharon Hoogstraten; **B78** U.S. Department of the Interior; **B79, B80** © Martin Miller/University of Oregon, Eugene, Oregon; **B81** © Tim Hauf Photography/Visuals Unlimited; **B82** Photograph by Sharon Hoogstraten; **B83** © Martin Miller/ University of Oregon, Eugene, Oregon; **B84** © Phil Schermeister/Corbis; **B85** © William Ervin/Photo Researchers; **B86, B88** Photograph by Sharon Hoogstraten; **B90** © G.R. Roberts Photo Library; **B91** *left* © Tom Bean/Corbis; *right* © Krafft-Explorer/Photo Researchers; **B92** © F. Gohier/Photo Researchers; **B93** NASA/Carnegie Mellon University; **B94** *top* © Krafft-Explorer/Photo Researchers; *bottom left, right* Photographs by Sharon Hoogstraten; **B96** *top* © James A. Sugar/Corbis; *bottom* © Mark E. Gibson/Corbis; **B97** *top* © Stephen and Donna O'Meara/Volcano Watch International/Photo Researchers; *bottom* © Sid Balatan/Black Star Publishing/PictureQuest; **B98** U.S. Department of the Interior, U.S. Geological Survey, Reston, Virginia; **B99** Photograph by Sharon Hoogstraten; **B100** © The Image Bank/Getty Images; **B101** © Simon Fraser/Photo Researchers; **B102** © Peter Ryan/Photo Researchers; **B103** *top right* © James Leynse/Corbis; *top left* © Raymond Gehman/Corbis; *center* Courtesy of the General Libraries, The University of Texas at Austin; *bottom* © Jeff Foott/Panoramic Images/National Geographic Image Collection; **B104** *bottom left* © Sid Balatan/Black Star Publishing/PictureQuest; *bottom center* © The Image Bank/Getty Images; bottom right © Simon Fraser/Photo Researchers; **B106** © Roger Ressmeyer/Corbis; **B108–B109** © Louis Psihoyos/psihoyos.com; **B109** *top right* © Digital Vision; *center right* Photograph by Sharon Hoogstraten; *bottom right* © Chris Butler/Photo Researchers; **B111** Photograph by Sharon Hoogstraten; **B112** *top left* Latreille-Cerpolex; *center left* © Alfred Pasteka/Photo Researchers; *bottom left* © Dominique Braud/Animals Animals; **B113** *bottom left, bottom right* Courtesy, American Museum of Natural History; **B114** © 2001 Tom Bean; **B115** *background* © Images Ideas, Inc./PictureQuest; *top left* © Dorling Kindersley; *top right* © John Elk III; *center right* © Kaj R. Svensson/Photo Researchers; *bottom right* © Francesc Muntada/Corbis; **B116** © Doug Wilson/Corbis; **B117** *top left* © B & C Alexander; *top right* © Maria Stenzel/National Geographic Image Collection; **B118** © Chris Butler/Photo Researchers; *inset* © Robert Dowling/Corbis; **B119** *left* Courtesy of The Bicycle Museum of America; *center* © Softride, Inc.; *right* © Photodisc/Getty Images; **B120** *bottom left* © Tom Bean 1993; *bottom right* © Dr. Morley Read/Photo Researchers; **B121** *top right* © Asa C. Thoresen/Photo Researchers; *bottom right* © Sinclair Stammers/Photo Researchers; **B122** *bottom* Photograph by Sharon Hoogstraten; **B124** *background* © G. Brad Lewis/ Getty Images; **B126** *left* © Jonathan Blair/Corbis; *inset* AP Wide World Photos; **B127** Photograph by Sharon Hoogstraten; **B128** © Sime s.a.s./eStock Photography/PictureQuest; **B129** *left, right* © John Marshall Photography; **B130** *bottom left* Mural by Peter Sawyer © National Museum of Natural History, Smithsonian Institution, Washington, D.C.; *bottom right* Exhibit Museum of Natural History, The University of Michigan, Ann Arbor, Michigan; **B131** *bottom left* © Ludek Pesek/Photo Researchers; *bottom right* © Steve Vidler/SuperStock; **B132** © Tom Bean; **B133** © Sisse Brimberg/National Geographic Image Collection; **B134** *top* © Jonathan Blair/Corbis; *left, right* Photographs by Sharon Hoogstraten; **B136** *center left* © Asa C. Thoresen/Photo Researchers; **B140** *top* The Granger Collection; *bottom* © Tom Bean/Corbis; **B141** *top* © Gianni Dagli Orti/Corbis; *center* The Natural History Museum, London; *bottom* Courtesy British Geological Survey; **B142** *top left* © Sally A. Morgan/Ecoscene/Corbis; *top right* © Bettmann/Corbis; *bottom* © James King-Holmes/ Photo Researchers; **B143** *top* © Mark A. Klinger/Carnegie Museum of Natural History; *bottom* © The Field Museum; **B144–B145** © Richard Folwell/Photo Researchers; **B145** *top right,center right* Photographs by Sharon Hoogstraten; **B147** © Corbis; **B149** *top* © SuperStock; *bottom* © Gunter Marx Photography/Corbis; **B153** Photograph by Sharon Hoogstraten; **B154** *left* Diane Moore/Icon SMI; *top right* © Corbis; *bottom right* © Photodisc/Getty Images; **B155** *left* © Photolink/Photodisc/PictureQuest; *inset* © Dr. Tony Braun/Photo Researchers; **B156, B157** Photograph by Sharon Hoogstraten; **B158** *top* Photograph by Sharon Hoogstraten; bottom © David Young-Wolff/PhotoEdit; **B159** José Azel/Aurora; **B160** *top* © Dick Luria/Index Stock/PictureQuest; *bottom* © Johnston Images/Picturesque/ PictureQuest; **B161** Photograph by Sharon Hoogstraten; **B163** © Steve Allen/Brand X Pictures/PictureQuest; **B164** © Beth Davidow/Visuals Unlimited; **B165** © Martin Bond/Photo Researchers; **B166** © James Stilling/Getty Images; **B167** © Lynne Ledbetter/Visuals Unlimited; **B168** Andrew Carlin/Tracy Operators; **B169** © California Fuel Cell Partnership; **B170** *top* © M.L. Sinibald/Corbis; *bottom left, right* Photograph by Sharon Hoogstraten; **B171** Photograph by Sharon Hoogstraten; **B172** *top left* (1) © SuperStock; *top left* (2) © Gunter Marx Photography/Corbis; *bottom* José Azel/Aurora.

Earth's Waters
Divider © Denis Scott/Corbis; **C2–C3** © Ralph White/Corbis; **C3** *center* © Roger Steene/imagequestmarine.com; *bottom* Wolcott Henry/National Geographic Image Collection; **C4** *top* NOAA/Pacific Marine Environmental Laboratory; *bottom* © The Chedd-Angier Production Company; **C5** © Orbital Imaging Corporation and processing by NASA Goddard Space Flight Center. Image provided by ORBIMAGE; **C6–C7** © John Lawrence/Getty Images; **C7** *top* © Anderson Ross/Getty Images; bottom Photograph by Sharon Hoogstraten; **C9, C12** Photograph by Sharon Hoogstraten; **C14** © Jagdish Agarwal/Alamy Images; **C15** *left, inset* AP/WideWorld Photos/NASA Jet Propulsion Laboratories; **C16** Photograph by Sharon Hoogstraten; **C18** *center inset* © NASA/Getty Images; *bottom* © Claver Carroll/photolibrary/ PictureQuest; **C20** © Bruce Heinemann/Photodisc/PictureQuest; **C21** Photograph by Sharon Hoogstraten; **C22** © The Image Bank/Getty Images; **C23** © Ron Erwin Photography; **C24, C27** Photograph by Sharon Hoogstraten; **C28** Peter Essick/Aurora; **C30** © Michael S. Lewis/Corbis; **C31** *left, right* © Jon Arnold/Jon Arnold Images/Alamy Images; **C32** *top* Peter Essick/Aurora; *bottom* Photograph by Sharon Hoogstraten;

C36 Photograph by Sharon Hoogstraten; C38–C39 © Photographer's Choice/Getty Images; C39 *top, bottom* Photograph by Sharon Hoogstraten; C41 AP/Wide World Photos; C42 © Charles E. Rotkin/Corbis; C43 *top* Photograph by Sharon Hoogstraten; *bottom* © Michael Andrews/Animals Animals/Earth Scenes; C44 *top* © Geoff Tompkinson/Photo Researchers; *bottom* AP/Wide World Photos; C45 © Macduff Everton/Corbis; C46 © Shubroto Chattopadhyay/Index Stock Imagery/PictureQuest; C47 © 1987 Tom Bean; C48 AP/Wide World Photos; C49 © J.C. Carton/Bruce Coleman, Inc./PictureQuest; C50 Photograph by Sharon Hoogstraten; C51 AP/Wide World Photos; C56 *left* © Brand X Pictures; *right* © Photodisc/Getty Images; C57 AP/Wide World Photos; C58 *top* © William Taufic/Corbis; *bottom left, right* Photograph by Sharon Hoogstraten; C60 © Dieter Melhorn/Alamy Images; C61 AP/Wide World Photos; C62 *top left* © Digital Vision; *top right* © Bob Melnychuk/Getty Images; *center left* © Photodisc/Getty Images; *center right* © Digital Vision; *bottom* AP/Wide World Photos; C63 Photograph by Sharon Hoogstraten; C65 NASA Goddard Space Flight Center Scientific Visualization Studio; C67 *left* © Denny Eilers/Grant Heilman Photography; *left inset* © Bob Rowan/Progressive Image/Corbis; *right* AP/WideWorld Photos; C68 *top* AP/Wide World Photos; *bottom* NASA Goddard Space Flight Center Scientific Visualization Studio; C72–C73 © Darrell Jones/Getty Images; C73 *top, center* Photograph by Sharon Hoogstraten; C75 Photograph by Sharon Hoogstraten; C77 © Roger Antrobus/Corbis; C78 *top* Photograph by Sharon Hoogstraten; *bottom* © Jane Burton/Bruce Coleman, Inc.; C79 *bottom* NASA/Photo Researchers; C81 Emory Kristof/National Geographic Image Collection; C83 Walter H. F. Smith/NOAA; C84 Photograph by Sharon Hoogstraten; C85 © AFP/Corbis/NASA; C86 © Dan Gair Photographic/Index Stock Imagery/PictureQuest; C87 Photograph by Sharon Hoogstraten; C88 *left* Ron Erwin Photography; *right* © Bettmann/Corbis; C89 Photograph by Sharon Hoogstraten; C92 © C.C. Lockwood/Bruce Coleman, Inc.; C93 © Buddy Mays/Corbis; C94 *top* AP/Wide World Photos; *bottom left, right* Photograph by Sharon Hoogstraten; C96 *top, bottom* © M. H. Black/Bruce Coleman, Inc.; C98 Photograph by Sharon Hoogstraten; C101 *left* © Attar Maher/Corbis; C104 Photograph by Sharon Hoogstraten; C106 *top* NOAA/OAR/National Undersea Research Program; *bottom* NOAA; C107 *top left* NOAA/OAR/ National Undersea Research Program; *top right* The Granger Collection, New York; *bottom* NOAA Central Library; C108 *top* AP Wide World Photos; *center* © Silva Joao/Corbis Sygma; *bottom* Alan Schietzch/ARSTI/NOAA; C109 *top* OAR/National Undersea Research Program/Fairleigh Dickinson University; *bottom* Photograph by Ben Allsup/Webb Research Corporation; C110–C111 © Brandon Cole; *top right* © Maximilian Weinzierl/Alamy Images; *center right* Photograph by Sharon Hoogstraten; C113 © Eric and David Hosking/Corbis; C115 *top, bottom* © Brandon Cole; C116 *top* Photograph by Sharon Hoogstraten; *bottom* © Robert Perron; C117 © W.K. Almond/Stock Boston/PictureQuest ; C118 *top* © Lee Foster/Bruce Coleman, Inc.; *right inset* © Masa Ushioda/V&W/Bruce Coleman, Inc.; C119 AP/Wide World Photos; C120 *left, inset* © Lowell Georgia/Corbis; C121 Photograph by Sharon Hoogstraten; C122, C124 © Stone/Getty Images; C125 *top* © Mark A. Johnson/Alamy; *bottom* Photograph by Sharon Hoogstraten; C127 © Norbert Wu; C128 *top* © Dr. Ken Mac Donald/Photo Researchers; *center left* © The Natural History Museum, London; *bottom* © John Burbidge/Photo Researchers; C129 *left* © B. Murton/Southampton Oceanography Centre/Photo Researchers; *inset* © NSF Oasis Project/Norbert Wu Productions; C130 Photograph by Sharon Hoogstraten; C131 © Stephen Frink Collection/Alamy Images; C132 *top* © Norbert Wu; *bottom* © Dani/Jeske/Animals Animals/Earth Scenes; C133 *bottom* Jan Stromme/Strom/Bruce Coleman, Inc.; C134 © Institute of Oceanographic Sciences/NERC/Photo Researchers; C135 *top* © James Marshall/Corbis; *bottom* © Dr. Morley Read/Photo Researchers; C136 © Simon Fraser/Photo Researchers; C137 *top left* © Richard A. Cooke/Corbis; *top right* © Dorling Kindersley; C138 *top* © Gary Bell/Alamy Images; *bottom* Photograph by Sharon Hoogstraten; C140 *bottom left* © Norbert Wu; *bottom right* Jan Stromme/Strom/Bruce Coleman, Inc.; C142 © Lawson Wood/Corbis.

Earth's Atmosphere
Divider © Bill Ross/Corbis; D2–D3 © Bruce Byers/Getty Images; D3 © D. Faulkner/Photo Researchers; D4 *top left* Luiz C. Marigo/Peter Arnold, Inc.; *top center* Image courtesy Norman Kuring, SeaWiFS Project/NASA; *top right* Norbert Wu; *bottom center* © The Chedd-Angier Production Company; D6–D7 © Peter Griffith/Masterfile frontiers; D7 *top, center* Photograph by Sharon Hoogstraten; D10 *top* © Didrik Johnck/Corbis Sygma; *bottom* Photograph by Sharon Hoogstraten; D11 NASA; D13 © Michael K. Nichols/NGS Image Collection; D14 *top left, top right* Provided by the SeaWiFS Project, NASA/Goddard Space Flight Center, and ORBIMAGE; D15 M. Thonig/Robertstock.com; D16 David Young-Wolff/PhotoEdit; D17 Photograph by Sharon Hoogstraten; D19 © Gerald and Buff Corsi/Visuals Unlimited, Inc.; D22, D24 Photographs by Sharon Hoogstraten; D26 *top, bottom* PhotoDisc/Getty Images; *background* © Pulse Productions/SuperStock/ PictureQuest; D27 Photograph by Sharon Hoogstraten; D28 © P.G. Adam/Publiphoto/ Photo Researchers; D29 AP/WideWorld Photos; D30 *background, center left* PhotoDisc/Getty Images; *centerright* © Corbis/PictureQuest; D32 © Mug Shots/Corbis; D33 *top left, bottom left* NASA/Goddard Space Flight Center; D34 *top left* © Still Pictures/Peter Arnold, Inc.; *left, right* Photographs by Sharon Hoogstraten; D36 NASA; D37 © Tom Branch/Photo Researchers; D40–D41 © Catherine Karnow/Corbis; D41, D45, D47 Photographs by Sharon Hoogstraten; D54 *top left, top right* Earth Vistas; D55 *top* NASA/Corbis; *background* © Lester Lefkowitz/Corbis; D56 *center right* Photograph by Sharon Hoogstraten; *bottom right* © Japack Company/Corbis; D57 © Kristi Bressert/Index Stock Imagery/PictureQuest; D59 Photograph by Sharon Hoogstraten; D60 GrantHeilman/Grant Heilman Photography, Inc.; D62 *top* © John Mead/Photo Researchers; *center* © Royalty-free/Corbis; *bottom* Fred Whitehead/Animals Animals/Earth Scenes; D63 © Tom Till; D64 *top* © Gunter Marx Photography/Corbis; *bottom left, bottom right, center* Photographs by Sharon Hoogstraten; D66 © Stockbyte/PictureQuest; D67 Photograph by Sharon Hoogstraten; D69 *bottom left* © Larry West/Photo Researchers; *bottom right* © Astrid & Hanns-Frieder Michler/Photo Researchers; D70 © Will McIntyre/Photo Researchers; D71 © 1990 Warren Faidley/Weatherstock; D74 © Dorling Kindersley; D76–D77 AP/WideWorld Photos; D77, D81 Photographs by Sharon Hoogstraten; D83 © PhotoDisc/Getty Images; D86 © Stephen J. Krasemann/Photo Researchers; D87 Photograph by Sharon Hoogstraten; D88 Image by Marit Jentoft-

Nilsen/NASA GSFC; **D89** *top, center* Courtesy of U.S. Geological Survey; **D90** Photograph by Sharon Hoogstraten; **D91** AP/WideWorld Photos; **D92, D94** *top* Photographs by Sharon Hoogstraten; *bottom left* © PhotoDisc/Getty Images; **D95** *left, center, right* © David K. Hoadley; **D96** © Reuters/New Media/Corbis; **D97** *background* © Waite Air Photos, Inc.; *top left, top right* © Fletcher & Baylis/Photo Researchers; **D98** Used with permission © January 9, 2003 Chicago Tribune Company, Chicago, Illinois. Photograph by Sharon Hoogstraten; **D101** Provided by Space Science & Engineering Center, University of Wisconsin-Madison; **D102** WSBT-TV, South Bend, Indiana; **D104** *top left* Mary Kate Denny/PhotoEdit, Inc.; *center left, bottom right* Photographs by Sharon Hoogstraten; **D105** Photograph by Sharon Hoogstraten; **D106** Image by Marit Jentoft-Nilsen/NASA GSFC; **D108** Used with permission © January 9, 2003 Chicago Tribune Company, Chicago, Illinois. Photograph by Sharon Hoogstraten; **D110** *top right* © Joel W. Rogers/Corbis; *bottom* © Dorling Kindersley; **D111** *top left* © Snark/Art Resource, New York; *top right* Matthew Oldfield, Scubazoo/Photo Researchers; *bottom* Smithsonian Institution; **D112** *top left* © Mark A. Schneider/Photo Researchers; *top right* © Bettmann/Corbis; *right center* © Roger Ressmeyer/Corbis; *bottom* © Corbis; **D113** NASA; **D114–D115** © Ferrero-Labat/Auscape International; **D115** *top, center,* **D117, D119** Photographs by Sharon Hoogstraten; **D120** *left* Tony Freeman/PhotoEdit, Inc.; *right* © Duomo/Corbis; **D123** *top left, top right* Steve McCurry/Magnum Photos; **D124** *top left* © Dave G. Houser/Corbis; *center right* AP/WideWorld Photos; *center left, bottom* Glenn Murcutt; **D125** © The Image Bank/Getty Images; **D127** *center left* © Rick Schafer/Index Stock Imagery/PictureQuest; *top left* © Gerald D. Tang; *bottom* © Photodisc/Getty Images; *center right* © Willard Clay; *top right* © Bill Ross/Corbis; *bottom left* © John Conrad/Corbis; **D130** *top left* © Mark Lewis/Pictureque/PictureQuest; *center left* Photograph by Sharon Hoogstraten; **D132** Johner/Photonica; **D133** *top right* © Photodisc/Getty Images; *bottom right* Photograph by Sharon Hoogstraten; **D137** Lonnie G. Thompson, Ohio State University; **D139** Simon Fraser/Mauna Loa Observatory/Photo Researchers.

Space Science
Divider © David Nunuk/Photo Researchers; **E2–E3** © Charles O'Rear/Corbis; **E3** *top right* © D. Nunuk/Photo Researchers; **E4** © The Chedd-Angier Production Company; **E4–E5** © David Parker/Photo Researchers; **E5** *top center* NASA/JPL; **E6–E7** NASA; **E7, E9** Photographs by Sharon Hoogstraten; **E11** Johnson Space Center/NASA; **E12** Photograph by Sharon Hoogstraten; **E13** *top* © Roger Ressmeyer/Corbis; *bottom* Photograph by Sharon Hoogstraten; **E15** Photograph by Sharon Hoogstraten; **E16** *center left* Kapteyn Laboratorium/Photo Researchers; *center* National Optical Astronomy Observatories/Photo Researchers; *center right* A. Wilson (UMD) et al., CXC/NASA; **E18** © Roger Ressmeyer/Corbis; **E19** *top left* NASA Johnson Space Center; *top right* © STScl/NASA/ Photo Researchers; **E20** *top left* © ImageState-Pictor/PictureQuest; **E20–E21, E22** Photographs by Sharon Hoogstraten; **E23** *bottom, inset* NASA; **E24** Courtesy of NASA/JSC; **E25** *top* NASA; *bottom* Photograph by Sharon Hoogstraten; **E27** Photograph by Bill Ingalls/NASA; **E30** *left, inset* Chris Butler/Photo Researchers; **E31** NASA; **E32** Courtesy of V.R. Sharpton University of Alaska-Fairbanks and the Lunar and Planetary Institute; **E33** Photograph by Sharon Hoogstraten; **E34** NASA; **E35** *background* © Jan Tove Johansson/Image State-Pictor/ PictureQuest; *left inset* Andy Fyon, Ontariowildflower.com (Division of Professor Beaker's Learning Labs); *right inset* NASA; **E36** *top* Photograph by Sharon Hoogstraten; *center* © Roger Ressmeyer/Corbis; *bottom* NASA; **E40–E41** © Roger Ressmeyer /Corbis; **E41** *top right, center right* Photographs by Sharon Hoogstraten; *bottom right* NASA Goddard Space Flight Center; **E43** *left* NASA; *right* Photograph by Sharon Hoogstraten; **E44** *top* © 2003 The Living Earth Inc.; *bottom* Photograph by Sharon Hoogstraten; **E45** Photograph by Sharon Hoogstraten; **E47** NASA/JSC; **E49** © Arnulf Husmo/Getty Images; **E50** *top* © Christian Perret/jump; *bottom left, bottom right* Photograph by Sharon Hoogstraten; **E51, E52** Photographs by Sharon Hoogstraten; **E53** Courtesy of NASA and the Lunar and Planetary Institute; **E54** USGS Flagstaff, Arizona; **E55** *top right* Photograph by Sharon Hoogstraten; *bottom right* NASA; *right inset* NASA and the Lunar and Planetary Institute; **E58** Photograph by Steve Irvine; **E59** © DiMaggio/Kalish/ Corbis; **E61** *background* Lunar Horizon View/NASA; **E62** Photograph by Sharon Hoogstraten; **E63** *top* © Roger Ressmeyer/Corbis; *bottom* Photograph by Jean-Francois Guay; **E64** *center* NASA/Getty Images; *bottom left* © Fred Espenak; **E65** *top* © Jeff Greenberg/MRP/Photo Researchers; *bottom* © 1999 Ray Coleman/Photo Researchers; **E67** *top left* © Peter Duke; *right inset* © David Parker/Photo Researchers; *bottom left* Public Domain; *bottom center* Barlow Aerial Photography, Ignacio, CO; **E68** *top left* © 2003 The Living Earth, Inc.; *center left* Photograph courtesy of NASA and the Lunar and Planetary Institute; **E70** *left* USGS Flagstaff, Arizona; *right* NASA Goddard Space Flight Center; **E72** Courtesy of Adler Planetarium & Astronomy Museum, Chicago, Illinois; **E73** *top left* © Stapleton/Corbis; *center* © Science Museum/Science & Society Picture Library; *right* provided by Roger Bell, University of Maryland, and Michael Briley, University of Wisconsin, Oshkosh; *bottom* Courtesy of Adler Planetarium & Astronomy Museum, Chicago, Illinois; **E74** *top left* © Harvard College Observatory/Photo Researchers; *top right* Robert Williams and the Hubble Deep Field Team (STScl) and NASA; *bottom* © Fermi National Accelerator Laboratory/Photo Researchers; **E75** *top* Ann Feild (STScl); *bottom* © NASA/Photo Researchers; **E76–E77** Courtesy of NASA/JPL/University of Arizona; **E77** *top right, center right* Photographs by Sharon Hoogstraten; **E79, E82** Photographs by Sharon Hoogstraten; **E83** *left* Photo © Calvin J. Hamilton; *right* Courtesy of NASA/JPL/Caltech; **E84** NASA; **E85** *top* Photograph by Sharon Hoogstraten; *bottom* Johnson Space Center NASA; **E87** *background* Mark Robinson/Mariner 10/NASA; *top right* NASA; *top left* © Walt Anderson/Visuals Unlimited; *bottom left* NASA/ JPL/Malin Space Science Systems; **E88** Photograph by Sharon Hoogstraten; **E89** *top* USGS; *bottom* Courtesy of NASA/JPL/ Northwestern University; **E90** *top, center, bottom* NASA; **E91** NASA/JSC; **E92** Courtesy of NASA/JPL/Caltech; **E93** *left* Courtesy of NASA/JPL/Malin Space Science Systems; *right* MAP-A-Planet/NASA; *right inset* NASA/Goddard Space Flight Center Scientific Visualization Studio; **E94, E95** Courtesy of NASA/JPL/Caltech; **E96** *top* Courtesy of NASA/JPL/Caltech; *bottom* Photograph by Sharon Hoogstraten; **E97** *top* NASA; *bottom* NASA and the Hubble Heritage Team (STScl/AURA); **E98** *top* E. Karkoschka(LPL) and NASA; *bottom* © Calvin J. Hamilton; **E99** *top* Courtesy of NASA/JPL/Caltech; *center* NASA; **E100** near.jhuapl.edu; **E101** Hubble Space Telescope, STScl-PR96-09a/NASA; **E102** *top left, inset* NASA; *bottom left* Courtesy of NASA/JPL/Caltech; *bot-*

tom left inset NASA; *top right* © NASA/ JPL/Photo Researchers; *top right inset, bottom right, bottom right inset* NASA; **E103** Courtesy of NASA/JPL/Caltech; **E104** *background* © 1997 Jerry Lodriguss; *right* Courtesy of NASA/JPL/ Caltech; **E105** Fred R. Conrad/The New York Times; **E106** *top left* © James L. Amos/Corbis; *bottom left* Photograph by Sharon Hoogstraten; **E107** Photograph by Sharon Hoogstraten; **E108** *top* NASA; *bottom* Courtesy of NASA/JPL/Caltech; **E112–E113** David Malin Images/Anglo- Australian Observatory; **E113** *top left* © Jerry Schad/Photo Researchers; *center left* Photograph by Sharon Hoogstraten; **E115** Photograph by Sharon Hoogstraten; **E117** Photograph by Jay M. Paschoff, Bryce A. Babcock, Stephan Martin, Wendy Carlos, and Daniel B. Seaton © Williams College; **E118** *left* © John Chumack/Photo Researchers; *right* © NASA/Photo Researchers; **E119** © Patrick J. Endres/Alaskaphotographics.com; **E120** *top* © Dave Robertson/ Masterfile; *left bottom, right bottom* Photograph by Sharon Hoogstraten; **E121, E122, E123** Photographs by Sharon Hoogstraten; **E125** *top* © Dorling Kindersley; *bottom* ESA and J. Hester (ASU),NASA; **E126** J. Hester et al./NASA/CXC/ASU; **E127** Hubble Heritage Team/AURA/STScI/NASA; **E129** © MPIA-HD, Birkle, Slawik/Photo Researchers; **E130** Photograph by Sharon Hoogstraten; **E131** *top* Allan Morton/Dennis Milon/Photo Researchers; *bottom* Photograph by Sharon Hoogstraten; **E132** David Malin Images /Anglo-Australian Observatory; **E133** Walter Jaffe/Leiden Observatory, Holland Ford/JHU/STScI, and NASA; **E134** *left* NASA and Hubble Heritage Team (STScI); *center* NASA, H. Ford (JHU), G. Illingworth (UCSC/LO), M. Clampin (STScI), G. Hartig (STScI), the ACS Science Team, and ESA; **E135** Photograph by Sharon Hoogstraten; **E136** © Jason Ware; **E138** Photograph by Sharon Hoogstraten; **E139** N. Benitez (JHU), T. Broadhurst (The Hebrew University), H. Ford (JHU), M. Clampin (STScI), G. Hartig (STScI), G. Illingworth (UCO/Lick Observatory), the AGS Science Team and ESA/NASA; **E140** *top* David Malin Images/Anglo-Australian Observatory; *bottom* N. Benitez (JHU), T. Broadhurst (The Hebrew University), H. Ford (JHU), M. Clampin (STScI), G. Hartig (STScI), G. Illingworth (UCO/Lick Observatory), the AGS Science Team and ESA/NASA; **E142** *left* Hubble Heritage Team (AURA/STScI/NASA); *right* Anglo-Australian Observatory/David Malin Images.

Backmatter
R28 © Photodisc/Getty Images.

Illustrations and Maps
Accurate Art Inc. **A39, A107, A175, B139, C143, D75, D109, E106**
Ampersand Design Group **C93**
Argosy **B165, B167, B169, D46, D119**
Julian Baum **E57, E117, E127, E128, E131, E140**
Richard Bonson/Wildlife Art Ltd. **A83, B10–B11, B38, B40, B72, B79, B81, B83, B87, B101, B104, C13, C19, C25, C26, C29, C34, D44, D72**
Peter Bull/Wildlife Art Ltd. **A160, A162, A167, A169, B17, B40, B52, B58, B70, B122, C52, C53, C55, C68, D99, D106, E26, E27, E47, E48, E68**
Bill Cigliano **E67, E137**
Steve Cowden **C91, E48**
Stephen Durke **A45, A53, B24, B65, B67, B70, C11, C31, C47, C54, C66, C133, D17, D18, D25, D36, E12, E14, E18**
Chris Forsey **A99, B55, C17, C20, C34, D129**
Luigi Galante **A127, A138**
David A. Hardy **A12, A84, A86, A104, E11, E32, E80, E83, E95, E108**
Gary Hincks **A63, A79, A80, A149, A153, B23, B24, B26, B28, B31, B34, B35, B38, B90–B91, B104, B132, C80–C81, D20, D36, D48, D51**
Ian Jackson **C115, C123, C127, C140**
Dan Maas/Maas Digital **E28, E36**
Mapquest.com, Inc. **A17, A18, A23, A32, A33, A34, A36, A64, A88, A110, A125, A166, A170, B13, B16, B19, B23, B27, B28, B31, B32, B34, B35, B36, B38, B46, B57, B63, B64, B65, B70, B78, B81, B89, B113, B128, B129, B132, C10, C30, C42, C44, C45, C47, C56, C61, C64, C65, C76, C77, C85, C88, C98, C101, C113, C117, C118, C122, , C132, C134, D3, D14, D49, D52, D54, D55, D80, D83, D84, D85, D86, D88, D89, D93, D97, D118, D120, D121, D123, D126, D133, D134, D135, D136, D140, D143, E64, R58–R59, R62–R63**
Janos Marffy **B115, B124, B136, B151**
Morgan, Cain & Assoc. **A128, C77, C82, C85, C100, C133**
Mike Saunders **A117, A120, A138, D61, D69, D72**
NOAA/NGDC (National Geophysical Data Center) **R60–R61**
Precision Graphics **B48, B49, B70, B92, B152, D53, D59, D72**
SlimFilms **B67, B70, B150, B162, B164, B166**
Space.comCanada.Inc. **R71–R74**
Space Science and Engineering Center, University of Wisconsin-Madison **D84, D100, D101, D102, D106**
Dan Stuckenschneider **C101, E17, E36, R11–R19, R22, R32**
Raymond Turvey **A159, C86, C90–C92, D83, D106**
Rob Wood **A117, A154**
Ron Wood/Wood Ronsaville Harlin **B121, B138, E56, E68**